NEW PERSPECTIVES ON

# Microsoft® Office 2010

## SECOND COURSE

Ann Shaffer
Patrick Carey
Katherine T. Pinard

Roy Ageloff
June Jamrich Parsons
Dan Oja

S. Scott Zimmerman
Brigham Young University

Beverly B. Zimmerman
Brigham Young University

Joseph J. Adamski
Grand Valley State University

COURSE TECHNOLOGY
CENGAGE Learning™

Australia • Brazil • Japan • Korea • Mexico • Singapore • Spain • United Kingdom • United States

COURSE TECHNOLOGY
CENGAGE Learning

**New Perspectives on Microsoft Office 2010, Second Course**

Vice President, Publisher: Nicole Jones Pinard
Executive Editor: Marie L. Lee
Associate Acquisitions Editor: Brandi Shailer
Senior Product Manager: Kathy Finnegan
Product Manager: Leigh Hefferon
Associate Product Manager: Julia Leroux-Lindsey
Editorial Assistant: Jacqueline Lacaire
Director of Marketing: Cheryl Costantini
Senior Marketing Manager: Ryan DeGrote
Marketing Coordinator: Kristen Panciocco
Developmental Editors: Kim T. M. Crowley, Jessica Evans, Robin M. Romer, Mary Pat Shaffer
Senior Content Project Managers: Jill Braiewa, Jennifer Goguen McGrail
Content Project Manager: Jennifer Feltri
Composition: GEX Publishing Services
Art Director: Marissa Falco
Text Designer: Althea Chen
Cover Designer: Roycroft Design
Cover Art: © Masterfile
Copyeditor: Suzanne Huizenga
Proofreader: Andrea Schein
Indexer: Alexandra Nickerson



Library of Congress Control Number: 2010934338

International Edition:

ISBN-13: 978-0-538-47050-6

ISBN-10: 0-538-47050-X

Cengage Learning International Offices

**Asia**
www.cengageasia.com
tel: (65) 6410 1200

**Australia/New Zealand**
www.cengage.com.au
tel: (61) 3 7685 4111

**Brazil**
www.cengage.com.br
tel.: (011) 3665 9900

**India**
www.cengage.co.in
tel: (91) 11 30484837/38

**Latin America**
www.cengage.com.mx
tel: +52 (55) 1500 6000

**UK/Europe/Middle East/Africa**
www.cengage.co.uk
tel: (44) 207 067 2500

**Represented in Canada by**
**Nelson Education, Ltd.**
tel: (416) 752 9100 / (800) 668 0671
www.nelson.com

Cengage Learning is a leading provider of customized learning solutions with office locations around the globe, including Singapore, the United Kingdom, Australia, Mexico, Brazil, and Japan. Locate your local office at: **www.cengage.com/global**

For product information: **www.cengage.com/international**
Visit your local office: **www.cengage.com/global**
Visit our corporate website: **www.cengage.com**



Printed in the United States of America
1 2 3 4 5 6 7 16 15 14 13 12 11 10

# Preface

**The New Perspectives Series' critical-thinking, problem-solving approach is the ideal way to prepare students to transcend point-and-click skills and take advantage of all that Microsoft Office 2010 has to offer. In developing the New Perspectives Series, our goal was to create books that give students the software concepts and practical skills they need to succeed beyond the classroom. We've updated our proven case-based pedagogy with more practical content to make learning skills more meaningful to students.**

**With the New Perspectives Series, students understand *why* they are learning *what* they are learning, and are fully prepared to apply their skills to real-life situations.**

*"The new Visual Overviews give students valuable insight into what they will learn in each tutorial session. Clearly seeing what's ahead will engage students from the start."*

—Diane Shingledecker
Portland Community College

## About This Book

This book provides complete coverage of introductory-to-advanced concepts and skills for Microsoft Office 2010, and includes the following:

- Three Word 2010 tutorials on working with templates, themes, and styles; performing a mail merge; and collaborating with others
- Four Excel 2010 tutorials plus two Appendices that cover creating Excel tables and PivotTables; managing multiple workbooks; using conditional formatting; developing an Excel application; and working with advanced functions, custom formats, and filters
- Four Access 2010 tutorials plus one Appendix that cover creating advanced queries and enhancing table design; creating custom forms and reports; sharing, integrating, and analyzing data; and understanding relational databases and database design
- Two PowerPoint 2010 tutorials on adding and customizing media and charts; integrating PowerPoint with other programs; and collaborating with others

*New for this edition!*

- Each session begins with a Visual Overview, a new two-page spread that includes colorful, enlarged screenshots with numerous callouts and key term definitions, giving students a comprehensive preview of the topics covered in the session, as well as a handy study guide.
- New ProSkills boxes provide guidance for how to use the software in real-world, professional situations, and related ProSkills exercises integrate the technology skills students learn with one or more of the following soft skills: decision making, problem solving, teamwork, verbal communication, and written communication.
- Important steps are highlighted in yellow with attached margin notes to help students pay attention to completing the steps correctly and avoid time-consuming rework.

## System Requirements

This book assumes a typical installation of Microsoft Office 2010 and Microsoft Windows 7 Ultimate using an Aero theme. (You can also complete the material in this text using another version of Windows 7, such as Home Premium, or earlier versions of the Windows operating system. You will see only minor differences in how some windows look.) The browser used for any steps that require a browser is Internet Explorer 8.

*"The clear step-by-step instructions, real-world data files, and helpful figures make New Perspectives texts excellent for courses taught in the classroom, the hybrid/blended format, or entirely online."*
—Sylvia Amito'elau
Coastline Community College

# The New Perspectives Approach

**Context**
Each tutorial begins with a problem presented in a "real-world" case that is meaningful to students. The case sets the scene to help students understand what they will do in the tutorial.

**Hands-on Approach**
Each tutorial is divided into manageable sessions that combine reading and hands-on, step-by-step work. Colorful screenshots help guide students through the steps. **Trouble?** tips anticipate common mistakes or problems to help students stay on track and continue with the tutorial.

VISUAL OVERVIEW

**Visual Overviews**
*New for this edition!* Each session begins with a Visual Overview, a new two-page spread that includes colorful, enlarged screenshots with numerous callouts and key term definitions, giving students a comprehensive preview of the topics covered in the session, as well as a handy study guide.

PROSKILLS

**ProSkills Boxes and Exercises**
*New for this edition!* ProSkills boxes provide guidance for how to use the software in real-world, professional situations, and related ProSkills exercises integrate the technology skills students learn with one or more of the following soft skills: decision making, problem solving, teamwork, verbal communication, and written communication.

KEY STEP

**Key Steps**
*New for this edition!* Important steps are highlighted in yellow with attached margin notes to help students pay close attention to completing the steps correctly and avoid time-consuming rework.

INSIGHT

**InSight Boxes**
InSight boxes offer expert advice and best practices to help students achieve a deeper understanding of the concepts behind the software features and skills.

TIP

**Margin Tips**
Margin Tips provide helpful hints and shortcuts for more efficient use of the software. The Tips appear in the margin at key points throughout each tutorial, giving students extra information when and where they need it.

REVIEW

APPLY

**Assessment**
Retention is a key component to learning. At the end of each session, a series of Quick Check questions helps students test their understanding of the material before moving on. Engaging end-of-tutorial Review Assignments and Case Problems have always been a hallmark feature of the New Perspectives Series. Colorful bars and brief descriptions accompany the exercises, making it easy to understand both the goal and level of challenge a particular assignment holds.

REFERENCE

TASK REFERENCE

GLOSSARY/INDEX

**Reference**
Within each tutorial, Reference boxes appear before a set of steps to provide a succinct summary and preview of how to perform a task. In addition, a complete Task Reference at the back of the book provides quick access to information on how to carry out common tasks. Finally, each book includes a combination Glossary/Index to promote easy reference of material.

**www.cengage.com/ct/newperspectives**

# Our Complete System of Instruction

BRIEF
INTRODUCTORY
COMPREHENSIVE

**Coverage To Meet Your Needs**

Whether you're looking for just a small amount of coverage or enough to fill a semester-long class, we can provide you with a textbook that meets your needs.

- Brief books typically cover the essential skills in just 2 to 4 tutorials.
- Introductory books build and expand on those skills and contain an average of 5 to 8 tutorials.
- Comprehensive books are great for a full-semester class, and contain 9 to 12+ tutorials.

So if the book you're holding does not provide the right amount of coverage for you, there's probably another offering available. Go to our Web site or contact your Course Technology sales representative to find out what else we offer.

COURSECASTS

**CourseCasts – Learning on the Go. Always available...always relevant.**

Want to keep up with the latest technology trends relevant to you? Visit our site to find a library of podcasts, CourseCasts, featuring a "CourseCast of the Week," and download them to your mp3 player at http://coursecasts.course.com.

Our fast-paced world is driven by technology. You know because you're an active participant—always on the go, always keeping up with technological trends, and always learning new ways to embrace technology to power your life.

Ken Baldauf, host of CourseCasts, is a faculty member of the Florida State University Computer Science Department where he is responsible for teaching technology classes to thousands of FSU students each year. Ken is an expert in the latest technology trends; he gathers and sorts through the most pertinent news and information for CourseCasts so your students can spend their time enjoying technology, rather than trying to figure it out. Open or close your lecture with a discussion based on the latest CourseCast.

Visit us at http://coursecasts.course.com to learn on the go!

**Instructor Resources**

We offer more than just a book. We have all the tools you need to enhance your lectures, check students' work, and generate exams in a new, easier-to-use and completely revised package. This book's Instructor's Manual, ExamView testbank, PowerPoint presentations, data files, solution files, figure files, and a sample syllabus are all available on a single CD-ROM or for downloading at http://www.cengage.com/coursetechnology.

**SAM: Skills Assessment Manager**

SAM is designed to help bring students from the classroom to the real world. It allows students to train and test on important computer skills in an active, hands-on environment.

SAM's easy-to-use system includes powerful interactive exams, training, and projects on the most commonly used Microsoft Office applications. SAM simulates the Office application environment, allowing students to demonstrate their knowledge and think through the skills by performing real-world tasks, such as bolding text or setting up slide transitions. Add in live-in-the-application projects, and students are on their way to truly learning and applying skills to business-centric documents.

Designed to be used with the New Perspectives Series, SAM includes handy page references, so students can print helpful study guides that match the New Perspectives textbooks used in class. For instructors, SAM also includes robust scheduling and reporting features.

**Content for Online Learning**

Course Technology has partnered with the leading distance learning solution providers and class-management platforms today. To access this material, visit www.cengage.com/webtutor and search for your title. Instructor resources include the following: additional case projects, sample syllabi, PowerPoint presentations, and more. For students to access this material, they must have purchased a WebTutor PIN-code specific to this title and your campus platform. The resources for students might include (based on instructor preferences): topic reviews, review questions, practice tests, and more. For additional information, please contact your sales representative.

# BRIEF CONTENTS

# TABLE OF CONTENTS

### Tutorial 7 Collaborating with Others and Creating Web Pages



## EXCEL LEVEL II TUTORIALS

### Tutorial 5 Working with Excel Tables, PivotTables, and PivotCharts

## POWERPOINT LEVEL II TUTORIALS

TUTORIAL 5

# Working with Templates, Themes, and Styles

*Creating a Site Selection Report*

## OBJECTIVES

**Session 5.1**

- Create a new document from a template
- Insert a Word file into a document
- Customize the document theme
- Select a style set
- Change character and paragraph spacing
- Modify a style

**Session 5.2**

- Create a new style
- Inspect and compare styles
- Create a table of contents
- Use the Research task pane
- Translate text
- Create and use a new template

## Case | *Department of City Planning*

Clarenbach, Tennessee is a rapidly growing suburb of Nashville. Clarenbach's Department of City Planning prepares reports on many public projects that contribute to this growing community. Sam Hooper, a senior member of the department, has asked you to help prepare a report on possible sites for a new public swimming pool. He'd like you to use a Word template as the basis for the new report. He also wants you to create a template that can be used for all reports produced by the department. You will create a custom theme for the reports, and you will work with creating and modifying style sets.

## STARTING DATA FILES

**Word5** →

**Tutorial**
Placeholder.docx
Report.docx
Willow Grove.docx

**Review**
Consultants.docx
Template Text.docx
Water.docx

**Case1**
Characteristics.docx
Crab Apple.jpg
Height.docx
Plant Headings.docx
Requirements.docx

**Case2**
Star.docx

**Case3**
Text.docx

**Case4**
(none)

# SESSION 5.1 VISUAL OVERVIEW

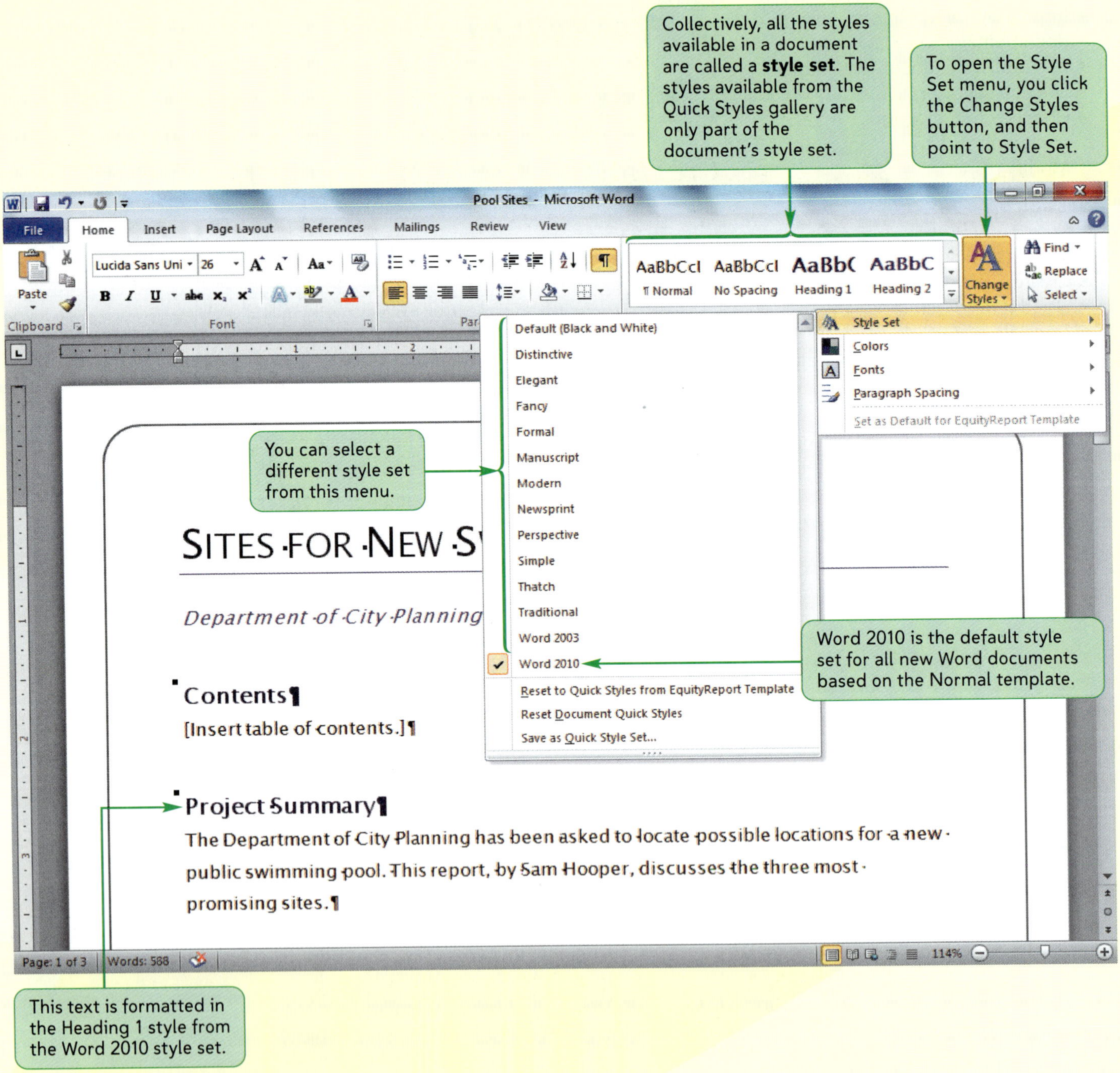

# CUSTOM THEMES AND STYLE SETS

The buttons in the Themes group on the Page Layout tab allow you to customize a document's theme by selecting a new set of theme colors, fonts, or effects, which control the theme's graphical elements.

The Themes gallery displays the available themes on your computer, including any custom themes you have created and saved in the default location of Templates\Document Themes.

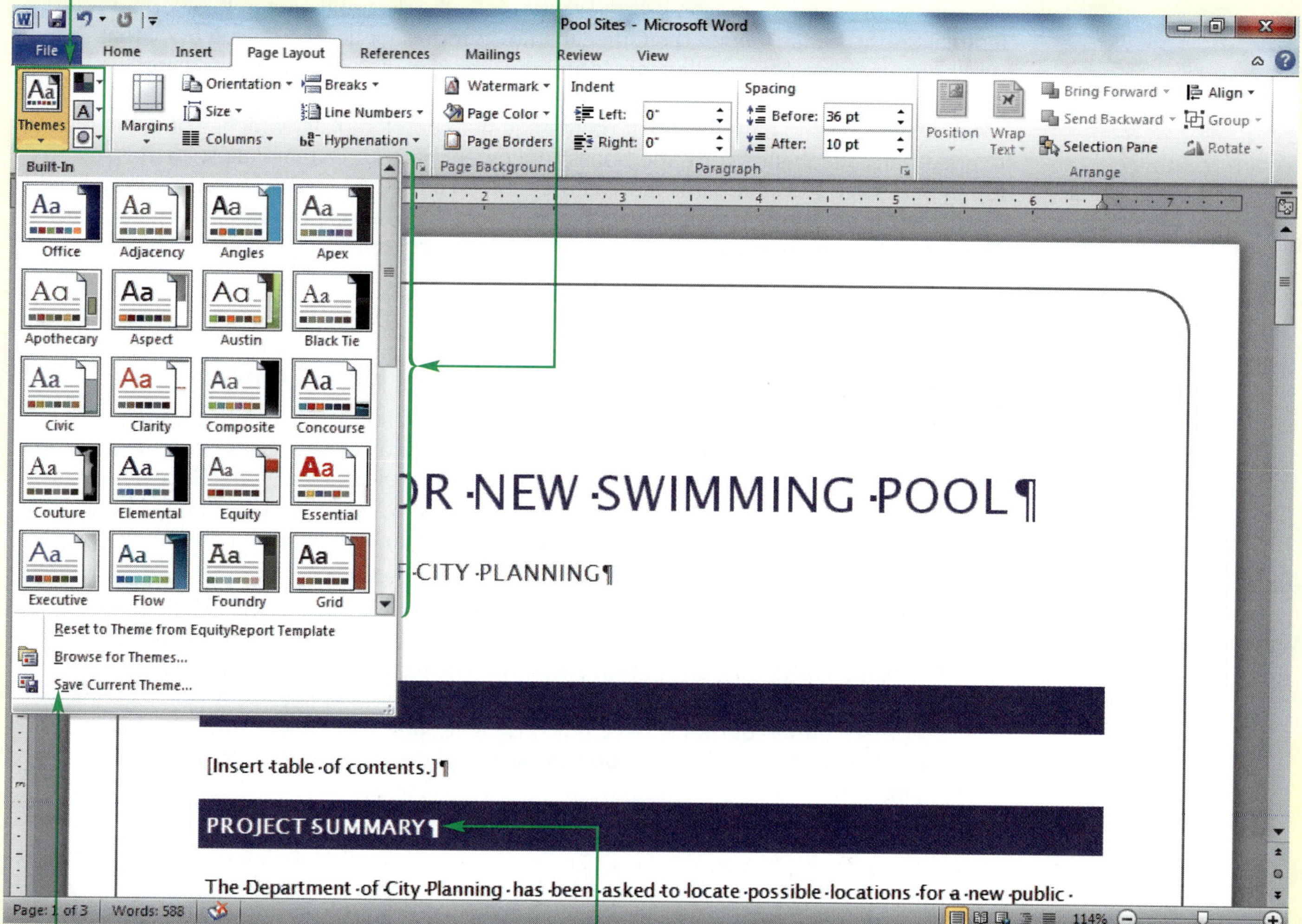


After you modify a theme, you can save it as a new theme, with a new name. By default, your custom theme will be saved in the Document Themes subfolder inside Word's Template folder, unless you specify another save location.

This text is formatted in the Heading 1 style from the Modern style set.

# Creating a New Document from a Template

A **template** is a file that you use as a starting point for a series of similar documents so that you don't have to re-create formatting and text for each new document. A template can contain customized styles, text, graphics, or any other element that you want to repeat from one document to another. Word includes templates that you can use to create reports, fax cover sheets, letters, and other types of documents. For an even wider selection of templates, you can look online, where you'll find templates for certificates, contracts, brochures, and greeting cards, just to name a few. You can also create your own templates to suit your specific needs.

**TIP**

Templates have the file extension .dotx to differentiate them from regular Word documents, which have the extension .docx.

Although you might not realize it, you already have experience working with templates. Every new, blank document that you open in Word is a copy of the Normal template. Unlike the other templates included with Word, the **Normal template** does not have any text, formatting, or graphics, but it does include all the default settings that you are accustomed to using in Word. For example, the default theme in the Normal template is the Office theme. The Office theme, in turn, supplies the default body font (Calibri) and the default heading font (Cambria). The default 1.15 line spacing and the paragraph spacing are also specified in the Normal template.

Sam would like to base his report on the Equity Report template, which is one of the templates installed with Word. You open a document based on a template from the New tab in Backstage view, the same tab you use to open a new, blank document. When you open a template, Word actually creates a document that is an exact copy of the template. The template itself remains unaltered, so that you can continue to use it as the basis for other documents.

### To open a new document based on the Equity Report template:

1. In Word, click the **File** tab to open Backstage view, and then click the **New** tab in the navigation bar. The left pane of the New tab gives you access to templates that are stored on your computer and templates available online at Office.com. The default selection, Blank document, opens a new, blank document based on the Normal template. In this case, you want to open a document based on a different template.
2. In the Home section, click **Sample templates.** The left pane of the New tab displays thumbnails of the templates that were installed with Word. Scroll down, if necessary, and then click **Equity Report**. The right pane of the New tab displays a preview of the first page of the selected template. Below the preview, the Document option button is selected by default, indicating that Word will create a new document that is a copy of the template, *not the template itself*. See Figure 5-1.

**Figure 5-1** Selecting the Equity Report template

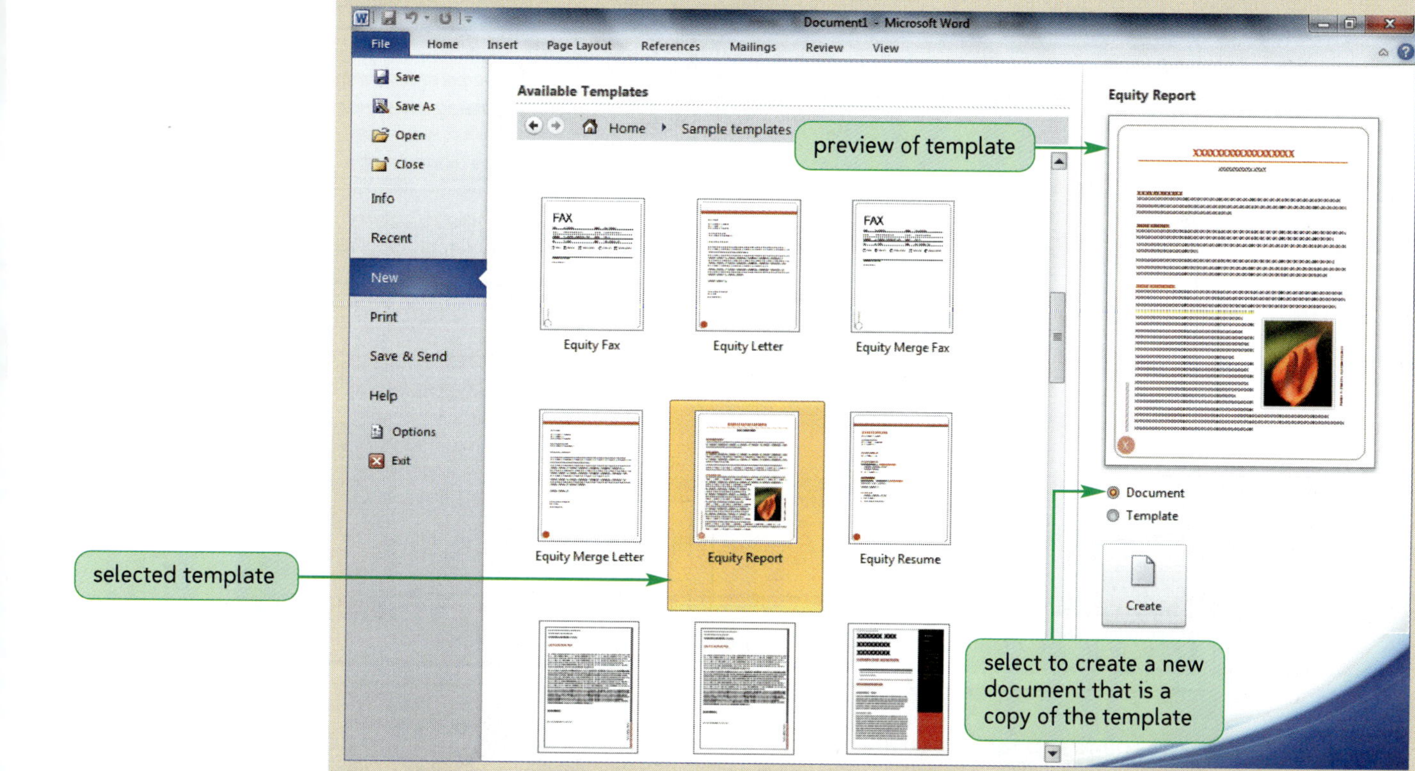


3. Click the **Create** button. A new document, named Document2, opens. It contains a number of content controls designed specifically for the Equity Report template.

4. Switch to **Print Layout** if necessary, change the Zoom setting to **Page Width**, display nonprinting characters if necessary, and then scroll down and review the parts of the document. Figure 5-2 shows all the elements of the Equity Report template.

**TIP**

The sample text in the Equity Report is actually a helpful summary of techniques for working with templates, rather than text one might use in a report.

**Figure 5-2** **Equity Report template**

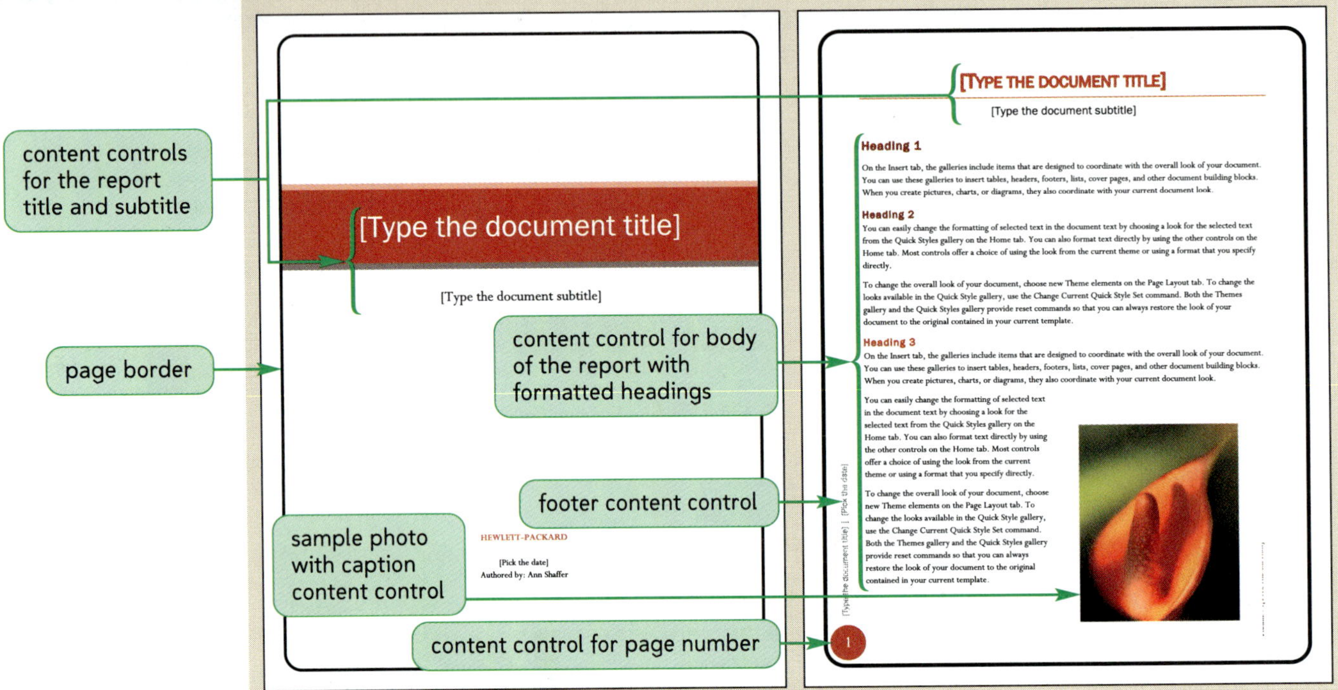


The first page is a cover page with several content controls for the document title, subtitle, and other elements. The second page contains similar content controls as well as a sample photograph with a content control for a caption. Each page is surrounded by a border with rounded corners. The colors, fonts, and other elements you see in the document are specified by the Equity theme, which is the default theme for the Equity Report template.

5. Save the document as **Pool Sites** in the Word5\Tutorial folder included with your Data Files.

After you use a template to create a new document, you can delete the elements you don't want to use, type appropriate text in the content controls that you want to keep, and then replace the sample body text with text that is specific to your document. In this case, you do not need the cover page, so you can begin by deleting that from the Pool Sites document, and then enter the appropriate text for this report into the content controls.

### To modify the document created from the Equity template:

1. Click the **Insert** tab, click the **Cover Page** button in the Pages group, and then click **Remove Current Cover Page**. The cover page is removed from the document, leaving only the page with the sample photograph, which is now page 1.
2. Press the **Delete** key to delete the blank paragraph at the top of the remaining page.
3. Replace the **[Type the document title]** placeholder text with **Sites for New Swimming Pool**. The new title replaces the placeholder text. Next, you need to enter the subtitle.

4. Replace the **[Type the document subtitle]** placeholder text with **Department of City Planning**. The new subtitle appears in the control. Next, you need to add the date to the vertical footer. To do this, you need to switch to Header and Footer view.

5. In the Header & Footer group, click the **Footer** button, and then, under the Footer gallery, click **Edit Footer**. The document switches to Header and Footer view and scrolls down to display the vertical footer in the lower-left corner of the page. The Document Title content control in the footer displays the document title, "Sites for New Swimming Pool," which you entered earlier. The Date content control contains the [Pick the date] placeholder.

**TIP**

To remove the preformatted footer from the document, you click Remove Footer on the Footer menu.

6. Click the **[Pick the date]** placeholder text to display the content control, click the **Date button arrow** to display the calendar, and then click the current date. The calendar closes and the current date is displayed in the Date content control.

7. On the Header & Footer Tools Design tab, click the **Close Header and Footer** button in the Close group. You return to Page Layout view. The Subtitle content control is still active, because it was active when you switched to Header and Footer view.

Sam wants the report to begin with the heading "Contents" followed by a table of contents. You'll insert the heading now, and then insert the table of contents information later in this tutorial.

## To enter the Contents heading:

1. Move the mouse pointer over the text in the body of the report, which begins with "Heading 1." The text area is highlighted in light blue.

2. Click anywhere in the body of the report. The blue highlight darkens and now covers only the text itself. A blue tag above the highlighted text indicates that the body of the report is actually a content control. See Figure 5-3. Unlike with other content controls, you can delete this one simply by typing something new.

**Figure 5-3** **Document with sample text highlighted**

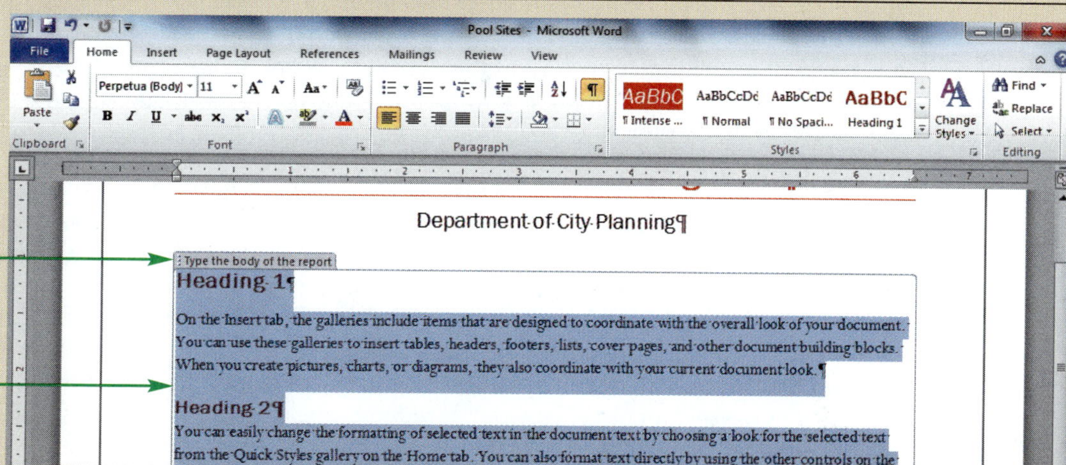

3. Type **Contents**. The content control is removed, along with the sample text and the sample photograph. The new text is formatted in the Perpetua font, which is the default body font for the Equity Report template.
4. In the Styles group, click the **Heading 1** style. The Contents heading is formatted in 14-point Franklin Gothic Book font with a dark orange color.
5. Press the **Enter** key to start a new paragraph, type **[Insert table of contents.]**, and then press the **Enter** key again. This placeholder text will remind Sam to insert a table of contents later, after his report is created. The new text is formatted in the Normal style, not in the Heading 1 style. A new paragraph after a heading is formatted in the Normal style by default. See Figure 5-4.

**Figure 5-4 Report with new heading**

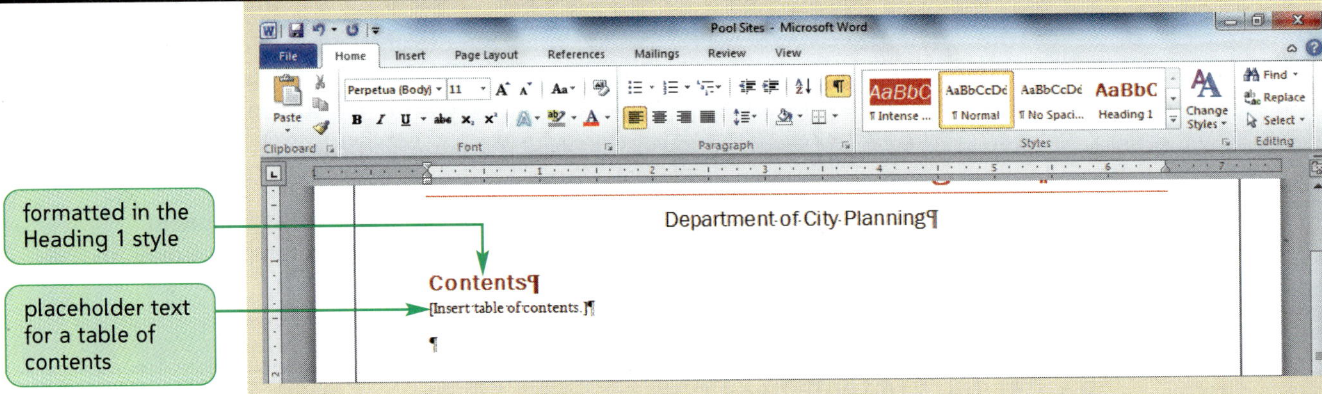


PROSKILLS

### *Decision Making: Using Templates from Other Sources*

The templates installed with Word are only a small sample of the templates available to you. The Microsoft Office Online Web site offers a huge variety of templates that are free to registered Microsoft Office users. Countless other sites offer templates for free, for individual sale, as part of a subscription service, or a combination of all three. However, you need to be wary when searching for templates online. Keep in mind the following when deciding what sites to use:

- Files downloaded from the Internet can infect your computer with viruses and spyware, so make sure your computer is up-to-date with antivirus and antispyware software before attempting to download any templates.
- Evaluate a site carefully to verify that it is a reputable source of virus-free templates. Verifying the site's legitimacy is especially important if you intend to pay for a template with a credit card. Search for the Web site's name and Web address on several different search engines (such as Bing and Google) to see what other people say about it. The Better Business Bureau's Web site at *www.bbb.org* allows you to search for complaints against an online business by entering its URL (Web address).
- Some Web sites claim to offer templates for free, when in fact the offer is primarily a lure to draw visitors to sites that are really just online billboards, with ads for any number of businesses completely unrelated to templates or Word documents. You should avoid downloading templates from these Web sites.
- Many templates available online were created for earlier versions of Word that did not include themes or many other design features that you are accustomed to in Word 2010. Make sure you know what you're getting before you pay for an out-of-date template.

Sam has typed a draft of his report and saved it in a separate Word document. You can insert this Word file into the Pool Sites document.

## Inserting a File into a Word Document

To insert a file into a document, you start by clicking the Object button in the Text group on the Insert tab. When you insert a Word file into an open Word document, the text is inserted at the location of the insertion point, so you need to make sure the insertion point is at the correct location. Word always inserts a blank paragraph at the end of text inserted from another file. If you don't want to include this extra paragraph, you can delete it. Before inserting the file, you will open it and review the formatting.

### To insert a file into the Pool Sites document:

1. Open the file **Report** from the Word5\Tutorial folder included with your Data Files. As you can see, the document is formatted in the Office theme. It contains text formatted with the familiar blue color of the Office theme Heading 1 and Heading 2 styles.
2. Close the Report document and return to the Pool Sites document, verify that the insertion point is located in the blank paragraph below the [Insert table of contents.] text.
3. Click the **Insert** tab, and then in the Text group, click the **Object button arrow**. A menu appears with two options.

   **Trouble?** If the Object dialog box opens, you clicked the Object button instead of the Object button arrow. Close the dialog box, and then click the Object button arrow instead.
4. On the Object menu, click **Text from File**. The Insert File dialog box opens, which is very similar to the Open dialog box.
5. If necessary, navigate to the Word5\Tutorial folder included with your Data Files, click the **Report** document, and then click the **Insert** button. The text of the Report document is inserted in the Pool Sites document. It takes on the theme of the current document (the Equity theme), with the headings now formatted in a dark orange color.
6. Scroll up to review the beginning of the document, as shown in Figure 5-5.

**Figure 5-5** **Report document inserted into the Pool Sites document**

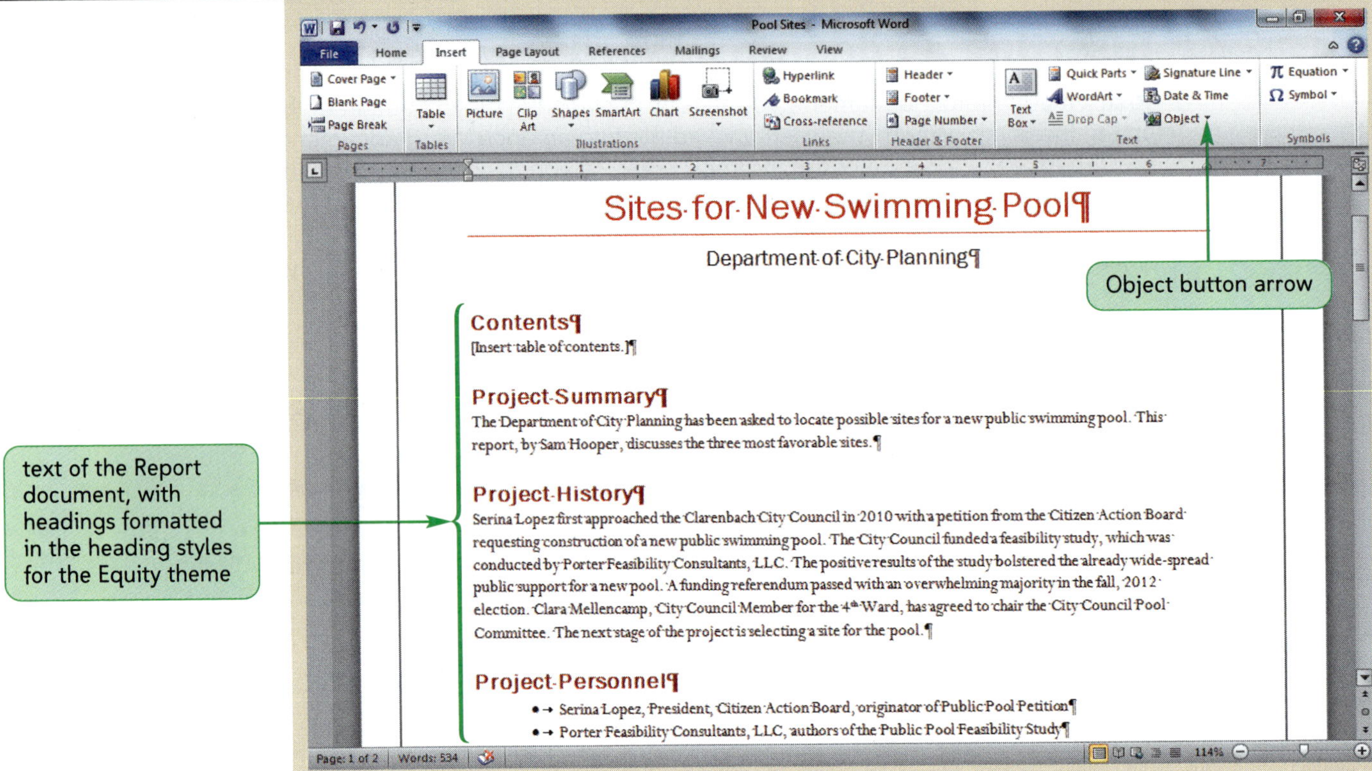


7. On page 1, in the second sentence below the "Project Summary" heading, replace "Sam Hooper" with your first and last name.
8. Save the document.

Now that the document contains the report text, Sam asks you to customize the formatting. You'll start with the document theme.

# Customizing the Document Theme

A document theme consists of three main components—theme colors, theme fonts, and theme effects. A specific set of colors, fonts, and effects is associated with each theme, but you can mix and match them to create a customized theme for your document.

As you saw in the Session 5.1 Visual Overview, you change the theme colors, fonts, and effects for a document using the options in the Themes group on the Page Layout tab. When you change the theme colors, fonts, and effects for a document, the changes affect only that document.

The Pool Sites document, which was based on the Equity Report template, is formatted with the Equity theme. Although Sam likes the overall layout of the document, he wants to select different theme colors and theme fonts. He doesn't plan to include any graphics, so there's no need to customize the theme effects. You'll start with the theme colors.

## Changing the Theme Colors

**Theme colors** are the coordinated colors used by a theme to format headings, body text, and other elements. For example, the Equity theme, which is currently applied to Sam's report, uses orange for the headings and the circle graphic in the footer, and a coordinating gray for the page border and footer text. Sam prefers something more neutral than the orange color used in the Equity theme. He asks you to apply a different set of theme colors.

### To change the theme colors in the Pool Sites document:

1. Click the **Page Layout** tab, and then click the **Theme Colors** button. A gallery of theme colors opens, with one coordinated set of colors for each theme. A pale orange outline indicates that the Equity theme color set is currently applied to the document. The gallery displays eight colors in each set of colors. The third color from the left is the color used for headings. For example, the third color from the left in the Equity theme color set is dark orange, which is currently applied to the headings in the document. The remaining colors are used for other types of elements, such as hyperlinks, page borders, shading, and so on. See Figure 5-6.

**Figure 5-6** Theme Colors gallery

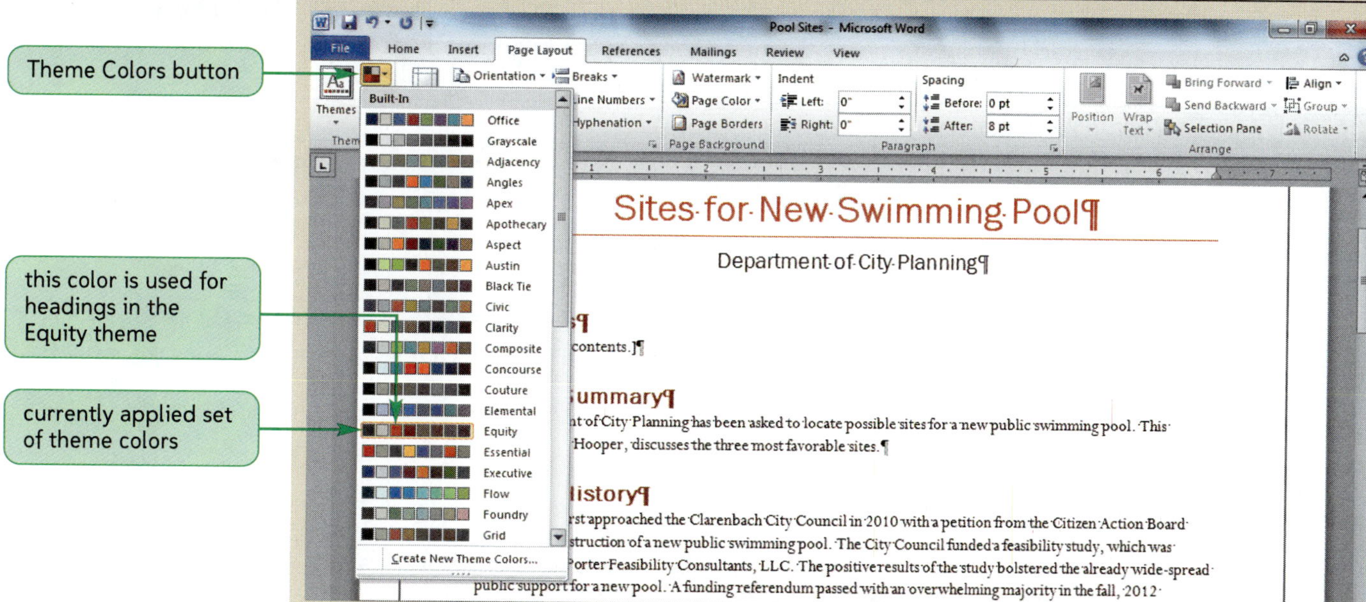


**Trouble?** If you see additional theme colors at the top of the menu under the heading "Custom," then custom theme colors have been created and stored on your computer.

2. Move the mouse pointer over the options in the gallery to observe the Live Preview of the colors in the document.
3. Scroll down, and then click the **Urban** color set, which is the third from the bottom. The document headings are now formatted in dark blue.
4. Save your work.

The new colors you just selected affect only the Pool Sites document. Your changes do not affect the Equity theme that was installed with Word and that is available to all new documents. Next, Sam asks you to customize the document theme further by changing the theme fonts.

## Changing the Theme Fonts

As with theme colors, you can change the **theme fonts** in a document to suit your needs. You know from Tutorial 2 that each theme uses two coordinating fonts or font styles—one for the headings and one for the body text. For example, the Equity theme in the Pool Sites document includes the Franklin Gothic Book font for headings, and Perpetua for body text. When changing the theme fonts, you can select from all the font combinations available in any of the themes installed with Word.

### To select a different set of theme fonts for the Pool Sites document:

1. In the Themes group, move the mouse pointer over the **Theme Fonts** button [A]. A ScreenTip appears, indicating that the current fonts are Franklin Gothic Book for headings and Perpetua for body text.
2. Click the **Theme Fonts** button [A]. The Theme Fonts gallery opens, displaying the heading and body font combinations for each theme.
3. Scroll down to review the fonts. Sam prefers the Lucida Sans Unicode font, which is used by the Concourse theme for both heading and body text. See Figure 5-7.

**Figure 5-7** Theme Fonts gallery

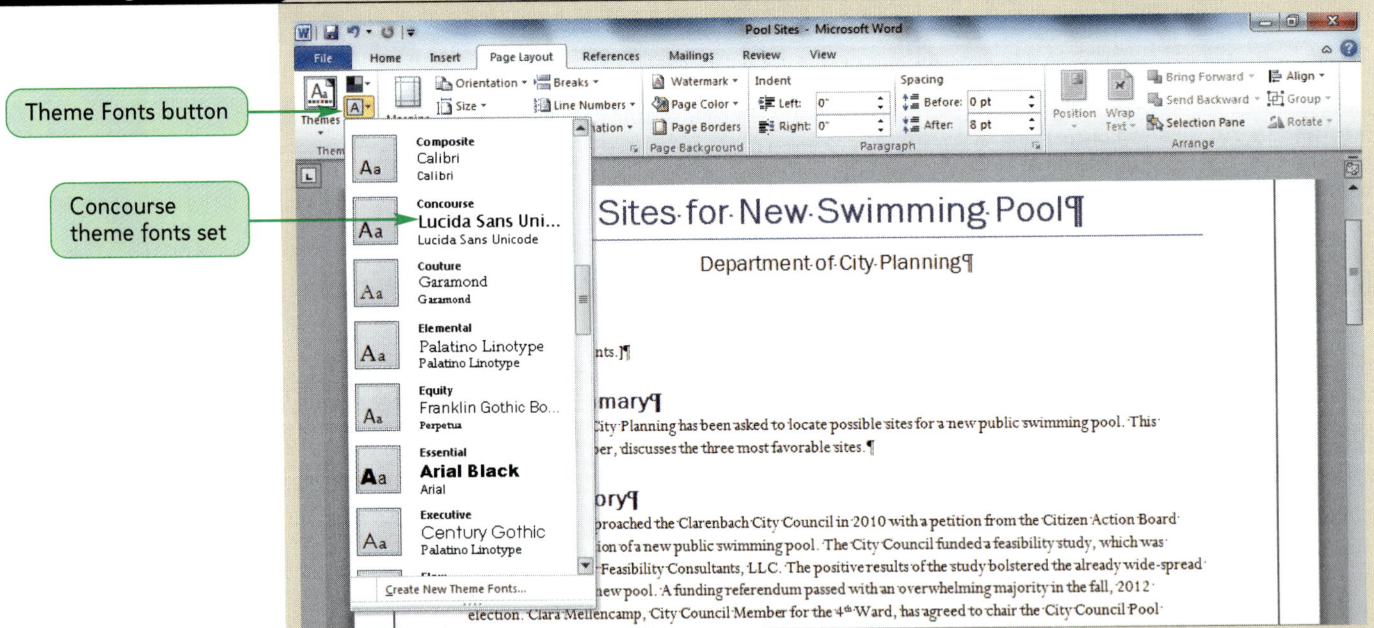


4. Scroll the gallery, and then click the **Concourse** theme fonts set. The Theme Fonts gallery closes, and the Lucida Sans Unicode Font is applied to the headings and body text in the Pool Sites document.
5. Save your work.

The changes you have made to the theme fonts for the Pool Site do not affect the original Equity theme that was installed with Word and that is available to all new documents. To make your new combination of theme fonts and theme colors available to other documents, you can save them as a new, custom theme.

INSIGHT

### *Creating Custom Theme Colors and Theme Fonts*

The theme colors and theme fonts installed with Word were created by Microsoft designers who are experts in creating harmonious-looking documents. It's always best to stick with these predesigned options, rather than trying to create your own set. However, in some specialized situations you might need to create customized sets of theme fonts and colors. When you create a customized set, the theme fonts and colors are saved as part of Word so that you can use them in other documents. To create a custom set of theme colors, you click the Theme Colors button in the Themes group on the Page Layout tab, click Create New Theme Colors to open the Create New Theme Colors dialog box, in which you can select colors for different theme elements, and enter a descriptive name for the new theme colors. The custom set of theme colors appears as an option in the Themes Color gallery.

To create a custom set of heading and body fonts, you click the Theme Fonts button in the Themes group on the Page Layout tab, click Create New Theme Fonts, select your custom heading and body, and then enter a descriptive name for the new set of fonts in the Name box. The custom set of theme fonts appears as an option in the Theme Fonts menu.

## Saving a Custom Theme

You can save a new custom theme to any folder, but when you save a custom theme to the default location—the Document Themes subfolder inside the Word Templates folder—it appears as an option in the Themes gallery. To save a custom theme, you click the Themes button in the Themes group on the Home tab, and then click Save Current Theme.

Sam asks you to save his combination of theme fonts and theme colors as a new theme.

### To save a new theme:

1. In the Themes group, click the **Themes** button, and then, in the menu below the Themes gallery, click **Save Current Theme**. The Save Current Theme dialog box opens. The Document Themes folder is the default location. The default theme name is "Theme1." You can select a different save location and enter a more meaningful theme name. See Figure 5-8.

**Figure 5-8** Save Current Theme dialog box

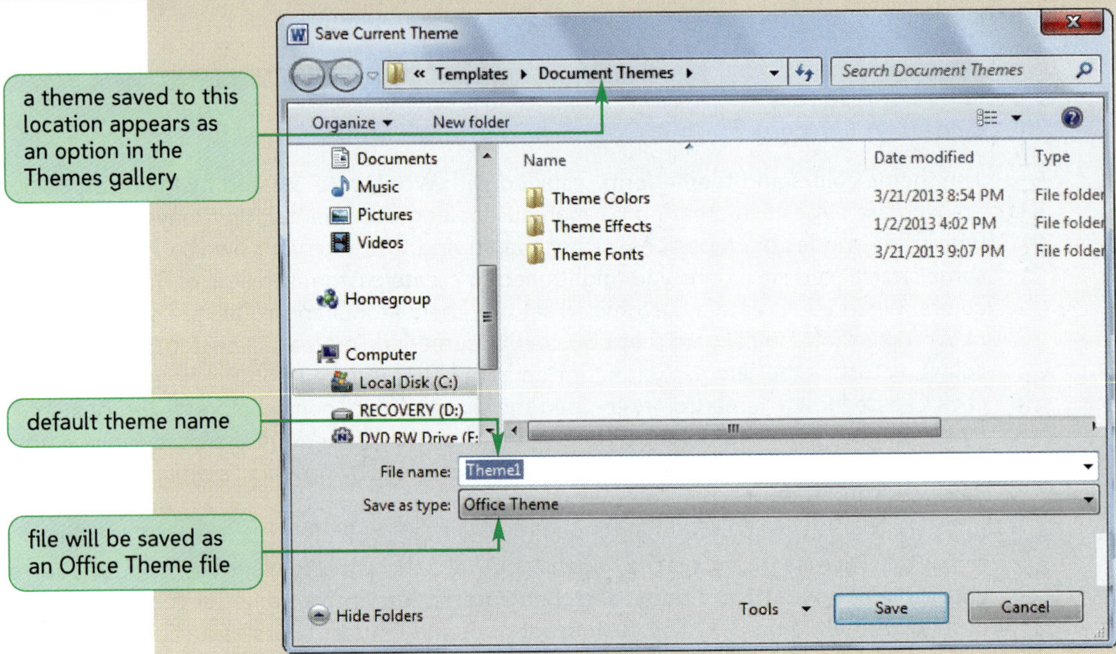


2. Navigate to the Word5\Tutorial folder included with your Data Files. Next you'll type the new filename, using "DCP," the acronym for "Department of City Planning," as part of the filename.

3. Click in the File name box, type **DCP Theme**, and then click the **Save** button. The Save Current Theme dialog box closes.

**TIP**

To delete a theme from the Document Themes folder and remove it from the Themes gallery, click the Themes button in the Themes group on the Page Layout tab, right-click the theme you want to delete, click Delete, and then click Yes.

Sam plans to use the new DCP theme later to help standardize the look of all documents created in his department. When he is ready to apply it to a document, he can click the Themes button in the Themes group on the Page Layout tab, click Browse for Themes, navigate to the folder containing the custom theme, and then select and open the theme.

## Selecting a Style Set

Recall that a style is a set of formatting options that you can apply to a specific text element in a document, such as a document's title, heading, or body text. A **style set** is a coordinated set of styles in a document. By default, the Quick Styles gallery displays styles from the Word 2010 style set, and this is the style set you see in the Quick Styles gallery when you open a new, blank document. You can choose from 12 additional style sets using the Change Styles button in the Styles group on the Home tab, as shown in the Session 5.1 Visual Overview.

Each style set has a Normal style, a Heading 1 style, a Heading 2 style, and so on. The styles in a style set are designed to convey a specific look. For example, the Thatch style set shown in Figure 5-9 has a bold, modern look. The Heading 1 style includes a thick band of color with an outline and a contrasting font color. The Heading 2 style in the Thatch style set has white letters that are outlined in the same color used as the background color in the Heading 1 style.

**TIP**

Once you have applied a style set, you can still change the theme. Changing the theme only affects the theme colors and theme fonts.

**Figure 5-9** Styles from two different style sets

| | |
|---|---|
| **Word 2010 style set** | Title style<br>Heading 1 style<br>Heading 2 style<br>Normal style |
| **Thatch style set** | Title style<br>Heading 1 style<br>Heading 2 style<br>Normal style |

Sam asks you to select a different style set for the Pool Sites document.

### To select a new style set for the Pool Sites document:

1. Click the **Home** tab, and then click the **Change Styles** button in the Styles group. The Change Styles menu opens. To select a new style set, you use the Style Set option.
2. Point to **Style Set**. The Style Set menu opens, displaying a list of style sets.
3. Drag the mouse pointer down the menu, and then point to **Modern**. As you drag the mouse pointer, a Live Preview shows some of the styles that make up the different style sets in the menu. In the Modern style set, the Heading 1 style applies a blue box that spans the left and right margins, with the heading text in white. Notice that the theme fonts you specified earlier—Lucida Sans Unicode for both headings and the body text—are still applied, as are the Concourse theme colors. See Figure 5-10.

**Figure 5-10** Live Preview of the Modern style set

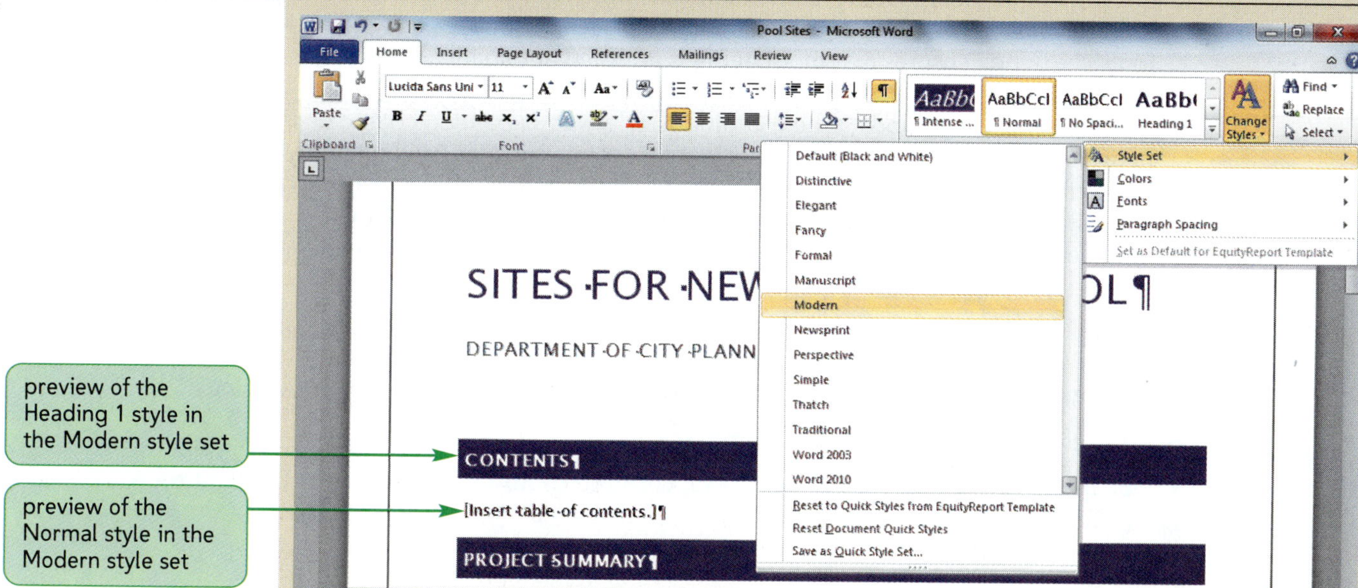

4. Click **Modern** on the Style Set menu. The styles in the document change to reflect the styles in the Modern style set, and the Quick Styles gallery in the Styles group displays the first four styles in the Modern Style set.
5. In the Styles group, click the **More** button to review the set of styles available in the Quick Styles gallery, and then click anywhere in the document to close the Quick Styles gallery.

The ability to select a new style set gives you a lot of flexibility when formatting a document. However, sometimes you will want to modify a style to better suit your particular needs.

# Modifying Styles

To modify a style, you select text formatted with the style you want to modify, apply new formatting, and then update the style by saving your changes. Sam asks you to modify the Heading 1 style for the report by increasing the character spacing and paragraph spacing and applying italics. You'll start by adjusting the character spacing.

## Changing Character Spacing

The term **character spacing** refers to the space between individual characters. To add emphasis to text, you can expand or contract the spacing between characters. As with line and paragraph spacing, space between characters is measured in points, with one point equal to 1/72 of an inch.

To adjust character spacing for selected text, click the Dialog Box Launcher in the Font group on the Home tab, and then click the Advanced tab in the Font dialog box. Of the numerous settings available on this tab, you'll find two especially useful.

First, the Spacing box allows you to choose Normal spacing (which is the default character spacing you normally see in documents), Expanded spacing (with the characters farther apart than with the Normal setting) and Condensed spacing (with the characters closer together than with the Normal setting). With both Expanded and Condensed spacing, you can specify the number of points between characters.

Secondly, the Kerning for fonts check box allows you to adjust the spacing between characters to make them look like they are spaced evenly. Kerning is helpful when you are working with large font sizes, which can sometimes cause characters to appear unevenly spaced even though they are in fact spaced evenly. Selecting the Kerning for fonts check box ensures that the spacing is adjusted automatically so that letters appear evenly spaced.

Sam wants you to update the Heading 1 style with expanded character spacing, and he wants the Heading 1 style to include italics formatting. You will begin by making these changes to a paragraph that is currently formatted with the Heading 1 style. Later, you will update the Heading 1 style to match the new formatting of the paragraph you modified and, as a result, all the paragraphs formatted with the Heading 1 style will be updated as well.

**To modify the character spacing of the Project Summary heading:**

1. Select the heading **Project Summary**.
2. In the Font group on the Home tab, click the **Dialog Box Launcher**. The Font dialog box opens.

**TIP**

The more advanced options, under "OpenType Features," allow you to fine tune the appearance of characters.

3. Click the **Advanced** tab. This tab includes several options for changing the space between characters. The Character Spacing settings at the top of this tab reflect the style settings for the currently selected text. The Spacing box is set to Expanded.
4. Click the **Spacing** arrow to see the available spacing options. If you wanted to move the selected characters closer together, you would click Condensed. In this case, you will keep the Expanded setting but increase the space between the characters by changing the setting in the By box next to the Spacing box.
5. Click the **Spacing** arrow again to close the menu without making any changes, and then next to the Spacing box, delete the contents in the By box, type **2** (you don't have to type "pt"), and then press the **Tab** key. The Preview section shows a sample of the expanded character spacing. See Figure 5-11.

**Figure 5-11** **Changing character spacing in the Font dialog box**

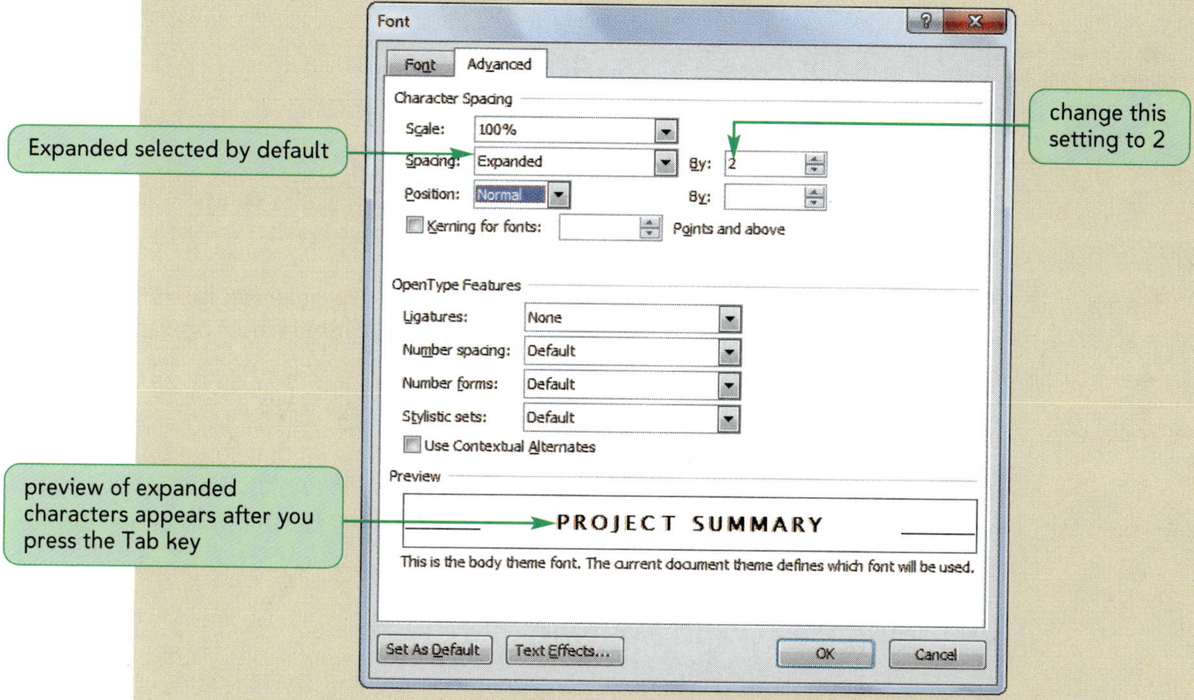


Next, you need to apply italics, which you can do from the Font tab.

6. In the Font dialog box, click the **Font** tab. Here you can make numerous changes affecting the appearance of the selected text, including adding special effects such as shadows or outlines.
7. In the Font style box, click **Bold Italic**. The Preview section of the Font tab shows a preview of the italics formatting applied to the Project Summary heading, which also has the Heading 1 style applied to it. See Figure 5-12.

**Figure 5-12** Applying italics to text formatted with the Heading 1 style

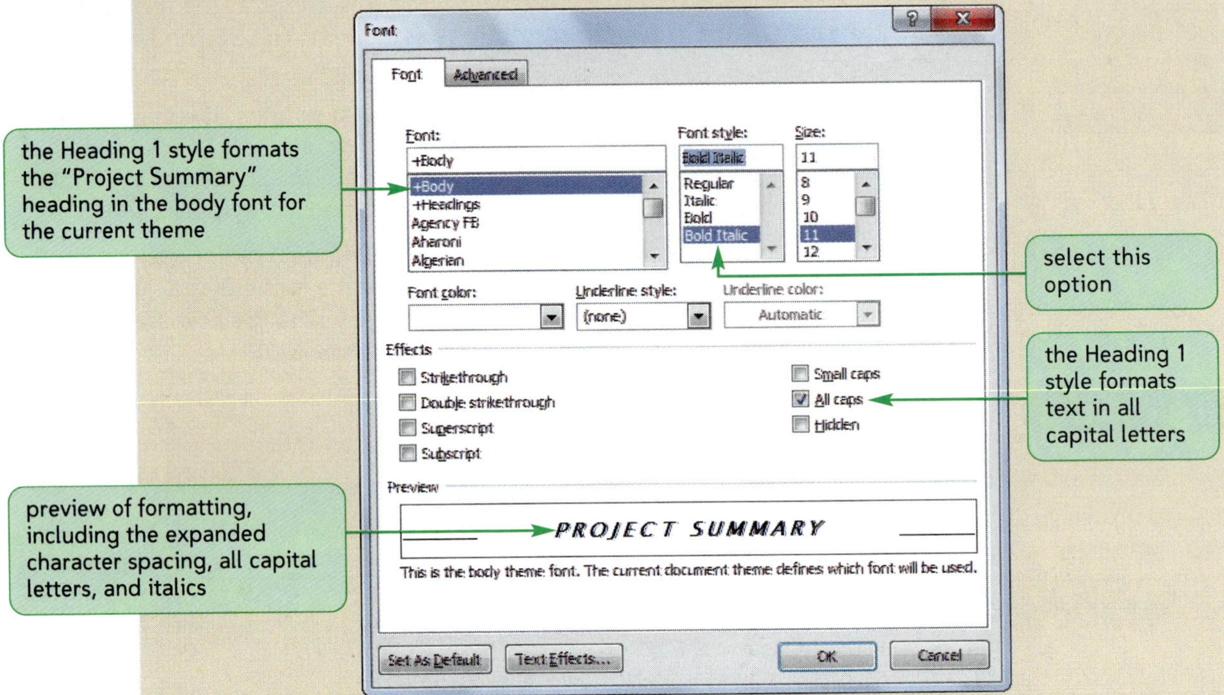


8. Click the **OK** button to close the Font dialog box. The selected heading is now italicized, with the individual characters spread slightly farther apart.
9. Save your work.

Next, you need to change the Project Summary heading so that some extra spacing appears below it. Then you will update the Heading 1 style to match the new formatting of the Project Summary heading. This will affect all the headings that are currently formatted with the Heading 1 style.

## Changing Paragraph Spacing

You already know how to add or delete a default amount of space before or after a paragraph using the Line and Paragraph Spacing button in the Paragraph group on the Home tab. To specify an exact amount of space, you use the options in the Paragraph group on the Page Layout tab. Sam wants 15 points of space after the Contents heading. The extra space will help further distinguish the heading from the body text that follows it.

### To increase the space after the Project Summary heading:

1. Verify that the Project Summary heading is still selected.
2. Click the **Page Layout** tab. Note that the Paragraph group on this tab includes settings for paragraph indents and paragraph spacing. You use the Spacing Before and After boxes to add space before or after the selected paragraph. Currently, the selected paragraph has 10 points of space before it and 0 points after it. Sam wants to change the After setting to 15.

**3.** In the Spacing section of the Paragraph group, click the **After** box, type **15,** and then press the **Enter** key to apply the change to the selected paragraph. See Figure 5-13.

**Figure 5-13** **Changing paragraph spacing**

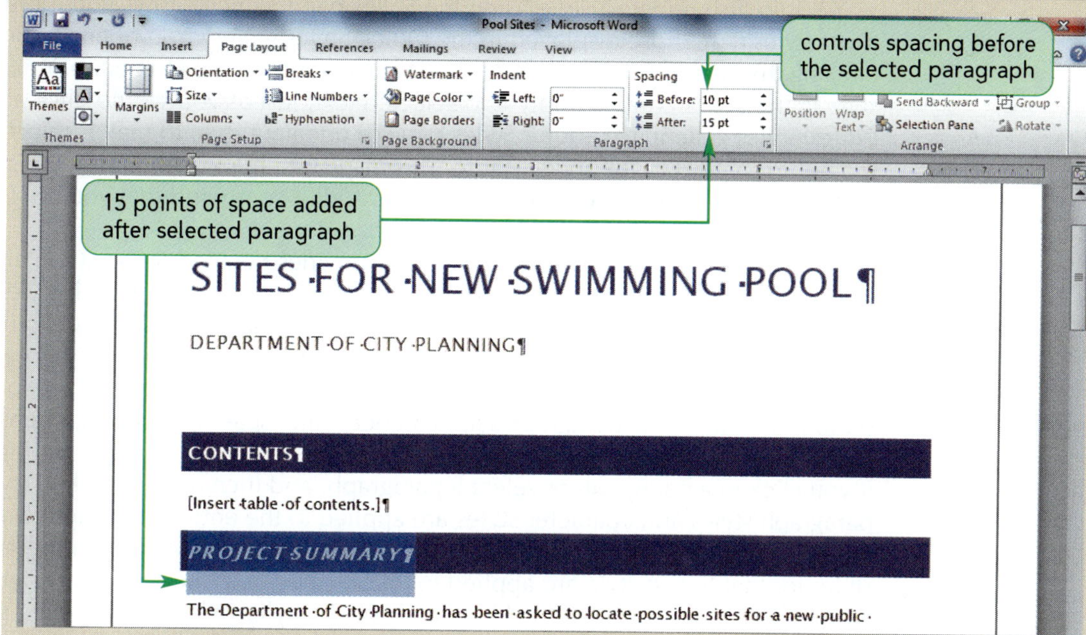


## Updating a Style

Now that the selected heading is formatted the way you want, you can update the Heading 1 style to match it. When updating a style, you need to decide whether you want to save the style to the current document or to the current template—that is, the template from which your document draws its default formatting settings. As you know, when you open a new blank document, it is based on the Normal template. In the case of Sam's Pool Site document, the current template is the Equity Report template. When you save a modified style to the current template, the modified version of the style appears in all new documents based on that template. Unless you have a very good reason for saving a modified style to the current template, you should save it to the current document instead.

INSIGHT

### *Modifying and Saving Styles to a Template*

Making changes to a template, especially to the Normal template, is not something you should do casually, because your changes will affect all future documents created from that template. Also, continually modifying or creating styles in the Normal template can result in a Quick Styles gallery that is disorganized, making it hard to find the styles you want. To avoid this problem, consider saving modified styles to the current document (rather than to the current template), and then saving the current document as a template. All future documents based on that template will contain your new styles. Meanwhile, the Normal template will remain unaffected by the new styles.

To update a style to match the currently selected text, you can right-click the style in the Quick Styles gallery and then click Update *Style* to Match Selection, where *Style* is the name of the style you want to update. For example, to update the Heading 1 style, you could right-click it and then click Update Heading 1 to Match Selection. This saves the updated style to the current document. To save a modified style to the current template, right-click the style, click Modify, and then, in the Modify Style dialog box, select the New documents based on this template option button.

You can also update a style using the Styles pane, which shows you more of the document styles than those displayed in the Quick Styles gallery. You open the Styles pane by clicking the Dialog Box Launcher in the Styles group on the Home tab. You can click a style in the Styles pane to apply it to selected text, just as you would click a style in the Quick Styles gallery. To use the Styles pane to update a style to match selected text, click the list arrow next to the style's name. This displays a menu containing the same Update *Style* to Match Selection command and the Modify command that you see when you right-click a style in the Quick Styles gallery.

The Styles pane can be useful because it provides detailed information about each style. In particular, it differentiates between character styles, paragraph styles, and linked styles. A **character style** contains formatting options that affect the appearance of individual characters, such as font style, font color, font size, bold, italics, and underline. A **paragraph style** contains all the character formatting options as well as formatting options that affect the paragraph's appearance—line spacing, text alignment, tab stops, and borders. A **linked style** contains both character and paragraph formatting options. If you click in a paragraph or select a paragraph, and then apply a linked style, both the paragraph styles and character styles are applied to the entire paragraph. If you apply a linked style to a selected word or group of words in a paragraph, then only the character styles for that linked style are applied to the selected text; the paragraph styles are not applied to the paragraph itself. All of the heading styles in Word are linked styles.

REFERENCE

*Modifying Styles Using the Style pane*

- In the document, select text formatted with the style you want to modify, and make the formatting changes you want to add to the style.
- In the Styles group on the Home tab, click the Dialog Box Launcher to open the Styles pane.
- With the text still selected in the document, move the mouse pointer over the style you want to modify in the Styles pane to display an arrow next to the style's name, and then click the arrow.
- To save the modified style to the current document, click Update *Style Name* to Match Selection (where *Style Name* is the name of the style you want to modify).
- To save the modified style to the current template, click Modify to open the Modify Style dialog box, click the New documents based on this template option button, and then click the OK button.

**To open the Styles pane and modify the Heading 1 style:**

1. Click the **Home** tab, and then, in the Styles group, click the **Dialog Box Launcher**. The Styles pane opens. It might be docked on the right side of the document window, or it might be floating over the document.

**TIP**

To change how the styles are displayed in the Styles pane, click the Options link in the bottom-right corner of the Styles pane to open the Style Pane Options dialog box.

2. If the Styles pane is not docked on the right side of the document window, double-click the title bar of the pane. The Styles pane attaches itself to the right side of the document window, and the document zoom adjusts so you can see the full width of the page next to the Styles pane. See Figure 5-14. The blue outline around the Heading 1 style in the Styles pane indicates that the currently selected text, the "Project Summary" heading, is formatted with the Heading 1 style. A paragraph symbol to the right of a style name indicates a paragraph style, a lowercase letter "a" indicates a character style, and a combination of both a paragraph symbol and a lowercase letter "a" indicates a linked style. You can display even more information about a style by moving the mouse pointer over the style name in the Styles pane.

**Figure 5-14** **Styles pane**

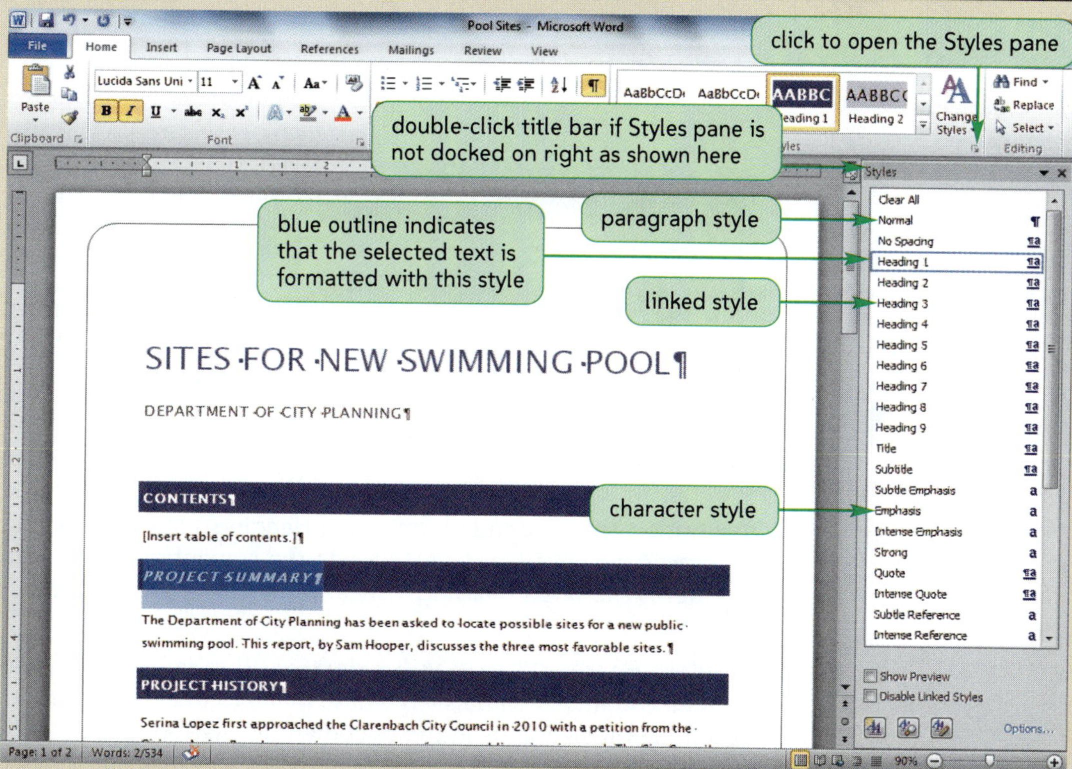


3. In the Styles pane, move the mouse pointer over **Heading 1**. An arrow next to the Heading 1 style name appears, and a ScreenTip with detailed information about the Heading 1 style opens below the style name. The information in the ScreenTip relates only to the formatting applied by default with the Heading 1 style; it makes no mention of italics, expanded character spacing, or the 15 points of space after the paragraph. Although you applied these formatting changes to the Project Summary heading, they are not yet part of the Heading 1 style.

4. Click the **Heading 1** arrow. A menu opens with options related to working with the Heading 1 style. See Figure 5-15.

**Figure 5-15** **Heading 1 style menu**

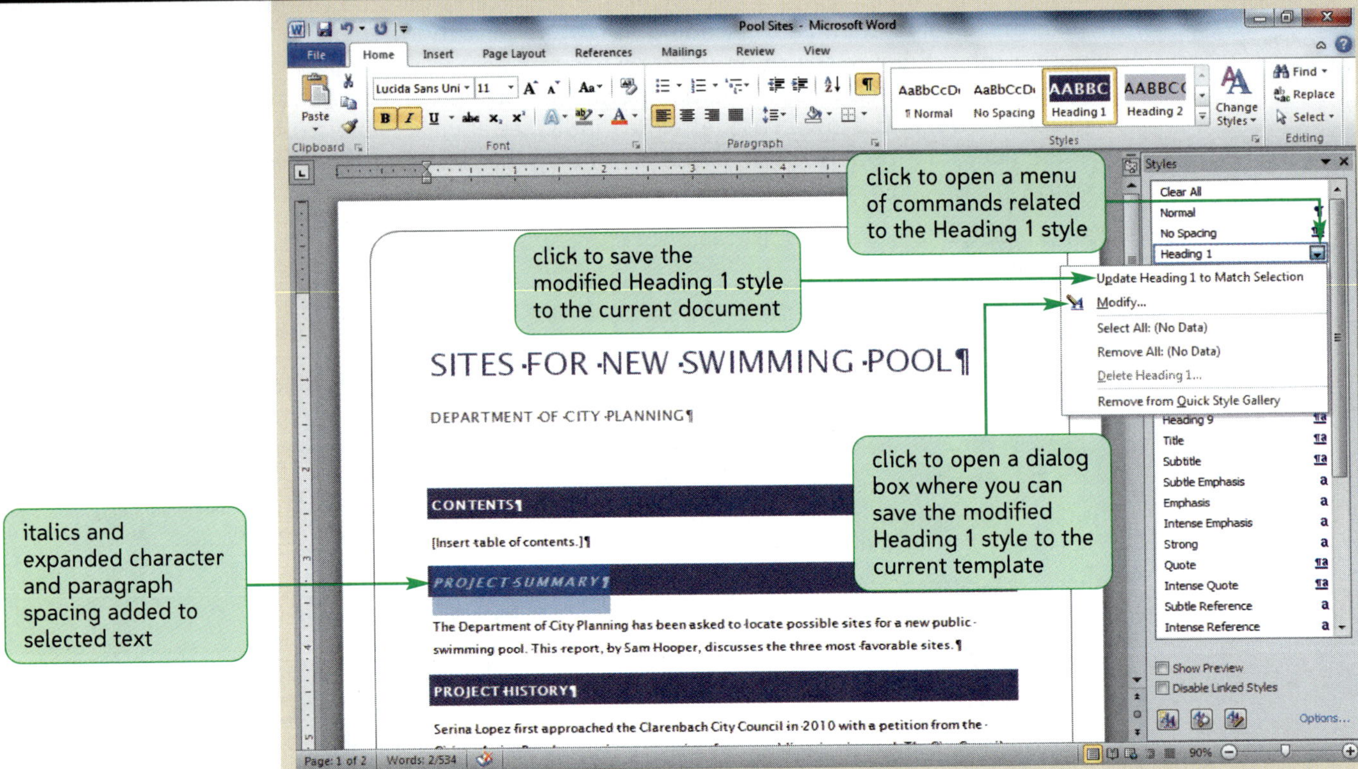


The first option on the menu modifies the Heading 1 style to match the selected text and saves the newly modified style to the current document. Sam wants to save the newly modified Heading 1 style to the current document, so you'll use the first option.

5. Click **Update Heading 1 to Match Selection**. The Heading 1 style changes to include all the changes Sam asked you to make to the Project Summary heading. As a result, all the headings in the document formatted in the Heading 1 style are now formatted with italics, expanded character spacing, and additional paragraph spacing.

6. In the Styles pane, click the **Close** button , and then save your work. The modified version of the Heading 1 style is saved along with the document. No other documents are affected by this change to the Heading 1 style.

You can also create a new style for a document, also from the Styles pane. You will do that in the next session.

REVIEW

## *Session 5.1 Quick Check*

1. What template is used when you create a new blank document?
2. Explain how to insert a Word file into a document.
3. What are the three main components of a document theme?
4. Explain how to save a new theme.
5. Explain how to select a new style set.
6. Explain how to display the dialog box tab where you can adjust the character spacing for selected text.
7. True or False. The Quick Styles gallery shows the same styles as the Styles pane.
8. Explain how to save a modified style to the current document using the Styles pane.

# SESSION 5.2 VISUAL OVERVIEW

You use the options in the Create New Style from Formatting dialog box to create a new style based on selected text.

You should give your new style a descriptive name.

By default, each new style is based on the style originally applied to the selected text.

You can use these options to add additional formatting to the new style.

The new style will consist of all the formatting applied to the selected text.

When creating a new style it's usually best to save the style only to the current document.

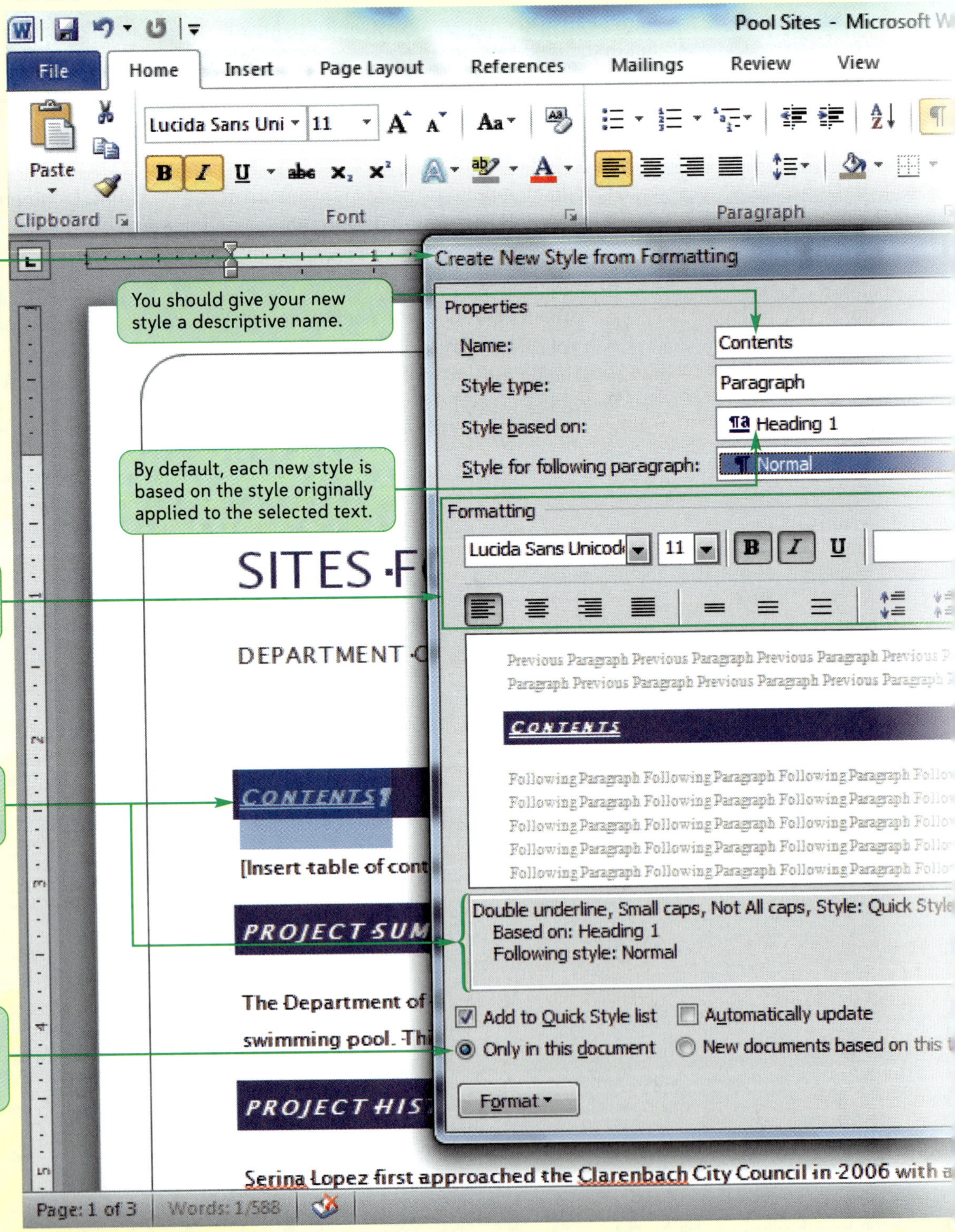

# CREATING A NEW STYLE

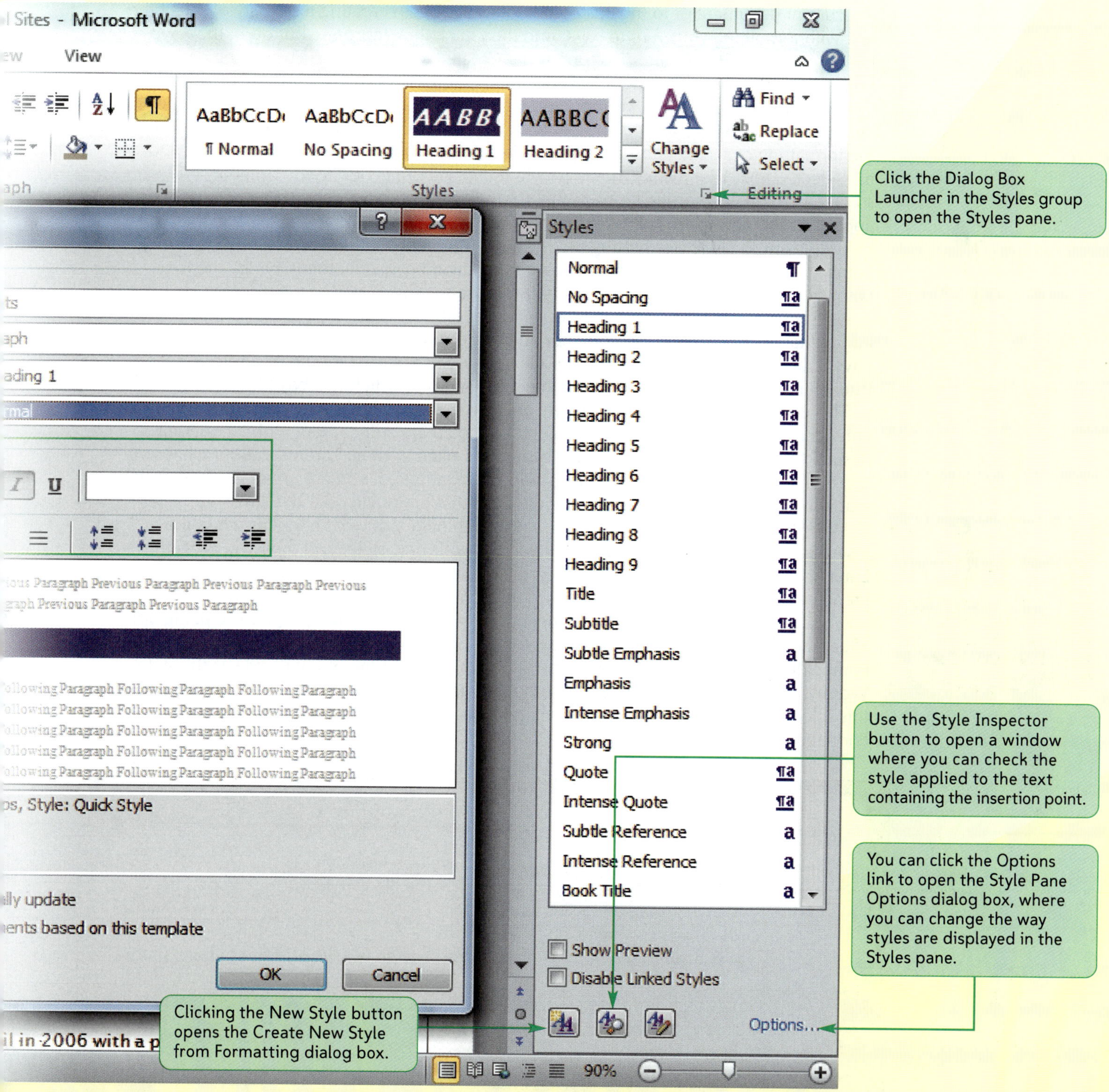

## Creating a New Style

Creating a new style is similar to the steps you followed in the previous session to modify a style, except that, instead of updating an existing style to match the formatting of selected text, you save the formatting of the selected text as a new style. As when modifying styles, when creating a new style you need to decide whether to save the style to the current document or to the current template. To begin creating a new style, select the text with formatting you want to save, and then click the New Style button in the lower-left corner of the Styles pane. This opens the Create New Style from Formatting dialog box, where you can assign the new style a name and adjust other settings.

Remember that all text in your document has a style applied to it, whether it is the default Normal style or a style you applied. When you create a new style based upon the formatting of selected text, the new style is based on the style originally applied to the selected text. That means the new style retains a connection to the original style, so that if you make modifications to the original style, these modifications will also be applied to the new style. For example, suppose you need to create a new style that will be used exclusively for formatting the heading "Budget" in all upcoming reports. You could start by selecting text formatted with the Heading 1 style, then change the font color of the selected text to purple, and then save the formatting of the selected text as a new style named "Budget." Later on, if you modify the Heading 1 style—perhaps by adding italics—the text in the document that is formatted with the Budget style will also have italics, because it is based on the Heading 1 style. Note that the opposite is not true: changes to the new style do *not* affect the style on which it is based.

This connection between a new style and the style on which it is based enforces a consistent look among styles, encouraging you to create a document with a coherent design. To take full advantage of this feature, you need to think carefully about what style you want to use as the basis for a new style. For example, if you are creating a new style that will be used as a heading, you should base that new style on a heading style.

**TIP**

To delete a new style, point to the style's name in the Styles pane, click the down arrow next to the style name, click Revert to *Style Name*, and then click Yes.

When creating a new style, you also need to think about what happens when the insertion point is in a paragraph formatted with your new style, and then you press the Enter key to start a new paragraph. With the default heading styles in Word, a new paragraph created in this way is formatted in the Normal style. That makes sense, because you typically only want to format a single paragraph with a heading style. The paragraph after a heading style is usually body text formatted in the Normal style. Unless you have compelling reason to do otherwise, you should also select the Normal style as the style Word will use to format a new paragraph following your new heading style. You make this selection using the Style for following paragraph box in the Create New Style from Formatting dialog box.

**REFERENCE**

### *Creating a New Style*

- Select text with the formatting you want to save as a new style.
- In the lower-left corner of the Styles pane, click the New Style button to open the Create New Style from Formatting dialog box.
- Type a name for the new style in the Name box.
- Verify that the Style based on box displays the style on which you want to base your new style.
- Click the Style for following paragraph arrow, and click Normal.
- To save the new style to the current document, verify that the Only in this document option button is selected.
- To save the style to the current template, click the New documents based on this template option button.
- Click the OK button.

Sam is ready for you to create a new style for the "Contents" heading. The new style will be based on the Heading 1 style. It will look just like the Heading 1 style, except that instead of formatting text in all capital letters, it will format text in smaller versions of capital letters known as **small caps**. Also, the new style will apply an underline.

**TIP**

To change the case of selected text, use the Change Case button in the Font group on the Home tab.

### To format the Contents heading with the options for the new style:

1. If you took a break after the last session, make sure the Pool Sites document is open in Print Layout view with the nonprinting characters and the ruler displayed.
2. Select the **Contents** heading. You use the Font dialog box to format text in small caps.
3. In the Font group on the Home tab, click the **Dialog Box Launcher** and then, in the Font dialog box, click the **Font** tab if necessary. In the Effects section, the All caps check box is currently selected. Instead of All caps (which formats text in regularly sized capital letters), you need to select Small caps.
4. In the Effects section, click the **Small caps** check box to add a check. The check is removed from the All caps check box.
5. Click the **Underline style** arrow, and click the **double underline** style. The Preview section of the Font dialog box displays a preview of the new formatting. See Figure 5-16.

**Figure 5-16** Formatting the Contents heading

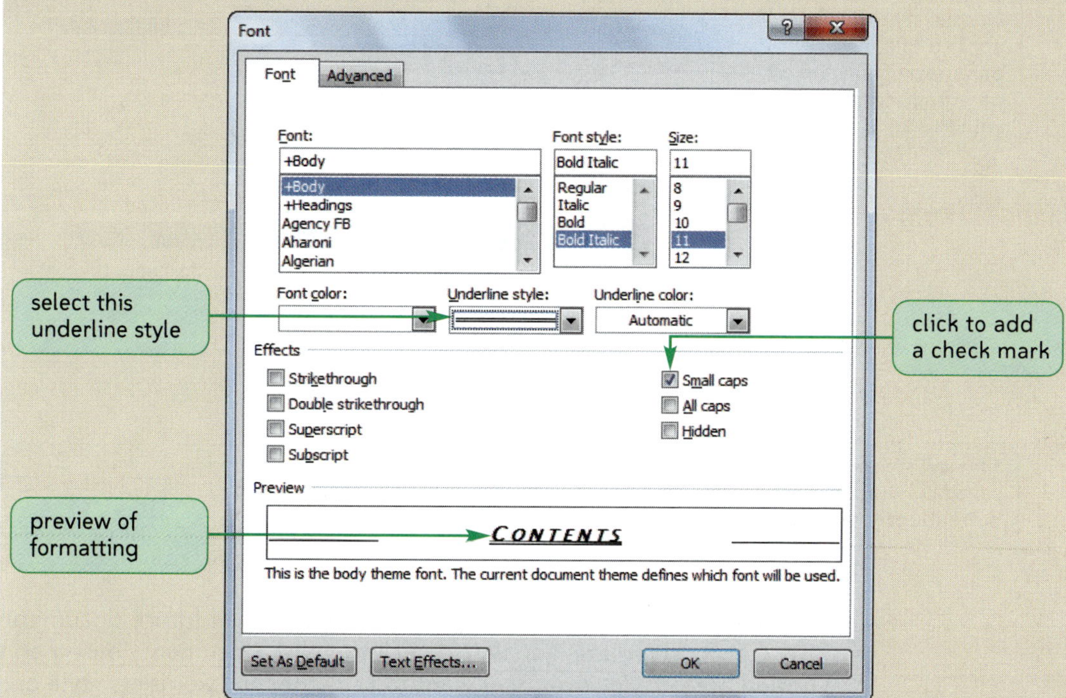


6. Click the **OK** button. The Font dialog box closes, and the "Contents" heading is formatted in small caps with a double underline.

Now that the text is formatted the way you want, you can save its formatting as a new style.

**To save the formatting of the Contents heading as a new style:**

1. In the Styles group, click the **Dialog Box Launcher** to open the Styles pane.
2. With the **Contents** heading still selected, click the **New Style** button in the lower-left corner of the Styles pane. The Create New Style from Formatting dialog box opens. A default name for the new style, "Style1," appears selected in the Name box. The name "Style1" also appears in the Style for following paragraph box.
3. Type **Contents**. The default style name is replaced with the new one. The Style based on box tells you that the new Contents style is based on the Heading 1 style, which is what you want. The Style for following paragraph box is now blank. You need to select the Normal style.
4. Click the **Style for following paragraph** arrow and then click **Normal**. See Figure 5-17.

**Figure 5-17 Creating a new style**

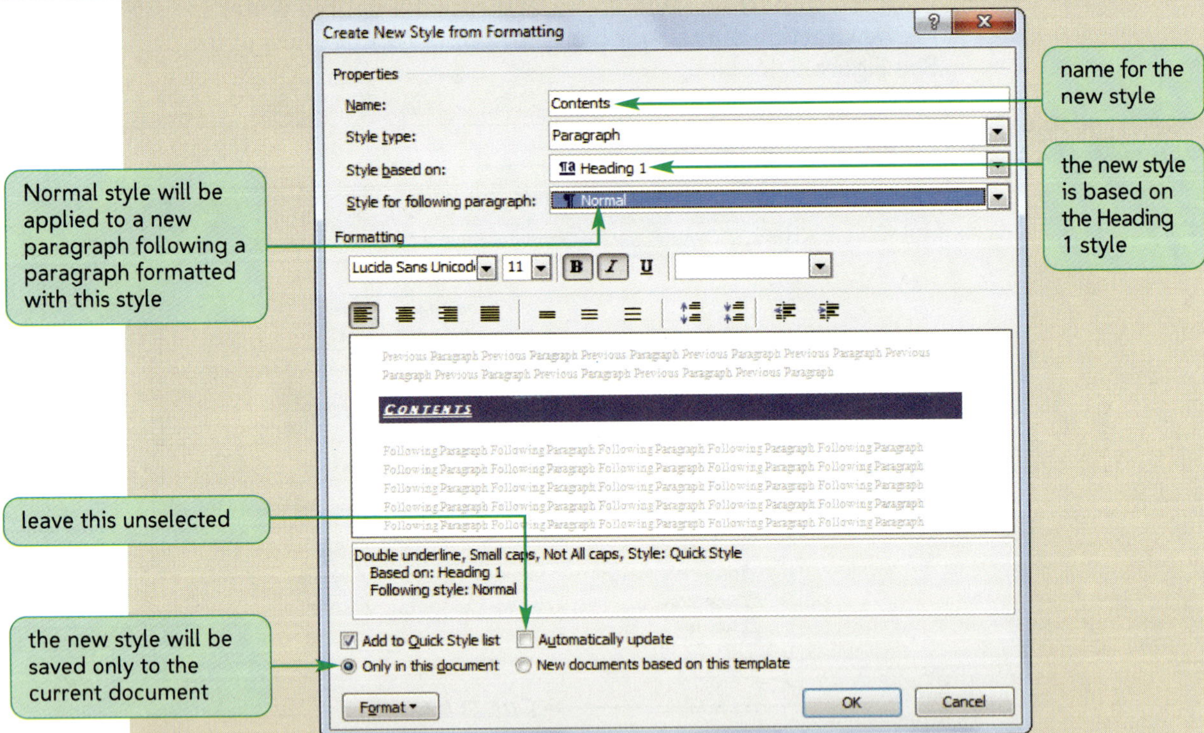


If you wanted to make the new style available to all future documents based on the current template, you would click the New documents based on this template option button. However, you want to save the new Contents style only to the current document, so you will accept that default setting, with the Only in this document option button selected. Note that, by default, the Automatically update check box is *not* selected. As a general rule, you should never select this check box, because it can produce unpredictable results in future documents based on the same template.

5. Click the **OK** button. The Create New Style from Formatting dialog box closes. The new Contents style is added to the Quick Styles gallery and to the Styles pane. If Sam needs to format additional headings with this new style, he can access it in either location. See Figure 5-18.

**Figure 5-18** **Contents style added to Quick Styles gallery and Styles pane**

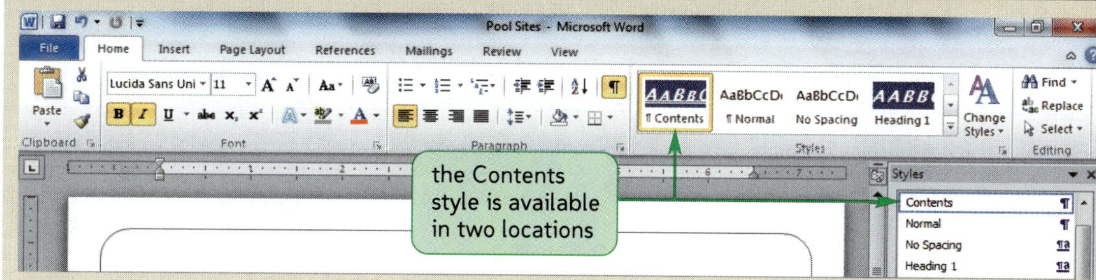


**TIP**

To remove a style from the Quick Styles gallery, right-click it in the Quick Styles gallery and then click Remove from Quick Style Gallery.

6. Save the document.

# Inspecting and Comparing Styles

If you create a document with many styles, it's easy to lose track of the style applied to each paragraph and the formatting associated with each style. To see a comparison of two styles, you can use the **Reveal Formatting pane**. To quickly determine which style is applied to a paragraph, you can click a paragraph, and then look to see which style is selected in the Styles Pane. However, if you need to check numerous paragraphs in a long document, it's easier to use the **Style Inspector pane**, which remains open while you scroll through the document and displays only the style for the paragraph that currently contains the insertion point.

Sam asks you to show him how to use the Style Inspector and the Reveal Formatting panes in order to learn more about the Normal and the Heading 2 styles.

### To use the Style Inspector and Reveal Formatting panes:

1. Click anywhere in the **[Insert table of contents.]** paragraph.
2. At the bottom of the Styles pane, click the **Style Inspector** button. The Style Inspector opens. The top pane displays the name of the style applied to the paragraph that currently contains the insertion point. See Figure 5-19.

**Figure 5-19** Style Inspector window

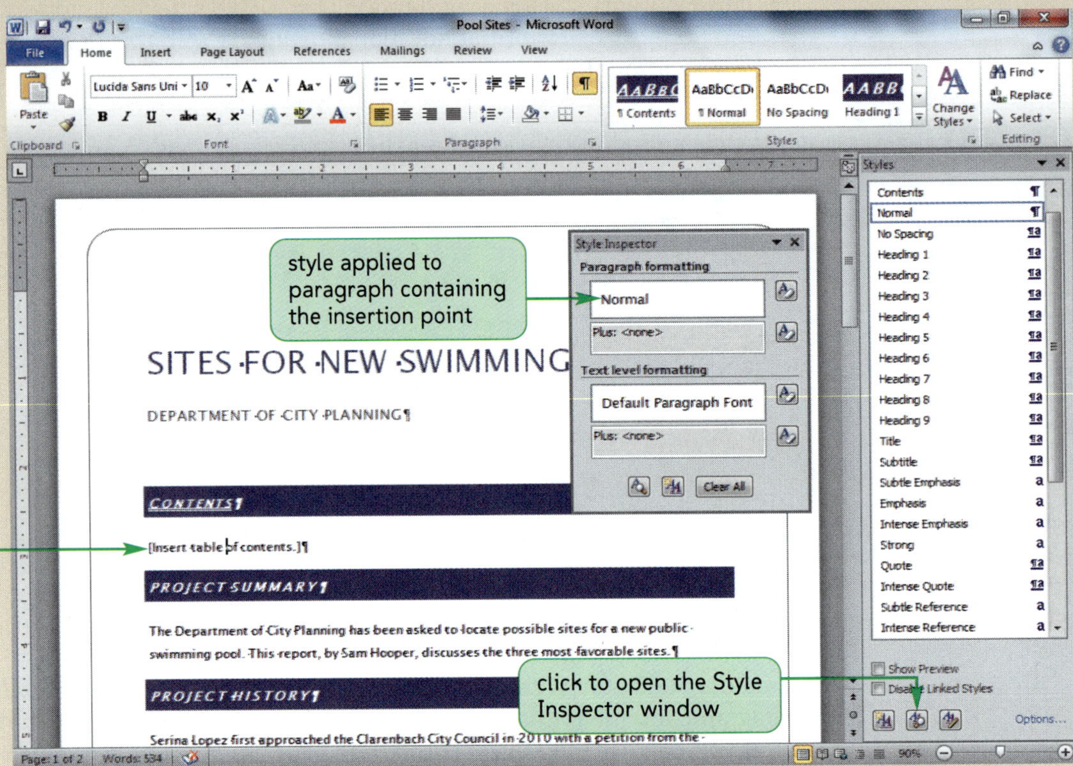


3. Press the **Ctrl+↓** keys. In the document, the insertion point moves down to the next paragraph. The Style Inspector tells you that this paragraph is formatted with the Heading 1 style.
4. Continue to use the **Ctrl+↓** key combination to move the insertion point down through the paragraphs of the document, observing the style names displayed in the Style Inspector.
5. Scroll up and select the paragraph **[Insert table of contents.]**, click the **Reveal Formatting** button at the bottom of the Style Inspector window to open the Reveal Formatting pane, and then close the Style Inspector. The Reveal Formatting pane displays detailed information about the Normal style, the style applied to the selected paragraph.
6. In the Reveal Formatting pane, click the **Compare to another selection** check box to select it. The options in the Reveal Formatting pane change to allow you to compare one style to another. Under Selected text, both text boxes display copies of the selected text, "[Insert a table of contents.]" This tells you that, currently, the style applied to the selected text (that is, the Normal style) is being compared to itself. Now you'll compare the Normal style to the Heading 2 style.
7. In the document, scroll down to page 2 and select the text **Villas Park**, which is formatted with the Heading 2 style. The text "Villas Park" appears in the Reveal Formatting pane, in the text box below "[Insert a table of contents.]" The Formatting differences section displays information about the styles applied to the two different text samples. The information in the Reveal Formatting pane contains a lot of detail. But, generally, if you see two settings separated by a hyphen and a greater than symbol, the item on the right relates to the text in the bottom box. For example, in the Font section, you see "10pt -> 11 pt." This tells you

**TIP**

Text formatted in a white font, such as the Contents heading, is not visible in the text boxes at the top of the Reveal Formatting pane. To use the Reveal Formatting pane with white text, temporarily format it in black.

that the item in the top text box, "[Insert a table of contents.]," is formatted in a 10-point font, whereas the item in the bottom text box, "Villas Park," is formatted in an 11-point font. See Figure 5-20.

**Figure 5-20** **Comparing two styles**

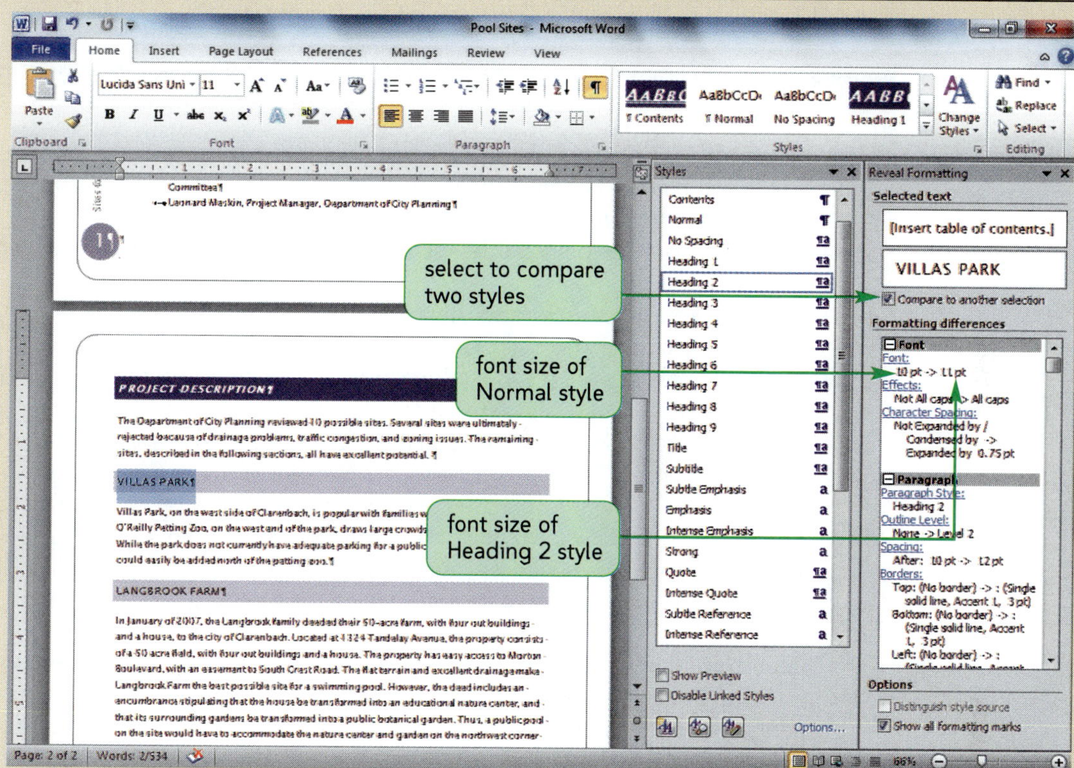


8. In the Reveal Formatting pane, click the **Close** button, and then click the **Close** button in the Styles pane.

You are finished formatting the Pool Sites report with themes and styles. Now Sam asks you to create a table of contents for the report.

# Creating a Table of Contents

You can use the Table of Contents button in the Table of Contents group on the References tab to generate a table of contents that includes any text to which you have applied heading styles. A table of contents is essentially an outline of the document. By default, Heading 1 text is aligned on the left, Heading 2 text is indented slightly to the right below the Heading 1 paragraphs, Heading 3 text is indented slightly to the right below the Heading 2 paragraphs, and so on.

The page numbers and headings in a table of contents in Word are hyperlinks that you can click to jump to a particular part of the document. If you add or delete a heading in the document, or add body text that causes one or more headings to move to a new page, you can quickly update the table of contents by clicking the Update Table button in the Table of Contents group on the References tab. To add text that is not formatted as a heading to the table of contents, you can select the text, format it as a heading, and then update the table of contents. However, if you already have the References tab displayed, it's more efficient to select the text in the document, use the Add Text button in the Table of Contents group to add a Heading style, and then update the table of contents.

When inserting a table of contents, you can insert one of the predesigned formats available from the Table of Contents button in the Table of Contents group on the References tab. If you prefer to select from more options, you can open the Table of Contents dialog box. From within the Table of Contents dialog box, you can adjust the level assigned to each style within the table of contents.

REFERENCE

### *Creating a Table of Contents*

- Apply the built-in heading styles, such as Heading 1, Heading 2, and Heading 3, to the appropriate text in the document.
- Move the insertion point to the location in the document where you want to insert the table of contents.
- Click the References tab, and then click the Table of Contents button in the Table of Contents group.
- To insert a predesigned table of contents, click one of the Automatic table of contents styles in the Table of Contents menu.
- To open a dialog box where you can choose from a variety of table of contents settings, click Insert Table of Contents to open the Table of Contents dialog box. Click the Formats arrow and select a style, change the Show levels setting to the number of heading levels you want to include in the table of contents, verify that the Show page numbers check box is selected, and then click the OK button.

The current draft of Sam's report is fairly short, but the final document will be much longer. He asks you to create a table of contents for the report now, just after the "Contents" heading. Then, as Sam adds sections to the report, he can update the table of contents.

### To insert the table of contents into the Pool Sites document:

1. On page 1, below the heading "Contents," delete the placeholder text **[Insert a table of contents.]**. Do not delete the paragraph mark after the placeholder text. Your insertion point should now be located in the blank paragraph between the "Contents" heading and the "Project Summary" heading.

**TIP**

To delete a table of contents, click the Table of Contents button, and then click Remove Table of Contents.

2. Click the **References** tab, and then click the **Table of Contents** button in the Table of Contents group. The Table of Contents menu opens, displaying a gallery of table of contents formats. See Figure 5-21. The Automatic options insert a table of contents made up of the first three levels of document headings, in a predefined format. Each of the Automatic options also includes a heading for the Table of Contents. Because Sam's document already contains the heading "Contents," you do not want to use either of the Automatic options. The Manual option is useful only in specialized situations, when you need to type the table of contents yourself—for example, when creating a book manuscript for an academic publisher. Instead of using one of the Automatic options, you will use the Insert Table of Contents command to open the Table of Contents dialog box.

Figure 5-21 Table of Contents gallery

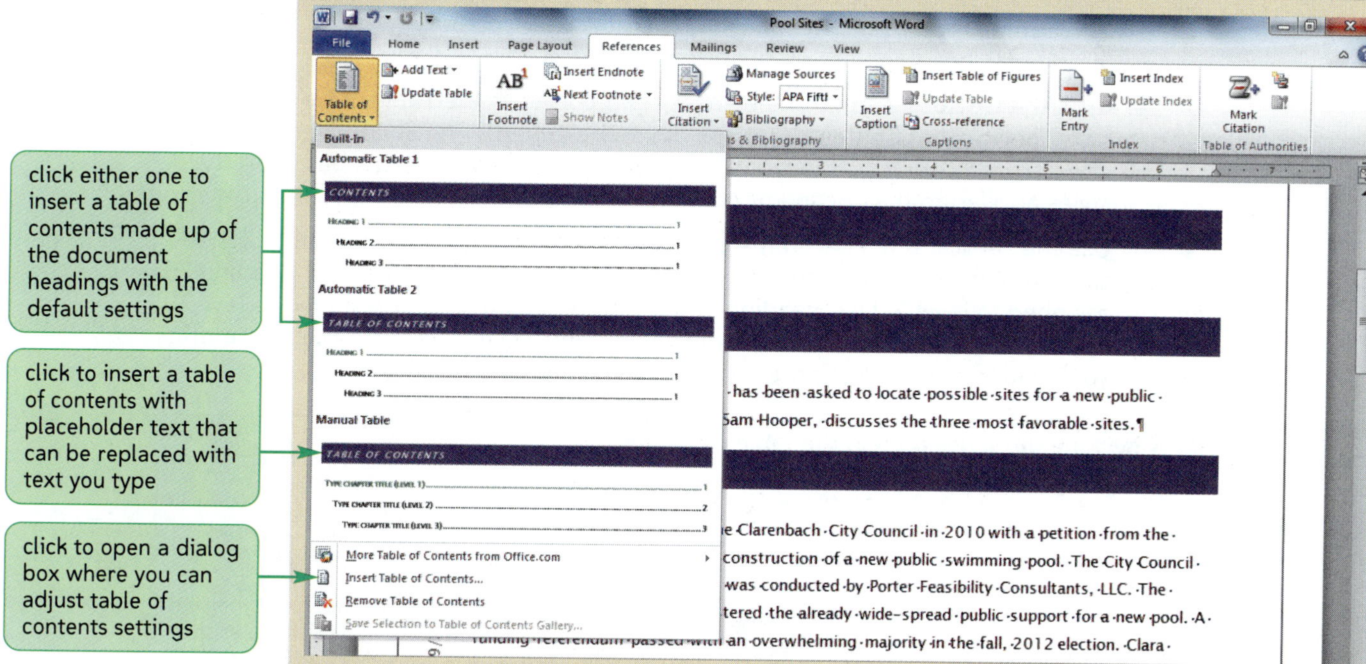


**3.** Below the Table of Contents gallery, click **Insert Table of Contents**. The Table of Contents dialog box opens, with the Table of Contents tab displayed. See Figure 5-22. The Print Preview on the left shows the appearance of the table of contents in a Print Layout view, while the Web Preview on the right shows what the table of contents would look like if you displayed it in Web Layout view. The Formats box shows the default option, From template, which applies the table of contents styles provided by the document's template.

Figure 5-22 Table of Contents dialog box

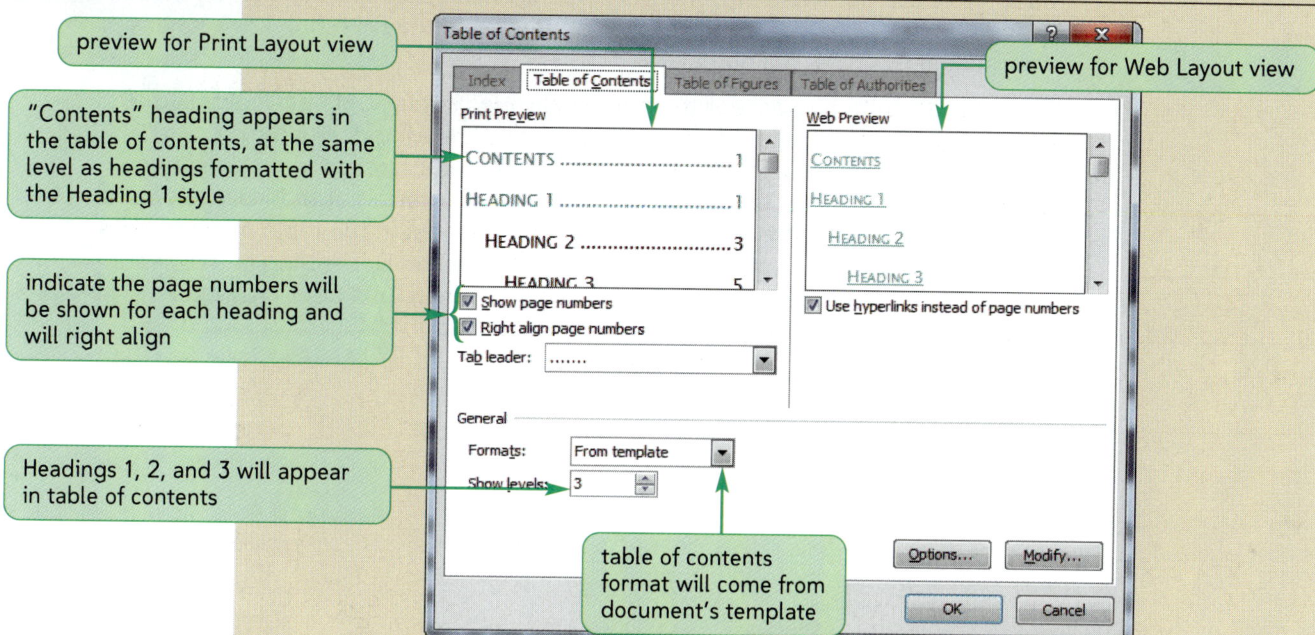

In the Print Preview section, notice that the Contents heading style, applied to the "Contents" heading you created in Session 5.1, is treated in the table of contents at the same level as the Heading 1 style. However, you don't want to include the "Contents" heading in the table of contents itself.

4. Click the **Options** button in the lower-right corner of the Table of Contents dialog box. The Table of Contents Options dialog box opens. The Styles check box is selected, indicating that Word will compile the table of contents based on the styles applied to the document headings.
5. Use the vertical scroll bar in the TOC level list to see the priority level assigned to each of the document styles. Heading 1 is assigned to level 1, and Heading 2 is assigned to level 2. Like Heading 1, the Contents style is also assigned to level 1. To remove any text formatted with the Contents style from the table of contents, you need to delete the Contents style level number. See Figure 5-23.

**Figure 5-23** **Checking the styles used in the table of contents**

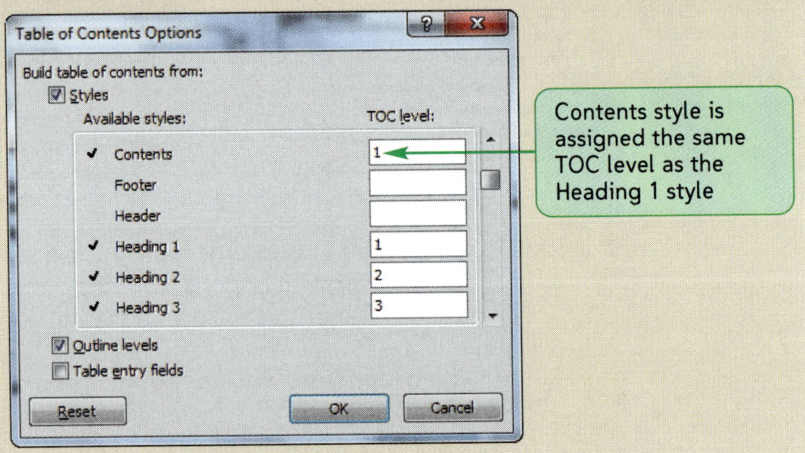


6. Delete the **1** from the TOC level box for the Contents style, and then click the **OK** button to close the Table of Contents Options dialog box. The "Contents" heading no longer appears in the sample table of contents in the Print Preview sections of the Table of Contents dialog box.
7. Click the **OK** button to accept the default settings in the Table of Contents dialog box. Word searches for text formatted with styles Heading 1, Heading 2, and Heading 3, and then places those headings and their corresponding page numbers in a table of contents. The table of contents is inserted at the insertion point, which appears below the "Contents" heading. The text in the table of contents is formatted with the TOC styles for the current template. Depending on how your computer is set up, the table of contents might appear on a light gray background. See Figure 5-24.

Figure 5-24 Table of contents inserted into document

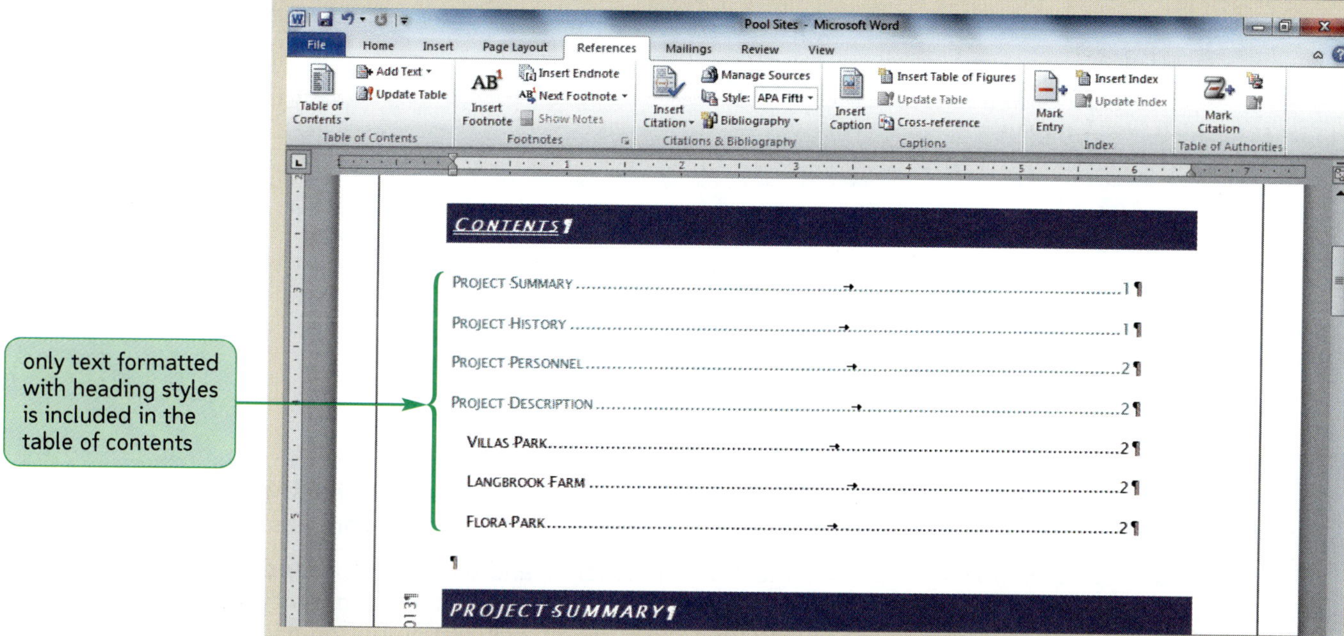


You can check the hyperlink formatting to make sure the headings really do function as links.

8. Press and hold the **Ctrl** key while you click **LANGBROOK FARM** in the table of contents. The insertion point moves to the beginning of the "Langbrook Farm" heading near the bottom of page 2.
9. Save the document.

Sam just finished compiling information on another potential pool site. He has the information saved as a Word file, which he asks you to insert at the end of the Pool Sites document. You will do this next, and then add the new heading to the table of contents.

## To add a section to the Pool Sites document and then update the table of contents:

1. Press the **Ctrl+End** keys to move the insertion point to the end of the document, and then insert the file **Willow Grove** from the Word5\Tutorial folder included with your Data Files.
2. Select the paragraph **Willow Grove**.
3. Click the **References** tab, and then click the **Add Text** button in the Table of Contents group. The Add Text menu opens. See Figure 5-25.

**Figure 5-25** **Add Text menu**

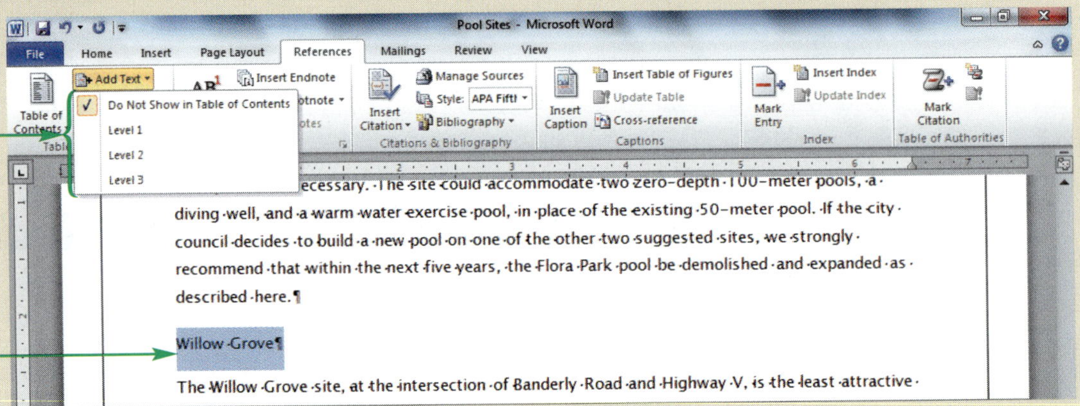


Add Text menu

selected text

**TIP**

You can also format new text with a heading style in the Quick Styles gallery, and then update the table of contents.

4. Click **Level 2**. The text is formatted with the Heading 2 style, to match the headings for the sections about the other possible pool sites. Now that the text is formatted with a heading style, you can update the table of contents.
5. Scroll up so you can see the table of contents, and then click the **Update Table** button in the Table of Contents group. The Update Table of Contents dialog box opens. You can use the Update page numbers only option button if you don't want to update the headings in the table of contents. In this case, you have added a new section, so you want to update the entire table of contents.
6. Click the **Update entire table** option button to select it, and then click the **OK** button. The table of contents is updated to include the Willow Grove heading. See Figure 5-26.

**Figure 5-26** **Updated table of contents**

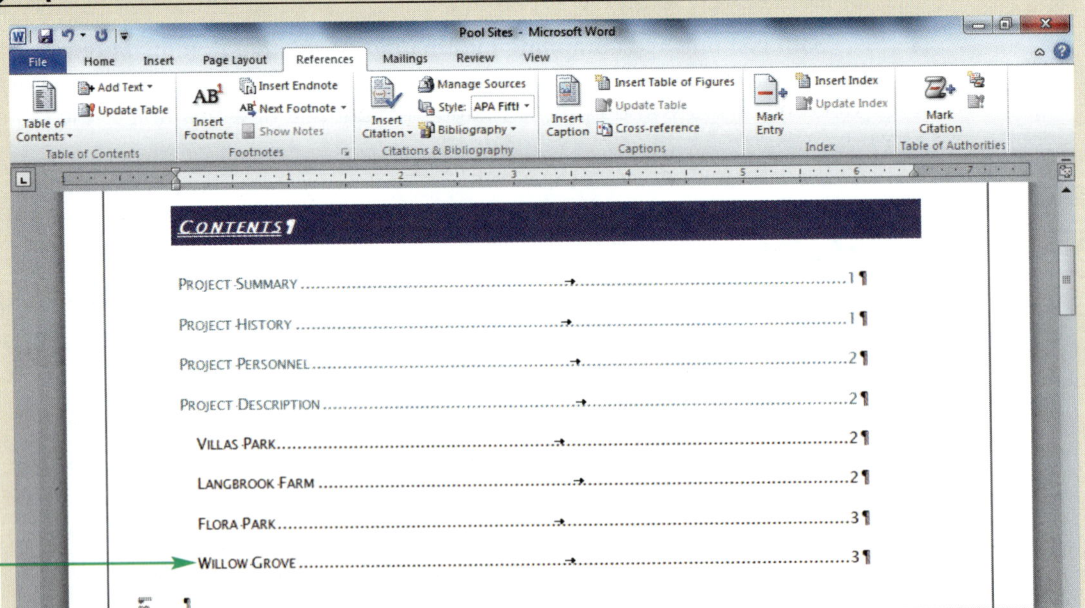


new heading

7. Save your work.

Now Sam needs you to perform a few research tasks, starting with looking up a definition and a synonym.

## Using the Research Task Pane

You can use the **Research task pane** to look up dictionary definitions in the Encarta Dictionary, which is installed with Word, and to search for synonyms in Word's thesaurus. In addition, you can search for information in online general interest encyclopedias and in sources devoted to particular topics, such as business and finance. If you prefer, you can use Microsoft's Bing search engine to search the entire Web from the Research task pane. The Research and Thesaurus buttons in the Proofing group both open the Research task pane. However, it's easiest to right-click the word or the selected phrase you want to look up, and then select an option on the shortcut menu.

First, Sam wants to make sure he understands the term *encumbrance*, in the paragraph at the bottom of page 2.

### To look up a definition in the Research task pane:

1. Find the word **encumbrance** in the last paragraph on Page 2, right-click **encumbrance**, and then point to **Look Up** on the shortcut menu. A submenu of research sources opens, as shown in Figure 5-27. Sam would like to look up the term "encumbrance" in Word's Encarta Dictionary.

Figure 5-27 **Look Up command in shortcut menu**

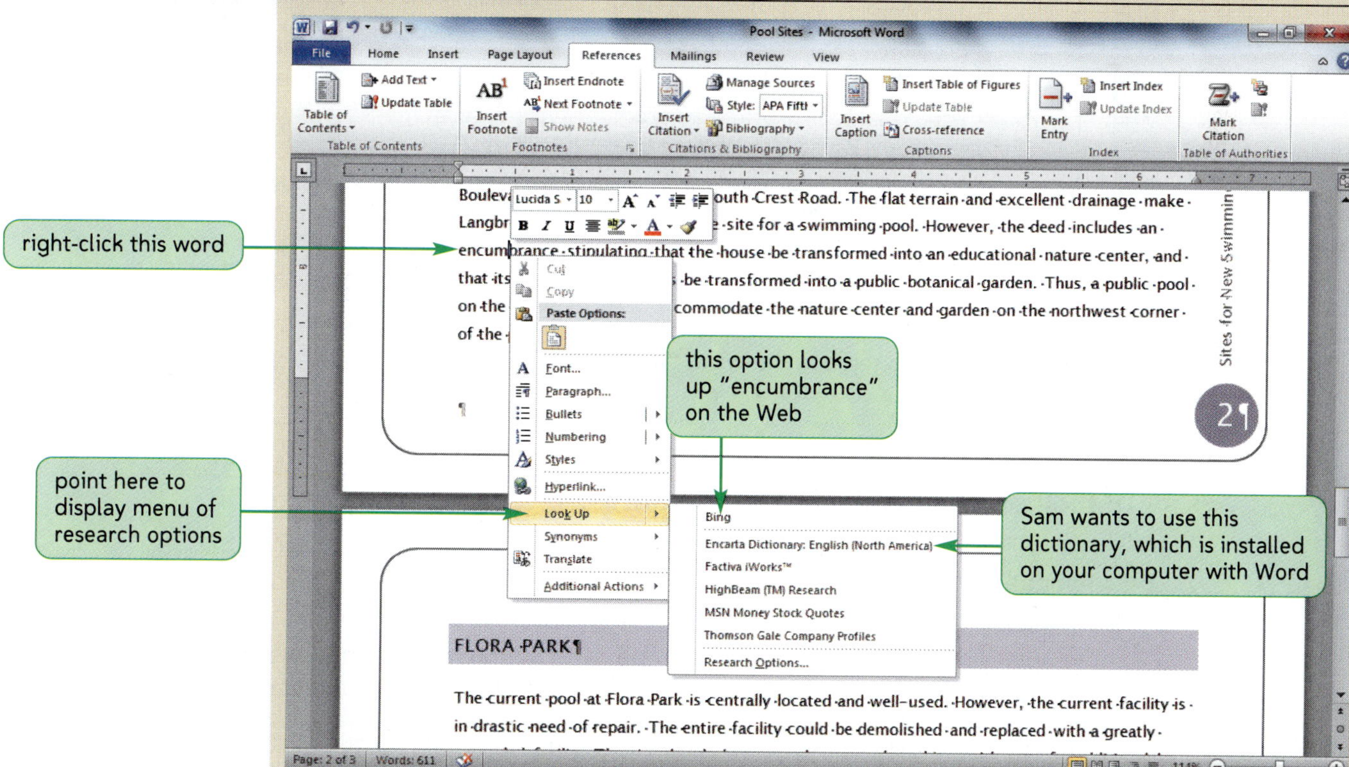

2. Click **Encarta Dictionary: English (North America)**. The Research task pane opens on the right side of the document window, displaying two definitions for the noun *encumbrance*. Definition 2, a "burden or claim on property" is the relevant definition in this case. See Figure 5-28. If you wanted to copy this definition to the Clipboard so you could use it in a document, you could right-click it in the Research task pane and then click Copy. Sam doesn't need you to do that in this case, however.

**Figure 5-28** **Definitions displayed in the Research task pane**

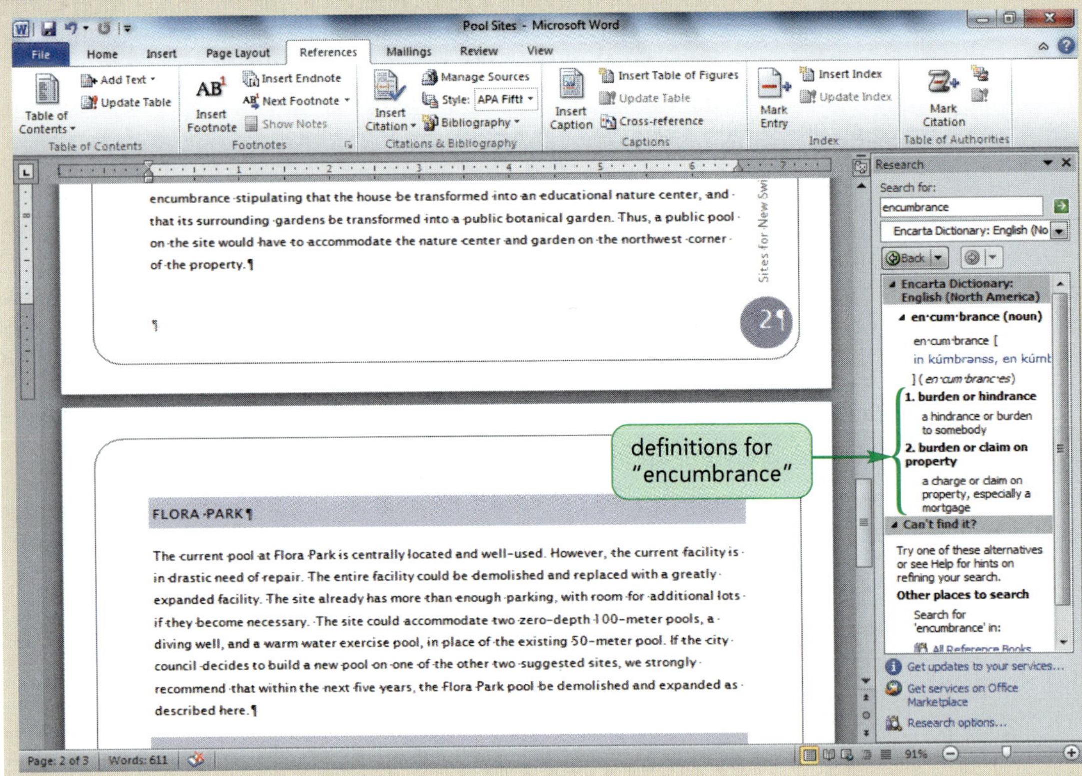


Next, Sam wants to replace the word "favorable" in the Project Summary section with a synonym.

## To look up a synonym in the thesaurus:

1. In the document, scroll up to display the "Project Summary" section on the first page.
2. In the last sentence of the "Project Summary" section, right-click the word **favorable** to open the shortcut menu, and then point to **Synonyms**. A menu of synonyms for "favorable" opens. See Figure 5-29. You can click any of the synonyms on the shortcut menu to insert it in the document as a replacement for "favorable." To display a more complete list of synonyms in the Research task pane, you could click Thesaurus at the bottom of the menu of synonyms. Sam likes the synonym "promising" on the shortcut menu, so there's no need to display more synonyms in the Research task pane.

Figure 5-29 Synonyms for "favorable"

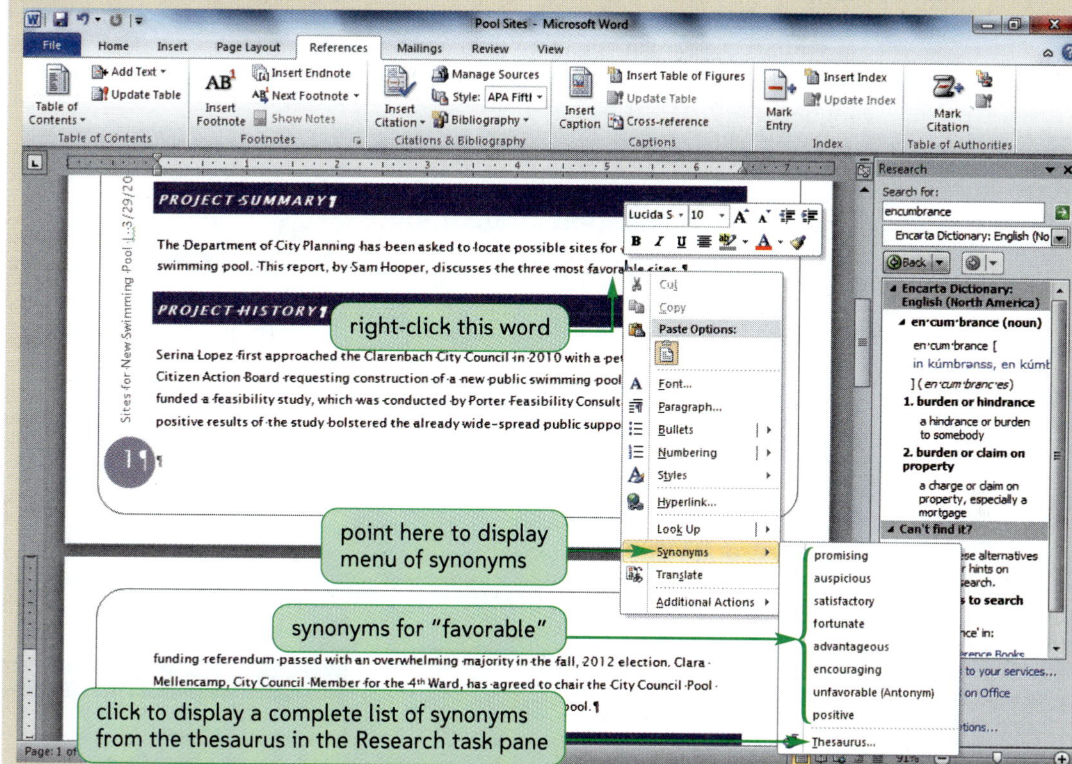


3. Click **promising**. The shortcut menus close and the word "promising" is inserted in the document, as a replacement for "favorable."
4. Close the Research task pane, and then save the document.

Next, Sam needs to view a Spanish translation of part of the document.

# Translating Text

The Translate button in the Language group on the Review tab offers three options for translating text into other languages. The Translate Document option sends your entire document to the Microsoft Translator Web site, which then displays your original document in a browser, side-by-side with the translated version. The Translate Selected Text option opens the Research task pane (if it is not already open), where you can select the language you want to translate your text into, and then read the translation in the Research task pane. The Mini Translator option opens a small window that displays a translation when you point to selected text in your document.

Before you can use the Translate Document option or the Mini Translator, you need to select the original language and the translation language. To do that, you click the Choose Translation Language command on the Translate menu to open the Translation Language Options dialog box. This dialog box includes two sections, one for the Translate Document option, and one for the Mini Translator, where you can select the language into which you want to translate the current text.

As you use Word's translation tools, keep in mind that the translations are generated by computer, so they are not necessarily perfect. That is, they might not sound exactly right to a native speaker. After you translate all or part of a document, make sure to have an expert in the language review the translation and make any necessary corrections.

Sam plans to distribute Spanish versions of his Pool Site report to the organization that provided a major donation for the new pool, the Association of Latino Businesses. He will ask a Spanish-speaking colleague to help him prepare a complete translation. For now, he wants to try out the translation tools. First you will select the translation languages.

## To select a translation language:

1. Click the **Review** tab, and then click the **Translate** button in the Language group. The Translate menu opens. You might see translation languages specified in brackets next to some of these options or you might not. See Figure 5-30.

**Figure 5-30** Translate menu

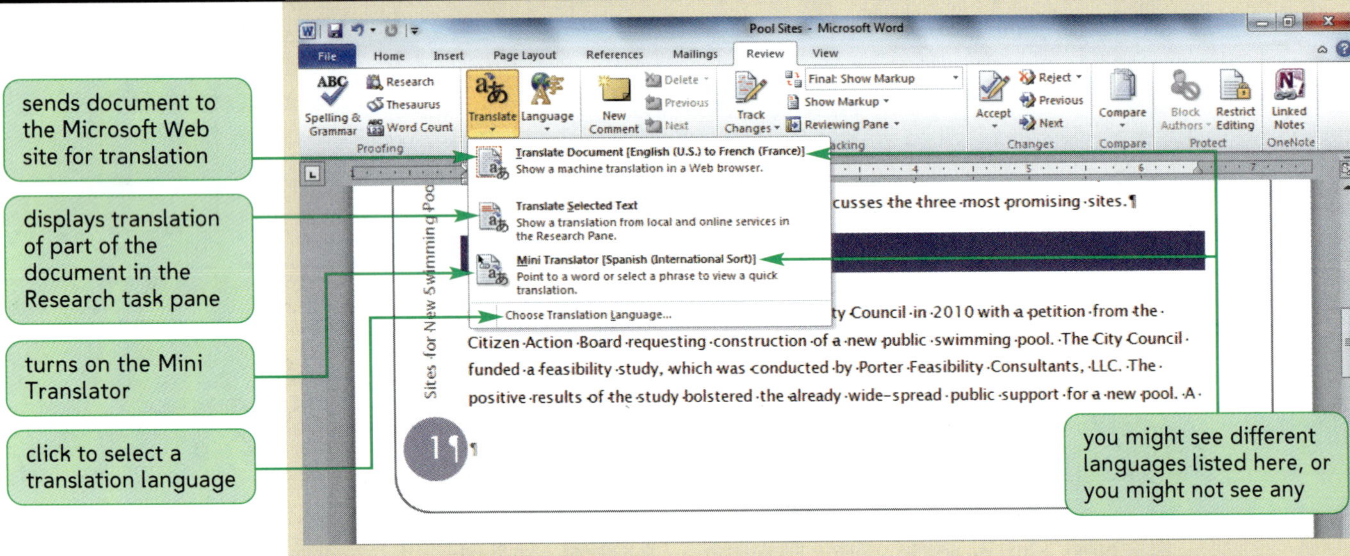


2. Click **Choose Translation Language**. The Translation Language Options dialog box opens. You can use the top box to select the language that the Mini Translator will translate the current document into. You can use the bottom two boxes to select the languages you want to translate to and from when using the Translate Document option on the Translate menu.
3. In the Choose Mini Translator language section, click the **Translate to** arrow to display a list of languages, scroll down the list if necessary, and then, if necessary, click **Spanish (International Sort)**.
4. In the Choose document translation languages section, click the **Translate from** arrow, select **English (U.S.)**, if necessary, click the **Translate to** arrow, and then click **Spanish (International Sort)**, if necessary. See Figure 5-31.

**Figure 5-31** Selecting the translation language for the Mini Translator

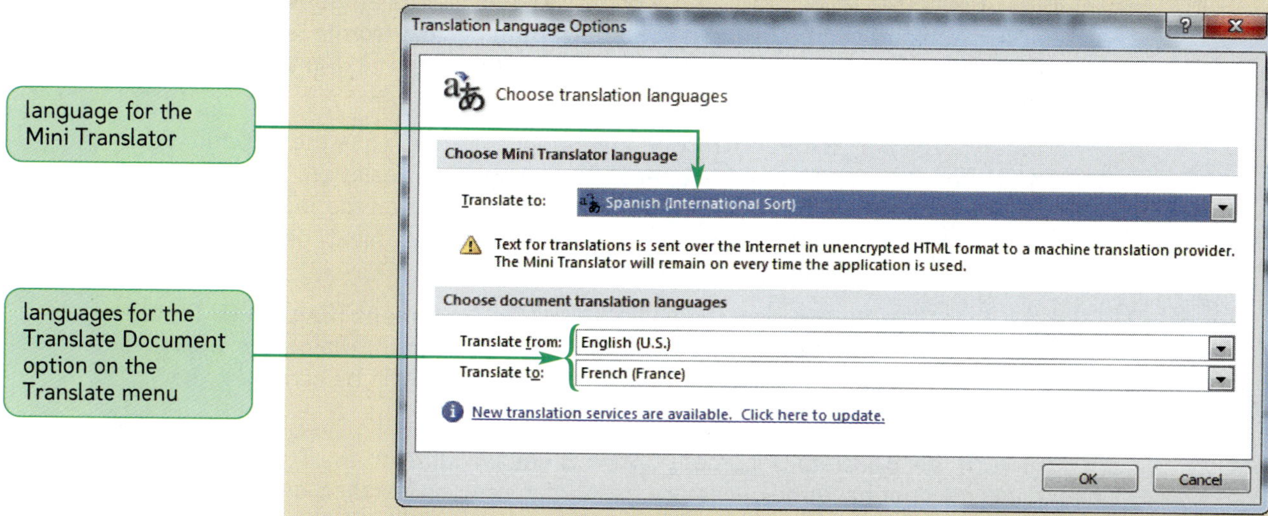


5. Click the **OK** button to close the dialog box and return to the document.

Once you have selected a translation language, you can begin translating text in your document. Next you will start the Mini Translator and translate some text.

*Note*: The following steps require an Internet connection. If your computer is not connected to the Internet, read the following steps but do not perform them.

### To use the translator to translate portions of the Pool Sites document:

1. In the Language group, click the **Translate** button, and then click **Mini Translator [Spanish (International Sort)]**. The Translate menu closes. To display the Mini Translator, you need to point to a word or a selected phrase.
2. In the "Project Summary" section, select the sentence that begins **The Department of City Planning...**
3. Position the mouse pointer over the selected text. A faint image of the Mini Translator appears.
4. Move the mouse pointer down or up over the Mini Translator window to display it fully. See Figure 5-32. If your computer has speakers installed, you can click the Mini Translator's Play button to hear the selected text read aloud.

**TIP**

To display a translation of a single word, click in the word and then use the mouse pointer to display the Mini Translator.

**Figure 5-32** Mini Translator window

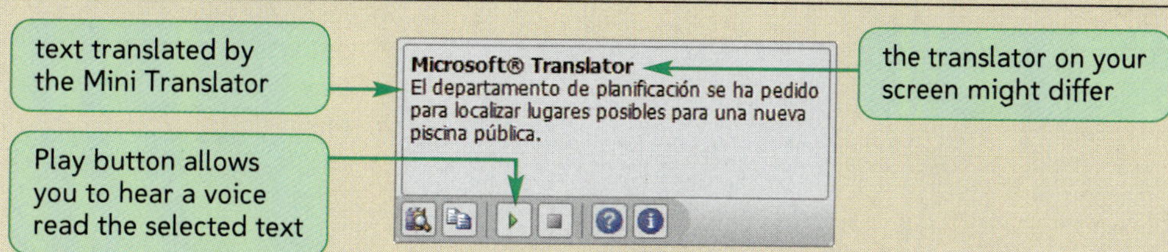

5. Click the **Play** button. If your computer has speakers installed, you hear a computer-generated voice reading the English sentence. The ability to hear a sentence read aloud can be useful if you are translating text from a language you don't understand very well, and you want to listen to the text in the original language.
6. If necessary, redisplay the Mini Translator window, and then click the **Expand** button. The Research task pane opens, displaying the translation. To replace the selected text with a copy of the translation, you could click the Insert button. However, Sam has no need for a copy of the translation now. Next, he wants to review a complete translation of the document.
7. Click the **Translate** button, and then click **Translate Document [English (U.S.) to Spanish (International Sort)]**. The Translate Whole Document dialog box opens. It displays a message explaining that the entire document will be sent over the Web to a translation service.

   **Trouble?** If the Translate Document option is not available on the Translate menu, you may not have the necessary translation options installed on your computer. In that case, read but do not attempt to complete Steps 7 through 9.
8. Click the **Send** button. Your computer's Web browser opens, displaying the original English document side-by-side with a Spanish translation. See Figure 5-33.

**Figure 5-33** Spanish translation side-by-side with original English text

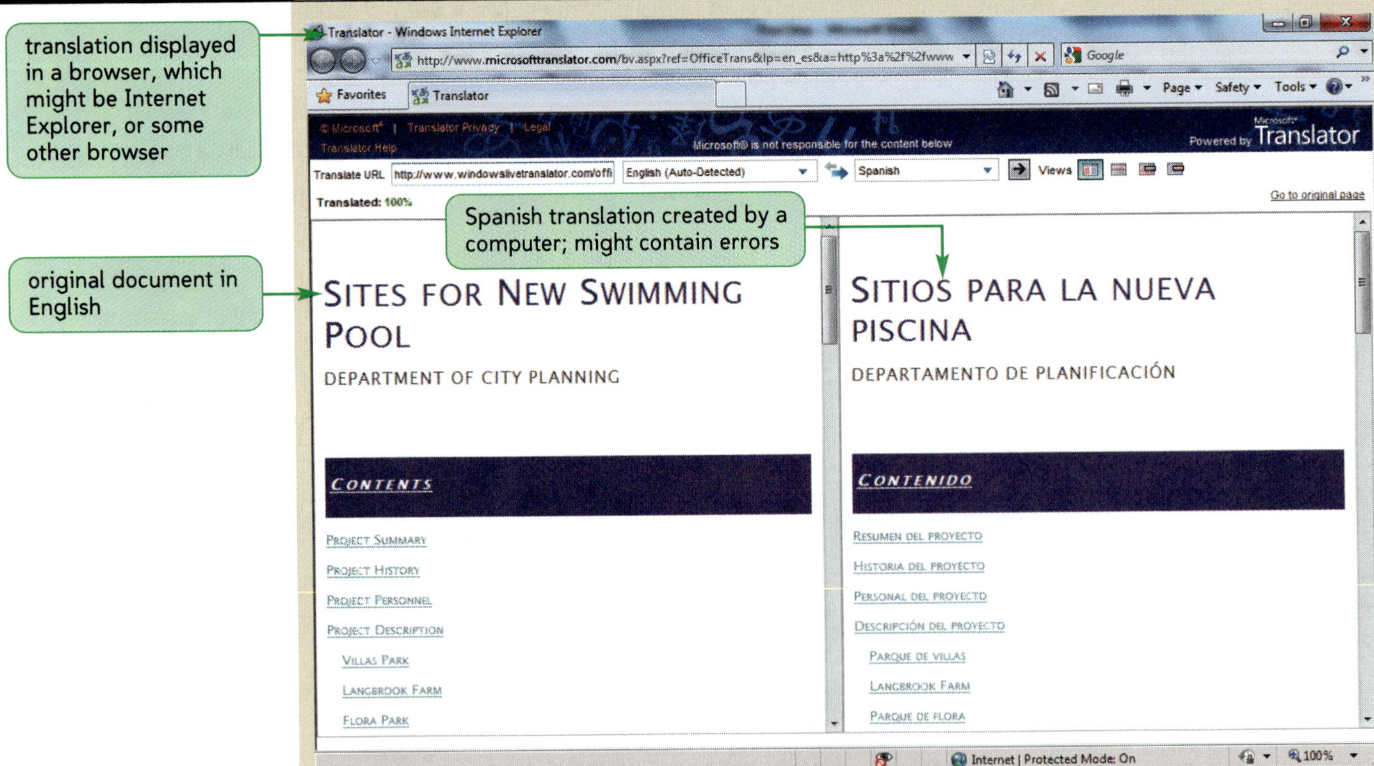

9. Close the browser window. You no longer need the Mini Translator, so you should turn it off.
10. In the Language group, click the **Translate** button, and then click **Mini Translator [Spanish (International Sort)]** to turn off the Mini Translator.

The Mini Translator will continue to appear and translate text until you turn it off.

11. Close the Research task pane, deselect the text, and then save your work.

You are finished working on the Pool Sites document. Sam thinks the document looks great, and would like to save it as a template to use for future department reports.

## Saving a Document as a Template

If you will frequently need to create a particular type of document, it's a good idea to create your own template for that type of document. In this case, Sam wants to create a template that will be used for all reports issued by the Department of City Planning. When creating a template, you can save it to any folder on your computer. However, if you save it to the Templates folder that is installed with Word, you can easily open the template later by clicking the My templates option on the New tab in Backstage view.

REFERENCE

*Saving a Document as a Template*

- Click the File tab, and then click Save As to open the Save As dialog box.
- Click the Save as type arrow, and then click Word Template.
- Navigate to the folder in which you want to save the template. To save the template to the Templates folder that is installed with Word, click the Templates folder in the Navigation pane of the Save As dialog box.
- In the File name box, type a name for the template.
- Click the Save button.

You will save the new template in the Word5\Tutorial folder, so that you can easily submit the completed tutorial files to your instructor.

**To save the Pool Sites document as a new template:**

1. Save the Pool Sites document to ensure that you have saved your most recent work.
2. Click the **File** tab, and then click **Save As**. The Save As dialog box opens.
3. Click the **Save as type** arrow, and then click **Word Template**.
4. If necessary, navigate to the Word5\Tutorial folder included with your Data Files. Next you'll type the new filename using "DCP," the acronym for "Department of City Planning."
5. Delete the default filename in the File name box, and then type **DCP Report**. See Figure 5-34.

**Figure 5-34** Saving a document as a template

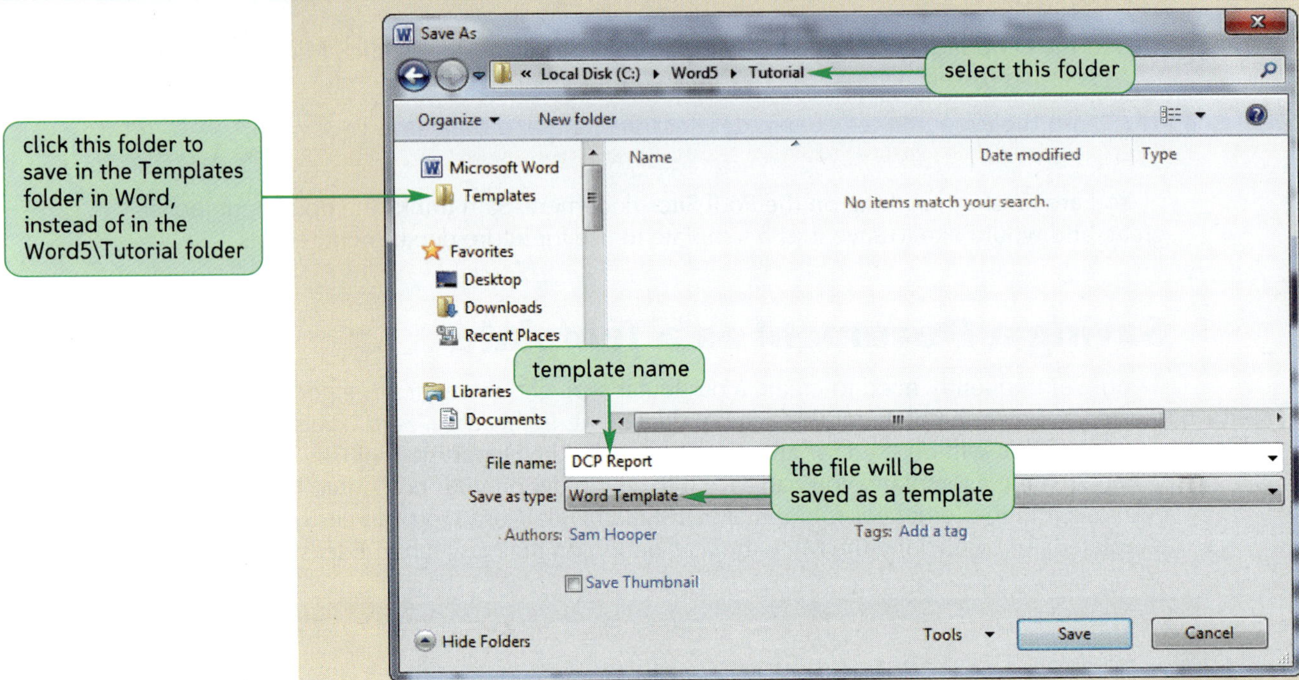


6. Click the **Save** button. The Save As dialog box closes, and the document, which is now a template with the .dotx file extension, remains open.

PROSKILLS

*Written Communication: Standardizing the Look of Your Documents*

Large companies often ask their employees to use a predesigned template for all corporate documents. If you work for an organization that does not require you to use a specific template, consider using one anyway in order to create a standard look for all of your documents. A consistent appearance is especially important if you are responsible for written communication for an entire department, because it ensures that colleagues and clients will immediately recognize documents from your department.

Take care to use a professional-looking template. If you decide to create your own, make sure to use document styles that make text easy to read, with colors that are considered appropriate in your workplace. Don't try to dazzle your readers with design elements. In nearly all professional settings, a simple, elegant look is ideal.

To make the new DCP Report template really useful to Sam's colleagues, you need to delete the specific information related to the Pool Sites report and replace it with placeholder text explaining the type of information required in each section. You'll start by editing the content controls. Then you will delete the body of the report and replace it with some placeholder text that Sam has already typed and saved as a separate Word document. Sam wants to use the current subtitle, "Department of City Planning," as the subtitle in all department reports, so there's no need to change it. However, the title will vary from one report to the next, so you need to replace it with a suitable placeholder. You'll retain the table of contents. When Sam's colleagues use the template to create future reports, they can update the table of contents to include the headings they add to their new documents.

**To replace the Pool Sites report information with placeholder text:**

1. Replace the report title "Sites for New Swimming Pool" with the text **[INSERT TITLE HERE.]**. Be sure to include the brackets, so it will be readily recognizable as placeholder text.
2. Switch to Header and Footer view, and then in the footer, replace the current date with the text **[Select current date.]**, making sure that you do not delete the Date Picker content control in the process.
3. Return to Print Layout view, and then delete everything in the document between the "Project Summary" heading and the final, blank paragraph, so all that remains is the Project Summary heading and a blank paragraph below it. Now you can insert a file containing placeholder text for the body of the report template.
4. In the blank paragraph under the Project Summary heading, insert the **Placeholder** file from the Word5\Tutorial folder included with your Data Files. See Figure 5-35. Scroll down to review the document and notice that the headings are all correctly formatted with the Heading 1 style. When Sam created the Placeholder document, he formatted the text in the default Heading 1 style provided by the Office theme. But when you inserted the file into the Pool Sites document, Word automatically reformatted the headings with your modified Heading 1 style. Now you can update the table of contents.

**Figure 5-35** Template with placeholder text

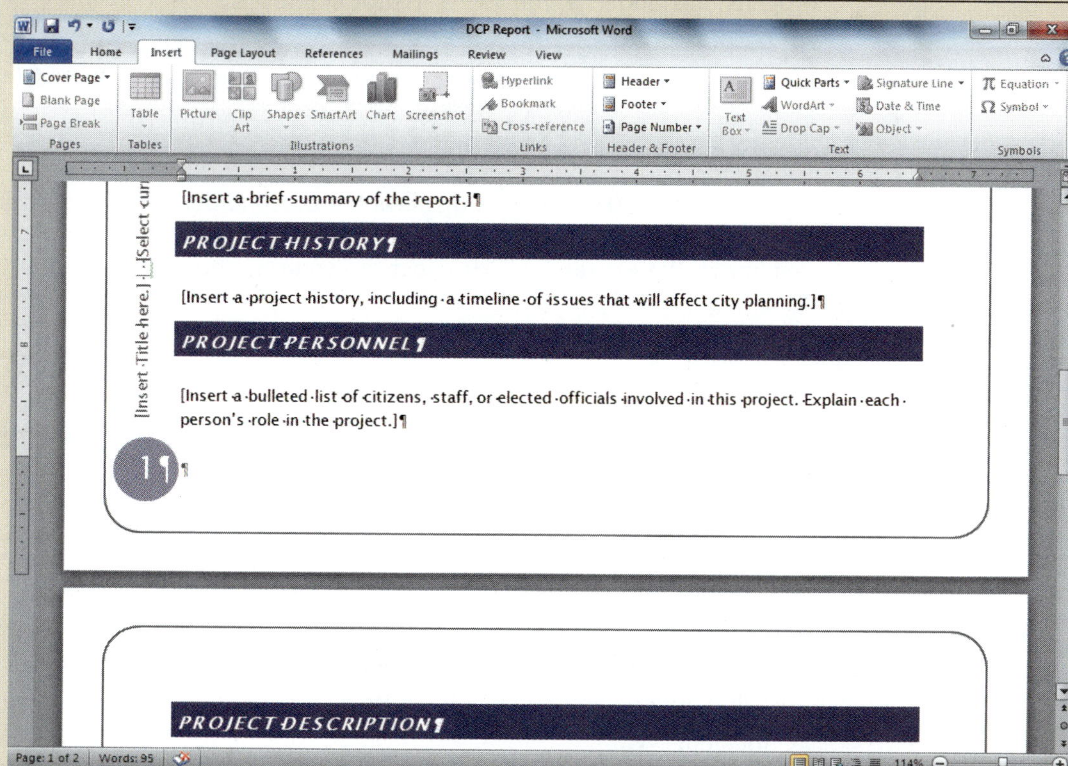


5. Click the **References** tab, and then click the **Update Table** button in the Table of Contents group. The table of contents is updated to include the headings currently in the template.
6. Save your work and close the template file.

The template you just created will simplify the process of creating new reports in Sam's department. Next you will use the template as the basis for a new document.

## Opening a New Document Based on Your Template

The new template is ready to be used by the Department of City Planning for all new reports. In fact, Sam would like to use it now to begin a report on possible sites for a new public library.

### To begin a new document based on the DCP Report template:

1. Click the **File** tab, and then click the **New** tab. The New tab in Backstage view displays a variety of template options.
2. Under "Home," click **New from existing**. The New from Existing Document dialog box opens. You can use this dialog box to open a copy of a template as a new document, or to open a copy of a regular document as a new document.
3. If necessary, navigate to the Word5\Tutorial folder included with your Data Files, click **DCP Report**, and then click the **Create New** button. A new document opens containing the text and formatting from the DCP Report template. Changes you make to this new document will not affect the DCP Report template file, which remains unchanged in the Word5\Tutorial folder.
4. Delete the placeholder **[Insert title here.]** and type **POSSIBLE SITES FOR NEW LIBRARY**, and then click anywhere outside the Title control to deselect it.
5. Save the document as **Library Sites** in the Word5\Tutorial folder included with your Data Files.

   **Trouble?** If the Title control displays the placeholder text "[Insert Title here.]" after you save the document, you didn't deselect the control before saving the document. Retype the title, deselect the control, and save your changes to the document.
6. Close the document.

REVIEW

### *Session 5.2 Quick Check*

1. Explain how to create a new style.
2. What tool do you use to see a quick comparison of two styles?
3. What is the advantage of saving a template to the Templates folder?
4. What do you have to do before you can create a table of contents?
5. What button can you click to revise a table of contents, and where is the button located?
6. How do you begin looking up a word in the dictionary or thesaurus?
7. What do you need to do before you can use the Mini Translator?

*Apply the skills you learned in the tutorial using the same case scenario.*

PRACTICE

## Review Assignments

**Data Files needed for the Review Assignments: Consultants.docx, Template Text.docx, Water.docx**

Sam's DCP Report template is now used for all reports created by employees of the Clarenbach Department of City Planning. Inspired by Sam's success with the template, the director of the Department of Water Utility (DWU), Heather Sheehan, wants you to help with a report on improving the city's water testing system. After you format the report, she'd like you to save the document as a new template. Finally, she'd like you to look up some terms using the Research task pane.

Complete the following steps:

1. Open a new Word document based on the **Oriel Report** template, and then save the document as **Water Testing** in the Word5\Review folder included with your Data Files.
2. Remove the cover page, and then delete the blank paragraph at the top of the new page 1.
3. Replace the title placeholder text with **Improving City Water Testing**. Replace the subtitle placeholder text with **Department of Water Utility**. Use the date control in the header to add the current date.
4. Delete the content control for the body of the report, and then select and delete the text box in the lower-right corner of the page.
5. In the blank paragraph below the subtitle, insert the file named **Water** from the Word5\Review folder included with your Data Files. This is just a skeletal draft of the report, but it includes the necessary headings.
6. At the end of the report, replace "Student Name" with your first and last name.
7. Change the theme colors to Newsprint, and then change the theme's fonts to the Apex fonts.
8. Save the new colors and fonts as a theme named **DWU Theme** in the Word5\Review folder included with your Data Files.
9. Select the Traditional style set.
10. Modify the Project Background heading by changing the character spacing to condensed, changing the paragraph spacing after the heading to 12 points, and adding italics.
11. Update the Heading 1 style to match the newly formatted Project Background heading.
12. Create a new style for the Contents heading that is based on the Heading 1 style. The style should be identical to the Heading 1 style, except that it should format text in 18-point font, with paragraph shading that uses the color Brown, Accent 3, Lighter 40%. Name the new style **Contents** and save it to the current document.
13. Open the Style Inspector and check the style applied to each paragraph in the document. Then use the Reveal Formatting pane to compare the Contents style with the Heading 1 style.
14. Insert a table of contents below the Table of Contents heading that does not include the "Contents" heading. Use the default settings in the Table of Contents dialog box.
15. At the end of the document, insert the Word file **Consultants** from the Word5\Review folder included with your Data Files, and then add the text "Outside Contributors" to the table of contents as a Level 1 heading.
16. Use the Mini Translator to display a Spanish translation of the paragraph below the "Project Background" heading.
17. Display the translation in the Research task pane, copy it to the Clipboard, and then paste it into a new document.

18. Save the new document as **Translation** in the Word5\Review folder included with your Data Files, close it, and then turn off the Mini Translator.
19. Find the word *aquifer* in the document, look up the term's meaning in the Encarta dictionary, copy the definition that begins "a layer of permeable rock…" to the Clipboard, click to the right of the word *aquifer* in the document, create a footnote that begins **According to the Encarta Dictionary, an aquifer is** and then insert the definition into the footnote, followed by a period.
20. In the "Project Background" section, find the first instance of the word *new*, and then replace it with an appropriate synonym.
21. Save your changes to the Water Testing document.
22. Save the Water Testing document as a template named **DWU Report** in the Word5\Review folder included with your Data Files.
23. On page 1, replace the title with the placeholder **[Insert title here.]**. Replace the current date with the placeholder **[Insert current date here.]**.
24. Delete everything in the report after the table of contents.
25. In the blank paragraph below the table of contents, insert the Word file **Template Text** from the Word5\Review folder included with your Data Files.
26. At the end of the template, replace "Student Name" with your first and last name, and then update the table of contents.
27. Save the template, and close it.
28. Open a new document based on the DWU Report template, enter **Estimate for New Wells** as the document title, save the new document as **New Wells** in the Word5\Review folder included with your Data Files, and close it.
29. Submit the finished documents to your instructor, either in printed or electronic form, as requested.

*Apply your skills to create a template for a handout.*

APPLY

## Case Problem 1

**Data Files needed for this Case Problem: Characteristics.docx, Crab Apple.jpg, Height.docx, Plant Headings.docx, Requirements.docx.**

***Bluestem Landscape Design*** Carla Niedenthal is the manager of the retail garden store owned by Bluestem Landscape Design. Customers often ask her for information about particular plants. Over the years, she has created fact sheets for some of the most popular plants, but now Carla would like to create a set of one-page plant descriptions. Her first step is to create a template that will serve as the basis of the handouts. As you'll see in the following steps, you can use templates intended for one purpose, such as a letter, for a different purpose, such as a handout.

Complete the following steps:

1. Open a new document based on the **Median Letter** template, and then save the document as **Plant** in the Word5\Case1 folder included with your Data Files. This document is set up as a table.
2. Use the View Gridlines button in the Table group on the Table Tools Layout tab to make sure the blue gridlines are visible.
3. Replace the placeholder text in the Company Name control with **Bluestem Landscape Design**. Replace the sender company address placeholder text with **Plant-at-a-Glance**.
4. Delete the date control, and then type **[Insert common plant name]** in the brown cell that used to contain the date control. Click the blue cell next to the brown cell and type **[Insert Latin plant name.]**.

5. Delete the contents of the bottom-right cell, including all the content controls and any blank paragraphs, and then delete the bottom row of the table, so that the table consists of only two rows with two cells each.
6. In the blank paragraph below the table, insert the file **Plant Headings** from the Word5\Case1 folder included with your Data Files.
7. Format the three headings, Characteristics, Mature Height, and Requirements, with the Heading 1 style. Remember that if you can't find a style in the Quick Styles gallery, you can look in the Styles pane.
8. Change the theme colors to Foundry.
9. Change the theme fonts to Verve.
10. Modify the Heading 1 style for the current document by changing the character spacing to Expanded, changing the paragraph spacing after the heading to 12 points, and adding italics.
11. At the bottom of the document, replace "STUDENT NAME" with your first and last name, and then save the document.
12. Save the Plant document as a template named **Plant Template** in the Word5\Case1 folder included with your Data Files, and then close the template.
13. Open a document based on your template. Save the new document as **Crab Apple** in the Word5\Case1 folder included with your Data Files.
14. For the common plant name, enter **Crab Apple**. For the Latin plant name, enter **Malus**.
15. Under the Characteristics heading, replace the placeholder text with the Word file **Characteristics** from the Word5\Case1 folder included with your Data Files. Delete the extra paragraph mark at the end of the new text.
16. Replace the placeholder text below the Mature Height heading and the Requirements heading with the files **Height** and **Requirements** from the Word5\Case1 folder included with your Data Files. Delete any extra new paragraphs.
17. At the bottom of the document, read the placeholder text about inserting a photograph. Delete the placeholder text (but not the paragraph mark at the end of it), and insert the photo named **Crab Apple.jpg** from the Word5\Case1 folder included with your Data Files. Format the photograph with the Drop Shadow Rectangle style.
18. Save and close the Crab Apple document.
19. Submit the finished documents to your instructor, either in printed or electronic form, as requested.

*Apply your skills to create a template for a consultant's report.*

APPLY

## Case Problem 2

### Data File needed for this Case Problem: Star.docx

***Star Avenue Consulting*** Steven Yang is a consultant for Star Avenue Consulting, a firm that helps retail chains evaluate and improve the organization of their retail floor space. Steven and his colleagues often have to produce reports that summarize their recommendations. Your job is to create a template they can use to generate these reports.

Complete the following steps:

1. Open the document **Star** from the Word5\Case2 folder included with your Data Files. In the third paragraph, replace "CONSULTANT NAME" with your first and last name, and then save it as **Star Report** in the same folder.
2. Change the document's theme to the Opulent theme, and change the theme colors to Flow. Change the style set to Traditional.

3. Format the "Assessment of Current Layout" heading by changing the character spacing to Expanded, changing the font size to 16 points, and changing the paragraph spacing after the paragraph to 18 points. Update the Heading 1 style for the current document to match the newly formatted heading.
4. Create a new style for the company name at the top of the document that is based on the Title style. The new style should be identical to the Title style, except that the text should be 20-point font, with bold and italic formatting and 6 points of space after the paragraph. Name the new style **Company**, select the Normal style as the style for following paragraphs, and save the new style to the current document.
5. In the blank paragraph above the heading "Assessment of Current Store Layout," insert a table of contents using the Automatic Table 2 format. Delete the blank paragraph after the content control that contains the table of contents.
6. In the placeholder text after the heading "Assessment of Current Store Layout," replace "current" with an appropriate synonym.
7. Save your changes to the Star Report document, and then save the Star Report document as a template named **Star Template** in the Word5\Case2 folder included with your Data Files. Close the template.
8. Open a document based on your new template. You will use this document as the basis of a new report for Gametron, a chain of video game stores. You will not complete the entire report; instead you'll leave the placeholder text in the body of the report for another consultant to replace.
9. Save the new document as **Gametron** in the Word5\Case2 folder included with your Data Files.
10. For the client name, insert **Gametron Inc. and Subsidiaries**.
11. Save and close the Gametron document.
12. Submit the finished documents to your instructor, either in printed or electronic form, as requested.

*Go beyond what you've learned to edit a business plan for a new Internet company.*

CHALLENGE

## Case Problem 3

### Data File needed for this Case Problem: Text.docx

***AllSecure, Inc.*** Camden Lui has written a business plan for his new Internet business, AllSecure, Incorporated. On its Web site, the company will publish security information on data storage and transmission services. Camden has written part of the report and needs help formatting it.

Complete the following steps:

1. Open a new document based on the Origin Report template and save it as **AllSecure Plan** in the Word5\Case3 folder included with your Data Files.
2. Remove the cover page, and then delete the blank paragraph at the top of the remaining page.
3. Use **AllSecure, Inc.** for the document title and **Business Plan** for the subtitle.
4. Delete the body control, and insert the file named **Text** from the Word5\Case3 folder included with your Data Files. At the end of the document, replace "Student Name" with your first and last name.
5. Create a new character style for the company name where it is used in the body of the report. (*Hint*: In the Create New Style from Formatting dialog box, click the Style type arrow and then click Character.) Base the style on the Intense Reference style. The new style should be identical to the Intense Reference style, except that it should format text in small caps. Name the style **Company Name** and save it to the current document.

EXPLORE 6. In the bottom-right corner of the Styles pane, click the Options link, and then review the Style Pane Options dialog box. Using Word Help as a reference, set up the Style pane to list the styles in the current document in alphabetical order.

EXPLORE 7. Replace all instances of "AllSecure" formatted in the Normal style with "AllSecure" formatted in the Company Name style. To do this, open the Find and Replace dialog box, type AllSecure in the Find what box, click the Format button, click Style, select the Normal style, and then click OK. Type AllSecure in the Replace with box, and then use the Format button to select the Company Name style. Continue the find and replace process as usual.

8. Insert a new paragraph before the Executive Summary heading, and then format the new paragraph with the Normal style.

EXPLORE 9. Use the Table of Contents dialog box to insert a table of contents without page numbers in the new, blank paragraph. Use the Distinctive format.

10. At the end of the document, change the heading Audience Needs to **Audience Requirements**, and then update the table of contents.

11. In the last paragraph on the first page, replace "crucial" with an appropriate synonym.

EXPLORE 12. Select the "Requirements for Success" heading, open the Paragraph dialog box, click the Line and Page Breaks tab, select the Keep with next check box, and then click the OK button. Update the Heading 1 style to match the newly formatted "Requirements for Success" heading, so that all text formatted with the Heading 1 style stays with the body text that follows it. This will prevent headings from being stranded at the bottom of a column, with the body text at the top of the next column.

13. Save and close the document.

14. Submit the finished documents to your instructor, either in printed or electronic form, as requested.

*Look up information about Web sites that offer Word 2010 templates.*

RESEARCH

## Case Problem 4

**There are no Data Files needed for this Case Problem.**

***Deca Publishing Associates*** You work as an editorial assistant at Deca Publishing Associates, a small firm that performs a variety of editorial tasks for larger publishing companies. Your supervisor would like to take advantage of the many Word templates available online from companies other than Microsoft. She asks you to do some research and write a short report summarizing your findings. She also asks you to include screenshots of sites that provide templates online. *Note:* To complete this case problem, you will need a connection to the Internet.

Complete the following steps:

1. Open a new document based on the Urban Report template, and then save the document as **Word Templates** in the Word5\Case4 folder included with your Data Files.
2. Remove the cover page.
3. Enter **Word Templates** as the document title and **A Sample of Online Sources** as the subtitle document control, and then delete the document control for the body of the report.
4. Enter your first and last name in the content control in the document header.
5. Open the Research task pane and use the Bing search engine to look up information about sites that offer Word 2010 templates. You can click View all results on Live Search to display the information in your browser, and then continue searching from there. Learn as much as you can about the various sites. Review the Microsoft site, as well as several other sites. Look for sites that offer templates for sale and for free.

6. Write a brief report describing the options available on the Microsoft site and on one other site. For each site, include the site's name formatted with the Heading 1 style, followed by a bulleted list that includes the site's Web address, a brief description of the types of templates available, and information about template prices. After you type a site's Web address, remember to press the spacebar or the Enter key to transform the Web address into a live hyperlink.
7. Add a blank paragraph formatted in the Normal style at the end of each bulleted list.
8. EXPLORE — Look up the term **screenshot** in Word Help and learn how to insert a screenshot of an open Window into a Word document. In the blank paragraph at the end of each bulleted list, insert a screenshot of the relevant Web site.
9. Save and close the document.
10. Submit the finished documents to your instructor, either in printed or electronic form, as requested

ASSESS

## SAM: Skills Assessment Manager

For current SAM information, including versions and content details, visit SAM Central (http://samcentral.course.com). If you have a SAM user profile, you may have access to hands-on instruction, practice, and assessment of the skills covered in this tutorial. Since various versions of SAM are supported throughout the life of this text, check with your instructor for the correct instructions and URL/Web site for accessing assignments.

### ENDING DATA FILES

Word5 →

**Tutorial**
DCP Report.dotx
DCP Theme.thmx
Library Sites.docx
Pool Sites.docx

**Review**
DWU Report.dotx
DWU Theme.thmx
New Wells.docx
Translation.docx
Water Testing.docx

**Case1**
Crab Apple.docx
Plant Template.dotx
Plant.docx

**Case2**
Gametron.docx
Star Report.docx
Star Template.dotx

**Case3**
AllSecure Plan.docx

**Case4**
Word Templates.docx

WORD

TUTORIAL 6

# Using Mail Merge

*Creating a Form Letter, Mailing Labels, and a Telephone Directory*

## OBJECTIVES

**Session 6.1**
- Learn about the mail merge process
- Select a main document
- Create a data source
- Insert mail merge fields into a main document
- Edit a main document
- Preview a merged document
- Complete a mail merge

**Session 6.2**
- Edit an existing data source
- Sort and filter records
- Create mailing labels and a phone directory
- Convert tables to text and text to tables
- Create multilevel lists

## Case | *Lily Road Yoga Studio*

Nina Ranabhat is the owner and chief instructor at Lily Road Yoga Studio in Boise, Idaho. The studio has just moved to a new, expanded location. Nina wants to invite clients to try out the new facility during free, open-studio days in the month of June. She plans to send a form letter to each client announcing the location and the open-studio days. The form letter will also contain specific details for individual clients, such as name, address, and each client's favorite class and instructor. Nina has already written the text of the form letter. She plans to use the mail merge process to add the personal information for each client. She asks you to complete the form letter using the Mail Merge feature in Word. She also needs a set of letters that will go just to the clients who like a particular teacher. After you create the merged letters, she'd like you to create the mailing labels for the envelopes and a telephone directory that lists a phone number for each teacher. Next, you will create an additional document with name and address information by converting text to a table, and converting a table to text. Finally, you will create and format an outline with information about the studio's teachers.

### STARTING DATA FILES

Word6 → Tutorial, Review, Case1, Case2, Case3, Case4

| Tutorial | Review | Case1 | Case2 | Case3 | Case4 |
|---|---|---|---|---|---|
| Client.docx | Bonus.docx | Gallery.docx | Mortgage Data.xlsx | Main.docx | Director.docx |
| Phone.docx | Contacts.docx | | Mortgage.docx | Pasta.txt | MAPH.docx |
| Yoga.docx | More.docx | | | | |

# SESSION 6.1 VISUAL OVERVIEW

To complete the merge, you click the Finish & Merge button. This creates a new document, the **merged document**, which contains a separate copy of the main document for each record in the data source.

Use the Start Mail Merge button to select the type of main document. Possible types of main documents include letters, envelopes, emails, labels, and directories.

The Select Recipients button allows you to select an existing data source or create a new one in the New Address List dialog box.

The Mailings tab contains four groups of options that, working left to right, walk you through the process of creating a mail merge.

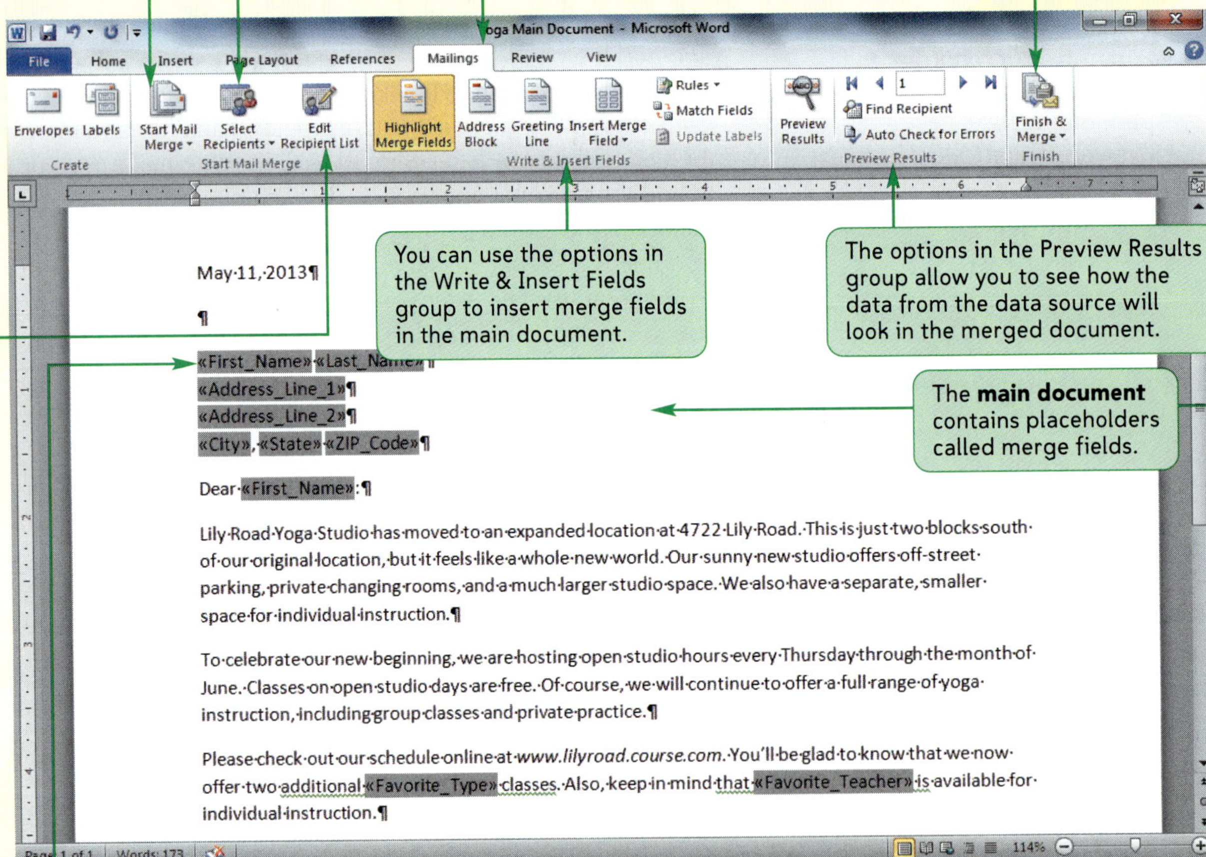


The Edit Recipient List button allows you to make changes to a data source.

You can use the options in the Write & Insert Fields group to insert merge fields in the main document.

The options in the Preview Results group allow you to see how the data from the data source will look in the merged document.

The **main document** contains placeholders called merge fields.

A **merge field** indicates what information you want to retrieve from the data source and display in the main document. For example, a merge field might retrieve a name or a zip code. A merge field is enclosed by angled brackets, or **chevrons**, like this: << >>.

# MAIL MERGE

A **data source** contains information, such as names and addresses, that is displayed in the main document by the merge fields. You can use a Word table, an Excel spreadsheet, or other types of files as data sources, or you can create a new one using the New Address List dialog box.

A **data source** stores information in a table.

The header row contains the names of the fields in the data source.

Each row, or **record**, contains a complete set of information, such as an address for a client.

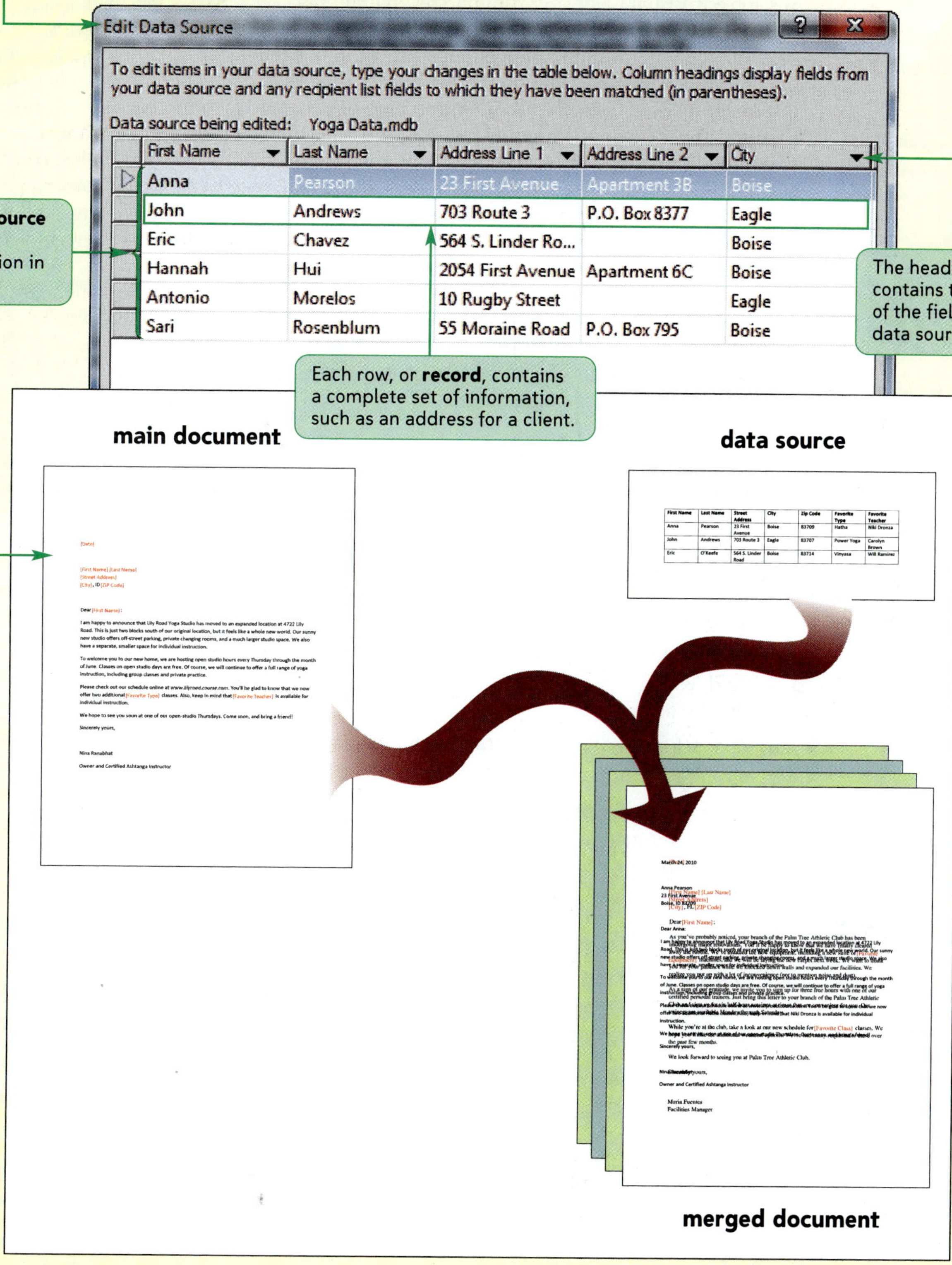

## Performing a Mail Merge

When you perform a mail merge, you insert individualized information from a data source into a main document. A main document can be a letter or any other kind of document containing merge fields that tell Word where to insert names, addresses, and other variable information from the data source. When you **merge** the main document with the data source, you produce a new document called a **merged document**. The Session 6.1 Visual Overview summarizes mail merge concepts.

Nina's main document is the letter shown in the Session 6.1 Visual Overview. In this session, you will insert the merge fields shown in this letter. You will also create Nina's data source, which will include the name and address of each client. It will also include information about each client's preferred type of class and favorite teacher.

You can perform a mail merge by using the Mail Merge task pane, which walks you through the steps of performing a mail merge. You can also use the options on the Mailings tab, which streamlines the process and offers more tools. In this tutorial you will work with the Mailings tab to complete the mail merge for Nina. The Mailings tab organizes the steps in the mail merge process so that you can move from left to right across the Ribbon using the buttons to complete the merge.

The first step is to open the document you want to use as the main document, and then use the Start Mail merge button in the Start Mail Merge group to select the type of document. Selecting the type of main document affects the commands that are available to you later as you continue through the mail merge process, so it's important to make the correct selection at the beginning. In this case, you will use a letter as the main document.

### To open the main document and begin the mail merge process:

1. Open the file **Yoga** from the Word6\Tutorial folder included with your Data Files, then save the document as **Yoga Main Document** in the same folder.
2. Display nonprinting characters, switch to Print Layout view, display the rulers, and set the zoom to Page Width.
3. Review the contents of the letter. Notice that the first paragraph includes a date field, which automatically updated to display the current date when you opened the document.
4. Scroll down to display the letter's closing, change "Nina Ranabhat" to your name, and then scroll back up to the beginning of the letter.
5. Click the **Mailings** tab on the Ribbon. Notice that most of the buttons in the groups on the Mailings tab are grayed out, indicating the options are unavailable. These options only become available after you begin the mail merge process by specifying a main document and a data source.
6. In the Start Mail Merge group, click the **Start Mail Merge** button. The Start Mail Merge menu opens. See Figure 6-1. The first five options on the menu allow you to specify the type of main document you will be creating. Most of the options involve print items, such as labels and letters, but you can also select an email as the type of main document. In this case, you will be creating a letter.

**TIP**

After you have completed a mail merge, you can break the connection between a main document and its data source by clicking Normal Word Document on the Start Mail Merge menu.

**Figure 6-1** Start Mail Merge menu

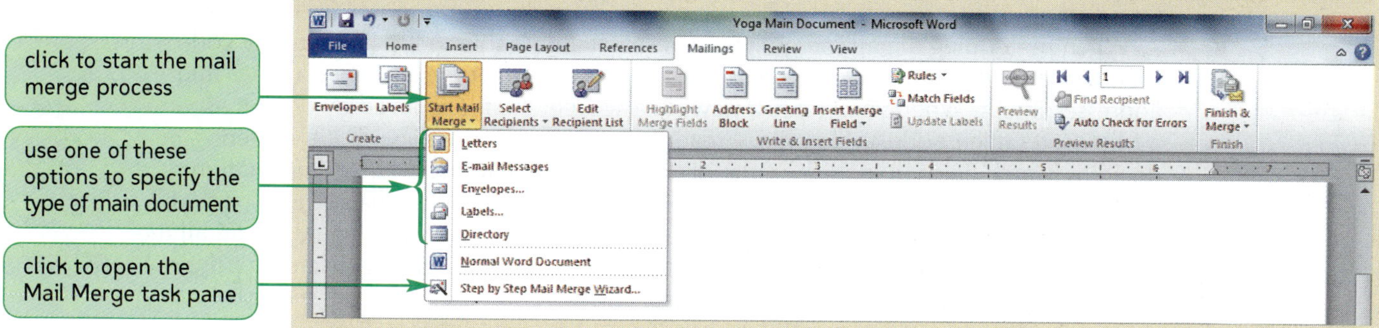


7. Click **Letters**. The Start Mail Merge menu closes.

   Next, you need to select the list of recipients for Nina's letter—the data source.

8. In the Start Mail Merge group, click the **Select Recipients** button. The Select Recipients menu allows you to use an existing list, select from Outlook Contacts (the address book in Outlook), or create a new recipient list. Because Nina hasn't had a chance to create a data source yet, she asks you to create one.

9. Click **Type New List**. The New Address List dialog box opens, as shown in Figure 6-2. The default fields for a data source appear in this dialog box. However, before you begin creating the data source, you need to identify the fields and records Nina wants you to include.

**Figure 6-2** New Address List dialog box

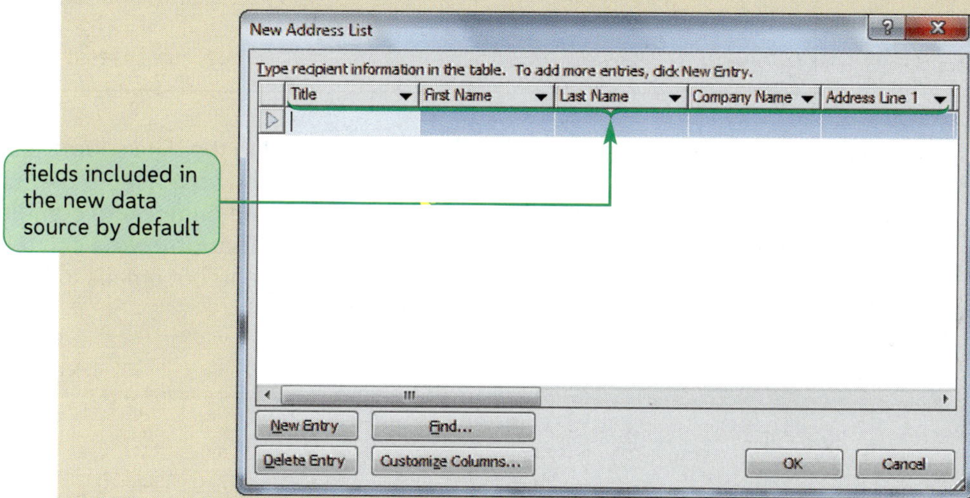


## Creating a Data Source

As described in the Session 6.1 Visual Overview, a data source is a file with information organized into fields and records. Typically, the data source for a mail merge contains a list of names and addresses, but it can also contain email addresses, telephone numbers, and other data. Various kinds of files can be used as the data source, including a simple text file, Word table, Excel worksheet, Access database, or a Microsoft Office Address

Lists file, which stores addresses for Microsoft Outlook and other Microsoft Office applications. (In Word Help, this type of file is sometimes called a Microsoft Office Contacts Lists file.) In this tutorial, you will create a Microsoft Office Address Lists file to use as your data source.

When performing a mail merge, you can select a data source file that already contains names and addresses, or you can create a new data source and enter names and addresses into it. When you create a new data source, the file is saved by default as a Microsoft Office Address Lists file. Creating a new data source involves two steps—deciding which fields to include in the data source and entering address information.

You need to create a data source that contains information on Nina's clients, including the name, address, preferred type of class, and favorite teacher. Nina collected all the necessary information by asking clients to fill out a form when they registered for their first yoga class. Figure 6-3 shows one of these forms.

**Figure 6-3** **Client information form**

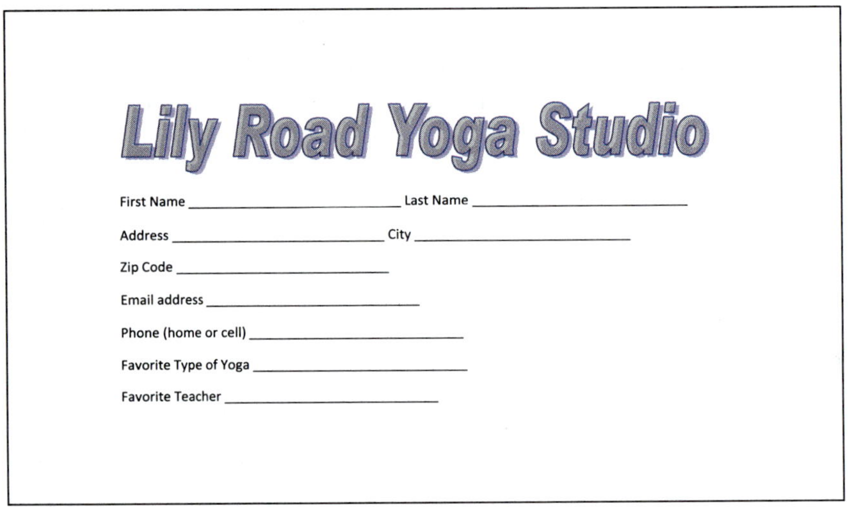

Lily Road Yoga Studio

First Name ________________ Last Name ________________

Address ________________ City ________________

Zip Code ________________

Email address ________________

Phone (home or cell) ________________

Favorite Type of Yoga ________________

Favorite Teacher ________________

The information on each form will make up one record in the data source. Each blank on the form translates into one field in the data source as shown in Figure 6-4. Even though you won't need the clients' email addresses or phone numbers to complete the mail merge, you can still include them in the data source. That way Nina can reuse the same data source in the future when using mail merge to send out emails to her clients, or when creating a directory of client phone numbers.

**Figure 6-4** **Fields to include in data source**

| Field Names | Description |
|---|---|
| First Name | Client's first name |
| Last Name | Client's last name |
| Address Line 1 | Client's street address |
| Address Line 2 | Additional address information, such as an apartment number |
| City | City |
| State | State |
| ZIP Code | Zip code |
| E-mail Address | Client's email address |
| Phone | Client's home or cell phone number |
| Favorite Type | Client's preferred type of yoga |
| Favorite Teacher | Client's preferred yoga teacher |

When you create a new data source, Word provides a number of default fields, such as First Name, Last Name, and Company. You can customize the data source by adding new fields and removing the default fields that you don't plan to use. As you create a data source, keep in mind that each field name must be unique; you can't have two fields with the same name.

REFERENCE

*Creating a Data Source for a Mail Merge*

- On the Mailings tab, click the Select Recipients button in the Start Mail Merge group, and then click Type New List to open the New Address List dialog box.
- To create the fields for your data source, click the Customize Columns button to open the Customize Address List dialog box.
- To delete an unnecessary field, select it, click the Delete button, and then click the Yes button.
- To add a new field, click the Add button, type the name of the field in the Add Field dialog box, and then click the OK button.
- To rearrange the order of the field names, click a field name, and then click the Move Up or Move Down button.
- To rename a field, click a field name, click the Rename button to open the Rename Field dialog box, type a new field name, and then click the OK button to close the Rename Field dialog box.
- Click the OK button to close the Customize Address List dialog box.
- In the New Address List dialog box, enter information for the first record, click the New Entry button, and type another record. Continue until you are finished entering information into the data source, and then click the OK button to open the Save Address List dialog box.
- Type a name for the data source in the File name box, and then click the Save button. The file is saved with the .mdb file extension.

You're ready to create the data source for Nina's form letter using information Nina has given you for three of her clients. You will use the New Address List dialog box to enter one record per client. However, before you begin entering information, you need to customize the list of fields to include only the fields Nina requires.

**To customize the list of fields before creating the data source:**

1. In the New Address List dialog box, click the **Customize Columns** button. The Customize Address List dialog box opens. Here you can delete the fields you don't need, add new ones, and arrange the fields in the order you want. You'll start by deleting fields.
2. In the Field Names box, verify that **Title** is selected, and then click the **Delete** button. A message appears asking you to confirm the deletion.
3. Click the **Yes** button. The Title field is deleted from the list of field names.
4. Continue using the Delete button to delete the following fields: **Company Name**, **Country or Region**, and **Work Phone**. Next, you need to add some new fields. When you add a new field, it is inserted below the selected field, so you will start by selecting the last field in the list.
5. In the Field Names box, click **E-mail Address**, and then click the **Add** button. The Add Field dialog box opens, asking you to type a name for your field.
6. Type **Favorite Type**, and then click the **OK** button. The field "Favorite Type" is added to the Field Names list.
7. Use the Add button to add a **Favorite Teacher** field below the Favorite Type field. Next, you need to move the E-mail Address field up above the Home Phone field, so that the fields are in the same order as they appear on the form shown previously in Figure 6-3.
8. Click **E-mail Address**, and then click the **Move Up** button. The E-mail Address field moves up, so it now appears just before the Home Phone field. Finally, because Nina's form asks clients to fill in a home or cell phone number, you need to change "Home Phone" to simply "Phone."
9. Click **Home Phone**, and then click the **Rename** button to open the Rename Field dialog box.
10. In the To box, replace "Home Phone" with **Phone**, and then click the **OK** button to close the Rename Field dialog box and return to the Customize Address List dialog box. See Figure 6-5.

**Figure 6-5** **Customized list of field names**

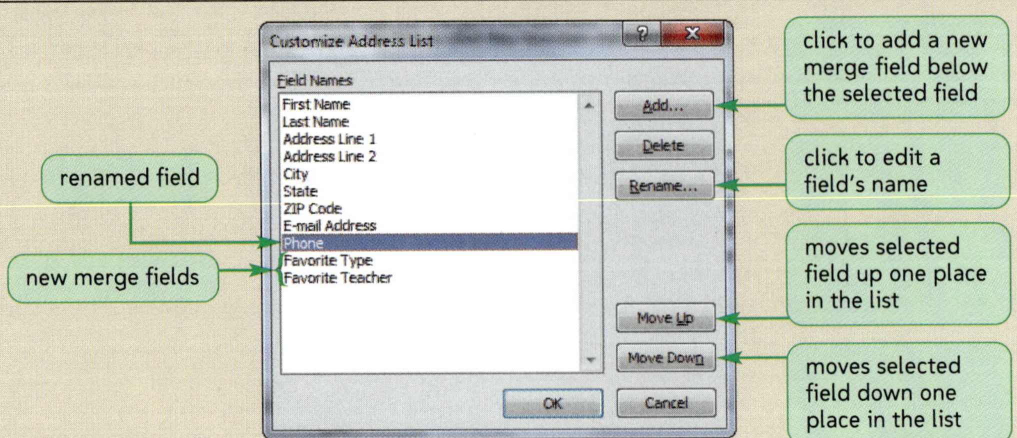

11. Click the **OK** button in the Customize Address List dialog box to close it and return to the New Address List dialog box. This dialog box reflects the changes you just made. For instance, it no longer includes the Title field. The fields are listed in the same order they appeared in the Customize Address List dialog box.

12. Use the horizontal scroll bar near the bottom of the New Address List dialog box to display the Favorite Type and Favorite Teacher fields. Although part of "Favorite Teacher" is cut off in the dialog box, the entire field name is stored as part of the data source. See Figure 6-6.

**Figure 6-6** **Changes made to New Address List dialog box**

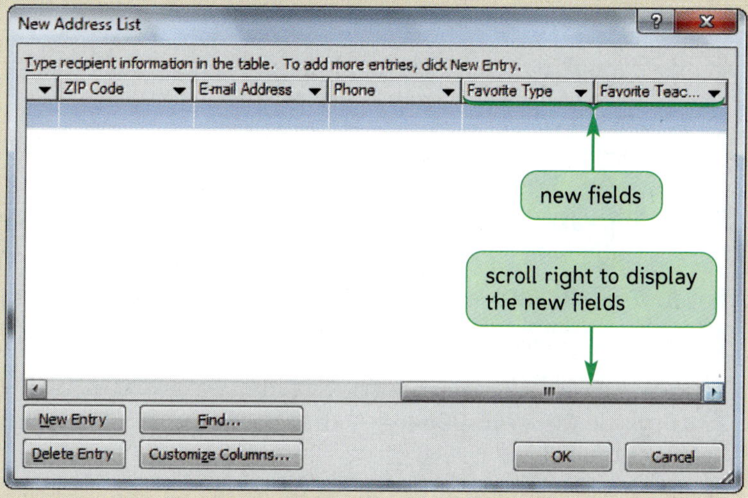


INSIGHT

### *Organizing Field Names*

Although the order of field names in the data source doesn't affect their placement in the main document, it's helpful to arrange field names logically in the data source so you can enter information quickly and efficiently. For example, you'll probably want the First Name field next to the Last Name field. To make it easier to transfer information from a paper form to a data source, it's a good idea to arrange the fields in the same order as on the form, just like you did in the preceding steps. Also, note that if you include spaces in your field names, Word will replace the spaces with underscores when you insert the fields into the main document. For example, Word transforms the field name First Name into First_Name.

Now that you have specified the fields you want to use, you are ready to enter the client information into the data source.

## Entering Data into a Data Source

Nina gives you three completed client information forms and asks you to enter the information from the forms into the data source. You'll use the New Address List dialog box to enter the information. As you press the Tab key to move right from one field to the next, the dialog box will scroll to display fields that are not currently visible.

**To enter data into a record using the New Address List dialog box:**

1. Scroll left to display the First Name field, click in the **First Name** field, if necessary, and then type **Anna** to enter the first name of the first client. Make sure you do not press the spacebar after you finish typing an entry in the New Address List dialog box. You should add spaces only in the text of the main document, not in the data source, to prevent too many or too few spaces between words.
2. Press the **Tab** key to move the insertion point to the Last Name field.
3. Type **Pearson**, and then press the **Tab** key to move the insertion point to the Address Line 1 field.
4. Type **23 First Avenue**, and then press the **Tab** key to move the insertion point to the Address Line 2 field.
5. Type **Apartment 3B**, and then press the **Tab** key to move the insertion point to the City field.
6. Type **Boise**, and then press the **Tab** key to move the insertion point to the State field.
7. Type **ID**, and then press the **Tab** key to move the insertion point to the ZIP Code field.
8. Type **83709**, and then press the **Tab** key to move to the E-mail Address field.
9. Type **pearson22@mount-tech.net**, and then press the **Tab** key to move to the Phone field.
10. Type **208-946-5264**, and then press the **Tab** key to move to the Favorite Type field.
11. Type **Hatha**, and then press the **Tab** key. The insertion point is now in the Favorite Teacher field, which is the last field in the data source.
12. Type **Niki Dronza**, but do *not* press the Tab key. See Figure 6-7.

**TIP**

You can press the Shift+Tab keys to move the insertion point to the previous field.

**Figure 6-7** **Completed record**

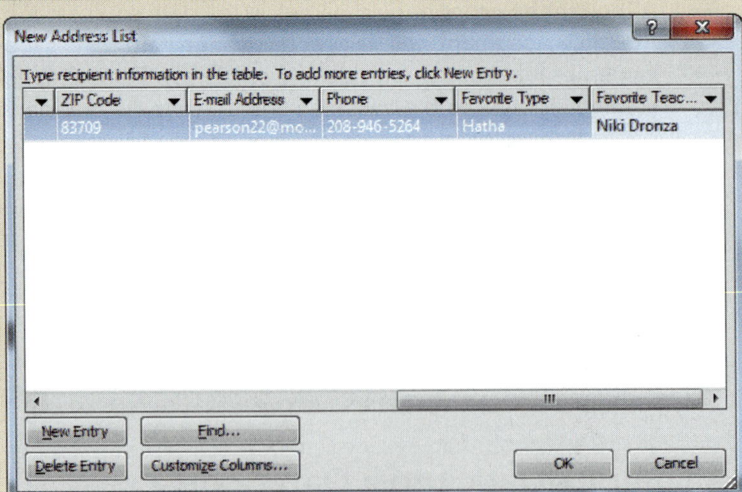

You have completed the information for the first record of the data source. Now you're ready to enter information for the next two records. You can create a new record by clicking the New Entry button, or by pressing the Tab key after you have finished entering information into the last field for a record. As you enter the next two records, you will use both methods. Note that, within a record, you can leave some fields blank. For example, only two of Nina's three clients included information for the Address Line 2 field.

### To add additional records to the data source:

1. In the New Address List dialog box, click the **New Entry** button. A new, blank record is created.
2. Enter the information shown in Figure 6-8 for the next two records in the data source. To create an Eric Chavez record, press the Tab key after entering the Favorite Teacher field for the John Andrews record. Also, leave the Address Line 2 field blank for the Eric Chavez record.

**Figure 6-8** **Information for records 2 and 3**

| First Name | Last Name | Address Line 1 | Address Line 2 | City | State | ZIP Code | E-mail Address | Phone | Favorite Type | Favorite Teacher |
|---|---|---|---|---|---|---|---|---|---|---|
| John | Andrews | 703 Route 3 | P.O. Box 8377 | Eagle | ID | 83707 | john23@world-org.org | 208-477-3843 | Power Yoga | Carolyn Ramirez |
| Eric | Chavez | 564 S. Linder Road | | Boise | ID | 83714 | chavez55@boise4quest.edu | 208-773-0990 | Vinyasa | Will Brown |

**Trouble?** If you create a fourth record by mistake, click the Delete Entry button to remove the blank fourth record.

You have entered the records for three clients. Nina's data source eventually will contain hundreds of records for Lily Road Yoga Studio clients. The current data source, however, contains only the records Nina wants to work with now. Next, you need to save the data source.

## Saving a Data Source

You have finished entering data, so you can close the New Address List dialog box. When you close this dialog box, the Save Address List dialog box opens, where you can save the data source as a Microsoft Office Address Lists file.

**To save the data source:**

1. In the New Address List dialog box, click the **OK** button. The New Address List dialog box closes, and the Save Address List dialog box opens, as shown in Figure 6-9. The Save as type box indicates that the data source will be saved as a Microsoft Office Address Lists file. The File name box is empty; you need to name the file before saving it.

**Figure 6-9** Saving the data source

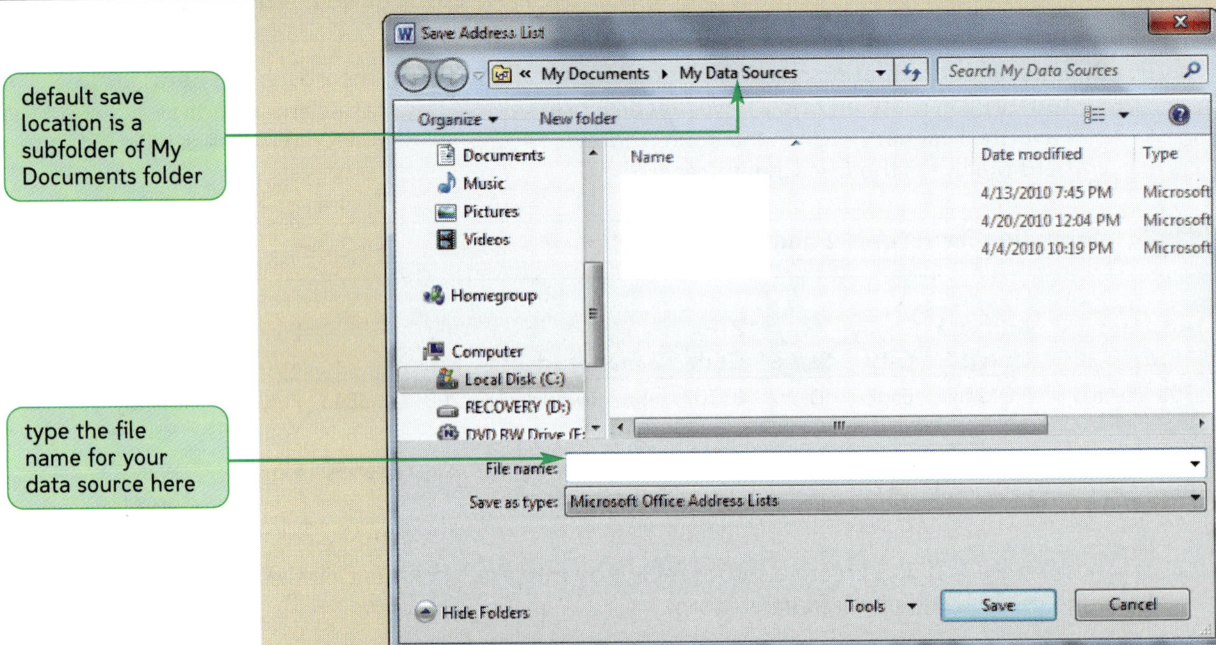


2. Click the **File name** box, and then type **Yoga Data**. By default, Word will save the file to the My Data Sources folder, which is a subfolder of the Documents folder, unless you specify another save location. In this case, you will save the data source in the Word6\Tutorial folder.
3. Navigate to the Word6\Tutorial folder included with your Data Files, and then click the **Save** button. The Save Address List dialog box closes, and you return to the main document.

PROSKILLS

*Decision Making: Planning Your Data Source*

When creating a data source, think beyond the current mail merge task to possible future uses for your data source. For example, Nina's data source includes both an E-Mail Address field and a Phone field, not because she wants to use that information in the current mail merge project, but because she can foresee needing these pieces of information at a later date as a means for communicating with her clients. Having all relevant client information in one data source will make it easier to retrieve and use the information effectively.

In some cases, you'll also want to include information that might seem obvious. For example, Nina's data source includes a State field even though all of her current clients live in or around Boise, Idaho. However, she included a state field because she knows that her pool of addresses might expand sometime in the future to include residents of other states.

Finally, think about the structure of your data source before you create it. Try to break information down into as many fields as seems reasonable. For example, it's always better to include a First Name field and a Last Name field, rather than simply a Name field, because including two separate fields makes it possible, later, to alphabetize the information in the data source by last name. If you entered first and last names in a single Name field, you could only alphabetize by first name, because the first name would appear first in the Name field.

If you're working with a very small data source, breaking information down into as many fields as possible is less important. However, it's very common to start with a small data source, and then, as time goes on, find that you need to continually add information to the data source, until you have a large file. If you failed to plan the data source adequately at the beginning, the expanded data source could become difficult to manage.

Next, you need to add the merge fields to the main document.

## Inserting Merge Fields

You have already learned how to insert merge fields using the Mail Merge task pane. In that instance you inserted an address block merge field for a letter's inside address. For this mail merge, you will build an inside address by inserting individual merge fields for the address elements. Nina's letter is a standard business letter, so you'll place merge fields for the client's name and address below the date. You must include proper spacing around the fields so that the information in the merged document will be formatted correctly. To insert a merge field, you move the insertion point to the location where you want to insert the merge field, and then click the Insert Merge Field button arrow in the Write & Insert Merge Fields group.

### To insert a merge field:

1. Click in the second blank paragraph below the date.
2. In the Write & Insert Fields group, click the **Insert Merge Field button arrow**. A menu containing all the merge fields in the data source opens. Note that the spaces in the merge field names have been replaced with underlines. See Figure 6-10.

**Figure 6-10** **Insert Merge Field menu**

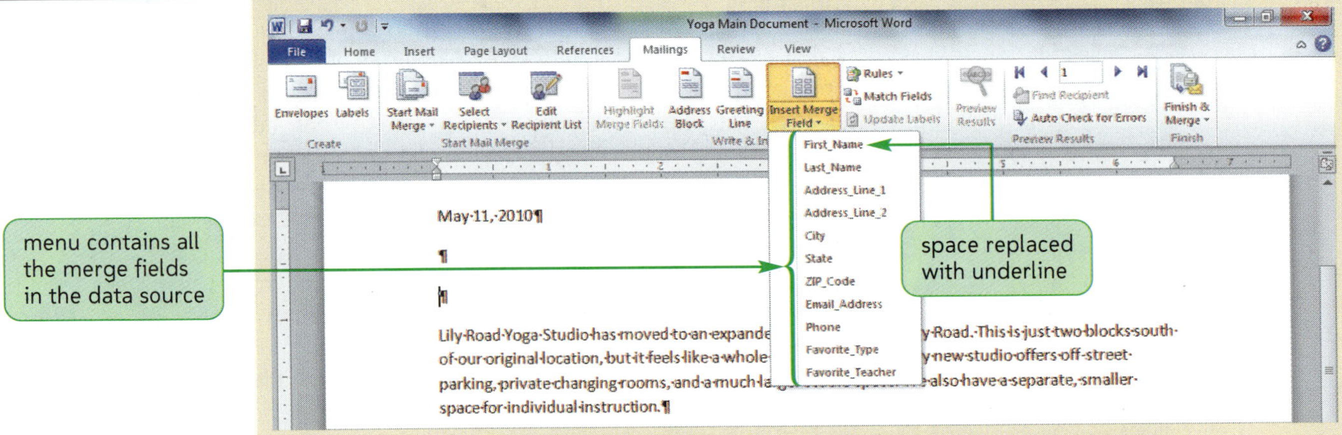


**Trouble?** If you see the Insert Merge Field dialog box instead, you clicked the Insert Merge Field button instead of the Insert Merge Field button arrow. Close the dialog box and repeat Step 2.

**TIP**

You can only insert merge fields into a main document by using the tools on the Mailings tab or in the Mail Merge task pane. You cannot simply type merge fields into the main document—even if you type the angled brackets.

3. Click **First_Name**. The Insert Merge Field menu closes, and the merge field is inserted into the document. The merge field consists of the field name surrounded by double angled brackets << >>, also called chevrons. In the Write & Insert Fields group, the Highlight Merge Fields button is now available, which means you can use it to display the merge field on a gray background.

   **Trouble?** If you make a mistake and insert the wrong merge field, click to the left of the merge field, press the Delete key to select the field, and then press the Delete key again to delete it.

4. In the Write & Insert Fields group, click the **Highlight Merge Fields** button. The First Name merge field is displayed on a gray background, making it easier to see in the document. See Figure 6-11.

**Figure 6-11** **First_Name merge field highlighted in main document**

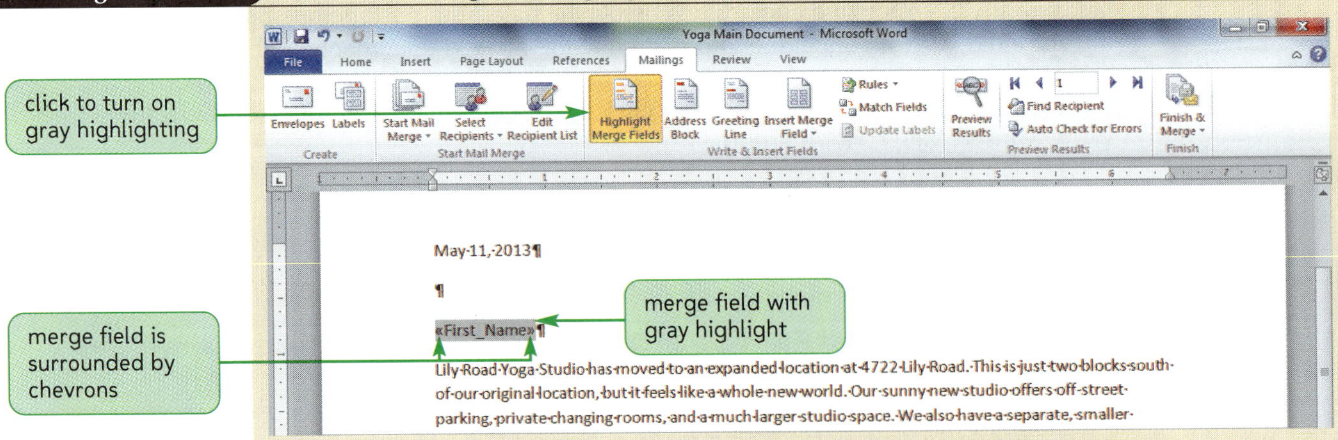


Later, when you merge the main document with the data source, Word will replace this merge field with information from the First Name field in the data source. Now, you're ready to insert the merge fields for the rest of the inside address. You'll add the necessary spacing and punctuation between the merge fields as well. You might be accustomed to pressing the Shift+Enter key combination to start a new line in an inside address without inserting paragraph spacing. However, because your data source includes a record in which one of the fields (the Address Line 2 field) is blank, you need to press the Enter key to start each new line. As you will see later in this tutorial, this ensures that, in the final merged document, Word hides the Address Line 2 field whenever it is blank. To maintain the proper spacing in the main document, you will adjust the paragraph spacing after you insert all the fields.

## To insert the remaining merge fields for the inside address:

1. Press the **spacebar** to insert a space after the First Name field, click the **Insert Merge Field button arrow**, and then click **Last_Name**.
2. Press the **Enter** key to start a new paragraph, click the **Insert Merge Field button arrow**, and then click **Address_Line_1**. Word inserts the Address Line 1 merge field into the form letter. Some of the records in the data source include an entry in the Address Line 2 field, so you will insert the Address Line 2 merge field next.
3. Press the **Enter** key, click the **Insert Merge Field button arrow**, and then click **Address_Line_2**. Word inserts the Address Line 2 merge field into the form letter.
4. Press the **Enter** key, insert the **City** merge field, type **,** (a comma), press the **spacebar** to insert a space after the comma, insert the **State** merge field, press the **spacebar**, and then insert the **ZIP_Code** merge field. The inside address now contains all the necessary merge fields. See Figure 6-12. Next you will adjust the paragraph spacing for the inside address.

**Figure 6-12** **Main document with merge fields for inside address**

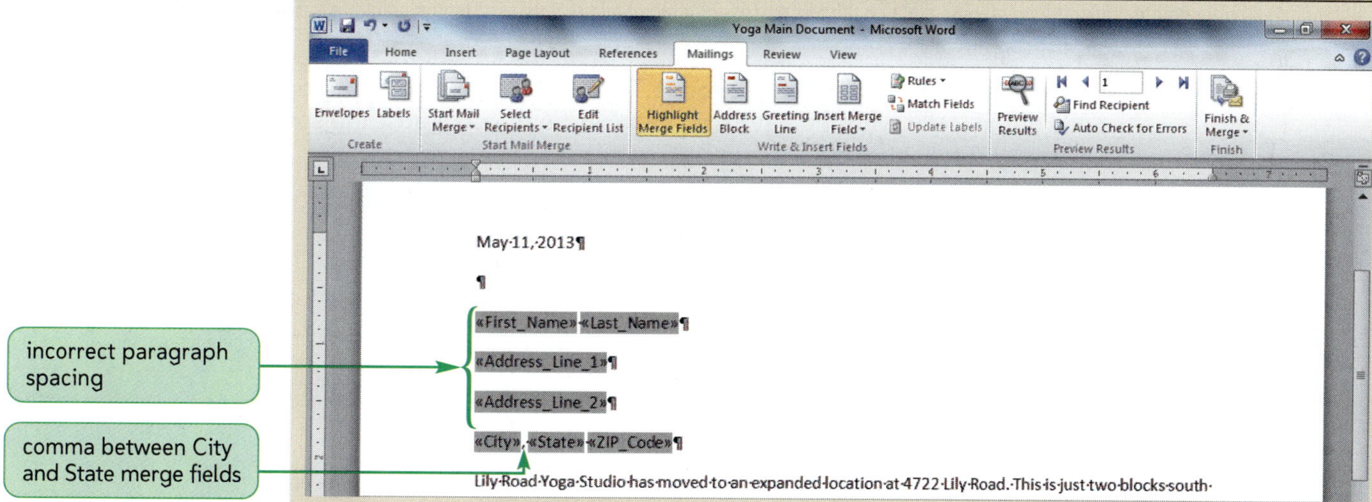


5. Select the first three paragraphs of the inside address, and then click the **Home** tab on the Ribbon.
6. In the Paragraph group, click the **Line and Paragraph Spacing** button, and then click **Remove Space After Paragraph.** The paragraph spacing is removed, so that the paragraphs of the inside address are now correctly spaced.

You can now add the salutation of the letter, which will contain each client's first name.

**To insert the merge field for the salutation:**

1. Insert a new paragraph after the ZIP_Code field, type **Dear**, and then press the **spacebar**.
2. Click the **Mailings** tab on the Ribbon.
3. In the Write & Insert Fields group, click the **Insert Merge Field** button, click **First_Name** to insert this field into the document, and then type **:** (a colon).
4. Save your work.

You'll further personalize the letter by including merge fields that will allow you to reference each client's favorite type of class and teacher.

**To add merge fields for each client's favorite type of class and teacher:**

1. Scroll down to display the third paragraph in the body of the letter, which begins "Please check out our schedule...."
2. In the third paragraph in the body of the letter, select the placeholder **[Favorite Type]**, including the brackets. You'll replace this phrase with a merge field. Don't be concerned if you also select the space following the closing bracket.
3. Insert the **Favorite_Type** merge field. Word replaces the selected text with the Favorite Type merge field.
4. Verify that the field has a single space before it and after it. Add a space on either side if necessary.
5. Replace the placeholder text **[Favorite Teacher]** in the third paragraph in the body of the letter with the **Favorite_Teacher** field, and adjust the spacing as necessary. See Figure 6-13.

   **Trouble?** The text before and after the inserted merge fields might appear with a wavy green underline. This is not a problem.

**Figure 6-13** Main document after inserting merge fields

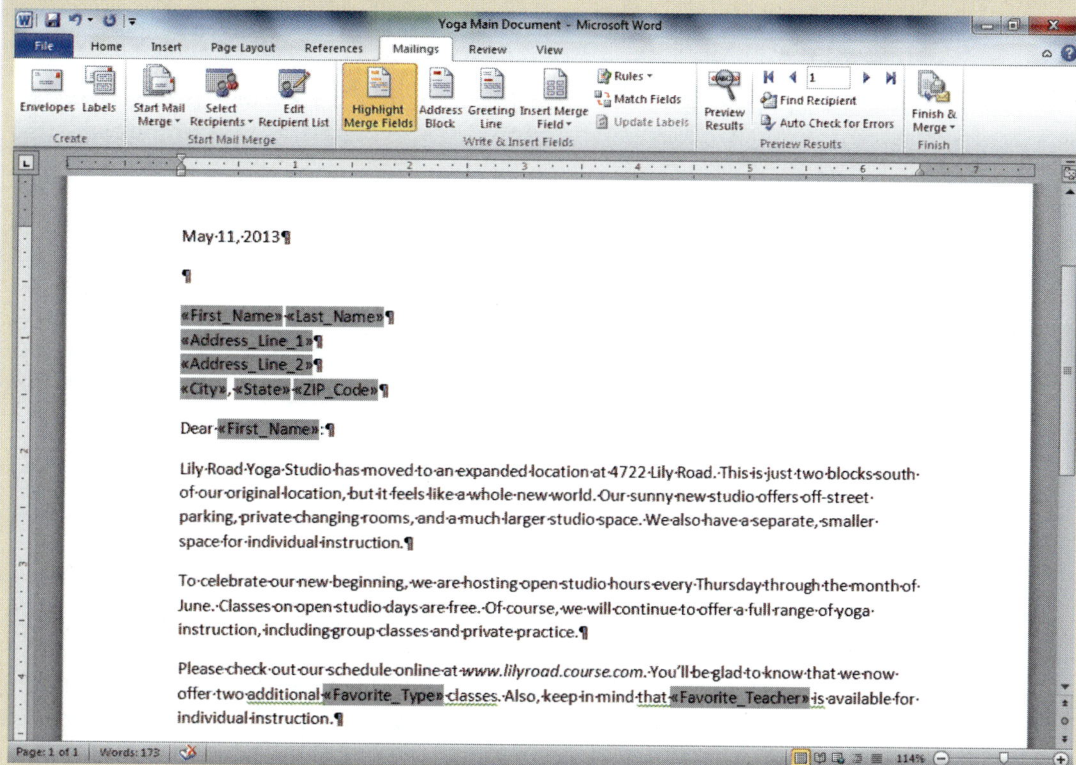

**6.** Save the document.

The main document now contains all the necessary merge fields. The next step is to merge the main document and the data source. Word allows you to preview the merged document before you complete the merge.

# Previewing the Merged Document

Your next step is to preview the merged document to see how the letter will look after Word inserts the information for each client. When you preview the merged document, you can check one last time for any missing spaces between the merge fields and the surrounding text. You can also look for any other formatting problems, and, if necessary, make final changes to the data source.

## To preview the merged document:

**1.** In the Preview Results group, click the **Preview Results** button. The data for the first record (Anna Pearson) replaces the merge fields in the form letter. The inside address for Anna Pearson includes information from the Address Line 2 field, for a total of four lines. The Go to Record box in the Preview Results group shows which record is currently displayed in the document. See Figure 6-14.

**Figure 6-14** First letter with merged data

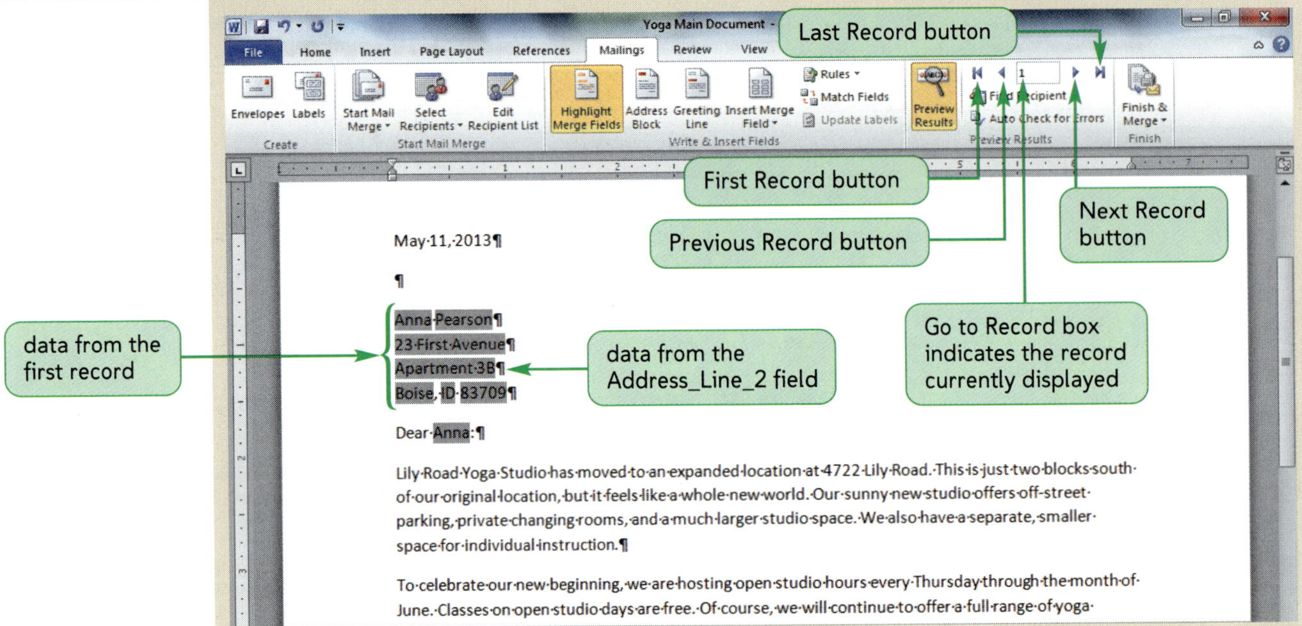


2. Carefully check the Anna Pearson letter to make sure the text and formatting are correct, and make any necessary corrections. In particular, check to make sure that the spaces before and after the merged data are correct; it is easy to accidentally omit spaces or add extra spaces around merge fields.
3. In the Preview Results group, click the **Next Record** button. The data for John Andrews is displayed in the letter. As with the preceding record, the inside address for this record includes four lines of information.
4. Click the **Next Record** button to display the data for Eric Chavez in the letter. In this case, the inside address includes only three lines of information. See Figure 6-15.

**Figure 6-15** Address for third record

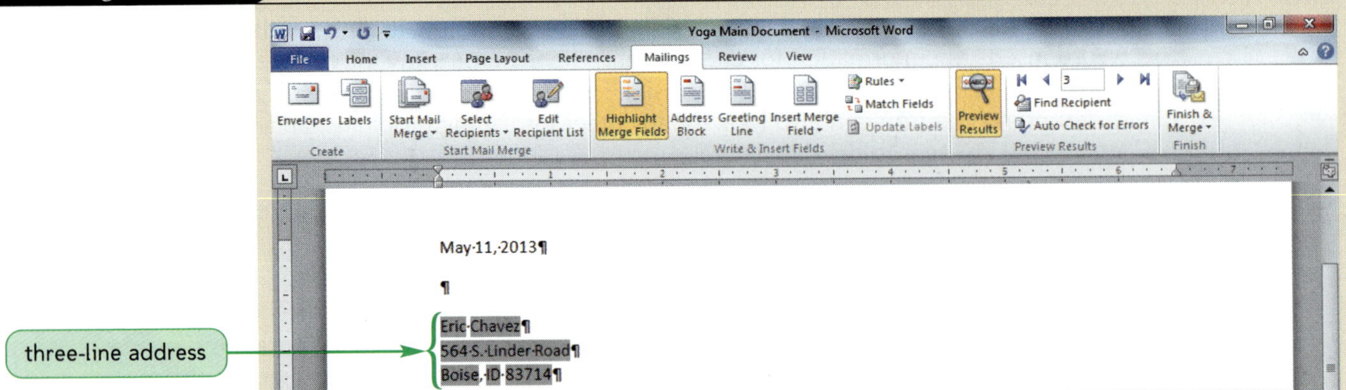


5. In the Preview Results group, click the **First Record** button to redisplay the first record in the letter (with data for Anna Pearson).

The main document of the mail merge is complete. Now that you have previewed the merged documents, you can finish the merge.

## Merging the Main Document and the Data Source

**TIP**

If your data source includes an E-mail Address field, you can merge to email, generating one email for every email address in the data source.

When you finish a merge, you can choose to merge directly to the printer. In other words, you can choose to have Word print the merged document immediately without saving it as a separate file. However, Nina wants to save an electronic copy of the merged document for her records. So you'll merge the data source and main document to a new document.

### To complete the mail merge:

1. In the Finish group, click the **Finish & Merge** button. As shown in Figure 6-16, the Finish & Merge menu displays the three merge options.

**Figure 6-16** Finishing the merge

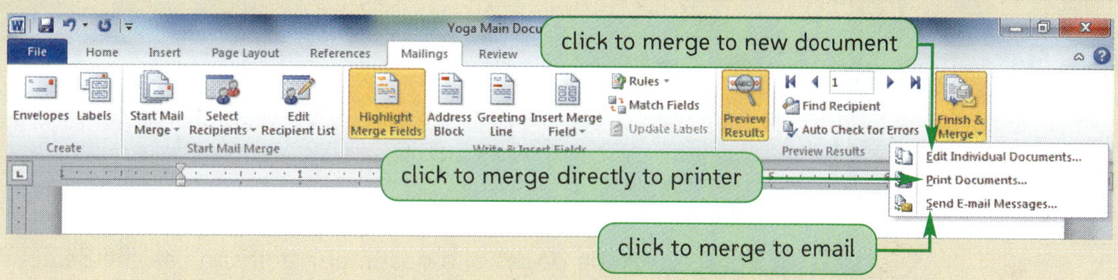


2. In the Finish & Merge menu, click **Edit Individual Documents**. The Merge to New Document dialog box opens. Here, you need to specify which records to include in the merge. You want to include all three records from the data source.
3. Verify that the **All** option button is selected, and then click the **OK** button. Word creates a new document named Letters1, which contains three pages, one for each record in the data source. In this new document, the merge fields have been replaced by the specific names, addresses, and so on, from the data source. See Figure 6-17. The date field appears at the top of every page, highlighted in gray. The gray highlighting will not print.

Figure 6-17 Merged document

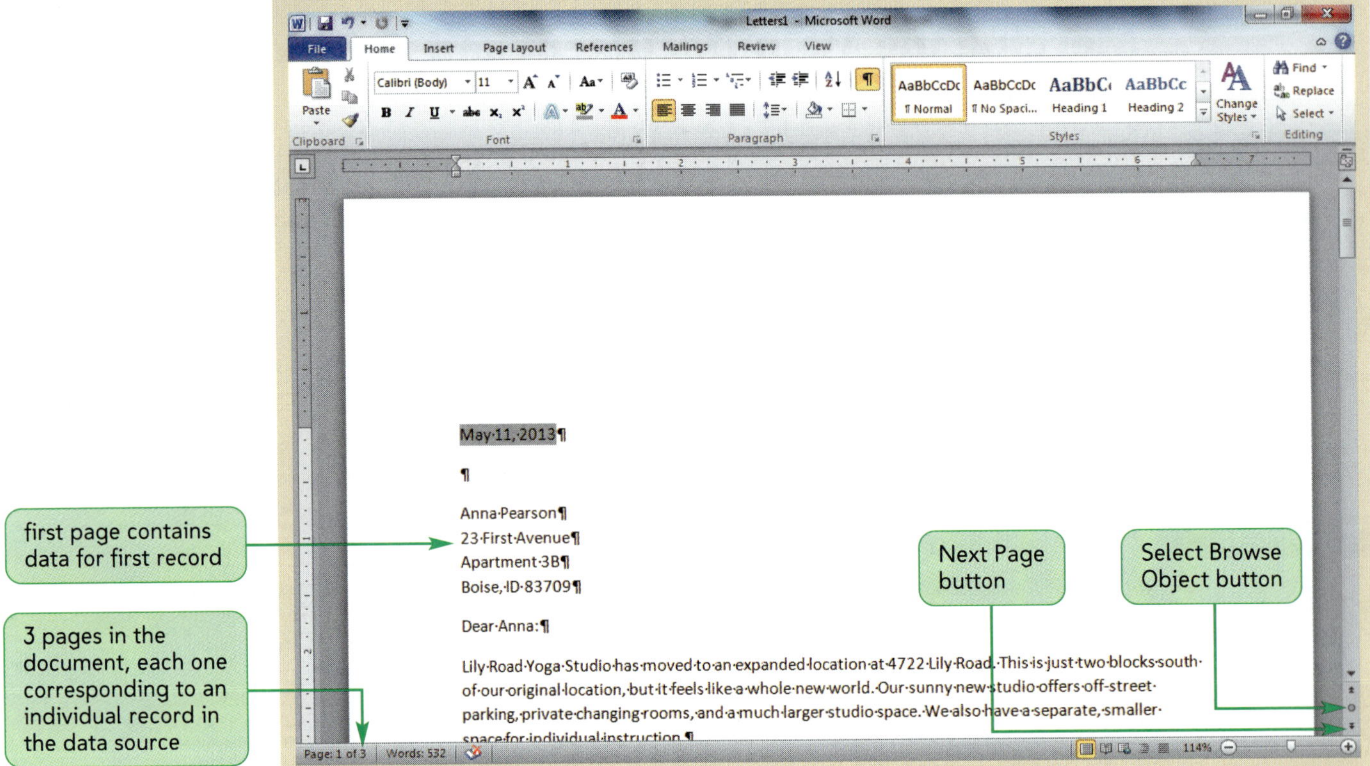


To quickly review the pages of a document, you can use the Select Browse Object button at the bottom of the vertical scroll bar.

4. Click the **Select Browse Object** button near the bottom of the vertical scroll bar, click the **Browse by Page** button on the palette to move to page 2, the letter for John Andrews, and then, below the Select Browse Object button, click the **Next Page** button to move to the letter addressed to Eric Chavez. Note that each letter is addressed to a different client and that the favorite type and teacher vary from one letter to the next.
5. Scroll back to the first page of the document, and as you scroll, notice that the letters are separated by page breaks.
6. Save the merged document in the Word6\Tutorial folder, using the filename **Yoga Merged Letters 1**.
7. Close the **Yoga Merged Letters 1** document. The document named "Yoga Main Document" is now the active document. After completing a merge, you need to save the main document. That ensures that any changes you might have made to the data source in the course of the mail merge are saved along with the main document.
8. Save and close the **Yoga Main Document** document.

Note that if you need to take a break while working on a mail merge, you can save the main document and close it. The data source and field information are saved along with the document. When you're ready to work on the merge again, you can open the main document and update the connection to the data source. You'll see how this works at the beginning of the next session, in which you will learn how to use additional Mail Merge features.

REVIEW

## *Session 6.1 Quick Check*

1. Define the following:
   a. date field
   b. main document
   c. merge field
   d. record
2. A ______________ is a file with information organized into fields and records.
3. True or False. You cannot use an Excel worksheet as a data source.
4. Explain how to use the options in the Mailings tab to insert a merge field into a main document.
5. List the three different ways to complete a merge.

# SESSION 6.2 VISUAL OVERVIEW

The Edit Recipient List button opens the Mail Merge Recipients dialog box.

In the Mail Merge Recipients dialog box, you can make changes that affect entire records or the structure and organization of the data source itself.

To sort a data source according to the contents of a particular field, click that field's column header. To sort in ascending order, click the field header once. To sort in descending order, click it twice.

A check mark indicates that a record will be included in the merge. By default, all records are checked. To omit a record in the merge, click its check box to delete the check mark.

To make changes to contents of individual records, select the data source in the Data Source box, and then click the Edit button to open the Edit Data Source dialog box.

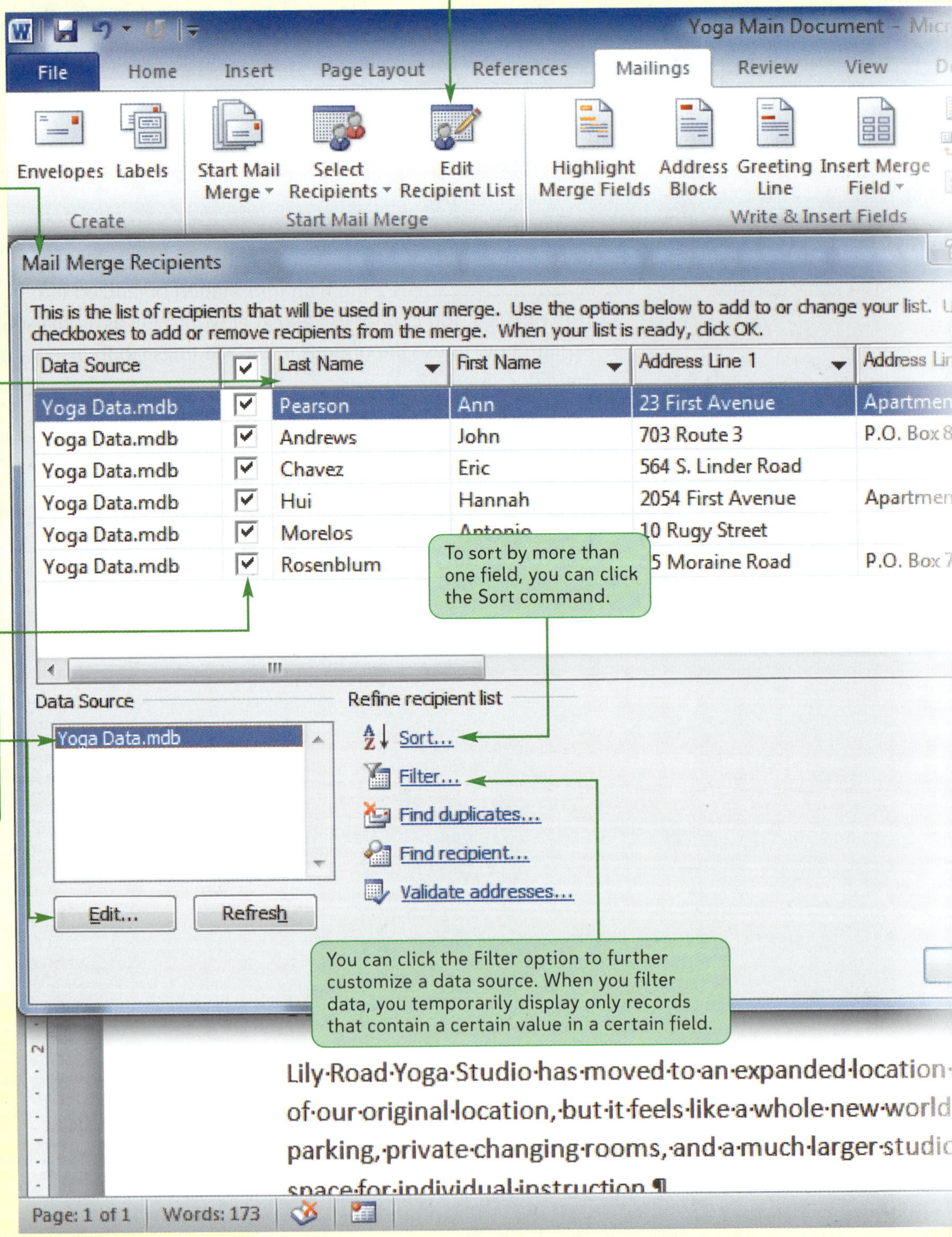


To sort by more than one field, you can click the Sort command.

You can click the Filter option to further customize a data source. When you filter data, you temporarily display only records that contain a certain value in a certain field.

# EDITING A DATA SOURCE

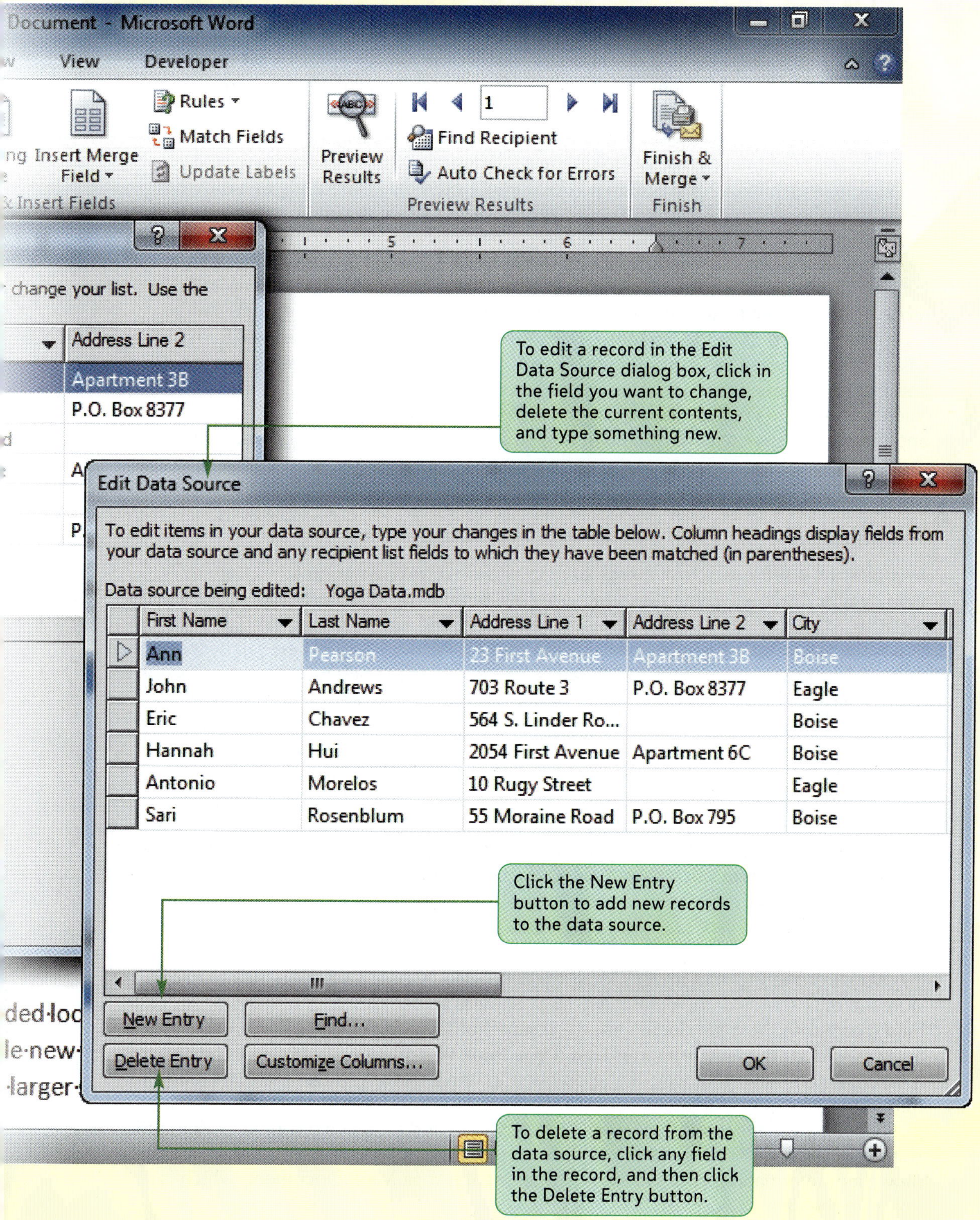

# Reopening a Main Document

After you complete a mail merge, a connection exists between the main document file and the data source file, even after you close the main document and exit Word. The connection is maintained as long as you keep both files in their original locations. The two files don't have to be in the same folder; each file just has to remain in the folder it was in when you first created the connection between the two files. When you reopen a main document, you see a warning dialog box explaining that data from a database (that is, the data source) will be placed in the document you are about to open. You can click Yes to open the document with its connection to the data source intact. If you click No, the main document opens with no connection to the data source. In that case, to perform a mail merge, you would have to select a data source using the Select Recipients button in the Start Mail Merge group on the Mailings tab.

What happens if you move the main document or the data source file to a different folder from the one in which they were originally saved? That depends on how your computer is set up and where you move the files. On most Windows 7 computers, you can't move the *data source* file on its own, but if you move the *main document* file to another location on the same computer, the connection is usually maintained. However, if you move the document to another computer on a network, or to a different storage media (say from the hard drive to a memory stick), the connection might be broken. In that case, when you open the main document, you'll see a series of message boxes informing you that the connection to the data source has been broken. Eventually, you will see a Microsoft Word dialog box with a button labeled Find Data Source, which you can click, and then use the Select Data Source dialog box to locate and select your data source.

PROSKILLS

### *Teamwork: Sharing Main Documents and Data Sources*

In professional settings, a mail merge project often involves files originating from multiple people. The best way to manage these files depends on your particular situation. For instance, at a small office supply company, the marketing manager might supply the text of a main document introducing monthly sales on printer supplies, while a sales representative might supply an updated list of names and addresses of potential customers every month. Suppose that you are the person responsible for performing the mail merge on the first of every month. You will be able to perform your work more efficiently if you, the marketing manager, and the sales representative know ahead of time where to store your contributions to the project. For example, you might have a special folder on the company network set up for storing these files.

In large companies, which maintain massive databases of customer information, a data source is typically stored at a fixed network location. In such cases, maintaining the security of the data is extremely important. You usually can't access such a data source without a password and the appropriate encryption software.

If you are creating mail merges for your own personal use, it's a good idea to either store the data source in the default My Data Sources folder and keep it there, or store the data source and the main document in the same folder (a folder other than the My Data Sources folder). The latter option is best if you think you might need to move the files to a different computer. That way, if you do need to move them, you can move the entire folder.

Nina has new client information she wants you to add to the data source used in the last mail merge, and she wants to perform another merge with the new data. To add the new client information, you will start by opening the Yoga Main Document, which is linked to the data source.

**To reopen the main document:**

1. Open the document named **Yoga Main Document** from the Word6\Tutorial folder included with your Data Files. A warning message appears, indicating that opening the document will run an SQL command. SQL is the database programming language that controls the connection between the main document and the data source.
2. Click the **Yes** button to open the main document with its link to the data source intact, and then click the **Mailings** tab on the Ribbon. The main document displays the data for the last record you examined when you previewed the merged document (Anna Pearson). You can alternate between displaying the merge fields and the client data by toggling the Preview Results button on the Mailings tab.

   **Trouble?** If you see the merge fields instead of the data for one of the yoga clients, skip to Step 4.
3. In the Preview Results group, click the **Preview Results** button to deselect it. The merge fields are displayed in the main document. The date field, at the beginning of the letter, displays the current date.
4. If necessary, highlight the merge fields by clicking the **Highlight Merge Fields** button in the Write & Insert Fields group.

# Editing a Data Source

After you complete a mail merge, you might find that you need to make some changes to the data source and redo the merge. You can edit a data source in two ways—from within the program used to create the data source, or via the Mail Merge Recipients dialog box in Word. If you are familiar with the program used to create the data source, the simplest approach is to edit the file from within that program. For example, if you were using an Excel worksheet as your data source, you could open the file in Excel, edit it (perhaps by adding new records), save it, and then reselect the file as your data source. To edit a Microsoft Office Address Lists file from within Word, you can use the Mail Merge Recipients dialog box.

REFERENCE

*Editing a Data Source in Word*

- Open the main document for the data source you want to edit.
- In the Start Mail Merge group on the Mailings tab, click the Edit Recipient List button.
- In the Data Source box in the Mail Merge Recipients dialog box, select the data source you want to edit, and then click the Edit button.
- To add a record, click the New Entry button, and then type a new record.
- To delete a record, click any field in the record, and then click the Delete Entry button.
- To add or remove fields from the data source, click the Customize Columns button, make any changes, and then click the OK button. Remember that if you remove a field, you will delete any data entered into that field.
- Click the OK button in the Edit Data Source dialog box, click the Yes button in the Microsoft Office Word dialog box, and then click the OK button in the Mail Merge Recipients dialog box.

Nina would like you to add information for three new clients to the data source.

**To edit the data source by adding records:**

1. In the Start Mail Merge group on the Mail Merge tab, click the **Edit Recipient List** button. The Mail Merge Recipients dialog box opens, displaying the three records you added when you first created the data source. The Data Source box in the lower-left corner allows you to select a data source to edit. If you had multiple data sources stored in the Word6\Tutorial folder, you would see them all in this list box.
2. In the Data Source box, click **Yoga Data.mdb**. The filename is selected.
3. Click the **Edit** button. The Edit Data Source dialog box opens.
4. Use the New Entry button to enter the information for the three new records shown in Figure 6-18. When you are finished, you will have a total of six records in the data source. Notice that the record for Antonio Morelos contains no Address Line 2 data.

**Figure 6-18** New client data

| First Name | Last Name | Address Line 1 | Address Line 2 | City | State | Zip Code | E-Mail Address | Phone | Favorite Type | Favorite Teacher |
|---|---|---|---|---|---|---|---|---|---|---|
| Hannah | Hiu | 2054 First Avenue | Apartment 6C | Boise | ID | 83709 | hiu@surgery.hospital.net | 208-775-3093 | Hatha | Niki Dronza |
| Antonio | Morelos | 10 Rugby Street | | Eagle | ID | 83707 | morelos-a@bfjorgen.com | 208-787-1000 | Hatha | Niki Dronza |
| Sari | Rosenblum | 55 Moraine Road | P.O. Box 795 | Boise | ID | 83710 | sari@rosenblum78.course.com | 208-987-0098 | Power Yoga | Carolyn Ramirez |

5. Click the **OK** button, and then click the **Yes** button in the message box that appears, asking if you want to update the Yoga Data.mdb file. You return to the Mail Merge Recipients dialog box, as shown in Figure 6-19.

   **Trouble?** If your records look different from those in Figure 6-19, select the data source, click the Edit button, edit the data source, and then click the OK button.

**Figure 6-19** **New records added to data source**

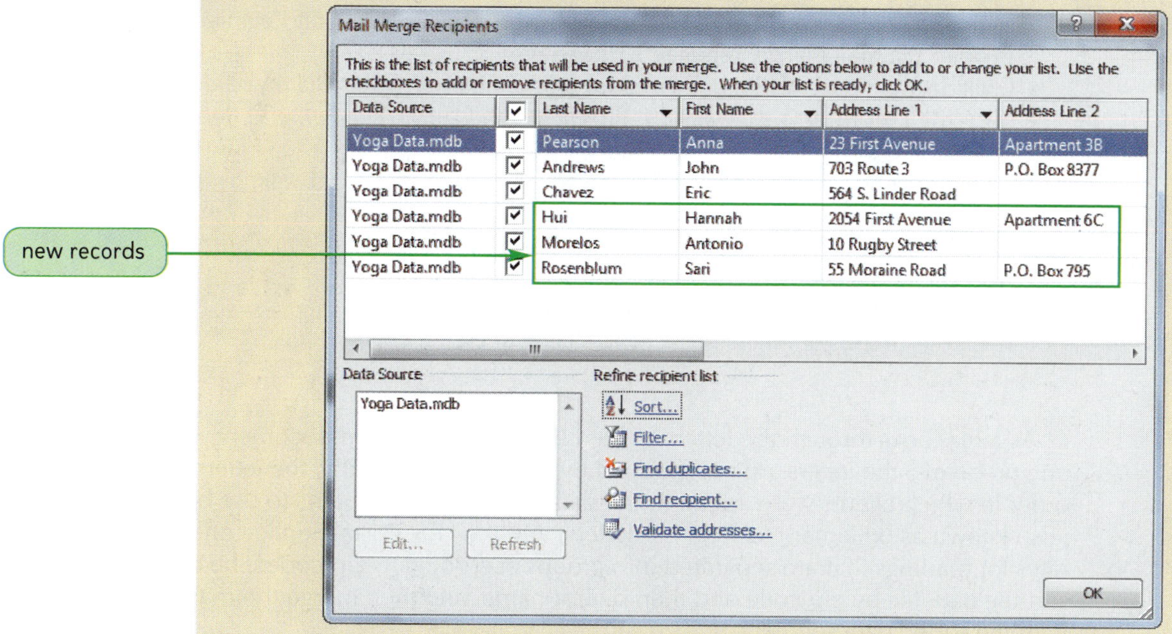


You'll leave the Mail Merge Recipients dialog box open so you can use it to make other changes to the data source.

## Sorting Records

You can sort information in a data source table just as you sort information in any other table. Recall that to sort means to rearrange a list or a document in alphabetical, numerical, or chronological order. To quickly sort information in ascending order (*A* to *Z*, lowest to highest, or earliest to latest) or in descending order (*Z* to *A*, highest to lowest, or latest to earliest), click a field's heading in the Mail Merge Recipients dialog box. The first time you click the heading, the records are sorted in ascending order. If you click it a second time, the records are sorted in descending order.

To perform a more complicated sort, you can click the Sort command in the Mail Merge Recipients dialog box. This opens the Filter and Sort dialog box, where you can choose to sort by more than one field. For example, you could sort records in ascending order by last name, and then in ascending order by first name, in which case the records would be organized alphabetically by last name, and then, in cases where multiple records contained the same last name, those records would be sorted by first name.

REFERENCE

## *Sorting a Data Source by Multiple Fields*

- In the Start Mail Merge group on the Mailings tab, click the Edit Recipient List button to open the Mail Merge Recipients dialog box.
- Click Sort to open the Sort Records tab of the Filter and Sort dialog box.
- Click the Sort by arrow, select the first field you want to sort by, and then select the Descending option button if necessary.
- Click the Then by arrow and select the second field you want to sort by, and then select the Descending option button if necessary.
- If necessary, click the Then by arrow and select the third field you want to sort by, and then select the Descending option button if necessary.
- Click the OK button to close the Filter and Sort dialog box.
- Click the OK button to close the Mail Merge Recipients dialog box.

As Nina looks through the letters to her clients in the merged document, she notices one problem—the letters are not grouped by zip codes. Currently, the letters are in the order in which clients were added to the data source file. She plans to use business mail (also known as bulk mail) to send her letters, and the U.S. Postal Service offers lower rates for mailings that are separated into groups according to zip code. She asks you to sort the data file by zip code and then by last name, and then merge the main document with the sorted data source.

### To sort the data source by zip code:

1. In the Mail Merge Recipients dialog box, click **Sort**. The Filter and Sort dialog box opens, with the Sort Records tab displayed.
2. Click the **Sort by** arrow, and then click **ZIP Code**.
3. Click the first **Then by** arrow, and then click **Last Name**. See Figure 6-20.

**Figure 6-20** **Sorting by zip code and by last name**

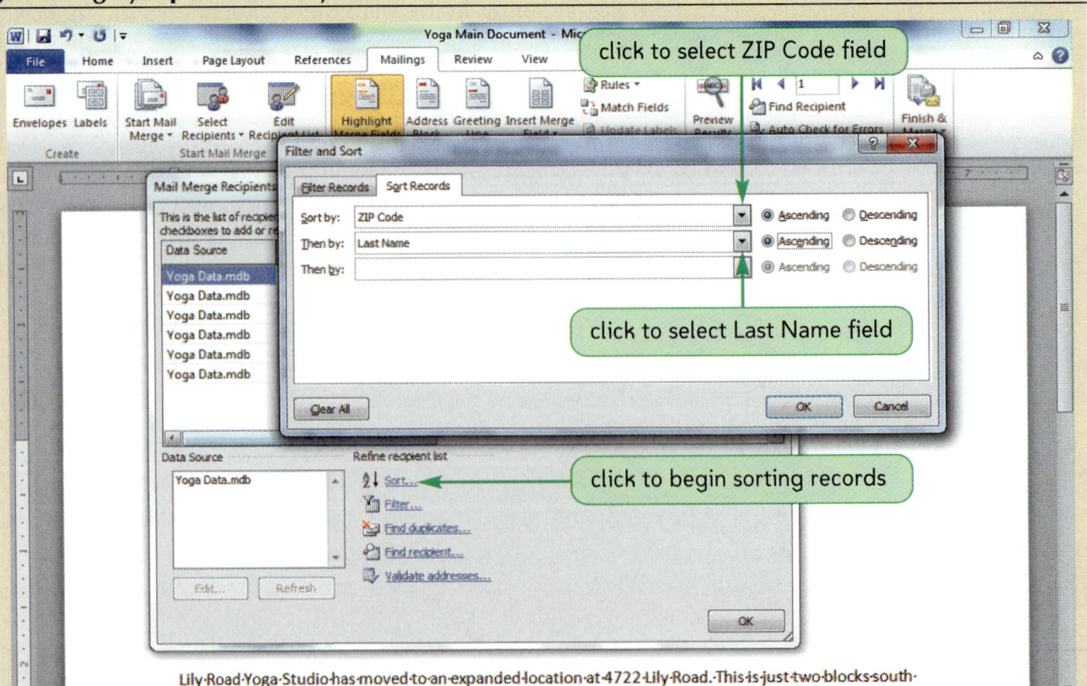

4. Click the **OK** button. Word sorts the records from lowest zip code number to highest, and then, within each zip code, it sorts the records by last name. In the Mail Merge Recipients dialog box, the record for John Andrews, with zip code 83707, is now at the top of the data source list. The record for Antonio Morelos, which also has a zip code of 83707, comes second. The remaining records are sorted similarly, with the record for Eric Chavez the last in the list. When you merge the data source with the form letter, the letters will appear in the merged document in this order.
5. Click the **OK** button. The Mail Merge Recipients dialog box closes.
6. In the Preview Results group, click the **Preview Results** button. The data for John Andrews is displayed in the main document.
7. In the Finish group, click the **Finish & Merge** button, click **Edit Individual Documents**, verify that the **All** option button is selected in the Merge to New Document dialog box, and then click the **OK** button. Word generates the new merged document with six letters, one letter per page as before—but this time the first letter is to John Andrews, who has the lowest zip code (83707) and a last name that comes before "Morelos" in the alphabet.
8. Use the Select Browse Object button to browse by page and verify that the letters in the newly merged document are arranged in ascending order by zip code.
9. Save the new merged document in the Word6\Tutorial folder, using the filename **Yoga Merged Letters 2**, and then close it. You return to the Yoga Main Document.
10. Save the Yoga Main Document file.

Next, Nina would like you to create a set of letters to just those clients who listed Carolyn Ramirez as their favorite teacher.

## Filtering Records

Nina wants to inform clients that the teacher Carolyn Ramirez is available for individual instruction only on Tuesdays and Thursdays. She asks you to modify the form letter and then merge it with the records of clients who have indicated that Carolyn is their favorite teacher. To select specific records in a data source, you **filter** the data source to temporarily display only the records containing a particular value in a particular field. To filter a data source, open the Mail Merge Recipients dialog box, click the arrow button in the column header for the field for which you want to specify a value to filter by, and then click the value you want to filter by.

### To filter the data source to select specific records for the merge:

1. In the Preview Results group, click the **Preview Results** button to deselect it and display the merge fields in the Yoga Main Document file instead of the data from the data source.
2. Scroll the document, and then in the body of the letter, click at the end of the third paragraph, which begins "Please check out our schedule online...."
3. Press the ← key to move the insertion point to the left of the period, insert a space, type **on Tuesdays and Thursdays**, and then verify that the sentence reads "...<<Favorite_Teacher>> is available for individual instruction on Tuesdays and Thursdays."

4. Save the Yoga Main Document with the new name, **Carolyn Main Document**, in the Word6\Tutorial folder included with your Data Files.

**TIP**

To remove an individual record from a merge, deselect the corresponding check box in the Mail Merge Recipients dialog box.

5. In the Start Mail Merge group, click the **Edit Recipient List** button to open the Mail Merge Recipients dialog box, and then scroll right so you can see the Favorite Teacher field.

6. Click the arrow button in the Favorite Teacher column header. A menu opens, listing all the entries in the Favorite Teacher field as well as a few other options. You can use the (All) option to redisplay all records after previously filtering a data source. See Figure 6-21.

**Figure 6-21** Filtering records in a data source

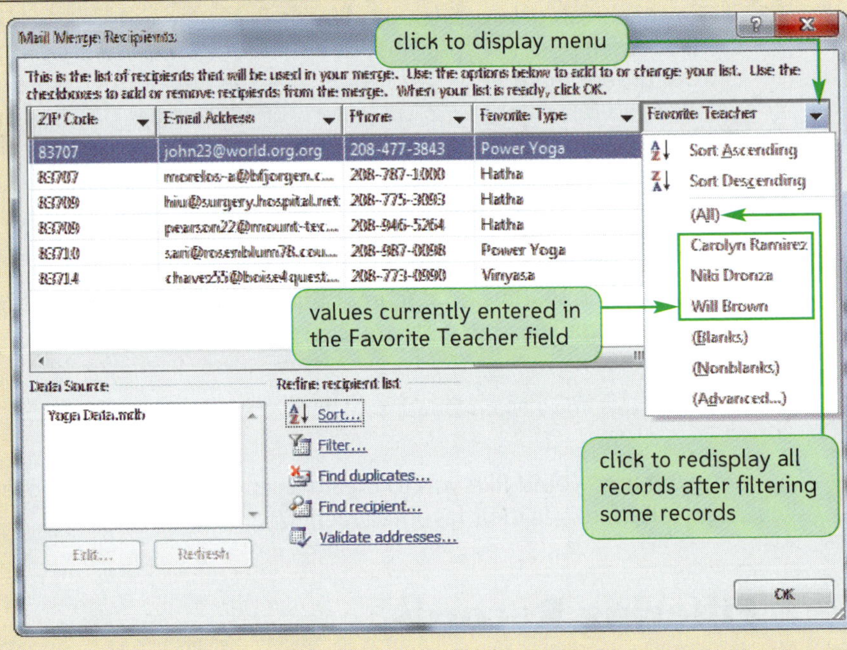


You can use the Advanced option in the Filter menu to open the Filter Records tab in the Filter and Sort dialog box, where you can perform complex filter operations that involve comparing the contents of one or more fields to a particular value to determine if a record should be displayed or not.

7. Click **Carolyn Ramirez**. Word temporarily hides all the records in the data source except those that contain "Carolyn Ramirez" in the Favorite Teacher field. See Figure 6-22. Now you can complete the merge.

**Figure 6-22** **Filtered data source**

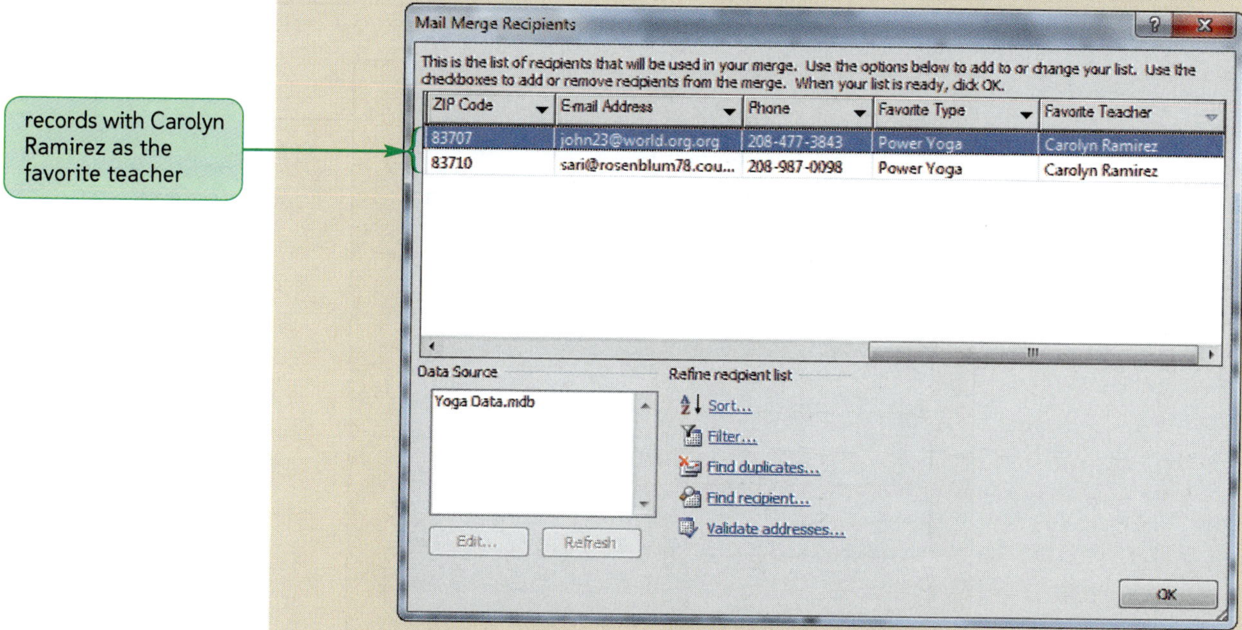


8. Click the **OK** button. The Mail Merge Recipients dialog box closes.
9. In the Preview Results group, click the **Preview Results** button, and then review the two records, for John Andrews and Sari Rosenblum, as they appear in the main document.
10. In the Finish group, click the **Finish & Merge** button, click **Edit Individual Documents**, in the Merge to New Document dialog box verify that the **All** option button is selected, and then click the **OK** button. Word generates the new merged document with two letters, one letter per page.
11. Save the merged document in the Word6\Tutorial folder using the filename **Yoga Merged Letters 3**, and then close it.
12. Save the **Carolyn Main Document** file, and then close it.

Next, you'll create and print mailing labels for the form letters.

## Creating Mailing Labels

Nina could print the names and addresses for the letters directly on envelopes, or she could perform a mail merge to create mailing labels. The latter method is easier because she can print 14 labels at once, rather than printing one envelope at a time.

Nina has purchased Avery® Laser Printer labels, which are available in most office-supply stores. Word supports most of the Avery label formats, allowing you to choose the layout that works best for you. Nina purchased labels in 8 1/2 × 11-inch sheets that are designed to feed through a printer. Each label measures 4 × 1.33 inches. Each sheet contains seven rows of labels, with two labels in each row, for a total of 14 labels. See Figure 6-23.

Figure 6-23 Layout of a sheet of Avery® labels

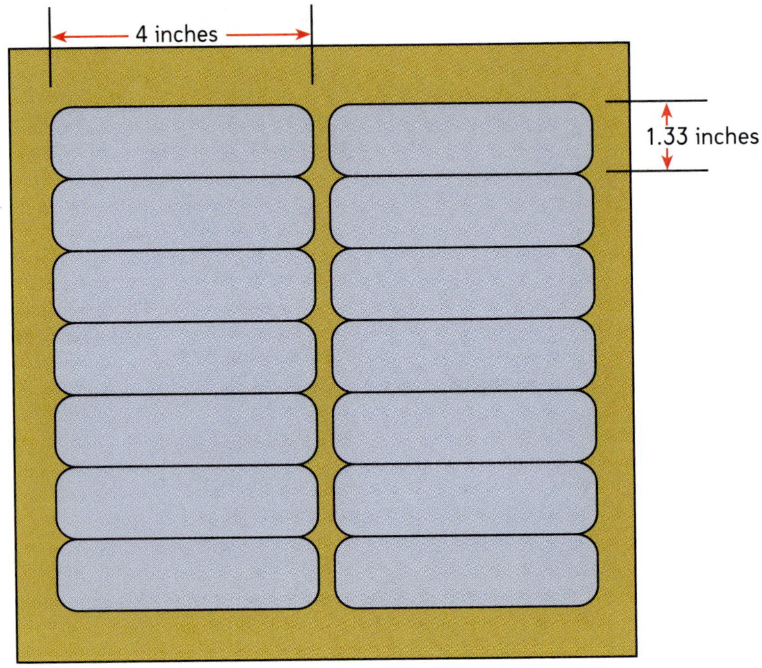


Performing a mail merge to create mailing labels is similar to performing a mail merge for a form letter. You begin by selecting Labels as the type of main document, and then you specify the brand and product number for the labels you are using. You will also need to specify a data source file. In this case you will use the Microsoft Office Address Lists data source file, Yoga Data.mdb, that you created and used in the form letter mail merges.

### To specify the main document for creating mailing labels:

1. Open a new, blank document, make sure nonprinting characters are displayed, and zoom out so you can see the whole page.
2. Save the document to the Word6\Tutorial folder using the filename **Yoga Labels Main Document**.
3. Click the **Mailings** tab on the Ribbon.
4. In the Start Mail Merge group, click the **Start Mail Merge** button, and then click **Labels**. The Label Options dialog box opens.
5. Click the **Label vendors** arrow, and then click **Avery US Letter**.
6. Scroll down the Product number box, and then click **5162 Easy Peel Address Labels**. See Figure 6-24.

**Figure 6-24** **Label Options dialog box**

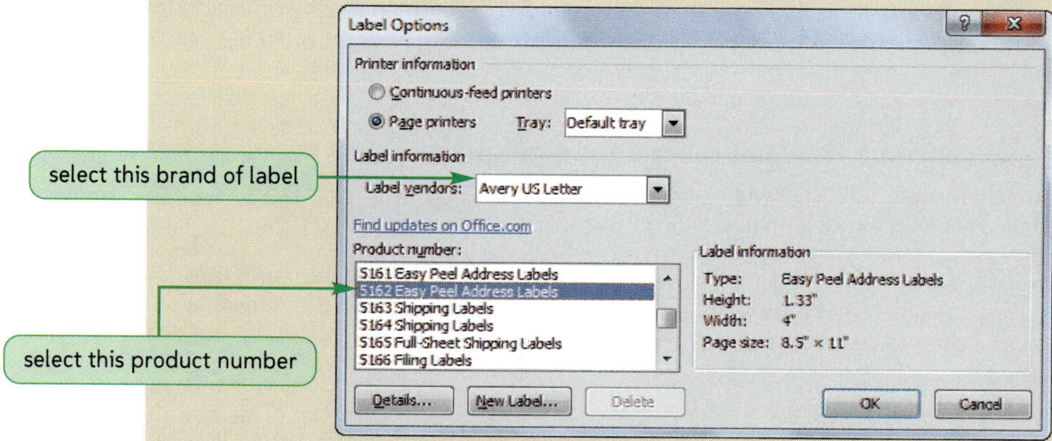


7. Click the **OK** button. The Label Options dialog box closes and Word inserts a table structure into the document, with one cell for each of the 14 labels on the page, as shown in Figure 6-25. The gridlines are visible only on the screen; they will not be visible on the printed labels.

**Figure 6-25** **Document ready for labels**

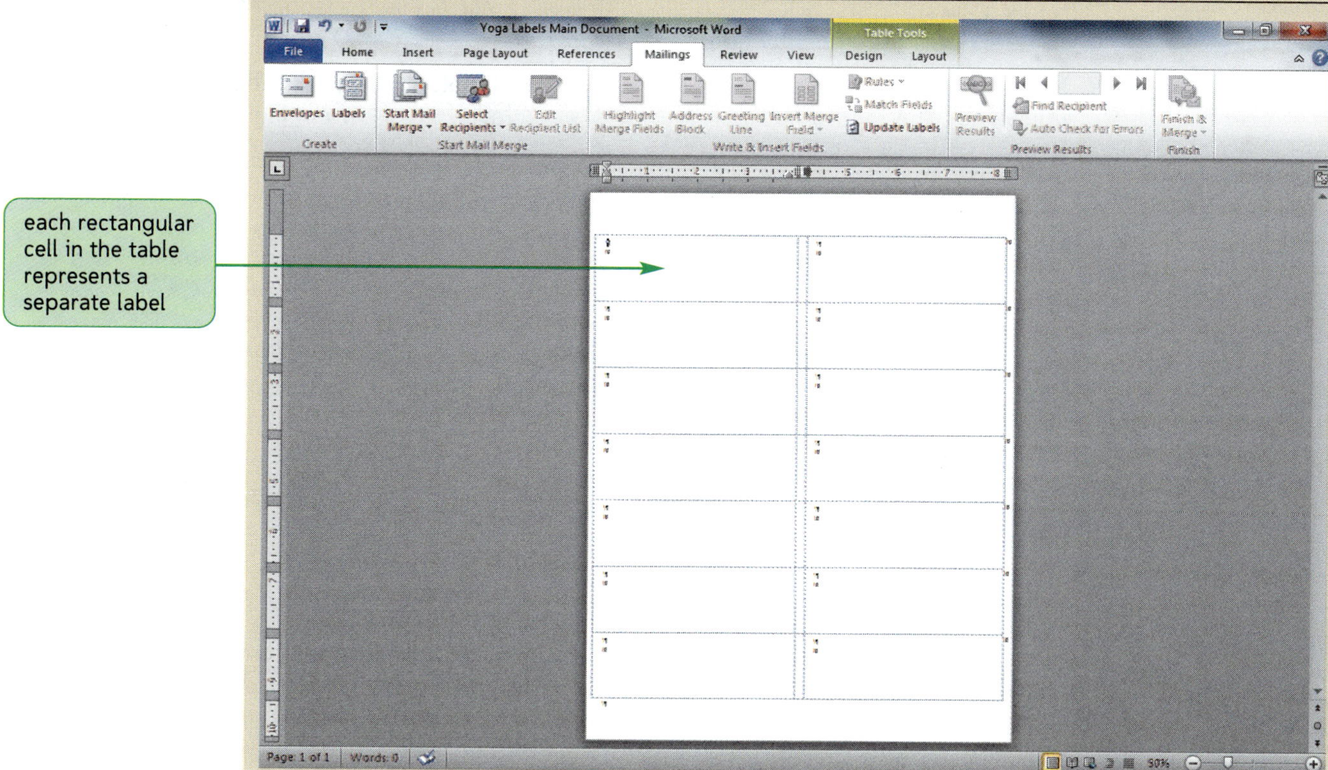


**Trouble?** If you don't see the table gridlines, click the Table Tools Layout tab, and then, in the Table group, click the View Gridlines button to select it.

You are finished setting up the document. Next, you need to select the data source you created earlier. Note that the changes you made to the data source as a whole earlier in this session (sorting the records and selecting only some records) have no effect on the data source in this new mail merge. However, the changes you made to individual records (such as editing individual records or adding new records) are retained.

## To continue the mail merge for the labels:

1. In the Start Mail Merge group on the Mailings tab, click the **Select Recipients** button and then click **Use Existing List**. The Select Data Source dialog box opens.
2. Navigate to the Word6\Tutorial folder, select the file named **Yoga Data**, and then click the **Open** button. The Select Data Source dialog box closes and you return to the main document.
3. Change the zoom to Page Width so you can read the document. In each label except the first one, the code <<Next Record>> appears. This code tells Word to retrieve the next record from the data source for each label.
4. Verify that the insertion point is located in the upper-left label, and then click the **Mailings tab** on the Ribbon.
5. In the Write & Insert Fields group, click the **Address Block** button. The Insert Address Block dialog box opens. The left pane displays possible formats for the name in the address block. The default format, "Joshua Randall Jr.," simply inserts the first and last name, which is what Nina wants. The Preview pane currently shows the first address in the data source, for Anna Pearson. You can click the Next button to display additional addresses.
6. In the Preview section of the Insert Address Field dialog box, click the **Next** button ▷. The record for John Andrews is displayed, as shown in Figure 6-26.

**TIP**

You can only use the Address Block merge field if you include a State field in your data source.

**Figure 6-26 Previewing addresses in the Insert Address Block dialog box**

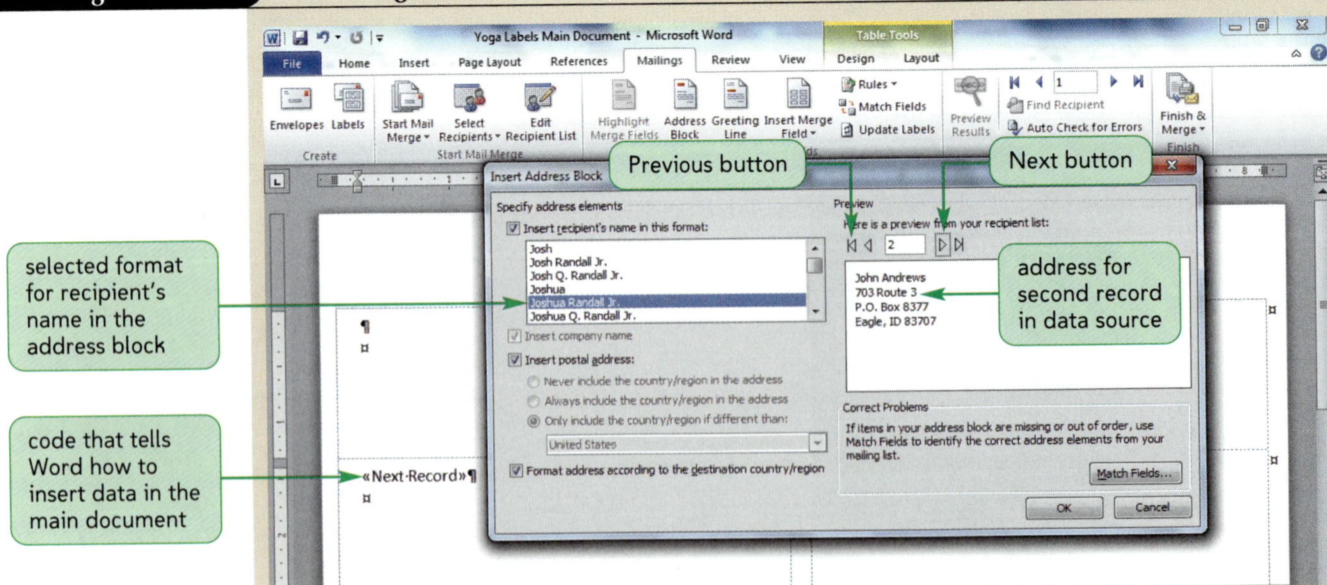


7. Click the **OK** button. The Insert Address Block dialog box closes, and an Address Block merge field appears in the upper-left label on the page. Next, you need to update the remaining labels to match the one containing the Address Block merge field.

8. In the Write & Insert Fields group, click the **Update Labels** button. The Address Block merge field is inserted into all the labels in the document, as shown in Figure 6-27. In all except the upper-left label, the Next Record code appears to the left of the Address Block merge field.

**Figure 6-27** Field codes inserted into document

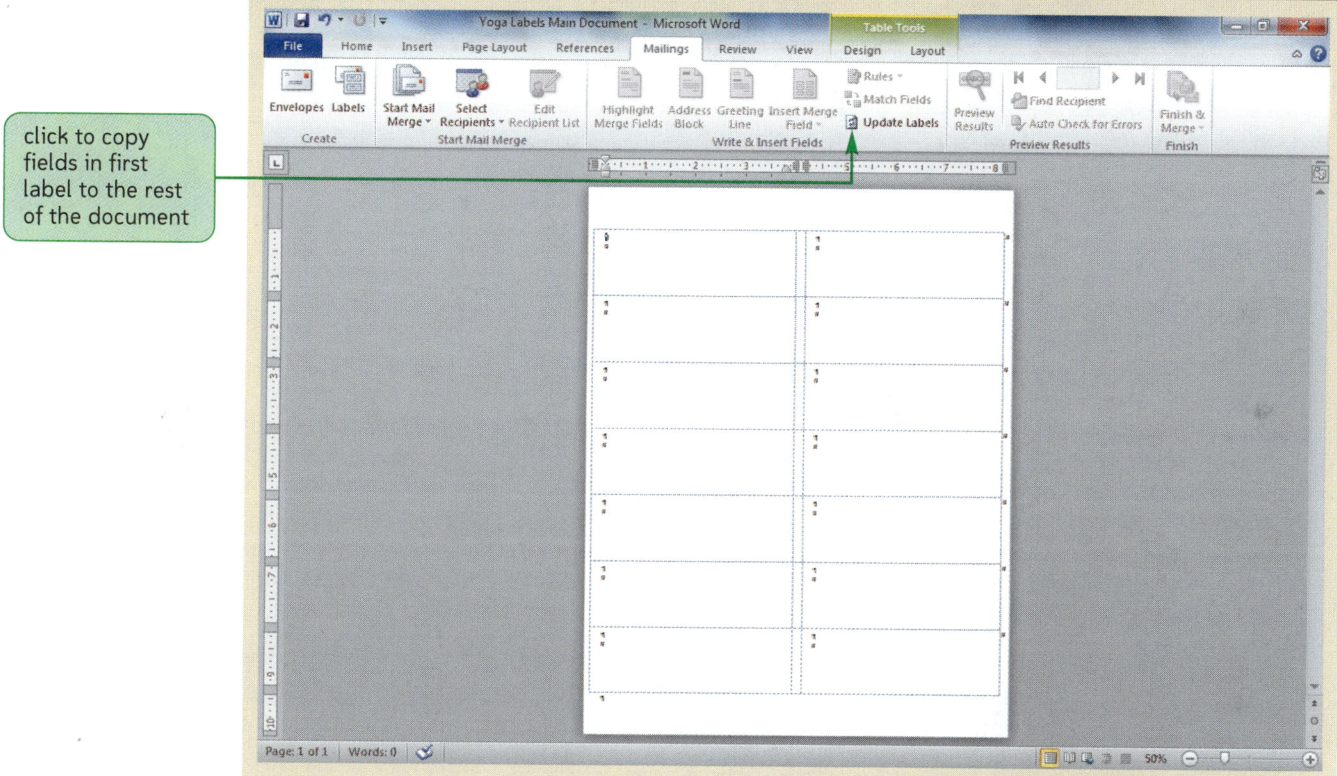


You are ready to preview the labels and complete the merge. To ensure that you see all the labels in the preview, make sure the Go to Records box in the Preview Results group displays the number "1".

## To preview the labels and complete the merge:

1. If necessary, click the **First Record** button in the Preview Results group to display "1" in the Go to Record box.
2. In the Preview Results group, click the **Preview Results** button. The data for Nina's six clients is displayed in the main document. See Figure 6-28.

**Figure 6-28** Previewing addresses in labels

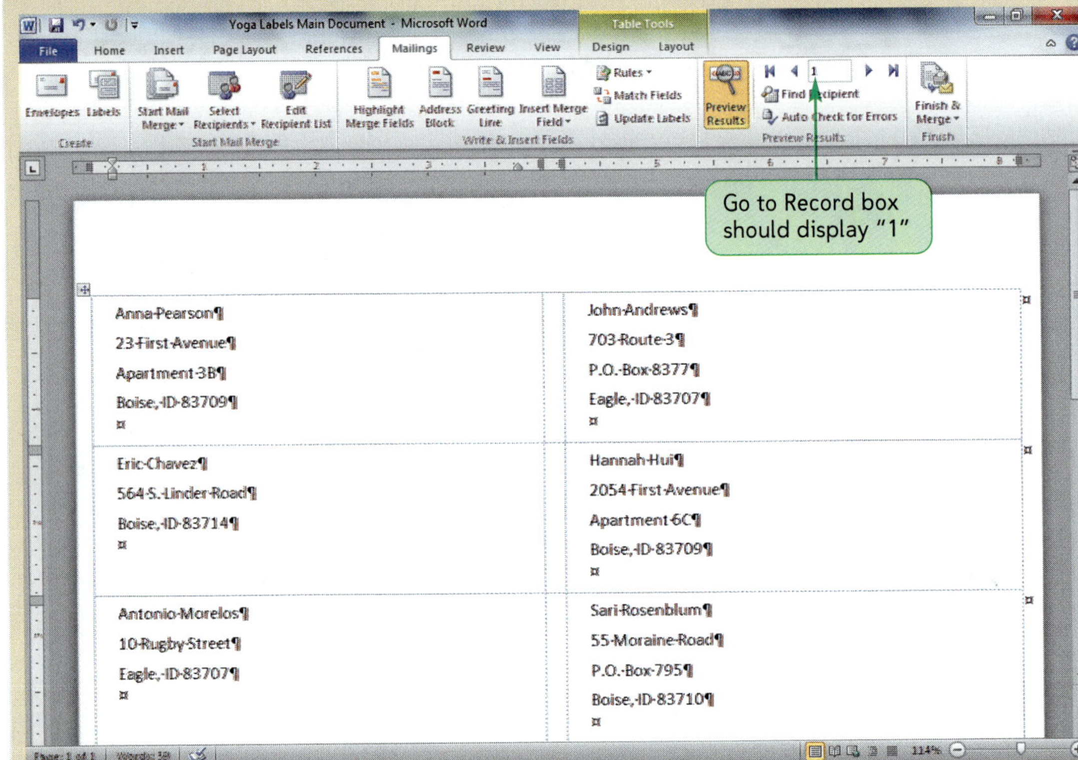


3. In the Finish group, click the **Finish & Merge** button, click **Edit Individual Documents**, verify that the **All** option button is selected in the Merge to New Document dialog box, and then click the **OK** button. The finished labels are inserted into a new document.
4. Scroll through the document. The document contains space for 14 labels, but because the data source contains only six records, the new document contains addresses for six labels.
5. In the upper-left label, change "Anna Pearson" to your name, and then save the merged document in the Word6\Tutorial folder using the filename **Yoga Merged Labels**.
6. Close the **Yoga Merged Labels** document, then save and close the Yoga Labels Main Document file.

**TIP**

It is a good idea to print one page of a label document on regular paper so you can check your work before printing on the more expensive sheets of adhesive labels.

## Creating a Telephone Directory

Next, Nina wants you to create a list of telephone numbers for all the teachers at Lily Road Yoga Studio. Nina has already created a Word document containing the phone numbers; you will use that document as the data source for the merge. You'll set up a mail merge as before, except this time you'll select Directory as the main document type. You'll start by examining the Word document that Nina wants you to use as the data source and then create the main document.

### To review the data source and create the main document for the merge:

1. Open the document named **Phone** from the Word6\Tutorial folder, and then save it as **Phone Data** in the same folder. The information in this document is arranged in a table with three column headings: "First Name," "Last Name," and "Phone." The information in the table has already been sorted in alphabetical order by last name.
2. In the bottom row, replace "Nina Ranabhat" with your first and last name, and then save and close the Phone Data document.
3. Open a new, blank document, display nonprinting characters and the rulers, if necessary, and change the Zoom to Page Width.
4. Save the main document in the Word6\Tutorial folder using the filename **Phone Directory with Merge Fields**.
5. Click the **Mailings** tab on the Ribbon.
6. In the Start Mail Merge group, click the **Start Mail Merge** button, and then click **Directory**.
7. In the Start Mail Merge group, click the **Select Recipients** button, and then click **Use Existing List** to open the Select Data Source dialog box.
8. Navigate to and select the file named **Phone Data** in the Word6\Tutorial folder, and click the **Open** button. The main document is still blank; you'll insert the merge fields next.

You're ready to insert the fields in the main document. Nina wants the telephone list to include the names at the left margin of the page and the phone numbers at the right margin. You'll set up the main document so that the phone number is preceded by a dot leader. A **dot leader** is a dotted line that extends from the last letter of text on the left margin to the beginning of the nearest text aligned at a tab stop.

### To set up the directory main document with dot leaders:

1. With the insertion point in the first line of the document, insert the **First_Name** merge field, insert a space, insert the **Last_Name** merge field, and then in the Write & Insert Fields group, click the **Highlight Merge Fields** button. The First Name and Last Name merge fields are displayed on a gray background. Now you'll set a tab stop at the right margin (at the 6-inch mark on the ruler) with a dot leader.
2. Click the **Home** tab on the Ribbon.
3. In the Paragraph group, click the **Dialog Box Launcher** to open the Paragraph dialog box, and then in the lower-left corner of the Indents and Spacing tab, click the **Tabs** button. The Tabs dialog box opens.
4. Type **6** in the Tab stop position box, click the **Right** option button in the Alignment section, and then click the **2 .......** option button in the Leader section. See Figure 6-29.

**TIP**

You can click the Clear All button in the Tabs dialog box to delete all the tab stops in the document.

Figure 6-29 **Creating a tab with a dot leader**

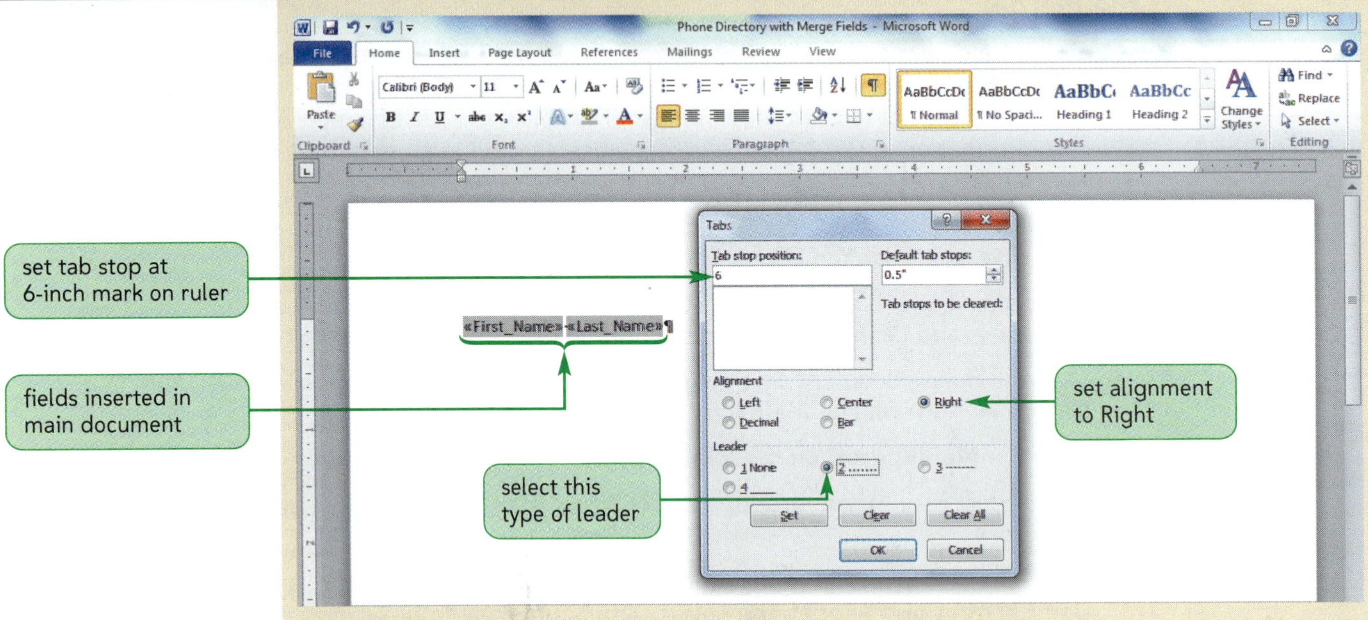


5. Click the **OK** button. Word clears the current tab stops and inserts a right-aligned tab stop at the 6-inch mark on the horizontal ruler.
6. Press the **Tab** key to move the insertion point to the new tab stop. A dotted line stretches across the page, from the Last Name field to the right margin.
7. Click the **Mailings** tab on the Ribbon, and then insert the **Phone** merge field at the insertion point. The dot leader shortens to accommodate the inserted merge field.
8. Press the **Enter** key. The completed main document should look like Figure 6-30.

You must insert a new paragraph here for each name and telephone number to appear on a separate line.

Figure 6-30 **Completed main document for telephone directory**

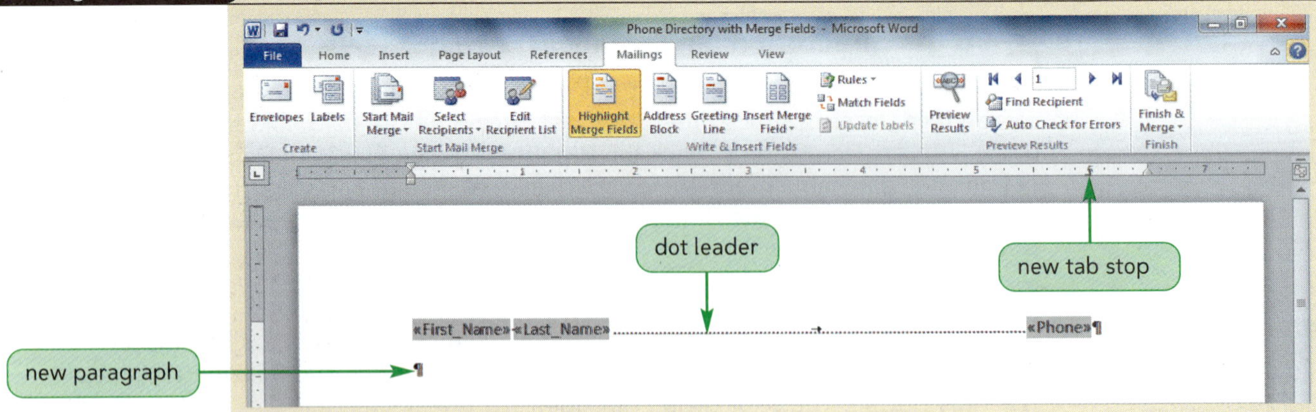


You are now ready to merge this file with the data source.

**To finish the merge for the phone list:**

1. In the Preview Results group, click the **Preview Results** button, and then review the data for the first record in the document.
2. In the Finish group, click the **Finish & Merge** button, click **Edit Individual Documents**, verify that the **All** option button is selected in the Merge to New Document dialog box, and then click the **OK** button. Word creates a new document named Directory1 that contains the completed telephone list. See Figure 6-31.

**Figure 6-31** Completed telephone directory

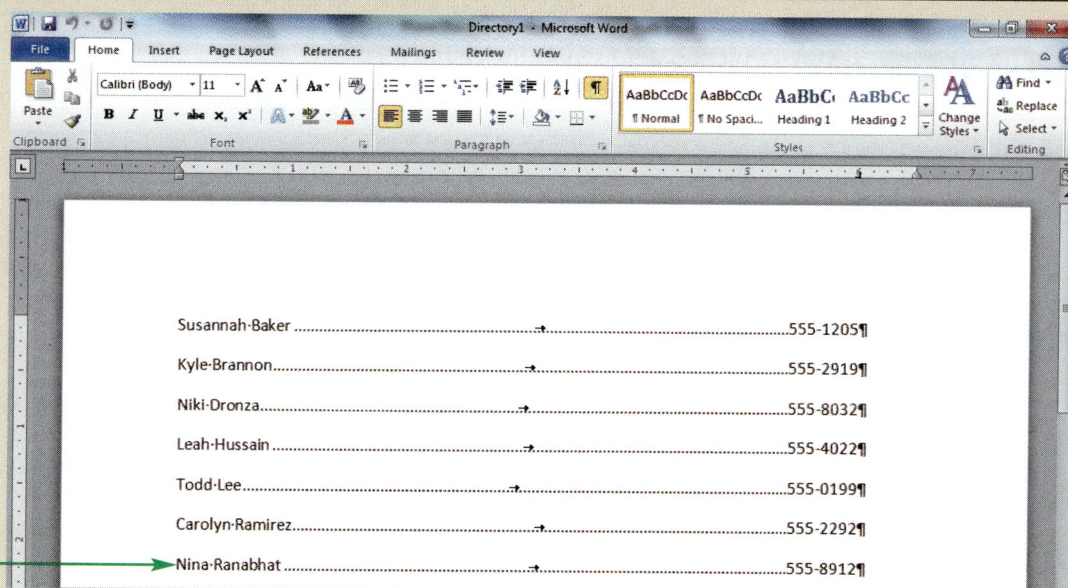


your name should appear here

3. Save the document as **Phone Directory** in the Word6\Tutorial folder, and then close it.
4. Save and close the **Phone Directory with Merge Fields** document.

# Converting Text to a Table

Nina needs your help with a few other tasks related to managing information about the teachers and clients at Lily Road Yoga Studio. First, she needs to prepare some information about new clients, which her assistant typed, to make it suitable for use as a data source. Because her assistant is not familiar with mail merge, she typed it as simple text in a Word document, instead of adding it to Nina's data source. Also, she forgot to include an email address and phone number for each client.

Nina can resolve these issues by converting the text to a Word table, and then adding columns for phone numbers and email addresses. Then, the next time she sees the clients she can get the missing information from them and add it to the table.

Before you can convert text into a table, you need to make sure it is set up correctly. That is, you need to make sure that **separator characters**—typically commas or tabs—are used consistently to divide the text into individual pieces of data to represent fields. Also, you need to make sure each paragraph in the document contains the same number of fields. Upon conversion, each field is formatted as a separate cell in a column, and each paragraph mark starts a new row, or record.

**TIP**

Address information exported from email and contact management programs often takes the form of a text file, with the fields separated by commas.

## To convert text into a table:

1. Open the document named **Client** from the Word6\Tutorial folder, and then save it as **Client Table** in the same folder. Display nonprinting characters, if necessary, and change the Zoom level to **Page Width**. See Figure 6-32. The document consists of three paragraphs, each of which contains a name, address, city, state, zip code, favorite type of yoga, and favorite teacher. Some of the fields are separated by commas (for example, the address and the city) but some are only separated by spaces (for example, the first and last name). Also, the favorite type of yoga and favorite teacher are enclosed in parentheses. You need to edit this information so that fields are separated by commas, with no parentheses enclosing the last two items.

**Figure 6-32** Text with inconsistent separator characters

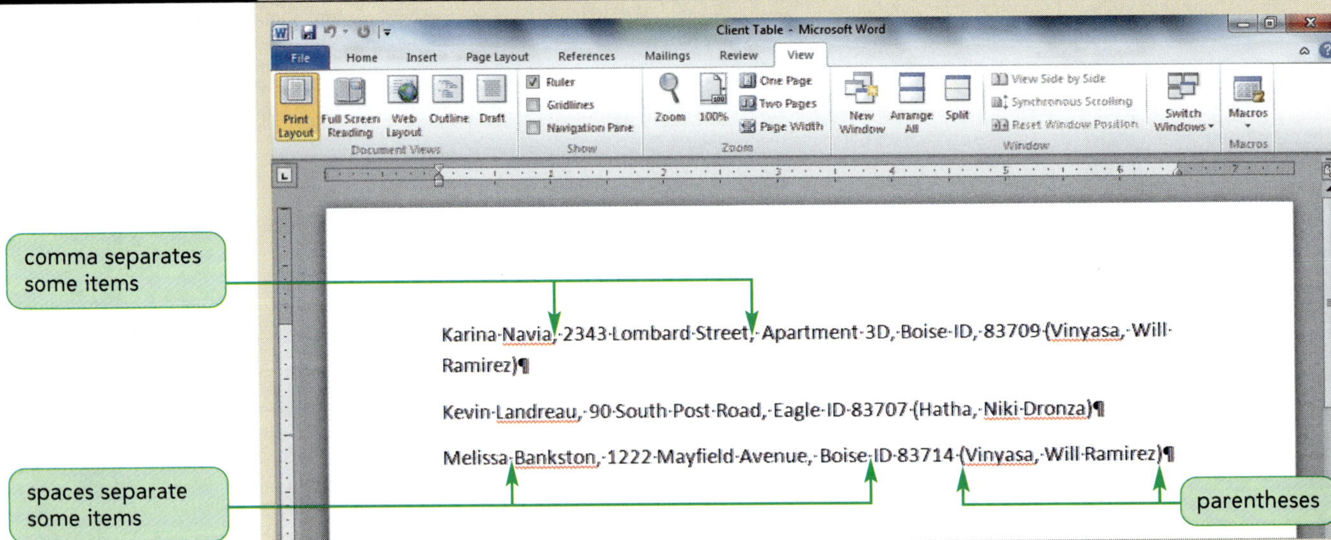


2. Edit the document to insert a comma after each first name, city, and zip code, and then delete the parentheses in each paragraph.

   In order to convert the text to a table, the paragraphs in the document must contain the same number of items that will become fields. The first paragraph includes two pieces of address information—a street address and an apartment number, which is equivalent to an Address Line 1 field and an Address Line 2 field. However, the other paragraphs only include an Address Line 1 field. Before you can convert the text into a table, you need to make sure each paragraph includes the same fields.

3. In the second paragraph, click to the right of the comma after "Road," press the **spacebar**, and then type **,** (a comma).

4. In the third paragraph, click to the right of the paragraph after "Avenue," press the **spacebar**, and then type **,** (a comma). Now the second two paragraphs each contain a blank field. See Figure 6-33.

**Figure 6-33** Text set up for conversion to a table

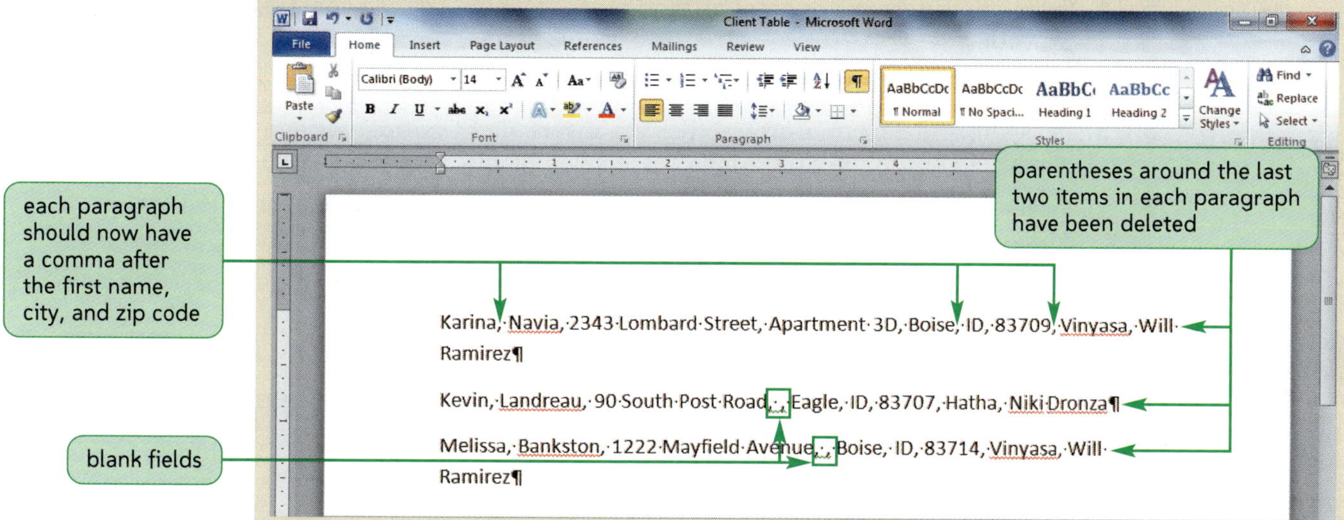


**TIP**

If a conversion does not turn out the way you expect, undo it and then review the text to make sure each paragraph contains the same number of data items, with the items divided by the same separator character.

5. Press the **Ctrl+A** keys to select the entire document, and then click the **Insert** tab on the Ribbon.
6. In the Tables group, click the **Table** button, and then click **Convert Text to Table**. The Convert Text to Table dialog box opens. Because the information in each paragraph is separated by commas, you need to select the Commas option button in the Separate text at section of the dialog box.
7. Click the **Commas** option button. See Figure 6-34. Note that the Number of columns setting is 9, and the Number of rows setting is 3. This corresponds to the nine fields in each of the three paragraphs.

**Figure 6-34** Converting text to a table

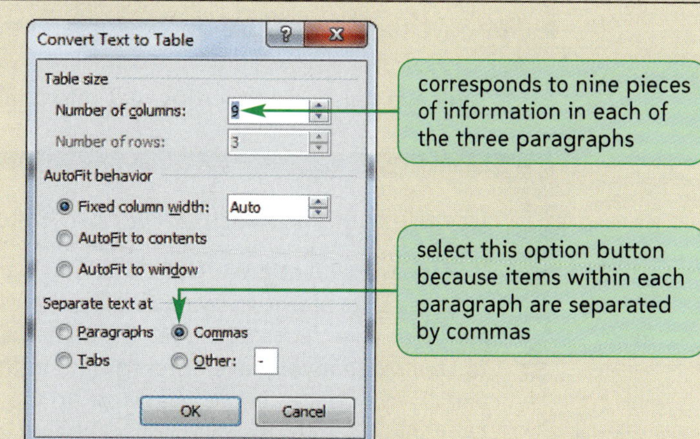


8. Click the **OK** button. The Convert Text to Table dialog box closes, and the text in the document is converted into a table consisting of nine columns and three rows.

Now that you have converted the text to a table, you need to finish the table by adding the columns for the phone number and email address, and adding a header row to identify the field names.

### To finish the table by adding columns and a header row:

1. Switch to Landscape orientation, and then select the column containing the zip codes.
2. Click the **Table Tools Layout** tab on the Ribbon.
3. In the Rows & Columns group, click the **Insert Right** button twice to add two blank columns to the right of the column containing zip codes.
4. Select the table's top row, and then in the Rows & Columns group, click the **Insert Above** button.
5. Enter the column headings shown in Figure 6-35 and format them in bold.

**Figure 6-35** Table with new columns and column headings

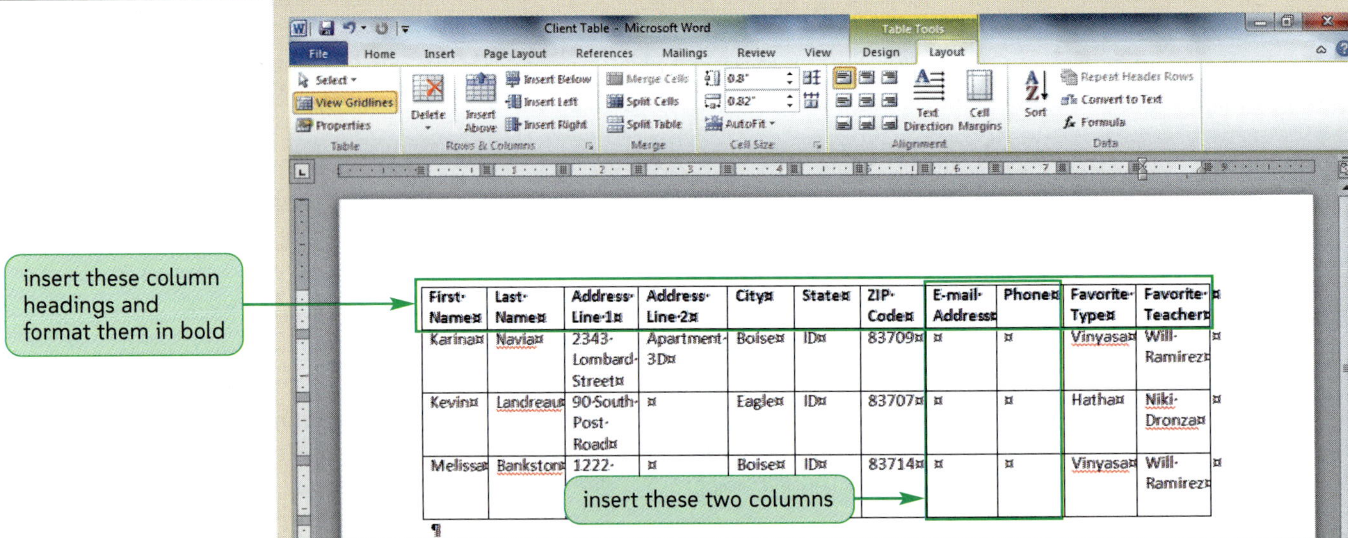


6. Save the Client Table document, and then close it.

You have finished converting text into a table.

## INSIGHT

### *Combining Data with a Microsoft Address Lists File*

If you have data in a Word file that you want to combine with data in a Microsoft Address Lists file, start by setting up the Word document as a table. That way you can be sure that each record includes the same fields. You can also check over the table quickly to confirm that you have entered data in the various fields in a consistent format. Once you are confident that you have set up the table correctly, you can begin the process of combining it with the Microsoft Address Lists file. First, delete the heading row, and then convert the table back to text, separating the fields with commas. Next, save the Word file as a text file, with the .txt file extension. Finally, open the Microsoft Office Address Lists file in Access, and then, on the Import & Link tab in the External Data group, click the Text File button to begin importing the text file into the Microsoft Address Lists file.

## Converting a Table to Text

At an upcoming open house, Nina plans to give a brief talk in which she introduces all the teachers at the studio. She wants to create a list of the teachers detailing their areas of specialty that she can refer to while she talks.

To create this list, Nina suggests you start with the Phone Data document that contained the table of yoga teachers and their phone numbers that you worked with earlier. You will begin by converting this table of information into text. As when you converted text into a table, you will need to specify how the individual pieces of information in the table will be separated in the document once it is removed from the table structure.

### To convert a table into text:

1. Open the document **Phone Data** from the Word6\Tutorial folder, and then save it as **Teacher List** in the same folder. Display nonprinting characters, if necessary, and change the Zoom to **Page Width**. You want to include only the names of Nina's teachers, so you will start by deleting the header row and the Phone column.
2. Delete the header row and the column of phone numbers from the table. The table now contains only the first and last name of each yoga teacher. You are ready to convert this table into text.
3. Select the entire table, click the **Table Tools Layout** tab, if necessary, to display this tab, and then in the Data group, click **Convert to Text**. The Convert to Text dialog box opens.
4. Click the **Other** option button. You want to separate the first and last names by a space.
5. In the Other box, delete the hyphen, verify that the insertion point is at the far-left edge of the text box, and then press the **spacebar** to insert a space. See Figure 6-36.

**Figure 6-36** Converting a table to text

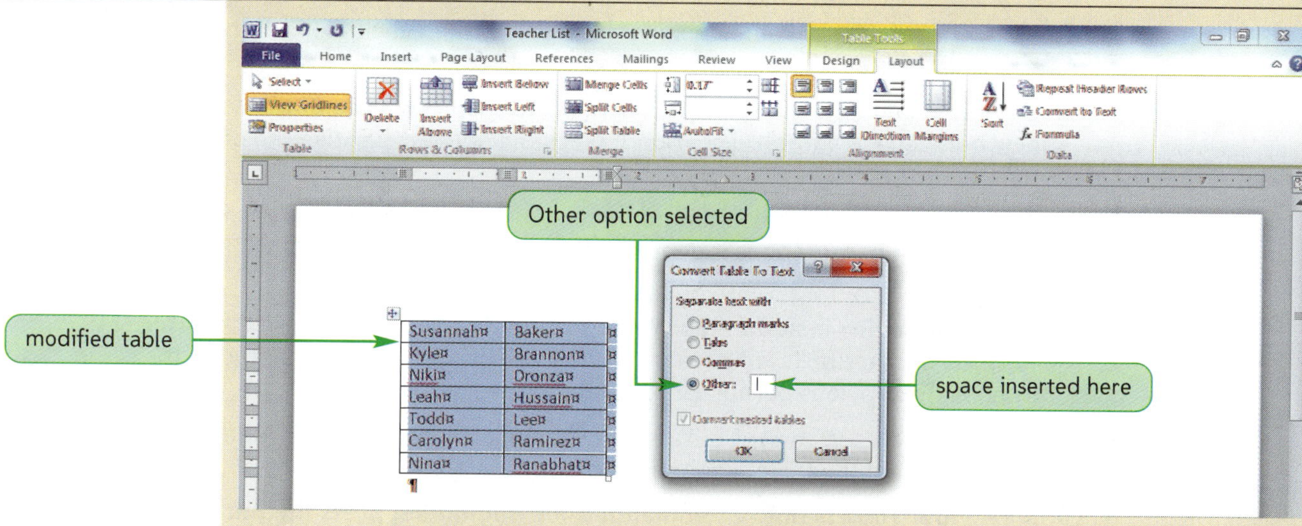


6. Click the **OK** button. The Convert Table to Text dialog box closes. The contents of the table are now formatted as seven separate paragraphs, one for each row in the table. Each first name is separated from its corresponding last name by a space.
7. Save the document.

## Working with Lists

Now that you have converted the table of information into text, you can work with it as you would any other text. For example, Nina wants you to create a detailed list of teachers and their classes. Because most people at the studio refer to the teachers by their first names, she asks you to first sort the list of teachers by first name.

### To sort the list:

1. If necessary, select the seven paragraphs containing the names of the yoga teachers, and then, in the Paragraph group, click the **Sort** button. The Sort Text dialog box opens. This is similar to the dialog box you've used before to sort tables. You want to sort the paragraphs in the list in ascending alphabetical order.
2. Verify that **Paragraphs** appears in the Sort by box and that the **Ascending** option button is selected, and then click the **OK** button. The Sort Text dialog box closes, and the paragraphs are arranged alphabetically. The list begins with Carolyn Ramirez, unless your first name comes alphabetically before "Carolyn," in which case your name appears at the top of the list.
3. Save the document.

Now that the list is sorted, you can use it to create an outline, or **multilevel list**. To create a multilevel list, first format text as a bulleted or numbered list, and then indent, or demote, some paragraphs within the list to create an outline structure. To demote a paragraph, click at the beginning of the paragraph and then press the Tab key or click the Increase Indent button in the Paragraph group on the Home tab. To promote, or unindent, a paragraph, click at the beginning of the paragraph and then press the Shift+Tab keys, or click the Decrease Indent button in the Paragraph group on the Home tab.

### To create a multilevel list:

1. Verify that the list of names is still selected, and then click the **Bullets** button to format it as a bulleted list.
2. Click at the end of Kyle Brannon's name, and then press the **Enter** key to insert a new bulleted paragraph. The round, black bullet looks just like the other bullets in the list.
3. In the Paragraph group on the Home tab, click the **Increase Indent** button. The bulleted paragraph is indented, and the bullet changes to a white circle with a black outline.
4. Type **Specialties include Flow Yoga and Pilates**, and then press the **Enter** key to insert another bulleted paragraph. The new paragraph is indented at the same level as the previous paragraph, with the same style of bullet.
5. Click the **Increase Indent** button. The bulleted paragraph is indented to the next level, and the bullet changes to a black square.
6. Type **Flow Yoga is not recommended for beginners**, press the **Enter** key, and then type **Pilates requires four hours of individual instruction**.
7. Press the **Enter** key to insert a new bulleted paragraph, and then click the **Decrease Indent** button in the Paragraph group to promote the new bulleted paragraph.
8. Type **His classes are generally considered very challenging**.

If you don't like the bullets or numbering styles that Word applies by default to a multilevel list, you can apply new styles by using the Multilevel List button in the Paragraph group on the Home tab. You can also use a multilevel list style to change a bulleted outline into a numbered outline. After looking over the list, Nina decides she would like to use a more eye-catching set of bullets.

## To apply a multilevel bullet style to the list:

1. Select the entire list, and then click the **Multilevel List** button to open a gallery of list styles. As shown in Figure 6-37, one of the list styles applies fancy bullets, two apply outline numbering, and three apply outline numbering and heading styles. The last is specially designed for creating a book outline. Finally, the None option retains any heading styles previously applied by one of the other multilevel list styles, but removes any outline numbering. Right now, Nina is interested in the bullets.

**Figure 6-37** Multilevel List menu

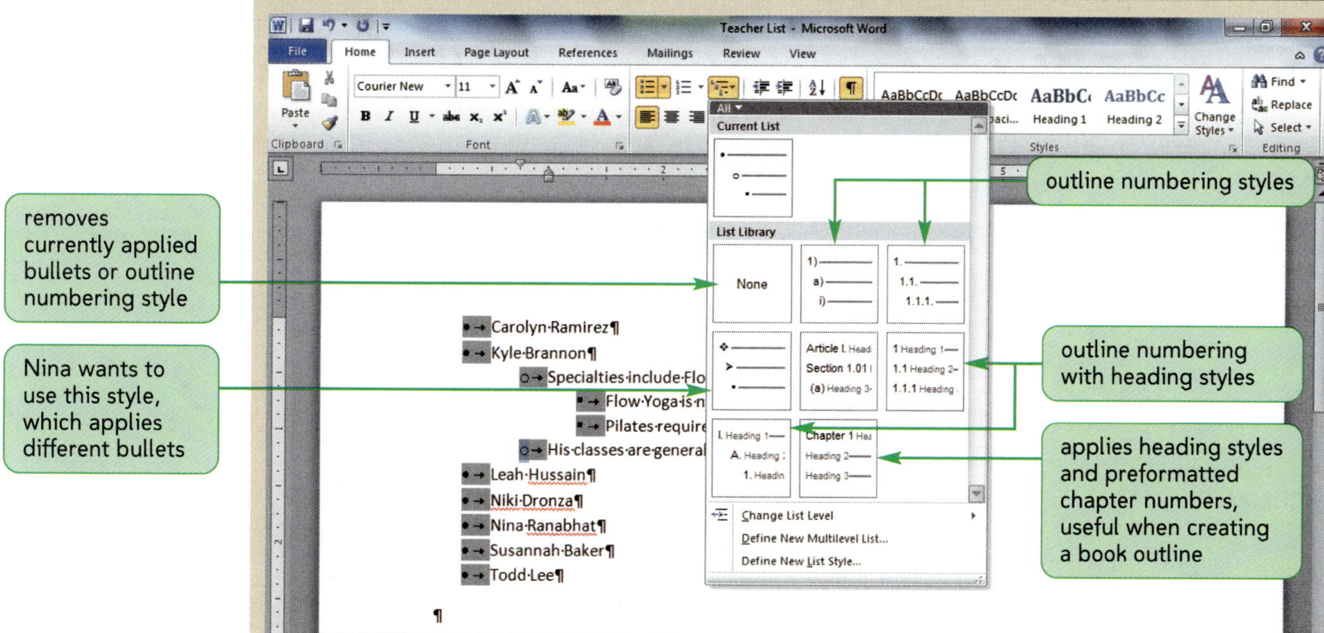


2. Click the bullet style in the second row of the List Library section, as shown in Figure 6-37. Your bulleted list should look like the list in Figure 6-38.

**Figure 6-38** Bulleted list with multiple levels

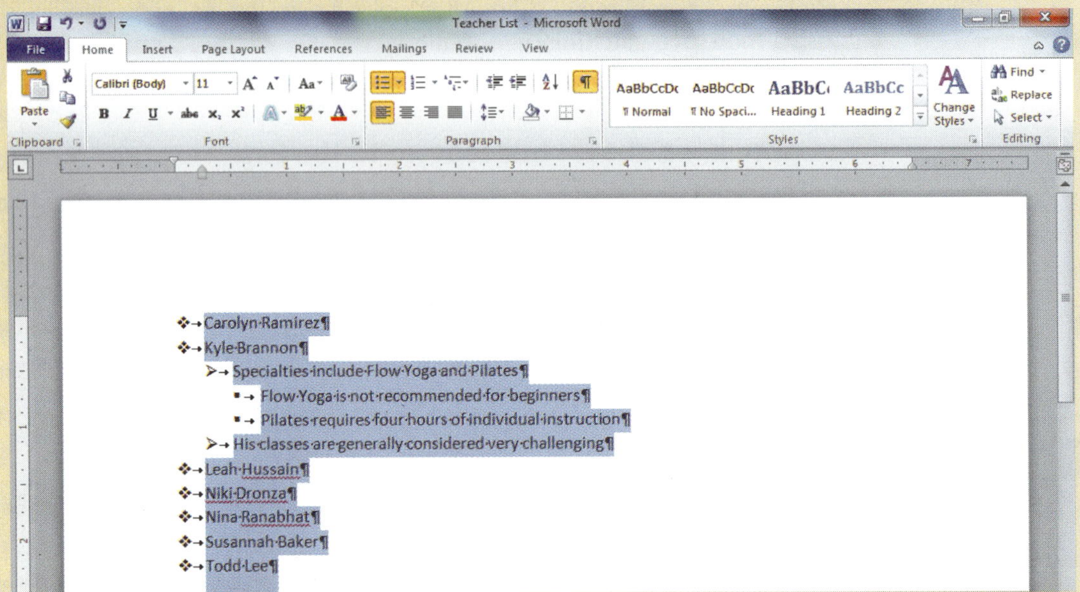


Nina decides the list would be more useful to her if it had outline numbering instead of bullets. You can make this change by applying a different multilevel list style.

**3.** With the list still selected, click the **Multilevel List** button to open the Multilevel List gallery, and then in the top row of the List Library section, click the middle style, which uses a combination of numbers and letters.

**4.** Deselect the list, and save the document. Your completed list should look like Figure 6-39.

**Figure 6-39** Multilevel list with outline numbering

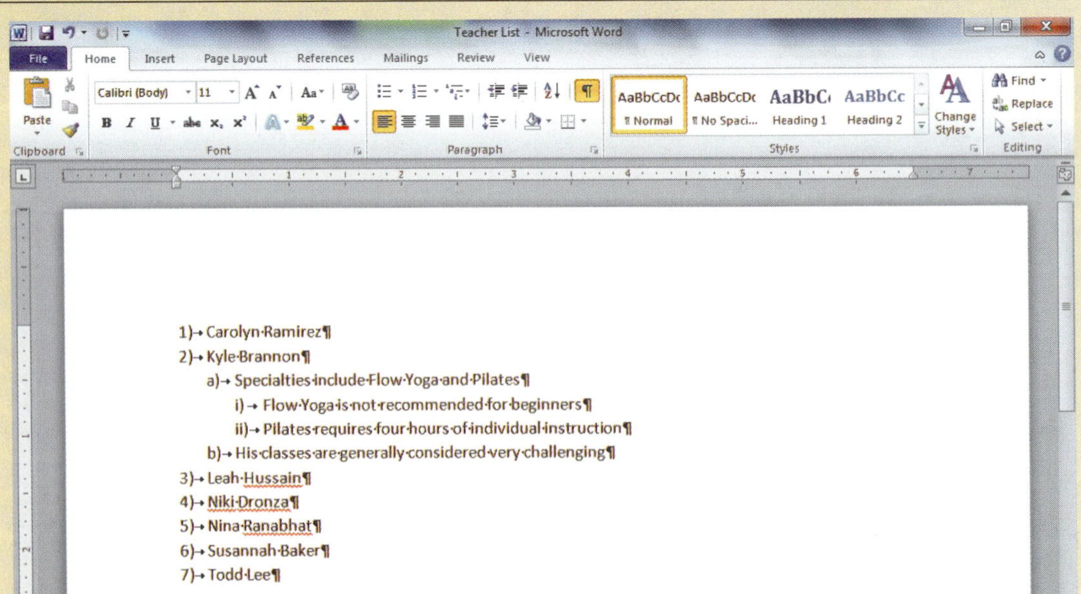

You have completed the mail merges Nina requested, and you have created an outline of yoga teachers she can use as she meets with potential new clients at the yoga studio open house.

REVIEW

## *Session 6.2 Quick Check*

1. True or False. After you complete a mail merge and close the main document, the connection between the main document file and the data source file is broken.
2. Explain how to edit a data source for a main document that is already open.
3. What's the quickest way to sort a data source by one field?
4. Explain how to filter a data source.
5. When you create a directory with a dot leader, what do you have to do after you insert the merge field on the right side of the page?
6. True or False. You can convert data in a document to a table only if the individual pieces of data are separated by tabs.

*Apply the skills you learned in the tutorial using the same case scenario.*

PRACTICE

## Review Assignments

**Data Files needed for the Review Assignments: Bonus.docx, Contacts.docx, More.docx**

Nina's clients are happy with the new facility, and the open-studio days she offered in June were a big success. Nina was pleased with how convenient it was to send out form letters with the Word Mail Merge feature. Now she wants to send a letter inviting clients who have purchased an annual membership to sign up for their membership bonus—either a massage or a meditation session, depending on which option they selected when they purchased their membership. Complete the following steps:

1. Open the file **Bonus** from the Word6\Review folder included with your Data Files, then save the document as **Bonus Main Document** in the same folder.
2. In the letter's closing, replace Nina's first and last name with your own.
3. Begin the mail merge by selecting Letters as the type of main document.
4. Create a new data source with the following fields in the following order: First Name, Last Name, Address Line 1, Address Line 2, City, State, ZIP Code, E-mail Address, Phone, and Bonus. Remove any extra fields. Rename fields as necessary.
5. Create four records using the information shown in Figure 6-40.

**Figure 6-40 Information for new data source**

| First Name | Last Name | Address Line 1 | Address Line 2 | City | State | ZIP Code | E-mail Address | Phone | Bonus |
|---|---|---|---|---|---|---|---|---|---|
| Jane | Cussler | 299 Hollister Street | Apartment 8D | Boise | ID | 83722 | cussler@curlygraphics.boise.net. | 208-399-1948 | massage |
| Carl | Hesse | 933 Wildway Avenue | | Beatty | ID | 83776 | yogaguy@world-net-global.com | 208-322-8294 | massage |
| William | Greely | 52 Eton Road | P.O. Box 9080 | Boise | ID | 83776 | william.greely@greely-productions.boise.org | 208-234-7766 | meditation session |
| Katya | Pushkin | 821 Ruby Road | | Boise | ID | 83722 | | 208-909-2893 | meditation session |

6. Save the data source as **Bonus Data** in the Word6\Review folder.
7. Edit the data source to replace "Carl Hesse" with your first and last name.
8. Sort the data source in ascending order by zip code and then by last name.
9. Create an inside address consisting of the necessary merge fields. Adjust the paragraph spacing in the inside address as necessary. Add a salutation that includes the First Name merge field. Insert the Bonus field into the body of the letter where indicated.
10. Save your changes to the main document, and then preview the merged document. Correct any formatting or spacing problems.
11. Merge to a new document, save the merged document as **Merged Bonus Letters**, and then close the file.
12. Filter the data source to display only records for clients interested in a massage, and then complete a second merge. Save the new merged document as **Merged Massage Letters**. Close all documents, saving all changes.
13. Open a new, blank document, and create a set of mailing labels using the vendor Avery US Letters and product number 5162. Save the main document as **Labels Main Document** in the Word6\Review folder.

14. Select the **Bonus Data** file you created earlier in this assignment as the data source.
15. Insert an Address Block merge field in the "Joshua Randall Jr." format and then update the labels.
16. Preview the merged labels, merge to a new document, and then save the new document as **Merged Labels** in the Word6\Review folder and close it. Save and close all open documents.
17. Create a telephone directory with a dot leader. Use the file named **Contacts** from the Word6\Review folder as the data source. Set a right tab at six inches and use a dot leader. Save the main document as **Directory Main Document** in the Word6\Review folder and the merged document as **Merged Directory** in the same folder. Save and close all open documents.
18. Open the document named **More** from the Word6\Review folder and save it as **More Bonus Data**. Convert the data in the document to a table with eight columns. Insert a header row with the following column headers formatted in bold: First Name, Last Name, Address Line 1, Address Line 2, City, State, ZIP Code, and Bonus. Replace "Daniel Einstein" with your name. Save and close the document.
19. Open the **Contacts** document from the Word6\Review folder and save it as **Contacts Info** in the same folder. Delete the header row and the phone number column, and then convert the table to four paragraphs of text.
20. In "Regent Property Management," change "Regent" to your last name.
21. Format the four paragraphs as a bulleted list, and then add the additional bullets and sub bullets of information shown in Figure 6-41.

**Figure 6-41** **List of company information**

- Clear Pane Window Cleaning
    - Scheduled for the first Monday of every month
        - In summer, may have to switch to the first Tuesday of every month
        - Move the table away from the front window before cleaners arrive
    - Paid by direct deposit
- Sampson Security
- Boise Federal Savings
    - Deposits must be in by 5 PM
    - Include a yellow deposit slip with every deposit
- Regent Property Management

22. Apply the bulleted multilevel list style.
23. Save the document as **Contacts Info Outline** in the Word6\Review folder, apply the multilevel list style that inserts outline numbering in the form 1), a), and i), then save the document again and close it.
24. Submit the documents to your instructor, either in printed or electronic form, as requested.

*Apply the skills you learned to create a letter to customers of an art gallery.*

APPLY

## Case Problem 1

**Data File needed for this Case Problem: Gallery.docx**

***Nightingale Gallery*** Nell Williams owns Nightingale Gallery, a purveyor of fine art photography in Saginaw, Michigan. She wants to send out a letter to past customers informing them of an upcoming show by a local photographer. Complete the following steps:

1. Open the document named **Gallery** from the Word6\Case1 folder, and then save it in the same folder as **Gallery Main Document**. In the closing, replace "Student Name" with your name.
2. Select Letters as the type of main document, and then create a data source with the following field names, in the following order: Title, First Name, Last Name, Street Address, City, State, ZIP Code, and E-mail Address.
3. Enter the following four records shown in Figure 6-42.

**Figure 6-42** **Four records for new data source**

| Title | First Name | Last Name | Street Address | City | State | ZIP Code | E-mail Address |
|---|---|---|---|---|---|---|---|
| Mr. | David | Joliet | 1577 Cooperville Drive | Saginaw | MI | 48601 | joliet@world-country5.net |
| Mr. | Paul | Robertson | 633 Wentworth | Bay City | MI | 48707 | d_roberts@p-m-c-57.org |
| Mrs. | Delia | Suyemoto | 4424 Bedford Avenue | Saginaw | MI | 48602 | d_suyemoto@filkins-incorporated.com |
| Ms. | Kira | Gascoyne | 844 Winter Way | Midland | MI | 33075 | gascoyne@saginaw.school65.edu |

4. Save the data source as **Gallery Data** in the Word6\Case1 folder, and then sort the records alphabetically by last name.
5. Edit the data source to replace "Kira Gascoyne" with your name. Change the title to "Mr." if necessary.
6. Build an inside address from separate merge fields, and then add a salutation using the Title and Last Name merge fields. Adjust paragraph spacing as necessary.
7. Save your changes to the Gallery Main Document file. Preview the merged document, and then merge to a new document.
8. Save the merged letters document as **Merged Gallery Letters** in the Word6\Case1 folder and then close it.
9. Save the **Gallery Main Document** document and close it.

EXPLORE

10. Open a new, blank document, save it as **Gallery Envelopes** in the Word6\Case1 folder. Assume Nell will be using envelopes with a preprinted return address, so you don't have to type a return address. Select Envelopes as the type of main document, select the 10 (4 ⅛ × 9 ½ in) size of envelopes in the Envelope Options dialog box, and use the **Gallery Data** file you created earlier as the data source. In the recipient address area of the envelope, insert the appropriate merge fields, and then merge to a new document.
11. Save the merged document as **Merged Gallery Envelopes** in the Word6\Case1 folder, and then close it. Save the main document and close it.

12. Create a customer email directory that includes first and last names but not titles. Use the file named **Gallery Data** (which you created earlier) as the data source. Do not include the record for David Joliet in the merge. Use a dot leader, with the right tab stop set at the 6-inch mark, to separate the name on the left from the email address on the right.
13. Save the main document for the email directory as **Directory Main Document** in the Word6\Case1 folder. Complete the merge to create the directory, and then save the merged document as **Merged Gallery Directory** in the Word6\Case1 folder.
14. Save and close all open documents. Submit the documents to your instructor, in either printed or electronic form, as requested.

*Apply your skills to create a form letter for a mortgage company.*

APPLY

## Case Problem 2

**Data Files needed for this Case Problem: Mortgage.docx, Mortgage Data.xlsx**

***Lensville Mortgage Corporation*** As an account manager at Lensville Mortgage Corporation, you need to send out letters to past customers asking them to consider refinancing. Your data for the mail merge is saved as an Excel file. Complete the following steps:

1. Open the document **Mortgage** from the Word6\Case2 folder, in the letter's closing, replace "Student Name" with your name, and then save it in the same folder as **Mortgage Main Document**.
2. Select Letters as the type of main document. In the closing, replace "Student Name" with your name.
3. EXPLORE For the data source, select the Excel file **Mortgage Data** from the Word6\Case2 folder. Click the OK button in the Select Table dialog box.
4. Edit the data source to replace "Barb Russ" with your name.
5. EXPLORE Insert an Address Block merge field for the inside address in the format "Joshua Randall Jr.," and format the Address block merge field using the No Spacing style. Insert a salutation using the First Name merge field. Add paragraph spacing before the salutation paragraph to account for the fact that the No Spacing style removed paragraph spacing after the preceding paragraph.
6. In the body of the letter, replace the placeholders [NUMBER OF YEARS], [CURRENT LOAN TERM], and [NEW LOAN TERM] with the appropriate merge fields.
7. Sort the records in the data source in ascending order by Current Loan Term.
8. Preview the merged document, and then merge to a new document. Save the merged document as **Merged Mortgage Letters** in the Word6\Case2 folder.
9. Close all open documents, saving all changes.
10. Create a main document for generating mailing labels on sheets of Avery US Letter Address labels, product number 5162, using the **Mortgage Data** file as your data source. Use the Address Block merge field in the format "Joshua Randall Jr.". Save the main document as **Labels Main Document** in the Word6\Case2 folder.
11. Preview the merged document, merge to a new document, and then save the merged document as **Merged Mortgage Labels** in the Word6\Case2 folder. Close all open documents, saving any changes.
12. Open the **Mortgage Main Document** file from the Word6\Case2 folder, maintaining the connection to its data source, and save it as **Mortgage Filtered**. Filter out all records in the data source except records for customers in Fort Myers.
13. Preview the merged document, and then complete the merge to a new document. Save the merged document as **Merged Fort Myers** in the Word6\Case2 folder.
14. Close all open documents, saving any changes. Submit the documents to your instructor, in either printed or electronic form, as requested.

*Convert a text file into a table, and then use the table as a data source for a mail merge.*

CHALLENGE

## Case Problem 3

### Data Files needed for this Case Problem: Letter.docx, Pasta.txt

***Fierenze Pasta*** Kayla Souza is manager of Fierenze, a manufacturer of fresh pasta in Racine, Wisconsin. Fierenze has just bought out a competitor, JD Pasta. Now Kayla wants to send a letter to JD Pasta's longtime customers, who she hopes will become Fierenze customers. She wants to use the mail merge feature in Word to create a letter that informs each customer of the price of his or her favorite type of pasta. The customer data has been saved in the form of a text file, with the data fields separated by commas. Kayla needs your help to convert the text file to a Word table, which she can then use as the data source for a mail merge. Complete the following steps:

1. In Word, open the text file named **Pasta.txt** from the Word6\Case3 folder included with your Data Files. (*Hint*: If the file is not listed in the Open dialog box, make sure All Files is specified in the box to the right of the File name box.) Save the Pasta.txt file as a Word document in the same folder using the filename **Pasta Data**.
2. Format the text in the document using the Normal style, and switch to Landscape orientation.
3. Convert the text to a table with the following nine columns: First Name, Last Name, Address Line 1, Address Line 2, City, State, Zip Code, Type, and Price. Insert your first and last name where indicated. Insert a header row with the appropriate column headers formatted in bold. Save the document and close it.
4. Open the file **Main** from the Word6\Case3 folder, and then save it as **Pasta Main Document** in the same folder. In the closing, replace "Student Name" with your first and last name.
5. Select Letter as the type of main document, select the **Pasta Data** document as the data source, and then sort the records in ascending alphabetical order by the Type field.
6. Insert an Address Block merge field for the inside address in the format "Joshua Randall Jr.," and format the Address block merge field using the No Spacing style.
7. EXPLORE For the salutation, experiment with the Greeting Line button on the Mailings tab. Use the Greeting Line dialog box to insert a salutation that includes "Dear" and the customer's first name, followed by a colon. Add paragraph spacing before the salutation paragraph.
8. Edit the body of the form letter to replace the placeholder text with the corresponding merge field names.
9. EXPLORE Use the Rules button in the Write & Insert Fields group on the Home tab to replace [PLACEHOLDER] with a merge field that displays "We hope to see you soon at our new Chicago location, opening early next year!" if the value in the State field is equal to IL; otherwise, the field should display "We hope to see you soon!" (*Hint*: Click If…Then…Else… in the Rules menu, select State as the Field name, select Equal to as the Comparison, and enter IL in the Compare to box. Insert the appropriate word in the Insert this text box and in the Otherwise insert this text box.)
10. EXPLORE Use the Filter command in the Mail Merge Recipients dialog box to display only the records that include either linguini or ravioli in the Type field. (*Hint:* In the Filter Records tab of the Query Options dialog box, you need to fill in two rows. Select Type in the Field box in both rows, select Equal to in the Comparison box for both rows, type the correct types of pasta in the Compare to boxes, and in the list box on the far left, select Or instead of And.)
11. Save the document and then finish the merge to a new document. Save the merged document as **Merged Pasta Letters** in the Word6\Case3 folder.
12. Save the main document and close it. Submit the documents to your instructor, in either printed or electronic form, as requested.

*Create the outline shown in Figure 6-43, to use as a basis for a report.*

CREATE

## Case Problem 4

**Data Files needed for this Case Problem: Director.docx, MAPH.docx**

***Public Health Report Outline*** Shakira Ankor is a communications specialist at the Municipal Association for Public Health (MAPH). Each year she begins her work on the association's annual report by creating an outline using the multilevel list feature in Word. She has asked you to help her create the outline. She also asks you to begin the report itself by inserting a Word file. Complete the following steps:

1. Open the document **MAPH** from the Word6\Case4 folder included with your Data Files, and then save it as **MAPH Outline** in the same folder.
2. Switch to Print Layout view, if necessary, and make sure nonprinting characters are displayed.
3. Replace "Student Name" with your first and last name, and then, in the paragraph below your name, create the outline shown in Figure 6-43. Format the list with the multilevel list style that numbers paragraphs 1, 1.1, 1.1.1, with heading styles.

**Figure 6-43 Outline for annual report**

1. A Message from the Director
2. Report Highlights
3. Summaries from Regional Committees
   3.1. Northeast Region
   3.2. Southeast Region
   3.3. Midwest Region
   3.4. West Region
4. National Health Information Campaigns
   4.1. Vaccinations for Adolescents and Young Adults
      4.1.1. Special Needs of High School Students
      4.1.2. Considerations for the College-Bound
   4.2. Childhood Obesity
   4.3. Geriatric Nutrition Needs
      4.3.1. Calcium Intake
      4.3.2. Protein Requirements

4. Save the MAPH Outline document, and then save it again as **MAPH Report** in the Word6\Case4 folder.
5. Select the list and apply the None Multilevel list style. Insert a new paragraph after the paragraph "A Message from the Director," and then insert the Word file **Director** from the Word6\Case4 folder. Delete the blank paragraph at the end of the newly inserted text.
6. Save and close the document.
7. Submit the finished documents to your instructor, either in printed or electronic form, as requested.

SAM

ASSESS

## SAM: Skills Assessment Manager

For current SAM information, including versions and content details, visit SAM Central (http://samcentral.course.com). If you have a SAM user profile, you may have access to hands-on instruction, practice, and assessment of the skills covered in this tutorial. Since various versions of SAM are supported throughout the life of this text, check with your instructor for the correct instructions and URL/Web site for accessing assignments.

## ENDING DATA FILES

**Word6** →

**Tutorial**
- Carolyn Main Document.docx
- Client Table.docx
- Phone Data.docx
- Phone Directory with Merge Fields.docx
- Phone Directory.docx
- Teacher List.docx
- Yoga Data.mdb
- Yoga Labels Main Document.docx
- Yoga Main Document.docx
- Yoga Merged Labels.docx
- Yoga Merged Letters 1.docx
- Yoga Merged Letters 2.docx
- Yoga Merged Letters 3.docx

**Review**
- Bonus Data.mdb
- Bonus Main Document.docx
- Contacts Info.docx
- Contacts Info Outline.docx
- Directory Main Document.docx
- Labels Main Document.docx
- Merged Bonus Letters.docx
- Merged Directory.docx
- Merged Labels.docx
- Merged Massage Letters.docx
- More Bonus Data.docx

**Case1**
- Directory Main Document.docx
- Gallery Data.mdb
- Gallery Envelopes.docx
- Gallery Letter.docx
- Gallery Main Document.docx
- Merged Gallery Directory.docx
- Merged Gallery Envelopes.docx
- Merged Gallery Letters.docx

**Case2**
- Labels Main Document.docx
- Merged Fort Myers.docx
- Merged Mortgage Labels.docx
- Merged Mortgage Letters.docx
- Mortgage Data.xlsx
- Mortgage Filtered.docx
- Mortgage Main Document.docx

**Case3**
- Merged Pasta Letters.docx
- Pasta Data.docx
- Pasta Main Document.docx

**Case4**
- MAPH Outline.docx
- MAPH Report.docx

TUTORIAL 7

# Collaborating with Others and Creating Web Pages

*Writing a Program Description*

## OBJECTIVES

**Session 7.1**
- Track changes in a document
- Insert and delete comments
- Accept and reject changes
- Compare and combine documents
- Embed and modify an Excel worksheet
- Link an Excel chart
- Modify and update a linked chart

**Session 7.2**
- Share files on SkyDrive
- Create bookmarks
- Insert and edit hyperlinks
- Save a Word document as a Web page
- Format a Web document
- View a Web document in a Web browser

## Case | *Green Fields Fresh Lunch Program*

Zoe Rios is the owner and president of Rios Communications in Dubuque, Iowa, a public relations company that specializes in developing publicity documents and Web sites in the field of public health. She is currently working on a program description for Green Fields, an organization that is devoted to improving the quality of meals served in area schools. She asked Henry Davis, a writer at Rios Communications, to review a draft of the program description. While Henry is revising the program description, Zoe has asked you to work on it, making additional changes. When you are finished, Zoe wants you to merge Henry's edited version of the document with your most recent draft.

After you create a new version of the document for Zoe, she wants you to add some budget figures from an Excel workbook. She also needs you to add a pie chart created by Henry. Finally, to make the program description available to the organization's members, she asks for your help to distribute it in electronic form and publish it on her company's Web site.

## STARTING DATA FILES

**Word7** →

| Tutorial | Review | Case1 | Case2 | Case3 | Case4 |
|---|---|---|---|---|---|
| Jorgenson Web Page_files (folder) | Salad Bar Web Page_files (folder) | Cook.docx | Kreelie.docx | Sunset.docx | FAQ.docx |
| Budget.xlsx | Expenses.xlsx | Statement.xlsx | Sun.docx | Survey.xlsx | |
| Chart.xlsx | Progress Henry.docx | | | | |
| Fields Henry.docx | Progress.docx | | | | |
| Fields.docx | Rates.xlsx | | | | |
| Jorgenson Web Page.htm | Salad Bar.docx | | | | |
| Resume.docx | Salad Bar Web Page.htm | | | | |

# SESSION 7.1 VISUAL OVERVIEW

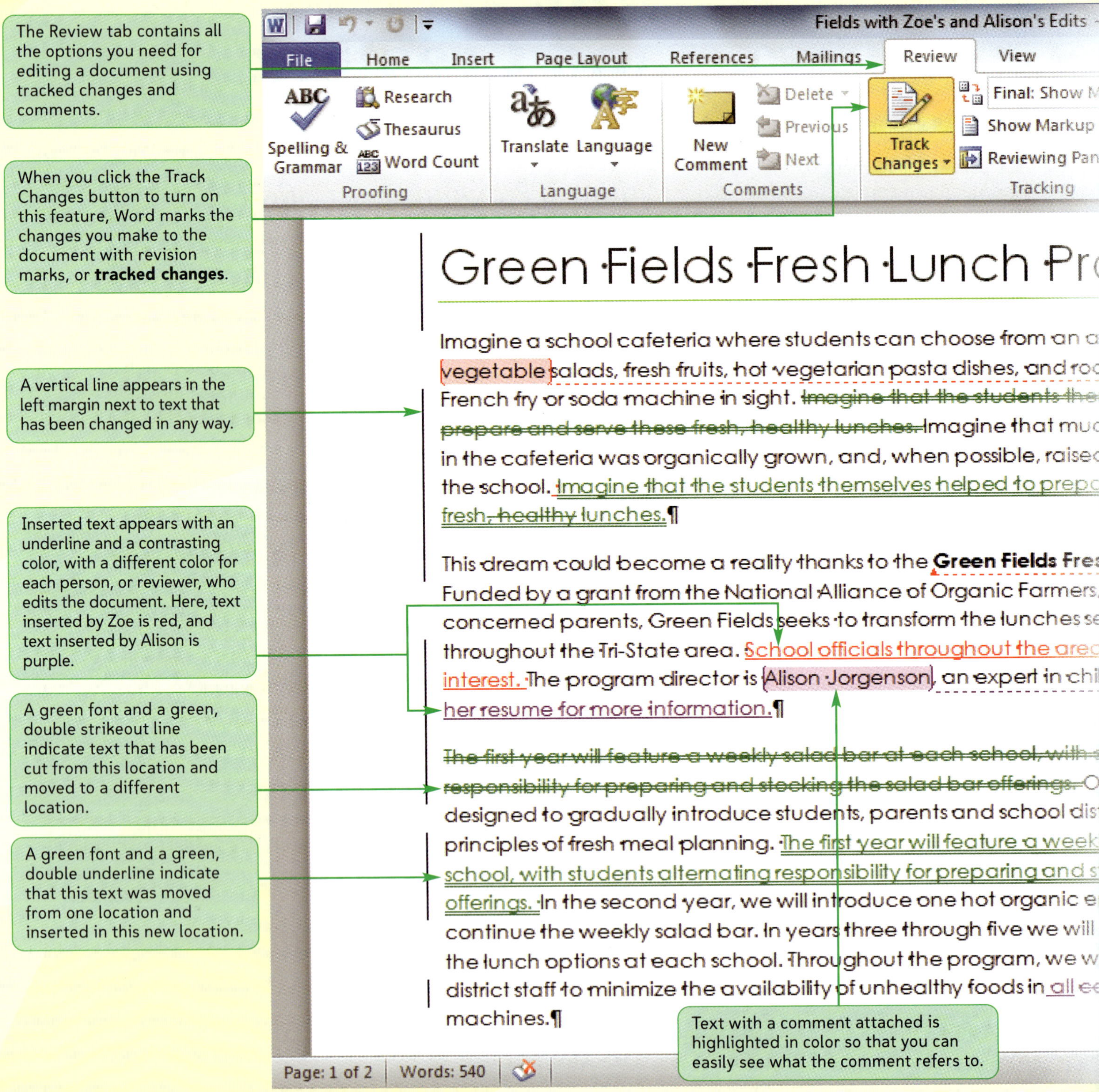

# TRACKING CHANGES

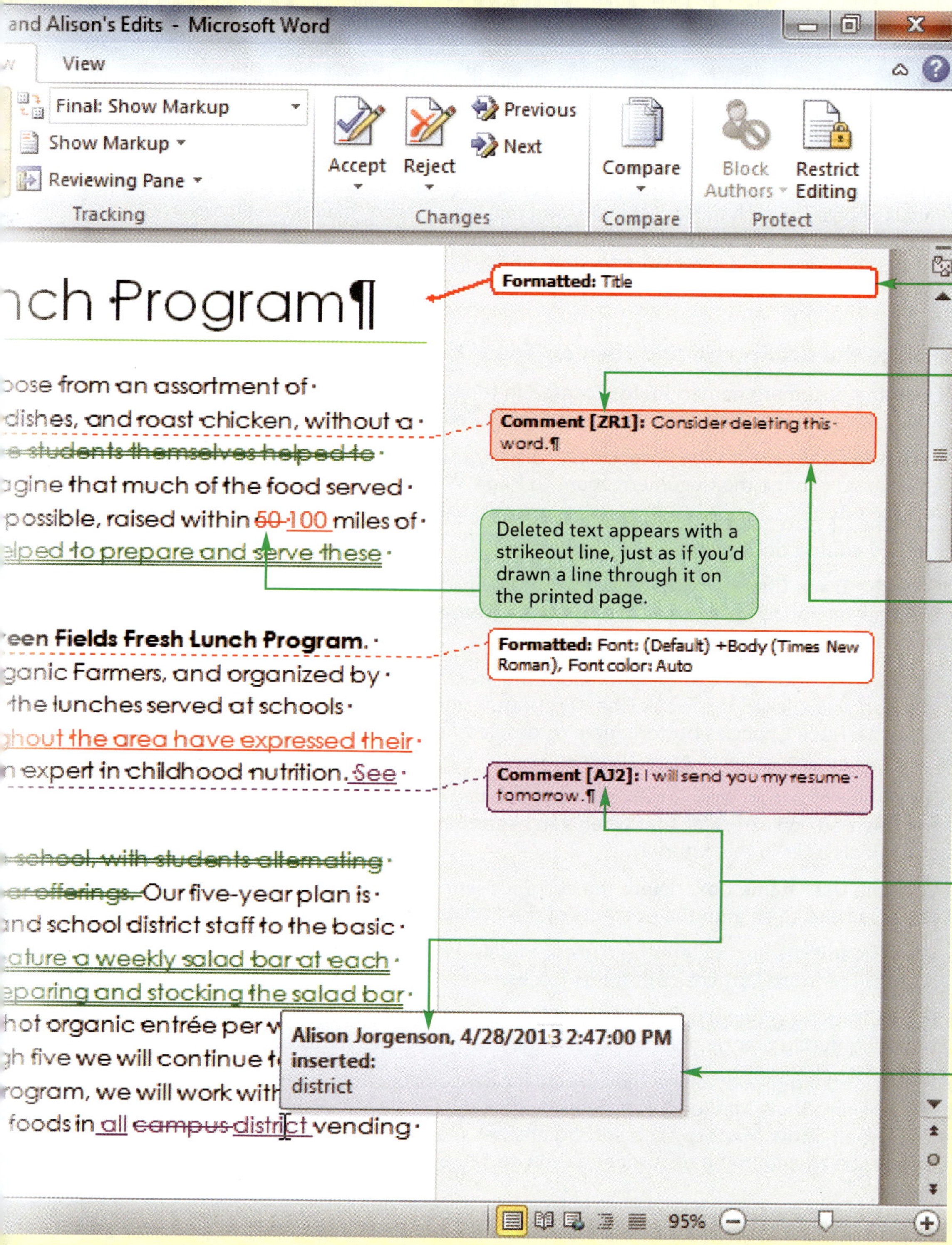


Formatting changes are listed in the margin in boxes known as **balloons** with a line connecting each balloon to the corresponding text in the document. This balloon indicates that a formatting change was made to the first paragraph; a reviewer applied the Title style.

A comment begins with the initials of the reviewer who inserted the comment, followed by a number indicating its position among all the comments in the document. This is the first comment in the document, and it was inserted by Zoe Rios (or ZR).

Deleted text appears with a strikeout line, just as if you'd drawn a line through it on the printed page.

Like formatting changes, **comments** appear in the margin in balloons. You can attach a comment to a selected word, phrase, or paragraph. A reviewer's comment balloons appear in the same color as the reviewer's tracked changes.

The names and initials associated with a tracked change or comment correspond to the user's name and initials as specified on the General tab of the Word Options dialog box.

When you point to a tracked change a ScreenTip appears indicating which reviewer made the change, when the change was made, and what the change was.

## Editing a Document with Tracked Changes

The Track Changes feature in Word simulates the process of marking up a hard copy of a document with a colored pen, but with many more advantages. Word keeps track of who makes each change, assigning a different color to each reviewer, and providing ScreenTips indicating details of the change, such as the reviewer's name and the date and time the change was made. Using the buttons in the Tracking group on the Review tab, you can move through the document quickly, accepting or rejecting changes with a click of the mouse. To turn on Track Changes, click the Track Changes button in the Tracking group on the Review tab.

Zoe is ready to revise her first draft of the lunch program description. In particular, she wants to make some changes to the first paragraph of the document. She asks you to turn on Track Changes before you begin making the edits for her. To ensure that her name and initials appear for each tracked change, and that your screens match the figures in this tutorial, you will temporarily change the user name on the General tab of the Word Options dialog box to "Zoe Rios" and the user initials to "ZR."

**To change the user name and turn on Track Changes:**

1. Open the document named **Fields** located in the Word7\Tutorial folder included with your Data Files, and then save it as **Fields Zoe** in the same folder.
2. Switch to Print Layout view if necessary, display the rulers and nonprinting characters, and change the document zoom to **Page Width**.
3. Click the **Review** tab on the Ribbon. The Review tab provides options for reviewing and editing documents.
4. Click the **Track Changes button arrow** in the Tracking group to open the Track Changes menu, and then click **Change User Name**. The General tab of the Word Options dialog box opens.

   **Trouble?** If you don't see a menu and if the Track Changes button is now selected, you clicked the Track Changes button rather than the arrow below it. Click the Track Changes button again to deselect it, and then click the Track Changes button arrow to open the menu.

**TIP**

You can also open the General tab of the Word Options dialog box by clicking the File tab and then clicking Options.

5. On a piece of paper, write down the current user name and initials, if they are not your own, so you can refer to it when you need to restore the original user name and initials later in this tutorial.
6. Click the **User name** box, delete the current user name, and then type **Zoe Rios**. You also need to change the contents of the Initials box.
7. Click the **Initials** box, delete the current initials, type **ZR**, and then click the **OK** button. The Word Options dialog box closes.
8. In the Tracking group, click the **Track Changes** button. The Track Changes button is highlighted in orange, indicating that the Track Changes feature is turned on.
9. In the Tracking group, locate the Display for Review box, and verify that it displays "Final: Show Markup." If it doesn't, click the Display for Review arrow and click **Final: Show Markup**. This setting ensures that tracked changes will appear on the screen and in the document as you edit it. See Figure 7-1.

**Figure 7-1** Track Changes turned on

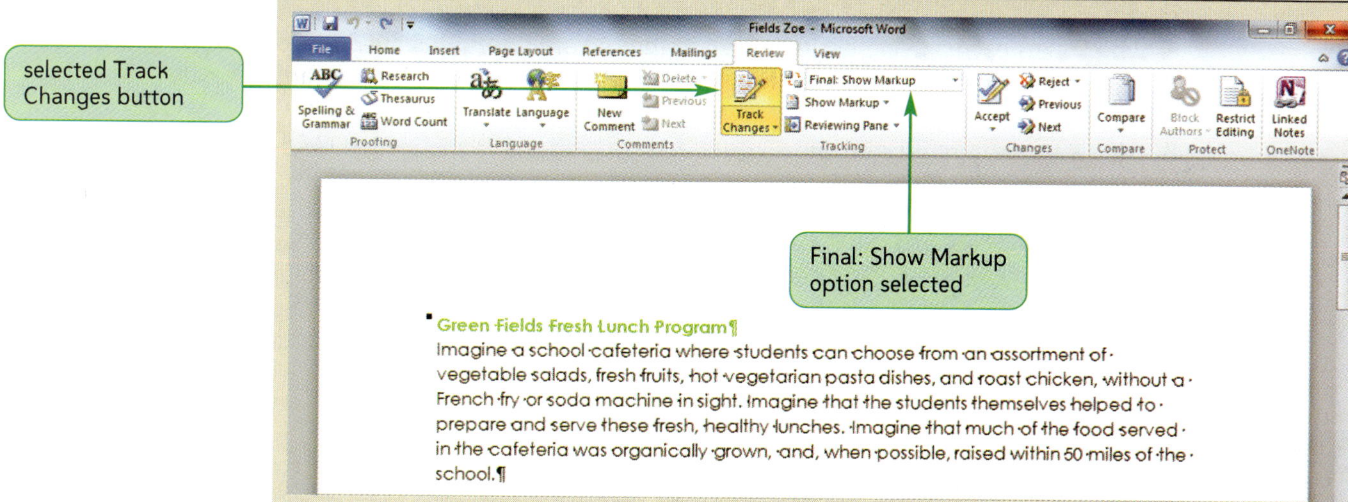


Now that Track Changes is turned on, you can begin editing Zoe's document. First, Zoe needs to change "50" in the last sentence of the second paragraph to "100."

**TIP**

Use the Word Count button in the Proofing group to display a document's total word count and other information about its contents.

## To edit Zoe's document:

1. In the paragraph below the first heading, select the number **50** in the last sentence, and then type **100**. A strikeout line appears through the number 50, and the new number, 100, appears in red. The new number is also underlined, and a vertical line appears in the left margin, drawing attention to the change.

   **Trouble?** If you see the number 100 in a color other than red, your computer is set up to display tracked changes in a different color.

2. Move the mouse pointer over the newly inserted number 100. A ScreenTip appears displaying the type of edit (an insertion), the user name associated with the edit, in this case "Zoe Rios," and the date and time the edit was made. See Figure 7-2.

**Figure 7-2** ScreenTip with user name and date

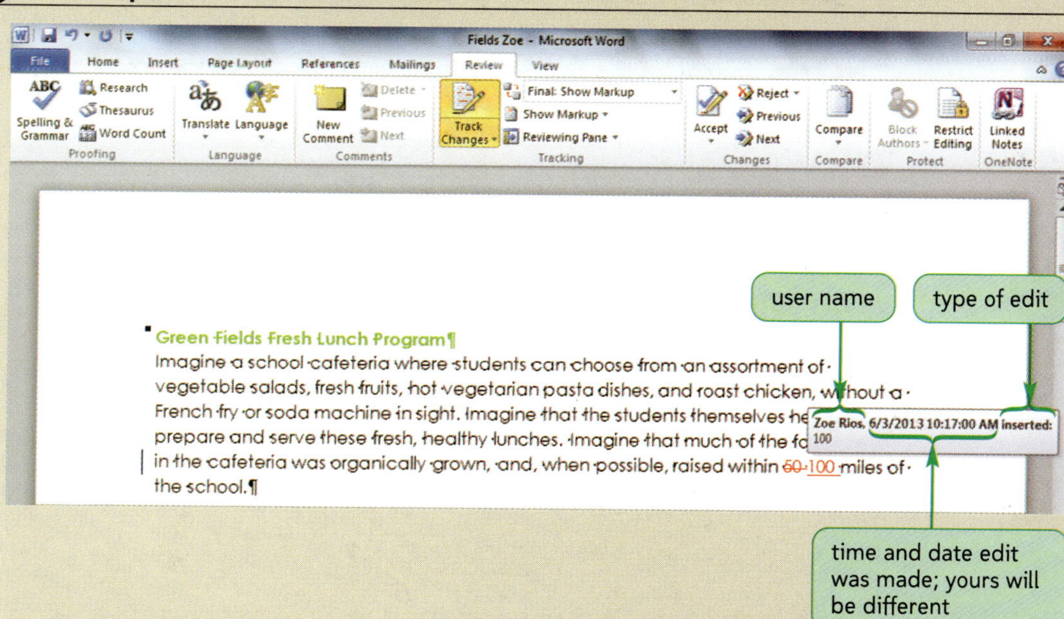

Next, Zoe wants you to move the second to last sentence in this paragraph to the end of the paragraph.

3. Press the **Ctrl** key, and then click in the sentence **Imagine that the students themselves helped to prepare and serve these fresh, healthy lunches.** The entire sentence is selected.

4. Drag the sentence down to insert it at the end of the paragraph, and then click anywhere in the document to deselect it. The sentence is inserted with a double underline, in green. The color is different from the one used for the number "100" earlier, because Word uses a separate color to denote moved text. See Figure 7-3. The sentence is still visible in its original location, but now it is displayed in green, with a double strikeout line through it. A vertical line appears in the left margin, next to the sentence in its original location, and also next to the sentence in its new location.

**Figure 7-3** **Tracked changes showing text moved to a new location**

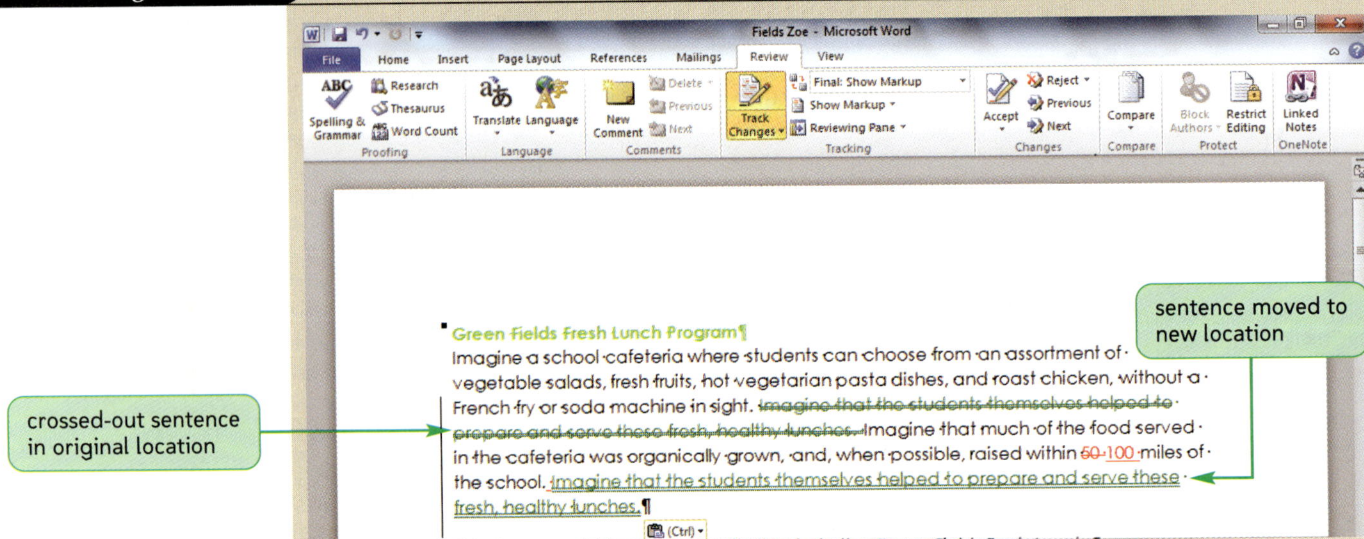


After reviewing the sentence in its new location at the end of the paragraph, Zoe decides she wants to delete the word "healthy" from the sentence.

5. In the sentence you moved in Step 4, click to the left of the comma after "fresh," and then press the **Delete** key nine times to delete the comma, the space after it, and the word **healthy**. The deleted text ", healthy" appears with a strikeout line through it, so that the sentence reads "...serve these fresh lunches."

Finally, you need to format the first heading in the document with the Title style.

6. Click in the heading **Green Fields Fresh Lunch Program**, and then click the **Home** tab.

7. In the Styles group, click the **More** button, and then click the **Title** style in the gallery. A vertical line appears in the left margin next to the heading, and a balloon appears in the right margin containing the text "Formatted: Title" indicating that you changed the formatting of the paragraph to the Title style. See Figure 7-4.

**Figure 7-4** Tracked changes showing formatted text

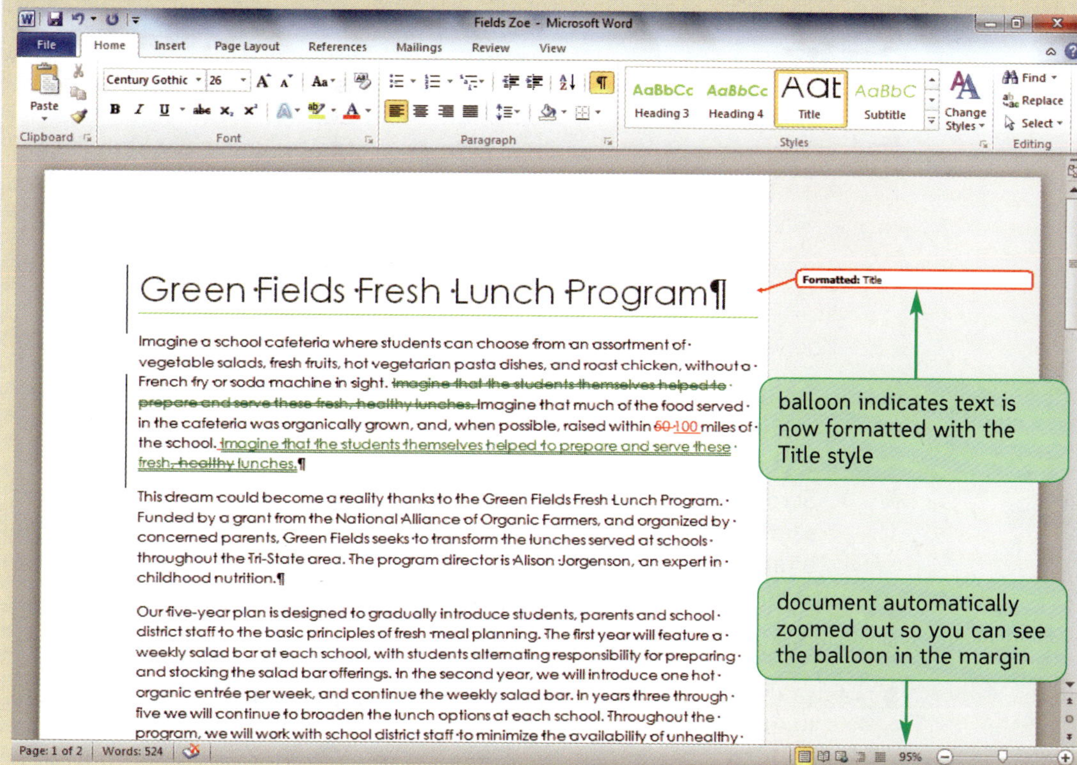


In addition to tracking changes, you can also add comments to the document you are editing.

## Inserting Comments

Comments are another useful revision tool. For example, you can use comments to insert notes to yourself as you create a document, or as a means of communicating ideas and feedback to coworkers who are also contributing to the same document. As shown earlier in the Session 7.1 Visual Overview, the text of your comment appears in a balloon in the right margin, along with the name of the person who made the comment and the date and time it was made.

Although comments are often used in conjunction with tracked changes, you don't have to turn on Track Changes to insert comments in a document. The buttons in the Comments group on the Review tab contain options for inserting, deleting, and navigating through comments in a document.

REFERENCE

*Inserting Comments*

- Select the text to which you want to attach a comment, or, to attach a comment to a single word, click in that word.
- Click the Review tab, and then click the New Comment button in the Comments group.
- Type the text of your comment in the balloon that appears in the margin.
- To display comments in the Reviewing Pane, click the Reviewing Pane button arrow in the Tracking group on the Review tab, and then click Reviewing Pane Vertical or Reviewing Pane Horizontal.

Zoe would like you to add a comment in the Budget section on page 2.

**To add a comment to page 2 of the document:**

1. Scroll down until you can see the Budget section at the top of page 2. The second sentence says that a complete budget will be available soon. Zoe wants to include a reminder to be more precise about exactly when the full budget will be ready.
2. At the end of the Budget section, click anywhere in the word **soon**.
3. Click the **Review** tab on the Ribbon.
4. In the Comments group, click the **New Comment** button. The word "soon" is highlighted in red, a balloon is inserted in the right margin, and the insertion point moves to the balloon, ready for you to begin typing the comment. See Figure 7-5. The default color for the highlighting and the balloon is red, but it might be a different color on your computer. In Figure 7-5, you see "Comment [ZR1]." The letters "ZR" are Zoe's initials; the number 1 after the initials tells you that this is the first comment in the document.

**Figure 7-5** **Inserting a comment**

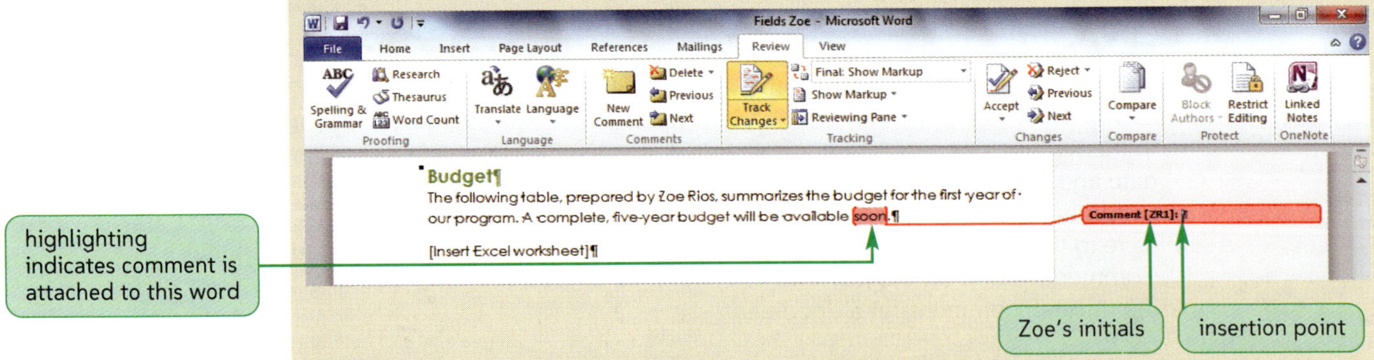


5. With the insertion point in the comment balloon, type **Insert precise date for new budget.** The comment is displayed in the balloon in the right margin. The insertion point remains in the comment balloon until you click in the document.
6. Click anywhere in the document. The comment balloon dims, but remains visible in the margin.
7. Save your work.

## Adjusting Track Changes Options

The default settings for Track Changes worked well as you edited Zoe's document. Note, however, that you can change these settings if you prefer. For instance, you could select a larger balloon for comments or a different color for inserted text. You could also change the user name that appears in the ScreenTip for each edit.

### To view the settings for the Track Changes options:

1. In the Tracking group on the Review tab, click the **Track Changes button arrow**. A menu appears below the Track Changes button.
2. Click **Change Tracking Options**. The Track Changes Options dialog box opens. As shown in Figure 7-6, you can use the options in the Balloons section to control the size and location of the balloons in the margins. Other options in this dialog box allow you to select the colors you want to use for various types of edits. For example, you can use the Color box next to the Insertions box to select a color to use for inserted text. Note that the default setting for Insertions, Deletions, Comments, and Formatting is By author. This means that Word assigns one color to each person who edits the document. You'll see the significance of that later in this tutorial, when you merge your copy of the document with Henry's. Right now there's no need to change any of the settings in the Track Changes Options dialog box, so you can close it.

**Figure 7-6** Examining the Track Changes Options dialog box

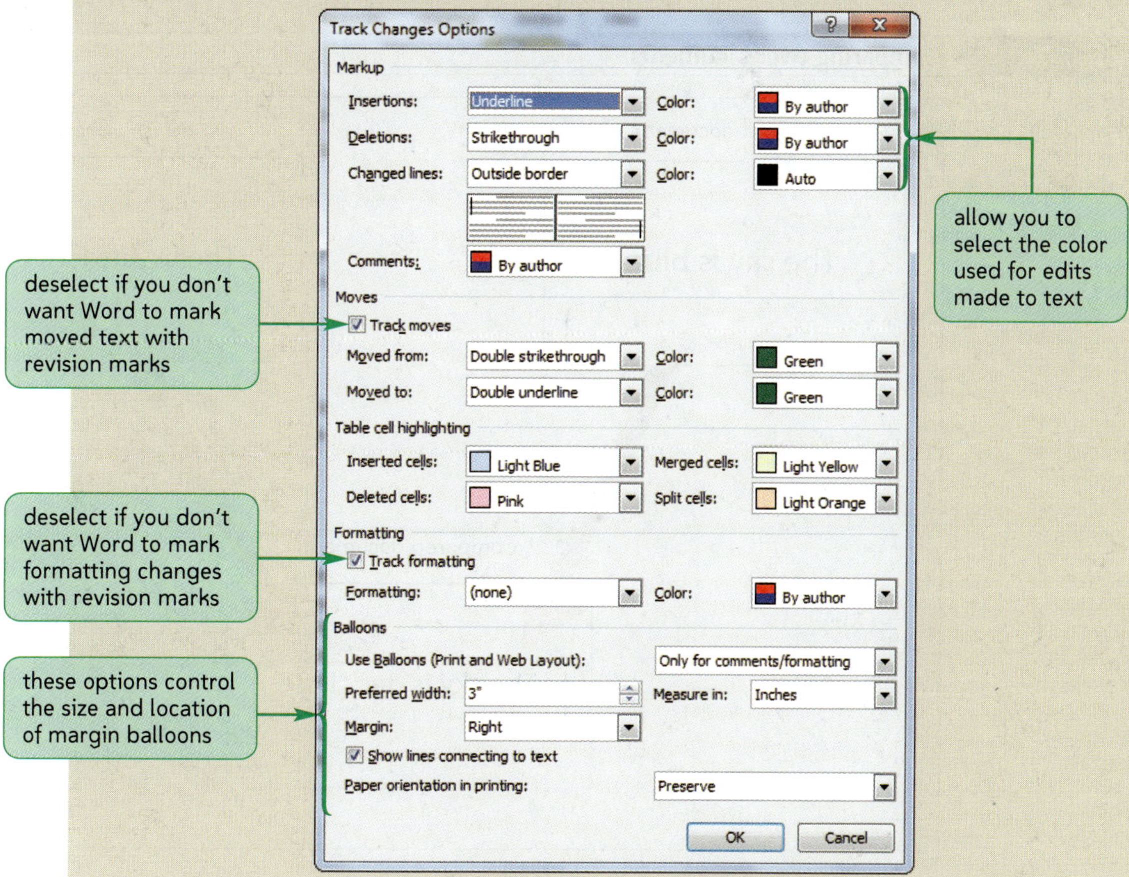


3. Click the **Cancel** button to close the Track Changes Options dialog box.

Zoe has received Henry's edited copy of the first draft via email, and now she'd like your help in combining her edited copy of the Fields Zoe document with Henry's.

## Comparing and Combining Documents

When you work in a collaborative environment with multiple people contributing to the same document, Word's Compare and Combine features are essential tools. They allow you to compare documents, with tracked changes highlighting the differences. The Compare and Combine features are similar, but they have different purposes.

Use the **Compare** feature when you have two different versions of a document and you want to see the differences between the two. Use the **Combine** feature when you have two or more versions of a document that you want to combine into a single document. Note that it's also common to use the term **merge** rather than "combine" when talking about combining documents. However, keep in mind that merging, when used in this context, is different from the mail merge process you learned about earlier.

When you compare two documents, you select one document as the original and one as the revised document. Word then creates a new, third document, which consists of the original document with tracked changes added to show how the revised document differs from the original. The original document and the revised document are left unchanged.

For example, suppose the original document contains the sentence "The sky is blue." Also, suppose that in the revised document, the sentence reads "The sky is dark blue." When you compare these two documents, you create a third document where the sentence looks as if you took the original document, turned on tracked changes, and inserted the word "dark." Figure 7-7 illustrates how this works.

**Figure 7-7 Comparing two documents**

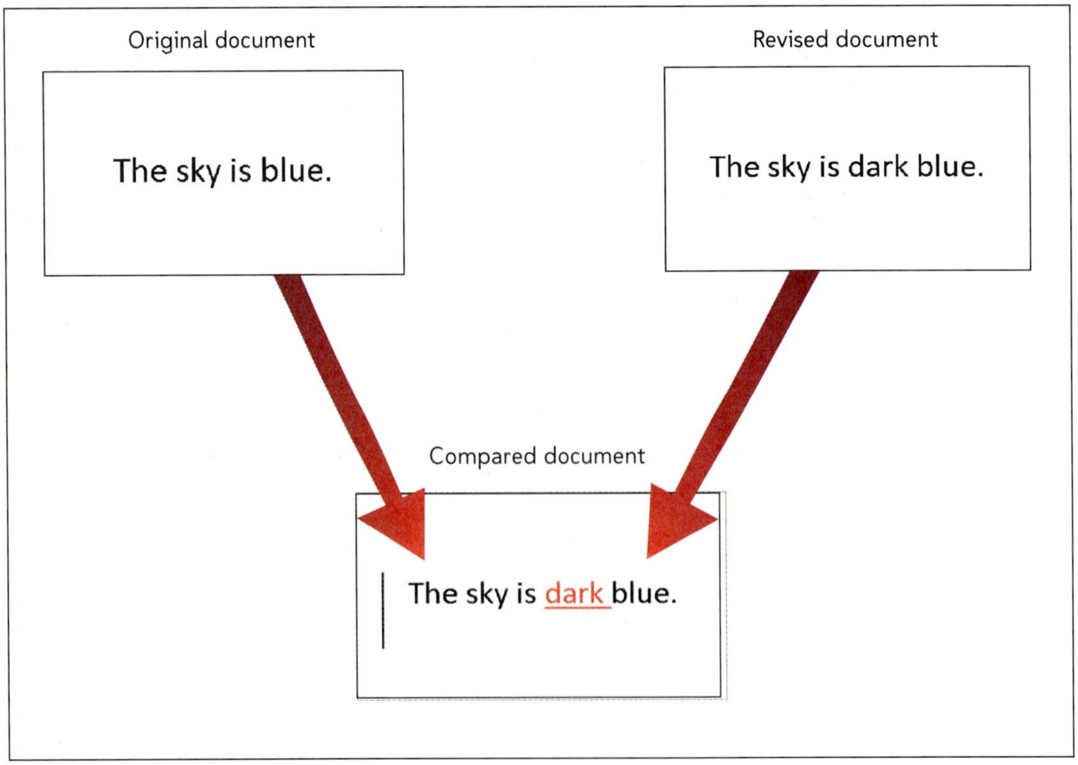

When combining documents, you also start by selecting one document as the original and the other document as the revised document. Word then creates a new document that contains the tracked changes from both the original document and the revised document. If you want, you can then take this new document and combine it with a third. You can continue using this process to incorporate changes from as many authors as you want.

When comparing or combining documents, it doesn't matter if they were originally edited with Tracked Changes turned on. Word marks all differences between the two documents using Tracked Changes, whether or not the original documents themselves contain tracked changes.

REFERENCE

*Comparing and Combining Documents*

- Click the Compare button in the Compare group on the Review tab.
- Click either Compare (to open the Compare Documents dialog box) or Combine (to open the Combine Documents dialog box).
- Next to the Original document box, click the Browse button, navigate to the location of the document, select the document, and then click the Open button.
- Next to the Revised document box, click the Browse button, navigate to the location of the document, select the document, and then click the Open button.
- Click the More button, if necessary, to display options that allow you to select which items you want marked with tracked changes, and then make any necessary changes.
- Click the OK button.

When you start combining or comparing documents, it's not necessary to have either the original document or the revised document open. In this case, the Fields Zoe document, which you will use as the original document, is currently open. You will combine this document with Henry's edited version of it.

### To combine Zoe's document with Henry's document:

1. Make sure you have saved your changes to the **Fields Zoe** document.
2. In the Compare group on the Review tab, click the **Compare** button. A menu opens with options for comparing or combining two versions of a document. You want to combine two documents.
3. Click **Combine**. The Combine Documents dialog box opens.
4. If necessary, click the **More** button. The dialog box expands to display check boxes, which you can use to specify the items you want marked with tracked changes.

   **Trouble?** If the dialog box has a Less button instead of a More button, the dialog box is already expanded to show the check boxes for selecting additional options. In this case, skip Step 4.

   In the Show changes section at the bottom of the dialog box, the New document option button is selected by default, indicating that Word will create a new, combined document rather than importing the tracked changes from the original document into the revised document, or vice versa. Now you need to specify the Fields Zoe document as the original document. Even though this document is currently open, you still need to select it.

5. Next to the Original document box, click the **Browse** button to open the Open dialog box.
6. If necessary, navigate to the Word7\Tutorial folder included with your Data Files, click **Fields Zoe** in the file list, and then click the **Open** button. You return to the Combine Documents dialog box, where the filename "Fields Zoe" now appears in the Original document box. The "Label unmarked changes with" box displays Zoe's name, indicating that any changes that have been made without tracked changes turned on will be labeled with Zoe's name in the combined document. Next, you need to select the document you want to use as the revised document.
7. Next to the Revised document box, click the **Browse** button, navigate to and select the file **Fields Henry** in the Word7\Tutorial folder included with your Data Files, and then click the **Open** button. The filename "Fields Henry" appears in the Revised document box, and Henry's first and last name appear in the Label unmarked changes with box. See Figure 7-8.

**Figure 7-8** **Selecting the original and revised documents**

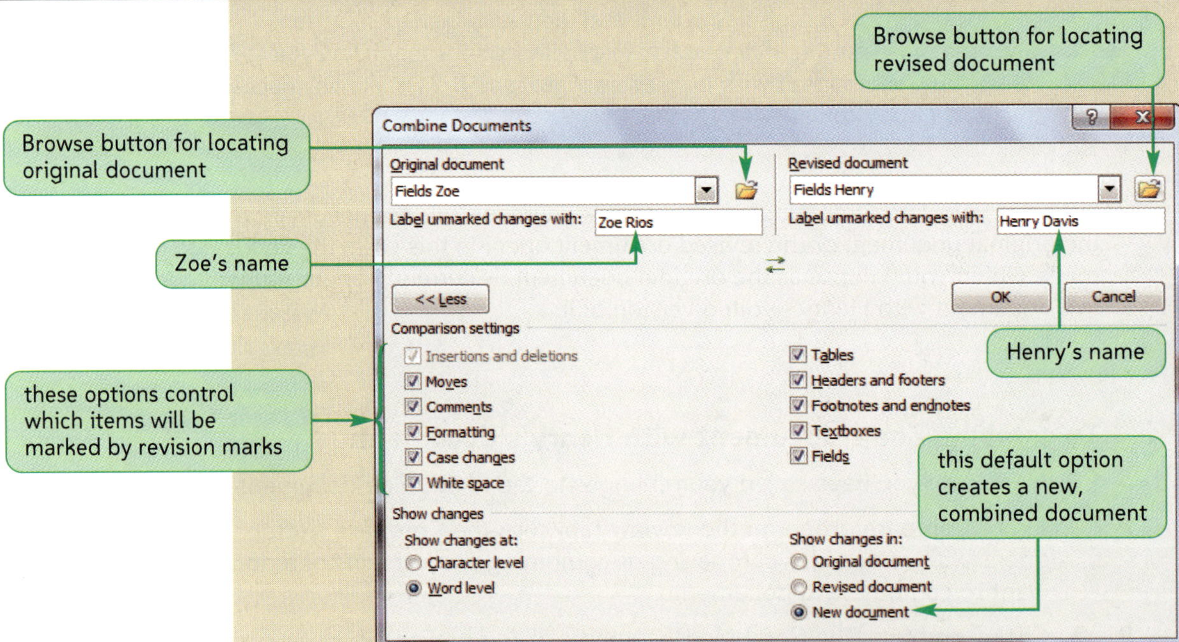


8. Click the **OK** button. The Combine dialog box closes, and a new document named either "Combine Result 1" or "Document1" opens. It contains the tracked changes from both the original document and the revised document. At this point, you might see only the new, combined document, or you might also see the original and revised documents open in separate windows, as shown in Figure 7-9. You might also see the Reviewing Pane, which lists each change in the new, combined document, also shown in Figure 7-9.

Figure 7-9 Two documents combined

You will make sure your screen is set up to show the original and revised documents and the Reviewing Pane.

9. In the Compare group, click the **Compare** button, point to **Show Source Documents**, and, if you do not see a check mark next to Show Both, click **Show Both**. If you do see a check mark next to Show Both, press the **Escape** key to close the menu.
10. If the Reviewing Pane shown in Figure 7-9 is not displayed, click the **Reviewing Pane** button in the Tracking group to display the Reviewing Pane. The Reviewing Pane will be displayed either in a horizontal window at the bottom of the screen or vertically on the left side of the screen.
11. If your Reviewing Pane is displayed horizontally, click the **Reviewing Pane button arrow** in the Tracking group, and then click **Reviewing Pane Vertical**. Your screen should now match Figure 7-9.

On a small screen, displaying the original and revised documents makes it harder to review the edits in the new, combined document. In that case, you can hide them.

### To hide the source documents and review the edits in the Reviewing Pane:

1. In the Compare group, click the **Compare** button, point to **Show Source Documents** button, and then click **Hide Source Documents**. The panes displaying the original and revised documents close.

2. Use the vertical scroll bar in the Reviewing Pane to scroll down and review the list of edits. Notice that the document contains the edits you made earlier as well as edits made by Henry Davis. By default, Word displays all the edits by all reviewers, but you can choose to display only the edits made by a specific reviewer or reviewers.
3. In the Tracking group, click the **Show Markup** button, and then point to **Reviewers**. A menu opens with check marks next to Henry's name and Zoe Rios. Also, the "All Reviewers" option is checked, indicating that all the edits from all the reviewers are displayed. To hide Zoe's edits, you need to deselect her name.
4. Click **Zoe Rios**. The menu closes, and the Reviewing Pane and document show only Henry's edits.
5. Scroll down through the document so you can see that the edits for Zoe Rios are no longer displayed in the document.
6. Click the **Show Markup** button again, point to **Reviewers**, and then click **All Reviewers**. Zoe's and Henry's edits are again displayed in the Reviewing Pane and in the document. You are finished with the Reviewing Pane, so you can close it.
7. In the Tracking group, click the **Reviewing Pane** button. The Reviewing Pane closes.
8. Save the document as **Fields Combined** in the Word7\Tutorial folder included with your Data Files.
9. Click the **Track Changes** button to turn off Track Changes. This ensures that you won't accidentally add any additional edit marks as you review the document.

Next you will review the edits to accept and reject the changes as appropriate.

## Accepting and Rejecting Changes

The document you just created contains all the edits from two different reviewers—Zoe's changes made in the original document, and Henry's changes as they appeared in the revised document. Each reviewer's edits appear in a different color, with ScreenTips, making it easy to see which reviewer has made each change.

When you review tracked changes in a document, the best approach is to move the insertion point to the beginning of the document, and then navigate through the document one change at a time using the Next and Previous buttons. In this way, you'll be sure not to miss any edits. As you review a tracked change, you can either accept the change or reject the change.

As you accept and reject changes, you often need to delete comments as well. To delete a comment, click in the comment balloon, and then click the Delete button in the Comment group. To delete all the comments in a document, click the Delete button arrow in the Comment group, and then click Delete All Comments in Document.

REFERENCE

### *Accepting and Rejecting Changes*

- Move the insertion point to the beginning of the document.
- In the Changes group on the Review tab, click the Next button to select the first edit or comment in the document.
- To accept a selected change, click the Accept button in the Changes group.
- To reject a selected change, click the Reject button in the Changes group.
- To accept all the changes in the document, click the Accept button arrow, and then click Accept All Changes in Document.
- To reject all the changes in the document, click the Reject button arrow, and then click Reject All Changes in Document.

Now you will review the document of combined changes.

## To accept and reject changes in the Fields Combined document:

1. Press the **Ctrl+Home** keys to move the insertion point to the beginning of the document.
2. In the Changes group on the Review tab, click the **Next** button. The heading "Green Fields Fresh Lunch Program" is selected, as shown in Figure 7-10. Recall that in the Fields Zoe document that you edited earlier, you formatted this heading with the Title style.

   **Trouble?** If the insertion point moves to Henry's comment at the bottom of page 1, you clicked the Next button in the Comments group instead of the Next button in the Changes group. Repeat Steps 1 and 2.

**Figure 7-10 First change in the document selected**

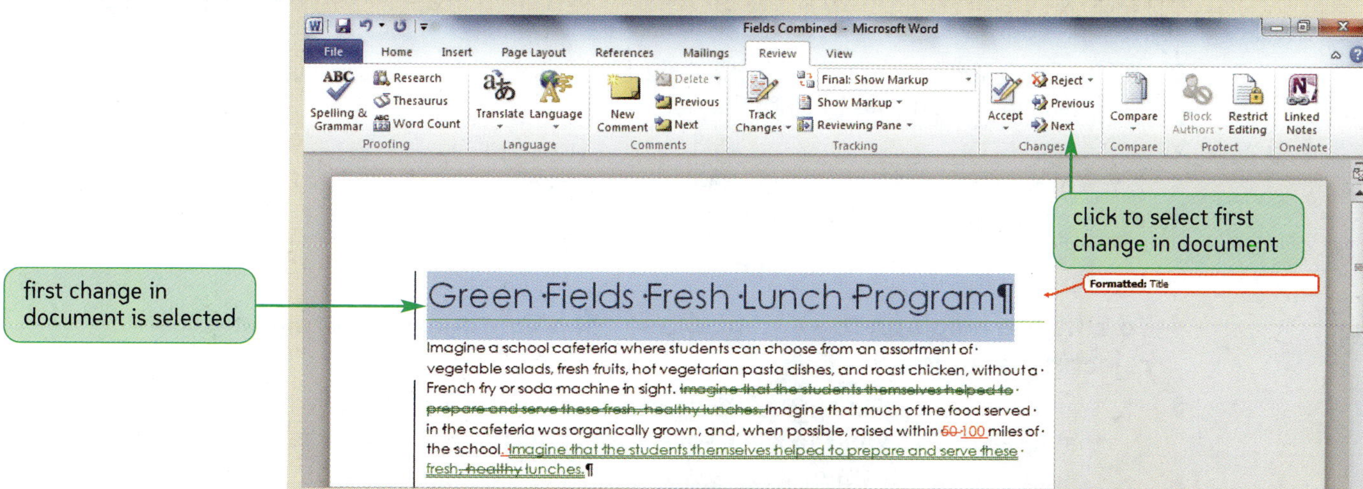


3. In the Changes group, click the **Accept** button. The margin balloon disappears, indicating that the change has been accepted. The next change in the document is now selected. This is the sentence that you moved to a new location at the end of the paragraph. Both the deleted sentence and the inserted copy of the sentence at the end of the paragraph appear in green. You need to accept the change of moving this sentence.

**Trouble?** If you see a menu below the Accept button, you clicked the Accept button arrow by mistake. Press the Escape key to close the menu, and then click the Accept button.

4. Click the **Accept** button. The sentence with the strikeout line through it is removed from the document, and the moved sentence in its new location at the end of the paragraph reverts to regular, black font. The next change in the document, the deleted number 50, is now selected.
5. Accept the deletion of the number 50 and the rest of the changes on page 1. At the top of page 2, the word "and" is selected as the next change. This is one of Henry's changes.
6. Scroll down to display the changes Henry made to page 2. See Figure 7-11.

**Figure 7-11** **Reviewing Henry's changes**

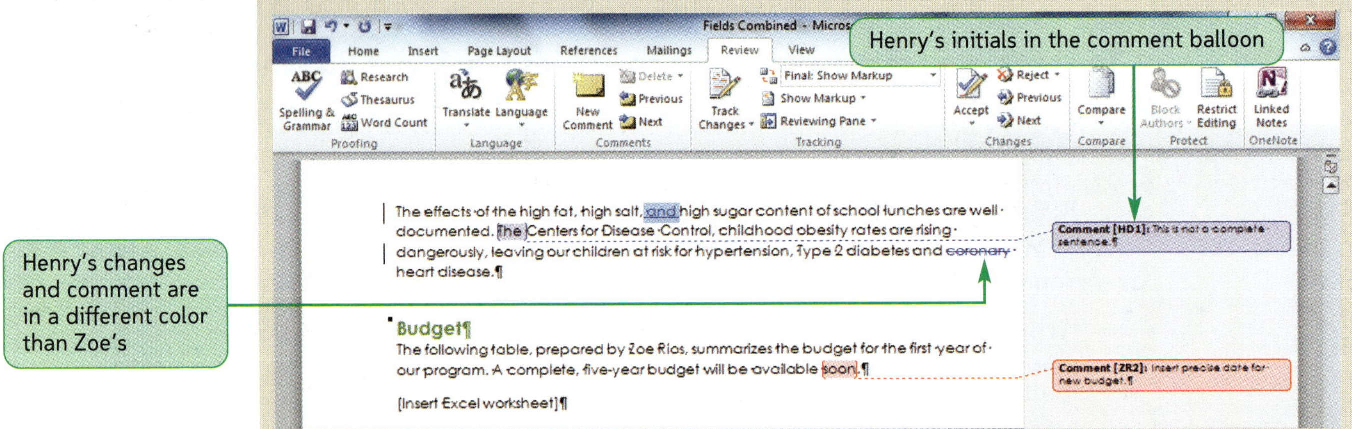


7. Click the **Accept** button to accept the insertion of the word "and." The insertion point moves to Henry's comment, which reads "This is not a complete sentence."
8. In the Comments group, click the **Delete** button. The comment is deleted and the insertion point moves back to the document.

You need to edit the sentence that Henry was concerned about, and then continue reviewing changes in the document.

## To edit the incomplete sentence, and then continue accepting and rejecting changes:

1. Edit the sentence that begins "The Centers for Disease Control, childhood…" so that it reads **According to the Centers for Disease Control, childhood….**
2. In the Changes group, click the **Next** button to select the next change in the document. The deleted word "coronary," which appears with a strikeout line through it, is highlighted. Zoe prefers to keep "coronary," so you will reject this change.
3. In the Changes group, click the **Reject** button. The word "coronary" is no longer marked for deletion, and the insertion point moves to the comment balloon in the margin containing Zoe's comment. See Figure 7-12.

**Figure 7-12** Rejected change

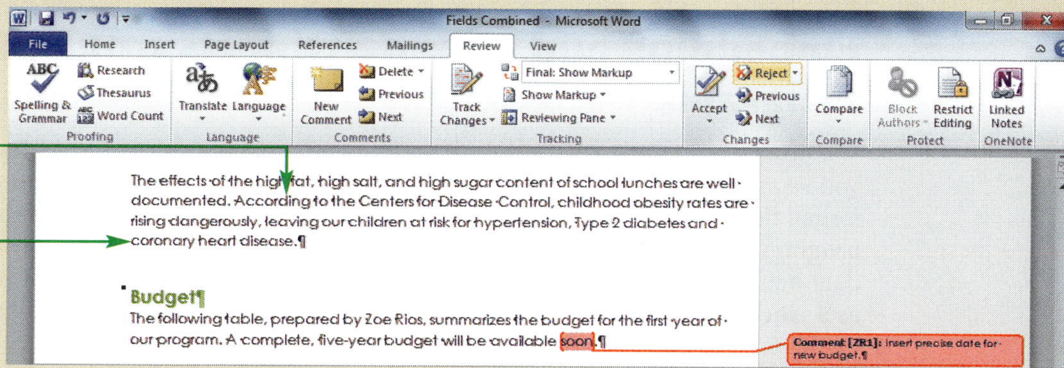


**TIP**

To delete all the comments in a document, click in any comment balloon, click the Delete button arrow in the Comments group, and then click Delete All Comments in Document.

4. Click anywhere in the comment balloon, and then click the **Delete** button in the Comments group. The comment is deleted, and the document zoom adjusts because the document no longer contains any tracked changes or comments in the margins.

5. Change the document view to Page Width, and then, in the first sentence under the "Budget" heading, replace "Zoe Rios" with your first and last name. Now that you are finished editing and reviewing the document with tracked changes, you need to restore your original user name and initials settings.

6. Click the **Review** tab, click the **Track Changes button arrow** in the Tracking group, click **Change User Name,** change the user name and initials back to their original settings on the General tab of the Word Options dialog box, and then click the **OK** button.

7. Click the **Word** button in the taskbar, click the **Fields Zoe – Microsoft Word** thumbnail to display the document, close the **Fields Zoe** document, and then save the **Fields Combined** document.

**INSIGHT**

## *Understanding Tracked Changes*

Once a document is finished, you want to make sure it does not contain any tracked changes or comments. You can't always tell if a document contains comments or tracked changes just by looking at it, because the comments or changes for some or all of the reviewers might be hidden. Also, the Display for Review box in the Tracking group on the Review tab might be set to Final instead of Final: Show Markup. In that case, the tracked changes would not be visible, but could easily be redisplayed by changing the Display for Review setting to Final: Show Markup. To determine whether or not a document contains any tracked changes or comments:

- In the Tracking group on the Review tab, verify that the Display for Review box is set to Final: Show Markup.
- In the Tracking group on the Review tab, click the Show Markup button, point to Reviewers, and confirm a check mark appears next to All Reviewers.
- Press the Ctrl+Home keys to move the insertion point to the beginning of the document, and then in the Changes group on the Review tab, click the Next button. This will either display a dialog box indicating the document contains no comments or tracked changes, or the insertion point will move to the next comment or tracked change.

Now that you have combined Henry's edits with Zoe's, you are ready to add the budget and Henry's pie chart to the document.

## Embedding and Linking Objects from Other Programs

The programs in Office 2010 are all designed to accomplish specific types of tasks. As you've seen with Word, you can use a word-processing program to create, edit, and format documents such as letters, reports, newsletters, and proposals. A **spreadsheet program**, on the other hand, allows you to organize, calculate, and analyze numerical data in a grid of rows and columns. A spreadsheet created in Microsoft Excel is known as a **worksheet**. Excel also has tools for analyzing and representing data graphically in charts.

Sometimes it is useful to combine information created in the different Office programs into one file. For example, in the Green Fields Fresh Lunch Program description, Zoe wants to include budget information that was created in an Excel worksheet. She also wants to include an Excel chart, created by Henry, that shows the percentage of fresh fruits and vegetables served in local schools. You can incorporate the Excel data and chart into Zoe's Word document by taking advantage of **object linking and embedding**, or **OLE**, a technology that allows you to share information between the Office programs. This process is commonly referred to as **integration**.

Recall that an object is anything that can be selected and modified as a whole, such as a table, picture, or block of text. When referring to OLE, the program used to create the original version of the object is called the **source program**. The program into which the object is integrated is called the **destination program.** Similarly, the original file that contains the object you are integrating is called the **source file**, and the file into which you integrate the object is called the **destination file**. You can integrate objects by either embedding or linking.

**Embedding** is a technique that allows you to insert a copy of an object into a destination document. In the destination document, you can double-click an embedded object to access the tools of the source program, allowing you to edit the object within the destination document using the tools of the source program. Because the embedded object is a copy, any changes you make to it are not reflected in the original source file, and vice versa. For instance, you could embed a worksheet named Itemized Expenses into a Word document named Travel Report. Later, if you change the Itemized Expenses file, those revisions would not appear in the Travel Report document. The opposite is also true; if you edit the embedded object from within the Travel Report file, those changes will not be reflected in the source file Itemized Expenses. The embedded object retains a connection to the source program, Excel, but not to the source file.

Figure 7-13 illustrates the relationship between an embedded Excel object in Zoe's Word document and the source file.

Figure 7-13 **Embedding an Excel worksheet in a Word document**

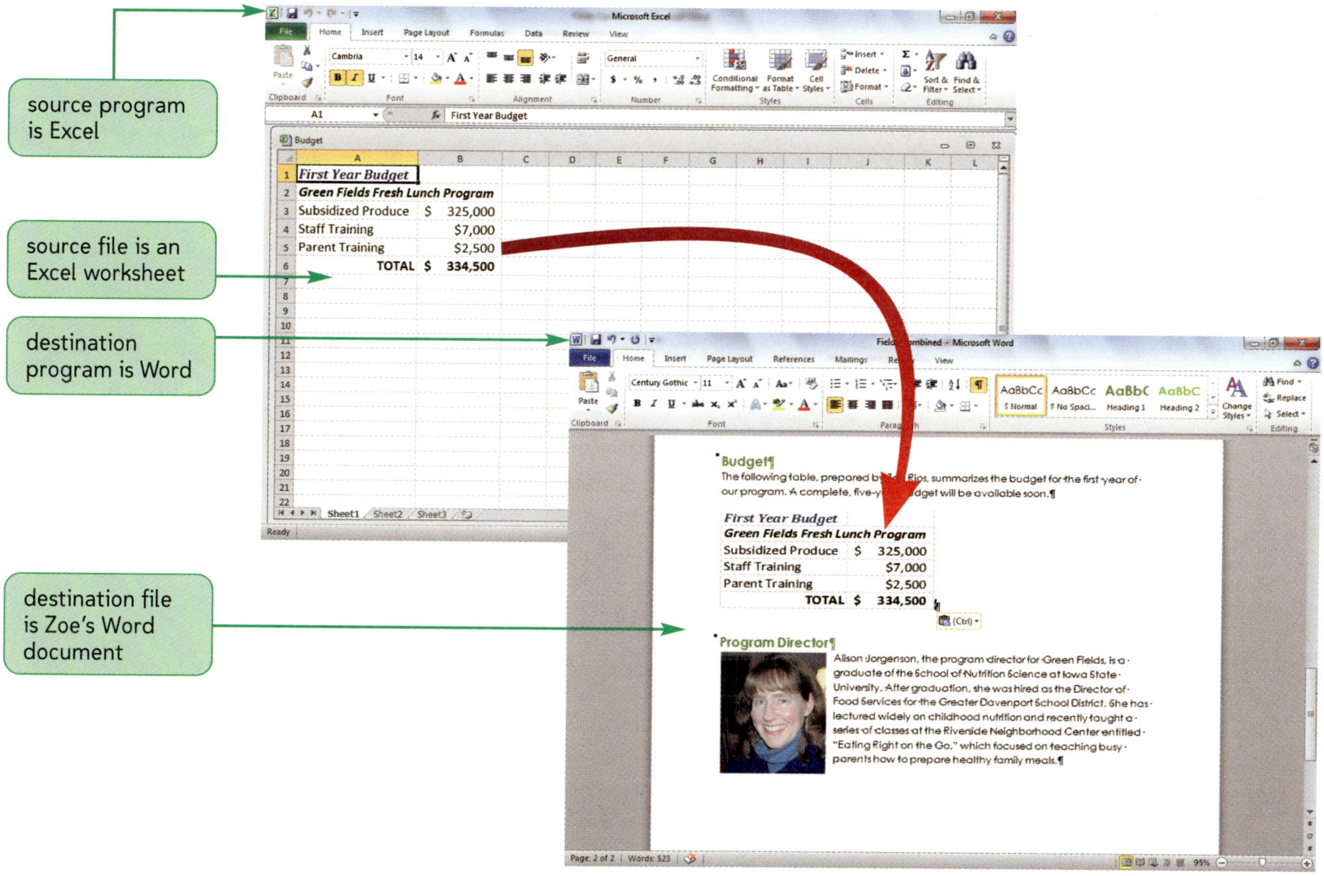


**TIP**

A document that contains a linked object takes up less space on a disk than does a document containing an embedded version of the same object.

**Linking** is similar to embedding, except that the object inserted into the destination file maintains a connection to the source file—not just the source program. Just as with an embedded object, you can double-click a linked object to access the tools of the source program. However, unlike with an embedded object, if you edit the source file in the source program, those changes appear in the linked object; likewise, if you change the object from the destination program, the changes will also appear in the file in the source program. The linked object in the destination document is not a copy; it is a shortcut to the original object in the source file.

**INSIGHT**

*Storing Linked Files*

When linking objects, it is important to keep the source and destination files in their original storage locations. If you move the files or the folders in which they are stored, you will disrupt the connection between the source file and the document containing the linked object, because the shortcut in the destination file will no longer have a valid path to the source file. For example, if you insert a linked Excel file into a Word document, close the Word document and the Excel file, and then later a colleague moves the source file (the Excel file) to a different folder or even deletes it, the next time you open the Word document containing the linked object, you will get an error message or you won't be able to update the linked object. To update the path for linked objects, click the File tab, click the Info tab in Backstage view, and then click Edit Links to Files in the right pane of the Info tab. In the Links dialog box that opens, click the link whose location has changed, click the Change Source button, and then navigate to the new location of the source file.

Figure 7-14 illustrates the relationship between the data in Henry's Excel chart and the linked object in Zoe's Word document.

**Figure 7-14** **Linking an Excel chart to a Word document**

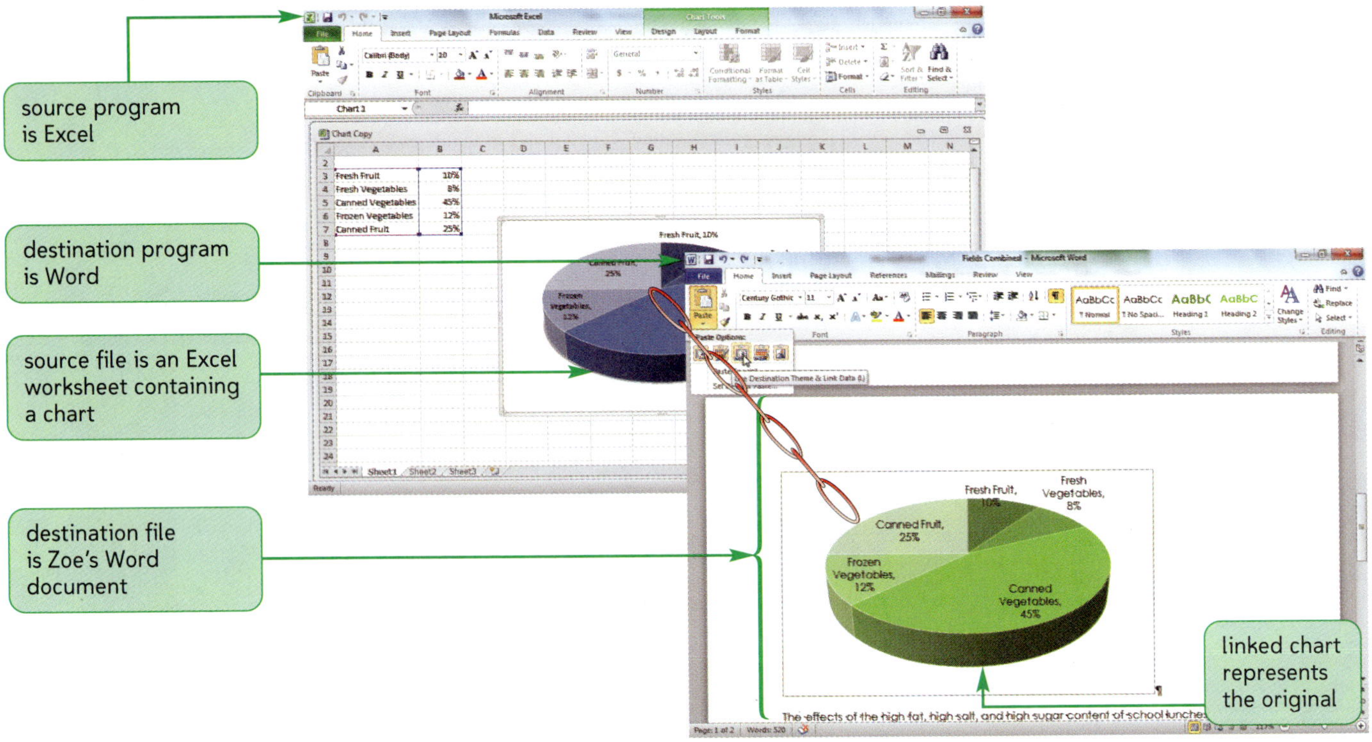


## PROSKILLS

### *Decision Making: Choosing Between Embedding and Linking*

Embedding and linking are both useful when you know you'll want to edit an object after inserting it into Word. But how do you decide whether to embed or link the object? Create an embedded object if you won't have access to the original source file in the future, or if you don't need to maintain the connection between the source file and the document containing the linked object. An advantage of embedding is that the source file is unaffected by any editing in the destination document, and the two files can be stored separately. You could even delete the source file from your disk without affecting the copy embedded in your Word document. A disadvantage is that the file size of the Word document containing the embedded object will be larger.

Create a linked object whenever you have data that is likely to change over time and when you want to keep the object in your document up to date. The advantage to linking is that the data in both the source file and destination file can reflect recent revisions. A disadvantage to linking is that you have to keep track of two files (the Excel file and the Word file) rather than just one.

## Embedding an Excel Worksheet

To embed an object from an Excel worksheet into a Word document, you start by opening the Excel worksheet (the source file) and copying the Excel object that you want to embed to the Office Clipboard. You then open the Word document (the destination file), click the Paste button arrow in the Clipboard group on the Home tab, and then click Paste Special to open the Paste Special dialog box. In this dialog box, you can choose to paste the copied Excel object in a number of different forms. To embed it, you select Microsoft Office Excel Worksheet Object.

Zoe wants to include the budget for the lunch program in her program description document. If she needs to adjust numbers in the budget later, she will need access to the Excel tools for recalculating the data. Therefore, you will embed the Excel object in the Word document, replacing the "[Insert Excel worksheet]" placeholder on page 2. Then you can use Excel commands to modify the embedded object from within Word.

### To embed the Excel data in the Word document:

1. On page 2, delete the placeholder **[Insert Excel worksheet]** that appears under the Budget heading, being careful not to delete the paragraph mark after it. The insertion point should now be located in a blank paragraph above the "Program Director" heading. Now you need to open Henry's Excel file and copy the budget.
2. Start Microsoft Excel 2010, open the file **Budget** located in the Word7\Tutorial folder included with your Data Files, and then maximize the Excel program window if necessary. See Figure 7-15.

**Figure 7-15** Budget file open in Excel

selected cell A1

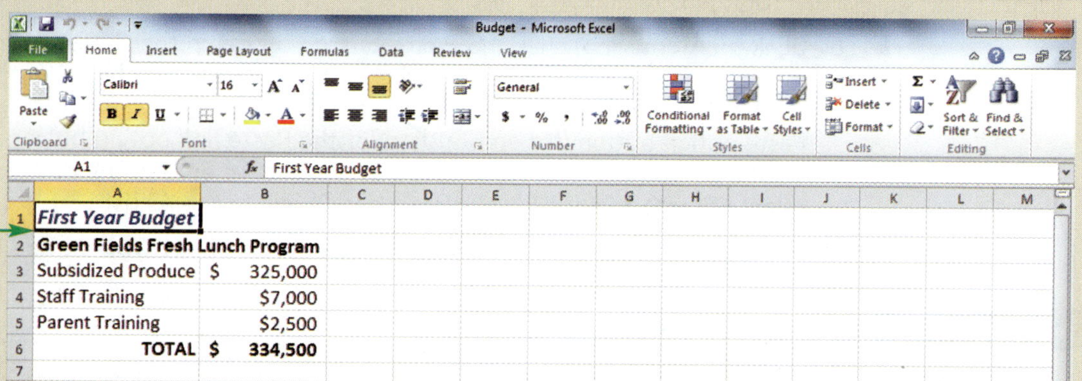


An Excel worksheet is arranged in rows and columns, just like a Word table. The intersection between a row and column is called a **cell**; an individual cell takes its name from its column letter and row number. For example, the intersection of column A and row 1 in the upper-left corner of the worksheet is referred to as cell A1, and it is currently selected, as indicated by its dark outline. To copy the budget data to the Office Clipboard, you need to select the entire block of cells containing the budget.

3. Click cell **A1** (the cell containing the text "First Year Budget"), press and hold the **Shift** key, and then click cell **B6** (the cell containing "$334,500"). See Figure 7-16.

**Figure 7-16** **Budget data selected in the worksheet**

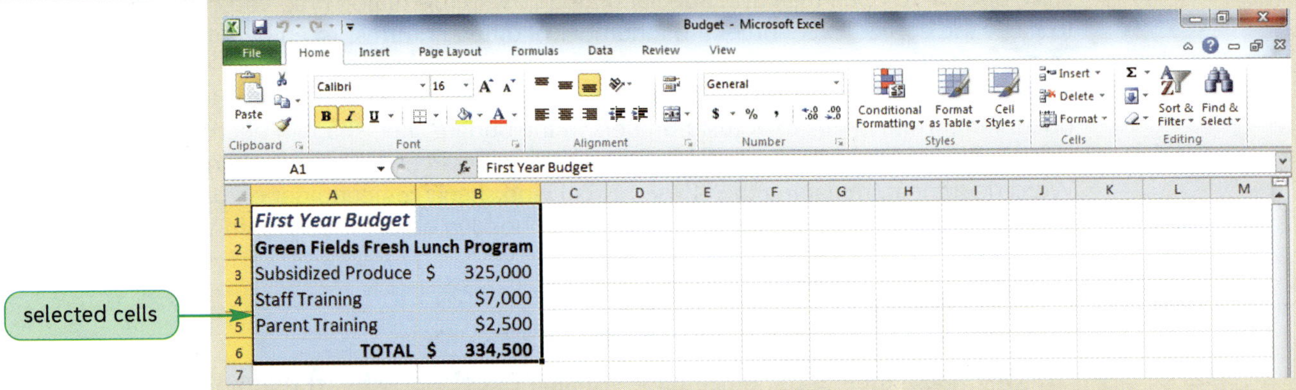


Now that the data is selected, you can copy it to the Office Clipboard, and return to Word. You need to keep Excel open, otherwise you will not have access to the commands for embedding the data in Word.

4. Press the **Ctrl+C** keys. The border around the selected cells is flashing, indicating that you have copied the data in these cells to the Office Clipboard.
5. Click the **Word** button in the taskbar. You return to the Fields Combined document, with the insertion point located in the blank paragraph above the heading "Program Director."
6. Click the **Home** tab, click the **Paste button arrow** in the Clipboard group, and then click **Paste Special** to open the Paste Special dialog box. Here you can choose to embed the Excel object or link it, depending on whether you select the Paste option button (for embedding) or the Paste link option button (for linking). The Paste option button is selected by default. To embed the data, you need to select Microsoft Office Excel Worksheet Object in the As list.
7. In the As list, click **Microsoft Office Excel Worksheet Object**. See Figure 7-17.

**Figure 7-17** **Paste Special dialog box**

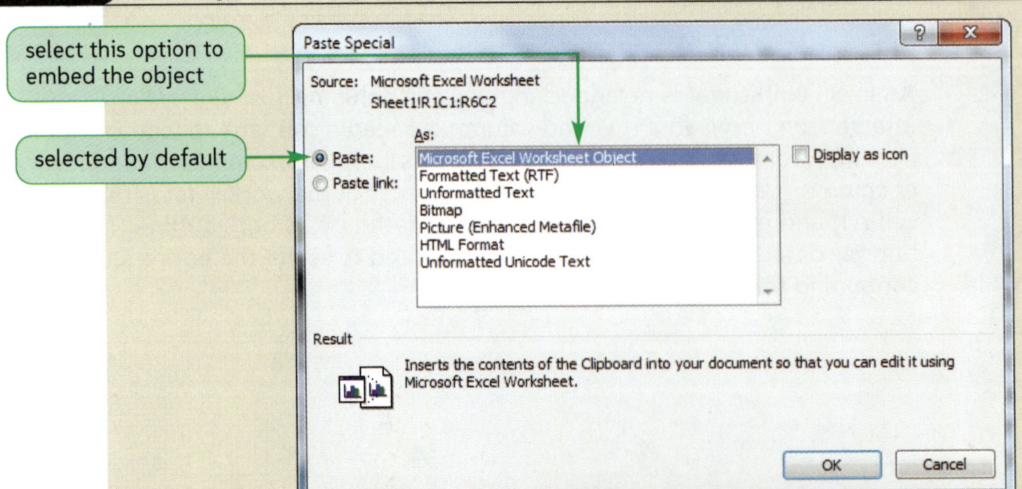

**8.** Click the **OK** button. The Excel object is inserted in the Word document, as shown in Figure 7-18.

**Figure 7-18** **Excel object embedded in the Word document**

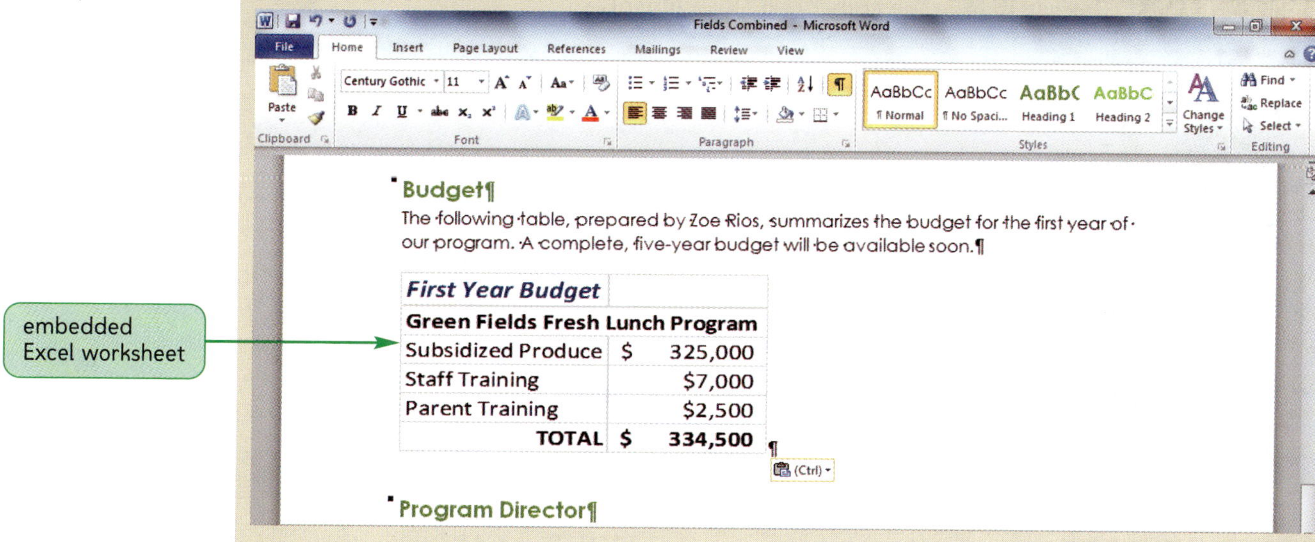


At this point, the Excel data looks like an ordinary table. But because you embedded it as an Excel worksheet object, you can modify it from within Word, using Excel tools and commands.

## Modifying the Embedded Worksheet

After you embed an object in Word, you can modify it two different ways. First, you can click the object to select it, and then move or resize it, just as you would a graphic object. Second, you can double-click the object to display the tools of the source program on the Word Ribbon, and then edit the contents of the object. After you modify the embedded object using the source program tools, you can click anywhere else in the Word document to deselect the embedded object and redisplay the usual Word tools on the Ribbon.

Zoe would like to center the Excel object on the page. She also explains that the value for Staff Training is incorrect, so she asks you to update the budget with the new data.

### To modify the Excel object:

**1.** Click anywhere in the embedded budget. Selection handles and a dotted blue outline appear around the Excel object, indicating that it is selected. With the object selected, you can center it as you would center any other selected item.

**2.** In the Paragraph group on the Home tab, click the **Center** button. The Excel object is aligned to the center of the page.

**3.** Double-click anywhere inside the Excel object. The object's border changes to resemble the borders of an Excel worksheet, with horizontal and vertical scroll bars, row numbers, and column letters. The Word tabs on the Ribbon are replaced with Excel tabs. You need to change the value for Staff Training from $7,000 to $6,000. This should also decrease the budget total by $1,000 because of the formula used in the worksheet to calculate this value.

4. Click cell **B4**, which contains the value $7,000, type **6000**, and then press the **Enter** key. The new value of "$6,000" replaces the old value of "$7,000." The budget total in cell B6 decreases from $334,500 to $333,500. See Figure 7-19.

**Figure 7-19** **Revised data in the embedded Excel object**

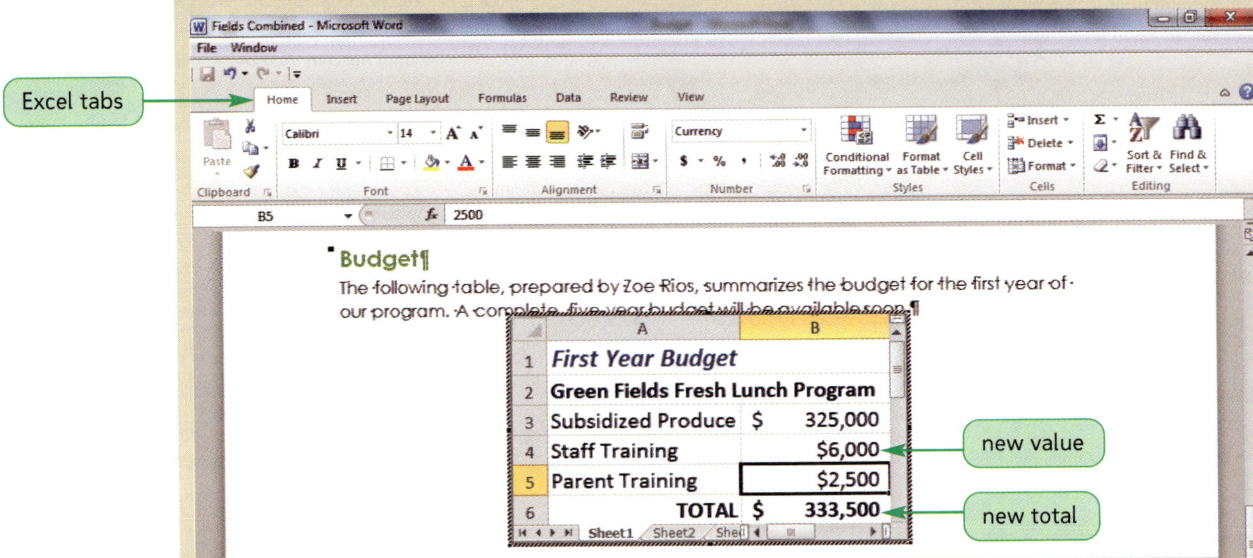


5. Click outside the borders of the Excel object to deselect it. The Word tabs are now visible on the Ribbon again.

6. Click the **Microsoft Excel** button in the taskbar to display the Excel window. Because you embedded the data from the Excel worksheet instead of linking it, the original Budget workbook, with the original Staff Training value of $7,000, remains unchanged.

7. Click the **File** tab, and then click **Close** in the navigation bar. The Budget workbook closes.

Next, Zoe wants you to insert Henry's Excel chart, which illustrates the percentage of fresh fruits and vegetables served in school lunches. Because Henry plans to revise the chart soon, Zoe decides to link the chart in the Excel file rather than embed it. That way, once Henry updates the chart in the source file, the new data will appear in Zoe's Word document as well.

## Linking an Excel Chart

When you link an object, you start by selecting it in the source program and copying it to the Office Clipboard. Then you return to Word and select one of the linking options from the Paste Options menu. The Paste Options menu displays different options depending on what you have copied to the Office Clipboard. Figure 7-20 describes some of the commands you will see on the Paste Options menu for different objects. Note that the ScreenTip (button name) for some of these buttons changes depending on the object you have selected to copy and paste.

**Figure 7-20** Commands on the Paste Options menu

| Button | Button Name | Function | Available when... |
|---|---|---|---|
| | Keep Text Only | Pastes formatted text as unformatted text; also, pastes text from a table as tabbed, unformatted text | You copy text to the Clipboard |
| | Use Destination Theme | Pastes or embeds copied element from another document or file using theme colors and fonts of destination document | You copy formatted text or a graphic from another document or file and the insertion point is located in a Word document |
| | Keep Source Formatting | Pastes or embeds copied item from Clipboard with the same formatting it had in source file | You copy text or a graphic from another document or file and the insertion point is located in a Word document |
| | Use Destination Theme & Link Data | Pastes copied element from another document or file using theme colors and fonts of destination document; also, retains link to source document or file | You copy formatted text or a graphic from another document or file and the insertion point is located in a Word document |
| | Keep Source Formatting & Link Data | Pastes copied item from Clipboard with the same formatting it had in source file; also retains link to source document or file | You copy formatted text or a graphic from another document or file and the insertion point is located in a Word document |
| | Picture | Pastes copied Excel data or chart as a picture | You copy data or a chart from an Excel workbook and the insertion point is located in a Word document |
| | Nest Table | Pastes multiple cells inside a single cell | You copy cells in a table to the Clipboard and the insertion point is located in a table |
| | Merge Table | Pastes copied table or rows at the bottom of the current table | You copy a table or table rows to the Clipboard and the insertion point is located in a table |
| | Insert as New Rows | Pastes copied rows as new rows in the current table | You copy table rows to the Clipboard and the insertion point is located in a table |
| | Insert as New Columns | Pastes copied columns as new columns in the current table | You copy table rows to the Clipboard and the insertion point is located in a table |

The chart Zoe wants to use is stored in a workbook named Chart, located in the Word7\Tutorial folder included with your Data Files. Because you'll make changes to the chart after you link it, you will make a copy of the Chart workbook before you link it. This leaves the original workbook file unchanged in case you want to repeat the tutorial steps later. Normally you don't need to copy a file before you link it to a Word document.

## To link an Excel chart to the program description document:

1. Open the Excel file named **Chart** from the Word7\Tutorial folder included with your Data Files, and then save the Excel file with the name **Chart Copy** in the same folder. The worksheet includes some data and the pie chart created from the data.
2. Click the chart border. Do not click any part of the chart itself. A selection border appears around the chart. The worksheet data is also outlined in color to indicate this is the data used to create the chart. See Figure 7-21.

**Figure 7-21** Pie chart selected in the worksheet

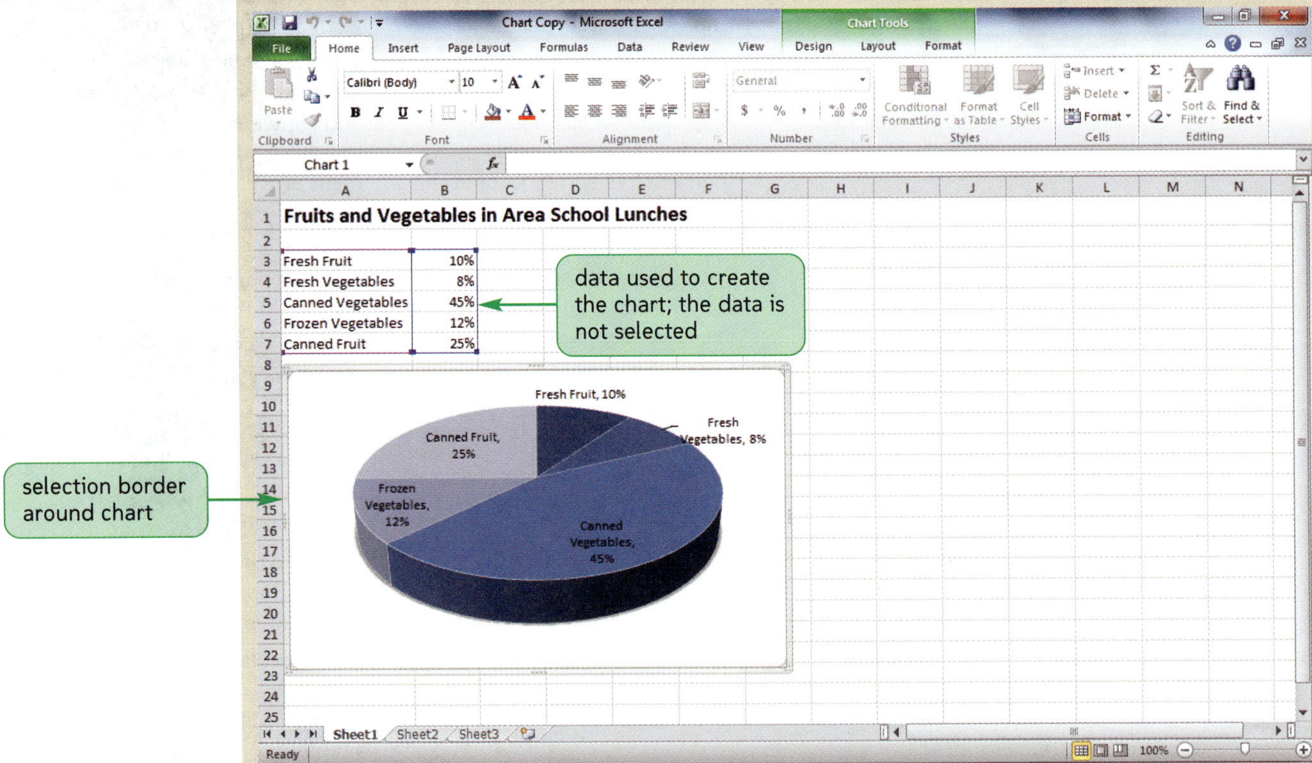


**Trouble?** If you see borders or handles around individual elements of the pie chart, click in the worksheet outside the chart border, and then repeat Step 2.

3. Press the **Ctrl+C** keys to copy the pie chart to the Office Clipboard, and then click the **Microsoft Word** button in the taskbar. The Fields Combined document is displayed in the Word window.
4. Scroll up to the bottom of page 1, delete the text **[Insert Excel chart]**, and verify that the insertion point is located in the blank paragraph at the bottom of page 1.
5. In the Clipboard group on the Home tab, click the **Paste button arrow** to display the Paste Options menu.

**6.** Move the mouse pointer over the icons in the Paste Options menu and notice the changing appearance of the chart, depending on which Paste Option you are previewing. Note that, for linking, you can choose between the Keep Source Formatting & Link Data option, which retains the font and blue colors from the Excel workbook, or Use Destination Theme & Link Data, which formats the chart with the font and green colors of the document's current theme. See Figure 7-22.

**Figure 7-22 Linking options in the Paste Options menu**

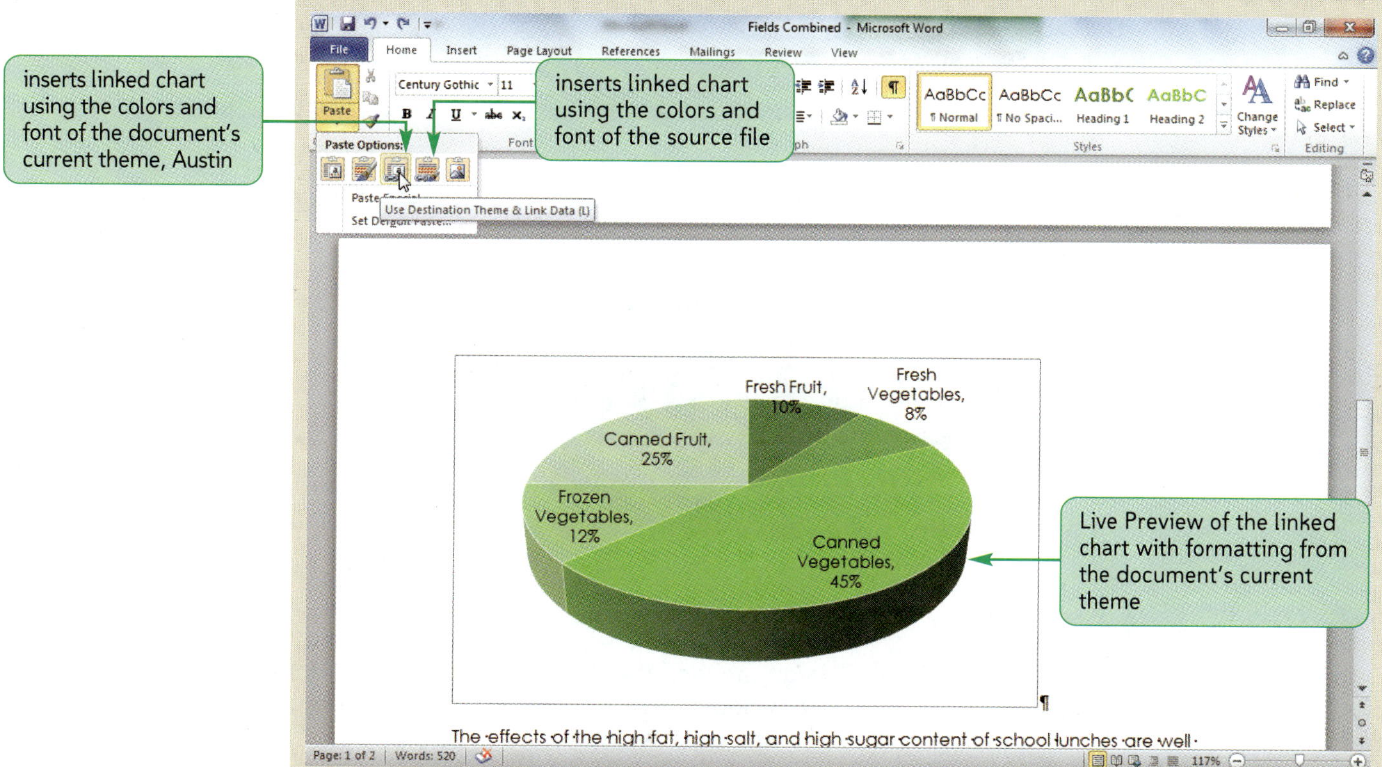


**7.** On the Paste Options menu, click the **Use Destination Theme & Link Data** button. The chart is inserted at the top of page 2. It is formatted with the green colors and font of the Austin theme used in the document.

## Modifying the Linked Chart

The advantage of linking compared to embedding is that you can update the data in the source file, and those changes will automatically be reflected in the destination file as well.

Zoe has received Henry's updated percentages of fruit and vegetables served, and she wants the chart in her program description to reflect this new information. You will update the data in the Excel chart in the source file. You start by selecting the chart, and then clicking the Edit Data button in the Data group on the Chart Tools Design tab. This displays the source and destination files side by side, so you can edit the source file and see the results in the destination file.

## To modify the chart in the source file:

1. Click anywhere in the white area inside the chart border. The gray chart border appears, and the three Chart Tools contextual tabs appear on the Ribbon, indicating that the chart is selected. See Figure 7-23.

**Figure 7-23** **Chart selected in Word**

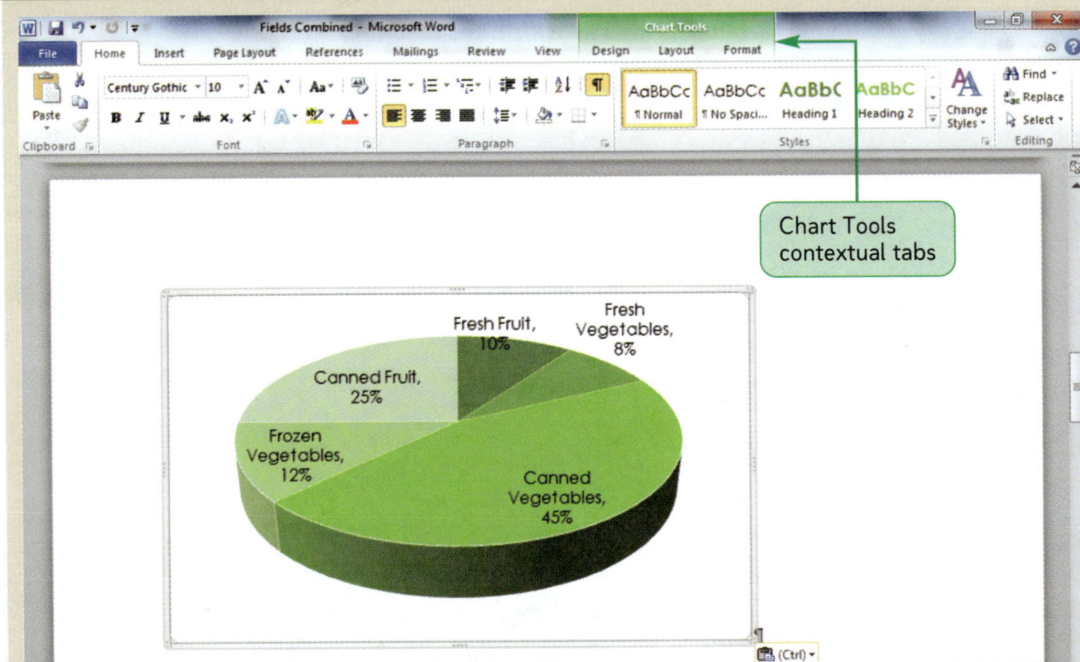


2. Click the **Chart Tools Design** tab, and then click the **Edit Data** button in the Data group. The Excel and Word windows are displayed side-by-side, with the Chart Copy workbook displayed in the Excel window on the right.
3. In the Excel window, click anywhere outside the chart to deselect it. To modify the chart, you need to edit the data in the worksheet.
4. In the Excel window, click cell **B5**, which contains the percentage for Canned Vegetables, type **40**, and then press the **Enter** key. The new percentage is entered in cell B5, and the label in the Canned Vegetables section of the pie chart changes from 45% to 40% in both the Excel workbook and the linked chart in the Word document.

   **Trouble?** If the chart in the Word document does not change to show the new value for Canned Vegetables, click the Refresh Data button in the Data group of the Chart Tools Design tab in the Word window.

5. In the Excel window, click cell **B7**, which contains the percentage for Canned Fruit, type **30**, and then press the **Enter** key. The new percentage is entered in cell B7, and the label in the Canned Fruit section of the pie charts in both the Excel and Word windows changes from 25% to 30%. See Figure 7-24.

**Figure 7-24 Modifying the chart in Excel**

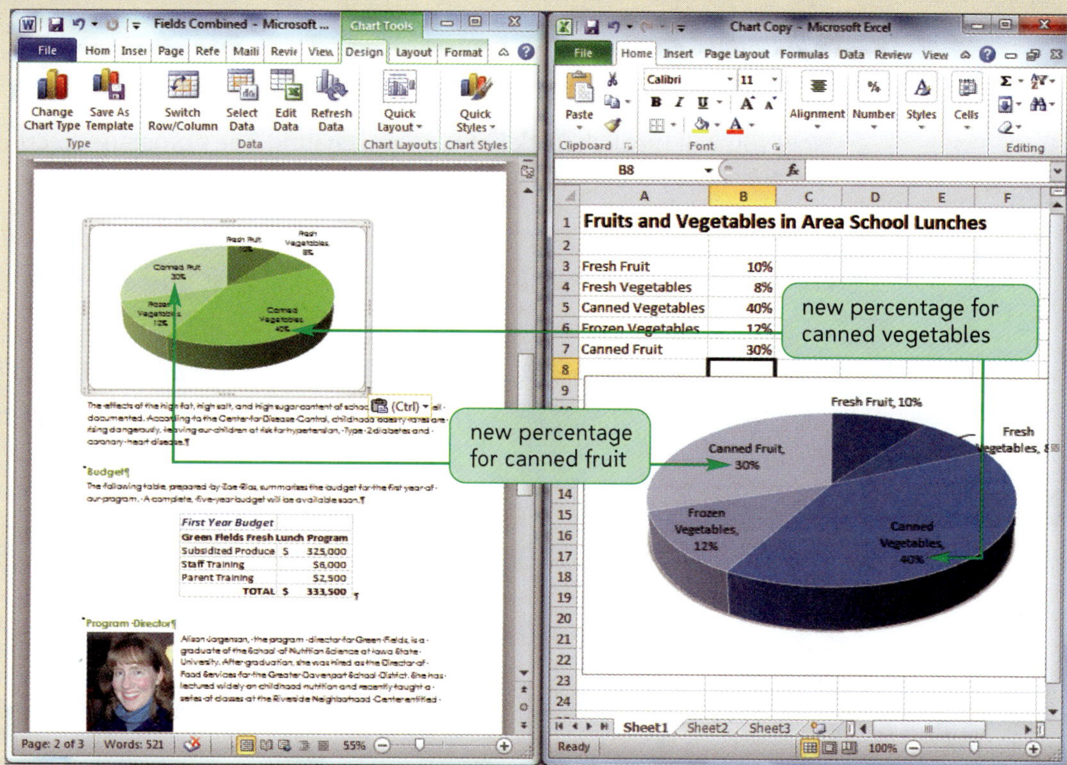


**Trouble?** If the chart in the Word document does not change to show the new value for Canned Vegetables, click the Refresh Data button in the Data group of the Chart Tools Design tab in the Word window.

6. On the Quick Access Toolbar in the Excel window, click the **Save** button, and then close the Chart Copy file and exit Excel. The Word window maximizes to fill the screen.

7. Click anywhere outside the chart to deselect it, and then save your work.

Zoe is finished with her work on the chart, and does not expect the data in it to change, so she decides to break the link between the Excel workbook and the Word document.

## Breaking Links

If you no longer need a link between files, you can break it. When you break a link, the object in the source file and the object in the destination file no longer have any connection to each other, and changes made to one object do not affect the other object.

REFERENCE

### *Breaking a Link to a Source File*

- Click the File tab to open Backstage view, and then click the Info tab, if necessary.
- Click Edit Links to Files in the right pane of the Info tab to open the Links dialog box.
- In the list of links in the document, click the link that you want to break.
- Click the Break Link button.
- Click the Yes button in the dialog box that opens asking you to confirm breaking the link.
- Click the OK button to close the Links dialog box.

Now you will break the link between the chart in Zoe's program description and the source chart in the Chart Copy workbook.

### To break the link between the Excel workbook and the Word document:

1. Click the **File** tab. Backstage view opens with the Info tab displayed.
2. At the bottom of the right pane of the Info tab, click **Edit Links to Files**. The Links dialog box opens with the only link in the document (the link to the Chart Copy Excel workbook) selected. See Figure 7-25.

**Figure 7-25** **Links dialog box**

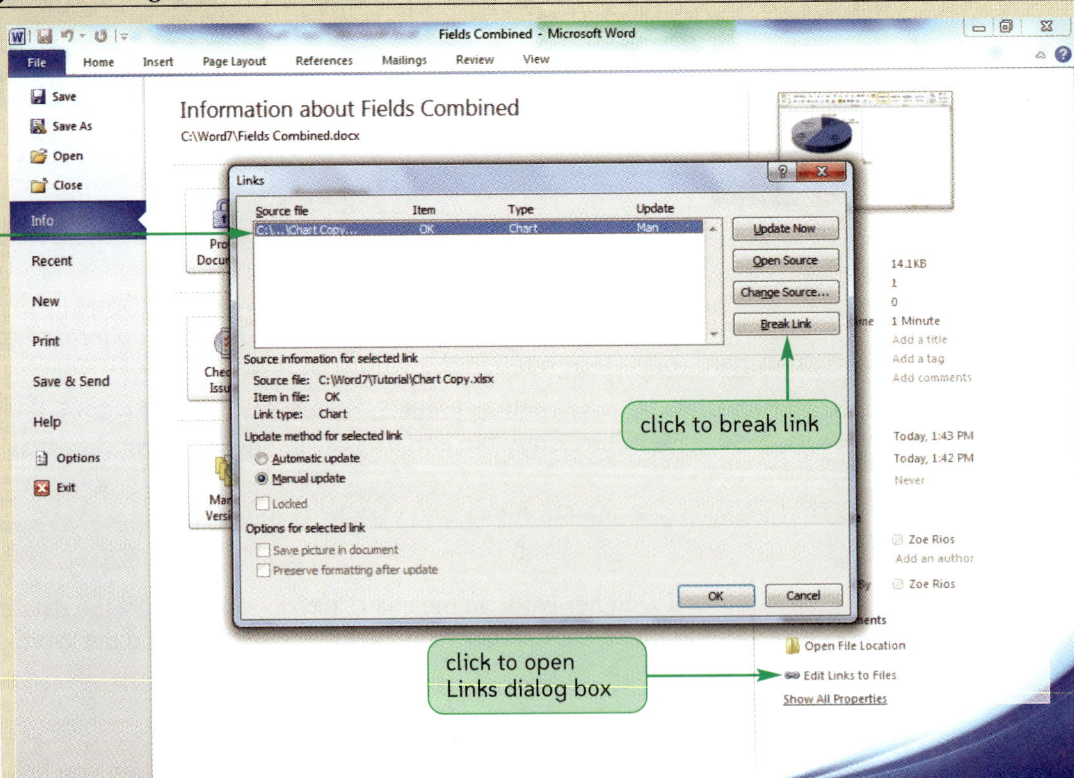

3. Click the **Break Link** button, and then click **Yes** in the dialog box that opens asking if you are sure you want to break the link. The list in the Links dialog box now indicates there is no source file for the chart in the document.
4. Click the **OK** button in the Links dialog box to close it. You return to the Info tab in Backstage view. With the link broken, you can no longer edit the Excel data from within Word. You can verify that by checking the Chart Tools Design tab.
5. Click the **Home** tab to display the document, click the white area inside the chart to select it, click the **Chart Tools Design** tab, and then notice that the Edit Data button in the Data group is grayed out, indicating this option is no longer available.
6. Click anywhere outside the chart to deselect it, and then save your work.

Zoe wants to focus on the task of distributing the document electronically, which you'll do in the next session.

REVIEW

## *Session 7.1 Quick Check*

1. Explain how to use Track Changes to edit a document.
2. What button do you use to insert a comment and on what tab is it located?
3. Explain the difference between comparing and combining documents.
4. True or False. You need to turn on Tracked Changes to insert a comment in a document.
5. Explain the difference between a linked object and an embedded object.
6. What button do you use in Word to embed or link an object from another program that you've copied to the Clipboard?
7. Explain how to break a link between a Word file and another file.

# SESSION 7.2 VISUAL OVERVIEW

You can use the Send Using E-mail command on the Save & Send tab when you want to email a document as an attachment.

The Save to Web command allows you to save a document to **SkyDrive**, an online storage service included with a Windows Live account. You can access files stored on SkyDrive from any computer with an Internet connection.

Before you can use SkyDrive, you need to create a Windows Live account at www.windowslive.com.

The My Documents folder is a private folder on SkyDrive that no one but you can access when you are signed into your Windows Live account.

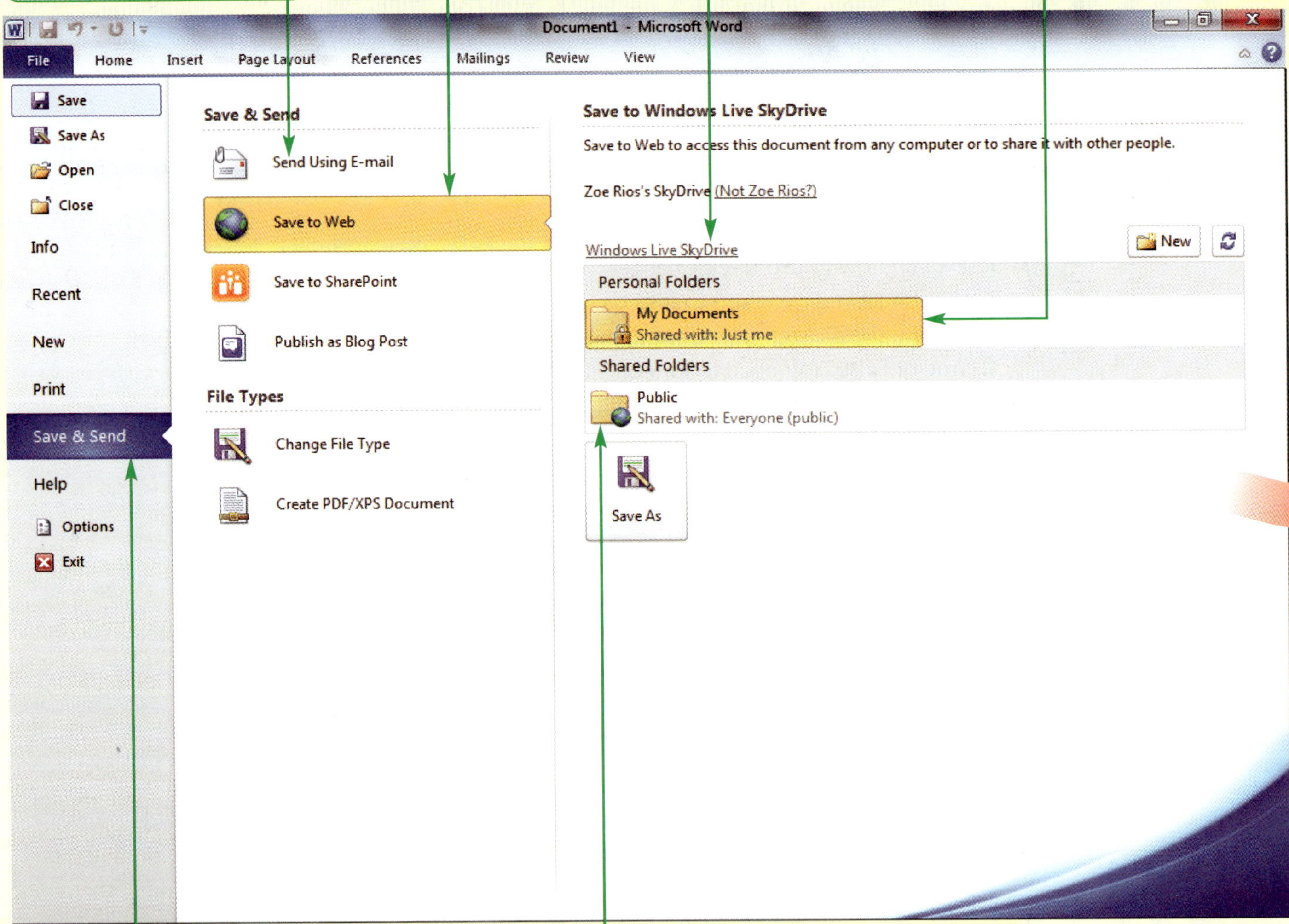


The Save & Send tab in Backstage view provides options for sharing documents with other people.

You can use the Public folder on SkyDrive when you want to make your documents available to other people.

# VIEWING A WORD DOCUMENT ON SKYDRIVE

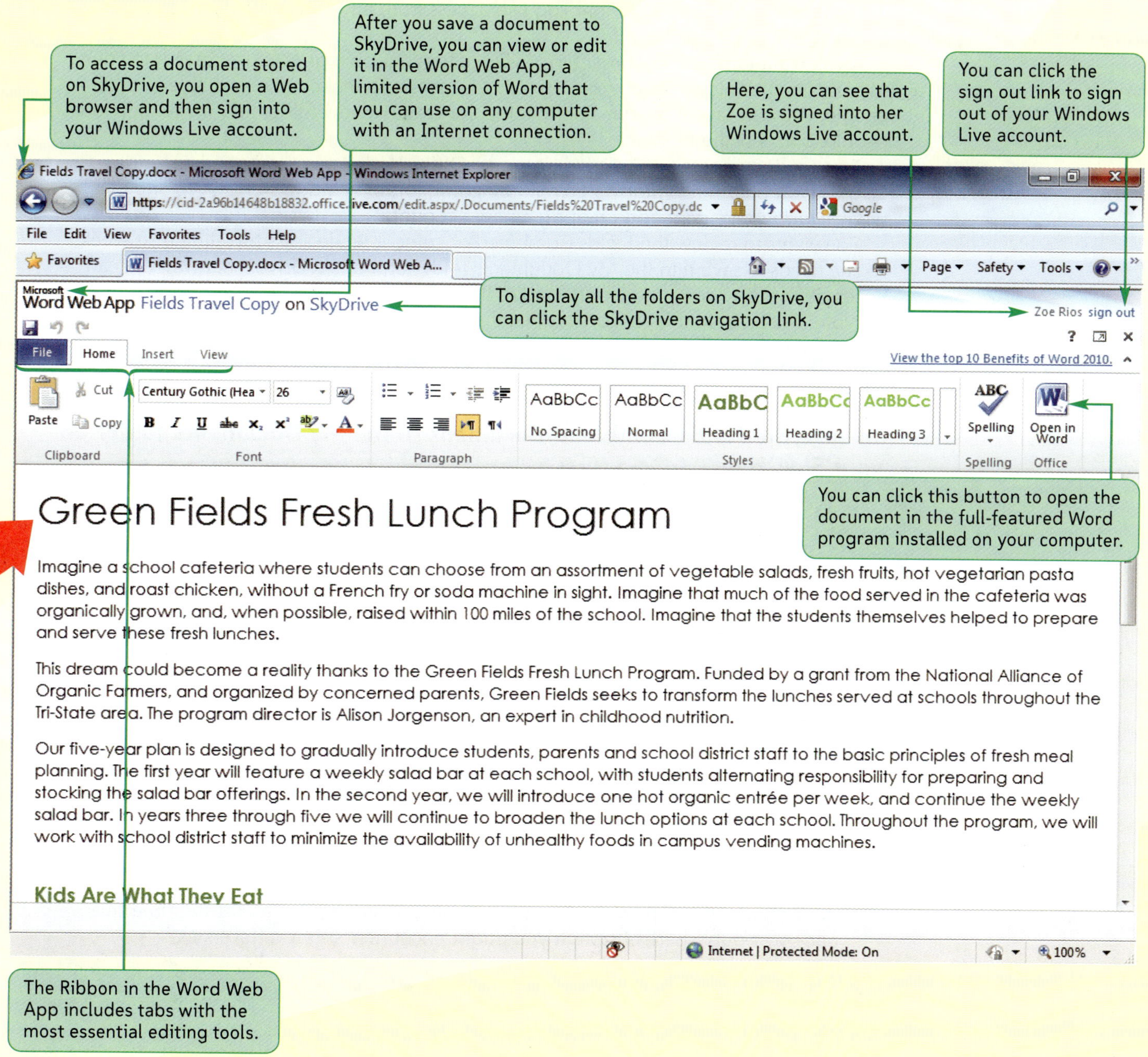

## Saving and Sharing Files on SkyDrive

SkyDrive is Microsoft's online storage and file sharing service, which you can access with a free Windows Live account. You upload files to SkyDrive so you can access the documents from another computer, share the documents with other people, or use SkyDrive's additional storage. Each Windows Live account comes with its own SkyDrive. After you have saved a document on SkyDrive, you can edit it in the Word Web App, which is a limited version of Word 2010 that you can access from any computer connected to the Internet.

If you want to save a document to SkyDrive for your own private use, save it to your My Documents folder, which no one else can access. To make a file available to other people, you can save it to your Public folder, or create a new folder and invite individual people to access the file.

To save documents to SkyDrive or to use Office Web Apps, you need a Windows Live ID. You obtain a Windows Live ID by going to the Windows Live Web site at *www.windowslive.com* and creating a new account.

Zoe wants to review the Fields Combined document while she's traveling next week, so she needs to save it to the My Documents folder on her SkyDrive. That way she can access it from any computer connected to the Internet.

**Note:** The steps in this section assume that you already have a Windows Live ID and account.

**To save the Fields Combined document to the My Documents folder on your SkyDrive:**

1. If you took a break after the previous session, make sure the Fields Combined document is open in Print Layout view.
2. Click the **File** tab, and then click the **Save & Send** tab in the navigation bar. The Save & Send options available in Word appear in Backstage view.
3. In the Save & Send section, click **Save to Web**. The right pane changes to display a Sign In button that you can use to sign into your Windows Live account. See Figure 7-26.

   **Trouble?** If you do not already have a Windows Live account, your screen will look different from the one in the figure. Before you can complete the rest of these steps, you need to set up a Windows Live account, which is free, by going to the Windows Live Web site at *www.windowslive.com* and following the steps on the site to create a new account.

   **Trouble?** SkyDrive and the Office Web Apps are dynamic Web pages and might change over time, including the way they are organized and how commands are performed. The steps and figures in this section were accurate at the time this book was published, although you might encounter slight differences.

**Figure 7-26** Save & Send tab in Backstage view

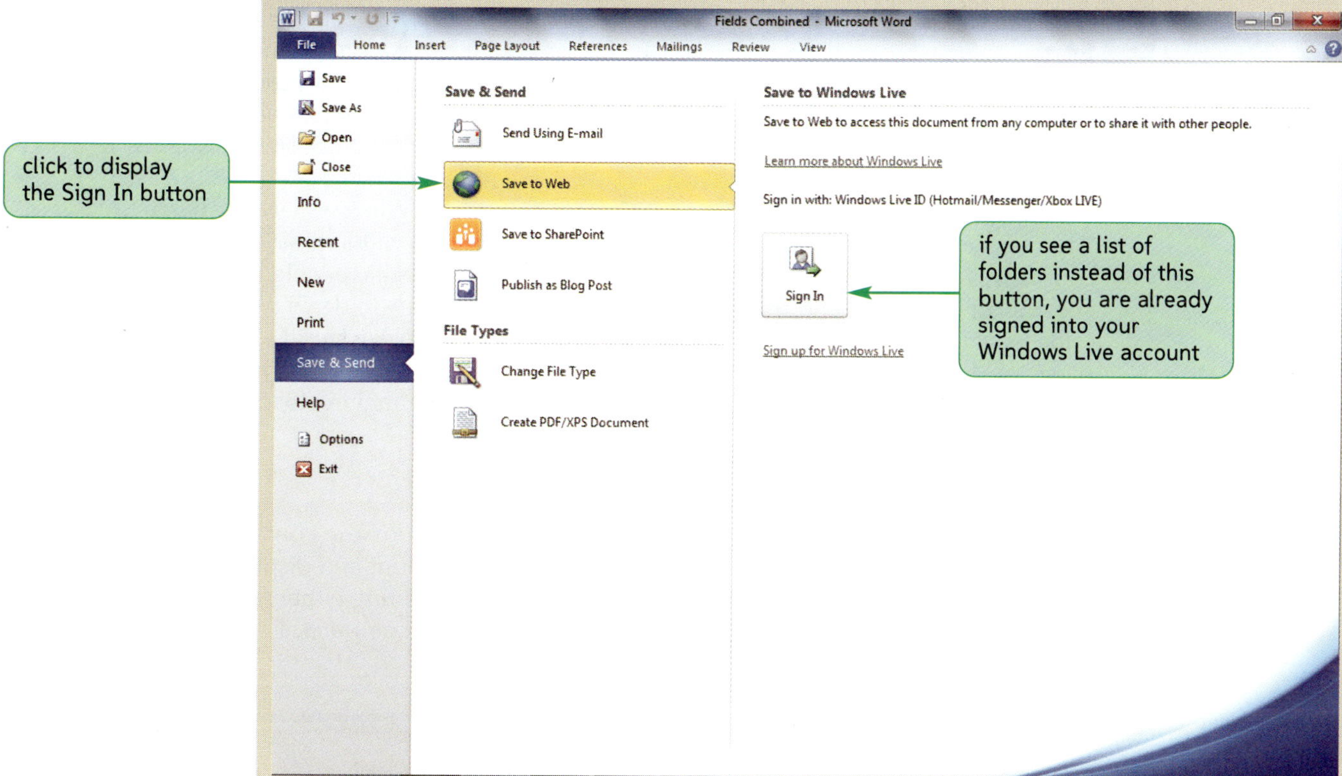


**Trouble?** If you are already signed into Windows Live, you see the folders in your SkyDrive account listed instead. Skip Steps 4–6 and continue with Step 7.

4. Click the **Sign In** button. The Connecting to docs.live.net dialog box opens.
5. In the E-mail address box, type the email address associated with your Windows Live account, press the **Tab** key, and then type the password associated with your Windows Live account in the Password box.
6. Click the **OK** button. The dialog box closes, and after a few moments, the right pane in Backstage view changes to list the folders on your SkyDrive, as shown earlier in the Session 7.2 Visual Overview.
7. In the right pane, click the **My Documents** folder to select it (if necessary), and then click the **Save As** button. Backstage view closes, and then after a few moments the Save As dialog box opens.
8. In the Save As dialog box, change the filename to **Fields Travel Copy**, and then click the **Save** button. The Save As dialog box closes. The Fields Travel Copy document is currently open on your computer, but it is stored on your SkyDrive.
9. Close the **Fields Travel Copy** document and exit Word.

INSIGHT

### *Sharing Files on SkyDrive*

After you save a document to your Public folder on SkyDrive, you can make it available to other people by emailing them the URL for the file. To copy a document's URL, display the document on SkyDrive, right-click the URL in the Address bar, click Copy on the shortcut menu, then open your email program and paste the URL into a new email message. Anyone who receives the email can click the URL to view the document, whether or not they are signed into Windows Live.

Another option is to invite people to join your network on Windows Live. By default, anyone in your network has access to your Public folder from within their own SkyDrive.

Finally, you can create a new folder on SkyDrive, grant specific people access to the contents of the folder, and then upload a document to the new folder. To create a new folder, sign in to Windows Live, display your Sky Drive, click New, click Folder, type a name for the folder, click Change, select the sharing options you want, click Next, click Add files, and then select documents from your computer to begin uploading them to your SkyDrive.

TIP

If your computer is part of a network that runs Microsoft SharePoint, you can use Word's co-authoring feature, which allows you and one or more colleagues to edit a document on SkyDrive simultaneously.

After you save a document to SkyDrive, you can access it from any computer connected to the Internet by logging into your Windows Live account and displaying your SkyDrive. You can simply view the document, or open it for editing either from within the Word Web App or from the Word program stored on your computer. In both cases, any changes are saved to the document on your SkyDrive.

REFERENCE

### *Accessing Files Stored on SkyDrive*

- Start Internet Explorer, go to *www.windowslive.com*, and sign into your Windows Live account.
- If you don't see the folders for your SkyDrive account, click Office.
- Click the folder in which you stored the document, and then click the document.
- To edit the document on your computer, click Open in Word.
- To edit the document online in the Word Web App, click Edit in Browser.

Zoe wants to view her document on SkyDrive.

### To view the Fields Travel Copy document on SkyDrive:

1. Click the **Internet Explorer** button on the taskbar, click in the Address bar, type **www.windowslive.com**, and then sign into your Windows Live account.
2. If you do not see your SkyDrive folders on the left side of the Windows Live page, click the **Office** link at the top of the page to display them. (Ignore the menu that opens when you move the mouse pointer over the Office link.) Your SkyDrive folders are divided into Personal folders (which only you can access), Shared folders (which other people can access), and Shared with me folders (which other people have shared with you). In Figure 7-27, the My Documents folder is the only Personal folder, and the Public folder is the only Shared folder. There are no Shared with me folders shown in Figure 7-27. In the center of the page you see information about documents you've worked with recently on your SkyDrive. In particular, you see a link for the Fields Travel Copy document. You could click that link now to display the file. However, to get some experience opening folders on SkyDrive, you'll click the My Documents link instead.

**Figure 7-27** SkyDrive folders

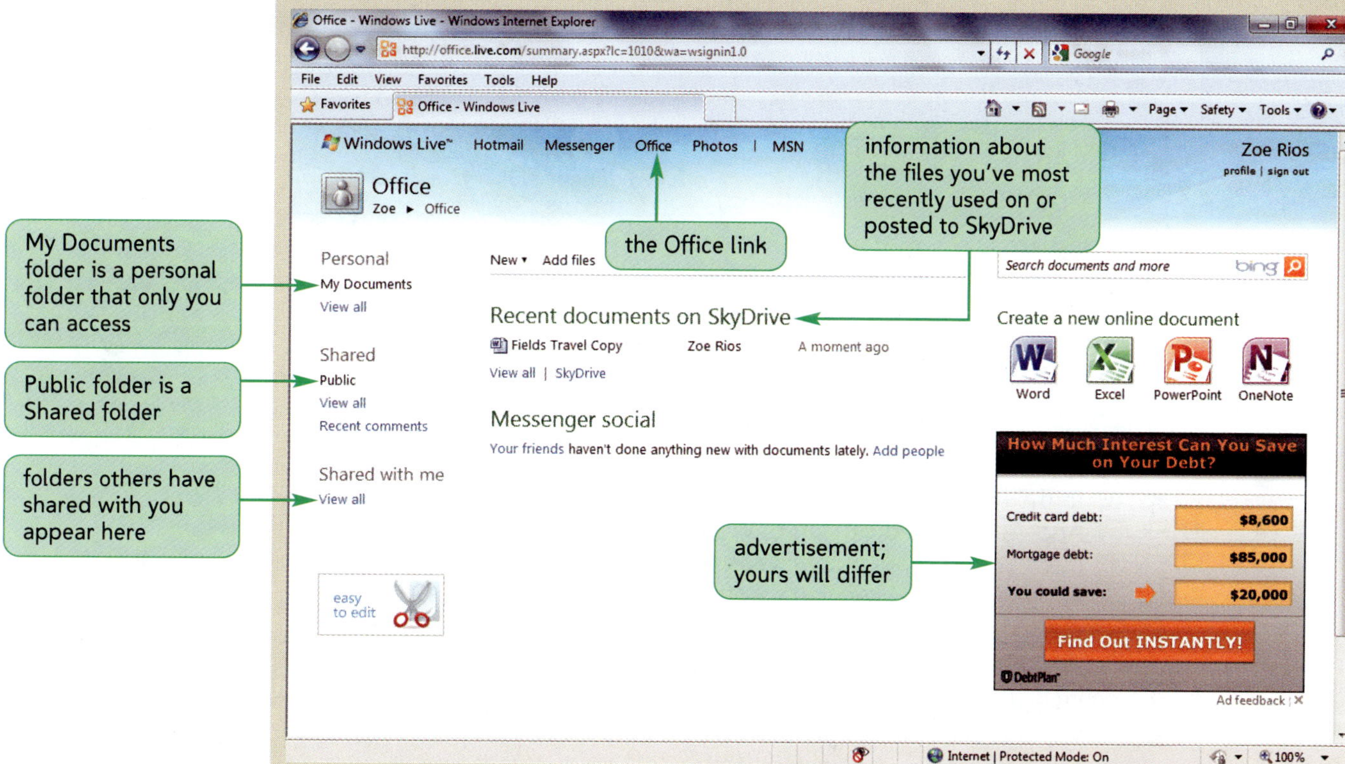


3. In the Personal section, click **My Documents**. You see the contents of the My Documents folder, which includes the Fields Travel Copy document.

4. Point to the **Fields Travel Copy** document to display the file management options shown in Figure 7-28. You could click the Delete button [X] on the far right to delete the Fields Travel Copy document from your SkyDrive.

**Figure 7-28** File Management options in SkyDrive

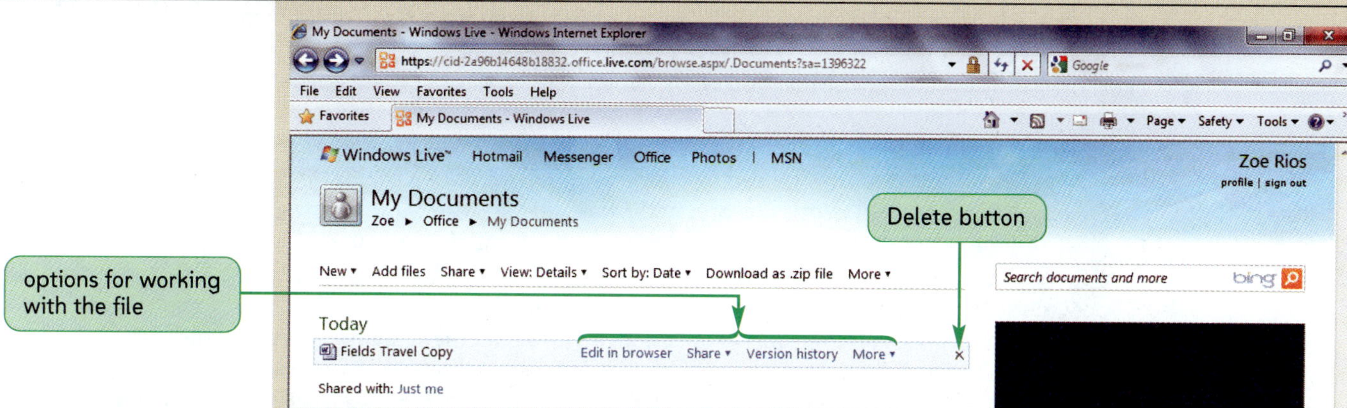


**TIP**

To open a new Word Web App file in your browser, point to Office and then click New Word document.

5. Click **Fields Travel Copy**. The document is displayed in the browser window for viewing only, with a menu bar above it, providing options for working with the document. If you want to open the document in Word on your computer, you can click Open in Word. If you want to open the document in your browser and edit it using the Web App version of Word, you can click Edit in Browser. See Figure 7-29.

**Figure 7-29** **Document displayed for viewing in SkyDrive**

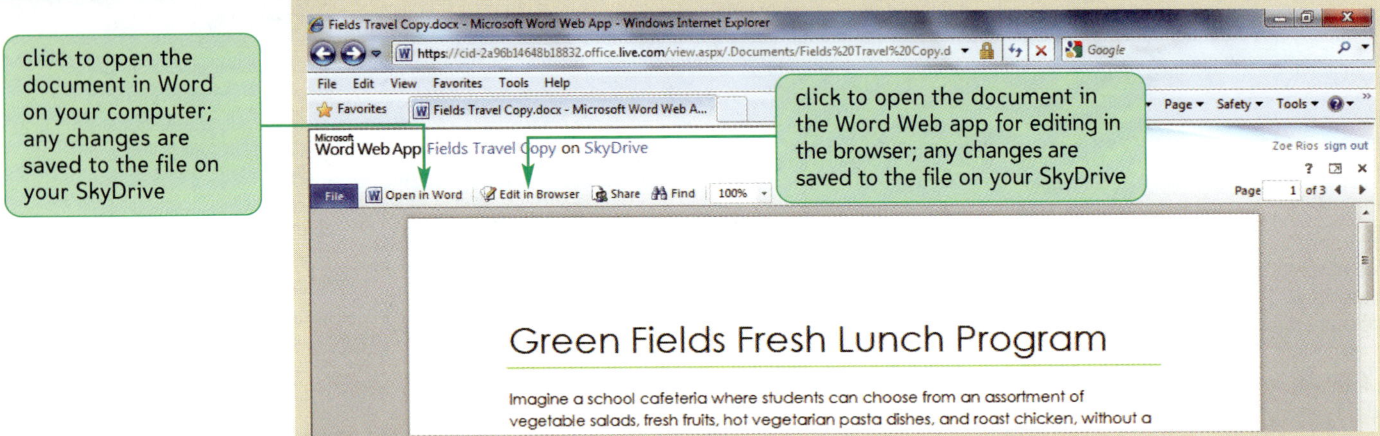


6. In the menu bar, click **Edit in Browser**. The document opens in the Word Web App. This limited version of Word is useful when you need to edit a Word document on a computer that does not have a copy of Word installed. Before you sign out of Windows Live, you can try out the navigation links.
7. In the navigation links at the top of the Windows Live page, click the **SkyDrive** link to return to the My Documents folder, and then, at the top of the page, click **Office** to display all your SkyDrive folders again. When you are finished using Windows Live, it's important to sign out, so another person using your computer can't gain access to your account.
8. In the upper-right corner of the page, click **sign out**, and then close Internet Explorer.

PROSKILLS

### *Teamwork: Emailing Word Documents*

SkyDrive is a powerful tool for sharing documents among co-workers. But sometimes emailing a document as an attachment is the simplest way to share a file. To get started emailing a document, click the File tab, click Save & Send, verify that Send Using E-mail is selected, and then select the email option you want. When you email documents, keep in mind a few basic rules:

- Many email services have difficulty handling attachments larger than 4 MB. Consider storing large files in a compressed (or zipped) folder to reduce their size before emailing.
- Other word-processing programs and early versions of Word might not be able to open files created in Word 2010. To avoid problems with conflicting versions, you have two options. You can save the Word document as a rich text file (using the Rich Text File document type in the Save As dialog box) before emailing it. All versions of Word can open rich text files. Another option is to convert the document to PDF format, which is essentially a picture of a Word document that can be read on any computer system using Adobe Acrobat Reader. To save a Word Document as a PDF file, use the Create PDF/XPS Document command from the Save & Send tab in Backstage view.
- If you plan to email a document that contains links to other files, remember to email all the linked files.
- Attachments, including Word documents, are sometimes used maliciously to spread computer viruses. Remember to include an explanatory note with any email attachment so that the recipient can be certain the attachment is legitimate. Also, it's important to have a reliable virus checker program installed if you plan to receive and open email attachments.

Next, Zoe turns her attention back to the Fields Combined document, which is stored on her computer. First, she asks you to add some hyperlinks. While hyperlinks are widely used in Web pages, you can also use them in ordinary Word documents.

## Using Hyperlinks in Word

**TIP**

Hyperlinks are commonly referred to as "links," but take care not to confuse them with the OLE links you worked with earlier in this tutorial.

A **hyperlink** is a word, phrase, or graphic that you can click to jump to another part of the same document, to a separate Word document, to a file created in another program, or to a Web page. You can also include email links, which you can click to create an email message from a document.

Zoe wants you to add two hyperlinks to the program description—one that jumps to a location within the program description and one that will open a different document.

### Inserting a Hyperlink to a Bookmark in the Same Document

Creating a hyperlink within a document is actually a two-part process. First, you need to mark the text you want the link to jump to—either by formatting the text with a heading style or by inserting a bookmark. A **bookmark** is an electronic marker that refers to a specific point in a document. Second, you need to select the text that you want users to click, format it as a hyperlink, and specify the bookmark or heading as the target of the hyperlink. The **target** is the place in the document to which the link connects. In this case, Zoe wants to create a hyperlink that targets the name of the Program Director, Alison Jorgenson, near the end of the document. Figure 7-30 illustrates this process.

**Figure 7-30** Hyperlink that targets a bookmark

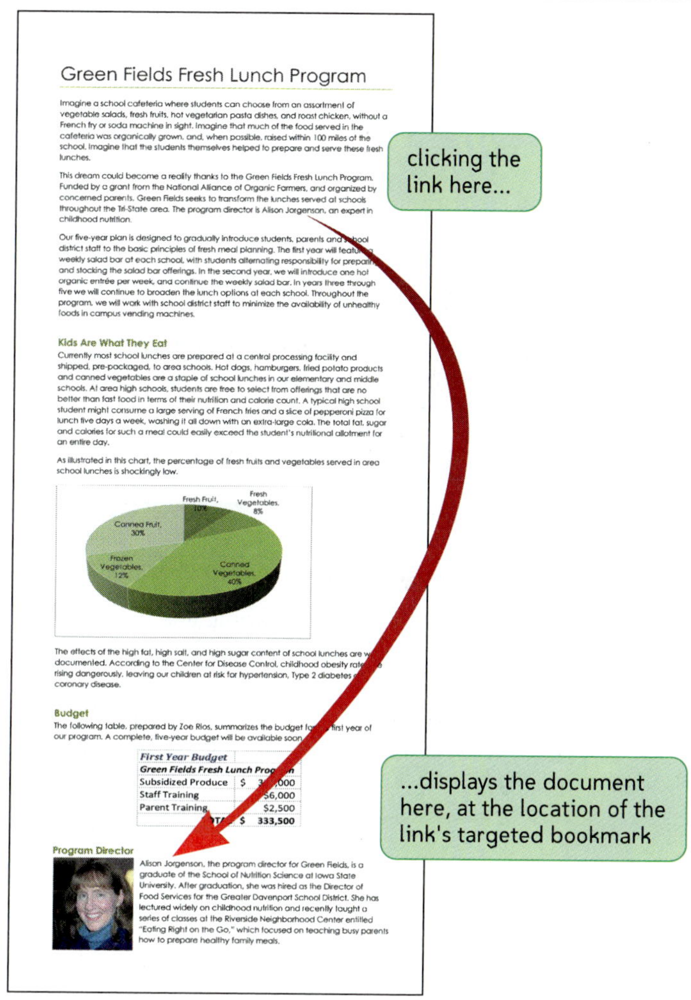

To create a hyperlink in Zoe's document, you'll need to insert a bookmark in the Program Director section.

**To insert a bookmark:**

1. Start Word and open the **Fields Combined** document from the Word7\Tutorial folder included with your Data Files. Switch to Print Layout view if necessary, display the rulers and nonprinting characters, and change the document zoom to Page Width.
2. Scroll down and select the name **Alison Jorgenson** at the beginning of the Program Director section, near the bottom of page 2.
3. Click the **Insert** tab, and then click the **Bookmark** button in the Links group. The Bookmark dialog box opens. You can now type the bookmark name, which cannot contain spaces.
4. Type **Director**. See Figure 7-31.

Figure 7-31 Creating a bookmark

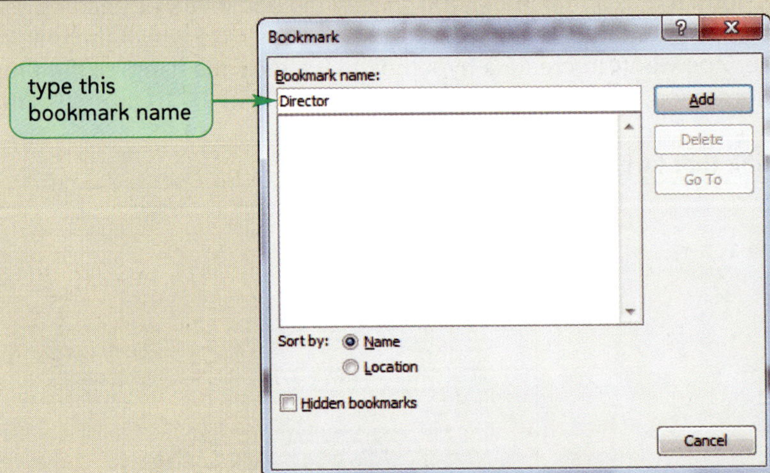


**TIP**

The Bookmark dialog box lists all the document's bookmarks. To delete a bookmark, click it in the dialog box and then click the Delete button.

5. Click the **Add** button. The Bookmark dialog box closes. Although you can't see it, a bookmark has been inserted before Alison's name.

The bookmark you just created will be the target of the hyperlink you will create next.

REFERENCE

*Creating a Hyperlink to a Location in the Same Document*

- Select the text or graphic you want to format as the hyperlink.
- In the Links group on the Insert tab, click the Hyperlink button to open the Insert Hyperlink dialog box.
- In the Link to pane, click Place in This Document.
- In the list displayed, click the bookmark or heading you want to link to and then click the OK button.

Zoe wants you to create a hyperlink from the program director's name (Alison Jorgenson) on the first page of the document that will target the bookmark you created at the beginning of the program director's description on the second page.

### To create a hyperlink to the bookmark:

1. Scroll up to page 1, and then, in the last sentence of the second paragraph under the heading "Green Fields Fresh Lunch Program," select the name **Alison Jorgenson**.
2. In the Links group on the Insert tab, click the **Hyperlink** button. The Insert Hyperlink dialog box opens.
3. In the Link to pane, click **Place in This Document**. The Select a place in this document list shows the headings and bookmarks in the document. Here you can click the bookmark or heading you want as the target for the hyperlink.
4. Under "Bookmarks," click **Director**. See Figure 7-32.

**Figure 7-32 Inserting a hyperlink**

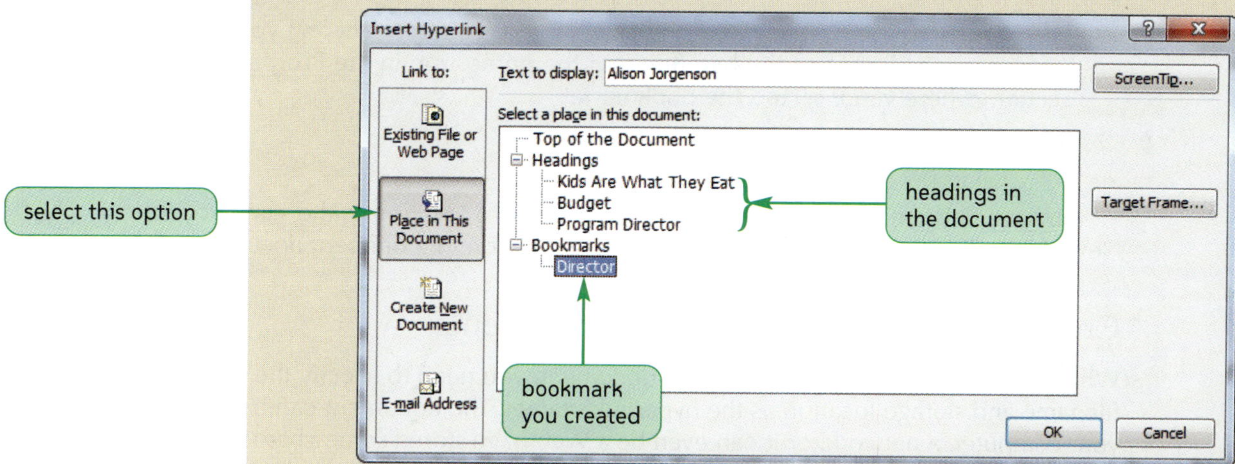


5. Click the **OK** button. The name "Alison Jorgenson" is formatted in the hyperlink style for the Austin theme, which applies an orange font color with an underline. The hyperlink now targets the Director bookmark that you created in the last set of steps.

After inserting a hyperlink into a document, you should test it.

### To test the hyperlink in your document:

1. Move the mouse pointer over the hyperlink, **Alison Jorgenson**. A ScreenTip appears with the name of the bookmark (Director) and instructions for following the link. See Figure 7-33.

**TIP**

To edit the text that appears in a hyperlink's ScreenTip, click the ScreenTip button in the Insert Hyperlink dialog box, type the text you want for a ScreenTip, and then click the OK button.

**Figure 7-33** **Displaying the ScreenTip for a hyperlink**

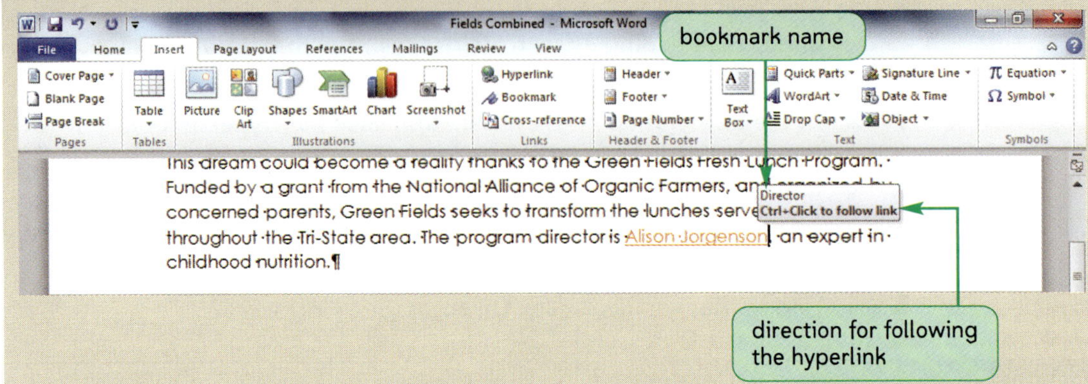


2. Press and hold the **Ctrl** key, and then click the **Alison Jorgenson** hyperlink. The insertion point jumps to the beginning of the paragraph in the Program Director section, where you inserted the bookmark.
3. Save your work.

You have finished creating a hyperlink that jumps to a location in the same document. Next, you will create a hyperlink that jumps to a location in a different document.

## Creating Hyperlinks to Other Documents

When you create a hyperlink to another document, you need to specify the document's filename and storage location as the hyperlink's target. The document can be stored on your computer, a network, or it can even be a Web page stored somewhere on the Web. In that case, you need to specify the Web page's URL (Web address) as the target. When you click a hyperlink to another document, the document opens on your computer, with the beginning of the document displayed. Keep in mind that if you move the source or target documents after you create a hyperlink, the hyperlink will no longer work.

REFERENCE

### *Creating a Hyperlink to Another Document*

- Select the text you want to format as a hyperlink.
- In the Links group on the Insert tab, click the Hyperlink button to open the Insert Hyperlink dialog box.
- In the Link to pane, click Existing File or Web Page.
- To target a specific file on your computer or network, use the Look in arrow to open the folder containing the file, and then click the file in the file list.
- To target a Web page, type its URL in the Address box.

Zoe wants to insert a hyperlink that, when clicked, will open a Word document containing Alison's resume. Because she wants the hyperlink to take users to the beginning of the resume, you don't need to insert a bookmark. Instead, you can specify just the name and location of the target document.

### To create a hyperlink to the resume document:

1. Press the **Ctrl+End** keys to move the insertion point to the blank paragraph at the end of the document. This is where you'll insert text, some of which will become the hyperlink.
2. Type **See Alison's resume.**
3. Select the word **resume** in the text you just typed.
4. In the Links group on the Insert tab, click the **Hyperlink** button. The Insert Hyperlink dialog box opens.
5. In the Link to pane, click **Existing File or Web Page**. The dialog box displays options related to selecting a file or a Web page.
6. Navigate to the Word7\Tutorial folder included with your Data Files (if necessary), and then click **Resume** in the file list. See Figure 7-34.

**Figure 7-34** Inserting a hyperlink to a different document

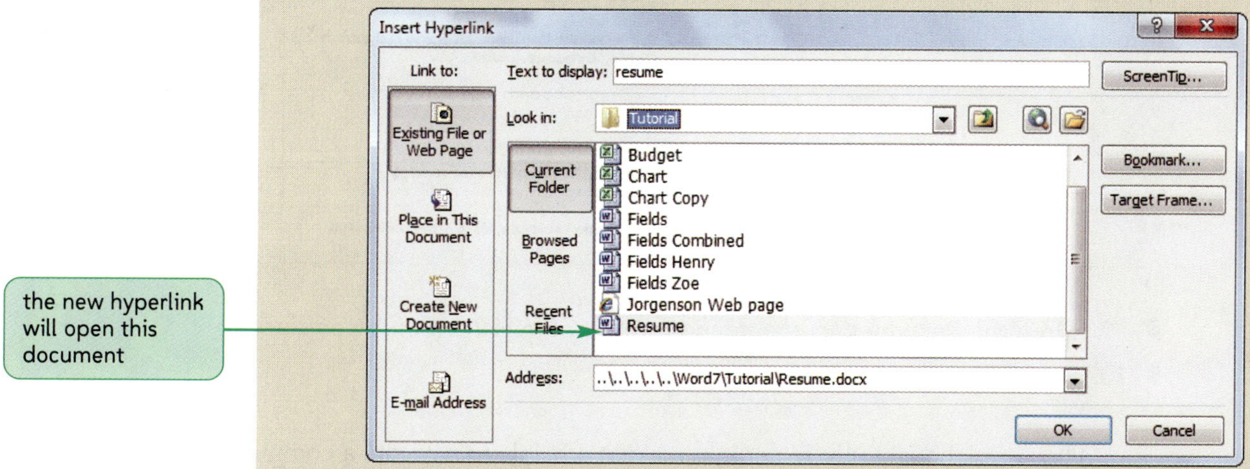


7. Click the **OK** button. The word "resume" is now formatted as a hyperlink. Now you will test the hyperlink.
8. Press and hold the **Ctrl** key, and then click the **resume** hyperlink. The Resume document opens. See Figure 7-35.

**Figure 7-35** Resume document

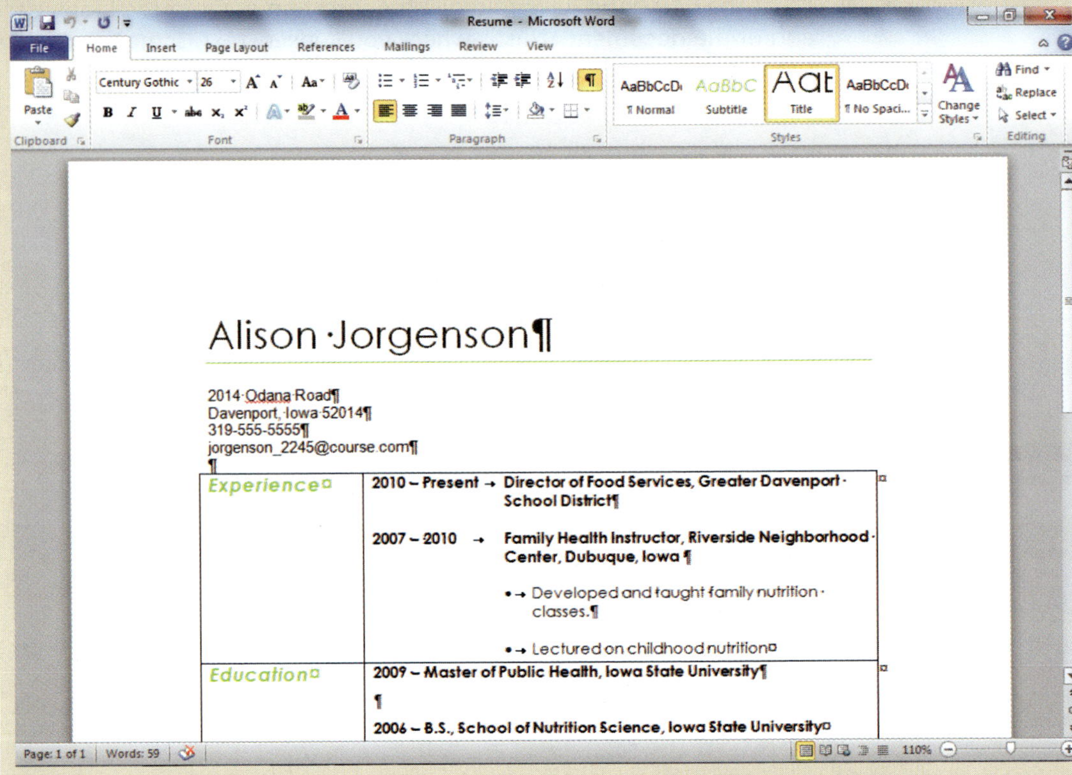


9. Close the **Resume** document, and return to the Fields Combined document.
10. Save your work.

When used thoughtfully, hyperlinks make it possible to navigate a complicated document or a set of files quickly and easily. Next, you need to save the document as a Web page.

## Saving a Word Document as a Web Page

**Web pages** are special documents designed to be viewed in a program called a **browser**. One widely used browser is Internet Explorer 8. Because Web pages include code written in the **Hypertext Markup Language**, or **HTML**, they are often referred to as **HTML documents**.

To create sophisticated Web pages (or a complete Web site), you'll probably want to use a dedicated HTML editor, such as Adobe Dreamweaver. However, in Word you can create a simple Web page from an existing document by saving it as a Web page. When you do so, Word inserts HTML codes that tell the browser how to format and display the text and graphics. Fortunately, you don't have to learn the Hypertext Markup Language to create Web pages with Word. When you save the document as a Web page, Word creates all the necessary HTML codes (called tags). This process is transparent to you, so you won't actually see the HTML codes in your Web page.

When you save a document as a Web page, Word saves the document as an HTML file and places the graphics that appear in the document in a separate folder. A group of smaller files travels across the Web faster than one large file, so this division of files makes it easier to share your documents on the Web.

You can choose from three different Web page file types in Word. The main differences among these file types are file size and the way special elements, such as WordArt or embedded or linked objects, are treated when they are displayed in a browser:

- **Single File Web Page**—Saves the document as an MHTML file, which is similar to an HTML file, with all graphics stored in the file along with the text. A Single File Web Page can be more than three or four times the size of the original Word document.
- **Web Page**—Saves the document as an HTML file, with a separate folder containing graphics and other elements that control the page's formatting. The HTML file created using the Web Page file type is approximately the same size as the original Word document, but the total size of the accompanying files can be two or three times the size of the Word document.
- **Web Page, Filtered**—Saves the document as an HTML file, with graphics stored in a separate folder. This file type retains less information than the other two formats. Any formatting differences are apparent only when you open the filtered Web page in a browser, or the next time you open the file in Word. Before you save a Word document as a filtered Web page, Word displays a dialog box warning you that some Office features (typically formatting) may not be available when you reopen the page. The total file size of a filtered Web page and its accompanying graphics files is smaller than the Word document from which it is created.

The Single File Web Page file type is a good choice when you plan to share your Web page only over a small network and not over the Internet. Having to manage only one file is more convenient than having to keep track of a group of files. But when you want to share your files over the Internet, it's better to use the Web Page, Filtered option. This will keep your overall file size as small as possible. Note that the folder Word creates to store the accompanying files has the same name as your Web page, plus an underscore and the word "files." For instance, a Web page saved as "Finance Summary" would be accompanied by a folder named "Finance Summary_files."

REFERENCE

### *Saving a Word Document as a Web Page*

- Click the File tab, and then click Save As to open the Save As dialog box.
- Click the Save as type arrow, and then click Single File Web Page; Web Page, Filtered; or Web Page.
- If desired, type a new filename in the File name box.
- Click the Change Title button to open the Enter Text dialog box, type a title for the Web page in the Page title box, and then click the OK button.
- Click the Save button in the Save As dialog box. If you saved the document using the Web Page, Filtered option, click Yes in the warning dialog box.

After you save a document as a Web page, Word displays it in **Web Layout view**, which displays the document similarly to the way it would appear in a Web browser. For example, in Web Layout View, the text spans the width of the screen (as it would in a browser), with no page breaks, and without any margins or headers and footers. Also, text wrapping around graphics often changes in Web Layout view, as the text expands to fill the wider area of the screen. For example, on the second page of the Fields Combined document, some text currently wraps below the Program Director's photograph, flowing onto a third page. When this document is saved as a Web page, the text wrapping will adjust to the wider page.

## To save the Fields Combined document as a Web page:

1. Click the **File** tab, and then click **Save As**. The Save As dialog box opens.
2. Navigate to the Word7\Tutorial folder included with your Data Files (if necessary), click the **Save as type** arrow, and then click **Web Page, Filtered**.
3. In the File name box, change the filename to **Fields Web Page**.
4. Click the **Change Title** button to open the Enter Text dialog box, and then type **Green Fields Fresh Lunch Program** in the Page title box. This title will appear in the browser title bar. See Figure 7-36.

**Figure 7-36 Web page title in the Enter Text dialog box**

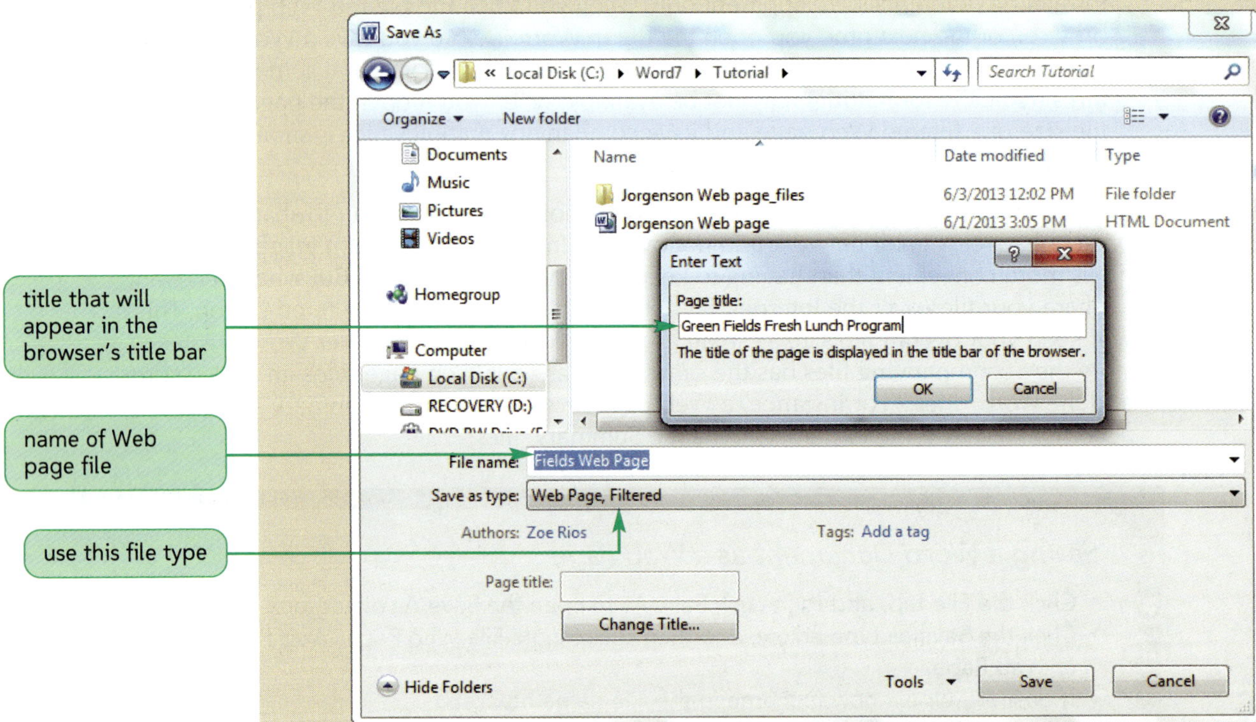


5. Click the **OK** button in the Enter Text dialog box.
6. Click the **Save** button in the Save As dialog box. A dialog box opens warning you that using the Web Page, Filtered file type will remove Office-specific tags that control how the document is displayed in Word.
7. Click the **Yes** button. The document is converted into a Web page and displayed in Web Layout view. The text spans the document window, no longer constrained by the page margins. The revised filename, "Fields Web Page," appears in the Word title bar, as usual. The title you specified in Step 4 won't be visible until you open the Web page in a browser, at which point it will be displayed in the browser's title bar. You need to zoom to make the text easier to read.
8. Drag the Zoom slider to change the document zoom to **100%**. The text wrapping adjusts to the new zoom setting.
9. Scroll down and review the Web page. Note the lack of page breaks and the way the text wraps next to the photo, near the end of the Web page. Because the text spans all the way to the edge of the Word window, it all fits to the right of the photograph, without wrapping below. See Figure 7-37.

Figure 7-37 New Web page displayed in Web Layout view

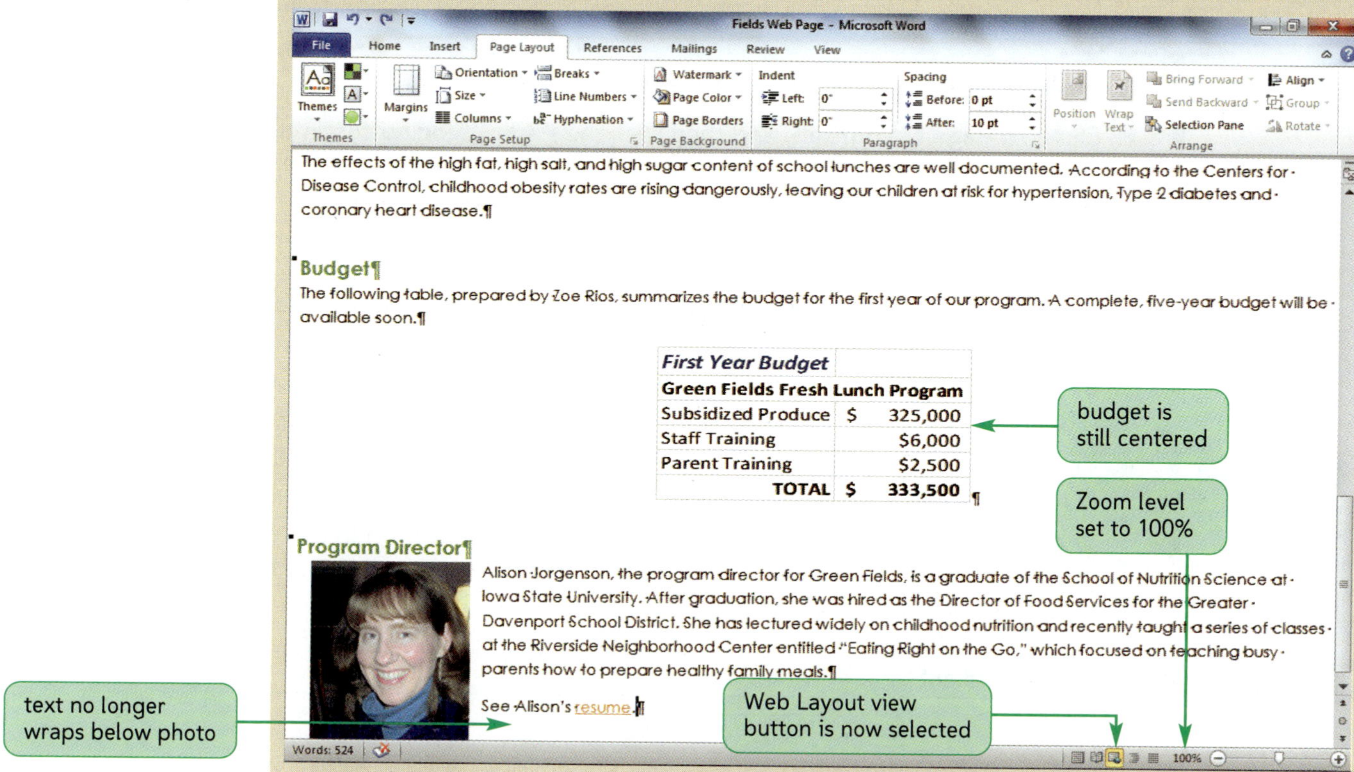


The total file size for the new Web page plus the accompanying files is 38 KB, compared to 50 KB for the Fields Combined document. This smaller size, plus the fact that the graphics files are stored separately from the text, means the Fields Web Page can travel more quickly over the Web than the Fields Combined document file.

Next, you'll make some changes to the Fields Combined document that will improve its online appearance.

# Formatting a Web Page

You can edit and format text and graphics in a Web page the same way you edit and format a normal Word document.

## Applying a Background Effect

To make the document more visually interesting for online viewers, Zoe would like to add a background effect. You can apply one of the following background effects:

- Solid color
- Gradient—a single color combined with gray, or a combination of colors that varies in intensity
- Texture—a design that mimics the look of various textured materials, including linen and marble
- Pattern—a repetitive design such as checks, polka dots, and stripes, in colors you specify
- Picture—a single image

Note that backgrounds do not appear in printed documents. After you apply a background, you should make sure your text is still easy to read. Zoe wants to use a gradient background with varying shades of green and gray.

**To apply a background effect to a document:**

1. Click the **Page Layout** tab, and then click the **Page Color** button in the Page Background group. The Page Color gallery opens, with a menu at the bottom. You could click a color in the gallery to select it as a background color for the page. To select any other type of background effect, you need to click Fill Effects.
2. Click **Fill Effects**, and then click the **Gradient** tab (if necessary). Note that you could use other tabs in this dialog box to add a textured, patterned, or picture background.
3. In the Colors section, click the **One color** option button. The Color 1 box and scroll bar appear. You can use them to select the color and specify its intensity.
4. Click the **Color 1** arrow and then click **Light Green, Background 2, Lighter 60%,** in the third row, third color from the left.
5. In the Shading Styles section, click the **Vertical** option button to change the gradient pattern so it stretches vertically up and down the page. Compare your dialog box to Figure 7-38.

**TIP**

You can use the scroll bar below the Color 1 box to increase or decrease the intensity of the gradient color.

**Figure 7-38** Selecting a gradient

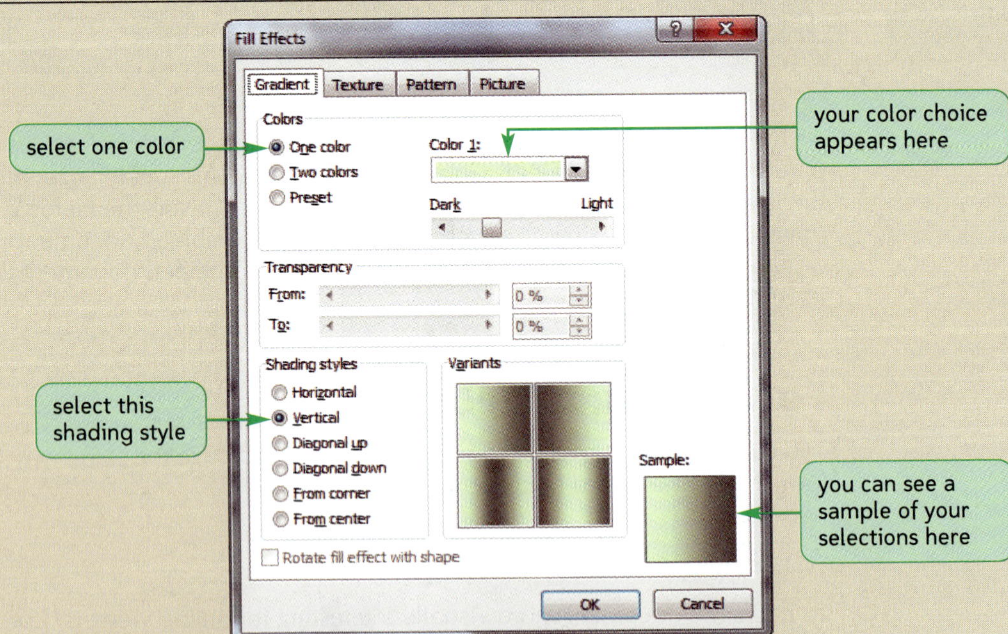


6. Click the **OK** button. The document's background is now a gradient that varies between shades of green. On the new background, the gridlines of the Excel worksheet data appear white.
7. Save the document, clicking **Yes** in the warning dialog box.

The background is attractive and light enough to make the document text easy to read. Next, you will add lines to separate the various sections of the Web page.

## Inserting Horizontal Lines

Horizontal lines allow you to see at a glance where one section ends and another begins. You can also add horizontal lines to regular Word documents. If you don't like a horizontal line after you insert one into a document, you can delete it by clicking the line and then pressing the Delete key.

Zoe wants you to add a horizontal line at the end of each section except the last one. To add a horizontal line using a simple, default style, click the Border button in the Paragraph group on the Home tab, and select the Horizontal Line command. To add a more elaborate horizontal line, you need to use the Horizontal Line dialog box.

### To insert horizontal lines into the Web page:

1. Click at the beginning of the heading "Kids Are What They Eat" on the first page of the document, and then click the **Home** tab on the Ribbon.
2. In the Paragraph group, click the **Border button arrow** to open the Borders menu. You could click the Horizontal Line command to insert a default gray line, but Zoe wants to select a line that will work better on the gradient background.
3. At the bottom of the Border menu, click **Borders and Shading**. The Borders and Shading dialog box opens, with the Borders tab displayed.
4. Click the **Horizontal Line** button. The Horizontal Line dialog box opens, displaying several styles of horizontal lines.
5. Scroll down and click the olive green line, ninth from the top in the right column, as shown in Figure 7-39.

**Figure 7-39** **Selecting a horizontal line style**

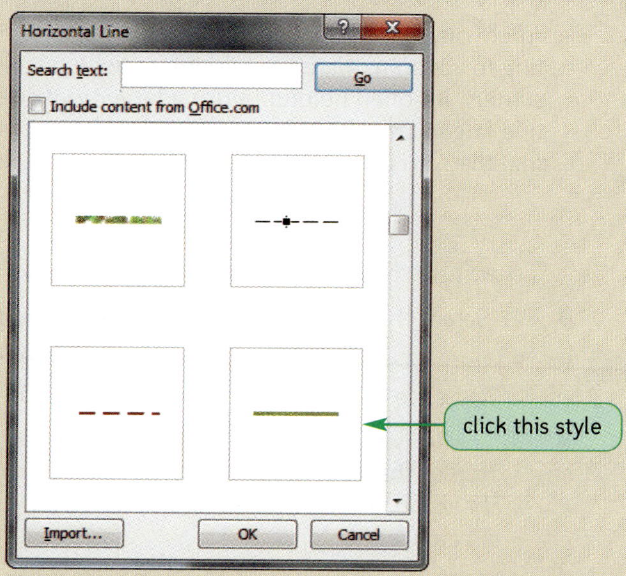


6. Click the **OK** button. An olive green line is inserted into the Web page above the "Kids Are What They Eat" heading. Your Web page should look similar to Figure 7-40.

**Figure 7-40** **Newly inserted horizontal line**

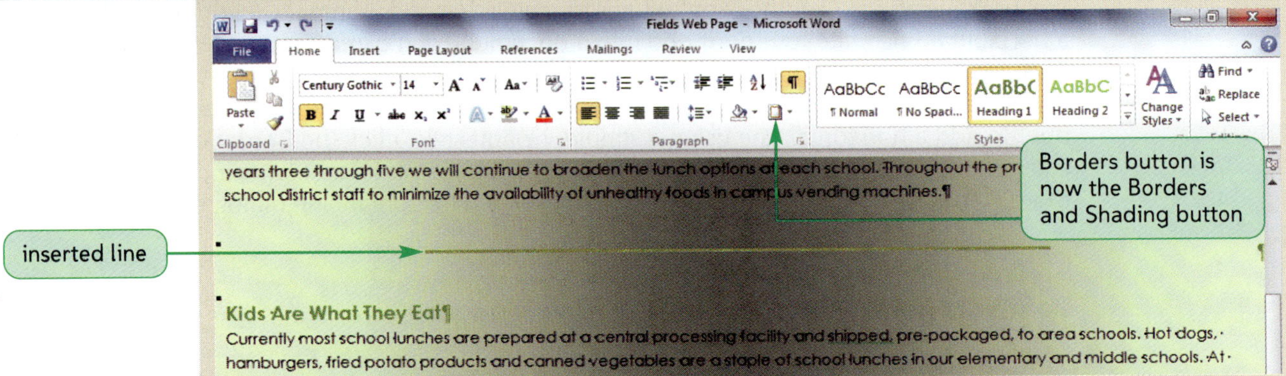


7. Scroll down, click to the left of the "B" in the "Budget" heading, and repeat Steps 2 through 6 to insert a horizontal line above the Budget heading.
8. Click to the left of the "Program Director" heading, and repeat Steps 2 through 6 to insert a horizontal line above the Program Director heading.
9. Scroll back to the top of the document, save your work, and click the **Yes** button in the warning dialog box.

Now that you've used horizontal lines to help organize the Web page, you decide to improve the appearance of the Web page's text.

## Formatting Text and Hyperlinks in a Web Page

After you convert a Word document to a Web page, you often need to adjust the formatting to accommodate the wider text, which spans the width of the viewer's screen. For starters, it's often helpful to use a larger font size for headings. Zoe asks you to make the title larger. She also asks you to center it. Then she asks you to format the hyperlinks so that they are easier to read on the gradient background.

**TIP**

You can use the Shrink Font button to reduce the font size of selected text.

### To adjust the formatting for the page title and hyperlinks:

1. Select the title **Green Fields Fresh Lunch Program** at the top of the Web page.
2. In the Font group on the Home tab, click the **Grow Font** button A˄ twice to increase the font size from 26-point to 36-point.
3. In the Paragraph group, click the **Center** button ≡ to center the heading at the top of the document, and then click anywhere in the document to deselect the heading. To make the hyperlinks easier to read, you can format them in bold and in a darker color.
4. In the second paragraph below the title, select the **Alison Jorgenson** hyperlink, format it in bold, then change the font color to Orange, Accent 6, Darker 50%. Do the same for the resume hyperlink at the bottom of the Web page.
5. Save your work, clicking the **Yes** button in the warning dialog box.

Next, you'll create a new hyperlink and edit the existing one.

## Editing Hyperlinks

Zoe's Web page contains two hyperlinks—the Alison Jorgenson link, which jumps to the Program Director section at the end of the Web page, and the resume link, which jumps to a Word document containing Alison's resume. You originally created these hyperlinks in Zoe's Word document, but they remained functional after you saved the document as a Web page. Now that Zoe is ready to publish her program description on the Web, she has also saved the Resume document as a Web page. She asks you edit the Resume hyperlink to jump to this new Web page, rather than to the original Resume.docx file.

### To edit a hyperlink:

1. Position the pointer over the **resume** hyperlink at the end of the Web page. A ScreenTip appears indicating that the link will jump to a document named Resume.docx.
2. Right-click the **resume** hyperlink, and then click **Edit Hyperlink** on the shortcut menu. The Edit Hyperlink dialog box opens. This looks just like the Insert Hyperlink dialog box, which you have already used. To edit the hyperlink, you simply select a different target file.
3. In the Link to pane, verify that the **Existing File or Web Page** option is selected.
4. If necessary, navigate to the Word7\Tutorial folder, click **Jorgenson Web Page** in the file list, and then click the **OK** button. You return to the Fields Web Page.
5. Place the mouse pointer over the **resume** hyperlink. A ScreenTip appears, indicating that the link will now jump to a Web page named Jorgenson Web Page.htm.

The edited hyperlink in the program description Web page now correctly targets the Web page with Alison's resume. After users read the resume, they most likely will want to return to the program description, so Zoe asks you to insert a hyperlink in the Jorgenson Web Page file containing Alison's resume, that jumps back to the Fields Web Page file. You insert hyperlinks into Web pages just as you do in Word documents. To open the Jorgenson Web Page file, you might be tempted to click the "resume" hyperlink in the Fields Web Page. However, if you do, the Web page would open in Internet Explorer. Instead, you need to open it using the Open command in Backstage view.

### To insert a hyperlink in the Jorgenson Web page:

1. Click the **File** tab, click **Open**, navigate to the Word7\Tutorial folder included with your Data Files if necessary, click the **Jorgenson Web Page** file, and then click the **Open** button.
2. Press the **Ctrl+End** keys, and then at the bottom of the resume, select the text **Return to Green Fields Fresh Lunch Program page.**
3. Click the **Insert** tab, click the **Hyperlink** button, and then, in the Link to pane of the Insert Hyperlink dialog box, click **Existing File or Web Page** if it is not already selected.
4. If necessary, navigate to the Word7\Tutorial folder included with your Data Files, click **Fields Web Page**, and then click the **OK** button. Word formats the selected text as a hyperlink.
5. Save the Jorgenson Web page, and then close the Web page. You return to the Fields Web Page.
6. Save and close the Fields Web Page.

The resume now contains a hyperlink that takes users back to the Fields Web Page.

INSIGHT

*Keeping Track of Documents Containing Hyperlinks*

When your documents or Web pages include hyperlinks to other documents or Web pages, you must keep track of where you store the target files. If you move a target file to a different location, hyperlinks to it will not function properly. In this case, you created a hyperlink in the Fields Web Page file that links to the Jorgenson Web Page file, and vice versa. Both Web pages are stored in the Word7\Tutorial folder, which is most likely located on your computer's hard disk. To ensure that these hyperlinks continue to function, you must store the two Web pages in the same folder as when you created the link. If you have to move a target Web page, then be sure to edit the hyperlink to select the target Web page in its new location.

Now Zoe suggests you view both Web pages in a browser, and test the hyperlinks.

## Viewing the Web Page in a Browser

You're now ready to view the finished Web pages in Internet Explorer, a Web browser. In the browser, you can test the hyperlinks and verify that the formatting looks the way you intended. In a browser, you don't have to press the Ctrl key to use a hyperlink. Instead, you simply click the link.

**To view the Web pages in a Web browser:**

1. Click the **Internet Explorer** button on the taskbar.
2. If the program window does not fill the screen entirely, click the **Maximize** button on the Internet Explorer title bar.
3. If you do not see a menu bar directly below the title bar, right-click a blank area of the Favorites bar to open the shortcut menu, and then click **Menu Bar** to place a check next to this option.
4. On the menu bar, click **File**, and then click **Open**. The Open dialog box opens.
5. Click the **Browse** button, navigate to the Word7\Tutorial folder, click **Fields Web Page**, and then click the **Open** button. You return to the Open dialog box.
6. Click the **OK** button. The Open dialog box closes, and Zoe's Web page is displayed in the browser window. The title "Green Fields Fresh Lunch Program," appears in the Internet Explorer title bar. See Figure 7-41.

**Figure 7-41** Web page displayed in Internet Explorer 8

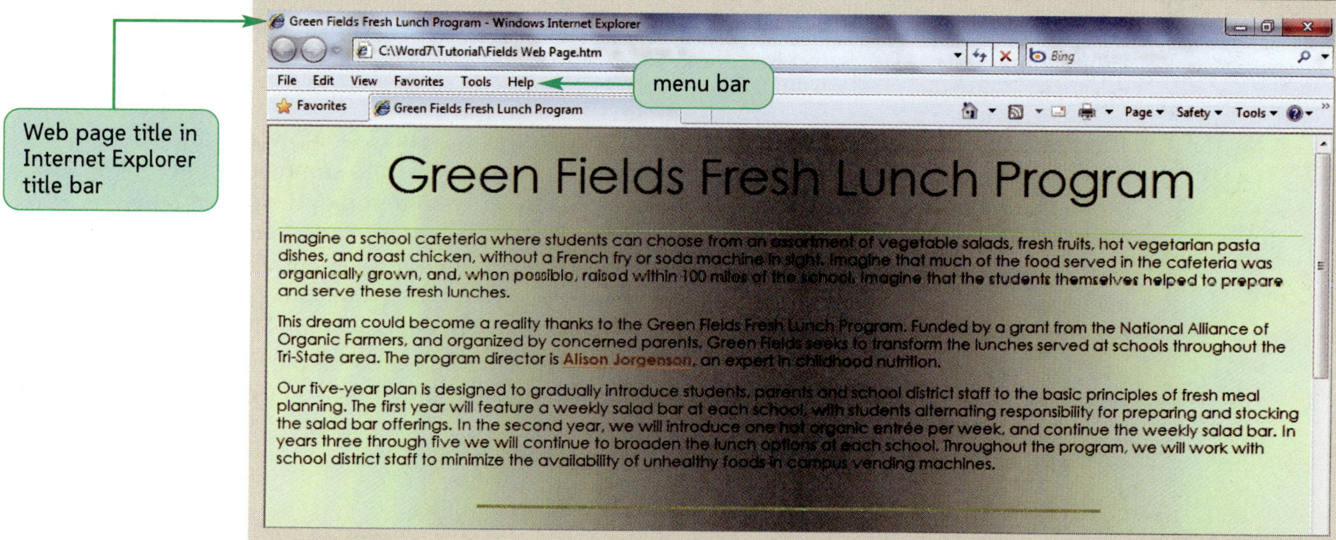


7. Scroll down and review the Web page, then scroll back up and click the **Alison Jorgenson** hyperlink. The Program Director section is displayed in the browser window.
8. In the last paragraph of the document, click the **resume** hyperlink. The browser opens the Jorgenson Web page.
9. Scroll down to review the resume.
10. At the bottom of the resume, click the **Return to Green Fields Fresh Lunch Program page.** hyperlink. The browser displays the Fields Web Page.

    **Trouble?** If any of the hyperlinks don't work properly, close the browser, return to Word, edit the hyperlinks so they link to the proper files, and then test the links again in Internet Explorer.

11. Close Internet Explorer.

REVIEW

## *Session 7.2 Quick Check*

1. If you want to save a file to SkyDrive for your own private use, what folder can you save it in?
2. True or False. A Web page is the same thing as an HTML document.
3. What is the first step in creating a hyperlink to a location in the same document?
4. What kind of page backgrounds can you apply using the Fill Effects dialog box?
5. True or False. When you save a document as a Web page, Word automatically displays it in Print Layout view.
6. Explain how to insert a horizontal line in a document or Web page in a simple, default style.
7. Explain how to edit a hyperlink.

*Apply the skills you learned in the tutorial using the same case scenario.*

PRACTICE

## Review Assignments

**Data Files needed for the Review Assignments: Expenses.xlsx, Progress.docx, Progress Henry.docx, Rates.xlsx, Salad Bar.docx, Salad Bar Web Page.htm, Salad Bar Web Page_Files (folder)**

The first year of the Green Fields Fresh Lunch program was a success. Now Zoe and the staff of Rios Communications need to create a progress report to summarize the program's effectiveness. Zoe has written a draft of the progress report and emailed it to Henry. While he reviews it, Zoe plans to turn on Track Changes and continue work on the document. Then she can combine her edited version of the document with Henry's, accepting or rejecting changes as necessary. Next, she needs to insert some data from an Excel worksheet as an embedded object and insert an Excel chart as a linked object. She then wants to create a version of the document with hyperlinks, format the document for viewing as Web page, save it as a Web page, and view it in a browser. Complete the following steps:

1. Open the file named **Progress** from the Word7\Review folder included with your Data Files. Save the file as **Progress Zoe** in the same folder.
2. Change the user name to "Zoe Rios" and the user initials to "ZR," and then turn on Track Changes.
3. Format the first heading with the Title style.
4. Delete **concerned** in the first sentence below the title.
5. In the third line below the title, insert the word **generous** before the word "grant," so the sentence reads "...by a generous grant...."
6. In the third paragraph below the title, select the word "thirty" and insert a comment that reads **Remember to verify this number**.
7. In the Current Membership section at the end of the document, replace "Marti Sundra" with your name. Save your work.
8. Combine the **Progress Zoe** document with Henry's edited version, named **Progress Henry**, located in the Word7\Review folder included with your Data Files. Use the Progress Zoe document as the Original document.
9. Turn off Track Changes, accept the formatting change on the document title, then accept all the remaining changes in the document except Henry's deletion of "extremely." Review the comments, and then delete all comments in the document.
10. Change the user name and initials back to their original settings.
11. Save the new document as **Progress Combined** in the Word7\Review folder included with your Data Files, and then save it as **Progress Sky Drive** to the My Documents folder on your Sky Drive and close it.
12. Close the **Progress Zoe** document, and then reopen the **Progress Combined** document from the Word7\Review folder.
13. Replace the placeholder [Insert Excel worksheet] on the second page with the budget in the **Expenses.xlsx** file in the Word7\Review folder included with your Data Files. Insert the budget as an embedded object, and then close Excel.
14. Center the embedded object, and then edit it to change the Parent Training value from $2,500 to **$3,000**.
15. Open the workbook named **Rates.xlsx** file in the Word7\Review folder included with your Data Files, save it as **Rates Copy.xlsx,** and then copy the chart to the Office Clipboard.
16. Return to the Progress Combined document, and replace the placeholder [Insert Excel chart] at the bottom of the first page with a linked copy of the chart in the Rates Copy workbook using the destination theme. Save your work.

17. Edit the data in the Rates Copy workbook by changing the Last Month participation rate for middle schools from 35% to **80%**. Save and close the **Rates Copy.xlsx** file and close Excel.
18. Save your work, and then save the document with the new name **Progress No Links** in the same folder.
19. Break the link to the Excel workbook, and then save your work.
20. In the list of board members at the end of the document, select the word Chair and insert a bookmark named **Board**. In the second line of the document, format the word "parents" as a hyperlink that targets the Board bookmark. Test the hyperlink to make sure it works.
21. In the line below the heading "Year One: What Went Right?" format **salad bars** as a hyperlink that targets the Word document named **Salad Bar** in the Word7\Review folder included with your Data Files. Test the hyperlink to make sure it works, and then close the Salad Bar document. Save the Progress Combined document.
22. Save the document as a Web page in the Word7\Review folder using the Web Page, Filtered file type. Use **Progress Web Page** for the filename and **Green Fields First Year Progress** as the page title.
23. Add a gradient page color using Indigo, Accent 1, Lighter 80% as the color, with the Dark/Light scroll box at its default setting, and the shading style set to From center.
24. Before every heading except the title, insert a black horizontal line with circles on each end.
25. Increase the font size for the first heading, "Green Fields Progress Report," to 36-point, and then center the heading. Save the Web page.
26. Edit the "salad bar" hyperlink to open the **Salad Bar Web Page** file stored in the Word7\Tutorial folder included with your Data Files.
27. Open the **Salad Bar Web Page** file in Word, and format the last paragraph as a hyperlink that targets the **Progress Web Page** file.
28. Save all files, close Word, start Internet Explorer, and then open the **Progress Web Page**. Review the Web page in the browser, test the hyperlinks, and then close the browser.
29. Submit the documents to your instructor in printed or electronic form, as requested.

*Apply the skills you learned to create an investment statement.*

APPLY

## Case Problem 1

**Data Files needed for this Case Problem: Cook.docx, Statement.xlsx**

***KingFish Financial Planning*** You have just started work as a certified financial planner at KingFish Financial Planning. At the end of every quarter, you need to send a letter to each client containing a statement that summarizes the client's investment portfolio. The letter is a Word document, and the investment data for each client is stored in an Excel file. You need to insert the Excel data in the Word document as an embedded object. In the following steps, you will create a statement for a client named Isabella Cook.

1. Open the file named **Cook** from the Word7\Case1 folder included with your Data Files. Save the file as **Cook Letter** in the same folder.
2. In the signature line, replace "Student Name" with your name.
3. Delete the placeholder "[Insert Excel worksheet.]."
4. Start Excel and open the file named **Statement** from the Word7\Case1 folder included with your Data Files.
5. Copy the two columns of account names and current holdings to the Clipboard and insert it into the Word document in the blank paragraph that previously contained the placeholder text. Insert the data as an embedded Microsoft Excel Worksheet Object.

6. Return to the **Statement** worksheet and close Excel.
7. In the Cook Letter document, change the value for the Roth IRA to **$27,000.00**, and then save the document.
8. Save the document as **Cook Letter Sky Drive** to the My Documents folder on your SkyDrive and close it.
9. Submit the finished documents to your instructor, either in printed or electronic form, as requested.

*Apply the skills you learned to create a Web page for a dog kennel.*

APPLY

## Case Problem 2

**Data Files needed for this Case Problem: Kreelie.docx, Sun.docx**

***Kreelie Kennels Web Page*** Brianna Kreelie is the owner of Kreelie Kennels, an upscale dog boarding facility in Knoxville, Kentucky. She would like your help in creating a Web page for her business. She has created a first draft and saved it as a Word document. In the document, she included some comments explaining the edits she would like you to make. After you edit the document and remove the comments, she would like you to format it and save it as a Web page. Complete the following steps:

1. Open the file **Kreelie** from the Word7\Case2 folder included with your Data Files, and then save it as **Kreelie Edited** in the same folder.
2. Turn on Track Changes, review the comments, and make the changes requested in the comments. When you are finished, delete the comments. At the end of the document, attach a comment to the word "pool" that reads **I made all the changes you requested**.
3. Save the **Kreelie Edited** document.
4. Save the document as **Kreelie Final** in the Word7\Case2 folder.
5. Turn off Track Changes, and then accept all your changes in the document. Delete your comment at the end of the document, and then save your work.
6. Open the document named **Sun** from the Word7\Case2 folder, save it as **Sundeck** in the same folder, and then close it.
7. In the **Kreelie Final** document, at the end of the "Fun in the Sun" section, format the word "here" as a hyperlink that opens the **Sundeck** document.
8. Test the link, and then, in the Sundeck document, format the text **Back to main page.** as a hyperlink that jumps to the **Kreelie Final** document. Test the link.
9. Format the page background for the **Kreelie Final** document and the **Sundeck** document with the Parchment texture. (*Hint*: On the Texture tab of the Fill Effects dialog box, click a texture to see its name in the box.) Save the **Kreelie Final** and **Sundeck** documents.
10. Save the Kreelie Final document as **Kreelie Web Page** in the Word7\Case2 folder, using the Web Page, Filtered file type. Use **Kreelie Kennels** as the page title. Save the Sundeck document as **Sundeck Web Page** in the same folder, using the same file type. Use **Kreelie Kennels Sundeck** as the page title.
11. Edit the hyperlinks so they target the correct files, and then save the files.
12. In the Kreelie Web Page file, add a wavy orange horizontal line before each paragraph formatted with the Heading 1 style.
13. Save your work, close Word, open the **Kreelie Web Page** file in Internet Explorer, and note the formatting applied to the kennel name at the top of the page. Test the hyperlink. Close the browser.
14. Open the **Kreelie Edited** document and attach a comment to the Kreelie Kennels title at the top of the page, explaining how the title's formatting differs when the page is saved as a Web page and displayed in a browser.

15. Save and close the document. Submit the finished file to your instructor, either in printed or electronic form, as requested.

*Use the Web to find a copyright-free, public domain photo to use in a Web page.*

RESEARCH

## Case Problem 3

**Data Files needed for this Case Problem: Sunset.docx, Survey.xlsx**

***Sunset Optical Web Page*** You have been asked to create a Web page for Sunset Optical, a supplier of high-quality eyeglasses in Bellingham, Washington. Complete the following steps:

1. Open the file **Sunset** from the Word7\Case3 folder included with your Data Files, and then save it as **Sunset Optical** in the same folder.
2. In the second to last line, replace "Student Name" with your name.
3. Review the comments and delete them.
4. Use the Research task pane to look up information on the Web about public domain, copyright-free photos. Click the link to one of the sites listed in the Research task pane to open the Web site offering public domain, copyright-free photos, and then search the site to locate a public domain photo of a sunset. If the photo is displayed as a thumbnail image, click it to display it in a larger size.
5. Right-click the photo, and then, on the shortcut menu, click Save Picture As. Save the photo file to the Word7\Case3 folder included with your Data Files. Leave the browser open with the photo displayed.
6. Delete the [Insert Photo] placeholder text at the beginning of the Word document, and insert the photo. Crop or resize it as necessary so the photo is approximately 6 inches wide and between 3 and 4 inches tall.

EXPLORE

7. Return to the browser, select the URL for the photo in the browser's address bar, and then press Ctrl+C to copy the address to the Clipboard. Return to the Word document, right-click the photo, and then click Hyperlink on the shortcut menu to format the photo as a hyperlink. In the Address box at the bottom of the Insert Hyperlink dialog box, paste the URL from your browser. Close your browser, test the link in the Word document, and then close the browser again.
8. Open the Excel file named **Survey** from the Word7\Case3 folder included with your Data Files, and then save it as **Survey Copy**.
9. Delete the [Insert chart] placeholder text, and in its place insert a linked copy of the chart from the Survey Copy file in the Word document. Use the formatting of the destination file. Close Excel.
10. Revise the linked chart to change the value for "Surprised to find they needed glasses" to **200**. Change the value for "Have worn glasses most of their life" to **275**. Save your changes to the **Survey Copy** workbook and close Excel.
11. In Word, drag the border of the chart until it is small enough to fit on the same page as the document text and the document is only one page long.
12. Apply a theme with theme colors that complement your photo.

EXPLORE

13. Format the page background using a two-color gradient with a horizontal style. Choose colors that match your photo and make the text easy to read.
14. Save the **Sunset Optical** document, and then save it again as a Web page using the Single File Web Page file type. Use **Sunset Web Page** as the filename and **Sunset Optical** as the page title.
15. Close Word, open the Web page in a browser, test the photo hyperlink, and then close your browser.
16. Submit the finished files to your instructor, either in printed or electronic form, as requested.

*Go beyond the skills you've learned to create a FAQ Web page.*

CHALLENGE

## Case Problem 4

**Data File needed for this Case Problem: FAQ.docx**

***Great Falls Health Resource*** Sebastian Morey is publications director at Great Falls Health Resource, a county agency in Great Falls, Montana, that helps county residents manage health and health insurance-related issues. Sebastian asks you to help create a FAQ (Frequently Asked Questions) page that answers some basic questions related to health insurance. So far, he has created the basic structure of the FAQ and inserted a few questions. He wants you to add the necessary hyperlinks. Complete the following steps:

1. Open the file named **FAQ** from the Word7\Case4 folder included with your Data Files, and then save it as a Word document using the name **Insurance FAQ** in the same folder.
2. At the bottom of the document, replace "Student Name" with your name. Replace "Date" with the current date.
3. **EXPLORE** Create a system of hyperlinks that makes it possible for a user to click a topic in the Table of Contents and jump immediately to the relevant heading in the document. Use a heading as the target of each hyperlink rather than a bookmark. Add hyperlinks to the "Back to top" text that jump to the "Table of Contents" heading at the beginning of the document.
4. At the bottom of page 1, delete the placeholder "[Insert chart here.]," and then verify that the insertion point is located in a blank paragraph between two other blank paragraphs.
5. **EXPLORE** In the Illustrations group on the Insert tab, use the Chart button to insert the default type of column chart. In the Excel workbook, drag the lower-right corner of the blue selection box so that it only encloses rows 1 through 4 in columns A and B. Drag the border between column headers for columns A and B to the right to make Column A about four times wider than its default width.
6. **EXPLORE** Replace "Category 1" with the **No employee contribution**, replace "Category 2" with **Required for family coverage**, and then replace "Category 3" with **Required for employee coverage**. Enter the following data in Column B:
   - No employee contribution: 5%
   - Required for family coverage: 60%
   - Required for employee coverage: 80%

   Replace "Series1" with **Employee Contributions**. Close Excel. There's no need to save the data because it will be saved with the Word document.
7. **EXPLORE** Select the chart in the Word document, and then examine the various Chart Tools tabs. Use a button on the Chart Tools Layout tab to turn off the chart legend. Use the Edit Data button on the Design tab to edit the data, changing the percentage for "Required for family coverage" from 60% to 93%. Close Excel.
8. Near the end of page 2, in the section on finding health insurance statistics on the Web, format the word "here" as a hyperlink that targets the Web site for the U.S. Census Bureau. In the Address box of the Insert Hyperlink dialog box, enter the following URL: **www.census.gov**. (Do not include the period at the end.) If your computer is connected to the Internet, test the hyperlink, and then close the browser. Save the document.
9. Save the document as **Insurance FAQ Sky Drive** to the My Documents folder on your SkyDrive and close it.
10. Open the **Insurance FAQ** document from the Word7\Case4 folder, and then save the document as a Web page using the Single File Web Page file type. Use **FAQ Web Page** as the filename and **Frequently Asked Questions** as the page title.
11. Close Word and open the **FAQ Web Page** in a browser. Test all the table of contents and "Back to top" hyperlinks, and then test the U.S. Census Bureau hyperlink.
12. Submit the finished files to your instructor, either in printed or electronic form, as requested.

## ENDING DATA FILES

**Word7** →

**Tutorial**

- Fields Web Page_files (folder)
- Jorgenson Web Page_files (folder)
- Chart Copy.xlsx
- Fields Combined.docx
- Fields Web Page.htm
- Fields Zoe.docx
- Jorgenson Web Page.htm
- Resume.docx

**Review**

- Progress Web Page_files (folder)
- Salad Bar Web Page_files (folder)
- Progress Combined.docx
- Progress No Links.docx
- Progress Web Page.htm
- Progress Zoe.docx
- Rates Copy.xlsx
- Salad Bar.docx
- Salad Bar Web Page.htm

**Case1**

- Cook Letter.docx

**Case2**

- Kreelie Web Page_files (folder)
- Sundeck Web Page_files (folder)
- Kreelie Edited.docx
- Kreelie Final.docx
- Kreelie Web Page.htm
- Sundeck Web Page.htm
- Sundeck.docx

**Case3**

- Sunset Optical.docx
- Sunset Web Page.mht
- Survey Copy.xlsx
- [public domain photo from the Web]

**Case4**

- FAQ Web Page.mht
- Insurance FAQ.docx

ProSkills

# Teamwork

## Collaborating with Others to Create Documents

Collaboration means working together to achieve a specific goal through teamwork.

Organizations establish collaborative teams for completing a wide variety of tasks, with long- or short-term goals. Sometimes team members collaborate on projects by working side-by-side. However, it's increasingly common for the members of a team to collaborate from different corporate or geographical locations, using telecommunications technologies and social networks to complete tasks. When forming a team, it is important to understand the skills each team member has, and how these skills can best be used as the team collaborates to achieve its goals. An effective team is made up of people with abilities and talents that are complementary, and well-suited to the tasks at hand. It's also essential that each member of the team understand his or her responsibilities. On a truly integrated team, team members support each other, agreeing to share new responsibilities when they arise, rather than waiting around for someone else to pick up the slack.

## The Structure of a Team

When structuring a team it is important to identify team leaders, work coordinators, idea people, and critics. Each member must recognize the significance of their individual contributions to the team's overall success in meeting its goals. Some team members will serve specific roles on the team. For example, task specialists spend a lot of time and effort ensuring that the team achieves its goals  by presenting ideas, sharing opinions, collecting information, sorting details, and motivating the team to keep on track. When stresses occur due to time constraints or heavy workloads, positive team morale and a sense of shared focus and camaraderie can become essential. Some team members hold the role of managing social satisfaction by strengthen the team's social bonds through encouragement, empathy, conflict resolution, compromise, and tension reduction through humor or organizing social activities outside of the work environment. Oftentimes, the individual team members will serve more than one role on the team. For example, the task specialist might also be the team leader, and the idea person might also fill the social satisfaction role.

In this exercise you will work with a team to create documents. As you structure your team to complete these tasks, consider the roles you need the team members to fill. Before beginning, you might want to discuss the roles each member is comfortable assuming, and determine how complementary your collective abilities might be.

To ensure your team works effectively to complete tasks and achieve its goals:

- Recognize that everyone brings something of value to the team.
- Respect and support each other as you work toward the common goal.
- Try to see things from the other person's perspective when conflict or criticisms arise.
- Encourage or support team members that might need assistance.
- Address negative or unproductive attitudes immediately so they don't damage team energy and attitude.
- Seek outside help if the team gets stuck and can't move forward.
- Provide periodic positive encouragement or rewards for contributions.

ProSkills

## Using Technology in Teamwork

Team members often work together from separate locations. Also, most of the time, teams need to produce work on accelerated schedules, and therefore need to do so efficiently. In these instances, teams depend on technology to accomplish work tasks. For example, corporate intranets and networks, email and voice mail, texting and instant messaging, teleconferencing and software collaboration tools, social networks, and cell phones can support teamwork. Before beginning a team project, identify the most appropriate technology tools the team will use to communicate and document work activities. Then you should determine how the team will organize, combine, and make available the documents and files the team produces.

PROSKILLS

### Create a Report Template, Directory, and Web Page

At this point, you should feel confident that you have the word-processing skills required to create, revise, and distribute useful documents in your professional and personal life. But there's no need to wait to use these new skills. You can create some practical documents right now, starting with a template for a report that you need to create routinely. In the following exercise, work with your team members to create documents using the Word skills and features presented in Tutorials 5 through 7.

**Note:** Please be sure *not* to include any personal information of a sensitive nature in the documents you create to be submitted to your instructor for this exercise. Later on, you can update the documents with such information for your own personal use.

1. Meet with your team to plan a new report template to use for school reports or another type of report that you might have to create on a regular basis. Work with your group to select an appropriate template installed with Word, delete or edit document controls as necessary, insert placeholder text as necessary, and customize the theme. Select an appropriate style set, and create at least one new style that will be useful in your report. As a group, take the time to plan your template to ensure that it will be useful for a series of similar documents.
2. Use your template as the basis for a new report. Insert a file containing the text of a report you or a team member wrote for one of your classes, or insert appropriate text of your choosing, and then format the text using the template styles. Remember to include a table of contents in the report. At the end of the report, include a hyperlink that jumps to the beginning of the report.
3. If you or a team member are familiar with Excel, open a new workbook, enter some data that supports one of the points in the team's report, and then embed the worksheet data in the report. If you don't know how to enter data in Excel, you can embed the data from the Budget file in the Word7\Tutorial folder included with your Data Files, and then edit the data as necessary. Note that you can widen a column in Excel by dragging the right border of the column's header (the letter at the top of the column).
4. Email a copy of your report to a team member. Have him or her edit the document with Track Changes turned on and then send the report back to you.

# ProSkills

5. Combine your edited copy of the document with the copy edited by your team member. Accept or reject changes as necessary. Save the new, combined document with a new name.
6. Meet with your team and choose a type of information, such as email addresses or birthdays, that the group would like to organize in a single document. Create a Word table, and then enter fictitious versions of the information into the table. You can replace this with real information later for your personal use, after you've handed in your assignments. Sort the information based on one of the columns.
7. Create a main document for a directory that includes a dot leader. Use the group's Word table from Step 6 as the data source. Insert the necessary merge codes into the main document and complete the merge.
8. Format the merged document with a gradient page color and add a title. Format the title appropriately. Save the document as a Web page that consists of only one file.
9. Submit your team's completed documents to your instructor in electronic or printed form, as requested. Also, save a copy of the documents to the My Documents folder on your SkyDrive.

TUTORIAL 5

# Working with Excel Tables, PivotTables, and PivotCharts

*Tracking Museum Art Objects*

## OBJECTIVES

**Session 5.1**
- Explore a structured range of data
- Freeze rows and columns
- Plan and create an Excel table
- Rename and format an Excel table
- Add, edit, and delete records in an Excel table
- Sort data

**Session 5.2**
- Filter data
- Insert a Total row to summarize an Excel table
- Split a worksheet into two panes
- Insert subtotals into a range of data
- Use the Outline buttons to show or hide details

**Session 5.3**
- Create and modify a PivotTable
- Apply PivotTable styles and formatting
- Filter and sort a PivotTable
- Insert a slicer to filter a PivotTable
- Group PivotTable items
- Create a PivotChart

## Case | *LaFouch Museum*

Henry LaFouch, a rancher in Missoula, Montana, amassed a huge collection of North American art, particularly art of the West. Henry was a well-respected, active member of the community, and he often donated art to the town. Similarly, he loaned the town artwork to place in public locations and community centers. Upon his death, Henry donated his art collection to the town of Missoula and its people. They established an art museum in his name.

Mary Littlefield was recently hired as the curator and director of the LaFouch Museum. She is responsible for assessing the current holdings and using the endowment set aside by Henry to purchase additional art in keeping with his vision for the collection. One of Mary's first tasks was to establish an accurate inventory of the museum's holdings. For each piece of artwork, she identified the title, the artist, the date acquired, the type of art, and other pertinent facts such as its location in the museum, its condition, and its appraised value. Then, she entered all this data in an Excel worksheet.

You will help Mary maintain this data so she can provide current and accurate information to the administration and board of directors about the art objects. You'll work with the data using Excel table features. You will sort the data and add, modify, and delete the data to ensure it is current. You'll also filter the information to display only data that meets certain criteria. Finally, you'll summarize the data using a PivotTable and a PivotChart.

### STARTING DATA FILES

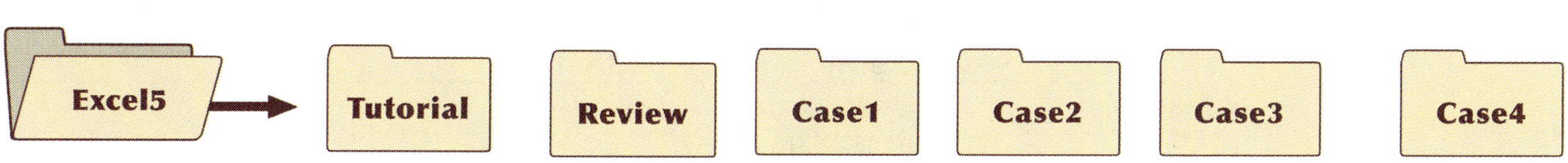


Museum.xlsx | Art.xlsx | Pledges.xlsx | Ring.xlsx | CustLoans.xlsx | Bowls.xlsx

# SESSION 5.1 VISUAL OVERVIEW

Every Excel table has a table name, which you can change to a descriptive name.

Each column represents a **field**, which describes some characteristic of a person, place, or thing such as a last name, address, city, or state.

The first row of the range contains field names called the **header row**. Although the header row often is row 1, it can begin in any row.

Each row represents a **record**, which is a collection of related fields that are grouped together.

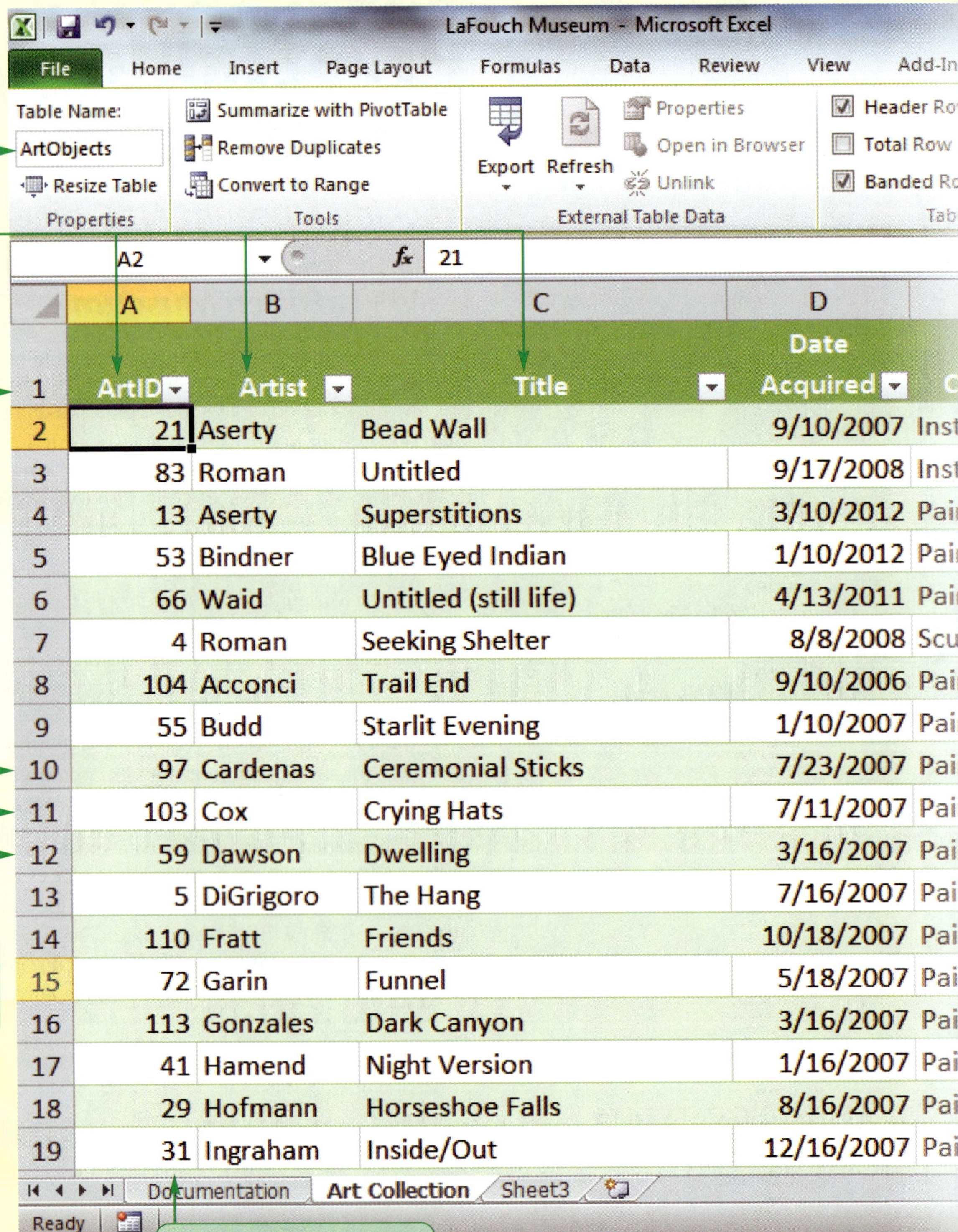


You can rearrange, or **sort**, the records in a table or range based on one or more fields.

# AN EXCEL TABLE

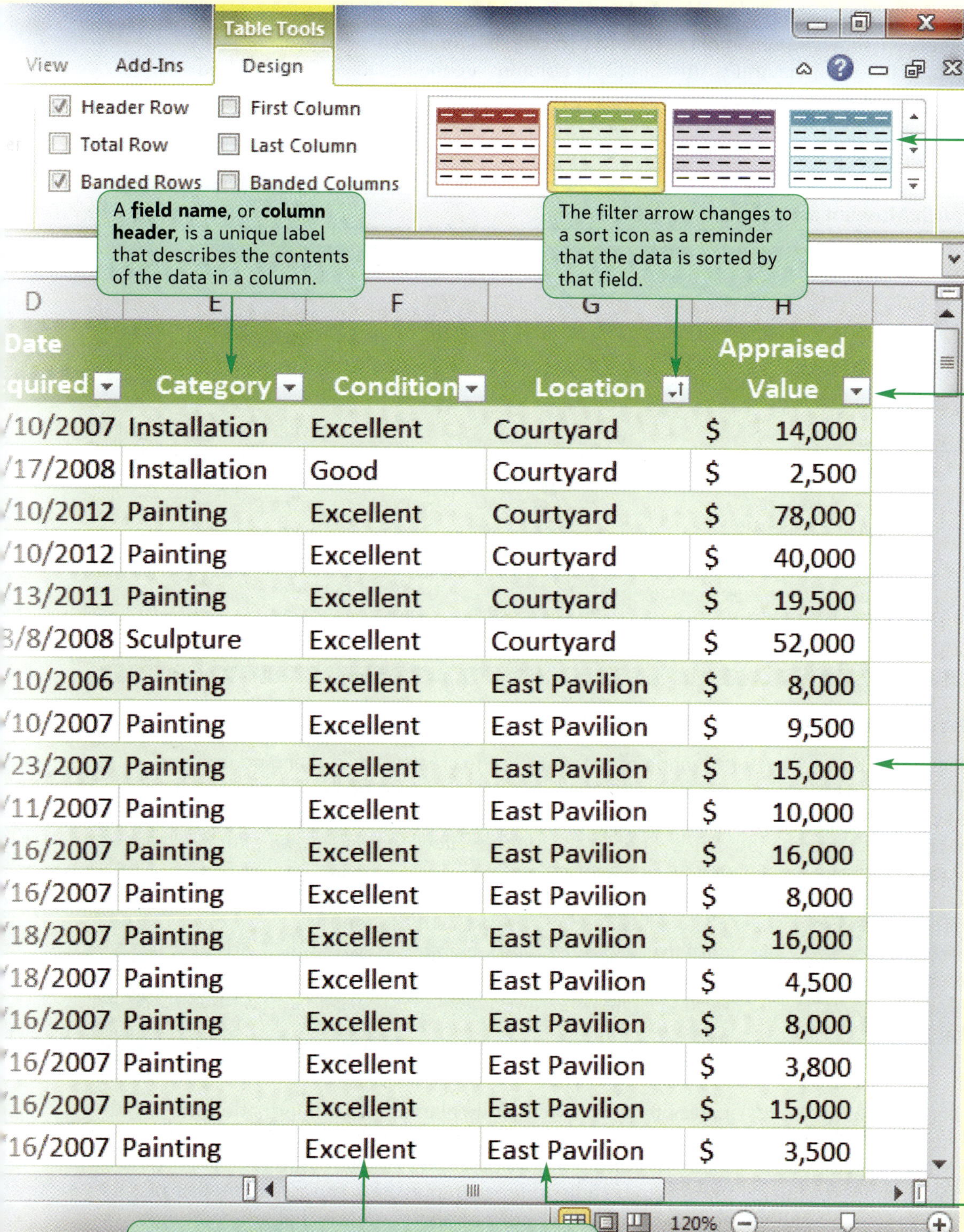


A **field name**, or **column header**, is a unique label that describes the contents of the data in a column.

The filter arrow changes to a sort icon as a reminder that the data is sorted by that field.

Table styles provide a way to quickly format an entire table using a preset style definition.

You can click a filter arrow to sort the table by data in that column.

An Excel table is a range of related data that is managed independently from data in other rows and columns in the worksheet.

The fields that you use to order data are called **sort fields**. This data is sorted by Location, the sort field.

You can create a custom list to sort data in the order you specify, such as art objects by their condition rankings: Excellent, Good, Fair, and Poor.

# Planning a Structured Range of Data

One of the more common uses of a worksheet is to manage data, such as lists of clients, products, and transactions. Using Excel, you can store and update data, sort data, search for and retrieve subsets of data, summarize data, and create reports. In Excel, a collection of similar data can be structured in a range of columns and rows, representing fields and records, respectively.

Figure 5-1 shows a portion of the data Mary compiled for the LaFouch Museum's art objects. In this data, the ArtID, Artist, and Title columns are the first three fields. Each row is a record that stores the data for each art object—art ID, artist name, title, date acquired, category, condition, location, and appraised value. All the art object records make up the *structured range of data*. A structured range of data is commonly referred to as a list or table.

**Figure 5-1** **LaFouch Museum art objects data**

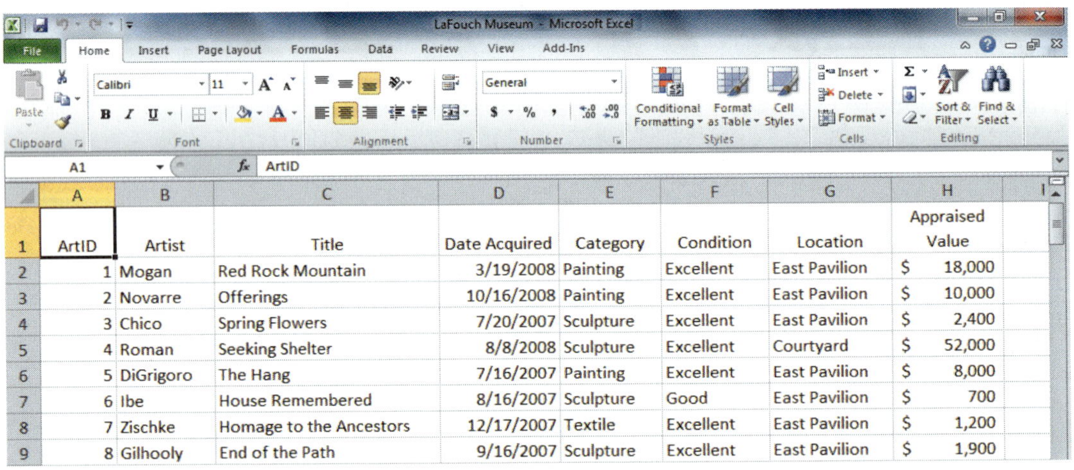


| ArtID | Artist | Title | Date Acquired | Category | Condition | Location | Appraised Value |
|---|---|---|---|---|---|---|---|
| 1 | Mogan | Red Rock Mountain | 3/19/2008 | Painting | Excellent | East Pavilion | $ 18,000 |
| 2 | Novarre | Offerings | 10/16/2008 | Painting | Excellent | East Pavilion | $ 10,000 |
| 3 | Chico | Spring Flowers | 7/20/2007 | Sculpture | Excellent | East Pavilion | $ 2,400 |
| 4 | Roman | Seeking Shelter | 8/8/2008 | Sculpture | Excellent | Courtyard | $ 52,000 |
| 5 | DiGrigoro | The Hang | 7/16/2007 | Painting | Excellent | East Pavilion | $ 8,000 |
| 6 | Ibe | House Remembered | 8/16/2007 | Sculpture | Good | East Pavilion | $ 700 |
| 7 | Zischke | Homage to the Ancestors | 12/17/2007 | Textile | Excellent | East Pavilion | $ 1,200 |
| 8 | Gilhooly | End of the Path | 9/16/2007 | Sculpture | Excellent | East Pavilion | $ 1,900 |

PROSKILLS

## *Decision Making: The Importance of Planning*

Before you create a structured range of data, be sure to create a plan. Planning involves gathering relevant information about the data and deciding your goals. The end results you want to achieve will help you determine the kind of data to include in each record and how to divide that data into fields. Specifically, do the following to create an effective plan:

- Spend time thinking about how you will use the data.
- Consider what reports you want to create for different audiences (supervisors, customers, directors, and so forth) and the fields needed to produce those reports.
- Think about the various questions, or *queries*, you want answered and the fields needed to create these results.

Careful and thorough planning will help you avoid having to redesign a structured range of data later.

Before creating the list of art objects, Mary carefully planned what information she needs and how she wants to use it. Mary plans to use the data to track where each art object is located in the museum, its condition, the date it was acquired, its art category, and its appraised value. She wants to be able to create reports that show specific lists of art objects, such as all the objects by a specific artist or all the objects that are paintings. Based on her needs, Mary developed a **data definition table**, which is documentation that lists the fields to be maintained for each record (in this case, each art object) and a description of the information each field will include. Figure 5-2 shows Mary's completed data definition table.

**Figure 5-2** Data definition table for the art objects

| Field | Description |
|---|---|
| ArtID | Unique number |
| Artist | Name of artist |
| Title | Title of art object |
| Date Acquired | Date of purchase or donation of art object |
| Category | Painting, Sculpture, Installation, Textile |
| Condition | Excellent, Good, Fair, Poor |
| Location | Location of art object |
| Appraised Value | Current value of art object |

After you determine the fields and records you need, you can enter the data in a blank worksheet or use a range of data that is already entered in a worksheet. You can then work with the data in many ways, including the following common operations:

- Add, edit, and delete data in the range.
- Sort the data range.
- Filter to display only rows that meet specified criteria.
- Insert formulas to calculate subtotals.
- Create summary tables based on the data in the range (usually with PivotTables).

You'll perform many of these operations on the art objects data.

INSIGHT

### *Creating an Effective Structured Range of Data*

For a range of data to be used effectively, it must have the same structure throughout. Keep in mind the following guidelines:

- Enter field names in the top row of the range.
- Use short, descriptive field names. Shorter field names are easier to remember and enable more fields to appear in the workbook window at once.
- Format field names to distinguish the header row from the data. For example, apply bold, color, and a different font size.
- Enter the same kind of data for a State field in each record. For example, enter CA, AZ, or IL for State, but not cities such as Los Angeles, Tucson, or Chicago.
- Separate the data (including the header row) from other information in the worksheet by *at least* one blank row and one blank column. The blank row and column enable Excel to accurately determine the range of the data.

You'll open the workbook in which Mary entered the art objects data according to the data definition table.

### To open and review the Museum workbook:

1. Open the **Museum** workbook located in the Excel5\Tutorial folder included with your Data Files, and then save the workbook as **LaFouch Museum**.
2. In the Documentation sheet, enter your name in cell B3 and the date in cell B4.

3. Switch to the **Art Collection** worksheet. This worksheet (which was shown in Figure 5-1) contains data about the museum's art objects. Currently, the worksheet lists 115 art objects. Each art object record is a separate row (rows 2 through 116) and contains eight fields (columns A through H). The top row, the header row, contains labels that describe the data in each column.
4. Scroll the worksheet to row **116**, the last record. The column headers, in the top row, are no longer visible.
5. Press the **Ctrl+Home** keys to return to cell A1.

## Freezing Rows and Columns

You want to see the column headers as you scroll the art objects data. Without the column headers visible, it is difficult to know what the data entered in each column represents. You can select rows and columns to remain visible in the workbook window as you scroll around the worksheet. **Freezing** a row or column lets you keep headings visible as you work with the data in a large worksheet. As you scroll the data, the first row remains on the screen so the column headers are visible, making it easier to identify the data in each record.

You'll freeze the first row, which contains the column headers.

### To freeze the top row in the worksheet:

1. Click the **View** tab on the Ribbon. The Ribbon displays the View options.
2. In the Window group, click the **Freeze Panes** button, and then click **Freeze Top Row**. A dark, horizontal line appears below the column headers to indicate which row is frozen.
3. Scroll the worksheet to row **99**. This time, the column headers remain visible as you scroll. See Figure 5-3.

**Figure 5-3** Top row of the worksheet is frozen

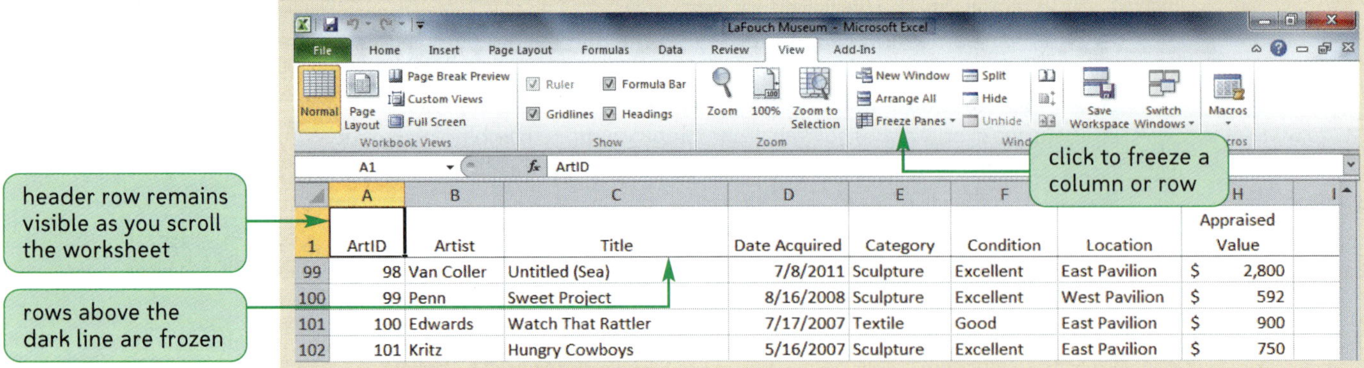


4. Press the **Ctrl+Home** keys to return to cell A2, the cell directly below the frozen row.

After you freeze panes, the first option on the Freeze Panes menu changes to Unfreeze Panes. This option releases the frozen headers, which means that all the columns and rows in worksheet shift when you scroll the worksheet. You will use a different method to keep the column headers visible, so you will unfreeze the top row of the worksheet.

**To unfreeze the top row of the worksheet:**

1. In the Window group on the View tab, click the **Freeze Panes** button. The first Freeze Panes option is now Unfreeze Panes.
2. Click **Unfreeze Panes**. The headers are no longer frozen and the dark, horizontal line below the column headers is removed. You can now scroll all the rows and columns in the worksheet.

# Creating an Excel Table

You can convert a structured range of data, such as the art objects data in the range A1:H116, to an Excel table. An Excel table makes it easier to identify, manage, and analyze the groups of related data. You can create more than one Excel table in a worksheet. Although you can perform all of the tasks in this section without creating an Excel table, there are many advantages to creating a table rather than leaving the art collection data as a range of data.

INSIGHT

*Saving Time with Excel Table Features*

Excel tables provide many advantages to structured ranges of data. When you create an Excel table, you can perform the same operations as you can for a structured range of data. In addition, you can use Excel tables to do the following to be more productive and reduce the chance of error:

- Format the Excel table quickly using a table style.
- Add new rows and columns to the Excel table that automatically expand the range.
- Add a Total row to calculate the summary function you select, such as SUM, AVERAGE, COUNT, MIN, and MAX.
- Enter a formula in one table cell that is automatically copied to all other cells in that table column.
- Create formulas that reference cells in a table by using table and column names instead of cell addresses.

These Excel table features let you focus on analyzing and understanding the data, leaving the more time-consuming tasks for the program to perform.

Next, you'll create an Excel table from the art objects data in the Art Collection worksheet. By doing so, you'll be able to take advantage of the many features and tools for working with Excel tables to analyze data effectively.

**TIP**

If the first row of data does not contain column headers, uncheck the My table has headers check box. Excel adds headers with the default names Column1 and so on.

**To create an Excel table from the art objects data:**

1. Verify that the active cell is cell **A2**, which is in the range of art objects data.
2. Click the **Insert** tab on the Ribbon. The Ribbon displays the Insert options.
3. In the Tables group, click the **Table** button. The Create Table dialog box opens. The range of data for the table is entered in the dialog box.

4. Click the **OK** button. The dialog box closes, and the range of data is converted to an Excel table. Filter arrows appear in the header row, the table is formatted with a predefined table style, and the Table Tools Design contextual tab appears on the Ribbon. See Figure 5-4.

**Figure 5-4** **Excel table created for the art objects data**

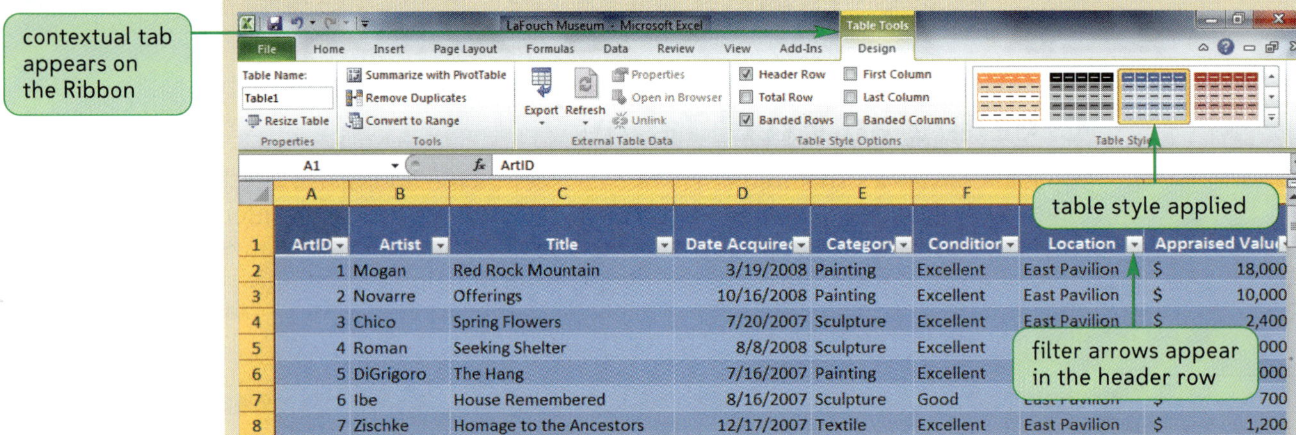


5. Scroll the table down. The text of the header row replaces the standard lettered column headings (A, B, C, and so on) as you scroll so that you don't need to freeze panes to keep the header row visible. See Figure 5-5.

**Figure 5-5** **Art objects table scrolled**

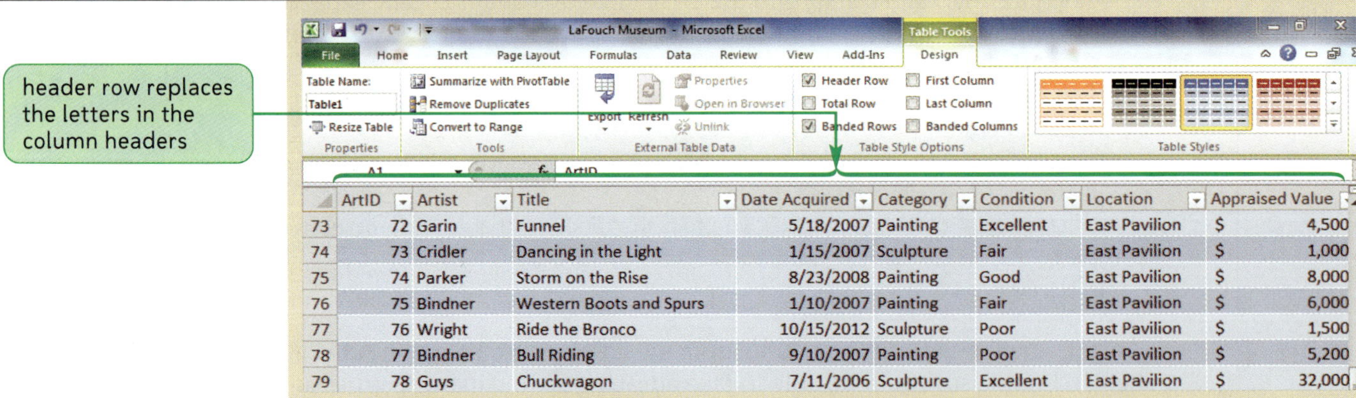


6. Press the **Ctrl+Home** keys to make cell A1 active. The column headings return to the standard display, and the header row scrolls back into view as row 1.

## Renaming an Excel Table

**TIP**

You can use the underscore character instead of spaces to separate words in a table name.

Excel assigns the name Table1 to the first Excel table created in a workbook. Any additional Excel tables you create in the workbook are named consecutively, Table2, Table3, and so forth. You can assign a more descriptive name to a table, making it easier to identify a particular table by its content. Descriptive names are especially useful when you create more than one Excel table in the same workbook. Table names must start with a letter or an underscore and can use any combination of letters, numbers, and underscores for the rest of the name. Table names cannot include spaces.

You will change the name of the Excel table you just created from the art objects data.

**To rename the Table1 table:**

1. In the Properties group on the Design tab, select **Table1** in the Table Name box. See Figure 5-6.

**Figure 5-6** Table Name box

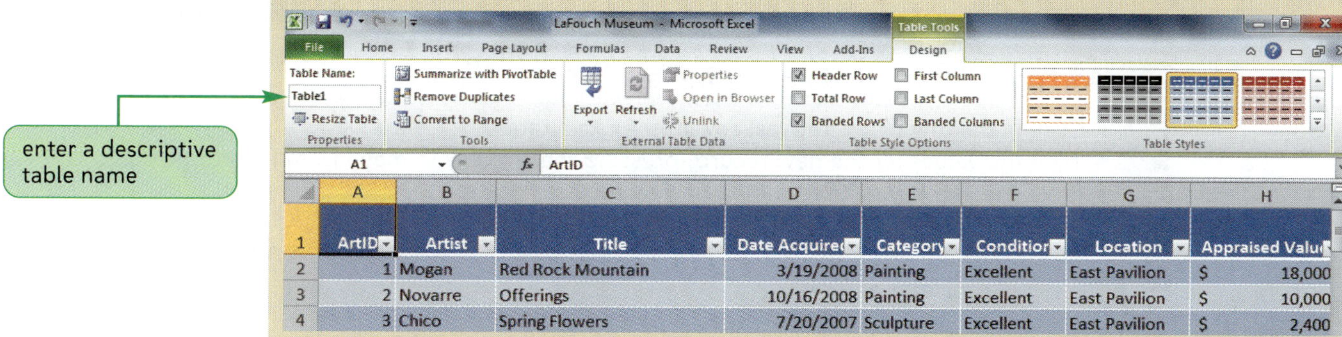


2. Type **ArtObjects**, and then press the **Enter** key. The Excel table is renamed as "ArtObjects."

## Formatting an Excel Table

The check boxes in the Table Style Options group on the Design tab enable you to quickly and easily add or remove table elements or change the table's formatting. For example, you can display or hide the header row and select whether to format the table with banded rows, banded columns, or neither. You can also apply a table style.

You will format the table by selecting which table style options are applied to the Excel table.

**To format the ArtObjects table:**

1. In the Table Style group on the Table Tools Design tab, click the **More** button. A gallery of table styles opens.
2. In the Table Styles gallery, click **Table Style Medium 4**. The table now has a green theme.
3. Change the width of column D to **12** characters. The width of the Date Acquired column better fits the dates.
4. Change the width of columns E, F, and H to **12** characters.
5. If cell A1 is not already the active cell, click cell **A1**.

# Maintaining Data in an Excel Table

Mary has several changes you need to make to the data in the ArtObjects table. First, the museum acquired a new painting and received a sculpture from an anonymous donor; both art objects need to be added to the table. Second, the condition of the Moonlight painting has deteriorated and requires repairs; its condition needs to be changed from "Fair" to "Poor." Finally, one of the paintings has been sold to raise money for new acquisitions; the record for this art object needs to be deleted from the table. You will update the ArtObjects table to reflect these changes.

## Adding Records

As you maintain data in an Excel table, you often need to add new records. You add a record to an Excel table in a blank row. The simplest and most convenient way to add a record to an Excel table is to enter the data in the first blank row below the last record. You can then sort the data to arrange the table in the order you want. If you want the record in a specific location, you can also insert a row within the table for the new record.

REFERENCE

### *Adding a Record to an Excel Table*

- Click in the row below the last row of the Excel table.
- Type the values for the new record, pressing the Tab key to move from field to field.
- Press the Tab key to create another new record.

  *or*

  Press the Enter key if this is the last record.

Next, you'll add records for the new painting and sculpture to the ArtObjects table.

### To add two records to the ArtObjects table:

1. Press the **End+↓** keys to make cell A116 the active cell. This cell is in the last row of the table.
2. Press the **↓** key to move the active cell to cell A117. This is the first blank row below the table.
3. In cell A117, type **116**, and then press the **Tab** key. Cell B117 in the Artist column becomes the active cell. The table expands to include a new row in the table structure with the same formatting as the rest of the table. The AutoCorrect Options button appears so you can undo the table formatting if you hadn't intended the new data to be part of the existing table. The sizing handle in the lower-right corner of the table indicates the last row and column in the table. You can use the sizing handle to add columns or rows to the Excel table to expand it, or remove them to make the table smaller. See Figure 5-7.

**Figure 5-7** New row added to the ArtObjects table

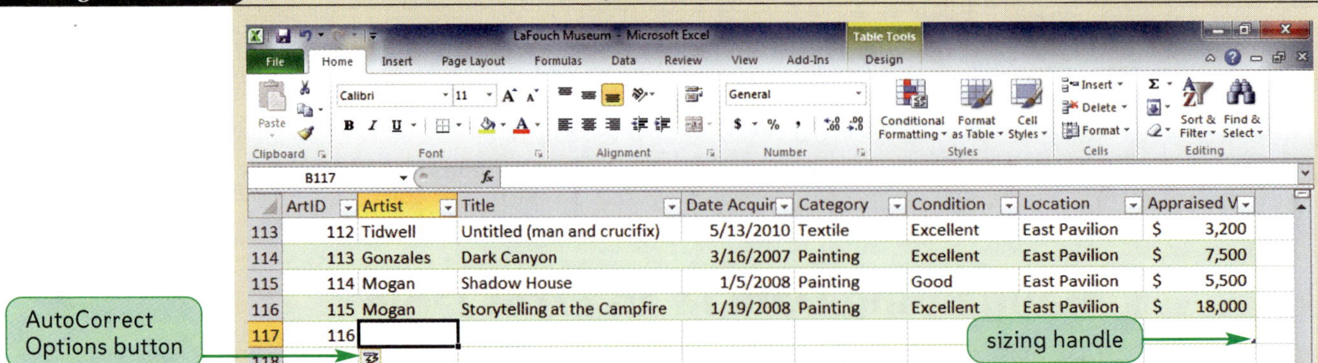


**Trouble?** If cell A118 is the active cell, you probably pressed the Enter key instead of the Tab key. Click cell B117 and then continue entering the data in Step 4.

**TIP**

As you type in a cell, AutoComplete displays any existing entry in the column that matches the characters you typed. Press the Tab key to accept the entry; continue typing to replace it.

4. In the range B117:H117, enter **Giama** for the artist, **Starry Night** for the title, **4/3/2013** for the date acquired, **Painting** for the category, **Excellent** for the condition, **South Pavilion** for the location, and **8500** for the appraised value, pressing the **Tab** key after each entry. Cell A118 becomes the active cell and the table expands to incorporate row 118.
5. In the range A118:H118, enter **117** for the art ID, **Higgins** for the artist, **Apache Warrior** for the title, **4/5/2013** for the date acquired, **Sculpture** for the category, **Excellent** for the condition, **Garden** for the location, and **23000** for the appraised value, press the **Enter** key, and then click cell **A119** after the last entry. The record for the sculpture is added to the table. See Figure 5-8.

**Figure 5-8** Records added to the ArtObjects table

two new records

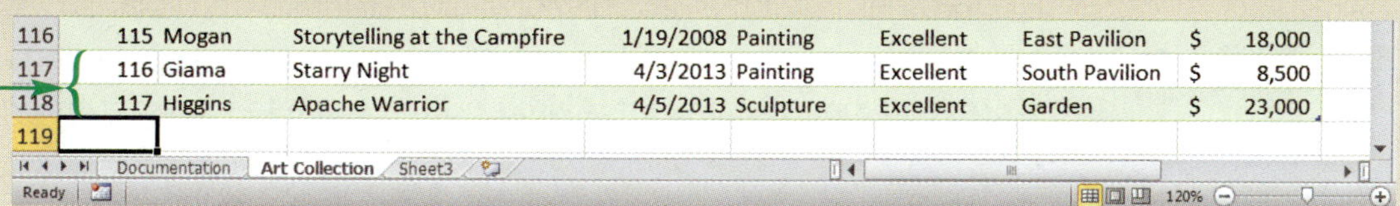


**Trouble?** If a new row is added to the table, you probably pressed the Tab key instead of the Enter key after the last entry in the record. On the Quick Access Toolbar, click the Undo button to remove the extra row.

## Finding and Editing Records

You need to update the condition for the art object with the title "Moonlight." Although you can manually scroll through the table to find a specific record, a quicker and more accurate way to locate a record is to use the Find command. You edit the data in a field the same way as you edit data in a worksheet cell. You'll use the Find command to locate the record for the Moonlight painting, which has deteriorated to poor condition. Then, you'll edit the record in the table to change the condition to "Poor."

### To find and edit the record for the Moonlight painting:

1. Press the **Ctrl+Home** keys to move to the top of the worksheet, and then click cell **C2** to make it the active cell.
2. In the Editing group on the Home tab, click the **Find & Select** button, and then click **Find**. The Find and Replace dialog box opens.
3. Type **Moonlight** in the Find what box, and then click the **Find Next** button. Cell C69, which contains the title "Moonlight," is selected. This is the record you want. If it wasn't, you would click the Find Next button again to display the next record that meets the search criteria.
4. Click the **Close** button. The Find and Replace dialog box closes.
5. Press the **Tab** key three times to move the active cell to the Condition column, and then type **P**. AutoComplete displays "Poor" in the cell, which is the condition text you want to enter.
6. Press the **Tab** key to enter the AutoComplete entry. The painting's condition is changed in the table.
7. Press the **Ctrl+Home** keys to make cell A1 active.

## Deleting a Record

The final update you need to make to the ArtObjects table is to delete the record for the Trappers painting (ArtID 90), which was sold. You'll use the Find command to locate the painting's record. Then, you'll delete the record from the table.

**TIP**

You can find fields whose contents match a value (such as 90) exactly by clicking the Options button in the Find and Replace dialog box, and checking the Match entire cell contents check box.

Be sure to verify that you selected the correct record before you delete; a dialog box does *not* open to confirm the delete operation.

**To find and delete the Trappers painting record:**

1. In the Editing group on the Home tab, click the **Find & Select** button, and then click **Find**. The Find and Replace dialog box opens.
2. Type **90** in the Find what box, and then click the **Find Next** button. Because Excel searches the entire worksheet (not just the current column), and because it finds the search value even if it is part of another value, the appraised value $1,900 is selected. This is not the record you want to delete.
3. Click the **Find Next** button to highlight the appraised value $1,900 for a different record, and then click the **Find Next** button again to highlight the value 90 in the ArtID column. This is the record you need to delete.
4. Click the **Close** button. The Find and Replace dialog box closes.
5. In the Cells group on the Home tab, click the **Delete button arrow**, and then click **Delete Table Rows**. The record for the Trappers painting is deleted from the table.

   **Trouble?** If a different record was deleted, the active cell was not in the record for the Trappers painting. On the Quick Access Toolbar, click the Undo button to restore the record, and then repeat Steps 1 through 5.
6. Press the **Ctrl+Home** keys to make cell A1 active.

# Sorting Data

The records in the ArtObjects table appear in the order that Mary entered them. As you work, however, you'll want to view the same records in a different order, such as by the artist name or by the art object's location in the museum. For example, if you want to arrange the art objects by artist name, you can sort the data using the Artist column as the sort field.

You can sort data in ascending or descending order. **Ascending order** arranges text alphabetically from A to Z, numbers from smallest to largest, and dates from oldest to newest. **Descending order** arranges text in reverse alphabetical order from Z to A, numbers from largest to smallest, and dates from newest to oldest. In both ascending and descending order, blank fields are placed at the end of the table.

## Sorting One Column Using the Sort Buttons

You can quickly sort data with one sort field using the Sort A to Z button or the Sort Z to A button. Mary wants you to sort the art objects in ascending order by the artist. This will rearrange the table data so that the records appear in alphabetical order by the artist name.

**TIP**

You can also click the Sort & Filter button in the Editing group on the Home tab, and then click a sort option.

**To sort the ArtObjects table in ascending order by the artist name:**

1. Click any cell in the Artist column. You do not need to select the entire ArtObjects table, which consists of the range A1:H117. Excel determines the table's range when you click any cell in the table.
2. Click the **Data** tab on the Ribbon. The Data options appear on the Ribbon.

3. In the Sort & Filter group, click the **Sort A to Z** button. The data is sorted in ascending order by Artist. The Artist filter arrow indicates the data is sorted by that column. See Figure 5-9.

**Figure 5-9** ArtObjects table sorted by Artist

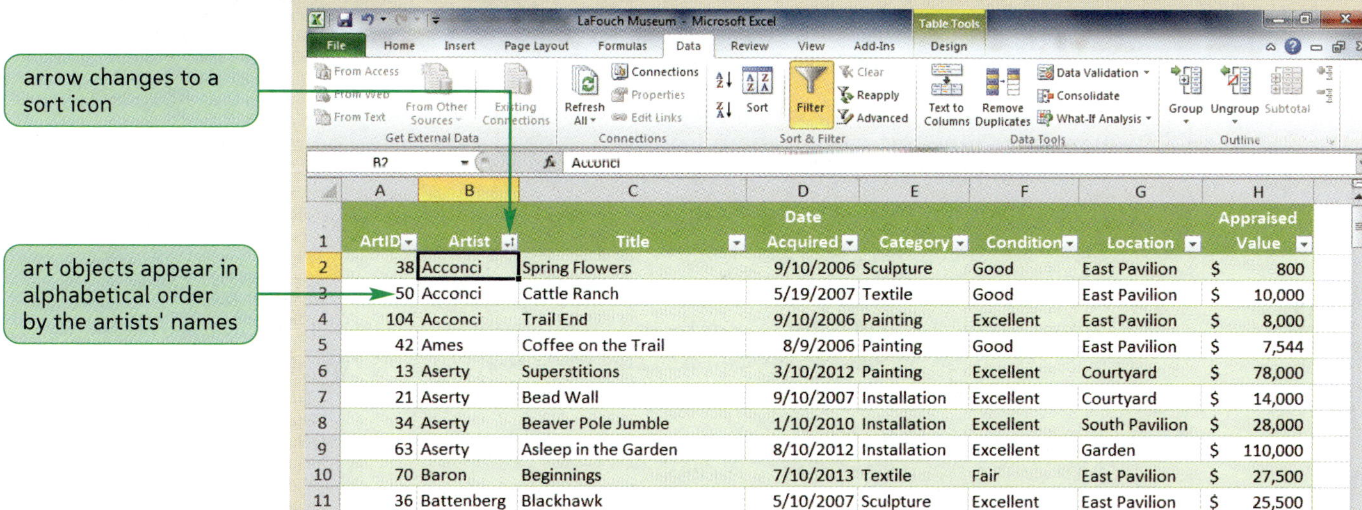


| | ArtID | Artist | Title | Date Acquired | Category | Condition | Location | Appraised Value |
|---|---|---|---|---|---|---|---|---|
| 2 | 38 | Acconci | Spring Flowers | 9/10/2006 | Sculpture | Good | East Pavilion | $ 800 |
| 3 | 50 | Acconci | Cattle Ranch | 5/19/2007 | Textile | Good | East Pavilion | $ 10,000 |
| 4 | 104 | Acconci | Trail End | 9/10/2006 | Painting | Excellent | East Pavilion | $ 8,000 |
| 5 | 42 | Ames | Coffee on the Trail | 8/9/2006 | Painting | Good | East Pavilion | $ 7,544 |
| 6 | 13 | Aserty | Superstitions | 3/10/2012 | Painting | Excellent | Courtyard | $ 78,000 |
| 7 | 21 | Aserty | Bead Wall | 9/10/2007 | Installation | Excellent | Courtyard | $ 14,000 |
| 8 | 34 | Aserty | Beaver Pole Jumble | 1/10/2010 | Installation | Excellent | South Pavilion | $ 28,000 |
| 9 | 63 | Aserty | Asleep in the Garden | 8/10/2012 | Installation | Excellent | Garden | $ 110,000 |
| 10 | 70 | Baron | Beginnings | 7/10/2013 | Textile | Fair | East Pavilion | $ 27,500 |
| 11 | 36 | Battenberg | Blackhawk | 5/10/2007 | Sculpture | Excellent | East Pavilion | $ 25,500 |

**Trouble?** If the data is sorted in the wrong order, you might have clicked in a different column than the Artist column. Repeat Steps 1 through 3.

## Sorting Multiple Columns Using the Sort Dialog Box

Sometimes, sorting by one sort field is not adequate for your needs. For example, Mary wants you to arrange the ArtObjects table so that all the art objects in each location are together, and then all the objects for each artist within each location are together, and then each artist's work is arranged by the date acquired. You must sort on more than one column to accomplish this. The first sort field is called the **primary sort field**, the second sort field is called the **secondary sort field**, and so forth. You can use up to 64 sort fields in a single sort, although you most typically will use one to three sort fields. In this case, the Location field is the primary sort field, the Artist field is the secondary sort field, and the Date Acquired field is the tertiary sort field. When you have more than one sort field, you should use the Sort dialog box to specify the sort criteria.

REFERENCE

### *Sorting Data Using Multiple Sort Fields*

- Click any cell in a table or range.
- In the Sort & Filter group on the Data tab, click the Sort button.
- If necessary, click the Add Level button to insert the Sort by row.
- Click the Sort by arrow, select the column heading for the primary sort field, click the Sort On arrow to select the type of data, and then click the Order arrow to select the sort order.
- To sort by a second column, click the Add Level button. Click the Then by arrow, select the column heading for the secondary sort field, click the Sort On arrow to select the type of data, and then click the Order arrow to select the sort order.
- To sort by additional columns, click the Add Level button and select appropriate Then by, Sort On, and Order values.
- Click the OK button.

You will sort the art objects by location, and then within location by artist, and then within artist by date acquired, with the most recently acquired objects for the artist appearing before the older ones. This will make it faster for Mary to find information about the location and the creator of the art objects in each location.

## To sort the ArtObjects table by multiple sort fields:

1. Click cell **A1** in the ArtObjects table. Cell A1 is the active cell, although you can click any cell in the table to sort the table data.
2. In the Sort & Filter group on the Data tab, click the **Sort** button. The Sort dialog box opens. Any sort specifications (sort field, type of data sorted on, and sort order) from the last sort appear in the dialog box.
3. Click the **Sort by** arrow to display the list of the column headers in the ArtObjects table, and then click **Location**. The primary sort field is set to Location.
4. If necessary, click the **Sort On** arrow to display the type of sort, and then click **Values**. Typically, you want to sort by the numbers, text, or dates stored in the cells, which are all values. You can also sort by formats such as cell color, font color, and cell icon (a graphic that appears in a cell due to a conditional format).
5. If necessary, click the **Order** arrow to display sort order options, and then click **A to Z**. The sort order is set to ascending.
6. Click the **Add Level** button. A Then by row is added below the primary sort field.
7. Click the **Then by** arrow and click **Artist**, and then verify that **Values** appears in the Sort On box and **A to Z** appears in the Order box.
8. Click the **Add Level** button to add a second Then by row.
9. Click the second **Then by** arrow, click **Date Acquired**, verify that **Values** appears in the Sort On box, click the **Order** arrow, and then click **Newest to Oldest** to specify a descending sort order for the Date Acquired values. See Figure 5-10.

**Figure 5-10** Sort dialog box with complete sort specifications

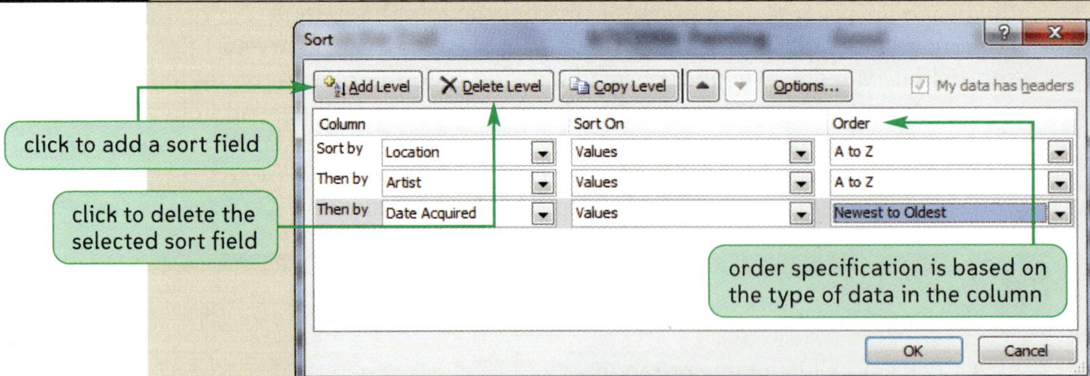


10. Click the **OK** button. Excel sorts the table records first in ascending order by the Location field, then within each location by the Artist field (again, in ascending order), and then within each artist by the Date Acquired field. For example, notice the three works by Acconci located in the East Pavilion; the works are arranged in descending order by the value in the Date Acquired column, so that the newer works appear before the older works. See Figure 5-11.

**Figure 5-11** Art objects sorted by Location, then by Artist, and then by Date Acquired

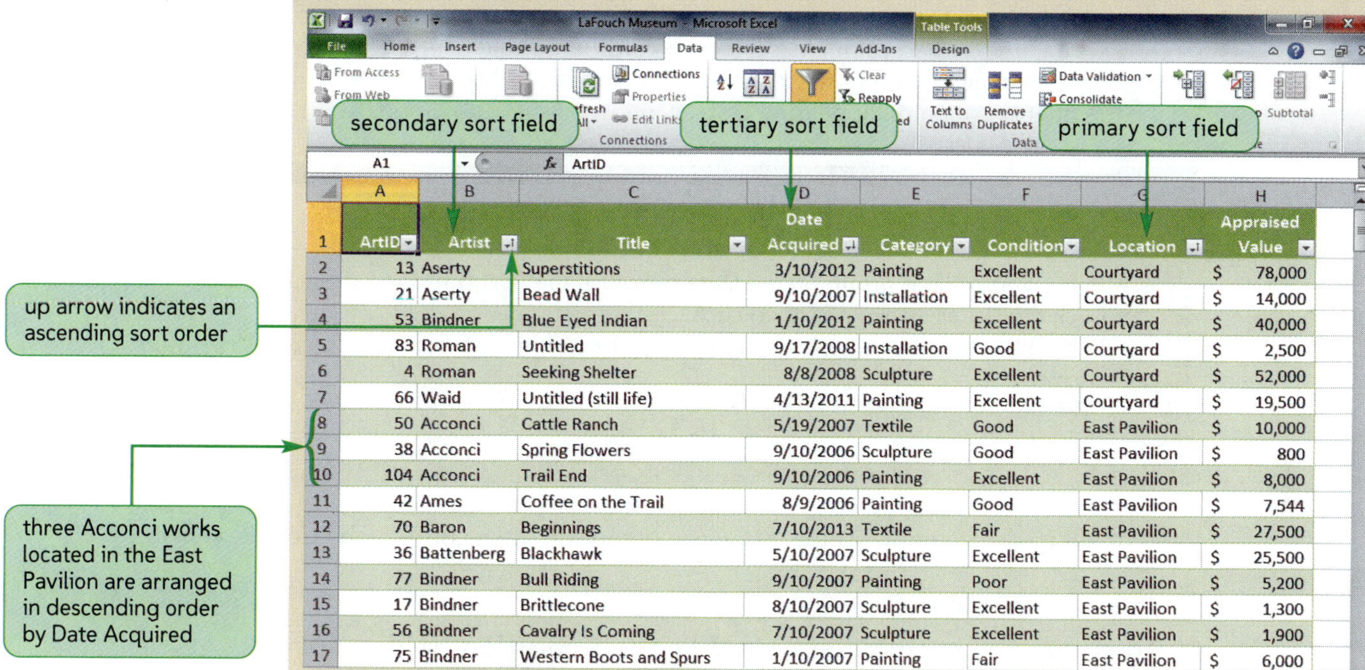


| | ArtID | Artist | Title | Date Acquired | Category | Condition | Location | Appraised Value |
|---|---|---|---|---|---|---|---|---|
| 2 | 13 | Aserty | Superstitions | 3/10/2012 | Painting | Excellent | Courtyard | $ 78,000 |
| 3 | 21 | Aserty | Bead Wall | 9/10/2007 | Installation | Excellent | Courtyard | $ 14,000 |
| 4 | 53 | Bindner | Blue Eyed Indian | 1/10/2012 | Painting | Excellent | Courtyard | $ 40,000 |
| 5 | 83 | Roman | Untitled | 9/17/2008 | Installation | Good | Courtyard | $ 2,500 |
| 6 | 4 | Roman | Seeking Shelter | 8/8/2008 | Sculpture | Excellent | Courtyard | $ 52,000 |
| 7 | 66 | Waid | Untitled (still life) | 4/13/2011 | Painting | Excellent | Courtyard | $ 19,500 |
| 8 | 50 | Acconci | Cattle Ranch | 5/19/2007 | Textile | Good | East Pavilion | $ 10,000 |
| 9 | 38 | Acconci | Spring Flowers | 9/10/2006 | Sculpture | Good | East Pavilion | $ 800 |
| 10 | 104 | Acconci | Trail End | 9/10/2006 | Painting | Excellent | East Pavilion | $ 8,000 |
| 11 | 42 | Ames | Coffee on the Trail | 8/9/2006 | Painting | Good | East Pavilion | $ 7,544 |
| 12 | 70 | Baron | Beginnings | 7/10/2013 | Textile | Fair | East Pavilion | $ 27,500 |
| 13 | 36 | Battenberg | Blackhawk | 5/10/2007 | Sculpture | Excellent | East Pavilion | $ 25,500 |
| 14 | 77 | Bindner | Bull Riding | 9/10/2007 | Painting | Poor | East Pavilion | $ 5,200 |
| 15 | 17 | Bindner | Brittlecone | 8/10/2007 | Sculpture | Excellent | East Pavilion | $ 1,300 |
| 16 | 56 | Bindner | Cavalry Is Coming | 7/10/2007 | Sculpture | Excellent | East Pavilion | $ 1,900 |
| 17 | 75 | Bindner | Western Boots and Spurs | 1/10/2007 | Painting | Fair | East Pavilion | $ 6,000 |

11. Scroll the table to view the sorted table data.

Mary wants to review the condition of each art object to determine how many objects need repairs. It is easier to do this with the objects sorted by their condition. Because you need to sort by only one field, you'll use the Sort A to Z button.

### To sort the art objects by condition:

1. Click any cell in the **Condition** column.
2. In the Sort & Filter group on the Data tab, click the **Sort A to Z** button. The previous sort is removed and the art objects are now sorted in ascending order by condition.
3. Scroll the table to see the reordered art objects.

The table data is sorted in alphabetical order by the condition of the art objects: Excellent, Fair, Good, and Poor. This default sort order for fields with text values is not appropriate for the condition ratings. Instead, Mary wants you to base the sort on quality ranking rather than alphabetical order. You'll use a custom sort list to set up the sort order Mary wants.

## Sorting Using a Custom List

Text is sorted in ascending or descending alphabetical order unless you specify a different order using a custom list. A **custom list** indicates the sequence in which you want data ordered. Excel provides four predefined custom sort lists. Two days-of-the-week custom lists (Sun, Mon, Tues, ... and Sunday, Monday, Tuesday, ...) and two months-of-the-year custom lists (Jan, Feb, Mar, Apr, ... and January, February, March, April, ...). If a column consists of day or month labels, you can sort them in their correct chronological order using one of these predefined custom lists.

You can also create custom lists to sort records in a sequence you define. In this case, you want to create a custom list to arrange the art objects based on their condition, with the top quality condition appearing first, as follows: Excellent, Good, Fair, Poor.

REFERENCE

*Creating a Custom List*

- In the Sort & Filter group on the Data tab, click the Sort button.
- Click the Order arrow, and then click Custom List.
- In the List entries box, type each entry for the custom list, pressing the Enter key after each entry.
- Click the Add button.
- Click the OK button.

You'll create a custom list that Mary can use to sort the records by the Condition field.

### To create the custom list based on the Condition field:

1. Make sure the active cell is in the table, and then, in the Sort & Filter group on the Data tab, click the **Sort** button. The Sort dialog box opens, showing the sort specifications from the previous sort.
2. If necessary, click the **Sort by** arrow, click **Condition** to select the sort field (if necessary), and then verify that **Values** appears in the Sort On box.
3. Click the **Order** arrow to display the sort order options, and then click **Custom List**. The Custom Lists dialog box opens.
4. In the Custom lists box, click **NEW LIST** to place the insertion point in the List entries box.

   Next, you'll enter the condition values in the order you want them sorted. You must press the Enter key after each entry.

**TIP**

You can also use commas to separate entries in a custom list.

5. Type **Excellent**, press the **Enter** key to move the insertion point to the next line, type **Good**, press the **Enter** key, type **Fair**, press the **Enter** key, type **Poor**, and then press the **Enter** key. The four items appear in the List entries box.
6. Click the **Add** button. The custom list entries are added to the Custom lists box. See Figure 5-12.

**Figure 5-12** **Custom Lists dialog box with custom list defined**

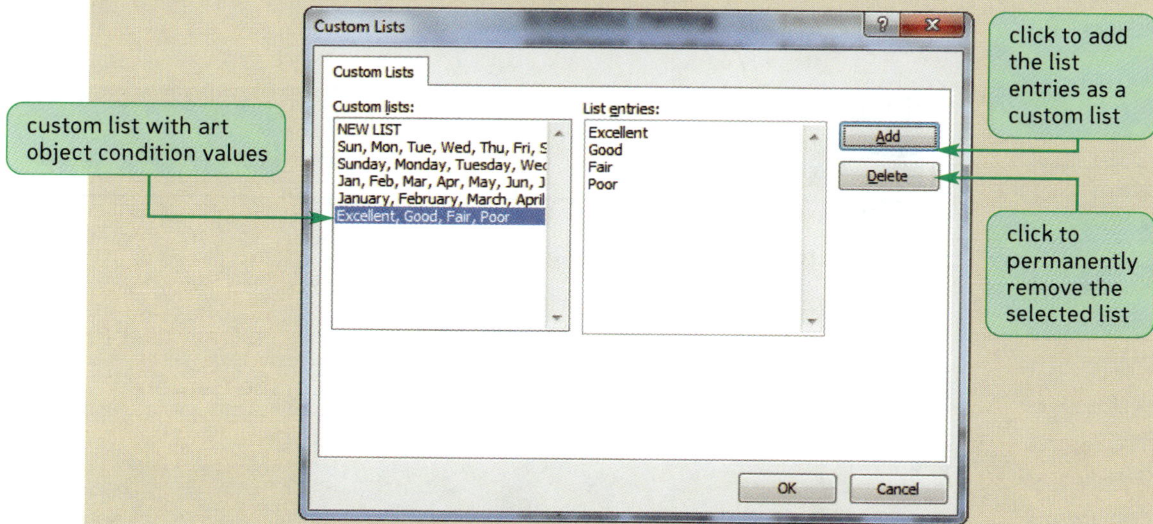


7. Click the **OK** button to return to the Sort dialog box. The custom sort list—Excellent, Good, Fair, Poor—appears in the Order box.
8. Click the **OK** button. The table is sorted based on the custom list.
9. Scroll the sorted table to verify that the art objects are sorted by their condition rankings: Excellent, Good, Fair, and Poor. Six art objects are in poor condition.

So far, you created an Excel table for the art objects, and then named and formatted the table. You updated the table by adding, editing, and deleting records. You also sorted the records and created a custom list to sort the Condition field by its quality ratings. In the next session, you will filter the ArtObjects table to retrieve specific information on some of the art objects.

REVIEW

## *Session 5.1 Quick Check*

1. What is the purpose of the Freeze Panes button in the Window group on the View tab? Why is this feature helpful?
2. What three elements indicate an Excel table is created in the worksheet?
3. A field that you use to order data is referred to as a(n) ______________ field.
4. An Excel table of college students tracks each student's first name, last name, major, and year of graduation. How can you order the table so that students graduating in the same year appear together in alphabetical order by the student's last name?
5. How do you enter a new record in an Excel table?
6. An Excel table of faculty data includes the Rank field with the values Full, Associate, Assistant, and Instructor. How can you sort the data by rank in the following order: Full, Associate, Assistant, and Instructor?
7. If you sort table data from the most recent purchase date to the oldest purchase date, in what order have you sorted the data?

# SESSION 5.2 VISUAL OVERVIEW

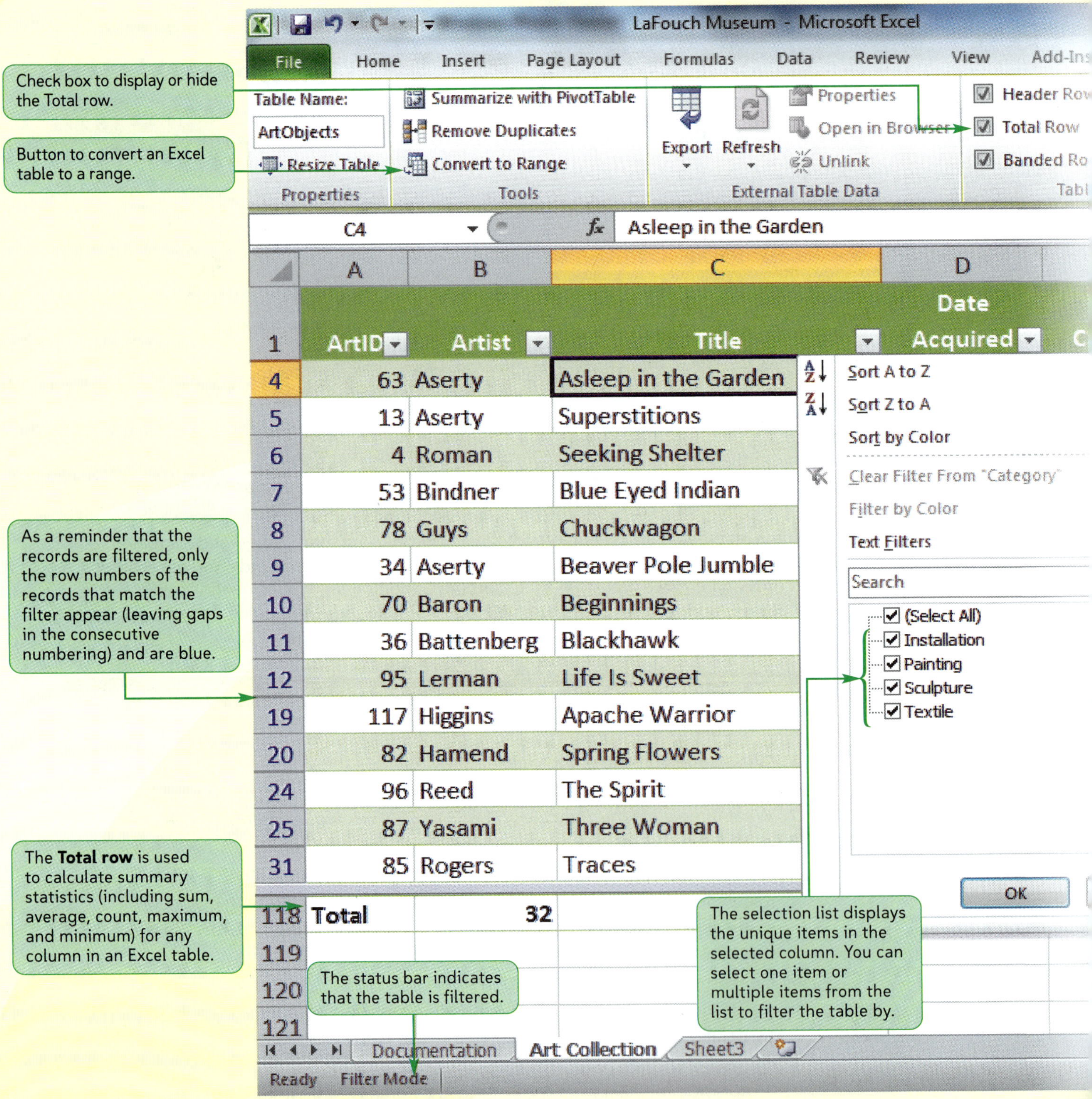

# FILTERING TABLE DATA

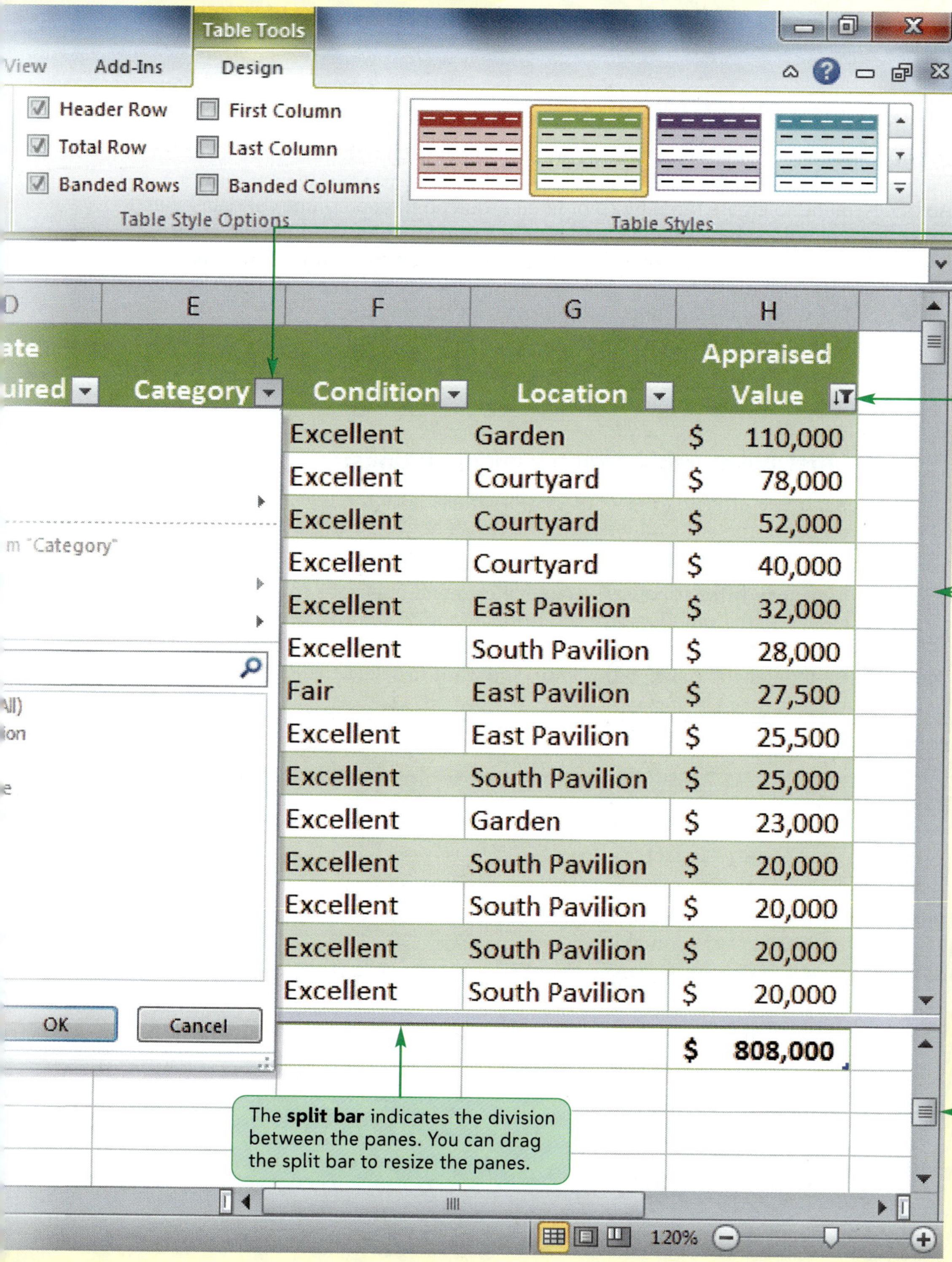


The filter arrow opens the Filter menu, which includes options to sort and filter the table based on the data in that column.

**Filtering** is the process of displaying a subset of rows in an Excel table that meets the criteria you specify. In this case, the table is filtered to show art objects in with an appraised value of $20,000 or higher.

To view different areas of a large worksheet, you can split the window into two or four resizable areas. Each area is called a **pane**.

Each pane has its own set of scroll bars for shifting different parts of the worksheet into view in each pane.

The **split bar** indicates the division between the panes. You can drag the split bar to resize the panes.

# Filtering Data

Mary needs to determine which art objects the museum can afford to repair this year. She asks you to prepare a list of all paintings in poor condition. Although you could sort the list of paintings by condition to group those in poor condition, you are still working with the entire table. A better solution is to display only the specific records you want. Filtering the data temporarily hides any records that do not meet the specified criteria. After data is filtered, you can sort, copy, format, chart, and print it.

## Filtering Using One Column

**TIP**

You can display or hide filter arrows for an Excel table or a range of data by using the Filter button in the Sort & Filter group on the Data tab.

When you create an Excel table, a filter arrow appears in each column header. You click a filter arrow to open the AutoFilter menu for that field. You can use options on the AutoFilter menu to create three types of filters. You can filter a column of data by its cell colors or font colors; by a specific text, number, or date filter, although the choices depend on the type of data in the column; or by selecting the exact values by which you want to filter in the column. After you filter a column, the Clear Filter command becomes available so you can remove the filter and redisplay all the records.

Mary wants to see only paintings in poor condition. First, you'll filter the ArtObjects table to show only those records with the value "Paintings" in the Category column.

### To filter the ArtObjects table to show only paintings:

1. If you took a break after the previous session, make sure the LaFouch Museum workbook is open, the Art Collection worksheet is active, and the ArtObjects table is active.
2. Click the **Category filter arrow**. The AutoFilter menu opens, as shown in Figure 5-13, listing the unique entries in the Category column: Installation, Painting, Sculpture, and Textile. All the items are selected initially, but you can set which items to use to filter the data. In this case, you want to select the Painting item.

**Figure 5-13** Filter menu for the Category column

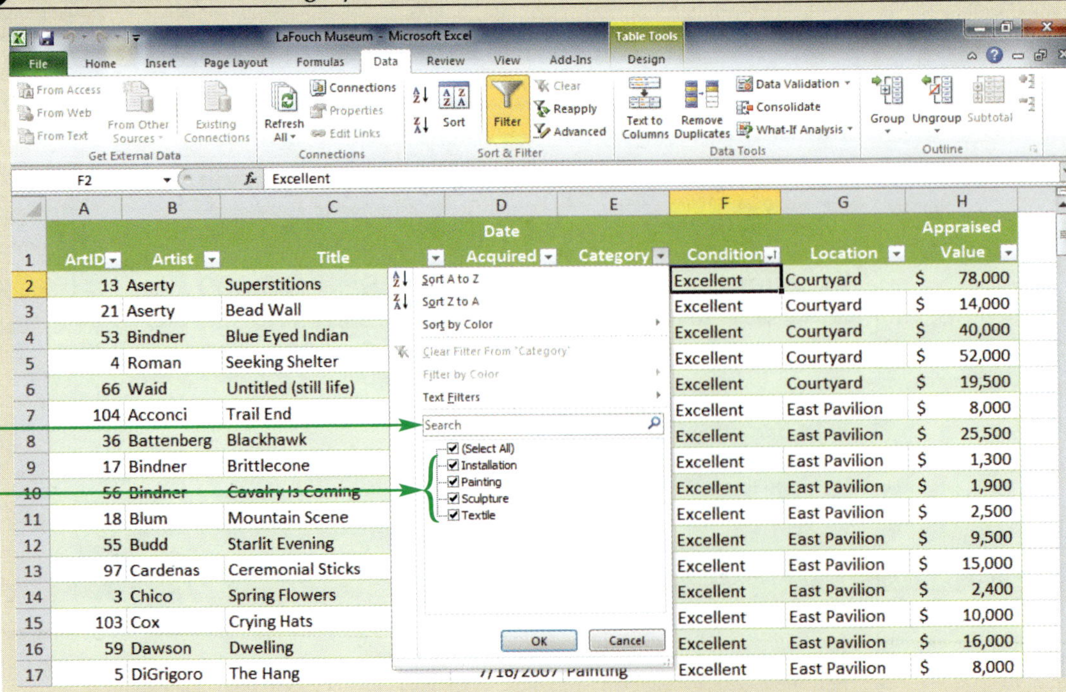


If the list is long you can enter the item you want to find in the Search box

unique items in the Category column

3. Click the **(Select All)** check box to remove the check marks from all the Category items, and then click the **Painting** check box to insert a check mark. The filter will show only those records that match the checked item and hide records that contain the unchecked items.

4. Click the **OK** button. The filter is applied. The status bar lists the number of paintings found in the entire table. Fifty-seven of the 116 records in the table are displayed. See Figure 5-14.

**Figure 5-14** ArtObjects table filtered to show only paintings

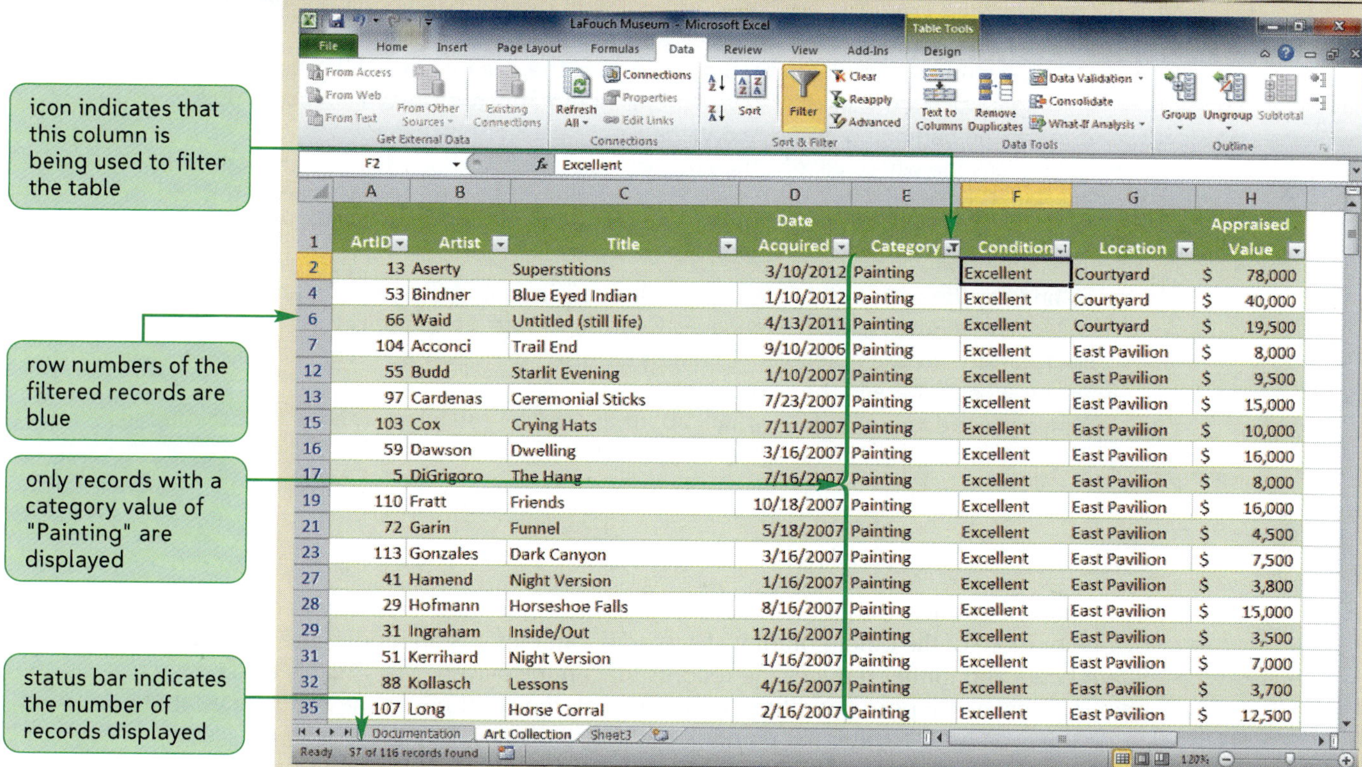


5. Review the records to verify that only records with a value equal to "Painting" in the Category column are visible. All records that do not have the value "Painting" in this column are hidden, leaving gaps in the row numbers.

6. Point to the **Category filter arrow**. A ScreenTip—Category: Equals "Painting"—describes the filter applied to the column.

The AutoFilter menu includes options to Sort by Color and Filter by Color. These options enable you to filter and sort data using color, one of many cell attributes. Suppose that Mary used specific cell background colors for certain works of art in the ArtObjects table. For example, she might want to highlight the works given to the museum by its two most generous donors, using yellow for one and red for the other. So the cells in the Title column for the two donors would be formatted with these colors. You could then click the Sort by Color option in the AutoFilter menu to display a list of available colors by which to sort, and then click the specific color so that all the records for the first donor (formatted with yellow) would appear together, and all the records for the second donor (formatted with red) would appear together. Similarly, you could click the Filter by Color option to display a submenu with the available colors by which to filter, and then click a color. In this example, if you selected yellow, only the records for the first donor would be displayed in the table, allowing you to focus on just those records.

INSIGHT

*Exploring Text Filters*

You can use different text filters to display the records you want. If you know only part of a text value or if you want to match a certain pattern, you can use the Begins With, Ends With, and Contains operators to filter a text field to match the pattern you specify.

The following examples are based on a student directory table that includes First Name, Last Name, Address, City, State, and Zip fields:

- To find a student named Smith, Smithe, or Smythe, create a text filter using the Begins With operator. In this example, use "Begins With Sm" to display all records that have "Sm" at the beginning of the text value.
- To Find anyone whose Last Name ends in "son" (such as Robertson, Anderson, Dawson, Gibson, and so forth), create a text filter using the Ends With operator. In this example, use "Ends With son" to display all records that have "son" as the last characters in the text value.
- To find anyone whose street address includes "Central" (such as 101 Central Ave., 1024 Central Road, or 457 Avenue De Central), create a text filter using the Contains operator. In this example, use "Contains Central" to display all records that have "Central" anywhere in the text value.

When you create a text filter, think about the results you want. Then, consider what text filter you can use to best achieve those results.

## Filtering Using Multiple Columns

If you need to further restrict the records that appear in a filtered table, you can filter by one or more of the other columns. Each additional filter is applied to the currently filtered data and further reduces the records that are displayed. Mary wants to see only paintings that are in poor condition, rather than all the paintings in the ArtObjects table. To do this, you need to filter the painting records to display only those with the value "Poor" in the Condition column. You'll use the filter arrow in the Condition column to add this second filter criterion to the filtered data.

**To filter the painting records to show only those in poor condition:**

1. Click the **Condition filter arrow**. The AutoFilter menu opens.
2. Click the **Excellent**, **Fair**, and **Good** check boxes to remove the check marks. The Poor check box remains checked, so only paintings in poor condition will be displayed.
3. Click the **OK** button. The ArtObjects table is further filtered and shows the three paintings that are in poor condition. See Figure 5-15.

**Figure 5-15** ArtObjects table filtered to show only paintings in poor condition

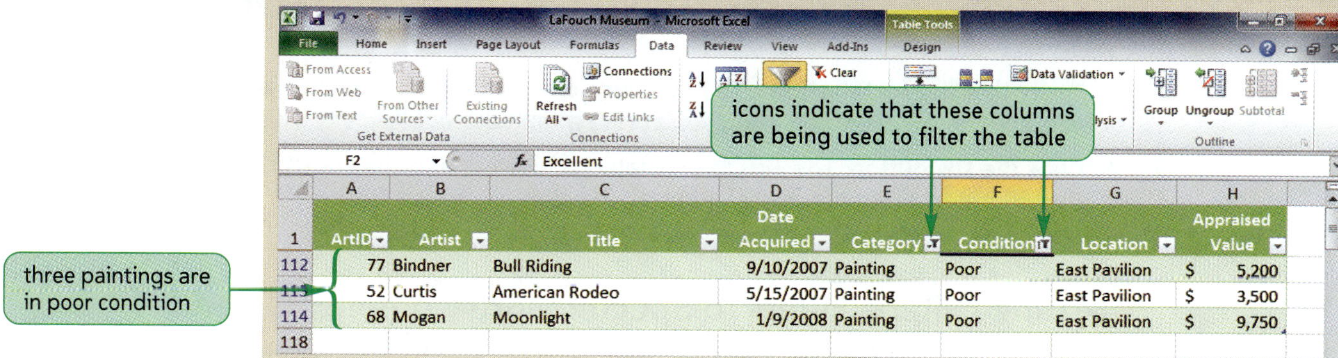


## Clearing Filters

When you want to redisplay all of the data in a filtered table, you need to **clear** (or remove) the filters. When you clear a filter from a column, any other filters are still applied. For example, in the ArtObjects table, you would see all the paintings in the table if you cleared the filter from the Condition field, or you would see all the art objects in poor condition if you cleared the filter from the Category field. To redisplay all the art objects in the table, you need to clear both the Condition filter and the Category filter. You will do this now to redisplay the entire table of art objects.

### To clear the filters to show all the records in the ArtObjects table:

1. Click the **Condition filter arrow**, and then click **Clear Filter From "Condition"**. The Condition filter is removed from the table. The table shows only paintings because the Category filter is still in effect.
2. Click the **Category filter arrow**, and then click **Clear Filter From "Category"**. The Category condition is removed, and all the records in the ArtObjects table are displayed again.

## Selecting Multiple Filter Items

You can often find the information you need by selecting a single filter item from a list of filter items. Sometimes, however, you need to specify a more complex set of criteria to find the records you want. Earlier, you selected one filter item for the Category column and one filter item for the Condition column to display the records whose Category field value equals Painting AND whose Condition field value equals Poor. The records had to contain both values to be displayed. The AND condition requires that all of the selected criteria be true for the record to be displayed.

Now you want to select two filter items for the Category column to display records whose Category field value equals Installation OR whose Category field value equals Sculpture. The records must have at least one of these values to be displayed. A filter that selects more than one item from the list of items in a single column uses the OR condition, which requires that only one of the selected criteria be true for a record to be displayed. For example, if you check the Installation and Sculpture check boxes in the Category filter items, you create the filter condition "Category equals Installation" OR "Category equals Sculpture."

The museum's board of directors wants a list of all installations or sculptures valued at more than $20,000. You will create a list of these holdings.

**To select multiple filter items:**

1. Click the **Category filter arrow**, and then click the **Painting** and **Textile** check boxes to remove the check marks.
2. Verify that the **Installation** and **Sculpture** check boxes remain checked. When you select more than one item, you create a multiselect filter.
3. Click the **OK** button. The ArtObjects table is filtered, and the status bar indicates that 51 out of 116 records are either an installation or a sculpture.

## Creating Criteria Filters to Specify More Complex Criteria

Filter items enable you to filter a range of data or an Excel table based on exact values in a column. However, many times you need broader criteria. **Criteria filters** enable you to specify various conditions in addition to those that are based on an "equals" criterion. For example, you might want to find all art objects with an appraised value greater than $20,000 or those that were acquired after 7/1/2011. You use criteria filters to create these conditions.

The type of criteria filters available change depending on whether the data in a column contains text, numbers, or dates. Figure 5-16 shows some of the options for text, number, and date criteria filters.

**Figure 5-16** **Options for text, number, and date criteria filters**

| Filter | Criteria | Records Displayed |
|---|---|---|
| Text | Equals | Exactly match the specified text string |
| | Does Not Equal | Do not exactly match the specified text string |
| | Begins With | Begin with the specified text string |
| | Ends With | End with the specified text string |
| | Contains | Have the specified text string anywhere |
| | Does Not Contain | Do not have the specified text string anywhere |
| Number | Equals | Exactly match the specified number |
| | Greater Than or Equal to | Are greater than or equal to the specified number |
| | Less Than | Are less than the specified number |
| | Between | Are greater than or equal to *and* less than or equal to the specified numbers |
| | Top 10 | Are the top or bottom 10 (or the specified number) |
| | Above Average | Are greater than the average |
| Date | Today | Have the current date |
| | Last Week | Are in the prior week |
| | Next Month | Are in the month following the current month |
| | Last Quarter | Are in the previous quarter of the year (quarters defined Jan, Feb, Mar; Apr, May, June; and so on) |
| | Year to Date | Are since January 1 of the current year to the current date |
| | Last Year | Are in the previous year (based on the current date) |

PROSKILLS

## *Problem Solving: Using Filters to Find Appropriate Data*

Problem solving often requires finding information from a set of data to answer specific questions. When you're working with a range of data or an Excel table that contains hundreds or thousands of records, filters help you find that information without having to review each record in the table. For example, a human resources manager can use a filter to narrow the search for a specific employee of the 2,500 working at the company knowing only that the employee's first name is Elliot.

Filtering limits the data to display only the specific records that meet the criteria you set, enabling you to more effectively analyze the data. The following examples further illustrate how filtering can help people to quickly locate the data they need to answer a particular question:

- A customer representative can use a filter to search a list of 10,000 products to find all products priced between $500 and $1,000.
- A donations coordinator can use a filter to prepare a report that shows the donations received during the first quarter of the current year.
- A professor who has 300 students in a psychology class can use a filter to develop a list of potential student assistants for next semester from the names the professor has highlighted in blue because their work was impressive. Filtering by the blue color generates a list of students to interview.
- The author of a guide to celebrity autographs can use a filter to determine whether an entry for a specific celebrity already exists in an Excel table and, if it does, determine whether the entry needs to be updated. If the entry does not exist, the author will know to add the autograph data to the autograph price table.

As these example show, filtering is a useful tool for locating the answers to a wide variety of questions. You then can use this information to help you resolve problems.

You will modify the filtered ArtObjects table to add a criteria filter that includes only objects that have values greater than $20,000.

### To create a number filter:

1. Click the **Appraised Value filter arrow**, and then point to **Number Filters**. A menu opens, displaying the comparison operators available for columns of numbers.
2. Click **Greater Than**. The Custom AutoFilter dialog box opens. The upper-left box lists *is greater than*, the comparison operator you want to use to filter the Appraised Value column. You enter the value you want to use for the filter criteria in the upper-right box, which, in this case, is $20,000.
3. Type **20000** in the upper-right box. See Figure 5-17. You use the lower set of boxes if you want the filter to meet a second condition. You click the And option button to display rows that meet both criteria. You click the Or option button to display rows that meet either of the two criteria. You only want to set one criterion for this filter, so you'll leave the lower boxes empty.

**Figure 5-17** **Custom AutoFilter dialog box**

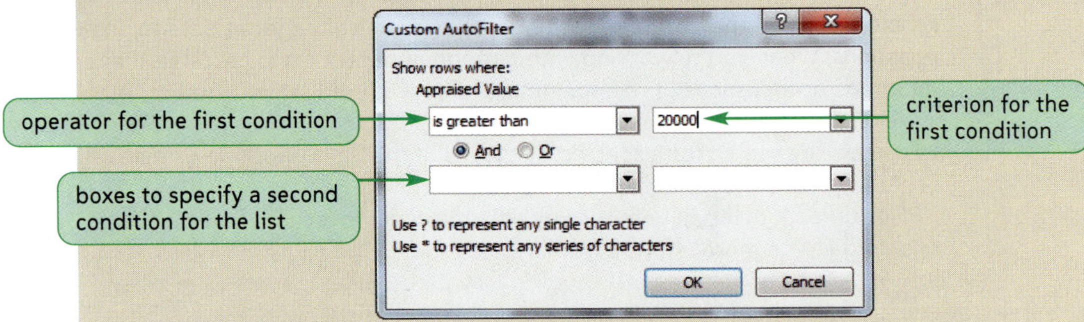


4. Click the **OK** button. The status bar indicates that 7 of 116 records were found. The seven records that appear in the ArtObjects table are either installations or sculptures and have an appraised value greater than $20,000.

Before Mary sends this list to the board of directors, you'll sort the filtered data to show the largest appraised value first. Although you can sort the data using Sort buttons, as you did earlier, these sort options are also available on the AutoFilter menu for your convenience. If you want to perform a more complex sort, you still need to use the Sort dialog box.

### To sort the filtered table data:

1. Click the **Appraised Value filter arrow**. The AutoFilter menu opens. The sort options are at the top of the menu.
2. Click **Sort Largest to Smallest**. The filtered table now displays installations and sculptures with an appraised valued greater than $20,000 sorted in descending order. See Figure 5-18.

**Figure 5-18** **Filtered ArtObjects table**

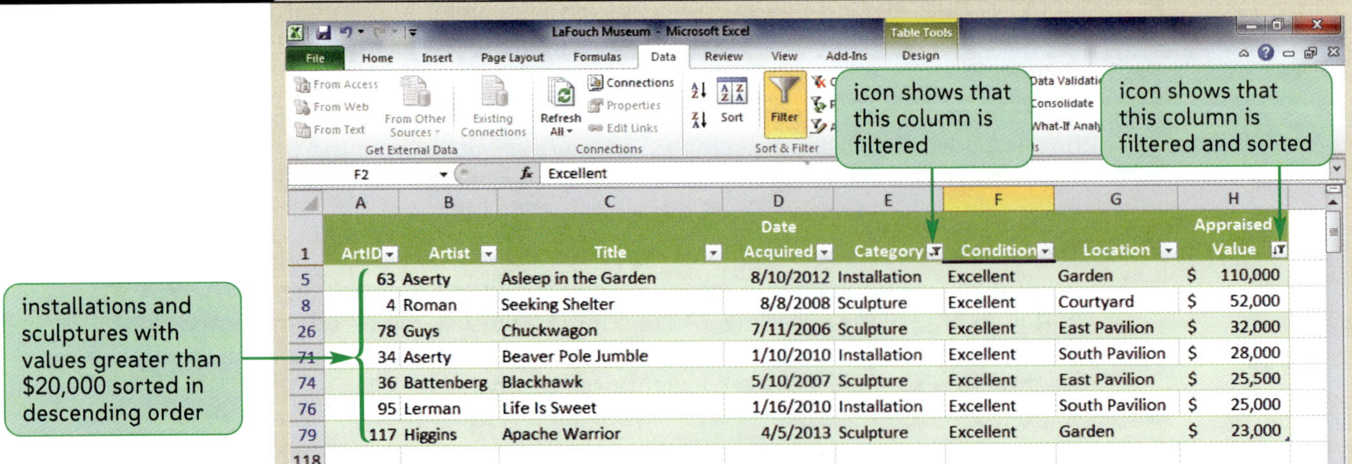


Mary will send this list to the board of directors. You need to restore the entire table of art objects, which you can do by clearing all the filters at one time.

**To clear all the filters from the ArtObjects table:**

1. Click the **Data** tab on the Ribbon, if necessary.
2. In the Sort & Filter group, click the **Clear** button. All the records appear in the table.

# Using the Total Row to Calculate Summary Statistics

You can calculate summary statistics (including sum, average, count, maximum, and minimum) on all the columns in an Excel table or on a filtered table in a Total row, which you can display at the end of the table. When you click in each cell in the Total row, an arrow appears that you can click to open a list of the most commonly used functions.

Mary is creating a brochure for an upcoming fund-raising event, and wants to know the number and value of the items in the current museum collection, excluding art objects in poor condition. You will filter the table to display art objects that are in excellent, good, and fair condition (art objects in poor condition will not be displayed). Then, you will display the Total row for the ArtObjects table to count the number of art objects in excellent, good, and fair condition, and add their total appraised value.

**To add a Total row and select summary statistics:**

1. Click the **Condition filter arrow**, click the **Poor** check box to remove the check mark, and then click the **OK** button. The ArtObjects table displays objects that are in excellent, good, or fair condition. The status bar indicates that 110 of 116 records remain in the filtered table.
2. Click the **Table Tools Design** tab on the Ribbon, and then click the **Total Row** check box in the Table Style Options group to insert a check mark.
3. Scroll to the end of the table. The Total row is the last row of the table, the word "Total" appears in the far-left cell, and the total appraised value $1,118,723 appears in the far-right cell. By default, the Total row adds the numbers in the last column of the Excel table or counts the number of records if the data in the last column contains text. See Figure 5-19.

**Figure 5-19** Total row added to the ArtObjects table

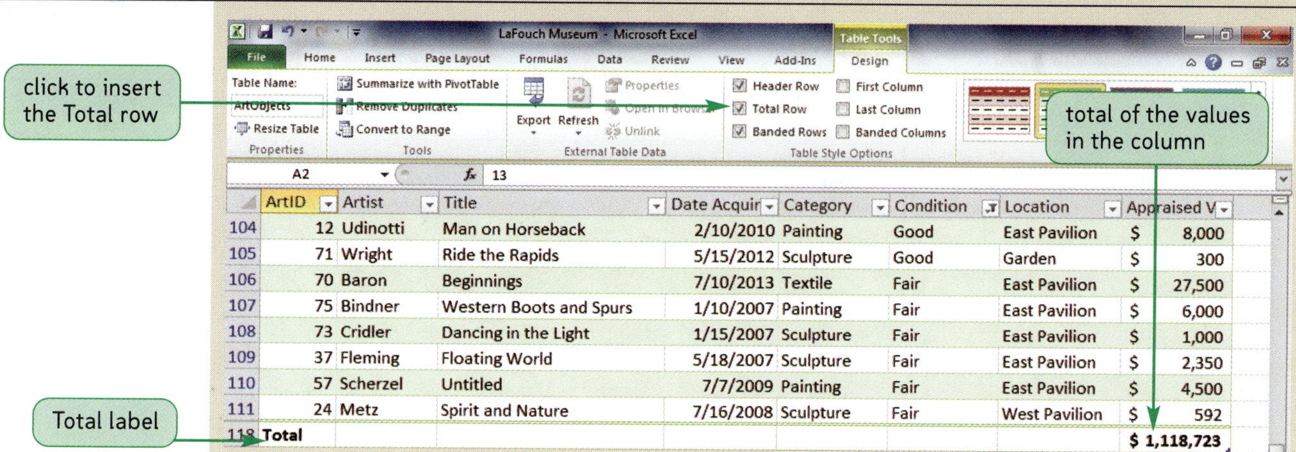

In the Artist cell of the Total row, you want to count the number of records whose appraised values were added in the last column.

4. Click cell **B118** (the Artist cell in the Total row), and then click the **arrow button** to display a list of functions. "None" is the default function in all columns except the last column. See Figure 5-20.

**Figure 5-20** Total row functions

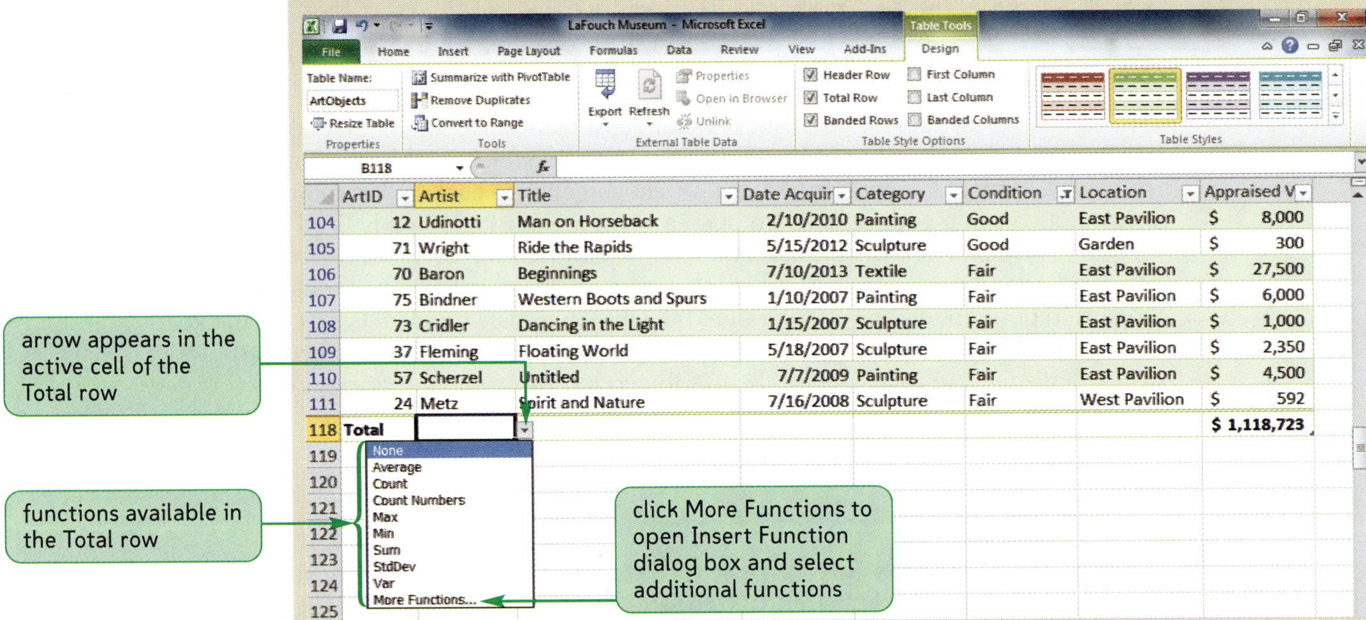


5. Click **Count**. The number 110, which is the number of records in the filtered ArtObjects table, appears in the cell. See Figure 5-21.

**Figure 5-21** Count of records in the filtered table

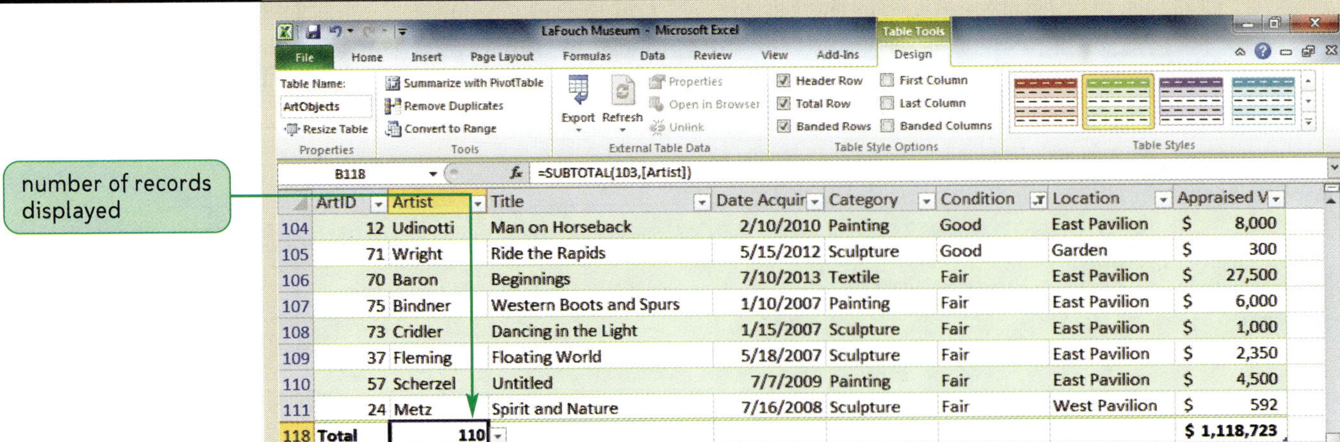

## Splitting the Worksheet Window into Panes

You can split the worksheet window into two or four separate panes. This allows you to easily view data from several areas of the worksheet at the same time. Each pane has its own scroll bars so you can navigate easily within one pane or display different parts of the worksheet. You can move between panes using the mouse. To create two panes, select a cell in row 1 or column A; to create four panes, select any other cell.

Mary wants to view the art collection summary totals at the same time she views the data on individual art objects. You will divide the worksheet into two horizontal panes to view the art object records in the top pane and the totals in the bottom pane.

### To split the Art Collection worksheet window into panes:

1. Press the **Ctrl+Home** keys to jump to the top of the table, and then click cell **A17**.
2. Click the **View** tab on the Ribbon, and then click the **Split** button in the Window group. The worksheet window splits into two panes. Each pane has its own set of scroll bars. See Figure 5-22.

**Figure 5-22** Worksheet split into two panes

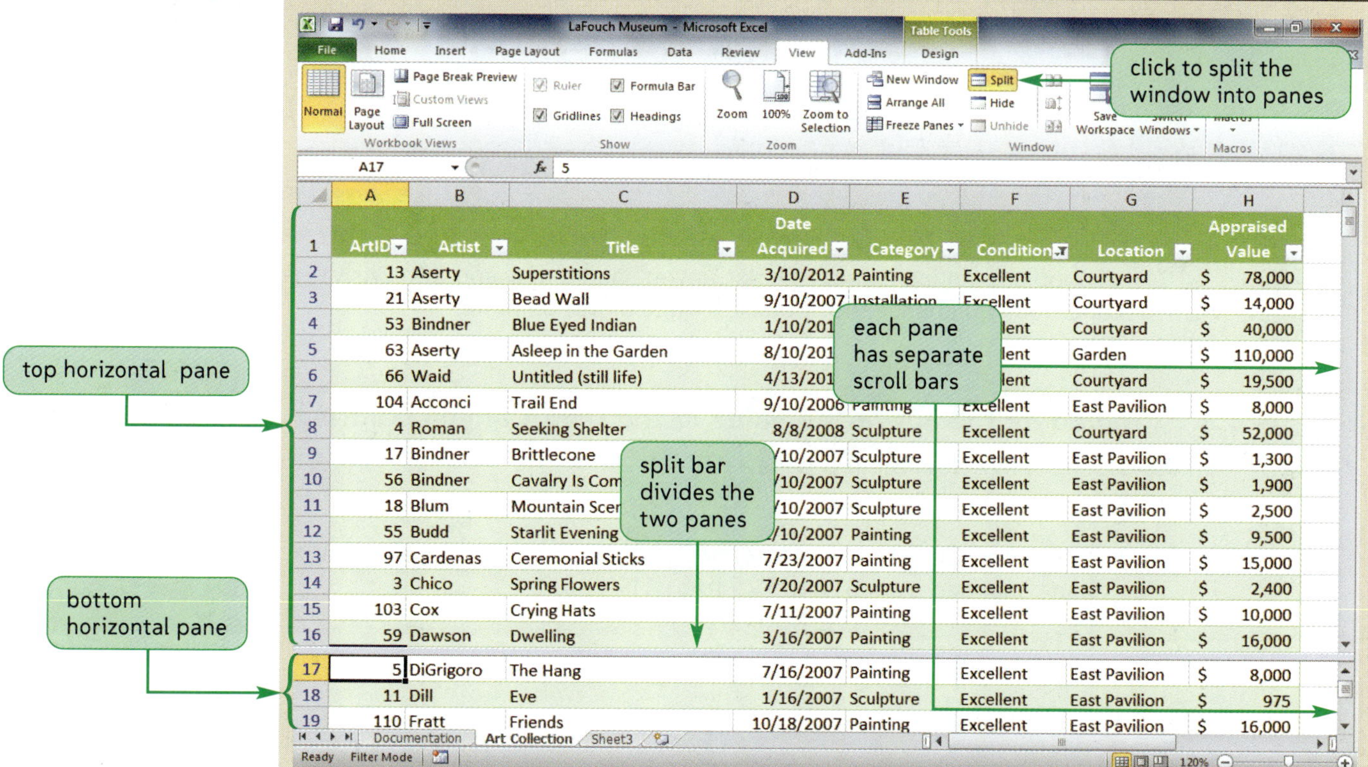


3. If necessary, click cell **A17** to activate the bottom pane.
4. Using the lower scroll bar, scroll down until row 118, the Total row, appears immediately below the split bar. See Figure 5-23.

**Figure 5-23** Total row displayed in the bottom pane

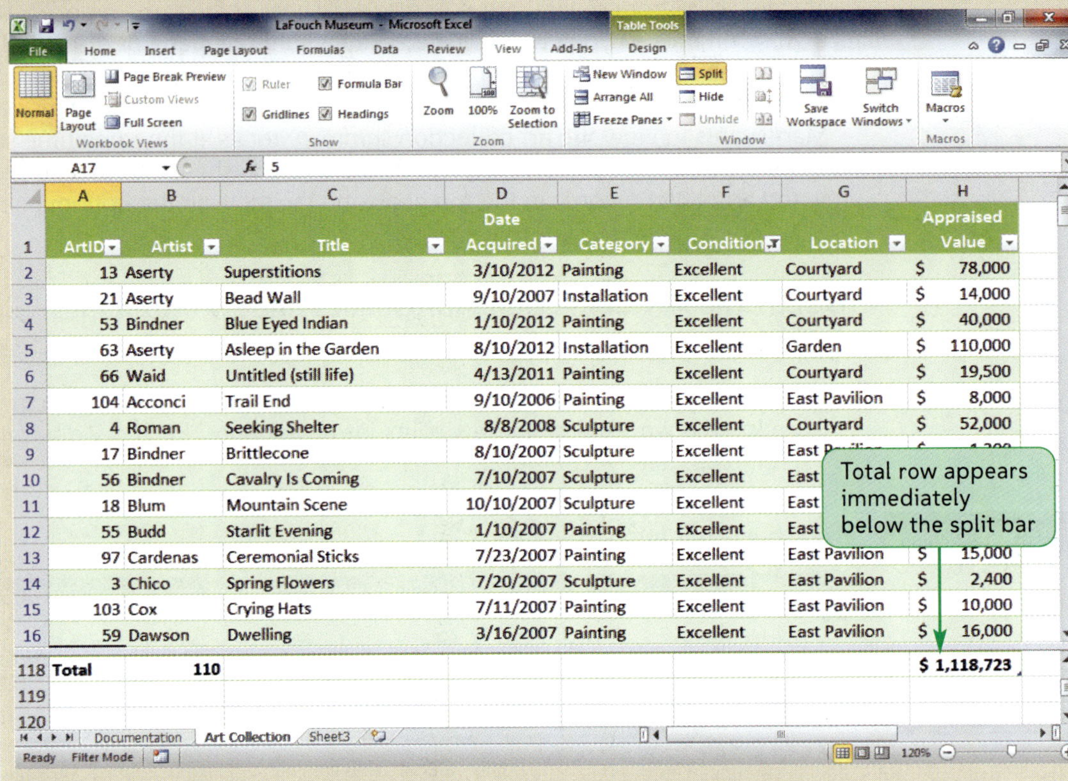


A popular painting named "Dark Canyon" had a new appraisal. Its value is now $8,000. You will change the appraised value of this painting.

### To update the appraised value of the Dark Canyon painting:

1. Click any cell in the top pane.
2. Use the Find command to locate the art object with ArtID **113**.
3. In the Appraised Value cell, enter **8000**. The total appraised value in the bottom pane changed from $1,118,723 to $1,119,223.

Next, you will remove the split panes from the worksheet window.

### To remove the split panes from the Art Collection worksheet window:

1. If necessary, click the **View** tab on the Ribbon.
2. In the Window group, click the **Split** button. The split bar is removed, and the worksheet is again a single window.

**TIP**

You can also double-click the split bar to remove the panes.

Now, you will remove the Total row and clear the filter.

**To remove the Total row and clear the filter from the ArtObjects table:**

1. Click the **Table Tools Design** tab on the Ribbon.
2. In the Table Style Options group, click the **Total Row** check box to remove the check mark. The Total row is no longer visible.
3. Click the **Condition filter arrow**, and then click **Clear Filter From "Condition"**. The ArtObjects table displays all the art objects.
4. Press the **Ctrl+Home** keys to return to cell A1.

**TIP**

If you redisplay the Total row, the functions you last used will appear even after you save, close, and then reopen the file.

The board of directors asked Mary to create a report that shows all the museum's art objects sorted by Category with the total appraised value of the art objects in each category. The board also wants to see the total appraised value for each category after the last item of that category. Although you could use the Total row in the Excel table to calculate the results, you would need to filter, total, and print the data for each category separately. A faster way to provide the information Mary needs is to use the Subtotal command.

## Inserting Subtotals

You can summarize data in a range by inserting subtotals. The Subtotal command offers many kinds of summary information, including counts, sums, averages, minimums, and maximums. The Subtotal command inserts a subtotal row into the range for each group of data and adds a grand total row below the last row of data. Because Excel inserts subtotals whenever the value in a specified field changes, you need to sort the data so that records with the same value in a specified field are grouped together *before* you use the Subtotal command. The Subtotal command cannot be used in an Excel table, so you must first convert the Excel table to a range.

REFERENCE

*Calculating Subtotals for a Range of Data*

- Sort the data by the column for which you want a subtotal.
- If the data is in an Excel table, in the Tools group on the Table Tools Design tab, click the Convert to Range button, and then click the Yes button to convert the Excel table to a range.
- In the Outline group on the Data tab, click the Subtotal button.
- Click the At each change in arrow, and then click the column that contains the group you want to subtotal.
- Click the Use function arrow, and then click the function you want to use to summarize the data.
- In the Add subtotal to box, click the check box for each column that contains the values you want to summarize.
- To calculate another category of subtotals, click the Replace current subtotals check box to remove the check mark, and then repeat the previous three steps.
- Click the OK button.

To produce the results Mary needs, you will sort the art objects by category and calculate subtotals in the Appraised Value column for each category grouping. You will also convert the Excel table to a normal range.

**TIP**

Be sure to sort the table and then convert the table to a range before calculating subtotals.

## To sort the art objects and convert the table to a range:

1. Click the **Category filter arrow**, and then click **Sort A to Z** on the AutoFilter menu. The ArtObjects table is sorted in ascending order by the Category field. This ensures one subtotal is created for each category.
2. In the Tools group on the Table Tools Design tab, click the **Convert to Range** button. A dialog box opens, asking if you want to convert the table to a normal range.
3. Click the **Yes** button. The Excel table is converted to a range. You can tell this because the filter arrows and the Table Tools Design tab disappear, and the Home tab on the Ribbon is selected.

Next, you'll calculate the subtotals.

## To calculate appraised values subtotals for each category of art object:

1. Click the **Data** tab on the Ribbon, and then, in the Outline group, click the **Subtotal** button. The Subtotal dialog box opens. See Figure 5-24.

**Figure 5-24** Subtotal dialog box

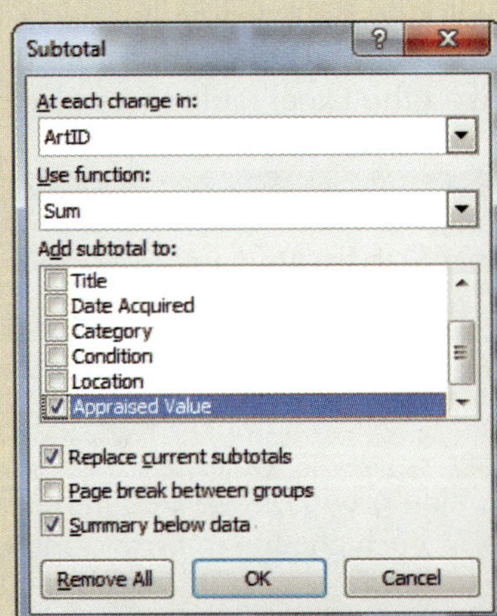


2. Click the **At each change in** arrow, and then click **Category**. This is the column you want Excel to use to determine where to insert the subtotals; it's the column you sorted. A subtotal will be calculated at every change in the Category value.
3. If necessary, click the **Use function** arrow, and then click **Sum**. The Use function list provides several options for subtotaling data, including counts, averages, minimums, maximums, and products.

4. In the Add subtotal to list box, make sure only the **Appraised Value** check box is checked. This specifies the Appraised Value field as the field to be subtotaled. If the data already included subtotals, you would check the Replace current subtotals check box to replace the existing subtotals or uncheck the option to display the new subtotals on separate rows above the existing subtotals. Because the data has no subtotals, it makes no difference whether you select this option.
5. Make sure the **Summary below data** check box is checked. This option places the subtotals below each group of data, instead of above the first entry in each group, and places the grand total at the end of the data, instead of at the top of the column just below the row of column headings.
6. Click the **OK** button. Excel inserts rows below each category group and displays the subtotals for the appraised value of each art category. A series of Outline buttons appears to the left of the worksheet so you can display or hide the detail rows within each subtotal.

   **Trouble?** If each item has a subtotal following it, you probably forgot to sort the data by Category. Click the Undo button on the Quick Access Toolbar, sort the data by Category, and then repeat Steps 1 through 6.
7. Scroll through the data to see the subtotals below each category and the grand total at the end of the data. See Figure 5-25.

**Figure 5-25** **Subtotals and grand total added to the art objects data**

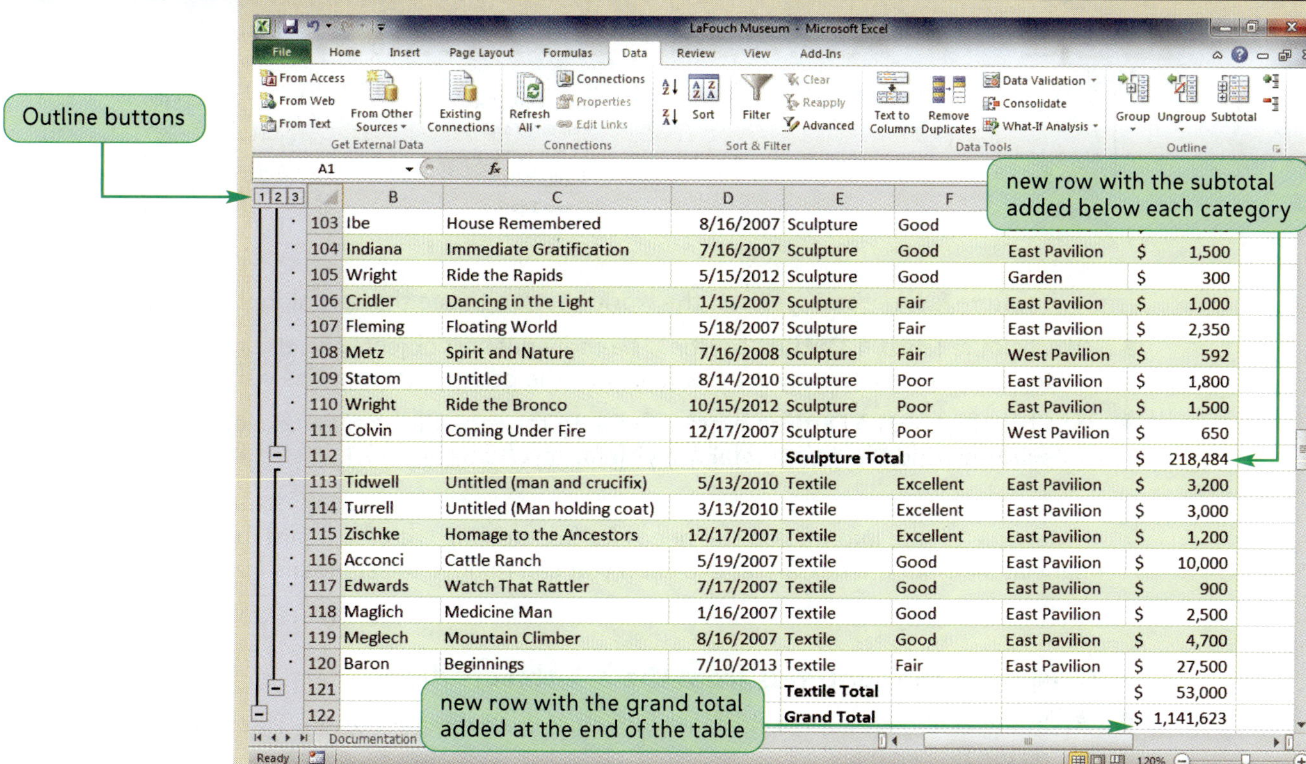


| | B | C | D | E | F | G | H |
|---|---|---|---|---|---|---|---|
| 103 | Ibe | House Remembered | 8/16/2007 | Sculpture | Good | | |
| 104 | Indiana | Immediate Gratification | 7/16/2007 | Sculpture | Good | East Pavilion | $ 1,500 |
| 105 | Wright | Ride the Rapids | 5/15/2012 | Sculpture | Good | Garden | $ 300 |
| 106 | Cridler | Dancing in the Light | 1/15/2007 | Sculpture | Fair | East Pavilion | $ 1,000 |
| 107 | Fleming | Floating World | 5/18/2007 | Sculpture | Fair | East Pavilion | $ 2,350 |
| 108 | Metz | Spirit and Nature | 7/16/2008 | Sculpture | Fair | West Pavilion | $ 592 |
| 109 | Statom | Untitled | 8/14/2010 | Sculpture | Poor | East Pavilion | $ 1,800 |
| 110 | Wright | Ride the Bronco | 10/15/2012 | Sculpture | Poor | East Pavilion | $ 1,500 |
| 111 | Colvin | Coming Under Fire | 12/17/2007 | Sculpture | Poor | West Pavilion | $ 650 |
| 112 | | | | **Sculpture Total** | | | $ 218,484 |
| 113 | Tidwell | Untitled (man and crucifix) | 5/13/2010 | Textile | Excellent | East Pavilion | $ 3,200 |
| 114 | Turrell | Untitled (Man holding coat) | 3/13/2010 | Textile | Excellent | East Pavilion | $ 3,000 |
| 115 | Zischke | Homage to the Ancestors | 12/17/2007 | Textile | Excellent | East Pavilion | $ 1,200 |
| 116 | Acconci | Cattle Ranch | 5/19/2007 | Textile | Good | East Pavilion | $ 10,000 |
| 117 | Edwards | Watch That Rattler | 7/17/2007 | Textile | Good | East Pavilion | $ 900 |
| 118 | Maglich | Medicine Man | 1/16/2007 | Textile | Good | East Pavilion | $ 2,500 |
| 119 | Meglech | Mountain Climber | 8/16/2007 | Textile | Good | East Pavilion | $ 4,700 |
| 120 | Baron | Beginnings | 7/10/2013 | Textile | Fair | East Pavilion | $ 27,500 |
| 121 | | | | **Textile Total** | | | $ 53,000 |
| 122 | | | | **Grand Total** | | | $ 1,141,623 |

## Using the Subtotal Outline View

In addition to displaying subtotals, the Subtotal feature "outlines" your worksheet so you can control the level of detail that is displayed. The three Outline buttons at the top of the outline area, as shown in Figure 5-25, allow you to show or hide different levels of detail in the worksheet. By default, the highest level is active; in this case, Level 3. Level 3 displays the most detail—the individual art object records, the subtotals, and the grand total. Level 2 displays the subtotals and the grand total, but not the individual records. Level 1 displays only the grand total.

The subtotals are useful, but Mary wants you to isolate the different subtotal sections so that she can focus on them individually. You will use the Outline buttons to prepare a report for Mary that includes only subtotals and the grand total.

### To use the Outline buttons to hide records:

1. Click the **Level 2 Outline** button, and then scroll up to view all the category subtotals, if necessary. The individual art object records are hidden, and you see only the subtotals for each category and the grand total. See Figure 5-26.

**Figure 5-26** Table displaying only subtotals and grand total

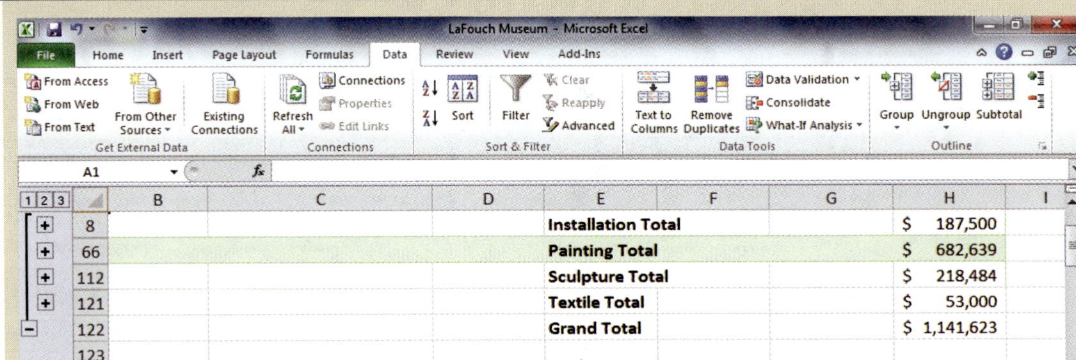


**Trouble?** If necessary, scroll the worksheet up to see the complete Level 2 list.

2. Click the **Level 1 Outline** button. The individual art object records and the subtotals for each category are hidden. Only the grand total remains visible.
3. Click the **Level 3 Outline** button. Scroll to the top. All the records along with the subtotals and the grand total are visible.

Mary has all the information she needs for her meeting with the board to review financial plans for the next fiscal cycle. So you can remove the subtotals from the data.

### To remove the subtotals from the art objects data:

1. In the Outline group on the Data tab, click the **Subtotal** button. The Subtotal dialog box opens.
2. Click the **Remove All** button. The subtotals are removed from the data, and only the records appear in the worksheet.

   You'll reset the art objects data as an Excel table.

3. Make sure the active cell is a cell within the structured range of data.

4. Click the **Insert** tab on the Ribbon, and then click the **Table** button in the Tables group. The Create Table dialog box opens.
5. Click the **OK** button to create the Excel table, and then click any cell in the table. The table structure is active.
6. In the Properties group on the Table Tools Design tab, type **ArtObjects** in the Table Name box, and then press the **Enter** key. The Excel table is again named "ArtObjects."

In this session, you filtered the table data and determined totals and subtotals for the data. Mary needs to generate information for a board meeting about the appraised values of the museum's art objects. You will work with PivotTables and PivotCharts in the next session to gather the information that Mary needs.

REVIEW

## *Session 5.2 Quick Check*

1. Explain the relationship between the Sort and Subtotal commands.
2. An Excel table includes records for 500 employees. What can you use to calculate the average salary of employees in the finance department?
3. How can you display a list of marketing majors with a GPA of 3.0 or greater from an Excel table with records for 300 students?
4. After you display subtotals, how can you change the amount of detail displayed?
5. True or False. The COUNT function is a valid subtotal function when using the Subtotal command.
6. An Excel table of Major League Baseball players includes the column Position (pitchers, catchers, infielders, outfielders, and so forth). What feature can you use to display only pitchers and catchers in the table?
7. If you have a list of employees that includes fields for gender and salary, among others, how can you determine the average salary for females using the Total row feature?

# SESSION 5.3 VISUAL OVERVIEW

A **PivotTable** is an interactive table used to group and summarize either a range of data or an Excel table into a concise, tabular format for easier reporting and analysis.

This PivotTable uses the data from the Location field as row labels.

You can add many levels of subtotals and totals to a PivotTable.

**Values fields** are the fields that contain summary data in a PivotTable. This PivotTable uses the total of the Appraised Value as the values field.

A **PivotChart** is a graphical representation of the data in a PivotTable.

Button to filter the PivotChart.

This PivotTable uses the data from the Category field as column labels.

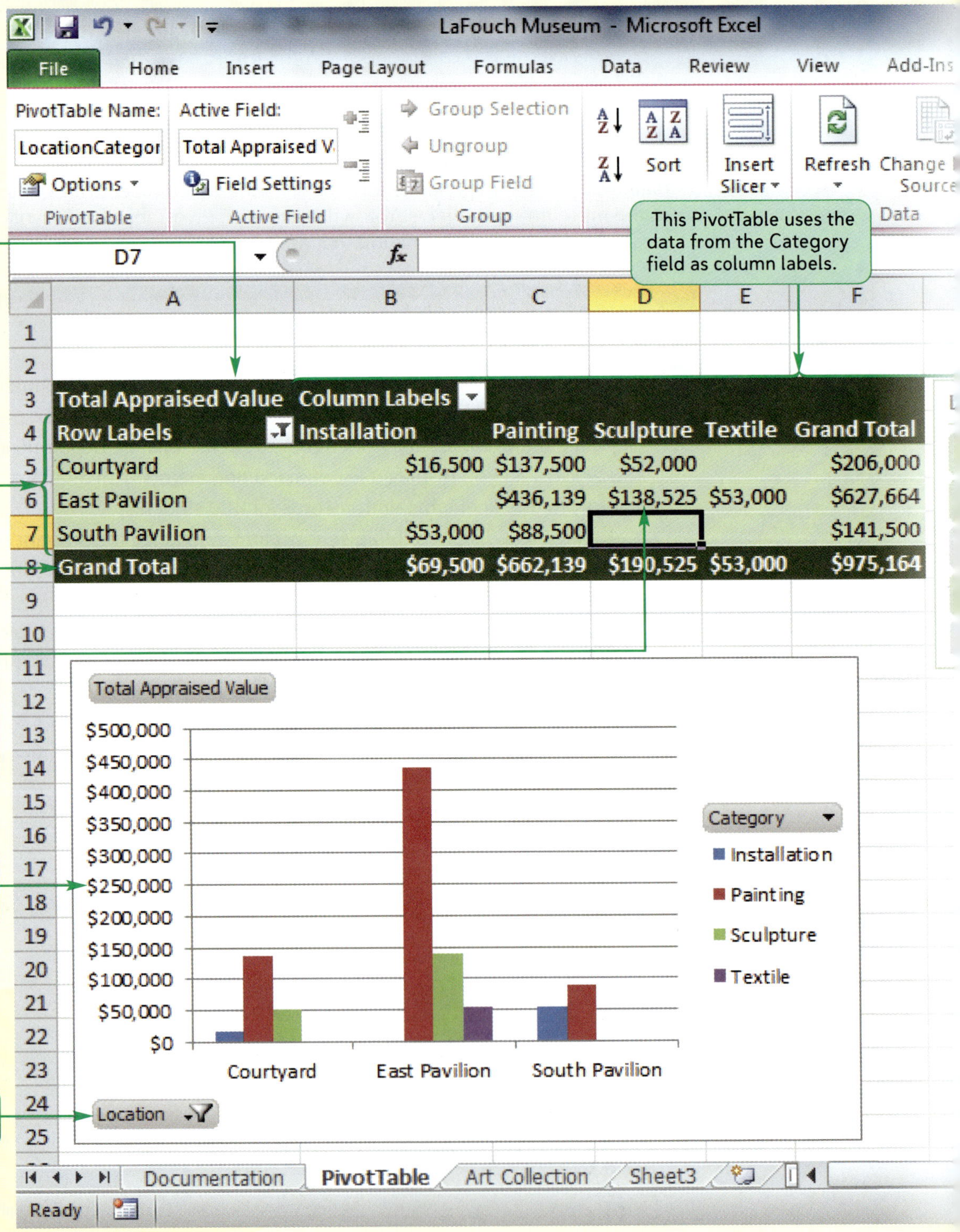

# PIVOTTABLE AND PIVOTCHART

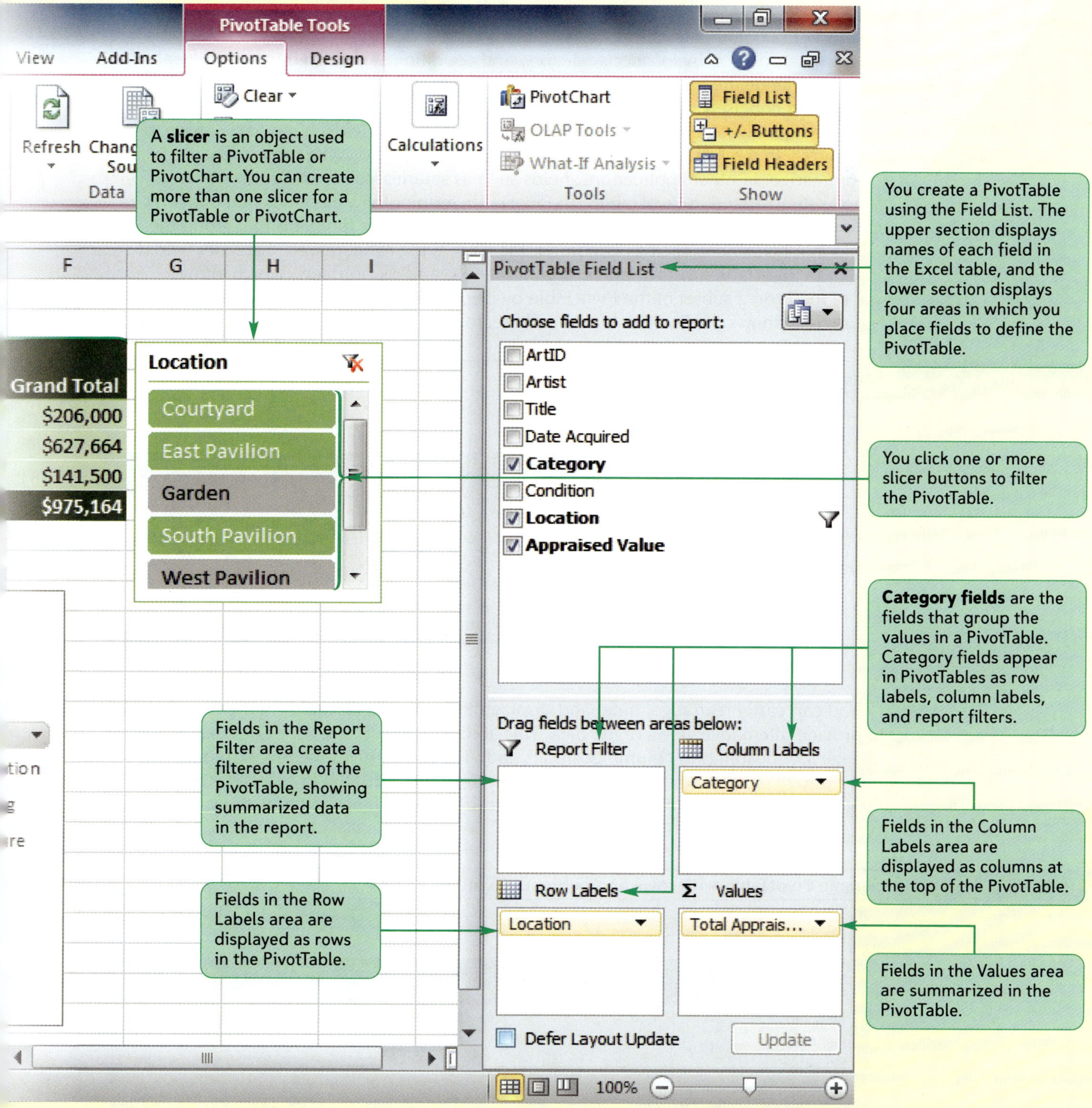

# Analyzing Data with PivotTables

An Excel table can contain a wealth of information. However, the large amounts of detailed data it contains often make it difficult to form a clear, overall view of that information. You can use a PivotTable to help organize the data into a meaningful summary. A PivotTable summarizes data into categories using functions such as COUNT, SUM, AVERAGE, MAX, and MIN. For example, Mary is preparing a presentation for the museum's board of directors that will include a report of the appraised value of the museum's art objects by location, category, and condition. Although there are several ways to generate the information Mary needs, a PivotTable can generate this information quickly and concisely.

To create a PivotTable report, you need to specify which fields in the data source to summarize. In the ArtObjects table, the Appraised Value field is the most likely field to summarize. In other applications, fields such as salaries, sales, and costs are frequently summarized in PivotTables. In PivotTable terminology, the fields that contain summary data are known as values fields. Category fields are the fields that group the values in a PivotTable, such as condition, location, and year acquired. Category fields appear in PivotTables as row labels, column labels, and report filters, which allows you to focus on a subset of the PivotTable by displaying one, several, or all items. Figure 5-27 shows the PivotTable you will create.

**Figure 5-27 Sample PivotTable**

| | A | B | C | D | E | F |
|---|---|---|---|---|---|---|
| 2 | | | | | | |
| 3 | Total Appraised Value | | | | | |
| 4 | | Installation | Painting | Sculpture | Textile | Grand Total |
| 5 | East Pavilion | | $436,639 | $141,525 | $53,000 | $631,164 |
| 6 | Courtyard | $16,500 | $137,500 | $52,000 | | $206,000 |
| 7 | Garden | $118,000 | | $24,100 | | $142,100 |
| 8 | South Pavilion | $53,000 | $88,500 | | | $141,500 |
| 9 | West Pavilion | | $20,000 | $3,859 | | $23,859 |
| 10 | Grand Total | $187,500 | $682,639 | $221,484 | $53,000 | $1,144,623 |

You can easily rearrange, hide, and display different category fields in the PivotTable to provide alternative views of the data. This ability to "pivot" the table—for example, change row headings to column positions and vice versa—gives the PivotTable its name and makes it a powerful analytical tool. In Figure 5-28, the PivotTable is rearranged so that the Category items appear as row labels and the Location items appear as column labels.

**Figure 5-28 Sample PivotTable with rows and columns pivoted**

| | A | B | C | D | E | F | G |
|---|---|---|---|---|---|---|---|
| 1 | | | | | | | |
| 2 | Total Appraised Value | | | | | | |
| 3 | | Courtyard | East Pavilion | Garden | South Pavilion | West Pavilion | Grand Total |
| 4 | Installation | $ 16,500 | | $ 118,000 | $ 53,000 | | $ 187,500 |
| 5 | Painting | $ 137,500 | $ 436,639 | | $ 88,500 | $ 20,000 | $ 682,639 |
| 6 | Sculpture | $ 52,000 | $ 141,525 | $ 24,100 | | $ 3,859 | $ 221,484 |
| 7 | Textile | | $ 53,000 | | | | $ 53,000 |
| 8 | Grand Total | $ 206,000 | $ 631,164 | $142,100 | $ 141,500 | $ 23,859 | $1,144,623 |

To conceptualize the layout of a PivotTable and convey your ideas to others who might implement them, a useful first step in creating a PivotTable is to sketch its layout. Mary's sketch, shown in Figure 5-29, illustrates the PivotTable you will create to show the appraised value of the art objects organized by location, category, and condition.

**Figure 5-29** **PivotTable sketch**

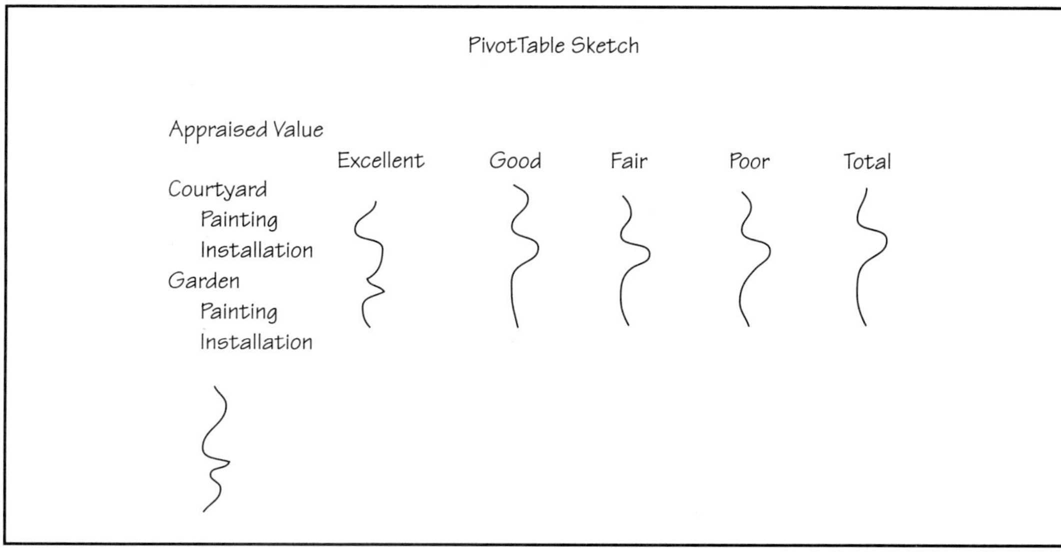


You are ready to create a PivotTable summarizing the total appraised value of art objects by location, category, and condition.

PROSKILLS

### *Written Communication: Summarizing Data with a PivotTable*

PivotTables are a great way to summarize data from selected fields of an Excel table or range, which can help you back up or support specific points in written documents. The PivotTable omits all the detailed data, enabling readers to focus on the bigger picture. This makes it easier for readers to understand the results and gain insights about the topic.

You can show summaries in written documents based on function results in PivotTables. The SUM function is probably the most frequently used function. For example, you might show the total sales for a region. However, you can use many other functions to summarize the data, including COUNT, AVERAGE, MIN, MAX, PRODUCT, COUNT NUMBERS, STDEV, STDEVP, VAR, and VARP. For example, you might show the average sales for a region, the minimum price of a product, or a count of the number of products sold.

When you write a report, you want supporting data to be presented in the way that best communicates your points. With PivotTables, you display the values in different views. For example, to compare one item to another item in the PivotTable, you can show the values as a percentage of a total. You can display the data in each row as a percentage of the total for the row. You can also display the data in each column as a percentage of the total for the column or display the data as a percentage of the grand total of all the data in the PivotTable. Viewing data as a percentage of the total is useful for analyses such as comparing product sales with total sales within a region or comparing expense categories to total expenses for the year

As you can see, PivotTables provide great flexibility in how you analyze and display data. This makes it easier to present data in a way that highlights and supports the points you are communicating, making your written documents much more effective.

## Creating a PivotTable

To create the PivotTable that will provide the information Mary needs, you will use the PivotTable dialog box to select the data to analyze and the location of the PivotTable report. Often when creating a PivotTable, you begin with data stored in a worksheet, although a PivotTable can also be created using data stored in an external database file such as one in Access. In this case, you will use the ArtObjects table to create the PivotTable and place the PivotTable in a new worksheet.

REFERENCE

*Creating a PivotTable*

- Click in the Excel table or select the range of data for the PivotTable.
- In the Tables group on the Insert tab, click the PivotTable button.
- Click the Select a table or range option button and verify the reference in the Table/Range box.
- Click the New Worksheet option button or click the Existing Worksheet option button and specify a cell.
- Click the OK button.
- Click the check boxes for the fields you want to add to the PivotTable (or drag fields to the appropriate box in the layout section).
- If needed, drag fields to different boxes in the layout section.

When you create a PivotTable, you need to specify where to find the data for the PivotTable. The data can be in an Excel table or range in the current workbook or an external data source such as an Access database file. You also specify whether to place the PivotTable in a new or an existing worksheet. If you place the PivotTable in an existing worksheet, you must also specify the cell in which you want the upper-left corner of the PivotTable to appear. For the appraised value PivotTable report, you will use the ArtObjects table and place the PivotTable in a new worksheet.

**TIP**

You can also create a PivotTable by clicking the Summarize with PivotTable button in the Tools group on the Table Tools Design tab.

### To create a PivotTable using the ArtObjects table:

1. If you took a break after the previous session, make sure the LaFouch Museum workbook is open, the Art Collection worksheet is active, and the Excel table is active.
2. Click the **Insert** tab on the Ribbon, and then, in the Tables group, click the **PivotTable** button. The Create PivotTable dialog box opens. See Figure 5-30.

**Figure 5-30 Create PivotTable dialog box**

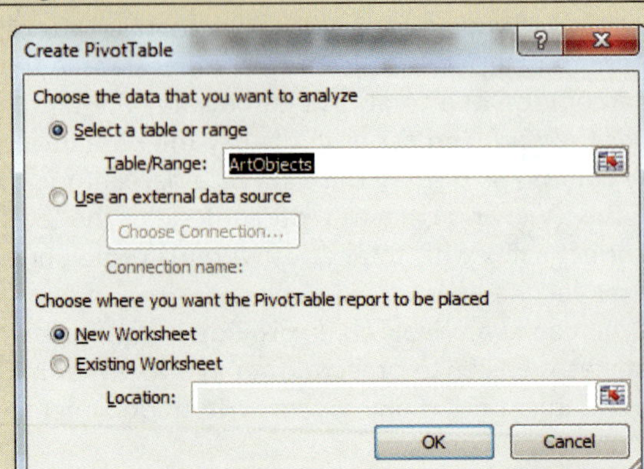

3. Make sure the **Select a table or range** option button is selected and **ArtObjects** appears in the Table/Range box.
4. Click the **New Worksheet** option button, if necessary. This sets the PivotTable report to be placed in a new worksheet.
5. Click the **OK** button. A new worksheet, Sheet1, is inserted to the left of the Art Collection worksheet. The empty PivotTable report area is where the finished PivotTable will be placed. You use the PivotTable Field List to build the PivotTable by adding, removing, and arranging fields, or columns. The PivotTable Tools contextual tabs appear on the Ribbon. See Figure 5-31.

**Figure 5-31** PivotTable report area and PivotTable Field List

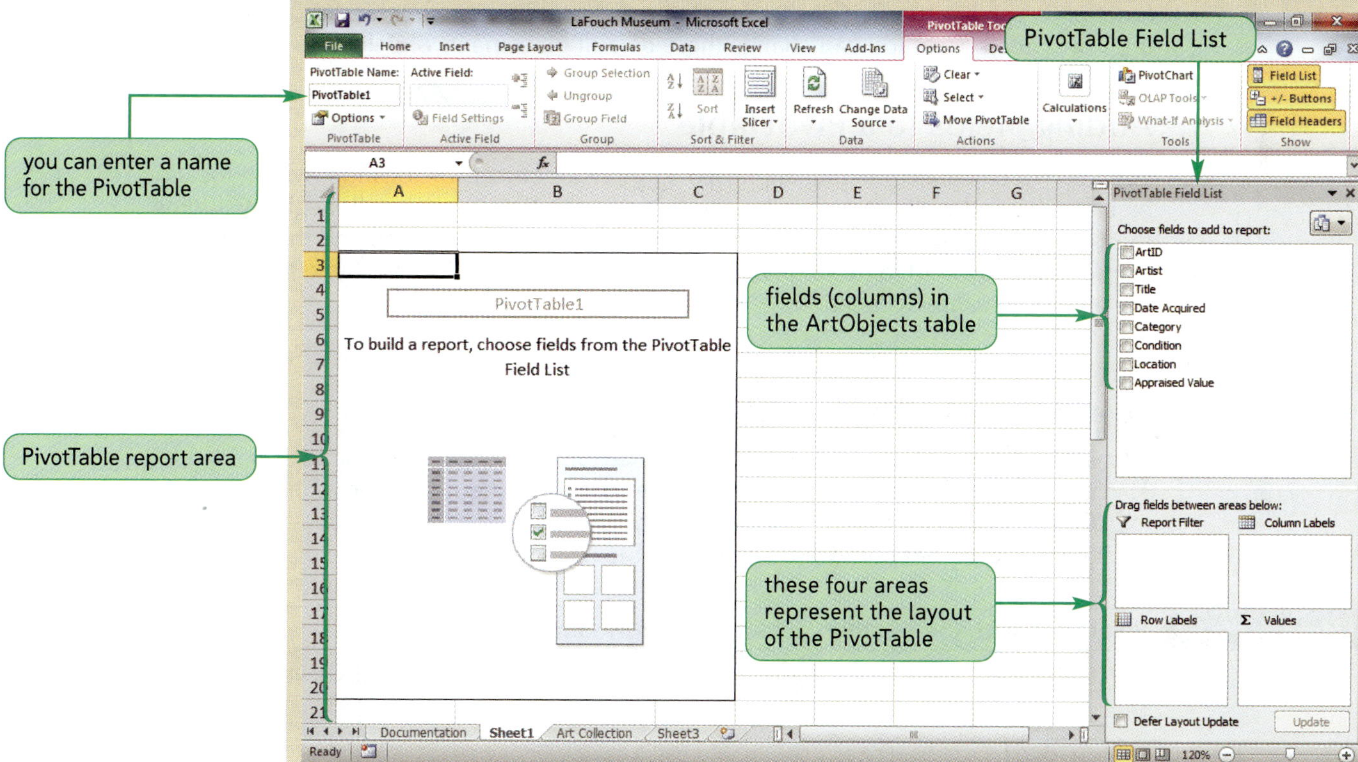


The PivotTable Field List is divided into two sections. The upper field list section displays the names of each field in the ArtObjects table. You check a field check box to add that field to the PivotTable. The lower layout section includes boxes for the four areas in which you can place fields: Report Filter, Row Labels, Column Labels, and Values. Figure 5-32 describes the function of each area.

**Figure 5-32** Layout areas for a PivotTable

| Layout Area | Description |
|---|---|
| Row Labels | The fields you want to display as the rows in the PivotTable. One row is displayed for each unique item in this area. You can have nested row fields. |
| Column Labels | The fields you want to display as columns at the top of the PivotTable. One column is displayed for each unique item in this area. You can have nested column fields. |
| Report Filter | A field used to filter the report by selecting one or more items, enabling you to display a subset of data in a PivotTable report. |
| Values | The fields you want to summarize. |

Initially, selected fields with numeric data are placed in the Values area and the SUM function is used to summarize the PivotTable. Fields with nonnumeric data are placed in the Row Labels area. You can change these default placements of fields.

## Adding Fields to a PivotTable

You need to calculate the total appraised value of art objects by location, within location by category, and within category by condition. In the PivotTable, you'll begin by adding the Location, Category, and Condition fields to appear as row labels, and the data in the Appraised Value field to be summarized. First, you will create a PivotTable summarizing the appraised value by location.

### To add fields to the PivotTable:

1. In the PivotTable Field List, click the **Location** check box. The Location field is added to the Row Labels box and the unique values in the Location field—Courtyard, East Pavilion, Garden, South Pavilion, and West Pavilion—appear in the PivotTable report area. See Figure 5-33.

**Figure 5-33** PivotTable with the Location field items as row labels

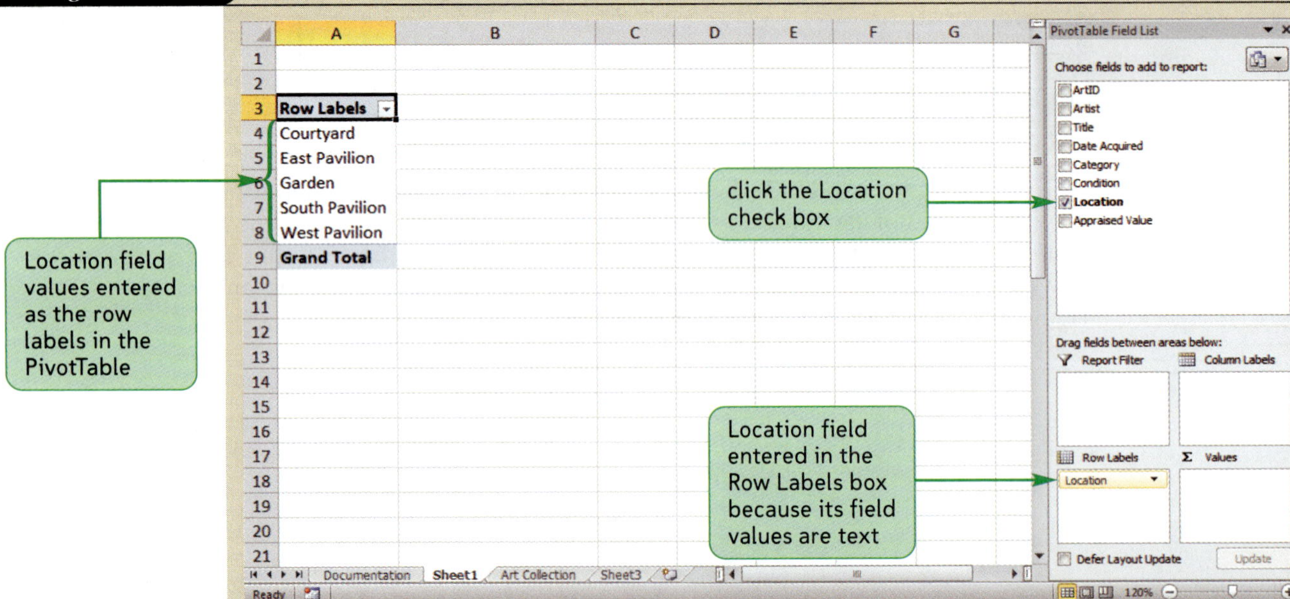

2. In the PivotTable Field List, click the **Appraised Value** check box. The Sum of Appraised Value button appears in the Values box. The PivotTable groups the items from the ArtObjects table by location, and calculates the total appraised value for each location. The grand total appears at the bottom of the PivotTable. See Figure 5-34.

**Figure 5-34 PivotTable of the appraised value of art objects by location**

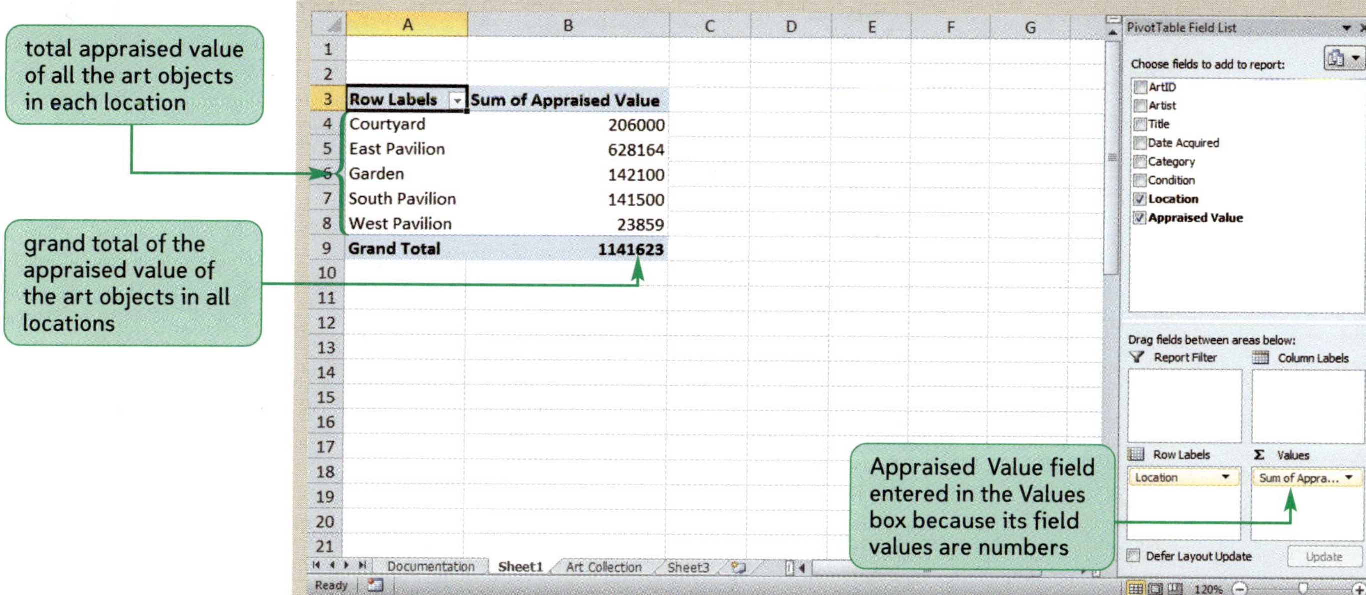


3. Rename the worksheet as **Appraised Value Summary**.

By default, the PivotTable report uses the SUM function for numbers in the Values area and the COUNT function for text and other nonnumeric values. If you want a different summary function, such as AVERAGE, MAX, or MIN, click the appropriate button in the Values box (in this case, the button is called "Sum of Appraised Value") in the PivotTable Field List, and then click Value Field Settings. The Value Field Settings dialog box opens. You can then select the type of calculation you want from the list of available functions, and then click the OK button.

Next, you'll add the Category and Condition fields to the PivotTable.

## To add the Category and Condition fields to the PivotTable:

1. In the PivotTable Field List, click the **Category** check box. The Category field appears in the Row Labels box below the Location field, and the unique items in the Category field are indented below each location field item in the PivotTable.

   **Trouble?** If the PivotTable Field List is not visible, the active cell is probably not in the PivotTable. Click any cell within the PivotTable to redisplay the PivotTable Field List.

2. In the PivotTable Field List, click the **Condition** check box. The Condition field appears in the Row Labels box below the Category field, and its unique items are indented below the Location and Category fields already in the PivotTable. See Figure 5-35.

**Figure 5-35** PivotTable with Location, Category, and Condition field items as row labels

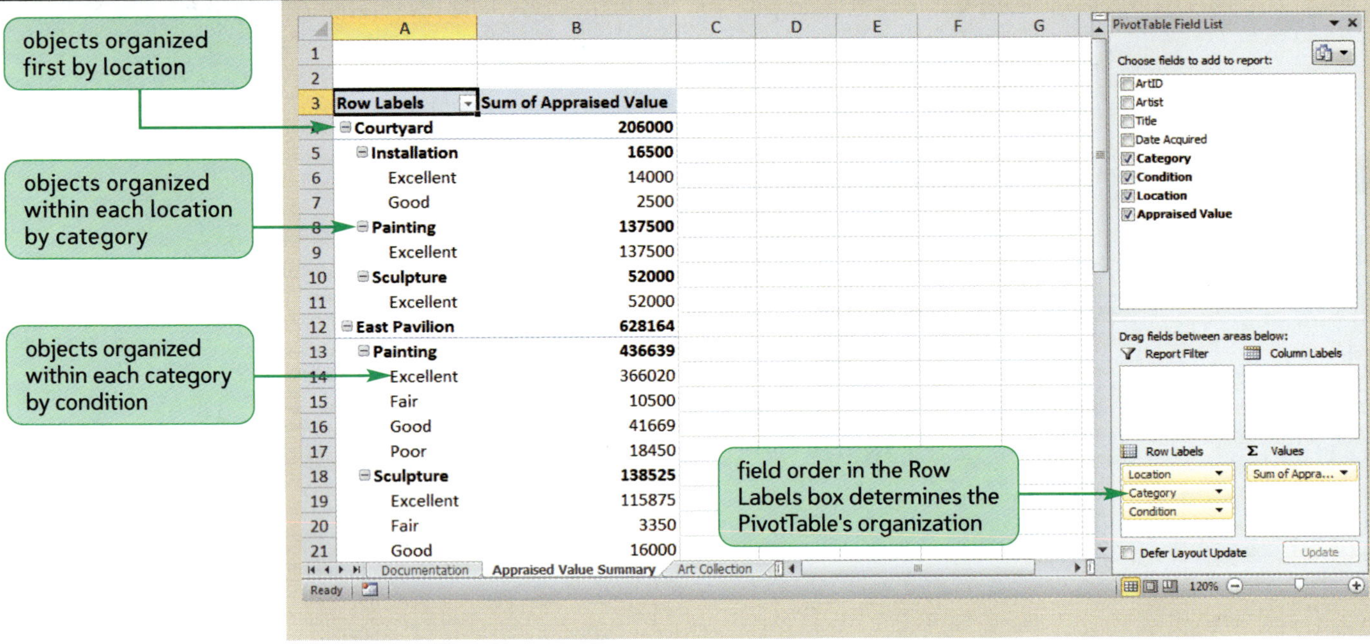


## Applying PivotTable Styles

As with worksheet cells and Excel tables, you can quickly format a PivotTable report using a preset style. You can choose from a gallery of PivotTable styles similar to the gallery of Table styles. You can point to any style in the gallery to see a Live Preview of the PivotTable with that style applied. You also can modify the appearance of PivotTables by adding or removing banded rows, banded columns, row headers, and column headers.

You will apply the Dark 4 style, which makes each group in the PivotTable stand out and subtotals in the report easier to find.

### To apply a PivotTable style to the PivotTable report:

1. Make sure the active cell is in the PivotTable, and then click the **PivotTable Tools Design** tab on the Ribbon.
2. In the PivotTable Styles group, click the **More** button to open the PivotTable Styles gallery.
3. Move the pointer over each style to see the Live Preview of the PivotTable report with that style.
4. Click the **Pivot Style Dark 4** style (the fourth style in the Dark section). The style is applied to the PivotTable.

## Formatting PivotTable Values Fields

Applying PivotTable styles does not change the numeric formatting in the PivotTable. Mary wants the numbers in the PivotTable to be quickly recognized as currency. You can format cells in a PivotTable the same way as you do cells in the worksheet. You'll change the total appraised values in the PivotTable to Currency style.

**To format the appraised value numbers in the PivotTable:**

1. Click any cell in the **Sum of Appraised Value** column of the PivotTable report.
2. Click the **PivotTable Tools Options** tab on the Ribbon, and then click the **Field Settings** button in the Active Field group. The Value Field Settings dialog box opens. See Figure 5-36.

Figure 5-36 **Value Field Settings dialog box**

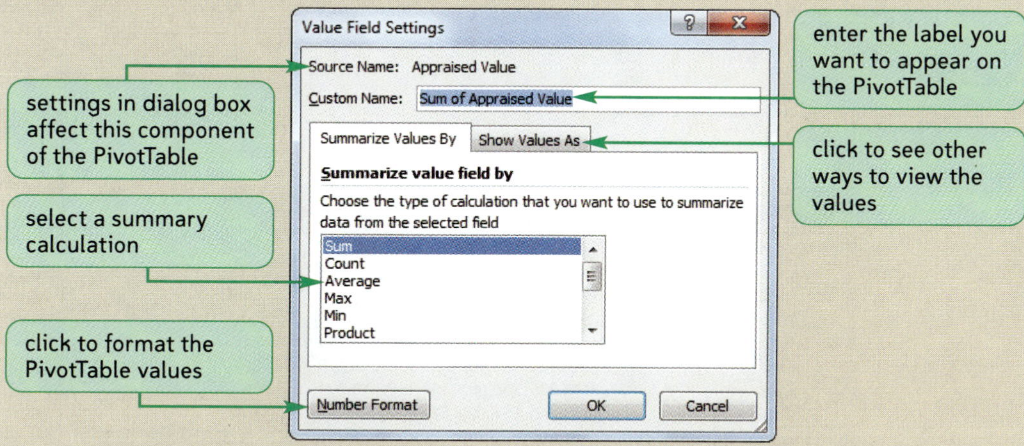


**TIP**

You can use the Summarize Values By tab to change the SUM function to a different summary function, such as AVERAGE. The name is updated to reflect your selection.

3. Click the **Number Format** button. The Format Cells dialog box opens. This is the same dialog box you've used before to format numbers in worksheet cells.
4. Click **Currency** in the Category box, and then type 0 in the Decimal places box.
5. Click the **OK** button. The numbers in the PivotTable will be formatted as currency with no decimal places.
6. In the **Custom Name** box, replace "Sum Of Appraised Value" with **Total Appraised Value**.
7. Click the **OK** button. The Value Field Settings dialog box closes, and the name used to describe the calculations in the PivotTable report is changed to the custom name you entered.

## Rearranging a PivotTable

You can add, remove, and rearrange fields to change the PivotTable's layout. Recall that the benefit of a PivotTable is that it summarizes large amounts of data into a readable format. After you create a PivotTable, you can view the same data in different ways. The PivotTable Field List enables you to change, or pivot, the view of the data in the PivotTable by dragging the field buttons to different areas in the layout section.

Refer back to Mary's PivotTable sketch in Figure 5-29. As illustrated in the sketch, the Condition field items should be positioned as column labels instead of row labels in the PivotTable. You'll move the Condition field now to produce the format Mary wants.

**To move the Condition field:**

1. In the layout section of the PivotTable Field List, locate the Condition field button in the Row Labels box.

2. Drag the **Condition** field button from the Row Labels box to the Column Labels box. The PivotTable is rearranged so that the Condition field is a column label instead of a row label. See Figure 5-37. Each time you make a change in the PivotTable Field List, the PivotTable layout is rearranged.

**Figure 5-37** PivotTable rearranged with Condition as a column label

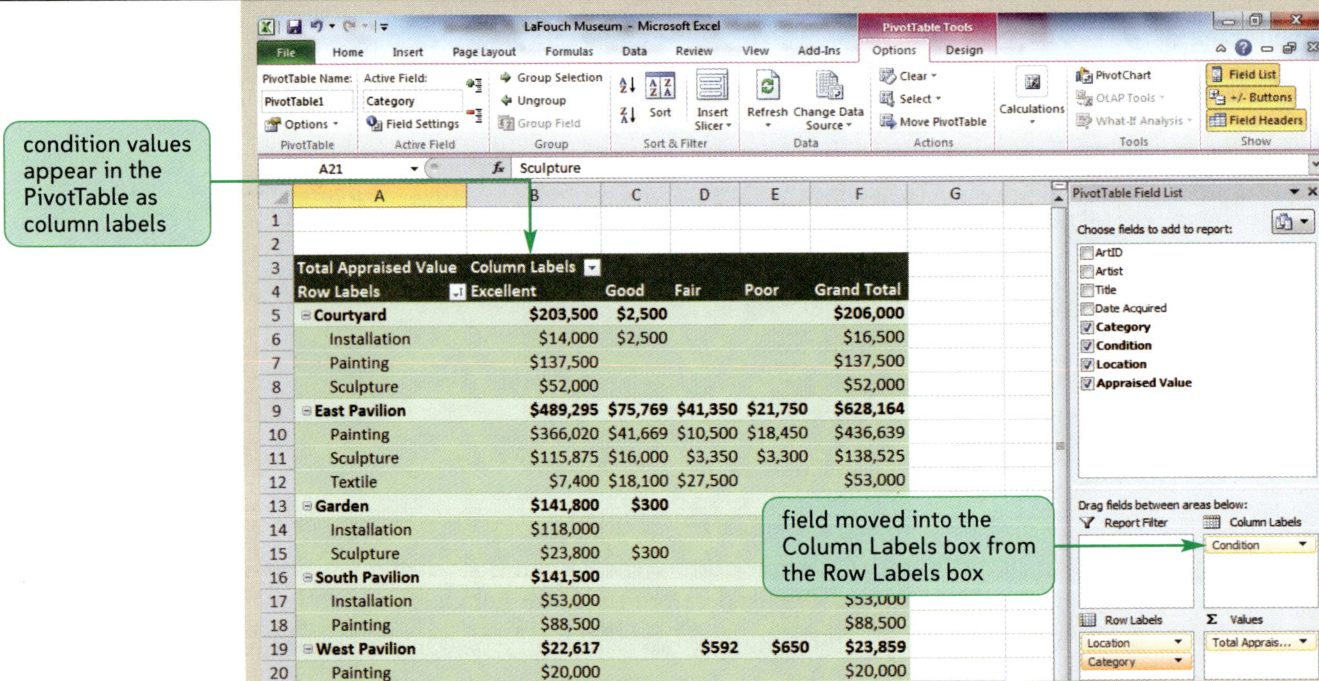


## Changing the PivotTable Report Layout Options

The Compact report layout, shown in Figure 5-37, places all fields from the row area in a single column and indents the items from each field below the outer fields. This is the default layout for PivotTable reports. You can choose two other layouts. In the Outline report layout, each field in the row area takes a column in the PivotTable. By default, the outline form shows the subtotals for each group at the top of every group. The Tabular report layout displays one column for each field and leaves space for column headers. A total for each group appears at the bottom of each group. You can find these report layout options on the PivotTable Tools Design tab in the Layout group.

You will see how the PivotTable looks in these alternative layouts.

### To display the PivotTable in Outline and Tabular layouts:

1. Click the **PivotTable Tools Design** tab on the Ribbon.
2. In the Layout group, click the **Report Layout** button, and then click **Show in Outline Form**. The PivotTable layout changes to the Outline report layout. See Figure 5-38.

**Figure 5-38** Outline PivotTable report layout

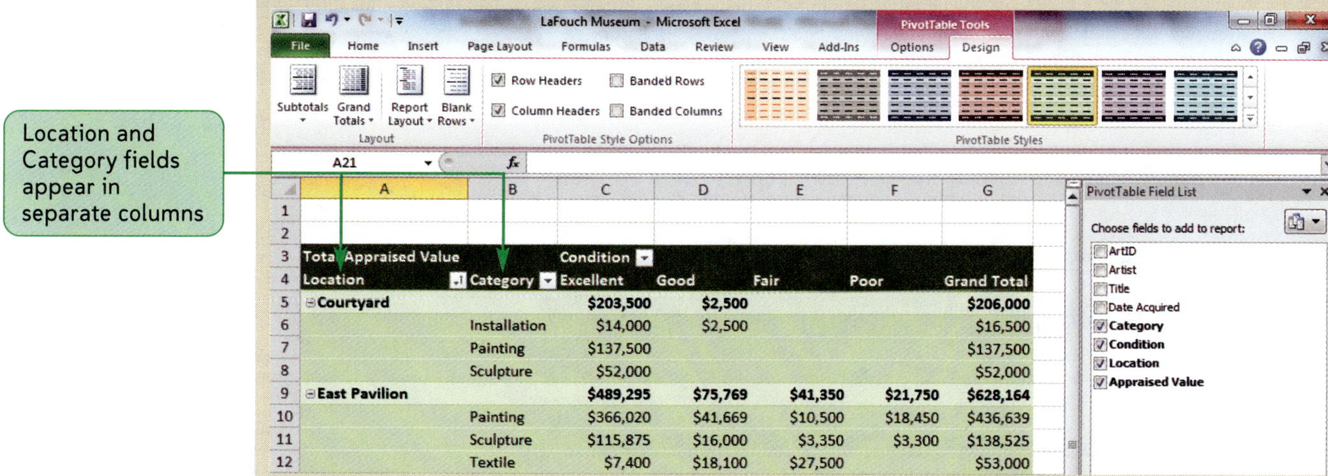


3. In the Layout group, click the **Report Layout** button, and then click **Show in Tabular Form**. The PivotTable layout changes to the Tabular report layout. See Figure 5-39.

**Figure 5-39** Tabular PivotTable report layout

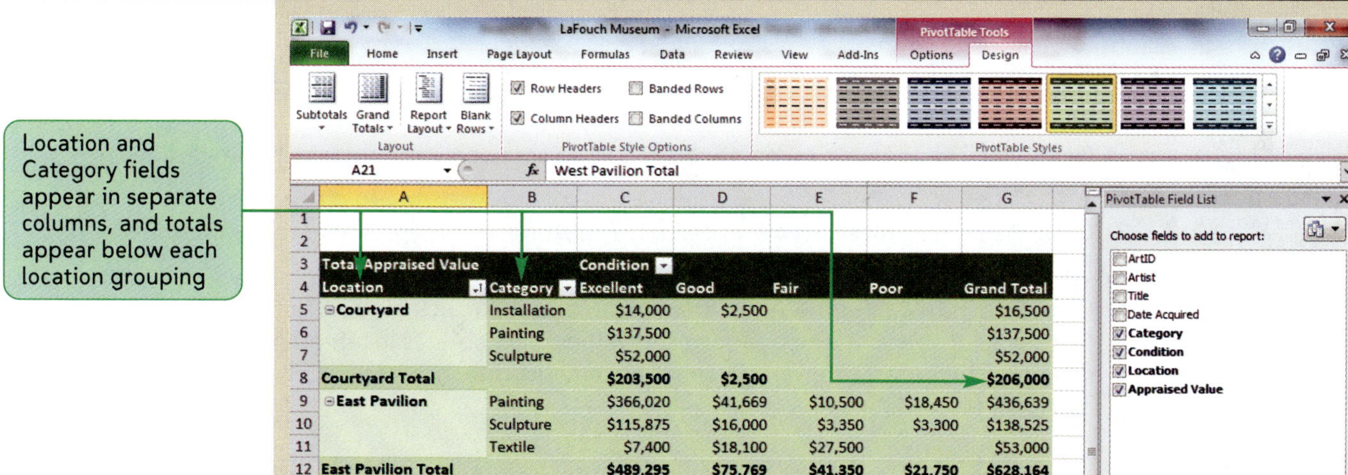


4. In the Layout group, click the **Report Layout** button, and then click **Show in Compact Form**. The PivotTable returns to the original layout, the Compact form.

## Adding a Report Filter to a PivotTable

You can drag a field to the Report Filter area to create a filtered view of the PivotTable report. A report filter is used to filter the PivotTable to display summarized data for one or more field items or all field items in the Report Filter area. For example, creating a report filter for the Location field allows you to view or print the total appraised value for all locations or for specific locations such as the Courtyard.

You will add a report filter for the Location field to see if displaying the information in this way adds value to the report.

### To add a report filter for the Location field:

1. In the PivotTable Field List, drag the **Location** button from the Row Labels box to the Report Filter box. The Report Filter field item shows "All" to indicate that the PivotTable report displays all the summarized data associated with the Location field. See Figure 5-40.

**Figure 5-40** **PivotTable with the Location report filter applied**

PivotTable shows all the values in the Location field

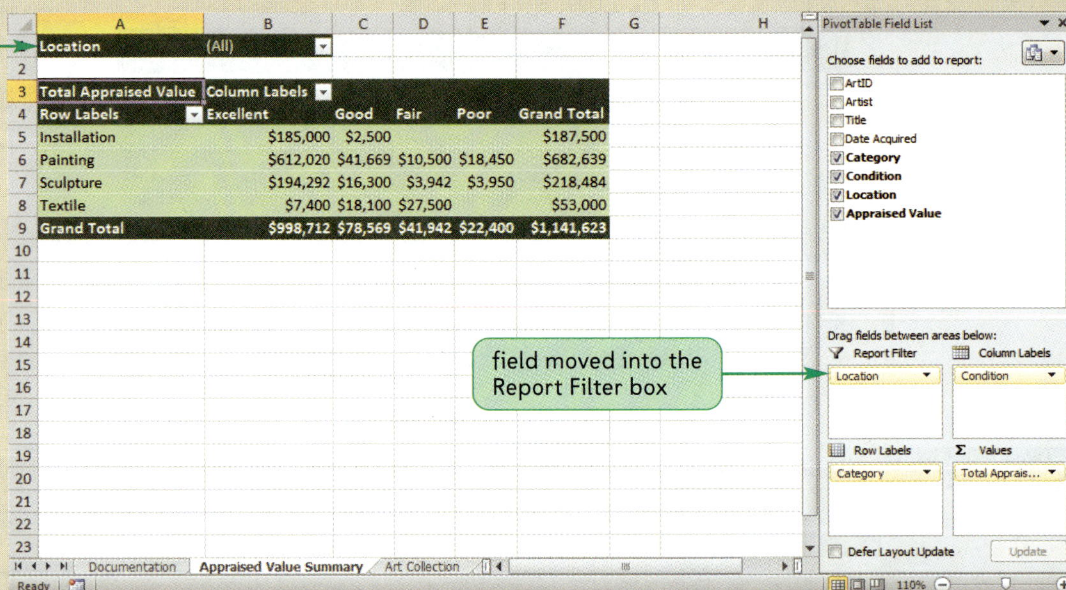


field moved into the Report Filter box

**TIP**

To filter more than one location at a time, click the Select Multiple Items check box in the AutoFilter menu to add a check mark next to each item, and then uncheck items you don't want to include.

Next, you'll change the summarized report to show only art objects in the East Pavilion.

2. Click the **report filter arrow** in cell B1. The AutoFilter menu opens, showing the field items displayed.
3. Click **East Pavilion** in the AutoFilter menu, and then click the **OK** button. The PivotTable displays the total appraised value of art objects located only in the East Pavilion. The report filter arrow changes to an icon to indicate the PivotTable is currently filtered. See Figure 5-41.

**Figure 5-41** **Report filter view for art objects in the East Pavilion**

filtered PivotTable shows the appraised values of art objects located in the East Pavilion

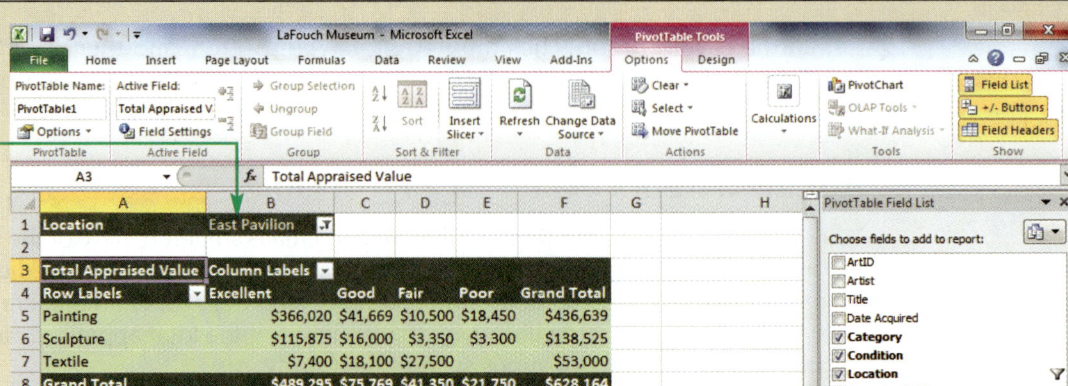

4. In the PivotTable Field List, drag the **Location** button from the Report Filter box to the top of the Row Labels box. The Location field is positioned above the Category field, and the PivotTable returns to its previous layout.

   **Trouble?** If the PivotTable report is arranged differently, the Location field is not the top field in the Row Labels box. Drag the Location button in the Row Labels box above the Category button.

## Filtering PivotTable Fields

Filtering a field lets you focus on a subset of items in that field. You can filter field items in the PivotTable by clicking the field arrow button in the PivotTable that represents the data you want to hide, and then uncheck the check box for each item you want to hide. To show hidden items, you click the field arrow button and check the check box for the item you want to show.

Mary wants to focus her analysis on art objects in excellent, good, and fair condition. She asks you to remove art objects in poor condition from the PivotTable. You will hide the art objects in poor condition from the PivotTable report.

### To filter the Condition field items from the PivotTable:

1. In the PivotTable, click the **Column Labels filter arrow**. The AutoFilter menu displays the list of items in the Condition field.
2. Click the **Poor** check box to remove the check mark. The Select All check box is deselected as well.
3. Click the **OK** button. The Poor column is removed from the PivotTable. The PivotTable includes only art objects in excellent, good, and fair condition. See Figure 5-42. You can show the hidden objects by clicking the Column Labels arrow and checking the Poor check box.

**Figure 5-42** PivotTable report filtered by condition

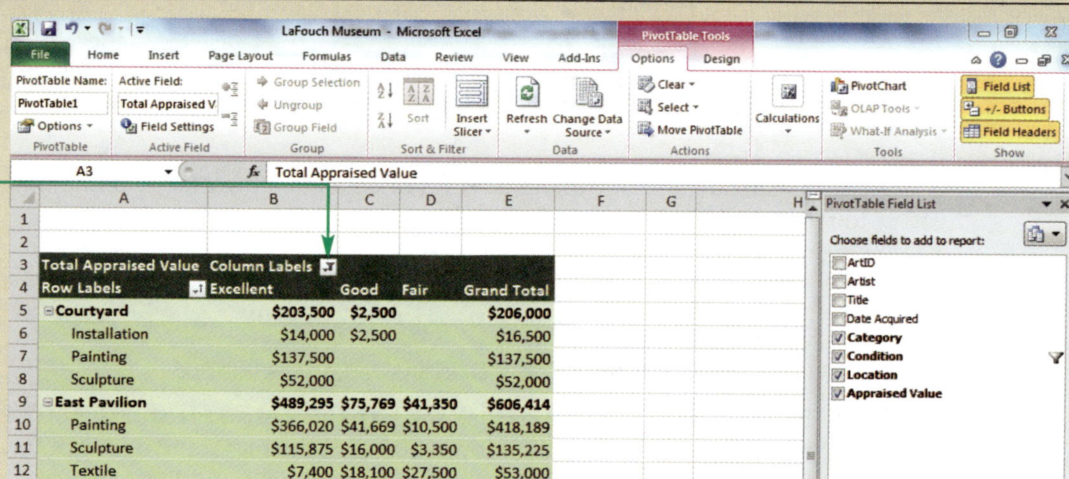


**TIP**

You can change the alignment of the column headings for better placement and readability.

## Collapsing and Expanding Items

You can expand and collapse items in the row labels of the PivotTable to view fields at different levels of detail. The Expand and Collapse buttons identify where more details exist. The Expand button [+] indicates you can show more details for that item, and the Collapse button [−] indicates you can hide details for that item. The lowest level of the hierarchy does not have Expand and Collapse buttons because there is no data to expand or collapse. These buttons are helpful when you have complex PivotTables where you want to switch quickly between a detailed view and an overview.

Mary wants to see the total appraised value for each location without the Category items in the PivotTable. You will collapse the level of detail so that only the Location items are showing. Currently, all items are expanded.

### To collapse the Courtyard items in the PivotTable:

1. Point to the **Collapse** button [−] next to Courtyard until the pointer changes to the arrow pointer.
2. Click the **Collapse** button [−] next to Courtyard. The detail items below Courtyard are hidden, and the Collapse button changes to an Expand button.
3. Click the **Collapse** button [−] next to East Pavilion, Garden, South Pavilion, and West Pavilion. The details for these four locations are hidden, and only the Location items are displayed. The PivotTable provides a higher level summary without displaying the Category details. See Figure 5-43.

**Figure 5-43** PivotTable with all locations collapsed and categories hidden

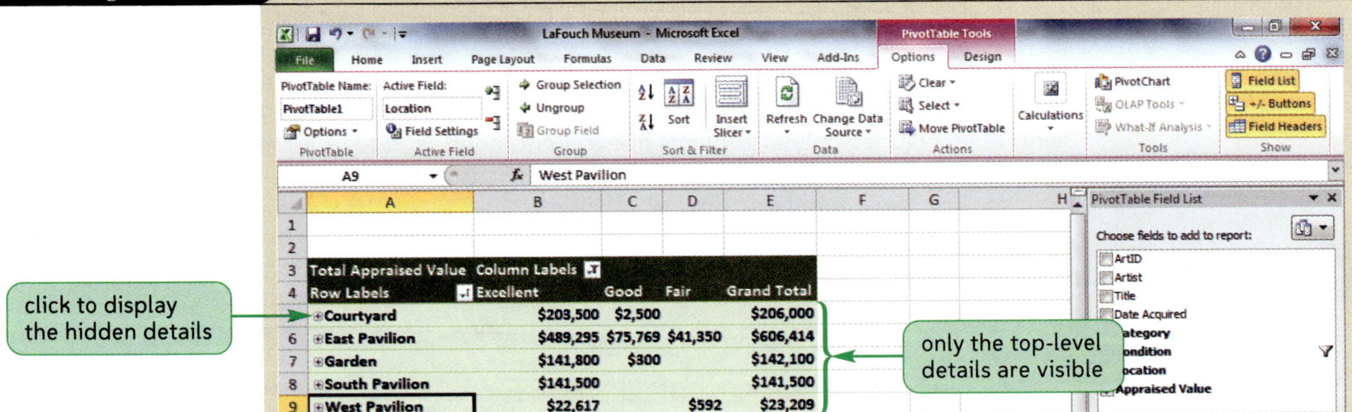


You can collapse or expand all level of detail in a PivotTable at one time. You'll do this to return to the original level of detail.

### To expand all items in the PivotTable:

1. Click the **PivotTable Tools Options** tab on the Ribbon.
2. In the Active Field group, click the **Expand Entire Field** button. The detail items for all levels reappear. The lowest level of the hierarchy does not have Expand and Collapse buttons.

## Sorting PivotTable Fields

You can sort a PivotTable field either by its own items—for example, alphabetizing fields such as Location and Category—or by the values in the body of the PivotTable. To sort a PivotTable field, you can use any of the Sort buttons on the Options tab to sort the information in a PivotTable report. These options are similar to the sort options you used earlier in the tutorial.

The PivotTable might be more informative if the appraised values in each location were sorted in descending order. You will sort the PivotTable so that the location with the highest total appraised value is displayed first.

### To sort the PivotTable:

1. Click cell **E5**, which contains the Grand Total for Courtyard. This is the field total you want to sort.
2. In the Sort & Filter group on the PivotTable Tools Options tab, click the **Sort Largest to Smallest** button. The Location field is sorted based on the total appraised value for each location. For example, the East Pavilion location appears first in the PivotTable because it has the highest total appraised value, $606,414. The Courtyard location appears next because it has the second highest total appraised value, $206,000, and so on. See Figure 5-44.

**Figure 5-44** PivotTable results sorted by location

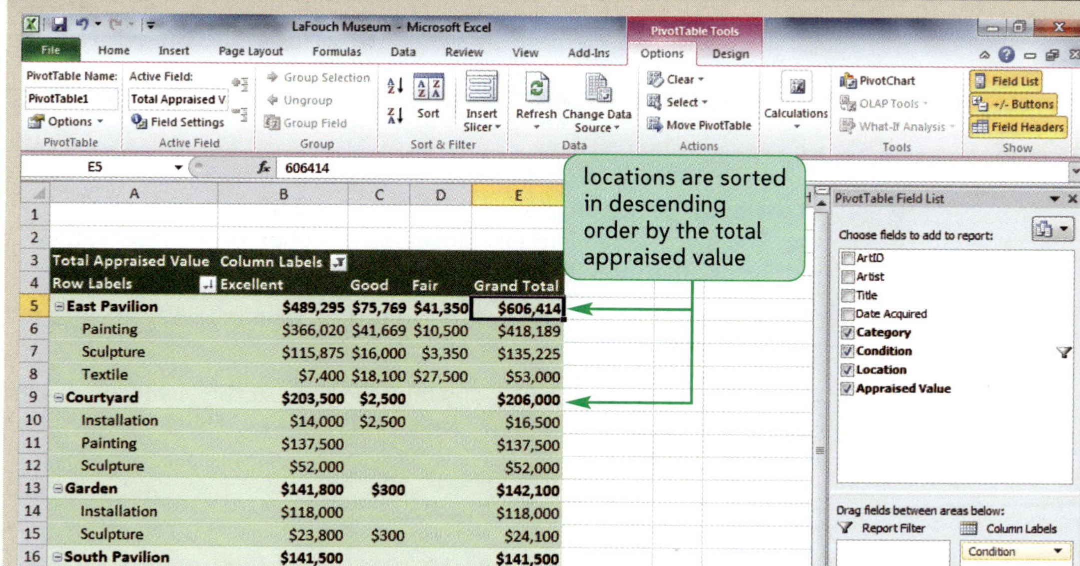


## Adding a Second Values Field to a PivotTable

You can expand a PivotTable to create a more informative table by adding fields to the Values layout area. For example, Mary believes that a more accurate presentation of the art objects would include the number of objects corresponding to the total value in each cell of the PivotTable. Adding the Title field to the Values box would count the number of art objects in each location-category-condition combination (because the title is a non-numeric field). You will add the Title field to the PivotTable.

### To add the Title field to the Values box:

1. In the PivotTable Field List, drag **Title** from the field area to immediately below the Total Appraised Value button in the Values box. The PivotTable displays the number of art objects as well as the total appraised value. The Values box in the layout area includes a second button, Count of Title, and fields from the Values box are added to the Column Labels box. See Figure 5-45.

**Figure 5-45** Count of art objects added to the PivotTable

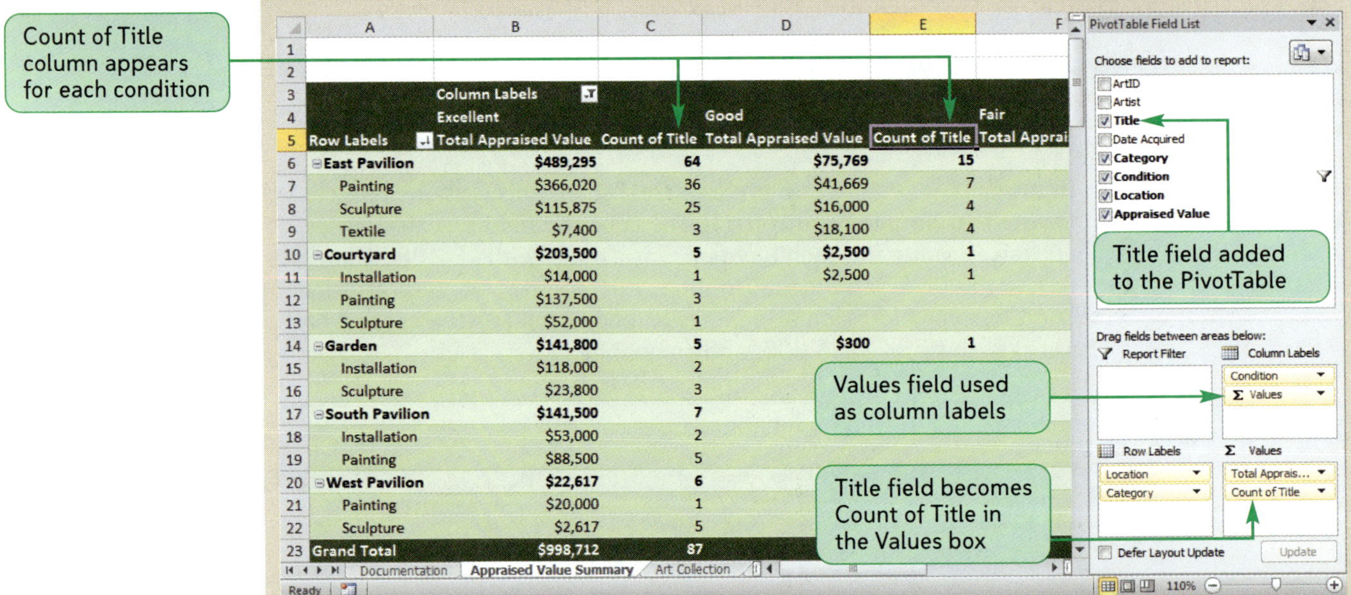


2. In the Show group on the PivotTable Tools Options tab, click the **Field List** button. The PivotTable Field List closes, so a section of the PivotTable is no longer hidden. More of the PivotTable is now visible.
3. In the PivotTable, click any of the **Count of Title** labels. You want to change the "Count of Title" label to "Count."
4. On the PivotTable Tools Options tab, click the **Active Field** box in the Active Field group, type **Count**, and then press the **Enter** key. The Count label replaces the Count of Title label.

## Removing a Field, Field Headers, and Buttons from a PivotTable

The PivotTable report with the Count column looks cluttered and is difficult to read. You will remove the Title field from the PivotTable. Removing a field from the PivotTable has no effect on the underlying Excel table.

### To remove the Title field from the PivotTable:

1. In the Show group on the PivotTable Tools Options tab, click the **Field List** button to display the PivotTable Field List.
2. In the PivotTable Field List, click the **Title** check box in the field area. The Count column is removed from the PivotTable, which returns to its previous layout. The Title field is still in the ArtObjects table.

The PivotTable is almost complete. Mary wants you to improve the appearance of the PivotTable by removing the field headers (Row Labels and Column Labels) and hiding the Expand/Collapse buttons.

### To remove the field headers and hide the Expand/Collapse buttons:

1. In the Show group on the PivotTable Tools Options tab, click the **+/- Buttons** button. The Expand/Collapse buttons disappear from the PivotTable.
2. In the Show group, click the **Field Headers** button. The Column Labels and Row Labels headers are hidden. See Figure 5-46.

**Figure 5-46** **PivotTable without field headers and the Expand/Collapse buttons**

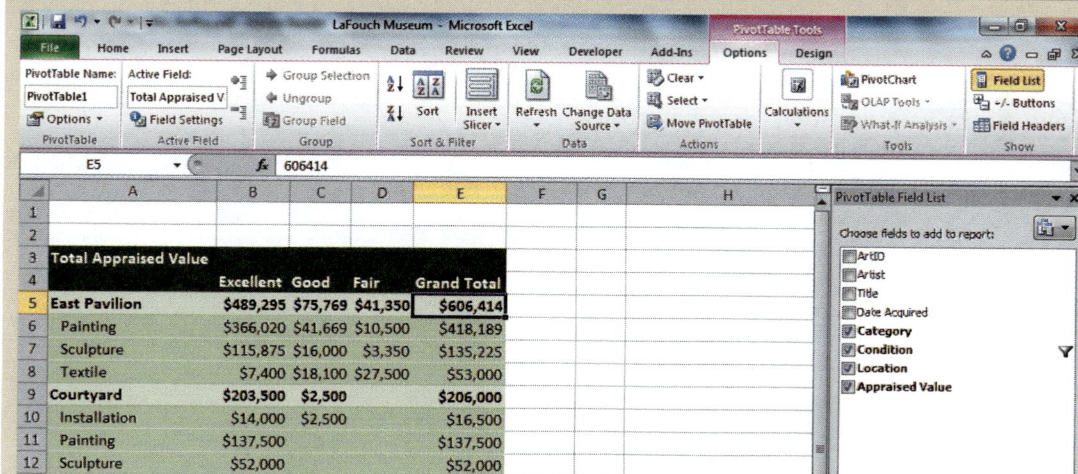


## Using a Slicer to Filter a PivotTable

Although you can filter a PivotTable using the report filter arrow, column label arrows, and row label arrows, a slicer provides a quicker and easier way to filter a PivotTable or PivotChart. You can create a slicer for any field in a range or an Excel table. Every slicer consists of an object that contains a button for each unique value in that field. You can format the slicer and its buttons, changing its style, height, and width. You also can create more than one slicer at a time. For example, you can have a slicer for Category that has a button for each unique category value and a second slicer for Condition. This allows you to filter a PivotTable report so that it displays the results for all paintings in Excellent or Good condition by clicking the corresponding slicer buttons.

You will add a Location slicer to the current PivotTable so that Mary can have more flexibility in making changes to the PivotTable.

### To add the Location slicer to the PivotTable:

1. In the Sort & Filter group on the PivotTable Tools Options tab, click the **Insert Slicer** button. The Insert Slicers dialog box opens, displaying a list of available PivotTable fields. You can select any or all of the fields.

2. Set the width of column F to **8**.
3. Click the **Location** check box to insert a check mark, and then click the **OK** button. The Location slicer control appears on the worksheet.
4. Drag the **Location slicer control** to the right of the PivotTable, placing its upper-left corner in cell G3.
5. If necessary, click the **Location** slicer to select the slicer object. The Slicer Tools Options tab appears on the Ribbon.
6. In the Size group on the Slicer Tools Options tab, change the height to **1.9"** and change the width to **1.3"**. The slicer object is resized, eliminating the extra space below the buttons and to the right of the labels.
7. In the Slicer Styles group, click the **More** button, and then click **Slicer Style Dark 3**. The slicer colors now match the PivotTable. See Figure 5-47.

**Figure 5-47** Location slicer control

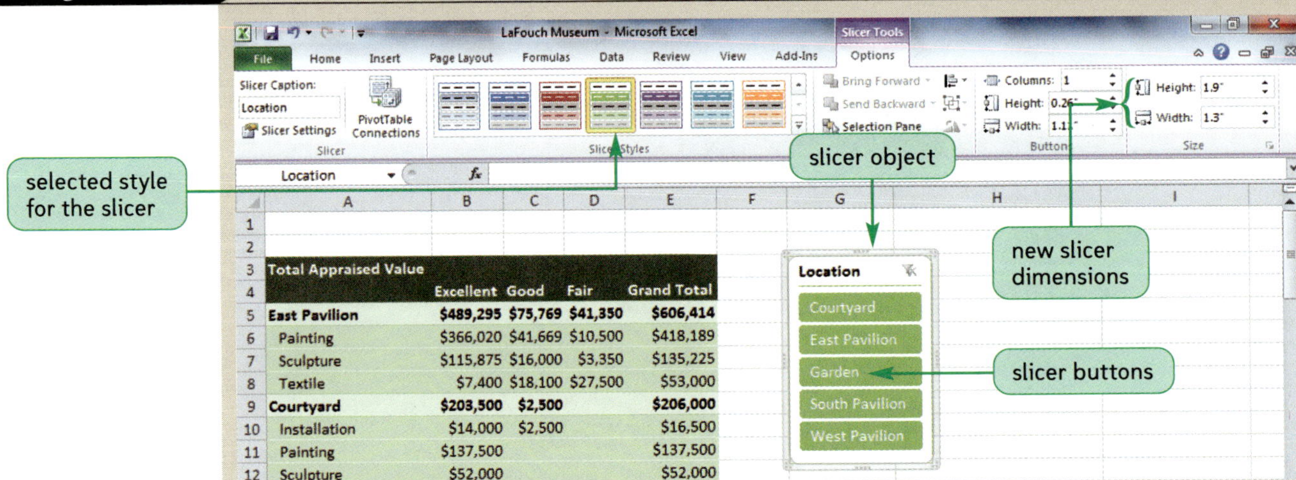


Mary wants you to display the results of the PivotTable for all the pavilion rooms—East, South, and West. You can do this quickly using the Location slicer.

### To filter the PivotTable using the Location slicer:

1. In the Location slicer control, click the **East Pavilion** button. The PivotTable is filtered to display only the results for the East Pavilion. The other slicer buttons are gray because those locations have been filtered and are not part of the report.
2. Press and hold the **Ctrl** key, click the **South Pavilion** button, and then release the Ctrl key. The South Pavilion data also appears in the PivotTable.
3. Press and hold the **Ctrl** key, click the **West Pavilion** button, and then release the Ctrl key. The West Pavilion data is added to the PivotTable. See Figure 5-48.

**Figure 5-48** Location slicer used to filter the PivotTable

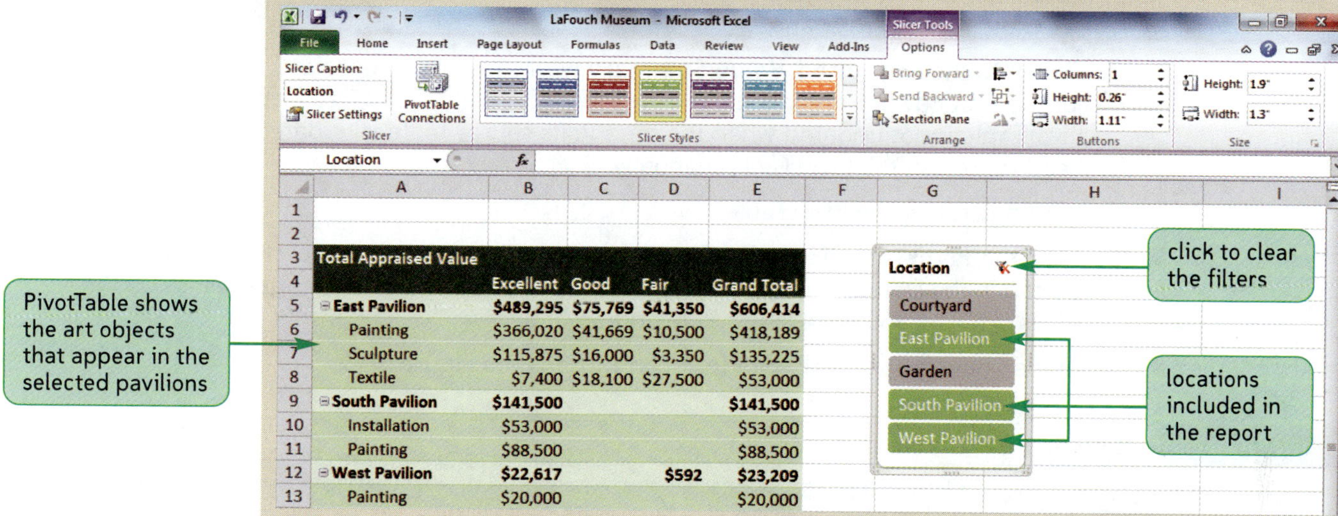


Next, you will remove all the filters so that Mary can view the PivotTable with all locations.

### To remove the filters from the PivotTable:

1. In the Location slicer, click the **Clear Filter** button. The filters are removed and all locations appear in the PivotTable.
2. In the Location slicer, notice that all the buttons are deselected, indicating that no filters are being used.

## Refreshing a PivotTable

The art object titled "Dancing in the Light" by Cridler has been reappraised and is now valued at $4,000 (not $1,000 as indicated in its current listing). You cannot change data directly in the PivotTable. Instead, you must edit the Excel table, and then **refresh**, or update, the PivotTable to reflect the updated data—in this case, the current state of the art objects list.

You'll edit the record for Dancing in the Light in the ArtObjects table. This sculpture is located in the East Pavilion and is in fair condition. This one change will affect the PivotTable in several locations. For example, currently the Total value of objects in the East Pavilion is $606,414; the sculptures in the East Pavilion are valued at $135,225; and sculptures in the East Pavilion in fair condition are valued at $3,350. After you update the appraised value of this art object in the Excel table, all these values in the PivotTable will increase by $3,000.

### To update the ArtObjects table:

1. Switch to the **Art Collection** worksheet, and then find **Cridler, Dancing in the Light** (ArtID 73).

2. Click the record's Appraised Value cell, and then enter **4000**. The sculpture's appraised value is updated in the table. You'll return to the PivotTable report to see the effect of this change.
3. Switch to the **Appraised Value Summary** worksheet. The appraised value totals for the East Pavilion are still $606,414, $135,225, and $3,350, respectively. The PivotTable is not updated when the data in its source table is updated, so you need to refresh the PivotTable manually.
4. Click any cell in the PivotTable.
5. Click the **PivotTable Tools Options** tab on the Ribbon, and then click the **Refresh** button in the Data group. The PivotTable report is updated. The appraised value totals are now $609,414, $138,225, and $6,350.
6. In the Show group, click the **Field List** button. See Figure 5-49.

**Figure 5-49** **Refreshed PivotTable**

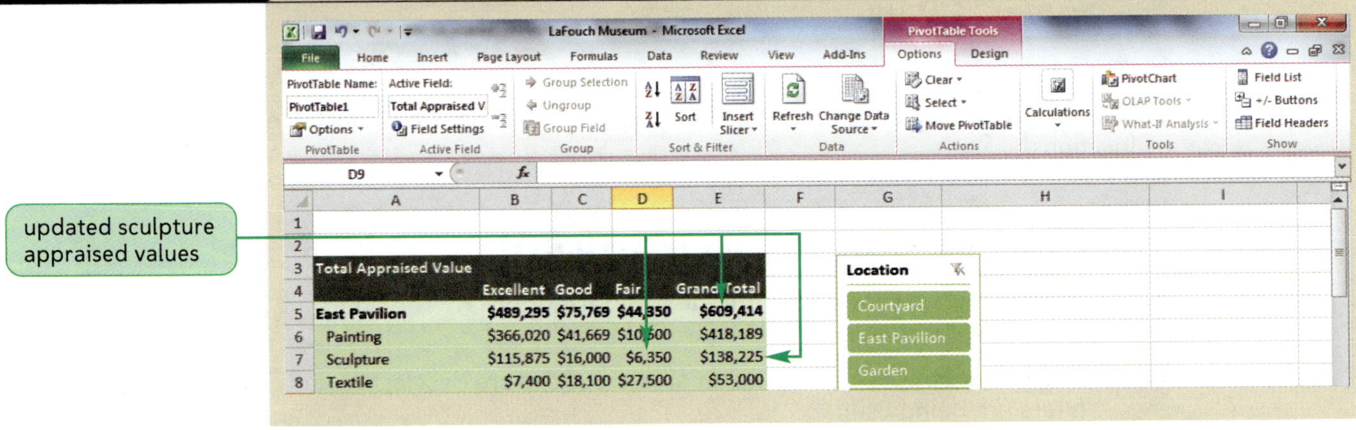


# Grouping PivotTable Items

When a field contains numbers, dates, or times, you can combine items in the rows of a PivotTable and combine them into groups automatically. Mary thinks a PivotTable that displays the number of objects acquired each year would be of interest to the board of directors. This report involves using the Date Acquired field as a row label and ArtID as the values field, although you could us any field as the values field. When using a date field as a row label in a PivotTable, each date initially appears as a separate item.

Typically, you want to analyze date data by month, quarter, or year. To do that, you need to group the data in the Date Acquired field. Grouping items combines dates into larger groups such as months, quarters, or years so that the PivotTable can include the desired level of summarization. You can also group numeric items, typically into equal ranges. For example, you can calculate the number of art objects in appraised value groups based on increments of any amount you specify (for example, 1–25,000, 25,001–50,000, and so on).

You'll add a second PivotTable in a new worksheet.

**To create a PivotTable based on the Date Acquired field:**

1. Switch to the **Art Collection** worksheet, and then click any cell in the Excel table. The table is active.

2. Click the **Insert** tab on the Ribbon, and then click the **PivotTable** button in the Tables group. The Create PivotTable dialog box opens.
3. Verify that the Table/Range box shows **ArtObjects** and the **New Worksheet** option button is selected, and then click the **OK** button. The PivotTable report area and PivotTable Field List appear in a new worksheet.
4. In the PivotTable Field List, click the **Date Acquired** check box. The Date Acquired field appears in the Row Labels box. Each unique date appears in the PivotTable report area. Mary wants each year to appear as a row label. You will correct that shortly.
5. Click the **ArtID** check box in the PivotTable Field List. "Sum of ArtID" appears in the Values box in the layout area because the ArtID field contains numeric data. See Figure 5-50.

**Figure 5-50** PivotTable with Sum of ArtID for each date

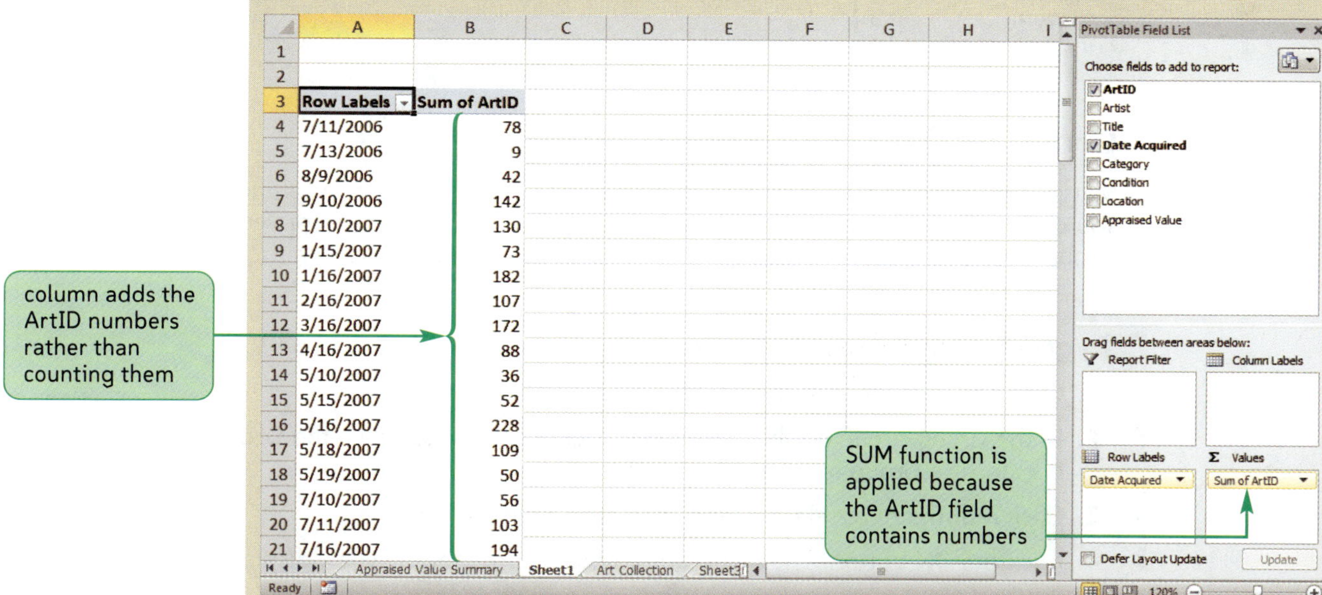


The PivotTable includes the sum of ArtIDs instead of a count of art objects, as Mary requested. This occurs because fields that contain numbers placed in the Values area are summed. Adding all the ArtIDs together to get a total is meaningless; you need to count the number of ArtIDs in each year. To do this, you need to change the SUM function to the COUNT function so Excel will *count* the number of objects in each group.

## To count the number of objects in each group:

1. Click any value in the **Sum of ArtID** column, and then click the **PivotTable Tools Options** tab on the Ribbon.
2. Click the **Calculations button arrow**, click the **Summarize Values By** button, and then click **Count**. The label indicating the type of summary in the PivotTable changes to Count of ArtID, and the PivotTable report displays the number of art objects acquired by date. See Figure 5-51.

Figure 5-51 **PivotTable report with count**

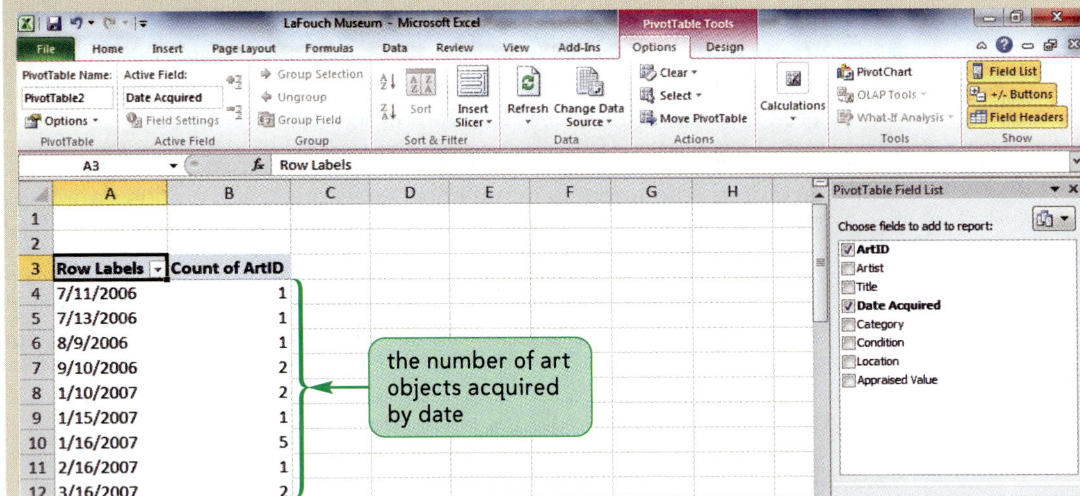


## Grouping Date Fields

Mary wants the PivotTable layout to show a count of acquisitions by year, not by date. You can group a range of dates into periods such as months, quarters, or years using the Group Field command. You will group the Date Acquired dates by year.

### To group acquisitions by year:

1. Click any date value in the Row Labels column of the PivotTable.
2. In the Group group on the PivotTable Tools Options tab, click the **Group Field** button. The Grouping dialog box opens.
3. Click **Months** to deselect it, and then click **Years** to select it.
4. Click the **OK** button. The PivotTable report is grouped by year, displaying the number of art acquisitions in each year. See Figure 5-52.

Figure 5-52 **PivotTable report of annual acquisitions**

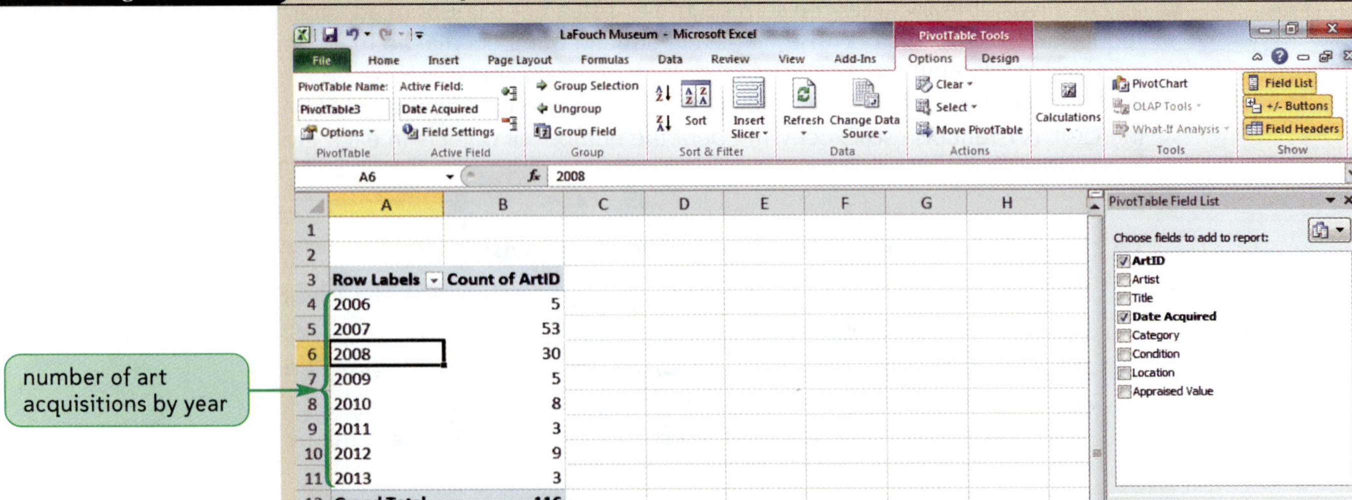


5. Rename the worksheet as **Acquired By Year**.

INSIGHT

*Creating Different Types of PivotTable Reports*

This tutorial only scratched the surface of the variety of PivotTable reports you can create. Here are a few more examples:

- Most PivotTable summaries are based on numeric data, but PivotTables can also contain only nonnumeric data. You cannot add nonnumeric data, so you must use the COUNT function to produce summaries. For example, you could count the number of art objects by Location and Category.
- You can use PivotTables to combine items into groups. Items that appear as row labels or column labels can be grouped. If items are numbers or dates, they can be grouped automatically using the Grouping dialog box, or they can be grouped manually using the Ctrl key to select items in a group and choosing Group from the shortcut menu. For example, you can manually combine the Courtyard and Garden locations into an Outdoor group, combine the three pavilion locations into an Indoor group, and then provide counts or total appraised values by these groups within the PivotTable. Being able to combine categories that aren't part of your original data using the grouping feature gives you flexibility to summarize your PivotTables in a way that meets your analysis requirements.
- You can develop PivotTables using the value filter, which allows you to filter one of your row or column fields in the PivotTable based on numbers that appear in the Values area of the PivotTable. For example, a PivotTable can show the total value of art objects for each artist and be filtered to display only artists whose total is greater than $25,000. Filtering provides you with a more precise way to view the PivotTable results by enabling you to include or remove data from the report.

# Creating a PivotChart

Mary wants you to add a PivotChart next to the PivotTable. A PivotChart allows you to interactively add, remove, filter, and refresh data fields in the PivotChart similar to working with a PivotTable. PivotCharts can have all the same formatting as other charts, including layouts and styles. You can move and resize chart elements, or change formatting of individual data points.

You will prepare a clustered column chart next to the new PivotTable report. You can create a PivotChart from the PivotTable.

**TIP**

You can also create a PivotChart based directly on an Excel table, in which case both a PivotTable and a PivotChart are created.

### To create the PivotChart:

1. Click any cell in the PivotTable.
2. In the Tools group on the PivotTable Tools Options tab, click the **PivotChart** button. The Insert Chart dialog box opens.
3. Click the **Clustered Column** chart (the first chart in the first row of the Column section), if necessary, and then click the **OK** button. A PivotChart appears next to the PivotTable along with the PivotTable Field List.
4. Click the **PivotChart Tools Layout** tab, click the **Legend button arrow** in the Labels group, and then click **None**. The legend is removed from the PivotChart. You do not need a legend because the PivotChart has only one series.
5. In the PivotChart, right-click the **chart title**, and then click **Edit Text**. The insertion point appears in the title so you can edit it.
6. Select the title, type **Number Acquired By Year** as the new title, and then click the chart area to deselect the title.

7. Drag the **PivotChart** so its upper-left corner is in cell C3. The PivotChart is aligned with the PivotTable. See Figure 5-53.

**Figure 5-53** PivotChart added to the PivotTable report

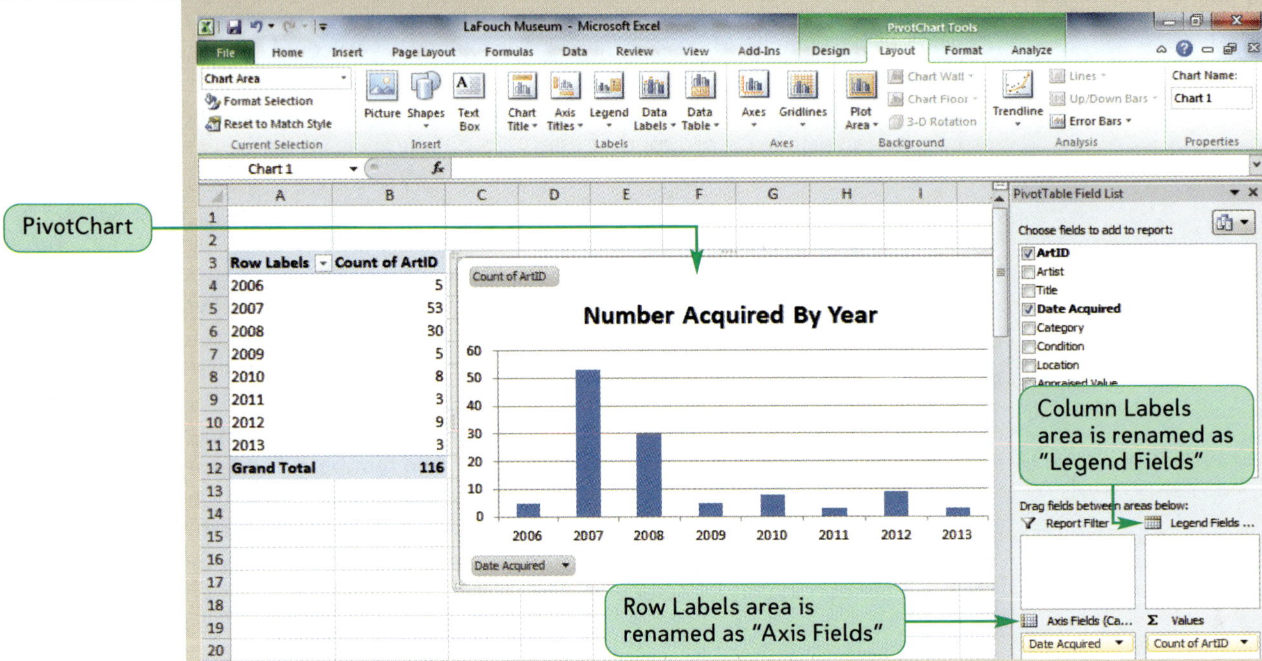


The PivotChart Tools contextual tabs enable you to manipulate and format the selected PivotChart the same way as an ordinary chart. A PivotChart and its associated PivotTable are linked. When you modify one, the other also changes.

You can quickly display different chart views of the PivotChart using the chart filter button on the PivotChart to filter the data. Mary wants you to display only art acquisitions after 2009.

### To filter items in the PivotChart:

1. Make sure the PivotChart is selected, and then click the **Date Acquired** axis field button in the PivotChart. The AutoFilter menu opens.
2. Click the **Select All** check box. All the check boxes are deselected.
3. Click the **2010**, **2011**, **2012**, and **2013** check boxes. The years after 2009 are selected.
4. Click the **OK** button. The PivotChart displays only art objects acquired after 2009. The PivotTable is also filtered to display the same results.
5. Click cell **A1**. See Figure 5-54.

**Figure 5-54** **Filtered PivotChart**

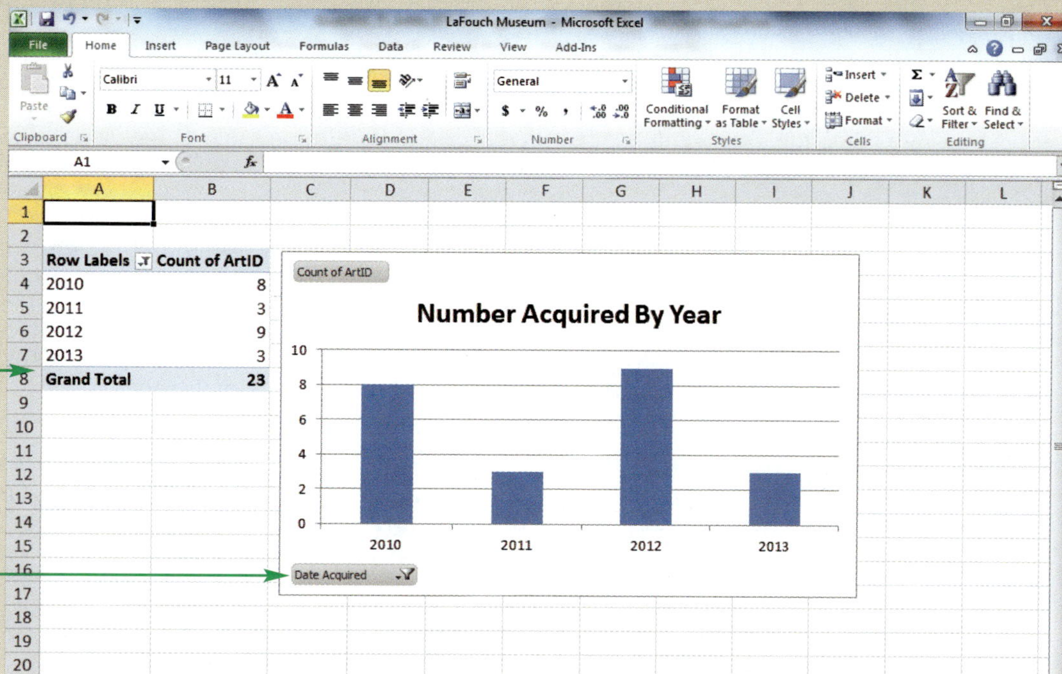


PivotTable shows the filtered results

click to filter the items in the PivotChart

6. Save the LaFouch Museum workbook, and then close it.

Mary is pleased with the PivotTable and PivotChart. Both show the number of art objects acquired by year, which will be important information for her upcoming board meeting.

REVIEW

## *Session 5.3 Quick Check*

1. What is the default summary function for numeric data in a PivotTable?
2. When creating a PivotTable, what do you use to lay out the fields in the PivotTable report?
3. After you update data in an Excel table, what must you do to a PivotTable based on that Excel table?
4. How are fields such as region, state, and country most likely to appear in a PivotTable?
5. How are fields such as revenue, costs, and profits most likely to appear in a PivotTable?
6. A list of college students includes a code to indicate the student's gender (male or female) and a field to identify the student's major. Which tool—Filter or PivotTable—would you use to (a) create a list of all females majoring in history, and (b) count the number of males and females in each major?
7. When the Date Acquired field is displayed in a row of a PivotTable by month or year, you have ______________ the Date Acquired field.
8. A PivotChart displays the number of art objects in each Location. How would you exclude the art objects in the Courtyard from the PivotTable?

*Practice the skills you learned in the tutorial using the same case scenario.*

PRACTICE

## Review Assignments

### Data File needed for the Review Assignments: Art.xlsx

Mary has another art object to enter in the art objects list. She wants to sort the data by the date acquired. She wants to filter data to retrieve all art with the word "cowboy" in the title. She wants to use a PivotTable to determine the average value of the artwork for each artist. Complete the following:

1. Open the **Art** workbook located in the Excel5\Review folder included with your Data Files, and then save the workbook as **Art Museum** in the same folder.
2. In the Documentation sheet, enter your name and the date.
3. Switch to the ArtObjects worksheet. Create an Excel table for the art objects data, and then change the table style to Medium 25. Format the Appraised Value field using the Accounting number format with no decimal places.
4. Rename the Excel table as **Collection**.
5. Make a copy of the ArtObjects worksheet, and then rename the copied worksheet as **Q5** (for "Question 5"). (*Hint*: To make a copy of the worksheet, press and hold the Ctrl key and drag the sheet tab to the right of the ArtObjects sheet tab.) Sort the art objects by date acquired to display the newest objects first.
6. Make a copy of the ArtObjects worksheet, and then rename the copied worksheet as **Q6**. Sort art objects by category (Z to A), location (A to Z), artist (A to Z), and date acquired (showing the oldest first).
7. Make a copy of the ArtObjects worksheet, and then rename the copied worksheet as **Q7**. Filter the Collection table to produce a list of art objects with the word "cowboy" in the title.
8. Make a copy of the ArtObjects worksheet, and then rename the copied worksheet as **Q8**. Use the Total row to calculate the average value of objects acquired between 2009 and 2013. Change the label in the Total row from Total to **Average**. Sort the filtered data by date acquired (newest first).
9. Make a copy of the ArtObjects worksheet, and then rename the copied worksheet as **Q9**. Use the Subtotal command to count how many art objects there are in each location, displaying the count in the ArtID column.
10. Create a PivotTable to show the average value of art objects by artist. Format the Value column appropriately. Rename the worksheet with the PivotTable as **Q10-11**.
11. Sort the PivotTable showing the artist with the highest average value first.
12. Create a PivotTable to show the number of art objects and the total value by category. Include location as a Report Filter field, and then filter the report so the number and total value by category is based on the Courtyard location. Rename the worksheet with the PivotTable as **Q12**.
13. Save and close the workbook. Submit the finished workbook to your instructor, either in printed or electronic form, as requested.

*Use the skills you learned to analyze and summarize donation data.*

APPLY

## Case Problem 1

### Data File needed for this Case Problem: Pledges.xlsx

***Hewart Zoo*** Marvis Chennard is the director of fund-raising for the Hewart Zoo. The zoo relies on donations to fund operations, temporary exhibits, and special programs. Marvis created an Excel table to track information about donors and their pledges. You will analyze the data in the list. Complete the following:

1. Open the **Pledges** workbook located in the Excel5\Case1 folder included with your Data Files, and then save the workbook as **Zoo Pledges** in the same folder.

2. In the Documentation worksheet, enter your name and the date, and then switch to the Pledges worksheet.
3. Create an Excel table, apply the Medium 7 table style, and then rename the table as **PledgeData**.
4. Make a copy of the Pledges worksheet, and then rename the copied worksheet as **Q4-6** (for "Question 4-6"). (*Hint*: Press the Ctrl key and drag the sheet tab to the right of the Pledges sheet tab to make a copy of the worksheet.) Sort the data in ascending order by donor type and fund name, and in descending order by amt pledged (largest first).
5. In the Q4-6 worksheet, insert a Total row. Display the number of pledges in the Donor Name column, the average pledge in the Amt Pledged column, the total received in the Amt Received column, and the total owed in the Amt Owed column.
6. In the Q4-6 worksheet, split the worksheet into two horizontal panes at row 23. In the top pane, display the pledge transactions. In the bottom pane, display the Total row.
7. Make a copy of the Pledges worksheet, and then rename the copied worksheet as **Q7**. Filter the data to display individual donors whose amt owed is greater than zero. Sort the filtered data by pledge date, with the oldest date displayed first.
8. Make a copy of the Pledges worksheet, and then rename the copied worksheet as **Q8**. Filter the data to display records that have a pledge date in October through December. Sort the filtered data by amt pledged (largest first).
9. Make a copy of the Pledges worksheet, and then rename the copied worksheet as **Q9**. Filter the data to display only records with an amt received greater than zero. Then use the Subtotal command (SUM) to display the total amt received by fund name.
10. Create a PivotTable that displays the total and average amt owed by each donor type and fund name. Place the PivotTable in a new worksheet, and then rename the worksheet as **Q10**. Select an appropriate report layout and format. Insert a Donor Type slicer and filter using the Organization donor type.
11. Using Figure 5-55 as a guide, create a PivotTable in a new worksheet that shows the amt pledged by month and fund name. Format the PivotTable appropriately, and then rename the worksheet as **Q11**.

**Figure 5-55** **PivotTable for the amount pledged**

| | A | B | C | D | E | F |
|---|---|---|---|---|---|---|
| 1 | | | | | | |
| 2 | | | | | | |
| 3 | Total Pledged | | | | | |
| 4 | | Bird Sanctuary | General Support | ZooMobile | Children's Zoo | Grand Total |
| 5 | Jan | | $1,000 | | $100 | $1,100 |
| 6 | Feb | | | $150 | $1,100 | $1,250 |
| 7 | Mar | | | $1,000 | $100 | $1,100 |
| 8 | Apr | $75 | $500 | | $425 | $1,000 |
| 9 | Jun | | | $50 | $1,000 | $1,050 |
| 10 | Jul | $1,000 | $1,000 | | | $2,000 |
| 11 | Sep | $100 | $25 | $150 | $250 | $525 |
| 12 | Oct | $200 | $200 | | | $400 |
| 13 | Nov | | $250 | | | $250 |
| 14 | Dec | | | $750 | $150 | $900 |
| 15 | **Grand Total** | **$1,375** | **$2,975** | **$2,100** | **$3,125** | **$9,575** |

12. Save and close the workbook. Submit the finished workbook to your instructor, either in printed or electronic form, as requested.

*Use the skills you learned to analyze and summarize expenditure data.*

APPLY

## Case Problem 2

**Data File needed for this Case Problem: Ring.xlsx**

***Ring Family Farm*** Fred and Alesia Ring own a small family farm outside Abita Springs, Louisiana. The couple wants to better organize their financial records. They created an Excel workbook to record their expenses. Typical expenses include those associated with hay production (seed, fertilizer, and irrigation), animal husbandry, fence maintenance, veterinary services, vehicles and maintenance, and so forth. The workbook includes categories associated with these expenses as well as an area to record how much is spent, the purpose of the expenditure, the check number, and the date paid. Complete the following:

1. Open the **Ring** workbook located in the Excel5\Case2 folder included with your Data Files, and then save the workbook as **Ring Farm** in the same folder.
2. Insert a new worksheet. Enter the company name, your name, the date, and a purpose statement, and then rename the worksheet as **Documentation**.
3. Create an Excel table in the Expenditures worksheet. Rename the table as **Checkbook**.
4. Replace the category code "Farm" in each record with **Payroll**.
5. Make a copy of the Expenditures worksheet, and then rename the copied worksheet as **Q5**. (*Hint*: Press the Ctrl key and drag the Expenditures sheet tab to the right of the Expenditures sheet tab to make a copy of the worksheet.) Sort the Checkbook table in ascending order by category, then by payee, and then by date paid (newest first).
6. Make a copy of the Expenditures worksheet, and then rename the copied worksheet as **Q6**. Filter the Checkbook table to display all expenditures for equipment and repairs in December, and then sort by amount (smallest first).
7. Make a copy of the Expenditures worksheet, and then rename the copied worksheet as **Q7**. Filter the Checkbook table to display all checks that include the word "vet" in the payee's name. Include the total amount at the bottom of the table.
8. Make a copy of the Expenditures worksheet, and then rename the copied worksheet as **Q8**. Use conditional formatting to apply a yellow fill with dark yellow text to all outstanding checks. (*Hint*: "Yes" appears in the Outstanding column.)
9. Make a copy of the Expenditures worksheet, and then rename the copied worksheet as **Q9**. Use the Subtotal command to display the total amount for each category, displaying the subtotal in the Amount column.
10. Create a PivotTable that summarizes expenditures by category and month. Place the PivotTable in a new worksheet, and then rename the worksheet as **Q10-11**. Format the PivotTable appropriately and choose a layout.
11. Insert a PivotChart with the Clustered Column chart type on the Q10-11 worksheet.
12. Create the PivotTable shown in Figure 5-56 in a new worksheet, rename the worksheet as **Q12**, and then sort the Total Amount column in descending order. (*Hint*: Click the Show Values As button in the Calculations group on the PivotTable Tools Options tab on the Ribbon to calculate the Pct Of Total column.)

**Figure 5-56** **PivotTable for the amount by category**

| | A | B | C |
|---|---|---|---|
| 1 | **Category** | **Total Amount** | **Pct Of Total** |
| 2 | Equipment | $6,575.00 | 37.05% |
| 3 | Payroll | $2,638.27 | 14.87% |
| 4 | Vet | $2,320.57 | 13.08% |
| 5 | Repairs | $2,003.44 | 11.29% |
| 6 | Feed | $2,002.24 | 11.28% |
| 7 | Medicine | $1,249.32 | 7.04% |
| 8 | Administration | $958.09 | 5.40% |
| 9 | **Grand Total** | **$17,746.93** | **100.00%** |

13. Save and close the workbook. Submit the finished workbook to your instructor, either in printed or electronic form, as requested.

*Use the skills you learned to analyze and summarize loan data for a bank.*

APPLY

## Case Problem 3

**Data File needed for this Case Problem: CustLoans.xlsx**

***High Desert Bank*** Eleanor Chimayo, loan manager for High Desert Bank, is getting ready for the bank's quarterly meeting. Eleanor is expected to present data on the status of different types of loans within three New Mexican cities. Eleanor asks you to summarize and analyze the data for her presentation. Complete the following:

1. Open the **CustLoans** workbook located in the Excel5\Case3 folder included with your Data Files, and then save the workbook as **High Desert Bank** in the same folder.
2. In the Documentation sheet, enter your name and the date.
3. In the Loans worksheet, create an Excel table, and then rename the table as **LoanData**.
4. Format the Amount and Interest Rate fields so that it is clear that these fields contain dollars and percentages, respectively.
5. Format the table using the table style of your choice.
6. To the right of the Type column, insert a new column named **Monthly Payment**. Use the PMT function to calculate the monthly payment for each loan. Adjust the formula so that each loan is displayed as a positive amount, and then improve the formatting.
7. Make a copy of the Loans worksheet, and then rename the copied worksheet as **Q7-8**. (*Hint*: Press the Ctrl key and drag the sheet tab to the right of the current sheet tab to make a copy of the worksheet.) Sort the loan data in ascending order by type, within type by city, and within city by last name.
8. Use conditional formatting to display all loans in Taos using a format of your choice to highlight these loans.
9. Make a copy of the Loans worksheet, and then rename the copied worksheet as **Q9-10**. Filter the LoanData table to display loans made during April and May of 2013.
10. Insert a Total row in the Q9-10 worksheet. Display the average amount of loans and the total monthly payment for the filtered data in Question 9.
11. Make a copy of the Loans worksheet, and then rename the copied worksheet as **Q11**. Sort the loans in ascending order by city, then by type of loan, and then by amount of loan (largest loan first). Insert subtotals (Average) for the loan amount and monthly payment by city and type of loan. Prepare the worksheet for printing. Include the worksheet name in the center of the custom header. Include your name in the left section of the custom footer and page numbers in the right section of the custom footer. Fit all columns on one page.
12. Create a PivotTable that displays the number (Count) and average loan by type and city. Place the PivotTable in a new worksheet, and then rename the PivotTable worksheet as **Q12 Loans-Type And City**. Remove the Other loan type from the PivotTable. Format the PivotTable appropriately.
13. Create a second PivotTable, as shown in Figure 5-57, in a new worksheet, and then rename the PivotTable worksheet as **Q13 Loans-Type and Date**. The PivotTable shows three calculations: number of loans, total loan amount, and average monthly payment categorized by type of loan. Insert a report filter based on the loan date, grouped so you can filter by month. Insert a Loan Date slicer and filter the PivotTable report for March and April.

**Figure 5-57** PivotTable for loans by type and date

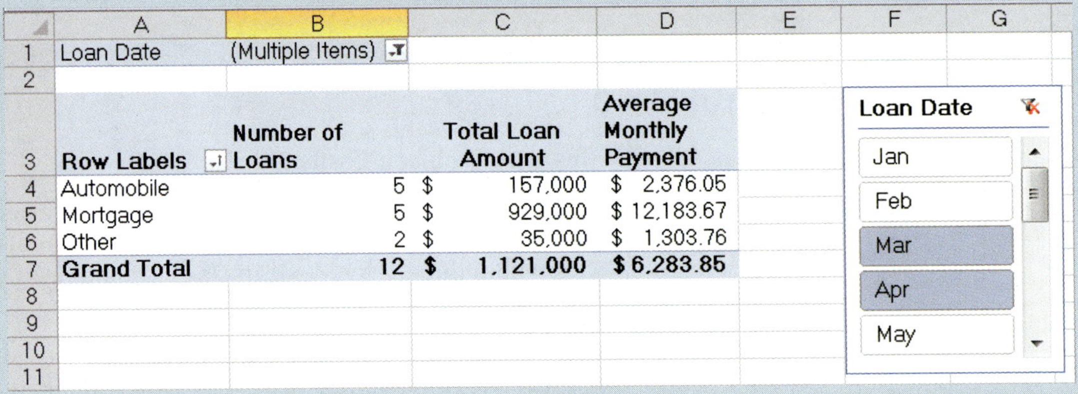

| Loan Date | (Multiple Items) | | |
|---|---|---|---|
| | | | |
| Row Labels | Number of Loans | Total Loan Amount | Average Monthly Payment |
| Automobile | 5 | $ 157,000 | $ 2,376.05 |
| Mortgage | 5 | $ 929,000 | $ 12,183.67 |
| Other | 2 | $ 35,000 | $ 1,303.76 |
| **Grand Total** | **12** | **$ 1,121,000** | **$ 6,283.85** |



14. Save and close the workbook. Submit the finished workbook to your instructor, either in printed or electronic form, as requested.

*Explore how to summarize data by creating subtotals, PivotTables, and PivotCharts.*

CHALLENGE

## Case Problem 4

### Data File needed for this Case Problem: Bowls.xlsx

***Bowls Department Stores*** Bowls Department Stores, with corporate headquarters in Portland, Oregon, operates department stores in midsize towns in selected areas of the Northwest. Although the organization maintains a large computer system for its accounting operations, the sales department often downloads data to complete additional analysis of its operations. Daniel Partner, analyst for the corporate sales department, regularly downloads data by territories and product areas including automotive, electronics, garden centers, and sporting goods. He often presents reports based on his analysis of sales by product areas and territory, best- and worst-performing product group periods, and total sales for certain regions and product groups. You will help Daniel compile and summarize the data. Complete the following:

1. Open the **Bowls** workbook located in the Excel5\Case4 folder included with your Data Files, and then save the workbook as **Bowls Stores** in the same folder.
2. In the Documentation sheet, enter your name, the date, and an appropriate purpose statement.
3. In the SalesData worksheet, create an Excel table. Rename the table as **ProductSales**. Format the Sales column in the Currency number format with no decimal places.
4. Make a copy of the SalesData worksheet, and then rename the copied worksheet as **Q4**. (*Hint*: Press the Ctrl key and drag the sheet tab to the right of the SalesData sheet tab to make a copy of the worksheet.) Sort the table in ascending order by territories, then by product group, then by year, and then by month. Month should be sorted in chronological order (Jan, Feb, Mar, ...), not in alphabetical order.
5. Make a copy of the SalesData worksheet, and then rename the copied worksheet as **Q5**. Display records for Automotive and Electronics products in 2013, excluding sales in Vancouver. Sort this data by sales in descending order. Add a Total row and calculate the average sales for the filtered data. Change the label in the Total row to **Average**. Split the worksheet into two panes. In the top pane, display all the rows except the last row on your screen. In the bottom pane, display the Total row.

EXPLORE

6. Make a copy of the SalesData worksheet, and then rename the copied worksheet as **Q6**. Display subtotals for sales (Sum) by year, month (Jan, Feb, Mar, ...), and territory.

7. Make a copy of the SalesData worksheet, and then rename the copied worksheet as **Q7**. Display the five lowest periods based on sales. Assume each row represents a period. Sort the sales so lowest sales appears first.

**EXPLORE**

8. Create a PivotTable similar to the one shown in Figure 5-58, displaying percentage of sales by product group, territories, and year. Omit the columnar grand totals. Use a tabular layout, inserting subtotals at the bottom of each product group and excluding the Toy product group. Rename the worksheet as **Q8**.

**Figure 5-58** Sample PivotTable showing percentage of sales

| | A | B | C | D |
|---|---|---|---|---|
| 1 | | | | |
| 2 | | | | |
| 3 | **Pct of Sales** | | **Year** | |
| 4 | **Product Group** | **Territories** | **2012** | **2013** |
| 5 | **Automotive** | Oregon | 10.05% | 8.85% |
| 6 | | Vancouver | 7.32% | 9.71% |
| 7 | | Washington | 6.88% | 9.94% |
| 8 | **Automotive Total** | | **24.25%** | **28.50%** |
| 9 | **Electronics** | Oregon | 7.53% | 8.67% |
| 10 | | Vancouver | 7.61% | 6.88% |
| 11 | | Washington | 8.05% | 9.22% |
| 12 | **Electronics Total** | | **23.20%** | **24.78%** |
| 13 | **Gardening** | Oregon | 8.19% | 6.85% |
| 14 | | Vancouver | 8.46% | 5.89% |
| 15 | | Washington | 9.77% | 9.91% |
| 16 | **Gardening Total** | | **26.42%** | **22.66%** |
| 17 | **Houseware** | Oregon | 6.86% | 5.01% |
| 18 | | Vancouver | 8.20% | 7.67% |
| 19 | | Washington | 11.07% | 11.39% |
| 20 | **Houseware Total** | | **26.14%** | **24.07%** |
| 21 | **Grand Total** | | **100.00%** | **100.00%** |

**EXPLORE**

9. Using Figure 5-59 as a guide, create a PivotChart of total sales by product group. Create a second PivotChart of total sales by territory in the same worksheet. Rename the worksheet as **Q9**.

**Figure 5-59** Sample PivotChart of total sales by product group

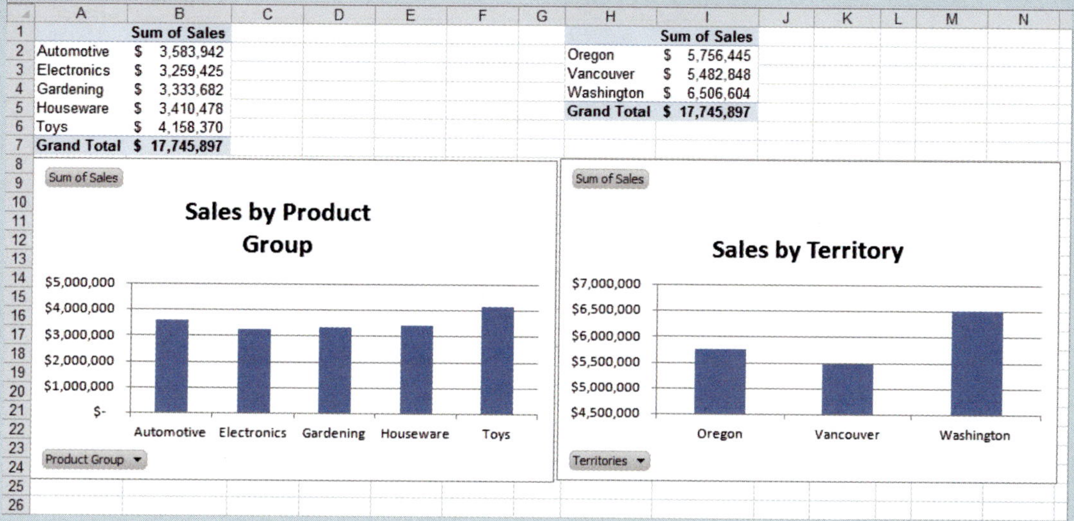

**EXPLORE** 10. Using Figure 5-60 as a guide, create a PivotTable to show four calculations: average, total, minimum, and maximum sales, categorized by territories and product group, and filtered by year and territories using two slicer filters. Display the results for 2013 and the Vancouver and Washington territories. Rename the worksheet as **Q10**.

**Figure 5-60** **Sample PivotTable showing calculations**

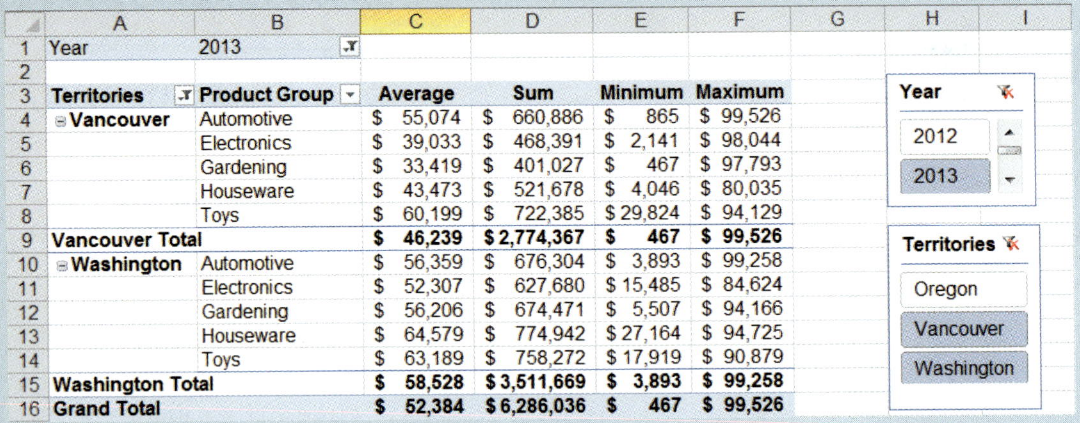

| | A | B | C | D | E | F |
|---|---|---|---|---|---|---|
| 1 | Year | 2013 | | | | |
| 2 | | | | | | |
| 3 | **Territories** | **Product Group** | **Average** | **Sum** | **Minimum** | **Maximum** |
| 4 | **Vancouver** | Automotive | $ 55,074 | $ 660,886 | $ 865 | $ 99,526 |
| 5 | | Electronics | $ 39,033 | $ 468,391 | $ 2,141 | $ 98,044 |
| 6 | | Gardening | $ 33,419 | $ 401,027 | $ 467 | $ 97,793 |
| 7 | | Houseware | $ 43,473 | $ 521,678 | $ 4,046 | $ 80,035 |
| 8 | | Toys | $ 60,199 | $ 722,385 | $ 29,824 | $ 94,129 |
| 9 | **Vancouver Total** | | **$ 46,239** | **$ 2,774,367** | **$ 467** | **$ 99,526** |
| 10 | **Washington** | Automotive | $ 56,359 | $ 676,304 | $ 3,893 | $ 99,258 |
| 11 | | Electronics | $ 52,307 | $ 627,680 | $ 15,485 | $ 84,624 |
| 12 | | Gardening | $ 56,206 | $ 674,471 | $ 5,507 | $ 94,166 |
| 13 | | Houseware | $ 64,579 | $ 774,942 | $ 27,164 | $ 94,725 |
| 14 | | Toys | $ 63,189 | $ 758,272 | $ 17,919 | $ 90,879 |
| 15 | **Washington Total** | | **$ 58,528** | **$ 3,511,669** | **$ 3,893** | **$ 99,258** |
| 16 | **Grand Total** | | **$ 52,384** | **$ 6,286,036** | **$ 467** | **$ 99,526** |



11. Save and close the workbook. Submit the finished workbook to your instructor, either in printed or electronic form, as requested.

ASSESS

## SAM: Skills Assessment Manager

For current SAM information, including versions and content details, visit SAM Central (http://samcentral.course.com). If you have a SAM user profile, you may have access to hands-on instruction, practice, and assessment of the skills covered in this tutorial. Because various versions of SAM are supported throughout the life of this text, check with your instructor for the correct instructions and URL/Web site for accessing assignments.

### ENDING DATA FILES

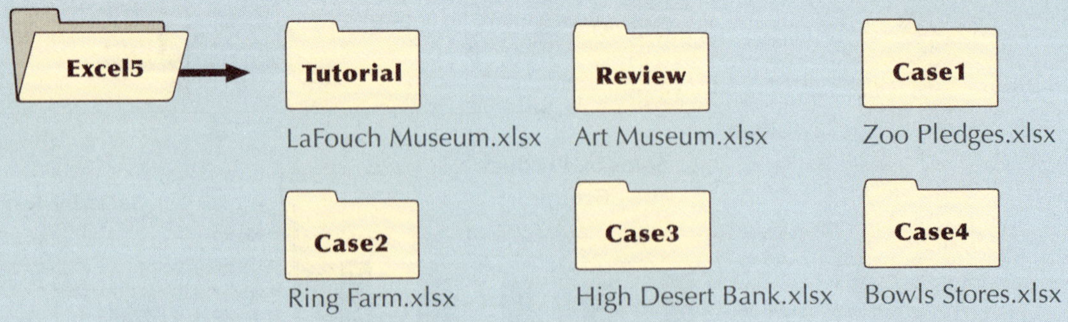

TUTORIAL 6

# Managing Multiple Worksheets and Workbooks

*Summarizing Ticket Sales*

## OBJECTIVES

**Session 6.1**
- Create a worksheet group
- Format and edit multiple worksheets at once
- Create cell references to other worksheets
- Consolidate information from multiple worksheets using 3-D references
- Create and print a worksheet group

**Session 6.2**
- Create a link to data in another workbook
- Create a workbook reference
- Learn how to edit links
- Create and use an Excel workspace

**Session 6.3**
- Insert a hyperlink in a cell
- Create a custom template
- Save a workbook to SkyDrive and use the Excel Web App

## Case | *Global Travel*

Global Travel, a member-owned organization, provides a variety of services ranging from travel assistance to insurance programs to discounted vacation packages. The company also offers special services and discounts to one-time entertainment events. Global Travel purchases tickets to selected theme and amusement parks to resell to its members. Each local office of Global Travel markets and sells these tickets to its members. Theme and amusement park sales account for more than 10 percent of Global Travel's sales.

Rhohit Gupta, accountant for Global Travel in New Mexico, is responsible for tracking ticket sales within the state and preparing an analysis for Alvin Alton, the corporate controller. Rhohit asks you to create a summary report that shows the quarterly sales in New Mexico for the past year. He already entered each quarter's values in separate worksheets, but wants you to summarize all the quarterly information in one worksheet.

Alvin has already received workbooks with the quarterly sales for Colorado and Utah. After Alvin receives the New Mexico workbook, you will create a workbook that summarizes the annual totals from each state workbook in the Southwest region.

### STARTING DATA FILES

**Excel6** →

**Tutorial**
Colorado.xlsx
NM.xlsx
Sales 2013.docx
TravelTotals.xlsx
Utah.xlsx

**Review**
Idaho.xlsx
OR.xlsx
NW Totals 2013.xlsx
NW Travel.xltx
Washington.xlsx

**Case1**
Cafe.xlsx

**Case2**
Carson.xlsx
Reno.xlsx
Vegas.xlsx

**Case3**
Infusion.xlsx

**Case4**
Europe.xlsx
North America.xlsx
Pluto Template.xltx
South America.xlsx

# SESSION 6.1 VISUAL OVERVIEW

Anything you do in the active sheet—such as entering formulas, adding labels, and formatting—is automatically done to all sheets in the worksheet group, saving you time and ensuring consistency.

When worksheets are grouped, the workbook is in group-editing mode and "[Group]" appears in the title bar.

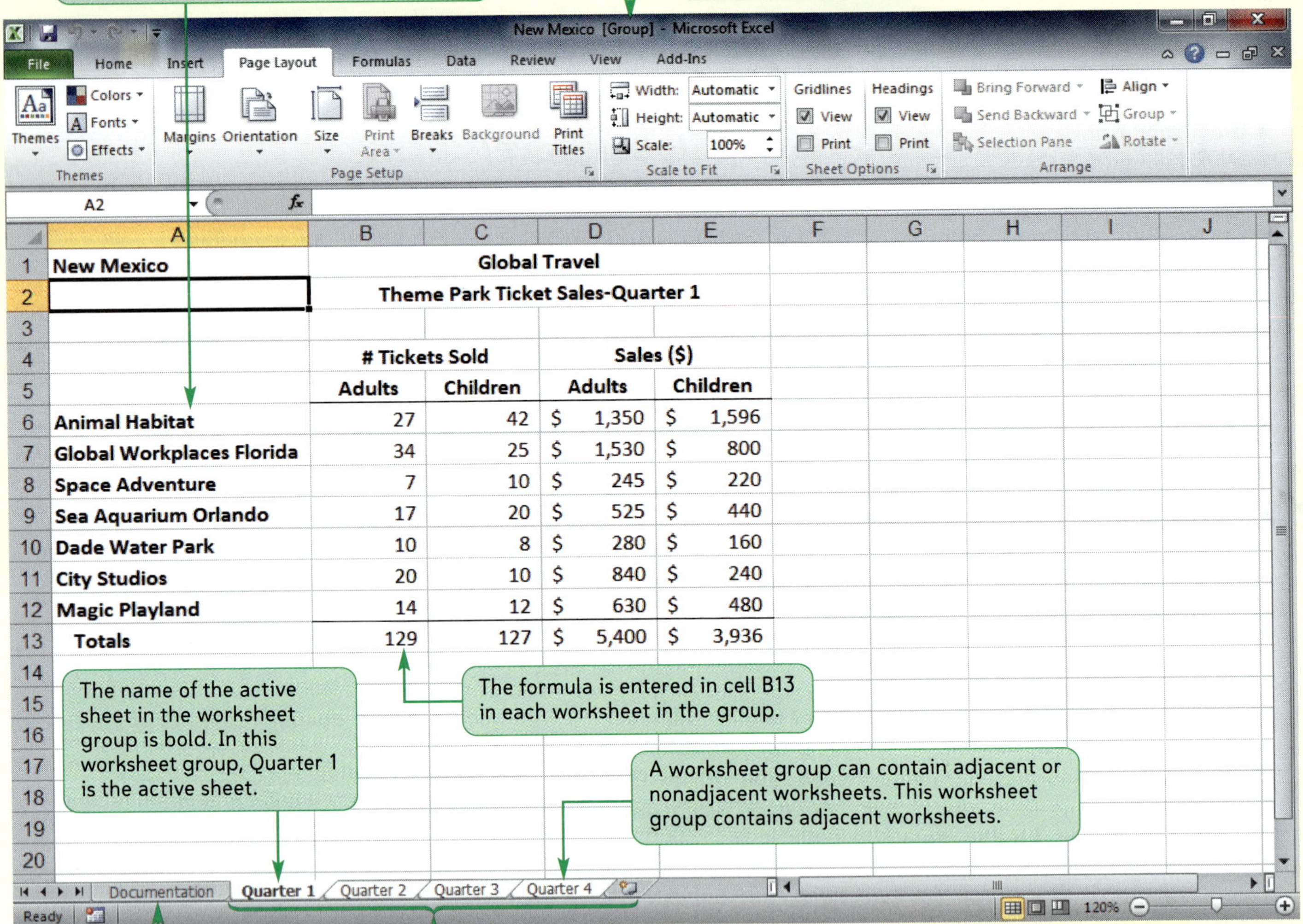


The name of the active sheet in the worksheet group is bold. In this worksheet group, Quarter 1 is the active sheet.

The formula is entered in cell B13 in each worksheet in the group.

A worksheet group can contain adjacent or nonadjacent worksheets. This worksheet group contains adjacent worksheets.

You can click any tab outside the worksheet group to exit group-editing mode. In this case, clicking the Documentation sheet tab ungroups the worksheets.

A **worksheet group** is a collection of two or more selected worksheets. This worksheet group includes four worksheets.

# WORKSHEET GROUPS AND 3-D REFERENCES

A **3-D reference** is a reference to the same cell or range in multiple worksheets in the same workbook. This 3-D reference refers to cell B6 in the Quarter 1, Quarter 2, Quarter 3, and Quarter 4 worksheets.

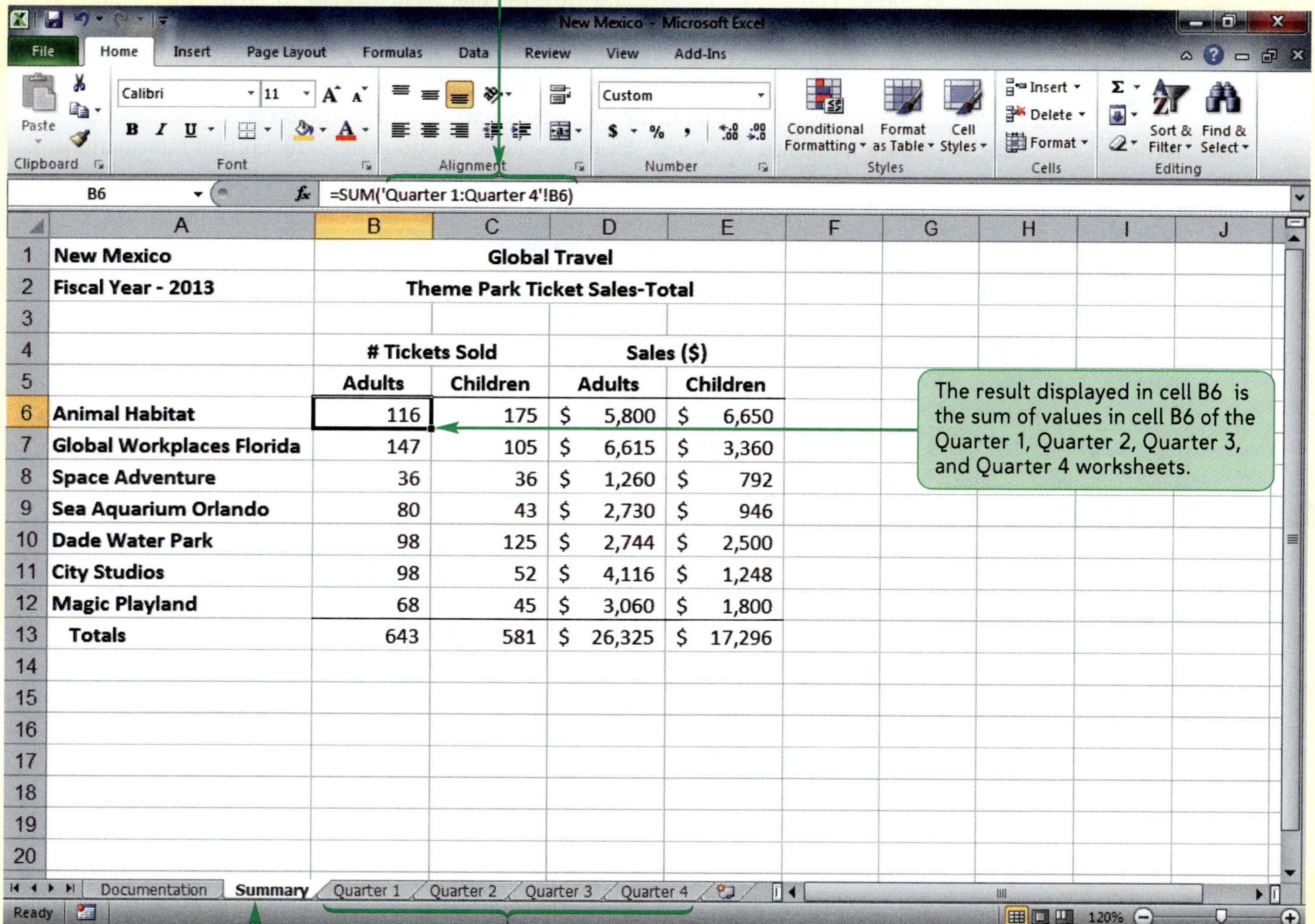


The result displayed in cell B6 is the sum of values in cell B6 of the Quarter 1, Quarter 2, Quarter 3, and Quarter 4 worksheets.

When two or more worksheets have identical row and column layouts, as the quarterly worksheets in this workbook do, you can enter formulas with 3-D references to summarize those worksheets in another worksheet.

The Summary worksheet uses 3-D references to summarize data from four worksheets—Quarter 1 , Quarter 2, Quarter 3, and Quarter 4.

# Grouping Worksheets

**TIP**

If a worksheet group includes all the worksheets in a workbook, you can edit only the active worksheet; any changes will be made to all the worksheets in the group. Clicking another sheet tab ungroups the worksheets.

Workbook data is often placed in several worksheets. Using multiple worksheets makes it easier to group and summarize data. For example, a company such as Global Travel with branches in different geographic regions can place sales information for each region in separate worksheets. Rather than scrolling through one large and complex worksheet that contains data for all regions, users can access sales information for a specific region simply by clicking a sheet tab in the workbook.

Using multiple worksheets enables you to place summarized data first. Managers interested only in an overall picture can view the first worksheet of summary data without looking at the details available in the other worksheets. Others, of course, might want to view the supporting data in the individual worksheets that follow the summary worksheet. In the case of Global Travel, Rhohit used separate worksheets to summarize the number of tickets sold and sales in dollars for the New Mexico branch offices for each quarter of the 2013 fiscal year. You will open Rhohit's workbook and review the current information.

## To open and review the Global Travel workbook:

1. Open the **NM** workbook located in the Excel6\Tutorial folder included with your Data Files, and then save the workbook as **New Mexico** in the same folder.
2. In the **Documentation** worksheet, enter your name and the date.
3. Switch to the **Quarter 1** worksheet, and then view the number of tickets sold and sales for the first quarter of the year. See Figure 6-1.

**Figure 6-1** Quarter 1 worksheet for Global Travel – New Mexico

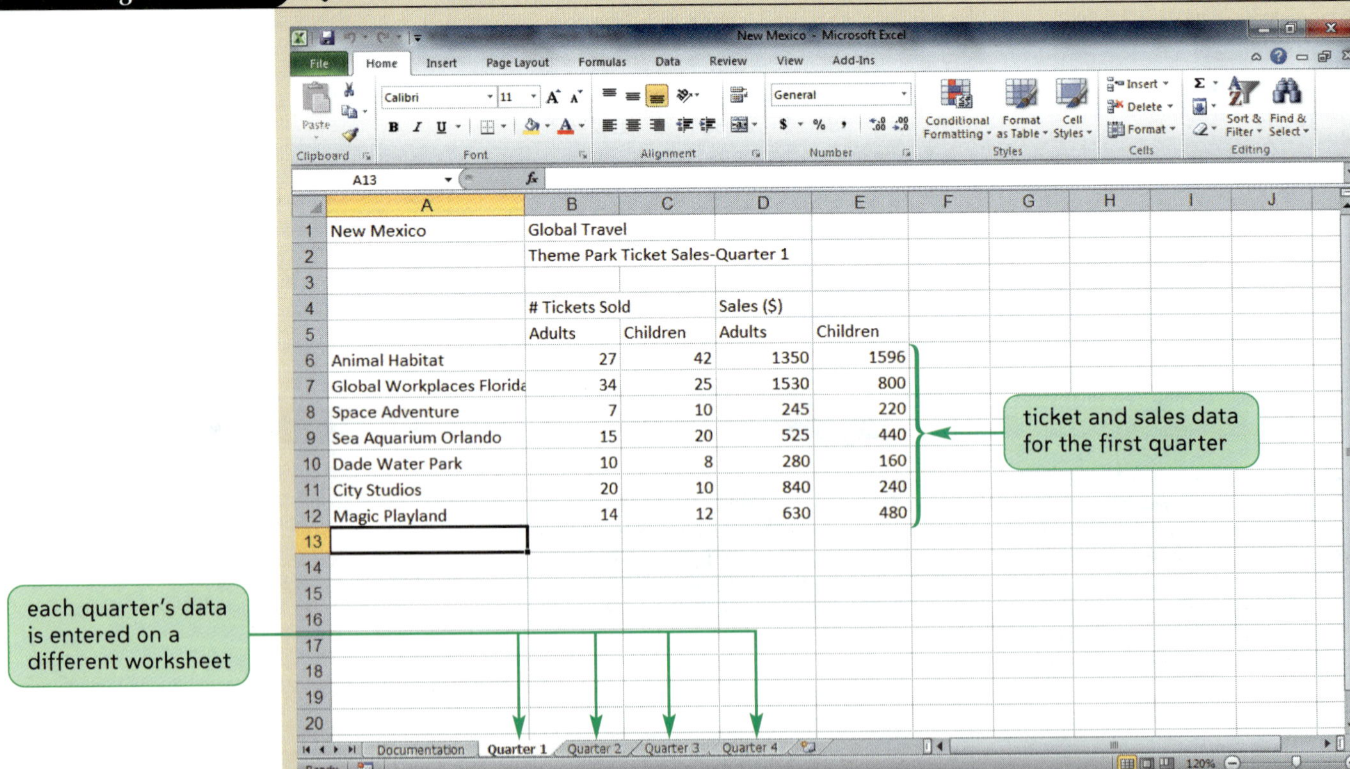


4. Review the **Quarter 2**, **Quarter 3**, and **Quarter 4** worksheets. The layout for all four worksheets is identical.

Rhohit didn't enter any formulas in the workbook. You need to enter formulas to calculate the total number of tickets and sales for each column (B through E) in all four worksheets. Rather than retyping the formulas in each worksheet, you can enter them all at once by creating a worksheet group. A worksheet group, like a range, can contain adjacent or nonadjacent worksheets. In group-editing mode, most editing tasks that you do to the active worksheet also affect the other worksheets in the group. By forming a worksheet group, you can:

- Enter or edit data and formulas in the active worksheet to enter or edit the data and formulas in the same cells in all the worksheets in the group. Find and replace can also be used with a worksheet group.
- Apply formatting to the active worksheet to format all the worksheets in the group, including changing row heights or column widths and applying conditional formatting.
- Insert or delete rows and columns of the active worksheet to make the same changes to all the worksheets in the group.
- Set the page layout options in one worksheet to apply the settings to all worksheets in the group, such as changing the orientation, scaling to fit, and inserting headers and footers.
- Apply view options such as zooming, showing and hiding worksheets, and so forth to all worksheets in the group.
- Print all the worksheets in the worksheet group at the same time.

Worksheet groups save you time and help improve consistency among the worksheets because you can perform an action once, yet affect multiple worksheets.

REFERENCE

### *Grouping and Ungrouping Worksheets*

- To select an adjacent group, click the sheet tab of the first worksheet in the group, press and hold the Shift key, click the sheet tab of the last worksheet in the group, and then release the Shift key.
- To select a nonadjacent group, click the sheet tab of one worksheet in the group, press and hold the Ctrl key, click the sheet tabs of the remaining worksheets in the group, and then release the Ctrl key.
- To ungroup the worksheets, click the sheet tab of a worksheet not in the group.

  *or*
- Right-click the sheet tab of one worksheet in the group, and then click Ungroup Sheets on the shortcut menu.

In the New Mexico workbook, you'll group an adjacent range of worksheets: the Quarter 1 worksheet through the Quarter 4 worksheet.

### To group the quarterly worksheets:

1. Click the **Quarter 1** sheet tab to make the worksheet active. This is the first worksheet you want to include in the group.
2. Press and hold the **Shift** key, and then click the **Quarter 4** sheet tab. This is the last worksheet you want to include in the group.
3. Release the **Shift** key. The sheet tabs for Quarter 1 through Quarter 4 are white, indicating they are all selected. The text "[Group]" appears in the title bar to remind you that a worksheet group is selected in the workbook. See Figure 6-2.

**TIP**

If you cannot see the sheet tab of a worksheet you want to include in a group, use the sheet navigation controls to display it.

**Figure 6-2** Grouped worksheets

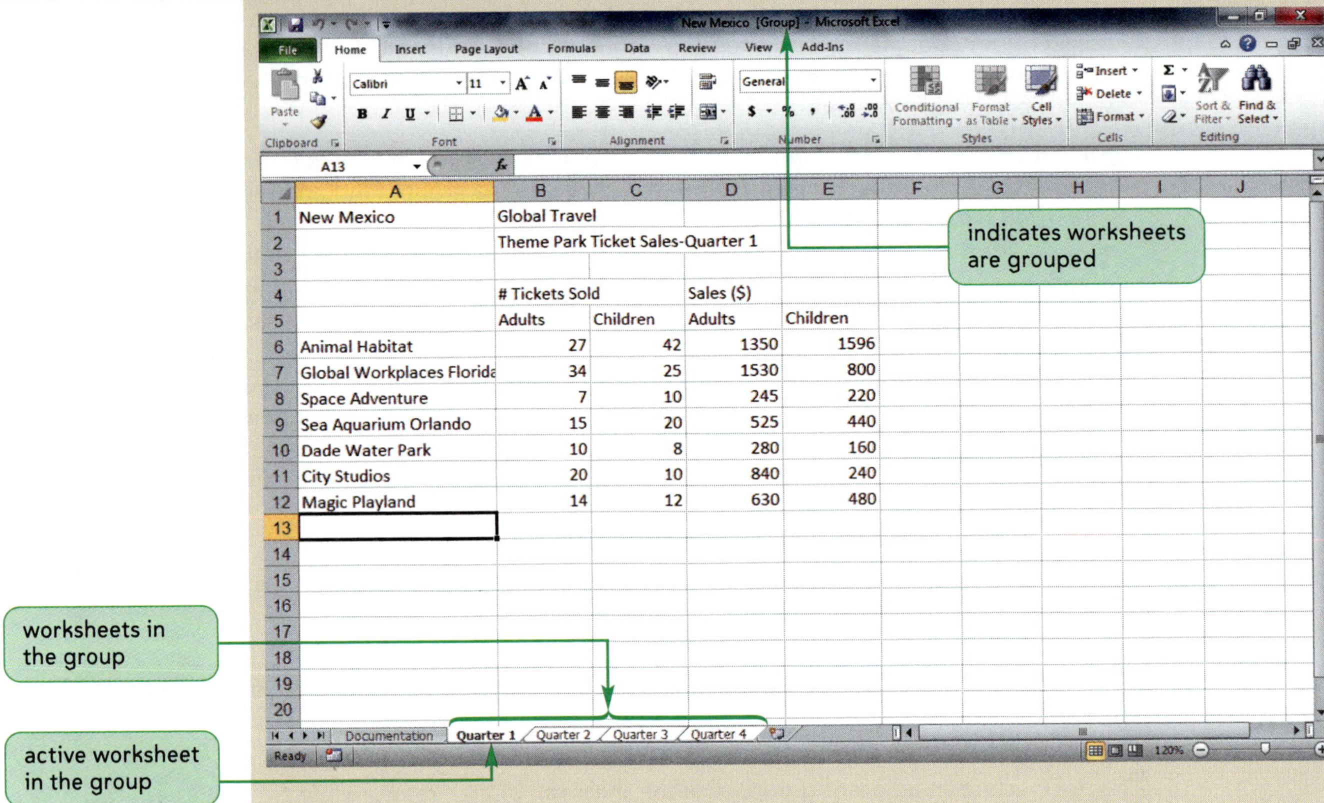


## Entering Formulas in a Worksheet Group

When you enter a formula in the active worksheet (in this case, the Quarter 1 worksheet), the formula is entered in the same cells in all the worksheets in the group. The grouped worksheets must have the exact same organization and layout (rows and columns) for this to work. Otherwise, any formulas you enter in the active sheet will be incorrect in the other worksheets in the group and could overwrite existing data. With the quarterly sheets grouped, you will enter the formulas to calculate the total number of tickets sold and total sales.

### To enter formulas in the worksheet group:

1. Click cell **B13**. You want to enter the formula in cell B13 in each of the four worksheets in the group.
2. In the Editing group on the Home tab, click the **Sum** button Σ, and then press the **Enter** key. The formula =SUM(B6:B12) is entered in the cell, adding the total number of adult tickets sold in the quarter, which is 127.
3. Copy the formula in cell B13 to the range **C13:E13**. The formula calculates the total number of children's tickets sold (127), the total adult ticket sales ($5400), as well as the total children's ticket sales ($3936).
4. In cell A13, enter **Totals**, and then click the **Increase Indent** button in the Alignment group on the Home tab. The label shifts to the right.

   The formulas and label you entered in the Quarter 1 worksheet were entered in the Quarter 2, 3, and 4 worksheets at the same time.

5. Click the **Quarter 2** sheet tab, and then click cell **B13**. The value 174 appears in the cell and the formula =SUM(B6:B12), which adds the number of adult tickets sold in Quarter 2, appears in the formula bar.
6. Click the **Quarter 4** sheet tab, and then make sure that cell **B13** is the active cell. The value 177 appears in the cell, and the same formula used in cell B13 in the Quarter 1 and Quarter 2 worksheets appears in the formula bar. See Figure 6-3.

**Figure 6-3** **Formulas entered in all worksheets in the group**

formula in cell B13 is the same in all the grouped worksheets

Quarter 4 worksheet has same layout as the Quarter 1, 2, and 3 worksheets

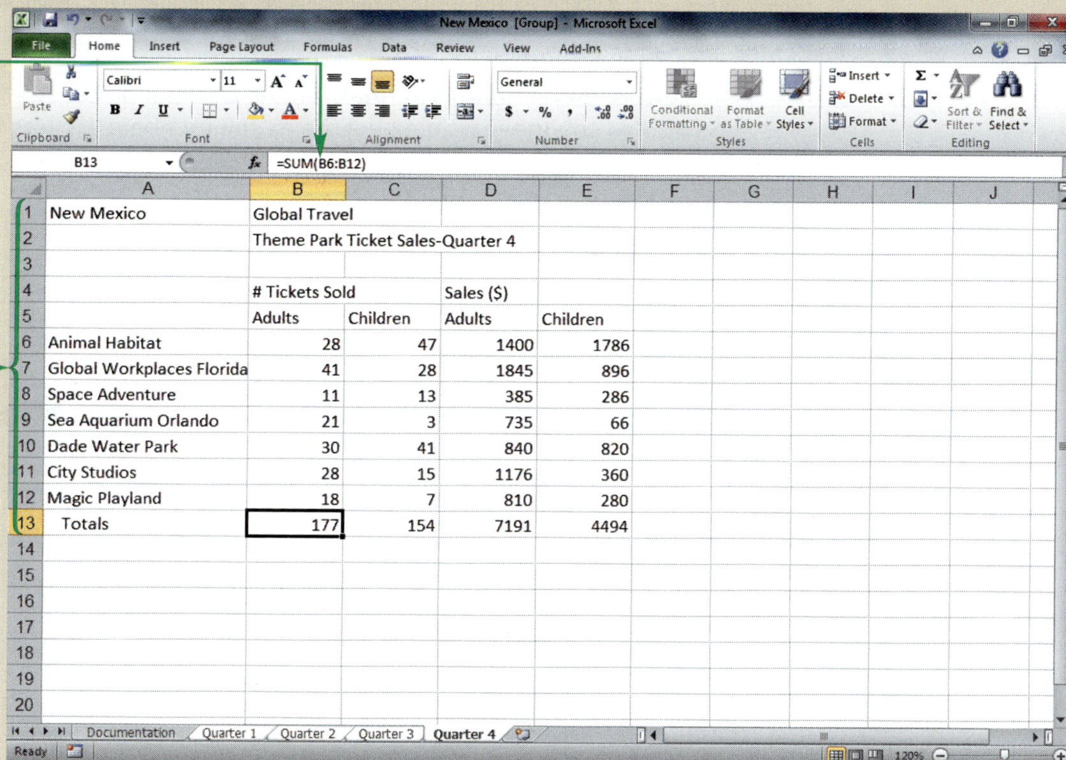


7. Click the **Quarter 1** sheet tab to redisplay the Quarter 1 results.

INSIGHT

### *Editing Grouped Worksheets*

When you enter, edit, or format cells in a worksheet group, the changes you make to one worksheet are automatically applied to the other worksheets in the group. For example, if you delete a value from one cell, the content is also deleted from the same cell in all the worksheets in the group. Be cautious when editing a worksheet that is part of a group. If the layout and structure of the other grouped worksheets are not exactly the same, you may inadvertently overwrite data in some of the worksheets. Also, remember to ungroup the worksheet group after you finish entering data, formulas, and formatting. Otherwise, changes you intend to make in one worksheet will be made to all the worksheets in the group, potentially producing incorrect results.

## Formatting a Worksheet Group

As with inserting formulas and text, any formatting changes you make to the active sheet are applied to all sheets in the group. You will format the quarterly worksheets.

### To apply formatting to the worksheet group:

1. Bold the text in the nonadjacent range **A1:B2;A6:A13;B4:E5**.
2. Increase the width of column A to **24**.
3. Merge and center each of the following ranges: **B1:E1**, **B2:E2**, **B4:C4**, and **D4:E4**.
4. Center the text in the range **B5:E5**.
5. Apply the **Comma Style** number format with no decimal places to the range B6:C13. No change is visible because all the numbers are less than 1000.
6. Apply the **Accounting** number format with no decimal places to the range D6:E13 so the values appear with a dollar sign and no decimal places.
7. Add a **bottom border** to the ranges B5:E5 and B12:E12.
8. Click cell **A1**. All the worksheets in the group are formatted. See Figure 6-4.

**Figure 6-4** Formatting applied to the worksheet group

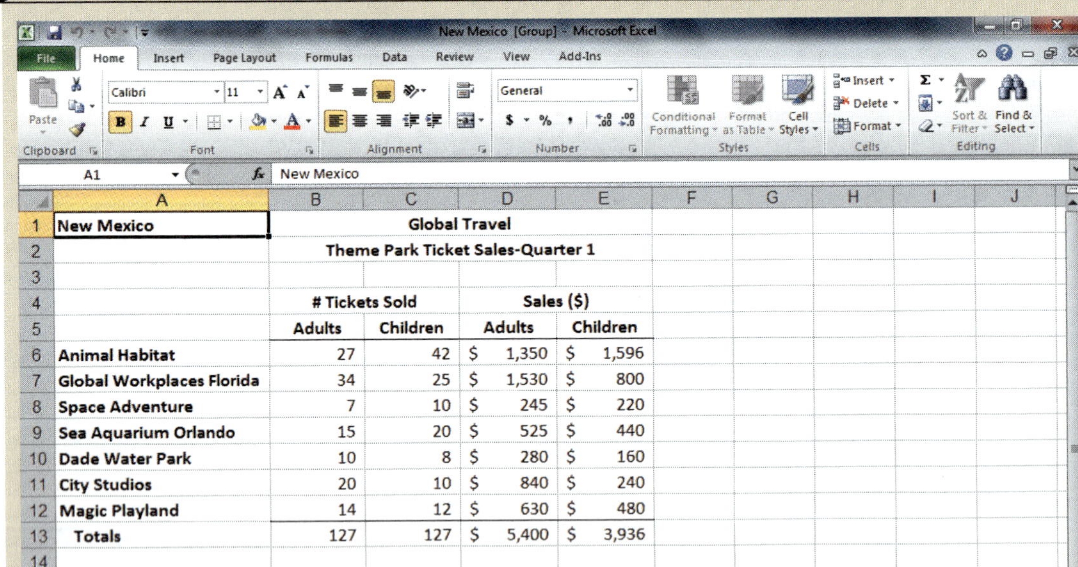


| | A | B | C | D | E |
|---|---|---|---|---|---|
| 1 | New Mexico | Global Travel | | | |
| 2 | | Theme Park Ticket Sales-Quarter 1 | | | |
| 3 | | | | | |
| 4 | | # Tickets Sold | | Sales ($) | |
| 5 | | Adults | Children | Adults | Children |
| 6 | Animal Habitat | 27 | 42 | $ 1,350 | $ 1,596 |
| 7 | Global Workplaces Florida | 34 | 25 | $ 1,530 | $ 800 |
| 8 | Space Adventure | 7 | 10 | $ 245 | $ 220 |
| 9 | Sea Aquarium Orlando | 15 | 20 | $ 525 | $ 440 |
| 10 | Dade Water Park | 10 | 8 | $ 280 | $ 160 |
| 11 | City Studios | 20 | 10 | $ 840 | $ 240 |
| 12 | Magic Playland | 14 | 12 | $ 630 | $ 480 |
| 13 | Totals | 127 | 127 | $ 5,400 | $ 3,936 |
| 14 | | | | | |

9. Click each sheet tab in the worksheet group and review the formatting changes, and then click the **Quarter 1** sheet tab.

## Ungrouping Worksheets

When you ungroup the worksheets, each worksheet functions independently again. If you forget to ungroup the worksheets, any changes you make in one worksheet will be applied to all the worksheets in the group. So be sure to ungroup worksheets when you are finished with changes that apply to multiple worksheets.

You will ungroup the quarterly worksheets so you can work in each worksheet separately.

**To ungroup the quarterly worksheets:**

Be sure to ungroup the worksheets; otherwise, any changes you make will affect all worksheets in the group.

1. Click the **Documentation** sheet tab. The worksheets are ungrouped because the Documentation worksheet was not part of the worksheet group. The text "[Group]" no longer appears in the Excel title bar.
2. Verify that the worksheets are ungrouped and the word "[Group]" no longer appears in the title bar.

PROSKILLS

*Written Communication: Using Multiple Worksheets with Identical Layouts*

Using multiple worksheets to organize complex data can help make it simpler to understand and analyze as well as to navigate to specific data. For example, a workbook that contains data about a variety of products, stores, or regions could use a different worksheet for each product, store, or region. This organization provides a way to view discrete units of data that can be combined and summarized in another worksheet.

When you use multiple worksheets to organize similar types of data, the worksheets should have identical layouts. You can quickly group the worksheets with the identical layouts, and then enter the formulas, formatting, and labels in all of the grouped worksheets at once. This helps to ensure consistency and accuracy among the worksheets as well as make it faster to create the different worksheets needed.

Using multiple worksheets with identical layouts enables you to use 3-D references to quickly summarize the data in another worksheet. The summary worksheet provides an overall picture of the data that is detailed in the other worksheets. Often, managers are more interested in this big picture view. However, the supporting data is still available in the individual worksheets when a deeper analysis is needed.

So, when you are working with a large and complex worksheet filled with data, consider the different ways to organize it in multiple worksheets. Not only will you save time when entering and finding data, but also the data becomes more understandable, and connections and results become clearer.

# Working with Multiple Worksheets

Rhohit wants the workbook to include a Summary worksheet that adds the annual totals of tickets and sales from the quarterly worksheets. Rather than starting from scratch, you will copy one of the quarterly worksheets as a starting point. The formulas you create in the Summary worksheet will reference cells in each quarterly worksheet using 3-D references. You can then group the completed worksheets to develop a consistent page setup in all worksheets and then print them all at once.

## Copying Worksheets

Often, after spending a lot of time developing a worksheet, you can use the existing worksheet as a starting point for creating another, saving you time and energy compared to building a new worksheet from scratch. Copying a worksheet duplicates all the values, formulas, and formats into the new worksheet, leaving the original worksheet intact. You can then edit, reformat, and enter new content as needed to create the exact worksheet you need.

Next, you'll create the Summary worksheet to provide an overall picture of the data included in the detailed quarterly worksheets. The Summary worksheet needs the same formatting and structure as the quarterly worksheets. To ensure consistency among worksheets, you will copy the Quarter 1 worksheet, and then modify its contents.

REFERENCE

*Copying Worksheets*

- Select the sheet tabs of the worksheets you want to copy.
- Right-click the sheet tabs, and then click Move or Copy on the shortcut menu.
- Click the To book arrow, and then click the name of an existing workbook or click (new book) to create a new workbook for the worksheets.
- In the Before sheet box, click the worksheet you want to insert the new worksheet before.
- Click the Create a copy check box to insert a check mark to copy the worksheets.
- Click the OK button.

*or*

- Select the sheet tabs of the worksheets you want to copy.
- Press and hold the Ctrl key as you drag the selected sheet tabs to a new location in the sheet tabs, and then release the Ctrl key.

You'll copy the Quarter 1 worksheet to the beginning of the workbook, and then modify the new copy to create the Summary worksheet.

**TIP**

To move a worksheet or worksheet group to another location in the same workbook, select the worksheets and then drag and drop them by the selected sheet tabs.

**To copy the Quarter 1 worksheet and create the Summary worksheet:**

1. Click the **Quarter 1** sheet tab, and then press and hold the **Ctrl** key as you drag the worksheet to the left of the Documentation sheet. The pointer changes to and a triangle indicates the drop location.
2. Release the mouse button, and then release the **Ctrl** key. An identical copy of the Quarter 1 worksheet appears in the new location. The sheet tab shows "Quarter 1 (2)" to indicate that this is the copied sheet.
3. Rename the Quarter 1 (2) worksheet as **Summary**.
4. Move the **Summary** worksheet between the Documentation worksheet and the Quarter 1 worksheet.
5. Make sure the **Summary** worksheet is the active sheet. You will modify the Summary worksheet.
6. In cell A2, enter **2013**. This is the year to which the summary refers.
7. In cell B2, enter **Theme Park Ticket Sales-Total**. The new title reflects this worksheet's content.
8. Select the range **B6:E12**, and then press the **Delete** key. The Quarter 1 sales data is removed, but the formatting remains intact and will apply to the combined sales data for all four quarters that you will enter shortly.

## Referencing Cells and Ranges in Other Worksheets

When you use multiple worksheets to organize related data, you can reference a cell or range in another worksheet in the same workbook. For example, the Summary worksheet references cells in the four quarterly worksheets to calculate the total sales for the entire year. The syntax to reference a cell or range in a different worksheet is as follows:

```
=SheetName!CellRange
```

In this formula, *SheetName* is the worksheet's name as listed on the sheet tab and *CellRange* is the reference for the cell or range in that worksheet. An exclamation mark (!) separates the worksheet reference from the cell or range reference. For example, you could enter the following formula in the Summary worksheet to reference cell D10 in the Quarter1 worksheet:

```
=Quarter1!D10
```

If the worksheet name contains spaces, you must enclose the sheet name in single quotation marks. For example, the following formula references cell D10 in the Quarter 1 worksheet:

```
='Quarter 1'!D10
```

You can use these references to create formulas that reference cells in different locations in different worksheets. For example, to add sales from two worksheets—cell E12 in the Quarter 1 worksheet and cell D12 in the Quarter 2 worksheet—you would enter the following formula:

```
='Quarter 1'!E12+'Quarter 2'!D12
```

You could type the formula directly in the cell, but it is faster and more accurate to use the point-and-click method to enter references to other worksheets.

REFERENCE

### *Entering a Formula with References to Another Worksheet*

- Click the cell where you want to enter the formula.
- Type = and begin entering the formula.
- To insert a reference from another worksheet, click the sheet tab for the worksheet, and then click the cell or select the range you want to reference.
- When the formula is complete, press the Enter key.

Rhohit wants you to enter a formula in cell A2 in each quarterly worksheet that displays the fiscal year from cell A2 in the Summary worksheet. All four quarterly worksheets will use the formula =Summary!A2 to reference the fiscal year in cell A2 of the Summary sheet.

### To enter the formula that references the Summary worksheet:

1. Click the **Quarter 1** sheet tab, press and hold the **Shift** key, and then click the **Quarter 4** worksheet. The Quarter 1 through Quarter 4 worksheets are grouped.
2. Click cell **A2**. This is the cell in which you want to enter the formula to display the fiscal year.
3. Type **=** to begin the formula, click the **Summary** sheet tab, and then click cell **A2**. The reference to cell A2 in the Summary worksheet is added to the formula in cell A2 in the grouped worksheets.
4. On the formula bar, click the **Enter** button ✓. The formula =Summary!A2 is entered in cell A2 in all the worksheets in the group. The formula appears in the formula bar and 2013 appears in cell A2. See Figure 6-5.

Figure 6-5 **Formula with a worksheet reference**

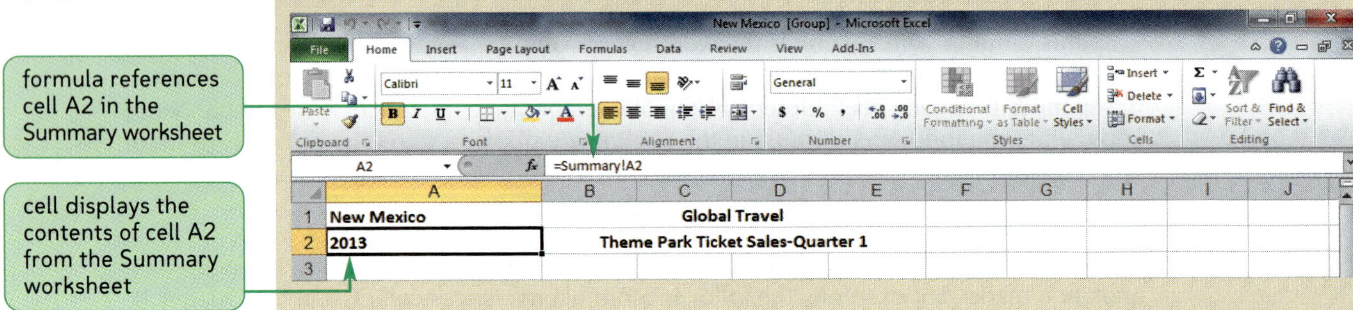


5. In each worksheet in the group, verify that the formula =Summary!A2 appears in the formula bar and 2013 appears in cell A2.
6. Switch to the **Summary** worksheet. The quarterly worksheets are ungrouped.
7. In cell A2, enter **Fiscal Year - 2013**. The descriptive label in cell A2 is entered in the Summary worksheet, and is also displayed in the quarterly worksheets because of the formula you entered.
8. Verify that the label "Fiscal Year - 2013" appears in cell A2 in the Quarter 1 through Quarter 4 worksheets.

## Using 3-D References to Add Values Across Worksheets

You need to calculate the number of tickets sold and the total sales for each theme park for the year, and display the totals for the fiscal year in the Summary worksheet. To calculate the totals for the year, you can add the results from each quarterly worksheet and place the sum in the Summary worksheet. For example, in cell B6 of the Summary worksheet, you can enter the formula:

```
='Quarter 1'!B6+'Quarter 2'!B6+'Quarter 3'!B6+'Quarter 4'!B6
```

This formula calculates the number of Adult tickets sold to Animal Habitat by adding the values in cell B6 in each of the quarterly worksheets. Continuing this approach for the entire worksheet is time consuming and error prone.

Instead, when two or more worksheets have *identical* row and column layouts, as do the quarterly worksheets in the New Mexico workbook, you can enter formulas with 3-D references to summarize those worksheets in another worksheet. The 3-D reference specifies not only the range of rows and columns, but also the range of worksheet names in which the cells appear. The general syntax of a 3-D cell reference is:

```
WorksheetRange!CellRange
```

In this syntax, *WorksheetRange* is the range of worksheets you want to reference and is entered as *FirstSheetName:LastSheetName* with a colon separating the first and last worksheets in the worksheet range. *CellRange* is the same cell or range in each of those worksheets that you want to reference. An exclamation mark (!) separates the worksheet range from the cell or range. For example, the following formula adds the values in cell E13 in the worksheets between Quarter1 and Quarter4, including Quarter1 and Quarter4:

```
=SUM(Quarter1:Quarter4!E13)
```

If worksheets named Quarter1, Quarter2, Quarter3, and Quarter4 are included in the workbook, the worksheet range Quarter1:Quarter4 references all four worksheets. Although the Quarter2 and Quarter3 worksheets aren't specifically mentioned in this 3-D reference, all worksheets positioned within the starting and ending names are included in the calculation.

INSIGHT

### *Managing 3-D References*

The results of a formula using a 3-D reference reflect the current worksheets in the worksheet range. If you move a worksheet outside the referenced worksheet range or remove a worksheet from the workbook, the formula results will change. For example, consider a workbook with four worksheets named Quarter1, Quarter2, Quarter3, and Quarter4. If you move the Quarter3 worksheet after the Quarter4 worksheet, the worksheet range Quarter1:Quarter4 includes only the Quarter1, Quarter2, and Quarter4 worksheets. Similarly, if you insert a new worksheet or move an existing worksheet within the worksheet range, the formula results reflect the change. To continue the example, if you insert a Quarter5 worksheet before the Quarter4 worksheet, the 3-D reference Quarter1:Quarter4 includes the Quarter5 worksheet.

When you create a formula, make sure that the 3-D cell reference reflects the appropriate worksheets. Also, if you later insert or delete a worksheet within the 3-D reference, be aware of how doing so will affect the formula results.

3-D references are often used in formulas that contain Excel functions, including SUM, AVERAGE, COUNT, MAX, MIN, STD, and VAR.

REFERENCE

### *Entering a Function That Contains a 3-D Reference*

- Click the cell where you want to enter the formula.
- Type = to begin the formula, type the name of the function, and then type ( to indicate the beginning of the argument.
- Click the sheet tab for the first worksheet in the worksheet range, press and hold the Shift key, and then click the tab for the last worksheet in the worksheet range.
- Select the cell or range to reference, and then press the Enter key.

In the New Mexico workbook, you'll use 3-D references in the Summary worksheet to add the total number of tickets sold and sales for the year. You will begin by entering a formula to add the number of tickets sold to adults for the Animal Habitat theme park in all four quarters of the year. Then, you'll copy this formula to calculate the tickets sold to adults and children for each theme park as well as the sales generated.

### To enter a formula with a 3-D reference to the quarterly worksheets:

1. In the Summary worksheet, click cell **B6**, and then type **=SUM(** to begin the formula. A ScreenTip shows the SUM function syntax. See Figure 6-6. You'll enter a 3-D reference to cell B6 in the four quarterly worksheets.

**Figure 6-6** **Formula for the 3-D reference**

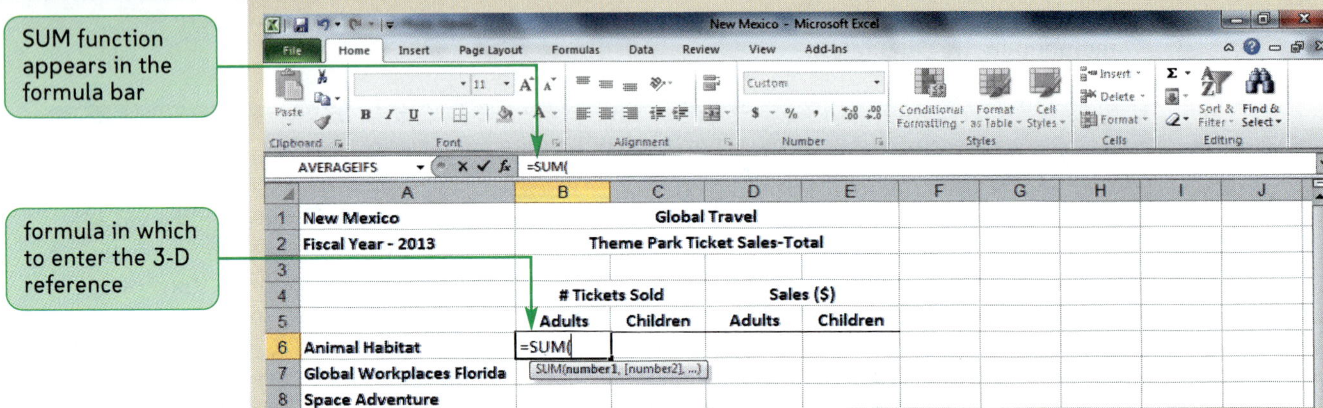


2. Click the **Quarter 1** sheet tab, press and hold the **Shift** key, click the **Quarter 4** sheet tab, and then release the **Shift** key. The worksheet range is selected and added to the SUM function as 'Quarter 1:Quarter 4'. Single quotation marks appear around the worksheet range because the worksheet names include spaces.
3. In the Quarter 1 worksheet, click cell **B6**. The cell is selected and added to the function. See Figure 6-7.

**Figure 6-7** **SUM function with a 3-D reference**

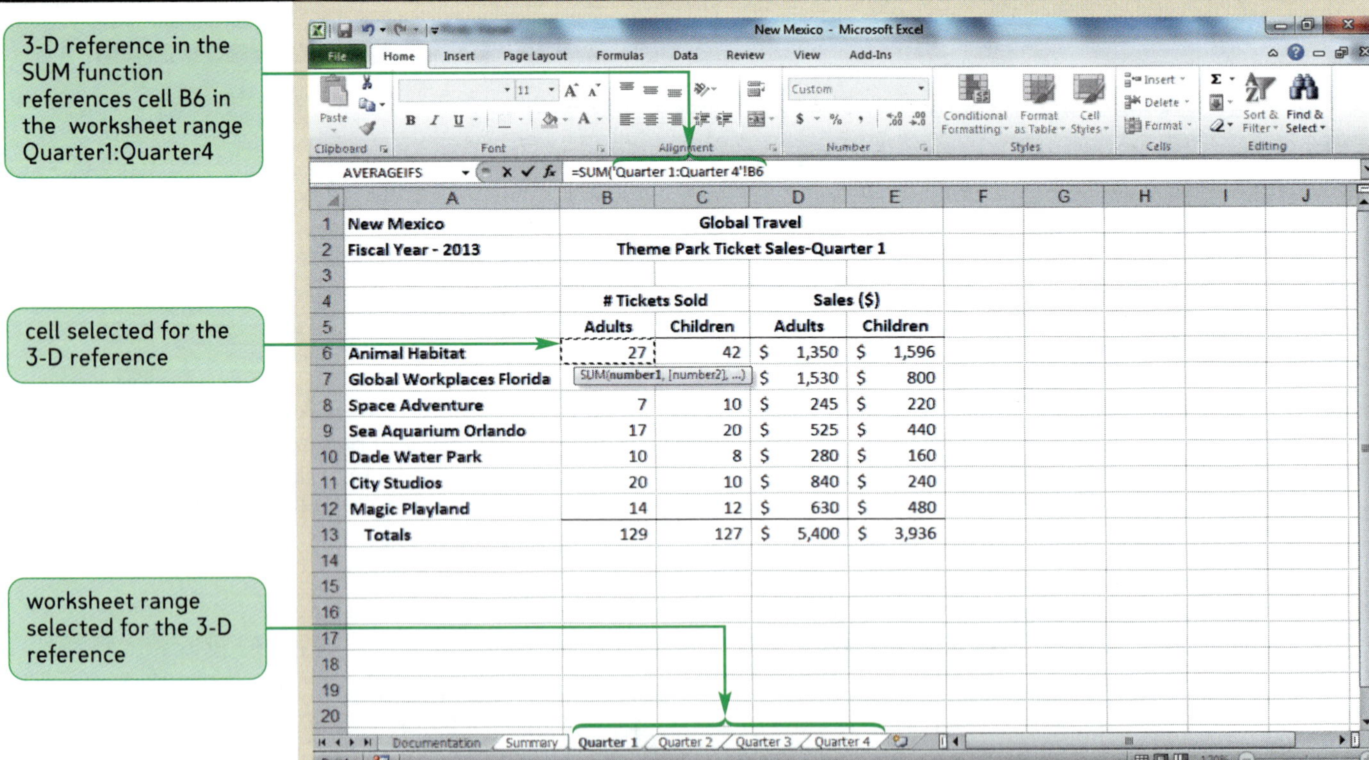


4. Press the **Enter** key to complete the formula. The closing right parenthesis is automatically inserted at the end of the formula.

5. In the Summary worksheet, click cell **B6**. The completed formula =SUM('Quarter 1:Quarter 4'!B6) appears in the formula bar. The total number of tickets for Animal Habitat sold to adults in 2013—116—appears in cell B6.

You'll repeat the process to enter a 3-D reference in cell C6 that adds the total number of tickets sold to children for Animal Habitat in 2013.

**TIP**

You could also copy the formula in cell B6 to cells C6 to E6.

### To enter another formula with a 3-D reference:

1. In the Summary worksheet, click cell **C6**, and then type **=SUM(** to begin the formula.
2. Click the **Quarter 1** sheet tab, press and hold the **Shift** key, click the **Quarter 4** sheet tab, and then release the **Shift** key. The quarterly worksheets are grouped.
3. In the Quarter 1 worksheet, click cell **C6** to select the cell, and then press the **Enter** key to complete the formula and return to the Summary worksheet.
4. In the Summary worksheet, click cell **C6**. The formula =SUM('Quarter 1:Quarter 4'!C6) appears in the formula bar. Also, the value 175—the total number of tickets sold to children for Animal Habitat in 2013—appears in cell C6.

In cells D6 and E6, you'll enter the SUM function with a 3-D reference to calculate the total revenue from tickets sales for Animal Habitat.

### To calculate total sales revenue for Animal Habitat:

1. In the Summary worksheet, click cell **D6**, and then type **=SUM(** to begin the formula.
2. Group the **Quarter 1** through **Quarter 4** worksheets, and then click cell **D6**.
3. Press the **Enter** key. The SUM function with a 3-D reference to cell D6 in the quarterly worksheets is entered. The completed formula is =SUM('Quarter 1:Quarter 4'!D6) and the total revenue from ticket sales to adults for Animal Habitat in 2013 is $5,800.
4. In the Summary worksheet, click cell **E6**, and then enter the SUM function formula with a 3-D reference to cell **E6** in the quarterly worksheets. The completed formula is =SUM('Quarter 1:Quarter 4'!E6) and the total revenue from ticket sales to children for Animal Habitat in 2013 is $6,650.

Instead of entering the SUM function to create the totals for the remaining theme parks, you can copy the formulas to the rest of the range. You copy formulas with 3-D references the same way you copy other formulas—using copy and paste or AutoFill. You'll copy the formulas in the range B6:E6 to the range B7:E12 so you can calculate the total ticket sales and revenue in 2013 for the remaining theme parks.

### To copy the formulas with 3-D cell references:

1. Select the range **B6:E6**. This range contains the SUM functions with the 3-D references you already entered.

2. Drag the fill handle over the range B7:E12. The formulas are copied for the rest of the theme park rows. The Auto Fill Options button appears below the copied range.
3. Click the **Auto Fill Options** button, and then click the **Fill Without Formatting** option button. You don't want to copy the formatting in this case because you want to keep the bottom border formatting in the range B12:E12. The total values for the year appear in the range.
4. Click cell **B6** to deselect the range. The Summary worksheet now shows the totals for 2013 in New Mexico for each theme park as well as statewide totals. See Figure 6-8.

**Figure 6-8** **Summary worksheet with all the 3-D reference formulas**

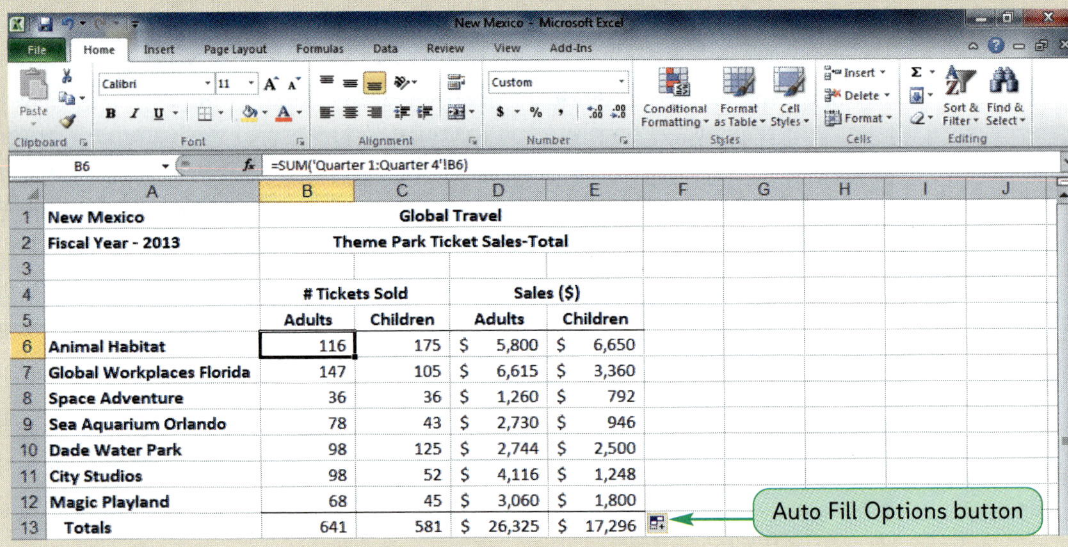


One benefit of summarizing data using 3-D reference formulas, like any other formula, is that if you change the value in one worksheet, the results of formulas that reference that cell reflect the change. Rhohit has discovered an error in the ticket sales data. Sea Aquarium Orlando sold 17 adult tickets in Quarter 1, not 15. You will correct the number of tickets sold for Sea Aquarium Orlando in Quarter 1.

## To change the ticket value in the Quarter 1 worksheet:

1. In the Summary worksheet, note that 78 adult tickets were sold for Sea Aquarium Orlando in 2013 and 641 total adult tickets were sold.
2. Switch to the **Quarter 1** worksheet, and then, in cell B9, enter **17**. The total adult tickets sold in Quarter 1 is now 129.

   The results in the Summary worksheet are also updated because of the 3-D references in the formulas.
3. Switch to the **Summary** worksheet. The total number of tickets sold to adults for Sea Aquarium Orlando in 2013 is now 80, and the total number of tickets sold to adults for all theme parks in 2013 is now 643. See Figure 6-9.

**Figure 6-9** Summary worksheet with the updated ticket data

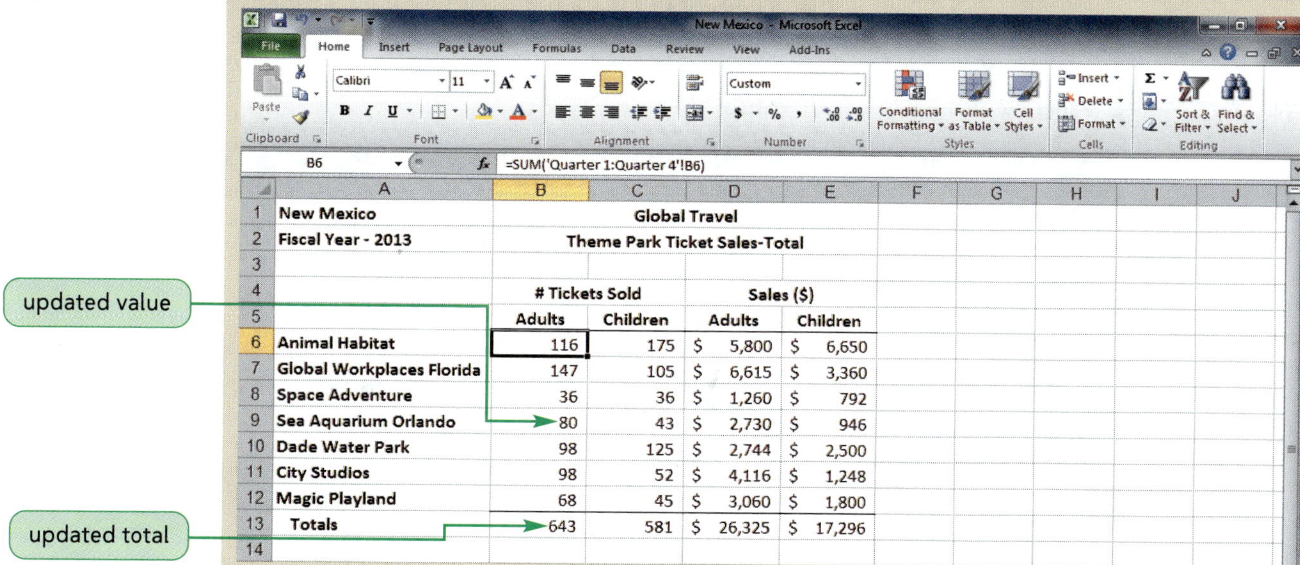


## Printing a Worksheet Group

By creating a worksheet group, you apply the same page layout settings to all the worksheets in the group at the same time. You can also print all the worksheets in the group at once.

Rhohit wants a printed copy of the five ticket sales worksheets to include in his report. Each page should have the same setup. Because the layout will be the same for all the quarterly worksheets in the New Mexico workbook, you can speed the page layout setup by creating a worksheet group before selecting settings.

### To print the Summary and quarterly worksheets with a custom header and footer:

Be sure to include all five worksheets in the group so that you can apply page layout settings and print the worksheets at once.

1. Group the **Summary**, **Quarter 1**, **Quarter 2**, **Quarter 3**, and **Quarter 4** worksheets. The five worksheets are grouped.
2. Click the **Page Layout** tab on the Ribbon, and then, in the Page Setup group, click the **Dialog Box Launcher**. The Page Setup dialog box opens with the Page tab active.
3. Click the **Margins** tab, and then, in the Center on page section, click the **Horizontally** check box to insert a check mark. The printed content will be centered horizontally on the page.
4. Click the **Header/Footer** tab, click the **Custom Header** button to open the Header dialog box, click in the **Center section** box, click the **Insert Sheet Name** button to add the &[Tab] code in the section box to insert the sheet tab name in the center section of the header, and then click the **OK** button. A preview of the header appears in the upper portion of the dialog box.
5. Click the **Custom Footer** button to open the Footer dialog box, type your name in the Left section box, click in the Right section box, click the **Insert Date** button to add the &[Date] code in the section box to insert the current date in the right section of the footer, and then click the **OK** button.

6. Click the **Print Preview** button. The preview of the Summary worksheet, the first worksheet in the group, appears on the Print tab in Backstage view. See Figure 6-10.

**Figure 6-10** **Preview of the worksheet group**

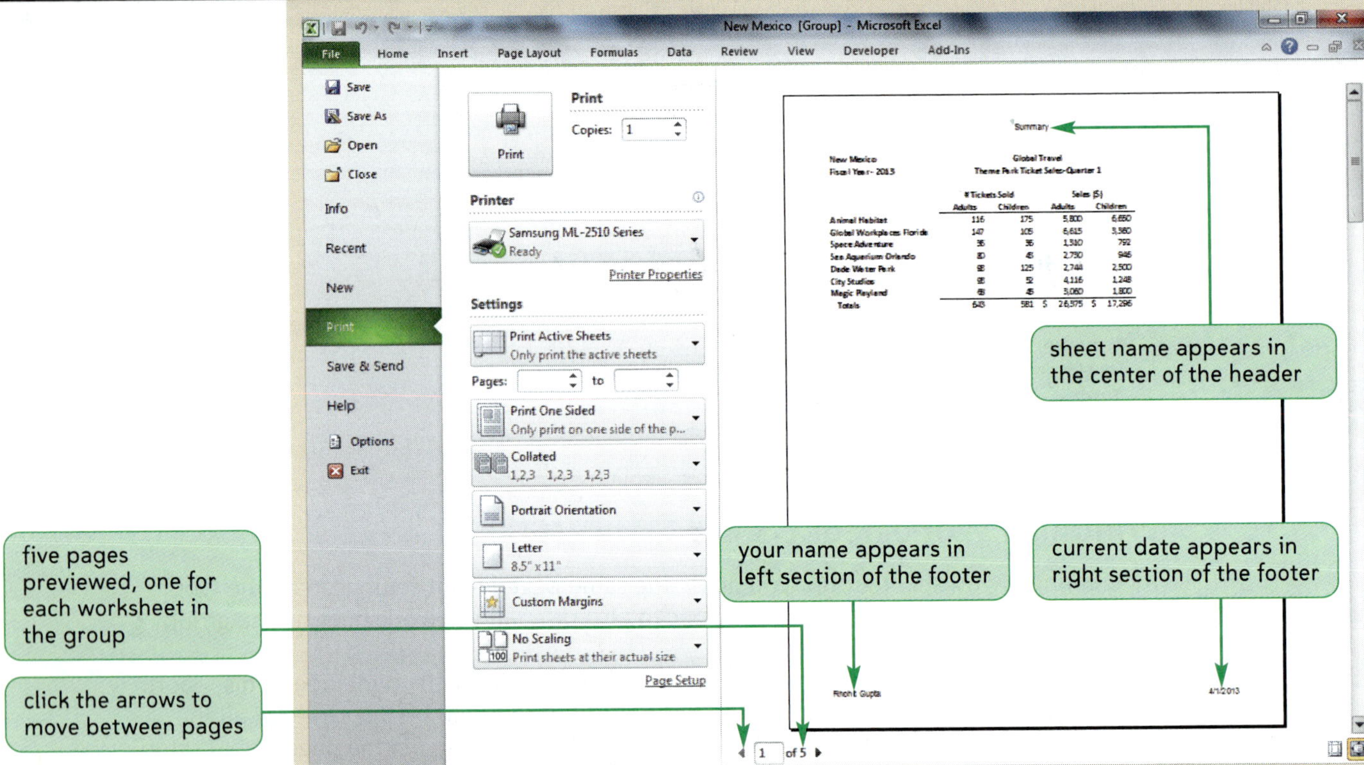


7. Below the preview, click the **Next Page** button four times to view the other worksheets in the group. Each page has the same page layout but the header shows the sheet tab names.

   **Trouble?** If only one page appears in the preview, the worksheets are not grouped. Click the File tab to exit Backstage view, and then repeat Steps 1 through 7.

8. Unless you are instructed to print, click the **Home** tab to exit Backstage view without printing the worksheet group. Otherwise, click the **Print** button.

9. Switch to the **Documentation** sheet to ungroup the worksheets, and then switch to the **Summary** worksheet.

In this session, you consolidated the data in Global Travel's New Mexico workbook in a Summary sheet, so that Rhohit and Alvin can quickly see the totals for the theme park sales. In the next session, you will help Alvin determine the annual totals for all of Global Travel's Southwest locations—New Mexico, Utah, and Colorado.

REVIEW

## *Session 6.1 Quick Check*

1. What is a worksheet group?
2. How do you select an adjacent worksheet group? How do you select a non-adjacent worksheet group? How do you deselect a worksheet group?
3. What formula would you enter in the Summary worksheet to reference cell A10 in the Quarter 2 worksheet?
4. What is the 3-D cell reference to cell A10 in the adjacent Summary 1, Summary 2, and Summary 3 worksheets?
5. Explain what the formula =MAX(Sheet1:Sheet4!B1) calculates.
6. If you insert a new worksheet named Sheet5 after Sheet4, how would you change the formula =MAX(Sheet1:Sheet4!B1) to include Sheet5 in the calculation?
7. If you insert a new worksheet named Sheet5 before Sheet4, how would you change the formula =MAX(Sheet1:Sheet4!B1) to include Sheet5 in the calculation?
8. How do you apply the same page layout to all of the worksheets in a workbook at one time?

# SESSION 6.2 VISUAL OVERVIEW

An **external reference** is a reference to cells or ranges in a worksheet from another workbook. For example, *'[New Mexico.xlsx]Summary'!$B6* references cell B6 in the Summary worksheet in the New Mexico workbook.

When two workbooks are linked, the **destination file** (sometimes referred to as the dependent file) is the workbook that receives data from another workbook. In this case, the Totals 2013 workbook is the destination file.

The total value shown in the destination file is calculated from values in the three source files.

Whenever a value in a source file changes, the destination is also updated to reflect the most recent information. For example, if Animal Habitat sales in New Mexico increase by four tickets, the changes are also reflected in the Totals 2013 workbook.

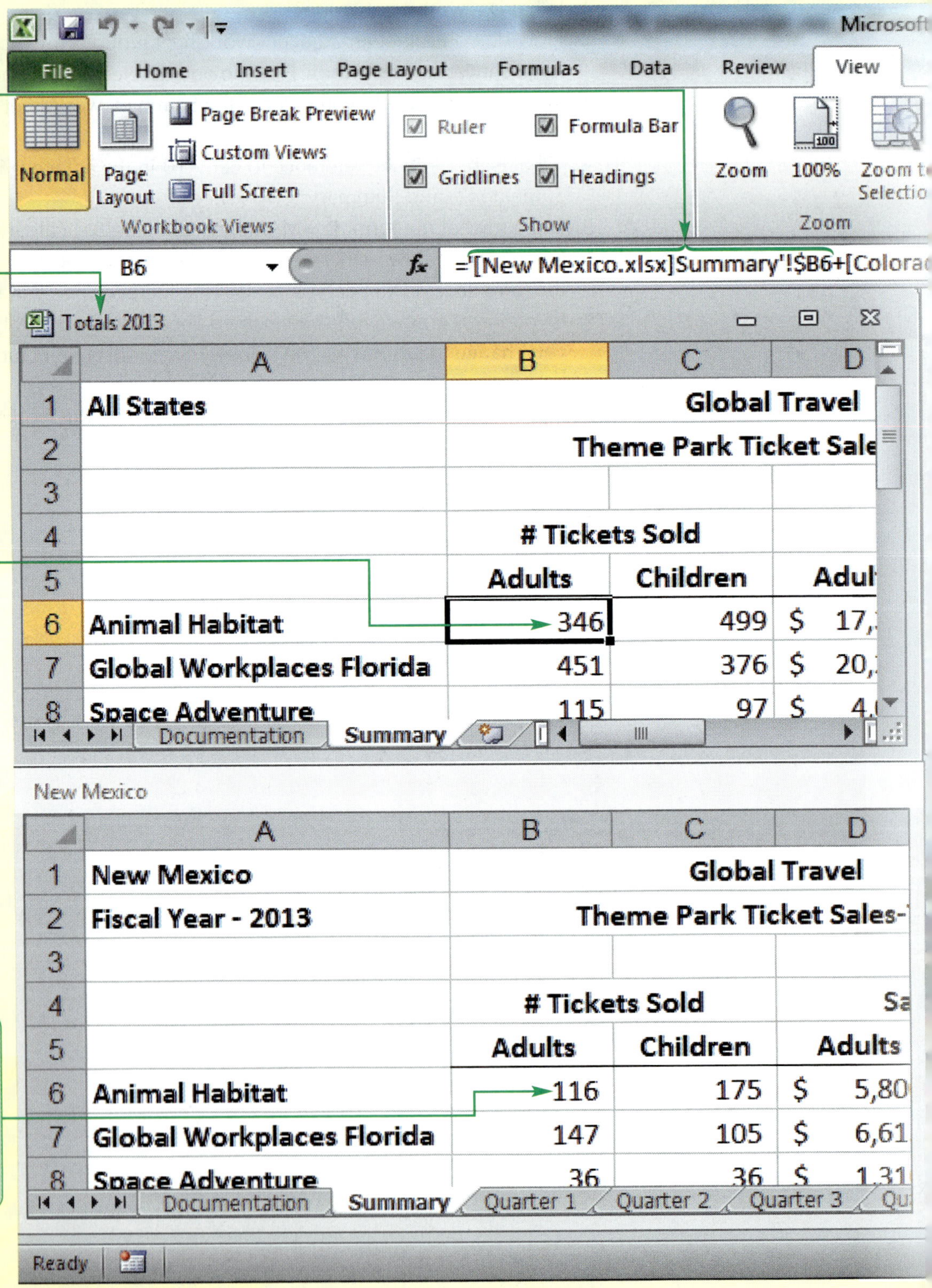

# LINKS AND EXTERNAL REFERENCES

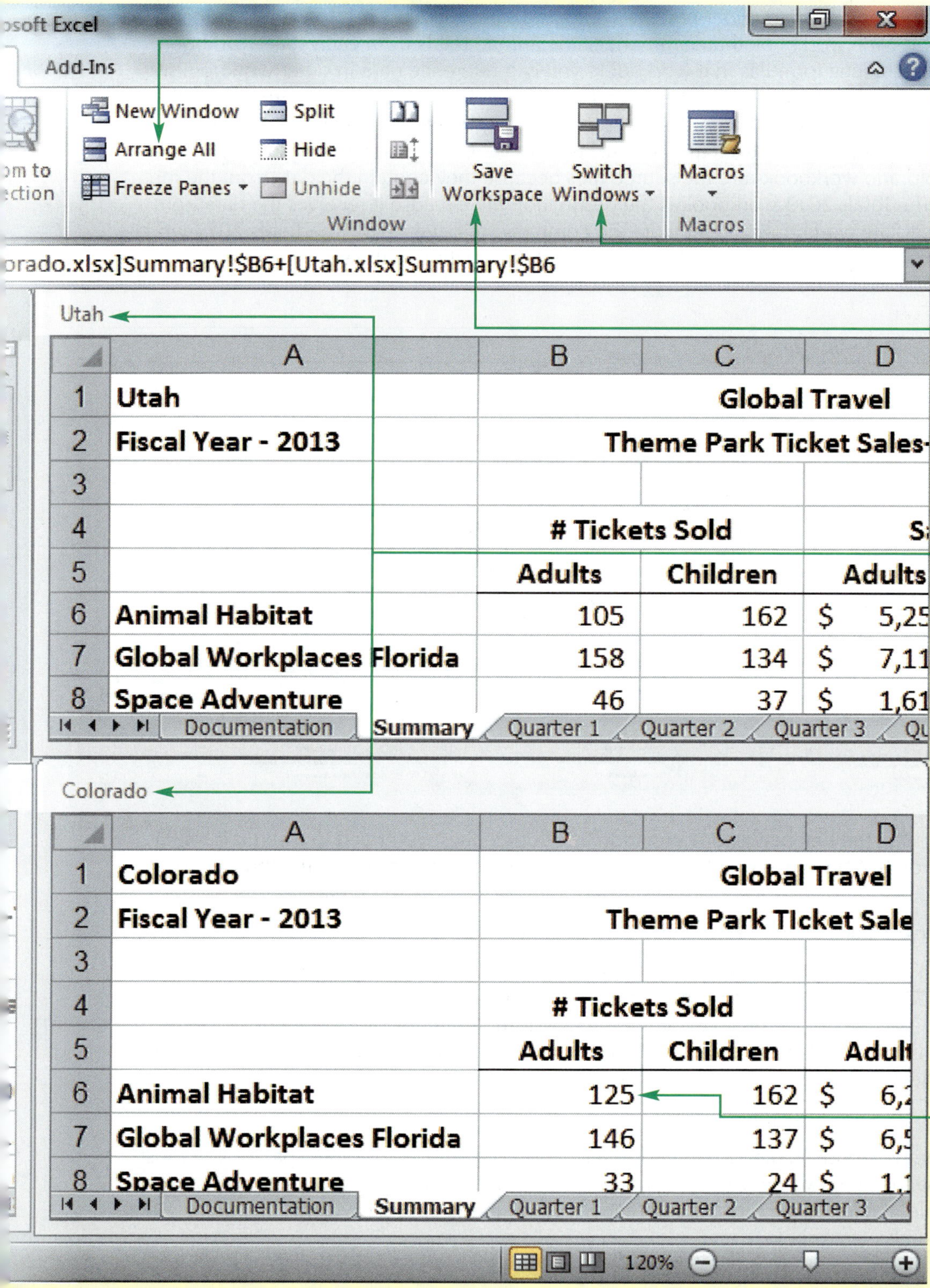


The Arrange All button displays all of the open workbooks in a tiled configuration within the program window.

The Switch Windows button lists each open workbook so you can change which workbook is active.

A **workspace** is an Excel file that saves information about all of the currently opened workbooks, such as their locations, window sizes, zoom level, and other settings. This workspace opens four workbooks in a tiled configuration.

When two or more workbooks are linked, the **source file** is a workbook that contains data to be used in the destination file. In this case, the New Mexico, Utah, and Colorado workbooks are source files.

These windows are arranged in a tiled configuration. Other options are horizontal, vertical, and cascade.

A **link** is a connection between files that allows data to be transferred from one file to the other.

# Linking Workbooks

Alvin has workbooks from the Colorado and Utah accountants similar to the one you helped Rhohit prepare. These three travel workbooks (named New Mexico, Colorado, and Utah) contain the number of tickets sold and sales for 2013. Alvin wants to create a company-wide workbook that summarizes the annual totals from each state workbook.

When creating formulas in a workbook, you can reference data in other workbooks. To do so, you must create a link between the workbooks. When two files are linked, the source file contains the data, and the destination file (sometimes called the *dependent* file) receives the data. In this case, as illustrated in Figure 6-11, the New Mexico, Utah, and Colorado workbooks are the source files because they contain the data from the three states. The Totals 2013 workbook is the destination file because it receives the data from the three state workbooks to calculate the company totals for 2013. The Totals 2013 workbook will always have access to the most recent information in the state workbooks because it can be updated whenever any of the linked values change.

**Figure 6-11 Source and destination files**

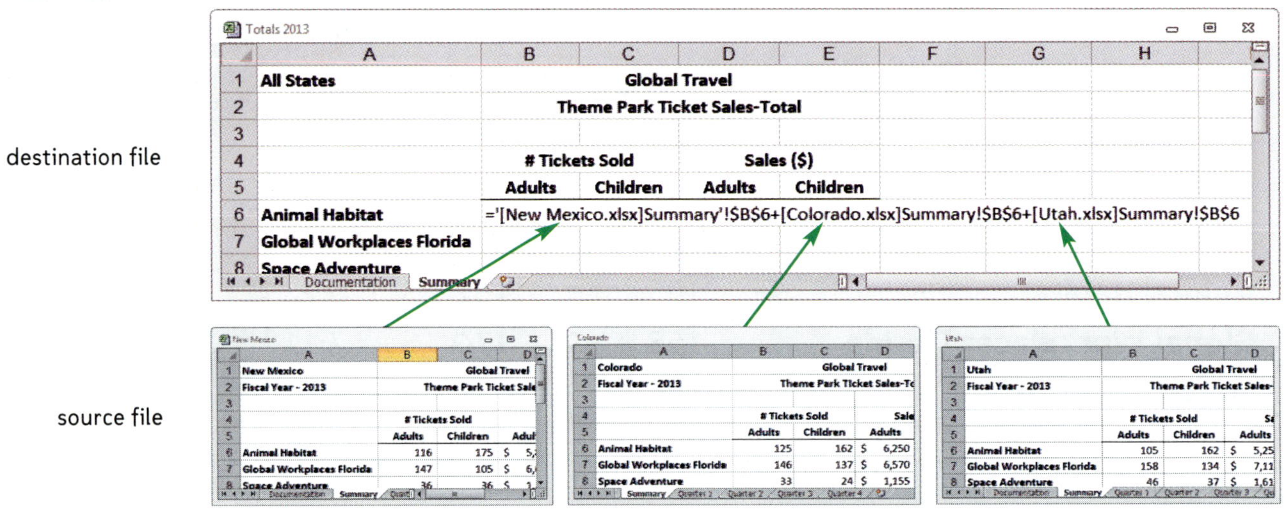


To create the link between destination and source files, you need to insert a formula in the Totals 2013 workbook that references a specific cell or range in the three state workbooks. That reference, called an external reference, has the syntax

```
[WorkbookName]WorksheetName!CellRange
```

where *WorkbookName* is the filename of the workbook (including the file extension) enclosed in square brackets; *WorksheetName* is the name of the worksheet that contains the data followed by an exclamation mark; and *CellRange* is the cell or range that contains the data. For example, the following formula references cell B6 in the Summary worksheet of the Colorado.xlsx workbook:

```
=[Colorado.xlsx]Summary!B6
```

**TIP**

When you use the point-and-click method to build formulas with external references, Excel enters all of the required punctuation, including quotation marks.

If the workbook name or the worksheet name contains one or more spaces, you must enclose the entire workbook name and worksheet name in single quotation marks. For example, the following formula references cell B6 in the Summary worksheet of the New Mexico.xlsx workbook:

```
='[New Mexico.xlsx]Summary'!B6
```

When the source and destination workbooks are stored in the same folder, you need to include only the workbook name in the external reference. However, when the source and destination workbooks are located in different folders, the workbook reference must include the file's complete location (also called the path). For example, if the destination file is stored in C:\TicketSales and the source file is stored in C:\TicketSales\Domestic Sales, the complete reference in the destination file would be:

```
='C:\TicketSales\Domestic Sales\[New Mexico.xlsx]Summary'!B6
```

The single quotation marks start at the beginning of the path and end immediately before the exclamation mark.

PROSKILLS

### *Decision Making: Understanding When to Link Workbooks*

More than one person is usually involved in developing information that will be used in an organization's decision-making process. If each person has access to only part of the data, everyone's ability to see the whole picture and make good decisions is limited. Linking workbooks provides one way to pull together all of the data being compiled by different people or departments to support the decision-making process.

When deciding whether to link workbooks, consider the following questions:

- **Can separate workbooks have the same purpose and structure?** With linked workbooks, each workbook can focus on a different store, branch office, or department with the same products or expenditure types and reporting periods (such as weekly, monthly, and quarterly).
- **Is a large workbook too unwieldy to use?** A large workbook can be divided into smaller workbooks for each quarter, division, or product and then linked to provide the summary information.
- **Can information from different workbooks be summarized?** Linked workbooks provide a way to quickly and accurately consolidate information from multiple source workbooks, and the summary worksheet will always contain the most current information even when information is later updated.
- **Are source workbooks received from another person or group continually updated?** With linked workbooks, an outdated source workbook can be replaced and the destination workbook will then reflect the latest information.

If you can answer yes to these questions, then linked workbooks are the way to go. Creating linked workbooks can help you analyze data better, leading to better decision making. It also provides greater flexibility as data becomes more expansive and complex.

## Navigating Multiple Workbooks

You'll combine the three state worksheets into one regional summary. You'll open all the workbooks you need to reference. Then, you'll switch between them to make each Summary worksheet the active sheet in preparation for creating the external references.

### To open the workbooks needed to create the regional summary:

1. If you took a break after the previous session, make sure the New Mexico workbook is open and the Summary worksheet is active.
2. Open the **TravelTotals** workbook located in the Excel6\Tutorial folder included with your Data Files, and then save the workbook as **Totals 2013**.
3. In the Documentation sheet, enter your name and the date, and then make the **Summary** worksheet active.
4. Open the **Utah** and **Colorado** workbooks located in the Excel6\Tutorial folder included with your Data Files.

You'll need to move between open workbooks when you create the external reference formulas in the Totals 2013 workbook. The Switch Windows button in the Window group on the View tab lists each open workbook so you can change which workbook is active. Another method is to click the Excel program button on the taskbar and then click the thumbnail of the workbook you want to make active.

**To switch between the open workbooks:**

1. Click the **View** tab on the Ribbon, and then, in the Window group, click the **Switch Windows** button to display a list of all the workbooks that are currently open.
2. Click **Utah** to make it the active workbook, and then make the **Summary** sheet active.
3. In the Window group, click the **Switch Windows** button, click **Colorado** to switch to the Colorado workbook, and then make the **Summary** worksheet active.
4. Make the **Totals 2013** workbook the active workbook.

## Arranging Multiple Workbooks

You might also want to display all the open workbooks on your screen at the same time. This way, you can easily click among the open workbooks to create links without having to continually change the active workbook, as well as quickly compare the contents of worksheets in different workbooks. You can arrange workbooks in the following layouts:

- **Tiled**, which divides the open workbooks evenly on the screen.
- **Horizontal**, which divides the open workbooks into horizontal bands.
- **Vertical**, which divides the open workbooks into vertical bands.
- **Cascade**, which layers the open workbooks on the screen.

The layout you select will depend on the contents being displayed and your purpose.

REFERENCE

*Arranging Workbooks*

- On the View tab, in the Window group, click the Arrange All button.
- Select the layout in which you want to arrange the open workbooks.
- When arranging multiple workbooks, uncheck the Windows of active workbook option. When arranging multiple worksheets within one workbook, check the option.
- Click the OK button.

Currently, four workbooks are open but only one is visible. You'll arrange the workbooks using the tiled arrangement.

**To tile the open workbooks:**

1. In the Window group on the View tab, click the **Arrange All** button. The Arrange Windows dialog box opens so you can select the layout arrangement you want.
2. Click the **Tiled** option button, if necessary. The Tiled option arranges the four Global Travel workbooks evenly on the screen.
3. Click the **OK** button. The four open workbooks appear in a tiled layout.

4. Click in the **Totals 2013** workbook to make it the active workbook, if necessary. In the tiled layout, the active workbook has darker text in the title bar, a gray background, scroll bars, and the active cell. See Figure 6-12.

**Figure 6-12** **Four workbooks arranged in a tiled layout**

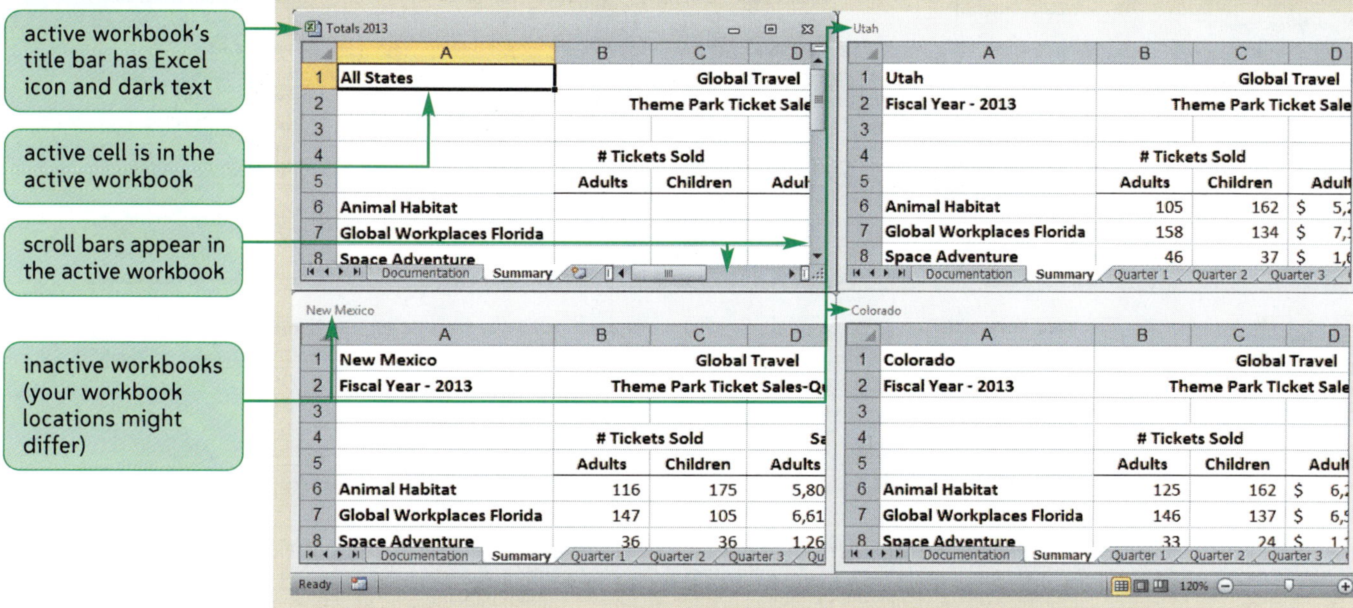


## Creating Formulas with External References

A formula can include a reference to another workbook (called an external reference), which creates a set of linked workbooks. The process for entering a formula with an external reference is the same as entering any other formula using references within the same worksheet or workbook. You can enter the formulas by typing them or using the point-and-click method. In most situations, you will use the point-and-click method to switch between the source files and destination files so that Excel enters the references to the workbook, worksheet, and cell using the correct syntax.

You need to enter the external reference formulas in the Totals 2013 workbook to summarize the states' totals into one workbook for Alvin. You'll start by creating the formula that adds the total number of adult tickets to Animal Habitat sold in New Mexico, Utah, and Colorado. You cannot use the SUM function with 3-D references here because you are referencing multiple workbooks and 3-D references can only be used to reference multiple worksheets in the same workbook.

### To create the external reference formula to total adult tickets for Animal Habitat:

1. In the Summary worksheet in the Totals 2013 workbook, click cell **B6**, and then type = to begin the formula.

As you create the formula, be sure to verify each external reference before going to the next step.

2. Click anywhere in the **New Mexico** workbook, and then, in the Summary worksheet, click cell **B6**. The external reference to cell B6 in the Summary worksheet of the New Mexico workbook—'[New Mexico.xlsx]Summary'!$B$6—is added to the formula in the Totals 2013 workbook. See Figure 6-13.

**Figure 6-13** External reference entered in the formula

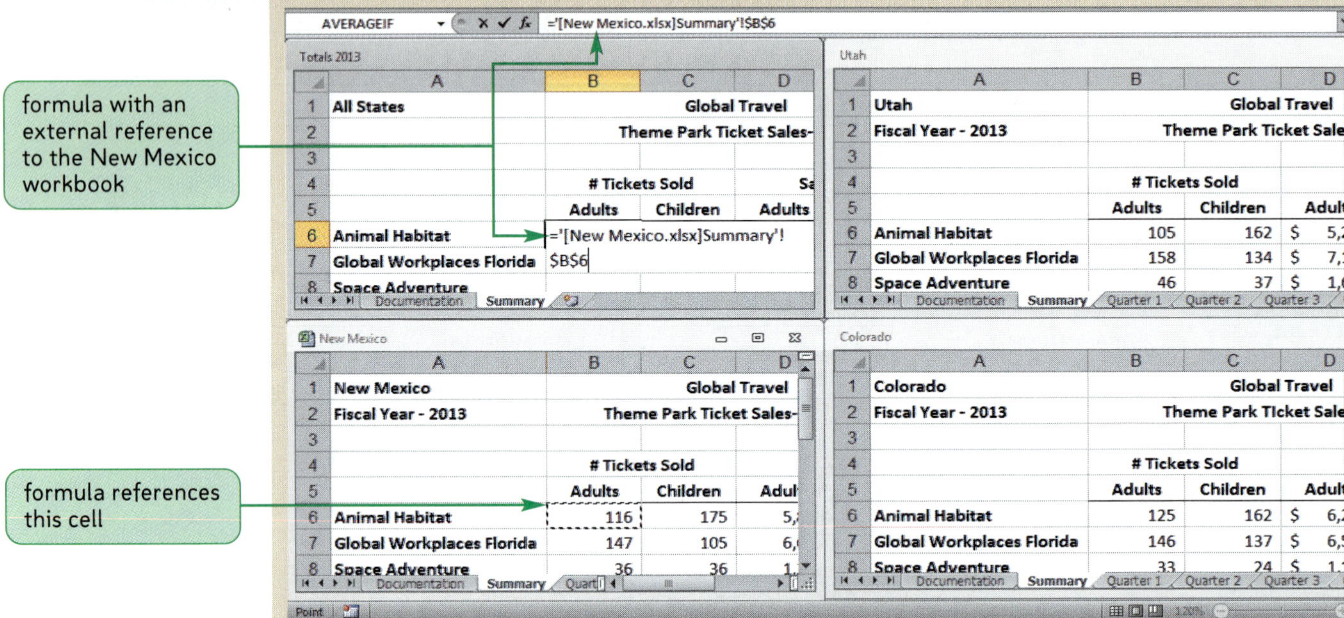


3. Type **+**. The Totals 2013 workbook becomes active and you can continue entering the formula. You need to create an external reference to the Colorado workbook.
4. Click anywhere in the **Colorado** workbook, click cell **B6** in the Summary worksheet, and then type **+**. The formula in the Totals 2013 workbook includes the external reference to the cell that has the total number of adult tickets to Animal Habitat sold in Colorado.
5. Click anywhere in the **Utah** workbook, click cell **B6** in the Summary worksheet, and then press the **Enter** key. The formula with three external references is entered in the Summary sheet in the Totals 2013 workbook.
6. In the Totals 2013 workbook, in the Summary sheet, click cell **B6**. The complete formula appears in the formula bar and the formula results appear in cell B6, showing that 346 adult tickets to Animal Habitat were sold in the three states: 116 in New Mexico, 105 in Utah, and 125 in Colorado. See Figure 6-14.

**Figure 6-14** Complete formula with external references

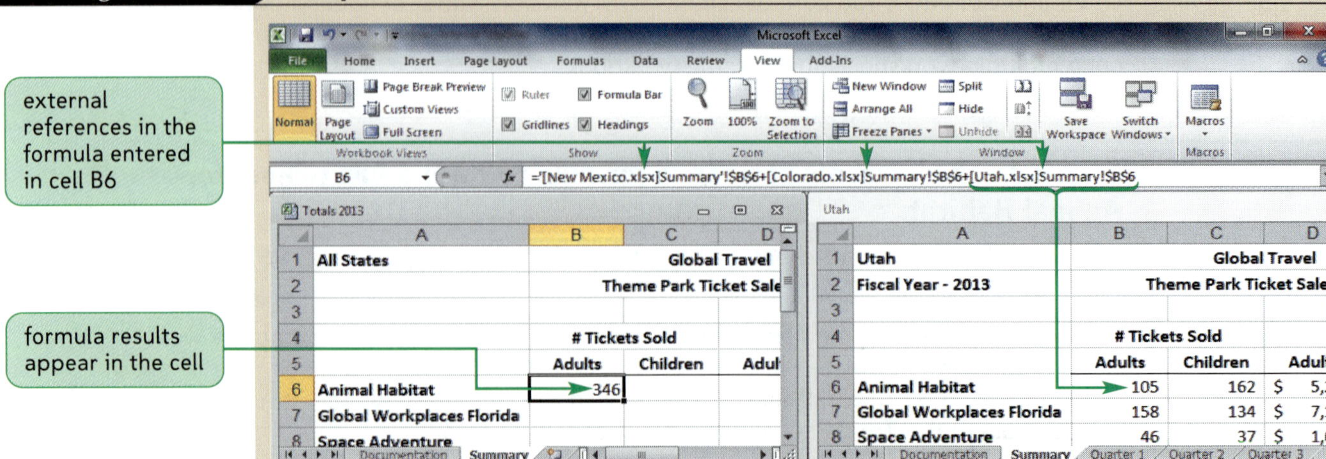

**Trouble?** If 346 doesn't appear in cell B6 in the Summary sheet in the Totals 2013 workbook, you might have clicked an incorrect cell for an external reference in the formula. Repeat Steps 1 through 6 to correct the formula.

You'll use the same process to enter the external reference formula for cell C6, which is the number of children's tickets to Animal Habitat sold in the three states. Then you'll do the same to create the formulas to calculate the total sales from all three states.

### To create the remaining external reference formulas:

1. In the Totals 2013 workbook, in the Summary worksheet, click cell **C6**, and then type = to begin the formula.
2. Click the **New Mexico** workbook, click cell **C6** in the Summary worksheet, and then type **+**. The formula in the Totals 2013 workbook includes the external reference to cell C6 in the Summary worksheet in the New Mexico workbook.
3. Click the **Colorado** workbook, click cell **C6** in the Summary worksheet, and then type **+**. The formula includes an external reference to cell C6 in the Summary worksheet in the Colorado workbook.
4. Click the **Utah** workbook, click cell **C6** in the Summary worksheet, and then press the **Enter** key. The external reference formula is complete.
5. In the Totals 2013 workbook, click cell **C6** in the Summary sheet. Cell C6 displays 499, the total children's tickets sold to Animal Habitat, and the following formula appears in the formula bar: ='[New Mexico.xlsx]Summary'!$C$6+[Colorado.xlsx]Summary!$C$6+[Utah.xlsx]Summary!$C$6.

   Next, you'll enter the external reference formulas in cells D6 and E6 to add the total sales from adult and children's tickets to Animal Habitat.
6. Use the same procedure in Steps 1 through 4 to enter the formula in cell **D6** in the Summary worksheet in the Totals 2013 workbook. The formula results displayed in cell D6 are 17300—the total sales from adult tickets to Animal Habitat in New Mexico, Colorado, and Utah.
7. Use the same procedure in Steps 1 through 4 to enter the formula in cell **E6** in the Summary worksheet in the Totals 2013 workbook. You may need to scroll each worksheet to see cell E6. The formula results displayed in cell E6 are 18962—the total sales from children's tickets to Animal Habitat in New Mexico, Colorado, and Utah.

You need to enter the remaining formulas for the other six theme parks. Rather than creating the rest of the external reference formulas manually, you can copy the formulas in row 6 to rows 7 through 12. The formulas created using the point-and-click method contain absolute references. Before you copy them to other cells, you need to change them to use mixed references because the rows in the formula need to change.

### To edit the external reference formulas to use mixed references:

1. Maximize the Totals 2013 workbook. The Totals 2013 workbook fills the program window. The other workbooks are still open but are not visible.
2. In the Summary worksheet, double-click cell **B6** to enter Edit mode and display the formula in the cell.

**TIP**

You can also create the mixed reference by deleting the $ symbol from the row references in the formula.

3. Click in the first absolute reference in the formula, and then press the **F4** key twice to change the absolute reference $B$6 to the mixed reference $B6.
4. Edit the other two absolute references in the formula to be mixed references with absolute column references and relative row references.
5. Press the **Enter** key. The formula is updated to include mixed references, but the formula results aren't affected. Cell B6 still displays 346, which is correct.
6. Edit the formulas in cells C6, D6, and E6 to change the absolute references to the mixed references $C6, $D6, and $E6, respectively. The formulas are updated, but the cells in the range C6:E6 still correctly display 499, 17300, and 18962, respectively.

With the formulas corrected to include mixed references, you can now copy the external reference formulas in cells B6:E6 to the other rows. Then, you'll enter the SUM function to total the values in each column.

## To copy and paste the external reference formulas:

1. Select the range **B6:E6**, and then drag the fill handle to select the range **B7:E12**. The formulas are copied to the range B7:E12 and the formula results appear in the cells. The Auto Fill Options button appears in the lower-right corner of the selected range, but you do not need to use it.
2. In cell B13, enter the SUM function to add the range **B6:B12**. A total of 2035 adult tickets were sold for all theme parks.
3. Copy the formula in cell B13 to the range **C13:E13**. The totals are 1855, 81889, and 55704, respectively.
4. Format the range B6:C13 with the **Comma** style and no decimal places, and then format the range D6:E13 with the **Accounting** number format and no decimal place.
5. Format the range B12:E12 with a **bottom border**, and then click cell **A1** to deselect the range. See Figure 6-15.

**Figure 6-15** Completed formulas in the Summary worksheet in the Totals 2013 workbook

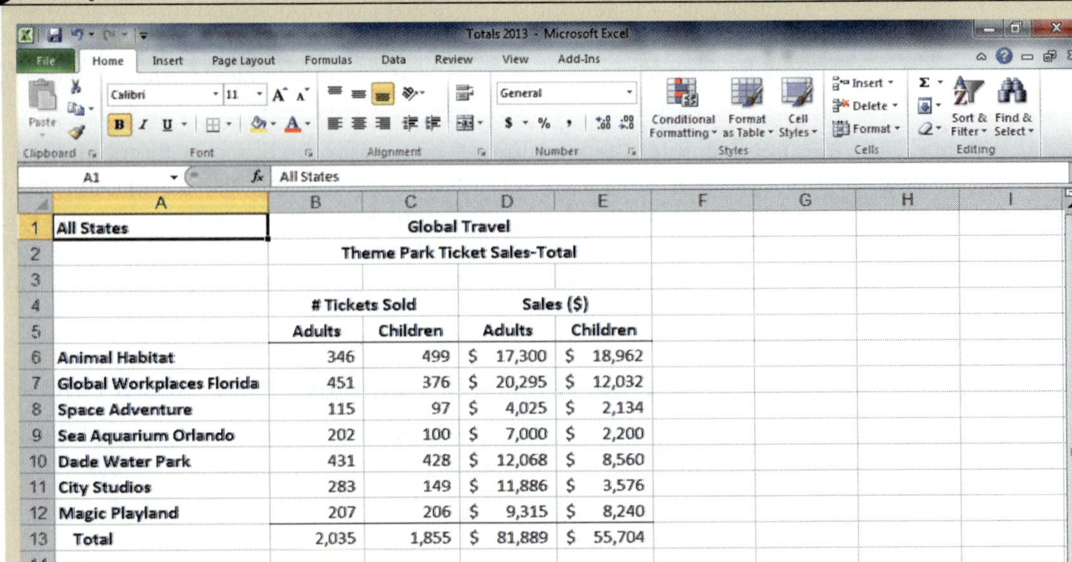

| | A | B | C | D | E |
|---|---|---|---|---|---|
| 1 | All States | Global Travel | | | |
| 2 | | Theme Park Ticket Sales-Total | | | |
| 3 | | | | | |
| 4 | | # Tickets Sold | | Sales ($) | |
| 5 | | Adults | Children | Adults | Children |
| 6 | Animal Habitat | 346 | 499 | $ 17,300 | $ 18,962 |
| 7 | Global Workplaces Florida | 451 | 376 | $ 20,295 | $ 12,032 |
| 8 | Space Adventure | 115 | 97 | $ 4,025 | $ 2,134 |
| 9 | Sea Aquarium Orlando | 202 | 100 | $ 7,000 | $ 2,200 |
| 10 | Dade Water Park | 431 | 428 | $ 12,068 | $ 8,560 |
| 11 | City Studios | 283 | 149 | $ 11,886 | $ 3,576 |
| 12 | Magic Playland | 207 | 206 | $ 9,315 | $ 8,240 |
| 13 | Total | 2,035 | 1,855 | $ 81,889 | $ 55,704 |
| 14 | | | | | |

Alvin is pleased; the regional summary results match the executive team's expectations.

INSIGHT

*Managing Linked Workbooks*

As you work with a linked workbook, you might need to replace a source file or change where you stored the source and destination files. However, replacing or moving a file can affect the linked workbook. Keep in mind the following guidelines to manage your linked workbooks:

- If you rename a source file, the destination workbook won't be able to find it. A dialog box opens, indicating "This workbook contains one or more links that cannot be updated." Click the Continue button to open the workbook with the most recent values, or click the Change Source button in the Edit Links dialog box to specify the new name of that linked source file.
- If you move a source file to a different folder, the link breaks between the destination and source files. Click the Change Source button in the Edit Links dialog box to specify the new location of the linked workbook.
- If you receive a replacement source file, you can swap the original source file with the replacement file. No additional changes are needed.
- If you receive a destination workbook but the source files are not included, Excel will not be able to find the source files, and a dialog box opens with the message "This workbook contains one or more links that cannot be updated." Click the Continue button to open the workbook with the most recent values, or click the Break Link button in the Edit Links dialog box to replace the external references with the existing values.
- If you change the name of a destination file, you can open that renamed version destination file without affecting the source files or the original destination file.

# Updating Linked Workbooks

When workbooks are linked, it is important that the data in the destination file accurately reflects the contents of the source file. When data in a source file changes, you want the destination file to reflect those changes. If both the source and destination files are open when you make a change, the destination file is updated automatically. If the destination file is closed when you make a change in a source file, you choose whether to update the link to display the current values, or continue to display the older values from the destination file when you open the destination file.

## Updating a Destination Workbook with Source Workbooks Open

When both the destination and source workbooks are open, any changes you make in a source workbook appear in the destination workbook. Rhohit tells Alvin that the total New Mexico children's sales for Animal Habitat in Quarter 4 is actually $1,000 more than recorded. After you correct the value in the Quarter 4 worksheet, the amount in the Summary worksheet of the New Mexico workbook and the regional total in the Totals 2013 workbook also change if both the source and destination files are open.

**To update the source workbook with the destination file open:**

1. Switch to the **New Mexico** workbook, and then make the **Quarter 4** worksheet active. You'll update the value of the Animal Habitat children's dollar amount in this worksheet.

2. In cell E6, enter **2786**. The Animal Habitat children's sales are updated.
3. Switch to the **Summary** worksheet in the New Mexico workbook, and then verify that the total Animal Habitat children's sales is now $7,650.
4. Switch to the **Totals 2013** workbook, and then, in the Summary worksheet, verify that the value in cell E6 is $19,962 and the total dollar amount from sales of children's tickets is $56,704, reflecting the new value you entered in the New Mexico workbook. Because both the destination and source files are open, Excel updated the destination file automatically.
5. Save the New Mexico and Totals 2013 workbooks, and then close the Utah, Colorado, and Totals 2013 workbooks. The New Mexico workbook remains open.

## Updating a Destination Workbook with Source Workbooks Closed

When you save a workbook that contains external reference formulas, such as Totals 2013, Excel stores the most recent results of those formulas in the destination file. Source files, such as the New Mexico, Colorado, and Utah workbooks, are often updated while the destination file is closed. In that case, the values in the destination file are not updated at the same time the source files are updated. The next time you open the destination file, the cells containing external reference formulas still display the old values. Therefore, some of the values in the edited source workbooks are different from the values in the destination workbook.

To update the destination workbook with the current data, you must specify that you want the update to occur. As part of the Excel security system that attempts to protect against malicious software, links to other workbooks are not updated without your permission. When you open a workbook with external reference formulas (the destination file), a Security Warning appears in the Information Bar, notifying you that the automatic update of links has been disabled. If you "trust" the provider of the source file(s), you can enable the content, which allows the external reference formulas to function and updates the links in the destination workbook. If you do not "trust" the provider of the source files or do not want the destination file updated at that time, do not enable the content. The old values in the destination workbook are displayed and the links to the source files remain disabled.

Rhohit informs Alvin that the New Mexico workbook needs a second correction. Space Adventure adult sales in Quarter 4 are $435, not $385, which is the current value in the New Mexico workbook. You will increase the amount of the Space Adventure adult sales in Quarter 4 by $50. As a result, sales in the Summary sheet of the New Mexico workbook and the regional total in the Totals 2013 workbook will both increase by $50. You'll edit the source file, the New Mexico workbook, while the destination file is closed.

### To update the source workbook with the destination file closed:

1. In the New Mexico workbook, make the **Quarter 4** worksheet active.
2. In cell D8, enter **435**. The sales total for adults in Quarter 4 increases to $7,241.
3. Switch to the **Summary** worksheet. The sales total for 2013 in cell D8 is $1,310 and the adult sales total is $26,375. See Figure 6-16.

Figure 6-16 **Summary worksheet with revised Quarter 4 sales for Space Adventure**

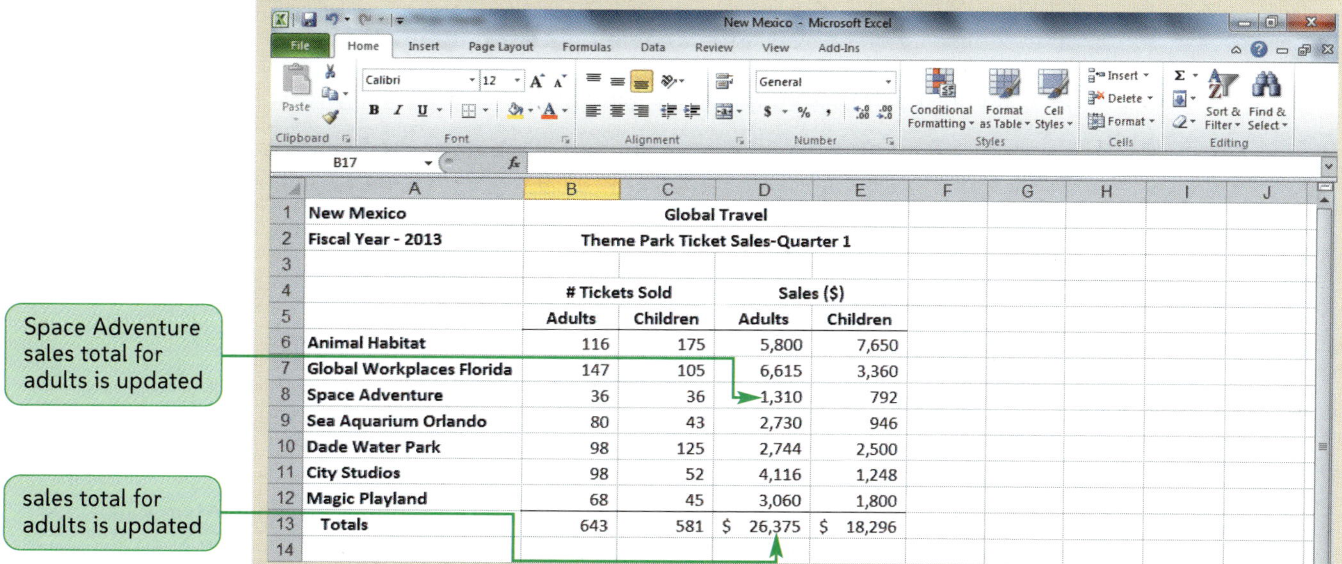


4. Save and close the New Mexico workbook.

Now you'll open the destination file (the Totals 2013 workbook). The total adult sales calculated from the source workbooks won't be updated until you specify that they should. When the destination file is open and the source files are closed, the complete file path is included as part of the external reference formula that appears in the formula bar.

## To open and update the destination workbook:

1. Open the **Totals 2013** workbook, and then switch to the **Summary** worksheet, if necessary. The value in cell D8 has *not* changed; it still is $4,025. A Security Warning message appears in the Information Bar, indicating that automatic update of links has been disabled. See Figure 6-17.

Figure 6-17 **Security Warning in the Information Bar**

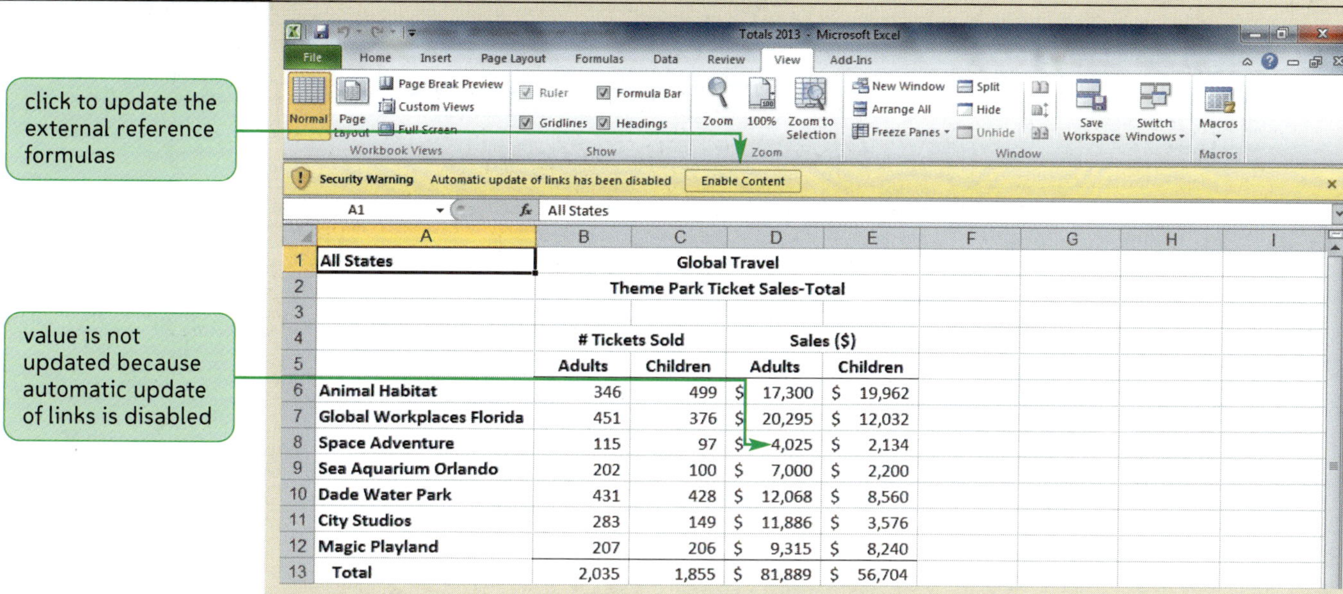

You want the current values in the source files to appear in the destination workbook.

2. In the Information Bar, click the **Enable Content** button. The values in the destination file are updated. The sales total in cell D8 of the Totals 2013 workbook increases to $4,075 and the total in cell D13 increases to $81,939.
3. Click cell **D8**, and then look at the complete file path for each external reference in the formula. The full path appears because the source workbooks are closed.
4. Save the workbook.

## Managing Links

When workbooks are linked, the Edit Links dialog box provides ways to manage the links. You can review the status of the links, update the data in the files, repair broken links, open the source file, and break the links, which converts all external reference formulas to their most recent values.

After the fiscal year audit is completed and the source workbooks are final, Alvin will archive the summary workbook and move the files to an off-site storage location as part of his year-end backup process. You will save a copy of the Totals 2013 workbook and then break the links to the source files in the copy.

### To save a copy of the Totals 2013 workbook and open the Edit Links dialog box:

1. Save the Totals 2013 workbook as **Audited 2013** in the Excel6\Tutorial folder included with your Data Files. The Totals 2013 workbook closes and the Audited 2013 workbook remains open.
2. Click the **Data** tab on the Ribbon.
3. In the Connections group, click the **Edit Links** button. The Edit Links dialog box opens. See Figure 6-18.

Figure 6-18 Edit Links dialog box

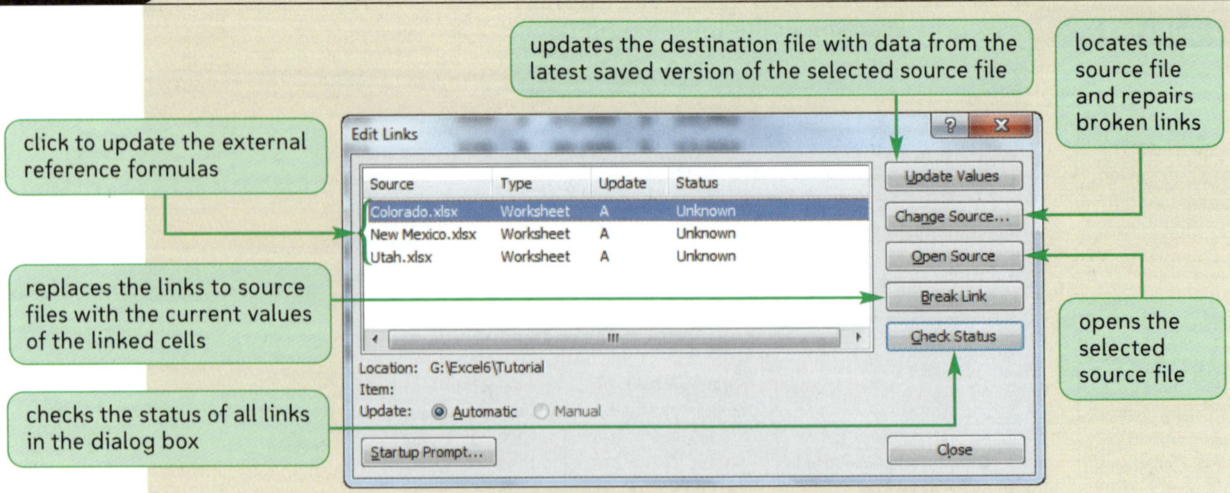

The Edit Links dialog box lists all of the files that the destination workbook is linked to so that you can update, change, open, or remove the links. You can see that the destination workbook, Audited 2013, has links to the Colorado, New Mexico, and Utah workbooks. The dialog box shows the following information about each link:

- **Source** indicates the file to which the link points. The Audited 2013 workbook contains three links pointing to the New Mexico.xlsx, Colorado.xlsx, and Utah.xlsx workbooks.
- **Type** identifies the type of each source file. In this case, the type is an Excel worksheet but it could also be a Word document, a PowerPoint presentation, or some other type of file.
- **Update** specifies the way values are updated from the source file. The letter *A* indicates the link is updated automatically when you open the workbook or when both the source and destination files are open simultaneously. The letter *M* indicates the link must be updated manually by the user, which is useful when you want to see the older data values before updating to the new data. To manually update the link and see the new data values, click the Update Values button.
- **Status** shows whether Excel successfully accessed the link and updated the values from the source document (status is OK), or Excel has not attempted to update the links in this session (status is Unknown). The status of the three links in the Audited 2013 workbook is Unknown.

You'll break the links so that the Audited 2013 workbook contains only the updated values (and is no longer affected by changes in the source files). Then you'll save the Audited 2013 workbook for Alvin to archive. This allows Alvin to store a "snapshot" of the data at the end of the fiscal year.

**To convert all external reference formulas to their current values:**

1. Click the **Break Link** button. A dialog box opens, alerting you that breaking links in the workbook permanently converts formulas and external references to their existing values.
2. Click the **Break Links** button. No links appear in the Edit Links dialog box.
3. Click the **Close** button. The Audited 2013 workbook now contains values instead of formulas with external references.
4. Click cell **B6**. The value 346 appears in the cell and the formula bar; the link (the external reference formula) was replaced with the data value. All cells in the range B6:E12 contain values rather than external reference formulas.
5. Save and close the Audited 2013 workbook. The Totals 2013 workbook has external reference formulas, and the Audited 2013 workbook has current values.

**TIP**

You cannot undo the break link action. To restore the links, you must reenter the external reference formulas.

## Creating an Excel Workspace

When working with multiple related workbooks, such as Alvin's four workbooks that contain the ticket sales data, you may want to access all of the workbooks at one time. Rather than having to open each workbook individually, you can create a workspace to open multiple workbooks at one time, saving time and avoiding having to remember all the filenames and folder locations.

A workspace is an Excel file that saves information about all of the currently opened workbooks, such as their locations, window sizes, zoom magnifications, and other settings. The workspace file has the file extension .xlw. The workspace does not contain the workbooks themselves—only information about them. To use that set of workbooks, you open the workspace file. Excel then opens the workbooks and settings in the same configuration they were in when you saved the workspace file. Even if a workbook is included in a workspace file, you can still open that workbook separately.

You will create a workspace file for Alvin that includes the four workbooks in a cascade layout, which arranges the open workbooks so that they overlap each other with all the title bars visible. Alvin prefers this layout because he can see more of the active workbook.

### To create the Theme Parks workspace file:

**TIP**

The workspace file contains only the location and name of each file, not the actual workbooks and worksheets. To use the workspace on another computer, you must copy the workspace file *and* the workbook files.

1. Open the **Colorado**, **New Mexico**, **Utah**, and **Totals 2013** workbooks located in the Excel6\Tutorial folder included with your Data Files, clicking the **Don't Update** button in the dialog that opens indicating that the workbook contains links. Four workbooks are open.
2. Make sure the **Summary** worksheet is the active worksheet in each workbook.
3. Switch to the **Totals 2013** workbook.
4. Click the **View** tab on the Ribbon, and then click the **Arrange All** button in the Window group. The Arrange Windows dialog box opens.
5. Click the **Cascade** option button, and then click the **OK** button. The four workbooks overlap each other, with the title bars visible. See Figure 6-19.

**Figure 6-19** Workbooks arranged in cascade layout

cascade arrangement (your workbook order might differ)

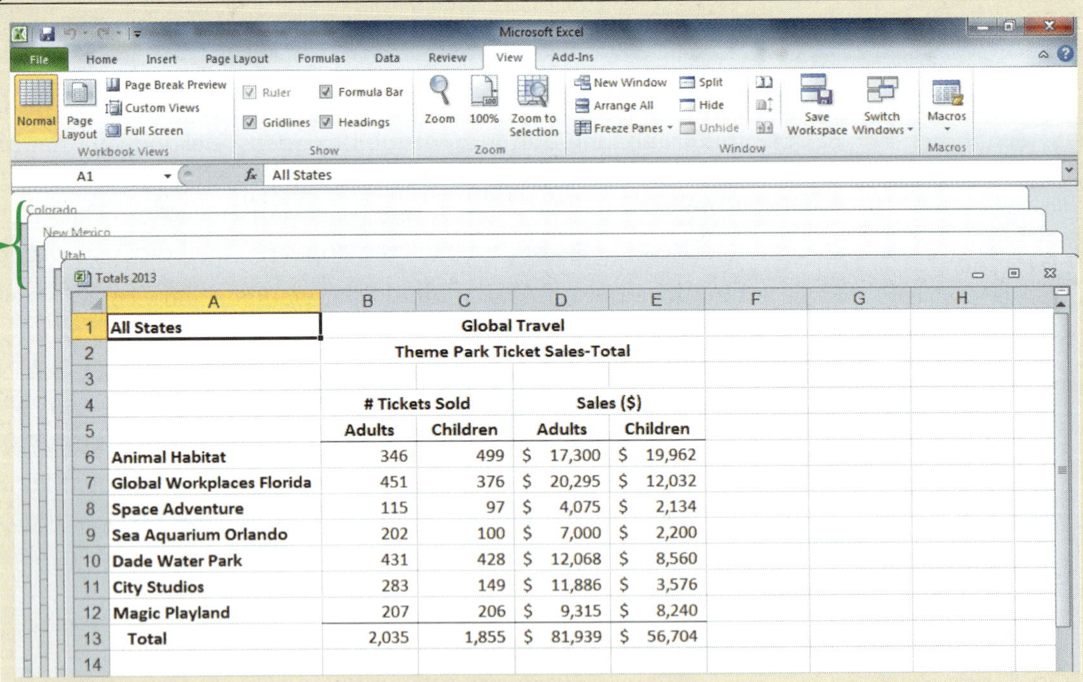


6. In the Window group, click the **Save Workspace** button. The Save Workspace dialog box opens and functions similarly to the Save As dialog box.
7. Type **Theme Parks** in the File name box, verify that **Workspaces** is selected in the Save as type box, verify that the save location is the Excel6\Tutorial folder, and then click the **Save** button. A dialog box might open, prompting you to save your changes to the open workbook files, if you haven't already done so.
8. If prompted to save changes, click the **Save** button. The Theme Parks workspace file is saved. The workspace file has the file extension .xlw.

You will test the workspace file you created to make sure it opens all four Global Travel workbooks.

**To open the Theme Parks workspace:**

1. Close all four workbooks.
2. Click the **File** tab on the Ribbon, and then click the **Open** command in the navigation bar. The Open dialog box opens, displaying the Excel6\Tutorial folder. The icon for the Theme Parks workspace file is different from the Excel workbook file icon.
3. Click the **Theme Parks** workspace file, and then click the **Open** button. A dialog box opens, indicating that the workbook contains links.
4. Click the **Don't Update** button. The four travel workbooks open and are arranged in a cascade layout, the same layout in which you saved them. You can work with the workbooks as usual.
5. Click the **Colorado** workbook title bar to bring it to the front of the cascaded workbooks. Colorado is now the active workbook.

   The workspace file provides a quick way to open a series of workbooks in a specific display. Because it doesn't actually contain the workbooks, you must close each workbook separately, saving as needed.
6. Close the New Mexico, Utah, Colorado, and Totals 2013 workbooks without saving any changes.

In this session, you worked with multiple worksheets and workbooks, summarizing data and linking workbooks. This ensures that the data in the summary workbook is accurate and remains updated with the latest data in the source files. In the next session, you will create templates, hyperlinks, and a Web page.

REVIEW

*Session 6.2 Quick Check*

1. What is the external reference to the range A1:A10 in the Sales Info worksheet in the Product Report workbook located in the Reports folder on drive D?
2. What is a source file?
3. What is a destination file?
4. How are linked workbooks updated when both the destination and source files are open?
5. How are linked workbooks updated when the source file is changed and the destination file is closed?
6. How would you determine to what workbooks a destination file is linked?
7. What is a workspace?
8. Explain how creating a workspace file can help you organize your work.

# SESSION 6.3 VISUAL OVERVIEW

This Travel expense report workbook was created from one of the templates available from Office.com. Microsoft provides many other templates that you can download.

From Backstage view, you can save the open workbook to your SkyDrive and then use the Exel Web App to work on that file from any computer with an Internet connection.

A **template** is a workbook with labels, formats, and formulas already built into it with data removed. In other words, a template includes everything but the variable data.

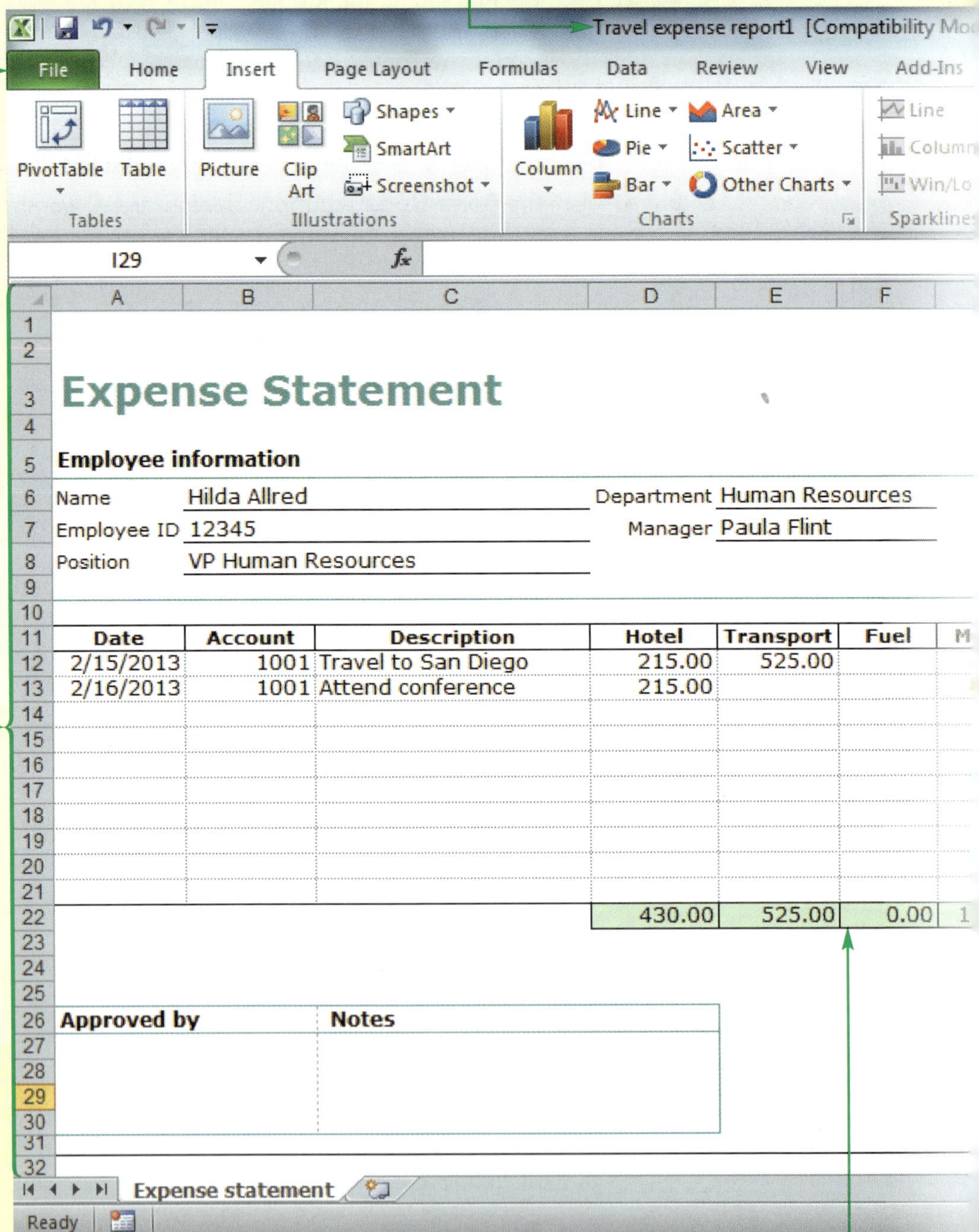


A template can use any Excel feature, including formatting, formulas, charts, data validation, cell protection, and macros. The template used to create this workbook includes labels, formatting, and formulas.

# TEMPLATES AND HYPERLINKS

The Hyperlink button is used to create a hyperlink.

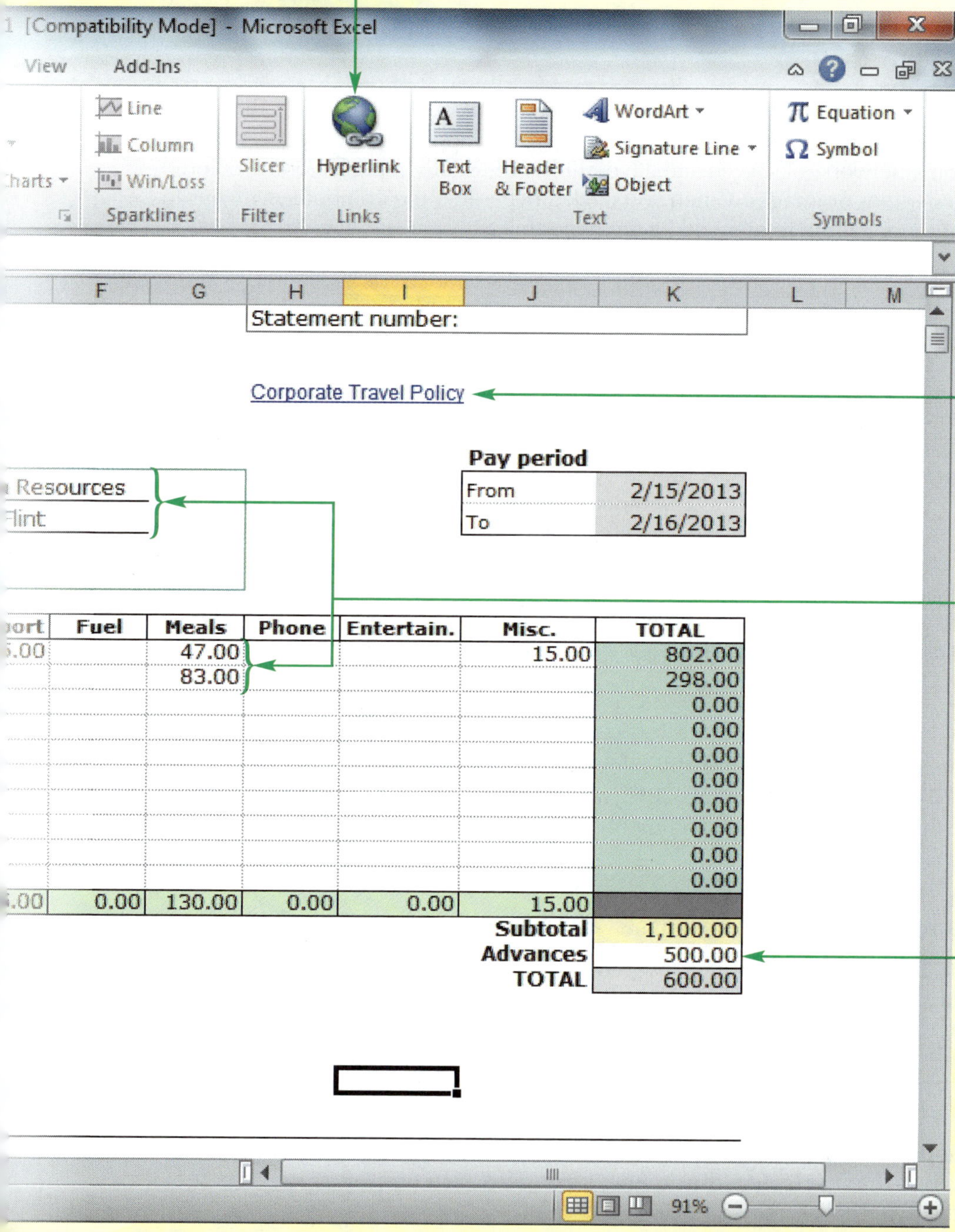


A **hyperlink** is a link in a file, such as a workbook, to information within that file or another file. In this case, the link opens a document created in Word that is stored in the same folder as the workbook.

Variable data is entered in the workbook created from the template. In this workbook, employee data was entered to fill out the expense report.

These formulas to calculate the total expenses and amount owed based on the values entered in the range D12: J21 were included in the template.

# Creating a Hyperlink

A hyperlink is a link in a file, such as a workbook, to information within that file or another file. Although hyperlinks are most often found on Web pages, they can also be placed in a worksheet and used to quickly jump to a specific cell or range within the active worksheet, another worksheet, or another workbook. Hyperlinks can also be used to jump to other files, such as a Word document or a PowerPoint presentation, or sites on the Web.

## Inserting a Hyperlink

You can insert a hyperlink directly in a workbook file to link to information in that workbook, another workbook, or a file associated with another application on your computer, a shared file on a network, or a Web site. Hyperlinks are usually represented by colored words with underlines or images. When you click a hyperlink, the computer switches to the file or portion of the file referenced by the hyperlink.

REFERENCE

*Inserting a Hyperlink*

- Select the text, graphic, or cell in which you want to insert the hyperlink.
- In the Links group on the Insert tab, click the Hyperlink button.
- To link to a file or Web page, click Existing File or Web Page in the Link to list, and then select the file or Web page from the Look in box.
- To link to a location in the current workbook, click Place in This Document in the Link to list, and then select the worksheet, cell, or range in the current workbook.
- To link to a new document, click Create New Document in the Link to list, and then specify the filename and path of the new document.
- To link to an email address, click E-mail Address in the Link to list, and then enter the email address of the recipient and a subject line for the message.
- Click the OK button.

Alvin wrote a memo summarizing the sales results for New Mexico, Utah, and Colorado in 2013. He wants the Totals 2013 workbook to include a link to this memo that points to the Sales 2013 Word document.

**To insert a hyperlink into the Totals 2013 workbook:**

1. Open the **Totals 2013** workbook located in the Excel6\Tutorial folder included with your Data Files, but don't update the links.
2. Maximize the Totals 2013 worksheet window.
3. Switch to the **Documentation** worksheet, and then click cell **A8**. You want to create the hyperlink in this cell.
4. Click the **Insert** tab on the Ribbon, and then click the **Hyperlink** button in the Links group. The Insert Hyperlink dialog box opens. You use this dialog box to define the hyperlink.

5. If necessary, click the **Existing File or Web Page** button in the Link to bar and click the **Current Folder** button in the Look in area. All the existing files and folders in the Tutorial folder, which is the folder where the Totals 2013 workbook is stored, are displayed. See Figure 6-20.

**Figure 6-20** **Insert Hyperlink dialog box**

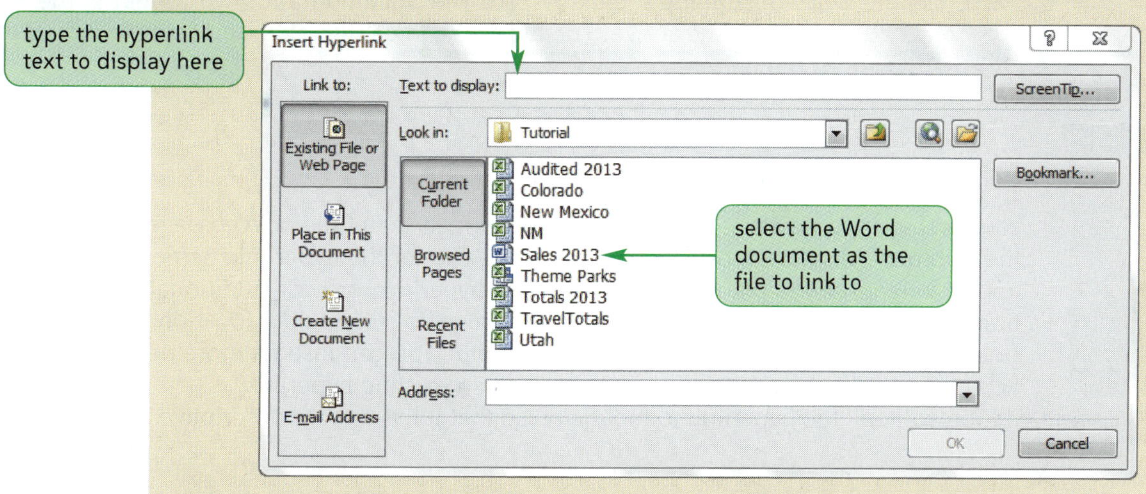


6. Click the **Text to display** box, and then type **Click here to read Executive Memo**. This is the hyperlink text that will appear in cell A8 in the Documentation worksheet.
7. Click the **Sales 2013** Word document in the list of files. This is the file you want to open when the hyperlink is clicked.
8. Click the **OK** button. As shown in Figure 6-21, the hyperlink text entered in cell A8 is underlined and in a blue font, indicating that the text within the cell is a hyperlink.

**Figure 6-21** **Hyperlink to the Sales 2013 document**

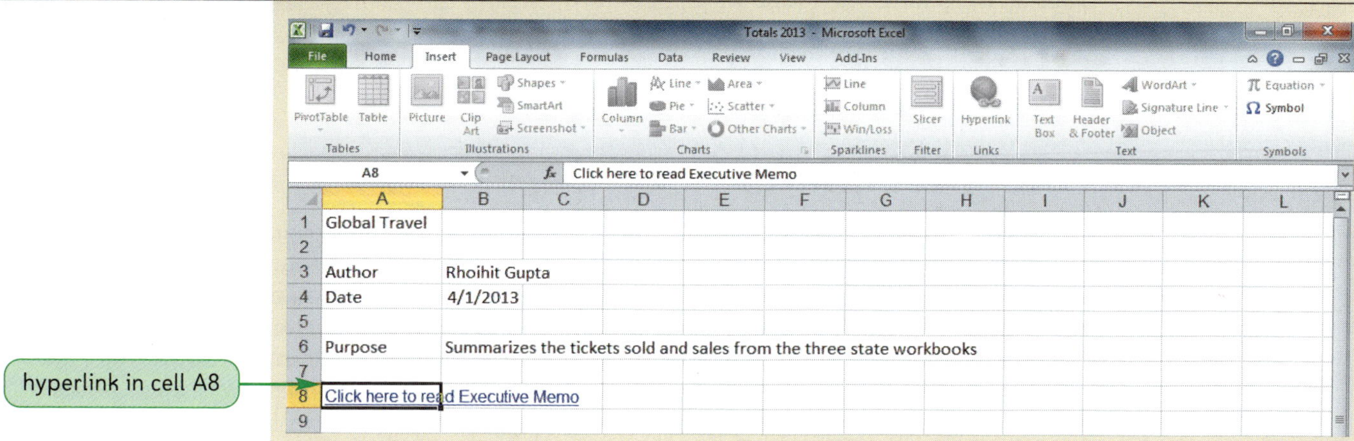


You will test the hyperlink that you just created to ensure it works correctly. To use a hyperlink in a worksheet, you must click the text inside the cell that contains the link. If you click white space in the cell or any text that flows into an adjacent cell, the hyperlink does not work.

**To test the hyperlink:**

1. Point to the text in cell **A8** until the pointer changes to 👆, and then click the hyperlink. The Sales 2013 document opens in Word.

   **Trouble?** If the hyperlink doesn't work, you might have clicked the text that overflows cell A8. Point to the text within cell A8, and then click the hyperlink.

2. Close the Word document and exit Word. The Documentation worksheet in the Totals 2013 workbook is active. The hyperlink in cell A8 changed color to indicate that you used the link.

**TIP**

To delete a hyperlink, right-click the hyperlink cell and then click Clear Contents. To delete the hyperlink but keep the text, right-click the hyperlink cell, and then click Remove Hyperlink.

## Editing a Hyperlink

You can modify an existing hyperlink by changing its target file or Web page, modifying the text that is displayed, or changing the ScreenTip for the hyperlink. ScreenTips, which appear whenever you place the pointer over a hyperlink, provide additional information about the target of the link. The default ScreenTip is the folder location and filename of the file you will link to, which isn't very helpful. You can insert a more descriptive ScreenTip when you create a hyperlink or edit an existing hyperlink.

You will edit the hyperlink to the memo so that it has a more descriptive ScreenTip.

**To edit the hyperlink:**

1. In the Documentation worksheet, right-click cell **A8**, and then click **Edit Hyperlink** on the shortcut menu. The Edit Hyperlink dialog box opens; it has the same layout and information as the Insert Hyperlink dialog box.
2. Click the **ScreenTip** button. The Set Hyperlink ScreenTip dialog box opens.
3. Type **Click to view sales analysis for 2013** in the ScreenTip text box, and then click the **OK** button.
4. Click the **OK** button to close the Edit Hyperlink dialog box.
5. Point to the text in cell **A8**, and then confirm that the ScreenTip "Click to view sales analysis for 2013" appears just below the cell.
6. Save and close the Totals 2013 workbook.

# Creating Templates

If you want to create a new workbook that has the same format as an existing workbook, you could save the existing workbook with a new name and replace the values with new data or blank cells. The potential drawback to this method is that you might forget to rename the original file and overwrite data you intended to keep. A better method is to create a template workbook that includes all the text (row and column labels), formatting, and formulas but does not contain any data. The template workbook is a model from which you create new workbooks. When you create a new workbook from a template, an unnamed copy of the template opens. You can then enter data as well as modify the existing content or structure as needed. Any changes or additions you make to the new workbook do not affect the template file; the next time you create a workbook based on the template, the original text, formatting, and formulas will be present.

The three state workbooks for 2013 have the same format. Alvin wants to use this workbook format for data collection and analysis for next year. You will create a template from one of the state workbooks.

PROSKILLS

*Teamwork: Using Excel Templates*

A team working together will often need to create the same types of workbooks. Rather than each person or group designing a different workbook, each team member should create a workbook from the same template. The completed workbooks will then all have the same structure with identical formatting and formulas. Not only does this ensure consistency and accuracy, it also makes it easier to compile and summarize the results. Templates help teams work better together and avoid misunderstandings.

For example, a large organization may need to collect the same information from several regions. By creating and distributing a workbook template, each region knows what data to track and where to enter it. The template already includes the formulas, so the results are calculated consistently.

The following are just some of the advantages of building and using templates to create multiple workbooks with the same features:

- Templates save time and ensure consistency in the design and content of workbooks because all labels, formatting, and formulas are entered once.
- Templates ensure accuracy because formulas can be entered and verified once, and then be used with confidence in all workbooks.
- Templates standardize the appearance and content of workbooks.
- Templates prevent data from being overwritten when an existing workbook is inadvertently saved with new data rather than saved as a new workbook.

If you are part of a team that needs to create the same type of workbook repeatedly, it's a good idea to use a template to both save time and ensure consistency in the design and content of the workbooks.

## Creating a Workbook Based on an Existing Template

The blank Book1 workbook that opens when you start Excel is based on the **default template**. The default template contains no text or formulas, but it includes all the formatting available in every new workbook: General number format applied to numbers, Calibri 11-point font, labels aligned to the left side of a cell, values and the formula results aligned to the right side of a cell, column width set to 8.43 characters, three worksheets inserted in the workbook, and so forth.

Excel has many other templates available. Some are automatically installed on your hard drive when you install Excel. Other templates are available to download from the Office.com site. These templates provide commonly used worksheet formats, saving you from "reinventing the wheel." Some of the task-specific templates available from the Office.com site include:

- **Monthly Family Budget.** This template builds projections and actual expenditures for items such as housing, transportation, and insurance.
- **Inventory List.** This template tracks the cost and quantity reorder levels of inventory.
- **Team Roster.** This template organizes a list with each player's name, phone number, email address, and so forth.
- **Time sheets.** This template creates an online time card to track employees' work hours.

You will create a new workbook based on one of the Excel templates provided by Microsoft.

REFERENCE

## *Creating a Workbook Based on a Template*

- Click the File tab on the Ribbon, and then click the New tab in the navigation bar.
- In the center pane, click a template category for the type of workbook you want to create, and then click a template.
- In the right pane, check the preview, and then click the Download button.
- Save the workbook with a new filename.

You'll download the Employee Timecard template. Note that you need an Internet connection to complete the following set of steps. If you don't have an Internet connection, you should read but not complete the steps involving creating and using the online template.

### To create a workbook based on the Employee Timecard template:

1. Click the **File** tab on the Ribbon, and then click the **New** tab in the navigation bar. The center pane shows the available templates on your computer and template categories on Office.com.
2. Click the **Time sheets** folder. All the available templates in this category appear in the center pane. There are several time sheet templates.

   **Trouble?** If you cannot find the Time sheets folder, you can search for the folder. In the search box to the ri ght of the Office.com Templates header, type **Employee timecard**, and then click the Start searching arrow.
3. Click the **Employee timecard (daily, weekly, monthly, and yearly)** template. A preview of a worksheet based on the selected template appears in the right pane. See Figure 6-22.

**Figure 6-22** Preview of the Employee timecard template

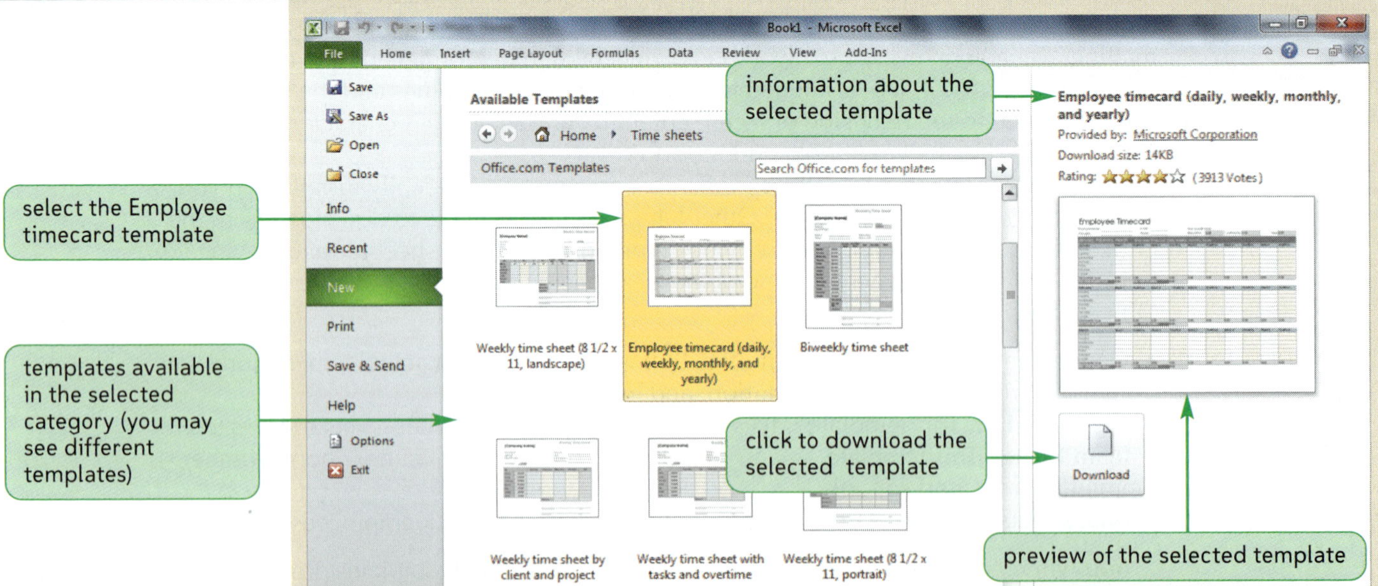


4. Click the **Download** button in the right pane. A new workbook based on the selected template opens. See Figure 6-23.

**Figure 6-23** **Workbook created from the Employee timecard template**

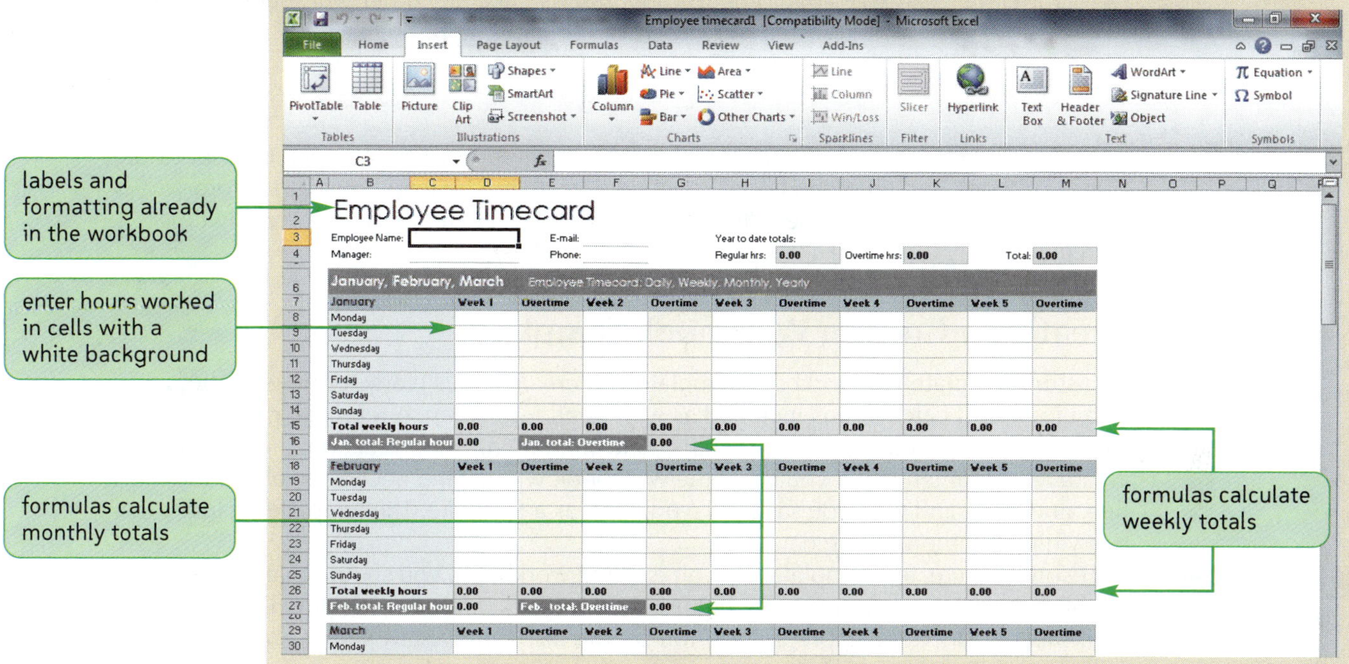


A workbook based on a specific template always displays the name of the template followed by a sequential number. Just as a blank workbook that you open is named Book1, Book2, and so forth, the workbook based on the Employee timecard template is named "Employee timecard1" in the title bar, not "Employee timecard." Any changes or additions to data, formatting, or formulas that you make affect only this workbook and not the template (in this case, the Employee timecard template). If you want to save your changes, you must save the workbook with a new name, the same way you save any new workbook.

Look at the labels and formatting already included in the Employee timecard workbook. Some cells have descriptive labels, others are blank so you can enter data in them, and still other cells contain formulas where calculations for total hours worked each day and pay category will be automatically displayed as data is entered.

You'll enter data for Ed Hoot, the student assisting Alvin, in the worksheet based on the Employee timecard template.

## To enter data in the Employee timecard1 workbook:

1. In cell C3, enter **Ed Hoot**.
2. In cell D8, enter **8**. This is the total regular hours Ed worked on Monday. Totals appear in cells D15, D16, I4, and M4 because formulas are already entered into these cells. Cell D15 shows 8 hours worked that week, cell D16 shows the number of hours worked in January, cell I4 shows the number of regular hours worked that year, and cell M4 shows the number of total hours worked that year.
3. In cell D9, enter **8** as the regular hours Ed worked on Tuesday, and then, in cell E9, enter **2** as the overtime hours Ed worked on Tuesday. The totals are updated to 16 regular hours worked that week, 2 overtime hours worked that week, and 18 total hours worked that year.

4. Save the workbook as **Hoot Time Card** in the Excel6\Tutorial folder included with your Data Files. The Hoot Time Card workbook, like any other workbook, is saved with the .xlsx file extension. It does not overwrite the template file.
5. Close the workbook.

Each day Ed Hoot works at Global Travel, he or his supervisor can open the Hoot Time Card workbook and enter the hours Ed worked that day. The total hours are automatically updated. You can see how useful templates with formulas can produce a weekly time card that is fully formatted.

## Creating a Custom Workbook Template

A **custom template** is a workbook template you create that is ready to run with the formulas for all calculations included as well as all formatting. A template can use any Excel feature, including formulas, charts, data validation, cell protection, and macros. To create a custom template, you build the workbook with all the necessary labels, formatting, and data, and then you save the workbook as a template. The template includes everything but the variable data.

Before you create a template from an existing workbook, you should make sure that all the formulas work as intended, the numbers and text are entered correctly, and the worksheet is formatted appropriately. You should also remove any values and text that will change in each workbook created from the custom template. Be careful not to delete the formulas. When you are sure the workbook is complete and accurate, you save it as an Excel template file. You can store template files in any folder, but keep in mind that custom template files stored in the Templates folder are available on the New tab in Backstage view.

**TIP**

It may be helpful to replace variable data values with spaces and apply a background color to cells in which users enter data to differentiate them from other cells in the worksheet.

**REFERENCE**

*Creating a Custom Template*

- Prepare the workbook: enter values, text, and formulas as needed; apply formatting; and replace data values with zeros or blank cells.
- Click the File tab on the Ribbon, and then click the Save As command in the navigation bar.
- In the File name box, enter the template name.
- Click the Save as type button, and then click Excel Template.
- Save the file in the Templates folder or select an alternative folder location.
- Click the Save button.

Alvin wants you to use the New Mexico workbook as the basis for creating a custom template. Then, Alvin can create new workbooks based on that template and distribute them to the accountants preparing the state workbooks. You'll reopen the workbook and clear the data values in the worksheets, leaving all of the formulas intact. After completing these modifications, you will save the workbook as a template.

**To replace the data values in the New Mexico workbook:**

1. Open the **New Mexico** workbook located in the Excel6\Tutorial folder included with your Data Files.
2. Group the **Quarter 1** through **Quarter 4** worksheets. The worksheet group includes the four quarterly worksheets but not the Summary and Documentation worksheets.

3. Select the range **B6:E12**. This range includes the specific ticket and sales data for each theme park. You want to delete these values.
4. Right-click the selected range, and then click **Clear Contents** on the shortcut menu. The data values are cleared from the selected range in each of the quarterly worksheets, but the formulas and formatting remain intact. The cleared cells are blank. The range B13:E13 displays dashes, representing zeros, where there are formulas.
5. Apply an orange fill color (the third color in the Standard Colors section of the Fill Color gallery) to the selected range. The range B6:E12 has an orange fill to indicate where users should enter data for the number of tickets sold and the sales amount in the quarterly worksheets.
6. In cell A1, enter **=Summary!A1**. This formula inserts the contents of cell A1 in the Summary worksheet into cell A1 in the quarterly worksheets. The text "New Mexico" is still displayed because that text is currently in cell A1 in the Summary worksheet.
7. Switch to the **Summary** worksheet. The quarterly worksheets are ungrouped, and dashes, representing zeros, appear in the cells in the range B6:E13, which contain formulas.
8. In cell A1, enter **Enter state name here** and then, in cell A2, enter **Enter Fiscal Year – yyyy**. This text will remind users to enter the correct state name and year. See Figure 6-24.

**TIP**

To delete the data values, you can also click the Clear button in the Editing group on the Home tab, and then click Clear Contents.

**Figure 6-24** Worksheet with formatting and formulas but no data

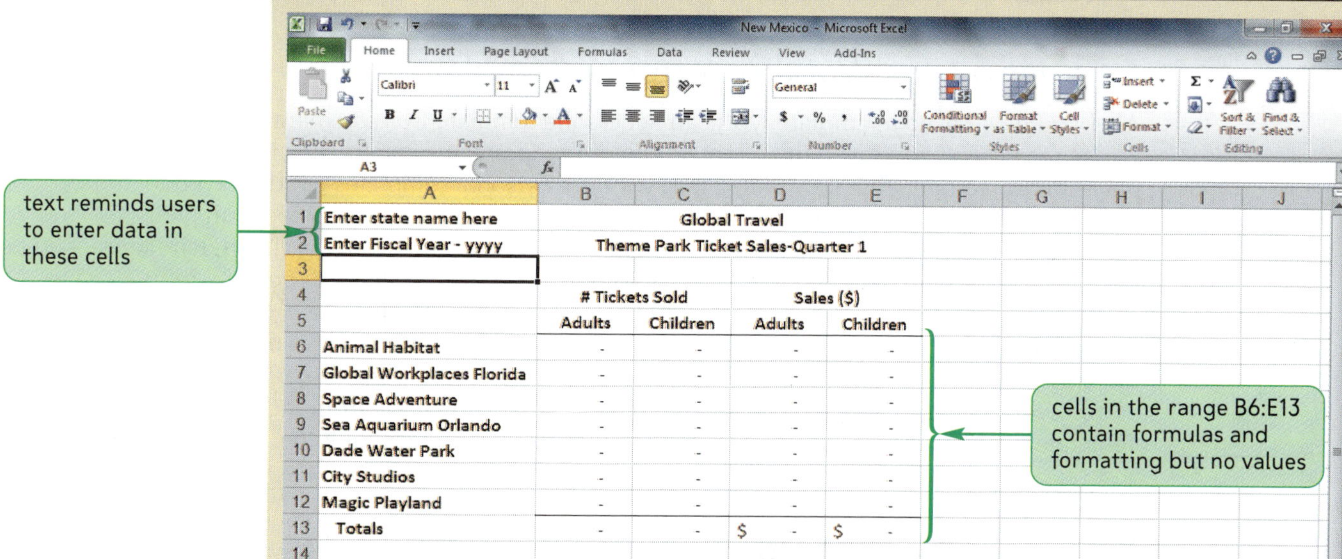


9. Switch to the **Documentation** worksheet, delete your name and the date from the range B3:B4, enter **Theme park ticket sales** in cell B6, and then click cell **A1**. The Documentation sheet is updated to reflect the purpose of the workbook.

When you save the workbook as a template, the save location opens to the Templates folder, which is where custom template files are often stored. Excel, by default, looks for template files in this folder. However, you can store templates in other folders as well. Because you might not have access to the Templates folder, you will save the template file with the other Data Files. All template files have the .xltx file extension. This extension differentiates template files from workbook files, which have the .xlsx file extension.

After you have saved a workbook in a template format, you can make the template accessible to other users.

The New Mexico workbook no longer contains any specific data, but the formulas and formatting will still be in effect when new data is entered. It is ready to save in template format.

**To save the New Mexico workbook as a template:**

1. Click the **File** tab on the Ribbon to open Backstage view, and then click the **Save As** command in the navigation bar. The Save As dialog box opens.
2. Type **Travel Template** in the File name box.
3. Click the **Save as type** button, and then click **Excel Template**. The Address bar displays the Templates folder on your computer. You will change this location.
4. Navigate to the **Excel6\Tutorial** folder included with your Data Files.
5. Click the **Save** button. The Travel Template is saved in the same folder as your Data Files.
6. Close the Travel Template workbook template.

Make sure the save location and save as type are accurate so that you can locate and use the template file later in this session.

Alvin will use the Travel Template file to create the workbooks to track next year's sales for each state and then distribute the workbooks via email to each accountant. By basing these new workbooks on the template file, Alvin has a standard workbook with identical formatting and formulas for each accountant to use. He also avoids the risk of accidentally changing the workbook containing the 2013 data when preparing for 2014.

## Creating a New Workbook from a Template

After you have saved a template, you can access the template from the New tab in Backstage view. If you saved the template file in the Templates folder, click the My templates button to open the New dialog box with the Personal Templates tab displayed to select the template you want to use. If you saved the template to another location, you can use the New from existing button to create a new workbook from the file, much like creating a workbook based on a template found in the Templates folder. The New from existing button opens a copy of the selected file, not the selected file. Also, the copy of the workbook that opens has a number at the end of the filename, and is considered an unnamed file, which prevents anyone from inadvertently overwriting the original file.

You will use the New from existing button to create a workbook from the Travel Template file because you saved the template in your Excel6\Tutorial folder.

**To create a new workbook based on the Travel Template file:**

1. Click the **File** tab on the Ribbon to open Backstage view, and then click the **New** tab in the navigation bar. The New tab appears in Backstage view.
2. Click the **New from existing** button. The New from Existing Workbook dialog box opens, with All Excel Files displayed.

**TIP**

The active worksheet in the new workbook is the same worksheet that was active when you saved the template file.

3. Click **Travel Template** located in the Excel6\Tutorial folder included with your Data Files, and then click the **Create New** button. A copy of the Travel Template workbook opens named "Travel Template1" to indicate this is the first copy of the Travel Template workbook created during the current Excel session.
4. Click the **Summary** sheet tab, enter **New Mexico** in cell A1, and then enter **Fiscal Year - 2014** in cell A2.
5. Switch to the **Quarter 1** worksheet. The text "New Mexico" appears in cell A1, and the text "Fiscal Year - 2014" appears in cell A2.
6. Enter the following test data in the data area (range B6:E6, which has the orange background fill color), and then review the column totals in the range B13:E13 (the cells that contain formulas to sum each column):

   cell B6: **120**
   cell C6: **150**
   cell D6: **3000**
   cell E6: **2850**

7. Enter the following test data in the range B7:E7, and then notice that the formulas in the range B13:E13 are updated. See Figure 6-25.

   cell B7: **180**
   cell C7: **200**
   cell D7: **3500**
   cell E7: **3150**

**Figure 6-25** **New workbook based on the Travel Template**

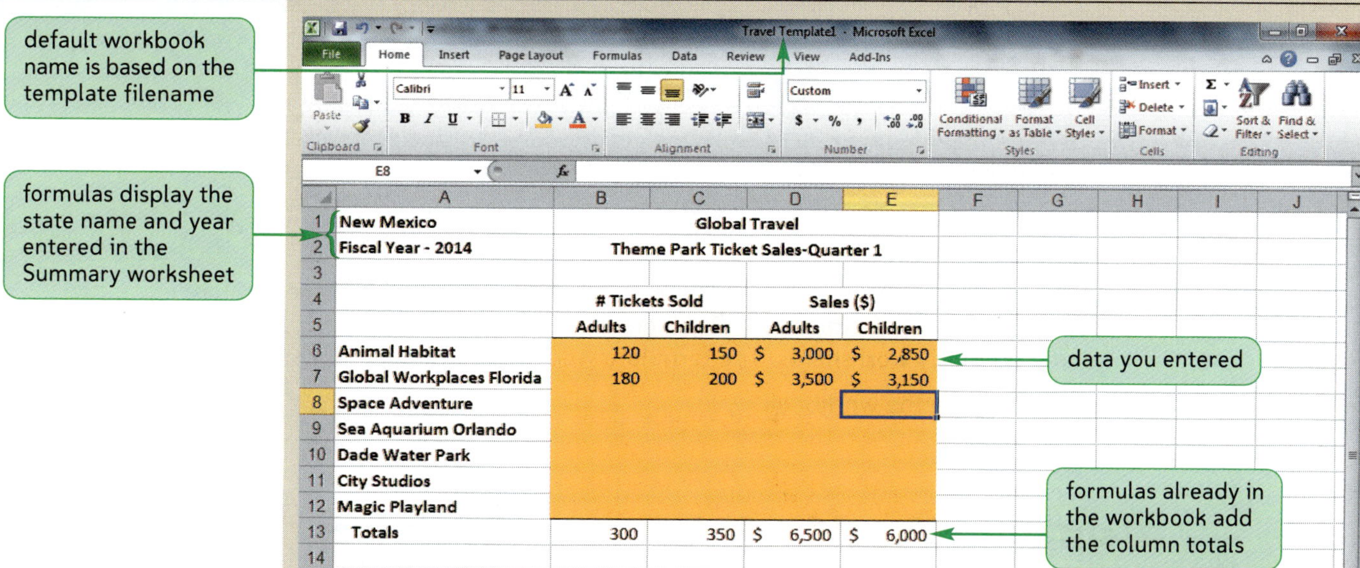


8. Switch to the **Summary** worksheet. Totals appear in the ranges B6:E7 and B13:E13 as a result of the formulas in this worksheet. See Figure 6-26.

**Figure 6-26** Summary worksheet after data is entered

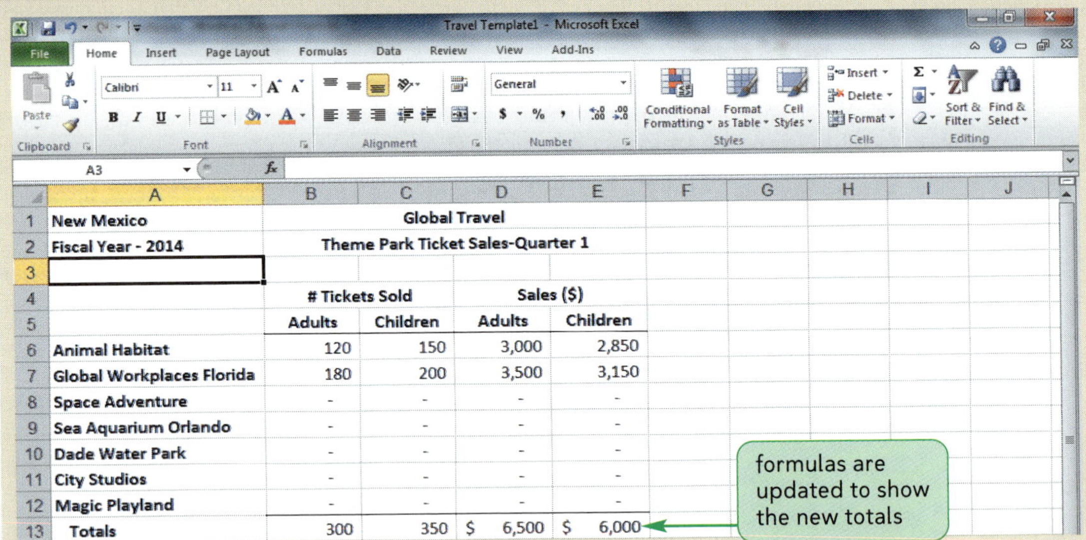


9. Save the workbook as **New Mexico 2014** in the Excel6\Tutorial folder included with your Data Files, and then close the workbook. The copy of the template is saved as a workbook with the .xlsx file extension. The original template file is not changed.

You'll add data to the Quarter 2, Quarter 3, and Quarter 4 worksheets to verify that the Summary worksheet is correctly adding numbers from the four worksheets.

**To test the New Mexico 2014 workbook:**

1. Open the **New Mexico 2014** workbook located in the Excel6\Tutorial folder included with your Data Files.
2. Group the **Quarter 2**, **Quarter 3**, and **Quarter 4** worksheets, enter **120** in cell B6, and then, enter **150** in cell C6.
3. Switch to the **Summary** worksheet. The total in cell B6 is 480 and the total in cell C6 is 600. The formulas in the Summary worksheet correctly add values from all the quarterly worksheets. The template workbook is functioning as intended.
4. Save and close the workbook.

# Using the Excel Web App and SkyDrive

**TIP**

**Cloud computing** refers to data, applications, and even resources that are stored on servers that you access over the Internet rather than on your own computer.

**Office Web Apps** are Web-based versions of Microsoft Excel, Word, PowerPoint, and OneNote. These Web apps allow you to create, view, and edit Office files directly from a Web browser as well as share files and collaborate with other users online. Office Web Apps are a part of **Windows Live**, which is a collection of services and Web applications that you can use to be more productive. For example, you can use Windows Live to upload Office files to an online storage and file sharing service called SkyDrive. The service requires a Windows Live ID, allowing you to keep your files private, share them with individuals you specify, or make the files public. You can save your files directly from Microsoft Office 2010 onto SkyDrive from Backstage view.

Note: SkyDrive and Office Web Apps are dynamic Web pages, and might change over time, including the way they are organized and how commands are performed. The steps and figures in this tutorial were accurate at the time this book was published.

## Obtaining a Windows Live ID

To save files to SkyDrive or use the Office Web Apps, you need a Windows Live ID. You obtain a Windows Live ID by going to the Windows Live Web site and creating a new account. Once you have a Windows Live ID, you can access your SkyDrive and use it to store files, create new files, and share your files with others.

*Note:* If you already have a Windows Live ID, you can skip this set of steps.

**To obtain a Windows Live ID:**

1. Start your Web browser, and then go to **www.windowslive.com**. The page where you can sign into Windows Live opens.

   **Trouble?** If the URL doesn't bring you to the page where you can sign into Windows Live, use a search engine to search for "Windows Live."
2. Click the **Sign up** button. The Create your Windows Live ID page opens.
3. Follow the instructions on the screen to create a Windows Live ID.
4. Sign out of Windows Live, exit your browser, and return to Excel.

## Saving a Workbook to SkyDrive

After you have a Windows Live ID, you can access your SkyDrive and the Office Web Apps. You can access your SkyDrive from the Windows Live page in your browser after you signed in with your Windows Live ID, or from Backstage view in Excel. You can save a file to a private or public folder on your SkyDrive.

REFERENCE

*Saving a Workbook to SkyDrive*

- Open the workbook you want to save to SkyDrive.
- Click the File tab, click Save & Send in the navigation pane, and then click the Save to Web command in the center pane.
- In the right pane, click the Sign In button, and then complete the sign-in process.
- Click the folder in which to save the workbook, and then click the Save As button.
- Enter a filename in the File name box, and then click the Save button.

You'll save the New Mexico 2014 workbook to the My Documents folder on your SkyDrive. This is a private folder that only you can access.

**To save the workbook from Excel to the My Documents folder on your SkyDrive:**

1. In Excel, open the **New Mexico 2014** workbook located in the Excel6/Tutorial folder.
2. Click the **File** tab, and then click **Save & Send** in the navigation bar. The Save & Send options appear in Backstage view.
3. Under Save & Send, click the **Save to Web** button. A Sign in button appears that you use to sign in to your Windows Live account. See Figure 6-27.

**Figure 6-27** Save to Web options on the Save & Send tab in Backstage view

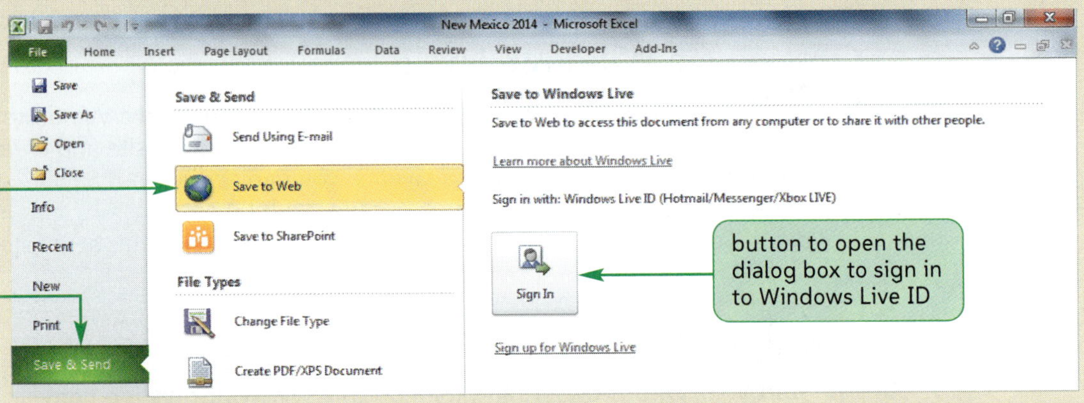


**Trouble?** If you're already signed into Windows Live, you'll see the folders in your SkyDrive account and the Save As button (see Figure 6-28). Continue with Step 8.

4. Click the **Sign In** button. The Connecting to docs.live.net dialog box opens.
5. In the E-mail address box, type the email address associated with your Windows Live ID, and then press the **Tab** key.
6. In the Password box, type the password associated with your Windows Live ID.
7. Click the **OK** button. The dialog box closes, and another dialog box appears while you connect to the Windows Live server. After you connect to Windows Live, the right pane in Backstage view lists the folders on your SkyDrive and a Save As button appears. See Figure 6-28.

**Figure 6-28** Save & Send tab after connecting to Windows Live

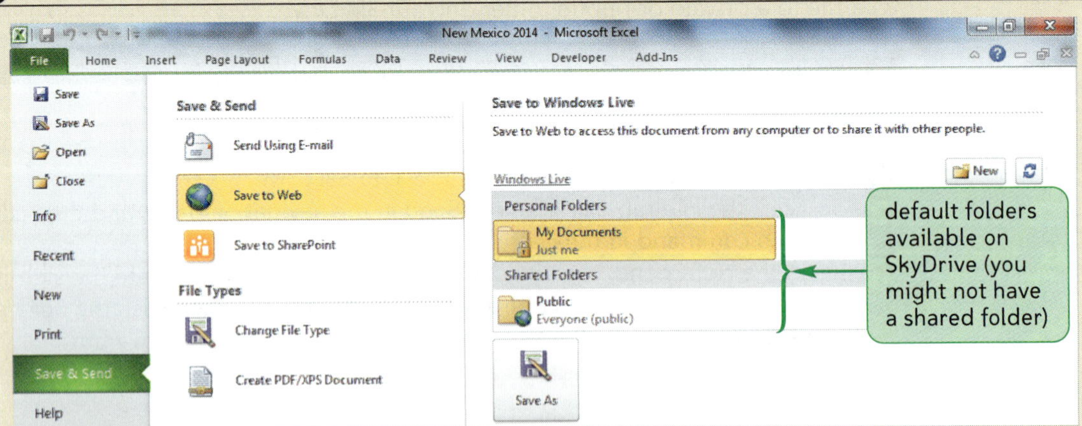


8. In the right pane, click the **My Documents** folder, if necessary, and then click the Save As button. Backstage view closes, and the **Save As** dialog box opens.
9. Click the **Save** button. The workbook is saved in the My Documents folder on your SkyDrive. In Excel, close the workbook.

## Editing a Workbook with the Excel Web App

You can view and edit workbooks in the Excel Web App. The interface for the Excel Web App is similar to the interface of the full-featured program on your computer; however, only a limited number of commands are available.

You'll sign in to your Windows Live account and use the Excel Web App to update the New Mexico 2014 workbook on your SkyDrive.

## To edit the workbook using the Excel Web App:

1. Start your browser, and then go to **www.windowslive.com** and sign in to your SkyDrive using your Windows Live ID.
2. If your SkyDrive account is not open, click the **Office** link at the top of the Windows Live page, and then click **Your documents**.
3. Click **My Documents**, and then point to **New Mexico 2014**. See Figure 6-29.

**Figure 6-29** New Mexico 2014 Information page on SkyDrive

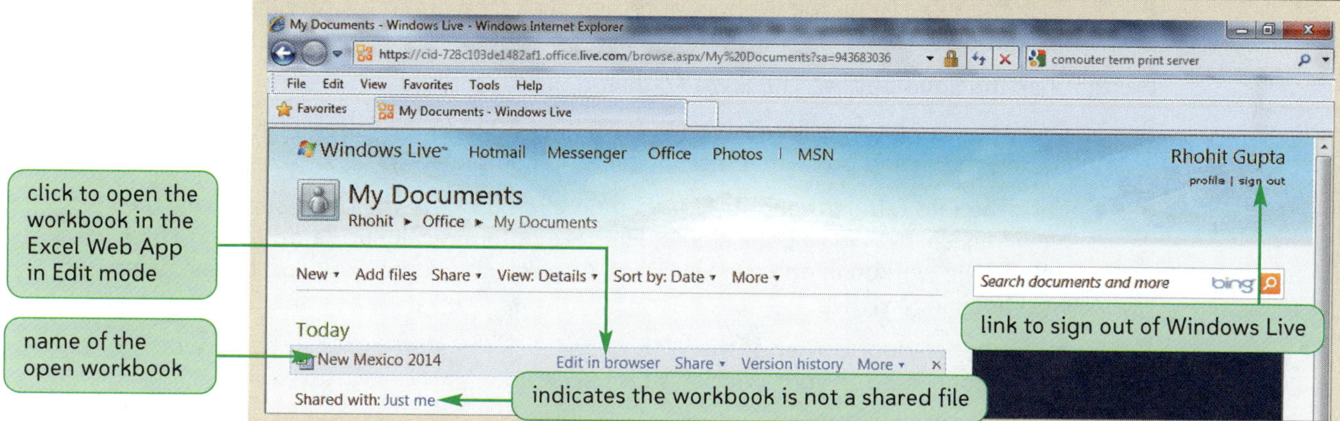


4. Click the **Edit in browser** link. The New Mexico 2014 workbook opens in the Excel Web App in Edit mode so you can make changes to the file.

   **Trouble?** If this is the first time you have opened a file in SkyDrive file, you might be asked to read and accept the user agreement in order to continue. Accept the user agreement, and then continue with Step 5.

5. Click the **Quarter 1** sheet tab, and then enter **200** in cell B8, **1500** in cell C8, **1500** in cell D8, and **4000** in cell E8. See Figure 6-30.

**Figure 6-30** Edited New Mexico 2014 workbook in the Excel Web App

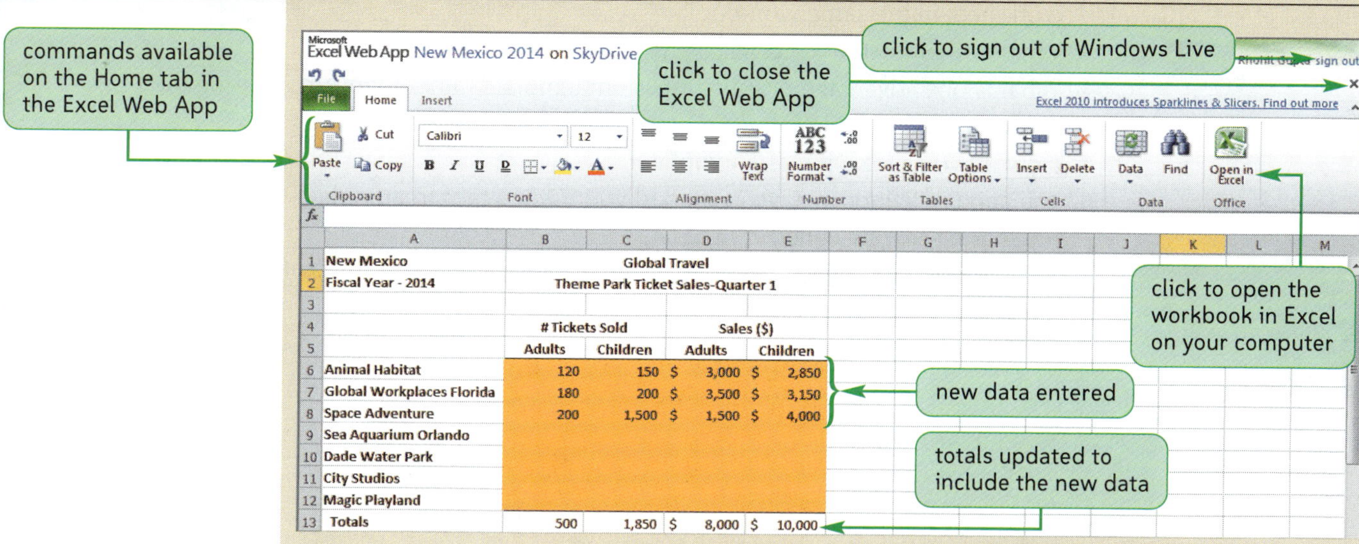

6. Switch to the **Summary** worksheet and verify that the data on the Summary worksheet was also updated.

**TIP**

To open the file in Excel on your computer, click the Open in Excel button in the Office group on the Home tab of the Excel Web App (refer to Figure 6-30).

The Excel Web App in Edit mode does not have all of the features of the program installed on your computer available. To use the other features, you need to open the workbook in the full-featured program on your computer. You can save a workbook from SkyDrive to your computer and then continue working in the full version of Excel. You'll save the updated the version of the New Mexico 2014 workbook to your computer.

### To save the workbook from SkyDrive to your computer:

1. Click the **File** tab on the Ribbon, and then click **Download a Copy** in the navigation bar. The File Download dialog box opens.
2. Click the **Save** button. The Save As dialog box opens.
3. Save the workbook as **SkyDrive New Mexico 2014** in the Excel6/Tutorial folder, closing the dialog box when the download is complete.
4. Click the **File** tab on the Ribbon, and then **click** Close in the navigation bar. The New Mexico 2014 workbook closes. Files are automatically updated as you enter data in the workbook on your SkyDrive. As a result, you do not need to save your workbook in SkyDrive.
5. In the upper-right corner of the Web page, click the **sign out** link. You are no longer connected to your Windows Live account.
6. Close your Web browser.

With the ability to edit a workbook from any computer, Rhohit can be sure that his workbooks are always updated. The templates you created will ensure that all regions enter data consistently, making it simpler for Alvin to track ticket sales for Global Travel.

**REVIEW**

## *Session 6.3 Quick Check*

1. How do you insert a hyperlink into a worksheet cell?
2. True or False. A hyperlink in a worksheet cell can be used to jump to another worksheet in the same workbook.
3. What is a template?
4. What is one advantage of using a custom template rather than simply using the original workbook file to create a new workbook?
5. How do you save a file as a template?
6. You can use Windows Live to upload your Office files to an online storage and file sharing service called ______________.
7. True or False. You need a Windows Live ID to save files to your SkyDrive and use the Office Web Apps.

*Practice the skills you learned in the tutorial using the same case scenario.*

PRACTICE

## Review Assignments

**Data Files needed for the Review Assignments: OR.xlsx, Idaho.xlsx, Washington.xlsx, NW Totals 2013.xlsx, and NW Travel.xltx**

Elaine Dennerson, accountant for Global Travel in Oregon, needs your help. Global Travel has added Oregon to its Northwest territory, which already includes Washington and Idaho. You will complete the Summary worksheet in the Oregon workbook, and then enter the formulas in the NW Totals 2013 workbook to summarize the regional totals in one workbook. Complete the following:

1. Open the **OR** workbook located in the Excel6\Review folder included with your Data Files, and then save the workbook as **Oregon** in the same folder.
2. In the Documentation sheet, enter your name and the date, and then review the worksheets in the workbook.
3. Create a worksheet group that contains the Qtr 1 through Qtr 4 worksheets.
4. In the worksheet group, insert formulas in the range B13:E13 to total each column.
5. Format the quarterly worksheets as specified below, and then ungroup the worksheets:
   a. Bold the range A1:B2;A6:A13; and B4:E5.
   b. Merge and center the ranges B1:E1, B2:E2, B4:C4, and D4:E4.
   c. Format the range A6:A12 in italic.
   d. Add a top and double bottom border to the range B13:E13.
   e. Add a fill color to the range B1:E2 using the Orange color in the Standard Colors section.
   f. Apply the Accounting number format with no decimal places to the range D6:E13.
6. Make a copy of the Qtr 1 worksheet, rename it as **Summary**, and place it after the Documentation worksheet.
7. In the Summary worksheet, remove the data from the range B6:E12, change the heading in cell B2 to **Theme Park Ticket Sales – Total** and then enter the label **Fiscal Year – 2013** in cell A2.
8. In worksheets Qtr 1 through Qtr 4, enter formulas to reference the labels in cells A1 and A2 of the Summary worksheet.
9. In the Summary worksheet, create 3-D reference formulas to calculate annual totals for theme park tickets sold and sales.
10. Prepare all worksheets except the Documentation sheet for printing. Display the name of the workbook and the name of the worksheet on separate lines in the right section of the header. Display your name and the date on separate lines in the right section of the footer. Preview the five worksheets.
11. Ungroup the worksheets and save the workbook.
12. Open the regional **NW Totals 2013** workbook located in the Excel6\Review folder included with your Data Files, and then save the workbook as **Northwest Totals 2013**. In the Documentation worksheet, enter your name and the date.
13. In the Summary worksheet, enter external reference formulas to create a set of linked workbooks to summarize the totals for Oregon, Washington, and Idaho in the Northwest Totals 2013 workbook.
14. In the Northwest Totals 2013 workbook, switch to the Documentation sheet. In the range A10:A12, enter the name of each state (**Idaho**, **Oregon**, and **Washington**). Create hyperlinks from each state label to its corresponding workbook. Add appropriate text for the ScreenTip to each hyperlink. Test each hyperlink.

15. Create a workspace with the following four workbooks in a tiled layout: Idaho, Oregon, Washington, and Northwest Totals 2013. Make the Summary worksheet in each workbook the active worksheet, and make the Northwest Totals 2013 workbook the active workbook. Save the workspace as **NW Workspace**.
16. Create a new workbook based on the **NW Travel** template located in the Excel6\Review folder included with your Data Files. Save the workbook as **Oregon 2014** in the same folder. In the Documentation worksheet, enter your name and the date.
17. In the Summary worksheet, enter **Oregon** in cell A1 and **Fiscal Year – 2014** in cell A2. In the Qtr 1 worksheet, enter **2000** in each cell of the range B6:C12. In the Qtr 2 worksheet, enter **3000** in each cell of the range B6:C12. Confirm that the values entered in this step were correctly totaled in the Summary worksheet. Save the Oregon 2014 workbook.
18. Save the Oregon 2014 workbook to the My Documents folder on your SkyDrive using the same name. In the Qtr 3 worksheet, enter **4000** in each cell in the range B6:C12. Download the file to your computer using the name **SkyDrive Oregon 2014**.
19. Close all the workbooks. Submit the finished files to your instructor, either in printed or electronic form, as requested.

*Use the skills you learned to summarize sales data.*

APPLY

## Case Problem 1

**Data File needed for this Case Problem: Cafe.xlsx**

***Java Café*** Java Café currently has three stores in the Southwest: Tucson, Arizona; Las Cruces, New Mexico; and Dallas, Texas. Jayne Mitchell manages the three stores and uses Excel to summarize sales data from these stores. She asks you to total the sales by product group and store for each quarter and then format each worksheet. Jayne also needs you to add another worksheet to calculate Summary sales for the stores and product groups. Complete the following:

1. Open the **Cafe** workbook located in the Excel6\Case1 folder included with your Data Files, and then save the workbook as **Java Cafe** in the same folder.
2. In the Documentation worksheet, enter your name and the date, and then switch to the Quarter 1 worksheet.
3. Group the four quarterly worksheets. For each quarter, calculate the product totals in the range B8:F8 and the store locations in the range F5:F7. Improve the look of the quarterly worksheets using the formatting of your choice. Ungroup the worksheets.
4. Place a copy of one of the quarterly worksheets between the Documentation and Quarter 1 worksheets, rename the new worksheet as **Summary Sales**, and then delete the values in the range B5:E7. The Summary Sales worksheet is identical in appearance to the quarterly worksheets.
5. In the Summary Sales worksheet, in the range B5:E7, insert the formulas that add the sales in the corresponding cells of the four quarterly worksheets. Use 3-D references to calculate the totals for each product group and store.
6. Set up the Summary Sales and four quarterly worksheets for printing. Each worksheet should be centered horizontally, fit on one page, display the name of the worksheet centered in the header, and display your name and the date on separate lines in the right section of the footer.
7. Save the Java Cafe 2014 workbook to the My Documents folder on your SkyDrive using the same name. In the Quarter 1 worksheet, change coffee sales in Tucson to **$30,000**. Download the file to your computer using the name **SkyDrive Java Cafe 2014**.
8. Save the Java Cafe workbook, and then remove the sales data, but not the formulas, from each of the quarterly worksheets.

9. Return to the Documentation worksheet, and then save the workbook as an Excel template with the name **Java Template** in the Excel6\Case1 folder included with your Data Files.
10. Use the Java Template file to create a new workbook. Save the workbook as **Java Cafe 2014** in the Excel6\Case1 folder. In the range B5:E7 of all four quarterly worksheets, enter **1**. Verify that the formulas in each worksheet summarize the data accurately.
11. Save and close the workbook. Submit the finished files to your instructor, either in printed or electronic form, as requested.

*Link workbooks to summarize sales data for a car dealership.*

APPLY

## Case Problem 2

### Data Files needed for this Case Problem: Carson.xlsx, Reno.xlsx, and Vegas.xlsx

***UTE Auto Sales & Services*** Hardy Ute is founder and operator of UTE Auto Sales & Services, which has dealerships in Las Vegas, Reno, and Carson City, Nevada. His dealerships sell new and used cars, hybrids, SUVs, and trucks, as well as service customers' vehicles. To analyze sales and service at each of his three dealerships, Hardy wants his staff to prepare a report that shows the unit and dollar sales of new and used vehicles by type as well as service by vehicle type. Complete the following:

1. Open the **Carson** workbook located in the Excel6\Case2 folder included with your Data Files, and then save the workbook as **UTE Carson City** in the same folder.
2. In the Documentation worksheet, enter your name, the date, and an appropriate purpose statement, and then switch to the Quarter 1 worksheet.
3. Group the four quarterly worksheets. For each quarter, calculate the totals in the range B10:G10, and then improve the formatting of the quarterly worksheets by merging and centering cells B4:C4, cells D4:E4, and cells F4:G4, and then center aligning the range B5:G5. Ungroup the worksheets.
4. Insert a new worksheet between the Documentation and Quarter 1 worksheets, and then rename this worksheet as **Summary**. Format the worksheet identically to the quarterly worksheets except leave the range B6:G9 blank. (*Hint*: Copy one of the quarterly worksheets, and then modify it as needed.)
5. In the Summary worksheet, in the range B6:G9, insert formulas that add the sales in the corresponding cells of the four quarterly worksheets.
6. Prepare the Summary and four quarterly sales worksheets for printing. Center the worksheets horizontally, center the worksheet name in the header, and place your name and the current date on separate lines in the right section of the footer.
7. Save and close the workbook.
8. Open the **Reno** workbook located in the Excel6\Case2 folder included with your Data Files, and then save the workbook as **UTE Reno**. Repeat Steps 2 through 7 for this workbook.
9. Open the **Vegas** workbook located in the Excel6\Case2 folder, and then save the workbook as **UTE Vegas**. Repeat Steps 2 through 7 for this workbook.
10. Create a new workbook, and then use Figure 6-31 as a guide to create a summary of the three dealerships' workbooks. Save the workbook as **UTE Summary**.

**Figure 6-31** UTE sales for all dealers

| | A | B | C | D | E | F | G |
|---|---|---|---|---|---|---|---|
| 1 | UTE Auto Sales & Service | | | | | | |
| 2 | Sales - All Dealers | | | | | | |
| 3 | | | | | | | |
| 4 | | New | | Pre-owned | | Service | |
| 5 | | Units | Sales ($) | Units | Sales ($) | Units | Sales ($) |
| 6 | Cars | 733 | $ 14,940,828 | 203 | $ 1,476,397 | 5405 | $ 1,058,958 |
| 7 | Hybrids | 288 | $ 7,979,268 | 76 | $ 478,632 | 1798 | $ 492,525 |
| 8 | SUVs | 166 | $ 3,928,990 | 87 | $ 750,758 | 1007 | $ 328,662 |
| 9 | Trucks | 113 | $ 1,639,386 | 64 | $ 341,907 | 691 | $ 117,874 |
| 10 | Totals | 1300 | $ 28,488,472 | 430 | $ 3,047,694 | 8901 | $ 1,998,019 |

11. Use the UTE Carson City workbook to create an Excel template with the name **UTE Template** in the Excel6\Case2 folder included with your Data Files. Add appropriate formatting of your choice and remove the date in cell B4 from the Documentation worksheet.
12. Create a new workbook using the UTE Template. Add appropriate test data for Quarter 1. Save the workbook as **Carson City 2014** in the Excel6\Case2 folder included with your Data Files. In the Documentation sheet, enter the date in cell B4.
13. Save the Carson City 2014 workbook to the My Documents folder on your SkyDrive using the same name. In the Quarter 2 worksheet, enter **75** new cars at a value of **$825,000**. Download the file to your computer using the name **SkyDrive Carson City 2014**.
14. Close any open workbooks. Submit the finished files to your instructor, either in printed or electronic form, as requested.

*Create a worksheet to summarize sales data.*

CREATE

## Case Problem 3

### Data File needed for this Case Problem: Infusion.xlsx

***Infusion Blend*** Micki Goldstein is a sales representative for Infusion Blend, a specialty soft drink producer. Micki is based in Tampa, and she travels around Florida to meet and make product presentations to managers of stores ranging from major supermarket chains to small corner markets. Although Micki does not personally make the deliveries, she often works closely with the delivery staff to assure quality service to her customers.

Micki must report her sales progress to her regional manager in Atlanta, Georgia. These reports include the overall sales volume, the types of products sold, locations, and stores where the products were delivered. For the larger markets, she must prepare a separate workbook for each chain store. Complete the following:

1. Open the **Infusion** workbook located in the Excel6\Case3 folder included with your Data Files, and then save the workbook as **Infusion 2013** in the same folder.
2. In the Documentation worksheet, enter your name and the date, and then switch to the January worksheet.
3. Group the 12 monthly worksheets. For each month (January through December), enter formulas to calculate the total sales for each product and store, and then improve the formatting of the monthly worksheets using the formatting of your choice. Ungroup the worksheets.

4. Insert a new worksheet between the Documentation and January worksheets that has the same content as the monthly worksheets except the range B6:G12 is blank, rename the worksheet as **YTD Summary**, and then format this worksheet identically to the monthly worksheets.
5. Use 3-D reference formulas to calculate the total number of cases sold for each product by store from January through December. For example, in cell B6, the formula results in 1335 cases of the Popgo product sold in the Elteron store.
6. Insert formulas that calculate total cases sold by product for all stores in column G, and total cases of all products sold by store in row 12. Calculate the Summary total for all products sold in all stores.

EXPLORE

7. Insert a new worksheet following the Documentation worksheet, and then rename this worksheet as **Annual Recap**. Using Figure 6-32 as a guide, create three summaries on this worksheet by product, store, and month, using the following formulas:
   a. Insert formulas that add the total cases sold of each product in the range C7:C12 (column G in the monthly worksheets). Calculate the total for all products.
   b. Insert formulas that add the total cases sold at each store in the range G7:G11 (row 12 in the monthly worksheets). Calculate the total for all stores.
   c. Insert formulas that add the total cases sold each month in the range K7:K18 (cell G12 in each monthly worksheet). Calculate the total for all months.
   d. Insert formulas in column D to calculate the percentage of cases sold for each product to the total cases sold for all products. Calculate the percentage of each product's total to the total cases sold for all products.
   e. Insert formulas in column H to calculate the percentage of cases sold by each store total to the total cases sold by all stores. Calculate the percentage of each store's total to the total for all stores.
   f. Insert formulas in column L to calculate the percentage of cases sold each month to the total cases sold for the year. Calculate the percentage of each month's total to the total for the year.

**Figure 6-32** **Infusion Blend's sales by product, store, and month**

| | A | B | C | D | E | F | G | H | I | J | K | L |
|---|---|---|---|---|---|---|---|---|---|---|---|---|
| 1 | | Infusion Blend Sales by Product, Store and Month | | | | | | | | | | |
| 2 | | Cases Sold | | | | | | | | | | |
| 3 | | | | | | | | | | | | |
| 4 | | | | | | | | | | | | |
| 5 | | Breakdown by Product | | | | Breakdown by Store | | | | Breakdown by Month | | |
| 6 | | Products | Cases Sold | Percent | | Store | Cases Sold | Percent | | Month | Cases Sold | Percent |
| 7 | | Popgo | 7,065 | 30.7% | | Elteron | 4,700 | 20.5% | | January | 8,975 | 39.1% |
| 8 | | Diet Popgo | 4,760 | 20.7% | | Everett | 4,600 | 20.0% | | February | 7,120 | 31.0% |
| 9 | | Mt. Spring | 3,360 | 14.6% | | Franklin | 4,700 | 20.5% | | March | 3,905 | 17.0% |
| 10 | | Red Burst | 1,675 | 7.3% | | Grant | 4,625 | 20.1% | | April | 2,980 | 13.0% |
| 11 | | Dr Selsa | 3,135 | 13.6% | | Grover | 4,355 | 19.0% | | May | - | 0.0% |
| 12 | | L & L | 2,985 | 13.0% | | Totals | 22,980 | 100.0% | | June | - | 0.0% |
| 13 | | Totals | 22,980 | 100% | | | | | | July | - | 0.0% |
| 14 | | | | | | | | | | August | - | 0.0% |
| 15 | | | | | | | | | | September | - | 0.0% |
| 16 | | | | | | | | | | October | - | 0.0% |
| 17 | | | | | | | | | | November | - | 0.0% |
| 18 | | | | | | | | | | December | - | 0.0% |
| 19 | | | | | | | | | | Totals | 22,980 | 100.0% |

8. Save the Infusion 2013 workbook, and then use the Save As command to save a copy of the Infusion 2013 workbook with the name **Infusion with May 2013**.
9. In the Infusion with May 2013 workbook, insert the May results, shown in Figure 6-33, into the May worksheet.

**Figure 6-33** **Infusion Blend's May sales**

| | A | B | C | D | E | F | G |
|---|---|---|---|---|---|---|---|
| 1 | Infusion Blend Sales by Store and Product | | | | | | |
| 2 | Cases Sold | | | | | | |
| 3 | | | | | | | |
| 4 | | Stores | | | | | |
| 5 | Products | Elteron | Everett | Franklin | Grant | Grover | Totals |
| 6 | Popgo | 515 | 545 | 560 | 670 | 510 | 2,800 |
| 7 | Diet Popgo | 435 | 445 | 435 | 430 | 410 | 2,155 |
| 8 | Mt. Spring | 235 | 275 | 240 | 240 | 205 | 1,195 |
| 9 | Red Burst | 125 | 125 | 150 | 150 | 325 | 875 |
| 10 | Dr Selsa | 160 | 145 | 150 | 160 | 125 | 740 |
| 11 | L & L | 325 | 240 | 175 | 245 | 225 | 1,210 |
| 12 | Totals | 1,795 | 1,775 | 1,710 | 1,895 | 1,800 | 8,975 |

10. In the Documentation worksheet, in the range A8:A19, type the months **January** through **December**. Create hyperlinks from each cell to its corresponding worksheet. Test the hyperlinks.
11. Save and close the workbook. Submit the finished workbooks to your instructor, either in printed or electronic form, as requested.

*Explore using worksheet groups, 3-D and external references, workspaces, and templates.*

CHALLENGE

## Case Problem 4

**Data Files needed for this Case Problem: Europe.xlsx, North America.xlsx, South America.xlsx, and PlutoTemplate.xltx**

***Pluto Pharmaceuticals*** Pluto Pharmaceuticals is a multinational manufacturer of healthcare products. The chief financial analyst, Kevin Cross, asks you to prepare the first quarter revenue summary based on workbooks from the regions of North America, South America, and Europe. Each workbook has monthly worksheets displaying forecasted and actual revenues of the major product groups for the first quarter. Kevin wants you to calculate the difference between forecasted and actual sales (Difference) and the percent change between forecasted and actual sales (% Change). He also wants you to summarize each workbook, reporting the quarterly forecasted and actual totals for revenues in a new worksheet. After you have added this information to each workbook, Kevin wants you to consolidate the information from the three regional workbooks, reporting in a single workbook the summarized information for each region. Complete the following:

1. Open the **Europe**, **North America**, and **South America** workbooks located in the Excel6\Case4 folder included with your Data Files. Save the Europe workbook as **PlutoEU**, save the North America workbook as **PlutoNA**, and save the South America workbook as **PlutoSA**. In the Documentation worksheet in each regional revenue workbook, enter your name and the date.
2. Each regional workbook contains a Documentation worksheet, a first quarter summary worksheet, and three monthly worksheets. Complete the monthly worksheets in each region's workbook by doing the following:
   a. Calculate the difference for each product group: Actual–Forecast.
   b. Calculate the % change for each product group: Difference/Forecast.
   c. Calculate the total revenue for the Forecast, Actual, and Difference columns, and then calculate the total % change.
   d. Format the numbers to improve the appearance of the worksheets.

3. In each workbook, complete the Quarter 1 worksheet by first summarizing the forecasted and actual totals for product groups for the first three months of the year, then calculating the difference and the % change, and, finally, summarizing the forecasted, actual, difference, and % change values for the quarter. (*Hint*: The Total Revenue % change in cell E10 is not the sum of the column; it is the percent change between the forecasted and actual totals.) Use Figure 6-34 as a guide as you complete the worksheet.

**Figure 6-34** **First quarter North America revenue**

| | A | B | C | D | E |
|---|---|---|---|---|---|
| 1 | Pluto Pharmaceuticals-North America | | | | |
| 2 | Revenue - Quarter 1 | | | | |
| 3 | | | | | |
| 4 | Product Group | Forecast | Actual | Difference | % Change |
| 5 | Personal Care | $ 2,295,600 | $ 2,363,891 | $ 68,291 | 3.0% |
| 6 | Beauty | $ 340,500 | $ 363,536 | $ 23,036 | 6.8% |
| 7 | Animal Healthcare | $ 2,079,100 | $ 2,101,693 | $ 22,593 | 1.1% |
| 8 | Prescription Medicine | $ 522,300 | $ 526,672 | $ 4,372 | 0.8% |
| 9 | Photo | $ 1,006,200 | $ 976,096 | $ (30,104) | -3.0% |
| 10 | Total Revenue | $ 6,243,700 | $ 6,331,888 | $ 88,188 | 1.4% |

4. Format the Quarter 1 worksheet for each regional workbook with the same formatting used for the monthly worksheets, and then save the workbooks.
5. Create a new workbook, and save it as **PlutoSummary** in the Excel6\Case4 folder included with your Data Files. Rename the Sheet1 worksheet as **Documentation**, and in column A enter the same labels used in the Documentation worksheets in the other workbooks. In column B, enter **Corporate** as the region, your name as the author, the current date as the date created, and **To report on revenue for all regions** as the purpose. Format the Documentation worksheet to match the Documentation worksheet formatting in the PlutoNA, PlutoSA, and PlutoEU workbooks.
6. Switch to the Sheet2 worksheet, and then enter the text shown in Figure 6-35. Enter formulas to total the Forecasted and Actual revenue for each product group. Compute the difference and % change for each product group. Include the totals for the Forecast, Actual, and Difference columns, and calculate the % change for the total revenue for the quarter. Rename the worksheet as **Quarter 1**.

**Figure 6-35** **First quarter corporate revenue**

| | A | B | C | D | E |
|---|---|---|---|---|---|
| 1 | Pluto Pharmaceuticals-Corporate | | | | |
| 2 | Revenue - Quarter 1 | | | | |
| 3 | | | | | |
| 4 | Product Group | Forecast | Actual | Difference | % Change |
| 5 | Personal Care | $ 5,670,800 | $ 5,913,673 | $ 242,873 | 4.3% |
| 6 | Beauty | $ 1,210,500 | $ 1,250,000 | $ 39,500 | 3.3% |
| 7 | Animal Healthcare | $ 4,632,300 | $ 4,662,070 | $ 29,770 | 0.6% |
| 8 | Prescription Medicine | $ 1,432,900 | $ 1,507,357 | $ 74,457 | 5.2% |
| 9 | Photo | $ 2,707,600 | $ 2,657,288 | $ (50,312) | -1.9% |
| 10 | Total Revenue | $ 15,654,100 | $ 15,990,388 | $ 336,288 | 2.1% |

EXPLORE

7. Insert a bar chart similar to Figure 6-36 that compares the actual and forecast sales by product group. Place the chart beneath the data you entered in the Quarter 1 worksheet. Change the axis so the sales (Displayed Units) are displayed in millions of dollars.

**Figure 6-36** **Chart of first quarter corporate revenue**

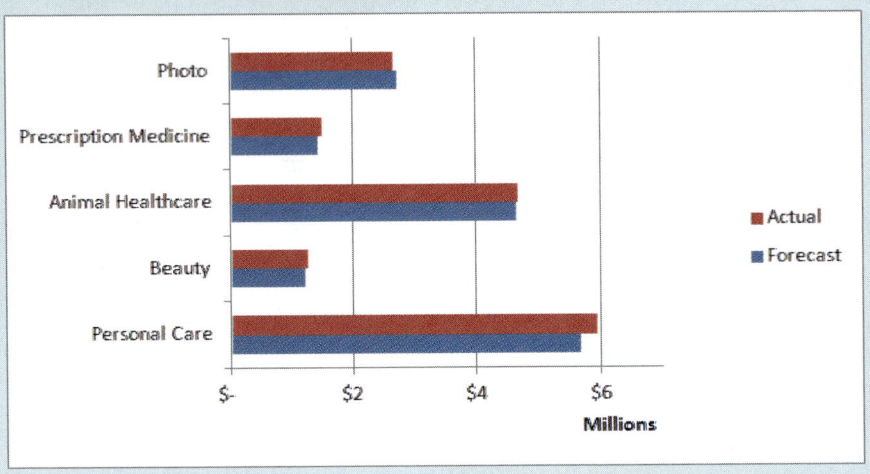


8. Prepare the three regional and corporate workbooks for printing. On each page, include the worksheet name in the center section of the header and your name in the left section of the footer.
9. Create a workspace that opens with the Quarter 1 worksheet active in each of the four workbooks using a horizontal layout for the four workbooks, and then save it as **Quarter1 Files** in the Excel6\Case4 folder included with your Data Files.
10. Save a copy of the **PlutoSummary** workbook located in the Excel6\Case4 folder as **Pluto Yearend** in the same folder. For year-end backup, break the links in the Pluto Yearend workbook.

EXPLORE

11. You receive a new source file to substitute for the original source file. The new source file has a different name.
    a. Open the **PlutoSummary** workbook, save the workbook as **PlutoSummaryTest** in the Excel6\Case4 folder, and then close the workbook.
    b. Open the **PlutoNA** workbook, and then save the workbook as **PlutoNorth**. In the PlutoNorth workbook in the March worksheet, change the actual personal care revenue in cell C5 to **$863,298**. Save and close the PlutoNorth workbook.
    c. Open the **PlutoSummaryTest** workbook, and change the link to the source workbook from PlutoNA to **PlutoNorth**. (*Hint*: Use the Edit Links dialog box.) Save and close the PlutoSummaryTest workbook.

EXPLORE

12. Update the source file but not the destination file.
    a. Open the **PlutoEU** workbook, and then save the workbook as **PlutoEurope**.
    b. Open the **PlutoSummaryTest** workbook, and change the link to the source workbook from PlutoEU to **PlutoEurope**. Note the actual total revenue in the Quarter 1 worksheet (cell C10). Close the PlutoSummaryTest workbook.
    c. In the PlutoEurope workbook, switch to the March worksheet and change the actual animal healthcare revenue in cell C7 to **$275,569**. Save and close the PlutoEurope workbook.
    d. Open the **PlutoSummaryTest** workbook and click the Don't Update button. How does this affect the Quarter 1 total actual revenue (cell C10) in the PlutoSummaryTest workbook (compare the current value to the value you noted in Step b)?
    e. Use the Edit Links dialog box to update the PlutoSummaryTest workbook. How does this affect the Quarter 1 total actual revenue (cell C10) in the PlutoSummaryTest workbook (compare the current value to the value you noted in Step d)?

EXPLORE 13. Modify the template named **PlutoTemplate** located in the Excel6\Case4 folder. Make the following two changes to the template, and then save the modified template as **PlutoTemplateRevised**:

   a. In the quarterly and monthly worksheets, change the formula in column E to display 0.0% when no values are entered in column B (Forecast) instead of #DIV/0!.

   b. In the monthly worksheets, apply a fill color of your choice to the range B5:C9 to identify where to enter data.

14. Create a new workbook from the PlutoTemplateRevised template. In the Documentation worksheet, enter your name and the date. In each monthly worksheet, enter **$500,000** in the range B5:B9 and enter **$550,000** in the range C5:C9. Save the workbook as **Pluto2014**.

15. Save and close all workbooks. Submit the finished workbooks to your instructor, either in printed or electronic form, as requested.

ASSESS

## SAM: Skills Assessment Manager

For current SAM information, including versions and content details, visit SAM Central (http://samcentral.course.com). If you have a SAM user profile, you may have access to hands-on instruction, practice, and assessment of the skills covered in this tutorial. Since various versions of SAM are supported throughout the life of this text, check with your instructor for the correct instructions and URL/Web site for accessing assignments.

## ENDING DATA FILES

**Excel6**

### Tutorial

Audited 2013.xlsx
Colorado.xlsx
Hoot Time Card.xlsx
New Mexico.xlsx
New Mexico 2014.xlsx
Sales 2013.docx
SkyDrive New Mexico 2014.xlsx
Theme Parks.xlw
Totals 2013.xlsx
Travel Template.xltx
Utah.xlsx

### Review

Idaho.xlsx
Northwest Totals 2013.xlsx
NW Workspace.xlw
Oregon.xlsx
Oregon 2014.xlsx
SkyDrive Oregon 2014.xlsx
Washington.xlsx

### Case1

Java Cafe.xlsx
Java Cafe 2014.xlsx
Java Template.xltx
SkyDrive Java Cafe 2014.xlsx

### Case2

Carson City 2014.xlsx
SkyDrive Carson City 2014.xlsx
UTE Carson City.xlsx
UTE Reno.xlsx
UTE Summary.xlsx
UTE Template.xltx
UTE Vegas.xlsx

### Case3

Infusion 2013.xlsx
Infusion with May 2013.xlsx

### Case4

Pluto2014.xlsx
PlutoEU.xlsx
PlutoEurope.xlsx
PlutoNA.xlsx
PlutoNorth.xlsx
PlutoSA.xlsx
PlutoSummary.xlsx
PlutoSummaryTest.xlsx
PlutoTemplateRevised.xltx
PlutoYearend.xlsx
Quarter1 Files.xlw

TUTORIAL 7

# Using Advanced Functions and Conditional Formatting

## *Calculating Employee Benefits*

### OBJECTIVES

**Session 7.1**

- Use the IF function
- Use the AND function
- Use the OR function
- Use structured references in formulas

**Session 7.2**

- Nest the IF function
- Use the VLOOKUP function
- Review the HLOOKUP function
- Use the IFERROR function

**Session 7.3**

- Use conditional formatting to highlight duplicate values
- Summarize data using the COUNTIF, SUMIF, and AVERAGEIF functions

## Case | *Talent Tracs*

Rita Corvales started Talent Tracs, a software development company for the music and entertainment business that is located in Austin, Texas. Talent Tracs sells EasyTracs, a software program that matches venues with artists, and then schedules the performances. As the company's reputation grew, the business expanded rapidly. Today, Talent Tracs has nearly 100 employees, ranging from software developers to online customer relations staff. Rita uses Excel to track basic employee information such as each employee's name, gender, birth date, hire date, health plan, job status, pay type (hourly or salaried), pay grade, and annual salary.

Rita needs to track employee enrollment in and costs related to the benefit programs offered by the company. She wants to calculate each employee's life insurance premium and how much the company contributes to each employee's 401(k) retirement account and health plan. Rita also needs to calculate the amount Talent Tracs spends on bonuses, which are based on employee pay grades and performance. To provide Rita with all this information, you'll use a variety of logical functions, filters, and conditional formatting. After you calculate those values, Rita wants you to summarize information in the Employee Summary worksheet so she can quickly see the impact of the compensation and benefits package on the company. You will use functions to calculate counts, sums, and averages based on search criteria.

### STARTING DATA FILES

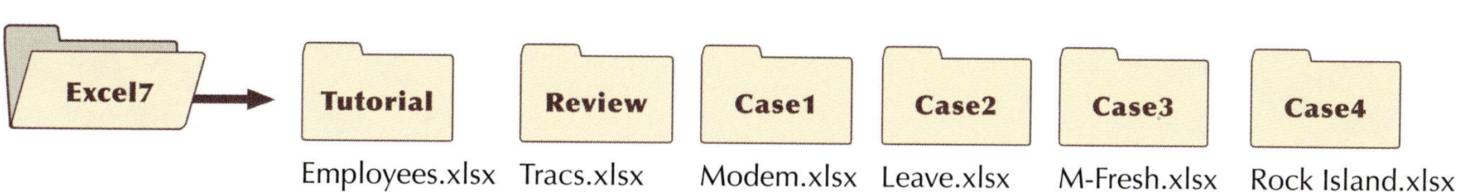

# SESSION 7.1 VISUAL OVERVIEW

When you create a formula that references all or parts of an Excel table, you can replace a specific cell or range address with a **structured reference**, which is the actual table name or column header.

The **AND function** is a logical function that returns a TRUE value if all of the logical conditions are true, and a FALSE value if any or all of the logical conditions are false.

The Function Arguments dialog box makes it simpler to build an IF function with a nested AND function (shown here) or a nested OR function for the logical test.

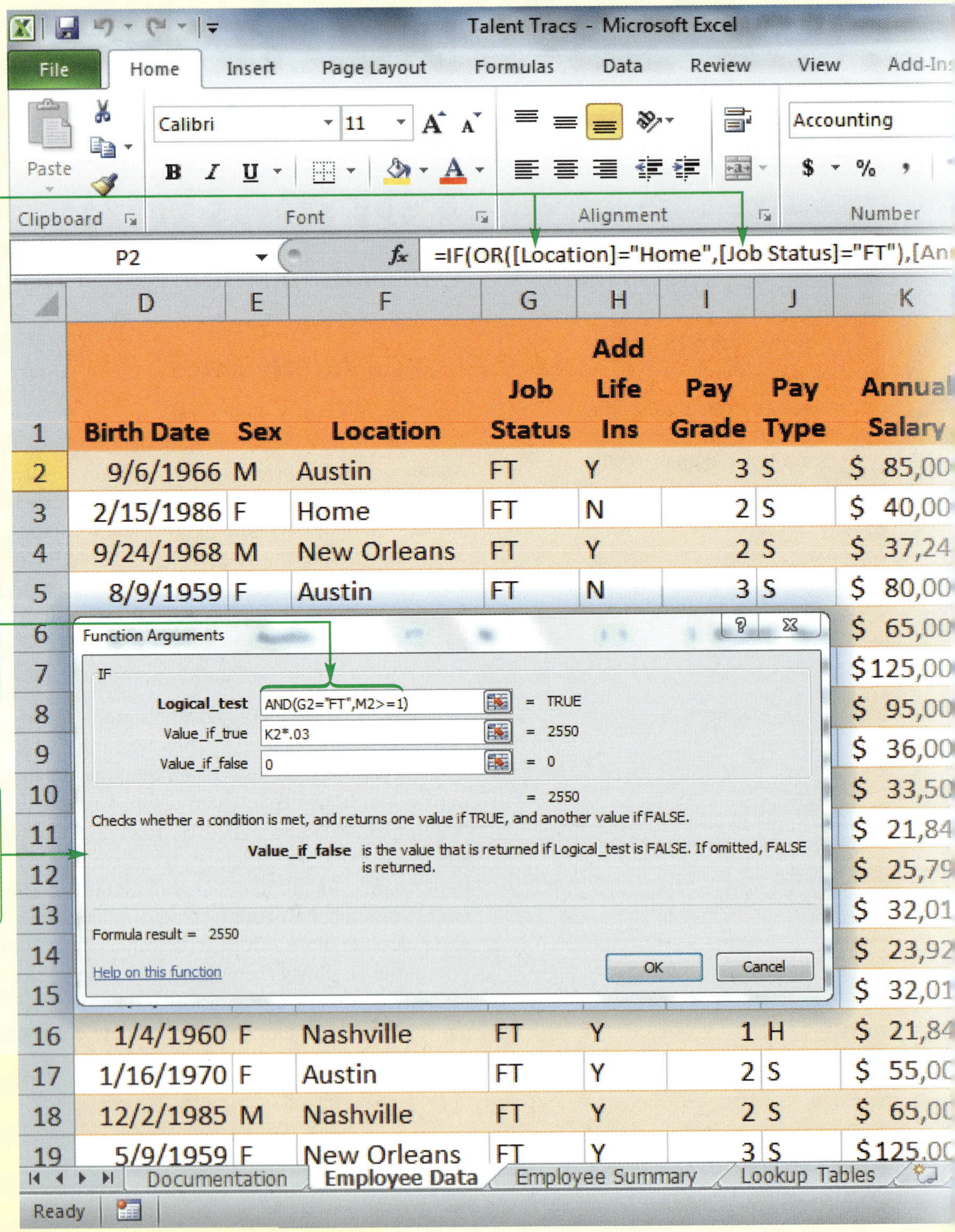

# LOGICAL FUNCTIONS

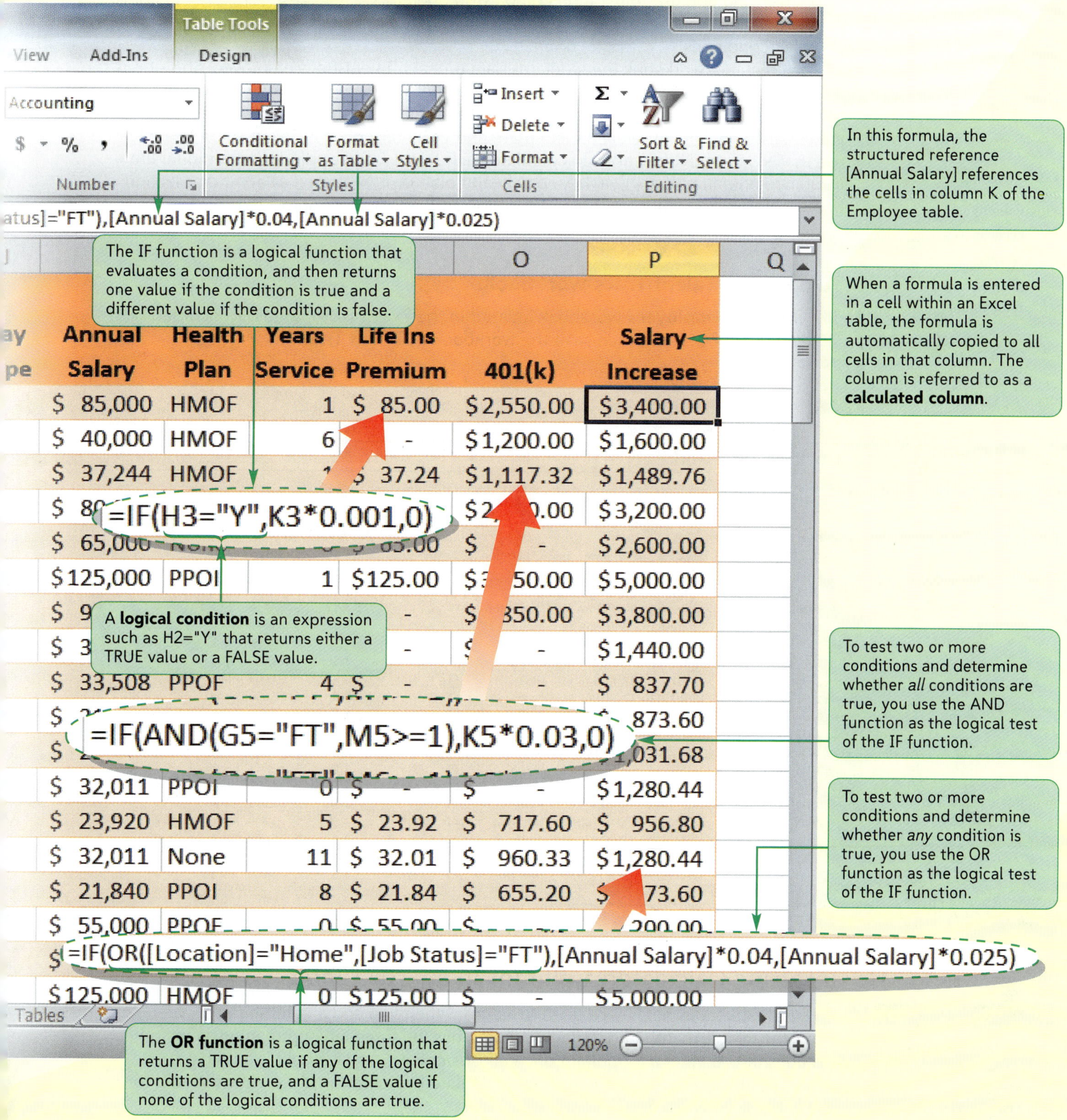

# Working with Logical Functions

Logical functions such as IF, AND, and OR determine whether a condition is true or false. The condition uses one of the comparison operators <, <=, =, <>, >, or >= to compare two values. You can combine two or more functions in one formula, creating more complex conditions.

Rita created a workbook that contains data for each Talent Tracs employee. She stored this information in an Excel table. The table includes each employee's ID, last name, hire date, birth date, gender, location, job status, additional life insurance coverage, pay grade, pay type, annual salary, health plan, and years of service at Talent Tracs. You will use IF, AND, and OR functions to calculate each Talent Tracs employee's additional life insurance premium (if any), 401(k) cost, health plan cost, proposed salary increase, and bonus amount. You will open Rita's workbook and review the employee data.

### To open the Talent Tracs workbook:

1. Open the **Employees** workbook located in the Excel7\Tutorial folder included with your Data Files, and then save the workbook as **Talent Tracs**.
2. In the Documentation worksheet, enter your name and the date.
3. Switch to the **Employee Data** worksheet. See Figure 7-1.

**Figure 7-1 Employee Data worksheet**

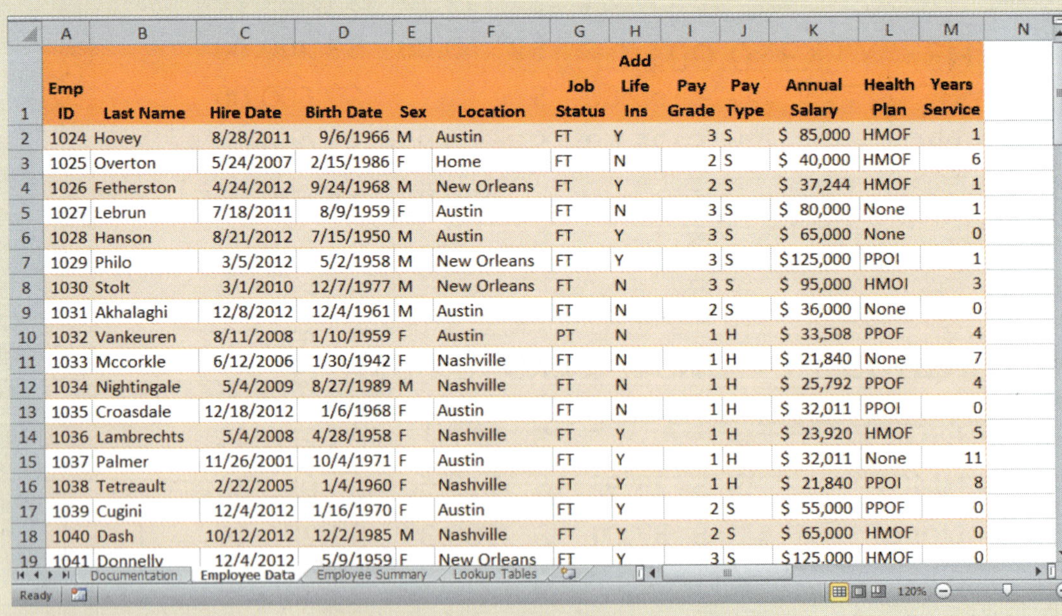

| | Emp ID | Last Name | Hire Date | Birth Date | Sex | Location | Job Status | Add Life Ins | Pay Grade | Pay Type | Annual Salary | Health Plan | Years Service |
|---|---|---|---|---|---|---|---|---|---|---|---|---|---|
| 2 | 1024 | Hovey | 8/28/2011 | 9/6/1966 | M | Austin | FT | Y | 3 | S | $ 85,000 | HMOF | 1 |
| 3 | 1025 | Overton | 5/24/2007 | 2/15/1986 | F | Home | FT | N | 2 | S | $ 40,000 | HMOF | 6 |
| 4 | 1026 | Fetherston | 4/24/2012 | 9/24/1968 | M | New Orleans | FT | Y | 2 | S | $ 37,244 | HMOF | 1 |
| 5 | 1027 | Lebrun | 7/18/2011 | 8/9/1959 | F | Austin | FT | N | 3 | S | $ 80,000 | None | 1 |
| 6 | 1028 | Hanson | 8/21/2012 | 7/15/1950 | M | Austin | FT | Y | 3 | S | $ 65,000 | None | 0 |
| 7 | 1029 | Philo | 3/5/2012 | 5/2/1958 | M | New Orleans | FT | Y | 3 | S | $125,000 | PPOI | 1 |
| 8 | 1030 | Stolt | 3/1/2010 | 12/7/1977 | M | New Orleans | FT | N | 3 | S | $ 95,000 | HMOI | 3 |
| 9 | 1031 | Akhalaghi | 12/8/2012 | 12/4/1961 | M | Austin | FT | N | 2 | S | $ 36,000 | None | 0 |
| 10 | 1032 | Vankeuren | 8/11/2008 | 1/10/1959 | F | Austin | PT | N | 1 | H | $ 33,508 | PPOF | 4 |
| 11 | 1033 | Mccorkle | 6/12/2006 | 1/30/1942 | F | Nashville | FT | N | 1 | H | $ 21,840 | None | 7 |
| 12 | 1034 | Nightingale | 5/4/2009 | 8/27/1989 | M | Nashville | FT | N | 1 | H | $ 25,792 | PPOF | 4 |
| 13 | 1035 | Croasdale | 12/18/2012 | 1/6/1968 | F | Austin | FT | N | 1 | H | $ 32,011 | PPOI | 0 |
| 14 | 1036 | Lambrechts | 5/4/2008 | 4/28/1958 | F | Nashville | FT | Y | 1 | H | $ 23,920 | HMOF | 5 |
| 15 | 1037 | Palmer | 11/26/2001 | 10/4/1971 | F | Austin | FT | Y | 1 | H | $ 32,011 | None | 11 |
| 16 | 1038 | Tetreault | 2/22/2005 | 1/4/1960 | F | Nashville | FT | Y | 1 | H | $ 21,840 | PPOI | 8 |
| 17 | 1039 | Cugini | 12/4/2012 | 1/16/1970 | F | Austin | FT | Y | 2 | S | $ 55,000 | PPOF | 0 |
| 18 | 1040 | Dash | 10/12/2012 | 12/2/1985 | M | Nashville | FT | Y | 2 | S | $ 65,000 | HMOF | 0 |
| 19 | 1041 | Donnelly | 12/4/2012 | 5/9/1959 | F | New Orleans | FT | Y | 3 | S | $125,000 | HMOF | 0 |



## Inserting Calculated Columns in an Excel Table

**TIP**

Calculated columns work only in Excel tables. To achieve the same results in a range of data, you must copy and paste the formula or use the AutoFill feature.

An Excel table does not have a fixed structure. When you add a column to an Excel table, the table expands and the new column has the same table formatting as the other columns. If you enter a formula in one cell of a column, the formula is automatically copied to all cells in that column. These calculated columns are helpful as you add formulas to an Excel table.

If you need to modify the formula in a calculated column, you edit the formula in any cell in the column and the formulas in all the cells in that table column are also modified. If you want to edit only one cell in a calculated column, you need to enter a value or a formula that is different from all the others in that column. A green triangle appears in the upper-left corner of the cell with the custom formula in the calculated column, making the inconsistency easy to find. After a calculated column contains one inconsistent formula or value, any other edits you make to that column are no longer automatically copied to the rest of the cells in that column. Excel does not overwrite custom values.

PROSKILLS

### *Written Communication: Creating Excel Table Fields*

Excel tables should be easy to use as well as understand. This requires labeling and entering data in a way that effectively communicates a table's content or purpose. If a field is entered in a way that is difficult to use and understand, it becomes more difficult to find and present data in a meaningful way.

To effectively communicate a table's function, keep the following guidelines in mind when creating fields in an Excel table:

- **Create fields that require the least maintenance.** For example, hire date and birth date require no maintenance after entered, unlike age and years of service, whose values change each year. If you need to know the specific age or years of service, use calculations to determine them based on values in the Hire Date and Birth Date columns.
- **Store the smallest unit of data possible in a field.** For example, use three separate fields for City, State, and Zip code rather than one field. Using separate fields for each unit of data enables you to sort or filter each field. If you want to display data from two or more fields in one column, you can use a formula to reference the City, State, and Zip code columns. For example, you can use the & operator to combine the city, state, and zip code in one cell as follows: `=C2&D2&E2`.
- **Apply a text format to fields with numerical text data.** For example, formatting fields such as zip codes and Social Security numbers as text ensures that leading zeros are stored as part of the data. Otherwise, the zip code 02892 is stored as a number and displayed as 2892.

Using these guidelines means that you and others will spend less time interpreting data and more time analyzing results. This lets you more effectively communicate the data in an Excel table.

## Using the IF Function

In many situations, the value you store in a cell depends on certain conditions. Consider the following examples:

- An employee's gross pay depends on whether that employee worked overtime.
- An income tax rate depends on the taxpayer's adjusted taxable income.
- A shipping charge depends on the size of an order.

To evaluate these types of conditions, you use the IF function. Recall that the IF function is a logical function that evaluates a condition, and then returns one value if the condition is true and another value if the condition is false. The IF function has the syntax

```
IF(logical_test, [value_if_true,] [value_if_false])
```

where *logical_test* is a condition that is either true or false, *value_if_true* is the value returned by the function if the condition is true, and *value_if_false* is the value returned by the function if the condition is false. The IF function results in only one value—either the *value_if_true* or the *value_if_false*.

For example, the following IF function tests whether the value in cell A5 is equal to "Yes." If it is, the *value_if_true* argument, C5+B5, is calculated and its value is displayed in the cell. Otherwise, the *value_if_false* argument, B5–C5, is calculated and its value is displayed in the cell.

```
=IF(A5="Yes",C5+B5,B5-C5)
```

You will use the IF function to calculate the additional life insurance premiums in the Employee table. Talent Tracs employees can elect to purchase additional life insurance coverage. This is indicated in the Add Life Ins column with Y for yes and N for no. The premium amount is equal to the employee's annual salary multiplied by the premium rate (.001). Rita sketched the flowchart shown in Figure 7-2 to illustrate the logic for calculating an employee's additional life insurance premium. The flowchart shows that if the employee elected additional life insurance (Add Life Ins = "Y" is True), the premium is calculated using the formula Salary*.001. If the employee did not elect additional life insurance (Add Life Ins = "Y" is False), the premium is 0.

**Figure 7-2** **Flowchart with logic for the additional life insurance premium**

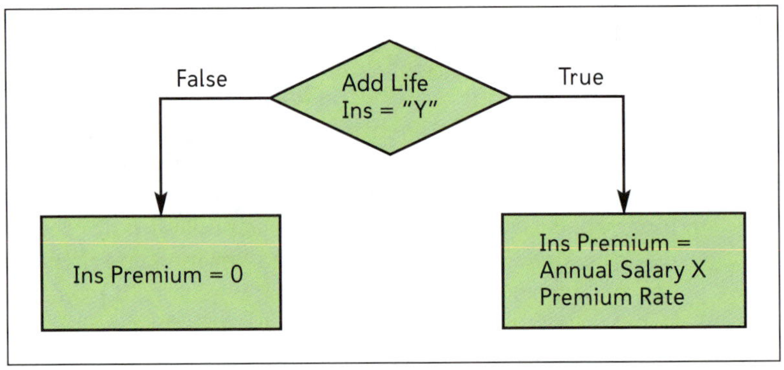


You'll add a column to the Employee table to display the results of the IF function that calculates the premium employees will pay if they elect additional life insurance coverage.

### To calculate the life insurance premium using an IF function:

1. In cell N1, enter **Life Ins Premium**. The Excel table expands to include this column and applies the table formatting to all the rows in the new column.
2. Make sure cell **N2** is the active cell, and then click the **Insert Function** button in the formula bar. The Insert Function dialog box opens.
3. Click **Logical** in the Or select a category list, click **IF** in the Select a function box, and then click the **OK** button. The Function Arguments dialog box for the IF function opens.
4. In the Logical_test box, type **H2="Y"** and then press the **Tab** key. This sets the logical test to evaluate whether the employee wants additional life insurance, indicated by "Y" for Yes or "N" for No in cell H2. TRUE appears to the right of the Logical_test argument box, indicating the result for the employee in row 2 is true. That is, the employee wants additional life insurance.
5. In the Value_if_true box, type **K2*0.001**. This argument specifies that if the condition is true (the employee wants additional life insurance), the result of the employee's current salary (listed in cell K2) is multiplied by 0.1% and displayed in cell N2. The value to the right of the Value_if_true argument box is 85, which is the premium the employee will pay for additional life insurance if the condition is true.
6. In the Value_if_false box, type **0**. This argument specifies that if the condition is false (the employee does not want additional life insurance), 0 is displayed in cell N2. The value to the right of the Value_if_false argument box is 0, which is the value that will appear in cell N2 if the condition is false. See Figure 7-3.

**Figure 7-3** **Function Arguments dialog box for the IF Function**

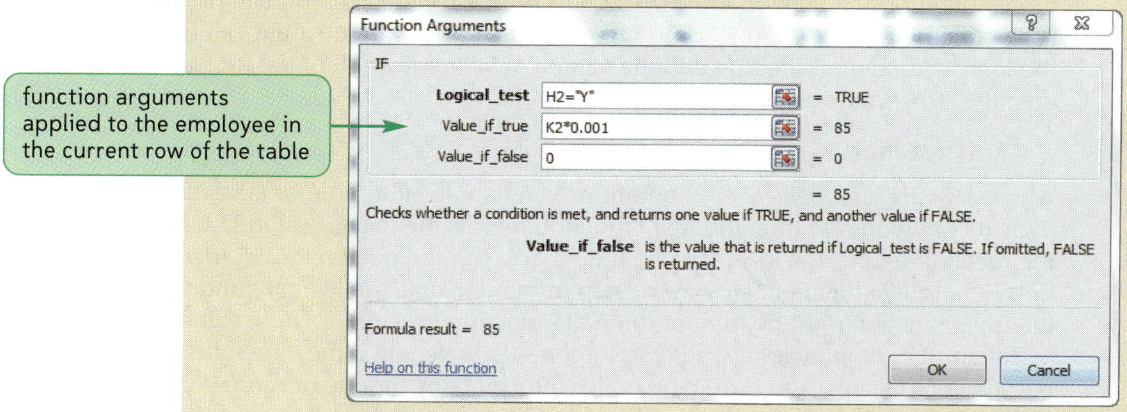


7. Click the **OK** button. The formula =IF(H2="Y",K2*0.001,0) appears in the formula bar, and 85 appears in cell N2 because the condition is true. The formula is automatically copied to all the cells in column N of the table.
8. Position the pointer just above cell **N1** until the pointer changes to ⬇, and then click to select the range N2:N101. The data in the Life Ins Premium column is selected, but not the column header.
9. Format the selected range N2:N101 with the **Accounting** number format, which includes the dollar sign and two decimal places. The Life Ins Premium column shows the additional life insurance premiums employees will pay formatted as currency.
10. Click cell **N2** to deselect the column. See Figure 7-4.

> **TIP**
> Click just above a cell in the header row of an Excel table (not the worksheet column heading) to select the column data but not the header; double-click to select the entire column including the column header.

**Figure 7-4** **Life Ins Premium column added to the Employee table**

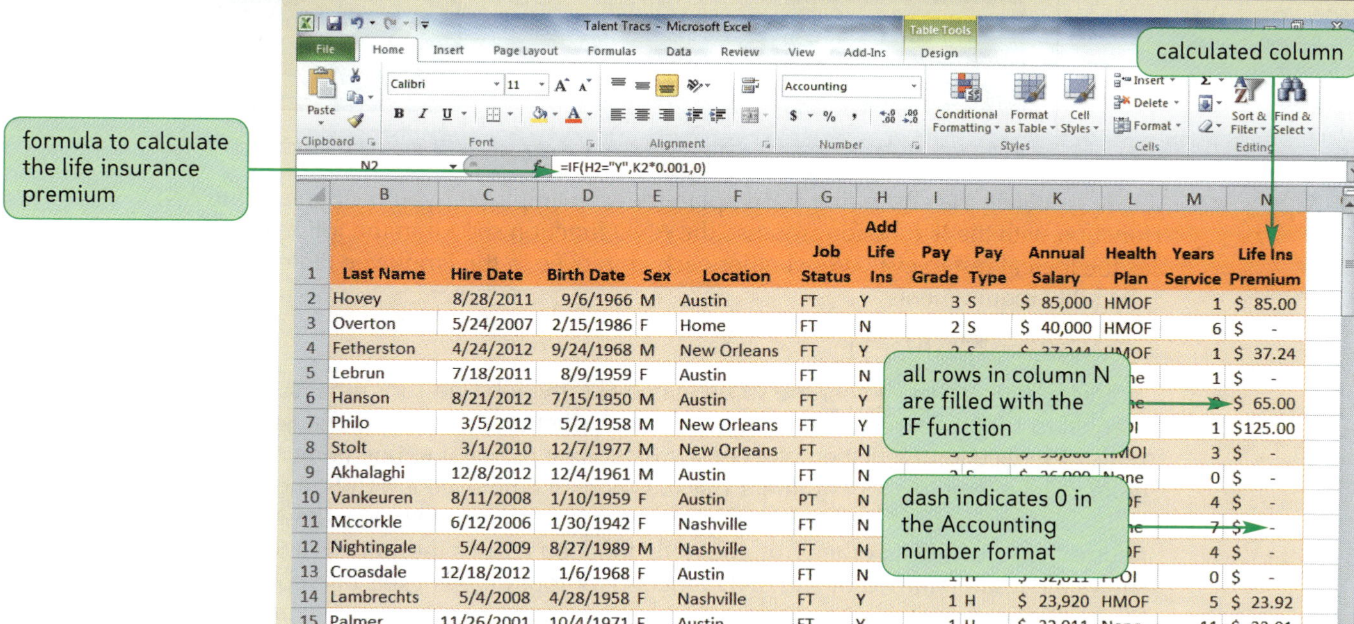

## Using the AND Function

The IF function evaluates a single condition. However, you often need to test two or more conditions and determine whether *all* conditions are true. You can do this with the AND function. The AND function is a logical function that returns the value TRUE if all the logical conditions are true and the value FALSE if any or all of the logical conditions are false. The syntax of the AND function is

```
AND(logical1 [,logical2,]...)
```

where *logical1* and *logical2* are conditions that can be either true or false. If all of the logical conditions are true, the AND function returns the logical value TRUE; otherwise, the function returns the logical value FALSE. You can include up to 255 logical conditions in an AND function. However, keep in mind that *all* the logical conditions listed in the AND function must be true for the AND function to return a TRUE value.

Talent Tracs employees are eligible for the 401(k) benefit if they are full-time employees (FT in Job Status) *and* have worked for the company for one or more years (1 or greater in Years Service). As long as *both* conditions are true, the company contributes an amount equal to 3 percent of the employee's salary to the employee's 401(k). If neither condition is true or if only one condition is true, the employee is not eligible for the 401(k) benefit and the company's contribution is 0. Rita outlined these eligibility conditions in the flowchart shown in Figure 7-5.

**Figure 7-5 Flowchart illustrating AND logic for the 401(k) benefit**

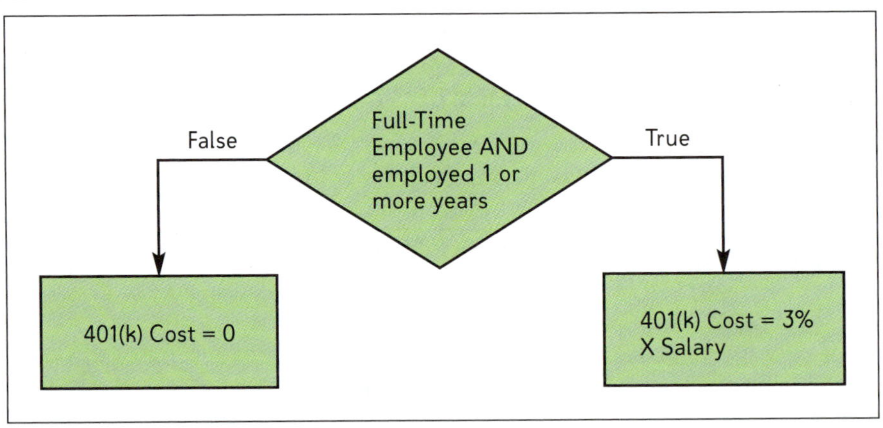


To calculate the cost of the 401(k) plan for each employee, you need to use the AND function with the IF function. You use the AND function shown in the following formula as the logical test to evaluate whether each employee in the Employee table fulfills the eligibility requirements:

```
=AND(G2="FT",M2>=1)
```

This formula tests whether the value in cell G2 (the job status for the first employee) is equal to FT (an abbreviation for full time) and whether the value in cell M2 (the years of service for the first employee) is greater than or equal to one (indicating one or more years of employment at Talent Tracs). When an employee is a full-time employee (G2="FT") *and* has worked one or more years at Talent Tracs (M2>=1), the AND function returns the value TRUE; otherwise, the AND function returns the value FALSE. Figure 7-6 shows the result returned by the AND function for four different sets of employee values for job status and years of service.

**Figure 7-6** Example of AND function results

**Purpose:** To determine employee eligibility for the company's 401(k) plan

**Logic Scenario:** An employee is eligible for the 401(k) plan if the employee's status is full time (FT) AND the employee's years of service total one or more years.

**Formula:** AND function with two conditions
`=AND(G2="FT",M2>=1)`

**Data:** cell G2 stores Employee Status
cell M2 stores Years Service

**Example:**

| Data | | Condition1 | Condition2 | Results |
|---|---|---|---|---|
| Cell G2 | Cell M2 | G2="FT" | M2>=1 | (Eligible?) |
| FT | 1 | True | True | True |
| FT | 0 | True | False | False |
| PT | 5 | False | True | False |
| PT | 0 | False | False | False |

The AND function shows only whether an employee is eligible for the 401(k) plan. It does not calculate how much Talent Tracs will contribute to that employee's 401(k) plan if the employee is eligible. To determine whether an employee is eligible *and* to calculate the amount of the 401(k) contribution, you use this AND function within an IF function. When the results of one function are used as the argument of another function, the functions are nested. In the following formula, the AND function (shown in red) is nested within the IF function and is used as the logical test that determines whether the employee is eligible for a 401(k) contribution. If the employee is eligible, the AND function returns the logical value TRUE and the IF function multiplies the employee's annual salary by 3 percent. If the AND function returns the logical value FALSE, the IF function displays the value 0.

```
=IF(AND(G2="FT",M2>=1),K2*0.03,0)
```

Figure 7-7 illustrates how the AND function is used to determine student eligibility for the dean's list. In this scenario, when students have 12 or more credits (stored in cell B1) *and* their GPA is greater than 3.25 (stored in cell B2), they are placed on the dean's list. Both conditions must be true for the AND function to return the logical value TRUE.

**Figure 7-7** Additional AND function example

**Purpose:** To determine dean's list requirements

**Logic Scenario:** 12 or more semester credits and GPA above 3.25

**Formula:** AND function with two conditions
`=AND(B1>=12,B2>3.25)`

**Data:** cell B1 stores number of credits
cell B2 stores student's GPA

**Example:**

| Data | | Condition1 | Condition2 | Results |
|---|---|---|---|---|
| Cell B1 | Cell B2 | B1>=12 | B2>3.25 | (Dean's List?) |
| 15 | 3.5 | True | True | True |
| 12 | 3.25 | True | False | False |
| 6 | 3.4 | False | True | False |
| 10 | 3.0 | False | False | False |

You'll insert a new column in the Employee table, and then enter the formula to calculate the 401(k) contribution.

## To use the IF and AND functions to calculate the 401(k) contribution:

1. In cell O1, enter **401(k)** as the column header. The Excel table expands to include the new column, and cell O2 is the active cell.
2. Make sure cell O2 is the active cell, and then click the **Insert Function** button in the formula bar. The Insert Function dialog box opens.
3. Click **IF** in the Select a function box, and then click the **OK** button. The Function Arguments dialog box opens.
4. In the Logical_test box, type **AND(G2="FT",M2>=1)** and then press the **Tab** key. This logical test evaluates whether the employee is full time, indicated by "FT" in cell G2, and has worked at Talent Tracs for one year or more. TRUE appears to the right of the Logical_test box, indicating the result for the employee in row 2 is true. This employee is eligible for the 401(k) plan.
5. In the Value_if_true box, type **K2*0.03** and then press the **Tab** key. This argument specifies that if the condition is true (the employee is eligible for the 401(k) plan as determined by the AND function), the amount in the employee's salary cell is multiplied by 3 percent. The amount of this employee's 401(k) contribution, 2550, appears to the right of the Value_if_true box.
6. In the Value_if_false box, type **0**. This argument specifies that if the condition is false (the employee is not eligible for the 401(k) as determined by the AND function), the amount displayed in cell O2 is 0, which appears to the right of the Value_if_false box. See Figure 7-8.

**Figure 7-8** Function Arguments dialog box for the IF function with the AND function

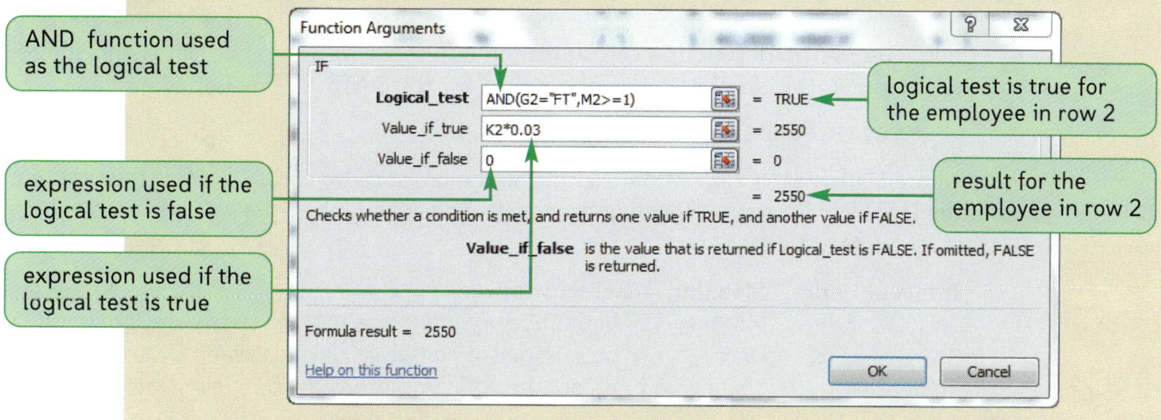


7. Click the **OK** button. The formula with the IF function that you just created is entered in cell O2 and copied to all rows in column O of the table.
8. Position the pointer at the top of cell **O1** until the pointer changes to ⬇, click to select the 401(k) data values, and then format the range using the **Accounting** number format.
9. Click cell **O2** to make it the active cell. The formula =IF(AND(G2="FT",M2>=1),K2*0.03,0) appears in the formula bar and $2,550.00 appears in cell O2 because the condition is true. See Figure 7-9.

**Figure 7-9** IF function with the AND function to calculate 401(k)

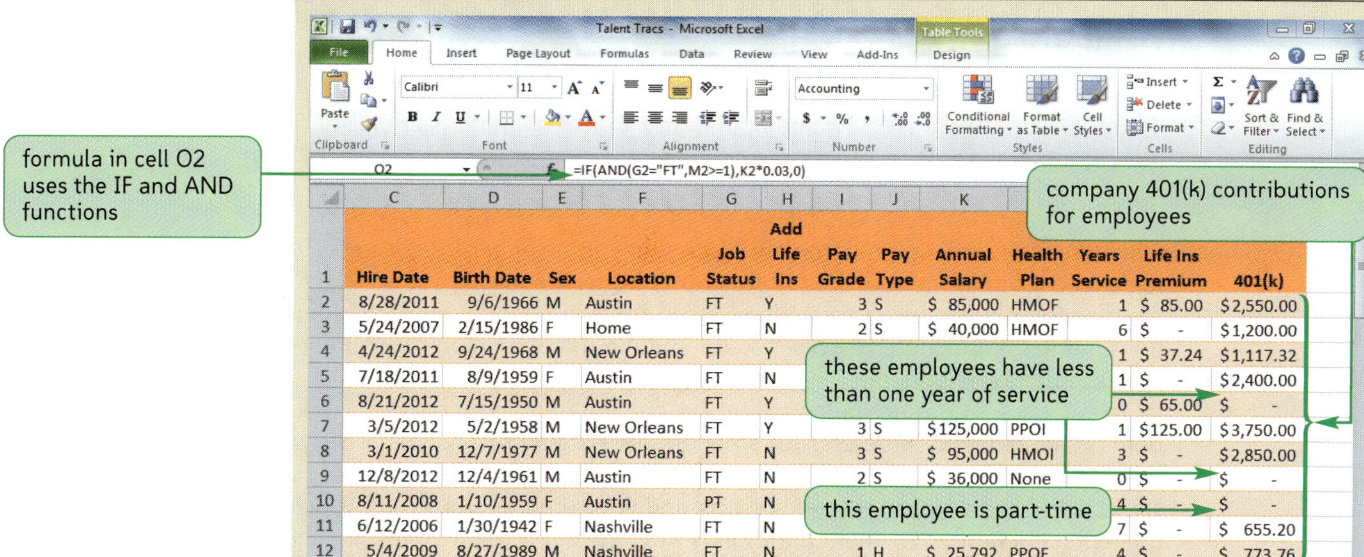

INSIGHT

### *Using the DATEDIF Function to Calculate Years of Service*

In the Employee table, the Years Service column was calculated using the DATEDIF function. The **DATEDIF function** calculates the difference between two dates and shows the result in months, days, or years. The syntax for the DATEDIF function is

```
DATEDIF(Date1,Date2,Interval)
```

where *Date1* is the earliest date, *Date2* is the latest date, and *Interval* is the unit of time the DATEDIF function will use in the result. You specify the *Interval* with one of the following interval codes:

| Interval Code | Meaning | Description |
|---|---|---|
| "m" | Months | The number of complete months between Date1 and Date2 |
| "d" | Days | The number of complete days between Date1 and Date2 |
| "y" | Years | The number of complete years between Date1 and Date2 |

For example, the following formula calculates years of service at Talent Tracs in complete years:

```
=DATEDIF(C2,$AB$1,"y")
```

The earliest date is located in cell C2, the hire date. The latest date is in cell $AB$1, which shows the date used to compare against the hire date—years of service as of a cut-off date. The Interval "y" indicates that you want to display the number of complete years between these two dates.

The DATEDIF function is undocumented in Excel, but it has been available since Excel 97. To learn more about this function, search the Web using "DATEDIF function in Excel" as the search text in your favorite search engine.

## Using the OR Function

The OR function is a logical function that returns a TRUE value if any of the logical conditions are true and a FALSE value if all of the logical conditions are false. The syntax of the OR function is

```
OR(logical1 [,logical2,]...)
```

where *logical1* and *logical2* are conditions that can be either true or false. If any of the logical conditions are true, the OR function returns the logical value TRUE; otherwise, the function returns the logical value FALSE. You can include up to 255 logical conditions in the OR function. However, keep in mind that if *any* logical condition listed in the OR function is true, the OR function returns a TRUE value.

Talent Tracs is considering awarding a 4 percent raise to employees working from home *or* working full-time (FT); all other employees will receive a 2.5 percent increase. The criteria for awarding a salary increase is based on two conditions—location and job status. If either condition is true or both conditions are true, the employee will receive the 4 percent raise. If neither condition is true, the employee will receive the 2.5 percent raise. Rita outlined these salary increase criteria in the flowchart shown in Figure 7-10.

**Figure 7-10** Flowchart of the OR function

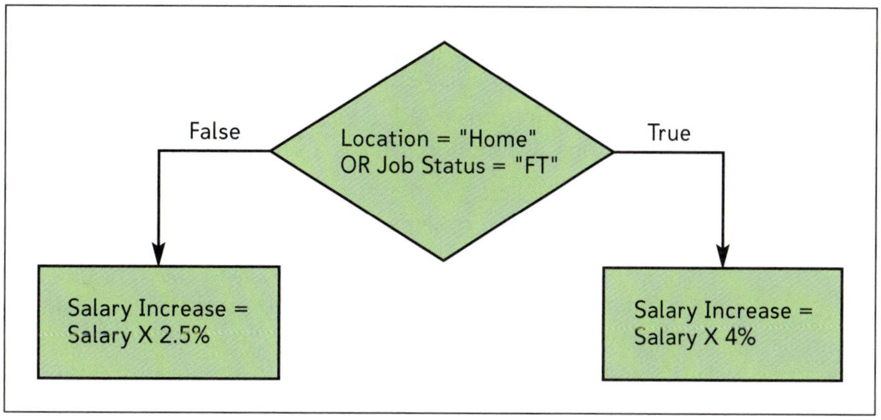


You need to use the OR function to test whether an employee meets the criteria for the 4 percent or 2.5 percent salary increase. The following formula uses the OR function to test whether the value in cell F2 (the work location for the first employee) is equal to "Home" or whether the value in cell G2 (the job status for the first employee) is equal to "FT." If the employee works from home *or* the employee works full time *or* the employee both works from home and works full time, the OR function returns the value TRUE; otherwise, the OR function returns the value FALSE.

```
=OR(F2="Home", G2="FT")
```

Figure 7-11 shows the results returned using the OR function for four different sets of values for employee work location and job status.

**Figure 7-11** Examples of OR function results

**Purpose:** To determine an employee's salary increase percentage

**Logic Scenario:** Proposed 4 percent salary increase to full-time (FT) employees or employees working from home

**Formula:** OR function with two conditions
`=OR(F2="Home",G2="FT")`

**Data:** cell F2 stores Location
cell G2 stores Job Status

**Example:**

| Data | | Condition1 | Condition2 | Results |
|---|---|---|---|---|
| Cell F2 | Cell G2 | F2="Home" | G2="FT" | (4% increase) |
| Home | FT | True | True | True |
| Austin | FT | False | True | True |
| Home | PT | True | False | True |
| Nashville | PT | False | False | False |

The OR function only determines which raise an employee is eligible for. It does not calculate the amount of the salary increase. To determine the amount of the salary increase, the OR function must be nested within an IF function. In the following formula, the logical test of the IF function uses the OR function (shown in red) to determine whether an employee is either working from home or working full-time or both. If the OR function returns a TRUE value, the IF function multiplies the annual salary by 4 percent. If the OR function returns a FALSE value, the IF function multiplies the annual salary by 2.5 percent.

```
=IF(OR(F2="Home",G2="FT"),K2*0.04,K2.*0.025)
```

Figure 7-12 illustrates how the OR function is used to determine eligibility for a 10 percent discount. In this scenario, anyone who is 65 years or older (stored in cell B1) *or* anyone who is a college student (stored in cell B2) receives a 10 percent discount. At least one condition must be true for the OR function to return the logical value TRUE.

**Figure 7-12** **Additional example of the OR function**

**Purpose:** To determine who is eligible for a discount

**Logic Scenario:** Discount is 10 percent for seniors (65 or older) or college students (Status = STU)

**Formula:** OR function with two conditions
`=OR(B1>=65,B2="STU")`

**Data:** cell B1 stores Age
cell B2 stores Status (STU, FAC, STF)

**Example:**

| **Data** | | **Condition1** | **Condition2** | **Results** |
|---|---|---|---|---|
| **Cell B1** | **Cell B2** | **B1>=65** | **B2="STU"** | **(Discount?)** |
| 22 | STU | False | True | True |
| 65 | FAC | True | False | True |
| 67 | STU | True | True | True |
| 45 | STF | False | False | False |

## Using Structured References to Create Formulas in Excel Tables

When you create a formula that references all or parts of an Excel table, you can replace the specific cell or range address with a structured reference, the actual table name or column header. This makes the formula easier to create and understand. The default Excel table name is Table1, Table2, and so forth unless you entered a more descriptive table name, as you did for the Employee table. Column headers provide a description of the data entered in each column. Structured references make it easier to create formulas that use portions or all of an Excel table because the names or headers are usually simpler to identify than cell addresses. For example, in the Employee table, the table name

**TIP**

If you are not sure of a table's name, click in the table, click the Table Tools Design tab on the Ribbon, and then check the Table Name box in the Properties group.

"Employee" refers to the range A2:N101, which is the range of data in the table excluding the header row and the Total row. When you want to reference an entire column of data in a table, you create a column qualifier, which has the syntax

```
Tablename[qualifier]
```

where *Tablename* is the name entered in the Table Name box in the Properties group on the Table Tools Design tab, and *qualifier* is the column header enclosed in square brackets. For example, the structured reference Employee[Annual Salary] references the annual salary data in the range K2:K101 of the Employee table.

You use structured references in formulas. The following formula adds the annual salary data in the range K2:K101 of the Employee table; in this case, [Annual Salary] is the column qualifier:

```
=SUM(Employee[Annual Salary])
```

When you create a calculated column, as you did to calculate life insurance premiums and 401(k) contributions in the Employee table, you can use structured references to create the formula. A formula that includes a structured reference can be fully qualified or unqualified. In a fully qualified structured reference, the table name precedes the column qualifier. In an unqualified structured reference, only the column qualifier appears in the reference. For example, you could have used either of the following formulas with structured references to calculate Life Ins Premium in the calculated column you added to the Employee table:

**Fully qualified**

```
=IF(Employee[Add Life Ins]="Y",Employee[Annual Salary]*.001,0)
```

**Unqualified**

```
=IF([Add Life Ins]="Y",[Annual Salary]*.001,0)
```

If you are creating a calculated column or formula within an Excel table, you can use either the fully qualified structured reference or the unqualified structured reference in the formula. If you use a structured reference outside the table or in another worksheet to reference an Excel table or portion of the table, you must use a fully qualified reference.

You'll use structured references to calculate the salary increases for Talent Tracs employees.

### To calculate the salary increase:

1. In cell P1, enter **Salary Increase** as the column header. The Excel table expands to include the new column, and cell P2 is the active cell.
2. Make sure cell P2 is the active cell, and then click the **Insert Function** button in the formula bar. The Insert Function dialog box opens.
3. Click **IF** in the Select a function box, and then click the **OK** button. The Function Arguments dialog box opens.
4. Next to the Logical_test box, click the **Collapse Dialog Box** button. The Function Arguments dialog box reduces to show only the Logical_test box.
5. In the Logical_test box, type **OR([Location]="Home",[Job Status]="FT")** to enter the OR function with structured references. This logical test evaluates whether the employee works from home or works full-time or both. See Figure 7-13.

Be sure to type square brackets around the structured references and use the exact spelling and location shown. Otherwise, the formula will return an error.

**Figure 7-13** Logical_test argument for the OR function

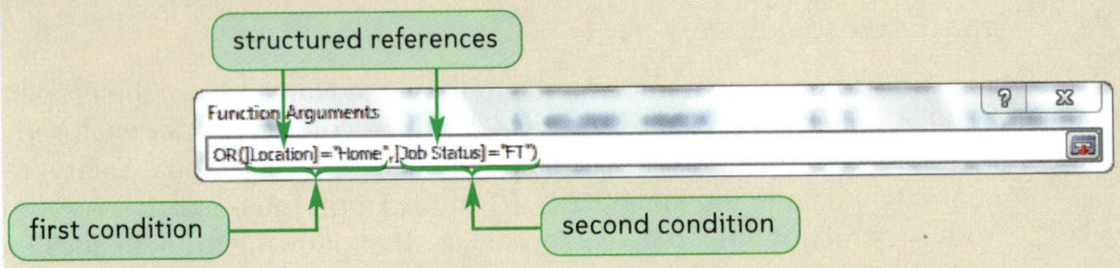


6. Click the **Expand Dialog Box** button to show the full Function Arguments dialog box, and then press the **Tab** key. TRUE appears to the right of the Logical_test box, indicating the result for the employee in the active row, row 2, is true. This employee is eligible for the 4 percent salary increase.

   **Trouble?** If "Invalid" appears instead of "TRUE" as the logical test results, you probably mistyped the logical test. Compare the function in your Logical_test box to the one shown in Figure 7-13, confirming that you used square brackets around the structured references [Location] and [Job Status] and typed all the text correctly.

7. In the Value_if_true box, type **[Annual Salary]*0.04** and then press the **Tab** key. This argument specifies that if the logical test is true (the employee is eligible for the 4 percent increase), the amount in the employee's salary cell is multiplied by 4 percent. The salary increases for all employees, beginning in row 2, whose logical test is true appear to the right of the Value_if_true box.

8. In the Value_if_false box, type **[Annual Salary]*0.025**. This argument specifies that if the logical test is false (the employee is not eligible for the 4 percent increase), the amount in the employee's salary cell is multiplied by 2.5 percent. The salary increases for all employees, beginning in row 2, whose logical test is false appear to the right of the Value_if_false box. See Figure 7-14.

**Figure 7-14** Function Arguments dialog box for the IF function with an OR function

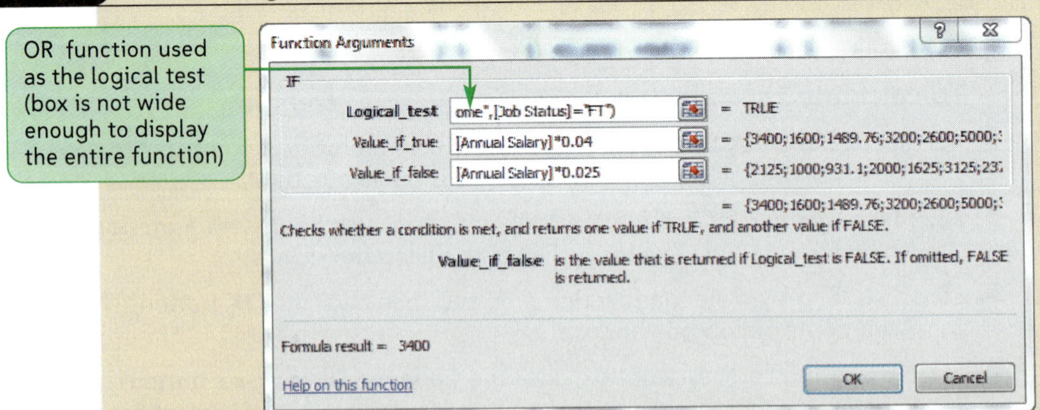


9. Click the **OK** button. The formula =IF(OR([Location]="Home",[Job Status]="FT"), [Annual Salary]*0.04,[Annual Salary]*0.025) appears in the formula bar and the value 3400 appears in cell P2 because the condition is true. The results are automatically copied to all rows in column P of the table.

10. Position the pointer at the top of cell **P1** until the pointer changes to ⬇, click to select the Salary Increase data values, and then format the range using the **Accounting** number format.

11. Click cell **P2** to deselect the column. See Figure 7-15.

**Figure 7-15** **IF function with the OR function calculates salary increase**

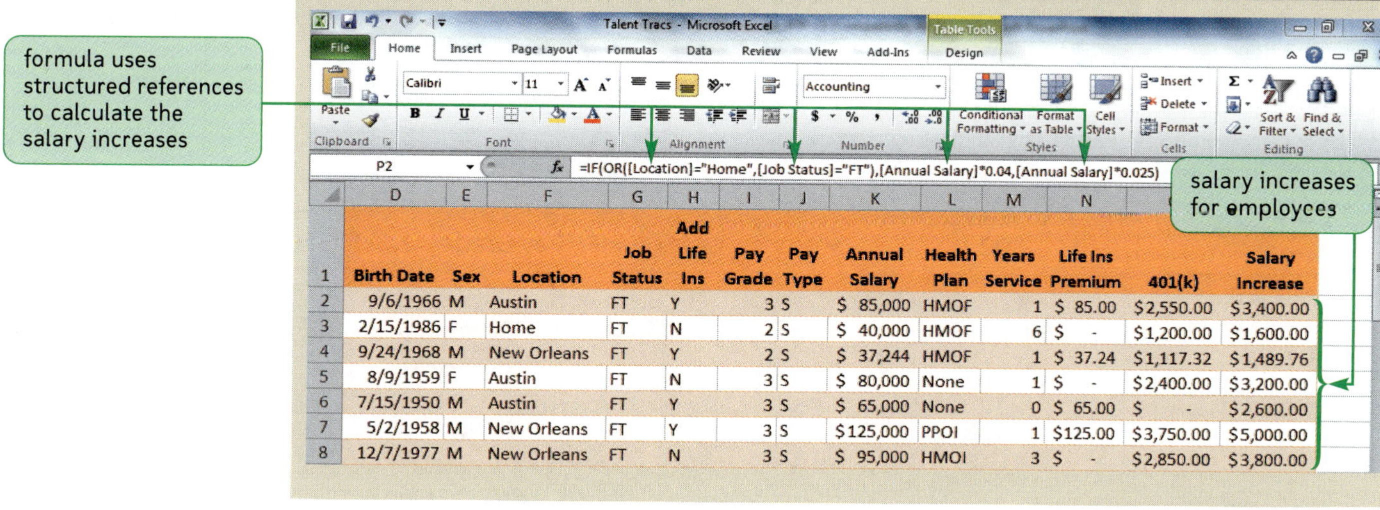


In this session, you used the IF, AND, and OR functions to calculate the additional life insurance premiums, 401(k) benefits, and next year's salary increases for Talent Tracs employees. Rita still needs to calculate the employee bonuses, health plan costs, and the employee recognition award for each employee. In the next session, you will create formulas with functions to perform these calculations.

REVIEW

## *Section 7.1 Quick Check*

1. What changes occur in the appearance and size of an Excel table after you enter a new column header named "Phone"?
2. Whenever you enter a formula in an empty column of an Excel table, Excel automatically fills the column with the same formula. What is this called?
3. If an Excel worksheet stores the cost per meal in cell Q5, the number of attendees in cell Q6, and the total cost of meals in cell Q7, what IF function would you enter in cell Q7 to calculate the total cost of meals (cost per meal times the number of attendees) with a minimum cost of $10,000?
4. True or False. The AND function is a logical function that returns a TRUE value if any of the logical conditions are true and a FALSE value if all of the logical conditions are false.
5. Write the formula that displays the label "Outstanding" if the amount owed (cell X5) is greater than 0 and the transaction date (cell R5) is before 3/15/2013, but otherwise leaves the cell blank.
6. When you create a formula that references all or parts of an Excel table, you can use ______________ to replace the specific cell or range addresses with the actual table or column header names.
7. If the formula `=IF(OR(B25="NY",B25="CA",B25="TX"),"Select","Ignore")` is entered in cell B26, and "PA" is entered in cell B25, what is displayed in cell B26?
8. What OR function represents the rule, "A potential enlistee in the Army is not eligible to enlist if younger than 17 or older than 42." The age is stored in cell B25.

# SESSION 7.2 VISUAL OVERVIEW

A **nested IF function** is when one IF function is placed inside another IF function to test an additional condition, such as calculating employee bonuses based on pay grade.

The **lookup value** is the value you are trying to find. In this case, the lookup value is the code in the Health Plan column.

The invalid code in the Health Plan column causes the IFERROR message to appear in the Health Cost column.

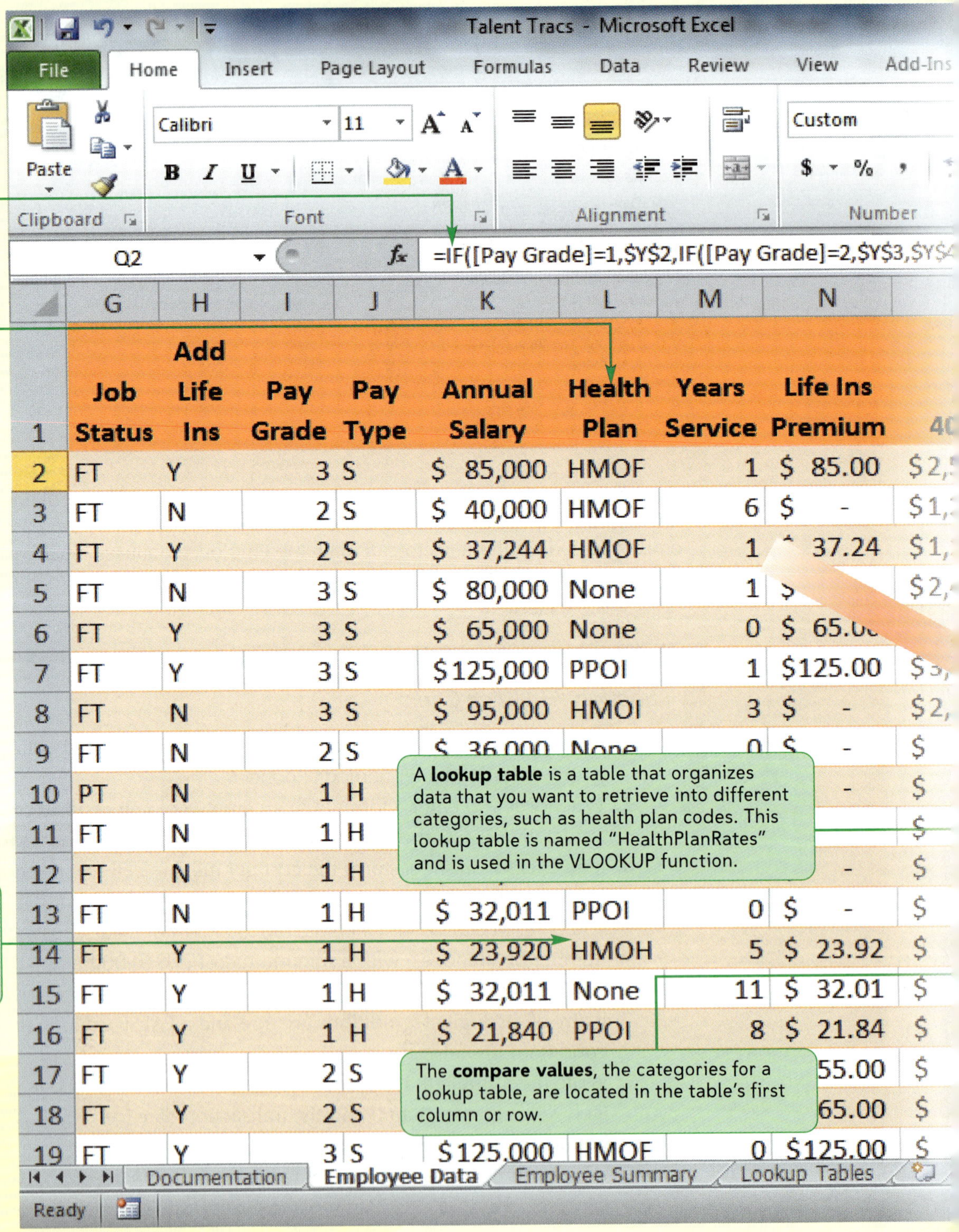


A **lookup table** is a table that organizes data that you want to retrieve into different categories, such as health plan codes. This lookup table is named "HealthPlanRates" and is used in the VLOOKUP function.

The **compare values**, the categories for a lookup table, are located in the table's first column or row.

# NESTED IFS AND LOOKUP TABLES

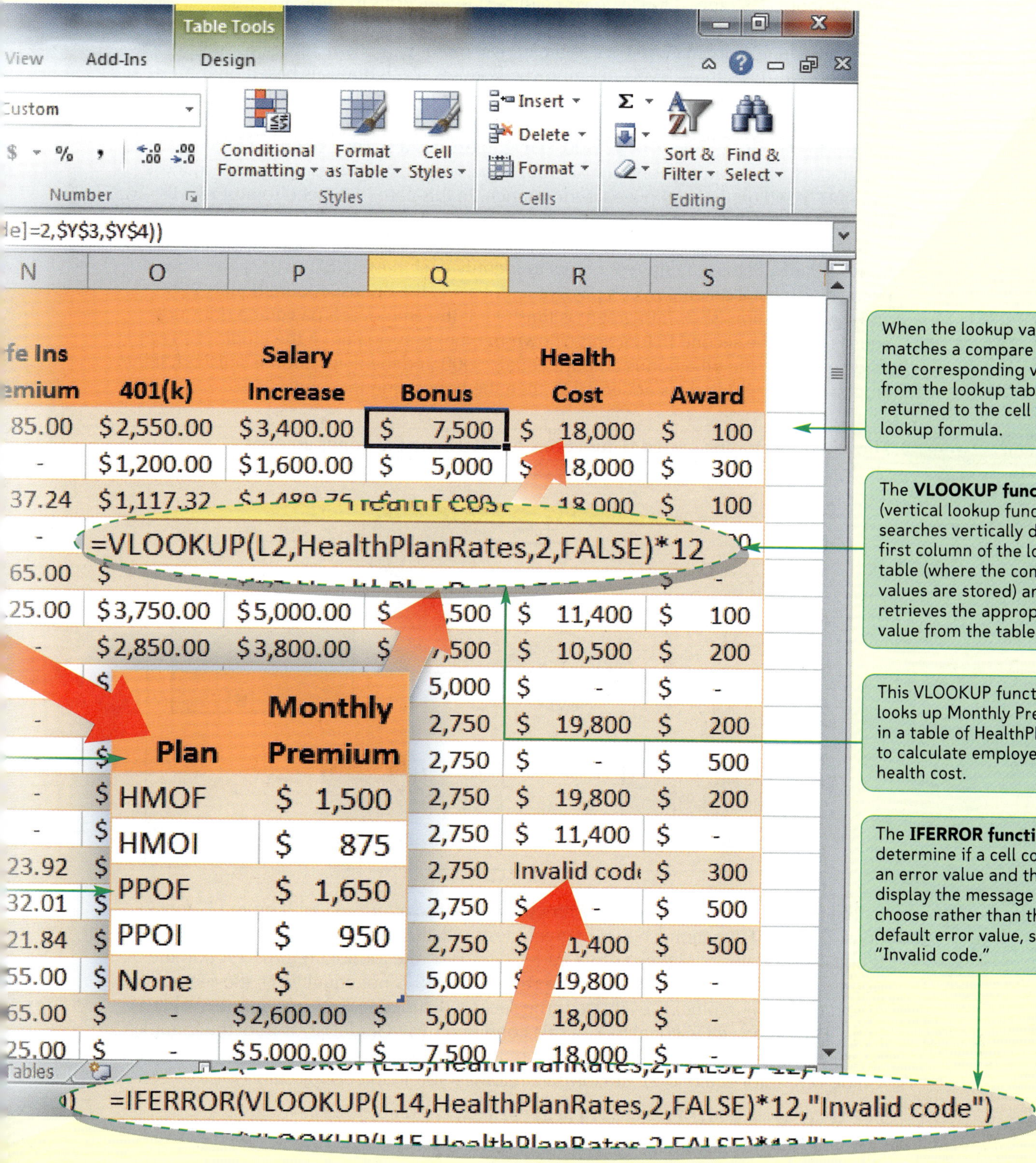


When the lookup value matches a compare value, the corresponding value from the lookup table is returned to the cell with the lookup formula.

The **VLOOKUP function** (vertical lookup function) searches vertically down the first column of the lookup table (where the compare values are stored) and retrieves the appropriate value from the table.

This VLOOKUP function looks up Monthly Premium in a table of HealthPlanRates to calculate employee health cost.

The **IFERROR function** can determine if a cell contains an error value and then display the message you choose rather than the default error value, such as "Invalid code."

## Creating Nested IFs

The IF function can choose between only two outcomes; it cannot choose from among three or more outcomes. However, you can nest IF functions to allow for three or more outcomes. A nested IF function is when one IF function is placed inside another IF function to test an additional condition. You can nest more than one IF function.

Talent Tracs pays three levels of employee bonuses. Each bonus is based on the employee's pay grade, which is a system Talent Tracs uses to group jobs based on difficulty and responsibility. Talent Tracs has three pay grade codes (1, 2, and 3). Pay grade 1 has a starting bonus of $2,500, pay grade 2 has a starting bonus of $5,000, and pay grade 3 has a starting bonus of $7,500. Supervisors can increase or decrease these amounts based on the employee's performance. In this case, you need to nest two IF functions to calculate the different series of outcomes for the employee bonuses.

Rita created the flowchart shown in Figure 7-16 to illustrate the logic for determining bonus awards. She used different colors to identify each nested IF function. The flowchart shows that if an employee's pay grade equals 1, the bonus amount equals 2500 and the IF function (shown in green) is finished. If the employee's pay grade does not equal 1, then the second IF function (shown in blue) is evaluated. If the employee's pay grade equals 2, then the bonus amount equals 5000 and the IF function is finished. If the employee's pay grade does not equal 2, then the bonus amount equals 7500.

**Figure 7-16** **Flowchart illustrating nested IF functions to determine the bonus amount**

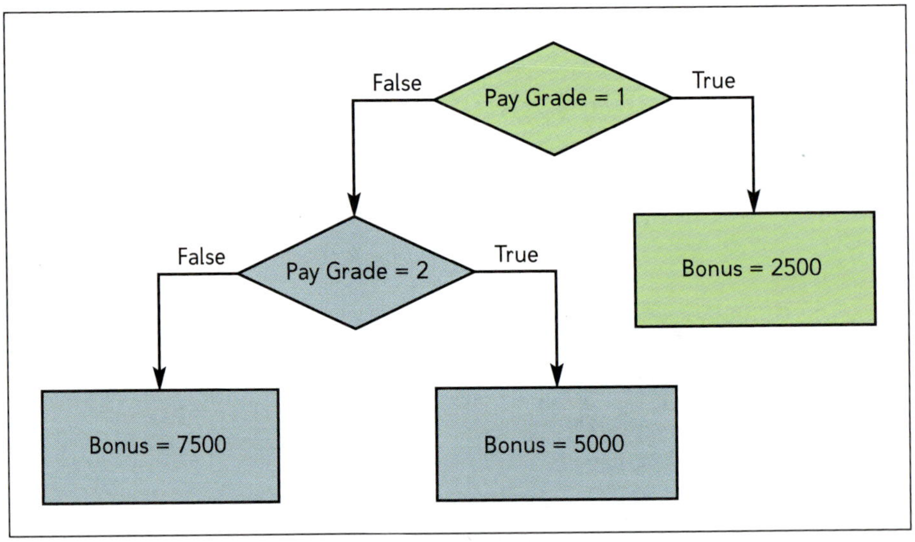


The following formula converts Rita's flowchart into a formula with nested IF functions. The first IF function (shown in green) tests whether the value in the Pay Grade cell is equal to 1. If this condition ([Pay Grade]=1) is true, the formula returns 2500 in the Bonus cell. If this condition is false (the Pay Grade cell is not equal to 1), the second IF function (shown in blue) is evaluated. The second IF function tests whether the value in the Pay Grade cell is equal to 2. If this condition ([Pay Grade]=2) is true, the formula returns 5000 in the Bonus cell. If this condition is false (the value in the current Pay Grade cell is not equal to 2), the formula returns 7500 in the Bonus cell.

```
=IF([Pay Grade]=1,2500,IF([Pay Grade]=2,5000,7500))
```

Figure 7-17 illustrates how one nested IF function is used to determine among three outcomes—whether the home football team won, lost, or tied a game. The first IF function evaluates whether the home team score (stored in cell B1) is greater than the visiting team score (stored in cell B2). If the home team score is higher, "Won" appears in the cell. If not, the nested IF function evaluates whether the visiting team score is greater than the home team score. If the visiting team score is higher, "Lost" appears in the cell. Otherwise, "Tie" appears in the cell.

**Figure 7-17** **Additional example of nested IF functions**

**Purpose:** To determine the outcome of football games for the home team

**Logic Scenario:** Display Won, Lost, or Tie based on home team and visitor team scores

**Formula:** Nested IF functions

```
=IF(B1>B2,"Won",IF(B2>B1,"Lost","Tie"))
```

**Data:** cell B1 stores the home team score
cell B2 stores the visitor team score

**Example:**

| Data | | Condition1 | Condition2 | Results |
|---|---|---|---|---|
| Cell B1 | Cell B2 | B1>B2 | B2>B1 | (Outcome) |
| 21 | 18 | True | Not evaluated | Won |
| 17 | 24 | False | True | Lost |
| 9 | 9 | False | False | Tie |

Figure 7-18 illustrates how two nested IFs are used to determine among four possible outcomes for a driver's license based on the applicant's age (stored in cell B1). The first IF function evaluates whether the applicant is less than 16 years old. If the applicant is younger than 16, "Too Young" appears in the cell. If not, the first nested IF function evaluates whether the applicant is 45 years old or younger. If so, 30 appears in the cell as the fee. If not, the second nested IF function evaluates whether the applicant is 60 years old or younger. If so, 25 appears in the cell as the fee. Otherwise, 20 appears in the cell as the fee.

**Figure 7-18** Additional example of nested IF functions

**Purpose:** To determine the fee for a driver's license

**Logic Scenario:** Driver's license fee varies by age

| | |
|---|---|
| Below 16 | "Too Young" |
| 16–45 | $30 |
| 46–60 | $25 |
| 61 and older | $20 |

**Formula:** Nested IF functions

`=IF(B1<16,"Too Young",IF(B1<=45,30,IF(B1<=60,25,20)))`

**Data:** cell B1 stores the driver's age

**Example:**

| Data | Condition1 | Condition2 | Condition3 | Results |
|---|---|---|---|---|
| Cell B1 | B1<16 | B1<=45 | B1<=60 | (Fee) |
| 15 | True | Not evaluated | Not evaluated | Too Young |
| 25 | False | True | Not evaluated | 30 |
| 55 | False | False | True | 25 |
| 65 | False | False | False | 20 |

PROSKILLS

## *Problem Solving: Finding and Fixing Errors in Formulas*

Errors occur in spreadsheets as illustrated in the following real-life incident: "City officials miscalculated the amount of sales taxes generated from a local sporting goods store. The mistake inflated the tax figures by tens of thousands of dollars, which, in turn, meant the total sales estimate was overblown by millions of dollars. The city believed the mistake was a result of an error in a spreadsheet formula...."

If formulas in a worksheet are returning errors or not working as expected, you need to find and fix the problems. Two common categories of formula errors in Excel are syntax errors and logic errors. A syntax error is an error in a statement that violates the rules of Excel. A syntax error might occur due to unmatched parentheses or a required argument that is omitted in a function. Logic errors occur in formulas that work but return an incorrect result. A logic error could occur because the formula uses the wrong calculation, the formula references the wrong cell, or the formula uses faulty reasoning, leading to incorrect results.

Some problem-solving approaches can help resolve these types of errors. First, examine the formulas in worksheet cells instead of the results by pressing the Ctrl+~ keys to show the formulas in each cell. Next, troubleshoot problem areas in the worksheet by pressing the F9 key to highlight part of a formula and temporarily display the actual value in the cell so you can check intermediate results. Press the Esc key to return the cell references. Finally, you can use the Formula Auditing tools on the Formulas tab to visually identify and trace cells used in a formula. This can help you locate and fix inaccurate cell references and faulty logic.

Carefully evaluating formulas and fixing any problems help to ensure that a worksheet is error-free and returns accurate results.

Next, you'll add a Bonus column to the Employee table and enter the formula to calculate the bonus amount. The bonus amounts for each pay grade are not yet final. To make the bonus calculation more flexible, Rita stored the three bonus amounts (2500, 5000, and 7500) in the Employee worksheet. You will reference these cells in the formula to calculate the employee bonus. This approach enables you to quickly update the calculated bonus amounts in the Employee worksheet without having to edit the bonus formula.

### To enter nested IFs to calculate employee bonuses:

1. If you took a break at the end of the previous session, make sure the Talent Tracs workbook is open and the Employee Data worksheet is active.
2. In cell Q1, enter **Bonus** as the column header. The Excel table expands to include the new column, and cell Q2 is the active cell.
3. Make sure cell Q2 is the active cell, and then click the **Insert Function** button *fx* in the formula bar. The Insert Function dialog box opens.
4. Click **IF** in the Select a function box, and then click the **OK** button. The Function Arguments dialog box opens.
5. In the Logical_test box, type **[Pay Grade]=1** and then press the **Tab** key to enter the logical test using a structured reference. This logical test evaluates whether the employee has a pay grade equal to 1. The values to the right of the Logical_test box are {False;False;..., indicating that the pay grades for the first few employees are not equal to 1.

   **Trouble?** If the value to the right of the Logical_test box is "Invalid," you probably mistyped the logical test. Select the text in the Logical_test box, and then repeat Step 5, typing the logical test exactly as shown, being sure to use square brackets around the structured reference.
6. In the Value_if_true box, type **$Y$2** and then press the **Tab** key. The value to the right of the Value_if_true argument box is 2500, which is the value in cell Y2. This argument specifies that if the logical test is true (the Pay Grade cell is equal to 1), the value stored in cell Y2 (the 2500 bonus amount) is displayed.
7. In the Value_if_false box, type **IF([Pay Grade]=2,$Y$3,$Y$4)**. This argument is a nested IF function that specifies if the logical condition is true (the Pay Grade cell is equal to 2), the value stored in cell Y3 (the 5000 bonus amount) is displayed; otherwise, the value stored in cell Y4 (the 7500 bonus amount) is displayed. The values to the right of the Value_if_false box are {7500;5000;5000;... indicating the bonus amounts for the employees in the first few rows. See Figure 7-19.

**TIP**

If you type a formula directly in a cell, the available structured references appear when you type the opening bracket. Double-click the structured reference to add it to the formula, and then type the closing bracket.

**Figure 7-19 Function Arguments dialog box with a nested IF**

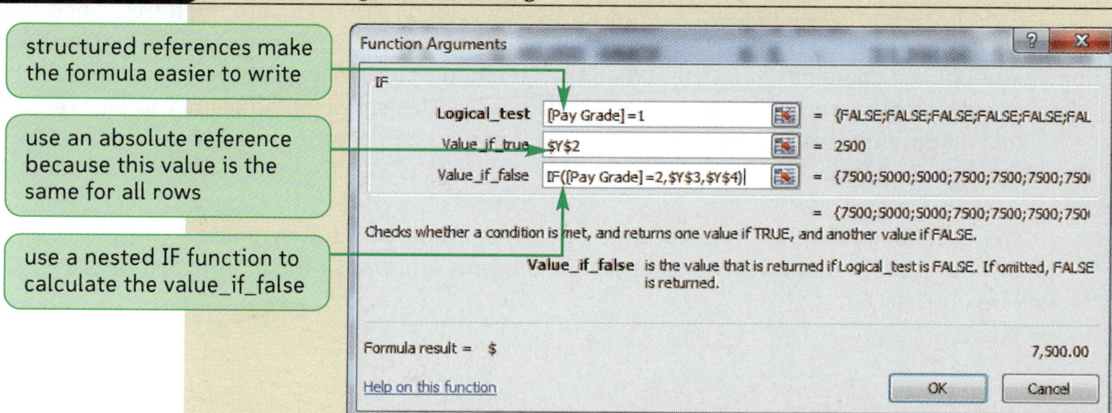

8. Click the **OK** button. The formula =IF([Pay Grade]=1,$Y$2,IF([Pay Grade]=2,$Y$3, $Y$4)) appears in the formula bar, and the value 7500 appears in cell Q2 because this employee has a pay grade of 3. The bonus formula is automatically copied to all other rows in the Bonus column. The references to cells Y2, Y3, and Y4 are absolute references and do not change from cell to cell in the Bonus column.
9. Select the Bonus values, and then format the selected range using the **Accounting** number format with no decimal places.
10. Click cell **Q2** to deselect the column. See Figure 7-20.

**Figure 7-20** **Nested IF function calculating the employee bonus amounts**

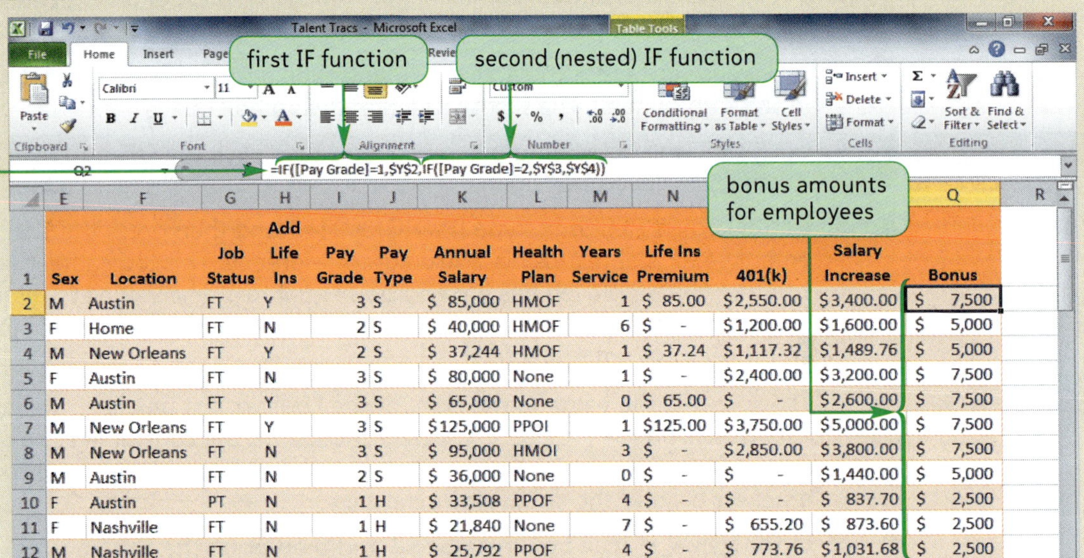


| | Sex | Location | Job Status | Add Life Ins | Pay Grade | Pay Type | Annual Salary | Health Plan | Years Service | Life Ins Premium | 401(k) | Salary Increase | Bonus |
|---|---|---|---|---|---|---|---|---|---|---|---|---|---|
| 2 | M | Austin | FT | Y | 3 | S | $ 85,000 | HMOF | 1 | $ 85.00 | $2,550.00 | $3,400.00 | $ 7,500 |
| 3 | F | Home | FT | N | 2 | S | $ 40,000 | HMOF | 6 | $ - | $1,200.00 | $1,600.00 | $ 5,000 |
| 4 | M | New Orleans | FT | Y | 2 | S | $ 37,244 | HMOF | 1 | $ 37.24 | $1,117.32 | $1,489.76 | $ 5,000 |
| 5 | F | Austin | FT | N | 3 | S | $ 80,000 | None | 1 | $ - | $2,400.00 | $3,200.00 | $ 7,500 |
| 6 | M | Austin | FT | Y | 3 | S | $ 65,000 | None | 0 | $ 65.00 | $ - | $2,600.00 | $ 7,500 |
| 7 | M | New Orleans | FT | Y | 3 | S | $125,000 | PPOI | 1 | $125.00 | $3,750.00 | $5,000.00 | $ 7,500 |
| 8 | M | New Orleans | FT | N | 3 | S | $ 95,000 | HMOI | 3 | $ - | $2,850.00 | $3,800.00 | $ 7,500 |
| 9 | M | Austin | FT | N | 2 | S | $ 36,000 | None | 0 | $ - | $ - | $1,440.00 | $ 5,000 |
| 10 | F | Austin | PT | N | 1 | H | $ 33,508 | PPOF | 4 | $ - | $ - | $ 837.70 | $ 2,500 |
| 11 | F | Nashville | FT | N | 1 | H | $ 21,840 | None | 7 | $ - | $ 655.20 | $ 873.60 | $ 2,500 |
| 12 | M | Nashville | FT | N | 1 | H | $ 25,792 | PPOF | 4 | $ - | $ 773.76 | $1,031.68 | $ 2,500 |

INSIGHT

## *Checking Formulas for Matching Parentheses*

A common problem when creating formulas is mismatched parentheses. As you write a formula, you should verify that you enclosed the correct argument, function, or term within the parentheses of the formula you are creating. This is especially important when you develop a complex formula that includes many parentheses, such as a nested IF function. Excel color-codes the parentheses as you build a formula so you can quickly determine whether you have complete pairs of them. You can also verify that the formula includes matching pairs of parentheses by selecting the cell with the formula and then clicking in the formula bar. Press the → key to move the insertion point through the formula one character at a time. When the insertion point moves across one parenthesis, its matching parenthesis is also highlighted briefly. This color coding helps you ensure that all parentheses in a formula are paired (opening and closing parentheses).

The executive team has increased the bonus for employees in pay grade 1 from $2,500 to $2,750. Rita asks you to update this bonus amount so the employee bonuses will be current.

**TIP**

Placing cell references to input values rather than constants in formulas makes a worksheet more flexible and easier to update.

**To update the bonus amount for Pay Grade 1:**

1. In cell Y2, enter **2750**.
2. Scroll to the **Bonus** column and observe that all employees with a pay grade equal to 1 show a bonus amount of $2,750.

# Using Lookup Tables and Functions

**Lookup functions** allow you to use tables of data to "look up" values and insert them in another worksheet location. For example, you might enter a product table in a worksheet that includes the product ID, product name, and price of all products a company sells. You could then use this product table to build an invoice in another worksheet by entering a product ID and having Excel look up the product name and price, and insert these values in the invoice.

The table that stores the data you want to retrieve is called a lookup table, and it organizes the data you want to retrieve into different categories, such as by product ID. The categories for the lookup table, called compare values, are located in the table's first column or row. To retrieve a particular value from the table, a lookup value (the value you are trying to find) needs to match one of the compare values. When a match is found, the corresponding value in the lookup table is displayed in the cell where the lookup formula is entered. Lookup values can also be used as part of a formula.

At Talent Tracs, all employees are eligible for the company's health plan. Employees can choose one of four health plans: an HMO for individuals (HMOI), an HMO for families (HMOF), a PPO for individuals (PPOI), or a PPO for families (PPOF). Each plan has a different cost, and Talent Tracs pays the entire health plan cost. If an employee shows evidence of coverage elsewhere, there is no health plan cost. You could calculate the health plan costs for each employee using several nested IF functions. However, a simpler approach is to use a lookup function.

You can use the HealthPlanRates table shown in Figure 7-21 as a lookup table. The lookup table shows the available plans and the corresponding monthly premiums. The health plan cost for each eligible employee is based on the plan the employee selected. The lookup value is the employee's health plan code, which is entered in column L of the Employee table. The compare values come from the first column of the HealthPlanRates table, which is in the range B3:C8 in the Lookup Tables worksheet. To retrieve the monthly cost for an employee, Excel moves down the first column in the HealthPlanRates lookup table until it finds the health plan code that matches the lookup value. Then it moves to the second column in the lookup table to locate the monthly cost, which is displayed in the cell where the lookup formula is entered or used as part of a calculation.

**Figure 7-21** **HealthPlanRates table used for an exact match lookup**

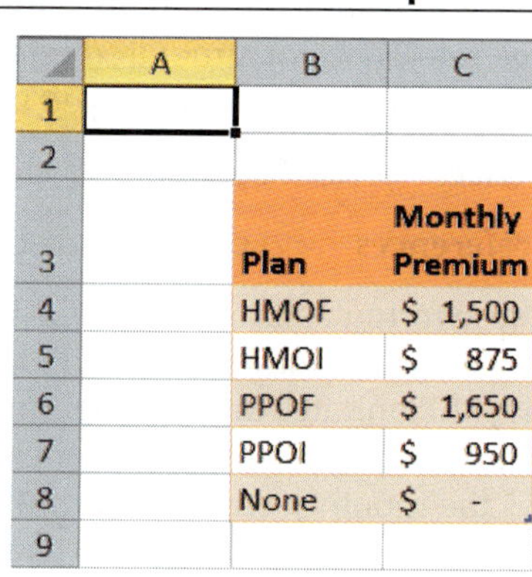

| | A | B | C |
|---|---|---|---|
| 1 | | | |
| 2 | | | |
| 3 | | Plan | Monthly Premium |
| 4 | | HMOF | $ 1,500 |
| 5 | | HMOI | $ 875 |
| 6 | | PPOF | $ 1,650 |
| 7 | | PPOI | $ 950 |
| 8 | | None | $ - |
| 9 | | | |

Lookup tables can be constructed as either exact match or approximate match lookups. An **exact match lookup** occurs when the value entered must match one of the values in the first column of the lookup table. The HealthPlanRates table in Figure 7-21 is an example of an exact match lookup because the health plan code must match one of the values in the HealthPlanRates table or a value is not returned. An **approximate match lookup** occurs when the value entered falls within a range of values in the first column of the lookup table. A discount based on the quantity of items purchased where each discount covers a range of units purchased is an example of an approximate match lookup. Figure 7-22 shows the approximate match lookup table for these quantity discounts. In this example, purchases of fewer than 25 units receive no discount, purchases of between 25 and 99 units receive a 2 percent discount, purchases of between 100 and 499 units receive a 3 percent discount, and purchases of 500 or more units receive a 4 percent discount.

**Figure 7-22** **Approximate match lookup table**

| Quantity | Discount Rate |
|---|---|
| 0 | 0% |
| 25 | 2% |
| 100 | 3% |
| 500 | 4% |

## Using the VLOOKUP Function to Find an Exact Match

To retrieve the correct value from the lookup table, you use the VLOOKUP function. This function searches a lookup table and, based on what you entered, retrieves the appropriate value from that table. The VLOOKUP function searches vertically down the first column of the lookup table. The VLOOKUP function has the syntax

```
VLOOKUP(lookup_value, table_array, col_index_num, [range_lookup])
```

where *lookup_value* is the value you want to use to search the first column of the lookup table, *table_array* is the range reference of the lookup table or its table name, *col_index_num* is the number of the column in the lookup table that contains the value you want to return, and *range_lookup* indicates whether the compare values are a range of values (for an approximate match) or an exact match. When you use a range of values (such as in a tax rate table), you set the *range_lookup* value to TRUE; when you want the *lookup_value* to exactly match a value in the first column of the *table_array* (such as in the HealthPlanRates table), you set the *range_lookup* value to FALSE. The *range_lookup* argument is optional; if you don't include a *range_lookup* value, the value is considered TRUE (an approximate match).

You'll use the VLOOKUP function to calculate the annual health plan cost for Talent Tracs because you want to search the values in the first column of the lookup table. You can use range references or structured references when you create the formula for the annual health plan cost for an employee from the HealthPlanRates table, as follows:

**Range references** `=VLOOKUP(L2,'Lookup Tables'!$B$4:$C$8,2,FALSE)*12`

**Structured references** `=VLOOKUP([HealthPlan],HealthPlanRates,2,FALSE)*12`

Both of these formulas use the VLOOKUP function to search for the code in the Health Plan column (column L) of the Employee table, in the first column of the lookup table (the HealthPlanRates table in the range B4:C8 in the Lookup Tables worksheet), and then return the value in the second column of the HealthPlanRates lookup table, which shows the monthly cost. The formulas use FALSE as the *range_lookup* argument because you want the lookup value to exactly match a value in the first column of the HealthPlanRates table.

## To find an exact match in the HealthPlanRates table:

1. In cell R1, enter **Health Cost**. The table expands to include the new column.
2. Make sure cell R2 is the active cell, and then click the **Insert Function** button *fx* in the formula bar. The Insert Function dialog box opens.
3. Click the **Or select a category** arrow, click **Lookup & Reference**, and then double-click **VLOOKUP** in the Select a function box. The Function Arguments dialog box opens.
4. Drag the Function Arguments dialog box below row 2 so you can see the column headers.
5. In the Lookup_value box, enter **L2** and then press the **Tab** key. The lookup value is the employee's health plan code, which is located in column L.
6. In the Table_array box, type **HealthPlanRates** and then press the **Tab** key. HealthPlanRates is the table name assigned to the range B4:C8 in the Lookup Tables worksheet. If the HealthPlanRates data was entered in a range of cells, the table_array argument would be entered as 'Lookup Tables'!B4:C8, and you would need to change the range to absolute references ('Lookup Tables'!$B$4:$C$8) so the formula would copy correctly to other cells.
7. In the Col_index_num box, type **2** and then press the **Tab** key. The number 2 indicates the monthly cost is stored in the second column of the HealthPlanRates lookup table.
8. In the Range_lookup box, type **FALSE**. This sets the function to find an exact match in the lookup table. See Figure 7-23.

**TIP**

For the col_index_num value, be sure to enter the number that corresponds to the column's position rather than its column letter; otherwise, the VLOOKUP formula may return #NAME? or #VALUE! as the result.

**Figure 7-23** Function Arguments dialog box for the VLOOKUP function

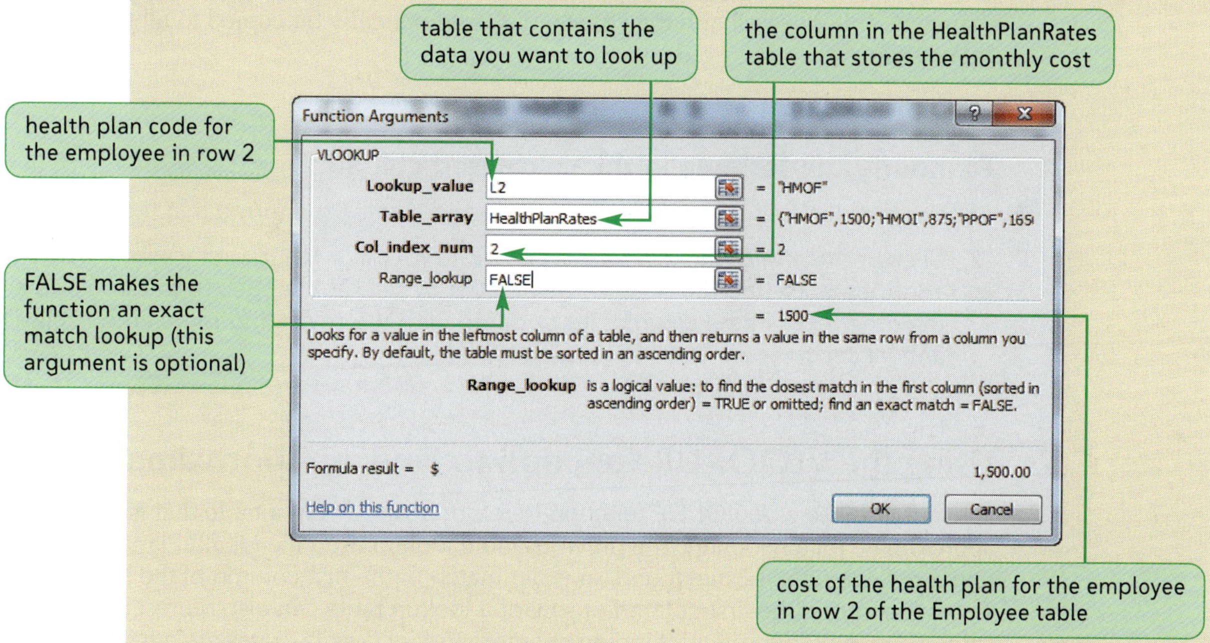


9. Click the **OK** button. The dialog box closes, 1500 appears in cell R2, and the formula VLOOKUP(L2,HealthPlanRates,2,FALSE) appears in the formula bar. The remaining rows in the Health Cost column are filled with the VLOOKUP function. If the value in column L does not match a value in the first column of the HealthPlanRates table, an exact match does not exist and the function returns #N/A in the cell.

10. Select the Health Cost values, and then format the range using the **Accounting** number format with no decimal places.
11. Click cell **R2** to deselect the column. See Figure 7-24.

**Figure 7-24** **VLOOKUP function calculating employee health costs**

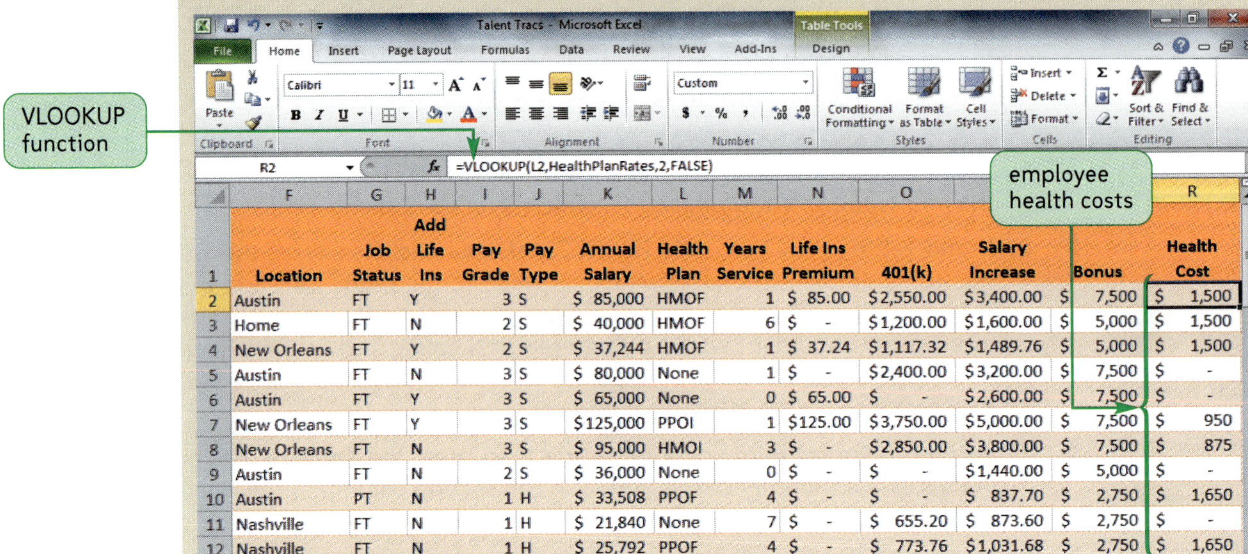


| | Location | Job Status | Add Life Ins | Pay Grade | Pay Type | Annual Salary | Health Plan | Years Service | Life Ins Premium | 401(k) | Salary Increase | Bonus | Health Cost |
|---|---|---|---|---|---|---|---|---|---|---|---|---|---|
| 2 | Austin | FT | Y | 3 | S | $ 85,000 | HMOF | 1 | $ 85.00 | $2,550.00 | $3,400.00 | $ 7,500 | $ 1,500 |
| 3 | Home | FT | N | 2 | S | $ 40,000 | HMOF | 6 | $ - | $1,200.00 | $1,600.00 | $ 5,000 | $ 1,500 |
| 4 | New Orleans | FT | Y | 2 | S | $ 37,244 | HMOF | 1 | $ 37.24 | $1,117.32 | $1,489.76 | $ 5,000 | $ 1,500 |
| 5 | Austin | FT | N | 3 | S | $ 80,000 | None | 1 | $ - | $2,400.00 | $3,200.00 | $ 7,500 | $ - |
| 6 | Austin | FT | Y | 3 | S | $ 65,000 | None | 0 | $ 65.00 | $ - | $2,600.00 | $ 7,500 | $ - |
| 7 | New Orleans | FT | Y | 3 | S | $125,000 | PPOI | 1 | $125.00 | $3,750.00 | $5,000.00 | $ 7,500 | $ 950 |
| 8 | New Orleans | FT | N | 3 | S | $ 95,000 | HMOI | 3 | $ - | $2,850.00 | $3,800.00 | $ 7,500 | $ 875 |
| 9 | Austin | FT | N | 2 | S | $ 36,000 | None | 0 | $ - | $ - | $1,440.00 | $ 5,000 | $ - |
| 10 | Austin | PT | N | 1 | H | $ 33,508 | PPOF | 4 | $ - | $ - | $ 837.70 | $ 2,750 | $ 1,650 |
| 11 | Nashville | FT | N | 1 | H | $ 21,840 | None | 7 | $ - | $ 655.20 | $ 873.60 | $ 2,750 | $ - |
| 12 | Nashville | FT | N | 1 | H | $ 25,792 | PPOF | 4 | $ - | $ 773.76 | $1,031.68 | $ 2,750 | $ 1,650 |

The health plan costs in the Employee table are monthly amounts rather than annual amounts. You need to modify the formula in the Health Cost column to reflect the annual amounts. Because the formula is in a calculated table column, you need to make the change in only one cell and the change will automatically be copied to all the cells in the column.

**To modify the formula in the calculated column:**

1. Double-click cell **R2** to enter Edit mode and display the formula in the cell.
2. Click at the end of the formula, type ***12** to multiply the monthly amount by 12, and then press the **Enter** key. The amount in cell Q2 changes to $18,000 and all the other cells in the column are updated with the revised formula and display the annual cost.

## Using the VLOOKUP Function to Find an Approximate Match

You can also use a VLOOKUP function to return a value from a table that is based on an approximate match lookup. The previous table lookup used the HealthPlanRates table to return a value only if Excel found an exact match in the first column of the lookup table. The categories in the first column or row of a lookup table can also represent a range of values. Quantity discounts, shipping charges, and income tax rates are a few examples of approximate match lookups.

As part of Talent Tracs' 10-year anniversary, management plans to give employee-recognition awards based on the number of years individuals have worked for Talent Tracs. Rita developed the criteria shown in Figure 7-25 to summarize how the company plans to distribute the recognition awards.

**Figure 7-25** **Recognition Awards table**

| Years of Service | Award |
|---|---|
| >=0 years and <1 year | 0 |
| >=1 year and <3 years | 100 |
| >=3 years and <5 years | 200 |
| >=5 years and <7 years | 300 |
| 7 years or more | 500 |

In the Recognition Awards table, you are not looking for an exact match for the lookup value. Instead, you need to use an approximate match lookup, which determines whether the lookup value falls within a range of values. You want to use the table lookup to determine what service range an employee falls into, and then return the recognition award based on the appropriate row. To accomplish this, you must rearrange the first column of the lookup table so that each compare value (row) in the table represents the low end of the category range, as shown in Figure 7-26.

**Figure 7-26** **Recognition Awards table**

| | F | G | H |
|---|---|---|---|
| 1 | | | |
| 2 | | | |
| 3 | | Years of Service | Recognition Award |
| 4 | | 0 | $ - |
| 5 | | 1 | $ 100 |
| 6 | | 3 | $ 200 |
| 7 | | 5 | $ 300 |
| 8 | | 7 | $ 500 |

To determine whether a lookup value falls within a range of values in the revised lookup table, Excel searches the first column of the table until it locates the largest value that is less than the lookup value. Then Excel moves across the row in the table to retrieve the corresponding value. For an employee working at Talent Tracs for six years, Excel would search the lookup table until the compare value is 5 (the largest value less than the lookup value) and retrieve 300 from column 2 of the corresponding row.

When a lookup table is used with a range of values, the compare values must be sorted in alphabetical order if they are text and in low-to-high order if they are numbers. When the compare values are arranged in a different order, Excel may not retrieve the correct value, leading to incorrect results. Even though the VLOOKUP function is accurate, the data in the lookup table is not organized the right way. The setup of the lookup table in an approximate match is critical for a VLOOKUP formula to work.

INSIGHT

### *Setting Up an Approximate Match Lookup Table*

Approximate lookup tables are commonly used to find a taxpayer's tax rate in a tax table, find a shipping charge based on the weight of a package in a shipping charges table, or determine a student's letter grade from a table of grading criteria. Setting up the lookup tables for an approximate match lookup can be tricky. Consider the following example, in which an instructor uses Excel to calculate grades. The instructor assigns final grades based on the following grading policy table:

| Score | Grade |
|---|---|
| 90–100 | A |
| 80–89 | B |
| 70–79 | C |
| 60–69 | D |
| 0–59 | F |

To set up the lookup table so it works in Excel, the leftmost column in the lookup table must represent the lower end of the range for each category, and the lookup table must be sorted in ascending order based on the value in the first column. Otherwise, Excel cannot retrieve the correct result. Following this structure, the lookup table for the instructor's grading policy would be arranged as follows:

| Score | Grade |
|---|---|
| 0 | F |
| 60 | D |
| 70 | C |
| 80 | B |
| 90 | A |

You'll create a formula in the Employee table to determine the recognition award for each employee. You will use an approximate match VLOOKUP formula because the years of service in the lookup table have a range of values.

## To insert an approximate match VLOOKUP formula:

1. In cell S1, enter **Award**. A new column is added to the table, and cell S2 is the active cell.
2. Click the **Insert Function** button *fx* in the formula bar. The Insert Function dialog box opens with the Lookup & Reference category active.
3. In the Select a function box, double-click **VLOOKUP**. The Function Arguments dialog box opens.
4. In the Lookup_value box, type **[Years Service]** and then press the **Tab** key. The lookup value is entered using the column header (structured reference) for the employee's years of service, which is located in column M. You can also enter the lookup value as M2. The number 1 appears as the lookup value for the current row.
5. In the Table_array box, type **Recognition** and then press the **Tab** key. Recognition is the table name assigned to the range G4:H8 in the Lookup Tables worksheet. If the Recognition data was entered in a range of cells, the table_array argument would be entered as 'Lookup Tables'!G4:H8, and you would need to change the range to absolute references ('Lookup Tables'!$G$4:$H$8) so that the formula would copy correctly to other cells.

6. In the Col_index_num box, type **2**. The number 2 indicates the column where the amount of the award is stored—in the second column of the Recognition table. See Figure 7-27. You do not need to enter the optional fourth argument in the VLOOKUP formula because Excel assumes the value to be TRUE and will use an approximate match table lookup.

**Figure 7-27** **Function Arguments dialog box for the VLOOKUP function**

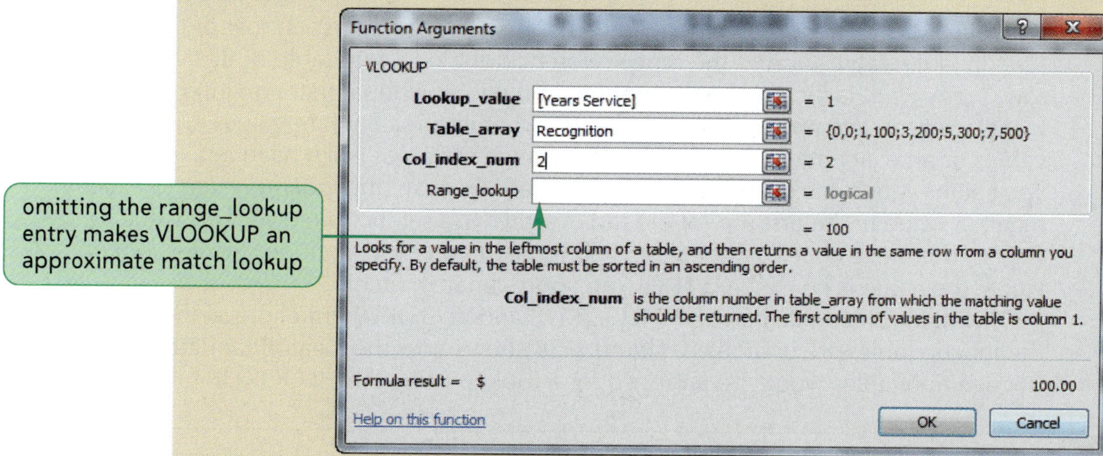


7. Click the **OK** button. All the cells in the Award calculated column are filled with the VLOOKUP formula and display the award amounts. The employee in row 2 has 1 year of service and will receive a recognition award of $100. The employee in row 3 has 6 years of service and will receive an award of $300. This second employee is a good illustration of the approximate match lookup, because 6 does not equal a value in the first column of the lookup table. Instead, it falls within two values in the table.

8. Select the values in the Award column, and then format the selected range using the **Accounting** number format with no decimal places.

9. Click cell **S2** to deselect the column. See Figure 7-28.

**Figure 7-28** **Award column**

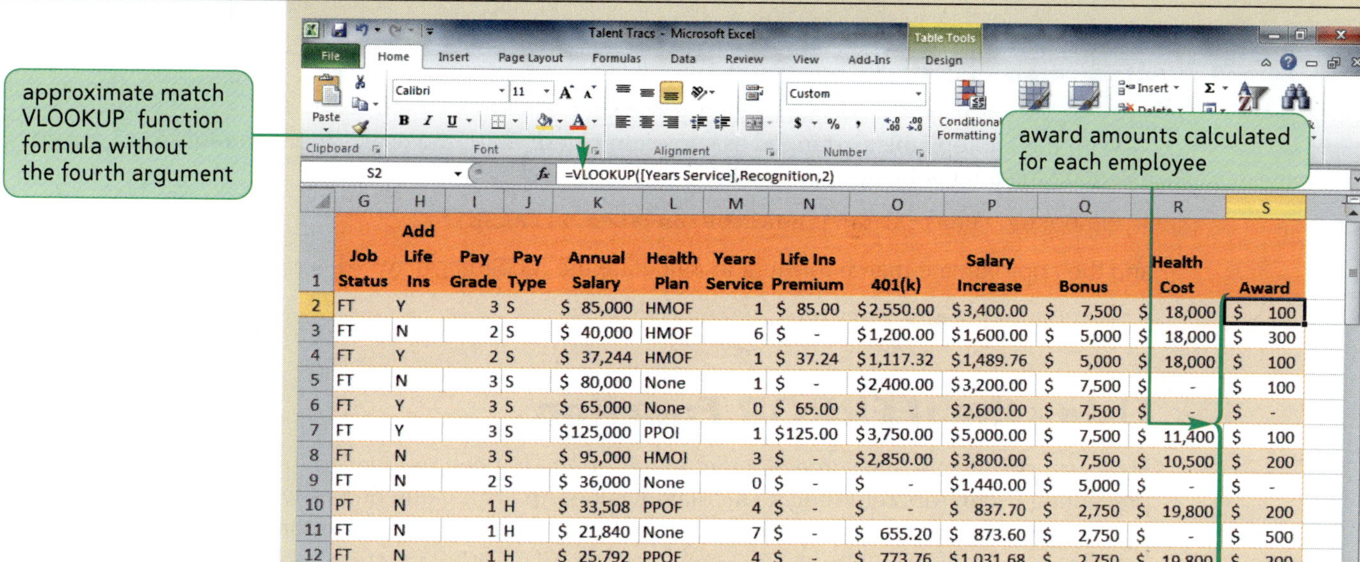


| | Job Status | Add Life Ins | Pay Grade | Pay Type | Annual Salary | Health Plan | Years Service | Life Ins Premium | 401(k) | Salary Increase | Bonus | Health Cost | Award |
|---|---|---|---|---|---|---|---|---|---|---|---|---|---|
| 2 | FT | Y | 3 | S | $ 85,000 | HMOF | 1 | $ 85.00 | $2,550.00 | $3,400.00 | $ 7,500 | $ 18,000 | $ 100 |
| 3 | FT | N | 2 | S | $ 40,000 | HMOF | 6 | $ - | $1,200.00 | $1,600.00 | $ 5,000 | $ 18,000 | $ 300 |
| 4 | FT | Y | 2 | S | $ 37,244 | HMOF | 1 | $ 37.24 | $1,117.32 | $1,489.76 | $ 5,000 | $ 18,000 | $ 100 |
| 5 | FT | N | 3 | S | $ 80,000 | None | 1 | $ - | $2,400.00 | $3,200.00 | $ 7,500 | $ - | $ 100 |
| 6 | FT | Y | 3 | S | $ 65,000 | None | 0 | $ 65.00 | $ - | $2,600.00 | $ 7,500 | $ - | $ - |
| 7 | FT | Y | 3 | S | $125,000 | PPOI | 1 | $125.00 | $3,750.00 | $5,000.00 | $ 7,500 | $ 11,400 | $ 100 |
| 8 | FT | N | 3 | S | $ 95,000 | HMOI | 3 | $ - | $2,850.00 | $3,800.00 | $ 7,500 | $ 10,500 | $ 200 |
| 9 | FT | N | 2 | S | $ 36,000 | None | 0 | $ - | $ - | $1,440.00 | $ 5,000 | $ - | $ - |
| 10 | PT | N | 1 | H | $ 33,508 | PPOF | 4 | $ - | $ - | $ 837.70 | $ 2,750 | $ 19,800 | $ 200 |
| 11 | FT | N | 1 | H | $ 21,840 | None | 7 | $ - | $ 655.20 | $ 873.60 | $ 2,750 | $ - | $ 500 |
| 12 | FT | N | 1 | H | $ 25,792 | PPOF | 4 | $ - | $ 773.76 | $1,031.68 | $ 2,750 | $ 19,800 | $ 200 |

## Looking Up Values Using the HLOOKUP Function

The HLOOKUP function is very similar to the VLOOKUP function. The **HLOOKUP function** (horizontal lookup function) searches horizontally across the top row of the lookup table and retrieves the value in the column you specify. You use the HLOOKUP function when the comparison values are located in the first row of the lookup table and you want to look down a specified number of rows to find the data to enter in another cell.

The HLOOKUP function has the syntax

```
HLOOKUP(lookup_value, table_array, row_index_num, [range_lookup])
```

where *lookup_value* is the value you want to use to search the first row of the lookup table, *table_array* is the range reference of the lookup table or its table name, *row_index_num* is the number of the row in the lookup table that contains the value you want to return, and *range_lookup* indicates whether the compare values are a range of values or an exact match. When you use a range of values (such as in a tax rate table), you set the *range_lookup* value to TRUE; when you want the *lookup_value* to exactly match a value in the first row of the *table_array*, you set the *range_lookup* value to FALSE. The *range_lookup* argument is optional; if you don't include a *range_lookup* value, the value is considered TRUE (an approximate match).

The major difference between HLOOKUP and VLOOKUP functions is the way the lookup tables are organized. Figure 7-28 shows how the HealthPlanRates and Recognition tables would be arranged for a lookup using the HLOOKUP function.

**Figure 7-29** **Lookup tables for the HLOOKUP function**

| | A | B | C | D | E | F | G |
|---|---|---|---|---|---|---|---|
| 1 | | **Health Rate Plans** | | | | | |
| 2 | | | | | | | |
| 3 | | **Plan** | HMOF | HMOI | PPOF | PPOI | None |
| 4 | | **Monthly Premium** | $ 1,500 | $ 875 | $ 1,650 | $ 950 | $ - |
| 5 | | | | | | | |
| 6 | | | | | | | |
| 7 | | **Recognition Award** | | | | | |
| 8 | | | | | | | |
| 9 | | **Years of Service** | 0 | 1 | 3 | 5 | 7 |
| 10 | | **Recognition Award** | $ - | $ 100 | $ 200 | $ 300 | $ 500 |
| 11 | | | | | | | |

With the lookup tables arranged as shown in Figure 7-29, the exact match formula to calculate the annual health plan cost is

```
=HLOOKUP([HealthPlan],HealthPlanRates,2,FALSE)*12
```

and the approximate match formula to calculate the recognition award is

```
=HLOOKUP([Years Service],Recognition,2)
```

# Using the IFERROR Function

**Error values** indicate that some element in a formula or a cell referenced in a formula is preventing Excel from returning a calculated value. An error value begins with a number sign (#) followed by an error name that indicates the type of error. For instance, the error value #N/A appears in a Health Cost cell when the VLOOKUP function cannot find the health plan code in the HealthPlanRates lookup table because it was entered incorrectly. Figure 7-30 describes common error values you might see in workbooks.

**Figure 7-30** **Excel error values**

| Error Value | Description of Error |
|---|---|
| #DIV/0! | The formula or function contains a number divided by 0. |
| #NAME? | Excel doesn't recognize text in the formula or function, such as when the function name is misspelled. |
| #N/A | A value is not available to a function or formula, which can occur when an invalid value is specified in the LOOKUP function. |
| #NULL! | A formula or function requires two cell ranges to intersect, but they don't. |
| #NUM! | Invalid numbers are used in a formula or function, such as text entered in a function that requires a number. |
| #REF! | A cell reference used in a formula or function is no longer valid, which can occur when the cell used by the function was deleted from the worksheet. |
| #VALUE! | The wrong type of argument is used in a function or formula. This can occur when you supply a range of values to a function that requires a single value. |

These error value messages are not particularly descriptive or helpful. To display a more descriptive message that helps users fix the problem, you can use the IFERROR function. The IFERROR function can determine if a cell contains an error value and then display the message you choose rather than the default error value. The IFERROR function has the syntax

```
IFERROR(expression, valueIfError)
```

where *expression* is the formula you want to check for an error, and *valueIfError* is the message you want displayed if Excel detects an error in the formula you are checking. If Excel does not detect an error, the result of the *expression* is displayed.

The IFERROR function enables you to easily find and handle formula errors. For example, you can enter the following formula to determine whether an invalid code was entered in the Health Plan column of the Employee table and then display a more descriptive message if Excel detects an error:

```
=IFERROR(VLOOKUP(L2,HealthPlanRates,2,False)*12,"Invalid code")
```

Based on this formula, if the value in cell L2 is HMOF, the result of the VLOOKUP formula is $1,500 (the corresponding value from the HealthPlanRates table), the first argument in the IFERROR function (shown in purple) is executed, and the health cost is displayed. On the other hand, if cell L2 has an invalid health plan code, such as HMOG, the VLOOKUP function returns the error value #N/A, the second argument in the IFERROR function (shown in red) is executed, and "Invalid code" is displayed.

You will scroll the Health Cost column to verify that all employees have an amount assigned to Health Cost.

**To check for an error value in the Health Cost column:**

1. Scroll to row **54** of the Health Plan column to see the error value #N/A in cell R54.
2. Click cell **R54**. See Figure 7-31.

**Figure 7-31** **Error value in the Health Cost column**

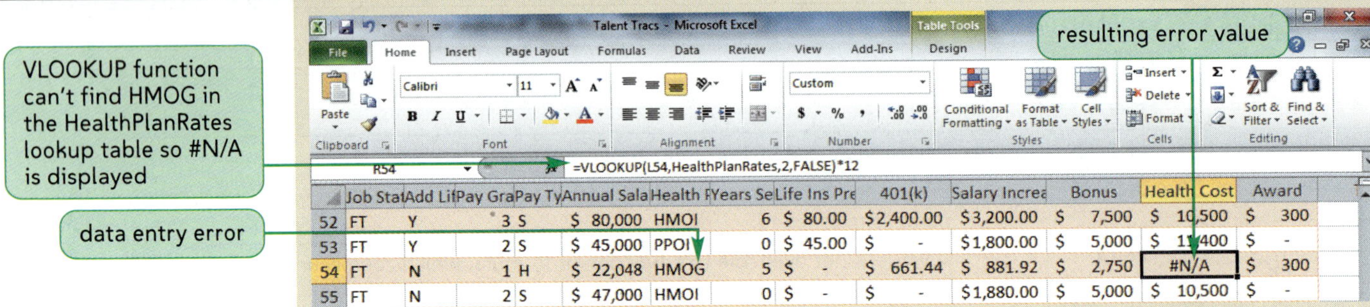


3. In row 54 in the Health Plan column, observe that the health plan code is HMOG, which is an invalid code.

Rita asks you to modify the formulas in the Health Cost column so that the descriptive error message "Invalid code" appears rather than the error value. The IFERROR function will check for errors in the formula, and display the error message you create rather than the error value if it finds an error.

You'll nest the VLOOKUP function within the IFERROR function to display the message "Invalid code" in the Health Cost column if Excel detects an error value.

### To nest the VLOOKUP function within the IFERROR function:

1. Double-click cell **R54** (the cell in row 54 of the Health Cost column) to enter Edit mode. The formula =VLOOKUP(L54,HealthPlanRates,2,False)*12 appears in the cell and the formula bar. You'll nest this formula within the IFERROR function.
2. Click to the right of **=** (the equal sign), and then type **IFERROR(** to begin entering the IFERROR function. The first argument in the IFERROR function is the formula you want to use if no error value is found; this is the VLOOKUP function already entered in the cell.
3. Move the insertion point to the right of the VLOOKUP formula, and then type **,"Invalid code")** to add the text you want to display if an error is found.
4. Press the **Enter** key. The error message "Invalid code" appears in cell R54, and the revised formula is automatically copied to all cells in the column. See Figure 7-32.

**Figure 7-32** **Invalid code message in the Health Cost column**

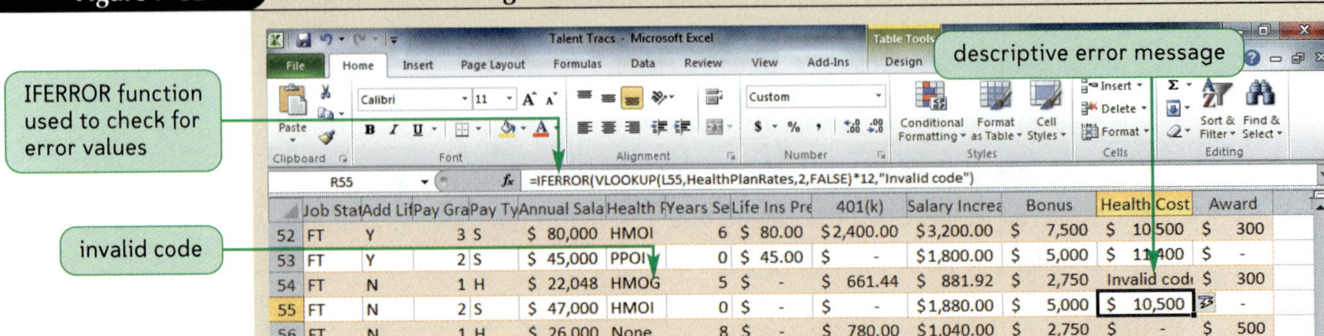

**Trouble?** If the error #NAME? appears in cell R54, you may have omitted quotation marks around the descriptive error message, "Invalid code." Correct the formula, and then continue with Step 5.

5. In cell L54 (the cell in row 54 of the Health Plan column), enter **HMOF**. The health plan code you entered is valid, so the health cost value $18,000 appears in cell R54.
6. Scroll to the top of the table, click cell **R2**, and observe in the formula bar that the IFERROR formula was copied to this cell.

In this session, you used nested IF functions to determine employee bonuses, the VLOOKUP function to calculate health cost and recognition award amounts, and the IFERROR function to display a descriptive message if invalid health plan codes are entered in the Employee table. In the next session, you will use conditional formatting and the COUNTIF, SUMIF, and AVERAGEIF functions to report on employee salaries.

REVIEW

## *Session 7.2 Quick Check*

1. When you include one IF function inside another IF function, you have created a(n) ______________.
2. If cell Y5 displays the value 24, cell Y6 displays the value 27, and cell Y7 contains the following formula, what is displayed in cell Y7?
   `=IF(Y5>Y6,"Older",IF(Y5<Y6,"Younger","Same Age"))`
3. Explain the difference between an exact match and an approximate match table lookup.
4. A customer table includes columns for name, street address, city, state abbreviation, and zip. A second table includes state abbreviations and state names from all 50 states (one state per row). You need to add a new column to the customer table with the state name. What is the most appropriate function to use to display the state name in this new column?
5. Convert the following table that shows the criteria used to determine a student's level to a table that can be used in a VLOOKUP function to display the level of each student:

| Earned Credits | Level |
|---|---|
| 0 but < 30 | Freshman |
| 30 but < 60 | Sophomore |
| 60 but < 90 | Junior |
| 90 or more | Senior |

6. In cell X5, the error value #DIV/0! appears when you divide by 0. Use the IFERROR function with the formula =W5/W25 so that instead of the error value #DIV/0! being displayed, the message "Dividing by zero" appears in the cell.
7. The following Sales Tax Rate table and the ______________ function could be used to display the sales tax rate for a customer in one of these four states.

| State | AZ | NM | OK | TX |
|---|---|---|---|---|
| Sales Tax Rate | 8.5% | 7% | 9% | 9.25% |

# SESSION 7.3 VISUAL OVERVIEW

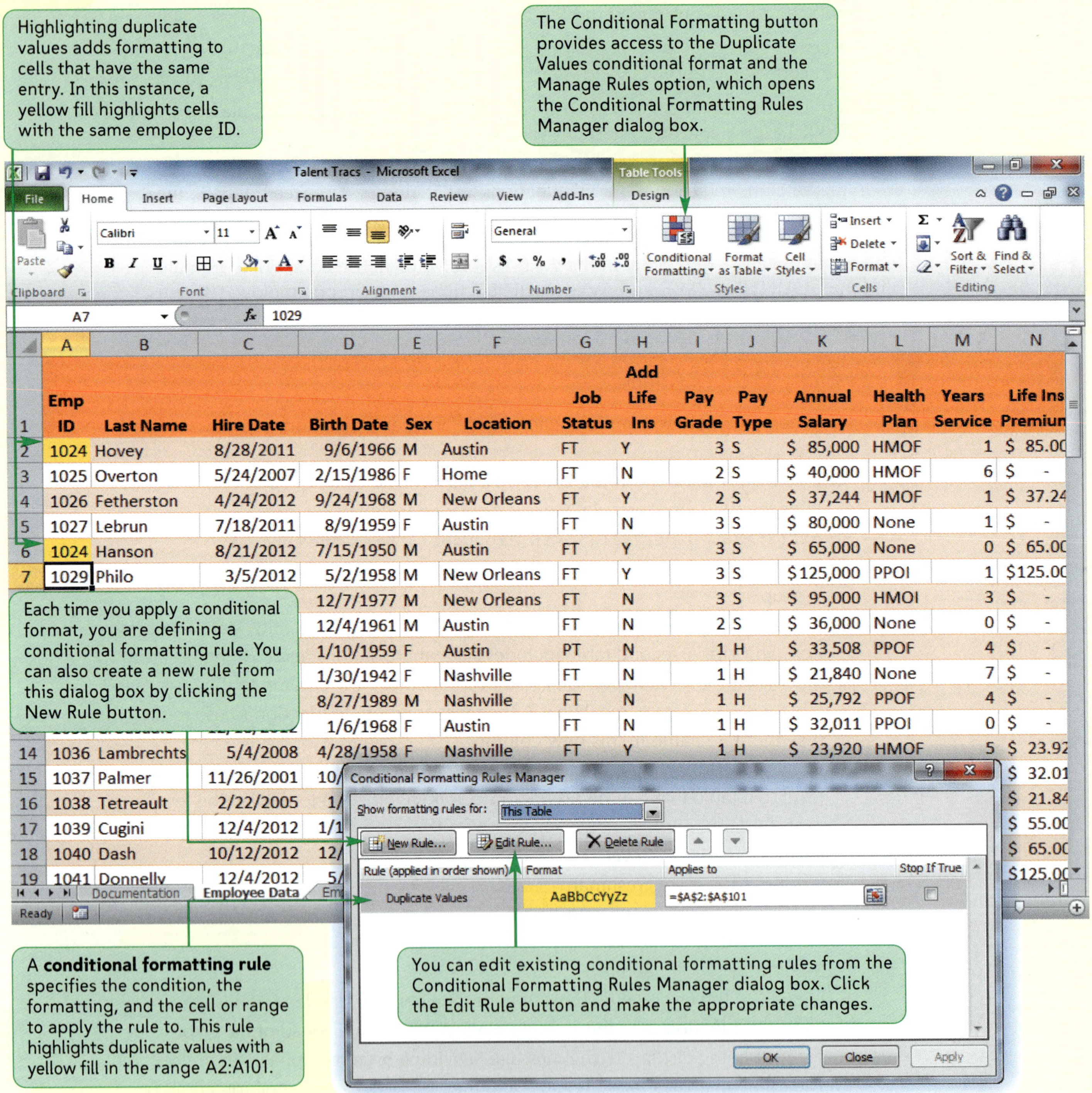

# CONDITIONAL FORMATTING

This formula must be fully qualified because the Employee table is located in a different worksheet.

These formulas use fully qualified structured references to make them easier to create and understand.

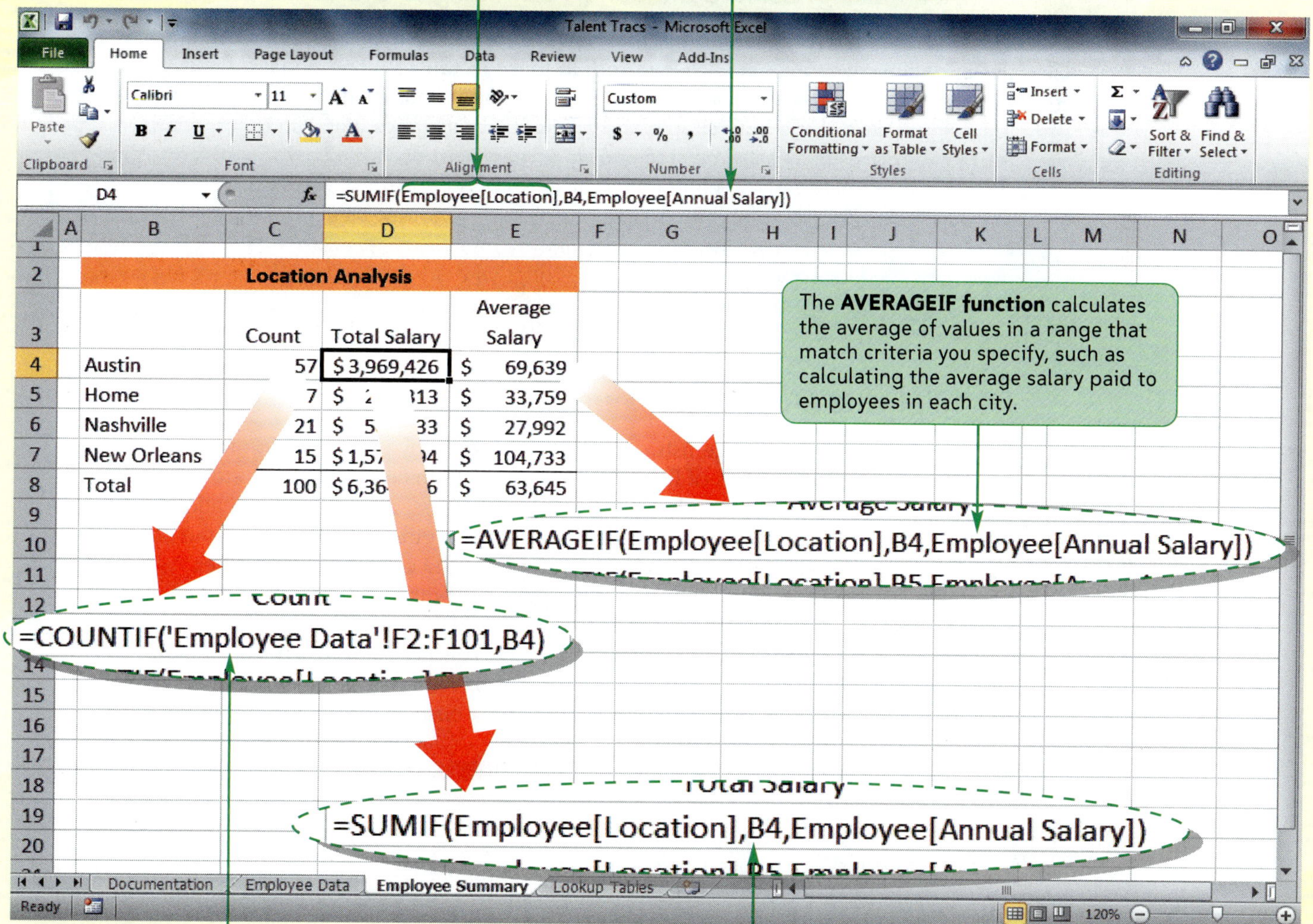


The **AVERAGEIF function** calculates the average of values in a range that match criteria you specify, such as calculating the average salary paid to employees in each city.

The **COUNTIF function** calculates the number of cells in a range that match criteria you specify, such as counting the number of company employees located in Austin.

The **SUMIF function** adds the values in a range that match criteria you specify, such as adding the total salary paid to Austin employees.

# Conditional Formatting

Conditional formatting changes a cell's formatting when its contents match a specified condition. You've already used conditional formatting to highlight cells based on their values and to add data bars that graph the relative values in a range. You can also use conditional formatting to highlight duplicate values in a column of data.

PROSKILLS

*Decision Making: Using Conditional Formatting to Evaluate Data*

Decisions are made by evaluating data. However, this becomes complex when large quantities of data or dynamic data are involved. In these instances, conditional formatting can be a useful tool to help with your decision making. Conditional formatting is designed to make searching a data range both simple and efficient. For instance, you can quickly find the latest market prices in a real-time stock quote spreadsheet by using conditional formatting to highlight them. You can use conditional formatting to find stocks whose price drops below the target buy price by highlighting the row of any stock that meets the buy criteria. You can use conditional formatting to quickly identify bank accounts with a bank balance that is overdrawn by highlighting accounts with a negative balance. Mastering the art of conditional formatting will help you make better decisions.

## Highlighting Duplicate Values

Excel is often used to manage lists of data, such as employee information, inventory, or phone numbers. These types of lists often include data that repeats in different records, such as the employee's state in his or her mailing address, a warehouse location for inventory, or an area code for phone numbers. On the other hand, some of the data is usually unique for each record, such as an employee ID or a product number. As the list of data becomes more extensive, duplicate entries may inadvertently occur. One way to identify unintended duplicate entries is to use conditional formatting to highlight duplicate values in a range with a font and/or fill color. This color coding makes it easier to identify the duplicates so you can then determine whether an entry needs to be corrected. In addition to the colors provided, you can create a custom format for the highlighting.

REFERENCE

*Highlighting Duplicate Values*

- Select the range in which to highlight duplicate values.
- In the Styles group on the Home tab, click the Conditional Formatting button, point to Highlight Cells Rules, and then click Duplicate Values.
- Select the appropriate formatting option.
- Click the OK button.

You will use duplicate value highlighting to verify that each cell in the employee ID column has a unique entry. Rita believes the current employee ID data in the Employee table is accurate, but wants you to use conditional formatting to ensure that there are no duplicate entries.

**To highlight duplicate employee IDs:**

1. If you took a break at the end of the previous session, make sure the Talent Tracs workbook is open and the Employee Data worksheet is active.

2. Scroll to column **A**, and then select the data in the Emp ID column. Rows 2 through 101 in the Emp ID column are selected.
3. Click the **Home** tab on the Ribbon, if necessary, and then click the **Conditional Formatting** button in the Styles group.
4. Point to **Highlight Cells Rules**, and then click **Duplicate Values**. The Duplicate Values dialog box opens.
5. Click the **values with** arrow to display a list of formatting options, and then click **Custom Format** to create a format that is not in the list. The Format Cells dialog box opens. You'll change the background fill color to red.
6. Click the **Fill** tab, and then, in the Background Color palette, click **red** (the second color in the last row).
7. Click the **OK** button in the Format Cells dialog box, and then click the **OK** button in the Duplicate Values dialog box. Any duplicate values in the ID column appear in a red cell.
8. Scroll the table to ensure that no duplicate values are found.

After you enter a formula, you should test all situations to verify how the formula performs in each case. In this case, you should test the column both with duplicate values and without duplicate values. No duplicate records appear in the Employee table, so you'll change the ID of the last record from 1123 to 1024, which is the ID of the first employee. The backgrounds of the cells with the duplicate IDs should turn red, which will confirm that the conditional formatting is working as intended. Then, you will return the ID to its original value and confirm that the duplicate value highlighting disappears.

### To test the duplicate value conditional formatting:

1. Click in the **Name** box, and then enter **A101**. The active cell moves to the last record in the Employee table.
2. In cell A101, enter **1024**. The ID changes from 1123 to 1024 and cell A101 is filled with a red background because it contains a duplicate ID. See Figure 7-33.

**Figure 7-33** **Duplicate record highlighted**

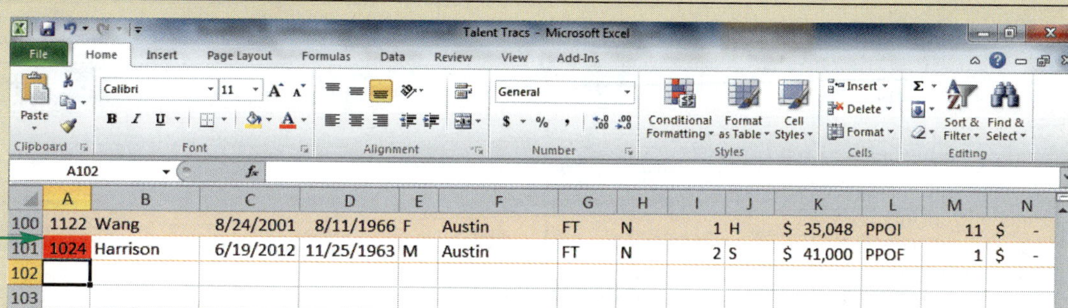


duplicate value is highlighted in red

3. Press the **Ctrl+Home** keys. Cell A1 becomes the active cell. Cell A2 has a red background fill because it has the same ID that you entered in cell A101. The conditional formatting correctly identified the duplicate values.

## Using the Conditional Formatting Rules Manager

Each time you apply a conditional format, you are defining a conditional formatting rule. A rule specifies the type of condition (such as formatting cells greater than a specified value), the type of formatting when that condition occurs (such as light red fill with dark red text), and the cell or range the formatting is applied to. You can edit existing conditional formatting rules from the Conditional Formatting Rules Manager dialog box.

REFERENCE

### *Editing a Conditional Formatting Rule*

- Select the range with the conditional formatting you want to edit.
- In the Styles group on the Home tab, click the Conditional Formatting button, and then click Manage Rules.
- Select the rule you want to edit, and then click the Edit Rule button.
- In the Select a Rule Type box, click a rule type, and then make the appropriate changes in the Edit the Rule Description section.
- Click the OK button in each dialog box.

The red background fill makes the cell content difficult to read. Rita asks you to use a yellow fill color to better contrast with the black text. You'll use the Conditional Formatting Rules Manager dialog box to edit the rule that specifies the formatting applied to duplicate values in the ID column.

### To change the duplicate values background fill color:

1. In the Styles group on the Home tab, click the **Conditional Formatting** button, and then click **Manage Rules**. The Conditional Formatting Rules Manager dialog box opens, listing all the formatting rules for the current selection, which, in this case, is the Employee table.
2. Verify that the Show formatting rules for box shows **This Table**. All the rules currently in effect in the Employee table are displayed. You can add new rules and edit or delete existing rules. You also can control which formatting rules are displayed in the dialog box, such as all rules in a specific worksheet or table. See Figure 7-34.

Figure 7-34 **Conditional Formatting Rules Manager dialog box**

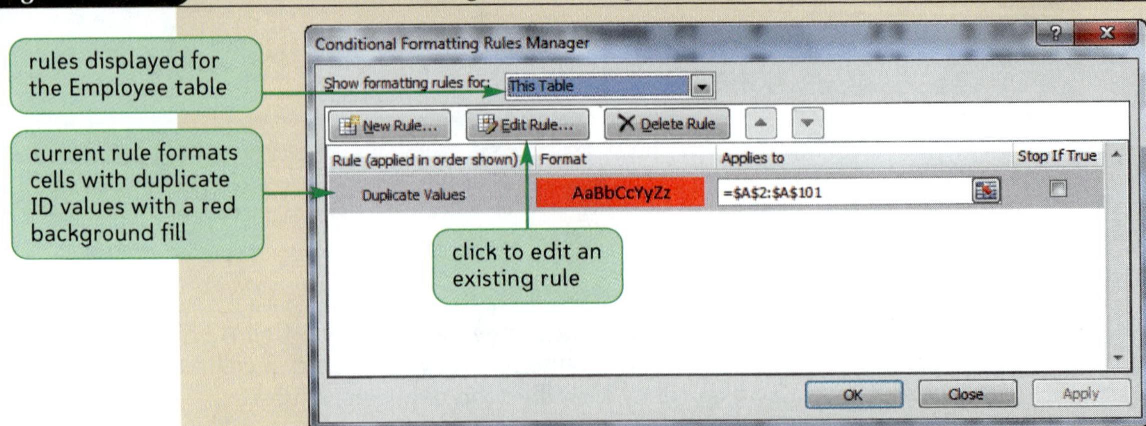

3. Click **Duplicate Values** in the Rule list to select the rule, and then click the **Edit Rule** button. The Edit Formatting Rule dialog box opens. See Figure 7-35.

**Figure 7-35 Edit Formatting Rule dialog box**

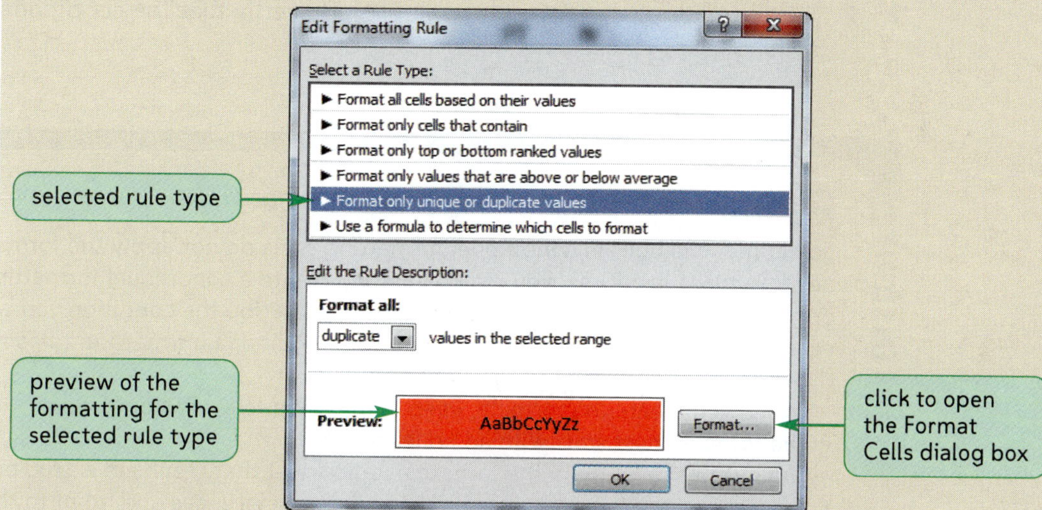


**TIP**

You can filter a table by color. Display the filter arrows, click a filter arrow, point to Filter by Color, and then click a color to display only cells with that fill or click No Fill to display only cells without a fill.

4. Click the **Format** button. The Format Cells dialog box opens.
5. Click the **Fill** tab, if necessary, and then, in the Background Color palette, click **yellow** (the fourth color in the last row).
6. Click the **OK** button in each dialog box. The duplicate records in the table are formatted with a yellow background color. See Figure 7-36.

**Figure 7-36 Revised conditional formatting for duplicate records**

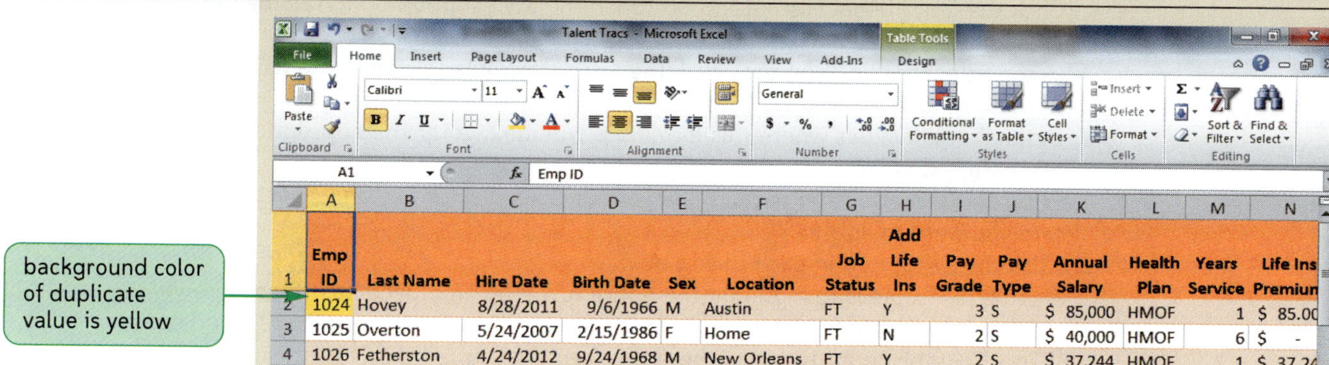


The cell text is easier to read on the yellow background. You'll correct the duplicate ID in cell A101 by entering the employee's actual ID number. The conditional format will remain active, and apply to any new records that Rita adds to the Employee table. Keep in mind that the Duplicate Values rule enables you to verify that each entry in the ID column is unique, but it does not ensure that each unique value is accurate.

**To correct the duplicate ID:**

1. Make cell **A101** the active cell, and then enter **1123**. The employee's ID is updated and the conditional formatting disappears because the value in the ID column is no longer a duplicate.
2. Scroll to the top of the Employee table, and verify that the conditional formatting no longer appears in cell A2.

INSIGHT

*Creating a Formula to Conditionally Format Cells*

Sometimes the built-in conditional formatting rules do not apply the formatting you need. In these instances, you may be able to create a conditional formatting rule based on a formula that uses a logical expression to describe the condition you want. For example, you can create a formula that uses conditional formatting to compare cells in different columns or to highlight an entire row.

When you create the formula, keep in mind the following guidelines:

- The formula must start with an equal sign.
- The formula must be in the form of a logical test that results in a True or False value.
- In most cases, the formula should use relative references and point to the first row of data in the table. If the formula references a cell or range outside the table, use an absolute reference.
- After you create the formula, enter test values to ensure the conditional formatting works in all situations that you intended.

For example, to use conditional formatting to highlight whether the hire date entered in column C is less than the birth date entered in column D, you need to enter a formula that applies conditional formatting that compares cells in different columns of a table. The following steps describe how to create this formula:

1. Select the range you want to format (in this case, the Hire Date column).
2. Click the Conditional Formatting button in the Styles group on the Home tab, and then click New Rule.
3. In the Select a Rule Type box, click the "Use a formula to determine which cells to format" rule.
4. In the Format values where this formula is true box, enter the appropriate formula (in this case, =C2<D2).
5. Click the Format button to open the Format Cells dialog box, and select the formatting you want to apply.
6. Click the OK button in each dialog box.

Another example is to highlight the entire row if an employee has 10 or more years of service. In this case, you would select the range of data, such as A2:S101, and enter =M$2>=10 in the Format values where this formula is true box. The other steps remain the same.

## Summarizing Data Conditionally

The COUNT function tallies the number of data values in a range, the SUM function adds the values in a range, and the AVERAGE function calculates the average of the values in a range. However, sometimes you need to calculate a conditional count, sum, or average using only those cells that meet a particular condition. In those cases, you need to use the COUNTIF, SUMIF, and AVERAGEIF functions. Rita wants you to create a report that shows the number, total, and average salaries for employees in Austin, New Orleans, and Nashville as well as for those employees who work from home.

## Using the COUNTIF Function

You can calculate the number of cells in a range that match criteria you specify using the COUNTIF function, which is sometimes referred to as a **conditional count**. The COUNTIF function has the syntax

```
COUNTIF(range, criteria)
```

where *range* is the range of cells you want to count, and *criteria* is an expression that defines which cells to count.

Rita wants to know how many employees are located in Austin. You can use the COUNTIF function to find this answer because you want a conditional count (a count of employees who meet a specified criterion; in this case, employees located in Austin). The location information is stored in column F of the Employee table. To count the number of employees in Austin, you can use either one of the following formulas:

**TIP**

You can use structured references or cell and range addresses to reference cells within an Excel table. If an Excel table has not been created for a range of data, you must use cell and range addresses.

**Cell references** `=COUNTIF('Employee Data'!F2:F101,"Austin")`

**Fully qualified structured references** `=COUNTIF(Employee[Location],"Austin")`

With either formula, Excel counts all the cells in the Location column of the Employee table that contain the text "Austin". Because Austin is text, you must enclose it within quotation marks. Numbers are not enclosed in quotation marks.

You will enter this formula using the COUNTIF function in the Employee Summary worksheet. You will use the Insert Function dialog box to help you build the formula using worksheet and range references to calculate the number of employees who work in Austin.

### To count employees located in Austin:

1. Switch to the **Employee Summary** worksheet.
2. Click cell **C4**, and then click the **Insert Function** button in the formula bar. The Insert Function dialog box opens.
3. Click the **Or select a category** arrow, and then click **Statistical**.
4. In the Select a function box, double-click **COUNTIF**. The Function Arguments dialog box opens.
5. In the Range box, type **'Employee Data'!F2:F101** to enter the range to search, and then press the **Tab** key. The range 'Employee Data'!F2:F101 refers to all data values in the range F2:F101 (Location column) in the Employee Data worksheet.
6. In the Criteria box, type **B4**. Cell B4 contains "Austin," which is the criterion you want Excel to use to determine which employee records to count. See Figure 7-37.

**Figure 7-37** Function Arguments dialog box for the COUNTIF function

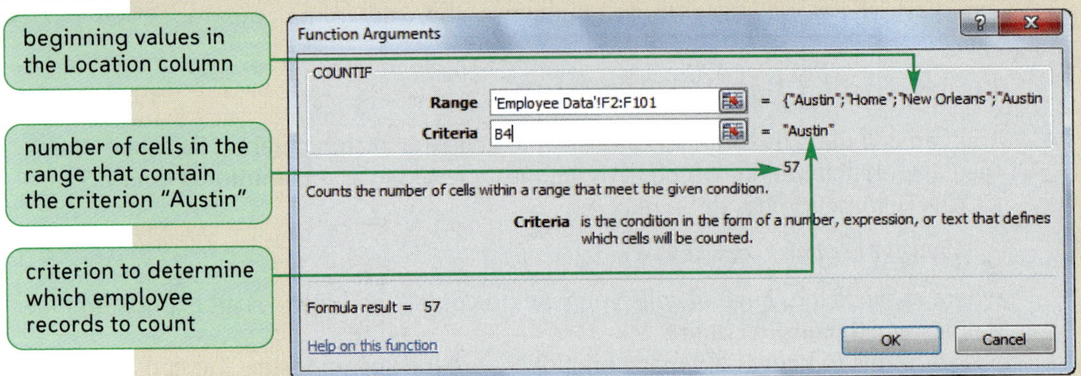


7. Click the **OK** button. Cell C4 remains active. The formula =COUNTIF('Employee Data'!F2:F101,B4) appears in the formula bar and 57 appears in cell C4, indicating that the company employs 57 workers in Austin. See Figure 7-38.

**Figure 7-38** Location Analysis with Austin workers

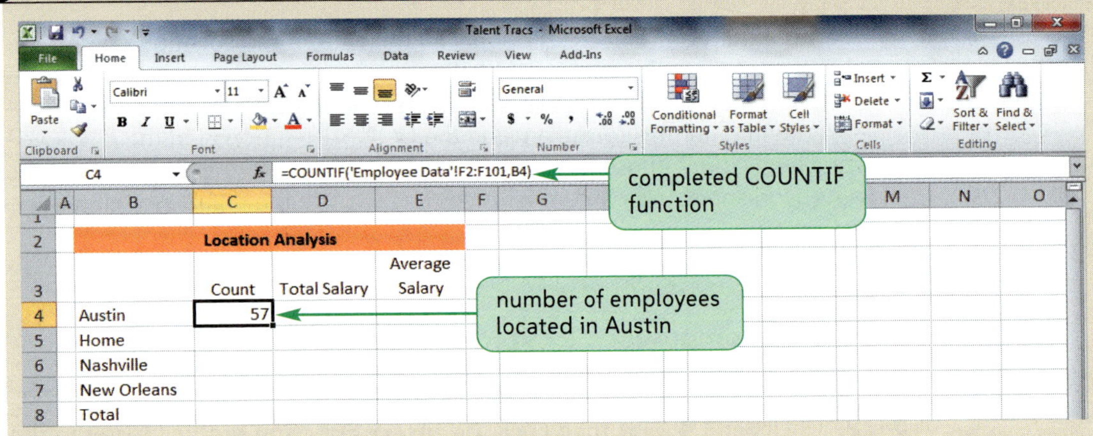


You will enter a similar formula to calculate the number of employees who work from home. This time, however, you will use structured references to specify the range to search.

### To count the number of employees who work from home:

1. Click cell **C5**, and then click the **Insert Function** button *fx* in the formula bar. The Insert Function dialog box opens with the Statistical category still selected.
2. In the Select a function box, double-click **COUNTIF**. The Function Arguments dialog box opens.
3. In the Range box, type **Employee[Location]** to enter the range to search, and then press the **Tab** key. The range Employee[Location] is a structured reference that refers to all data values in the Location column in the Employee table (range F2:F101). The beginning values in the Location column appear to the right of the Range box.

4. In the Criteria box, type **B5**. Cell B5 contains "Home" (the value shown to the right of the Criteria box), which is the criterion Excel will use to determine which employee records to count.
5. Click the **OK** button. Cell C5 remains active. The formula =COUNTIF(Employee[Location],B5) appears in the formula bar and 7 appears in cell C5, indicating 7 employees work from home.

You need to count employees at two other locations—Nashville and New Orleans. Rather than enter the COUNTIF formula, you'll copy the formula in cell C5 to cells C6 and C7.

**To copy the COUNTIF formula:**

1. Copy the formula in cell **C5** to cell **C6** and cell **C7** to calculate the number of employees for Nashville (cell B6) and New Orleans (cell B7). Talent Tracs has 21 employees working in Nashville and 15 employees working in New Orleans.
2. In cell C8, enter the **SUM** function to calculate the total number of employees working at Talent Tracs. Talent Tracs has a total of 100 employees.

## Using the SUMIF Function

The SUMIF function adds the values in a range that meet criteria you specify. The SUMIF function is also called a **conditional sum**. The syntax of the SUMIF function is

SUMIF(*range*, *criteria* [, *sum_range*])

where *range* is the range of cells you want to filter before calculating a sum, *criteria* is the condition used to filter the range, and *sum_range* is the range of cells to total. The *sum_range* is optional; if you omit it, Excel will total the values specified in the *range* argument. For example, if you want to total the salaries for all employees with salaries greater than $50,000, you do not use the optional third argument.

Rita wants to know the total salaries paid to employees at each location. She can use the SUMIF function to do this, because she wants to conditionally add salaries of employees at a specified location. Location is recorded in column F of the Employee Data worksheet, and the salary data is stored in column K. You can use either of the following formulas to calculate this value:

**Cell references**

```
=SUMIF('Employee Data'!F2:F101,"Austin", 'Employee Data'!K2:K101)
```

**Fully qualified structured references**

```
=SUMIF(Employee[Location],"Austin",Employee[Annual Salary])
```

Both of these formulas state that the salary of any employee whose location is Austin will be added to the total. Using the SUMIF function, you will insert the formula with structured references into the Employee Summary worksheet.

**To sum employee salaries in different locations:**

1. Click cell **D4**, and then click the **Insert Function** button *fx* in the formula bar. The Insert Function dialog box opens.
2. Click the **Or select a category** arrow, and then click **Math & Trig**.

3. In the Select a function box, double-click **SUMIF**. The Function Arguments dialog box opens.
4. In the Range box, type **Employee[Location]** to specify the range of data to filter, and then press the **Tab** key. The range Employee[Location] is a structured reference that refers to all data values in the Location column in the Employee table (range F2:F101).
5. In the Criteria box, type **B4** and then press the **Tab** key. Cell B4 contains "Austin" (shown to the right of the Criteria box), which is the criterion Excel will use to determine which employee records to sum.
6. In the Sum_range box, type the structured reference **Employee[Annual Salary]** to indicate that the Annual Salary column in the Employee table contains the data to sum in the filtered rows. The values to the right of the Sum_range box are the amounts in the filtered Annual Salary column. See Figure 7-39.

**Figure 7-39 Function Arguments dialog box for the SUMIF function**

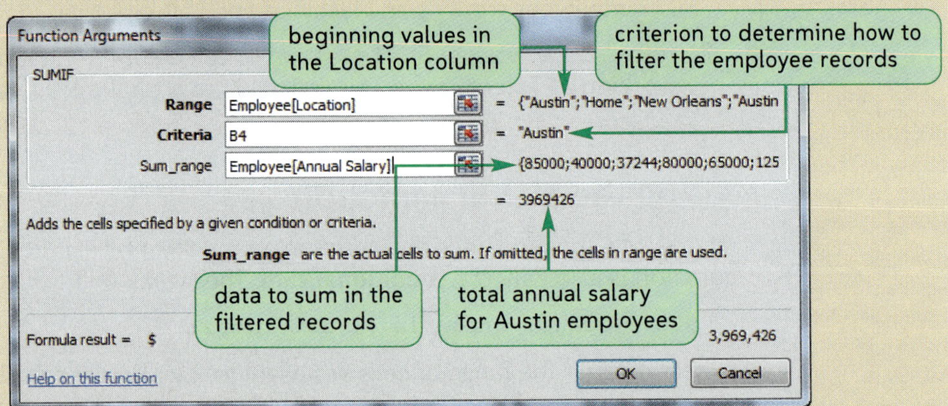


7. Click the **OK** button. Cell D4 is active. The formula =SUMIF(Employee[Location], B4,Employee[Annual Salary]) appears in the formula bar and $3,969,426 appears in cell D4, indicating the total annual salaries paid to Austin employees.
8. Copy the SUMIF formula in cell D4 to the range **D5:D7**. The total annual salary for employees working from home is $236,313. The total annual salary for Nashville employees is $587,833. The total annual salary for New Orleans employees is $1,570,994.
9. In cell D8, enter a SUM function to calculate the total salaries of all employees. The total salary of all Talent Tracs employees is $6,364,566.

## Using the AVERAGEIF Function

The AVERAGEIF function is similar to the SUMIF function. You use the AVERAGEIF function to calculate the average of values in a range that meet criteria you specify. The syntax of the AVERAGEIF function is

```
AVERAGEIF(range, criteria [, average_range])
```

where *range* is the range of cells you want to filter before calculating the average, *criteria* is the condition used to filter the range, and *average_range* is the range of cells to average. The *average_range* is optional; if you omit it, Excel will average the values specified in the *range* argument.

Rita wants to know the average salaries paid to employees at each location. Location is recorded in column F of the Employee Data worksheet, and the annual salary data is stored in column K. The formula to calculate this value is:

**Cell references**

```
=AVERAGEIF('Employee Data'!F2:F101,"Austin", 'Employee Data'!K2:K101)
```

**Fully qualified structured references**

```
=AVERAGEIF(Employee[Location],"Austin",Employee[Annual Salary])
```

Both of these formulas state that the annual salary of any employee whose location is Austin will be included in the average. You will enter the formula using the AVERAGEIF function with structured references into the Employee Summary worksheet.

## To average employee salaries in different locations:

1. Click cell **E4**, and then click the **Insert Function** button in the formula bar. The Insert Function dialog box opens.
2. Click the **Or select a category** arrow, and then click **Statistical.**
3. In the Select a function box, double-click **AVERAGEIF**. The Function Arguments dialog box opens.
4. In the Range box, type the structured reference **Employee[Location]** to specify the range of data to filter, and then press the **Tab** key. The range Employee[Location] is a structured reference that refers to all data values in the Location column in the Employee table (range F2:F101).
5. In the Criteria box, type **B4** and then press the **Tab** key. Cell B4 contains "Austin" (shown to the right of the Criteria box), which is the criterion Excel will use to determine which employee records to average.
6. In the Average_range box, type **Employee[Annual Salary]** to indicate that the Annual Salary column in the Employee table contains the data to average in the filtered rows. See Figure 7-40.

**Figure 7-40** Function Arguments dialog box for the AVERAGEIF function

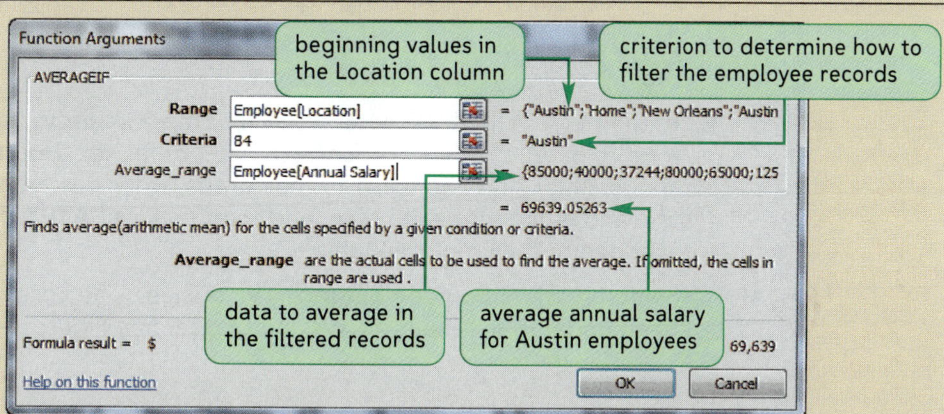


7. Click the **OK** button. Cell E4 remains active. The formula =AVERAGEIF(Employee [Location],B4,Employee[Annual Salary]) appears in the formula bar and $69,639 appears in cell E4, indicating the average salary paid to Austin employees.
8. Copy the formula in cell E4 to the range **E5:E7**. Talent Tracs pays an average of $33,759 to employees working at home, $27,992 to employees working in Nashville, and $104,733 to employees working in New Orleans.

9. In cell E8, enter **=D8/C8** to calculate the average salary at Talent Tracs by dividing the total salaries at Talent Tracs by the number of employees at the company. The average salary for all Talent Tracs employees is $63,646.
10. If necessary, format the range E4:E8 in the **Accounting** number format with no decimal places.
11. Add a bottom border to the range C7:E7, and then click cell **E4** to deselect the range. See Figure 7-41.

**Figure 7-41** Completed Location Analysis report

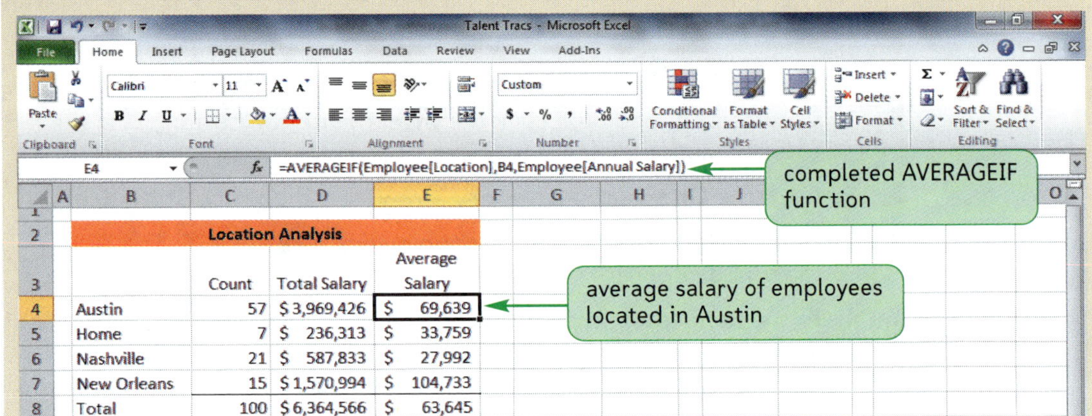


As Rita enters new employees or edits the location or annual salary values of current employees, the values in the Employee Summary worksheet will be automatically updated because the formulas reference the Employee table.

Rita has recently hired a new employee and asks you to add the new record to the Excel table.

## To add a record to the Employee table:

1. Switch to the **Employee Data** worksheet, and then click cell **A102**. You will enter the new employee record in this row.
2. In the range A102:L102 enter **1124** for Emp ID, **Joplin** for last name, **4/1/2013** for hire date, **11/15/1970** for birth date, **M** for sex, **Home** for location, **PT** for job status, **N** for Add Life Ins, **1** for pay grade, **H** for pay type, **23000** for annual salary, and **None** for health plan, and then click cell **A103**. The new employee record is added to the Employee table.
3. Switch to the **Employee Summary** worksheet. The Location Analysis report has been updated to reflect the new employee. See Figure 7-42.

**Figure 7-42** **Updated Location Analysis report**

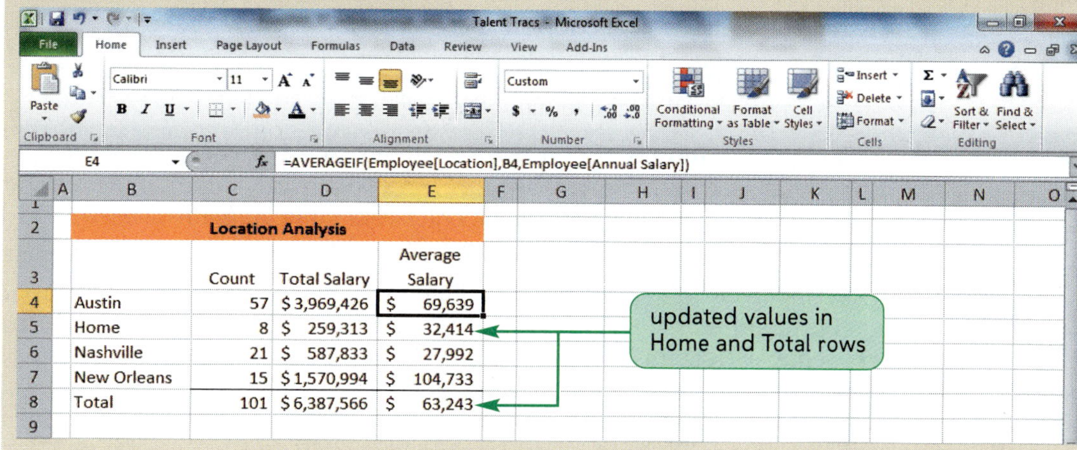


If the employee data had been stored as a range of data instead of an Excel table, the Location Analysis report would not have been automatically updated. Instead, you would have had to modify all the formulas in the report to reflect the expanded range of employee data. Rita is pleased with the formulas you added to the Employee Data and Employee Summary worksheets.

REVIEW

## *Session 7.3 Quick Check*

1. Would you apply the duplicate value conditional formatting rule to a table column of last names? Why or why not?
2. If you receive a worksheet that includes conditional formatting, which dialog box would you use to find out what criteria were used for the formatting?
3. Explain what the formula =COUNTIF(Employee[Sex],"F") calculates.
4. Explain what the formula =AVERAGEIF(Employee[Pay Type],"H",Employee [Annual Salary]) calculates.
5. Explain what the formula =SUMIF(Employee[Job Status],"FT",Employee[Annual Salary]) calculates.
6. Explain what the formula =COUNTIF(Employee[Annual Salary],">100000") calculates.
7. True or False. To display the number of females working from home, you could use the COUNTIF function.
8. True or False. Applying the duplicate value conditional formatting rule deletes the duplicate record.

*Practice the skills you learned in the tutorial using the same case scenario.*

PRACTICE

## Review Assignments

### Data File needed for the Review Assignments: Tracs.xlsx

Rita wants you to try some alternative calculations for bonuses and benefits for the Talent Tracs employees. Complete the following:

1. Open the **Tracs** workbook located in the Excel7\Review folder included with your Data Files, save the workbook as **Tracs Employees** in the same folder, and then, in the Documentation worksheet, enter your name and the date.
2. Go to the Employee Data worksheet, and then rename the Excel table as **EmpData**.
3. Employees who elect additional life insurance coverage (Add Life Ins) pay 0.1 percent times their annual salary. The life insurance premium rate of 0.1 percent is entered in cell Y5. Employees who do not elect additional coverage pay nothing. In the Life Ins Premium column, enter an IF function to calculate the life insurance premiums; use a reference to cell **Y5** to obtain the life insurance rate and enter **0** for employees who do not elect coverage.
4. All full-time (Job Status) employees over the age of 30 (Age) are eligible for the 401(k) benefit. In the 401(k) column, enter the IF and AND functions to calculate the 401(k) benefit as 3 percent of annual salary; use a reference to cell **Y6** to obtain the 401(k) matching percent rate (3 percent). If the employee is not eligible, enter **0**.
5. All employees with one or more years of service (Years Service) are eligible for a bonus. Pay Grade 1 employees receive $3,000 (cell Y2), Pay Grade 2 employees receive $6,000 (cell Y3), and Pay Grade 3 employees receive $8,000 (cell Y4). In the Bonus column, enter nested IF functions to calculate the bonus. For employees not eligible for a bonus, display the label **NE**.
6. In the Salary Increase column, enter IF and OR functions to insert the text **Not Eligible** if the individual's job status is a consultant (CN) or the pay grade is 4. Leave the cell blank if the individual is eligible for a salary increase.
7. In the Health Cost column, enter the HLOOKUP function to do an exact match lookup to calculate the health plan cost. The layout of HealthPlanRates data ($B$2:$F$3) in the Lookup Tables worksheet has been revised to work with the HLOOKUP function. Use the range address reference in the HLOOKUP function to reference HealthPlanRates data.
8. In the Award column, modify the VLOOKUP function to incorporate the IFERROR function and display the message **Invalid hire date**. Test the modified formula by changing the date in cell C2 from 3/13/2008 to **13/13/2008**. Increase the column width to view the entire message.
9. In the Emp ID column, change the format color of the duplicate value conditional formatting rule to Green (the sixth color in the last row of the Background Color palette) using the Conditional Formatting Rules Manager dialog box.
10. Go to the Reports worksheet, and then enter the COUNTIF function in cells C4 and C5 to count the number of female and male employees.
11. In cells D4 and D5, enter the AVERAGEIF function to calculate the average salary of female employees and the average salary of male employees.
12. Save and close the workbook. Submit the finished workbook to your instructor, either in printed or electronic form, as requested.

*Apply the skills you learned to analyze and summarize sales data.*

APPLY

## Case Problem 1

### Data File needed for this Case Problem: Modem.xlsx

***PC-Market Distribution*** Linda Klaussen works for PC-Market Distribution, a computer supply store. She needs your help with designing an Excel workbook to enter purchase order information. She has already entered the product information on PC-Market's line of modems. She wants you to insert a lookup function to look up data from the product table. The company also offers three shipping options—Standard, Express, and Overnight—that vary in price. She wants the purchase order worksheet to be able to calculate the total cost of the order, including the type of shipping the customer requests. Complete the following:

1. Open the **Modem** workbook located in the Excel7\Case1 folder included with your Data Files, save the workbook as **PC Modem** in the same folder, and then, in the Documentation worksheet, enter your name and the date.
2. Go to the Purchase Order worksheet. In cell B5, enter the Product ID **1050**. In cell C7, create a lookup function to display the product type. In cell C8, create a lookup function to display the model name. In cell C9, create a lookup function to display the price. Product information is displayed in the Product List worksheet.
3. If an incorrect Product ID is entered in cell B5, cells C7, C8, and C9 will display the #N/A error value. Modify the formula in these cells so that **Product ID not found** is displayed in the cell if the ID entered is not found.
4. In the range D40:E42, enter labels and shipping costs based on the following information: **Standard**, **$9.50**; **Express**, **$14.50**; and **Overnight**, **$18.50**. In cell B15, enter **Express**.
5. In cell C17, use nested IF functions to display the shipping costs for the option entered in cell B15. If the shipping option in cell B15 is blank, then cell C17 should be blank. (*Hint*: The IF functions should reference the cells in the range D40:E42.)
6. In cell C19, enter a formula to display the total cost of the product (price times quantity) plus shipping. In cell B12, enter **4**.
7. In cell C19, modify the formula so that if the cell equals an error value (#Value!), the message **Check Product ID, Quantity, or Shipping option** is displayed.
8. Go to the Product List worksheet, and then use conditional formatting to highlight all duplicate values in the ID column with the formatting you choose. To test that conditional formatting is working, temporarily change the Product ID in cell A119 to **1121**. When the test is completed, return the value in cell A119 to **1122**.
9. In the Product List worksheet, use conditional formatting to highlight all prices above $300 with the formatting you choose.
10. Go to the Summary worksheet, and then enter appropriate functions in the range B5:C7 to determine the average modem price and count for each modem type.
11. Save and close the workbook. Submit the finished workbook to your instructor, either in printed or electronic form, as requested.

*Apply the skills you learned to track employee vacation and family leave.*

APPLY

## Case Problem 2

### Data File needed for this Case Problem: Leave.xlsx

***Town of Baltic Administrative Office*** Alan Welton, HR Generalist at the Town of Baltic Administrative Office in Baltic, Indiana, wants to create a workbook that tracks the amount of vacation time and family leave used by each employee of the town. The workbook needs to calculate how much vacation and family leave each employee is eligible for. Then it should subtract the time already used from that amount. It should also calculate the total number of vacation and family leave days used by all employees, as well as the total number of days remaining. The eligibility requirements for the different vacation and family leave plans are as follows:

For vacation:

- 15 days for full-time employees
- 10 days for part-time employees
- 0 days for everyone else

For family leave:

- 5 days for full-time employees who have worked 1 or more years
- 0 days for everyone else

Use these eligibility requirements to calculate the available vacation and family leave time for each employee. Complete the following:

1. Open the **Leave** workbook located in the Excel7\Case2 folder included with your Data Files, save the workbook as **Baltic Leave** in the same folder, and then, in the Documentation worksheet, enter your name and the date.
2. Go to the LeaveData worksheet. Create an Excel table in the range A5:J107, name the Excel table **Leave**, and then remove the filter arrows. Set the column width for columns B through J to **10**.
3. In column D, enter a formula to calculate Years Employed. Use the Date Hired cell and the current date (assume 7/1/2013, which is stored in cell Z6), and express the length of time employed in years. (*Hint*: Use the formula **(current date–Date Hired)/365**.)
4. In column E, enter a formula using a nested IF function to determine the number of vacation days (based on the vacation rules above) each employee is eligible for based on the employee's job status in column B.
5. In column G, enter a formula to subtract the amount of vacation used from the available vacation time, which displays the remaining vacation time for each employee.
6. In column H, enter a formula to determine each employee's total family leave time (based on the Family leave rules above).
7. In column J, enter a formula to subtract used family leave from the total family leave to determine the remaining family leave available for each employee.
8. In column J, apply conditional formatting that highlights the remaining family leave of any employee who has not used any family leave days. You decide the formatting.
9. Go to the Leave Summary worksheet. In the range C4:C6, use a function to count the total number of employees eligible for each vacation plan. (*Hint*: Any employee who is eligible for 15 vacation days will have the value 15 in column E of the LeaveData worksheet.)
10. In the range D4:D6, use functions to calculate the total number of vacation days for each vacation plan.
11. In the range E4:E6, use functions to calculate the total vacation days remaining for each vacation plan.
12. In the range C7:E7, calculate totals for Number Eligible, Total Days, and Days Remaining.
13. Save and close the workbook. Submit the finished workbook to your instructor, either in printed or electronic form, as requested.

*Create reports for a water company that determine different billing plans.*

CHALLENGE

## Case Problem 3

### Data File needed for this Case Problem: M-Fresh.xlsx

***M-Fresh Water Company*** M-Fresh Water Company is a small independent water company in Miami, Oklahoma, that provides water to commercial customers throughout the region, delivering the water supply through pipelines, on-demand storage tanks, and bottles. Customers of M-Fresh Water range from government offices to nonprofit organizations to commercial retail shops and markets. Town regulations tax the latter group of commercial customers based on their usage, whereas nonprofit and government offices are not taxed. Furthermore, M-Fresh Water will occasionally waive a water bill based on its charitable-giving policy. Dawes Cado is in charge of the billing system that must take into account these business rules and assure accurate and on-time billing, which occurs quarterly. Complete the following:

1. Open the **M-Fresh** workbook located in the Excel7\Case3 folder included with your Data Files, save the workbook as **Water Bill** in the same folder, and then, in the Documentation worksheet, enter your name and the date.
2. In the Quarterly Data worksheet, create an Excel table for the range A1:F73, and name the table **WaterData**. Remove the filter arrows. Format the data in the Gal Used column with the Comma Style number format and no decimal places.
3. Add a column named **Gal Billed** to the table, and then enter a formula to calculate the number of gallons billed based on the following rules: If a customer's bill is waived (Bill Waived column) or the number of gallons used is less than 25,000 (Gal Used column), display **0** in Gal Billed column; otherwise, display the value from the Gal Used column in the Gal Billed column.
4. Add a column named **Water Bill** to the table, and then enter a formula to calculate the water bill based on the following rules: The billing rate varies based on the type of customer (Cust Type column). The billing rate is $3, $2, or $1.50 per *thousand* gallons billed, depending on the customer type (see the lookup table in cells B2:C5 of the Billing Rate worksheet). For example, a commercial customer using 75,000 gallons has a water bill of $225 (75 X $3), whereas a government customer using 100,000 gallons pays $150 (100 X $1.50). A commercial customer using 15,000 gallons has a water bill of $0 (see Gal Used rule in question 3).
5. Add a column named **Tax** to the table, and then enter a formula to calculate the tax based on the following rule: If a customer pays tax (Taxable column), then multiply the Water Bill by 3.5 percent; otherwise, the tax is 0. The tax rate is stored in cell T1.
6. Add a column named **Total Bill** to the table, and then enter a formula to calculate the bill amount by adding the Water Bill column and the Tax column.
7. Improve the formatting of the number fields in the WaterData table.
8. Make a copy of the Quarterly Data worksheet, rename the copied worksheet as **Q2-Q8**, and then add a Totals row to the Excel table displaying totals for the Gal Used, Gal Billed, Tax, and Total Bill columns.

EXPLORE

9. Make another copy of the Quarterly Data worksheet, rename the copied worksheet as **Q9**, and then use conditional formatting to highlight the top 15 percent of the Total Bill amounts with a yellow background color. Filter the table so that only the top 15 percent are displayed. Sort the filtered table by largest to smallest.
10. Insert a new worksheet, rename the worksheet as **Billing Summary**, and then create the report shown in Figure 7-43, using COUNTIF, AVERAGEIF, and SUMIF functions to prepare the report.

**Figure 7-43** **Water usage and billing by customer type**

| | A | B | C | D | E |
|---|---|---|---|---|---|
| 1 | | | | | |
| 2 | | | | | |
| 3 | | | | | |
| 4 | | | | | |
| 5 | | **Customer Type** | **Nbr Customers** | **Avg Gallons Used** | **Total Billed** |
| 6 | | Commercial | 37 | 322,437 | $37,043.12 |
| 7 | | Nonprofit | 11 | 87,661 | $ 224.18 |
| 8 | | Government | 24 | 774,532 | $27,901.44 |
| 9 | | Total | 72 | 437,267 | $65,168.74 |

**EXPLORE** 11. Make another copy of the Quarterly Data worksheet, and then rename the copied worksheet as **Q11**. Add a custom filter to the table to display only those organizations that have "church" or "center" as part of the customer name.

**EXPLORE** 12. Make another copy of the Quarterly Data worksheet, and then rename the copied worksheet as **Q12**. Use the lookup table in cells E2:H3 of the Billing Rate worksheet and the HLOOKUP function to modify the formula to calculate the Water Bill column (column H).

13. Save and close the workbook. Submit the finished workbook to your instructor, either in printed or electronic form, as requested.

*Create a worksheet that compiles and summarizes reports for a newspaper.*

CREATE

## Case Problem 4

### Data File needed for this Case Problem: Rock Island.xlsx

***Rock Island Home Sales*** Tim Derkson is a reporter for *Rock Island Times*, a newspaper in Rock Island, Illinois. He is compiling a quarterly real estate sales analysis for his newspaper. He obtained data on home sales from the local real estate association and county records. He wants to create a worksheet that will display summary information on the home sales in Rock Island. Tim has already set up and formatted the workbook, but he wants you to insert the correct formulas. Tim stored the housing data in the Home Sales Data worksheet. He wants to use the Home Summary worksheet to search for information about the homes. Complete the following:

1. Open the **Rock Island** workbook located in the Excel7\Case4 folder included with your Data Files, save the workbook as **Home Sales** in the same folder, and then, in the Documentation worksheet, enter your name and the date.
2. In the Home Sales Data worksheet, create an Excel table in the range A1:K118. Remove the filter arrows. Rename the Excel table as **SalesData**.
3. In column L, add a calculated column named **Days on Market**, and then enter a formula to verify that the date sold occurs after the date listed. If it does not, display the message **Check Dates**; otherwise, calculate the number of days on the market. (*Hint*: You might need to format this column in the General number format.)
4. An incentive bonus of $1,000 is awarded if the sales price is above the asking price or the number of days on the market is less than 25 days. In column M, add a calculated column named **Incentive**, and then enter a formula to calculate the bonus amount.
5. Use conditional formatting to highlight records in the Days on Market column where the house was on the market for 300 or more days.
6. Display the Total row in the SalesData table. In this row, display a count of homes sold (place in Listing ID), average asking price, average taxes, average sales price, and average days on the market.

7. Split the Home Sales Data worksheet so that the top pane shows rows in the SalesData table and the bottom pane displays the Total row.
8. Insert a new worksheet, and then rename it as **Sales Summary**. Create a report on home sales based on the style sold and the average sales price, as shown in Figure 7-44.

**Figure 7-44** **Home sales by type of home**

| | A | B | C | D |
|---|---|---|---|---|
| 1 | | Rock Island Home Sales | | |
| 2 | | Overall Data | | |
| 3 | | | | |
| 4 | | By Style of Home | | |
| 5 | | | | |
| 6 | | Style | Number Sold | Average Sales Price |
| 7 | | Condo | 23 | $ 90,347.83 |
| 8 | | Ranch | 46 | $ 91,842.39 |
| 9 | | Victorian | 48 | $ 113,567.71 |
| 10 | | Total | 117 | $ 100,461.54 |
| 11 | | | | |

EXPLORE 9. Create a PivotTable report with the information shown in Figure 7-45. Rename the worksheet as **DaysOnMarket**.

**Figure 7-45** **Days on Market PivotTable report**

| | A | B | C |
|---|---|---|---|
| 1 | Days on Market | | |
| 2 | | | |
| 3 | | | |
| 4 | | Values | |
| 5 | Days | Number Sold | Average Sales Price |
| 6 | 1-100 | 31 | $ 94,452 |
| 7 | 101-200 | 27 | $ 106,880 |
| 8 | 201-300 | 37 | $ 103,939 |
| 9 | 301-400 | 22 | $ 95,205 |
| 10 | Grand Total | 117 | $ 100,462 |
| 11 | | | |

EXPLORE 10. Make a copy of the Home Sales Data worksheet, and then rename the worksheet as **Q10**. Remove the current conditional formatting, and then add conditional formatting to highlight records in the Sales Price column where the sales price was above the asking price. Use appropriate formatting. (*Hint*: Create a new rule by selecting the Use formula to determine which cells to format rule type, and then editing the rule description to enter a formula with a conditional statement that compares the first data row between the two columns of interest.)

11. Save and close the workbook. Submit the finished workbook to your instructor, either in printed or electronic form, as requested.

ASSESS

## SAM: Skills Assessment Manager

For current SAM information, including versions and content details, visit SAM Central (http://samcentral.course.com). If you have a SAM user profile, you may have access to hands-on instruction, practice, and assessment of the skills covered in this tutorial. Since various versions of SAM are supported throughout the life of this text, check with your instructor for the correct instructions and URL/Web site for accessing assignments.

### ENDING DATA FILES

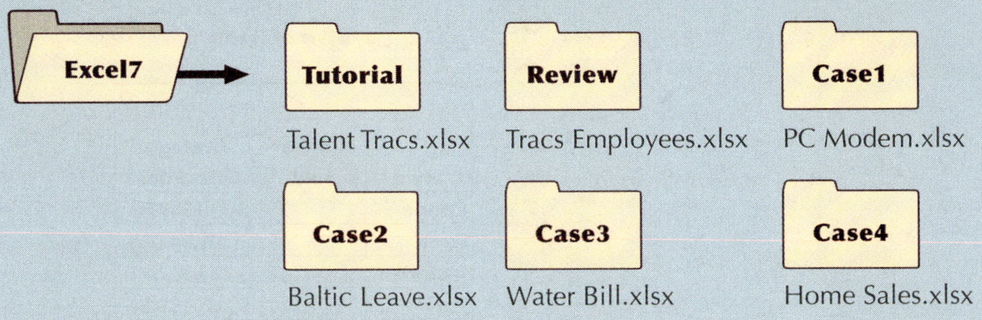

TUTORIAL 8

# Developing an Excel Application

*Creating an Invoice*

## OBJECTIVES

**Session 8.1**
- Create an application
- Create, edit, and delete defined names for cells and ranges
- Paste a list of defined names as documentation
- Use defined names in formulas
- Add defined names to existing formulas

**Session 8.2**
- Create validation rules for data entry
- Protect the contents of worksheets and workbooks
- Add, edit, and delete comments

**Session 8.3**
- Learn about macro viruses and Excel security features
- Add the Developer tab to the Ribbon
- Create and run a macro
- Edit a macro using the Visual Basic Editor
- Assign a macro to a keyboard shortcut and a button
- Save and open a workbook in macro-enabled format
- Minimize the Ribbon

## Case | *Eugene Community Theatre*

Ellen Jefferson, business manager for the Eugene Community Theatre in Eugene, Oregon, is automating several processes for the theatre's business office. Each year, the theatre mails a brochure to patrons and other interested individuals showcasing the upcoming season's offerings. Then, theatre-goers make their selections and mail in the order form. Ellen wants to automate the process of invoicing, capturing the order, calculating the charges, and printing an invoice. She also wants the invoice system to reflect specific requests for tickets (number, series, and location in theatre).

Many of these tasks can be accomplished in Excel. But without validating data entry, protecting cells with formulas from accidental deletion, and reducing repetitious keystrokes and mouse clicks, Ellen realizes too many opportunities for errors exist. In addition, as a nonprofit organization, the theatre relies on numerous volunteers who have varying degrees of computer experience and skill. To accommodate these varying skill levels and reduce potential errors, Ellen wants to create a custom interface for this project that does not rely exclusively on the Ribbon, galleries, and so forth. You will help Ellen create a unique Excel application that can resolve these issues and help ensure accurate data entry.

### STARTING DATA FILES

Excel8 →

| Tutorial | Review | Case1 | Case2 | Case3 | Case4 |
|---|---|---|---|---|---|
| Theatre.xlsx | Rentals.xlsx | MediTrax.xlsx | Popcorn.xlsx | Cookin.xlsx | (none) |

# SESSION 8.1 VISUAL OVERVIEW

A **defined name** (often called a **range name**) is a word or string of characters associated with a single cell or a range.

The Name box displays the cell reference or the defined name of the selected cell.

Click the Name box to display a list of all the defined names in the workbook.

An application includes an input area to enter and edit data. You can set what types of values can be entered and where the user can enter data.

An **Excel application** is a spreadsheet written or tailored to meet specific needs. It typically includes reports and charts, a data entry area, a custom interface, as well as instructions and documentation.

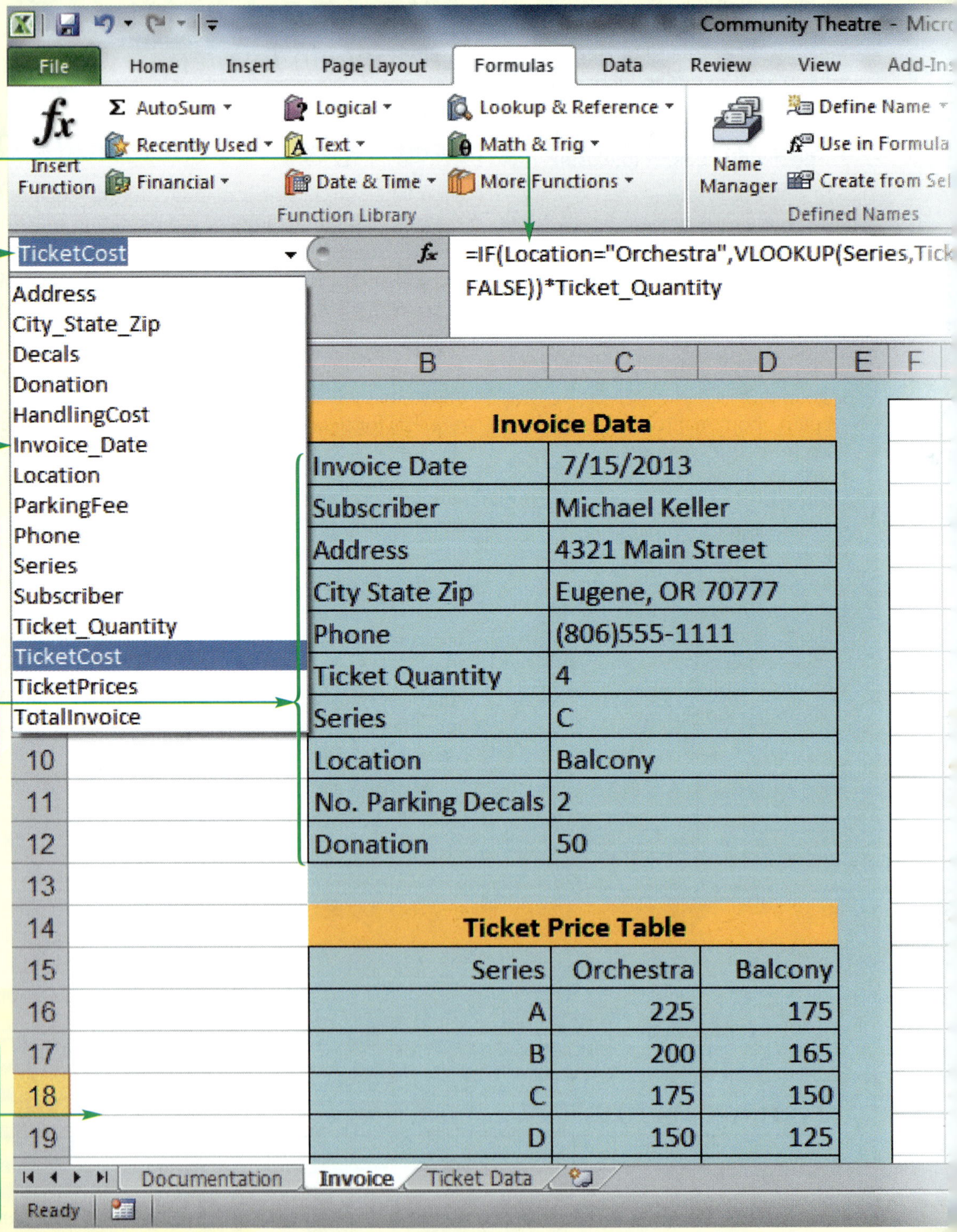

# EXCEL APPLICATION AND DEFINED NAMES

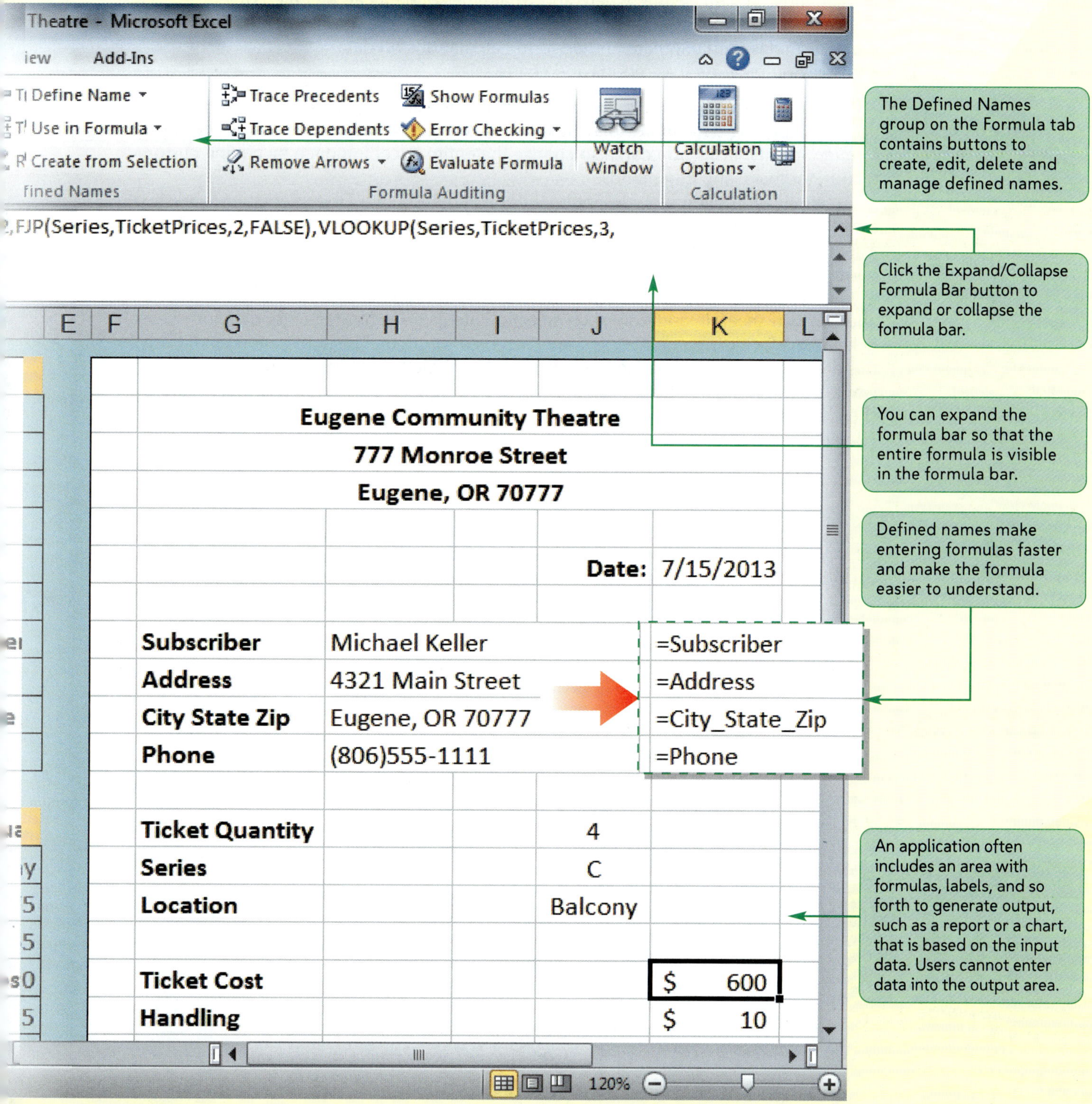

# Planning an Excel Application

Planning an Excel application includes designing how the worksheet(s) will be organized. You can include different sections for each function, depending on the complexity of the project. For example, an application often includes separate sections to:

- Enter and edit data (setting where and what types of data can be entered)
- Store data after it has been entered
- Use formulas to manipulate and perform calculations on data
- Display outputs, such as reports and charts

An application's interface helps others use it. For example, you can have separate sections for inputting data and displaying outputs. You can create special buttons for performing specific tasks. You can also change the entire Excel interface by adding custom menus, toolbars, and commands.

An application often includes internal documentation in a Documentation worksheet as well as comments to explain cell contents and provide instructions. It can also include a set of clearly written instructions. All of these help you and others use the workbook correctly and accurately.

Ellen wants to be able to easily print the invoice and transfer the invoice items to another worksheet. In addition, she wants volunteers to be able to enter data for a season ticket in a specific area of the worksheet reserved for input. The application would use this data to automatically generate and print the invoice. To keep the process simple, she wants users to be able to click buttons to print a single invoice, print the entire worksheet, and transfer the data from one worksheet to another. You'll open the workbook Ellen created.

## To open and review the Theatre workbook:

1. Open the **Theatre** workbook located in the Excel8\Tutorial folder included with your Data Files, and then save the workbook as **Community Theatre**.
2. In the Documentation worksheet, enter your name and the date.
3. Review the contents of the workbook, and then switch to the **Invoice** worksheet. See Figure 8-1.

**Figure 8-1** Initial Invoice worksheet

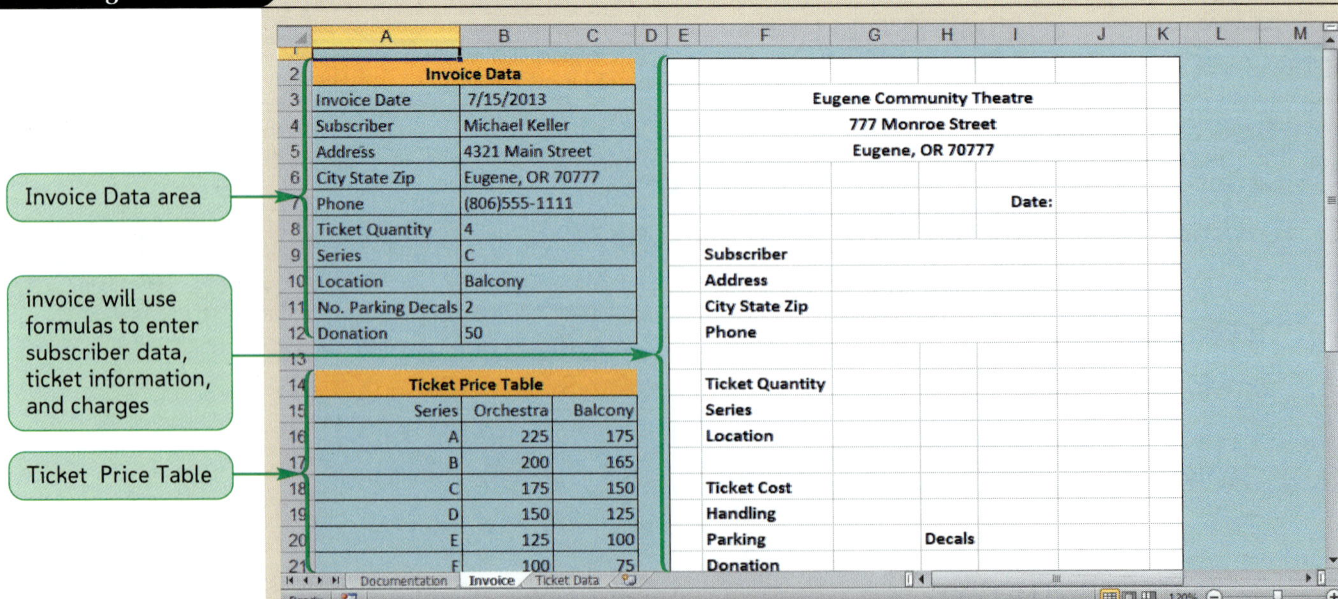

**TIP**

Larger and more complex applications often place the input and output sections in separate worksheets.

In addition to the Documentation worksheet, the Community Theatre workbook includes two other worksheets: Invoice and Ticket Data. The Invoice worksheet contains input, output, and transfer sections. The input section is divided into the following three areas:

- Invoice Data contains items that change for each subscriber transaction such as the subscriber name, address, phone number, ticket quantity, series, and location of seats.
- Ticket Price Table contains the table with ticket prices for the upcoming season.
- Invoice Constants contains charges for items that will not change during the upcoming season, such as the cost for parking ($15/decal) and the handling charge ($10/invoice).

The output section contains formulas and labels used to generate the invoice based on data in the input section. The invoice in the output section will be printed. The transfer section gathers selected data from the invoice in one area before the data is transferred to the Ticket Data worksheet for storage. The transfer section makes it simpler to move the data to the Ticket Data worksheet.

## Naming Cells and Ranges

So far, you have referred to a cell or range by its address except when you entered formulas within an Excel table. Cell and range references do not indicate what data is stored in those cells. Instead, you can use a defined name to assign a meaningful, descriptive name to a cell or range. For example, if the range D1:D100 contains sales data for 100 transactions, you can define the name "Sales" to refer to the range of sales data.

A defined name enables you to quickly navigate within a workbook to the cell with the defined name. You can also use defined names to create more descriptive formulas.

In the Invoice worksheet, the range B3:B12 contains the data values for each request for season tickets. As you can see, this range includes many variables. It will be simpler to remember where different data is stored by assigning a descriptive name to each cell or range rather than using its cell address. For example, the name Subscriber better identifies what is stored in the cell than cell B4.

**PROSKILLS**

### *Written Communication: Saving Time with Defined Names*

Words can be more descriptive than numbers. This is especially true in cell references. Instead of using the letter and number references for cells, you can create defined names to provide more intuitive references. Defined names have several advantages over cell references, especially as a worksheet becomes longer and more complex. Some advantages include:

- Names, such as TaxRate and TotalSales, are more descriptive than cell references, making it easier to remember what a cell or range contains.
- Names can be used in formulas, making it easier for users to understand the calculations being performed. For example, =GrossPay–Deductions is more understandable than =C15–C16.
- When you move a named cell or range within a worksheet, its name moves with it. Any formulas that contain the name automatically reference the new location.
- In a formula, referencing a named cell or range is the same as referencing the cell or range's absolute reference. So, if you move a formula that includes a defined name, the reference remains pointed to the correct cell or range.

By using defined names, you'll often save time and everyone reviewing the worksheet will have a clearer understanding of what a formula is calculating.

## Creating Defined Names

Creating defined names for cells or ranges makes building an application more intuitive and easier to document. When you define a name for a cell or range, keep in mind the following rules:

- The name must begin with a letter or _ (an underscore).
- The name can include letters and numbers as well as periods and underscores, but not other symbols or spaces. To distinguish multiword names, use an underscore between the words or capitalize the first letter of each word. For example, the names *Net_Income* and *NetIncome* are valid, but *Net Income* and *Net-Income* are not.
- The name cannot be a valid cell address (such as FY2013), function name, or reserved word (such as *Print_Area*).
- The name can include as many as 255 characters, although short, meaningful names of 5 to 15 characters are more practical.
- The name is not case sensitive. For example, both *Sales* and *SALES* refer to the same cell or range.

REFERENCE

### *Creating a Defined Name for a Cell or Range*

- Select the cell or range to which you want to assign a name.
- Click in the Name box on the formula bar, type the name, and then press the Enter key.
  *or*
  In the Defined Names group on the Formulas tab, click the Define Name button, type a name in the Name box, and then click the OK button.

*or*

- Select the range with labels and blank cells in the top row or first column to which you want to assign a name.
- In the Defined Names group on the Formulas tab, click the Create from Selection button.
- Specify whether to create the ranges based on the top row, bottom row, left column, or right column in the list.
- Click the OK button.

The fastest way to create a defined name is to use the Name box. You'll use the Name box to define names for the cells and ranges in the worksheet.

**To create defined names using the Name box:**

1. Click cell **B24** to make it active, and then click the **Name box** on the formula bar. The cell reference for the active cell, B24, is selected in the Name box.
2. Type **HandlingCost** and then press the **Enter** key. Cell B24 remains active, and "HandlingCost" appears in the Name box instead of the cell reference. See Figure 8-2.

**Figure 8-2** **Defined name for cell B24**

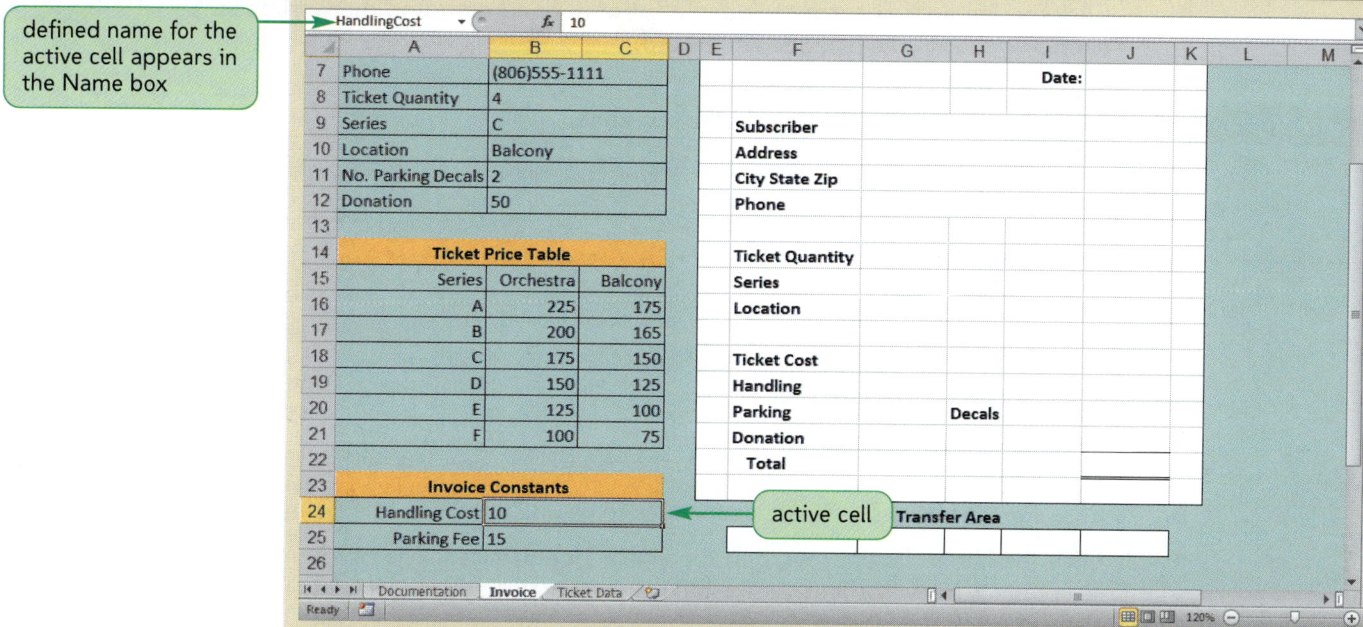


**Trouble?** If "HandlingCost" appears in cell B24, you probably did not click the Name box before typing the name. On the Quick Access Toolbar, click the Undo button, and then repeat Steps 1 and 2.

**Trouble?** If "cell B24" appears in the Name box instead of "HandlingCost," you probably didn't press the Enter key. Repeat Steps 1 and 2 being sure to press the Enter key to assign the defined name to cell B24.

3. Click cell **B25** to make it active, click the **Name box** to select the cell reference, type **ParkingFee** and then press the **Enter** key. Cell B25 remains active, and ParkingFee appears in the Name box instead of the cell reference.
4. Select the range **A16:C21**. The cell reference for the active cell in the range appears in the Name box.
5. Click the **Name box**, type **TicketPrices** and then press the **Enter** key. The name TicketPrices is assigned to the range A16:C21.
6. Select the range **F25:J25**, click the **Name box**, type **TransferArea** and then press the **Enter** key. The name TransferArea is assigned to the range F25:J25.
7. Click cell **J18** to make it active, click the **Name box** to select the cell reference, type **TicketCost** and then press the **Enter** key. Cell J18 remains active, and TicketCost appears in the Name box instead of the cell reference.
8. Click cell **J22** to make it active, click the **Name box** to select the cell reference, type **TotalInvoice** and then press the **Enter** key. Cell J22 remains active, and TotalInvoice appears in the Name box instead of the cell reference.

The Name box displays all of the names in a workbook. You can select a name in the Name box to quickly select the cell or range referenced by the name. You'll view the defined names you added to the workbook.

## To select cells and ranges with the Name box:

1. Click the **Name box arrow** to open a list of defined names in the workbook. Six names appear in the list. See Figure 8-3.

**Figure 8-3** Name box with the defined names in the workbook

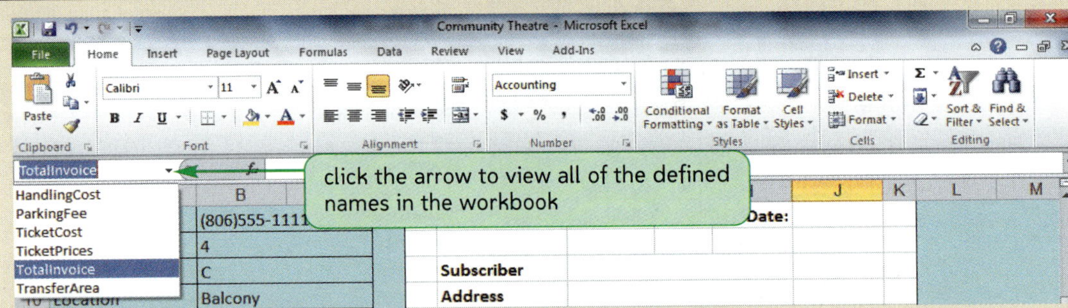


2. Click **ParkingFee**. The active cell moves to cell B25.
3. Click the **Name box arrow**, and then click **TicketPrices**. The range A16:C21 is selected in the worksheet, and cell A16 is the active cell.

You can quickly define names without typing them if the data is organized in a table format with labels in the first or last column or top or bottom row. The names are based on the row or column labels. Any blank or parenthesis in the labels are changed to an underscore (_) in the defined name.You will create names for each cell in the Invoice Data area, using the labels in the range A3:A11.

## To create defined names by selection for the Invoice Data area:

Select only the range A3:B12 though text extends into column C; otherwise, formulas you create later in this tutorial will not work.

1. Select the range **A3:B12**. In this range, column A contains the labels you want to use as the defined names, and column B contains the cells you want to name.
2. Click the **Formulas** tab on the Ribbon, and then click the **Create from Selection** button in the Defined Names group. The Create Names from Selection dialog box opens. See Figure 8-4.

**Figure 8-4** Create Names from Selection dialog box

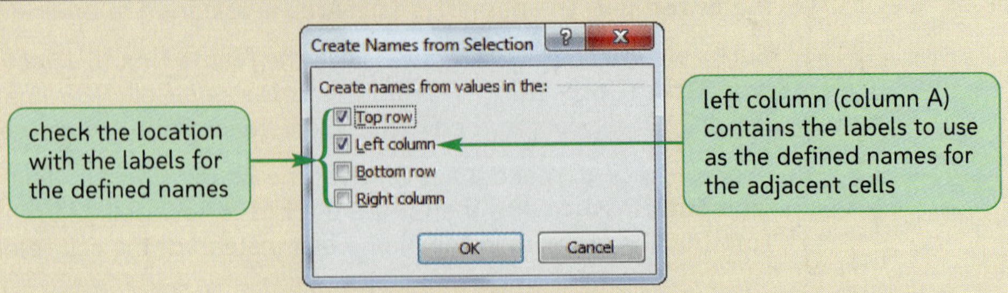


3. Click the **Top row** check box to remove the check mark because this range doesn't include labels at the top, and then verify that the **Left column** check box contains a check mark. The labels in the left column will be used to create the defined names.
4. Click the **OK** button. Each cell in the range B3:B12 is named based on its label in column A.

5. Click the **Name box arrow** to see the 16 defined names in the list.
6. Press the **Esc** key to close the list of defined names.

Although you can use the Name box to verify the names were created, the Name Manager dialog box lists all of the names currently defined in the workbook, including Excel table names. You can also use the Name Manager dialog box to create a new name, edit or delete existing names, and filter the list of names.

The name No._Parking_Decals is too long, so you'll change it to Decals. You will also delete the TransferData defined name, which Ellen decides is not needed.

**TIP**

The Name Manager dialog box also lists Excel table names.

## To edit and delete defined names with the Name Manager dialog box:

1. In the Defined Names group on the Formulas tab, click the **Name Manager** button. The Name Manager dialog box opens, listing the 16 defined names based on the labels in the range A3:A12 in the Invoice Data area, as well as the six names you defined with the Name box. See Figure 8-5.

**Figure 8-5** Name Manager dialog box

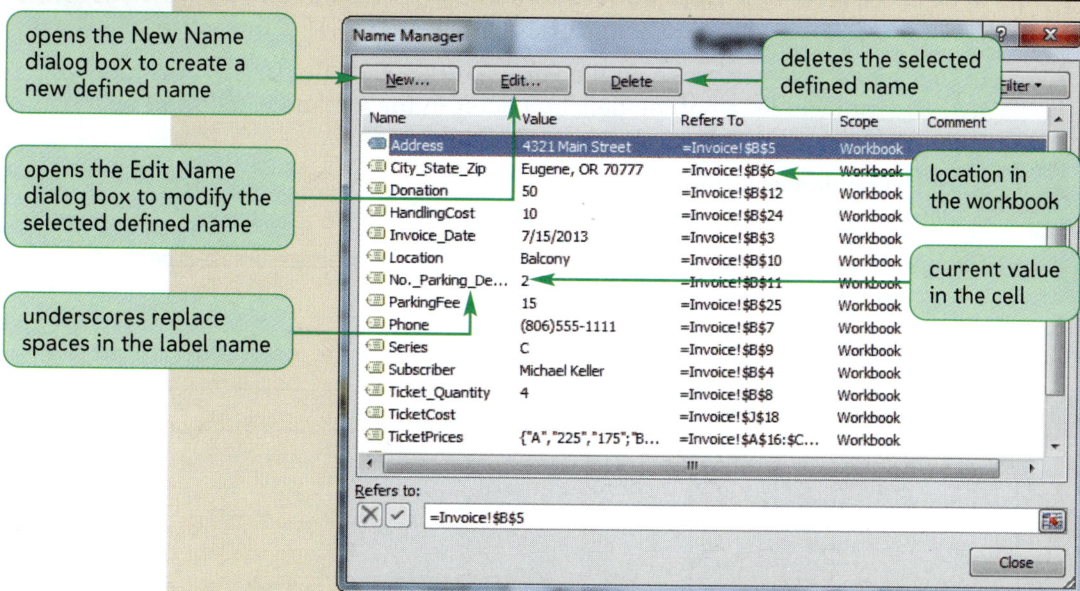


2. Click **No._Parking_Decals** in the Name list, and then click the **Edit** button. The Edit Name dialog box opens. See Figure 8-6.

**Figure 8-6** Edit Name dialog box

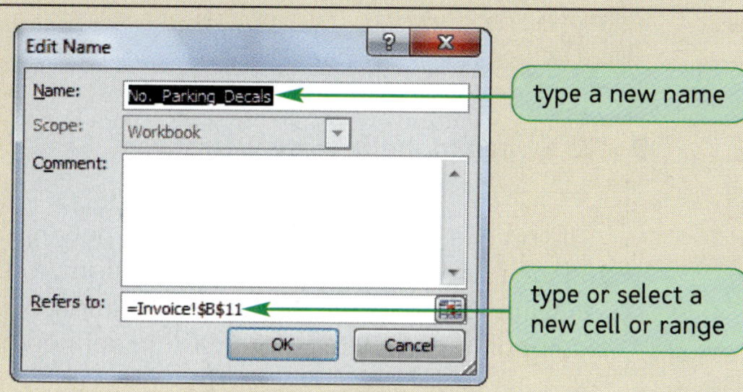

3. In the Name box, type **Decals** and then click the **OK** button. The edited name appears in the list in the Name Manager dialog box.
4. Scroll to find the TransferArea name, click **TransferArea**, and then click the **Delete** button. A dialog box opens to confirm that you want to delete the selected name.
5. Click the **OK** button. The name is removed from the list.
6. Click the **Close** button. The Name Manager dialog box closes.

## Using the Paste Names Command

When a workbook contains many defined names, it can be helpful to list all of the defined names and their corresponding cell addresses in the workbook's documentation. You can generate a list of names using the Paste Names command.

### To create a list of defined names in the Documentation worksheet:

1. Switch to the **Documentation** worksheet.
2. Click in cell **A10**, type **Defined Names** and then press the **Enter** key. The label for the list of defined names appears in cell A10, and cell A11 is the active cell.
3. In the Defined Names group on the Formulas tab, click the **Use in Formula** button. The list includes all of the defined names in the workbook followed by the Paste Names command.
4. Click **Paste Names**. The Paste Name dialog box opens. You can paste any selected name, or you can paste the entire list of names.
5. Click the **Paste List** button. The defined names and their associated cell references are pasted into the range A11:B25.
6. Deselect the range. See Figure 8-7.

**Figure 8-7** **Defined names in the Community Theatre workbook**

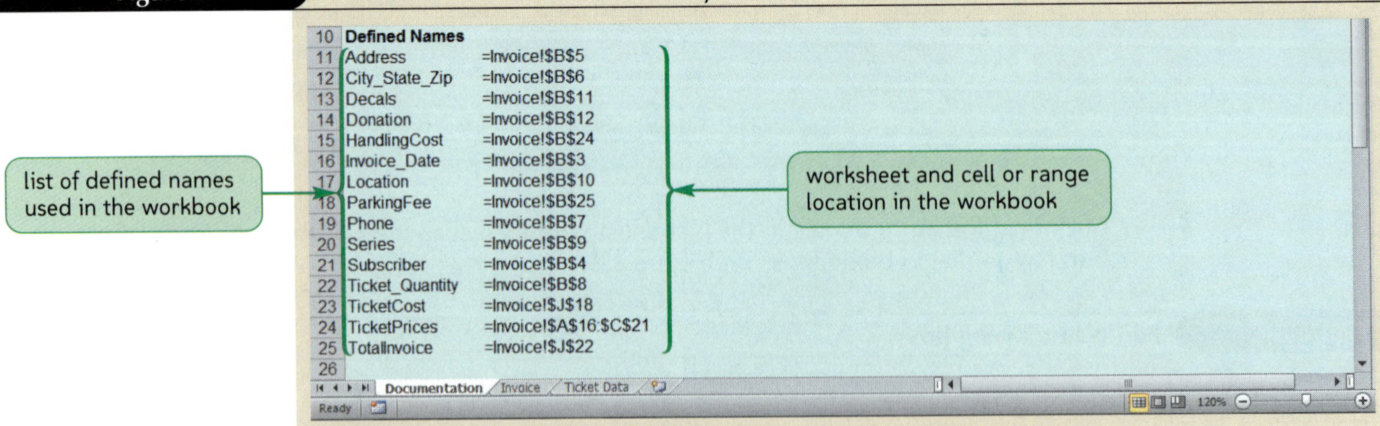


7. Switch to the **Invoice** worksheet.

If you edit a defined name or add a new defined name, the list of defined names and their addresses in the Documentation worksheet is not updated. You must paste the list again to update the names and locations. Usually, it is a good idea to wait until the workbook is complete before pasting defined names in the Documentation worksheet.

## Using Defined Names in Formulas

You can create more descriptive formulas by using defined names instead of cell or range references in formulas. For example, in the following formulas, the defined name Sales replaces the range reference D1:D100 in a formula to calculate average sales:

| | |
|---|---|
| **Range reference** | `=AVERAGE(D1:D100)` |
| **Defined name** | `=AVERAGE(Sales)` |

Keep in mind that if you enter a formula using a range reference rather than a defined name, the defined names do *not* automatically replace the range reference in the formula.

You need to enter the formulas required to generate the invoice. You'll start by entering formulas to display the invoice date, the subscriber's name, and the subscriber's address entered in the Invoice Data area in the invoice.

### To enter formulas to display the subscriber's name and address:

1. In cell J7, enter **=B3**. The invoice date recorded in the Invoice Data area, 7/15/2013, appears in the cell.
2. In cell G9, enter **=B4**. Michael Keller, the subscriber's name, appears in the cell.
3. In cell G10, enter **=B5**. The subscriber's address, 4321 Main Street, appears in the cell.
4. Click cell **G10**. The formula =B5 appears in the formula bar.

You entered these formulas using cell addresses rather than defined names. Although you defined names for cells B3, B4, and B5, the names do not automatically replace the cell addresses in the formula. Because defined names make formulas simpler to enter and understand, you will use named cells and ranges in the remaining formulas.

As you type a defined name in a formula, the Formula AutoComplete box lists functions and defined names that begin with the letters you typed. As you type additional letters, the list narrows. You can double-click the name you want in the Formula AutoComplete box or press the Tab key to enter the selected name. You can also just continue to type the rest of the name.

### To type defined names in formulas:

1. In cell G11, type **=C** to display a list of functions and defined names that begin with the letter "C."
2. Type **i** to narrow the list to the defined name =City_State_Zip.
3. Press the **Tab** key to enter the defined name in the formula, and then press the **Enter** key. The subscriber's city, state, and zip code appear in the cell.
4. Click cell **G11**. The data from cell B6 appears in the cell, and the formula with the defined name, =City_State_Zip, appears in the formula bar.
5. In cell G12, enter **=Phone** and then click cell **G12**. The sample data from cell B7 appears in the cell, and the formula with the defined name, =Phone, appears in the formula bar.

You can also use the point-and-click method to create a formula with defined names. When you click a cell or select a range, Excel substitutes the defined name for the cell reference in the formula. You'll use this method to enter formulas that display the ticket quantity, series, and theatre location from the input area in the invoice.

**To enter formulas with defined names using the point-and-click method:**

1. Click cell **I14**, type **=** and then click cell **B8**. The formula uses the defined name Ticket_Quantity rather than the cell reference B8.
2. Click the **Enter** button ✓ on the formula bar. The number 4, which is the number of tickets the subscriber ordered, appears in cell I14. See Figure 8-8.

**Figure 8-8** **Formula with a defined name**

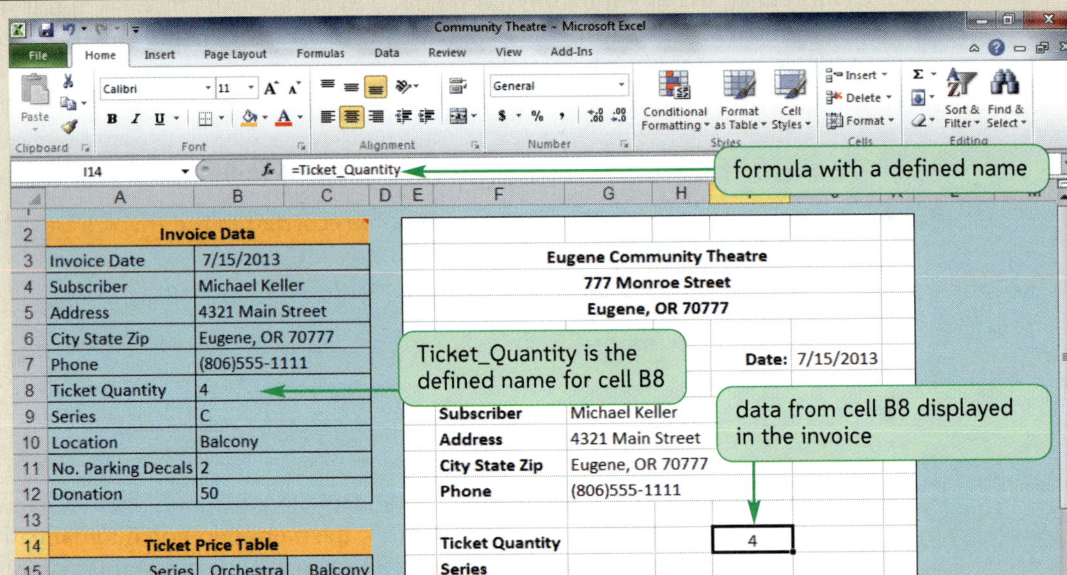


3. In cell I15, type **=** and then click cell **B9**. The formula uses the defined name Series rather than the cell reference B9.
4. Press the **Enter** key. The letter "C," indicating the series the subscriber selected, appears in cell I15.
5. In cell I16, type **=**, click **B10**, and then click the **Enter** button ✓ on the formula bar. The subscriber's preferred seat location, Balcony, appears in cell I16, and the formula with the defined name, =Location, appears in the formula bar.

Next, you will enter the formula to calculate the ticket cost to the subscriber. You need to combine two VLOOKUP functions within an IF function to create the formula to calculate ticket costs. The VLOOKUP functions will find the ticket price. The lookup value is the Series the subscriber selects (A, B, C, D, E, or F). Recall that the lookup value searches the first column of the lookup table to find the appropriate row. In this case, the lookup table is the Ticket Price Table (the range you earlier named TicketPrices), which contains two columns of ticket prices. Column 2 of the table lists the prices for the Orchestra, and column 3 of the table lists the prices for the Balcony. The column used to return the ticket prices depends on the Location the subscriber selected. You need to use an IF function to determine whether to search the second or third column for the ticket price.

### To enter the formula to determine ticket cost:

1. Click cell **J18** to make it the active cell. The defined name, TicketCost, appears in the Name box.
2. In the Function Library group on the Formulas tab, click the **Logical** button, and then click **IF**. The Function Arguments dialog box opens.
3. In the Logical_test box, type **Location="Orchestra"**. This logical test evaluates whether the subscriber wants to sit in the Orchestra. If the value in cell B10 equals Orchestra, then the condition is true. False appears to the right of the Logical_test box, indicating the subscriber wants to sit in the Balcony.
4. In the Value_if_true box, type **VLOOKUP(Series,TicketPrices,2,FALSE)**. This argument specifies that if the logical_test is true (the customer wants to sit in the Orchestra), the ticket price is determined using a VLOOKUP function, returning a value from column 2 (Orchestra prices) in the TicketPrices range. The first argument of the VLOOKUP function, Series, is the defined name that stores the Series code (A, B, C, and so on) used to look up a value in the second argument, TicketPrices (range A16:C21). The third argument, 2, returns a ticket price from the second column (Orchestra) of the TicketPrices table. The fourth argument, FALSE, indicates an exact match lookup.
5. In the Value_if_false box, type **VLOOKUP(Series,TicketPrices,3,FALSE)**. This argument specifies that if the logical_test is false (the customer wants to sit in the Balcony), the ticket price is determined using a VLOOKUP function, returning a value from column 3 (Balcony prices) in the TicketPrices range.
6. Click the **OK** button. The following formula appears in the formula bar, and 150 appears in cell J18 because the condition is false: =IF(Location="Orchestra", VLOOKUP(Series,TicketPrices,2,FALSE),VLOOKUP(Series,TicketPrices,3,FALSE)).

   **Trouble?** If #Name?, #Value?, or VLOOKUP appears in cell J18, you probably mistyped the formula. Click cell J18, compare the formula you entered with the complete formula in Step 6, and then edit the formula in the formula bar as needed. Also, make sure the references in your defined names are correct (refer to Figure 8-7 for the list of defined names used in the workbook).

   Next, you will complete the formula by multiplying the cost for one ticket by the number of tickets purchased.

7. Double-click cell **J18** to enter Edit mode and display the formula in the cell.
8. Click at the end of the formula, type ***Ticket_Quantity** and then press the **Enter** key. The amount in cell J18 changes to $600.
9. Click cell **J18**, and then click the **Expand Formula Bar** button on the right side of the formula bar. The entire formula is visible in the expanded formula bar. The IF function determines which column in the TicketPrices range to use to return the ticket price. If Location in the Invoice Data area is Orchestra, then the condition Location="Orchestra" is TRUE and the VLOOKUP function returns a ticket price from column 2. If the Location in the Invoice Data area is Balcony, then the VLOOKUP function searches column 3 for the ticket price. The price for one ticket, as determined by the IF and VLOOKUP functions, is then multiplied by the ticket quantity to calculate the total ticket cost for this transaction. See Figure 8-9.

**Figure 8-9** Formula to calculate the ticket cost

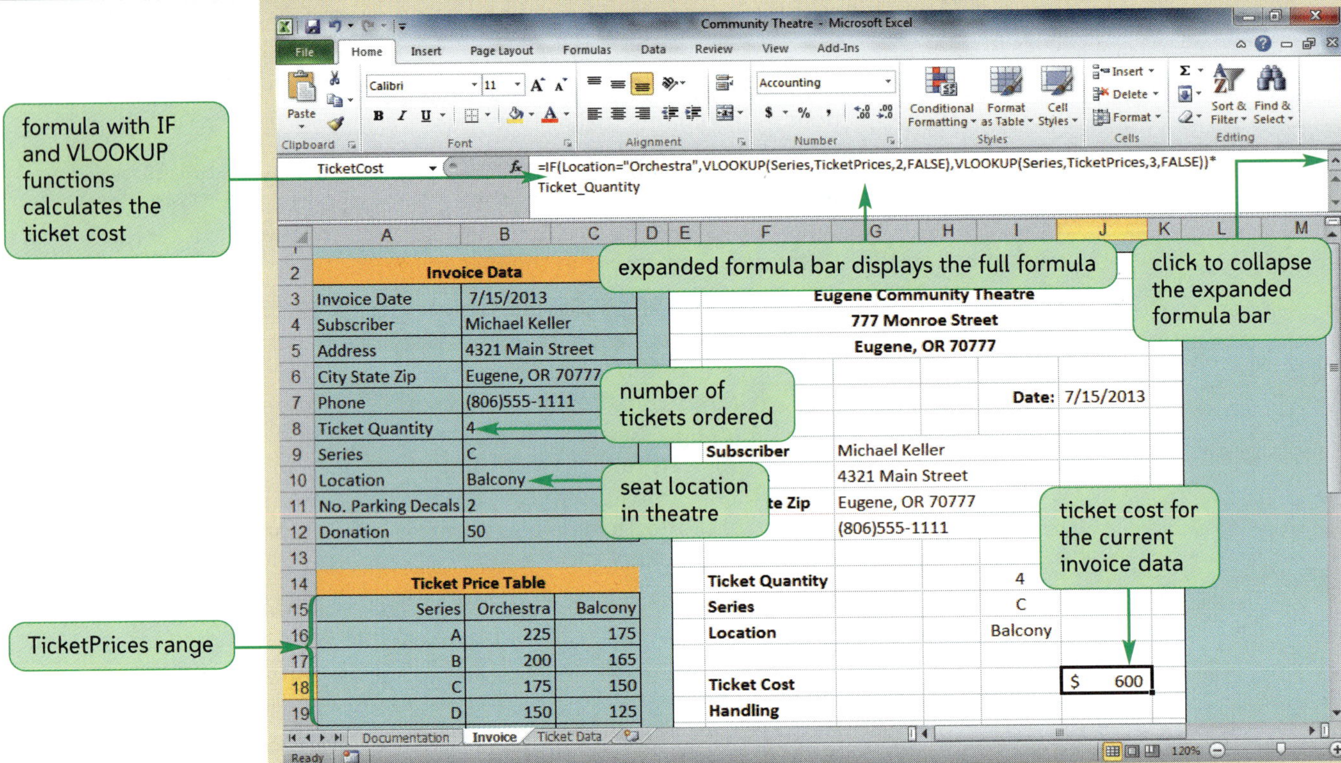


- **10.** Click the **Collapse Formula Bar** button on the formula bar. The formula bar returns to its usual height.

You'll enter the remaining formulas needed to complete the invoice.

**TIP**

If a formula uses a defined name that doesn't exist, #NAME? appears in the cell. Verify the defined name spelling and that the name wasn't deleted from the worksheet.

## To enter the remaining formulas in the invoice:

- **1.** In cell J19, enter **=HandlingCost**. The handling cost is $10, which is the amount in cell B24 in the Invoice Constants area.
- **2.** In cell I20, enter **=Decals**. The number of parking decals ordered is 2, which is the number listed in cell B11 in the Invoice Data area.
- **3.** In cell J20, enter **=Decals*ParkingFee**. The parking cost is $30, which is the number of parking decals listed in cell B11 multiplied by the parking fee in cell B25. The defined names make entering this calculation faster and the formula easier to understand.
- **4.** In cell J21, enter **=Donation**. The donation amount is $50, which is listed in cell B12.
- **5.** In cell J22, enter **=SUM(J18:J21)**. The SUM function adds all of the costs to determine the total invoice amount of $690. See Figure 8-10.

**Figure 8-10** **Invoice with all formulas entered**

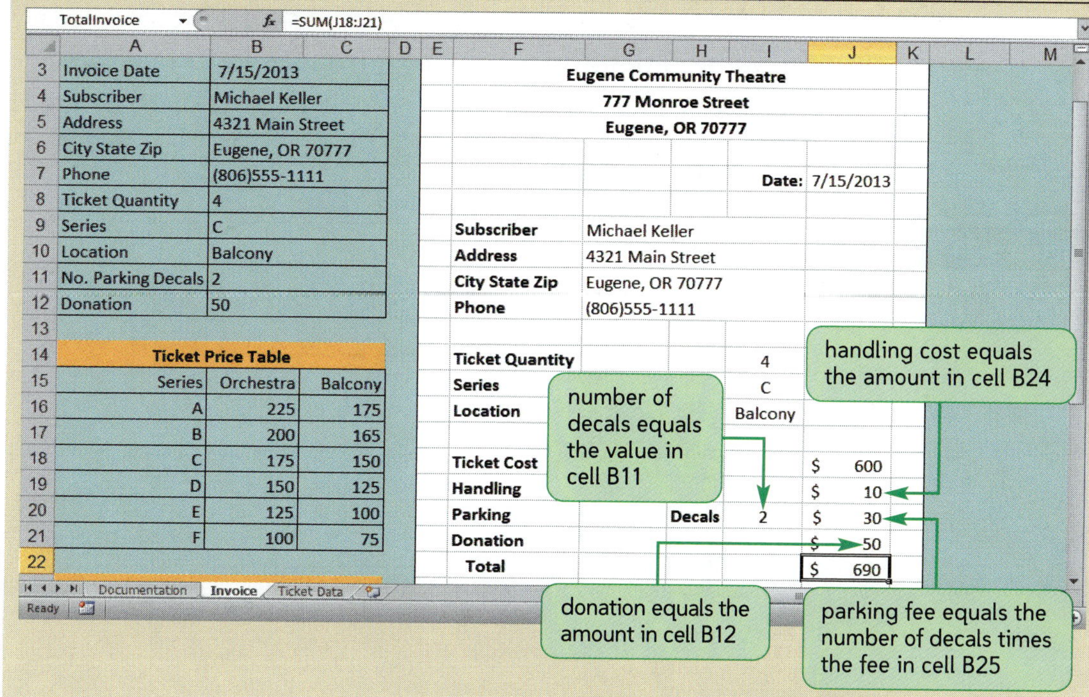


## Adding Defined Names to Existing Formulas

Sometimes, you might name cells after creating formulas in the worksheet. Other times, you might not use the defined names when you create formulas (as with the first three formulas you created in the invoice for the invoice date, subscriber name, and address). Because defined names are not automatically substituted for the cell addresses in a formula, you can replace cell addresses in existing formulas in the worksheet with their defined names to make the formulas more understandable.

REFERENCE

### *Adding Defined Names to Existing Formulas*

- In the Defined Names group on the Formulas tab, click the Define Name button arrow, and then click Apply Names (if the cell reference and defined name are in the same worksheet).
- In the Apply Names dialog box, select the names you want to apply.
- Click the OK button.

*or*

- Edit the formula by selecting the cell reference and typing the defined name or clicking the appropriate cell.

You'll change the two formulas you created to display the subscriber name and address in the invoice to use defined names instead of cell references.

### To add defined names to existing formulas in the invoice:

1. In the Defined Names group on the Formulas tab, click the **Define Name button arrow**, and then click **Apply Names**. The Apply Names dialog box opens. See Figure 8-11.

Figure 8-11 Apply Names dialog box

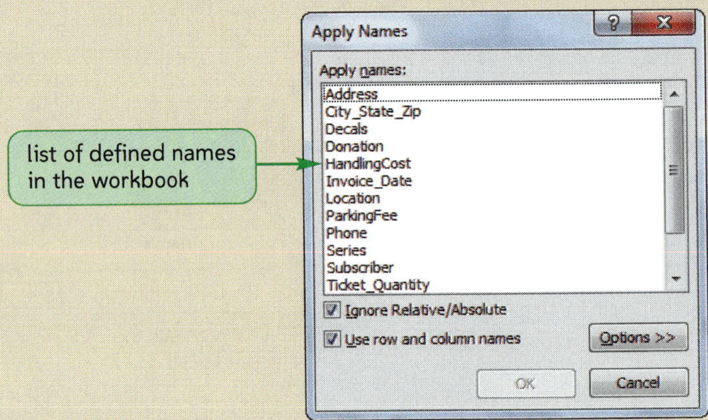


You want to select only the names you need for the existing formulas with cell references.

2. If any name is selected in the Apply names list, click that name to deselect it.
3. In the Apply names list, click **Address**, **Invoice_Date**, and **Subscriber**. The three names you want to apply to the formulas are selected.
4. Click the **OK** button. The three selected names are applied to the formulas.
5. Click cell **J7** and verify that the formula changed to =Invoice_Date.
6. Click cell **G9** and verify that the formula changed to =Subscriber.
7. Click cell **G10** and verify that the formula changed to =Address.

Ellen wants to store the following items in the Ticket Data worksheet: subscriber name, transaction date, ticket quantity, ticket cost, and total amount owed from the invoice. Displaying these data items in the Transfer Area enables you to copy and paste all of the items to the Ticket Data worksheet at once. You'll enter formulas to display the appropriate items in this section of the worksheet.

### To enter formulas to display data in the Transfer Area:

1. In cell F25, enter **=Subscriber**. The formula displays the subscriber name in this cell.
2. In cell G25, enter **=Invoice_Date**. The formula displays the current date.
3. In cell H25, enter **=Ticket_Quantity**. The formula displays the number of tickets.
4. In cell I25, enter **=TicketCost**. The formula displays the ticket cost.
5. In cell J25, enter **=TotalInvoice**. The formula displays the total cost.

The worksheet contains all of the formulas required to create the invoice based on the subscriber information. Because Ellen relies on volunteers to enter season ticket requests into the worksheet and print invoices, she wants to be sure the values entered are correct. You will continue to work on Ellen's application by creating validation checks, which are designed to prevent users from inserting incorrect data values. You will also protect cells so that volunteers cannot accidentally overwrite or delete the formulas. You'll do both of these tasks in the next session.

REVIEW

## *Session 8.1 Quick Check*

1. What is a defined name?
2. What are two advantages of using names in workbooks?
3. Describe three ways to create a name.
4. Which of the following is a valid defined name?
   a. Annual_Total
   b. 3rdQtr
   c. Annual total
5. How can you quickly select a cell or range using its name?
6. In the Report workbook, the defined name "Expenses" refers to a list of expenses stored in the range D2:D100. Currently, the total expenses are calculated by the formula =SUM(D2:D100). Change this formula to use the defined name.
7. True or False. If you create a defined name for a range referenced in an existing formula, you cannot change the formula to use the new name.

# SESSION 8.2 VISUAL OVERVIEW

A red triangle indicates that the cell contains a comment. Point to the cell to display the comment box.

You can use **data validation** to create a set of rules that determine what users can enter in a specific cell or range.

An **input message** appears when the cell becomes active, and can be used to specify the type of data the user should enter in that cell.

An **error alert** appears if a user tries to enter a value in the cell that does not meet the validation rule, as is the case when a user enters a ticket quantity of 20 in cell B8.

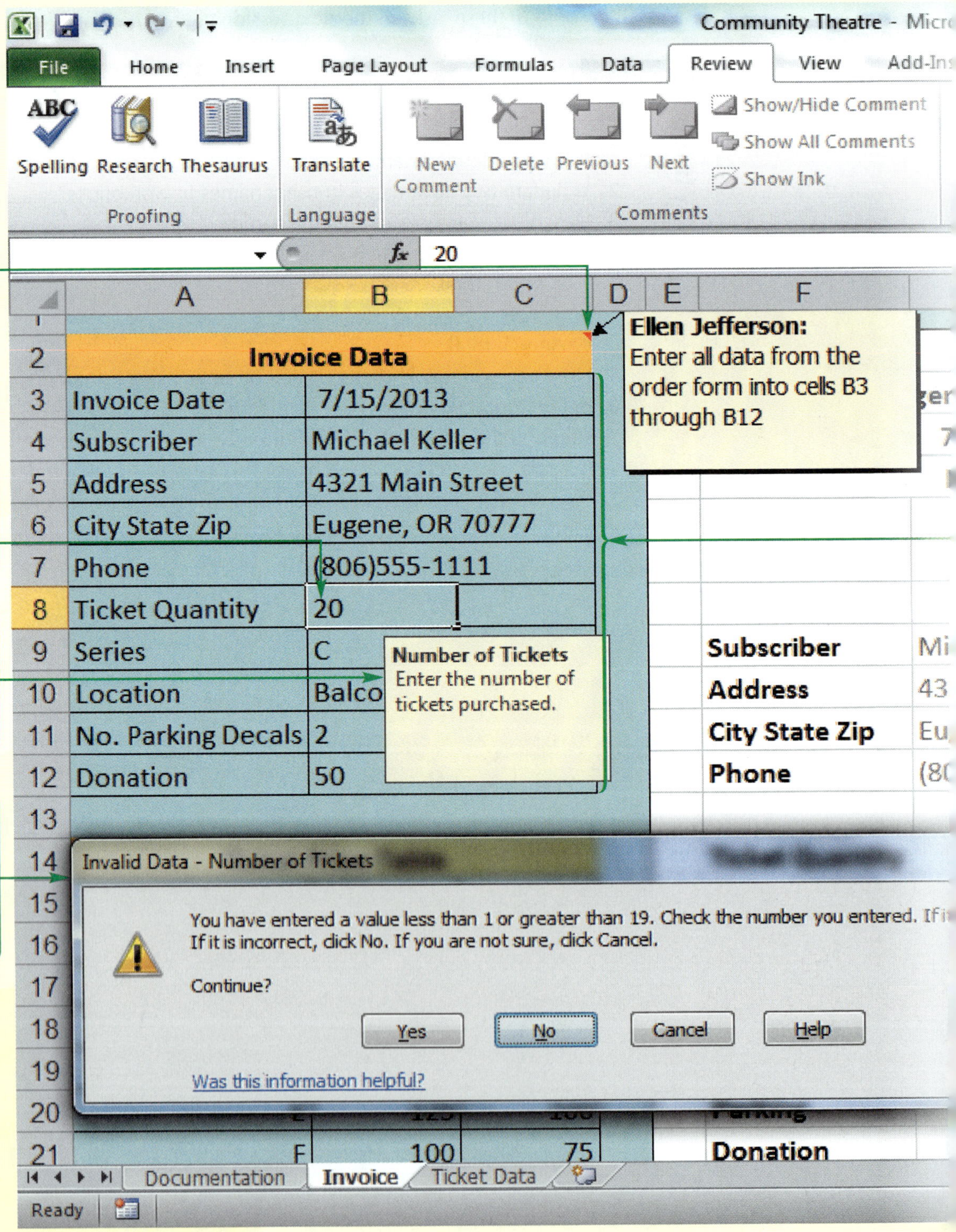

# DATA VALIDATION AND PROTECTION

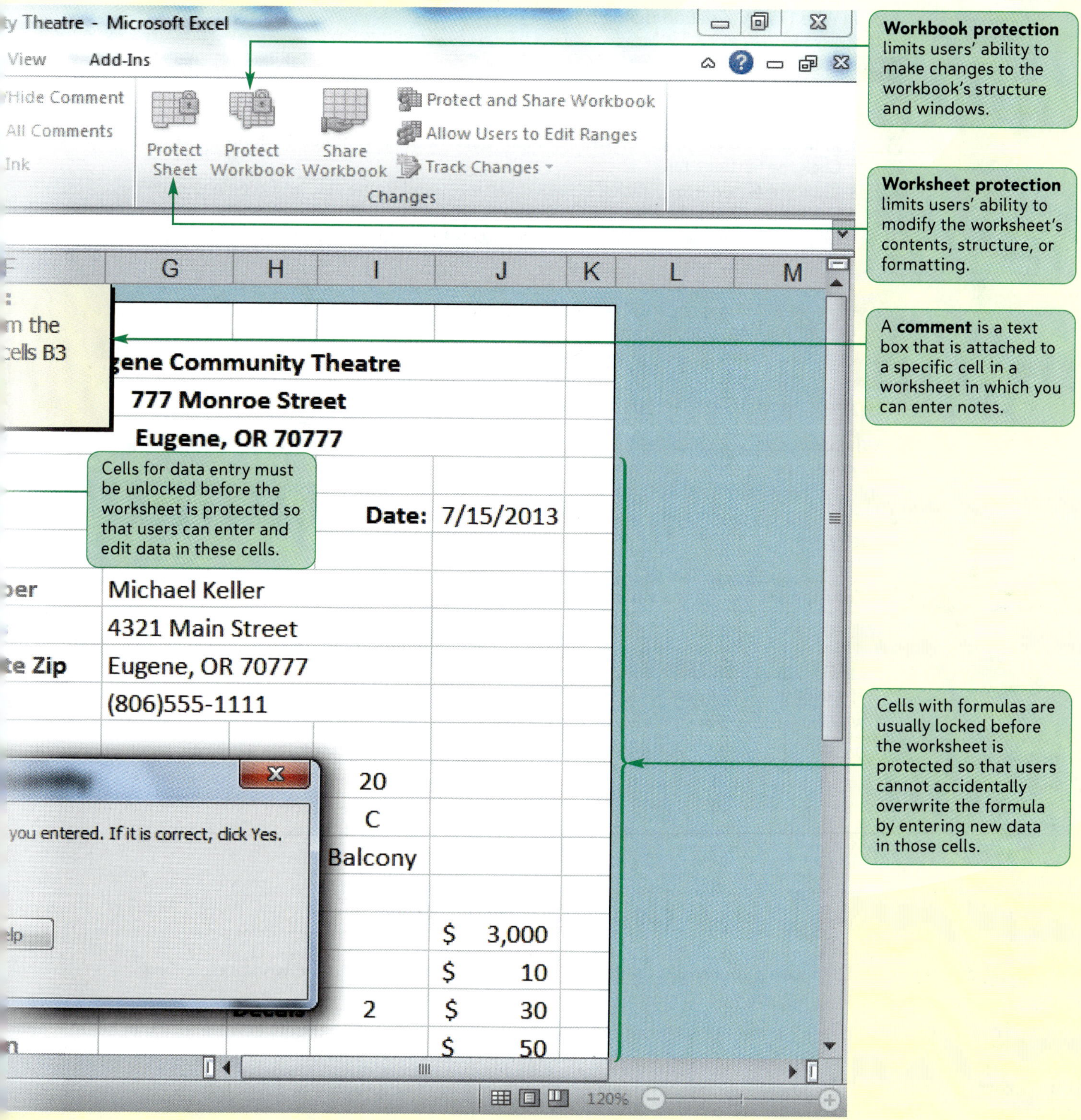

# Validating Data Entry

**TIP**

Each cell can have only one validation rule. Creating a second validation rule for a cell replaces the existing rule.

To ensure that correct data is entered and stored in a worksheet, you can use data validation. Each **validation rule** defines criteria for the data that can be stored in a cell or range. You can also add input and error alert messages for the user to that cell or range. You specify the validation criteria, the input message, and the error alert for the active cell in the Data Validation dialog box.

REFERENCE

*Validating Data*

- In the Data Tools group on the Data tab, click the Data Validation button.
- Click the Settings tab.
- Click the Allow arrow, click the type of data allowed in the cell, and then enter the validation criteria for that data.
- Click the Input Message tab, and then enter a title and text for the input message.
- Click the Error Alert tab, and then, if necessary, click the Show error alert after invalid data is entered check box to insert a check mark.
- Select an alert style, and then enter the title and text for the error alert message.
- Click the OK button.

## Specifying Validation Criteria

When you create a validation rule, you specify the type of data allowed as well as a list or range of acceptable values (called validation criteria). For example, you might specify integers between 1 and 100, or a list of codes such as Excellent, Good, Fair, and Poor. Figure 8-12 describes the types of data you can allow and the acceptable values for each type.

**Figure 8-12** **Allow options for the validation**

| Type | Acceptable Values |
|---|---|
| Any value | Any number, text, or date; removes any existing data validation |
| Whole number | Integers only; you can specify the range of acceptable integers |
| Decimal | Any type of number; you can specify the range of acceptable numbers |
| List | Any value in a range or entered in the Data Validation dialog box separated by commas |
| Date | Dates only; you can specify the range of acceptable dates |
| Time | Times only; you can specify the range of acceptable times |
| Text length | Text limited to a specified number of characters |
| Custom | Values based on the results of a logical formula |

**TIP**

To apply a validation rule to all of the cells in an Excel table column, select the column of data to which the validation rule will be applied, and then create the validation rule.

Ellen wants you to add the following three validation rules to the workbook to help ensure that volunteers enter valid data in the Invoice worksheet:

- In cell B8, the Ticket Quantity value should be a whole number between 1 and 19. In previous years, 19 was the maximum number of tickets purchased.
- In cell B9, the Series value should be one of the following list: A, B, C, D, E, or F.
- In cell B10, the Location value should be one of the following list: Orchestra or Balcony.

You will define the validation rule for the number of season tickets. Cell B8, which records the ticket quantity, requires an integer that is greater than 0 and less than 20.

## To create the validation rule for the Ticket Quantity cell:

1. If you took a break after the previous session, make sure the Community Theatre workbook is open and the Invoice worksheet is active.
2. Click cell **B8**. You will enter a whole number validation rule for this cell.
3. Click the **Data** tab on the Ribbon, and then click the **Data Validation** button in the Data Tools group. The Data Validation dialog box opens. You use the Settings tab to enter the validation rule for the active cell.
4. On the Settings tab, click the **Allow** arrow, and then click **Whole number**. The Data Validation dialog box expands to display the options specific to whole numbers. The Ignore blank check box is checked, which means the validation rule is not applied when the cell is empty. If you uncheck the option, users are required to make an entry in the cell.
5. If necessary, click the **Data** arrow, and then click **between**. The dialog box reflects the selected criteria.
6. Click the **Minimum** box, and then type **1** to specify the smallest value a user can enter.
7. Press the **Tab** key to move to the Maximum box, and then type **19** to specify the largest value a user can enter. See Figure 8-13.

**Figure 8-13** Settings tab in the Data Validation dialog box

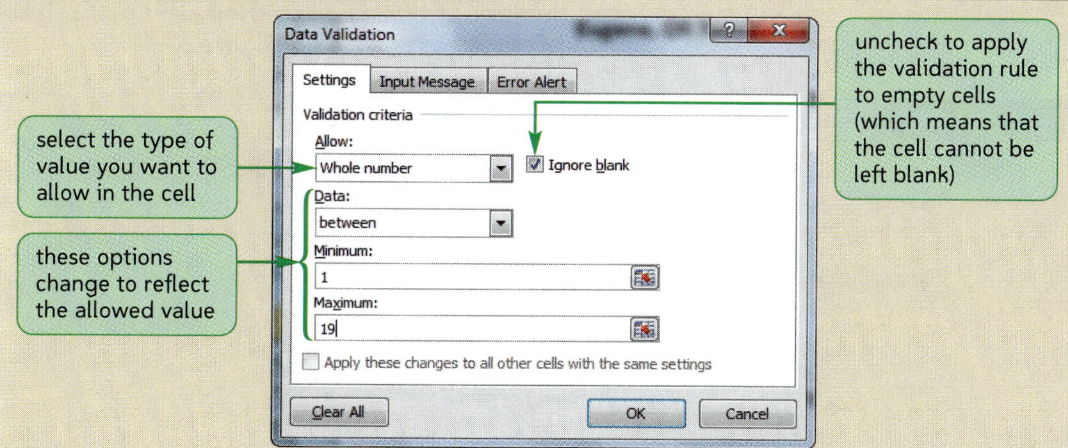


INSIGHT

### *Validating Existing Data*

Validation rules come into play only during data entry. If you add validation rules to a workbook that already contains data with erroneous values, Excel does not determine if any existing data is invalid. Instead, you can use the Circle Invalid Data command to help identify invalid data that is already in the workbook. (You'll learn about the Circle Invalid Data command later in this tutorial.)

## Creating an Input Message

One way to reduce the chance of a data-entry error is to display an input message when a user makes the cell active. An input message provides additional information about the type of data allowed for that cell. Input messages appear as ScreenTips next to the cell when the cell is selected. You can add an input message to a cell even if you don't set up a rule to validate the data in that cell.

Before volunteers enter a value for the ticket quantity, Ellen wants them to see the acceptable values that can be entered in the cell. The input message will help minimize the chance of a volunteer entering an invalid value. You will create an input message for cell B8.

**To create an input message for the Ticket Quantity cell:**

1. In the Data Validation dialog box, click the **Input Message** tab. You enter the input message title and text on this tab.
2. Verify that the **Show input message when cell is selected** check box contains a check mark. If you uncheck this option, you cannot enter a new input message and any existing input message will not be displayed when the selected cell becomes active.
3. Click in the **Title** box, and then type **Number of Tickets**. This title will appear in bold at the top of the ScreenTip above the text of the input message.
4. Press the **Tab** key to move the insertion point to the Input message box, and then type **Enter the number of tickets purchased.** This text will appear in the ScreenTip when the cell becomes active. See Figure 8-14.

**TIP**

The maximum number of characters allowed in the Title box is 32.

**Figure 8-14** Input Message tab in the Data Validation dialog box

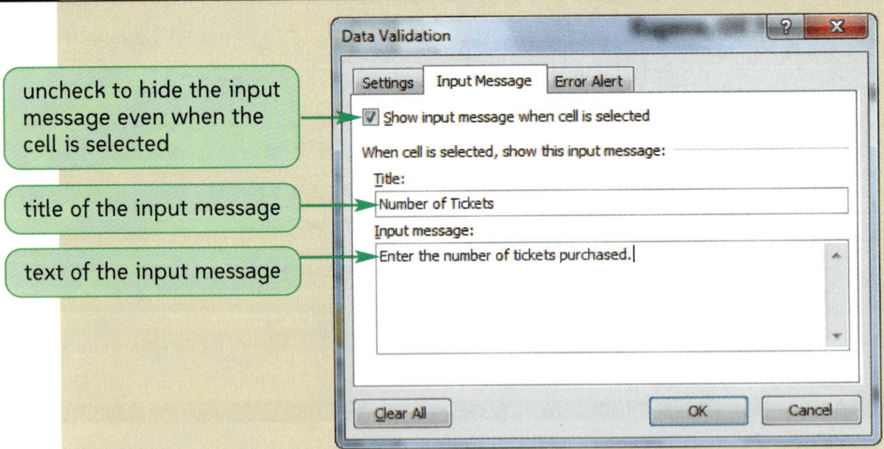


## Creating an Error Alert Style and Message

An error alert determines what happens after a user attempts to make an invalid entry in a cell that has a validation rule defined. The three error alert styles are Stop, Warning, and Information. The Stop alert prevents the entry from being stored in the cell. The Warning alert prevents the entry from being stored in the cell unless the user overrides the rejection and decides to continue using the data. The Information alert accepts the data value entered, but allows the user to choose to cancel the data entry.

Ellen wants to display an error alert if a volunteer enters data that violates the validation rule. Although ticket quantities between 1 and 19 are the norm for the theatre, occasionally a subscriber may want to purchase 20 or more tickets, and those entries should be allowed. To account for this possibility, you will create a Warning error alert that appears when a user enters a ticket quantity value greater than 20 or less than 1. The user can then verify the number entered. If the entry is correct, the user can accept the entry. If the entry is incorrect, the user can reenter the correct number.

You'll create the Warning error alert for the Ticket Quantity cell.

## To create the Warning error alert for the Ticket Quantity cell:

1. In the Data Validation dialog box, click the **Error Alert** tab. You use this tab to select the type of error alert and enter the message you want to appear.
2. Make sure that the **Show error alert after invalid data is entered** check box is checked. If unchecked, the error alert won't appear when an invalid value is entered in the cell.
3. Click the **Style** arrow, and then click **Warning**. This style allows the user to accept the invalid value, return to the cell and reenter a valid value, or cancel the data entry and restore the previous value to the cell.
4. Click in the **Title** box, and then type **Invalid Data - Number of Tickets**. This text will appear as the title of the error alert box.
5. Press the **Tab** key to move the insertion point to the Error message box, and then type **You have entered a value less than 1 or greater than 19. Check the number you entered. If it is correct, click Yes. If it is incorrect, click No. If you are not sure, click Cancel.** See Figure 8-15.

**TIP**

You might hide the input and error alert messages when only experienced users will enter data in the workbook by unchecking the Show check box. You can show them again if a new user will enter data.

**Figure 8-15** Error Alert tab in the Data Validation dialog box

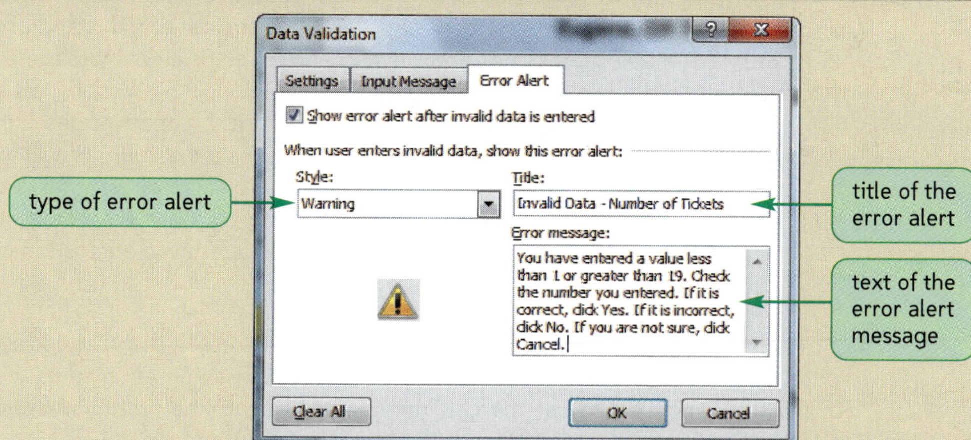


6. Click the **OK** button. The input message appears below cell B8 because the cell is active. See Figure 8-16.

**Figure 8-16** **Input message for cell B8**

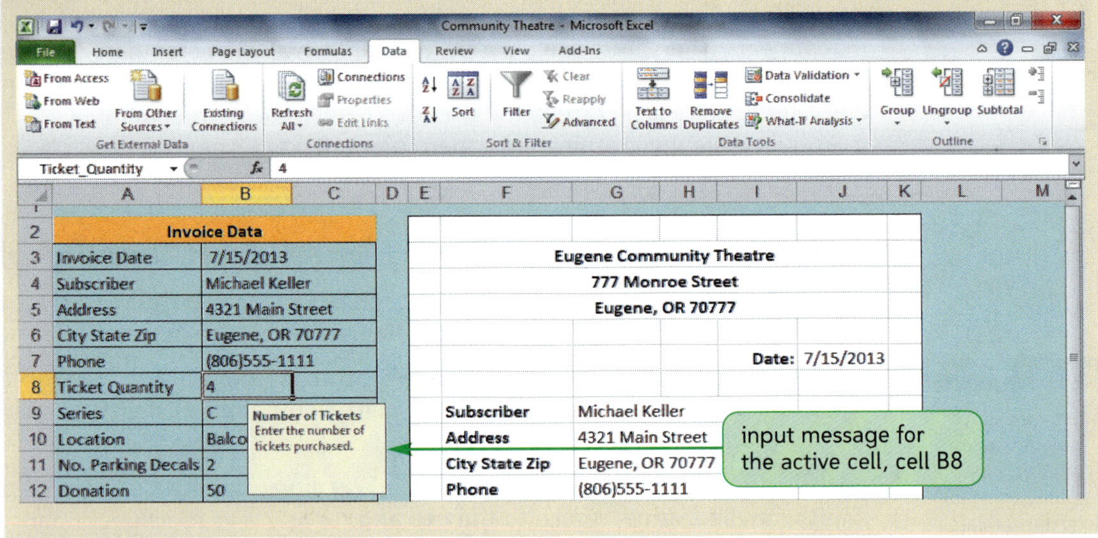


INSIGHT

### *Using Formulas to Define Complex Validation Criteria*

The built-in data validation rules are adequate for most simple needs. Sometimes, however, those rules just don't fit your specific worksheet. In those cases, you need to create a custom validation rule that includes a formula. To create a custom validation rule, open the Data Validation dialog box. On the Settings tab, click the Allow arrow, and then click Custom. You can then create the data validation formula.

The formula you specify must be in the form of a condition that returns either True or False. If True is returned, the data entered is considered valid and accepted. If False is returned, the entry is considered invalid and an error alert message is displayed. Consider two data validation examples.

The first example uses data validation to prevent the entry of dates that fall on Saturday or Sunday. The WEEKDAY function returns a number (1 to 7) for the date entered in the cell, and then you create a formula to display an error alert if values of 1 (Sunday) or 7 (Saturday) are detected. Assuming the date is entered in cell B2, the following formula returns False if either Saturday or Sunday is entered in cell B2:

```
=AND(WEEKDAY(B2)<>1,WEEKDAY(B2)<>7)
```

The second example uses data validation to ensure all product codes begin with the letter "C." To prevent any letter except a "C" from being entered as the first character in cell A2, you would use the LEFT function to extract the first character in the cell. The following formula returns True if the first character entered in cell A2 begins with a "C"; otherwise, an error alert message is displayed:

```
=LEFT(A2,1) = "C"
```

## Creating a List Validation Rule

You can use the data validation feature to restrict a cell to accept only entries that are on a list you create. You can create the list of valid entries in the Data Validation dialog box, or you can use a list of valid entries in a single column or row.

You will enter the validation rule for the Series being requested, which is one of the following six values: A, B, C, D, E, and F.

### To restrict the Series values to a list of entries:

1. Click cell **B9**. You will create a list validation rule for this cell.
2. In the Data Tools group on the Data tab, click the **Data Validation** button to open the Data Validation dialog box, and then click the **Settings** tab.
3. Click the **Allow** arrow, and then click **List**. The dialog box expands to display the Source box. You can enter values separated by commas directly in the Source box, or you can select a range of valid entries in the worksheet.
4. Click the **Collapse** button next to the Source box so you can see the entire worksheet.
5. Select the range **A16:A21**, which lists the valid six entry values, and then click the **Expand** button. The Data Validation dialog box returns to its full size and displays =$A$16:$A$21. Next, you'll enter an input message.
6. Click the **Input Message** tab, click in the **Title** box, and then type **Series** to enter the title of the input message.
7. Click in the Input message box, and then type **Click the arrow and select one of the choices listed.** to enter the text of the input message.
8. Click the **Error Alert** tab, and then verify that **Stop** appears in the Style box. You want to prevent a user from entering a value that is not included in the list of values you specified.
9. In the Title text box, type **Invalid Series** to enter the title of the error alert.
10. In the Error message box, type **An invalid series has been entered. Click Retry. Press the Esc key, and click the arrow to the right of cell B9. Select A, B, C, D, E, or F.** to enter the text of the error message.
11. Click the **OK** button. An arrow appears to the right of cell B9 and the input message appears in a ScreenTip.

You need to enter a data validation rule for cell B10, which indicates the subscriber's choice of seat location. This list validation rule will allow a user to select either Orchestra or Balcony and will include an error alert.

### To create a list validation rule for the Location cell:

1. Click cell **B10**. You will create a list validation rule for this cell.
2. In the Data Tools group on the Data tab, click the **Data Validation** button. The Data Validation dialog box opens.
3. Click the **Settings** tab, select **List** in the Allow box, click the **Source** box, and then select the range **B15:C15**. This range contains the two values you want to allow users to select for the seat location.
4. Click the **Input Message** tab, type **Location** in the Title box, and then type **Click the arrow and select Orchestra or Balcony.** in the Input message box.
5. Click the **Error Alert** tab, verify that **Stop** appears in the Style box, type **Invalid Location** in the Title box, and then type **An invalid location has been entered. Click Retry, press Esc, and click the arrow to the right of cell B10. Select Orchestra or Balcony.** in the Error message box.
6. Click the **OK** button. An arrow appears to the right of cell B10 and the input message appears in a ScreenTip.

After you create validation rules, you should test them. You do this by entering incorrect values that violate the validation rules. Keep in mind that the only way an error occurs in cells that have a list validation is if an incorrect entry is *typed* in the cell. Entering invalid data will ensure that validation rules work as expected. You will test the validation rules you've just created.

### To test the data validation rules:

1. Click cell **B8**. The input message appears in a ScreenTip, indicating the type of data allowed in the cell. You will enter an invalid value to test the validation rule for the Ticket Quantity field.
2. Type **30** and then press the **Tab** key. The Invalid Data - Number of Tickets message box opens, informing you that the value you entered might be incorrect. The entry 30 is incorrect; you'll enter a valid number.
3. Click the **No** button, type **4** in cell B8, and then press the **Enter** key. The data is entered in cell B8. Cell B9 is the active cell and the input message for Series appears.
4. Click the **arrow** to the right of cell B9, and then click **B**. The value is accepted. The only way an error occurs in cells that have a list validation is if an incorrect entry is *typed* in the cell. You'll try that method.
5. In cell B9, type **G**. The Invalid Series message box opens.
6. Click the **Retry** button to close the message box, and then press the **Esc** key to return the original value from the cell.
7. Click the **arrow** to the right of cell B9, and then click **C**.
8. In cell B10, enter **Mezzanine**. The Invalid Location message box opens, indicating that the location must be Orchestra or Balcony.
9. Click the **Retry** button, and then press the **Esc** key to return the original value entered. The three validation rules you entered work as you intended.

**TIP**

After the error alert appears, you must press the Esc key to return the original value to the cell; otherwise, the error alert will reappear when you click the arrow to make another selection.

**INSIGHT**

### *Validating Existing Data*

Validation rules come into play only during data entry. If you add validation rules to a workbook that already contains data with erroneous values, Excel does not determine if any existing data is invalid.

To ensure the entire workbook contains valid data, you need to also verify any data previously entered in the workbook. You can use the Circle Invalid Data command to find and mark cells that contain invalid data. Red circles appear around any data that does not meet the validation criteria, making it simple to scan a worksheet for errors. After you correct the data in a cell, the circle disappears.

To display circles around invalid data, perform the following steps:

1. Apply validation rules to existing range.
2. In the Data Tools group on the Data tab, click the Data Validation button arrow, and then click Circle Invalid Data. Red circles appear around cells that contain invalid data.
3. To remove the circle from a single cell, enter valid data in the cell.
4. To hide all circles, in the Data Tools group on the Data tab, click the Data Validation button arrow, and then click Clear Validation Circles.

To ensure an error-free workbook, you should use the Circle Invalid Data command to verify data entered before you set up the validation criteria or to verify data in a workbook you inherited from someone else, such as a coworker.

# Protecting a Worksheet and a Workbook

Another way to reduce data-entry errors is to limit access to certain parts of the workbook. Worksheet protection prevents users from changing cell contents, such as editing formulas in a worksheet. Workbook protection prevents users from changing the workbook's organization, such as inserting or deleting worksheets in the workbook. You can even keep users from viewing the formulas used in the workbook.

Ellen wants to protect the contents of the Invoice and Ticket Data worksheets. She wants volunteers to have access only to the range B3:B12 in the Invoice worksheet, where new invoice data is entered. She wants to prevent volunteers from editing the contents of any cells in the Ticket Data worksheet.

## Locking and Unlocking Cells

Every cell in a workbook has a **locked property** that determines whether changes can be made to that cell. The locked property has no impact as long as the worksheet is unprotected. However, after you protect a worksheet, the locked property controls whether the cell can be edited. You unlock a cell by turning off the locked property. By default, the locked property is turned on for each cell, and worksheet protection is turned off.

So, unless you unlock cells in a worksheet *before* protecting the worksheet, all of the cells in the worksheet will be locked, and you won't be able to make any changes in the worksheet. Usually, you will want to protect the worksheet, but leave some cells unlocked. For example, you might want to lock cells that contain formulas and formatting so they cannot be changed, but unlock cells in which you want to enter data.

To protect some—but not all—cells in a worksheet, you first turn off the locked property of cells in which data can be entered. Then, you protect the worksheet to activate the locked property for the remaining cells.

In the Invoice worksheet, users should be able to enter data in the range B3:B12 but not any other cell. To do this, you must unlock the cells in the range B3:B12.

**To unlock the cells in the range B3:B12:**

1. In the Invoice worksheet, select the range **B3:B12**. You want to unlock the cells in this range before you protect the worksheet.
2. Click the **Home** tab on the Ribbon, and then click the **Dialog Box Launcher** in the Font group. The Format Cells dialog box opens with the Font tab active.
3. Click the **Protection** tab, and then click the **Locked** check box to remove the check mark.
4. Click the **OK** button. The cells in the range B3:B12 are unlocked.
5. Click cell **A1** to deselect the range.

## Protecting a Worksheet

When you set up worksheet protection, you specify which actions are still available to users in the protected worksheet. For example, you can choose to allow users to insert new rows or columns, or to delete rows and columns. You can limit the user to selecting only unlocked cells, or allow the user to select any cell in the worksheet. These choices remain active as long as the worksheet is protected.

A protected worksheet can always be unprotected. You can also add a password to the protected worksheet that users must enter in order to turn off the protection. If you are concerned that users will turn off protection and make changes to formulas, you should use a password; otherwise, it's probably best to not specify a password.

REFERENCE

*Protecting a Worksheet*

- Select the cells and ranges to unlock so that users can enter data in them.
- In the Font group on the Home tab, click the Dialog Box Launcher.
- In the Format Cells dialog box, click the Protection tab, click the Locked check box to remove the check mark, and then click the OK button.
- In the Changes group on the Review tab, click the Protect Sheet button.
- Enter a password (optional).
- Select all of the actions you want to allow users to take when the worksheet is protected.
- Click the OK button.

Ellen wants to protect the Invoice and Ticket Data worksheets, but she doesn't want a password specified. You will enable worksheet protection that will allow users to select any cell in those worksheets, but enter data only in the unlocked cells.

## To protect the Invoice worksheet:

1. Click the **Review** tab on the Ribbon, and then click the **Protect Sheet** button in the Changes group. The Protect Sheet dialog box opens. See Figure 8-17.

**Figure 8-17** **Protect Sheet dialog box**

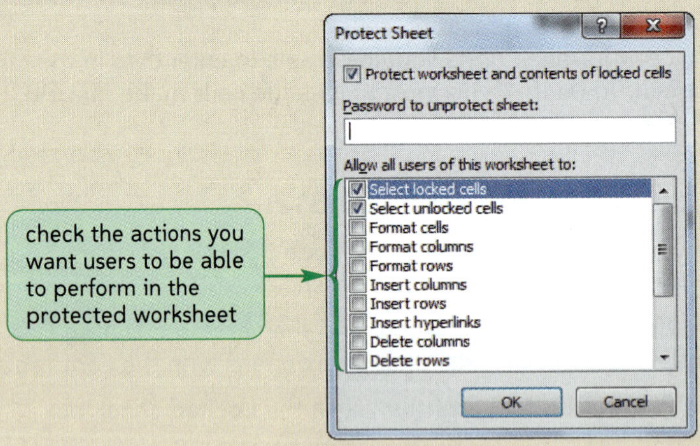


**TIP**

Keep passwords in a safe place. Remember, passwords are case sensitive. If you forget the password, it is very difficult to remove the worksheet protection.

You will leave the Password to unprotect sheet box blank because you do not want to use a password. By default, users can select locked and unlocked cells, which are all of the cells in the worksheet, but they can enter or edit values only in unlocked cells.

2. Click the **OK** button. The Protect Sheet dialog box closes.

Any time you modify a worksheet, you should test the worksheet to ensure that changes work as intended. You'll test the protection you added to the Invoice worksheet by trying to edit a locked cell and then trying to edit an unlocked cell in the Invoice worksheet.

### To test the Invoice worksheet protection:

1. Click cell **I14**, and then type **8**. As soon as you press any key, a dialog box opens, indicating that the cell is protected and cannot be modified. See Figure 8-18.

Figure 8-18 Message displayed after trying to change a protected cell

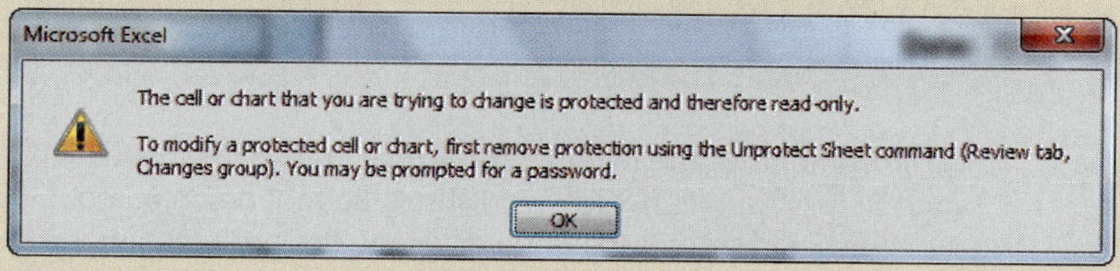


2. Click the **OK** button.
3. Click cell **B8**, type **8** and then press the **Enter** key. The ticket quantity is updated because you allowed editing in the range B3:B12. A user can enter and edit values in these cells. Although users can select any cell in the worksheet, they cannot make an entry in any other cell.
4. On the Quick Access Toolbar, click the **Undo** button to return the ticket quantity to 4.

You will repeat this process to protect all of the cells in the Ticket Data worksheet. Then you will test to see what would happen if someone tried to edit one of the cells in the Ticket Data worksheet.

### To protect and test the Ticket Data worksheet:

1. Switch to the **Ticket Data** worksheet.
2. In the Changes group on the Review tab, click the **Protect Sheet** button. The Protect Sheet dialog box opens.
3. Click the **OK** button to accept the default set of user actions.
4. Click cell **A2**, and then type **B**. A dialog box opens, indicating that the cell is protected and cannot be modified. All of the cells in this worksheet are protected because no cells have been unlocked.
5. Click the **OK** button to close the dialog box.

## Protecting a Workbook

Worksheet protection applies only to the contents of a worksheet, not to the worksheet itself. To keep a worksheet from being modified, you need to protect the workbook. You can protect both the structure and the windows of a workbook. Protecting the structure prohibits users from renaming, deleting, hiding, or inserting worksheets. Protecting the windows prohibits users from moving, resizing, closing, or hiding parts of the Excel window. The default is to protect only the structure of the workbook, not the windows used to display it.

You can also add a password to the workbook protection. However, the same guideline applies here as for protecting worksheets. Add a password only if you are concerned that others might unprotect the workbook and modify it. If you add a password, keep in mind that it is case sensitive and you cannot unprotect the workbook without it.

REFERENCE

*Protecting a Workbook*

- In the Changes group on the Review tab, click the Protect Workbook button.
- Click the check boxes to indicate whether you want to protect the workbook's structure, windows, or both.
- Enter a password (optional).
- Click the OK button.

The contents of the Invoice and Ticket Data worksheets, with the exception of the range B3:B12 in the Invoice worksheet, cannot be changed. However, a theatre volunteer could inadvertently rename or delete the protected worksheet. To keep the worksheets themselves from being modified, you will protect the workbook. Ellen doesn't want users to be able to change the structure of the workbook, so you will set workbook protection for the structure, but not the window.

**To protect the Community Theatre workbook:**

1. In the Changes group on the Review tab, click the **Protect Workbook** button. The Protect Structure and Windows dialog box opens. You can choose to protect the structure, protect the windows, or both. See Figure 8-19.

Figure 8-19 **Protect Structure and Windows dialog box**

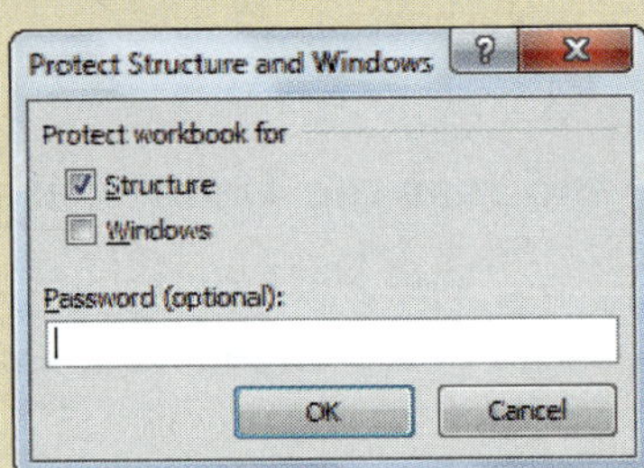


2. Make sure the **Structure** check box is checked, the **Windows** check box is unchecked, and the **Password** box is blank.
3. Click the **OK** button to protect the workbook without specifying a password.
4. Right-click the **Ticket Data** sheet tab. On the shortcut menu, notice that the Insert, Delete, Rename, Move or Copy, Tab Color, Hide, and Unhide commands are gray, indicating that the options that modify the worksheets are no longer available for the Ticket Data worksheet.
5. Press the **Esc** key to close the shortcut menu.

## Unprotecting a Worksheet and a Workbook

You can turn off worksheet protection at any time. This is often referred to as unprotecting the worksheet. You need to unprotect a worksheet to edit its contents. If you assigned a password when you protected the worksheet, you would need to enter the password to remove worksheet protection. Likewise, you can unprotect the workbook. If you need to insert a new worksheet or rename an existing worksheet, you can unprotect the protected workbook, make the changes to the structure, and apply workbook protection again.

At this point, you still have a lot of editing to do in the Invoice worksheet, so you'll turn off worksheet protection in that worksheet. Later, when you've completed your modifications, Ellen can turn worksheet protection back on.

**TIP**

To remove workbook protection, click the Protect Workbook button in the Changes group on the Review tab.

**To turn off worksheet protection for the Invoice worksheet:**

1. Switch to the **Invoice** worksheet.
2. In the Changes group on the Review tab, click the **Unprotect Sheet** button. Worksheet protection is removed from the Invoice worksheet. The button changes back to the Protect Sheet button.

## Inserting Comments

Comments are often used in workbooks to: (a) explain the contents of a particular cell, such as a complex formula; (b) provide instructions to users; and (c) share ideas and notes from several users collaborating on a project. The username for your installation of Excel appears in bold at the top of the comments box. If you collaborate on a workbook, the top of the comments boxes would show the name of each user who created that comment. A small red triangle appears in the upper-right corner of a cell with a comment. The comment box appears when you point to a cell with a comment.

REFERENCE

*Inserting a Comment*

- Click the cell to which you want to attach a comment.
- Right-click the cell, and then click Insert Comment on the shortcut menu.
  *or*
  In the Comments group on the Review tab, click the New Comment button.
- Type the comment into the box.

Ellen wants you to insert a note in cell A2 about entering data from the order form into the input section, and a note in cell J18 explaining how the IF and VLOOKUP functions are used to determine the cost of theatre tickets.

**TIP**

You can also add a comment by right-clicking the cell, and then clicking Insert Comment on the shortcut menu.

**To insert comments in cells A2 and J18:**

1. In the Invoice worksheet, click cell **A2**.
2. In the Comments group on the Review tab, click the **New Comment** button. A box opens to the right of cell A2. The username for your installation of Excel appears in bold at the top of the box. A small red triangle appears in the upper-right corner of the cell.
3. Type **Enter all data from the order form into cells B3 through B11** in the box. An arrow points from the box to cell A2, which contains the comment. A selection box with sizing handles appears around the box. See Figure 8-20.

**Figure 8-20** Comment added to cell A2

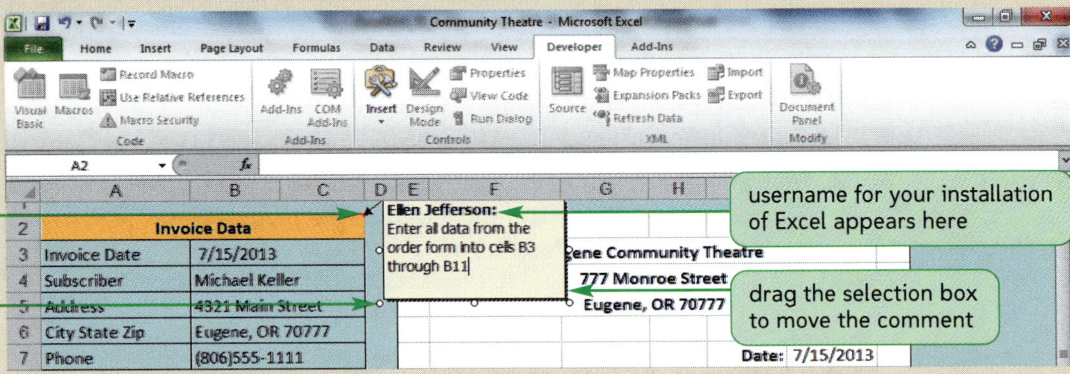


4. Click cell **B12** to hide the comment. The comment disappears. A small red triangle remains in the upper-right corner of cell A2 to indicate this cell contains a comment.
5. Move the pointer over cell **A2**. The comment appears.
6. Click cell **A2**.
7. In the Comments group on the Review tab, click the **Edit Comment** button. The comment appears with the insertion point at the end of the comment text, so you can edit the incorrect cell reference.
8. Select **B11** in the comment box, and then type **B12**. The comment in cell A2 now correctly references the range B3:B12.
9. Click any cell to hide the comment, and then point to cell **A2** to view the edited comment.
10. Click cell **J18**, and then click the **New Comment** button in the Comments group on the Review tab. A comment box opens to the right of cell J18.
11. Type **This IF function determines whether to use a VLOOKUP function referencing column 2 or 3 of the Ticket Price Table** in the box.
12. Drag the lower-right sizing handle down to increase the size of the box to fit the comment.
13. Click cell **I17** to hide the comment. A small red triangle remains in the upper-right corner of cell J18 to indicate it contains a comment.
14. Point to cell **J18** to see the comment. Ellen decides that the volunteers don't need to know how the ticket cost is calculated. You'll delete the comment in cell J18.
15. Click cell **J18**, and then click the **Delete** button in the Comments group on the Review tab. The comment is deleted, and the red triangle in the upper-right corner of cell J18 is removed.

**TIP**

To keep an active cell's comment on-screen, click the Show/Hide Comment button in the Comments group on the Review tab. Click the button again to hide the active cell's comment.

PROSKILLS

## Written Communication: Documenting a Spreadsheet

Providing documentation for a spreasheet is important because it provides instructions on the spreadsheet's use, defines technical terms, explains complex formulas, and identifies assumptions. By documenting a spreadsheet, you help users work more effectively. In addition, documentation helps you recall months or years from now what is in the spreadsheet that might otherwise be forgotten. Furthermore, when someone else becomes responsible for modifying the spreadsheet in the future, the documentation will help that person get up to speed quickly.

It is helpful for you to create a Documentation worksheet to provide an overview, definitions, assumptions, and instructions on how to use various parts of a workbook. Excel also offers many tools to help you document spreadsheets, including:

- Defined names and structured references to make formulas easier to create and understand
- Data validation including input messages specifying what to enter in a cell, and error messages providing instructions on what to do if the data entered is incorrect
- Cell comments to explain complex formulas, give reminders, and so on
- Formula mode to view all formulas in a worksheet at one time

Providing documentation will help users get a better understanding of the application, saving time and frustration.

In this session, you used data validation to help ensure that all values entered in the Invoice worksheet are valid. You created validation rules that included input messages and error alert messages. You learned how to protect and unprotect both the worksheet and the workbook. In addition, you used comments to add notes to specific cells. In the next session, you'll automate some of the steps in the application by recording macros.

REVIEW

## Session 8.2 Quick Check

1. Why do you want to validate data?
2. What is the purpose of the input message in the Data Validation command?
3. Describe the three types of error alert messages Excel can display when a user violates a validation rule.
4. What is a locked cell?
5. What is the difference between worksheet protection and workbook protection?
6. Can you rename a protected worksheet? Explain why or why not.
7. Give two reasons for adding a comment to a worksheet cell.

# SESSION 8.3 VISUAL OVERVIEW

The Record Macro button opens the Record Macro dialog box, which you use to start recording a macro.

The Macros button opens the Macro dialog box, which you use to run or edit existing macros in the open workbook.

The **macro security settings** control what Excel will do about macros in a workbook when you open that workbook. You can set the level of macro security.

In the Record Macro dialog box, you specify a name, shortcut key, location, and description of the macro.

You can automate any task you perform repeatedly with a macro. The macro recorder records keystrokes and mouse actions as you perform them.

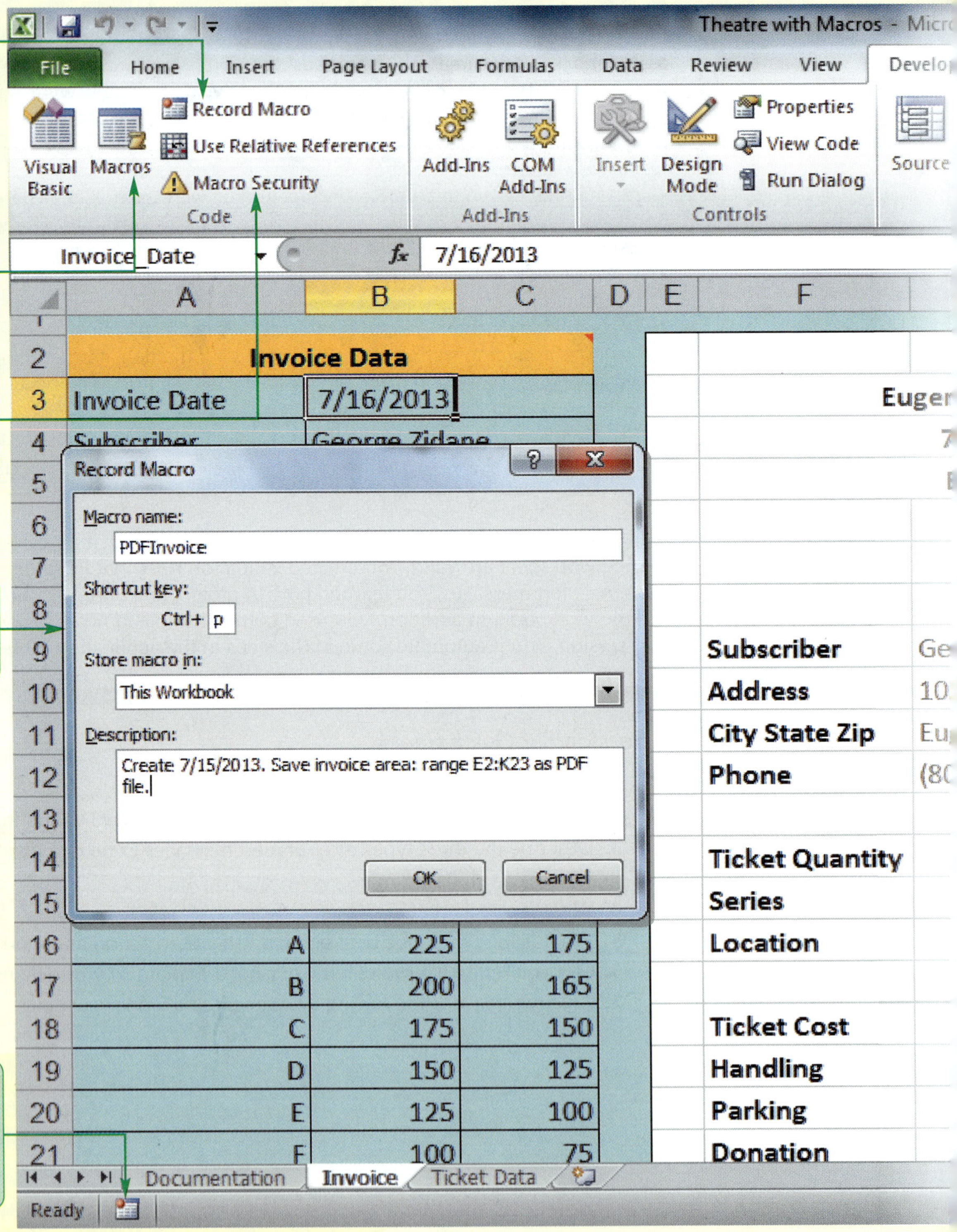

# WORKING WITH MACROS

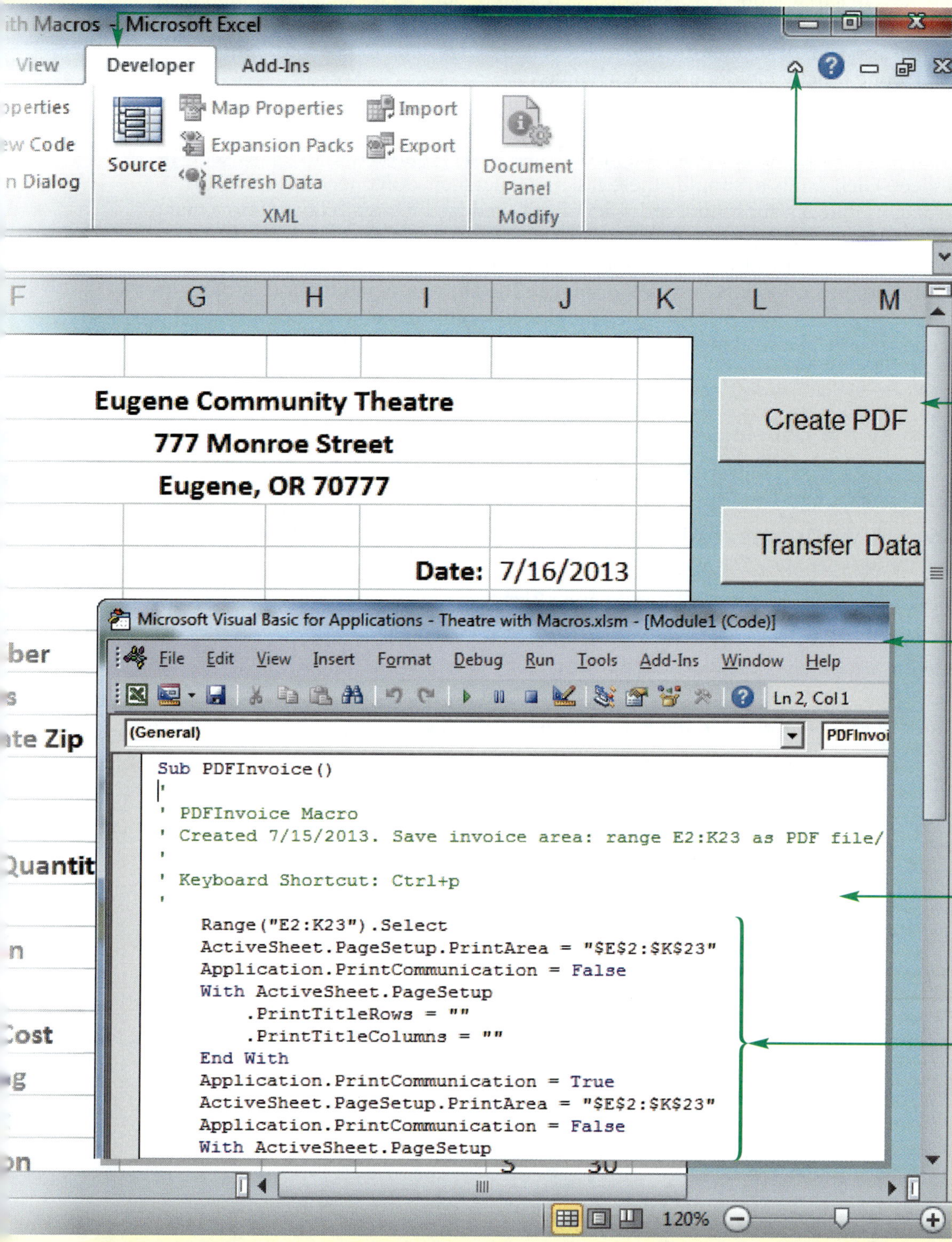


You can customize the Ribbon by showing or hiding tabs. You need to show the Developer tab to create macros.

You can minimize the Ribbon to make more space for a worksheet. When the Ribbon is minimized, only the Quick Access Toolbar and the tab names are displayed.

A macro button runs the assigned macro when clicked. Placing a macro button on the worksheet makes it easier for a user to run the macro.

To view the code of a macro, you need to open the **Visual Basic Editor (VBE)**, which is a separate application that works with Excel and all of the Office programs to view, debug, edit, and manage VBA code.

A **macro** is a series of stored commands that can be run whenever you need to perform the task. Commands can be viewed and/or edited in the Visual Basic Editor.

When you run a macro, Excel performs each of the recorded actions in the same order as when it was recorded. Macros perform repetitive tasks faster than you can.

## Automating Tasks with Macros

Using a macro, you can automate any task you perform repeatedly. For example, you can create a macro to print a worksheet, insert a set of dates and values, or import data from a text file and store it in Excel. Macros perform repetitive tasks consistently and faster than you can. And, after the macro is created and tested, you can be assured the tasks are done exactly the same way each time.

Ellen needs to save only the invoice as a PDF file so she can later send it as an attachment to the season subscriber along with an email confirming the ticket purchase transaction. In addition, data from the invoice needs to be transferred to the Ticket Data worksheet. Ellen wants to simplify these tasks so volunteers don't need to repeat the same actions for each subscriber order and also to reduce the possibility of errors being introduced during the repetitive process. You will create a macro for each action.

To create and run macros, you need to use the Developer tab. By default, this tab is not displayed on the Ribbon, so you'll display it. The Developer tab has four groups: one for code, one for controls, one for XML, and one to modify document controls. You'll use the Code group when working with macros. You'll add the Developer tab to the Ribbon.

### To display the Developer tab on the Ribbon:

1. If you took a break after the previous session, make sure the Community Theatre workbook is open and the Invoice worksheet is active.
2. Look for the **Developer** tab on the Ribbon. If you do not see the Developer tab, continue with Step 3. If you see the Developer tab, continue with Step 7.
3. Click the **File** tab on the Ribbon to open Backstage view, and then click the **Options** button in the navigation bar. The Excel Options dialog box opens.
4. In the left pane, click **Customize Ribbon**. See Figure 8-21.

**Figure 8-21** Customize Ribbon options in the Excel Options dialog box

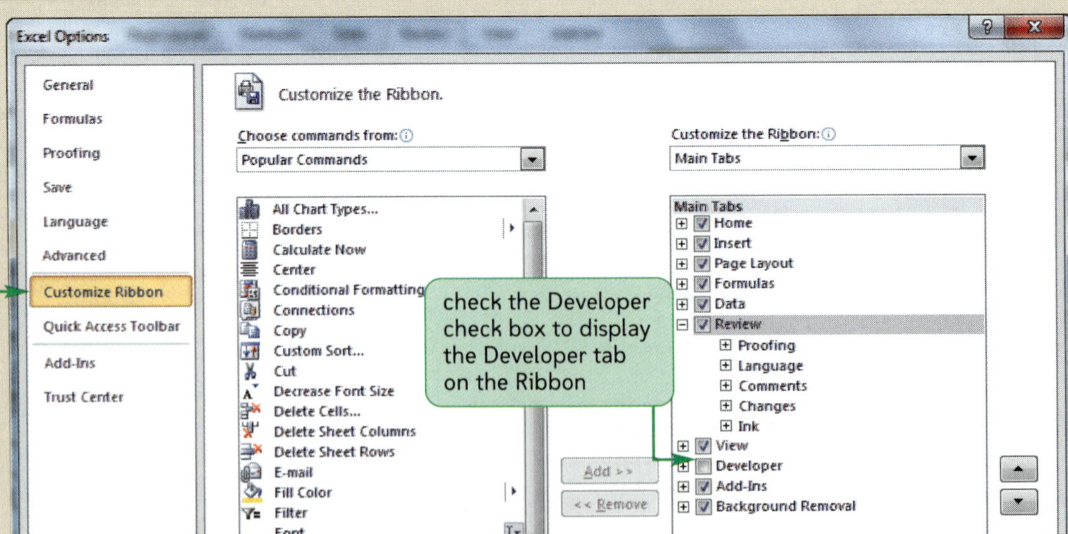


5. In the right pane, click the **Developer** check box to insert a check mark.
6. Click the **OK** button. The Developer tab appears on the Ribbon.

7. Click the **Developer** tab. See Figure 8-22.

**Figure 8-22** Developer tab on the Ribbon

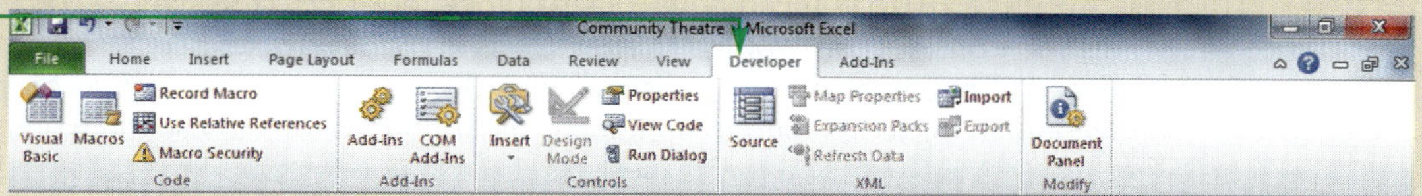


# Protecting Against Macro Viruses

In recent years, viruses have been attached as macros to files created in Excel and other Office programs. A **virus** is a computer program designed to copy itself into other programs with the intention of causing mischief or harm. When unsuspecting users opened these infected workbooks, Excel automatically ran the attached virus-infected macro. **Macro viruses** are a type of virus that uses a program's own macro programming language to distribute the virus. Most macro viruses are not harmful and do not affect data in any way. For example, one macro virus changed the title bar text from *Microsoft Excel* to *Microsofa Excel*. Occasionally, macro viruses are destructive and can modify or delete files that may not be recoverable. Because it is possible for a macro to contain a virus, Microsoft Office 2010 provides several options from which you can choose to set a security level you feel comfortable with.

## Macro Security Settings

The macro security settings control what Excel will do about macros in a workbook when you open that workbook. For example, one user may choose to run macros only if they are "digitally signed" by a developer who is on a list of trusted sources. Another user might want to disable all macros in workbooks and see a notification when a workbook contains macros. The user can then elect to enable the macros. Excel has four macro security settings, which are described in Figure 8-23.

**Figure 8-23** Macro security settings

| Setting | Description |
|---|---|
| Disable all macros without notification | All macros in all workbooks are disabled and no security alerts about macros are displayed. Use this setting if you don't want macros to run. |
| Disable all macros with notification | All macros in all workbooks are disabled, but security alerts appear when the workbook contains a macro. Use this default setting to choose on a case-by-case basis whether to run a macro. |
| Disable all macros except digitally signed macros | The same as the Disable all macros with notification setting except any macro signed by a trusted publisher runs if you have already trusted the publisher. Otherwise, security alerts appear when a workbook contains a macro. |
| Enable all macros | All macros in all workbooks run. Use this setting temporarily in such cases as when developing an application that contains macros. This setting is not recommended for regular use. |

You set macro security in the Trust Center. The **Trust Center** is a central location for all of the security settings in Office 2010. By default, all potentially dangerous content, such as macros and workbooks with external links, is blocked without warning. If content is blocked, the Message Bar (also called the trust bar) located under the Ribbon appears, notifying you that some content was disabled. You can click the Message Bar to enable that content.

In Office 2010, you can define a set of locations (file paths) where you can place files you consider trustworthy. This feature is known as Trusted Locations. Any workbook opened from a trusted location is considered safe, and content such as macros will work without having to respond to additional security questions to use the workbook.

REFERENCE

### *Setting Macro Security in Excel*

- In the Code group on the Developer tab, click the Macro Security button.
- Click the option button for the macro setting you want.
- Click the OK button.

*or*

- Click the File tab, and then click the Options button in the navigation bar.
- Click the Trust Center category, and then click the Trust Center Settings button.
- Click the Macro Settings category, and then click the option button for a macro setting.
- Click the OK button.

Ellen wants some protection against macro viruses, so she suggests you set the security level to "Disable all macros with notification." When you open a file with macros, this macro security level disables the macros and displays a security alert, allowing you to enable the macros if you believe the workbook comes from a trusted source. After the macros are enabled, you can run them.

### To set the macro security level:

1. In the Code group on the Developer tab, click the **Macro Security** button. The Trust Center dialog box opens with the Macro Settings category displayed.
2. In the Macro Settings section, click the **Disable all macros with notification** option button if it is not selected. See Figure 8-24.

**Figure 8-24** Macro Settings in the Trust Center dialog box

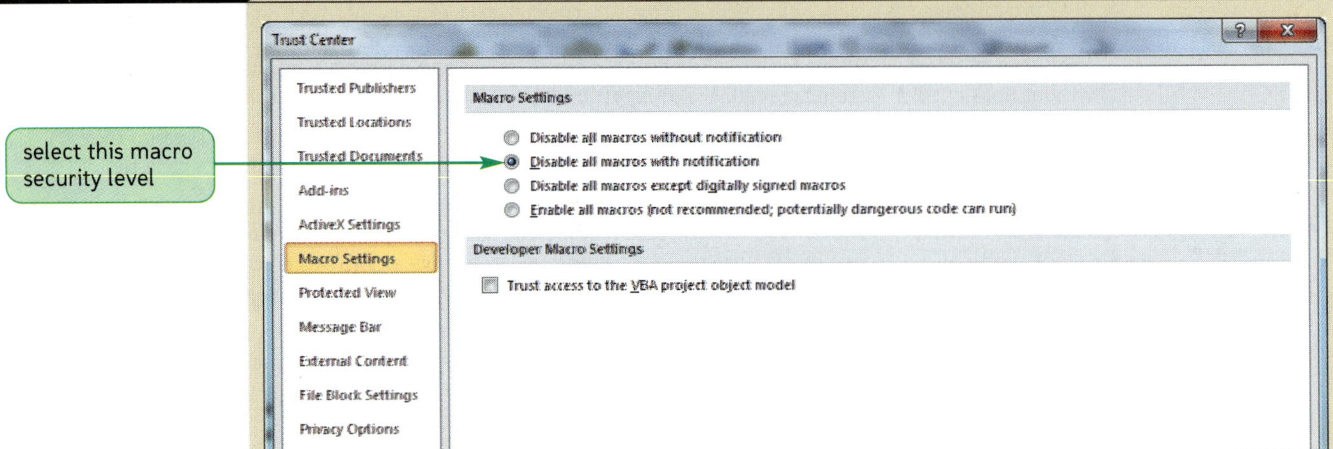


3. Click the **OK** button.

Each time you open a workbook that contains a macro detected by the Trust Center, the macro is disabled and a Message Bar containing the Security Warning that macros have been disabled appears below the Ribbon. If you developed the workbook or trust the person who sent you the workbook, click the Enable Content button to run the macros in the workbook. If you do not click the Enable Content button, you cannot run the macros in the workbook, but you can use the rest of the workbook.

INSIGHT

### *Using Digital Signatures with Macros*

A **digital signature** is like a seal of approval. It's often used to identify the author of a workbook that contains macros. You add a digital signature as the last step before you distribute a file. Before you can add a digital signature to a workbook, you need to obtain a digital ID (also called a digital certificate) that proves your identity. Digital certificates are typically issued by a certificate authority. After you have a digital certificate, do the following to digitally sign a workbook:

1. Click the File tab on the Ribbon, and then, in the navigation bar, click Info.
2. On the Info tab, click the Protect Workbook button, and then click the Add a Digital Signature button.
3. If a message dialog box opens, click the OK button. The Sign dialog box opens.
4. In the Purpose for signing this document box, enter a reason why you are adding a digital signature to this workbook.
5. Click the Sign button, and then click the OK button. The invisible digital signature does not appear within the workbook, but users will see the Signatures button on the status bar.

By digitally signing a workbook that contains a macro you intend to publicly distribute, you assure others of two things: (1) the identity of the creator of the macro, and (2) the macro has not been altered since the digital signature was created.

When you open a digitally signed file, you can see who the author is and decide whether the information in the file is authentic and whether you trust that the macros in the workbook are safe to run.

The digital signature is removed any time a file is saved after the signature has been added to the file. Therefore, no one (including the original workbook author) can open a digitally signed file, make changes to the workbook, save the workbook, and then send the file to another user with the digital signature intact. The original author must digitally sign the modified workbook.

## Recording a Macro

You can create an Excel macro in one of two ways: You can use the macro recorder to record keystrokes and mouse actions as you perform them, or you can enter a series of commands in the **Visual Basic for Applications (VBA)** programming language. The macro recorder can record only those actions you perform with the keyboard or mouse. The macro recorder is a good choice for creating simple macros. For more sophisticated macros, you might need to write VBA code directly in the Visual Basic Editor.

For Ellen's application, the tasks you need to perform can all be done with the keyboard and the mouse, so you will use the macro recorder to record the two macros. One macro will save the invoice as a PDF file, which is a file format created by Adobe Systems for document exchange. The second macro will transfer data from the Invoice worksheet to the Ticket Data worksheet.

PROSKILLS

*Decision Making: Planning and Recording a Macro*

Advance planning and practice help to ensure you create an error-free macro. First, decide what you want to accomplish. Then, consider the best way to achieve those results. Next, practice the keystrokes and mouse actions before you actually record the macro. This may seem like extra work, but it reduces the chance of error when you actually record the macro. As you set up the macro, consider the following:

- Choose a descriptive name that helps you recognize the macro's purpose.
- Weigh the benefits of selecting a shortcut key against its drawbacks. Although a shortcut key is an easy way to run a macro, you are limited to one-letter shortcuts, which can make it difficult to remember the purpose of each shortcut key. In addition, the macro shortcut keys will override the standard Office shortcuts for the workbook.
- Store the macro with the current workbook unless the macro can be used with other workbooks.
- Include a description that provides an overview of the macro and perhaps your name and contact information.

Good decision making includes thinking about what to do and what *not* to do as you progress to your goals. This is true when developing a macro as well.

Each macro must have a unique name that begins with a letter. The macro name can contain up to 255 characters, including letters, numbers, and the underscore symbol. The macro name cannot include spaces or special characters. It is helpful to use a descriptive name that describes the macro's purpose.

**TIP**

You can also use Ctrl+Shift+*letter* as the shortcut by entering the uppercase letter for the key.

You can assign a shortcut key to run the macro directly from the keyboard. Macro shortcut keys are used to run a macro. Assigning a shortcut key overrides the equivalent default Excel shortcut for the open workbook. For example, using the Ctrl+p keys to run a macro overrides the default Excel 2010 shortcut for printing a selected area while the workbook containing the macro is open. Some people find macro shortcut keys a quick way to run a macro; others dislike them because they override the original function of the shortcut key. It's a personal preference.

A macro needs to be stored somewhere. By default, the macro is stored in the current workbook, making the macro available in only that workbook when it is open. Another option is to store the macro in the **Personal Macro workbook**, a hidden workbook named Personal.xlsb that opens whenever you start Excel, making the macro available any time you use Excel. The Personal Macro workbook stores commonly used macros that apply to many workbooks. It is most convenient for users on stand-alone computers. Finally, you can store the macro in a new workbook. Keep in mind that the new workbook must be open to use the macro. For example, an accountant might store a set of macros that help with end-of-the-month tasks in a separate workbook.

You can also add a description of the macro to briefly explain what it does. You can also include the name of the person to contact and the date it was created.

REFERENCE

*Recording a Macro*

- In the Code group on the Developer tab, click the Record Macro button.
- Enter a name for the macro, and then specify the location to store the macro.
- Specify a shortcut key (optional).
- Enter a description of the macro (optional).
- Click the OK button to start the macro recorder.
- Perform the tasks you want to automate.
- Click the Stop Recording button.

Ellen provides you with the following outline of the actions needed for the macro to save the invoice as a PDF file:

1. Set the range E2:K23 as the print area.
2. Define the Page Layout setting with the custom heading "Customer Invoice."
3. Create the PDF file and name the PDF file "Invoice."
4. Make cell A1 the active cell.

You'll record the steps for this macro using a macro named "PDFInvoice" that is assigned a keyboard shortcut, has a description, and is stored in the Community Theatre workbook. You'll start the macro recorder.

If you make a mistake when recording the macro, you can close the workbook without saving, reopen the workbook, and then record the macro again.

### To start the macro recorder:

1. Save your workbook.
2. In the Code group on the Developer tab, click the **Record Macro** button. The Record Macro dialog box opens. The Macro name box displays a default name for the macro that consists of the word "Macro" followed by a number that is one greater than the number of macros already recorded in the workbook during the current Excel session. See Figure 8-25.

**Figure 8-25** Record Macro dialog box

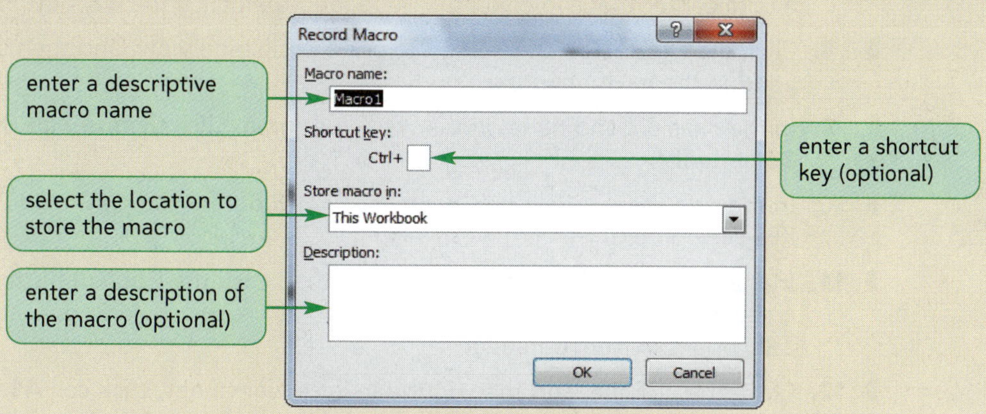


3. In the Macro name box, type **PDFInvoice** to change the default name to a more descriptive one, and then press the **Tab** key.
4. In the Shortcut key box, type **p** to set Ctrl+p as the shortcut to run the macro from the keyboard, and then press the **Tab** key.
5. Verify that the Store macro in box is set to **This Workbook** to store the macro in the Community Theatre workbook, and then press the **Tab** key.
6. In the Description box, type **Created 7/15/2013. Save invoice area: range E2:K23 as PDF file.** to enter notes about the macro.
7. Click the **OK** button. The workbook enters macro record mode. The Record Macro button in the Code group on the Developer tab changes to the Stop Recording button, which also appears on the status bar.

From this point on, *every* mouse click and keystroke you perform will be recorded and stored as part of the PDFInvoice macro. For that reason, it's very important to follow the instructions in the next steps precisely. Take your time as you perform each step, reading the entire step carefully first. After you finish recording the keystrokes, click the Stop Recording button to turn off the macro recorder.

**To record the PDFInvoice macro:**

1. Click the **Page Layout** tab on the Ribbon.
2. Select the range **E2:K23**. This range contains the invoice area.
3. In the Page Setup group, click the **Print Area** button, and then click **Set Print Area**. The invoice area is set as the print area. Next, you'll insert a custom header.
4. In the Page Setup group, click the **Dialog Box Launcher** to open the Page Setup dialog box.
5. Click the **Header/Footer** tab, and then click the **Custom Header** button to open the Header dialog box.
6. Click in the **Center section** box, type **Customer Invoice** and then click the **OK** button to close the Header dialog box.
7. In the Page Setup dialog box, click the **Margins** tab, click the **Horizontally** check box to center the invoice on the page, and then click the **OK** button.
8. Click the **File** tab on the Ribbon to open Backstage view, and then click **Save & Send** in the navigation bar.
9. In the Save & Send pane, in the File Types area, click **Create PDF/XPS Document**.
10. In the right pane, click the **Create PDF/XPS** button to open the Publish as PDF or XPS dialog box.
11. In the File name box, type **Invoice** and then click the **Publish** button. The invoice is saved as a PDF file in the same location as the Excel workbook, and automatically opens in Adobe Reader.
12. Close the PDF file, and then, in the Invoice worksheet, click cell **A1**.

    You've completed all of the steps in the PDFInvoice macro. You'll turn off the macro recorder.

13. Click the **Stop Recording** button on the status bar. The macro recorder turns off, and the button changes to the Record Macro button.

    **Trouble?** If you made a mistake while recording the macro, close the Community Theatre workbook without saving your changes. Reopen the workbook, and then repeat all of the steps beginning with the "To start the macro recorder" steps.

Be sure to turn off the macro recorder; otherwise, you'll continue to record your keystrokes and mouse clicks, leading to unintended consequences.

Be aware that the process for saving a workbook with a macro is different from saving one that does not contain a macro. If you need to save the workbook before you complete this session, refer to the section "Saving Workbooks with Macros" later in this session.

## Running a Macro

After you record a macro, you should run it to test whether it works as intended. Running a macro means Excel performs each of the steps in the same order as when it was recorded. To run the macro you created, you can either use the shortcut key you specified or select the macro in the Macro dialog box. The Macro dialog box lists all of the macros in the open workbooks. From this dialog box, you can select and run a macro, edit the macro with VBA, run the macro one step at a time so you can determine in which step an error occurs, or delete it.

REFERENCE

*Running a Macro*

- Press the shortcut key assigned to the macro.

*or*

- In the Code group on the Developer tab, click the Macros button.
- Select the macro from the list of macros.
- Click the Run button.

You will test the PDFInvoice macro.

## To run the PDFInvoice macro:

1. Click the **Developer** tab on the Ribbon, and then click the **Macros** button in the Code group. The Macro dialog box opens, listing all of the macros in the open workbooks. See Figure 8-26.

Figure 8-26 **Macro dialog box**

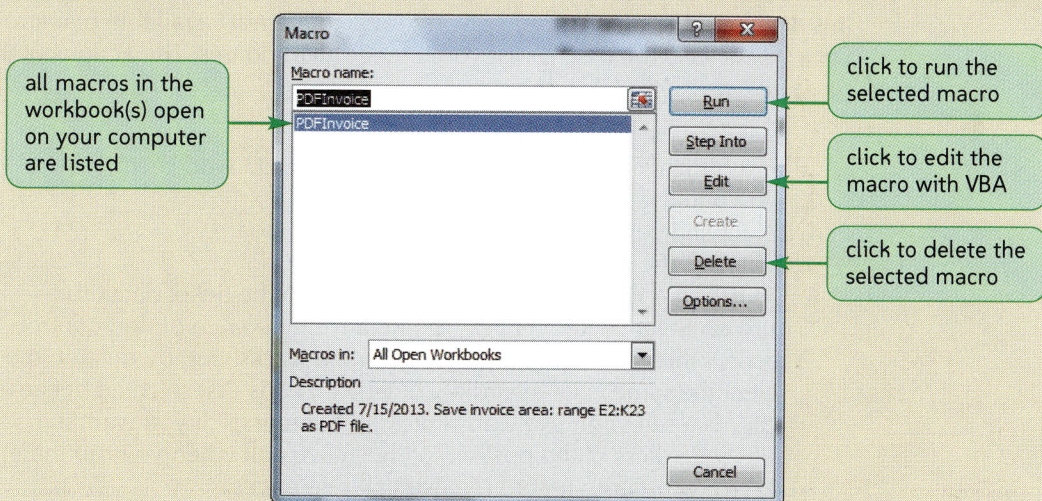


2. Verify that **PDFInvoice** is selected in the Macro name box, and then click the **Run** button. The PDFInvoice macro runs. The invoice is saved as a PDF file and the file is opened in Adobe Reader.
3. Close Adobe Reader. Cell A1 is the active cell in the Invoice worksheet.

   **Trouble?** If the PDFInvoice macro did not run properly, you might have made a mistake in the steps while recording the macro. Click the Developer tab, and then click the Macros button in the Code group. Select the PDFInvoice macro, and then click the Delete button. Click the OK button to confirm the deletion, and then repeat all of the steps beginning with the "To start the macro recorder" steps.

   Next, you will test the shortcut keys you used for the PDFInvoice macro.

4. Press the **Ctrl+p** keys. The PDFInvoice macro runs. The invoice is printed, and cell A1 in the Invoice worksheet is the active cell.

**5.** Close Adobe Reader.

**Trouble?** If your macro doesn't end on its own, you need to end it. Press the Ctrl+Break keys to stop the macro from running.

INSIGHT

*How Edits Can Affect Macros*

Be careful when making seemingly small changes to a workbook, as these can have a great impact on macros. If a run-time error (an error that occurs while running a macro) appears when you run a macro that has worked in the past, some part of the macro code no longer makes sense to Excel. For example, simply adding a space to a worksheet name can affect a macro that references the worksheet. If you recorded a macro that referenced a worksheet named "TicketData" (no spaces in the name) that you later changed to "Ticket Data" (space added to the name), the macro no longer works because the TicketData worksheet no longer exists. You could record the macro again, or you could edit the macro in VBA by changing "TicketData" to "Ticket Data."

## Creating the TransferData Macro

You need to record one more macro. The data you entered earlier in the input section of the Invoice worksheet was never added to the Ticket Data worksheet. Ellen wants to add this data from the purchase of season tickets to the next available blank row in the Ticket Data worksheet. The macro that you'll record will do this. The actions of this macro will be as follows:

1. Switch to the Ticket Data worksheet.
2. Turn off worksheet protection in the Ticket Data worksheet.
3. Switch to the Invoice worksheet.
4. Select and copy the Transfer Area to the Clipboard.
5. Switch to the Ticket Data worksheet.
6. Go to cell A1, and then go to the last row in the ticket data table.
7. Turn on Relative References. The Relative Reference button controls how Excel records the act of selecting a range in the worksheet. By default, the macro will select the same cells regardless of which cell is first selected because the macro records a selection using absolute cell references. If you want a macro to select cells regardless of the position of the active cell when you run the macro, set the macro recorder to record relative cell references.
8. Move down one row.
9. Turn off Relative References.
10. Paste values to the Ticket Data worksheet.
11. Go to cell A1.
12. Turn on worksheet protection.
13. Switch to the Invoice worksheet, and then make cell B3 the active cell.

Ellen wants you to name this new macro "TransferData" and assign the Ctrl+t keys as the shortcut.

### To record the TransferData macro:

1. Click the **Record Macro** button on the status bar to open the Record Macro dialog box, type **TransferData** in the Macro name box, type **t** in the Shortcut key box, type **Created 7/15/2013. Copy values in the transfer area in the Invoice worksheet to the Ticket Data worksheet.** in the Description box, and then click the **OK** button. The macro recorder is on.
2. Click the **Ticket Data** sheet tab, click the **Review** tab on the Ribbon, and then click the **Unprotect Sheet** button in the Changes group to turn off protection.
3. Click the **Invoice** sheet tab, and then select the range **F25:J25** in the Transfer Area.
4. Click the **Home** tab on the Ribbon, and then click the **Copy** button in the Clipboard group.
5. Click the **Ticket Data** sheet tab, click cell **A1**, and then press the **End+↓** keys to go to the last row with values.
6. Click the **Developer** tab on the Ribbon, and then click the **Use Relative References** button in the Code group. Relative references ensure that the invoice data being transferred is inserted in the next blank row (in this case, row 6) and not always in row 5 in the Ticket Data worksheet.
7. Click the ↓ key to move to the first blank cell in the worksheet.
8. In the Code group on the Developer tab, click the **Use Relative References** button. The Use Relative References button is toggled off.
9. Click the **Home** tab on the Ribbon.
10. In the Clipboard group, click the **Paste button arrow**, and then click the **Values** button in the Paste Values section. This option pastes the values rather than the formulas from the Transfer Area.

    **Trouble?** If #REF! appears in row 6 of the Ticket Data worksheet, you clicked the Paste button instead of the Paste Values button. Stop recording the macro. Delete the macro and begin recording the macro again.
11. Click cell **A1**, click the **Review** tab on the Ribbon, click the **Protect Sheet** button in the Changes group, and then click the **OK** button in the Protect Sheet dialog box.
12. Click the **Invoice** sheet tab, and then click cell **B3**.
13. Click the **Stop Recording** button on the status bar. The macro recorder turns off, and the button changes to the Record Macro button.

**TIP**

You can also turn off the macro recorder by clicking the Stop Recording button in the Code group on the Developer tab.

You've completed recording the TransferData macro. Next, you'll test whether it works. Ellen has a new season ticket subscription to add to the worksheet. You'll enter this data as you test the TransferData macro.

### To test the TransferData macro:

1. Enter the following data into the range B3:B12, pressing the **Enter** key after each entry:

   **7/15/2013**
   **Kate Holland**
   **186 Pinetop Drive**
   **Eugene, OR 70777**
   **(888) 555-1234**
   **2 tickets, D series, Balcony**
   **1 decal, 40 donation**

2. Press the **Ctrl+t** keys. The TransferData macro runs and the data transfers to the Ticket Data worksheet.
3. Switch to the **Ticket Data** worksheet, verify that the data for Kate Holland appears in row 7, and then return to the **Invoice** worksheet.

## Fixing Macro Errors

If a macro does not work correctly, you can fix it. Sometimes, you'll find a mistake when you test a macro you just created. Other times, you might not discover that error until later. No matter when you find an error in a macro, you have the following options:

- Rerecord the macro using the same macro name.
- Delete the recorded macro, and then record the macro again.
- Run the macro one step at a time to locate the problem, and then use one of the previous methods to correct the problem.

You can delete or edit a macro by opening the Macro dialog box (shown earlier in Figure 8-26), selecting the macro from the list, and then clicking the appropriate button. To rerecord the macro, simply restart the macro recorder and enter the same macro name you used earlier. Excel overwrites the previous version of the macro.

# Working with the Visual Basic Editor

To view the code of a macro, you need to open the Visual Basic Editor (VBE), which is a separate application that works with Excel and all of the Office programs to view, debug, edit, and manage VBA code. The VBE consists of several components, including the Code window that contains the VBA code, the Project Explorer window that displays a tree-like diagram consisting of every open workbook, and a menu bar with menus of commands you use to edit, debug, and run VBA statements. You can access the Visual Basic Editor through the Macro dialog box or the Visual Basic button in the Code group on the Developer tab.

REFERENCE

*Editing a Macro*

- In the Code group on the Developer tab, click the Macros button, select the macro in the Macro name list, and then click the Edit button.
  *or*
  In the Code group on the Developer tab, click the Visual Basic button.
- Use the Visual Basic Editor to edit the macro code.
- Click File on the menu bar, and then click Close and Return to Microsoft Excel.

Ellen wants the PDFInvoice macro to stop in cell B3 of the Invoice worksheet. Right now, the macro stops with cell A1 selected. Although you can delete the PDFInvoice macro and record it again, it is simpler to edit the existing macro. You will edit the VBA command in the macro.

## To view the code for the PDFInvoice macro:

1. Click the **Developer** tab on the Ribbon, and then click the **Macros** button in the Code group. The Macro dialog box opens.
2. Click **PDFInvoice** in the Macro name list, and then click the **Edit** button. The Visual Basic Editor opens as a separate program, consisting of two windows—the Project Explorer and the Code window.
3. If the Code window is not maximized, click the **Maximize** button on the Code window title bar. The Code window contains the VBA code generated by the macro recorder. See Figure 8-27 (your window may differ).

**Figure 8-27** Code window in the Visual Basic Editor

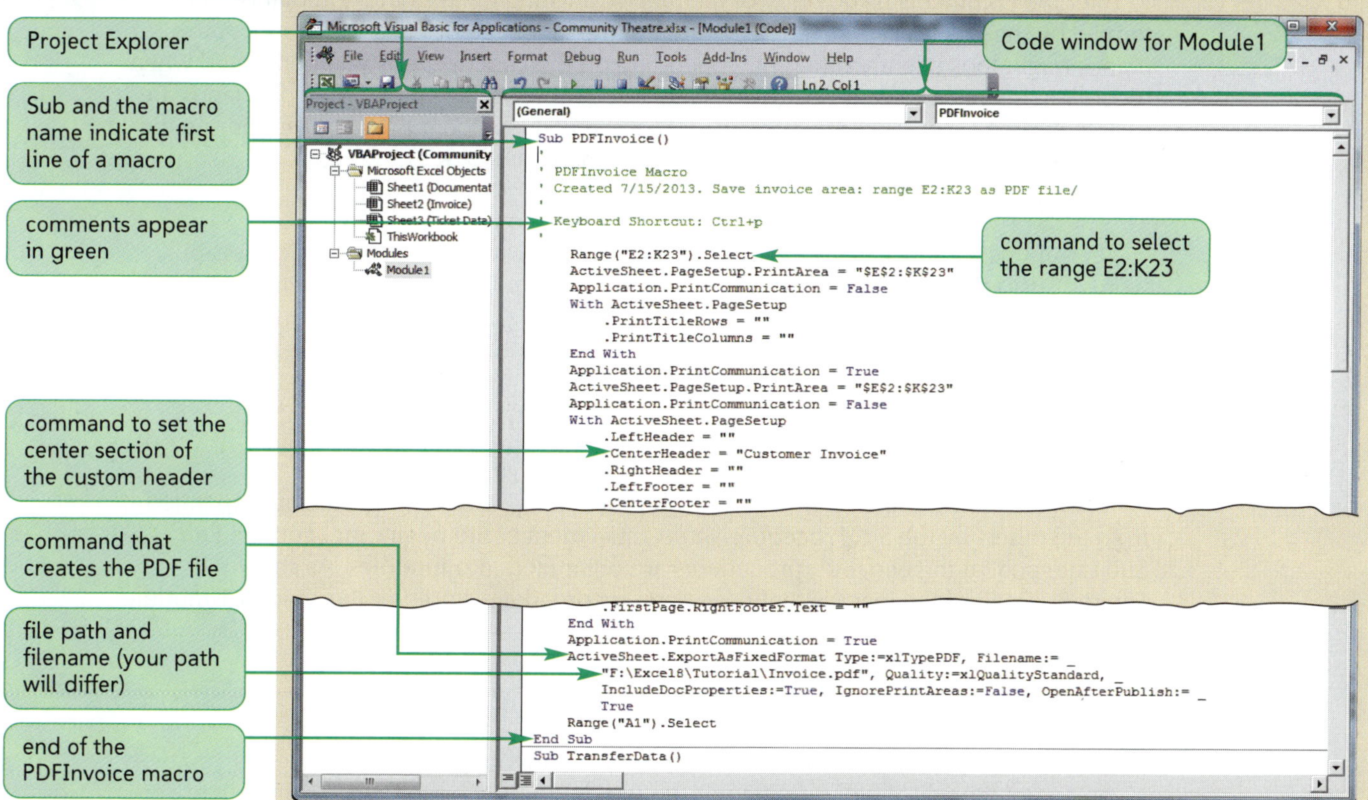


**Trouble?** If you see a different number of windows in the Visual Basic Editor, your computer is configured differently. You will be working with the Code window, so you can ignore any other windows.

## Understanding the Structure of Macros

The VBA code in the Code window lists all of the actions you performed when recording the PDFInvoice macro. In VBA, macros are called **sub procedures**. Each sub procedure begins with the keyword *Sub* followed by the name of the sub procedure and a set of parentheses. In this example, the code begins with

```
Sub PDFInvoice()
```

which provides the name of this sub procedure, PDFInvoice—the name you gave the macro. The parentheses are used to include any arguments in the procedure. These arguments pass information to the sub procedure and have roughly the same purpose as the arguments in an Excel function. If you write your own VBA code, sub procedure arguments are an important part of the programming process. However, they are not used when you create macros with the macro recorder.

Following the Sub PDFInvoice() statement are comments about the macro, taken from the macro name, shortcut key, and description you entered in the Record New Macro dialog box. Each line appears in green and is preceded by an apostrophe ('). The apostrophe indicates that the line is a comment and does not include any actions Excel needs to perform.

After the comments is the body of the macro, a listing of all of the commands performed by the PDFInvoice macro as written in the language of VBA. Your list of commands might look slightly different, depending on the exact actions you performed when recording the macro. Even though you might not know VBA, some of the commands are easy to interpret. For example, near the top of the PDFInvoice macro you should see the following command, which tells Excel to select the range E2:K23:

```
Range("E2:K23").Select
```

Several lines below this command you see the following command, which sets the words "Customer Invoice" at the top of the print page in the center of the custom header:

```
.CenterHeader = "Customer Invoice"
```

At the bottom of the macro is the following statement, which indicates the end of the PDFInvoice sub procedure:

```
End Sub
```

A Code window can contain several sub procedures, with each procedure separated from the others by the Sub*ProcedureName*() statement at the beginning, and the End Sub statement at the end. Sub procedures are organized into **modules**. As shown in Figure 8-27, all of the macros that have been recorded are stored in the Module1 module (your window may differ).

## Editing a Macro Using the Visual Basic Editor

The Visual Basic Editor provides tools to assist you in writing error-free code. As you type a command, the editor will provide pop-up windows and text to help you insert the correct code.

Ellen wants you to edit the following command in the PDFInvoice sub procedure, which sets the active cell to cell A1:

```
Range("A1").Select
```

You'll edit the command to the following to change the active cell from cell A1 to cell B3:

```
Range("B3").Select
```

### To edit a command in the macro:

1. Scroll down the Code window to the line immediately before End Sub in the PDFInvoice macro.
2. In the line with the command `Range("A1")`, select **A1**, and then type **B3**. The command in the macro is edited to select a different cell. See Figure 8-28.

**Figure 8-28** **Edited line in the PDFInvoice macro**

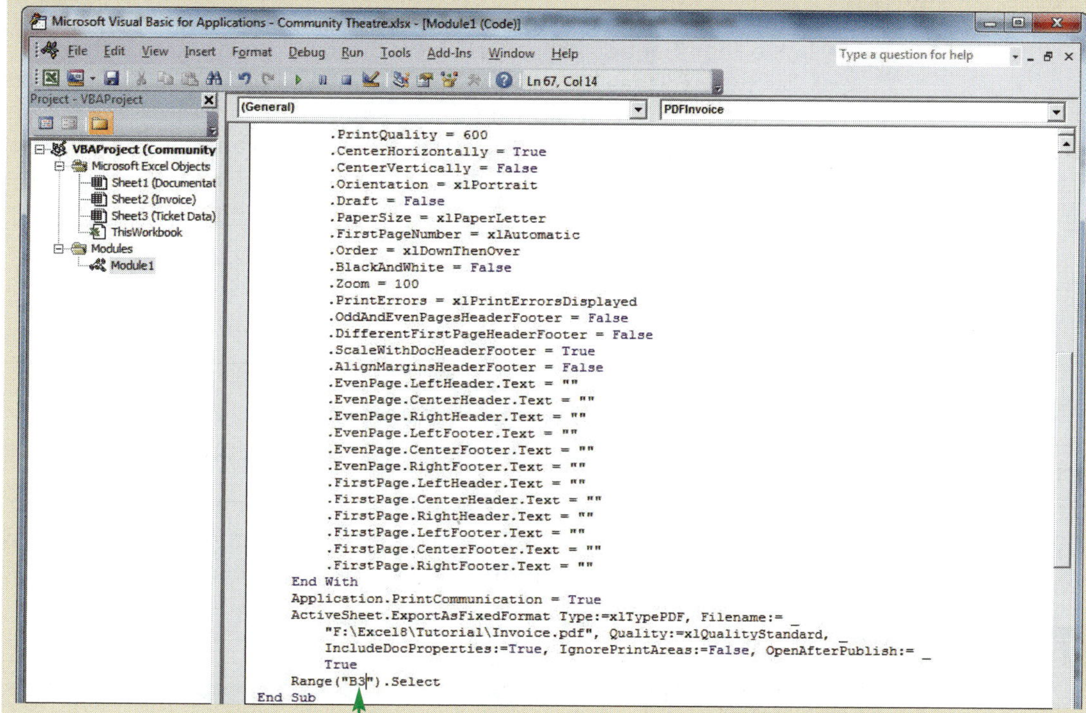


cell reference changed

3. On the menu bar, click **File**, and then click **Close and Return to Microsoft Excel**. The Visual Basic Editor closes, and the Community Theatre workbook is displayed.

Ellen wants you to test the macro. You'll check to see whether cell B3 is the active cell once the macro has run.

### To test the edited PDFInvoice macro:

1. Press the **Ctrl+p** keys. The PDFInvoice macro runs.

   **Trouble?** If a Microsoft Visual Basic message box appears with a run-time error, click the End button, click the Macros button, click PDFInvoice in the Macro name box, and then click the Edit button. In the Code window, find the line you edited (one line above End Sub), and then correct it to **Range("B3").Select**. On the menu bar, click File, and then click Close and Return to Microsoft Excel.
2. Close Adobe Reader. Cell B3 is the active cell.

# Creating Macro Buttons

Another way to run a macro is to assign it to a button placed directly in the worksheet. Macro buttons are often a better way to run macros than shortcut keys. Clicking a button (with a descriptive label) is often more intuitive and simpler for users than trying to remember different combinations of keystrokes.

REFERENCE

*Creating a Macro Button*

- In the Controls group on the Developer tab, click the Insert button.
- In the Form Controls section, click the Button (Form Control) button.
- Click the worksheet where you want the macro button to be located, drag the pointer until the button is the size and shape you want, and then release the mouse button.
- In the Assign Macro dialog box, select the macro you want to assign to the button.
- With the button still selected, type a new label.

Ellen wants you to add two macro buttons to the Invoice worksheet, one for each of the macros you've created.

## To insert a macro button in the worksheet:

1. Scroll to the right so that columns L and M are completely visible.
2. In the Controls group on the Developer tab, click the **Insert** button. The Form Controls appear, with a variety of objects that can be placed in the worksheet. You'll insert the Button form control. See Figure 8-29.

Figure 8-29 Form Controls

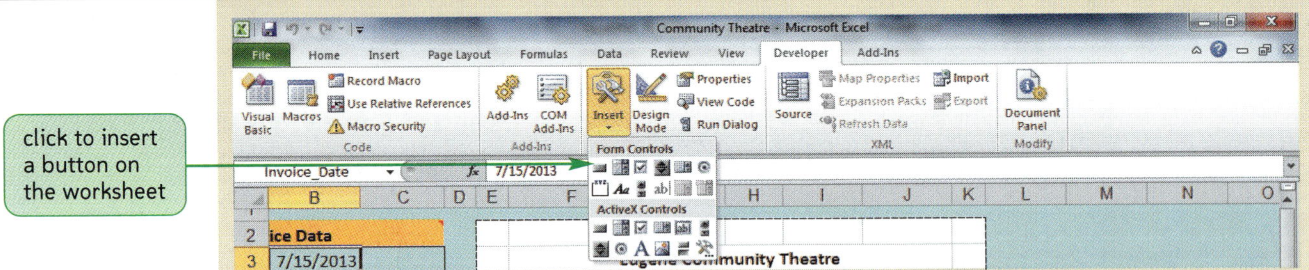


**Trouble?** If the Insert button is unavailable, the worksheet is protected. Click the Review tab on the Ribbon, click the Unprotect Sheet button in the Changes group to unprotect the Invoice worksheet, and then repeat Step 2.

3. In the Form Controls section, click the **Button (Form Control)** button, and then point to cell **L3**. The pointer changes to +.
4. Click and drag the pointer over the range **L3:M4**, and then release the mouse button. A button appears on the worksheet, and the Assign Macro dialog box opens with the button's default name in the Macro name box. See Figure 8-30.

**Figure 8-30** Assign Macro dialog box

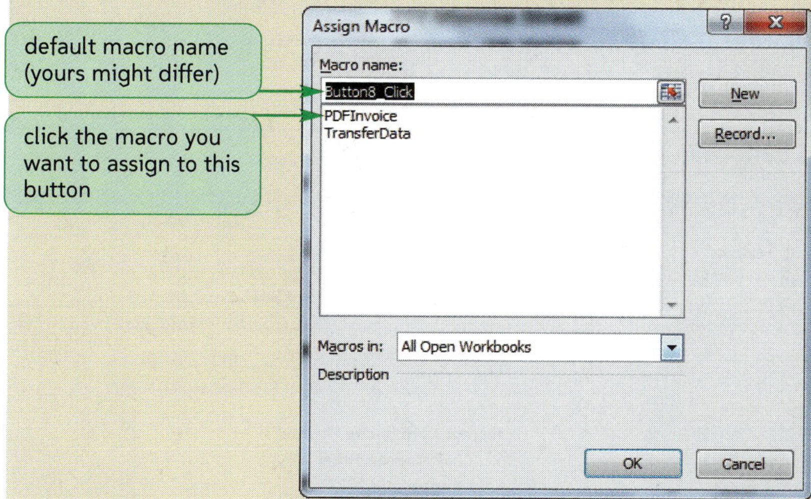


From the Assign Macro dialog box, you can assign a macro to the button. After you assign a macro to the button, the button appears with a default label. You can change the default label to a descriptive one that will indicate which macro will run when the button is clicked.

Ellen wants you to assign the PDFInvoice macro to this new button, and then rename the button with a label that reflects the PDFInvoice macro.

### To assign the PDFInvoice macro to the new button:

1. Click **PDFInvoice** in the Macro name box, and then click the **OK** button. The PDFInvoice macro is assigned to the selected button.
2. With the sizing handles still displayed around the button, type **Create PDF** (do not press the Enter key). The new label replaces the default label.

   **Trouble?** If no sizing handles appear around the button, the button is not selected. Right-click the button, click Edit Text to place the insertion point within the button, and then repeat Step 2.

   **Trouble?** If you pressed the Enter key after entering the label on the button, you created a new line in the button. Press the Backspace key to delete the line, and then continue with Step 3.
3. Click any cell in the worksheet to deselect the macro button.

At this point, if you click the Create PDF button, the PDFInvoice macro will run. Before you test the PDFInvoice button, you will add the other button.

### To add another macro button to the Invoice worksheet:

1. In the Controls group on the Developer tab, click the **Insert** button, click the **Button (Form Control)** button, and then drag the pointer over the range **L6:M7**.

2. Click **TransferData** in the Macro name box in the Assign Macro dialog box, and then click the **OK** button.
3. Type **Transfer Data** as the button label, and then click any cell in the worksheet to deselect the button. See Figure 8-31.

Figure 8-31 Macro buttons in the Invoice worksheet

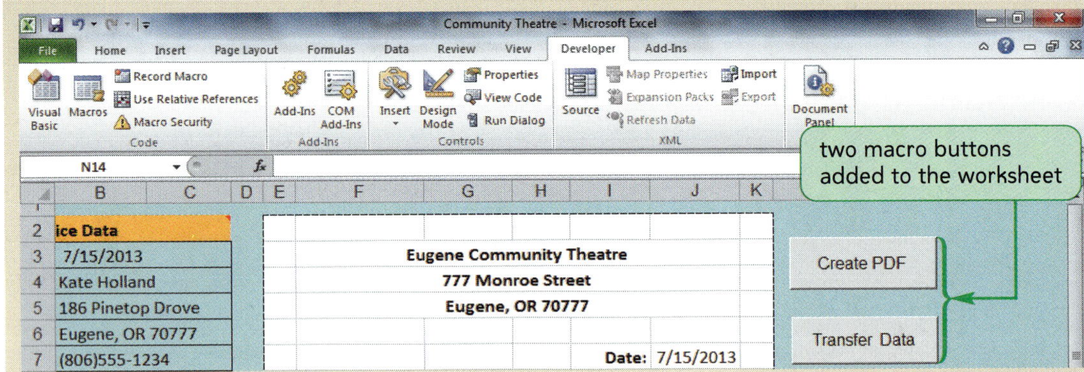


**TIP**

To move or resize a macro button, right-click the button to select it, press the Esc key to close the shortcut menu, and then drag a sizing handle or the selection box.

**Trouble?** If the macro buttons on your screen do not match the size and location of the buttons shown in the figure, right-click a button to select it, press the Esc key to close the shortcut menu, and then resize or reposition the button on the worksheet.

You have completed the application so you will reset worksheet protection.

4. Click the **Review** tab on the Ribbon, and then click the **Protect Sheet** button in the Changes group. The Protect Sheet dialog box opens.
5. Click the **OK** button to turn on worksheet protection.

Next, you will test the macro buttons to verify that they run the macros. Ellen received another subscriber order. You will use the new macro buttons as you enter this data.

## To test the macro buttons:

1. In the range B3:B12, enter the following subscriber order:

   **7/16/2013**
   **George Zidane**
   **105 Central Ave.**
   **Eugene, OR 70777**
   **(808) 555-5555**
   **3 tickets, E series, Balcony**
   **2 parking decals, 30 donation**

2. Click the **Create PDF** button to save the current invoice as a PDF file.
3. Close Adobe Reader to return to the Invoice worksheet.
4. Click the **Transfer Data** button to transfer data to the Ticket Data worksheet. Excel inserts the new transaction in the table.

5. Switch to the **Ticket Data** worksheet, and then verify the data was transferred. See Figure 8-32.

**Figure 8-32** Ticket Data worksheet with the new transaction record

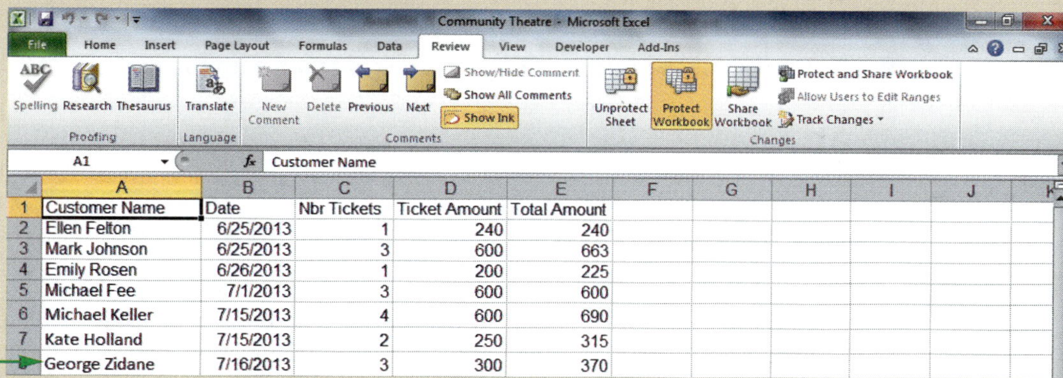


6. Switch to the **Documentation** worksheet.

## Saving Workbooks with Macros

When you save a workbook that contains macros, a dialog box opens indicating that the workbook you are trying to save contains features that cannot be saved in a macro-free workbook. The default Excel workbook does not allow macros to be stored as part of the file. If you want to save the workbook without the macros, click the Yes button. The workbook will be saved as a macro-free workbook, which means the macros you created will be lost. If you want to save the workbook with the macros, click the No button, and then save the workbook as a new file—one that allows macros to be saved as part of the file. The default Excel Workbook format, which is a macro-free workbook, has the .xlsx file extension. You need to change this to a macro-enabled workbook, which has the .xlsm file extension.

You've completed your work on the Excel application, so you will save and close the workbook and then exit Excel.

### To save the workbook with macros:

1. On the Quick Access Toolbar, click the **Save** button. A dialog box opens, indicating that the workbook you are trying to save contains features that cannot be saved in a macro-free workbook. See Figure 8-33.

**Figure 8-33** Macro warning dialog box

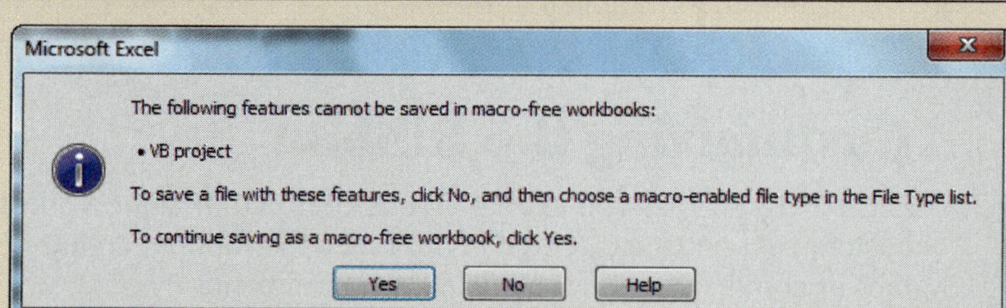

2. Click the **No** button. The Save As dialog box opens so you can save the workbook as a macro-enabled workbook.
3. In the File name box, type **Theatre with Macros** so you can easily determine which workbook contains macros.
4. Click the **Save as type** button, and then click **Excel Macro-Enabled Workbook**.
5. Click the **Save** button. The workbook is saved with the macros.
6. Close the workbook.

## Opening a Workbook with Macros

**TIP**

After you enable the content, the filename is added to a list of trusted files and the Security Warning will not reappear as long as the workbook name or location is not changed.

When you open a file with macros, Excel checks the opening workbook to see if it contains any macros. The response you see is based on the security level set on the computer. Earlier, you disabled all macros with notification. So, all of the macros will be disabled when the workbook opens. When the workbook opens the first time, a Security Warning appears in the Message Bar providing the option to enable the macros so they can be run, or to open the workbook with the macros disabled. If you know a workbook contains macros that you or a coworker created, you can enable them, which adds the filename to a list of trusted files so that you won't see the Security Warning when you open this file again. If you do not click the Enable Content button, the macros remain disabled and unavailable during the current session, but the other features of the workbook are still available.

You'll open the Theatre with Macros workbook and enable the macros.

**To open the Theatre with Macros workbook:**

1. Open the **Theatre with Macros** workbook. The workbook opens, and "Security Warning: Macros have been disabled" appears in the Message Bar below the Ribbon. See Figure 8-34.

**Figure 8-34** Security Warning appears when opening a workbook with macros

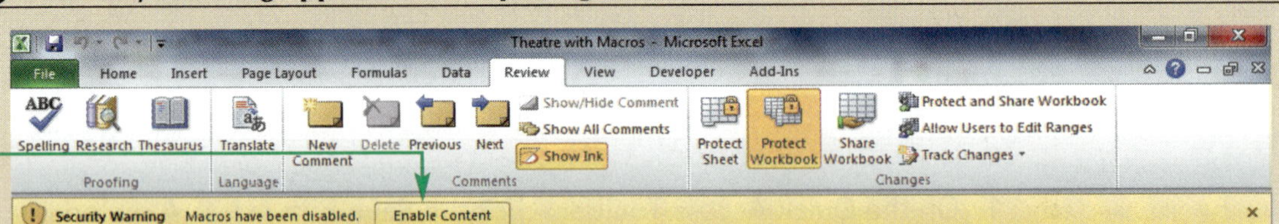


Security Warning that this workbook contains macros

2. In the Message Bar, click the **Enable Content** button. The macros in the workbook are available for use.
3. Switch to the **Invoice** worksheet.

## Customizing the Ribbon

Excel 2010 enables you to change the Ribbon to fit your work style. Among many other customization features, you can minimize the Ribbon, create new tabs and groups, hide tabs or commands, and rename tabs or commands.

## Minimize the Ribbon

You can minimize the Ribbon to make more space for a worksheet. When the Ribbon is minimized, only the Quick Access Toolbar and the tab names are displayed. To access a command from the Ribbon, click the appropriate tab. The Ribbon expands to show all of the groups and buttons on that tab. After you click a button on the Ribbon or a cell in the worksheet, the Ribbon returns to its minimized state.

Now that the application is complete, Ellen wants to provide more screen space for the input and output sections of the worksheet.

**TIP**

You can also minimize the Ribbon by double-clicking any tab on the Ribbon. Repeat to maximize the Ribbon.

### To minimize the Ribbon:

1. Near the upper-right corner of the Excel window, click the **Minimize the Ribbon** button. The Ribbon is minimized, leaving more room for the Invoice worksheet. See Figure 8-35.

**Figure 8-35 Minimized Ribbon**

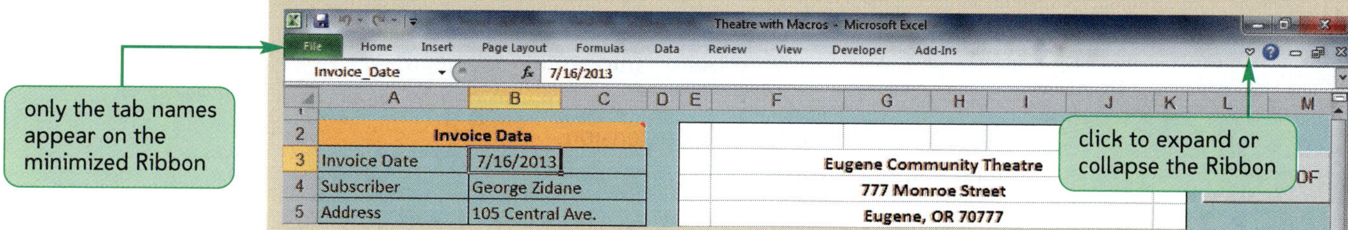


2. Click the **Home** tab. All of the buttons for this tab appear on the Ribbon.
3. Click cell **B3**. The Ribbon returns to its minimized state.

## Removing a Tab from the Ribbon

If you decide you don't want a tab displayed on the Ribbon, you can remove it. Now that the macros are completed, Ellen doesn't need the Developer tab to appear on the Ribbon. You will remove the Developer tab from the Ribbon.

### To remove the Developer tab from the Ribbon:

1. Click the **File** tab on the Ribbon, and then click the **Options** button in the navigation bar. The Excel Options dialog box opens.
2. Click **Customize Ribbon** in the left pane, and then click the **Developer** check box in the Customize the Ribbon box to remove the check mark.
3. Click the **OK** button. The Developer tab is removed from the Ribbon.

## Expanding the Ribbon

If worksheet space is not an issue and you prefer to view the maximized Ribbon, you can expand the Ribbon to show the tabs with all of the options displayed. You will expand the Ribbon so that all tab contents are visible.

**To expand the Ribbon:**

1. Near the upper-right corner of the Excel window, click the **Expand the Ribbon** button . The Ribbon is maximized.
2. Save and close the workbook.

Ellen is pleased with the Community Theatre workbook. The workbook protection and macros will streamline the data entry process for theatre volunteers.

REVIEW

## *Session 8.3 Quick Check*

1. The _______________ tab on the Ribbon is necessary to record a macro.
2. Discuss two ways of creating a macro.
3. What are the three places in which you can store a macro?
4. Identify two ways to run a macro.
5. What are the steps you follow to edit a macro?
6. How do you insert a macro button into your worksheet?
7. True or False. A workbook that contains a macro can be saved using the Excel Workbook format with the .xlsx extension.
8. How do you minimize the Ribbon?

*Practice the skills you learned in the tutorial using the same case scenario.*

PRACTICE

## Review Assignments

**Data File needed for the Review Assignments: Rentals.xlsx**

You did such a good job helping Ellen with the Community Theatre application that she recommended you to a friend who has a similar project. Ellen's friend wants to create an invoice system for his new car rental company, Eugene Discount Car Rental. Complete the following:

1. Open the **Rentals** workbook located in the Excel8\Review folder included with your Data Files, and then save the workbook as **Discount Rentals**.
2. In the Documentation worksheet, enter your name and the date.
3. In the Customer worksheet, define names for cells as follows:

| Cell | Defined Name | Cell | Defined Name |
|---|---|---|---|
| B4 | **Customer** | H9 | **ChargePerDay** |
| B5 | **TypeCar** | H10 | **ChargePerMile** |
| B6 | **DaysRented** | A12:C16 | **RentalRates** |
| B7 | **MilesDriven** | B19 | **SalesTaxRate** |

4. Create the validation rules for cells B5, B6, and B7 shown in Figure 8-36.

**Figure 8-36** **Validation rules for cells B5, B6, and B7**

| Cell | Settings | Input Message | Error Alert |
|---|---|---|---|
| B5 | List Source (A12:A16) | Title: Type of Car<br>Message: Click arrow to select the type of car. | Style: Stop<br>Title: Invalid Type<br>Message: Invalid Type. Use arrow to select Type. |
| B6 | Whole number between 1 and 29 | Title: Number of Days Rented<br>Message: Enter a whole number between 1 and 29. | Style: Warning<br>Title: Warning Days Rented<br>Message: Invalid entry. Enter whole number between 1 and 29. |
| B7 | Whole number between 1 and 5000 | Title: Number of Miles Driven<br>Message: Enter a whole number between 1 and 5000. | Style: Warning<br>Title: Warning Miles<br>Message: Invalid entry. Enter a value between 1 and 5000. |

5. Enter formulas based on the following using the defined names you created in Step 3 to calculate the Rental Bill:
   - Cell F6 is equal to the value in cell B4.
   - Cell F7 is equal to the value in cell B5.
   - Cell F9 is equal to the value in cell B6.
   - Cell F10 is equal to the value in cell B7.
   - Cell H9 is equal to the charge per day, which depends on the type of car entered in cell B5 and the rate table. (*Hint*: Use the VLOOKUP function.)
   - Cell H10 is equal to the charge per mile, which depends on the type of car entered in cell B5 and the rate table. (*Hint*: Use the VLOOKUP function.)

- Cell F12 is equal to the rental amount, which equals the number of days rented multiplied by the charge per day plus the miles driven multiplied by the charge per mile.
- Cell F13 is equal to the sales tax rate multiplied by the rental amount.
- Cell F14 is equal to the rental amount plus the sales tax.
- Use the IFERROR function in cells H9, H10, F12, F13, and F14 to test for an error value. If an error value is found, display a blank cell; otherwise, use the appropriate formula.

6. Test the worksheet using the following data: **Myles Fast**, **Intermediate**, **4**, **450**.
7. Protect the worksheet so a user can enter data only in the range B4:B7. Do not use a password to enable protection. Save the workbook.

   ***Note:*** In the following steps, you'll create one macro. Save your workbook before recording the macro. That way, if you make a mistake when recording the macro, you can close the workbook without saving the changes, and then reopen the workbook and try again. Be sure to read the list of tasks before you begin recording them.
8. Remove worksheet protection from the Customer worksheet.
9. Add the Developer tab to the Ribbon.
10. Save the workbook, then create a macro named **PDFBill** with the shortcut key **Ctrl+p** and the description **Created 7/15/2013. Macro saves the customer bill as a PDF file.**
11. Record the following macro steps to create a PDF file that displays only the bill portion of the worksheet:
    a. Select the range E3:H15, and set the range as the print area.
    b. Open the Page Layout dialog box, and then center the output horizontally on the page and insert your name in the right section of the custom footer.
    c. Create a PDF file using the Save & Send tab in Backstage view with **CustomerBill** as the filename.
    d. Close Adobe Reader.
    e. Stop the Macro Recorder.
12. Edit the PDFBill macro to set cell A1 in the Customer worksheet as the active cell when the macro stops running. Insert the following command immediately before the End Sub command:

    ```
    Range("A1").Select
    ```
13. Create a macro button, assign the PDFBill macro to the button, and then change the default label to **Create PDF**. Place the macro button in the range J3:K4.
14. Enter the following data for a new customer: **Ed Elders**, **Full**, **3** days, **2000** miles.
15. Test the PDFBill macro button using the customer bill for Ed Elders.
16. In the Documentation worksheet, use the Paste List command to document the defined names and their locations.
17. Turn on worksheet protection for the Customer worksheet. Do not assign a password.
18. Turn on workbook protection. Do not assign a password.
19. Remove the Developer tab from the Ribbon.
20. Save the workbook as **Rentals with Macros** in the macro-enabled workbook format, and then close it.
21. Submit the finished workbook to your instructor, either in printed or electronic form, as requested.

*Apply the macro skills you learned to produce monthly reports.*

APPLY

## Case Problem 1

### Data File needed for this Case Problem: MediTrax.xlsx

***MediTrax Controls*** MediTrax Controls, a U.S. subsidiary of a European multinational corporation, is testing an HVAC system designed to eliminate large temperature variances in its medical storage rooms. Lisa Goodman is a product tester for MediTrax. Each week, she records 25 temperature readings, five samples each day, in an Excel workbook. At the end of the month, Lisa sends the results to the parent company's Quality Department. Because many repetitive steps occur in developing the output requested by the parent company, Lisa asks you to create a macro to speed the creation of the report and reduce chances for error. Complete the following:

1. Open the **MediTrax** workbook located in the Excel8\Case1 folder included with your Data Files, and then save the workbook as **MediTrax Controls**.
2. In the Documentation sheet, enter your name and the date, and then review all of the worksheets in the workbook. Make Week 1 the active worksheet.
3. Create a macro to convert the worksheet to the one shown in Figure 8-37. Name the macro **ConvertData**, assign the shortcut key **Ctrl+d** to run the macro, and insert the macro description **Automate the weekly temperature reading report**. The macro performs the following steps:
   a. Formats the dates in the Date column using the date format type (3/14/2013).
   b. Formats the times in the Time column so they are displayed in 24-hour notation (format type 13:30).
   c. Types the title **Celsius** in cell D1.
   d. Converts the Fahrenheit temperatures to Celsius by entering the following formula in cell D2, and then copying the formula down the column: **=5/9*(C2–32)**.
   e. Formats the cells in column D using the Number format to 1 decimal place.
   f. Bolds the column heading and resizes the column to fully display Fahrenheit.
   g. Places the label **Average** in cell A27, computes the average Celsius temperature for the week in cell D27, and then bolds the row.
   h. Makes cell F1 the active cell.
   i. Stops recording the macro.
4. Switch to the Week 2 worksheet and test the macro using the shortcut key.
5. Edit the macro so that you end at cell A1 instead of ending at cell F1.
6. Switch to the Week 3 worksheet and test the revised macro using the shortcut key.
7. In the Week 1 worksheet, add the following comment to cell A1: **Use macro shortcut Ctrl+d to prepare a formatted report.**
8. Save the workbook as **MTC with Macros** as an Excel Macro-Enabled workbook, and then close it.
9. Submit the finished workbook to your instructor, either in printed or electronic form, as requested.

**Figure 8-37** Worksheet formatted by a macro

| | A | B | C | D |
|---|---|---|---|---|
| 1 | **Date** | **Time** | **Fahrenheit** | **Celsius** |
| 2 | 4/1/2013 | 1:05 | 60.5 | 15.8 |
| 3 | 4/1/2013 | 2:02 | 64.5 | 18.1 |
| 4 | 4/1/2013 | 6:42 | 63.8 | 17.7 |
| 5 | 4/1/2013 | 14:45 | 61.1 | 16.2 |
| 6 | 4/1/2013 | 21:12 | 60.2 | 15.7 |
| 7 | 4/2/2013 | 1:33 | 61.2 | 16.2 |
| 8 | 4/2/2013 | 2:25 | 62.9 | 17.2 |
| 9 | 4/2/2013 | 6:12 | 64.4 | 18.0 |
| 10 | 4/2/2013 | 15:35 | 62.3 | 16.8 |
| 11 | 4/2/2013 | 20:32 | 61.9 | 16.6 |
| 12 | 4/3/2013 | 1:56 | 63.9 | 17.7 |
| 13 | 4/3/2013 | 2:51 | 60.6 | 15.9 |
| 14 | 4/3/2013 | 6:55 | 62.6 | 17.0 |
| 15 | 4/3/2013 | 14:30 | 64.5 | 18.1 |
| 16 | 4/3/2013 | 22:18 | 63.2 | 17.3 |
| 17 | 4/4/2013 | 1:32 | 62.6 | 17.0 |
| 18 | 4/4/2013 | 2:58 | 62.7 | 17.1 |
| 19 | 4/4/2013 | 7:05 | 62.4 | 16.9 |
| 20 | 4/4/2013 | 14:12 | 63.5 | 17.5 |
| 21 | 4/4/2013 | 21:45 | 62.6 | 17.0 |
| 22 | 4/5/2013 | 1:22 | 64.8 | 18.2 |
| 23 | 4/5/2013 | 2:18 | 62.4 | 16.9 |
| 24 | 4/5/2013 | 6:50 | 61.9 | 16.6 |
| 25 | 4/5/2013 | 13:59 | 63.4 | 17.4 |
| 26 | 4/5/2013 | 22:03 | 64.2 | 17.9 |
| 27 | **Average** | | | **17.1** |

*Apply the skills you've learned to create a profit analysis workbook.*

APPLY

## Case Problem 2

### Data File needed for this Case Problem: Popcorn.xlsx

***Seattle Popcorn*** Seattle Popcorn is a small company located in Tacoma, Washington, that produces gourmet popcorn distributed in the Northwest. Steve Wilkes has developed a workbook that will allow him to perform a profit analysis for the company. Using this workbook, he wants to create formulas to determine the break-even point for the company—the sales volume needed so that revenues will match the anticipated monthly expenses. Three factors determine the break-even point: the sales price of each unit of Seattle Popcorn, the variable manufacturing cost to the company for each unit, and the fixed expenses (salaries, rent, insurance, and so on) that the company must pay each month. Steve wants to be able to explore a range of possible values for each of these factors, as follows:

- The sales price of each unit of Seattle Popcorn can vary from $5 to $15 (in whole numbers).
- The variable manufacturing cost of each unit can vary from $5 to $15 (in whole numbers).
- The fixed monthly expense for the company can vary from $15,000 to $30,000 (in whole numbers).

Complete the following:

1. Open the **Popcorn** workbook located in the Excel8\Case2 folder included with your Data Files, and then save the workbook as **Seattle Popcorn**. In the Documentation sheet, enter your name and the date.
2. Switch to the Profit Analysis worksheet, and then define names for cells, as follows:
   cell C15: **PricePerUnit**
   cell C16: **CostPerUnit**
   cell C17: **MonthlyExpenses**
3. In the range H3:H43, enter a formula using defined names to calculate the revenue, which is determined by the units sold multiplied by the price per unit.
4. In the range I3:I43, enter a formula using defined names to calculate the expenses, which are determined by the units sold multiplied by the cost per unit plus the fixed monthly expense.
5. In cell C18, enter a formula to calculate the break-even point, which is determined by the fixed monthly expense divided by the difference between the price per unit and the cost per unit. Use the IFERROR function to display a blank cell instead of an error value.
6. In cell C19, enter a formula to calculate the revenue at the break-even point, which is determined by the break-even point multiplied by the sales price per unit. Use the IFERROR function to display a blank cell instead of an error value.
7. Create the validation rules for cells C15, C16, and C17, as shown in Figure 8-38.

**Figure 8-38** **Validation rules for cells C15, C16, and C17**

| Cell | Settings | Input Message | Error Alert |
|---|---|---|---|
| C15 | Whole numbers between 5 and 15 | Title: Price per Unit<br>Message: *Enter an appropriate message.* | Style: Warning<br>Title: Invalid Price per Unit<br>Message: *Enter an appropriate message.* |
| C16 | Whole numbers between 5 and 15 | Title: Cost per Unit<br>Message: *Enter an appropriate message.* | Style: Warning<br>Title: Invalid Cost per Unit<br>Message: *Enter an appropriate message.* |
| C17 | Whole numbers between 15000 and 30000 | Title: Monthly Expenses<br>Message: *Enter an appropriate message.* | Style: Warning<br>Title: Invalid Monthly Expense<br>Message: *Enter an appropriate message.* |

8. Protect the worksheet so the user can enter data only in cells C15, C16, and C17. Everything else in the worksheet should remain locked.
9. Enter the following values in the worksheet to determine how many units Seattle Popcorn must sell each month in order to break even:
   - Sales Price per Unit = **$13**
   - Manufacturing Cost per Unit = **$10**
   - Fixed Monthly Expense = **$30,000**
10. In cell C16, add the following comment: **Call Joe Heller in Cost Accounting for unit cost data.**

    ***Note:*** In the following steps, you'll create a macro. Save your workbook before recording the macro. That way, if you make a mistake while recording the macro, you can close the workbook without saving the changes, and then reopen the workbook and try again. Also, read the list of tasks before you begin recording them.
11. Save the workbook.
12. Create a macro named **PrintChart** with the shortcut key **Ctrl+a** and an appropriate macro description that performs the following tasks:
    a. Set the print area to include the chart and input/output area (range A1:E20).
    b. Set the page layout to landscape orientation, centered horizontally on the page, with the text **Break-even Analysis** in the center section of the header, and your name in the right section of the footer.
    c. Print the chart and input area.
    d. Make cell A1 the active cell.
    e. Stop recording the macro.
13. Test the PrintChart macro by pressing the Ctrl+a keys. If the macro doesn't work, close the workbook without saving your changes, reopen the workbook, and record the macro again.
14. Edit the PrintChart macro, replacing the line `ActiveWindow.SelectedSheets.PrintOut Copies:=1, Collate:=True, IgnorePrintAreas:=False` with **`ActiveSheet.PrintPreview.`** (*Hint*: The line to edit is four lines above the end of the macro.)
15. Create a button in the range A22:B23, assign the PrintChart macro to the button, and change the default label to a more descriptive one.
16. Run the PrintChart macro to test the button and the revised macro.
17. Save the workbook as a macro-enabled workbook using the name **SP with Macros**, and then close it.
18. Submit the finished workbook to your instructor, either in printed or electronic form, as requested.

*Go beyond what you learned to design an Excel workbook to use as a data entry form.*

CHALLENGE

## Case Problem 3

### Data File needed for this Case Problem: Cookin.xlsx

***Cookin Good*** Cookin Good sells specialized home cooking products. The company employs individuals to organize "Cookin Good Parties" at which the company's products are sold. Cleo Benard is responsible for entering sales data from various Cookin Good Parties. She wants to design an Excel workbook to act as a data entry form. She has already created the workbook, but she needs your help with setting up data validation rules, creating a table lookup, and writing the macros to enter the data. Complete the following:

1. Open the **Cookin** workbook located in the Excel8\Case3 folder included with your Data Files, and then save the workbook as **Cookin Good**. In the Documentation sheet, enter your name and the date.
2. Go to the Sales Form worksheet. Create appropriate defined names for each cell in the range C3:C8. Assign the name **ProductInfo** to the range E4:G15.
3. In the Sales Form worksheet, create the following validation rules:
   a. The criteria allows only one of five regions (represented by the numbers 1, 2, 3, 4, and 5) to be entered in cell C3. Enter an appropriate input message and error alert.
   b. The criteria provides the list of 12 products (found in range E4:E15) in cell C4. Enter an appropriate input message and error alert.
   c. The criteria allows only whole numbers greater than 0 to be entered as the number of units sold in cell C7. Enter an appropriate input message and error alert.
4. In cells C5 and C6, enter a VLOOKUP function that automatically enters the product name and price into the sales form when the ProductID is entered. (*Hint*: Cells should be blank if an error value appears in a cell.)
5. In cell C8, enter a formula that automatically calculates the total sale for the order, which is determined by the number of units sold multiplied by the price of the product. Use the IFERROR function to display a blank cell if an error value occurs during the calculation of Total Sale.
6. Prevent users from entering data into any cell in the Sales Form worksheet other than cells C3, C4, and C7, and then protect the Sales Form worksheet.
7. Test the data entry form by entering the following new record: Region = **1**, Product ID = **CW**, Units Sold = **8**.
8. Save the workbook, and then create a macro named **AddData** with the shortcut key **Ctrl+d** that performs the following tasks:
   a. In the Sales Form worksheet, copy the values in the range C3:C8. (*Hint*: You'll paste later in the macro.)
   b. Switch from the Sales Form worksheet to the Sales Record worksheet. Click cell A1.
   c. Turn on Relative References.
   d. Use the End+↓ keys to locate the last used row in the first column. Then, press the ↓ key to move to the next row in the first column.
   e. Turn off Relative References.

   EXPLORE

   f. Paste the copied values from Step a into the blank row. (*Hint*: Use the Paste button arrow, and then click Paste Transpose button.)
   g. Switch to the Sales Table worksheet.
   h. Click inside the PivotTable and refresh the contents of the PivotTable to include the new data.
   i. Switch to the Sales Form worksheet and clear the values in cells C3, C4, and C7.

j. Make C3 the active cell.

k. Stop recording the macro.

9. Create a button in the range C11:C12 on the Sales Form worksheet and assign the AddData macro to the button. Change the button label to **Transfer Sales Data**.
10. Test the data entry form and AddData macro by entering the following new records:

| Region | Product ID | Units Sold |
|---|---|---|
| **3** | **HR** | **4** |
| **4** | **OEG** | **2** |

11. Create a macro named **ViewTable** with the **Ctrl+t** shortcut key that displays the contents of the Sales Table worksheet.
12. Create a macro named **ViewChart** with the **Ctrl+c** shortcut key that displays the Sales Chart worksheet.
13. Create a macro named **ViewForm** with the **Ctrl+f** shortcut key that displays the Sales Form worksheet. Test each macro using its shortcut keys.
14. In the Documentation worksheet, create three macro buttons below row 13 to view the Sales Table worksheet (Step 11), the Sales Chart worksheet (Step 12), and the Sales Form worksheet (Step 13). Assign the appropriate macro to each button, and change the labels on the buttons to be more descriptive.

**EXPLORE**

15. The Sales Table worksheet displays the total product sales in each region. Change the PivotTable to show the values in the cells as percentages of the Column Total. (*Hint*: On the Options tab, in the Calculations group, click the Show Values As button, and then click % of Column Total. You can return the original value by clicking No calculation.)

**EXPLORE**

16. Create two macros. The first displays the PivotTable as percentages of column totals (Step 15). Name this macro **ShowAsPercent**. The second macro displays the PivotTable as numbers (values shown as No Calculation). Name this macro **ShowAsNumber**.
17. Edit the ShowAsPercent macro to display the results with a percent style by adding the following three commands immediately before the End Sub statement:

```
Range("C5:H17").Select
Selection.Style = "Percent"
Range("A1").Select
```

18. Create two macro buttons below the PivotTable in the Sales Table worksheet to run each macro. Assign a macro to each button, and then change the button labels to be more descriptive.
19. Save the workbook as **CG with Macros**, and then close it. Submit the finished workbook to your instructor, either in printed or electronic form, as requested.

*Define names, apply worksheet protection, and create macros to prepare an invoice.*

**CREATE**

## Case Problem 4

**There are no Data Files needed for this Case Problem.**

***Alia's Senior Living Supplies*** Alia Moh left her job at a Chicago hospital to establish Alia's Senior Living Supplies, which provides products and services designed for seniors. Products offered by Alia on her Web site range from safety step ladders, doorknob grippers, and skid resistant surfaces to wheelchair ponchos. Alia has built up a large, steady client base—mainly seniors who find these uniquely designed products a great help in their daily lives. To ensure timely receipt of payments, Alia wants a billing/invoicing system to expedite that work. Figure 8-39 shows the finished application she has asked you to create.

**Figure 8-39** Completed Invoice worksheet

**Alia's Senior Living Supplies**
**2256 Central Avenue**
**Arlington, Illinois 60005**
**(555) 555-1212**

Print Invoice
Clear Inputs

**February 15, 2013**

Sold to:
Mark Kipper
123 Central Road
Arlington IL 60005

| Item | Qty | Per Unit | Total |
|---|---|---|---|
| Economy Patient Gowns | 4 | $ 6.95 | $ 27.80 |
| Doorknob Gripper | 5 | $ 4.95 | $ 24.75 |
| Giant TV Remote | 3 | $ 34.95 | $ 104.85 |

| | |
|---|---|
| Subtotal | $ 157.40 |
| Sales Tax | $ 11.81 |
| Shipping | $ 16.00 |
| **Total Due** | **$ 185.21** |

Complete the following:

1. Open a new workbook, and then save it as **AliaSupplies** in the Excel8\Case4 folder included with your Data Files.
2. Rename the first sheet as **Documentation**, and then enter the company name, your name, the date, and a purpose statement. Rename the second sheet as **Invoice**. Rename the third sheet as **Product Pricing and Shipping**.
3. In the Product Pricing and Shipping worksheet, enter the data for product pricing and shipping costs shown in Figure 8-40.

**Figure 8-40** Product pricing and shipping costs

| | A | B | C | D | E | F |
|---|---|---|---|---|---|---|
| 1 | **Product Pricing** | | | | | |
| 2 | | | | **Subtotal** | **Shipping Cost** | |
| 3 | Adjustable Home Bed Rail | 89.95 | | 0 | 6.00 | |
| 4 | Bed Cane | 81.95 | | 55 | 9.50 | |
| 5 | Doorknob Gripper | 4.95 | | 100 | 12.50 | |
| 6 | Easy Grip Utensils | 32.95 | | 150 | 16.00 | |
| 7 | Economy Patient Gowns | 6.95 | | | | |
| 8 | Full-Page Magnifier | 4.99 | | | | |
| 9 | Giant TV Remote | 34.95 | | | | |
| 10 | Inflatable Shampoo Basin | 39.95 | | | | |
| 11 | Jar Opener | 5.95 | | | | |
| 12 | Lamp Switch Enlarger | 4.95 | | | | |
| 13 | Medication Dispenser | 135.95 | | | | |
| 14 | No Rinse Shampoo | 34.95 | | | | |
| 15 | Tilting Overbed Table | 114.95 | | | | |
| 16 | Trolley Walker | 139.95 | | | | |
| 17 | Wheelchair Poncho | 51.95 | | | | |

4. Complete the following to build the invoice shown in Figure 8-39 on the Invoice worksheet. Use defined names and structured referencing to assist in creating formulas. (*Hint*: Review the steps below before you begin to enter the tables, labels, and formulas to build the invoice.)
   a. Adjust the column widths so column A is 2.57; column B is 6.14; column C is 20.86; column D is 6.14; column E is 13.57; column F is 8.71; column G is 12.71; column H is 13.71; column I is 3.43; and column J is 2.29.
   b. Insert labels with the company's name and contact information in rows 2 through 5, and then merge and center the ranges C2:H2, C3:H3, C4:H4, and C5:H5.
   c. Enter the current date in cell G7, merge and center G7:H7, and then format the cell with bold.
   d. Insert comments as a reminder as to what data should be entered in cells C10, C11, C12, D12, and E12.
   e. Enter the column headers in row 15.
   f. Create an Excel table in the range C15:H35. Remove the filter arrows.
   g. Enter the appropriate labels in the range G37:G40, and then format the range G40:H40 as bold.
   h. Use defined names for Product Pricing and Shipping Cost data.
   i. In the Item column (the range C16:C35), create a list of the different items, which are listed in the Product Pricing table in the Product Pricing and Shipping worksheet, that users might order. (*Hint*: Use the data validation list feature.)
   j. In the Qty column, create an error alert warning message that appears if the quantity entered is more than 50.
   k. In the Per Unit column, enter a formula that uses a table lookup in the Product Pricing table based on the value selected in the Item column. Use the IFERROR function to display a blank cell instead of the error value.
   l. In the Total column, enter a formula to calculate the total charge for that row: Qty × Per Unit. Use the IFERROR function to display a blank cell instead of the error value. Format the column appropriately.
   m. In the Subtotal cell (cell H37), enter a formula to sum the Total column. Format this cell appropriately.
   n. In the Sales Tax cell, enter a formula to calculate 7.5% of the subtotal in cell H37 if the customer's state is IL (cell D12); otherwise, enter 0 for the sales tax. Format this cell appropriately.
   o. In the Shipping cell, enter a formula that does the following: If the subtotal is $200 or more, the shipping cost is 0; otherwise, look up the shipping cost (from the Shipping Cost table in the Product Pricing and Shipping worksheet) based on the subtotal in cell H37. Format this cell appropriately.
   p. In the Total Due cell, calculate the invoice total by entering a formula that adds the values in the Subtotal, Sales Tax, and Shipping cells. Format this cell appropriately.
5. Protect the worksheet so a user can enter data in cells C10, C11, C12, D12, and E12; items in the range C16:C35; and quantities in the range F16:F35 but not in any other cells. Do not use a password.
6. Save the workbook.
7. Create a macro named **PrintInvoice** that prints the invoice. Assign the **Ctrl+p** shortcut key and type a macro description as you begin recording this macro. Center the worksheet horizontally and scale it to fit on one printed page. The heading has the label **I N V O I C E** in the center of the page. Create a macro button on the Invoice worksheet in column K, assign the PrintInvoice macro to the button, and then enter a descriptive label for the button.

8. Create a macro named **ClearInputs** that deletes the values from cells C10, C11, C12, D12, and E12; items in the range C16:C35; and quantities in the range F16:F35. Assign the **Ctrl+c** shortcut key and type a macro description as you begin recording this macro. Create a macro button on the Invoice worksheet in column K, assign the ClearInputs macro to the button, and then enter a descriptive label for the button. (*Hint*: Use the Delete key to clear a value from a cell.)
9. In the Documentation worksheet, paste a list of the defined names with their locations, and below this entry type a list of the macro names and their shortcut keys.
10. Test the worksheet using the data in Figure 8-39.
11. Use the PrintInvoice macro button to print the bill for the data you entered in Step 10, and then use the ClearInputs macro button to remove the input data.
12. Save the workbook as **Alia with Macros**, and then close it. Submit the finished workbook to your instructor, either in printed or electronic form, as requested.

ASSESS

## SAM: Skills Assessment Manager

For current SAM information, including versions and content details, visit SAM Central (http://samcentral.course.com). If you have a SAM user profile, you may have access to hands-on instruction, practice, and assessment of the skills covered in this tutorial. Since various versions of SAM are supported throughout the life of this text, check with your instructor for the correct instructions and URL/Web site for accessing assignments.

## ENDING DATA FILES

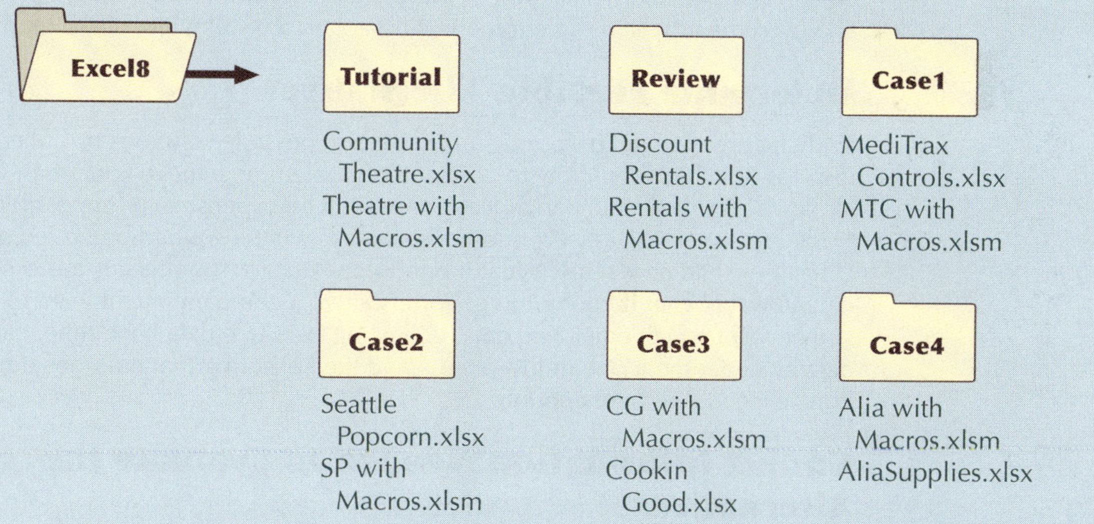

ProSkills

# Problem Solving

## Solving a Problem Using an Excel Table

Problem solving is the ability to identify a gap between an existing state and a desired state of being. A problem can be a one-time issue such as which car to purchase or a process-oriented dilemma such as how to track orders. The process of solving a problem follows a logical progression that consists of (1) recognizing and defining the problem, (2) determining feasible courses of action, (3) collecting information about those actions, and (4) evaluating the merits and drawbacks of each one in order to make a choice. Problem solving leads to decision making, and enables you to evaluate different courses of action and make an informed decision or select a good solution.

### Recognize and Define the Problem

A problem is the gap between a desired state and reality. In order to recognize and define a problem, ask questions to determine the real issue and identify your ultimate goal. For example, ask such questions as: Why do I think there is a problem? Where is it occurring? When and how frequently is it occurring? What is causing the problem? Who is involved? Why is it occurring? The answers to these questions help you define the problem and determine what information you need to solve the problem. For instance, a company might want to make sure that employee benefits and overtime payments don't exceed a certain amount, and needs to track the cost of each employee's benefit package, salary, and overtime as well as determine that the total costs fall within the intended levels.

### Determine Feasible Alternatives

With the problem defined, you can brainstorm possible solutions by collecting as many ideas as possible about how to correct the problem or achieve your goal. Write them all down. Don't discount any ideas as too radical, expensive, or impossible to achieve. Think creatively. Ask what-if questions, such as what if we had unlimited resources? What if we had new skills? What if our competitors or suppliers or customers acted in a certain way? What if I do nothing? For instance, a company might want to create a consistent way to track employee data, collecting the same data each time, categorizing the data by department or employee type, and then ensuring that paid benefits and overtime don't exceed a certain amount.

### Collect Information Needed to Evaluate the Alternatives

Data is crucial to problem solving. Collect data and information related to each possible solution or alternative. This information can include data expressed as currency or numbers, as well as data that cannot be measured numerically. All collected data should be organized in a way that provides information for effective decision-making and follow-up. For example, a business needs to collect data that enables it to write checks to employees, prepare reports about overtime, report payroll taxes to government agencies, provide premiums to health insurance companies, track Social Security payments, and so on. This requires an organized system to capture the appropriate data such as employee IDs, employee names, hours worked each day, salary or hourly rate, and insurance premium. You'll likely start to see relationships between the collected information that can provide insights into the feasibility of the possible solutions.

ProSkills

## Evaluate and Choose an Alternative

Document both the benefits and costs of all alternatives, whether numerical (cost savings) or other (employee morale). Spreadsheet software often helps problem solvers track and quantify merits and drawbacks. Consider the resources required—financial, human, equipment, and so on. Are they affordable? Is there enough time to implement the different solutions? What risks are associated with an alternative? What consequences would result if the solution didn't work? The best choice is to go with the solution that offers the greatest reward for the least amount of risk. In some cases, the solution may require developing a "Plan B" to fall back on in case the chosen solution fails to solve the problem. For instance, when collecting payroll data, it may become apparent that insurance premiums are higher percentage of payroll than previously thought, which requires further investigation and an alternative solution.

Don't try to select a solution that addresses every aspect of a problem, especially if it is complex. Solutions are rarely perfect. Instead, consider the overall effect each alternative may have. Will the resulting change generate positive results while solving the problem? Will the chosen alternative resolve the problem long-term? What is realistic, given the merits and drawbacks identified?

PROSKILLS

## Develop an Excel Table

In daily life, you solve all sorts of problems, such as which car purchase makes the most economic sense when comparing purchase price, mileage, and maintenance, or which software package will help your biking club manage its funds, plan road trips, and keep memberships up-to-date. To solve these and other problems, you need to collect data that tracks the current situation, determine your ultimate goal, and then follow a logical progression to the best solution. Developing an Excel table can help you to track the data you need to solve such problems.

In this exercise, you need to select an activity you participate in or an organization you belong to and identify a one-time or process-oriented problem that needs to be solved. Then, create a worksheet and develop an Excel table to track relevant data and create a solution to the problem, using the Excel skills and features presented in Tutorials 5 through 8.

**Note:** Please be sure *not* to include any personal information of a sensitive nature in any worksheets you create to submit to your instructor. Later, you can update the worksheets with such information for your own personal use.

1. Identify a problem to solve. This can be a one-time problem, such as a car purchase, or a process-oriented problem, such as tracking membership data for a club you belong to. Determine feasible alternatives to solve the problem, and then collect the data you need to evaluate these alternatives.
2. Plan the organization of your workbook and the Excel table you will develop based on how you will use the data. Consider the outputs you want to create, and the fields needed to produce those outputs. Decide what each record represents (such as data on a participant) and then identify the fields and field names (such as last name, first name, birth date, as so on) within each record. What calculations will you need to perform? How do you want to format the information?

ProSkills

3. Create a Documentation worksheet that includes your name, the date, and the purpose of your workbook. Format it appropriately.
4. Create an Excel table to track the data needed to solve the problem you identified. Enter an appropriate table name and column headers to track the data needed to create a solution to the problem. Add one or more calculated columns to the table to perform calculations on the data that you will use to solve the problem.
5. Improve the appearance of the table using appropriate formatting.
6. Apply validity checks to improve the accuracy of data entry.
7. Add records to the table.
8. Apply conditional formatting to at least one column in the table to highlight some aspect of the data that will help you evaluate and solve the problem.
9. Add a comment to the column with the conditional formatting to explain what the conditional formatting shows and how it will help you to evaluate and solve the problem.
10. Insert a Total row in the table and make appropriate summary calculations that you can use to evaluate and solve the problem.
11. Divide the table into two horizontal panes—one for the data and the second for the Total row.
12. Sort the data in a logical way.
13. Use a filter to answer a question about the data that you can use to evaluate and solve the problem.
14. Create a PivotTable and a PivotChart to analyze the data. Format, filter, and sort the PivotTable appropriately.
15. In a Word document, explain the problem you solved, identify the alternatives you considered, document the data you collected to evaluate the alternatives, and then describe the results of your analysis. Include the PivotChart in the Word document.
16. In an appropriate worksheet, insert a hyperlink that links to the Word document you created.
17. If you have a Windows Live ID, save the workbook to the My Documents folder on your SkyDrive. Modify the workbook by editing cell content. Save the workbook to your computer using a new filename.
18. Create at least one macro to automate a repetitive task you need to perform in the workbook, such as printing or saving a worksheet as a PDF file.
19. Prepare your workbook for printing. Include headers and footers that indicate the filename of your workbook, the workbook's author, and the date on which the report is printed. If a printed worksheet will extend across several pages, repeat appropriate print titles across all of the pages and include page numbers and the total number of pages on each printed page.
20. Save the workbook. Submit the completed files to your instructor in printed or electronic form, as requested.

APPENDIX **A**

# Working with Text Functions and Creating Custom Formats

*Cleaning Data in a Spreadsheet*

## OBJECTIVES

- Open a workbook in Compatibility Mode
- Use the LEN function
- Use the LEFT function
- Use the Paste Values command
- Use the PROPER function
- Use the & operator
- Use the Text to Columns command
- USE the UPPER function
- Use the SUBSTITUTE function
- Use a special format for phone numbers
- Create custom formats for numbers and dates
- Using the Compatibility Checker

## Case | *Zeus Engineering*

Growth in the town of Bayville has strained the capacity of local roads. Traffic increases have created delays, vehicular hazards, and pedestrian safety concerns. To address these issues, the town has contracted Zeus Engineering to develop a Transportation Improvement Program (TIP).

Myron Londale, traffic analyst at Zeus Engineering, will analyze data on private homes and commercial buildings located along the route being analyzed. He received the data from the Bayville Assessor's Office, which transferred the data to Excel. Before Myron begins his analysis, he needs to "clean" the data, and has asked for your help.

### STARTING DATA FILES

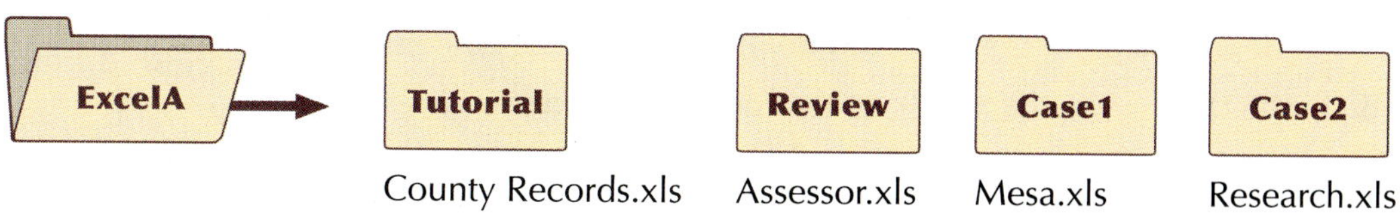

## Opening and Saving Workbooks Created in Earlier Versions of Excel

**TIP**

In the Open dialog box, point to a workbook file; the ScreenTip "Microsoft Excel Worksheet" appears for Excel 2007/2010 files and "Microsoft Excel 97-2003 Worksheet" appears for earlier files.

When you open a workbook that was created in an earlier version of Excel (Excel 2003 or earlier), Excel 2010 opens the workbook in Compatibility Mode. **Compatibility Mode** keeps the workbook in the older file format, making the workbook accessible for users who do not have the current version of Excel installed. The words "[Compatibility Mode]" appear in the title bar, indicating the file is not in the latest Excel format. You can work in Compatibility Mode, which keeps the workbook in the older file format with the .xls file extension. However, to have access to all the latest features and tools in Excel 2010, the workbook must be converted to the current file format, which has the .xlsx file extension. This is the file format you have used to save all workbooks in the tutorials.

The workbook Myron received from the Bayville Assessor's Office was created in Excel 2003. Myron wants you to convert the workbook to the current format.

### To save the workbook in the Excel 2007/2010 file format:

1. Open the **County Records** workbook located in the ExcelA\Tutorial folder included with your Data Files. The workbook opens in Compatibility Mode because the workbook was created in an earlier version of Excel. See Figure A-1.

Figure A-1 Workbook in Compatibility Mode

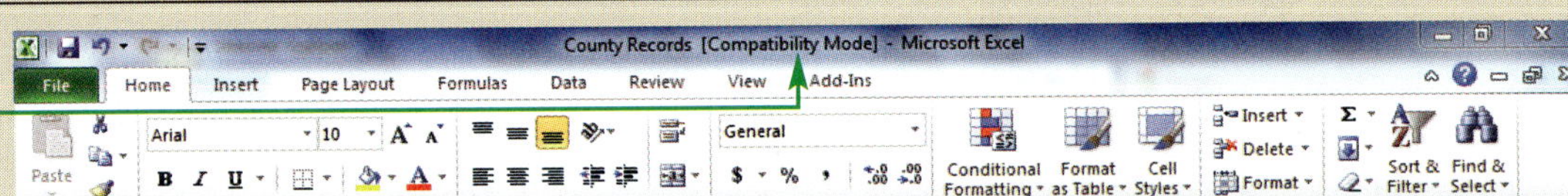


workbook was created in an earlier version of Excel

2. Click the **File** tab on the Ribbon to open Backstage view, and then click the **Save As** command in the navigation bar. The Save As dialog box opens.
3. In the File name box, type **Bayville County**. The Save as type box shows that the current file format is Excel 97-2003 Workbook, which is the earlier file format. You'll change this to the latest file format.
4. Click the **Save as type** button, and then click **Excel Workbook**. This is the file format for Excel 2007 and 2010.
5. Click the **Save** button. The workbook is saved with the new name and file type.

The workbook remains in Compatibility Mode, as you can see from the title bar. You can continue to work in Compatibility Mode, or you can close and then reopen the workbook in the new file format. You will open the workbook in the current file format.

### To open the Bayville County workbook in the current file format:

1. Close the **Bayville County** workbook.
2. Open the **Bayville County** workbook. The title bar no longer has "[Compatibility Mode]", indicating that the workbook is in the Excel 2007/2010 file format.
3. In the Documentation sheet, enter your name and the date.

The Data worksheet contains data obtained from the county assessor's office. Myron wants you to convert this data to an Excel table.

**To create an Excel table from the county records:**

1. Switch to the **Data** worksheet.
2. Click the **Insert** tab on the Ribbon, and then click the **Table** button in the Tables group. The Create Table dialog box opens with the range A1:H51 selected.
3. Click the **OK** button to create the Excel table.
4. In the Properties group on the Table Tools Design tab, enter **TIPData** in the Table Name box to rename the table.
5. Click the **Data** tab on the Ribbon, and then click the **Filter** button in the Sort & Filter group. The filter arrows are removed from the column headers.
6. Click any cell in the Excel table.

# Using Text Functions

If you receive a workbook from a coworker or obtain data from other software packages, you often have to edit (sometimes referred to as *clean* or *scrub*) and manipulate the data before it is ready to use. Many Text functions help users edit and correct the text values in their workbooks. Text, also referred to as a *text string* or *string*, contains one or more characters and can include spaces, symbols, and numbers as well as uppercase and lowercase letters. For example, Text functions are used to return the number of characters, remove extra spaces, and change the case of text strings. Figure A-2 reviews some of the common Text functions available in Excel.

**Figure A-2** Text functions

| Function | Syntax | Description | Example |
|---|---|---|---|
| LEFT | =LEFT(*text,nbr chars*) | Returns a specified number of characters at the left of the string | =LEFT("Michael",3) returns Mic |
| RIGHT | =RIGHT(*text,nbr chars*) | Returns a specified number of characters at the right of the string | =RIGHT("Michael",3) returns ael |
| MID | =MID(*text,start nbr, nbr chars*) | Returns a specified number of characters from a string, starting at a position you specify | =MID("Net Income",5,3) returns Inc |
| UPPER | =UPPER(*text*) | Converts all lowercase characters in a string to uppercase | =UPPER("kim") returns KIM |
| LOWER | =LOWER(*text*) | Converts all uppercase characters in a string to lowercase | =LOWER("KIM") returns kim |
| PROPER | =PROPER(*text*) | Capitalizes the first letter of each word in a string | =PROPER("JASON BAKER") returns Jason Baker |
| LEN | =LEN(*text*) | Returns the number of characters in a string | =LEN("Judith Tinker") returns 13 |
| SEARCH | =SEARCH(*find_text, within_text, start_nbr*) | Returns the number of the character at which the find_text is first found reading from left to right | =SEARCH("Main", "1234 Main St",1) returns 6 |
| TEXT | =TEXT(*value, format_text_code*) | Formats numbers within text using a specific number format | ="Total Revenue " & TEXT(SUM(D5:D75),"$#,0.00") returns Total Revenue $1,052.00 |
| TRIM | =TRIM(*text*) | Removes all spaces from a string except for single spaces between words | =TRIM("   Mary Eck") returns Mary Eck |

## Using the LEN and LEFT Functions

The Zip column includes zip codes in both five-digit and 10-digit formats. Myron wants only the five-digit component of the zip code. You will use the LEN and LEFT functions to convert all of the zip codes to the shorter form.

The **LEN function** returns the number of characters (length) of the specified string. Cell D4 stores the text *Narragansett, ri* so the formula =LEN(D4) returns the value 16, the number of characters, including spaces, in *Narragansett, ri*. You will use the LEN function to determine how many characters are in each cell of the Zip column.

The **LEFT function** returns a specified number of characters from the beginning of the string. To extract the five-digit zip code from the zip code 92975-0999 stored in cell G3, you use the formula =LEFT(G3,5) to return 92975.

You can use the IF function in the formula =IF(LEN([Zip])=10,LEFT([Zip],5),[Zip]) to display a five-digit zip code. The IF function uses the LEN function to test whether the zip code has 10 digits. If true (the zip code is 10 digits), the LEFT function displays the first five digits in the cell. If false (the code is not 10 digits), all the digits in the cell are displayed.

You'll insert a new column to the left of the Phone column in which to display the results.

### To extract the five-digit zip code from the Zip column:

1. Click cell **F2**. You'll insert the table column to the left of this column.
2. Click the **Home** tab on the Ribbon.
3. In the Cells group, click the **Insert button arrow**, and then click **Insert Table Columns to the Left**. A new column named Column1 is inserted with the Text number format, which is the same format as the Zip column (column E).
4. Select the range **F2:F51**. This range is formatted as Text.
5. In the Number group on the Home tab, click the **Number Format arrow**, and then click **General**. Now, you can enter the formula in cell F2.
6. Make sure cell **F2** is the active cell, and then click the **Insert Function** button *fx* on the formula bar. The Insert Function dialog box opens.
7. Click **Logical** in the Or select a category list, click **IF** in the Select a function box, and then click the **OK** button. The Function Arguments dialog box opens.
8. In the Logical_test box, type **LEN([Zip])=10**. The logical test tests whether the number of characters in the current cell of the Zip column equals 10.
9. In the Value_if_true box, type **LEFT([Zip],5)**. This argument specifies that if the condition is true, the first five characters from the cell are displayed.
10. In the Value_if_false box, type **[Zip]**. This argument specifies that if the condition is false, all the characters from the cell are displayed. See Figure A-3.

**TIP**

You cannot enter a formula in a cell formatted as Text.

**Figure A-3** IF function with the LEN and LEFT functions

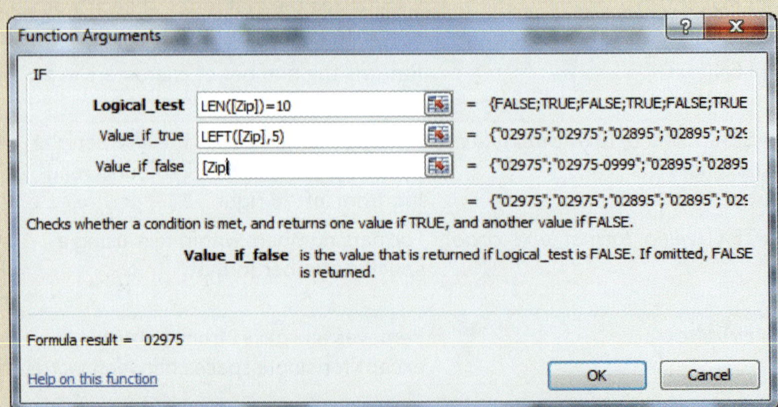

11. Click the **OK** button. The formula =IF(LEN([Zip])=10,LEFT([Zip],5),[Zip]) appears in the formula bar, and the value 02975 appears in cell F2 because the condition is false. The results are automatically copied to all rows in column F of the table. Each cell in column F displays the five-digit zip code. See Figure A-4.

**Figure A-4** **Table column with five-digit zip codes**

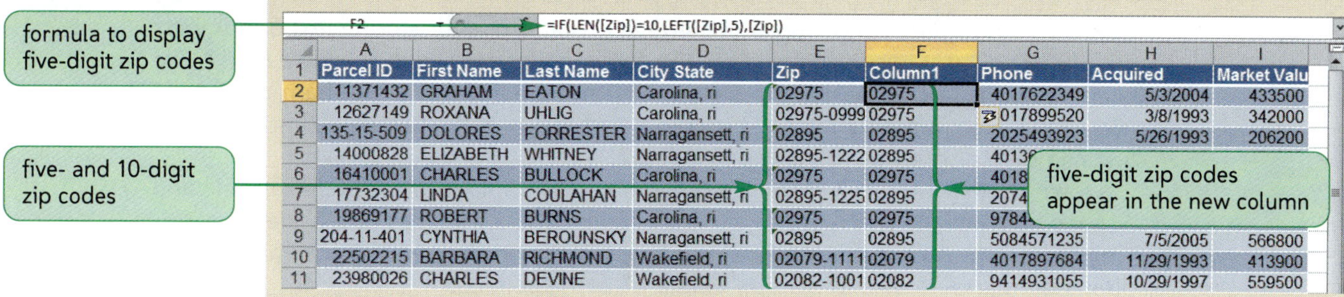


## Using the Paste Values Command

You now have two columns with zip codes (columns E and F). You need to keep only the column that displays the five-digit zip code. However, the data in column F is dependent on column E. If you delete column E, column F displays the #REF! error value. Therefore, before you delete column E, you need to convert the data in column F, which is based on a formula, to values. The easiest way to do that is to copy and paste the formula results, but not the actual formula, to a new column using the Paste Values command. Then, you can delete columns E and F.

### To convert the five-digit zip code formula results to values:

1. Click cell **G2**. In the Cells group on the Home tab, click the **Insert button arrow**, and then click **Insert Table Columns to the Left**. A new column named Column2 is inserted to the left of the Phone column.
2. Select the range **F2:F51**, which contains the formula results you want to convert to values.
3. In the Clipboard group on the Home tab, click the **Copy** button, and then click cell **G2**.
4. In the Clipboard group, click the **Paste button arrow**, and then click the **Values** button in the Paste gallery. The values from Column1 are pasted into Column2. The error button that appears indicates that the numbers in column G are stored as text; you want this to display leading zeros for zip codes.
5. Press the **Esc** key, and then click cell **F2**. The formula appears in the formula bar and the formula results appear in the cell.
6. Click cell **G2**. Both the formula bar and the cell display values because you pasted the range using the Paste Values command.
7. Select columns **E** and **F**, right-click the selected columns, and then click **Delete**. The two columns are removed.
8. In cell E1, enter **Zip**. Column E, which stores the five-digit zip code values, now has a descriptive column header.
9. Autofit the Zip column to fit the five-digit length.

## Using the PROPER Function and the & Operator

The **PROPER function** converts the first letter of each word to uppercase, capitalizes any letter that does not follow another letter, and changes all other letters to lowercase. The formula =PROPER("BOOTH") changes the word *BOOTH* to *Booth*.

The **& operator**, also called the Concatenation operator, concatenates or joins two or more text values. The syntax of the & operator is

```
Value1 & Value2 [& Value3 …]
```

where *Value1*, *Value2*, and *Value3* are string constants or cells storing text or numbers, and the & operator joins (or concatenates) these values to produce a single string. For example, if the last name "Eaton" is in cell B2 and the first name "Graham" is in cell C2, you can use the formula =B2 & C2 to join the contents of the two cells (last name and first name) to display the full name in cell D2.

However, this formula returns "EatonGraham" in cell D2. To include a comma and a space between the two names, you must change the formula to `=B2 & ", " & C2` which uses two & operators and a string constant (a comma and a space enclosed in quotation marks) to display "Eaton, Graham" in the cell.

Myron wants to combine the First Name and Last Name columns into one column. Because the names were entered in all uppercase letters, you need to combine the PROPER function and the & operator into the formula `=PROPER(B2)& ", " & PROPER(C2)`.

### To combine the names in one column with standard capitalization:

1. Click cell **D2**, and then insert a table column to the left. A new column named Column1 is inserted to the left of the Zip column.
2. In cell D2, type **=PR** and then double-click **PROPER** in the list of functions. The beginning of the formula, =PROPER(, appears in the cell and the formula bar, and a ScreenTip shows the function's syntax.
3. Type **[** to begin the column specifier, double-click **Last Name** in the list of the column qualifiers, type **]** to end the column specifier, and then type **)** to complete the PROPER function that converts the last name to uppercase and lowercase letters.
4. Type **&** to enter the operator, and then type **", "** to join the contents of cell D2 with a comma and space.
5. Type **&** to enter the operator, type **PR** and then double-click **PROPER** in the list of functions to begin the second PROPER function.
6. Type **[** to begin the column specifier, double-click **First Name** in the list of the column qualifiers, type **]** to end the column specifier, and then type **)** to complete the second PROPER function. The complete formula =PROPER([Last Name]) & ", "& PROPER([First Name]) appears in the cell and the formula bar.
7. Press the **Enter** key. Each cell in column D displays the owner's name in the form *Last name, First name* with the first letter of each name capitalized. See Figure A-5.

**Figure A-5** **Owner's name displayed in one column**

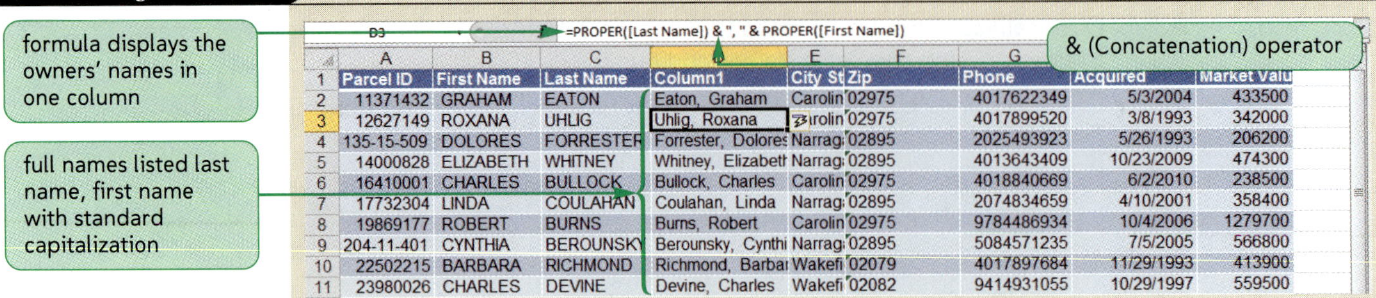


| | A | B | C | D | E | F | G | | |
|---|---|---|---|---|---|---|---|---|---|
| 1 | Parcel ID | First Name | Last Name | Column1 | City St | Zip | Phone | Acquired | Market Valu |
| 2 | 11371432 | GRAHAM | EATON | Eaton, Graham | Carolin | 02975 | 4017622349 | 5/3/2004 | 433500 |
| 3 | 12627149 | ROXANA | UHLIG | Uhlig, Roxana | arolin | 02975 | 4017899520 | 3/8/1993 | 342000 |
| 4 | 135-15-509 | DOLORES | FORRESTER | Forrester, Dolores | Narrag | 02895 | 2025493923 | 5/26/1993 | 206200 |
| 5 | 14000828 | ELIZABETH | WHITNEY | Whitney, Elizabeth | Narrag | 02895 | 4013643409 | 10/23/2009 | 474300 |
| 6 | 16410001 | CHARLES | BULLOCK | Bullock, Charles | Carolin | 02975 | 4018840669 | 6/2/2010 | 238500 |
| 7 | 17732304 | LINDA | COULAHAN | Coulahan, Linda | Narrag | 02895 | 2074834659 | 4/10/2001 | 358400 |
| 8 | 19869177 | ROBERT | BURNS | Burns, Robert | Carolin | 02975 | 9784486934 | 10/4/2006 | 1279700 |
| 9 | 204-11-401 | CYNTHIA | BEROUNSKY | Berounsky, Cynthi | Narrag | 02895 | 5084571235 | 7/5/2005 | 566800 |
| 10 | 22502215 | BARBARA | RICHMOND | Richmond, Barbai | Wakefi | 02079 | 4017897684 | 11/29/1993 | 413900 |
| 11 | 23980026 | CHARLES | DEVINE | Devine, Charles | Wakefi | 02082 | 9414931055 | 10/29/1997 | 559500 |

Now that the owners' names data is stored in column D, you no longer need the data in column B (Last Name) and column C (First Name). Because the results in column D are based on a formula, you need to convert the formula in column D to values before you delete columns B and C.

**To paste the formula results as values and delete the original data:**

1. Click cell **E2**, and then insert a table column to the left. A new column named Column2 is added to the table.
2. Select the range **D2:D51**, and then copy the range to the Clipboard.
3. Click cell **E2**, and then paste the values from the Clipboard to Column2.
4. Press the **Esc** key, and then autofit column E so you can see the owners' full names.
5. In cell E1, enter **Owners** as the column header.
6. Delete columns **B**, **C**, and **D**. The Owner column remains in the Excel table.

## Using the Text to Columns Command

When multiple pieces of data are stored in one cell, you can separate each piece of data into a different column using the Text to Columns command. This command starts the Convert Text to Column Wizard. You specify how to split the data based on how the data is stored. You can select what **delimits**, or separates, the data, such as a tab, a semicolon, a comma, or a space. For fixed-width data, you specify break locations. Each entry in a fixed-width field is the same length no matter how many characters are entered in the field. For example, a Last Name field with a fixed width of 20 characters always takes up 20 spaces in the record even though some last names contain a few characters and others contain many characters.

You'll split the city and state data into different columns.

**To split the city and state data into separate columns:**

1. Click cell **D2**, and then insert a table column to the left. A new column named Column1 is inserted to the left of the Zip column.
2. Select the range **C2:C51**. These cells contain the values you want to split.
3. Click the **Data** tab on the Ribbon, and then click the **Text to Columns** button in the Data Tools group. The Convert Text to Columns Wizard - Step 1 of 3 dialog box opens. You select how the data is organized in this step—delimited or a fixed width.
4. In the Original data type area, verify that the **Delimited** option button is selected, and then click the **Next** button. The Convert Text to Columns Wizard - Step 2 of 3 dialog box opens. You select the delimiter character in this step.
5. Click any check box with a check mark in the Delimiters section to remove the check mark, and then click the **Comma** check box. The data in the City State column is separated by a comma. The Data preview box shows the City and State data in separate columns. See Figure A-6.

**Figure A-6** Convert Text to Columns Wizard – Step 2 of 3 dialog box

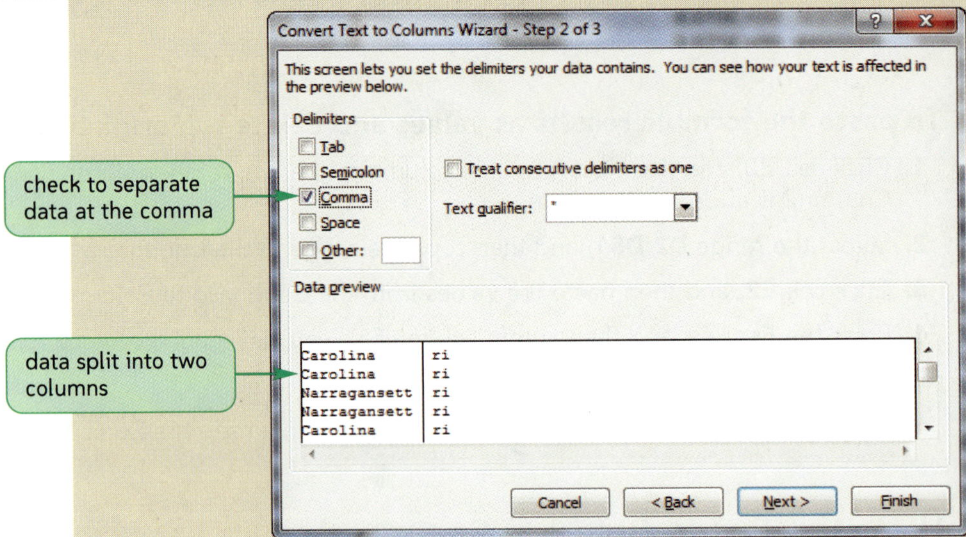


6. Click the **Next** button. The Convert Text to Columns Wizard - Step 3 of 3 dialog box opens so you can set the data format for each column. The Data preview box shows that each column is set to the General number format, which you want.
7. Click the **Finish** button. Cities remain in column C; states move to column D.
8. In cell C1, enter **City** and then, in cell D1, enter **State**.
9. Autofit the widths of columns C and D. See Figure A-7.

**Figure A-7** City and State in separate columns

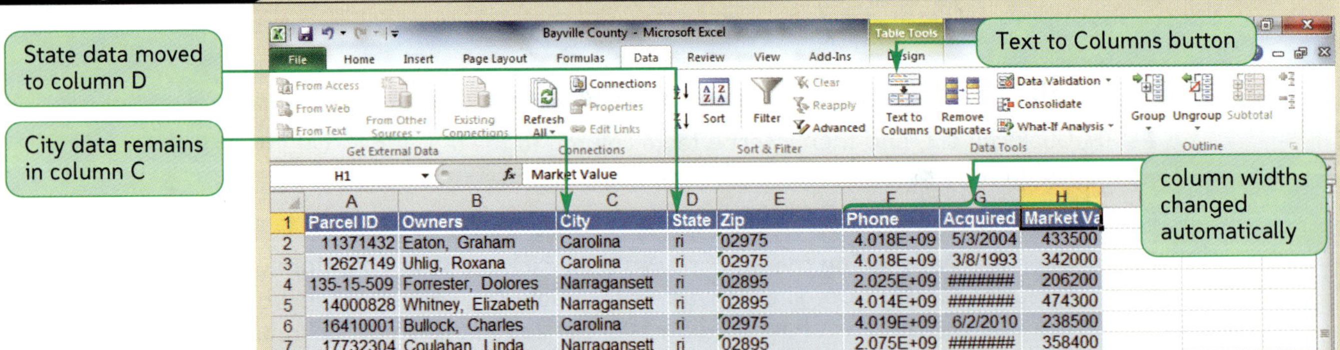


## Using the UPPER Function to Convert Case

The **UPPER function** converts all letters of each word in a text string to uppercase. The formula =UPPER("ri") returns RI. You'll use the UPPER function to change state abbreviations in column D from lowercase to uppercase.

### To use the UPPER function to capitalize the state abbreviations:

1. Click cell **E2**, and then insert a table column to the left. A new column named Column1 is inserted to the left of the Zip column.
2. In cell E2, type **=U** and then press the **Tab** key to select the UPPER function in the list. The beginning of the formula =UPPER( is in the cell and the formula bar.

3. Type **[** to begin the column specifier, double-click **State** in the list of the column qualifiers, type **]** to end the column specifier, and then type **)**. The formula =UPPER([State]) appears in the formula bar.
4. Press the **Enter** key. The state abbreviation appears in all uppercase letters in column E. See Figure A-8.

**Figure A-8** **UPPER function converted state abbreviations to uppercase**

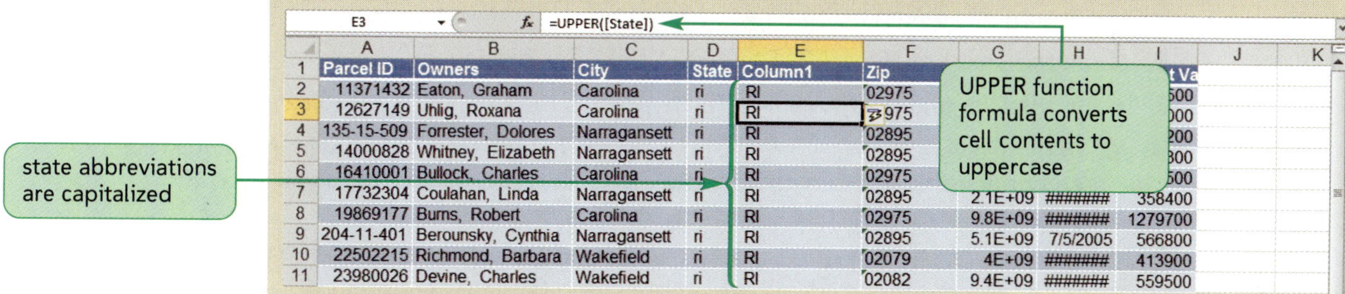


You want to keep only the data in column E. Because the results of column E are based on a formula, you again will convert the formula in column E to values before you delete columns D and E.

### To paste the state abbreviations as values:

1. Click cell **F2**, and then insert a table column to the left. A new column named Column2 is inserted to the left of the Zip column.
2. Select the range **E2:E51**, and then copy the range to the Clipboard.
3. Click cell **F2**, and then paste the values from the Clipboard. Verify that the formula bar displays a value and not a formula.
4. Delete columns **D** and **E**. Column D remains in the Excel table.
5. In cell D1, enter **State**. The column is renamed with a more descriptive header.

## Using the SUBSTITUTE Function

The **SUBSTITUTE function** replaces existing text with new text. The SUBSTITUTE function has the syntax

```
SUBSTITUTE (text,old_text,new_text,instance_num)
```

where *text* is a string constant or reference to a cell containing text you want to replace, *old_text* is the existing text you want to replace, *new_text* is the text you want to replace *old_text* with, and *instance_num* specifies which occurrence of *old_text* you want to replace. If you omit *instance_num*, every instance of *old_text* is replaced. The formula =SUBSTITUTE("164-45-890","-","") returns 16445890.

The entries in Parcel ID, column A, are inconsistent. Sometimes they are an eight-digit value, and other times hyphens separate the components of the Parcel (Book No., Map No., and Parcel No.). Myron wants you to remove the hyphens from the Parcel ID. You'll enter a formula with the SUBSTITUTE function to remove the hyphens from the Parcel ID data.

**To remove hyphens from the Parcel ID data and paste the values:**

1. Click cell **B2**, and then insert a table column to the left. A new column named Column1 is inserted to the left of the Owners column.
2. Click the **Insert Function** button *fx* on the formula bar. The Insert Function dialog box opens.
3. Click the **Or select a category** arrow, click **Text** to display the Text functions, and then double-click **SUBSTITUTE** in the Select a function box. The Function Arguments dialog box opens.
4. In the Text box, type **A2**. The text in cell A2 is displayed.
5. In the Old_text box, type **"-"**. The hyphen is the text you want to remove.
6. In the New_text box, type **""**. You want to replace the old text with nothing. You do not need to enter anything in the Instance_num box because you want to replace every instance of a hyphen.
7. Click the **OK** button. All of the Parcel IDs are changed to eight-digit numbers. The hyphens were replaced with an empty string (a blank, or nothing).
8. Click cell **B2**. See Figure A-9.

**Figure A-9** SUBSTITUTE function removed hyphens from the Parcel IDs

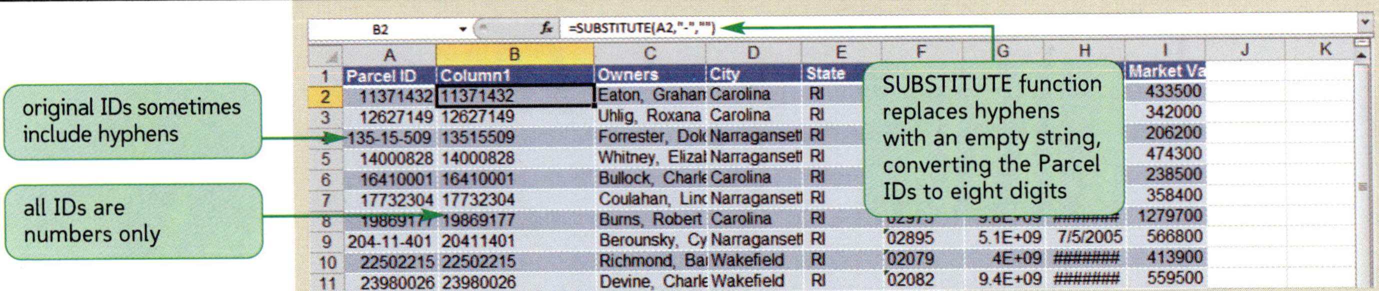


9. Click cell **C2**, and then insert a table column to the left. A new column named Column2 is inserted to the left of the Owners column.
10. Select the range **B2:B51**, and then copy this range to the Clipboard.
11. Click cell **C2**, and then paste the values from the Clipboard.
12. Delete columns **A** and **B**. The Parcel ID column remains in the Excel table.
13. In cell A1, enter **Parcel ID**.
14. Autofit the Parcel ID, Owners, City, State, Zip, Phone, Acquired, and Market Value columns.

## Using Special Formats

Four commonly used formats, referred to as special formats, are available: two zip code formats (five-digit and 10-digit), a phone number format (with the area code in parentheses and a hyphen between the prefix and the last four digits), and a Social Security number format. Using these special formats allows you to type a number without punctuation, yet still display that number in its common format.

Myron wants you to display the phone number using the common format of area code in parentheses and a hyphen between the prefix and the last four digits.

**To format the phone number with the Phone Number format:**

1. Select the range **F2:F51**. In the Number group on the Home tab, click the **Dialog Box Launcher**. The Format Cells dialog box opens with the Number tab active.
2. In the Category box, click **Special**. Four special formats appear in the Type list: Zip Code, Zip Code + 4, Phone Number, and Social Security Number.
3. In the Type box, click **Phone Number**. See Figure A-10.

**Figure A-10** Special category on the Number tab

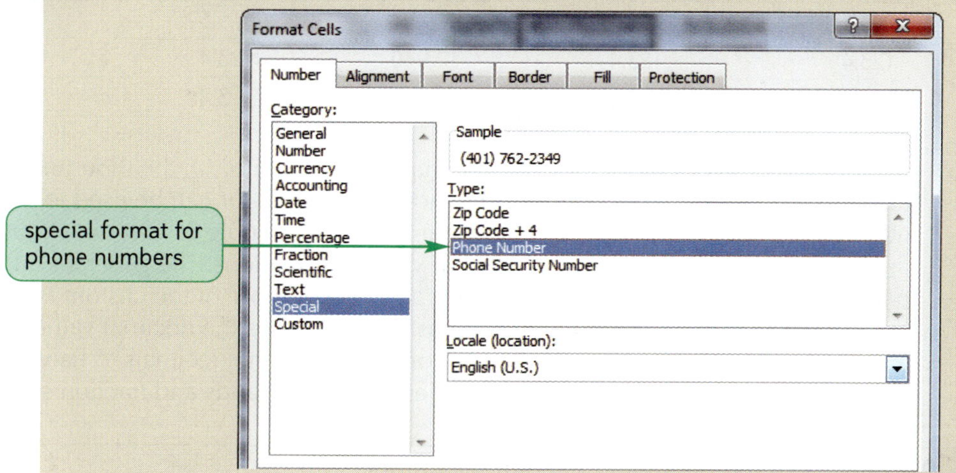


4. Click the **OK** button. The phone numbers are formatted in a standard format.

# Creating Custom Formats

**TIP**

Any custom format you create is stored only in the workbook in which it was created. To use it in another workbook, you must reenter it.

Excel supplies a generous collection of formats and styles to improve the appearance and readability of worksheets. However, sometimes you will need a format and style to accommodate a specific requirement. In these cases, you can create your own formats, called **custom formats**. Custom formats use **format codes**, a series of symbols, to describe exactly how Excel should display a number, date, time, or text string. You can use format codes to display text strings and spaces, and determine how many decimal places to display in a cell.

## Creating a Custom Number Format

Each number is composed of digits. In displaying these digits, Excel makes special note of **insignificant zeros**, which are zeros whose omission from the number does not change the number's value. For example, the number 0.1 is displayed in the General number format but changes to 0.10 when the cell is formatted as a number. To format a value, Excel uses the **placeholders** shown in Figure A-11 to represent individual digits.

**Figure A-11** Description of digit placeholders

| Placeholder | Description |
|---|---|
| # | Displays only significant digits; insignificant zeros are omitted. |
| 0 (zero) | Displays significant digits as well as insignificant zeros. |
| ? | Replaces insignificant zeros with spaces on either side of the decimal point so that decimal points align when formatted with a fixed-width font, such as Courier. |

A custom format can use combinations of these placeholders. For example, the custom format #.00 displays the value 8.9 as 8.90. If a value has more digits than placeholders in the custom format, Excel rounds the value to match the number of placeholders. Thus, the value 8.938 formatted with the custom format #.## is displayed as 8.94. Figure A-12 shows how the same series of numbers appears with different custom number formats.

**Figure A-12** **Examples of digit placeholders**

| | Custom Formats | | | |
|---|---|---|---|---|
| **Cell Value** | **#.##** | **0.00** | **?.??** | **#.#0** |
| 0.57 | .57 | 0.57 | .57 | .57 |
| 123.4 | 123.4 | 123.40 | 123.4 | 123.40 |
| 3.45 | 3.45 | 3.45 | 3.45 | 3.45 |

Number formats also include the decimal point separator (.), the thousands separator (,), and the fraction separator (/). The thousands separator can be used to separate the number in groups of 1000 or to scale a number by a multiple of 1000.

The fraction separator displays decimal values as fractions. The general syntax is *placeholder/placeholder,* where *placeholder* is one or more of the custom format placeholders. Excel displays the fraction that best approximates the decimal value. You can also specify the denominator for the fraction to convert the decimals to halves, quarters, and so forth. Figure A-13 provides examples of the thousands and fraction separators.

**Figure A-13** **Examples of thousands and fraction separators**

| **Value** | **Custom Format** | **Appearance** |
|---|---|---|
| 12000 | #,### | 12,000 |
| 12000 | #, | 12 |
| 12200000 | 0.0,, | 12.2 |
| 5.4 | # #/# | 5 2/5 |

All of the numeric format codes can be combined in a single custom format. If you don't specify a numeric code for data values, Excel uses the General format code, which hides all insignificant zeros.

You'll create a custom format to display the market values to the nearest thousand.

**To create a custom format for the market values:**

1. Select the range **H2:H51**.
2. In the Number group on the Home tab, click the **Dialog Box Launcher**. The Format Cells dialog box opens with the Number tab active.
3. In the Category box, click **Custom**. You will enter a custom format to display the numbers to the nearest thousand.
4. In the Type box, double-click **General** to select it, and then type **#,###,** as the custom format code. See Figure A-14.

Be sure to type a comma at the end of the format code so that the numbers will be displayed to the nearest thousand.

**Figure A-14** Custom category on the Number tab

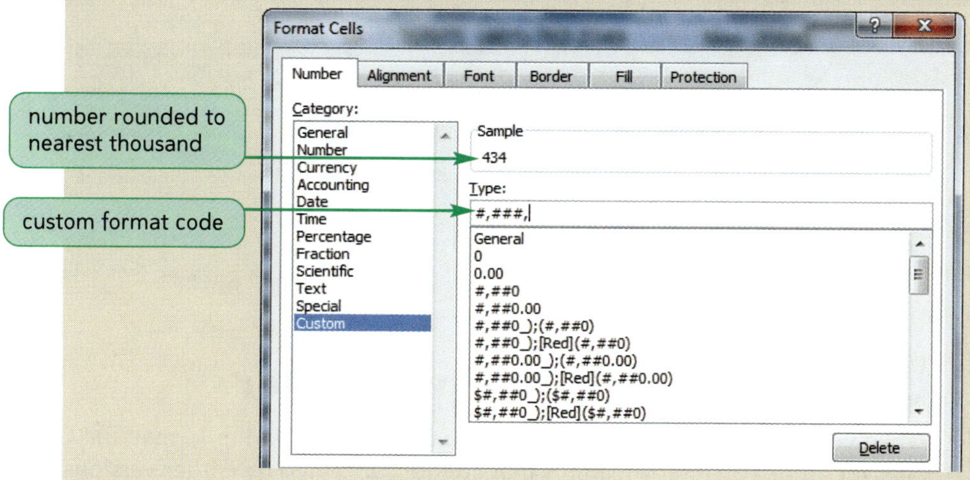


5. Click the **OK** button. The market values are displayed to the nearest thousand.

## Creating a Custom Date Format

When you have dates, times, or both in a workbook, you can use a predefined date and time format to display this information in a readable format. Although the predefined time and date formats are usually fine, you can also create your own custom date formats. Figure A-15 describes the format codes used for dates and times.

**Figure A-15** Date and Time format codes

| Symbol | To Display | Symbol | To Display |
|---|---|---|---|
| m | Months as 1 through 12 | dddd | Days as Sunday through Saturday |
| mm | Months as 01 through 12 | yy | Years as 00 through 99 |
| mmm | Months as Jan through Dec | yyyy | Years as 1900 through 9999 |
| mmmm | Months as January through December | h | Hours as 1 through 24 |
| d | Days as 1 through 31 | mm | Minutes as 01 through 60 (when immediately following h, mm signifies minutes; otherwise, months) |
| dd | Days as 01 through 31 | | |
| ddd | Days as Sun through Sat | ss | Seconds as 01 through 60 |

Myron wants the date values in the Acquired column to show the name of the month followed by the year (for example, 7/22/2013 should be displayed as July, 2013). You need to apply the custom format code *mmmm, yyyy* to do this.

### To apply a custom date format to the Acquired dates:

1. Select the range **G2:G51**.
2. In the Number group on the Home tab, click the **Dialog Box Launcher**. The Format Cells dialog box opens with the Number tab active.
3. In the Category box, click **Custom**.
4. In the Type box, select the current format, and then type **mmmm, yyyy**. The Sample box shows an example of the custom format you entered.
5. Click the **OK** button, and then click cell **A1** to deselect the range. See Figure A-16.

**Figure A-16** **Final formatted workbook**

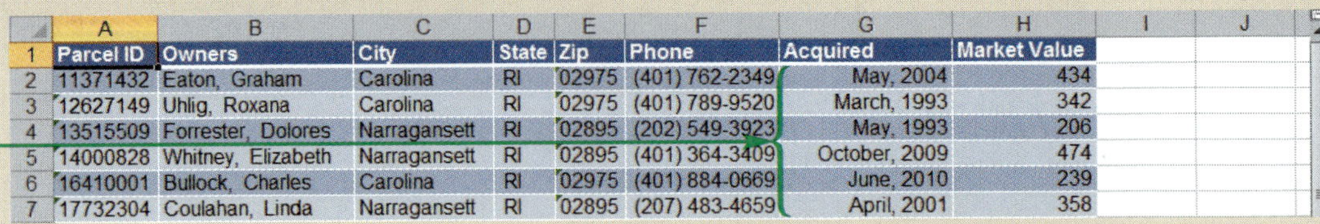

| Parcel ID | Owners | City | State | Zip | Phone | Acquired | Market Value |
|---|---|---|---|---|---|---|---|
| 11371432 | Eaton, Graham | Carolina | RI | 02975 | (401) 762-2349 | May, 2004 | 434 |
| 12627149 | Uhlig, Roxana | Carolina | RI | 02975 | (401) 789-9520 | March, 1993 | 342 |
| 13515509 | Forrester, Dolores | Narragansett | RI | 02895 | (202) 549-3923 | May, 1993 | 206 |
| 14000828 | Whitney, Elizabeth | Narragansett | RI | 02895 | (401) 364-3409 | October, 2009 | 474 |
| 16410001 | Bullock, Charles | Carolina | RI | 02975 | (401) 884-0669 | June, 2010 | 239 |
| 17732304 | Coulahan, Linda | Narragansett | RI | 02895 | (207) 483-4659 | April, 2001 | 358 |

dates with custom format

6. Save the workbook.

# Using the Compatibility Checker

When you save an Excel 2007 or 2010 workbook to an earlier format, the **Compatibility Checker** alerts you to any features that are not supported by earlier versions of Excel. You can click the Cancel button and redo the worksheet using a different approach, or you can click the Continue button to save the workbook in the earlier format. If you save the workbook in an earlier format, unsupported features will be lost.

You'll save a copy of the workbook in the Excel 2003 format.

### To convert the workbook to the Excel 2003 file format:

1. Open the Save As dialog box, and then change the filename to **Bayville County 2003**.
2. Click the **Save as type** button, and then click **Excel 97-2003 Workbook**. This is the earlier Excel file format you want to use.
3. Click the **Save** button. The Compatibility Checker dialog box opens, alerting you to features not supported by earlier versions of Excel. See Figure A-17.

**Figure A-17** **Compatibility Checker**

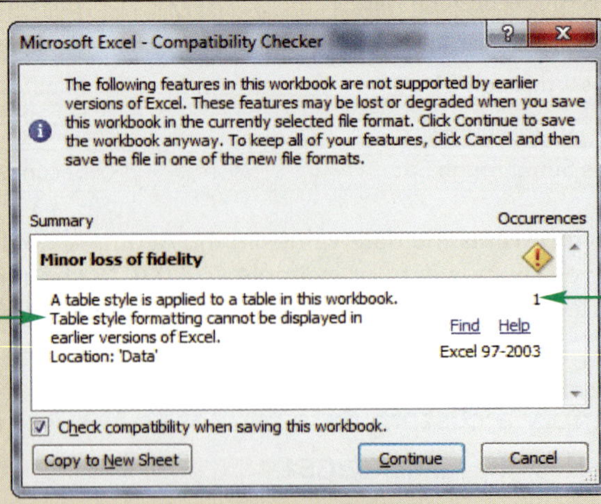


Excel tables are not supported in Excel 97-2003

number of times this problem occurs in the workbook

4. Read the message, and then click the **Continue** button. The workbook is saved in the earlier file format with the .xls file extension. Close the workbook.

The workbook data is clean and formatted in the best way for Myron. He'll analyze this data as he comes up with a proposal to address Bayville's traffic concerns.

*Practice the skills you learned by using the same case scenario.*

PRACTICE

## Review Assignments

### Data File needed for the Review Assignments: Assessor.xls

As part of the Transportation Improvement Program (TIP) study, Myron Londale obtained a second workbook from the Bayville Assessor's Office containing data on private homes and commercial buildings located along the route being reviewed. Myron asks you to clean and format the data. Complete the following:

1. Open the **Assessor** workbook located in the ExcelA\Review folder, and then save the workbook in the Excel Workbook (2007-2010) format as **Owners**.
2. Insert a new worksheet. Enter your name, the date, and a purpose statement in the worksheet, and then rename the worksheet as **Documentation**.
3. In the Owners worksheet, create an Excel table for the data in the range A1:G51. Apply the Table Style Medium 10 table style to the Excel table.
4. Use the Text to Columns command to split the Owner column into two columns named **Last Name** and **First Name**. Insert a blank column to the left of column C to store the first name, and leave the last name in column B.
5. In cell I1, enter the column header **Status**. In the Status column, use the IF and LEFT functions to display the word **Discard** if the address is a PO Box; otherwise, leave the cell blank.
6. In cell J1, enter the column header **Twn**. In cell J2, enter a formula to convert the data in the Town column to proper case.
7. In cell K1, enter the column header **St**. In column K, enter a formula to convert the data in the State column to uppercase.
8. In cell L1, enter the column header **Town State**. In column L, combine the town and state data from columns J and K into one column using the format *town, state*.
9. Format the data in the SSN column (column A) with the Social Security Number format.
10. Save and close the workbook. Submit the finished workbook to your instructor, either in printed or electronic form, as requested.

*Apply the skills you learned to clean and format data.*

APPLY

## Case Problem 1

### Data File needed for this Case Problem: Mesa.xls

***Mesa Senior Center*** Elliot Turner, director of the Mesa Senior Center, has begun compiling a list of its members. He's asked you to clean and format the data in the worksheet before he continues working on the project. Complete the following:

1. Open the **Mesa** workbook located in the ExcelA\Case1 folder, and then save the workbook in Excel Workbook (2007-2010) format as **Senior Center**.
2. Insert a new worksheet. Enter the company name, your name, the date, and a purpose statement in the worksheet, and then rename the worksheet as **Documentation**.
3. In the Members worksheet, apply the Social Security Number format to the data in the SSN column.
4. Split the Name data into two columns. Store the first name in column B and the last name in column C. Change the column headers to **First Name** and **Last Name**.
5. Insert two columns to the left of the CSZ column. In column D, apply the proper case to the first name data, and change the column header to **F Name**. In column E, apply the proper case to the last name data, and change the column header to **L Name**.
6. In the Member Since column, apply a custom format that displays only the year.
7. Split the CSZ column into three columns named **City**, **State**, and **Zip**. (*Hint*: Repeat the split twice.)

8. Sort the data by City and then within City by L Name.

EXPLORE

9. Name column J **UniqueID**. The senior center uses an ID that consists of the first three letters of the last name (L Name) followed by the first letter of first name (F Name). If the last name is fewer than three characters, the letter "Z" replaces each missing character. Use the LEN and LEFT functions and the & operator to display the proposed UniqueID.
10. Save the workbook. Submit the finished workbook to your instructor, either in printed or electronic form, as requested.

*Apply the skills you learned to calculate overhead.*

APPLY

## Case Problem 2

**Data File needed for this Case Problem: Research.xls**

***Steuben Institute*** Every two weeks, Elli Pjster processes payroll information for employees whose salaries are paid fully or partially from research grants. She downloads an Excel workbook from the Steuben Institute's Research and Grant Accounting system to calculate overhead. The overhead rate varies depending on the research grant. She asks you to clean and format the data in the worksheet. Complete the following:

1. Open the **Research** workbook located in the ExcelA\Case2 folder, and save the workbook in the Excel 2007/2010 format as **Grants**.
2. Insert a new worksheet. Enter the company name, your name, the date, and a purpose statement in the worksheet, and then rename the worksheet as **Documentation**.
3. In the Pay Period 10 worksheet, create an Excel table for the range A1:C51. Hide the filter arrows.
4. Split the data in column A into separate columns for the first name and the last name. Change the column headers to **First Name** and **Last Name**. Autofit the two columns, and then sort the table by the Last Name data.

EXPLORE

5. Use the MID function to extract the grant number from the ChartString column and display it in column E. Name the new column **Grant Nbr**. The Grant Nbr is a four-digit number that begins in position 10 of the ChartString column. (*Hint*: Research the MID function in the Help system.)
6. In the column to the right of the Grant Nbr column (column F), enter a VLOOKUP function to find the grant number in the lookup table in the Overhead Rates worksheet and display the grant name from the second column in the lookup table. Change the column header to **Grant Name**. Autofit the column.
7. In column G, enter the formula to calculate overhead (the Overhead Rate in the third column of the Overhead Rates worksheet multiplied by Salary). Use a VLOOKUP function to find the correct overhead rate for the grant. Name the column **Overhead**.
8. Format the Salary and Overhead columns using the Accounting number format.
9. Save and close the workbook. Submit the finished workbook to your instructor, either in printed or electronic form, as requested.

### ENDING DATA FILES

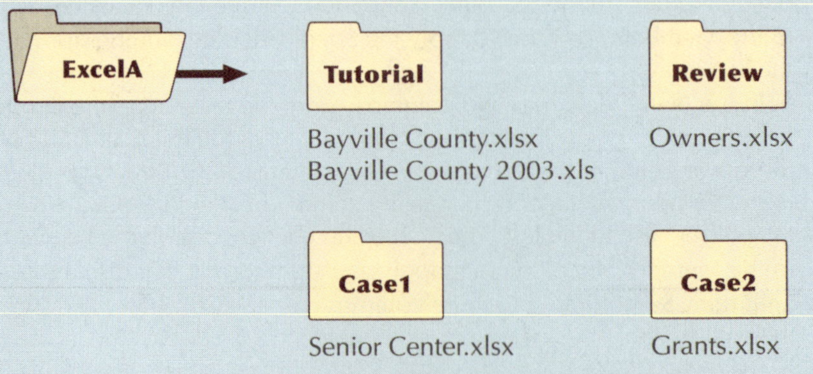

APPENDIX **B**

# Advanced Filters, Database, and Summary IFS Functions

*Generating a List of Eligible Employee Candidates*

## OBJECTIVES

- Use advanced filters
- Create a criteria range
- Use Database functions
- Summarize data using the COUNTIFS, SUMIFS, and AVERAGEIFS functions

## Case | *Talent Tracs*

Talent Tracs is growing rapidly and plans to hire additional full-time employees. Before searching outside the company, Rita Corvales wants to give preference to part-time employees and consultants at Talent Tracs who want to apply for the new full-time positions. Rita has established the following criteria to determine which part-time employees and consultants will be considered for full-time employment:

- Part-time employees who have worked for Talent Tracs for two or more years
- Consultants who have worked for Talent Tracs for more than three years earning less than $55,000

You will use advanced filters to generate the list of candidates who are eligible for the new positions.

## STARTING DATA FILES

TracEmployees.xlsx TracReview.xlsx World.xlsx Gifts.xlsx

# Using Advanced Filters

**Advanced filtering** displays a subset of the rows in an Excel table or a range of data that match the criteria you specify. With advanced filtering, you specify the filter criteria in a separate range, called the criteria range. Advanced filtering enables you to perform OR conditions across multiple fields, such as the criteria Rita wants you to use to find eligible candidates within Talent Tracs for the new full-time positions. You can also use advanced filtering to create complex criteria using functions and formulas. For example, Rita could use advanced filtering to find all female salaried employees whose salary falls below the median salary for all employees.

Rita created a workbook that contains data for each employee. You will open this workbook and filter the employee information to identify employees who are eligible for the new positions.

### To open the Talent Tracs workbook:

1. Open the **TracEmployees** workbook located in the ExcelB\Tutorial folder included with your Data Files, and then save the workbook as **TracSearch**.
2. In the Documentation worksheet, enter your name and the date.
3. Switch to the **Employee Data** worksheet. See Figure B-1.

**Figure B-1** Employee table

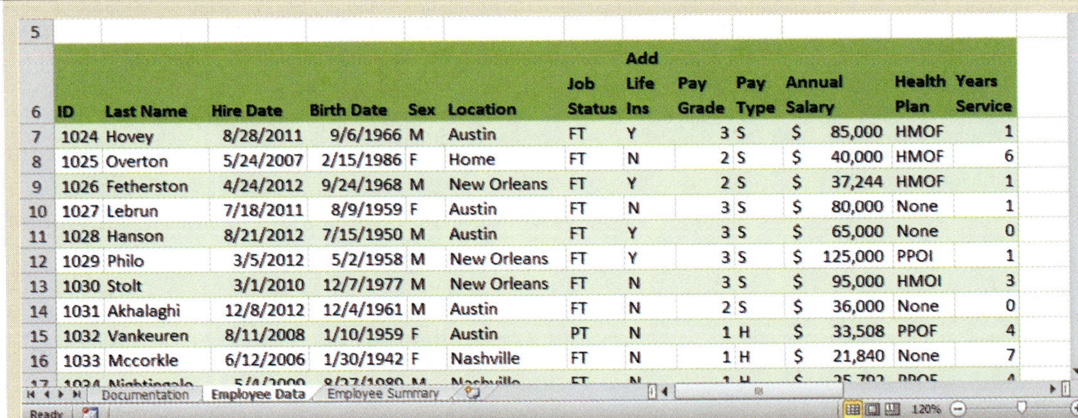

| | ID | Last Name | Hire Date | Birth Date | Sex | Location | Job Status | Add Life Ins | Pay Grade | Pay Type | Annual Salary | Health Plan | Years Service |
|---|---|---|---|---|---|---|---|---|---|---|---|---|---|
| 7 | 1024 | Hovey | 8/28/2011 | 9/6/1966 | M | Austin | FT | Y | 3 | S | $ 85,000 | HMOF | 1 |
| 8 | 1025 | Overton | 5/24/2007 | 2/15/1986 | F | Home | FT | N | 2 | S | $ 40,000 | HMOF | 6 |
| 9 | 1026 | Fetherston | 4/24/2012 | 9/24/1968 | M | New Orleans | FT | Y | 2 | S | $ 37,244 | HMOF | 1 |
| 10 | 1027 | Lebrun | 7/18/2011 | 8/9/1959 | F | Austin | FT | N | 3 | S | $ 80,000 | None | 1 |
| 11 | 1028 | Hanson | 8/21/2012 | 7/15/1950 | M | Austin | FT | Y | 3 | S | $ 65,000 | None | 0 |
| 12 | 1029 | Philo | 3/5/2012 | 5/2/1958 | M | New Orleans | FT | Y | 3 | S | $ 125,000 | PPOI | 1 |
| 13 | 1030 | Stolt | 3/1/2010 | 12/7/1977 | M | New Orleans | FT | N | 3 | S | $ 95,000 | HMOI | 3 |
| 14 | 1031 | Akhalaghi | 12/8/2012 | 12/4/1961 | M | Austin | FT | N | 2 | S | $ 36,000 | None | 0 |
| 15 | 1032 | Vankeuren | 8/11/2008 | 1/10/1959 | F | Austin | PT | N | 1 | H | $ 33,508 | PPOF | 4 |
| 16 | 1033 | Mccorkle | 6/12/2006 | 1/30/1942 | F | Nashville | FT | N | 1 | H | $ 21,840 | None | 7 |



## Understanding the Criteria Range

The **criteria range** is an area in a worksheet, separate from a range of data or an Excel table, used to specify the criteria for the data to be displayed after the filter is applied to the range or Excel table. The criteria range consists of a header row that lists field names from the table's header row, and at least one row with the specific filtering criteria for each field. The criteria range specifies which records from the data range will be included in the filtered data.

Criteria placed on the same row are considered to be connected with the logical operator AND. That means all criteria in the same row must be met before a record is included in the filtered data. Figure B-2 shows an AND criteria range filter to retrieve all employees from Nashville who earn more than $55,000.

**Figure B-2** Example of an AND filter specified in a criteria range

| | A | B | C | D | E | F | G | H | I | J | K | L | M |
|---|---|---|---|---|---|---|---|---|---|---|---|---|---|
| 1 | ID | Last Name | Hire Date | Birth Date | Sex | Location | Job Status | Add Life Ins | Pay Grade | Pay Type | Annual Salary | Health Plan | Years Service |
| 2 | | | | | | Nashville | | | | | >55000 | | |

Criteria placed on separate rows of the criteria range are treated as being connected by the logical operator OR. That means records that meet all the criteria on either row in the criteria range will be displayed. Figure B-3 shows an example of the OR filter to retrieve female employees or employees who are working in Austin and earning less than $50,000.

**Figure B-3** Example of an OR filter specified in a criteria range

| | A | B | C | D | E | F | G | H | I | J | K | L | M |
|---|---|---|---|---|---|---|---|---|---|---|---|---|---|
| 1 | ID | Last Name | Hire Date | Birth Date | Sex | Location | Job Status | Add Life Ins | Pay Grade | Pay Type | Annual Salary | Health Plan | Years Service |
| 2 | | | | | F | | | | | | | | |
| 3 | | | | | | Austin | | | | | <50000 | | |

To specify criteria between a range of values in the same field, you use the same field name repeated in separate cells within the same row to match a range of values (BETWEEN criteria). Figure B-4 shows a criteria range to retrieve all employees who were hired between 1/1/2008 and 12/31/2012.

**Figure B-4** Example of a Between filter specified in a criteria range

| | A | B | C | D | E | F | G | H | I | J | K | L | M |
|---|---|---|---|---|---|---|---|---|---|---|---|---|---|
| 1 | ID | Last Name | Hire Date | Hire Date | Sex | Location | Job Status | Add Life Ins | Pay Grade | Pay Type | Annual Salary | Health Plan | Years Service |
| 2 | | | >=1/1/2008 | <=12/31/2012 | | | | | | | | | |

## Creating a Criteria Range

Typically, you place a criteria range above the data range to keep it separate from the data. If you place a criteria range next to the data range, the criteria might be hidden when the advanced filtering causes rows to be hidden. You can also place a criteria range in a separate worksheet, particularly if you need to use several criteria ranges in different cells to perform calculations based on various sets of filtered records.

You will place the criteria range in rows 1 to 4 of the Employee Data worksheet to make it easier to locate. Because the field names in the criteria range must exactly match the field names in the Excel table or range except for capitalization, you should copy and paste the field names instead of retyping them. In row 2, you will enter an AND criteria range with the criteria for consultants (code CN) who earn less than $55,000 and have worked at Talent Tracs for more than three years. In row 3, you will enter the criteria for part-time employees who have more than two years of service.

### To create the criteria range to find eligible candidates:

1. Point to the left side of cell **A6** until the pointer changes to ➡, and then click the mouse button. The column headers in row 6 are selected.

2. Copy the field names to the Clipboard.
3. Click cell **A1**, and then paste the field names. The field names for the criteria range appear in row 1.
4. Press the **Esc** key to remove the copied data from the Clipboard.
5. In cell G2, enter **CN**. The condition specifies the criteria to retrieve all consultants (Pay Type code beginning with CN).
6. In cell K2, enter **<55000**. This condition specifies the criteria to retrieve all employees whose salaries are less than $55,000.
7. In cell M2, enter **>3**. This condition specifies the criteria to retrieve all employees who have more than 3 years of service. The criteria in row 2 select all consultants who earn less than $55,000 and have more than three years of service at Talent Tracs.
8. In cell G3, enter **PT**.
9. In cell M3, enter **>=2**. The criteria in row 3 select all employees who are part-time (Job Status is equal to PT) and who have two or more years of service at Talent Tracs (Years Service is greater than or equal to 2). See Figure B-5.

**Figure B-5** **Criteria range to filter records**

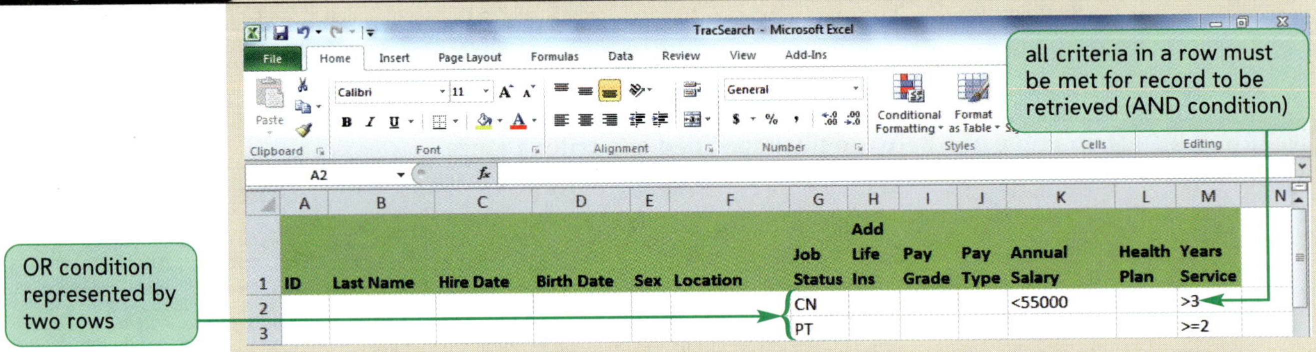


Now that the criteria range is established, you can use the Advanced Filter command to filter the Employee table. You can filter the records in their current location by hiding rows that don't match your criteria, as you have done with the Filter command. Or, you can copy the records that match your criteria to another location in the worksheet. Rita wants you to filter the records in their current location.

## To filter the Employee table in its current location:

1. Click any cell in the Employee table to make the table active.
2. Click the **Data** tab on the Ribbon.
3. In the Sort & Filter group, click the **Advanced** button. The Advanced Filter dialog box opens.
4. Make sure the **Filter the list, in-place** option button is selected and the range **$A$6:$M$106** appears in the List range box. The range $A$6:$M$106 is the current location of the Employee table, which is the table you want to filter.
5. Make sure the Criteria range box displays **$A$1:$M$3**. This range references the criteria range. See Figure B-6.

**Figure B-6** Completed Advanced Filter dialog box

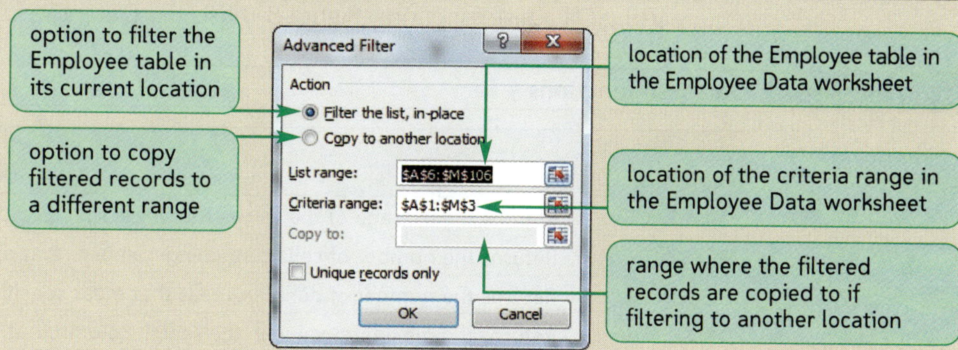


6. Click the **OK** button, and then scroll to the top of the worksheet. The list is filtered in its current location, and nine employee records match the criteria (as shown in the status bar). See Figure B-7.

**Figure B-7** Filtered employee data

| | A | B | C | D | E | F | G | H | I | J | K | L | M |
|---|---|---|---|---|---|---|---|---|---|---|---|---|---|
| 6 | ID | Last Name | Hire Date | Birth Date | Sex | Location | Job Status | Add Life Ins | Pay Grade | Pay Type | Annual Salary | Health Plan | Years Service |
| 15 | 1032 | Vankeuren | 8/11/2008 | 1/10/1959 | F | Austin | PT | N | 1 | H | $ 33,508 | PPOF | 4 |
| 41 | 1058 | Myette | 5/4/2009 | 6/28/1967 | M | Home | PT | N | 2 | S | $ 33,000 | HMOF | 4 |
| 65 | 1082 | Steyerl | 3/13/2008 | 5/12/1969 | M | Austin | CN | N | 3 | S | $ 54,000 | None | 5 |
| 75 | 1092 | Sherman | 11/26/2010 | 3/2/1955 | M | Austin | PT | N | 1 | H | $ 33,280 | HMOI | 2 |
| 76 | 1093 | Mulcahey | 8/25/2001 | 5/13/1964 | F | Austin | PT | N | 2 | S | $ 45,000 | None | 11 |
| 79 | 1096 | Silver | 9/6/2005 | 6/26/1967 | F | Austin | PT | N | 3 | S | $ 93,000 | None | 7 |
| 82 | 1099 | Reels | 6/15/2009 | 7/31/1963 | F | Austin | PT | N | 1 | H | $ 26,520 | None | 4 |
| 89 | 1106 | Tucker | 3/11/2007 | 3/3/1958 | F | Nashville | PT | N | 1 | H | $ 22,880 | PPOF | 6 |
| 100 | 1117 | Zunjic | 10/12/2010 | 1/17/1970 | F | Austin | PT | N | 1 | H | $ 36,004 | HMOI | 2 |

employees eligible to apply for the full-time position

**Trouble?** If all of the data in the table is filtered, the list range or criteria range might be incorrect. Click the Clear button in the Sort & Filter group on the Data tab, and then repeat Steps 1 through 6, making sure the list range is $A$6:$M$106 and the criteria range is $A$1:$M$3 in the Advanced Filter dialog box.

After providing the list of eligible employees to Rita, you remove the filter to display all of the records in the Employee table.

### To show all of the records in the table:

1. In the Sort & Filter group on the Data tab, click the **Clear** button. All of the records in the Employee table reappear.

## Using Database Functions to Summarize Data

**Database functions** (or **Dfunctions**) perform summary data analysis, such as sum, average, and count, on an Excel table or data range based on criteria specified in a criteria range. Although you can often use the SUMIF, AVERAGEIF, and COUNTIF functions;

the Total row of an Excel table; and PivotTables to achieve the same results as Database functions, some situations require Database functions. For example, the type of summary analysis, the placement of the summary results, or the complexity of the criteria might require using Database functions. Figure B-8 lists the Database functions.

**Figure B-8** **Database functions**

| Function | Description |
|---|---|
| DAVERAGE | Returns the average of the values that meet specified criteria |
| DCOUNT | Returns the number of cells containing numbers that meet specified criteria |
| DCOUNTA | Returns the number of nonblank cells that meet specified criteria |
| DMAX | Returns the maximum value in the search column that meets specified criteria |
| DMIN | Returns the minimum value in the search column that meets specified criteria |
| DSTDEV | Returns the estimate of standard deviation based on a sample of entries that meet the specified criteria |
| DSUM | Returns the sum of the values in the summary column that meet specified criteria |

Rita needs to prepare a report comparing the average salaries paid to employees by pay type (hourly and salaried) and by gender. To create this report, you must set up a criteria range to retrieve the appropriate records for each calculation. Consequently, a Database function is a good approach.

Database functions use a criteria range to specify the records to summarize. In a Database function, the criteria range is used as one of the arguments of the function. The general syntax for any Database function is

`DatabaseFunctionName(`*`table range, column to summarize, criteria range`*`)`

where *table range* refers to the cells where the data to summarize is located, including the column header, *column to summarize* is the column name of the field to summarize entered within quotation marks, and *criteria range* is the range where the criteria that determine which records are used in the calculation are specified.

You will use Database functions to complete the Employee Summary worksheet, summarizing the average salaries for employees by pay type and gender. First, you will set up a criteria range. Although the criteria range often includes all fields from the table, even those not needed to select records, you do not have to include all field names from the table when setting up a criteria range. In this case, you will use only the fields needed to specify the criteria.

You will create two criteria ranges for the Employee Pay Comparison report.

### To create criteria ranges for the Employee Pay Comparison report:

1. Switch to the **Employee Summary** worksheet. The column headers for the criteria range have already been copied from the Employee Data worksheet.
2. In cell G6, enter **F** and then, in cell H6, enter **S**. These are the criteria to find all salaried females.
3. In cell J6, enter **M** and then, in cell K6, enter **S**. These are the criteria to find all salaried males.
4. In cell G10, enter **F** and then, in cell H10, enter **H**. These are the criteria to find all hourly females.
5. In cell J10, enter **M** and then, in cell K10, enter **H**. These are the criteria to find all hourly males. See Figure B-9.

**Figure B-9** Criteria ranges for the report

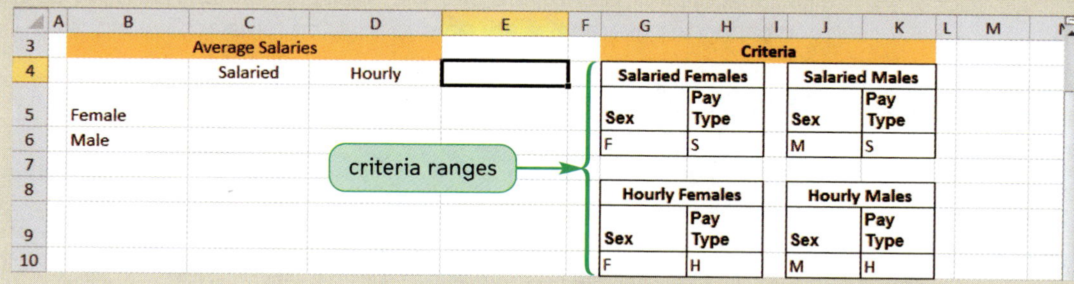


The criteria ranges are complete, so you can enter the formulas for the employee salary comparison. You will enter the DAVERAGE function to calculate the average salary in each group. In each function, the first two arguments are identical. The third argument, the criteria range, is different for each function so you can average a different subset of employees each time.

## To find average salaries for salaried males and salaried females:

1. Click cell **C5**, and then click the **Insert Function** button on the formula bar. The Insert Function dialog box opens.
2. Click the **Or select a category arrow**, and then click **Database**.
3. In the Select a function box, select **DAVERAGE**, if necessary, and then click the **OK** button. The Function Arguments dialog box opens.
4. In the Database box, type **'Employee Data'!$A$6:$M$106** to enter the range to search, and then press the **Tab** key. In this case, 'Employee Data'!$A$6:$M$106 refers to all data values in the range A6:M106 of the Employee Data worksheet.

   **Trouble?** If the error "Invalid" appears to the right of the Database box, you probably mistyped the range to search. Make sure you typed apostrophes (') and not quotation marks (") around the Employee Data worksheet name, included a space in the Employee Data worksheet name, and typed ! (an exclamation mark) before the criteria range.
5. In the Field box, type **"Annual Salary"** and then press the **Tab** key. The field specifies the table column that contains the data to be averaged.
6. In the Criteria box, type **G5:H6** to specify the criteria for salaried females. See Figure B-10.

**Figure B-10** DAVERAGE Function Arguments dialog box

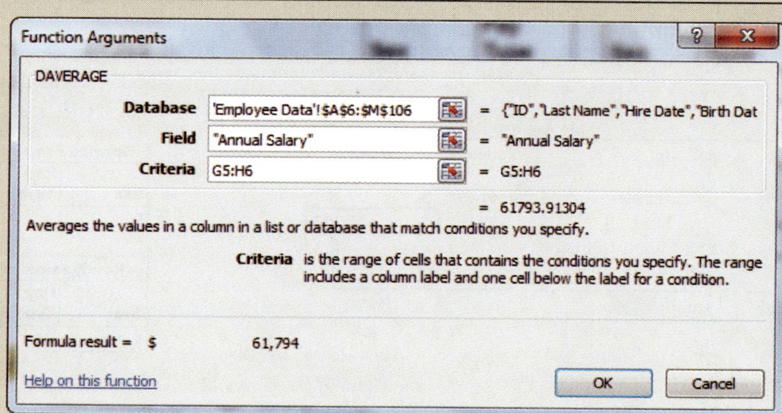

7. Click the **OK** button. The formula =DAVERAGE('Employee Data'!$A$6:$M$106, "Annual Salary",G5:H6) appears in the formula bar and $61,794 appears in cell C5, indicating the average salary paid to salaried females. See Figure B-11.

**Figure B-11** DAVERAGE function

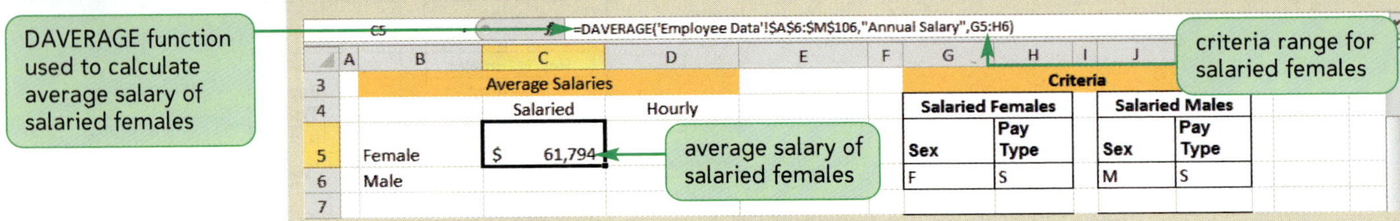


8. Click cell **C6**, and then click the **Insert Function** button on the formula bar.
9. Repeat Steps 2 through 5 to enter the first two arguments for the DAVERAGE function to calculate the average salary paid to male employees.
10. In the Criteria box, type **J5:K6** to specify the criteria for salaried males.
11. Click the **OK** button. The formula =DAVERAGE ('Employee Data'!$A$6:$M$106, "Annual Salary",J5:K6) appears in the formula bar and $95,081 appears in cell C6, indicating the average salary paid to salaried males.

For the last two cells in the salary comparison, you will copy the formulas in cells C5:C6 to cells D5 and D6 to calculate the average salaries paid to hourly females and hourly males.

## To find the average salaries for male and female hourly employees:

1. Copy the formula in cell **C5** to cell **D5**.
2. Click cell **D5**, and then change the criteria range (the third argument) from H5:I6 to **G9:H10**. The formula =DAVERAGE('Employee Data'!$A$6:$M$106,"Annual Salary",G9:H10) appears in the formula bar and $27,213 appears in cell D5, indicating the average salary paid to hourly females.
3. Copy the formula from cell **C6** to cell **D6**.
4. Click cell **D6**, and then change the criteria range (the third argument) from K5:L6 to **J9:K10**. The formula =DAVERAGE('Employee Data'!$A$6:$M$106,"Annual Salary",J9:K10) appears in the formula bar and $26,707 appears in cell D6, indicating the average salary paid to salaried males. See Figure B-12.

**Figure B-12** Completed Average Salaries report

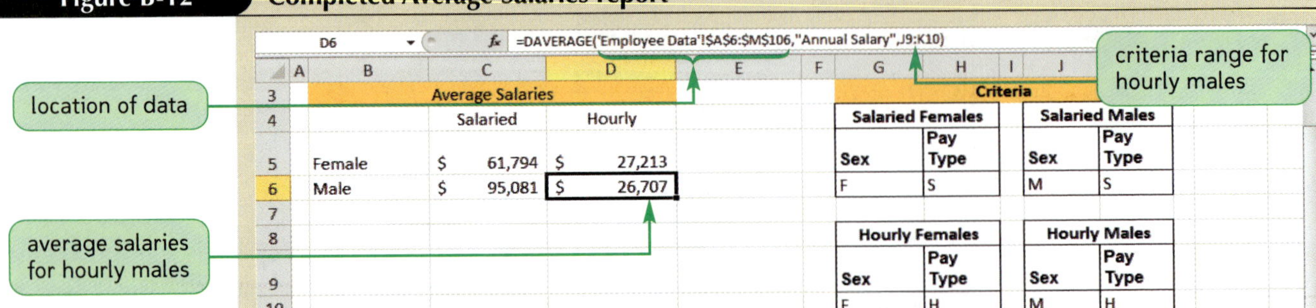

# Summarizing Data Using the COUNTIFS, SUMIFS, and AVERAGEIFS Functions

The COUNTIFS, SUMIFS, and AVERAGEIFS functions are similar to the COUNTIF, SUMIF, and AVERAGEIF functions except the latter functions enable you to specify only one condition to summarize the data, whereas the former functions enable you to summarize the data using several conditions.

The **COUNTIFS function** counts the number of cells within a range that meet multiple criteria. Its syntax is

```
COUNTIFS(,criteria_range1,criteria1[,criteria_range2,criteria2,…])
```

where *criteria_range1*, *criteria_range2*, and up represent up to 127 ranges (columns of data) in which to evaluate the associated criteria, and *criteria1*, *criteria2*, and up represent 127 criteria in the form of a number, an expression, a cell reference, or text that define which cells will be counted. Criteria can be expressed as a number such as 50 to find a number equal to 50, the expression ">10000" to find an amount greater than 10000, text such as "FT" to find a text value equal to FT, or the cell reference B4 to find the value equal to the value stored in cell B4. Each cell in a range is counted only if all of the corresponding criteria specified in the COUNTIFS function are true.

To count the number of full-time (FT) employees who are female (F) and earn more than $50,000, you can use the following function to count the full-time employees (Employee[Job Status],"FT") who are female (Employee[Sex],"F") and have a salary greater than 50,000 (Employee[Annual Salary],">50000"). The criteria are treated as if they are connected by an AND function, so all conditions must be true for a record to be counted.

```
=COUNTIFS(Employee[Job Status],"FT",Employee[Sex],"F",
Employee[Annual Salary],">50000")
```

The SUMIFS and AVERAGEIFS functions have a slightly different syntax. The **SUMIFS function** adds values in a range that meet multiple criteria using the syntax

```
SUMIFS(sum_range,criteria_range1,criteria1[,criteria_range2,
criteria2,…])
```

where *sum_range* is the range you want to add; *criteria_range1*, *criteria_range2*, and so on represent up to 127 ranges (columns of data) in which to evaluate the associated criteria; and *criteria1*, *criteria2*, and so on up to 127 criteria in the form of a number, expression, cell reference, or text define which cells will be added.

To calculate the total salary paid to full-time (FT) employees hired after 2012 who are living in Austin, you can use the following SUMIFS function to add the salaries (Employee[Annual Salary]) of employees located in Austin (Employee[Location],"Austin") who have a hire date on or later than 1/1/2012 (Employee[Hire Date],">=1/1/2012") and are full-time employees (Employee[Job Status],"FT"):

```
=SUMIFS(Employee[Annual Salary],Employee [Location],"Austin",
Employee[Hire Date],">=1/1/2012",Employee[Job Status],"FT")
```

The **AVERAGEIFS function** calculates the average of values within a range of cells that meet multiple conditions. Its syntax is

```
AVERAGEIFS(average_range,criteria_range1,criteria1[,criteria_range2,
criteria2,…])
```

where *average_range* is the range to average; *criteria_range1*, *criteria_range2*, and so on represent up to 127 ranges in which to evaluate the associated criteria; and *criteria1*, *criteria2*, and so on up to 127 criteria in the form of a number, an expression, a cell reference, or text define which cells will be averaged.

To calculate the average salary paid to males (M) who have worked at Talent Tracs for more than five years, you can use the following AVERAGEIFS function to average the salaries (Employee[Annual Salary]) of male employees (Employee[Sex],"M"), having more than five years of service (Employee[Years Service],">5"):

```
=AVERAGEIFS(Employee[Annual Salary],Employee[Sex],"M",
Employee[Years Service],">5")
```

Rita wants you to complete the Years' Service Summary report using the COUNTIFS, SUMIFS, and AVERAGEIFS functions to compute statistical information for Talent Tracs employees excluding employees working from home.

## To calculate employees with years of service between 0 and 4 years:

1. Click cell **C16**, and then click the **Insert Function** button on the formula bar. The Insert Function dialog box opens.
2. Click the **Or select a category arrow**, and then click **Statistical**.
3. In the Select a function box, click **COUNTIFS**, and then click the **OK** button. The Function Arguments dialog box opens.
4. In the Criteria_range1 box, enter **Employee[Location]** and then press the **Tab** key. This criterion selects employees not working from home.
5. In the Criteria1 box, type **"<>Home"** to specify employees not working from home, and then press the **Tab** key. The first condition is complete, and 93 appears as the total count in the middle of the Function Arguments dialog box.
6. In the Criteria_range2 box, enter **Employee[Years Service]** to enter the range referencing the number of years the employee has worked at Talent Tracs, and then press the **Tab** key.
7. In the Criteria2 box, type **">=0"** to select employees whose years of service are greater than or equal to 0, and then press the **Tab** key. The second condition is complete, and 93 appears as the total count.
8. In the Criteria_range3 box, enter **Employee[Years Service]** to enter the range referencing the number of years the employee has worked at Talent Tracs, and then press the **Tab** key.
9. In the Criteria3 box, type **"<=4"** to enter the criterion that employees' years of service are less than or equal to 4. The third condition is complete, and 57 appears as the total count. See Figure B-13.

**Figure B-13** Function Arguments box for the COUNTIFS function

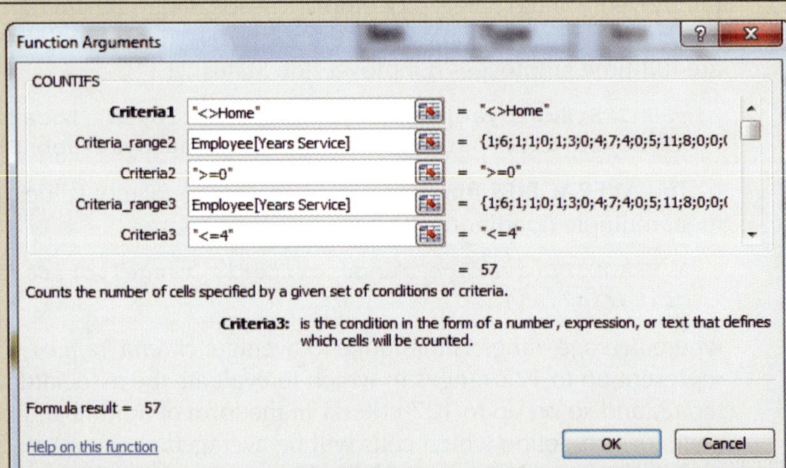

10. Click the **OK** button. The formula =COUNTIFS(Employee[Location],"<>Home", Employee[Years Service],">=0",Employee[Years Service],"<=4") appears in the formula bar and the value 57 appears in cell C16. See Figure B-14.

**Figure B-14** **Years' Service Summary report in process**

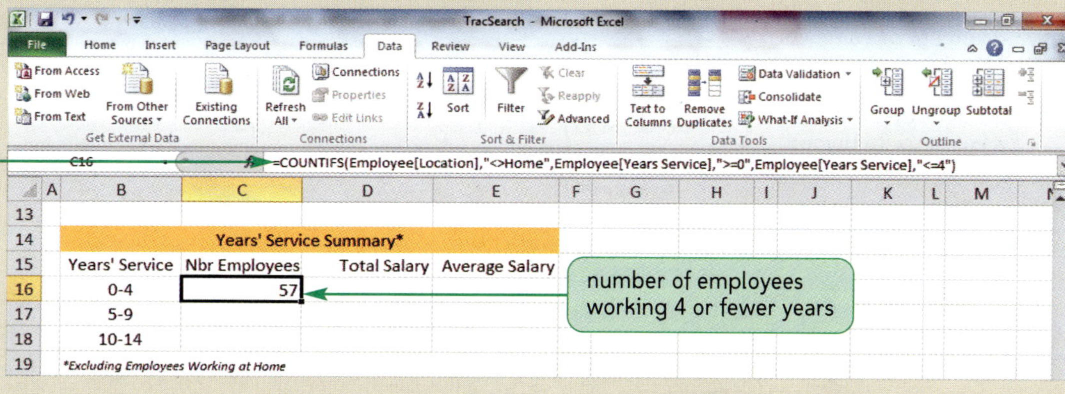


11. Copy the formula from cell **C16** to the range **C17:C18**.
12. In cell C17, change the second criteria argument from ">=0" to **">=5"** and change the third criteria argument from "<=4" to **"<=9"**. The criteria specify years of service greater than or equal to 5 and less than or equal to 9. The formula =COUNT IFS(Employee[Location],"<>Home",Employee[Years Service],">=5",Employee[Years Service],"<=9") appears in the formula bar and 26 appears in cell C17.
13. In cell C18, change the second criteria argument from ">=0" to **">=10"** and change the third criteria argument from "<=4" to **"<=14"**. The criteria specify years of service greater than or equal to 10 and less than or equal to 14. The formula =COUNTIFS(Employee[Location],"<>Home",Employee[Years Service], ">=10",Employee[Years Service],"<=14") appears in the formula bar and 10 appears in cell C18.

Next, you will calculate the total salary paid to employees based on years of service. To do this, you will use the SUMIFS function.

## To calculate the total salary paid to employees:

1. Click cell **D16**, and then click the **Insert Function** button *fx* on the formula bar. The Insert Function dialog box opens.
2. Click the **Or select a category arrow**, and then click **Math & Trig**.
3. In the Select a function box, click **SUMIFS**, and then click the **OK** button. The Function Arguments dialog box opens.
4. In the Sum_range box, type **Employee[Annual Salary]** to enter the range of data to sum, and then press the **Tab** key. In this case, a structured reference was used to reference all data values in the Annual Salary column.
5. In the Criteria_range1 box, enter **Employee[Location]** and then press the **Tab** key.

**TIP**

You could also have used the worksheet reference 'Employee Data'!K6:K106 to reference the annual salaries for all employees.

6. In the Criteria1 box, type **"<>Home"** to specify employees not working from home, and then press the **Tab** key. The first condition is complete. See Figure B-15.

**Figure B-15 Function Arguments dialog box for the SUMIFS function**

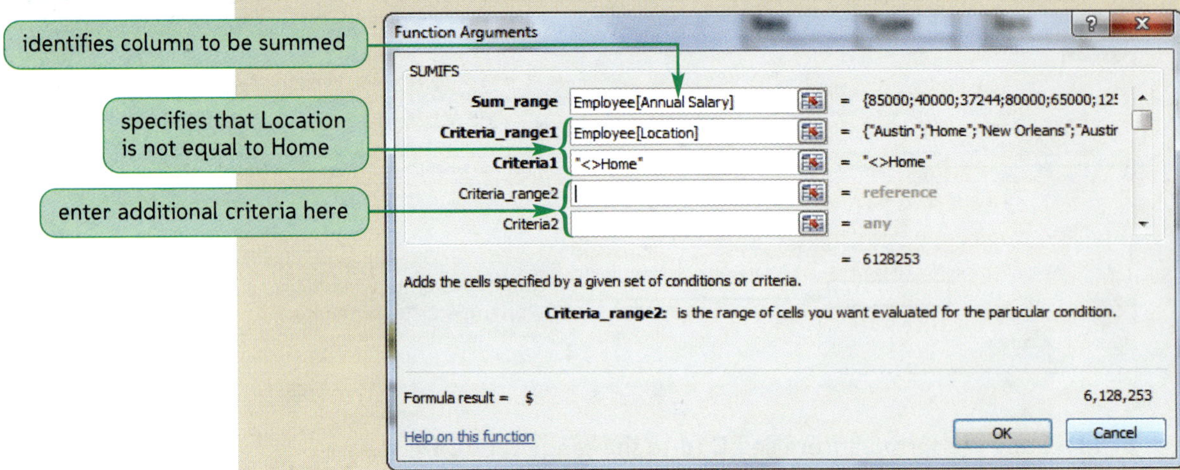


7. In the Criteria_range2 box, enter **Employee[Years Service]** for the range referencing the number of years the employee has worked at Talent Tracs, and then press the **Tab** key.
8. In the Criteria2 box, type **">=0"** to specify years of service that are greater than or equal to 0, and then press the **Tab** key.
9. In the Criteria_range3 box, type **Employee[Years Service]** for the range referencing the number of years the employee has worked at Talent Tracs, and then press the **Tab** key.
10. In the Criteria3 box, type **"<=4"** to specify years of service that are less than or equal to 4, and then press the **Tab** key.
11. Click the **OK** button. The formula =SUMIFS(Employee[Annual Salary],Employee [Location],"<>Home",Employee[Years Service],">=0",Employee[Years Service], "<=4") appears in the formula bar and 3,868,395 appears in cell D16.
12. Copy the formula from cell **D16** to the range **D17:D18**.
13. In cell D17, change the second criteria argument from ">=0" to **">=5"** and change the third criteria argument from "<=4" to **"<=9"**. The criteria specify years of service greater than or equal to 5 and less than or equal to 9. The formula =SUMIFS(Employee[Annual Salary],Employee[Location],"<>Home", Employee[Years Service],">=5",Employee[Years Service],"<=9") appears in the formula bar and 1,517,799 appears in cell D17.
14. In cell D18, change the second criteria argument from ">=0" to **">=10"** and then change the third criteria argument from "<=4" to **"<=14"**. The criteria specify years of service greater than or equal to 10 and less than or equal to 14. The formula =SUMIFS(Employee[Annual Salary],Employee[Location],"<>Home", Employee[Years Service],">=10",Employee[Years Service],"<=14") appears in the formula bar and 742,059 appears in cell D18.

Next, you will calculate the average salary paid to employees based on years of service. You will use the AVERAGEIFS function to do this.

## To calculate the average salary paid to employees:

1. Click cell **E16**, and then click the **Insert Function** button on the formula bar. The Insert Function dialog box opens.
2. Click the **Or select a category arrow**, and then click **Statistical**.
3. In the Select a function box, click **AVERAGEIFS**, and then click the **OK** button. The Function Arguments dialog box opens.
4. In the Average_range box, type **Employee[Annual Salary]** to enter the range to be averaged, and then press the **Tab** key.
5. In the Criteria_range1 box, enter **Employee[Location]** and then press the **Tab** key.
6. In the Criteria1 box, type **"<>Home"** to specify employees not working from home, and then press the **Tab** key. The first condition is complete.
7. In the Criteria_range2 box, enter **Employee[Years Service]** for the range referencing the number of years the employee has worked at Talent Tracs, and then press the **Tab** key.
8. In the Criteria2 box, type **">=0"** to specify years of service greater than or equal to 0, and then press the **Tab** key.
9. In the Criteria_range3 box, enter **Employee[Years Service]** for the range referencing the number of years the employee has worked at Talent Tracs, and then press the **Tab** key.
10. In the Criteria3 box, type **"<=4"** to specify years of service less than or equal to 4, and then press the **Tab** key.
11. Click the **OK** button. The formula =AVERAGEIFS(Employee[Annual Salary], Employee[Location],"<>Home",Employee[Years Service],">=0",Employee[Years Service],"<=4") appears in the formula bar and 67,867 appears in cell E16.
12. Copy the formula from cell E16 to the range **E17:E18**.
13. In cell E17, change the second criteria argument from ">=0" to **">=5"** and change the third criteria argument from "<=4" to **"<=9"**. The criteria specify years of service greater than or equal to 5 and less than or equal to 9. The formula =AVERAGEIFS(Employee[Annual Salary],Employee[Location],"<>Home", Employee[Years Service], ">=5",Employee[Years Service],"<=9") appears in the formula bar and 58,377 appears in cell E17.
14. In cell E18, change the second criteria argument from ">=0" to **">=10"** and change the third criteria argument from "<=4" to **"<=14"**. The criteria specify years of service greater than or equal to 10 and less than or equal to 14. The formula =AVERAGEIFS(Employee[Annual Salary],Employee[Location],"<>Home", Employee[Years Service],">=10",Employee[Years Service],"<=14") appears in the formula bar and 74,206 appears in cell E18.
15. Click cell **E18**, and then expand the formula bar. See Figure B-16.

Figure B-16 **Completed Years' Service Summary report**

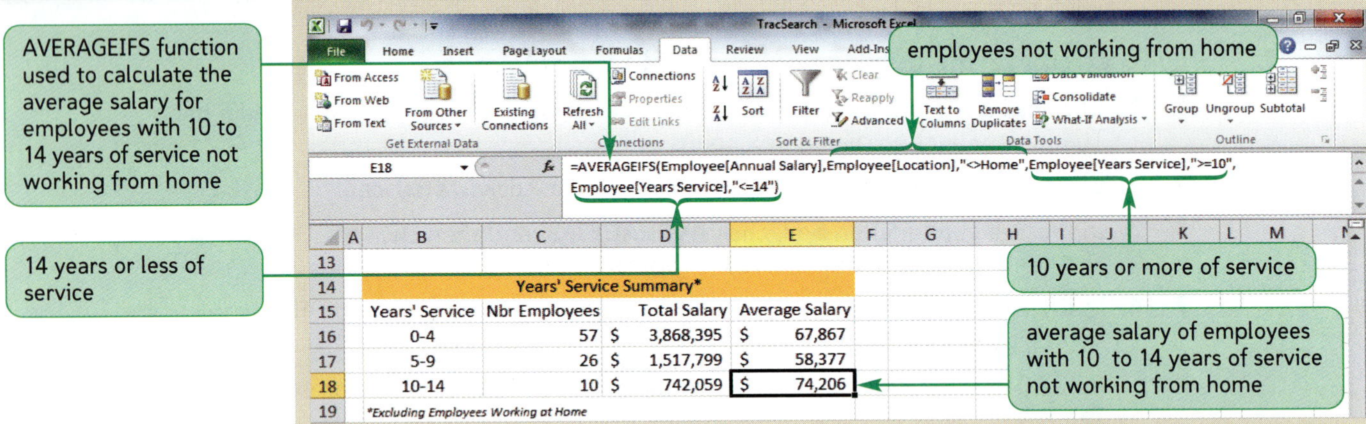


**16.** Save and close the workbook.

The Years' Service Summary report is complete. In this session, you used advanced filtering techniques to find potential candidates for a new full-time position. You also used the DAVERAGE and AVERAGEIFS functions to prepare a report calculating the average salary of employees broken down by pay type and gender.

*Practice the skills you learned in the tutorial using the same case scenario.*

PRACTICE

## Review Assignments

### Data File needed for the Review Assignments: TracReview.xlsx

Rita wants you to perform advanced filtering tasks to create a report about employee compensation and benefits. You need to set up a criteria range to generate the report. Complete the following:

1. Open the **TracReview** workbook located in the ExcelB\Review folder included with your Data Files, and then save the workbook as **TracReviewReport**. In the Documentation sheet, enter your name and the date.
2. Make a copy of the Employee Data worksheet, and then rename the copied worksheet as **Q2**. Complete the criteria range located in the range A1:M3 of the Q2 worksheet, and then use advanced filtering to display all part-time (PT) employees who have worked 2 or more years and earned more than $60,000 or consultants (CN). Filter the Employee table.
3. Make a copy of the Employee Data worksheet, and then rename the copied worksheet as **Q3**. Complete the criteria range located in the range A1:M3 of the Q3 worksheet so you can use advanced filtering to display all part-time (PT) employees working in Austin as well as all full-time (FT) employees working at home and earning $40,000 or more. Filter the Employee table.
4. Complete the Number of Employees by Sex and Health Plan report in the Employee Summary worksheet. Complete the criteria ranges (G4:K22) and then use the DCOUNT Database function to count the number of employees found in the range C5:D9 of the report. For example, in cell C5 count the number of employees with Health Plan PPOI that are female, in cell D5 count the number of employees with Health Plan PPOI that are male, and so on. Calculate totals in row 10 and column E to complete the report.
5. Complete the Total Salaries by Years Service and Sex in the Employee Summary worksheet. Use the SUMIFS function to calculate the total salary for each cell in the range C14:D16 of the Total Salaries by Years Service and Sex report. For example, in cell C14 calculate the total salary for female employees who have worked 0 to 4 years.
6. Save and close the workbook. Submit the finished workbook to your instructor, either in printed or electronic form, as requested.

*Apply the skills you learned by summarizing order data.*

APPLY

## Case Problem 1

### Data File needed for this Case Problem: World.xlsx

***World Foods*** Kerry Jeffries is analyzing orders from last year. She has already summarized orders by month for all customers. Complete the following:

1. Open the **World** workbook located in the ExcelB\Case1 folder included with your Data Files, and then save the workbook as **World Foods**.
2. In the Documentation worksheet, enter your name and the date.
3. Make a copy of the Orders worksheet, and then rename the copied worksheet as **Q3**. In the Q3 worksheet, use advanced filtering to display sales in the Scandinavian countries (Denmark, Finland, Norway, and Sweden). Set up the criteria range beginning in row 1 and use the filter the list in place option.
4. Make a copy of the Orders worksheet, and then rename the copied worksheet as **Q4**. In the Q4 worksheet, use advanced filtering to display all records for Laura Callahan with sales over $1,500 in September. Set up the criteria range beginning in row 1 and use the filter the list in place option.

5. In the Summary worksheet, complete the analysis for the South American countries (Argentina and Brazil). Use Database functions to count and sum orders totaling $150 or more in March for Argentina. Set up an appropriate criteria range in rows 1 and 2, and then build the formulas in row 11 for Argentina.
6. In the Summary worksheet, complete the analysis for the South American country Brazil. Use the COUNTIFS and SUMIFS functions to enter formulas in row 12 to count and sum orders that total $150 or more in March in Brazil.
7. Save and close the workbook. Submit the finished workbook to your instructor, either in printed or electronic form, as requested.

*Apply the skills you learned by analyzing donor gift data.*

APPLY

## Case Problem 2

### Data File needed for this Case Problem: Gifts.xlsx

***College Fund Raising*** Elliot Fastchow, the controller at ABC University, is analyzing gifts from several hundred donors. Complete the following:

1. Open the **Gifts** workbook located in the ExcelB\Case2 folder included with your Data Files, and then save the workbook as **ABC Gifts**.
2. In the Documentation worksheet, enter your name and the date.
3. Make a copy of the FundGifts worksheet, and then rename the copied worksheet as **Q3**. In the Q3 worksheet, use advanced filtering to display records from the current operating fund (FundType C) created after the year 2000 in the College of Nursing that have gifts totaling more than $1,000.
4. Make a copy of the FundGifts worksheet, and then rename the copied worksheet as **Q4**. In the Q4 worksheet, use advanced filtering to display records for funds in the College of Engineering with gifts of either $500 or less, or more than $50,000.
5. Sort the filtered data in the Gifts column from highest to lowest, and then format the Gifts column appropriately.
6. In the Summary worksheet, complete the analysis for Gifts from Endowment Funds. Use FundType E with Gifts over $1,000 to compare the gifts to the College of Arts & Science with gifts to the College of Pharmacy. Use Database functions to calculate the results for the college of Arts & Science. Use COUNTIFS, SUMIFS, and AVERAGEIFS to calculate the results for the College of Pharmacy.
7. Save and close the workbook. Submit the finished workbook to your instructor, either in printed or electronic form, as requested.

### ENDING DATA FILES

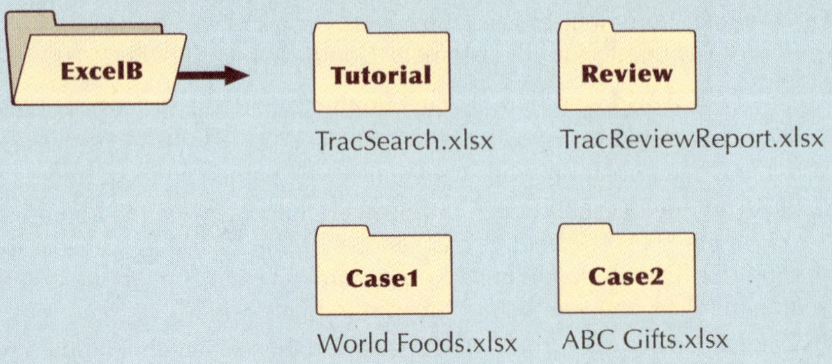

TUTORIAL 5

# Creating Advanced Queries and Enhancing Table Design

*Making the Panorama Database Easier to Use*

## OBJECTIVES

**Session 5.1**
- Review table and object naming standards
- Use the Like, In, Not, and & operators in queries
- Filter data using an AutoFilter
- Use the IIf function to assign a conditional value to a calculated field in a query
- Create a parameter query

**Session 5.2**
- Use query wizards to create a crosstab query, a find duplicates query, and a find unmatched query
- Create a top values query

**Session 5.3**
- Modify table designs using lookup fields, input masks, and data validation rules
- Identify object dependencies
- Review a Memo field's properties
- Designate a trusted folder

## Case | *Belmont Landscapes*

After graduating with a university degree in Landscape Architecture and then working for a firm that provides basic landscape services to residential customers, Oren Belmont started his own landscape architecture firm in Holland, Michigan. Belmont Landscapes specializes in landscape designs for residential and commercial customers and numerous public agencies. The firm provides a wide range of services—from site analyses and feasibility studies, to drafting and administering construction documents—for projects of various scales. Oren's company developed the Panorama database of customer, contract, and invoice data; and the employees use Microsoft Access 2010 (or simply Access) to manage it. The Panorama database contains tables, queries, forms, and reports that Sarah Fisher, office manager, and Taylor Sico, marketing manager, use to track customers and their landscape projects.

Oren, Sarah, and Taylor are interested in taking better advantage of the power of Access to make the database easier to use and to create more sophisticated queries. For example, Taylor wants to obtain lists of customers in certain cities, and Sarah needs a summarized list of invoice amounts by city. Sarah wants to change the design of the Customer and Contracts tables. In this tutorial, you'll modify and customize the Panorama database to satisfy these requirements.

## STARTING DATA FILES

Access2 →

| Folder | File |
|---|---|
| Tutorial | Panorama.accdb |
| Review | Products.accdb |
| Case1 | Contract.accdb |
| Case2 | Training.accdb |
| Case3 | Agency.accdb |
| Case4 | Vacation.accdb |
| Case5 | (none) |

# SESSION 5.1 VISUAL OVERVIEW

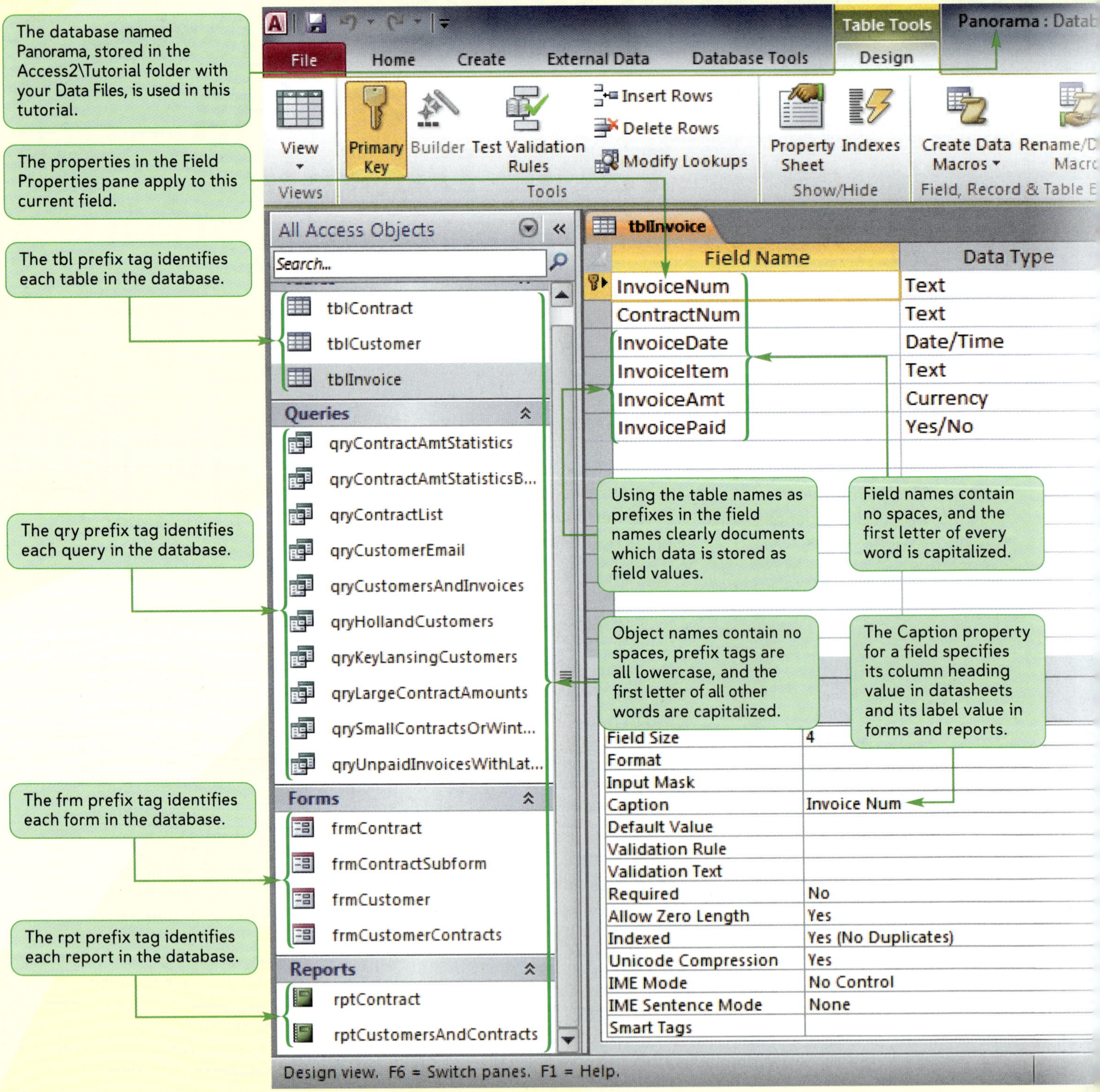

# DATABASE NAMING CONVENTIONS

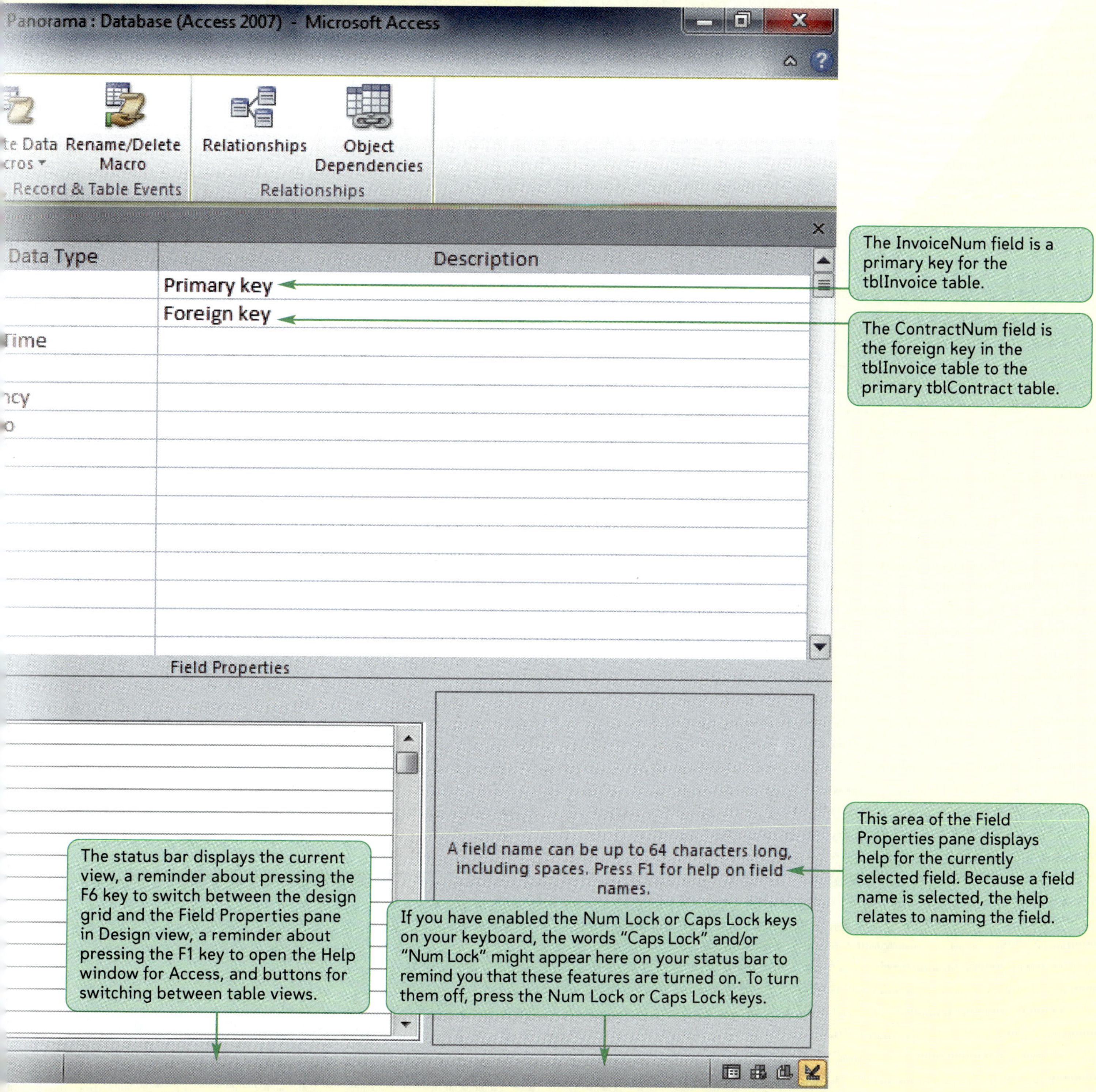

## Reviewing the Panorama Database

**TIP**

Read the Microsoft Access Naming Conventions section in the appendix titled "Relational Databases and Database Design" for more information about naming conventions.

Sarah and her staff had no previous database experience when they created the Panorama database; they simply used the wizards and other easy-to-use Access tools. As business continued to grow at Belmont Landscapes, Sarah convinced Oren that they needed to hire a computer expert to further enhance the Panorama database, and they hired Lucia Perez, who has a business information systems degree and nine years of experience developing database systems. Lucia spent a few days reviewing the Panorama database, making sure the database adhered to simple naming standards for the objects and field names to make her future work easier.

Before implementing the enhancements for Sarah and Taylor, you'll review the naming conventions for the object names in the Panorama database.

**To review the object naming conventions in the Panorama database:**

1. Make sure you have created your copy of the Access Data Files, and that your computer can access them.

   **Trouble?** If you don't have the Access Data Files, you need to get them before you can proceed. Your instructor will either give you the Data Files or ask you to obtain them from a specified location (such as a network drive). In either case, make a backup copy of the Data Files before you start so that you will have the original files available in case you need to start over. If you have any questions about the Data Files, see your instructor or technical support person for assistance.

2. Start Access, and then open the **Panorama** database in the Access2\Tutorial folder provided with your Data Files.

   **Trouble?** If the Security Warning is displayed below the Ribbon, click the Enable Content button next to the Security Warning.

The Navigation Pane displays the objects grouped by object type. Each object name has a prefix tag—a tbl prefix tag for tables, a qry prefix tag for queries, a frm prefix tag for forms, and a rpt prefix tag for reports. Using object prefix tags, you can readily identify the object type, even when the objects have the same base name—for instance, tblContract, frmContract, and rptContract. In addition, object names have no spaces, because other database management systems, such as SQL Server and Oracle, do not permit spaces in object and field names. If Belmont Landscapes needs to upscale to one of these other database management systems in the future, Lucia will have to do less work to make the transition.

PROSKILLS

*Teamwork: Following Naming Conventions*

Most Access databases have hundreds of fields, objects, and controls. You'll find it easier to identify the type and purpose of these database items when you use a naming convention or standard. Most companies adopt a standard naming convention, such as the one used for the Panorama database, so that multiple people can develop a database, troubleshoot database problems, and enhance and improve existing databases. When working on a database, a team's tasks are difficult, if not impossible, to perform if a standard naming convention isn't used. In addition, most databases and database samples on Web sites and in training books use standard naming conventions that are similar to the ones used for the Panorama database. By following the standard naming convention established by the company or organization you are a part of, you'll help to ensure smooth collaboration among all team members.

Now you'll create the queries that Sarah and Taylor need.

## Using a Pattern Match in a Query

You are already familiar with queries that use an exact match or a range of values (for example, queries that use the >= or < comparison operators) to select records. Access provides many other operators for creating select queries. These operators let you create more complicated queries that are difficult or impossible to create with exact match or range of values selection criteria.

Sarah and Taylor created a list of questions they want to answer using the Panorama database:

- Which customers have the 616 area code?
- What is the customer information for customers located in Holland, Rockford, or Saugatuck?
- What is the customer information for all customers *except* those located in Holland, Rockford, or Saugatuck?
- What is the customer and contract information for contracts that have values of less than $10,000 or that were signed during the winter *and* are located in Grand Rapids or East Grand Rapids?
- What are the names of Belmont Landscapes' customers? The customer name is either the company name for nonresidential customers or the last and first names for residential customers.
- What is the customer information for customers in a particular city? For this query, the user needs to be able to specify the city.

Next, you will create the queries necessary to answer these questions. Taylor wants to view the records for all customers located in the 616 area code. She plans to travel to this area next week and wants to contact customers ahead of time to schedule appointments. To answer Taylor's question, you can create a query that uses a pattern match. A **pattern match** selects records with a value for the designated field that matches the pattern of a simple condition value, in this case, customers with the 616 area code. You do this using the Like comparison operator.

The **Like comparison operator** selects records by matching field values to a specific pattern that includes one or more of these wildcard characters: asterisk (*), question mark (?), and number symbol (#). The asterisk represents any string of characters, the question mark represents any single character, and the number symbol represents any single digit. Using a pattern match is similar to using an exact match, except that a pattern match includes wildcard characters.

To create the new query, you must first place the tblCustomer table field list in the Query window in Design view.

### To create the new query in Design view:

1. If necessary, click the **Shutter Bar Open/Close Button** « at the top of the Navigation Pane to close it.
2. Click the **Create** tab on the Ribbon.
3. In the Queries group, click the **Query Design** button. Access opens the Show Table dialog box on top of the Query window in Design view.
4. Click **tblCustomer** in the Tables box, click the **Add** button, and then click the **Close** button. Access places the tblCustomer table field list in the Query window and closes the Show Table dialog box.

**TIP**

You can also double-click a table name to add the table's field list to the Query window.

5. Double-click the **title bar** of the tblCustomer field list to highlight all the fields, and then drag the highlighted fields to the first column's Field box in the design grid. Access places each field in a separate column in the design grid, in the same order that the fields appear in the table. See Figure 5-1.

**Figure 5-1** Adding the fields for the pattern match query

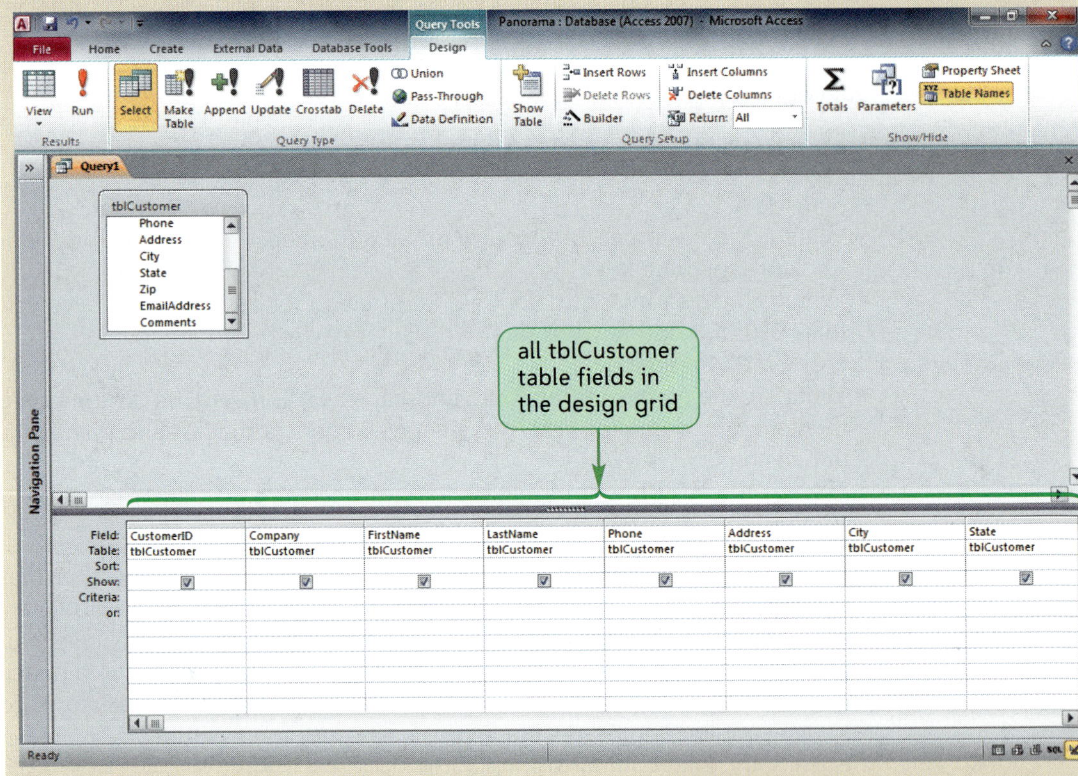


**Trouble?** If tblCustomer.* appears in the first column's Field box, you dragged the * from the field list instead of the highlighted fields. Press the Delete key, and then repeat Step 5.

Now you will enter the pattern match condition *Like "616*"* for the Phone field. Access will select records with a Phone field value of 616 in positions one through three. The asterisk wildcard character specifies that any characters can appear in the remaining positions of the field value.

**TIP**

If you omit the Like operator, Access automatically adds it when you run the query.

### To specify records that match the specified pattern:

1. Click the **Phone Criteria** box, and then type **L**. The Formula AutoComplete menu displays a list of functions beginning with the letter L, but the Like operator is not one of the choices in the list. You'll finish typing the condition.
2. Type **ike "616*"**. See Figure 5-2.

**Figure 5-2** Record selection based on matching a specific pattern

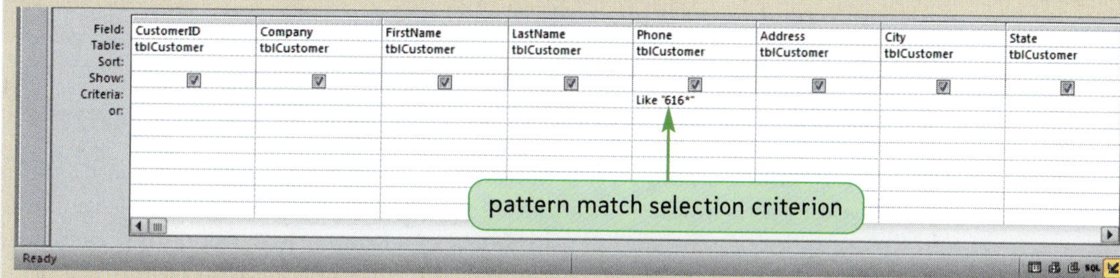


3. Click the **Save** button on the Quick Access Toolbar to open the Save As dialog box.
4. Type **qry616AreaCode** in the Query Name box, and then press the **Enter** key. Access saves the query and displays the name on the object tab.
5. In the Results group on the Design tab, click the **Run** button. The query results display the 24 records with the area code 616 in the Phone field. See Figure 5-3.

**Figure 5-3** tblCustomer table records for area code 616

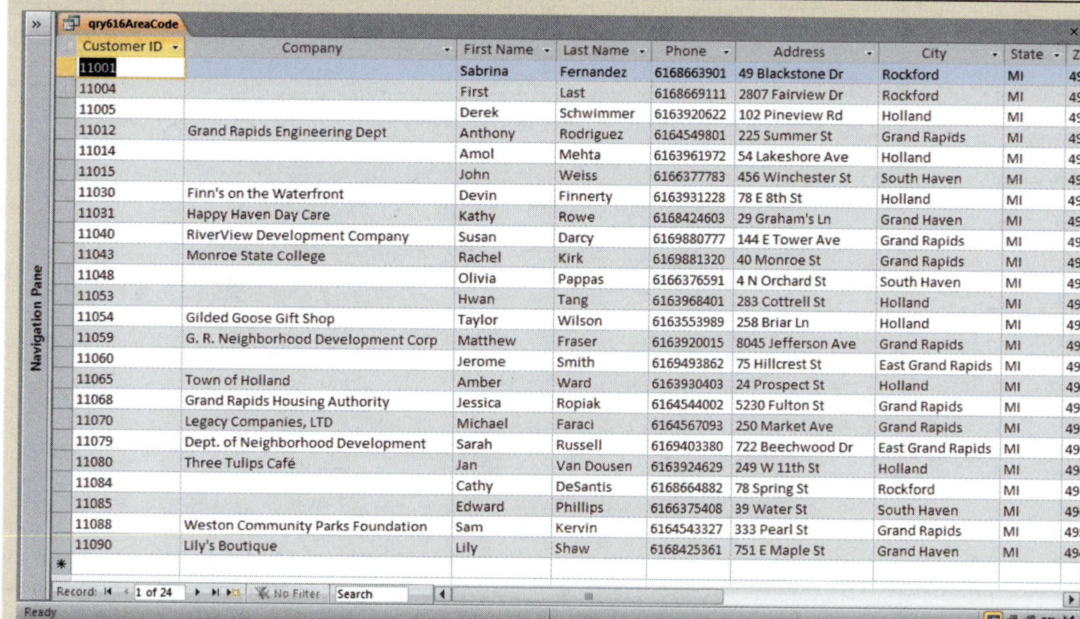


| Customer ID | Company | First Name | Last Name | Phone | Address | City | State |
|---|---|---|---|---|---|---|---|
| 11001 | | Sabrina | Fernandez | 6168663901 | 49 Blackstone Dr | Rockford | MI |
| 11004 | | First | Last | 6168669111 | 2807 Fairview Dr | Rockford | MI |
| 11005 | | Derek | Schwimmer | 6163920622 | 102 Pineview Rd | Holland | MI |
| 11012 | Grand Rapids Engineering Dept | Anthony | Rodriguez | 6164549801 | 225 Summer St | Grand Rapids | MI |
| 11014 | | Amol | Mehta | 6163961972 | 54 Lakeshore Ave | Holland | MI |
| 11015 | | John | Weiss | 6166377783 | 456 Winchester St | South Haven | MI |
| 11030 | Finn's on the Waterfront | Devin | Finnerty | 6163931228 | 78 E 8th St | Holland | MI |
| 11031 | Happy Haven Day Care | Kathy | Rowe | 6168424603 | 29 Graham's Ln | Grand Haven | MI |
| 11040 | RiverView Development Company | Susan | Darcy | 6169880777 | 144 E Tower Ave | Grand Rapids | MI |
| 11043 | Monroe State College | Rachel | Kirk | 6169881320 | 40 Monroe St | Grand Rapids | MI |
| 11048 | | Olivia | Pappas | 6166376591 | 4 N Orchard St | South Haven | MI |
| 11053 | | Hwan | Tang | 6163968401 | 283 Cottrell St | Holland | MI |
| 11054 | Gilded Goose Gift Shop | Taylor | Wilson | 6163553989 | 258 Briar Ln | Holland | MI |
| 11059 | G. R. Neighborhood Development Corp | Matthew | Fraser | 6163920015 | 8045 Jefferson Ave | Grand Rapids | MI |
| 11060 | | Jerome | Smith | 6169493862 | 75 Hillcrest St | East Grand Rapids | MI |
| 11065 | Town of Holland | Amber | Ward | 6163930403 | 24 Prospect St | Holland | MI |
| 11068 | Grand Rapids Housing Authority | Jessica | Ropiak | 6164544002 | 5230 Fulton St | Grand Rapids | MI |
| 11070 | Legacy Companies, LTD | Michael | Faraci | 6164567093 | 250 Market Ave | Grand Rapids | MI |
| 11079 | Dept. of Neighborhood Development | Sarah | Russell | 6169403380 | 722 Beechwood Dr | East Grand Rapids | MI |
| 11080 | Three Tulips Café | Jan | Van Dousen | 6163924629 | 249 W 11th St | Holland | MI |
| 11084 | | Cathy | DeSantis | 6168664882 | 78 Spring St | Rockford | MI |
| 11085 | | Edward | Phillips | 6166375408 | 39 Water St | South Haven | MI |
| 11088 | Weston Community Parks Foundation | Sam | Kervin | 6164543327 | 333 Pearl St | Grand Rapids | MI |
| 11090 | Lily's Boutique | Lily | Shaw | 6168425361 | 751 E Maple St | Grand Haven | MI |

Note that Lucia removed the hyphens from the Phone field values; for example, 6168663901 in the first record used to be 616-866-3901. You'll modify the Phone field later in this tutorial to format its values with hyphens.

6. Change the second record in the table so the First Name and Last Name columns contain your first and last names.
7. Close the qry616AreaCode query.

Next, Sarah asks you to create a query that displays information about customers in Holland, Rockford, or Saugatuck. She wants a printout of the customer data for her administrative aide, who will contact these customers. To produce the results Sarah wants, you'll create a query using a list-of-values match.

## Using a List-of-Values Match in a Query

A **list-of-values match** selects records whose value for the designated field matches one of two or more simple condition values. You could accomplish this by including several Or conditions in the design grid, but the In comparison operator provides an easier and clearer way to do this. The **In comparison operator** lets you define a condition with a list of two or more values for a field. If a record's field value matches one value from the list of defined values, then Access selects and includes that record in the query results.

To display the information Sarah requested, you want to select records if their City field value equals Holland, Rockford, or Saugatuck. These are the values you will use with the In comparison operator. Sarah wants the query to contain the same data as the qry616AreaCode query, so you'll make a copy of that query and modify it.

### To create the query using a list-of-values match:

1. Open the Navigation Pane, then in the Queries group on the Navigation Pane, right-click **qry616AreaCode**, and then click **Copy** on the shortcut menu.
2. In the Clipboard group on the Home tab, click the **Paste** button, type **qryHollandRockfordSaugatuckCustomers** in the Query Name box, and then press the **Enter** key.

   To modify the copied query, you need to open it in Design view.
3. In the Queries group on the Navigation Pane, right-click **qryHollandRockfordSaugatuckCustomers** to select it and display the shortcut menu.
4. Click **Design View** on the shortcut menu to open the query in Design view, and then close the Navigation Pane.

   You need to delete the existing condition from the Phone field.
5. Click the **Phone Criteria** box, press the **F2** key to highlight the entire condition, and then press the **Delete** key to remove the condition.

   Now you can enter the criterion for the new query using the In comparison operator. When you use this operator, you must enclose the list of values you want to match within parentheses and separate the values with commas. In addition, for fields defined using the Text data type, you enclose each value in quotation marks, although Access adds the quotation marks if you omit them. For fields defined using the Number or Currency data type, you don't enclose the values in quotation marks.

**TIP**

After clicking in a box, you can also open its Zoom dialog box by holding down the Shift key and pressing the F2 key.

6. Right-click the **City Criteria** box to open the shortcut menu, click **Zoom** to open the Zoom dialog box, and then type **In ("Holland","Rockford","Saugatuck")**. See Figure 5-4.

**Figure 5-4** Record selection based on matching field values to a list of values

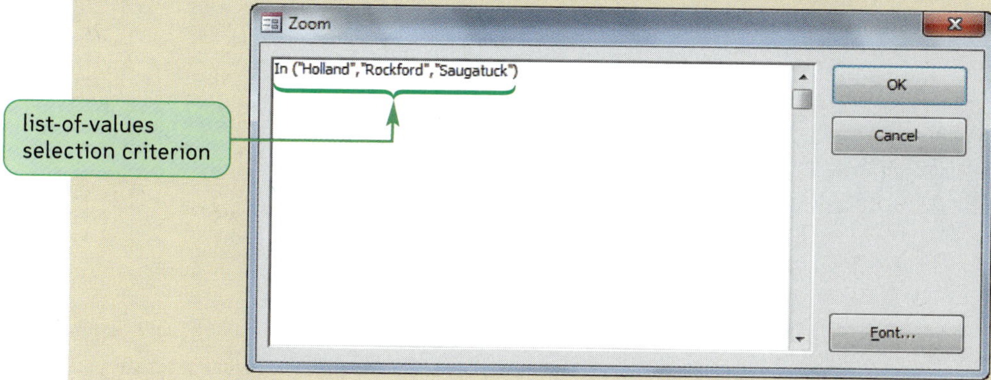


7. Click the **OK** button to close the Zoom dialog box, and then save and run the query. Access displays the recordset, which shows the 13 records with Holland, Rockford, or Saugatuck in the City field.
8. Close the query.

Sarah asks her assistant to contact Belmont Landscapes customers that are not in Holland, Rockford, and Saugatuck. You can provide Sarah with this information by creating a query with the Not logical operator.

## Using the Not Logical Operator in a Query

The **Not logical operator** negates a criterion or selects records for which the designated field does not match the criterion. For example, if you enter *Not "Holland"* in the Criteria box for the City field, the query results show records that do not have the City field value Holland, that is, records of all customers not located in Holland.

To create Sarah's query, you will combine the Not logical operator with the In comparison operator to select customers whose City field value is not in the list *("Holland","Rockford","Saugatuck")*. The qryHollandRockfordSaugatuckCustomers query has the fields that Sarah needs to see in the query results. Sarah doesn't need to keep the qryHollandRockfordSaugatuckCustomers query, so you'll rename and then modify the query.

**TIP**

You can rename any object type, including tables, in the Navigation Pane using the Rename command on the shortcut menu.

### To create the query using the Not logical operator:

1. Open the Navigation Pane, then in the Queries group on the Navigation Pane, right-click **qryHollandRockfordSaugatuckCustomers**, and then click **Rename** on the shortcut menu.
2. Position the insertion point after "qry," type **Non**, and then press the **Enter** key. The query name is now qryNonHollandRockfordSaugatuckCustomers.
3. Open the **qryNonHollandRockfordSaugatuckCustomers** query in Design view, and then close the Navigation Pane.

   You need to change the existing condition in the City field to add the Not logical operator.
4. Click the **City Criteria** box, open the Zoom dialog box, click at the beginning of the expression, type **Not**, and then press the **spacebar**. See Figure 5-5.

**Figure 5-5** Record selection based on not matching a list of values

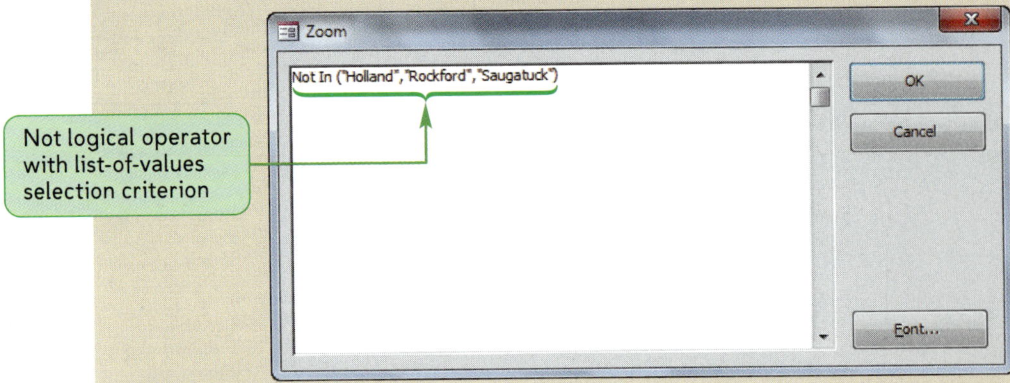


5. Click the **OK** button, and then save and run the query. The recordset displays only those records with a City field value that is not Holland, Rockford, or Saugatuck. The recordset includes a total of 29 customer records.
6. Scroll down the datasheet to make sure that no Holland or Rockford or Saugatuck customers appear in your results.

   Now you can close and delete the query, because Sarah does not need to run this query again.

**TIP**

You can delete any object type, including tables, in the Navigation Pane using the Delete command on the shortcut menu.

7. Close the query, and then open the Navigation Pane.
8. Right-click **qryNonHollandRockfordSaugatuckCustomers**, click **Delete** on the shortcut menu, and then click the **Yes** button when asked to confirm the query deletion. The query is permanently deleted from the database.

You now are ready to answer Taylor's question about Grand Rapids or East Grand Rapids customers that signed contracts for less than $10,000 or that signed contracts during the winter.

## Using an AutoFilter to Filter Data

Taylor wants to view the customer last and first names, company names, cities, contract amounts, signing dates, and contract types for customers in Grand Rapids or East Grand Rapids that have signed contracts for less than $10,000 or that signed contracts during the winter. The qrySmallContractsOrWinterSignings query contains the same fields Taylor wants to view. This query also uses the Or logical operator to select records if the ContractAmt field value is less than $10,000 or if the SigningDate field value is between 1/1/2014 and 3/1/2014. These are two of the conditions needed to answer Taylor's question. You could modify the qrySmallContractsOrWinterSignings query in Design view to further restrict the records selected to customers located only in Grand Rapids and East Grand Rapids. However, you can use the AutoFilter feature to choose the city restrictions faster and with more flexibility. You previously used the AutoFilter feature to sort records, and you previously used Filter By Selection to filter records. Now you'll show Taylor how to use the AutoFilter feature to filter records.

## To filter the records using an AutoFilter:

1. Open the **qrySmallContractsOrWinterSignings** query in Design view, and then close the Navigation Pane.

   The *<10000* condition for the ContractAmt field selects records whose contracts amounts are less than $10,000, and the *Between #1/1/2014# And #3/1/2014#* condition for the SigningDate field selects records whose contracts were signed during the first two months of 2014. Because the conditions are in two different rows, the query uses the Or logical operator. If you wanted to answer Taylor's question in Design view, you would add a condition for the City field, using either the Or logical operator—*"Grand Rapids" Or "East Grand Rapids"*—or the In comparison operator—*In ("Grand Rapids", "East Grand Rapids")*. You'd place this condition for the City field in both the Criteria row and in the or row. The query recordset would include a record only if both conditions in either row are satisfied. Instead, you'll show Taylor how to choose the information she wants using an AutoFilter.

2. Run the query, and then click the **arrow** on the City column heading to display the AutoFilter menu. See Figure 5-6.

**Figure 5-6** **Using an AutoFilter to filter records in the query recordset**

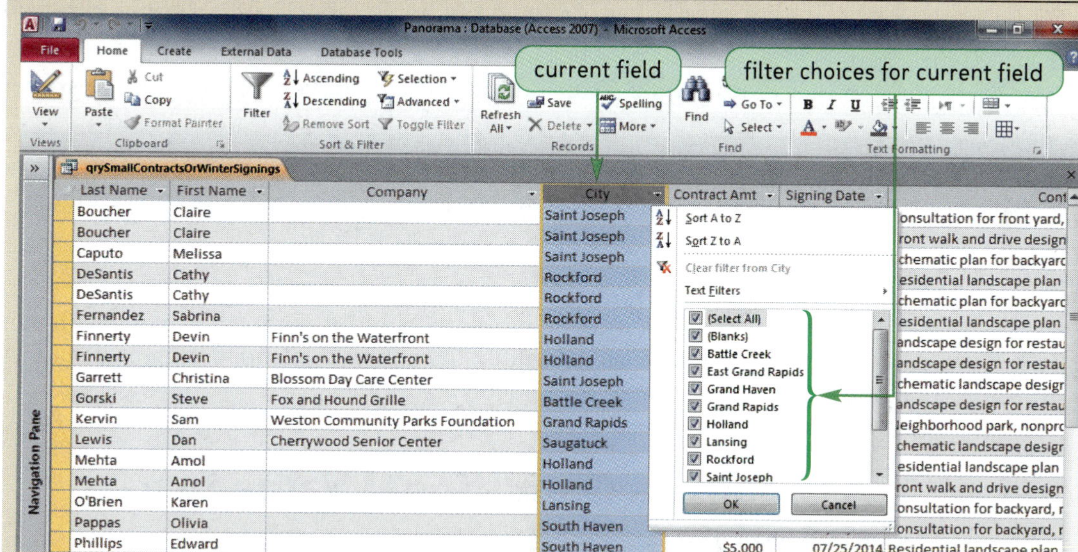


The AutoFilter menu lists all City field values that appear in the recordset. A check mark next to an entry indicates that records with that City field value appear in the recordset. To filter for selected City field values, you uncheck the cities you don't want selected and leave checked the cities you do want selected. You can click the "(Select All)" check box to select or deselect all field values. The "(Blanks)" option includes null values when checked and excludes null values when unchecked. (Recall that a null field value is the absence of a value for the field.)

3. Click the **(Select All)** check box to deselect all check boxes, click the **East Grand Rapids** check box, and then click the **Grand Rapids** check box.

   The two check boxes indicate that the AutoFilter will include only East Grand Rapids and Grand Rapids City field values.

4. Click the **OK** button. Access displays the four records for customers in East Grand Rapids and Grand Rapids with small contract amounts or with winter signing dates. See Figure 5-7.

Figure 5-7 **Using an AutoFilter to filter records in the query recordset**

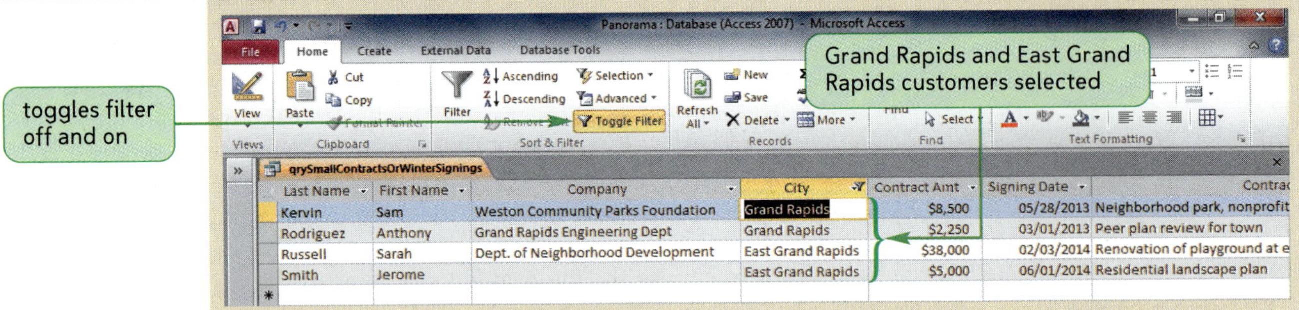


You click the Toggle Filter button in the Sort & Filter group on the Home tab to remove the current filter and display all records in the query. If you click the Toggle Filter button a second time, you reapply the filter.

5. In the Sort & Filter group on the Home tab, click the **Toggle Filter** button. Access removes the filter, and all 31 records appear in the recordset.
6. Click the **Toggle Filter** button. Access applies the City filter, displaying the four records for customers in East Grand Rapids and Grand Rapids.

   Taylor knows how to use the AutoFilter feature and has the information she needs. You can close the query without saving your query design changes.

7. Close the query without saving it.

Sarah wants to view all fields from the tblCustomer table, along with the customer name. The customer name is either the company name for nonresidential customers or the last and first names for residential customers.

## Assigning a Conditional Value to a Calculated Field

Records for residential customers have nonnull FirstName and LastName field values and null Company field values in the tblCustomer table, while records for all other customers have nonnull values for all three fields. Sarah wants to view records from the tblCustomer table in order by the Company field value, if it's nonnull, and at the same time in order by the LastName and then FirstName field values, if the Company field value is null. To produce the information for Sarah, you need to create a query that includes all fields from the tblCustomer table and then add a calculated field that will display the customer name—either the Company field value or the LastName and FirstName field values, separated by a comma and a space.

To combine the LastName and FirstName fields, you'll use the expression *LastName & ", " & FirstName*. The **& (ampersand) operator** is a concatenation operator that joins text expressions. If the LastName field value is Fernandez and the FirstName field value is Sabrina, for example, the result of the expression is *Fernandez, Sabrina*.

To display the correct customer value, you'll use the IIf function. The **IIf (Immediate If) function** assigns one value to a calculated field or control if a condition is true, and a second value if the condition is false. The IIf function has three parts: a condition that is true or false, the result when the condition is true, and the result when the condition is false. Each part of the IIf function is separated by a comma. The condition you'll use is *IsNull(Company)*. The **IsNull function** tests a field value or an expression for a null value; if the field value or expression is null, the result is true; otherwise, the result is false. The expression *IsNull(Company)* is true when the Company field value is null, and is false when the Company field value is not null.

For the calculated field, you'll enter *IIf(IsNull(Company),LastName & ", " & FirstName,Company)*. You interpret this expression as: If the Company field value is null, then set the calculated field value to the concatenation of the LastName field value and the text string *", "* and the FirstName field value. If the Company field value is not null, then set the calculated field value to the Company field value.

Now you are ready to create Sarah's query to display the customer name.

### To create the query to display the customer name:

1. Click the **Create** tab on the Ribbon and then, in the Queries group on the Create tab, click the **Query Design** button to open the Show Table dialog box on top of the Query window in Design view.
2. Click **tblCustomer** in the Tables box, click the **Add** button, and then click the **Close** button to place the tblCustomer table field list in the Query window and close the Show Table dialog box.

   Sarah wants all fields from the tblCustomer table to appear in the query recordset and the new calculated field to appear in the first column.
3. Double-click the **title bar** of the tblCustomer field list to highlight all the fields, and then drag the highlighted fields to the second column's Field box in the design grid. Access places each field in a separate column in the design grid starting with the second column in the design grid, in the same order that the fields appear in the table.

   **Trouble?** If you accidentally drag the highlighted fields to the first column in the design grid, click the CustomerID Field box, and then click the Insert Columns button in the Query Setup group on the Design tab. Continue with Step 4.
4. Right-click the blank Field box to the left of the CustomerID field, and then click **Build** on the shortcut menu to open the Expression Builder dialog box.

   Sarah wants to use "Customer" as the name of the calculated field, so you'll type that name, followed by a colon, and then you'll choose the IIf function.
5. Type **Customer:** and then press the **spacebar**.
6. Double-click **Functions** in the Expression Elements (left) column, click **Built-In Functions** in the Expression Elements column, scroll down the Expression Categories (middle) column and click **Program Flow**, and then double-click **IIf** in the Expression Values (right) column. Access adds the IIf function with four placeholders to the right of the calculated field name in the expression box. See Figure 5-8.

**TIP**

After clicking in a box, you can also open its Expression Builder dialog box by holding down the Ctrl key and pressing the F2 key.

Read the steps carefully, noting whether you should click or double-click the expression categories or expressions.

**Figure 5-8** IIf function inserted for the calculated field

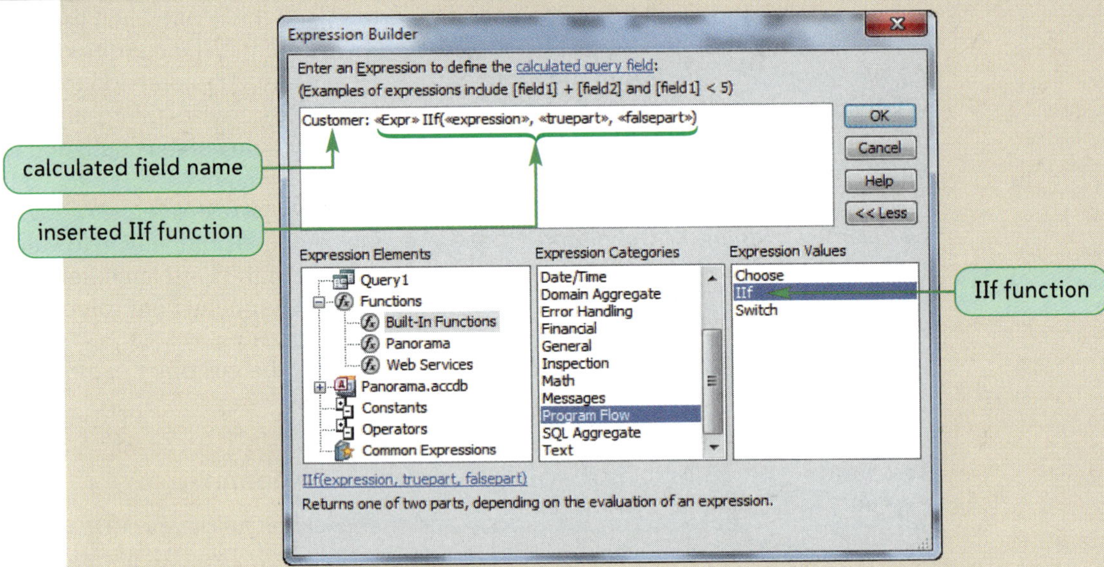


The expression you will create does not need the leftmost placeholder (<<Expr>>), so you'll delete it. You'll replace the second placeholder (<<expression>>) with the condition using the IsNull function, the third placeholder (<<truepart>>) with the expression using the & operator, and the fourth placeholder (<<falsepart>>) with the Company field name.

7. Click **<<Expr>>** in the expression box, and then press the **Delete** key to delete the first placeholder.

8. Click **<<expression>>** in the expression box, click **Inspection** in the Expression Categories (middle) column, double-click **IsNull** in the Expression Values (right) column, click **<<expression>>** in the expression box, and then type **Company**. You've completed the entry of the condition in the IIf function. See Figure 5-9.

**Figure 5-9** After entering the condition for the calculated field's IIf function

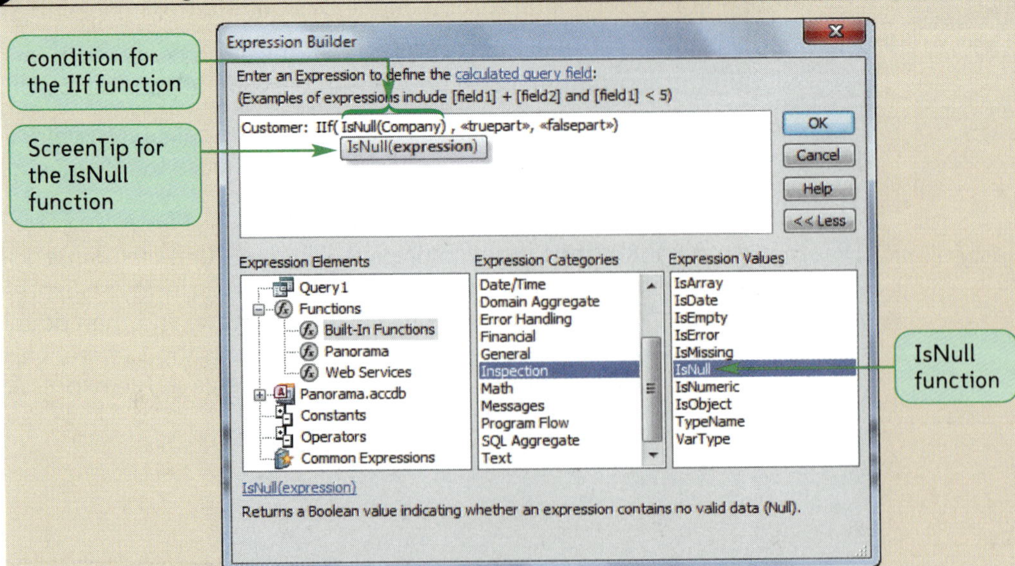

After you typed the first letter of *Company*, the Formula AutoComplete box displayed a list of functions beginning with the letter C, and a ScreenTip for the IsNull function appeared above the box. The box closed after you typed the third letter, but the ScreenTip remains on the screen.

Instead of typing the field name of Company in the previous step, you could have double-clicked Panorama.accdb in the Expression Elements column, double-clicked Tables in the Expression Elements column, clicked tblCustomer in the Expression Elements column, and then double-clicked Company in the Expression Elements column.

**TIP**

The expression *[tblCustomer]![Company]*, meaning the Company field in the tblCustomer table, is the same as *Company*.

Now you'll replace the fourth placeholder and then the third placeholder.

9. Click **<<falsepart>>** and then type **Company**.
10. Click **<<truepart>>**, and then type **LastName & ", " & FirstName** to finish creating the calculated field. Be sure you type a space after the comma within the quotation marks. See Figure 5-10.

**Figure 5-10 Completed calculated field**

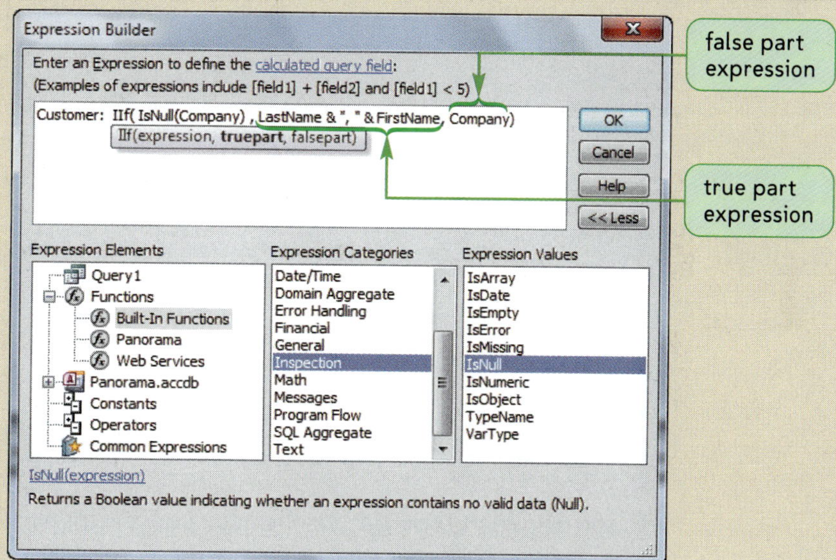


Sarah wants the query to sort records in ascending order by the Customer calculated field.

### To sort, save, and run the query:

1. Click the **OK** button in the Expression Builder dialog box to close it.
2. Click the right side of the **Customer Sort** box to display the sort order options, and then click **Ascending**. The query will display the records in alphabetical order based on the Customer field values.

The calculated field name of Customer consists of a single word, so you do not need to set the Caption property for it. However, you'll review the properties for the calculated field by opening its property sheet.

3. In the Show/Hide group on the Design tab, click the **Property Sheet** button. The property sheet opens and displays the properties for the Customer calculated field. See Figure 5-11.

**Figure 5-11 Property sheet for the Customer calculated field**

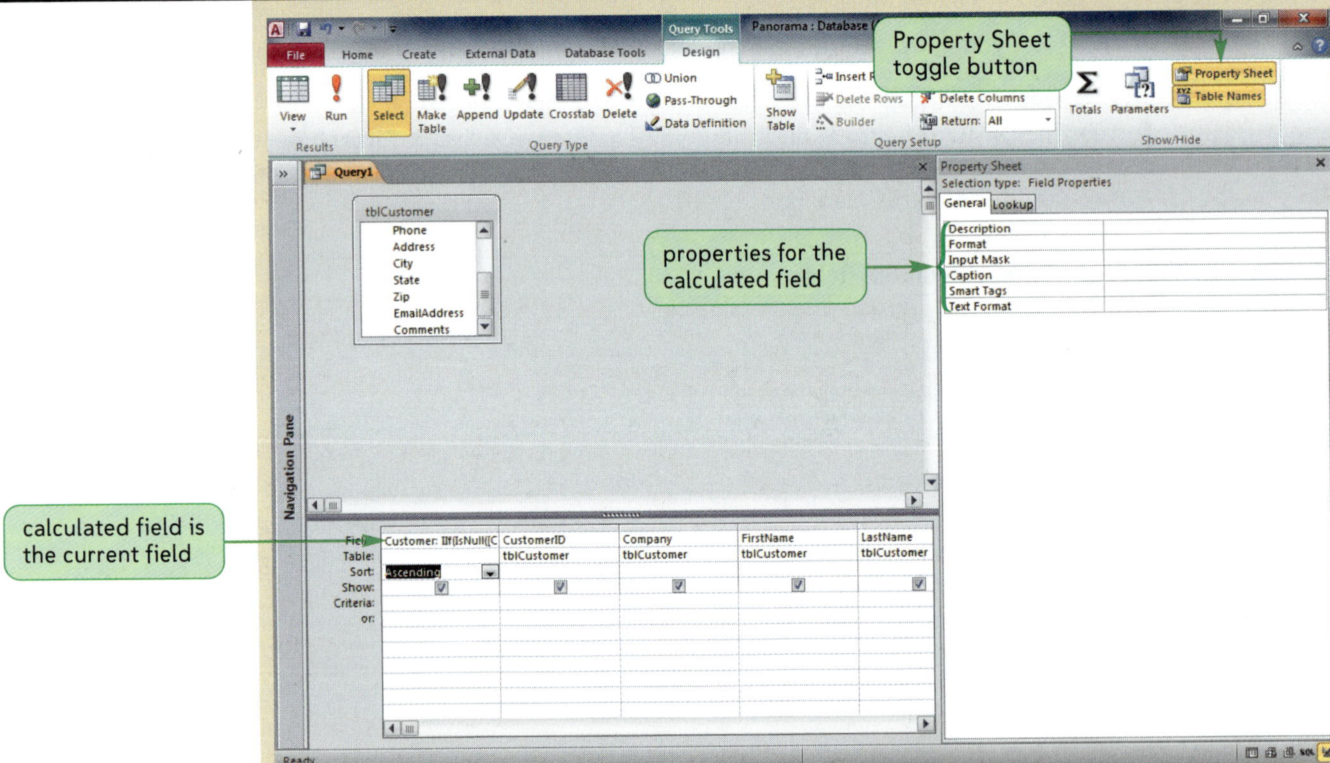


Among the properties for the calculated field, which is the current field, is the Caption property. Leaving the Caption property set to null means that the column name for the calculated field in the query recordset will be Customer, which is the calculated field name. The Property Sheet button is a toggle, so you'll click it again to close the property sheet.

4. Click the **Property Sheet** button to close the property sheet.

5. Save the query as **qryCustomersByName**, run the query, and then resize the Customer column to its best fit. Access displays all records from the tblCustomer table in alphabetical order by the Customer field. See Figure 5-12.

**Figure 5-12** Completed query displaying the Customer calculated field

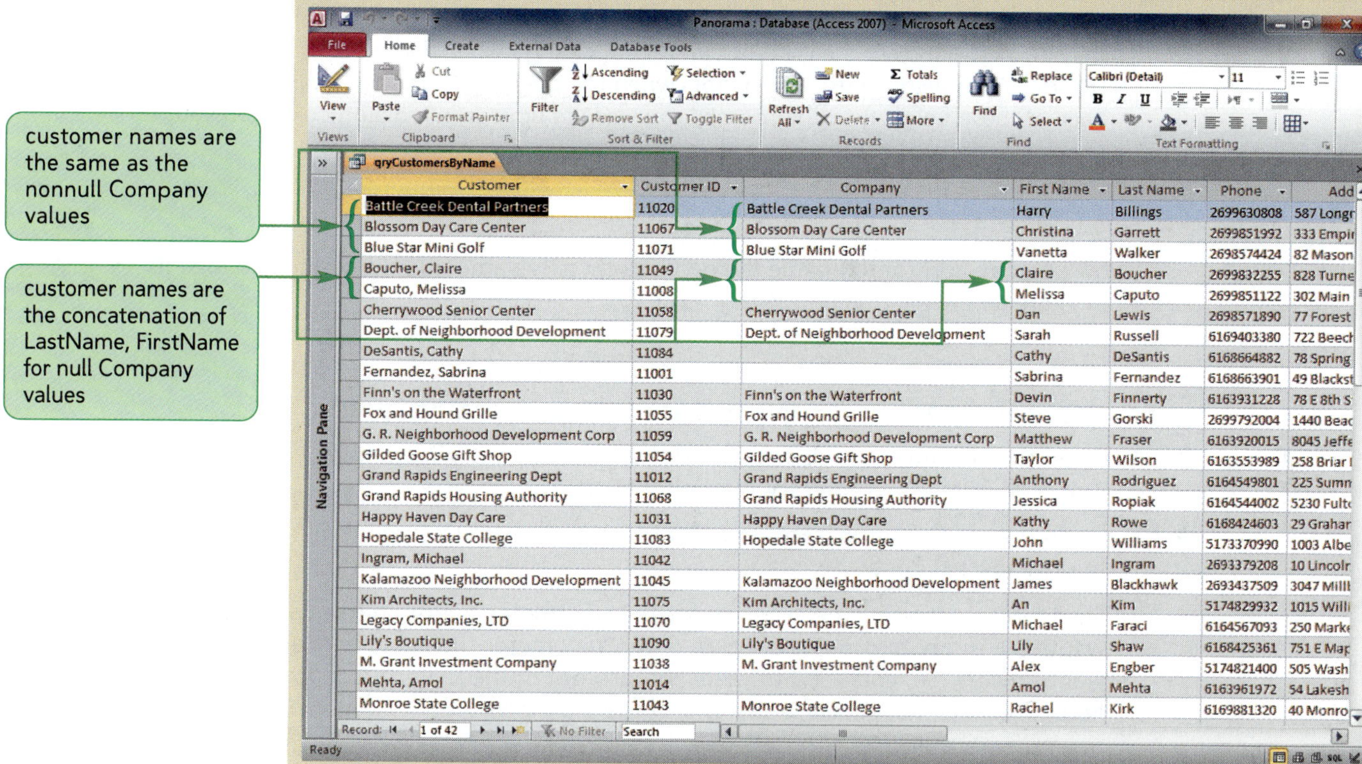


**6.** Save and close the query.

You are now ready to create the query to satisfy Sarah's request for information about customers in a particular city.

## Creating a Parameter Query

Sarah's next request is for records in the qryCustomersByName query for customers in a particular city. For this query, she wants to specify the city, such as Battle Creek or Holland, when she runs the query.

To create this query, you will copy, rename, and modify the qryCustomersByName query. You could create a simple condition using an exact match for the City field, but you would need to change it in Design view every time you run the query. Alternatively, Sarah or a member of her staff could filter the qryCustomersByName query for the city records they want to view. Instead, you will create a parameter query. A **parameter query** displays a dialog box that prompts the user to enter one or more criteria values when the query is run. In this case, you want to create a query that prompts for the city and selects only those customer records with that City field value from the table. You will enter the prompt in the Criteria box for the City field. When Access runs the query, it will open a dialog box and prompt you to enter the city. Access then creates the query results, just as if you had changed the criteria in Design view.

REFERENCE

### *Creating a Parameter Query*

- Create a select query that includes all fields to appear in the query results. Also choose the sort fields and set the criteria that do not change when you run the query.
- Decide which fields to use as prompts when the query runs. In the Criteria box for each of these fields, type the prompt you want to appear in a dialog box when you run the query, and enclose the prompt in brackets.

Now you can copy and rename the qryCustomersByName query, and then change its design to create the parameter query.

## To create the parameter query based on an existing query:

1. Open the Navigation Pane, copy and then paste the qryCustomersByName query, renaming it **qryCustomersByNameParameter**.
2. Open the **qryCustomersByNameParameter** query in Design view, and then close the Navigation Pane.

   Next, you must enter the criterion for the parameter query. In this case, Sarah wants the query to prompt users to enter the city for the customer records they want to view. So, you need to enter the prompt in the Criteria box for the City field. Brackets must enclose the text of the prompt.
3. Click the **City Criteria** box, type **[Type the city:]** and then press the **Enter** key. See Figure 5-13.

**Figure 5-13 Specifying the prompt for the parameter query**

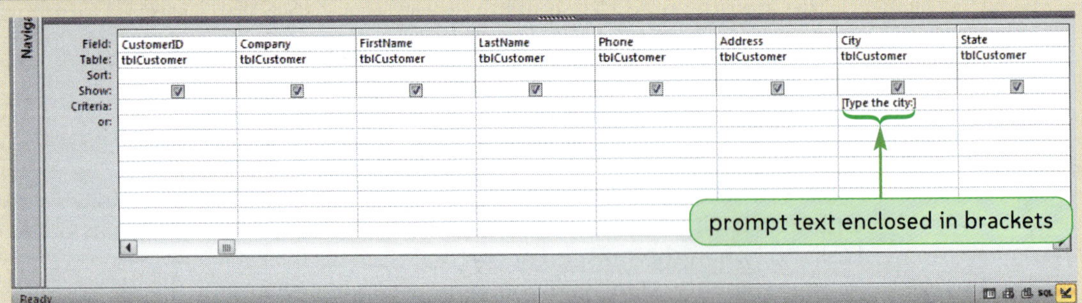


**TIP**

You must enter a value that matches the spelling of a City field value in the table, but you can use either lowercase or uppercase letters.

4. Save and run the query. Access displays a dialog box prompting you for the name of the city. See Figure 5-14.

**Figure 5-14 Enter Parameter Value dialog box**

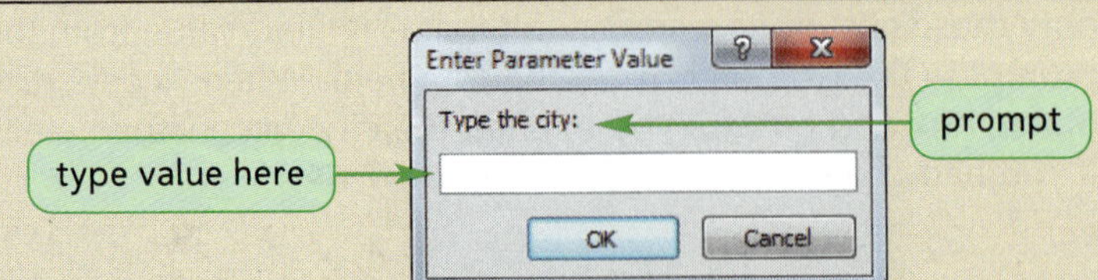

The bracketed text you specified in the Criteria box of the City field appears above a box, in which you must type a City field value. Sarah wants to see all customers in Holland.

5. Type **Holland**, press the **Enter** key, and then scroll the datasheet to the right, if necessary, to display the City field values. The recordset displays the data for the seven customers in Holland. See Figure 5-15.

**Figure 5-15** **Results of the parameter query**

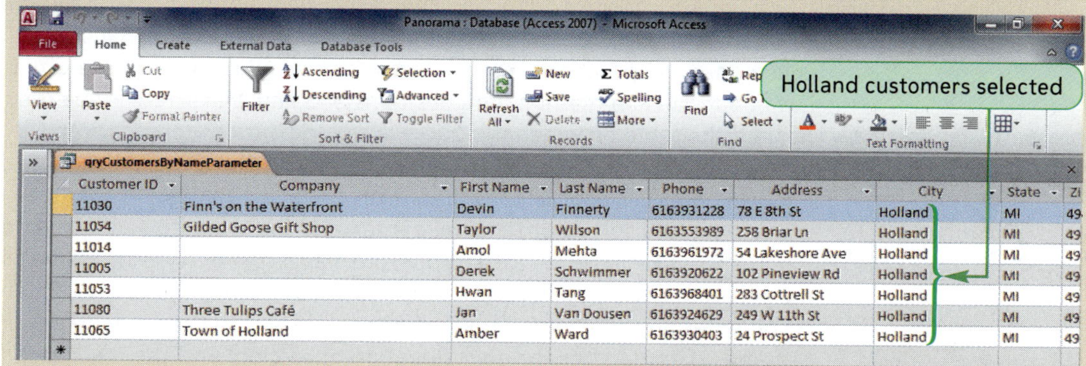


Sarah asks what happens if she doesn't enter a value in the dialog box when she runs the qryCustomersByNameParameter query. You can run the query again to show Sarah the answer to her question.

6. Switch to Design view, and then run the query. The Enter Parameter Value dialog box opens.

If you click the OK button or press the Enter key, you'll run the parameter query without entering a value for the City field criterion.

7. Click the **OK** button. Access displays no records in the query results.

When you run the parameter query and enter *Holland* in the dialog box, Access runs the query the same way as if you had entered *"Holland"* in the City Criteria box in the design grid by displaying all Holland customer records. When you do not enter a value in the dialog box, Access runs the query the same way as if you had entered *null* in the City Criteria box. Because none of the records has a null City field value, Access displays no records. Sarah asks if there's a way to display records for a selected City field value when she enters its value in the dialog box and to display all records when she doesn't enter a value.

INSIGHT

### *Creating a More Flexible Parameter Query*

Most users want parameter queries to display the records that match their entered parameter value or to display all records when they don't enter a parameter value. To provide this functionality, you can change the Criteria box in the design grid for the specified column. For example, you could change an entry for a City field from *[Type the city:]* to *Like [Type the city:] & "*"*. That is, you can prefix the Like operator to the original criterion and concatenate the criterion to a wildcard character. When you run the parameter query with this new entry, Access will display one of the following recordsets:

- If you enter a specific City field value in the dialog box, such as *Saugatuck*, the entry is the same as *Like "Saugatuck" & "*"*, which becomes *Like "Saugatuck*"* after the concatenation operation. That is, Access selects all records whose City field values have Saugatuck in the first nine positions and any characters in the remaining positions. If the table on which the query is based contains records with City field values of Saugatuck, Access displays only those records. However, if the table on which the query is based also contains records with City field values of Saugatuck City, then Access would display both the Saugatuck and the Saugatuck City records.
- If you enter a letter in the dialog box, such as *S*, the entry is the same as *Like "S*"*, and the recordset displays all records with City field values that begin with the letter S.
- If you enter no value in the dialog box, the entry is the same as *Like Null & "*"*, which becomes *Like "*"* after the concatenation operation, and the recordset displays all records.

Now you'll modify the parameter query to satisfy Sarah's request and test the new version of the query.

**To modify and test the parameter query:**

1. Switch to Design view.
2. Click the **City Criteria** box, and then open the Zoom dialog box.

   You'll use the Zoom dialog box to modify the value in the City Criteria box.

Be sure you type "*" at the end of the expression.

3. Click to the left of the expression in the Zoom dialog box, type **Like**, press the **spacebar**, press the **End** key, press the **spacebar**, and then type **& "*"**. See Figure 5-16.

**Figure 5-16** **Modified City Criteria value in the Zoom dialog box**

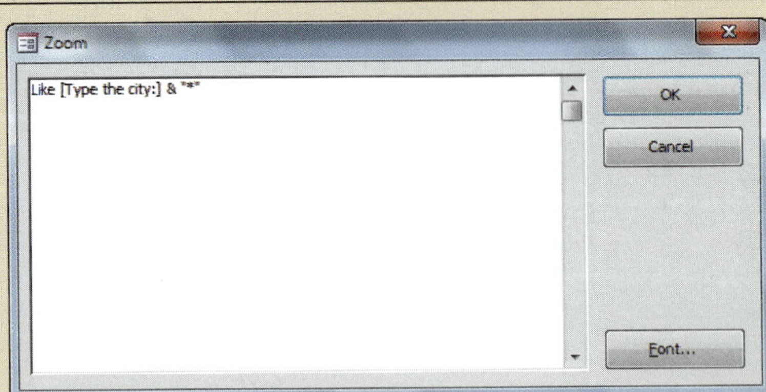

Now you can test the modified parameter query.

4. Click the **OK** button to close the Zoom dialog box, save your query design changes, and then run the query.

   First, you'll test the query to display customers in Saugatuck.

5. Type **Saugatuck**, and then press the **Enter** key. The recordset displays the data for the three customers in Saugatuck.

   Now you'll test the query without entering a value when prompted.

6. Switch to Design view, run the query, and then click the **OK** button. The recordset displays all 42 original records from the tblCustomer table.

   Finally, you'll test the query and enter S in the dialog box.

7. In the Records group on the Home tab, click the **Refresh All** button to open the Enter Parameter Value dialog box, type **S**, press the **Enter** key, and then scroll to the right, if necessary, to display the City field values. The recordset displays the 10 records for customers in Saint Joseph, Saugatuck, and South Haven.
8. Close the query.
9. If you are not continuing on to the next session, close the Panorama database and click the **Yes** button if necessary to empty the Clipboard.

The queries you created will make the Panorama database easier to use. In the next session, you will create a top values query and use query wizards to create three additional queries.

REVIEW

## *Session 5.1 Quick Check*

1. According to the naming conventions used in this session, you use the ______________ prefix tag to identify queries.
2. Which comparison operator selects records based on a specific pattern?
3. What is the purpose of the asterisk (*) in a pattern match query?
4. When do you use the In comparison operator?
5. How do you negate a selection criterion?
6. The ______________ function returns one of two values based on whether the condition being tested is true or false.
7. When do you use a parameter query?

# SESSION 5.2 VISUAL OVERVIEW

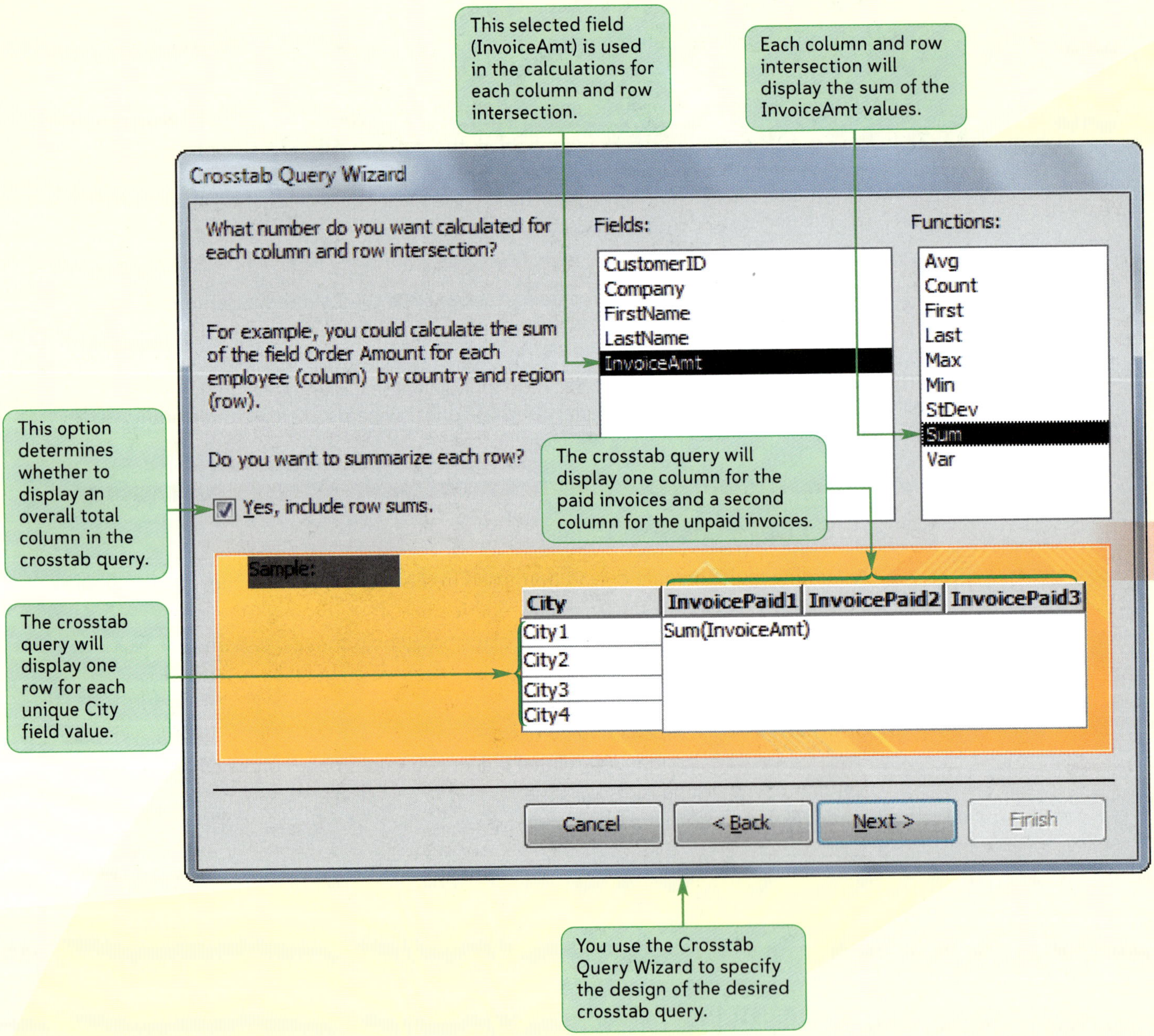

# CREATING A CROSSTAB QUERY

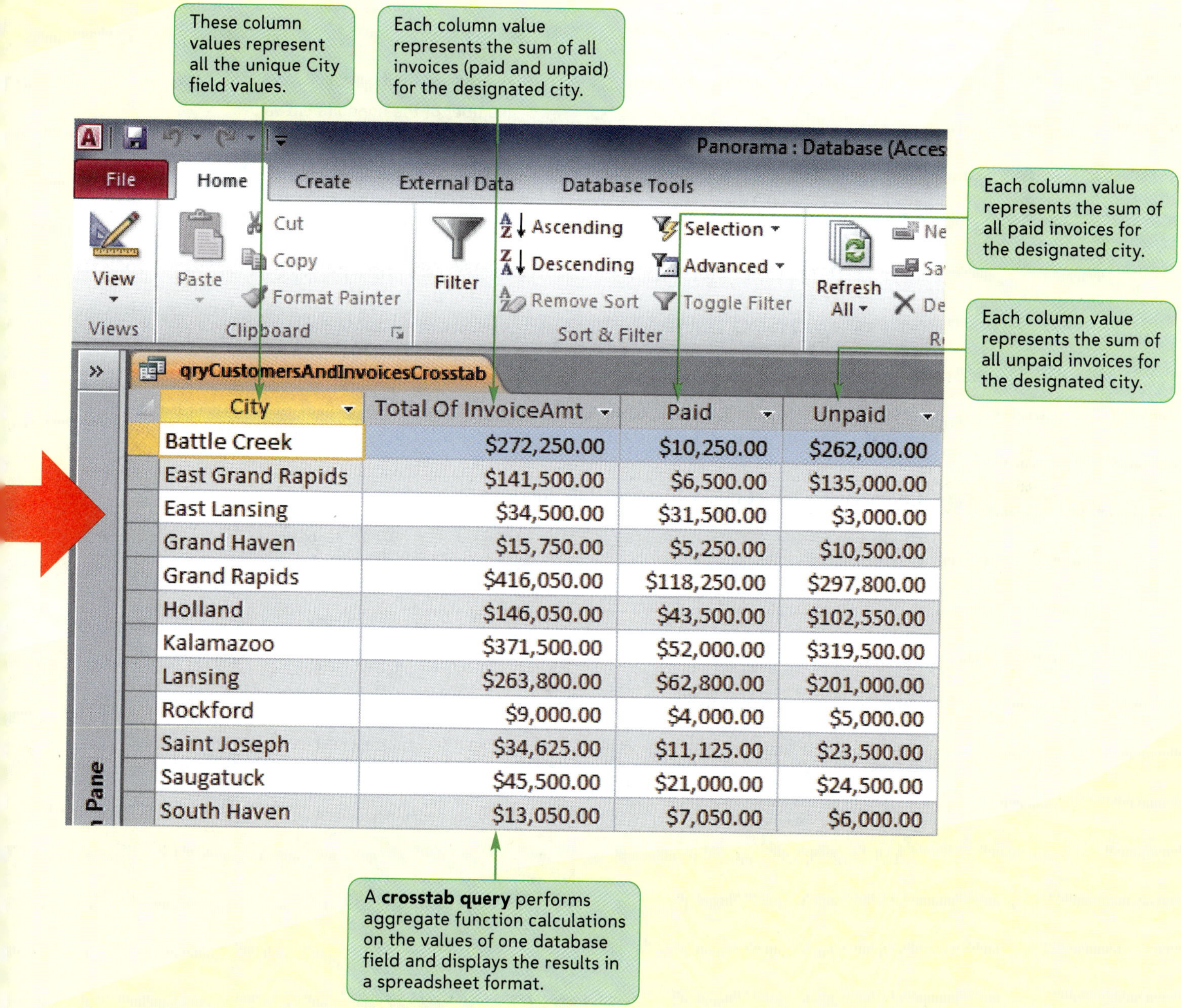

# Creating a Crosstab Query

Oren wants to analyze his company's invoices by city, so he can view the paid and unpaid contract amounts for all customers located in each city. Crosstab queries use the aggregate functions shown in Figure 5-17 to perform arithmetic operations on selected records. A crosstab query can also display one additional aggregate function value that summarizes the set of values in each row. The crosstab query uses one or more fields for the row headings on the left and one field for the column headings at the top.

**Figure 5-17** **Aggregate functions used in crosstab queries**

| Aggregate Function | Definition |
|---|---|
| Avg | Average of the field values |
| Count | Number of the nonnull field values |
| First | First field value |
| Last | Last field value |
| Max | Highest field value |
| Min | Lowest field value |
| StDev | Standard deviation of the field values |
| Sum | Total of the field values |
| Var | Variance of the field values |

Figure 5-18 shows two query recordsets—the recordset below (qryCustomersAndInvoices) is from a select query and the recordset on the next page (qryCustomersAndInvoicesCrosstab) is from a crosstab query based on the select query.

**Figure 5-18** **Comparing a select query to a crosstab query**

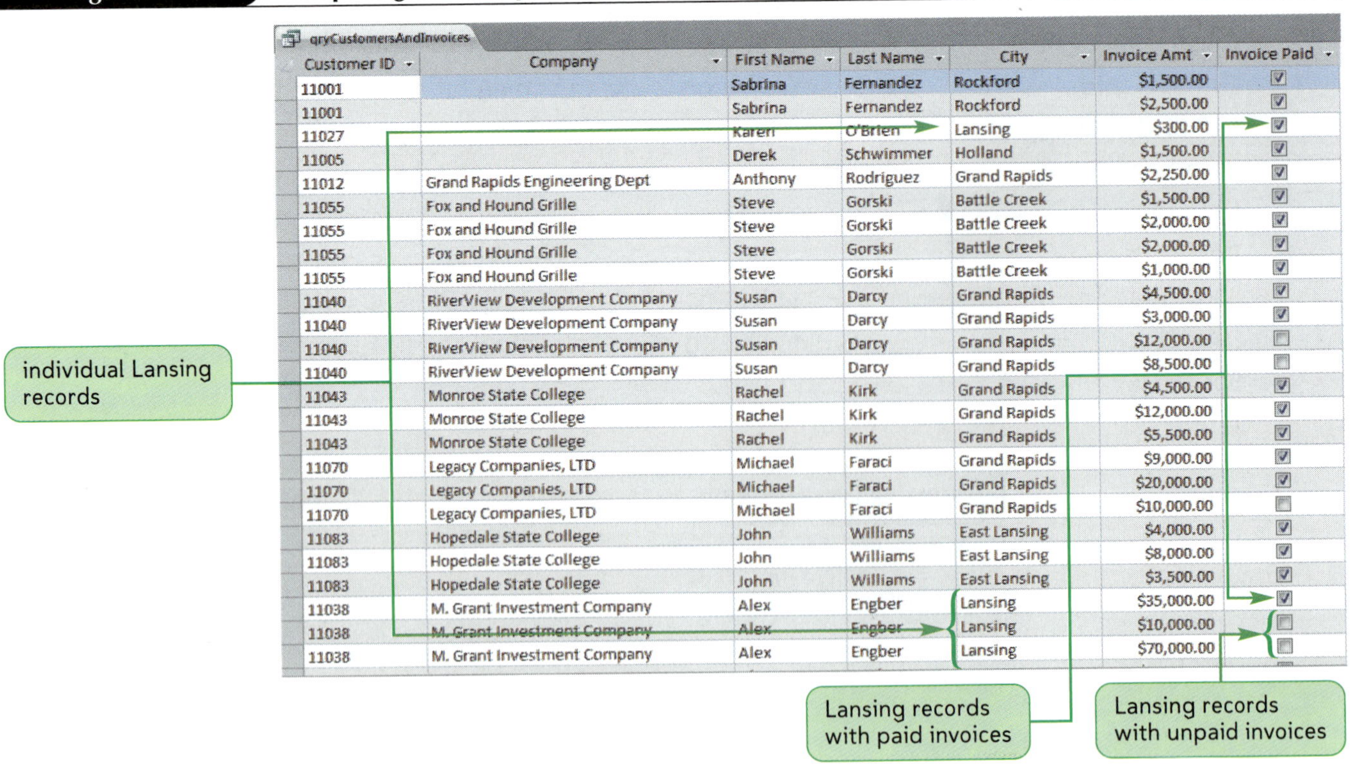


| Customer ID | Company | First Name | Last Name | City | Invoice Amt | Invoice Paid |
|---|---|---|---|---|---|---|
| 11001 | | Sabrina | Fernandez | Rockford | $1,500.00 | ☑ |
| 11001 | | Sabrina | Fernandez | Rockford | $2,500.00 | ☑ |
| 11027 | | Karen | O'Brien | Lansing | $300.00 | ☑ |
| 11005 | | Derek | Schwimmer | Holland | $1,500.00 | ☑ |
| 11012 | Grand Rapids Engineering Dept | Anthony | Rodriguez | Grand Rapids | $2,250.00 | ☑ |
| 11055 | Fox and Hound Grille | Steve | Gorski | Battle Creek | $1,500.00 | ☑ |
| 11055 | Fox and Hound Grille | Steve | Gorski | Battle Creek | $2,000.00 | ☑ |
| 11055 | Fox and Hound Grille | Steve | Gorski | Battle Creek | $2,000.00 | ☑ |
| 11055 | Fox and Hound Grille | Steve | Gorski | Battle Creek | $1,000.00 | ☑ |
| 11040 | RiverView Development Company | Susan | Darcy | Grand Rapids | $4,500.00 | ☑ |
| 11040 | RiverView Development Company | Susan | Darcy | Grand Rapids | $3,000.00 | ☑ |
| 11040 | RiverView Development Company | Susan | Darcy | Grand Rapids | $12,000.00 | ☐ |
| 11040 | RiverView Development Company | Susan | Darcy | Grand Rapids | $8,500.00 | ☐ |
| 11043 | Monroe State College | Rachel | Kirk | Grand Rapids | $4,500.00 | ☑ |
| 11043 | Monroe State College | Rachel | Kirk | Grand Rapids | $12,000.00 | ☑ |
| 11043 | Monroe State College | Rachel | Kirk | Grand Rapids | $5,500.00 | ☑ |
| 11070 | Legacy Companies, LTD | Michael | Faraci | Grand Rapids | $9,000.00 | ☑ |
| 11070 | Legacy Companies, LTD | Michael | Faraci | Grand Rapids | $20,000.00 | ☑ |
| 11070 | Legacy Companies, LTD | Michael | Faraci | Grand Rapids | $10,000.00 | ☐ |
| 11083 | Hopedale State College | John | Williams | East Lansing | $4,000.00 | ☑ |
| 11083 | Hopedale State College | John | Williams | East Lansing | $8,000.00 | ☑ |
| 11083 | Hopedale State College | John | Williams | East Lansing | $3,500.00 | ☑ |
| 11038 | M. Grant Investment Company | Alex | Engber | Lansing | $35,000.00 | ☑ |
| 11038 | M. Grant Investment Company | Alex | Engber | Lansing | $10,000.00 | ☐ |
| 11038 | M. Grant Investment Company | Alex | Engber | Lansing | $70,000.00 | ☐ |

**Figure 5-18** **Comparing a select query to a crosstab query (continued)**

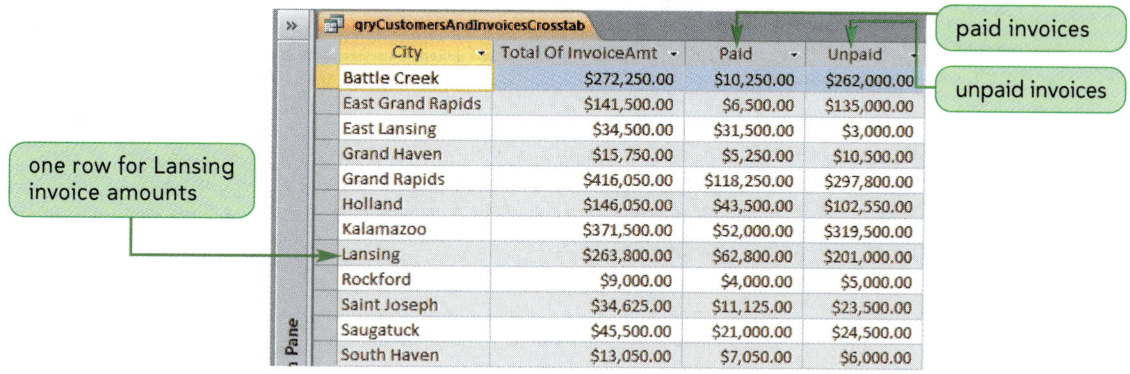


| City | Total Of InvoiceAmt | Paid | Unpaid |
|---|---|---|---|
| Battle Creek | $272,250.00 | $10,250.00 | $262,000.00 |
| East Grand Rapids | $141,500.00 | $6,500.00 | $135,000.00 |
| East Lansing | $34,500.00 | $31,500.00 | $3,000.00 |
| Grand Haven | $15,750.00 | $5,250.00 | $10,500.00 |
| Grand Rapids | $416,050.00 | $118,250.00 | $297,800.00 |
| Holland | $146,050.00 | $43,500.00 | $102,550.00 |
| Kalamazoo | $371,500.00 | $52,000.00 | $319,500.00 |
| Lansing | $263,800.00 | $62,800.00 | $201,000.00 |
| Rockford | $9,000.00 | $4,000.00 | $5,000.00 |
| Saint Joseph | $34,625.00 | $11,125.00 | $23,500.00 |
| Saugatuck | $45,500.00 | $21,000.00 | $24,500.00 |
| South Haven | $13,050.00 | $7,050.00 | $6,000.00 |

The qryCustomersAndInvoices query, a select query, joins the tblCustomer, tblContract, and tblInvoice tables to display selected data from those tables for all invoices. The qryCustomersAndInvoicesCrosstab query, a crosstab query, uses the qryCustomersAndInvoices query as its source query and displays one row for each unique City field value. The City column in the crosstab query identifies each row. The crosstab query uses the Sum aggregate function on the InvoiceAmt field to produce the displayed values in the Paid and Unpaid columns for each City row. An entry in the Total Of InvoiceAmt column represents the sum of the Paid and Unpaid values for the City field value in that row.

PROSKILLS

### *Decision Making: Using Both Select Queries and Crosstab Queries*

Companies use both select queries and crosstab queries in their decision making. A select query displays several records—one for each row selected by the select query—while a crosstab query displays only one summarized record for each unique field value. When management wants to analyze data at a high level to see the big picture, it might start with a crosstab query, identify which field values to analyze futher, and then look in detail at specific field values using select queries. Both select and crosstab queries serve as valuable tools in tracking and analyzing a company's business, and companies use both types of queries in the appropriate situations. By understanding how managers and other employees use the information in a database to make decisions, you can create the correct type of query to provide the information they need.

**TIP**

Microsoft Access Help provides more information on creating a crosstab query without using a wizard.

The quickest way to create a crosstab query is to use the **Crosstab Query Wizard**, which guides you through the steps for creating one. You could also change a select query to a crosstab query in Design view using the Crosstab button in the Query Type group on the Design tab.

REFERENCE

### *Using the Crosstab Query Wizard*

- In the Queries group on the Create tab, click the Query Wizard button.
- In the New Query dialog box, click Crosstab Query Wizard, and then click the OK button.
- Complete the Wizard dialog boxes to select the table or query on which to base the crosstab query, select the row heading field (or fields), select the column heading field, select the calculation field and its aggregate function, and enter a name for the crosstab query.

The crosstab query you will create, which is similar to the one shown in Figure 5-18, has the following characteristics:

- The qryCustomersAndInvoices query in the Panorama database is the basis for the new crosstab query. The base query includes the CustomerID, Company, FirstName, LastName, City, InvoiceAmt, and InvoicePaid fields.
- The City field is the leftmost column in the crosstab query and identifies each crosstab query row.
- The values from the InvoicePaid field, which is a Yes/No field, identify the rightmost columns of the crosstab query.
- The crosstab query applies the Sum aggregate function to the InvoiceAmt field values and displays the resulting total values in the Paid and Unpaid columns of the query results.
- The grand total of the InvoiceAmt field values appears for each row in a column with the heading Total Of InvoiceAmt.

Next you will create the crosstab query based on the qryCustomersAndInvoices query.

### To start the Crosstab Query Wizard:

1. If you took a break after the previous session, make sure that the Panorama database is open and the Navigation Pane is closed.

   **Trouble?** If the Security Warning is displayed below the Ribbon, click the Enable Content button next to the Security Warning.

2. Click the **Create** tab on the Ribbon and then, in the Queries group on the Create tab, click the **Query Wizard** button. The New Query dialog box opens.
3. Click **Crosstab Query Wizard**, and then click the **OK** button. The first Crosstab Query Wizard dialog box opens.

You'll now use the Crosstab Query Wizard to create the crosstab query for Oren.

### To finish the Crosstab Query Wizard:

1. Click the **Queries** option button in the View section to display the list of queries in the Panorama database, and then click **Query: qryCustomersAndInvoices**. See Figure 5-19.

**Figure 5-19** Choosing the query for the crosstab query

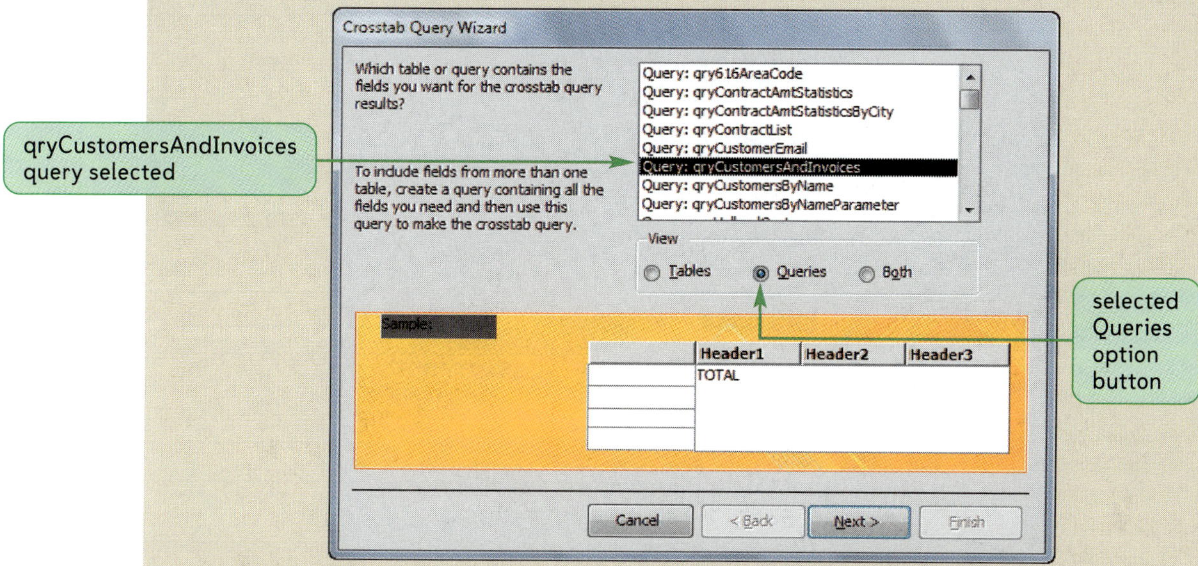


2. Click the **Next** button to open the next Crosstab Query Wizard dialog box, in which you choose the field (or fields) for the row headings. Because Oren wants the crosstab query to display one row for each unique City field value, you will select that field for the row headings.

**TIP**

When you select a field, Access changes the sample crosstab query in the dialog box to illustrate your choice.

3. In the Available Fields box, click **City**, and then click the > button to move the City field to the Selected Fields box.
4. Click the **Next** button to open the next Crosstab Query Wizard dialog box, in which you select the field values that will serve as column headings. Oren wants to see the paid and unpaid total invoice amounts, so you need to select the InvoicePaid field for the column headings.
5. Click **InvoicePaid** in the box, and then click the **Next** button.

   In the next Crosstab Query Wizard dialog box, you choose the field that will be calculated for each row and column intersection and the function to use for the calculation. The results of the calculation will appear in the row and column intersections in the query results. Oren needs to calculate the sum of the InvoiceAmt field value for each row and column intersection.

6. Click **InvoiceAmt** in the Fields box, click **Sum** in the Functions box, and then make sure that the **Yes, include row sums** check box is checked. The "Yes, include row sums" option creates a column showing the overall totals for the values in each row of the query recordset. See Figure 5-20.

**Figure 5-20 Completed crosstab query design**

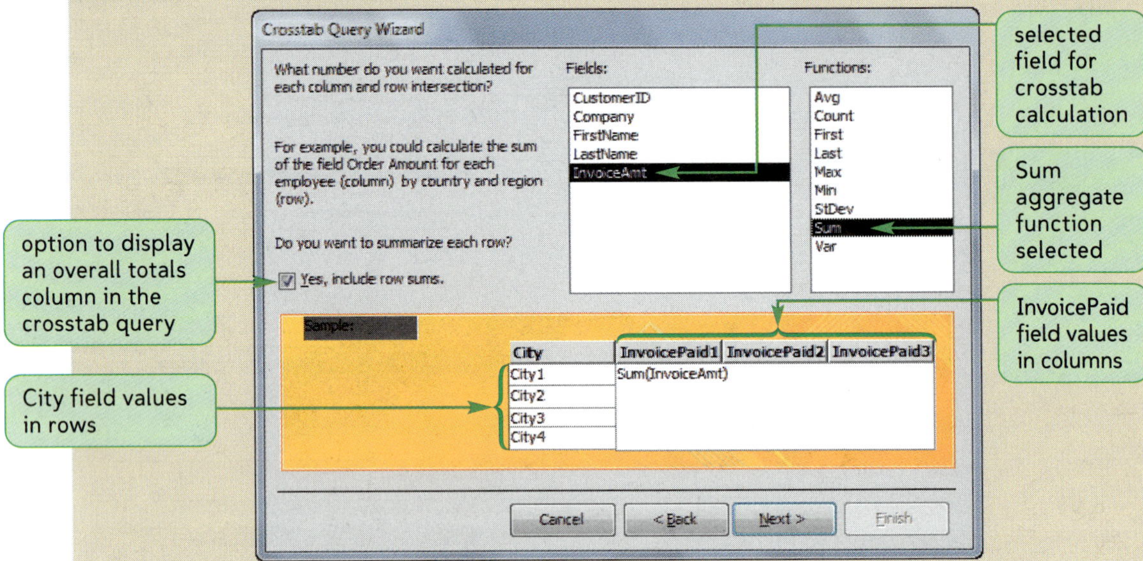


7. Click the **Next** button to open the final Crosstab Query Wizard dialog box, in which you choose the query name.
8. Click in the box, delete the underscore character so that the query name is qryCustomersAndInvoicesCrosstab, be sure the option button for viewing the query is selected, and then click the **Finish** button. Access saves the crosstab query, and then displays the query recordset.
9. Resize all the columns in the query recordset to their best fit, and then click the City field value in the first row (**Battle Creek**). See Figure 5-21.

**Figure 5-21 Crosstab query recordset**

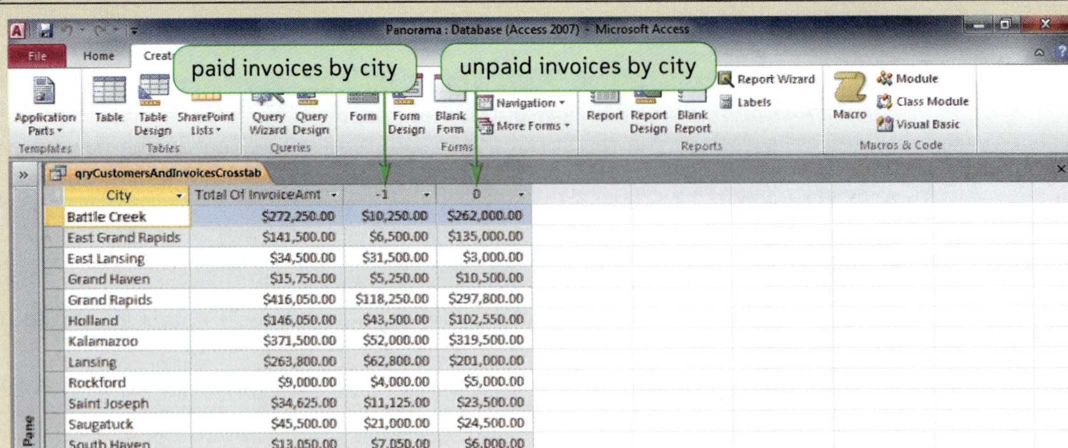


The query recordset contains one row for each City field value. The Total Of InvoiceAmt column shows the total invoice amount for the customers in each city. The columns labeled -1 and 0 show the total paid (-1 column) and unpaid (0 column) invoice amounts for customers in each city. Because the InvoicePaid field is a Yes/No field, by default, Access displays field values in datasheets, forms, and reports in a check box (either checked or unchecked), but stores a checked value in the database as a -1 and an unchecked value as a 0. Instead of displaying check boxes, the crosstab query displays the stored values as column headings.

Oren wants you to change the column headings of -1 to Paid and of 0 to Unpaid. You'll use the IIf function to change the column headings, using the expression *IIf (InvoicePaid,"Paid","Unpaid")*—if the InvoicePaid field value is true (because it's a Yes/No field or a True/False field), or is checked, use Paid as the column heading; otherwise, use Unpaid as the column heading. Because the InvoicePaid field is a Yes/No field, the condition *InvoicePaid* is the same as the condition *InvoicePaid = -1*, which uses a comparison operator and a value. For all data types except Yes/No fields, you must use a comparison operator in a condition.

### To change the crosstab query column headings:

1. Click the **Home** tab on the Ribbon, and then switch to Design view. The design grid has four entries. See Figure 5-22.

**Figure 5-22** Crosstab query in the design grid

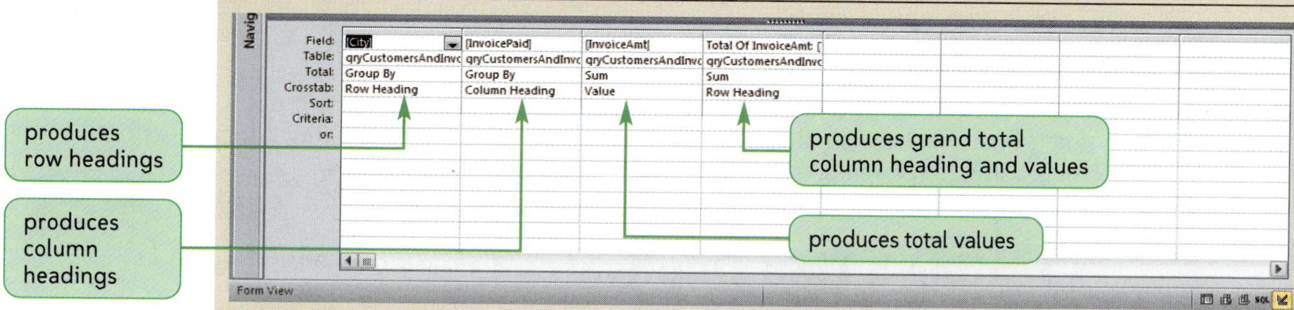


From left to right, the [City] entry produces the row headings, the [InvoicePaid] entry produces the column headings, the [InvoiceAmt] entry produces the totals in each row/column intersection, and the Total Of InvoiceAmt entry produces the row total column heading and total values. The field names are enclosed in brackets; the Total Of InvoiceAmt entry is the name of this calculated field, which displays the sum of the InvoiceAmt field values for each row.

You need to replace the Field box value in the second column with the IIf function expression to change the -1 and zero column headings to Paid and Unpaid. You can type the expression in the box, use Expression Builder to create the expression, or type the expression in the Zoom dialog box. You'll use the last method.

2. Click the **InvoicePaid Field** box, and then open the Zoom dialog box.
3. Delete the expression, and then type **IIf (InvoicePaid,"Paid","Unpaid")** in the Zoom dialog box. See Figure 5-23.

**Figure 5-23** IIf function for the crosstab query column headings

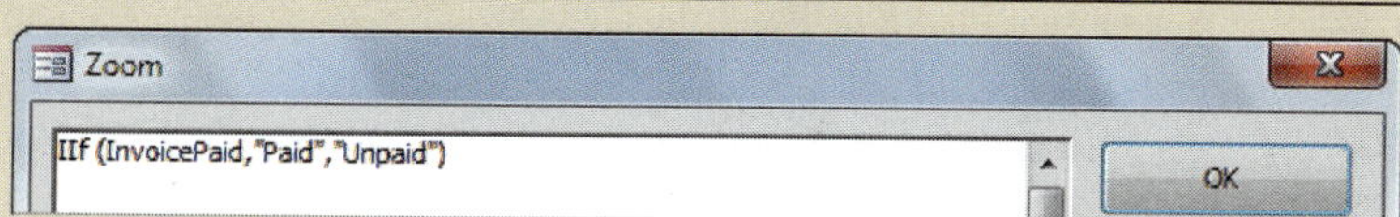


4. Click the **OK** button, and then save and run the query. Access displays the completed crosstab query with Paid and Unpaid as the last two column headings.
5. Close the query, and then open the Navigation Pane.

**TIP**

Point to an object in the Navigation Pane to display the full object name in a ScreenTip.

In the Navigation Pane, Access uses unique icons to represent different types of queries. The crosstab query icon appears in the Queries list to the left of the qryCustomersAndInvoicesCrosstab query. This icon looks different from the icon that appears to the left of the other queries, which are all select queries.

INSIGHT

*Using Special Database Features Cautiously*

When you create a query in Design view or with a wizard, Access automatically constructs an equivalent SQL statement and saves only the SQL statement version of the query. **SQL (Structured Query Language)** is a standard language used in querying, updating, and managing relational databases. If you learn SQL for one relational DBMS, it's a relatively easy task to begin using SQL for other relational DBMSs. However, differences exist between DBMSs in their versions of SQL, somewhat like having different dialects in English, and in what additions they make to SQL. The SQL statement equivalent that Access creates for a crosstab query is one such SQL-language addition. If you need to convert an Access database to SQL-Server, Oracle, or another DBMS, crosstab queries created in Access will not work in these other DBMSs. You'd have to construct a set of SQL statements in the other DBMS to replace the SQL statement automatically created by Access. Constructing this replacement set of statements is a highly technical process that only an experienced programmer can complete, so you should use special features of a DBMS judiciously.

Next, Oren wants to identify any contracts that have the same start dates as other contracts because these are the ones that might have potential scheduling difficulties. To find the information Oren needs, you'll create a find duplicates query.

## Creating a Find Duplicates Query

A **find duplicates query** is a select query that finds duplicate records in a table or query. You can create this type of query using the **Find Duplicates Query Wizard**. A find duplicates query searches for duplicate values based on the fields you select as you answer the Wizard's questions. For example, you might want to display all employers that have the same name, all students who have the same phone number, or all products that have the same description. Using this type of query, you can locate duplicates to avert potential problems (for example, you might have inadvertently assigned two different numbers to the same product), or you can eliminate duplicates that cost money (for example, you could send just one advertising brochure to all customers having the same address).

REFERENCE

*Using the Find Duplicates Query Wizard*

- In the Queries group on the Create tab, click the Query Wizard button.
- Click Find Duplicates Query Wizard, and then click the OK button.
- Complete the Wizard dialog boxes to select the table or query on which to base the query, select the field (or fields) to check for duplicate values, select the additional fields to include in the query results, enter a name for the query, and then click the Finish button.

You'll use the Find Duplicates Query Wizard to create and run a new query to display duplicate start dates in the tblContract table.

### To create the query using the Find Duplicates Query Wizard:

1. Close the Navigation Pane, click the **Create** tab on the Ribbon and then, in the Queries group, click the **Query Wizard** button to open the New Query dialog box.

2. Click **Find Duplicates Query Wizard**, and then click the **OK** button. The first Find Duplicates Query Wizard dialog box opens. In this dialog box, you select the table or query on which to base the new query. You'll use the tblContract table.
3. Click **Table: tblContract** (if necessary), and then click the **Next** button. Access opens the next Find Duplicates Query Wizard dialog box, in which you choose the fields you want to check for duplicate values.
4. In the Available fields box, click **StartDate**, click the > button to select the StartDate field as the field to check for duplicate values, and then click the **Next** button. In the next Find Duplicates Query Wizard dialog box, you select the additional fields you want displayed in the query results.

   Oren wants all remaining fields to be included in the query results.
5. Click the >> button to move all fields from the Available fields box to the Additional query fields box, and then click the **Next** button. Access opens the final Find Duplicates Query Wizard dialog box, in which you enter a name for the query. You'll use qryDuplicateContractStartDates as the query name.
6. Type **qryDuplicateContractStartDates** in the box, be sure the option button for viewing the results is selected, and then click the **Finish** button. Access saves the query, and then displays the 10 records for contracts with duplicate start dates. See Figure 5-24.

**Figure 5-24** **Query recordset for contracts with the same start dates**

qryDuplicateContractStartDates

| Start Date | Contract Num | Customer ID | Contract Amt | Signing Date | Contract Type |
|---|---|---|---|---|---|
| 07/12/2013 | 3025 | 11083 | $15,500 | 03/25/2013 | Landscape renovation for plaza |
| 07/12/2013 | 3023 | 11070 | $39,000 | 03/22/2013 | Renovation of large multifamily housing open space |
| 08/17/2013 | 3033 | 11005 | $2,250 | 07/08/2013 | Residential landscape plan for front yard |
| 08/17/2013 | 3021 | 11040 | $28,000 | 05/03/2013 | Landscape plans for multifamily housing site |
| 03/17/2014 | 3068 | 11049 | $4,500 | 02/07/2014 | Front walk and drive design, residential |
| 03/17/2014 | 3045 | 11064 | $25,000 | 08/20/2013 | Open space corridor planning at new transit station |
| 06/28/2014 | 3077 | 11058 | $6,500 | 05/17/2014 | Schematic landscape design for senior center |
| 06/28/2014 | 3072 | 11059 | $46,000 | 03/11/2014 | Landscape design for affordable housing site |
| 10/06/2014 | 3105 | 11084 | $5,000 | 08/24/2014 | Residential landscape plan |
| 10/06/2014 | 3100 | 11031 | $10,500 | 08/08/2014 | Schematic landscape design for daycare center |

7. Close the query.

Oren now asks you to find the records for customers with no contracts. These are customers that had contracts in the past, but have chosen not to sign a contract with Belmont Landscapes in the past year. Oren wants to contact these customers to see if there are any services that the company might be able to furnish. To provide Oren with this information, you need to create a find unmatched query.

## Creating a Find Unmatched Query

A **find unmatched query** is a select query that finds all records in a table or query that have no related records in a second table or query. For example, you could display all customers that have not signed recent contracts or all students who are not currently enrolled in classes. Such a query provides information for Oren to solicit business from the inactive customers and for a school administrator to contact the students to find out their future educational plans. You can use the **Find Unmatched Query Wizard** to create this type of query.

REFERENCE

## *Using the Find Unmatched Query Wizard*

- In the Queries group on the Create tab, click the Query Wizard button.
- Click Find Unmatched Query Wizard, and then click the OK button.
- Complete the Wizard dialog boxes to select the table or query on which to base the new query, select the table or query that contains the related records, specify the common field in each table or query, select the additional fields to include in the query results, enter a name for the query, and then click the Finish button.

Oren wants to know which customers have no open contracts. These customers are inactive, and he will contact them to determine their interest in doing further business with Belmont Landscapes. To create a list of inactive customers, you'll use the Find Unmatched Query Wizard to display only those records from the tblCustomer table with no matching CustomerID field value in the related tblContract table.

### To create the query using the Find Unmatched Query Wizard:

1. In the Queries group on the Create tab, click the **Query Wizard** button to open the New Query dialog box.
2. Click **Find Unmatched Query Wizard**, and then click the **OK** button. The first Find Unmatched Query Wizard dialog box opens. In this dialog box, you select the table or query on which to base the new query. You'll use the qryCustomersByName query.
3. Click the **Queries** option button in the View section to display the list of queries, click **Query: qryCustomersByName** in the box to select this query, and then click the **Next** button to open the next Find Unmatched Query Wizard dialog box, in which you choose the table that contains the related records. You'll select the tblContract table.
4. Click **Table: tblContract** in the box (if necessary), and then click the **Next** button to open the next dialog box, in which you choose the common field for both tables. See Figure 5-25.

**Figure 5-25** **Selecting the common field**

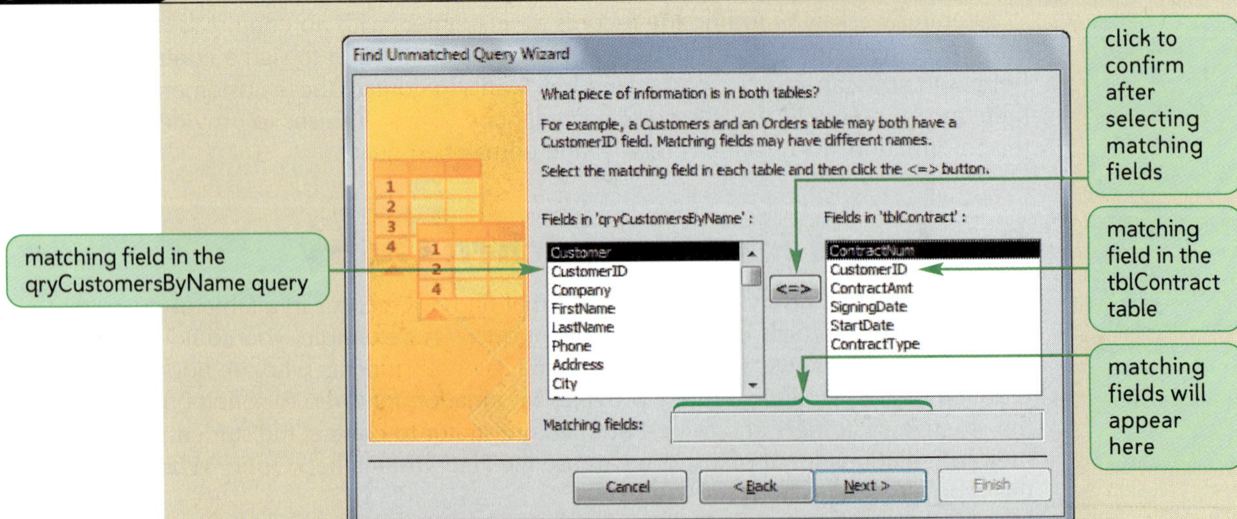

The common field between the query and the table is the CustomerID field. You need to click the common field in each box, and then click the symbol between the two boxes to join the two objects. The Matching fields box then will display CustomerID <=> CustomerID to indicate the joining of the two matching fields. If the two selected objects already have a one-to-many relationship defined in the Relationships window, the Matching fields box will join the correct fields automatically.

Be sure you click the CustomerID field in both boxes.

5. Click **CustomerID** in the Fields in 'qryCustomersByName' box, click **CustomerID** in the Fields in 'tblContract' box, click the <=> button to connect the two selected fields, and then click the **Next** button to open the next Find Unmatched Query Wizard dialog box, in which you choose the fields you want to see in the query recordset. Oren wants the query recordset to display all available fields.
6. Click the >> button to move all fields from the Available fields box to the Selected fields box, and then click the **Next** button to open the final dialog box, in which you enter the query name.
7. Type **qryInactiveCustomers**, be sure the option button for viewing the results is selected, and then click the **Finish** button. Access saves the query and then displays two records in the query recordset. See Figure 5-26.

**Figure 5-26** **Query recordset displaying two customers without contracts**

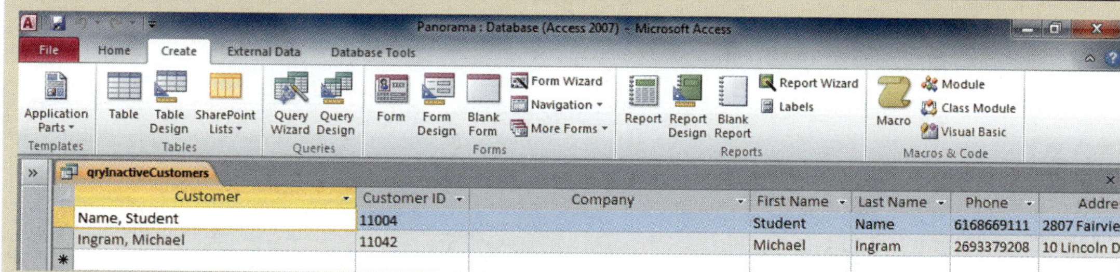


8. Close the query.

Next, Oren wants Taylor to contact those customers who have the highest contract amounts to make sure that Belmont Landscapes is providing satisfactory service. To display the information Taylor needs, you will create a top values query.

## Creating a Top Values Query

Whenever a query displays a large group of records, you might want to limit the number to a more manageable size by displaying, for example, just the first 10 records. The **Top Values property** for a query lets you limit the number of records in the query results. For the Top Values property, you can click one of the preset values from a list, or enter either an integer (such as 15, to display the first 15 records) or a percentage (such as 20%, to display the first fifth of the records), to find a specific number of records.

Suppose you have a select query that displays 45 records. If you want the query recordset to show only the first five records, you can change the query by entering a Top Values property value of either 5 or 10%. If the query contains a sort and the last record that Access can display is one of two or more records with the same value for the primary sort field, Access displays all records with that matching key value.

Taylor wants to view the same data that appears in the qryLargeContractAmounts query for customers with the highest 25% contract amounts. Based on the number or percentage you enter, a top values query selects that number or percentage of records starting from the top of the recordset. Thus, you usually include a sort in a top values query to display the records with the highest or lowest values for the sorted field. You will modify the query and then use the Top Values property to produce this information for Taylor.

## To set the Top Values property for the query:

1. Open the Navigation Pane, open the **qryLargeContractAmounts** in Datasheet view, and then close the Navigation Pane. Access displays 22 records, all with ContractAmt field values greater than $25,000, sorted in descending order by the ContractAmt field.
2. Switch to Design view.
3. In the Query Setup group on the Design tab, click the **Return** arrow (with the ScreenTip "Top Values"), and then click **25%**. See Figure 5-27.

Figure 5-27 **Creating the top values query**

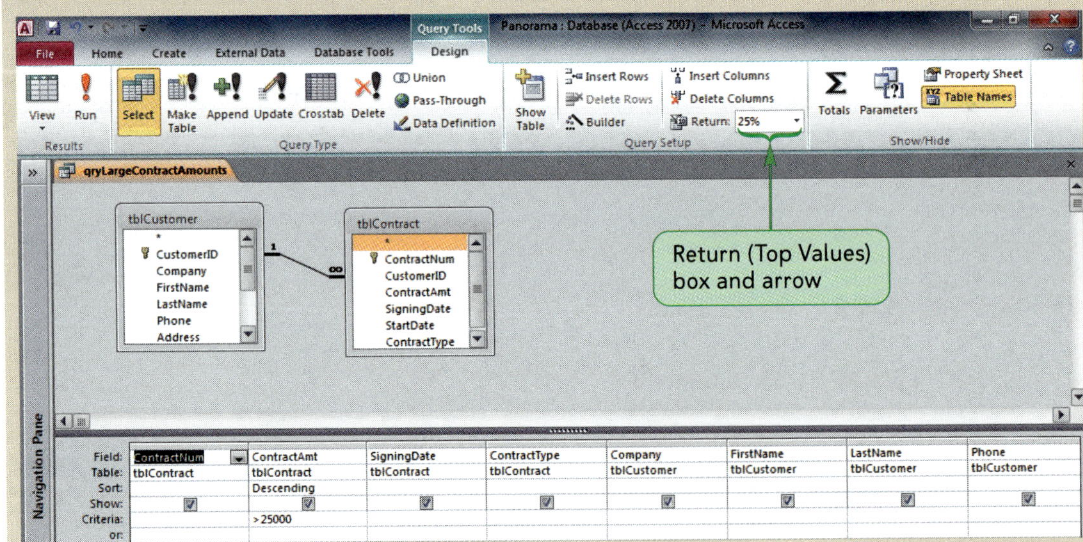


If the number or percentage of records you want to select, such as 15 or 20%, doesn't appear in the Top Values list, you can type the number or percentage in the Return box.

4. Run the query. Access displays six records in the query recordset; these records represent the customers with the highest 25% contract amounts (25% of the original 22 records). See Figure 5-28.

**Figure 5-28** Top values query recordset

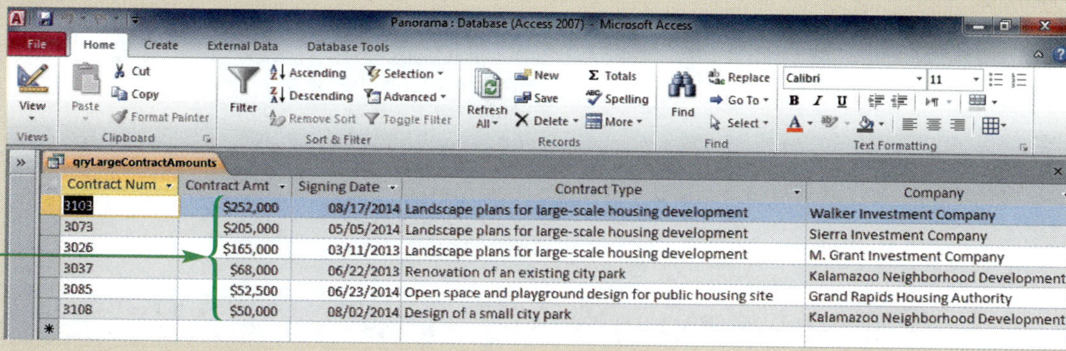


Because Taylor won't need to run this query again, you won't save it.

5. Close the query without saving it.
6. If you are not continuing on to the next session, close the Panorama database, and then click the **Yes** button if necessary to empty the Clipboard.

Oren and Taylor will use the information provided by the queries you created to analyze the business and to contact customers. In the next session, you will enhance the tblCustomer and tblContract tables.

REVIEW

## Session 5.2 Quick Check

1. What is the purpose of a crosstab query?
2. What are the four query wizards you can use to create a new query?
3. What is a find duplicates query?
4. What does a find unmatched query do?
5. What happens when you set a query's Top Values property?
6. What happens if you set a query's Top Values property to 2 and the first five records have the same value for the primary sort field?

# SESSION 5.3 VISUAL OVERVIEW

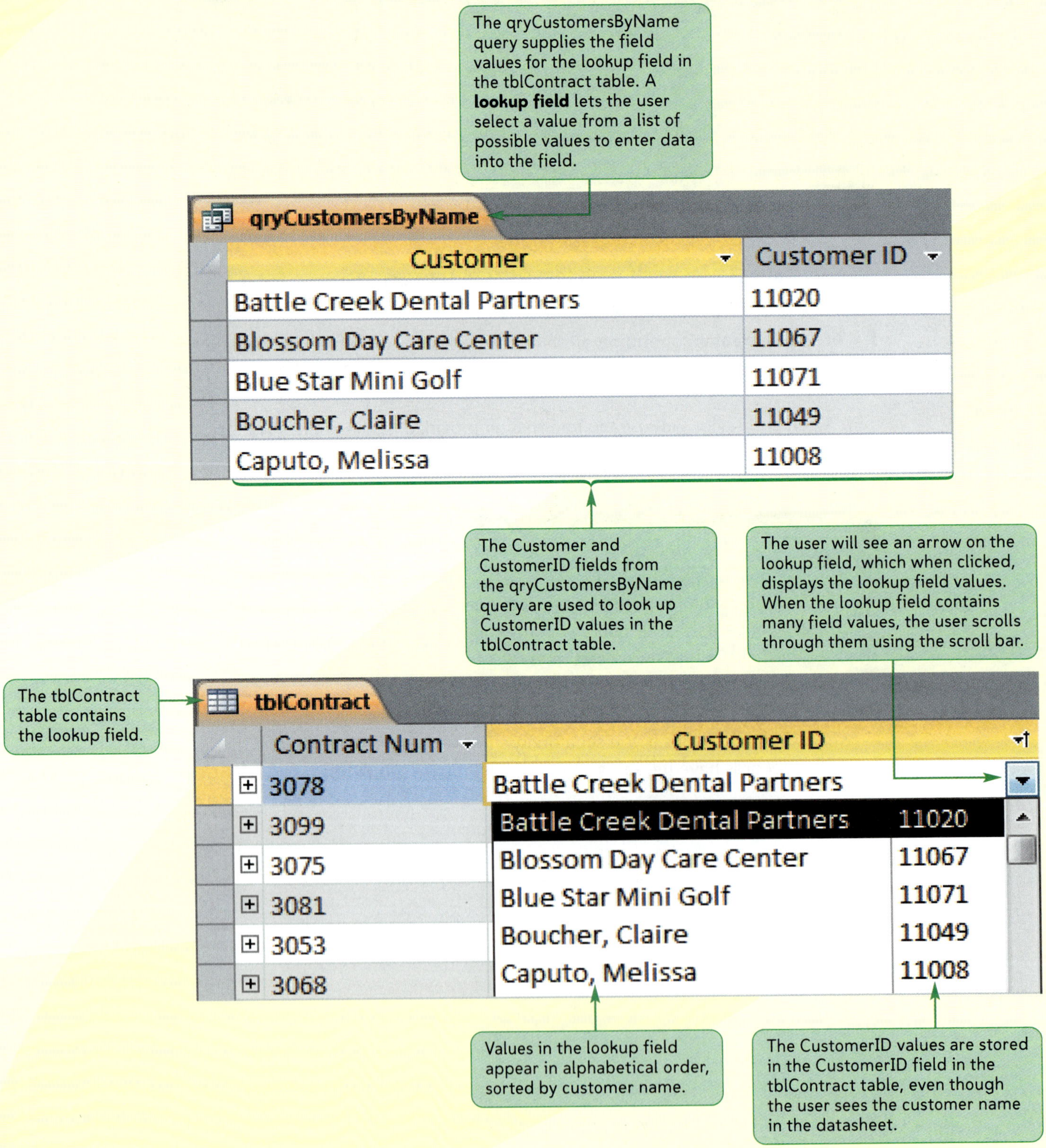

# LOOKUP FIELDS AND INPUT MASKS

The tblCustomer table contains the field that displays values with an input mask. An **input mask** is a predefined format that is used to enter and display data in a field. For example, the input mask displays a value entered as 9876543210 as 987-654-3210. The hyphens in the field value, called **literal display characters**, will not be stored in the database.

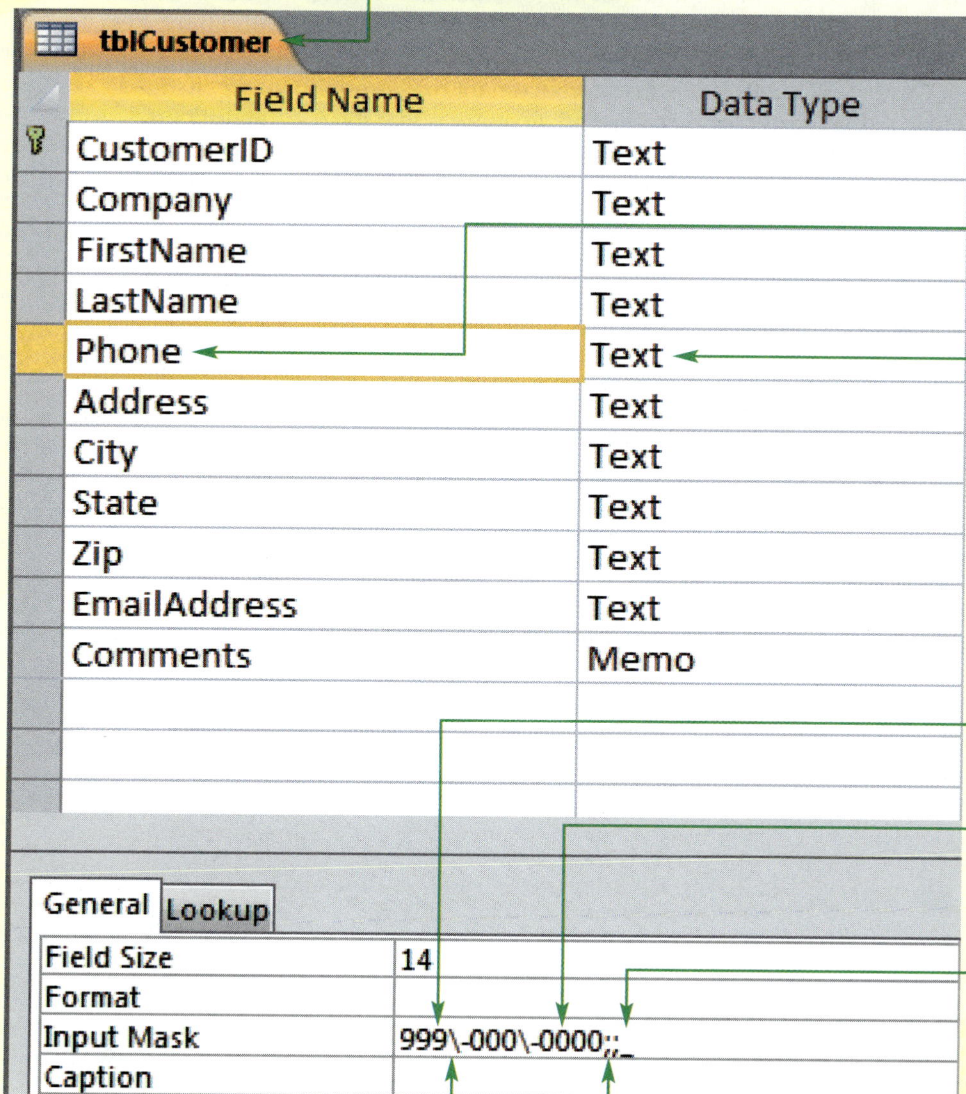


The Phone field uses an input mask to format displayed field values.

The Phone field uses the Text data type. You can create an input mask for field with the Text and Number data types.

A nine indicates a digit or space in the field value; entry is optional.

A zero indicates that only a digit can be entered in the field value; entry is required.

The character after the ;; indicates what to display as a field value is being entered. In this case, the underscore will be displayed as the user enters a phone number.

The backslash (\) indicates that the following character is treated as a literal display character. In this input mask, the backslash indicates that the hyphen that follows it is a literal display character.

Two semicolons (;;) indicate whether to store the literal display character in the database. In this case, ;; indicates not to store the literal display characters.

## Creating a Lookup Field

The tblContract table in the Panorama database contains information about the contracts Belmont Landscapes has signed with its customers. Sarah wants to make entering data in the table easier for her staff. In particular, data entry is easier if they do not need to remember the correct CustomerID field values for each customer. Because the tblCustomer and tblContract tables have a one-to-many relationship, Sarah asks you to change the tblContract table's CustomerID field, which is a foreign key to the tblCustomer table, to a lookup field. As noted earlier, a lookup field lets the user select a value from a list of possible values. For the CustomerID field, the user will be able to select a customer's ID number from the list of customer names in the qryCustomersByName query rather than having to remember the correct CustomerID field value. Access will store the CustomerID in the tblContract table, but both the customer name and the CustomerID field value will appear in Datasheet view when entering or changing a CustomerID field value. This arrangement makes entering and changing CustomerID field values easier for the user and guarantees that the CustomerID field value is valid. You use a **Lookup Wizard field** in Access to create a lookup field in a table.

Sarah asks you to change the CustomerID field in the tblContract table to a lookup field. You begin by opening the tblContract table in Design view.

### To change the CustomerID field to a lookup field:

1. If you took a break after the previous session, make sure that the Panorama database is open.

   **Trouble?** If the Security Warning is displayed below the Ribbon, click the Enable Content button next to the Security Warning.

2. If necessary, open the Navigation Pane, and then open the **tblContract** table in Design view.

3. Click the right side of the **Data Type** box for the CustomerID field to display the list of data types, and then click **Lookup Wizard**. A message box appears, warning you to delete the relationship between the tblCustomer and tblContract tables if you want to make the CustomerID field a lookup field. See Figure 5-29.

**TIP**

You can display the arrow and the menu simultaneously if you click the box near its right side.

**Figure 5-29** Warning message for an existing table relationship

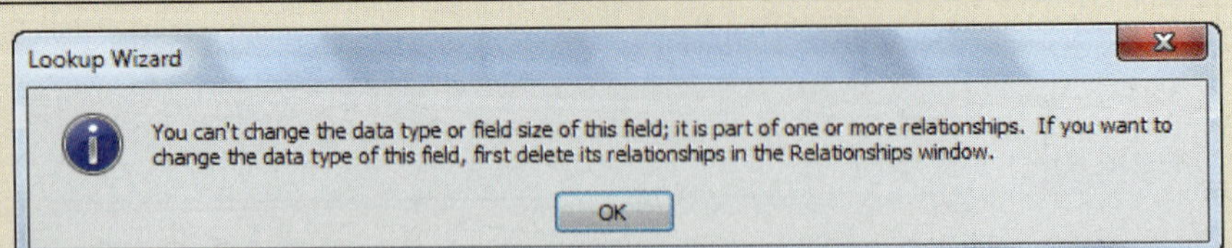


Access will use the lookup field to form the one-to-many relationship between the tblCustomer and tblContract tables, so you don't need the relationship you previously defined between the two tables.

4. Click the **OK** button, close the tblContract table, and then click the **No** button when asked if you want to save the table design changes.

5. Click the **Database Tools** tab on the Ribbon, and then in the Relationships group on the Database Tools tab, click the **Relationships** button to open the Relationships window.

6. Right-click the join line between the tblCustomer and tblContract tables, click **Delete**, and then click the **Yes** button to confirm the deletion.

**Trouble?** If the Delete command does not appear on the shortcut menu, click a blank area in the Relationships window to close the shortcut menu, and then repeat Step 6.

7. Close the Relationships window.

Now you can resume changing the CustomerID field to a lookup field.

## To finish changing the CustomerID field to a lookup field:

1. Open the **tblContract** table in Design view.
2. Click the right side of the **Data Type** box for the CustomerID field, and then click **Lookup Wizard**. The first Lookup Wizard dialog box opens.

   This dialog box lets you specify a list of allowed values for the CustomerID field in a record in the tblContract table. You can specify a table or query from which users select the value, or you can enter a new list of values. You want the CustomerID values to come from the qryCustomersByName query.
3. Make sure the option for looking up the values in another table or query is selected, and then click the **Next** button to display the next Lookup Wizard dialog box.
4. Click the **Queries** option button in the View section to display the list of queries, click **Query: qryCustomersByName**, and then click the **Next** button to display the next Lookup Wizard dialog box. See Figure 5-30.

**Figure 5-30** Selecting the lookup fields

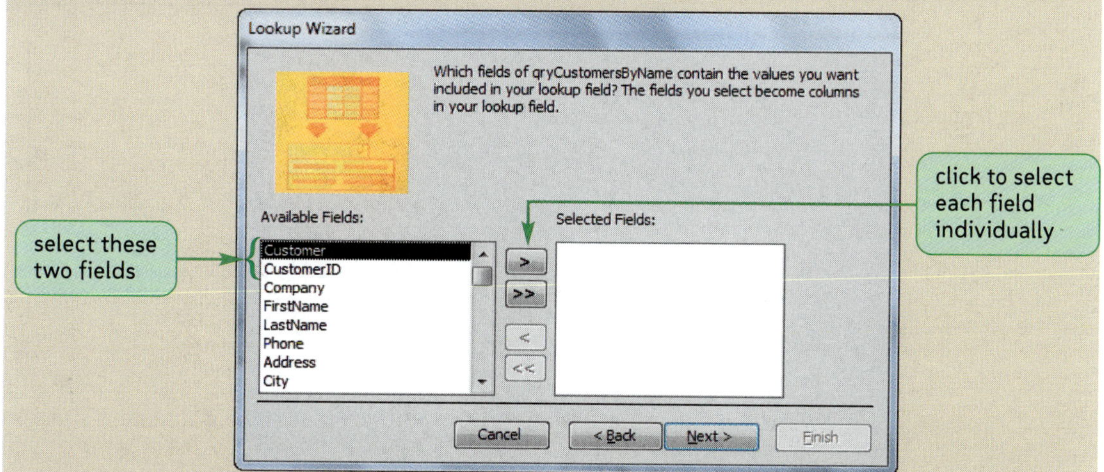


This dialog box lets you select the lookup fields from the qryCustomersByName query. You need to select the CustomerID field because it's the common field that links the query and the tblContract table. You also must select the Customer field because Sarah wants the user to be able to select from a list of customer names when entering a new contract record or changing an existing CustomerID field value.

5. Click **Customer** (if necessary), click the > button to move the Customer field to the Selected Fields box, click **CustomerID** (if necessary), click the > button to move the CustomerID field to the Selected Fields box, and then click the

**Next** button to display the next Lookup Wizard dialog box. This dialog box lets you choose a sort order for the box entries. Sarah wants the entries to appear in ascending Customer order. Note that ascending is the default sort order.

6. Click the **1** arrow, click **Customer**, and then click the **Next** button to open the next dialog box.

   In this dialog box, you can adjust the widths of the lookup columns. Note that when you resize a column to its best fit, Access resizes the column so that the widest column heading and the visible field values fit the column width. However, some field values that aren't visible in this dialog box might be wider than the column width, so you must scroll down the column to make sure you don't have to repeat the column resizing.

**TIP**

If you need to rearrange the columns in a lookup field, you can click a column heading and drag it to the left or right.

7. Click the **Customer** column selector, press and hold down the **Shift** key, click the **CustomerID** column selector to select both columns, release the **Shift** key, and then place the pointer on the right edge of the CustomerID field column heading. When the pointer changes to a ↔ shape, double-click to resize the columns to their best fit, and then scroll down the columns, and repeat the resizing as necessary. When you are finished, press **Ctrl + Home** to scroll back to the top of the Customer column. See Figure 5-31.

**Figure 5-31 Adjusting the widths of the lookup columns**

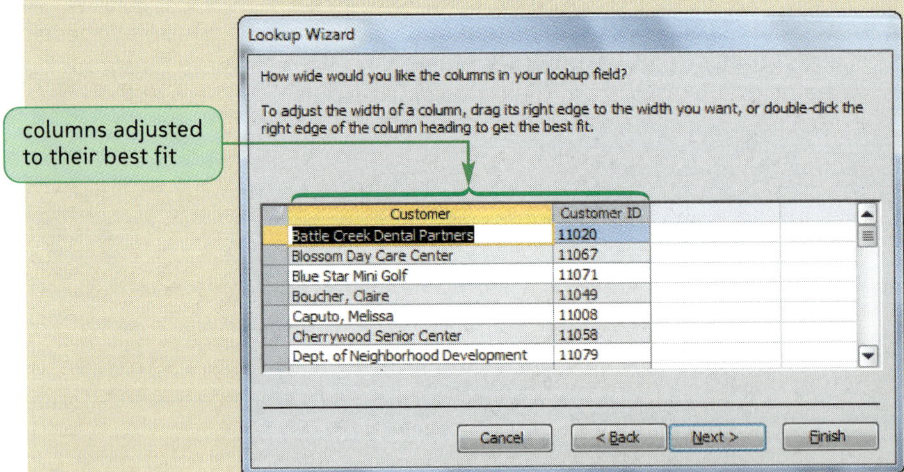


8. Click the **Next** button.

   In the next dialog box, you select the field you want to store in the table. You'll store the CustomerID field in the tblContract table because it's the foreign key to the tblCustomer table.

9. Click **CustomerID** in the Available Fields box, and then click the **Next** button.

   In the next dialog box, you specify the field name for the lookup field. Because you'll be storing the CustomerID field in the table, you'll accept the default field name, CustomerID.

10. Click the **Finish** button, and then save the table.

    The Data Type value for the CustomerID field is still Text because this field contains text data. However, when you update the field, Access uses the CustomerID field value to look up and display in the tblContract table datasheet both the Customer and CustomerID field values from the qryCustomersByName query.

In reviewing contracts recently, Sarah noticed that the CustomerID field value stored in the tblContract table for contract number 3030 is incorrect. She asks you to test the new lookup field to select the correct field value. To do so, you need to switch to Datasheet view.

## To change the CustomerID field value:

1. Switch to Datasheet view, and then resize the **CustomerID** column to its best fit.

   Notice that the Customer ID column displays Customer field values, even though the CustomerID field values are stored in the table.

2. For Contract Num 3030, click **Lily's Boutique** in the Customer ID column, and then click the **arrow** to display the list of Customer and CustomerID field values from the qryCustomersByName query. See Figure 5-32.

**Figure 5-32** List of Customer and CustomerID field values

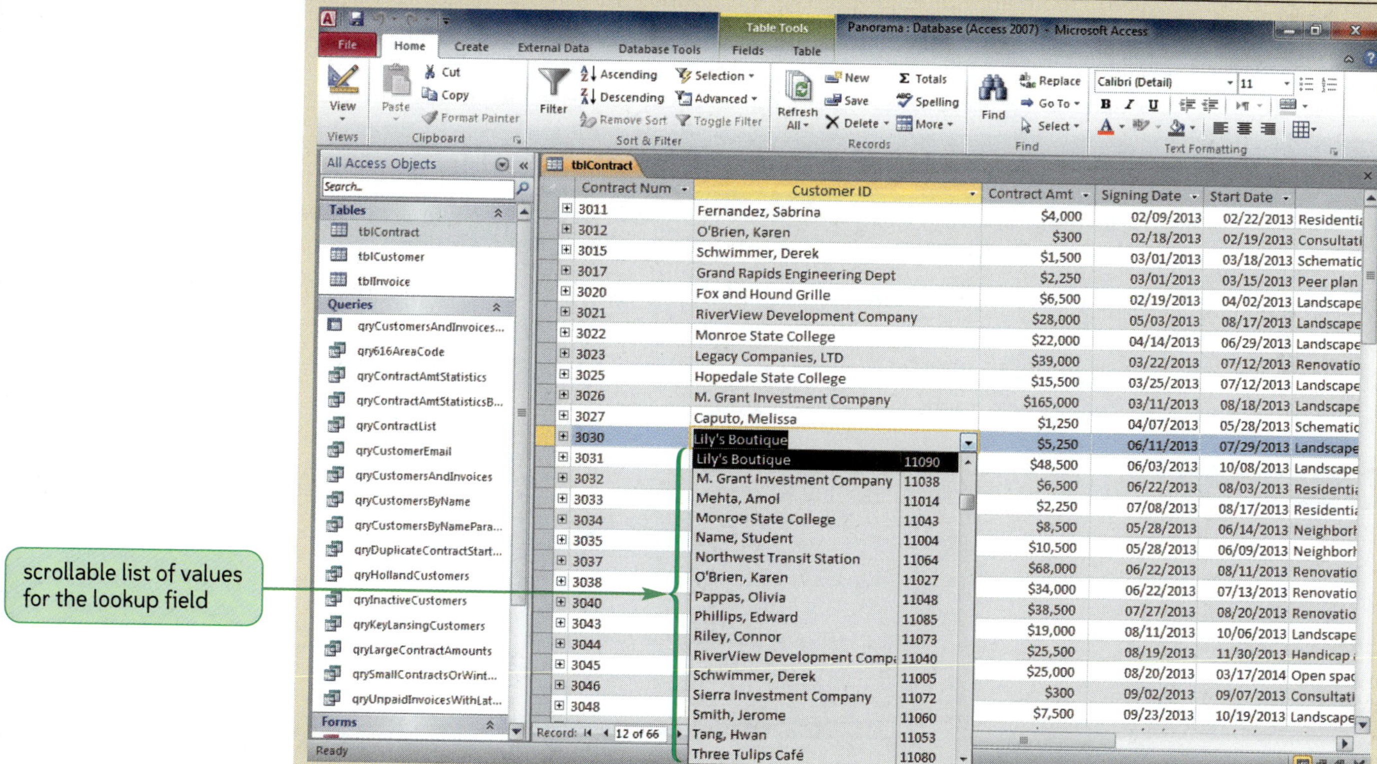


The customer for contract 3030 is Michael Ingram, so you need to select his entry in the list to change the CustomerID field value.

3. Scroll up the list, and then click **Ingram, Michael** to select that value to display in the datasheet and to store the CustomerID field value of 11042 in the table. The list closes and "Ingram, Michael" appears in the Customer ID column.

4. Save and close the tblContract table.

   Sarah wants you to make changes to the design of the tblCustomer table, so you'll open the table in preparation for the changes.

5. Open the **tblCustomer** table in Datasheet view, and then close the Navigation Pane.

Sarah asks you to change the appearance of the Phone field in the tblCustomer table to a standard telephone number format.

## Using the Input Mask Wizard

The Phone field in the tblCustomer table is a 10-digit number that's difficult to read because it appears with none of the special formatting characters usually associated with a telephone number. For example, the Phone field value for Sabrina Fernandez, which appears as 6168663901, would be more readable in any of the following formats: 616-866-3901, 616.866.3901, 616/866-3901, or (616) 866-3901. Sarah asks you to use the (616) 866-3901 style for the Phone field.

Sarah wants the parentheses and hyphens to appear as literal display characters whenever users enter Phone field values. As noted earlier, a literal display character is a special character that automatically appears in specific positions of a field value; users don't need to type literal display characters. To include these characters, you need to create an input mask, a predefined format used to enter and display data in a field. An easy way to create an input mask is to use the **Input Mask Wizard**, an Access tool that guides you in creating a predefined format for a field. You must use the Input Mask Wizard in Design view.

### To use the Input Mask Wizard for the Phone field:

1. Switch to Design view, and then click the **Phone Field Name** box to make that row the current row and to display its Field Properties options.
2. Click the **Input Mask** box in the Field Properties pane. A Build button [...] appears at the right edge of the Input Mask box.
3. Click the **Build** button [...] in the Input Mask box. The first Input Mask Wizard dialog box opens. See Figure 5-33.

Figure 5-33 Input Mask Wizard dialog box

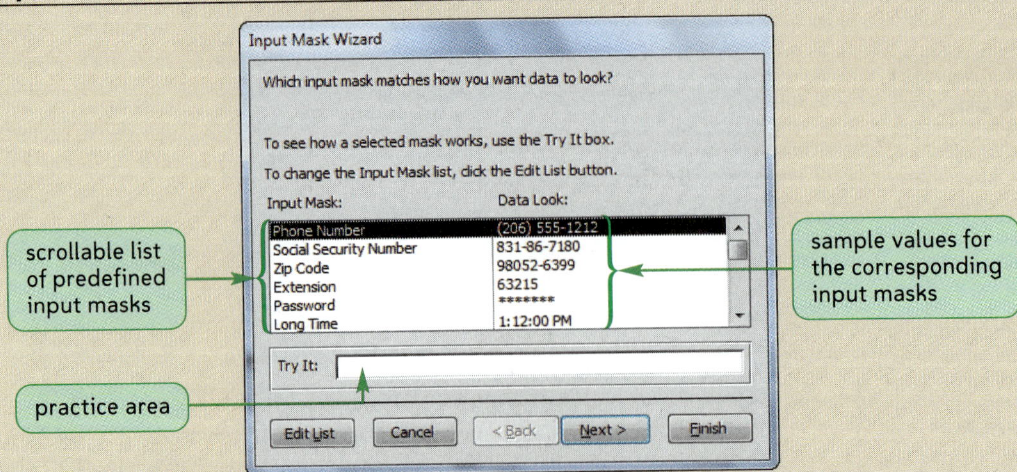


You can scroll the Input Mask box, select the input mask you want, and then enter representative values to practice using the input mask.

4. If necessary, click **Phone Number** in the Input Mask box to select it.
5. Click the far left side of the **Try It** box. (___) ___-____ appears in the Try It box. As you type a phone number, Access replaces the underscores, which are placeholder characters.

   **Trouble?** If your insertion point is not immediately to the right of the left parenthesis, press the ← key until it is.

6. Type **9876543210** to practice entering a sample phone number. The input mask formats the typed value as (987) 654-3210.
7. Click the **Next** button. The next Input Mask Wizard dialog box opens. In it, you can change the input mask and placeholder character. Because you can change an input mask easily after the Input Mask Wizard finishes, you'll accept all wizard defaults.
8. Click the **Finish** button, and then click to the right of the value in the Input Mask box. The Input Mask Wizard creates the phone number input mask, placing it in the Input Mask box for the Phone field. See Figure 5-34.

**Figure 5-34** **Phone number input mask created by the Input Mask Wizard**

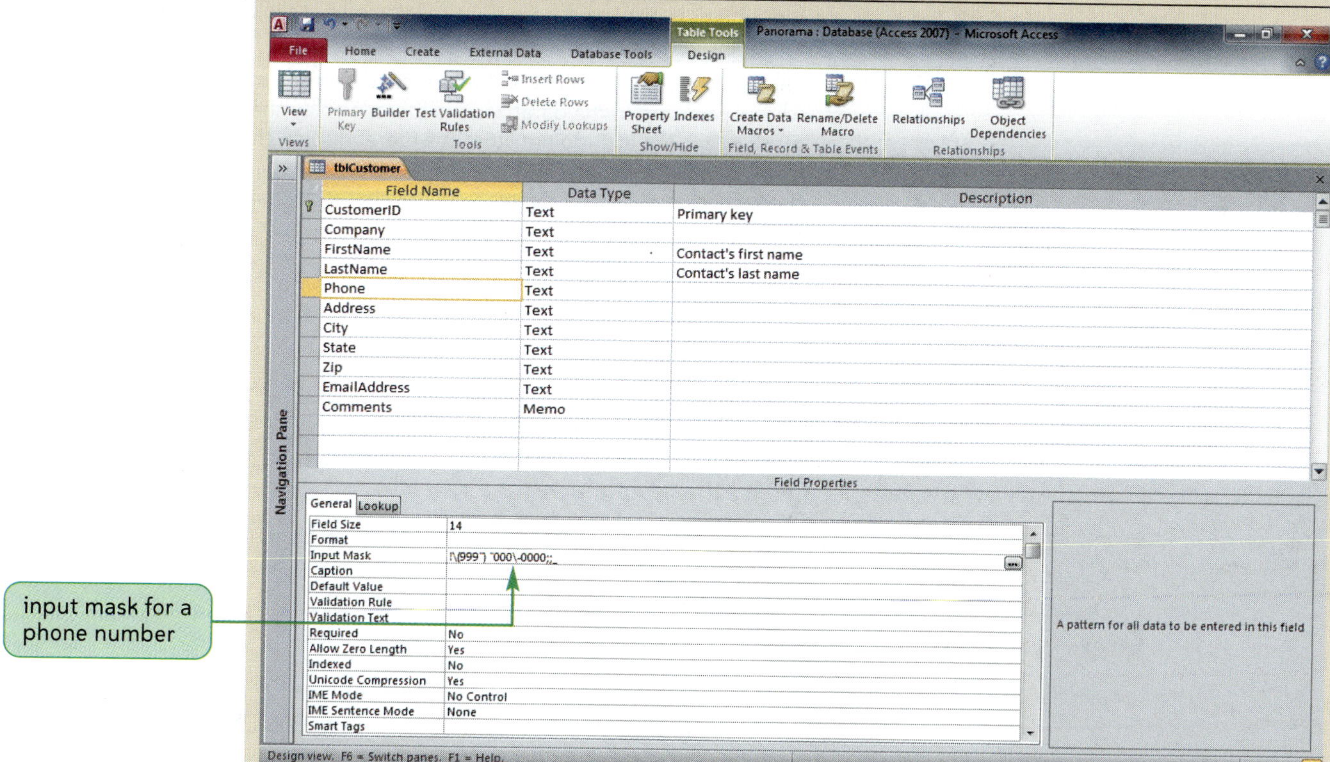


The characters used in a field's input mask restrict the data you can enter in the field, as shown in Figure 5-35. Other characters, such as the left and right parentheses in the phone number input mask, that appear in an input mask are literal display characters.

**Figure 5-35** **Input mask characters**

| Input Mask Character | Description |
|---|---|
| 0 | Digit only must be entered. Entry is required. |
| 9 | Digit or space can be entered. Entry is optional. |
| # | Digit, space, or a plus or minus sign can be entered. Entry is optional. |
| L | Letter only must be entered. Entry is required. |
| ? | Letter only can be entered. Entry is optional. |
| A | Letter or digit must be entered. Entry is required. |
| a | Letter or digit can be entered. Entry is optional. |
| & | Any character or a space must be entered. Entry is required. |
| C | Any character or a space can be entered. Entry is optional. |
| > | All characters that follow are displayed in uppercase. |
| < | All characters that follow are displayed in lowercase. |
| " | Enclosed characters treated as literal display characters. |
| \ | Following character treated as a literal display character. This is the same as enclosing a single character in quotation marks. |
| ! | Input mask is displayed from right to left, rather than the default of left to right. Characters typed into the mask always fill in from left to right. |
| ;; | The character between the first and second semicolon determines whether to store in the database the literal display characters. If left blank or a value of 1, do not store the literal display characters. If a value of 0, store the literal display characters. The character following the second semicolon is the placeholder character that will appear in the displayed input mask. |

Sarah wants to view the Phone field with the default input mask.

### To view and change the input mask for the Phone field:

1. Save the table, and then switch to Datasheet view. The Phone field values now have the format specified by the input mask.

   Sarah decides that she would prefer to omit the parentheses around the area codes and use only hyphens as separators in the displayed Phone field values, so you'll change the input mask in Design view.

2. Switch to Design view.

   The input mask is to !\(999") "000\-0000;;_. The backslash character (\) causes the character that follows it to appear as a literal display character. Characters enclosed in quotation marks also appear as literal display characters. (See Figure 5-35.)

   If you omit the backslashes preceding the hyphens, Access will automatically insert them when you press the Tab key. However, Access doesn't add backslashes automatically for other literal display characters, such as periods and slashes, so it's best to always type the backslashes.

3. Change the input mask to **999\-000\-0000;;_** in the Input Mask box for the Phone field, and then press the **Tab** key.

   Because you've modified a field property, the Property Update Options button appears to the left of the Input Mask property.

4. Click the **Property Update Options** button, and then click **Update Input Mask everywhere Phone is used**. The Update Properties dialog box opens. See Figure 5-36.

**Figure 5-36 Update Properties dialog box**

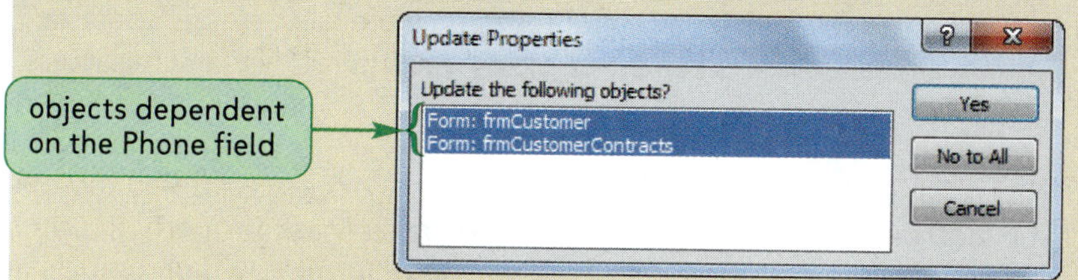


Because the frmCustomer and frmCustomerContracts forms display Phone field values from the tblCustomer table, Access will automatically change the Phone field's Input Mask property in these objects to your new input mask. This capability to update field properties in objects automatically when you modify a table field property is called **property propagation**. Although the Update Properties dialog box displays no queries, property propagation also does occur with queries automatically. Property propagation is limited to field properties such as the Decimal Places, Description, Format, and Input Mask properties.

5. Click the **Yes** button, save the table, switch to Datasheet view, and then resize the Phone column to its best fit. The Phone field values now have the format Sarah requested. See Figure 5-37.

**Figure 5-37 After changing the Phone field input mask**

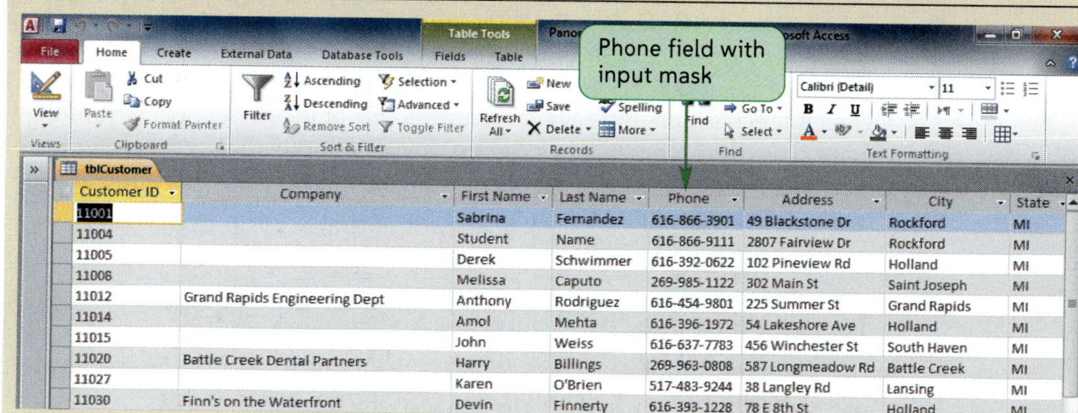


Because Sarah wants her staff to store only standard 10-digit U.S. phone numbers for customers, the input mask you've created will enforce the standard entry and display format that Sarah desires.

INSIGHT

*Understanding When to Use Input Masks*

An input mask is appropriate for a field only if all field values have a consistent format. For example, you can use an input mask with hyphens as literal display characters to store U.S. phone numbers in a consistent format of 987-654-3210. However, a multinational company would not be able to use an input mask to store phone numbers from all countries because international phone numbers do not have a consistent format. For another example, U.S. zip codes have a consistent format, and you could use an input mask of 00000#9999 to enter and display U.S. zip codes such as 98765 and 98765-4321, but you could not use an input mask if you need to store and display foreign postal codes in the same field. If you need to store and display phone numbers, zip/postal codes, and other fields in a variety of formats, it's best to define them as Text fields without an input mask so users can enter the correct literal display characters.

After the change to the Phone field's input mask, Access gave you the option to update, selectively and automatically, the Phone field's Input Mask property in other objects in the database. Sarah asks if there's an easy way to determine which objects are affected by changes made to other objects. To show Sarah how to determine the dependencies among objects in an Access database, you'll open the Object Dependencies pane.

# Identifying Object Dependencies

An **object dependency** exists between two objects when a change to the properties of data in one object affects the properties of data in the other object. Dependencies between Access objects, such as tables, queries, and forms, can occur in various ways. For example, the tblContract and tblInvoice tables are dependent on each other because they have a one-to-many relationship. As another example, because the tblContract table uses the qryCustomersByName query to obtain the Customer field to display along with the CustomerID field, these two objects have a dependency. Any query, form, or other object that uses fields from the tblCustomer table is dependent on the tblCustomer table. Any form or report that uses fields from a query is directly dependent on the query and is indirectly dependent on the tables that provide the data to the query. Large databases contain hundreds of objects, so it is useful to have a way to easily view the dependencies among objects before you attempt to delete or modify an object. The **Object Dependencies pane** displays a collapsible list of the dependencies among the objects in an Access database; you click the list's expand indicators to show or hide different levels of dependencies. Next, you'll open the Object Dependencies pane to show Sarah the object dependencies in the Panorama database.

**To open and use the Object Dependencies pane:**

1. Click the **Database Tools** tab on the Ribbon, and then, in the Relationships group, click the **Object Dependencies** button to open the Object Dependencies pane, and then drag the left edge of the pane to the left until the horizontal scroll bar at the bottom of the pane disappears. See Figure 5-38.

**Figure 5-38** After opening the Object Dependencies pane

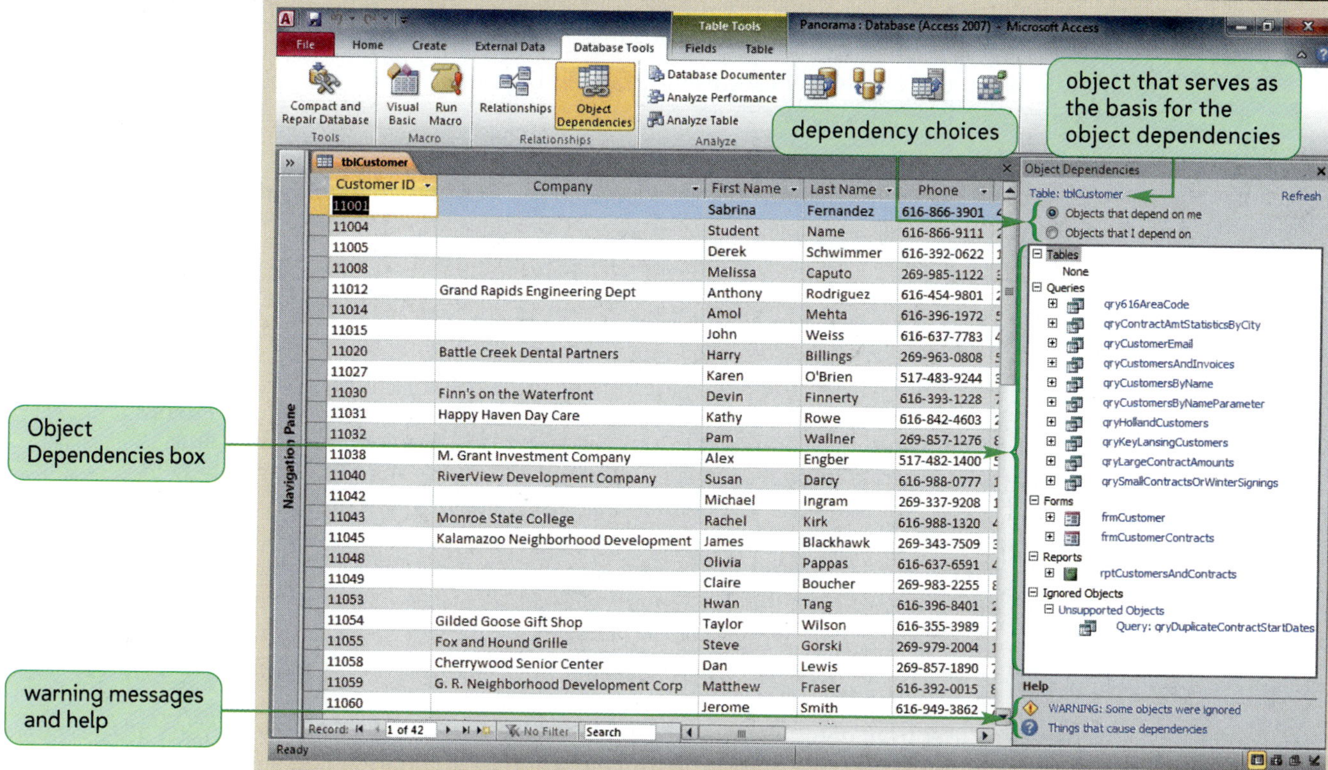


**Trouble?** If the "Objects that depend on me" option button is not selected, click the option button to select it.

The Object Dependencies pane displays the objects that depend on the tblCustomer table, the object name that appears at the top of the pane. If you change the design of the tblCustomer table, the change might affect objects in the pane. Changing a property for a field in the tblCustomer table that's also used by another listed object affects that other object. If the other object does not use the field you are changing, that other object is not affected.

Objects listed in the Ignored Objects portion of the box might, or might not, have an object dependency with the tblCustomer table, and you'd have to review them individually. The Help section at the bottom of the pane displays links for further information about object dependencies.

2. Click the **frmCustomer** link in the Object Dependencies pane. The frmCustomer form opens in Design view. All the fields in the form are fields from the tblCustomer table, which is why the form has an object dependency with the table.
3. Switch to Form view for the frmCustomer form. Note that the Phone field value displays using the input mask you applied to the field in the tblCustomer table. Access propagated this change from the table to the form.
4. Close the frmCustomer form, open the Navigation Pane, open the **tblContract** table in Datasheet view, and then click the **Refresh** link near the top of the Object Dependencies pane. The Object Dependencies box now displays the objects that depend on the tblContract table.
5. Click the **Objects that I depend on** option button near the top of the pane to view the objects that affect the tblContract table.

6. Click the **expand indicator** ⊞ for the qryCustomersByName query in the Object Dependencies pane. The list expands to display the tblCustomer table, which is another table that the query depends upon.
7. Close the tblContract table, close the Object Dependencies pane, and then save and close the tblCustomer table.

Sarah now better understands object dependencies and how to identify them by using the Object Dependencies pane.

# Defining Data Validation Rules

Sarah wants to limit the entry of InvoiceAmt field values in the tblInvoice table to values greater than $10 because Belmont Landscapes does not invoice customers for balances of $10 or less. In addition, Sarah wants to make sure that a SigningDate field value entered in a tblContract table record is chronologically earlier than the StartDate field value in the same record. She's concerned that typing errors might produce incorrect query results and cause other problems. To provide these data-entry capabilities, you'll set field validation properties for the InvoiceAmt field in the tblInvoice table and set table validation properties in the tblContract table.

## Defining Field Validation Rules

To prevent a user from entering an unacceptable value in the InvoiceAmt field, you can create a **field validation rule** that verifies a field value by comparing it to a constant or a set of constants. You create a field validation rule by setting the Validation Rule and the Validation Text field properties. The **Validation Rule property** value specifies the valid values that users can enter in a field. The **Validation Text property** value will be displayed in a dialog box if the user enters an invalid value (in this case, an InvoiceAmt field value of $10 or less). After you set these two InvoiceAmt field properties in the tblInvoice table, Access will prevent users from entering an invalid InvoiceAmt field value in the tblInvoice table and in all current and future queries and future forms that include the InvoiceAmt field.

You'll now set the Validation Rule and Validation Text properties for the InvoiceAmt field in the tblInvoice table.

### To create and test a field validation rule for the InvoiceAmt field:

1. Open the **tblInvoice** table in Design view, close the Navigation Pane, and then click the **InvoiceAmt Field Name** box to make that row the current row.

   To make sure that the only values entered in theInvoiceAmt field are greater than 10, you'll use the > comparison operator in the Validation Rule box.
2. In the Field Properties pane, click the **Validation Rule** box, type **>10**, and then press the **Tab** key.

You can set the Validation Text property to a value that appears in a dialog box that opens if a user enters a value not listed in the Validation Rule box.

3. Type **Invoice amounts must be greater than 10** in the Validation Text box. See Figure 5-39.

**Figure 5-39** Validation properties for the InvoiceAmt field

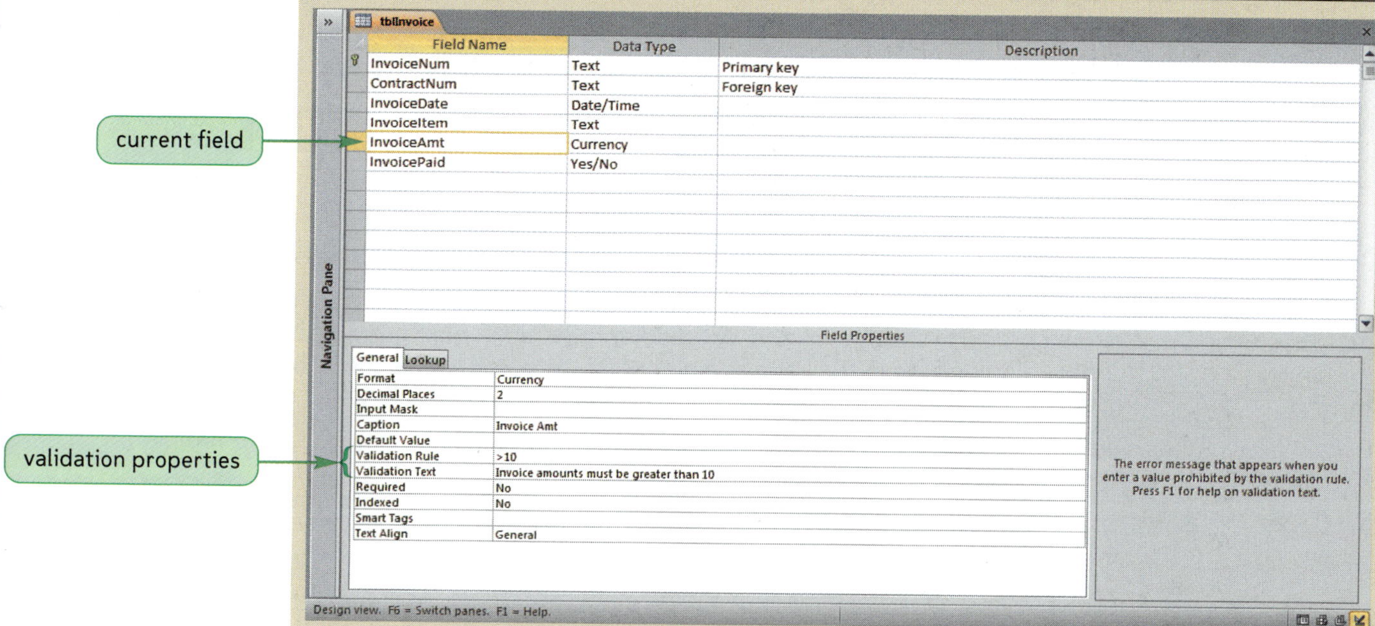


You can now save the table design changes and then test the validation properties.

4. Save the table, and then click the **Yes** button when asked if you want to test the existing InvoiceAmt field values in the tblInvoice table against the new validation rule.

   Access tests the existing records in the tblInvoice table against the validation rule. If any record violates the rule, you are prompted to continue testing or to revert to the previous Validation Rule property setting. Next, you'll test the validation rule.

5. Switch to Datasheet view, select **$1,500.00** in the first row's InvoiceAmt field box, type **5**, and then press the **Tab** key. A dialog box opens containing the message "Invoice amounts must be greater than 10," which is the Validation Text property setting you created in Step 3.

6. Click the **OK** button, and then press the **Esc** key. The first row's InvoiceAmt field value again has its original value, $1,500.00.

7. Close the tblInvoice table.

Now that you've finished entering the field validation rule for the InvoiceAmt field in the tblInvoice table, you'll enter the table validation rule for the date fields in the tblContract table.

## Defining Table Validation Rules

To make sure that a user enters a SigningDate field value in the tblContract table that is chronologically earlier than the record's StartDate field value, you can create a **table validation rule** that compares one field value in a table record to another field value in the same record to verify their relative accuracy. Once again, you'll use the Validation Rule and Validation Text properties, but this time you'll set these properties for the table instead of for an individual field.

### To create and test a table validation rule in the tblContract table:

Be sure "Table Properties" is listed as the selection type in the property sheet.

1. Open the Navigation Pane, open the **tblContract** table in Design view, and then, in the Show/Hide group on the Design tab, click the **Property Sheet** button to open the property sheet for the table.

   To make sure that each SigningDate field value is chronologically earlier than, or less than, each StartDate field value, you'll compare the two field values in the Validation Rule box for the table.

Be sure brackets enclose each of the two field names.

2. In the property sheet, click the **Validation Rule** box, type **Si**, press the **Tab** key to select SigningDate in the AutoComplete box, type **<St**, press the **Tab** key to select StartDate in the AutoComplete box, and then press the **Tab** key.

   **Trouble?** If necessary, drag the left edge of the property sheet to the left until you can see the entire value in the Validation Rule box.

3. Type **The signing date must be earlier than the start date** in the Validation Text box. See Figure 5-40.

**Figure 5-40** Setting table validation properties

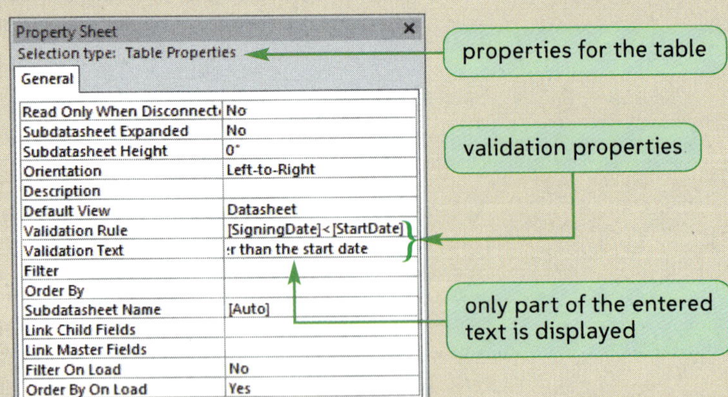


You can now test the validation properties.

4. Close the property sheet, save the table, and then click the **Yes** button when asked if you want to test the existing dates in the tblContract table against the new validation rule.

5. Close the Navigation Pane, switch to Datasheet view, click the Signing Date column value in the first record, click the **date picker** icon to the right of the date, click **27** in the calendar control to change the date to 2/27/2013, press the **Tab** key to advance to the Start Date column, and then press the **Tab** key two more times to complete your changes to the record. A dialog box opens containing the message "The signing date must be earlier than the start date," which is the Validation Text property setting you entered in Step 3.

Unlike field validation rule violations, which Access detects immediately after you finish a field entry and advance to another field, Access detects table validation rule violations when you finish all changes to the current record and advance to another record.

6. Click the **OK** button, and then press the **Esc** key to undo your change to the Signing Date column value.
7. Close the tblContract table.

PROSKILLS

*Problem Solving: Perfecting Data Quality*

It's important that you design accurate queries, forms, and reports and that you test them thoroughly. But the key to any database is the accuracy of the data stored in its tables. It's critical that the data be as error-free as possible. Most companies employ people who spend many hours tracking down and correcting errors and discrepancies in their data, and you can greatly assist and minimize their problem solving by using as many database features as possible to ensure the data is correct from the start. Among these features for fields are selecting the proper data type, setting default values whenever possible, restricting the permitted values by using field and table validation rules, enforcing referential integrity, and forcing users to select values from lists instead of typing the values. Likewise, having an arsenal of queries, such as find duplicates and top values queries, available to users will expedite the work they do to find and correct data errors.

Based on a request from Sarah, Lucia added a Memo field to the tblCustomer table, and now you'll review Lucia's work.

## Working with Memo Fields

You use a Memo field to store long comments and explanations. Text fields are limited to 255 characters, but Memo fields can hold up to 65,535 characters. In addition, Text fields limit you to plain text with no special formatting, but you can define Memo fields either to store plain text similar to Text fields or to store rich text, which you can selectively format with options such as bold, italic, and different fonts and colors.

You'll review the Memo field, named Comments, that Lucia added to the tblCustomer table.

### To review the Memo field in the tblCustomer table:

1. Open the Navigation Pane, open the **tblCustomer** table in Datasheet view, and then close the Navigation Pane.

   If you scroll to the right to view the Comments field, you'll no longer be able to identify which customer applies to a row because the Company, First Name, and Last Name columns will be hidden. You'll freeze those three columns so they remain visible in the datasheet as you scroll to the right.

2. Click the **Company** column selector, press and hold down the **Shift** key, click the **Last Name** column selector, and then release the **Shift** key to select the Company, First Name, and Last Name columns.

3. In the Records group on Home tab, click the **More** button, and then click **Freeze Fields**. The three selected columns shift to the left and are now the three leftmost columns in the datasheet.
4. Scroll to the right until you see the Comments column. Notice that the Company, First Name, and Last Name columns, the three leftmost columns, remain visible. See Figure 5-41.

**Figure 5-41** **Freezing three datasheet columns**

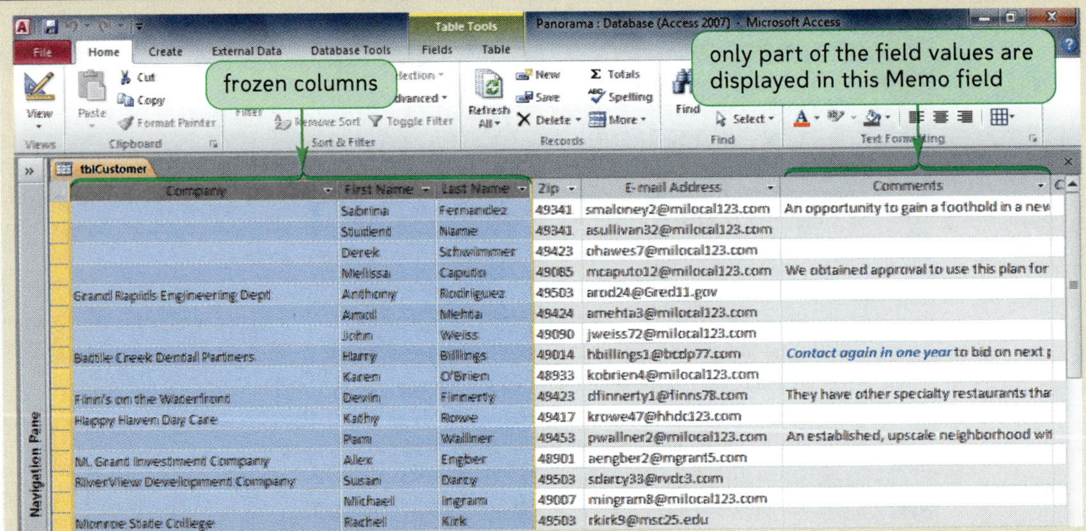


The Comments column is a Memo field that Belmont Landscapes staff members use to store notes, explanations, and other commentary about the customer. Notice that the Comments field value for Battle Creek Dental Partners displays rich text, using a bold, italic, and blue font. The Comments field values are partially hidden because the datasheet column is not wide enough. You'll view the first record's Comments field value in the Zoom dialog box.

5. Click the **Comments** box for the first record, hold down the **Shift** key, press the **F2** key, and then release the **Shift** key. The Zoom dialog box displays the entire Comments field value.
6. Click the **OK** button to close the Zoom dialog box.

INSIGHT

### *Table Datasheet Row and Column Resizing for Memo Fields*

For Memo fields that contain many characters, you can widen the field's column to view more of its contents by dragging the right edge of the field's column selector to the right or by using the Field Width command when you click the More button in the Records group on the Home tab. However, increasing the column width reduces the number of other columns you can view at the same time. Further, for Memo fields containing thousands of characters, you can't widen the column enough to be able to view the entire contents of the field at one time across the width of the screen. Therefore, increasing the column width of a Memo field seldom makes sense.

Alternatively, you can increase the row height of a datasheet by dragging the bottom edge of a row selector down or by using the Row Height command when you click the More button in the Records group on the Home tab. Increasing the row height causes the text in a Memo field to wrap to the next line, so that you can view multiple lines at one time. Once again, however, for Memo fields containing thousands of characters, you can't increase the row height enough to ensure viewing the entire contents of the field at one time on screen. Additionally, you'd view fewer records at one time, and the row height setting for a table propagates to all queries that have an object dependency with the table. Thus, you shouldn't increase the row height of a table datasheet to accommodate a Memo field.

What is the best way to view the contents of Memo fields that contain a large number of characters? It is best to use the Zoom dialog box in a datasheet, or to use a large scrollable box on a form.

Now you'll review the property settings for the Comments field Lucia added to the tblCustomer table.

#### To review the property settings of the Memo field:

1. Save the table, switch to Design view, click the **Comments Field Name** box to make that row the current row, and then use the scroll bar to scroll to the bottom of the list of properties in the Field Properties pane.
2. Click the **Text Format** box in the Field Properties pane, and then click its **arrow**. The list of available text formats appears in the box. See Figure 5-42.

**Figure 5-42** Viewing the properties for a Memo field

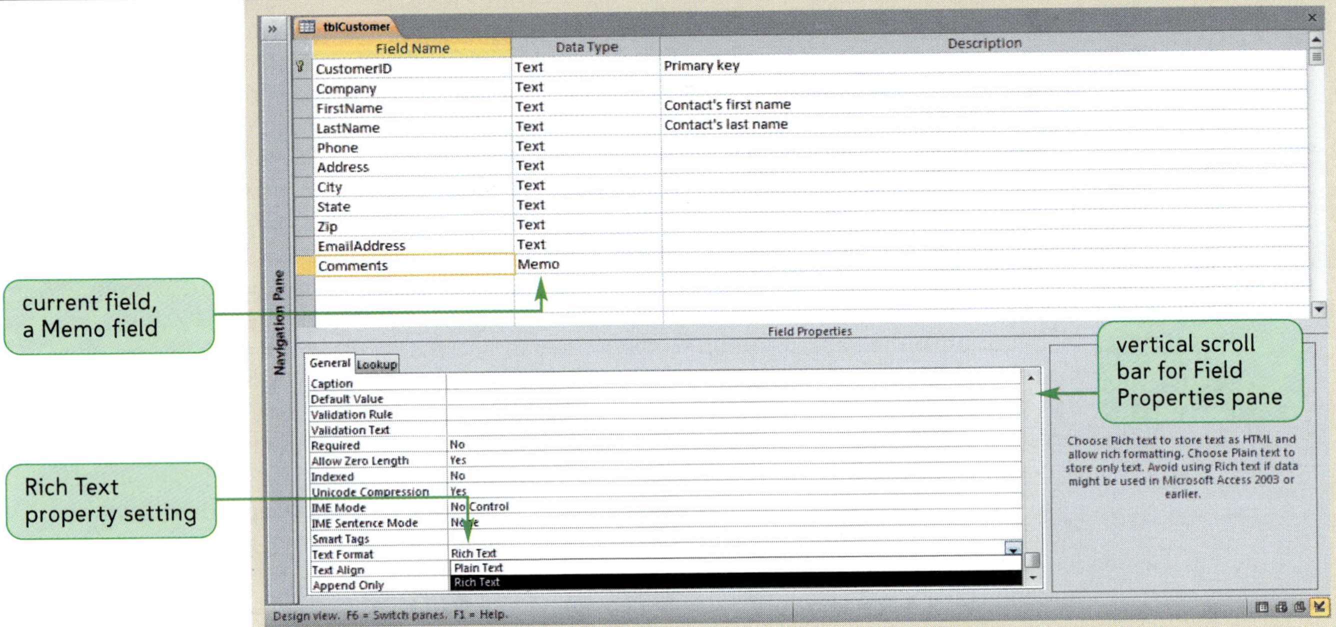


Lucia set the **Text Format property** for the Comments field to Rich Text, which lets you format the field contents using the options in the Font group on the Home tab. The default Text Format property setting for a Memo field is Plain Text, which doesn't allow text formatting.

3. Click the **arrow** on the Text Format box to close the list, and then click the **Append Only** box.

The **Append Only property**, which appears at the bottom of the list of properties, tracks the changes that you make to a Memo field. The default setting of No lets you edit the Memo field value in a normal way. Setting this property to Yes also lets you edit the Memo field value in a normal way but, additionally, causes Access to keep a historical record of all versions of the Memo field value. You can view each version of the field value, along with a date and time stamp of when each version change occurred.

You've finished your review of the Memo field, so you can close the table.

4. Close the tblCustomer table.

When employees at Belmont Landscapes open the Panorama database, a Security Warning might appear below the Ribbon, and they must "enable the content" of the database before beginning their work. Sarah asks if you can eliminate this extra step when employees open the database.

## Designating a Trusted Folder

A database is a file, and files can contain malicious instructions that can damage other files on your computer or files on other computers on your network. Unless you take special steps, Access treats every database as a potential threat to your computer. One such special step is to designate a folder as a trusted folder. A **trusted folder** is a folder on a drive or network that you designate as trusted and where you place databases you know are safe. When you open a database located in a trusted folder, Access treats it as a safe file and no longer displays a Security Warning. You can also place files used with other Microsoft Office programs, such as Word documents and Excel workbooks, in a trusted folder to eliminate warnings when you open them.

Because the Panorama database does not contain harmful instructions, you'll set up a trusted folder in which to store it to eliminate the security warning when a user opens the database.

## To designate a trusted folder:

1. Click the **File** tab on the Ribbon to display Backstage view, and then click **Options** in the navigation bar. The Access Options dialog box opens.
2. In the left section of the dialog box, click **Trust Center**, click the **Trust Center Settings** button in the window on the right to open the Trust Center dialog box, and then in the left section click **Trusted Locations**. The trusted locations for your installation of Access and other trust options are displayed on the right. See Figure 5-43.

**Figure 5-43 Designating a trusted folder**

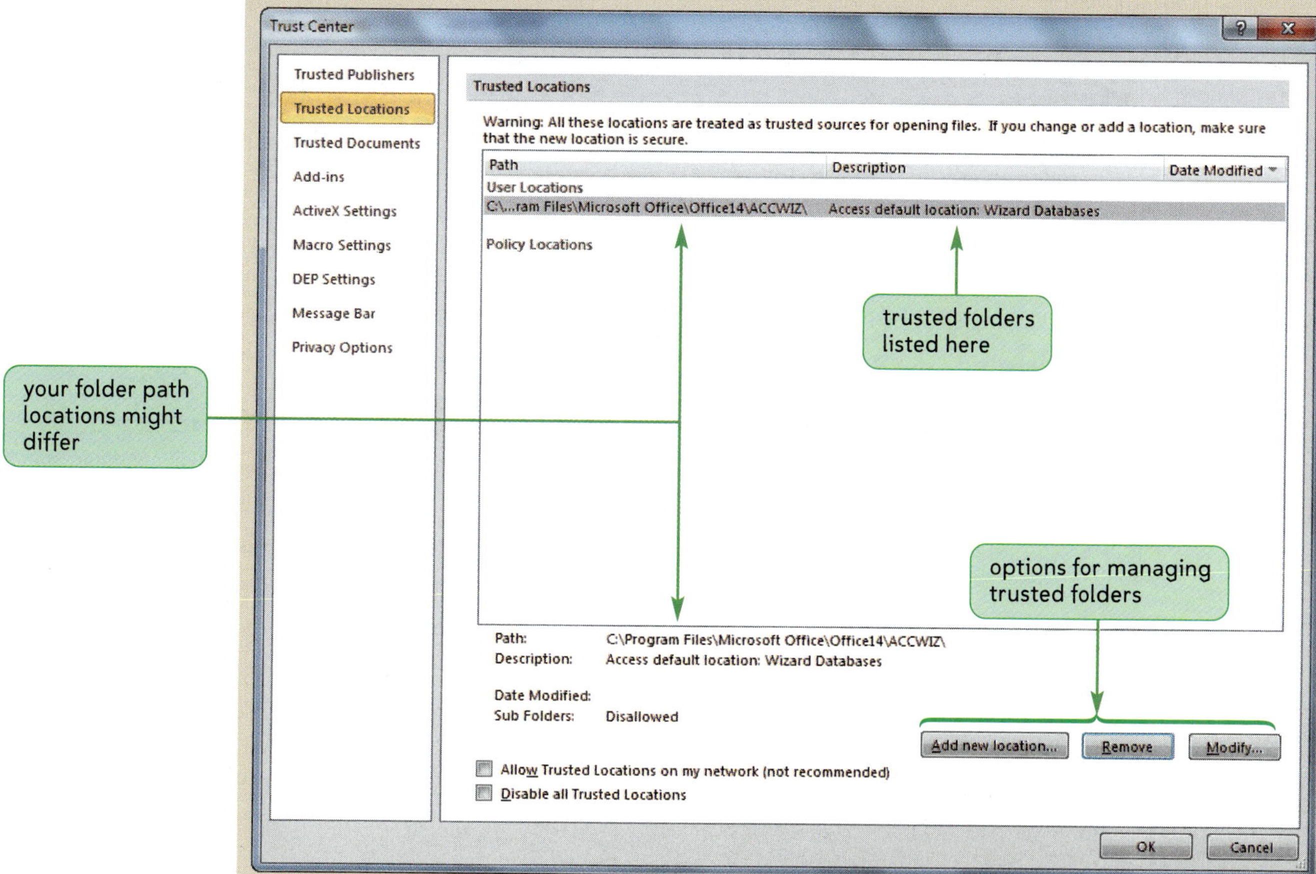


Existing trusted locations appear in the list at the top; and options to add, remove, and modify trusted locations appear at the bottom.

**Trouble?** Check with your instructor before adding a new trusted location. If your instructor tells you not to create a new trusted location, skip to Step 5.

3. Click the **Add new location** button to open the Microsoft Office Trusted Location dialog box, click the **Browse** button, navigate to the Access2\Tutorial folder where your Data Files are stored, and then click the **OK** button.

   You can also choose to designate subfolders of the selected location as trusted locations, but you won't select this option.

4. Click the **OK** button. Access adds the Access2\Tutorial folder to the list of trusted locations.

5. Click the **OK** button to close the Trust Center dialog box, and then click the **OK** button to close the Access Options dialog box.

You've created several queries and completed several table design changes, so you should compact and repair the Panorama database. Lucia doesn't use the Compact on Close option with the Panorama database because it's possible to lose the database if there's a computer malfunction when the Compact on Close operation runs. As a precaution, you'll make a backup copy of the database before you compact and repair it. Making frequent backup copies of your critical files safeguards your data from hardware and software malfunctions, which can occur at any time.

### To backup and compact and repair the Panorama database:

1. Click the **File** tab on the Ribbon, and then click the **Close Database** command to close the Panorama database.

2. Make a backup copy of the Panorama database, preferably to a USB drive or other external medium, using a filename of Backup Panorama_date, where *date* is the current date in the format 2013-02-15, for example, if you made the backup on February 15, 2013.

3. Make sure the Access window is the active window, and then click **Panorama.accdb** in the navigation bar. The database opens, and no Security Warning appears below the Ribbon because the database is located in the trusted location you designated.

   Next, you'll compact and repair the database.

4. Click the **File** tab on the Ribbon, and then click the **Compact & Repair Database** button.

   You've finished the work requested by Belmont Landscapes, so you can close the database and exit Access.

5. Close the Panorama database.

You've completed the table design changes to the Panorama database that will make working with it easier and more accurate.

REVIEW

## *Session 5.3 Quick Check*

1. What is a lookup field?
2. A(n) ______________ is a predefined format you use to enter and display data in a field.
3. What is property propagation?
4. Define the Validation Rule property, and give an example of when you would use it.
5. Define the Validation Text property, and give an example of when you would use it.
6. Setting a Memo field's Text Format property to ______________ lets you format its contents.
7. A(n) ______________ folder is a location in which you can place safe databases.

*Practice the skills you learned in the tutorial using the same case scenario.*

PRACTICE

## Review Assignments

**Data File needed for the Review Assignments: Products.accdb**

In the Review Assignments, you'll create several new queries and enhance the table design in a database that contains information about the suppliers that Belmont Landscapes works with on its landscape design projects. Complete the following steps:

1. Open the **Products** database, which is located in the Access2\Review folder provided with your Data Files.
2. Modify the first record in the **tblCompany** table datasheet by changing the ContactFirstName and ContactLastName field values to your first and last names. Close the table.
3. Create a query to find all records in the tblCompany table in which the City field value starts with the letter H. Display all fields in the query recordset, and sort in ascending order by CompanyName. Save the query as **qryHSelectedCities**, run the query, and then close it.
4. Make a copy of the qryHSelectedCities query using the new name **qryOtherSelectedCities**. Modify the new query to find all records in the tblCompany table in which the City field values are not Lansing, Rockford, or Zeeland. Save and run the query, and then close it.
5. Create a query to find all records from the tblProduct table in which the Color field value is Black, White, or Grey. Use a list-of-values match for the selection criteria. Display all fields in the query recordset, and sort in descending order by Price. Save the query as **qrySelectedColors**, run the query, and then close it.
6. Create a query to display all records from the tblCompany table, selecting the CompanyName, City, and Phone fields, and sorting in ascending order by CompanyName. Add a calculated field named **ContactName** as the first column that concatenates the ContactFirstName, a space, and the ContactLastName. Set the Caption property for the ContactName field to **Contact Name**. Save the query as **qryCompanyContacts**, run the query, resize the Contact Name column to its best fit, and then save and close the query.
7. Create a parameter query to select the tblProduct table records for a Color field value that the user specifies. If the user doesn't enter a Color field value, select all records from the table. Display the ProductType, Price, Color, and DiscountOffered fields in the query recordset, sorting in ascending order by Price. Save the query as **qryColorParameter**. Run the query and enter no value as the Color field value, and then run the query again and enter **Wood** as the Color field value. Close the query.
8. Create a find duplicates query based on the tblProduct table. Select ProductType as the field that might contain duplicates, and select the ProductID, CompanyID, Price, and DiscountOffered fields as additional fields in the query recordset. Save the query as **qryDuplicateProductTypes**, run the query, and then close it.
9. Create a find unmatched query that finds all records in the tblCompany table for which there is no matching record in the tblProduct table. Display the CompanyID, CompanyName, City, Phone, ContactFirstName, and ContactLastName fields from the tblCompany table in the query recordset. Save the query as **qryCompaniesWithoutMatchingProducts**, run the query, and then close it.

10. Make a copy of the qryPricesWithDiscountAmounts query using the new name **qryTopPricesWithDiscountAmounts**. Modify the new query to use the Top Values property to select the top 25% of records. Save and run the query, and then close it.
11. In the **tblProduct** table, change the CompanyID field to a lookup field. Select the CompanyName field and then the CompanyID field from the tblCompany table; sort in ascending order by the CompanyName field, do not hide the key column, make sure the Company Name column is the leftmost column, resize the lookup columns to their best fit, select CompanyID as the field to store in the table, and accept the default label for the lookup column. View the tblProduct table datasheet, resize the Company ID column to its best fit, test the lookup field without changing a value permanently, and then save and close the table.
12. Use the Input Mask Wizard to add an input mask to the Phone field in the **tblCompany** table. The ending input mask should use periods as separators, as in 987.654.3210 with only the last seven digits required; do not store the literal display characters, if you are asked to do so. Update the Input Mask property everywhere the Phone field is used. Resize all columns in the datasheet to their best fit, test the input mask by typing over an existing Phone field value, being sure not to change the value by pressing the Esc key after you type the last digit in the Phone field.
13. Add a Memo field named **CompanyComments** as the last field in the tblCompany table. Set the Caption property to **Company Comments** and the Text Format property to Rich Text. In the table datasheet, resize the new column to its best fit, and then add your city and state in bold, italic font to the Company Comments column in the first record. Save and close the tblCompany datasheet.
14. Designate the Access2\Review folder as a trusted folder. (*Note:* Check with your instructor before adding a new trusted location.)
15. Close the Products database without exiting Access, make a backup copy of the database, and compact and repair and then close the Products database.

*Use the skills you learned to work in a database for a small music school.*

APPLY

## Case Problem 1

**Data File needed for this Case Problem: Contract.accdb**

***Pine Hill Music School*** Yuka Koyama owns and runs the Pine Hill Music School in Portland, Oregon. She and the qualified teachers who work for her offer instruction in voice, violin, cello, guitar, percussion, and other instruments. Yuka created an Access database named Contract to store data about students, teachers, and contracts. You'll help Yuka create several new queries and make design changes to the tables. Complete the following steps:

1. Open the **Contract** database, which is located in the Access2\Case1 folder provided with your Data Files.
2. Change the first record in the **tblStudent** table datasheet so the First Name and Last Name columns contain your first and last names. Close the table.
3. Create a query to find all records in the tblStudent table in which the Phone field value begins with 541. Display the FirstName, LastName, City, and Phone fields in the query recordset; and sort in ascending order by LastName. Save the query as **qry541AreaCodes**, run the query, and then close it.

EXPLORE

4. Make a copy of the qryCurrentLessons query using the new name **qrySelectedLessons**. Modify the new query to delete the existing condition for the ContractEndDate field and to include a list-of-values criterion that finds all records in which the LessonType field value is Cello, Flute, or Violin. Save and run the query, and then close it.

5. Create a query to find all records in the tblStudent table in which the City field value is not equal to Portland. Display the FirstName, LastName, City, and Phone fields in the query recordset; and sort in ascending order by City. Save the query as **qryNonPortland**, run the query, and then close it.
6. Create a query to display all records from the tblTeacher table, selecting all fields, and sorting in ascending order by LastName and then in ascending order by FirstName. Add a calculated field named **TeacherName** as the second column that concatenates FirstName, a space, and LastName for each teacher. Set the Caption property for the TeacherName field to **Teacher Name**. Do not display the FirstName and LastName fields in the query recordset. Save the query as **qryTeacherNames**, run the query, resize the Teacher Name column to its best fit, and then save and close the query.
7. Create a parameter query to select the tblContract table records for a LessonType field value that the user specifies. If the user doesn't enter a LessonType field value, select all records from the table. Include all fields from the tblContract table in the query recordset. Save the query as **qryLessonTypeParameter**. Run the query and enter no value as the LessonType field value, and then run the query again and enter **Guitar** as the LessonType field value. Close the query.

EXPLORE

8. Create a crosstab query based on the tblContract table. Use the LessonType field values for the row headings, the LessonLength field values for the column headings, and the count of the ContractID field values as the summarized value, and include row sums. Save the query as **qryLessonTypeCrosstab**. Change the column heading for the row sum column to **Total Number of Lessons**, and change the column headings for the [LessonLength] columns to **Number of 30-Minute Lessons** and **Number of 60-Minute Lessons**. Resize the columns in the query recordset to their best fit, and then save and close the query.
9. Create a find duplicates query based on the tblContract table. Select StudentID and LessonType as the fields that might contain duplicates, and select all other fields in the table as additional fields in the query recordset. Save the query as **qryMultipleLessonsForStudents**, run the query, and then close it.
10. Create a find unmatched query that finds all records in the tblStudent table for which there is no matching record in the tblContract table. Display all fields from the tblStudent table in the query recordset. Save the query as **qryStudentsWithoutContracts**, run the query, and then close it.
11. In the **tblContract** table, change the TeacherID field data type to Lookup Wizard. Select the TeacherName and TeacherID fields from the qryTeacherNames query, sort in ascending order by TeacherName, resize the lookup columns to their best fit, select TeacherID as the field to store in the table, and accept the default label for the lookup column. View the tblContract table datasheet, resize the Teacher ID column to its best fit, and then save and close the table.
12. Use the Input Mask Wizard to add an input mask to the Phone field in the **tblStudent** table. The ending input mask should use periods as separators, as in 987.654.3210 with only the last seven digits required; do not store the literal display characters, if you are asked to do so. Update the Input Mask property everywhere the Phone field is used. Resize the Phone column to its best fit, test the input mask by typing over an existing Phone field value, being sure not to change the value permanently by pressing the Esc key after you type the last digit in the Phone field.

13. Define a field validation rule for the Gender field in the tblStudent table. Acceptable field values for the Gender field are F or M. Use the message "Gender values must be F or M" to notify a user who enters an invalid Gender field value. Save your table changes, test the field validation rule for the Gender field, making sure any tested field values are the same as they were before your testing, and then close the table.
14. Define a table validation rule for the **tblContract** table to verify that ContractStartDate field values precede ContractEndDate field values in time. Use an appropriate validation message. Save your table changes, test the table validation rule, making sure any tested field values are the same as they were before your testing, and then close the table.
15. Designate the Access2\Case1 folder as a trusted folder. (*Note:* Check with your instructor before adding a new trusted location.)
16. Close the Contract database without exiting Access, make a backup copy of the database, and compact and repair and then close the Contract database.

*Apply your skills to work in a database for a health and fitness center.*

APPLY

## Case Problem 2

### Data File needed for this Case Problem: Training.accdb

***Parkhurst Health & Fitness Center*** Martha Parkhurst owns and operates the Parkhurst Health & Fitness Center in Richmond, Virginia. The center offers the usual weight training equipment and fitness classes and also offers specialized programs designed to meet the needs of athletes who participate in certain sports or physical activities. Martha created the Training database to maintain information about the members who have joined the center and the types of programs offered. To make the database easier to use, Martha wants you to create several queries and to make changes to its table design. Complete the following steps:

1. Open the **Training** database, which is located in the Access2\Case2 folder provided with your Data Files.
2. Modify the first record in the **tblMember** table datasheet by changing the First Name and Last Name column values to your first and last names. Close the table.
3. Create a query to find all records in the tblProgram table in which the MonthlyFee field value is 20, 30, or 40. Use a list-of-values match for the selection criterion, and include all fields from the table in the query recordset. Sort the query in descending order by the ProgramID field. Save the query as **qrySelectedPrograms**, run the query, and then close it.
4. Make a copy of the qrySelectedPrograms query using the new name **qrySelectedProgramsModified**. Modify the new query to find all records in the tblProgram table in which the MonthlyFee field value is not 20, 30, or 40. Save and run the query, and then close it.
5. Create a query to display all records from the tblMember table, selecting the LastName, FirstName, Street, and Phone fields, and sorting in ascending order by LastName and then in ascending order by FirstName. Add a calculated field named **MemberName** as the first column that concatenates FirstName, a space, and LastName. Set the Caption property for the MemberName field to **Member Name**. Do not display the FirstName and LastName fields in the query recordset. Create a second calculated field named **CityLine**, inserting it between the Street and Phone fields. The CityLine field concatenates City, a space, State, two spaces, and Zip. Set the Caption property for the CityLine field to **City Line**. Save the query as **qryMemberNames**, run the query, resize all columns to their best fit, and then save and close the query.

**EXPLORE**

6. Create a query to display all matching records from the tblProgram and tblMember tables, selecting the ProgramType and MonthlyFee fields from the tblProgram table, and the FirstName and LastName fields from the tblMember table. Add a calculated field named **MonthlyFeeStatus** as the last column that equals Active if the MembershipStatus field is equal to Active and equals Not Active otherwise. Set the Caption property for the calculated field to **Monthly Fee Status**. Save the query as **qryMonthlyFeeStatus**, run the query, resize all columns to their best fit, and then save and close the query.
7. Make a copy of the qryRichmondOnHold query using the new name **qryRichmondAndChesterActive**. Modify the new query to select all records in which the City field value is Richmond or Chester and the MembershipStatus field value is Active. Save and run the query, and then close the query.
8. Create a parameter query to select the tblMember table records for a City field value that the user specifies. If the user doesn't enter a City field value, select all records from the table. Display all fields from the tblMember table in the query recordset. Save the query as **qryMemberCityParameter**. Run the query and enter no value as the City field value, and then run the query again and enter **Ashland** as the City field value. Close the query.
9. Create a crosstab query based on the qryMonthlyFeeStatus query. Use the ProgramType field values for the row headings, the MonthlyFeeStatus field values for the column headings, the sum of the MonthlyFee field values as the summarized value, and include row sums. Save the query as **qryMonthlyFeeCrosstab**, resize the columns in the query recordset to their best fit, and then save and close the query.
10. Create a find duplicates query based on the tblMember table. Select ExpirationDate as the field that might contain duplicates, and select all other fields in the table as additional fields in the query recordset. Save the query as **qryDuplicateMemberExpirationDates**, run the query, and then close it.
11. Create a find unmatched query that finds all records in the tblProgram table for which there is no matching record in the tblMember table. Select all fields from the tblProgram table. Save the query as **qryProgramsWithoutMembers**, run the query, and then close it.
12. Create a new query based on the tblMember table. Display the FirstName, LastName, Phone, ExpirationDate, MembershipStatus, and ProgramID fields, in this order, in the query recordset. Sort in ascending order by the ExpirationDate field, and then use the Top Values property to select the top 25% of records. Save the query as **qryUpcomingExpirations**, run the query, and then close it.

**EXPLORE**

13. Use the Input Mask Wizard to add an input mask to the JoinDate field in the **tblMember** table. Select the Short Date input mask, and then modify the default Short Date input mask by changing the two slashes to dashes. Next for the JoinDate field, set the Format property to **mm-dd-yyyy** to specify the date format with dashes instead of slashes. Test the input mask by typing over an existing Join Date column value, being certain not to change the value by pressing the Esc key after you type the last digit in the Join Date column. Finally, repeat the same procedure to add the same input mask and Format property setting to the ExpirationDate field, and then save and close the table.
14. Define a field validation rule for the MonthlyFee field in the **tblProgram** table. Acceptable field values for the MonthlyFee field are values between 15 and 55. Enter the message **Value must be between 15 and 55, inclusive** so it appears if a user enters an invalid MonthlyFee field value. Save your table changes and then test the field validation rule for the MonthlyFee field; be certain the field values are the same as they were before your testing, and then close the table.

15. Define a table validation rule for the **tblMember** table to verify that JoinDate field values precede ExpirationDate field values in time. Use an appropriate validation message. Save your table changes, test the table validation rule, making sure any tested field values are the same as they were before your testing.
16. Add a Memo field named **MemberComments** as the last field in the tblMember table. Set the Caption property to **Member Comments** and the Text Format property to Rich Text. In the table datasheet, resize the new column to its best fit, and then add a comment in the Member Comments column in the first record about the types of physical activities you pursue, formatting the text with blue, italic font. Save your table changes, and then close the table.
17. Designate the Access2\Case2 folder as a trusted folder. (*Note:* Check with your instructor before adding a new trusted location.)
18. Close the Training database without exiting Access, make a backup copy of the database, and compact and repair and then close the Training database.

*Explore some new skills to work with a database for a recycling agency.*

CHALLENGE

## Case Problem 3

### Data File needed for this Case Problem: Agency.accdb

***Rossi Recycling Group*** The Rossi Recycling Group is a not-for-profit agency in Salina, Kansas that provides recycled household goods to needy people and families at no charge. Residents of Salina and surrounding communities donate cash and goods, such as appliances, furniture, and tools, to the Rossi Recycling Group. The group's volunteers then coordinate with local human services agencies to distribute the goods to those in need. The Rossi Recycling Group was established by Mary and Tom Rossi, who live on the outskirts of Salina on a small farm. Mary and Tom organize the volunteers to collect the goods and store the collected items in their barn for distribution. Tom has created an Access database to keep track of information about donors, their donations, and the human services agencies. He wants you to create several queries and to make changes to the table design of the database. To do so, you'll complete the following steps:

1. Open the **Agency** database, which is located in the Access2\Case3 folder provided with your Data Files.
2. Modify the first record in the **tblDonor** table datasheet by changing the Title, First Name, and Last Name column values to your title and name. Close the table.
3. Create a query to find all records in the tblDonation table in which the AgencyID field value starts with either the letter R or the letter W. Display all fields in the query recordset, and sort in descending order by DonationValue. Save the query as **qryROrWAgencyDonations**, run the query, and then close it.
4. Make a copy of the qryAgenciesByCity query using the new name **qryNonAbileneSalinaAgencies**. Modify the new query to select all records in which the City field value is not Abilene or Salina. Save and run the query, and then close it.

EXPLORE

5. The existing qryDonationsAfterPickupCharge query displays the DonorID, AgencyName, DonationDesc, and DonationValue fields for all donations that require a pickup, along with the NetDonation calculated field that displays the results of subtracting the $8.75 delivery charge from the DonationValue field value. Make a copy of the qryDonationsAfterPickupCharge query using the new name **qryNetDonations**. Modify the new query to select *all* records, to display the PickupRequired field, and to sort only in descending order by NetDonation. Also, change the NetDonation calculated field to subtract the delivery charge of $8.75 from the DonationField value when a pickup is required and to otherwise use the DonationValue field value. Save and run the query, and then close it.

6. Create a query to display all records from the tblAgency table, selecting all the fields except the ContactFirstName and ContactLastName fields, and sorting in ascending order by AgencyName. Add a calculated field named **ContactName** as the third column that concatenates ContactFirstName, a space, and ContactLastName. Set the Caption property for the ContactName field to **Contact Name**. Save the query as **qryAgencyContactNames**, run the query, resize the new column to its best fit, and then save and close the query.
7. Create a parameter query to select the tblDonation table records for a DonationDesc (donation description) field value that the user specifies. If the user doesn't enter a DonationDesc field value, select all records from the table. Display all fields from the tblDonation table in the query recordset, and sort in ascending order by DonationValue. Save the query as **qryDonationDescParameter**. Run the query and enter no value as the DonationDesc field value, and then run the query again and enter **Cash** as the DonationDesc field value. Close the query.

**EXPLORE**

8. Create a crosstab query based on the qryNetDonations query. Use the AgencyName field values for the row headings, the PickupRequired field values for the column headings, and the sum of the NetDonation field values as the summarized value, and include row sums. Save the query as **qryNetDonationsCrosstab**. Change the column headings for the two rightmost columns to **No Pickup** and **Pickup Required**. Change the format of the displayed values (NetDonation and Total Of NetDonation columns in Design view) to Standard with two decimal places. Resize the columns in the query recordset to their best fit, and then save and close the query.
9. Create a find duplicates query based on the qryNetDonations query. Select DonorID and AgencyName as the fields that might contain duplicates, and select the remaining fields in the query as additional fields in the query recordset. Save the query as **qryMultipleDonorDonations**, run the query, and then close it.
10. Create a find unmatched query that finds all records in the tblDonor table for which there is no matching record in the tblDonation table. Select all fields from the tblDonor table in the query recordset. Save the query as **qryDonorsWithoutDonations**, run the query, and then close it.

**EXPLORE**

11. Make a copy of the qryNetDonations query using the new name **qryTopNetDonations**. Modify the new query by using the Top Values property to select the top 40% of the records. Save and run the query, and then close the query.
12. Use the Input Mask Wizard to add an input mask to the Phone field in the **tblDonor** table. The ending input mask should use hyphens as separators, as in 987-654-3210 with only the last seven digits required; do not store the literal display characters, if you are asked to do so. Update the Input Mask property everywhere the Phone field is used. Test the input mask by typing over an existing Phone field value, being sure not to change the value permanently by pressing the Esc key after you type the last digit in the Phone field. Close the table.
13. Designate the Access2\Case3 folder as a trusted folder. (*Note:* Check with your instructor before adding a new trusted location.)
14. Close the Agency database without exiting Access, make a backup copy of the database, and compact and repair and then close the Agency database.

*Explore some new skills to work with the data for a luxury property rental company.*

CHALLENGE

## Case Problem 4

**Data File needed for this Case Problem: Vacation.accdb**

***GEM Ultimate Vacations*** Griffin and Emma MacElroy own and operate their own agency, GEM Ultimate Vacations, which specializes in locating and booking luxury rental properties in Europe and Africa. To track their guests, properties, and reservations, they created the Vacation database. Griffin and Emma want you to create several queries and to make changes to the table design. To do so, you'll complete the following steps:

1. Open the **Vacation** database, which is located in the Access2\Case4 folder provided with your Data Files.
2. Modify the first record in the **tblGuest** table datasheet by changing the Guest First Name and Guest Last Name column values to your first and last names.
3. Create a query to find all records in the tblProperty table in which the PropertyName field value starts with the word Chateau. Display all fields except the Description field in the query recordset. Save the query as **qryChateauProperties**, run the query, and then close it.
4. Make a copy of the qryChateauProperties query using the new name **qryNonChateauProperties**. Modify the new query to find all records in the tblProperty table in which the PropertyName field value starts with a word other than Chateau, and sort in ascending order by PropertyName. Save and run the query, and then close it.
5. Create a query to find all records in the tblGuest table in which the City field value is Aurora, Chicago, or Crown Point. Use a list-of-values match for the selection criterion, and display all fields from the tblGuest table in the query recordset. Save the query as **qrySelectedGuests**, run the query, and then close it.

EXPLORE

6. Create a query to select all records from the tblProperty table with nightly rates of $1,700 or $2,000 in France or Italy. Display all fields except the Description field in the query recordset. Save the query as **qryFranceItalySelectedProperties**, run the query, and then close it.
7. Create a parameter query to select the tblProperty table records for a Country field value that the user specifies. If the user doesn't enter a Country field value, select all records from the table. Display all fields from the tblProperty table in the query recordset, and sort in ascending order by PropertyName. Save the query as **qryCountryParameter**. Run the query and enter no value as the Country field value, and then run the query again and enter **Scotland** as the Country field value. Close the query.
8. Create a query that contains all records from the tblGuest table and all matching records from the tblReservation table. Display all fields from the tblGuest table and all fields except GuestID from the tblReservation table. Save the query as **qryGuestsAndReservations**, run the query, and then close it. Create a crosstab query based on the qryGuestsAndReservations query. Use the City field values for the row headings, the People field values for the column headings, and the sum of the RentalRate field as the summarized value, and include row sums. Save the query as **qryReservationsCrosstab**, resize the columns in the query recordset to their best fit, and then save and close the query.
9. Create a find duplicates query based on the tblProperty table. Select Location and Country as the fields that might contain duplicates, and select the remaining fields in the table as additional fields in the query recordset. Save the query as **qryDuplicateLocations**, run the query, and then close it.

10. Create a find unmatched query that finds all records in the tblGuest table for which there is no matching record in the tblReservation table. Display the GuestFirstName, GuestLastName, City, and Phone fields from the tblGuest table in the query recordset. Save the query as **qryGuestsWithoutReservations**, run the query, and then close it.

**EXPLORE** 11. Modify the **qryTopRentalCost** query to use the Top Values property to select the top 30% of the records. Save and run the query, and then close it.

12. In the **tblReservation** table, change the PropertyID field data type to Lookup Wizard. Select the PropertyID, PropertyName, and Location fields from the tblProperty table, sort in ascending order by PropertyName, do not hide the key column, resize the lookup columns to their best fit, select PropertyID as the field to store in the table, and accept the default label for the look up column. View the tblReservation datasheet, resize the PropertyID column to its best fit, test the lookup field without changing a field value permanently, and then close the table.

**EXPLORE** 13. Open the **tblGuest** table in Design view. Change the StateProv field data type to Lookup Wizard using a list of values that you enter. In the Lookup Wizard dialog box, create two columns and type the following pairs of values: **Illinois** and **IL**, **Indiana** and **IN**, and **Ontario** and **ON**. Select Col2 as the field to store in the table, and accept the default label for the lookup column. View the tblGuest table datasheet, test the lookup field without changing permanently field values, and then save and close the table.

**EXPLORE** 14. Define a field validation rule for the Bedrooms field in the **tblProperty** table. Acceptable field values for the Bedrooms field are values between 3 and 25, including those two values. Display the message **Value must be between 3 and 25** when a user enters an invalid Bedrooms field value. Save your table changes and then test the field validation rule for the Bedrooms field; be certain the field values are the same as they were before your testing.

15. Define a table validation rule for the **tblReservation** table to verify that StartDate field values precede EndDate field values in time. Use an appropriate validation message. Save your table changes, test the table validation rule, making sure any tested field values are the same as they were before your testing, and then close the table.

16. Designate the Access2\Case4 folder as a trusted folder. (*Note:* Check with your instructor before adding a new trusted location.)

17. Close the Vacation database without exiting Access, make a backup copy of the database, and compact and repair and then close the Vacation database.

*Explore some new skills to create a database for an Internet service provider.*

CREATE

## Case Problem 5

**There are no Data Files needed for this Case Problem.**

***Always Connected Everyday*** Chris and Pat Dixon own and manage Always Connected Everyday (ACE), a successful Internet service provider (ISP) in your area. ACE provides Internet access to residential and business customers and offers a variety of access plans, from dial-up and DSL to wireless. Figure 5-44 shows the pricing options for the access plans ACE offers.

**Figure 5-44** **Pricing options for ACE access plans**

| Access Plan | Monthly | Annually | Setup Fee |
|---|---|---|---|
| Dial-up limited | $9.95 | | |
| Dial-up no e-mail | $14.95 | $149.50 | |
| Dial-up unlimited | $19.95 | $199.50 | |
| DSL pro | $29.95 | | $69.00 |
| DSL turbo | $49.95 | | $69.00 |
| DSL business | $89.95 | | $129.00 |
| Wireless city economy | $39.95 | | $99.00 |
| Wireless city basic | $49.95 | | $99.00 |
| Wireless city advanced | $64.95 | | $109.00 |
| Wireless city business | $99.95 | | $199.00 |
| Wireless rural basic | $59.95 | | $109.00 |

Dial-up plans are available in all communities served by ACE, and DSL and wireless access are limited by a customer's proximity to DSL phone lines or wireless towers. Within each type of service—dial-up, DSL, and wireless—ACE offers low-cost plans with either slower access speeds or fewer capabilities and more expensive plans with either higher access speeds or greater service and features.

Chris and Pat need you to create a database to track their plans, customers, and service calls. The process of creating a complete database—including all fields, tables, relationships, queries, forms, and other database objects—for ACE is an enormous undertaking. You will start with just a few database components, and then you will create additional objects and functionality in subsequent tutorials.

Complete the following steps to create the database and its initial objects:

1. Read the appendix titled "Relational Databases and Database Design" at the end of this text.
2. If you are not familiar with ISPs, use your Web browser to find out more about them, so that you know common terminology and offerings. (*Hint*: You might use Wikipedia as one of your starting points.)
3. The initial database structure includes the following tables and fields:
   a. The **tblAccessPlan** table includes the fields shown in Figure 5-44, along with a primary key field, which you can define as an AutoNumber field.
   b. The **tblCustomer** table includes a unique customer account number; an optional company name; and first name, last name, address, city, state, zip, phone, access plan ID (foreign key), next billing date, and e-mail address for the customer; and the customer's user ID and password for accessing ACE's Web site.
4. Building on Step 3, for each field, determine and set its attributes, such as data type, field size, and validation rules.
5. Create the database structure using Access. Use the database name **ACE**, and save the database in the Access2\Case5 folder provided with your Data Files. Create the tables with their fields, following the naming standards used in this tutorial. Be sure to set each field's properties correctly, including the Caption property. Select a primary key for each table, use an input mask for one field, and then define the relationships between the tables.
6. For each table, create a form that you'll use to view, add, edit, and delete records in that table.

7. For tables with one-to-many relationships, create a form with a main form for the primary table and a subform for the related table.
8. Design test data for each table in the database. Your tblCustomer table should contain at least 15 records. Make sure your test data covers common situations. For example, your test data should include at least two access plans with multiple customers using the plans; at least two access plans with no customers using the plans, multiple cities, phone prefixes, and next billing dates; residential customers with no company names; and commercial customers with company names and the first and last names of the company's contact. Use your first and last names for the first record in the tblCustomer table.
9. Add the test data to your tables using the forms you created in Steps 6 and 7.
10. Open each table datasheet, and resize all datasheet columns to their best fit.
11. For the foreign key field in the tblCustomer table, change the field's data type to Lookup Wizard. If necessary, resize the lookup column in the table datasheet.
12. Create a query named **qryCustomerNames** that contains all the fields from the tblCustomer table. Add a calcualted field named **CustomerName** as the first column that is either the company name or the concatenation of the last name, a comma, a space, and the first name; set its Caption property to **Customer Name**. Sort in ascending order by CustomerName.
13. Create one parameter query, one crosstab query, and one find unmatched query, and save them using appropriate object names.
14. Designate the Access2\Case5 folder as a trusted folder. (*Note:* Check with your instructor before adding a new trusted location.)
15. Close the ACE database without exiting Access, make a backup copy of the database, and compact and repair and then close the ACE database.

SAM

ASSESS

## SAM: Skills Assessment Manager

For current SAM information, including versions and content details, visit SAM Central (http://samcentral.course.com). If you have a SAM user profile, you may have access to hands-on instruction, practice, and assessment of the skills covered in this tutorial. Since various versions of SAM are supported throughout the life of this text, check with your instructor for the correct instructions and URL/Web site for accessing assignments.

### ENDING DATA FILES

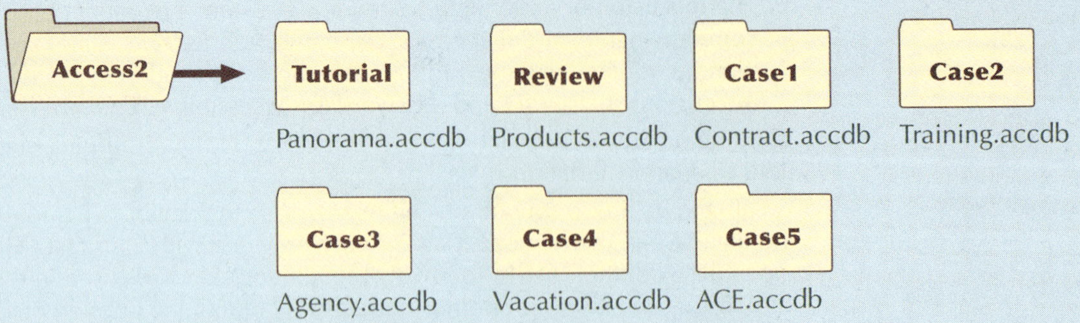

TUTORIAL 6

# Using Form Tools and Creating Custom Forms

## *Creating Forms for Belmont Landscapes*

### OBJECTIVES

**Session 6.1**
- Change a lookup field to a Text field
- View and print database documentation
- Create datasheet, multiple items, and split forms
- Modify a form and anchor form controls in Layout view

**Session 6.2**
- Plan, design, and create a custom form in Design view and in Layout view
- Select, move, align, resize, delete, and rename controls in a form
- Add a combo box to a form
- Add headers and footers to a form

**Session 6.3**
- Add a combo box to a form to find records
- Add a subform to a form
- Add calculated controls to a form and a subform
- Change the tab order in a form
- Improve the appearance of a form

## Case | ***Belmont Landscapes***

Oren Belmont hired Lucia Perez to enhance the Panorama database, and she initially concentrated on standardizing the table design and creating queries for Belmont Landscapes. Sarah Fisher and her staff created a few forms before Lucia's hiring, and Lucia's next priority is to work with Sarah to create new forms that will be more useful and easier to use.

In this tutorial, you will create new forms for Belmont Landscapes. In creating the forms, you will use many Access form customization features, such as adding controls and a subform to a form, using combo boxes and calculated controls, and adding color and special effects to a form. These features will make it easier for Sarah and her staff to interact with the Panorama database.

### STARTING DATA FILES

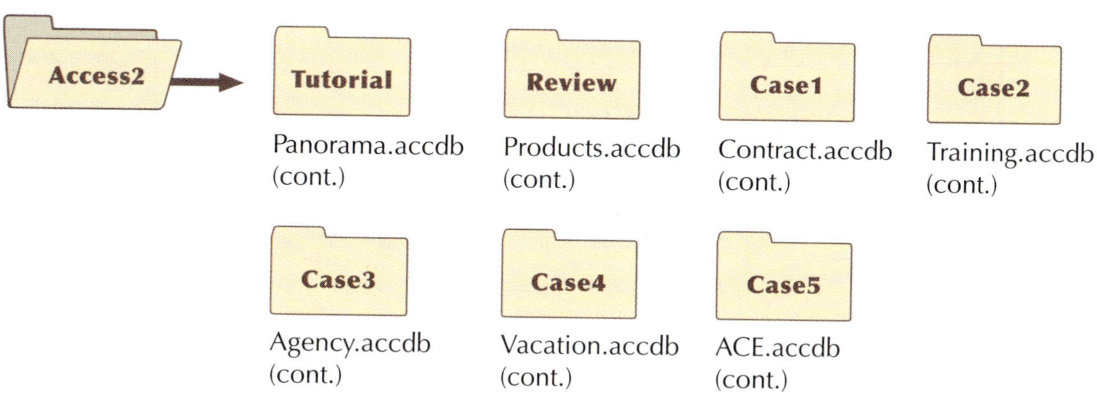

# SESSION 6.1 VISUAL OVERVIEW

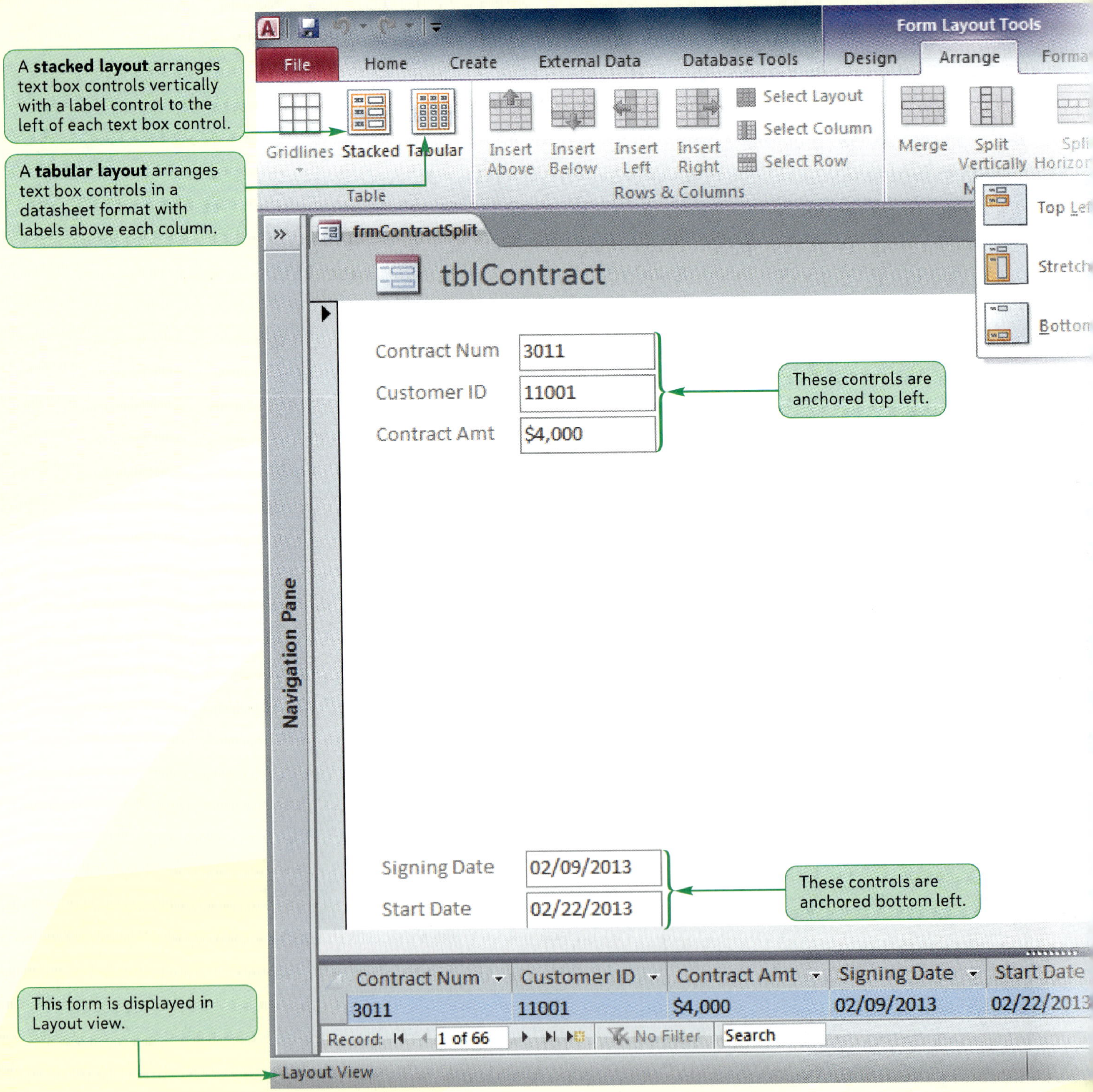

# ANCHORING CONTROLS

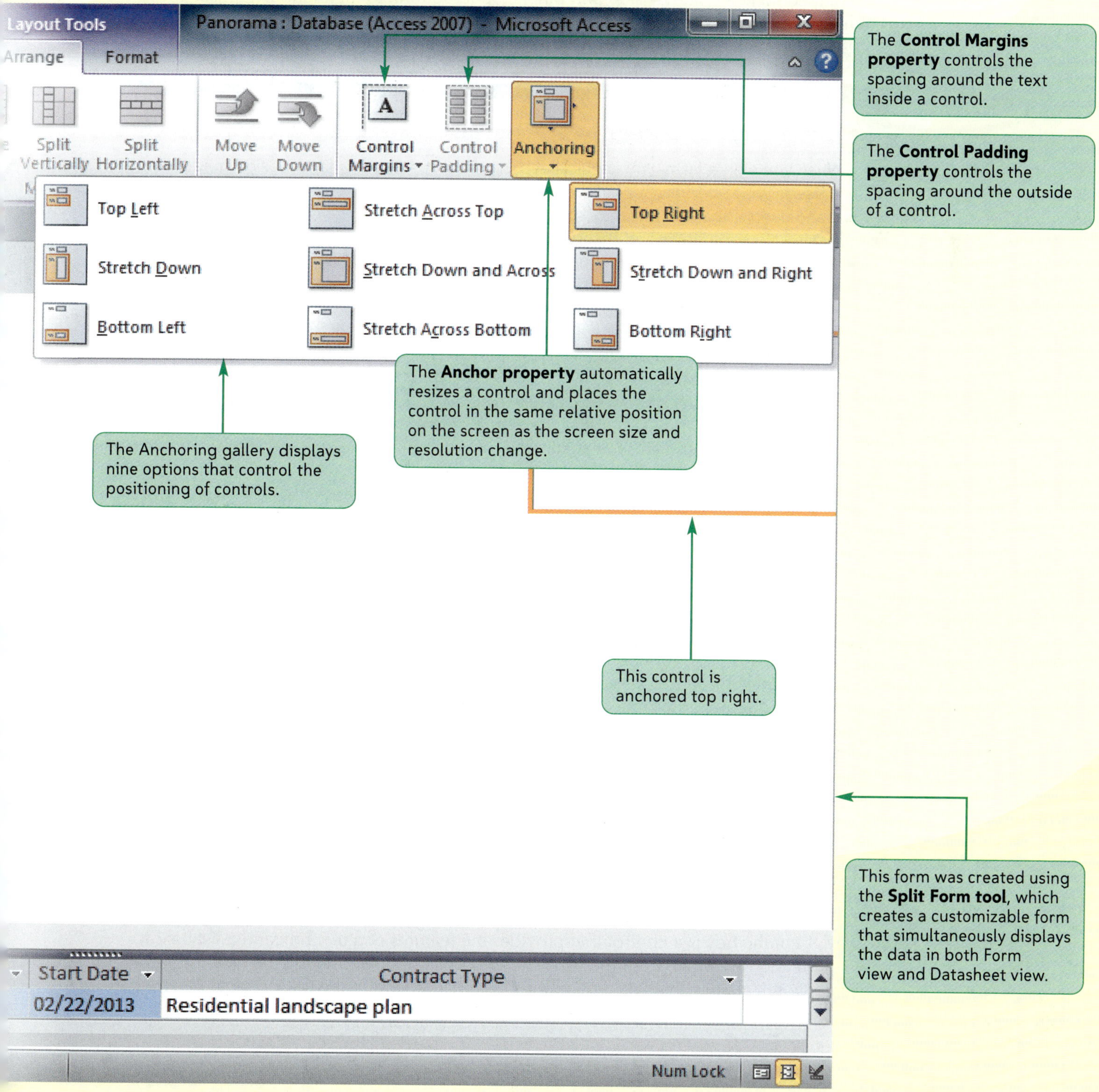

# Designing Forms

You've used wizards to create forms, and you've modified a form's design in Layout view to create a custom form. To create a **custom form**, you can modify an existing form in Layout view or in Design view, or you can design and create a form from scratch in Layout view or in Design view. You can design a custom form to match a paper form, to display some fields side by side and others top to bottom, to highlight certain sections with color, or to add visual effects. Whether you want to create a simple or complex custom form, planning the form's content and appearance is always your first step.

INSIGHT

### *Form Design Guidelines*

When you plan a form, you should keep in mind the following form design guidelines:

- Use forms to perform all database updates because forms provide better readability and control than do table and query recordsets.
- Determine the fields and record source needed for each form. A form's **Record Source property** specifies the table or query that provides the fields for the form.
- Group related fields and position them in a meaningful, logical order.
- If users will refer to a source document while working with the form, design the form to match the source document closely.
- Identify each field value with a label that names the field, and align field values and labels for readability.
- Size the width of each text box to fully display the values it contains and also to provide a visual clue to users about the length of those values.
- Display calculated fields in a distinctive way, and prevent users from changing and updating them.
- Use default values, list boxes, and other form controls whenever possible to reduce user errors by minimizing keystrokes and limiting entries. A **control** is an item, such as a text box or command button, that you place in a form or report.
- Use colors, fonts, and graphics sparingly to keep the form uncluttered and to keep the focus on the data.
- Use a consistent style for all forms in a database.

Sarah and her staff had created a few forms and made table design changes before learning about proper form design guidelines. These guidelines recommend performing all database updates using forms. As a result, Belmont Landscapes won't use table or query datasheets to update the database, and Sarah asks if she should reconsider any of the table design changes you made to the Panorama database in the previous tutorial.

## Changing a Lookup Field to a Text Field

The input mask and validation rule changes are important table design changes, but setting the CustomerID field to a lookup field in the tblContract table is an unnecessary change. A form combo box provides the same capability in a clearer, more flexible way. A **combo box** is a control that provides the features of a text box and a list box; it lets you choose a value from the list or type an entry. Before creating the new forms for Sarah, you'll change the data type of the CustomerID field in the tblContract table from a Lookup Wizard field to a Text field.

### To change the data type of the CustomerID field:

1. Start Access, and then open the **Panorama** database in the Access2\Tutorial folder provided with your Data Files.

   **Trouble?** If the Security Warning is displayed below the Ribbon, either the Panorama database is not located in the Access2\Tutorial folder or you did not designate that folder as a trusted folder. Make sure you opened the database in the Access2\Tutorial folder, and make sure that it's designated as a trusted folder.

**TIP**

You can press the F11 key to open or close the Navigation Pane.

2. Open the Navigation Pane, open the **tblContract** table in Design view, and then close the Navigation Pane.
3. Click the **CustomerID** Field Name box, and then click the **Lookup** tab in the Field Properties pane. The Field Properties pane now displays the lookup properties for the CustomerID field. See Figure 6-1.

**Figure 6-1** Lookup properties for the CustomerID field

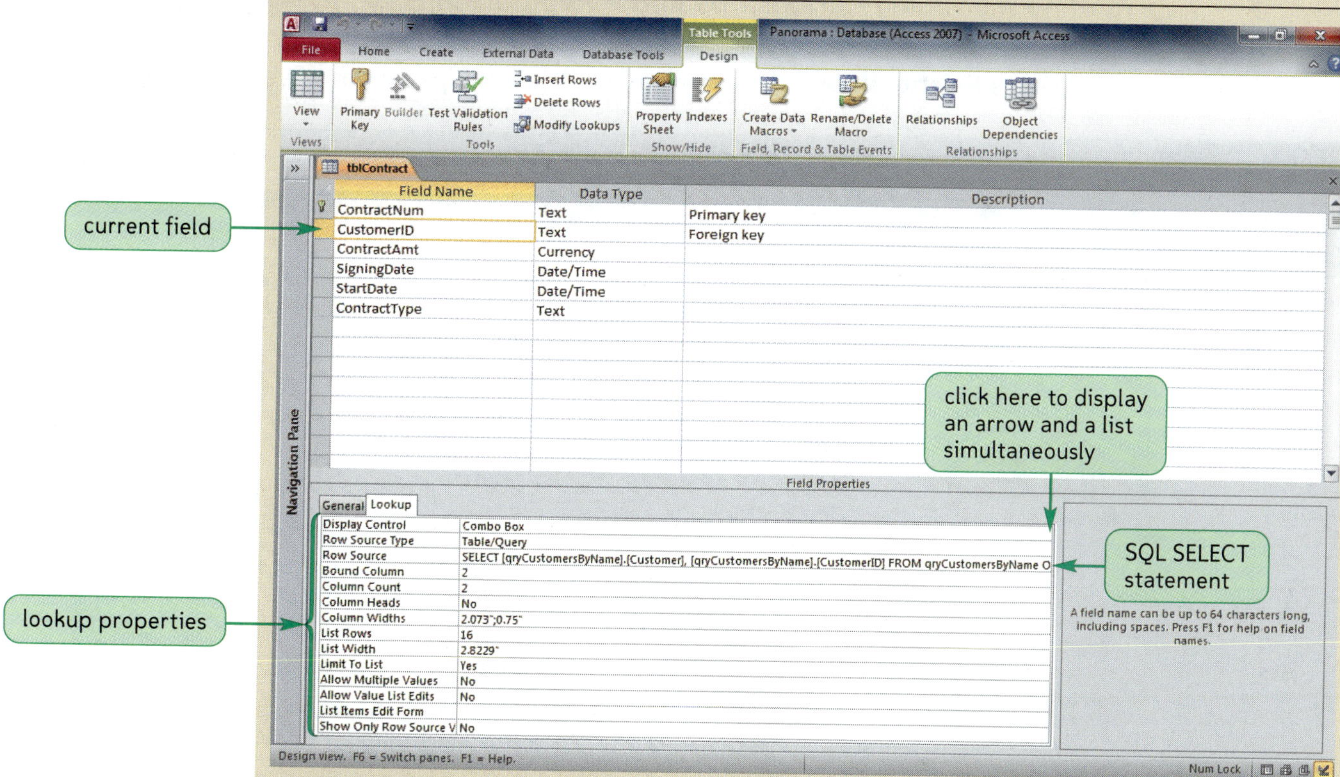


Notice the **Row Source property**, which specifies the data source for a control in a form or report or for a field in a table or query. The Row Source property is usually set to a table name, a query name, or an SQL statement. For the CustomerID field, the Row Source property is set to an SQL SELECT statement. You'll learn more about SQL later in this text.

To remove the lookup feature for the CustomerID field, you need to change the **Display Control property**, which specifies the default control used to display a field, from Combo Box to Text Box.

4. Click the right side of the **Display Control** box, and then click **Text Box**. All the lookup properties in the Field Properties pane disappear, and the CustomerID field changes back to a Text field without lookup properties.

5. Click the **General** tab in the Field Properties pane and notice that the properties for a Text field still apply to the CustomerID field.
6. Save the table, switch to Datasheet view, resize the Customer ID column to its best fit, and then click one of the **Customer ID** boxes. An arrow does not appear in the Customer ID box because the field is no longer a lookup field.
7. Save the table, and then close the tblContract table.

Before you could change the CustomerID field in the tblContract table to a lookup field in the previous tutorial, you had to delete the one-to-many relationship between the tblCustomer and tblContract tables. Now that you've changed the data type of the CustomerID field back to a Text field, you'll view the table relationships to make sure that the tables in the Panorama database are related correctly.

## To view the table relationships in the Relationships window:

1. On the Ribbon, click the **Database Tools** tab, and then in the Relationships group, click the **Relationships** button to open the Relationships window. See Figure 6-2.

**Figure 6-2** Panorama database tables in the Relationships window

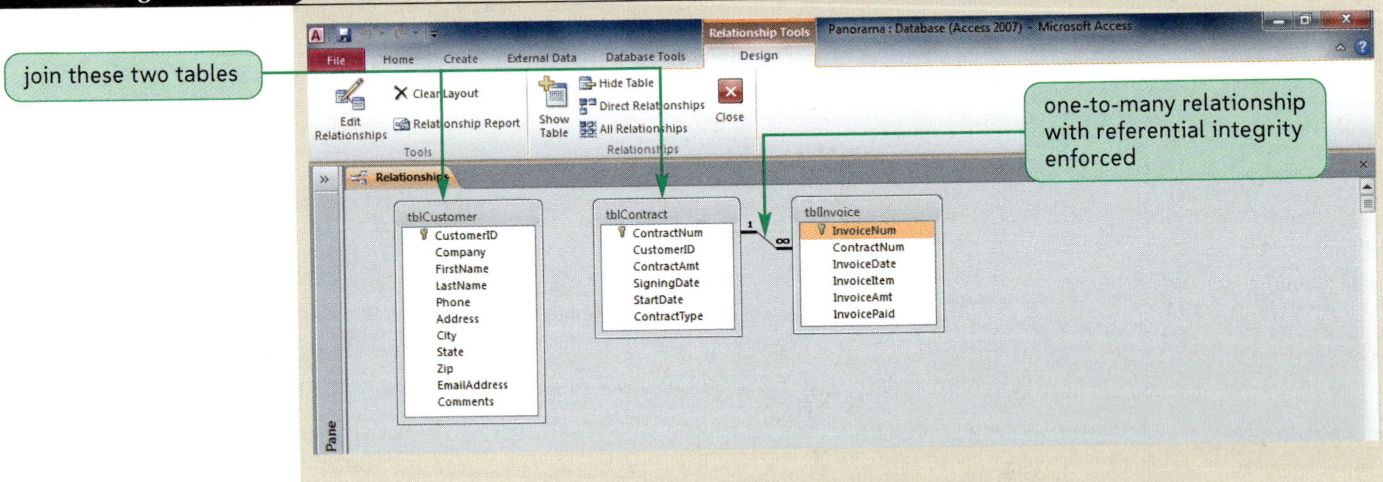


The primary tblContract table and the related tblInvoice table have a one-to-many relationship with referential integrity enforced. You need to establish a similar one-to-many relationship between the tblCustomer and tblContract tables.

2. Click **CustomerID** in the tblCustomer field list, drag it to **CustomerID** in the tblContract field list, and then release the mouse button to open the Edit Relationships dialog box.
3. Click the **Enforce Referential Integrity** check box, click the **Cascade Update Related Fields** check box, and then click the **Create** button to define the one-to-many relationship between the two tables and to close the dialog box. The join line connecting the tblCustomer and tblContract tables indicates the type of relationship (one-to-many) with referential integrity enforced (bold join line).

Sarah asks you to print a copy of the database relationships to use as a reference, and she asks if other Access documentation is available.

# Printing Database Relationships and Using the Documenter

You can print the Relationships window to document the fields, tables, and relationships in a database. You can also use the **Documenter**, another Access tool, to create detailed documentation of all, or selected, objects in a database. For each selected object, the Documenter lets you print documentation, such as the object's properties and relationships, and the fields used by the object and their properties. You can use the documentation to help you understand an object and to help you plan changes to that object.

REFERENCE

## *Using the Documenter*

- Start Access and open the database you want to document.
- In the Analyze group on the Database Tools tab, click the Database Documenter button.
- Select the object(s) you want to document.
- If necessary, click the Options button to select specific documentation options for the selected object(s), and then click the OK button.
- Click the OK button, print the documentation, and then close the Object Definition window.

Next, you'll print the Relationships window and use the Documenter to create documentation for the tblContract table. Sarah will show her staff the tblContract table documentation as a sample of the information that the Documenter provides.

### To print the Relationships window and use the Documenter:

1. In the Tools group on the Design tab, click the **Relationship Report** button to open the Relationships for Panorama report in Print Preview. See Figure 6-3.

**Figure 6-3** Relationships for Panorama report

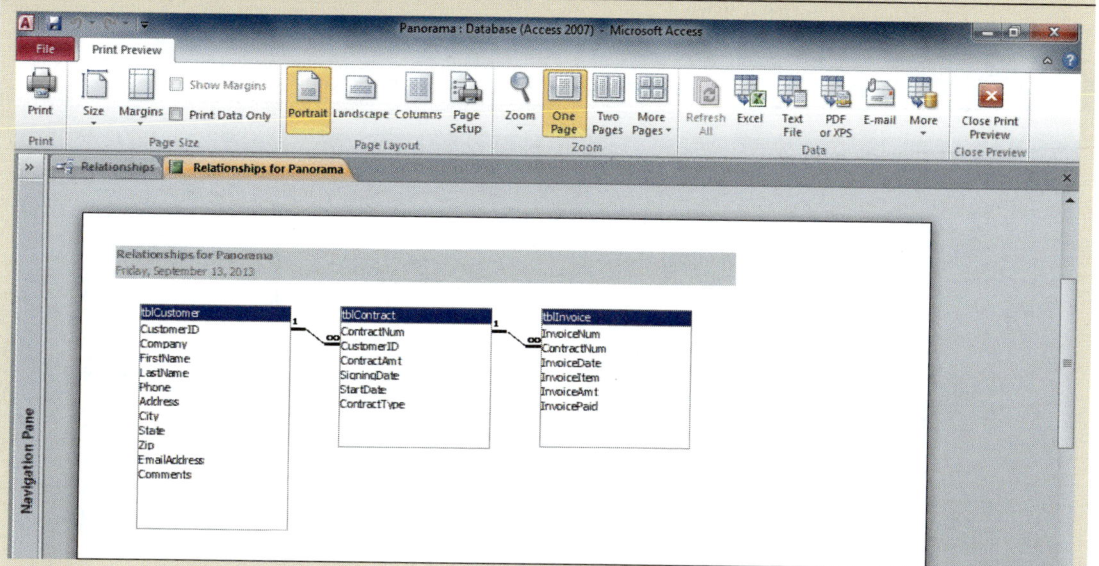

2. In the Print group on the Print Preview tab, click the **Print** button, select your printer in the Name box (if necessary), and then click the **OK** button. Access prints the Relationships for Panorama report.

3. Click the **Close 'Relationships for Panorama'** button on the Relationships for Panorama tab to close the window. A dialog box opens and asks if you want to save the report. Because you can easily create the report at any time, you won't save it.

4. Click the **No** button to close the report without saving changes, and then close the Relationships window.

   Now you'll use the Documenter to create detailed documentation for the tblContract table as a sample to show Sarah.

5. On the Ribbon, click the **Database Tools** tab. In the Analyze group, click the **Database Documenter** button, and then click the **Tables** tab (if necessary) in the Documenter dialog box. See Figure 6-4.

**Figure 6-4** **Documenter dialog box**

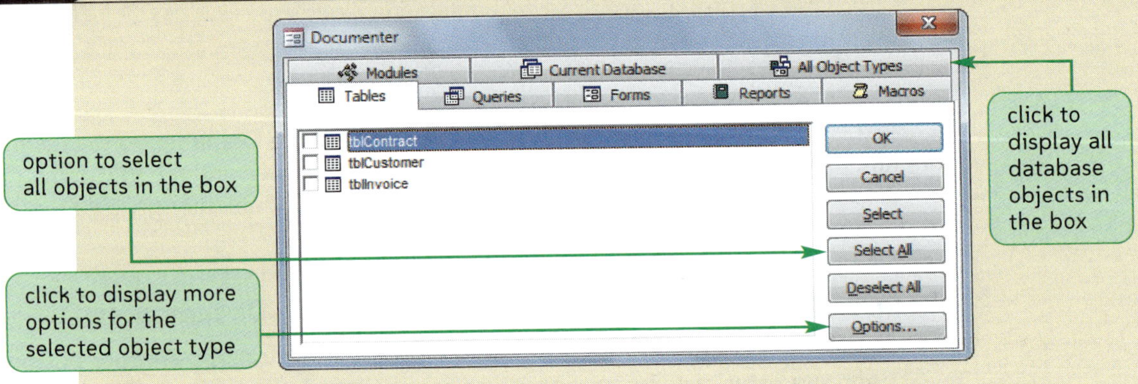


6. Click the **tblContract** check box, and then click the **Options** button. The Print Table Definition dialog box opens on top of the Documenter dialog box. See Figure 6-5.

**Figure 6-5** **Print Table Definition dialog box**

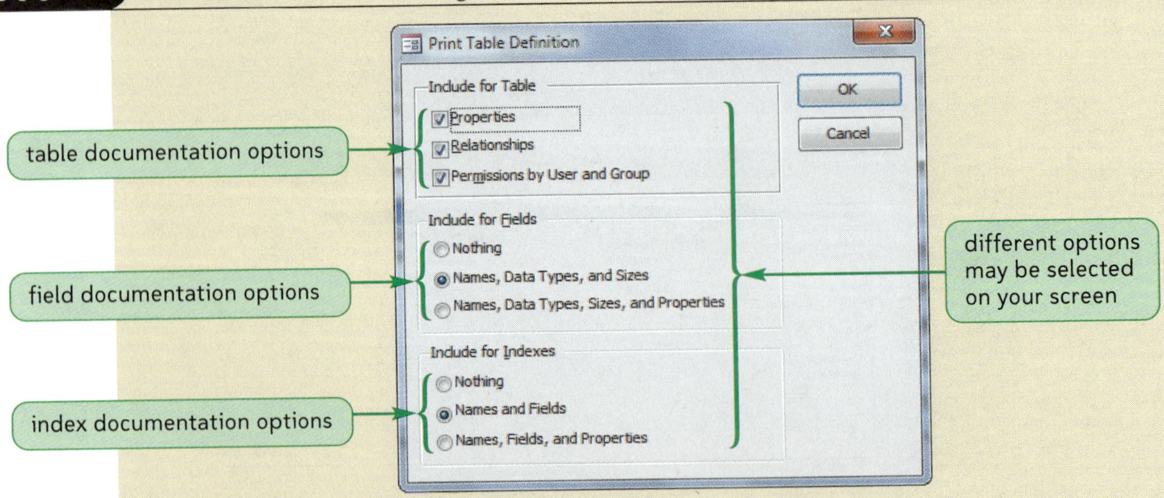

You select which documentation you want the Documenter to include for the selected table, its fields, and its indexes. Sarah asks you to include all table documentation and the second options for fields and for indexes.

7. Make sure all check boxes are checked in the Include for Table section, click the **Names, Data Types, and Sizes** option button in the Include for Fields section (if necessary), click the **Names and Fields** option button in the Include for Indexes section (if necessary), click the **OK** button, and then click the **OK** button. The Documenter dialog box closes and the Object Definition report opens in Print Preview.

8. In the Zoom group on the Print Preview tab, click the **Zoom button arrow**, and then click **Zoom 100%**.

When you need to view more of the horizontal contents of an open object, you can close the Navigation Pane. You can also minimize the Ribbon when you want to view more of the vertical contents of an open object. To minimize the Ribbon, double-click any tab on the Ribbon, or right-click a tab and then click Minimize the Ribbon on the shortcut menu. To restore the Ribbon, double-click any tab on the Ribbon, or right-click a tab and then click Minimize the Ribbon (it's a toggle option) on the shortcut menu.

**TIP**

If you click, instead of double-click, any tab on the minimized Ribbon, the full Ribbon appears until you click anywhere outside the Ribbon.

9. Double-click the **Print Preview** tab on the Ribbon to minimize the Ribbon, and then scroll down the report so you can see more of the report. See Figure 6-6.

**Figure 6-6** **Object Definition report for the tblContract table**

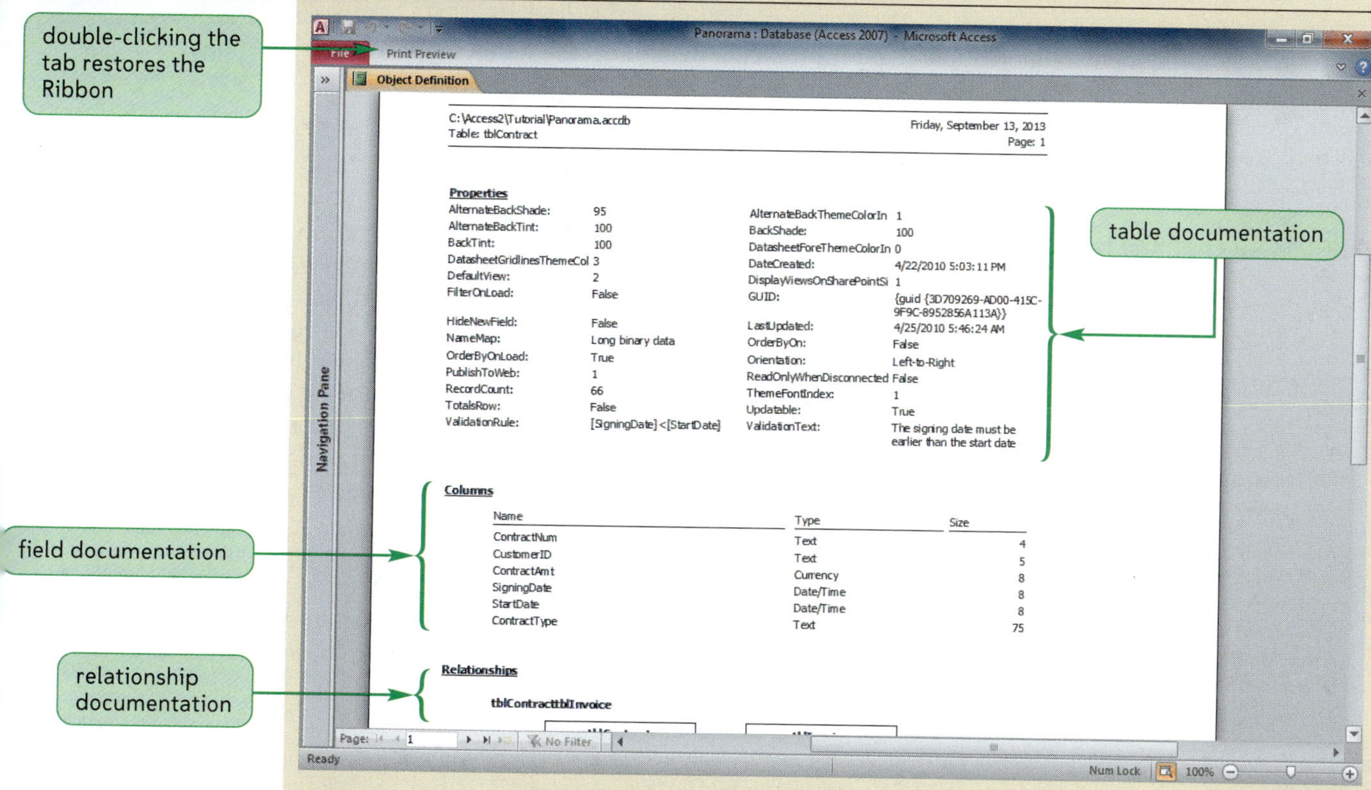


The Object Definition report displays table, field, and relationship documentation for the tblContract table.

**10.** Scroll down the Object Definition report to view the remaining information in the documentation, print the documentation if your instructor asks you to do so, and then close the Object Definition report. Notice that the Navigation Pane is closed and the Ribbon is minimized.

PROSKILLS

### *Written Communication: Satisfying User Documentation Requirements*

The Documenter produces object documentation that is useful to the technical designers, analysts, and programmers who develop and maintain Access databases and who need to understand the minutia of a database's design. Users who interact with databases have no interest in the documentation produced by the Documenter. Users need to know how to enter and maintain data using forms and how to obtain information using forms and reports, so they require special documentation that matches these needs, but this documentation isn't produced by the Documenter. Many companies assign one or more users the task of creating the documentation needed by users because they best know their company's procedures and what specific documentation users require. Databases with dozens of tables and with hundreds of other objects are complicated structures, so be sure you provide documentation that satisfies the needs of users separate from the documentation for the database developers.

Sarah and her staff will review the printout of the Relationships window and the documentation about the tblContract table and decide if they need to view additional documentation. Next, you'll create new forms for Sarah and her staff.

# Creating Forms Using Form Tools

The Panorama database currently contains four forms: the frmContract form was created using the Form tool, the frmCustomer form was created using the Form Wizard, and the frmCustomerContracts main form and its frmContractSubform subform were created using the Form Wizard. Only the frmCustomer form is a custom form. Design changes that were made to the frmCustomer form in Layout view include changing its theme, changing its form title color and its line type, adding a picture, and moving a field.

Sarah wants to view the forms that she can create using other types of form tools, so she can determine if any of the forms would be helpful to her when updating the database.

## Creating a Form Using the Datasheet Tool

The **Datasheet tool** creates a form in a datasheet format that contains all the fields in the source table or query. You'll use the Datasheet tool to create a form based on the tblContract table.

**TIP**

When you use the Datasheet tool, the record source (either a table or query) for the form must either be open or selected in the Navigation Pane.

**To create the form using the Datasheet tool:**

1. Open the Navigation Pane, and then click **tblContract** (if necessary) in the Navigation Pane.
2. Double-click the **Create** tab on the Ribbon to restore the Ribbon and to display the Create tab.

3. In the Forms group, click the **More Forms** button, and then click **Datasheet**. The Datasheet tool creates a form showing every field in the tblContract table in a datasheet format. See Figure 6-7.

**Figure 6-7** **Form created by the Datasheet tool**

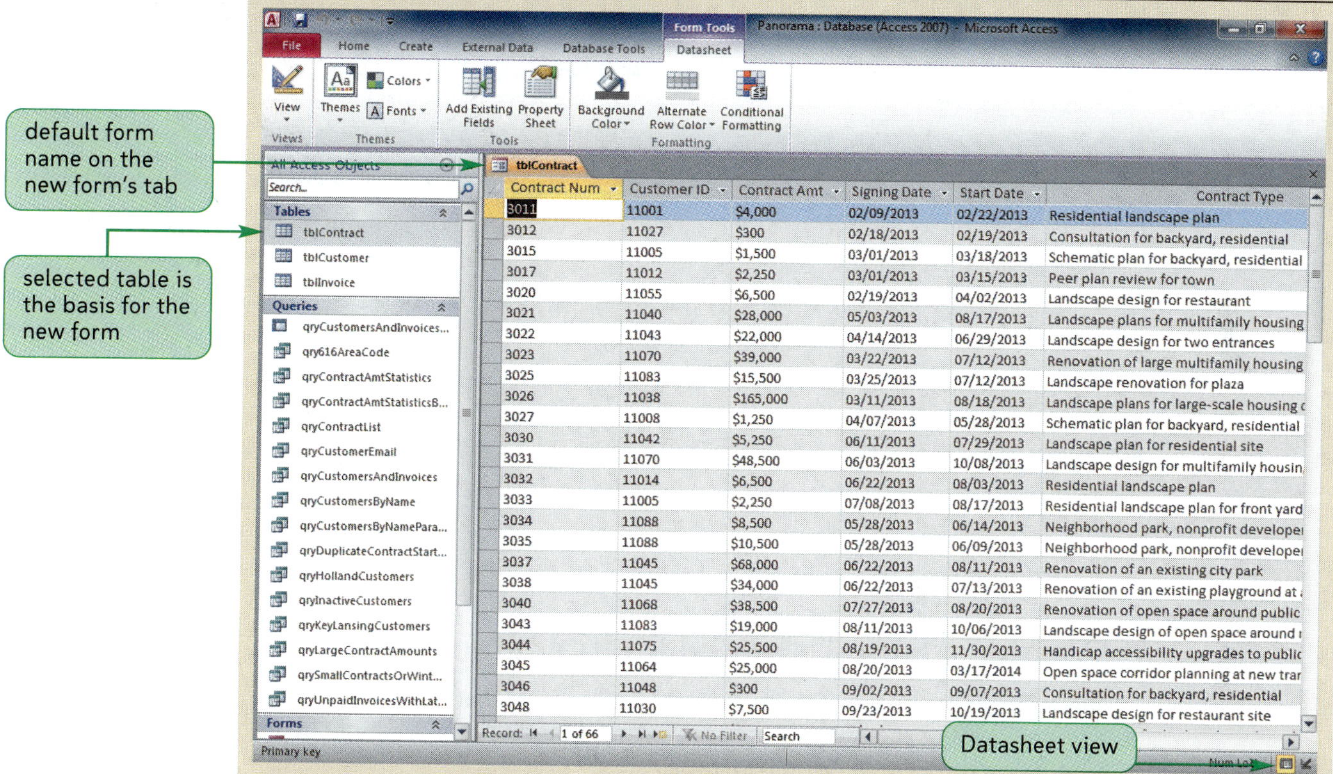


The new form displays all the records and fields from the tblContract table in Datasheet view and in the same format as a table or query recordset displayed in Datasheet view. On the right side of the status bar, two view icons appear, one for Datasheet view (selected) and the other for Design view. The form name, tblContract, is the same name as the table used as the basis for the form. Each table and query in a database must have a unique name. Although you could name a form or report the same as a table or query, it would cause confusion. Fortunately, using object name prefixes prevents this confusing practice, and you would change the name when you save the form.

When working with forms, you view and update data in Form view, you view and make simple design changes in Layout view, and you make simple and complex design changes in Design view. For the form created with the Datasheet tool, you'll check the available view options.

4. In the Views group on the Datasheet tab, click the **View button arrow**. See Figure 6-8.

**Figure 6-8** View options for a form created by the Datasheet tool

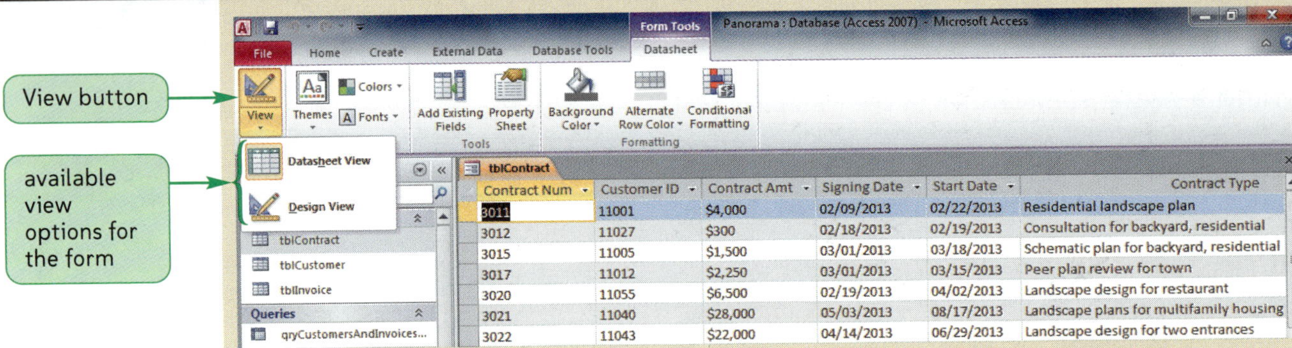


Form view and Layout view are not options in the list, which means that they are unavailable for this form type. Datasheet view allows you to view and update data, and Design view is the only other view option for this form.

Sarah and her staff don't have a need for a form with a datasheet format, so you won't save it.

5. Click the **View button arrow** to close the menu, and then close the form without saving it.

Next, you'll show Sarah a form created using the Multiple Items tool.

## Creating a Form Using the Multiple Items Tool

The **Multiple Items tool** creates a customizable form that displays multiple records from a source table or query in a datasheet format. You'll use the Multiple Items tool to create a form based on the tblContract table.

### To create the form using the Multiple Items tool:

1. Make sure that the tblContract table is selected in the Navigation Pane, and then click the **Create** tab on the Ribbon.
2. In the Forms group, click the **More Forms** button, and then click the **Multiple Items** button. The Multiple Items tool creates a form showing every field in the tblContract table and opens the form in Layout view. See Figure 6-9.

**Figure 6-9** Form created by the Multiple Items tool

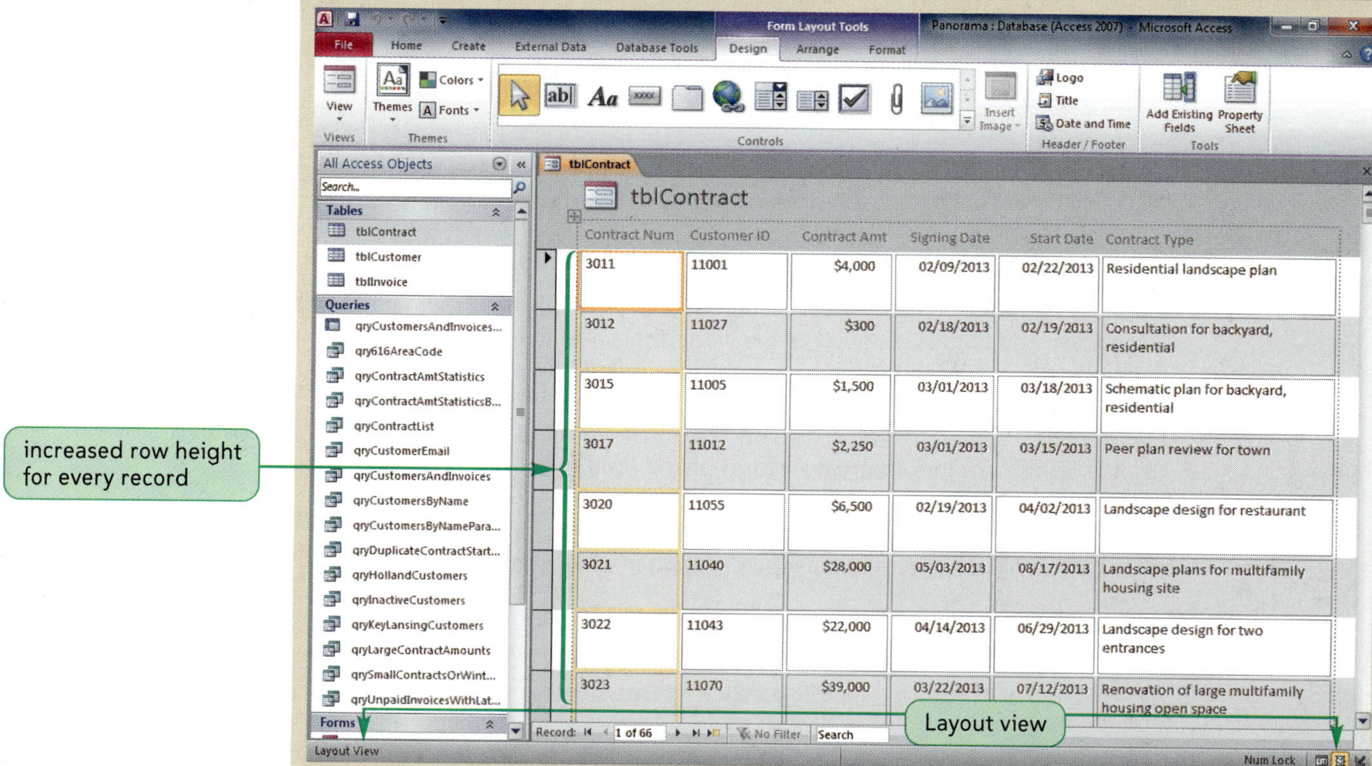


> **TIP**
>
> You can click one of the view buttons on the right side of the status bar to switch to another view.

The new form displays all the records and fields from the tblContract table in a format similar to a datasheet, but the row height for every record is increased compared to a standard datasheet. Unlike a form created by the Datasheet tool, which has only Datasheet view and Design view available, a Multiple Items form is a standard form that can be displayed in Form view, Layout view, and Design view, as indicated by the buttons on the right side of the status bar.

For the form created with the Multiple Items tool, you'll check the available view options.

3. In the Views group, click the **View button arrow**. Form view, Layout view, and Design view are the available views for this form. See Figure 6-10.

**Figure 6-10** View options for a form created by the Multiple Items tool

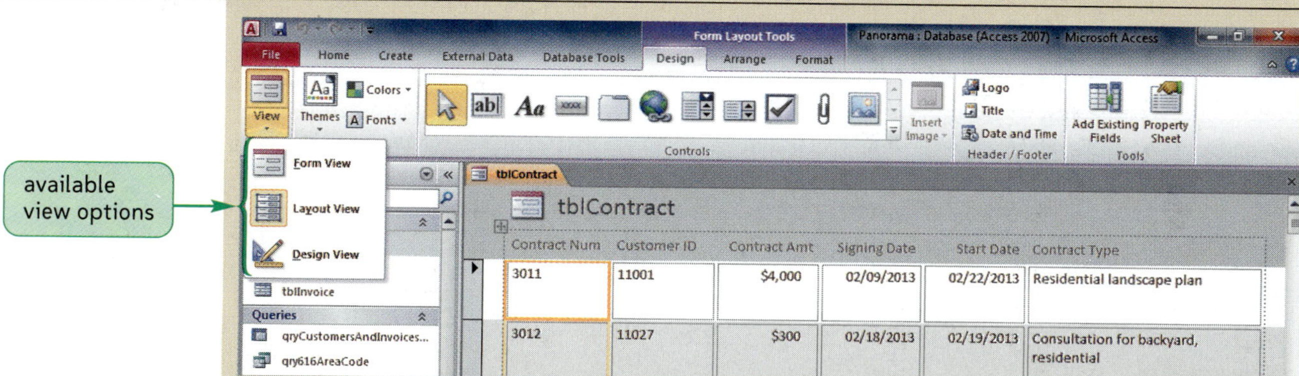

Sarah thinks this new form could be more useful than the form created by the Datasheet tool, but she doesn't have an immediate need for the form, so you won't save it.

4. Click the **View button arrow** to close the menu, and then close the form without saving it.

The final form tool you'll show Sarah is the Split Form tool.

## Creating a Form Using the Split Form Tool

The Split Form tool creates a customizable form that displays the data in a form in both Form view and Datasheet view at the same time. The two views are synchronized with each other at all times. Selecting a record in one view selects the same record in the other view. You can add, change, or delete data from either view. Typically, you'd use Datasheet view to locate a record, and then use Form view to update the record. You'll use the Split Form tool to create a form based on the tblContract table.

### To create the form using the Split Form tool:

1. Make sure that the tblContract table is selected in the Navigation Pane, and then click the **Create** tab on the Ribbon.
2. In the Forms group, click the **More Forms** button, click the **Split Form** button, and then close the Navigation Pane. The Split Form tool creates a split form that opens in Layout view and displays a form with the contents of the first record in the tblContract table on the top and a datasheet of the first several records in the tblContract table on the bottom. See Figure 6-11.

**Figure 6-11** Form created by the Split Form tool

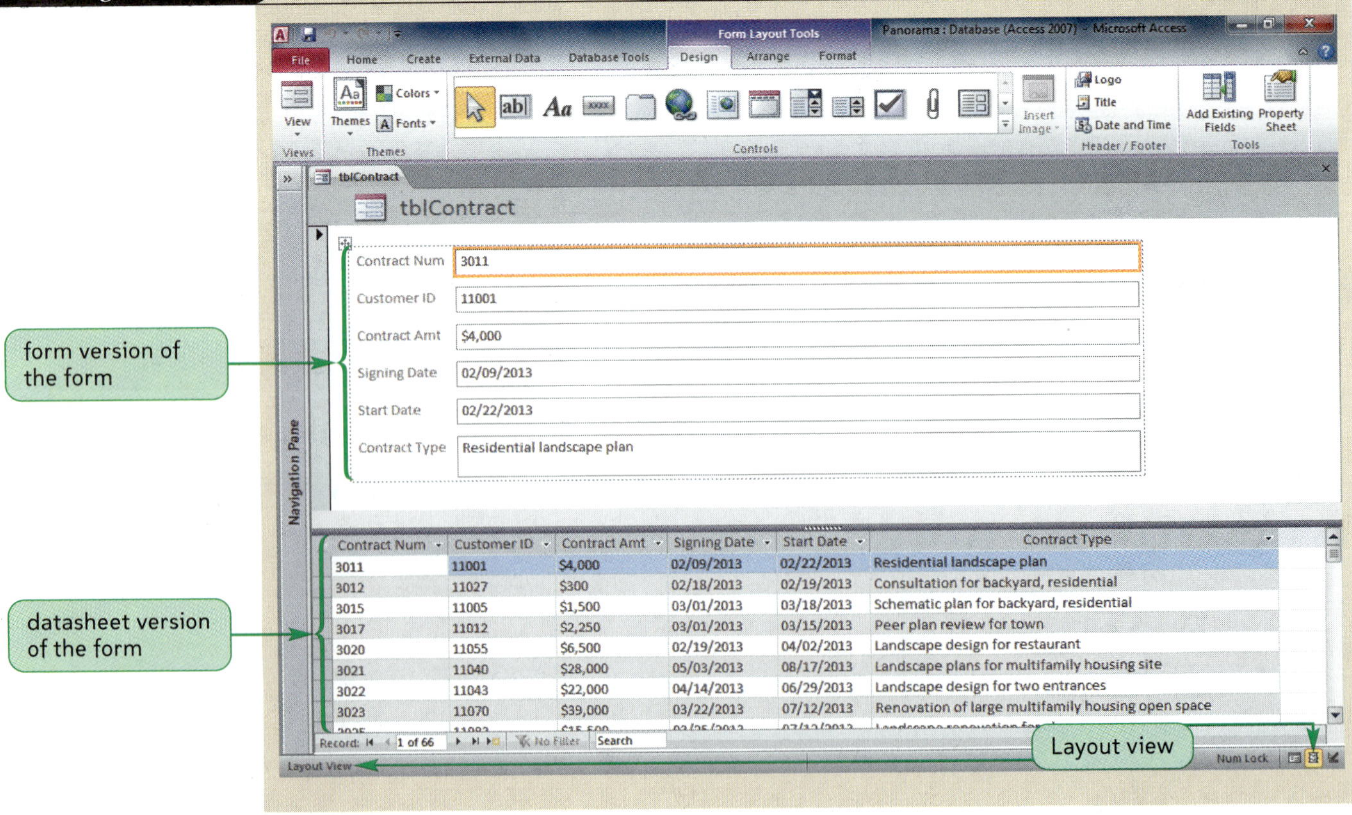

In Layout view, you can make layout and design changes to the form and layout changes to the datasheet. Sarah thinks the split form will be a useful addition to the Panorama database, and she wants you to show her the types of design modifications that are possible with a split form.

## Modifying a Split Form in Layout View

You use the options on the Design tab on the Ribbon to add controls and make other modifications to the form but not to the datasheet, and you'll use these options later in this tutorial. In previous tutorials, you've shown Sarah how to use some of the form modification options on the Format tab, and you'll use other options on this tab later in this tutorial, so you won't show her any Format tab options now. Instead, you'll show her some options on the Arrange tab. For a split form, options on the Arrange tab apply only to the form and do not apply to the datasheet.

### To modify the form in Layout view:

1. Click the **Arrange** tab on the Ribbon.

   The form's label and text box controls for the fields from the tblContract table are grouped in a control layout. A **control layout** is a set of controls grouped together in a form or report, so that you can manipulate the set as a single control. For example, you can move and resize all the controls in a control layout as a group—moving or resizing one control in the control layout moves or resizes all controls in the control layout. You also can rearrange fields and their attached labels within the control layout.

   All the text boxes in the control layout are the same width. The first five text boxes—from the ContractNum text box to the StartDate text box—are much wider than necessary. However, if you reduce the width of any text box in a control layout, all text boxes in the control layout are also resized. Sarah wants you to reduce the width of the first five text boxes and to move and resize the ContractType label and text box.

2. Click the **layout selector** ⊞, which is located at the top-left corner of the Contract Num label, to select all controls in the control layout. An orange outline, which identifies the controls that you've selected, appears around the labels and text boxes in the form. See Figure 6-12.

**Figure 6-12** **Control layout selected in the form**

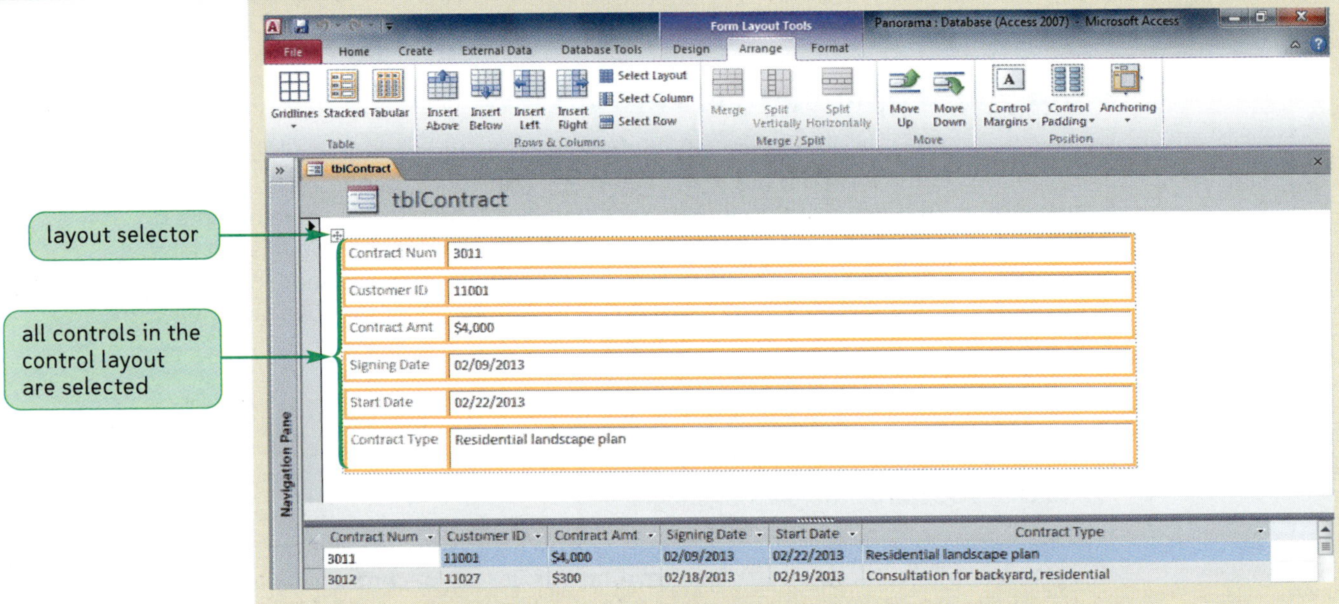


**Trouble?** If the layout selector wasn't visible, or if only one large orange outline appears outside the controls but not around each individual control, click the ContractNum text box, and then repeat Step 2.

Next, you'll resize the text boxes in the control layout.

3. Click the **SigningDate** text box (the text box that contains the value 02/09/2013) to deselect the control layout and select the SigningDate text box.
4. Position the pointer on the right edge of the SigningDate text box until the pointer changes to a ↔ shape, click and drag to the left until the right edge is just to the right of the SigningDate field value, and then release the mouse button. You've resized all six text boxes. See Figure 6-13.

**Figure 6-13** **After resizing the text boxes in the control layout**

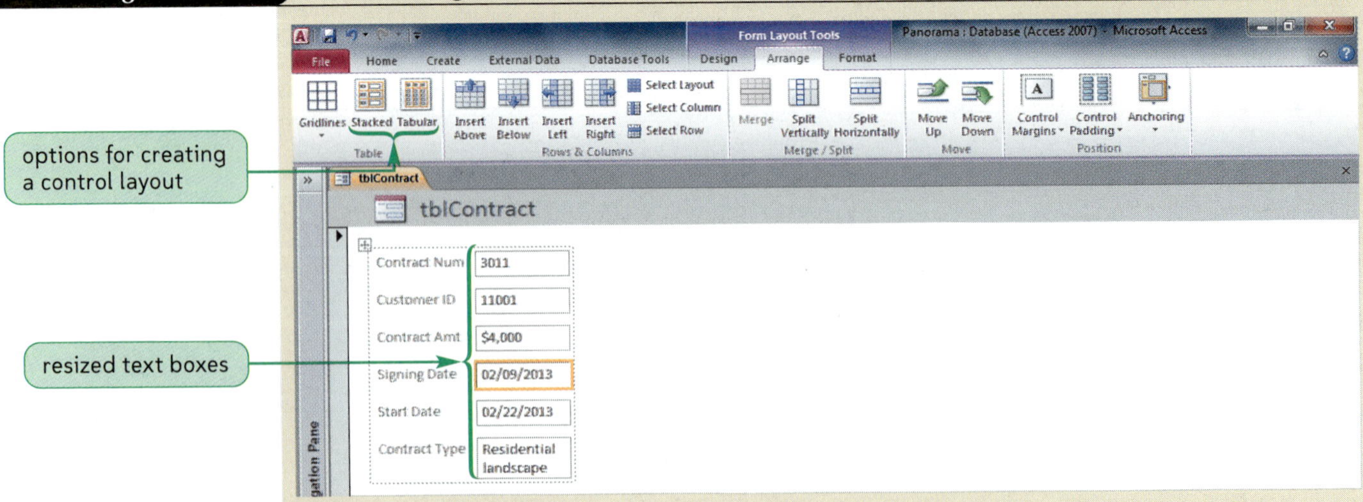

**Trouble?** If you resize the text boxes too far to the left, number signs appear inside the SigningDate and StartDate text boxes. Drag the right edge of the SigningDate text box slightly to the right and repeat the process until the date values are visible inside the text boxes.

The control layout for the form is a stacked layout, which arranges text box controls vertically with a label control to the left of each text box control; you click the Stacked button in the Table group to place selected controls in a stacked layout. You can also choose a tabular layout, which arranges text box controls in a datasheet format with labels above each column; you click the Tabular button in the Table group to place selected controls in a tabular layout.

You can now remove the ContractType text box and its label from the stacked layout, move the two controls, and then resize the text box.

5. Click the **ContractType** text box, hold down the **Shift** key, click the **Contract Type** label to select both controls, release the **Shift** key, right-click the **ContractType** text box to open the shortcut menu, point to **Layout**, and then click **Remove Layout**. You've removed the two selected controls from the stacked layout.
6. Make sure that the ContractType text box and its label are selected, and then drag the two controls up and to the right until their tops are aligned with the top of the ContractNum controls. See Figure 6-14. (Note: You will resize the ContractType text box in the next step.)
7. Click the **ContractType** text box so that it's the only selected control, and then drag the right edge of the control to the right and the bottom edge of the control down to the positions shown in Figure 6-14.

**Figure 6-14** After moving and resizing the ContractType controls

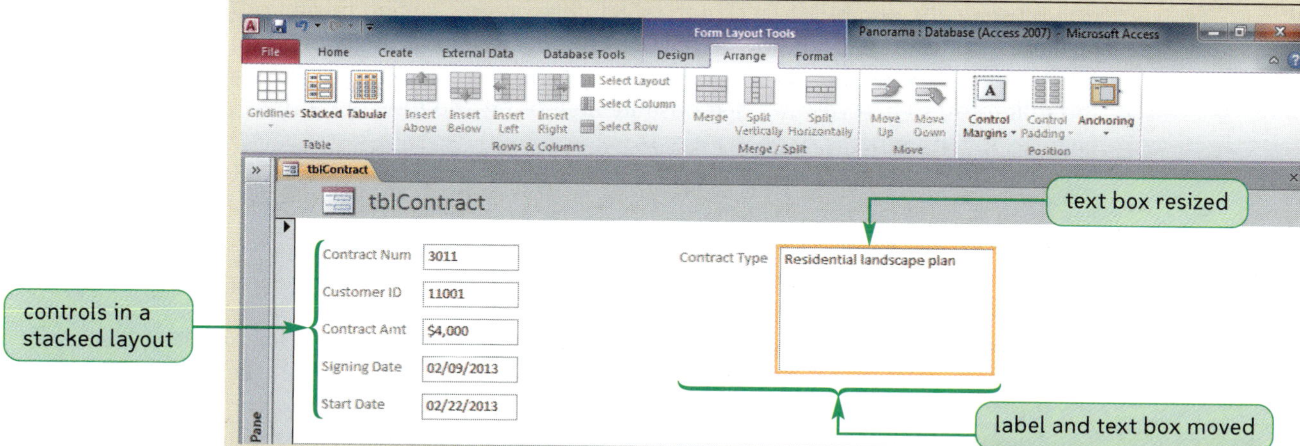


**Trouble?** It won't cause any problems if the two ContractType controls on your screen are in slightly different positions than the ones shown in the figure or if your ContractType text box is not exactly the same size.

You do not usually need to change the default settings for the Control Margins property, which controls the spacing around the text inside a control, and the Control Padding property, which controls the spacing around the outside of a control. However, you'll show Sarah the effects of changing these properties.

8. Click one of the controls in the stacked layout, click the **layout selector** to select all controls in the stacked layout, click the **Control Margins** button in the Position group, and then click **Medium**. The text inside the stacked layout controls moves down slightly.

9. Click the **Control Margins** button, click **Wide** and observe the effect of this setting on the text inside the controls, click the **Control Margins** button, click **None** and observe the effect of this setting, click the **Control Margins** button, and then click **Narrow**. Narrow is the default setting for the Control Margins property.

   Narrow is also the default setting for the Control Padding property.

10. In the Position group, click the **Control Padding** button, click **Medium** and observe the change to the spacing around the controls, and then repeat for the other settings of this property, making sure you set the property to **Narrow** as your final step.

Next, you'll show Sarah how to anchor controls.

## Anchoring Controls in a Form

You can design attractive forms that use the screen dimensions effectively when all the users of a database have the same sized monitors and use the same screen resolution. How do you design attractive forms when users have a variety of monitor sizes and screen resolutions? If you design a form to fit on large monitors using high screen resolutions, then only a portion of the controls in the form fit on smaller monitors with lower resolutions, forcing users to scroll the form. If you design a form to fit on smaller monitors with low screen resolutions, then the form displays on larger monitors in a small area in the upper-left corner of the screen, making the form look unattractively cramped. As a compromise, you can anchor the controls in the form. As shown in the Visual Overview for this session, the Anchor property for a control automatically resizes the control and places the control in the same relative position on the screen as the screen size and resolution change. Unfortunately, when you use the Anchor property, Access doesn't scale the control's font size to match the screen size and resolution.

Next, you'll show Sarah how to anchor controls in a form. Because all monitors at Belmont Landscapes are the same size and use the same resolution, first you'll save the split form, so that you can demonstrate anchoring and then discard the anchoring changes to the form.

### To anchor controls in the form:

1. Save the form as **frmContractSplit**.

   You can't anchor individual controls in a control layout; you can only anchor the entire control layout as a group. You've already removed the ContractType controls from the stacked layout, so you can anchor them separately from the stacked layout. You'll remove the SigningDate and StartDate controls from the stacked layout, so you'll have three sets of controls to anchor—the stacked layout is one set, the ContractType controls are in the second set, and the Signing Date and StartDate controls make up the third set.

2. Use **Shift+Click** to select the **SigningDate** and **StartDate** text boxes and labels, right-click the **SigningDate** text box, point to **Layout**, and then click **Remove Layout** to remove these two text boxes and their labels from the stacked layout.

   First, you'll anchor the selected SigningDate and StartDate controls.

3. In the Position group on the Arrange tab, click the **Anchoring** button to open the Anchoring gallery. See Figure 6-15.

**Figure 6-15** **Displaying the Anchoring gallery**

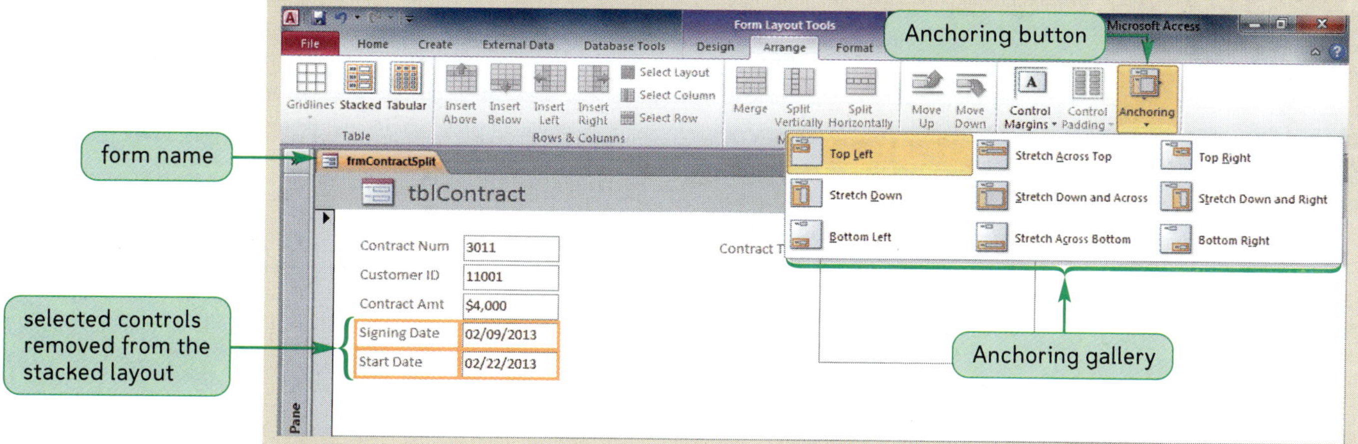


Four of the nine options in the Anchoring gallery fix the position of the selected controls in the top left (the default setting), bottom left, top right, or bottom right positions in the form. If other controls block the corner positions for controls you're anchoring for the first time, the new controls are positioned in relation to the blocking controls. The other five anchoring options resize (or stretch) and position the selected controls.

You'll anchor the SigningDate and StartDate controls in the bottom left and the ContractType controls in the top right.

4. Click **Bottom Left** in the Anchoring gallery, click the **ContractType** text box, click the **Anchoring** button, and then click **Top Right**. The SigningDate and StartDate controls shifted down, and the ContractType controls shifted to the right.

Next, you'll open the Navigation Pane, and then increase the height of the form to simulate the effect of a larger screen for the form.

5. Open the Navigation Pane. The two sets of controls on the left shift to the right because the horizontal dimensions of the form decreased from the left, and these two sets of controls are anchored to the left in the form. The ContractType controls remain in the same position in the form.

6. Position the pointer on the border between the form and the datasheet until the pointer changes to a ╪ shape, and then drag down until you see only the column headings and the first row in the datasheet. The bottom set of controls shift down, because it's anchored to the bottom, and the two sets of controls at the top remain in the same positions in the form. See Figure 6-16.

**Figure 6-16** **Anchored controls in a resized form**

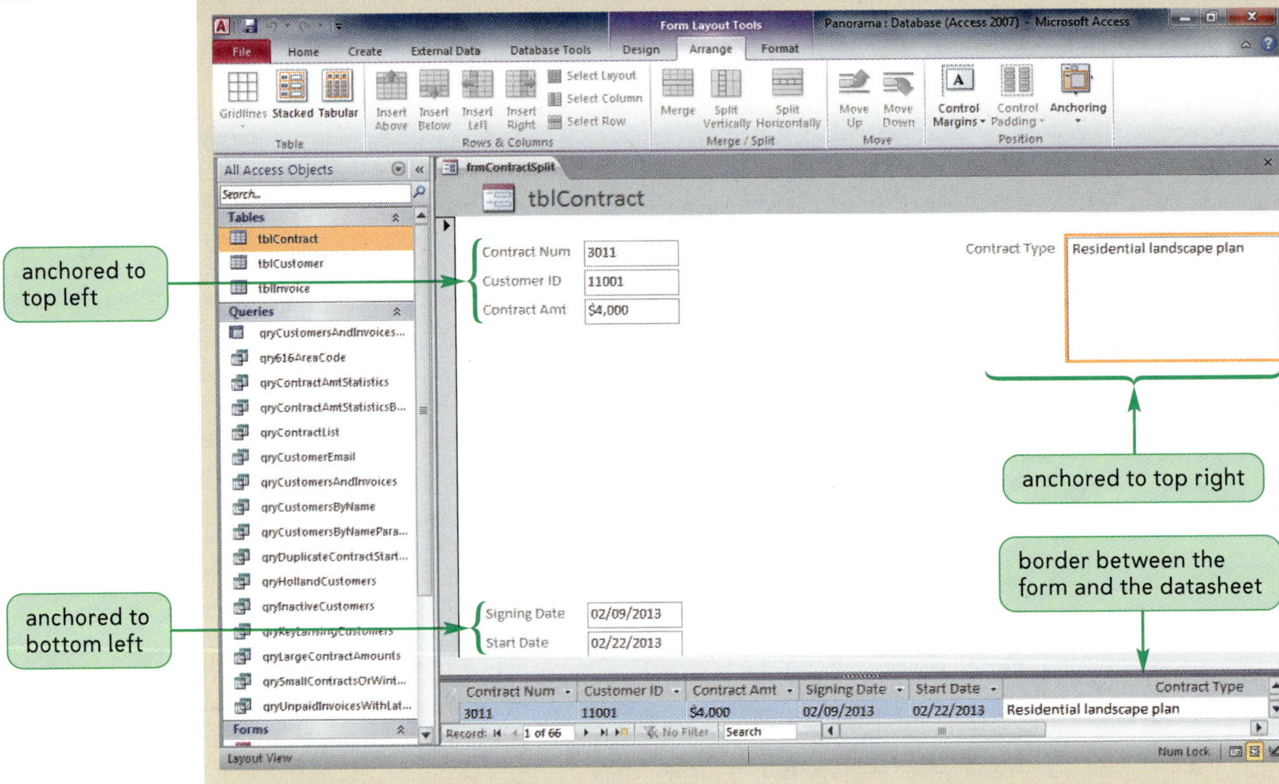


Finally, you'll show Sarah one of the anchoring options that resizes the ContractType text box as the form dimensions change.

7. Click the **ContractType** text box (if necessary), click the **Anchoring** button, and then click **Stretch Down and Right**. Because the ContractType text box is already anchored to the top right, it can't stretch any more to the right, but it does stretch down to increase the height of the text box.
8. Position the pointer on the border between the form and the datasheet until the pointer changes to a ╪ shape, and then drag up until you can see several rows in the datasheet. The bottom set of controls shifts up, and the bottom edge of the ContractType text box shifts up, reducing its height.

   You've finished showing Sarah the Layout view changes to the split form, so you can close the form without saving the anchoring changes.
9. Close the frmContractSplit form without saving your design changes.
10. If you are not continuing on to the next session, close the Panorama database.

You've used form tools to create forms, and you've modified forms in Layout view. In the next session, you will continue your work with forms, concentrating on the techniques, tools, and options available in Design view.

REVIEW

## *Session 6.1 Quick Check*

1. According to the form design guidelines, which object(s) should you use to perform all database updates?
2. The ____________ property specifies the data source for a control in a form or report or for a field in a table or query.
3. What is the Documenter?
4. What is the Multiple Items tool?
5. What is a split form?
6. The ____________ property for a control automatically resizes the control and places the control in the same relative position on the screen as the screen's size and resolution change.

# SESSION 6.2 VISUAL OVERVIEW

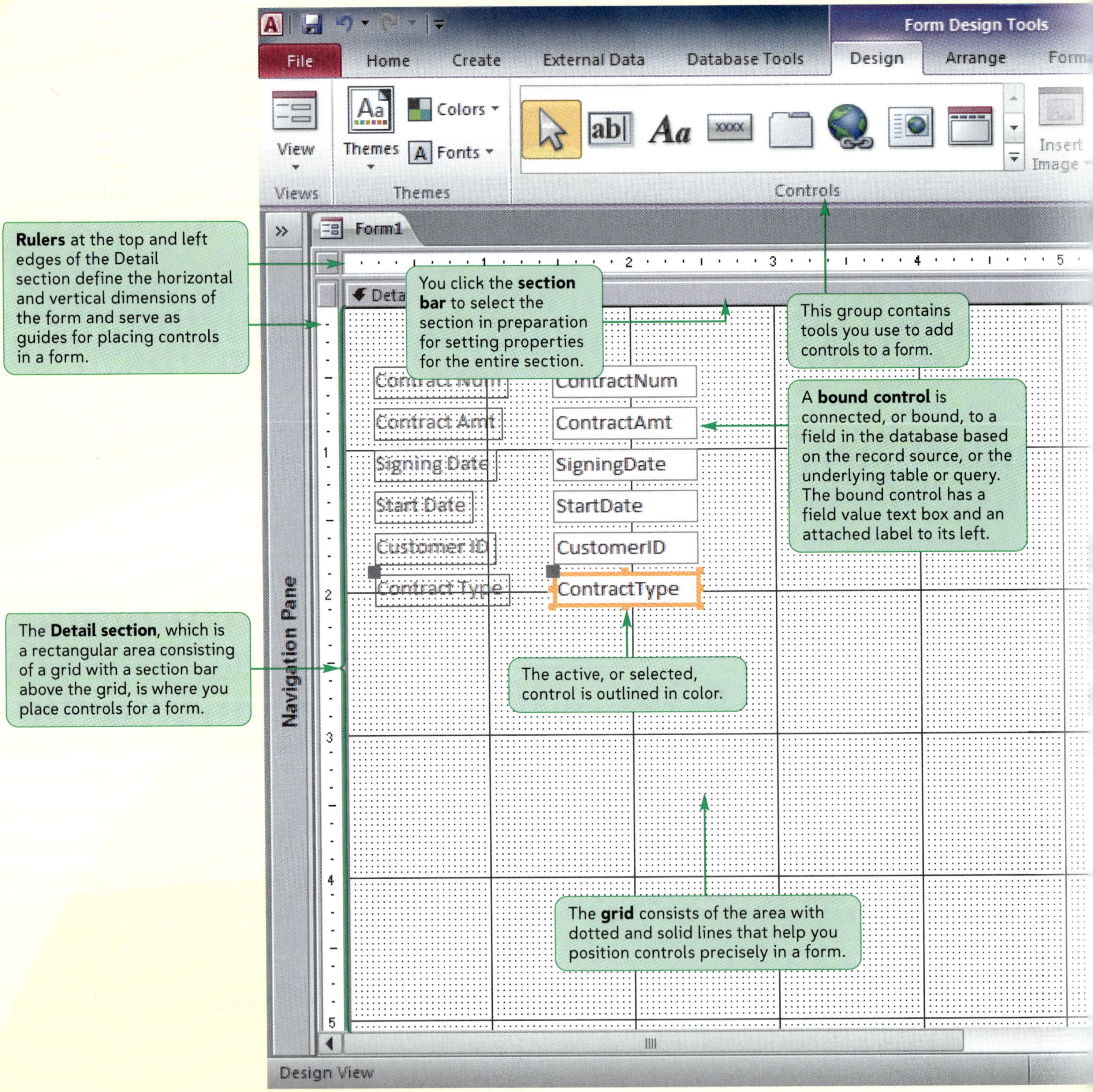

# FORM IN DESIGN VIEW

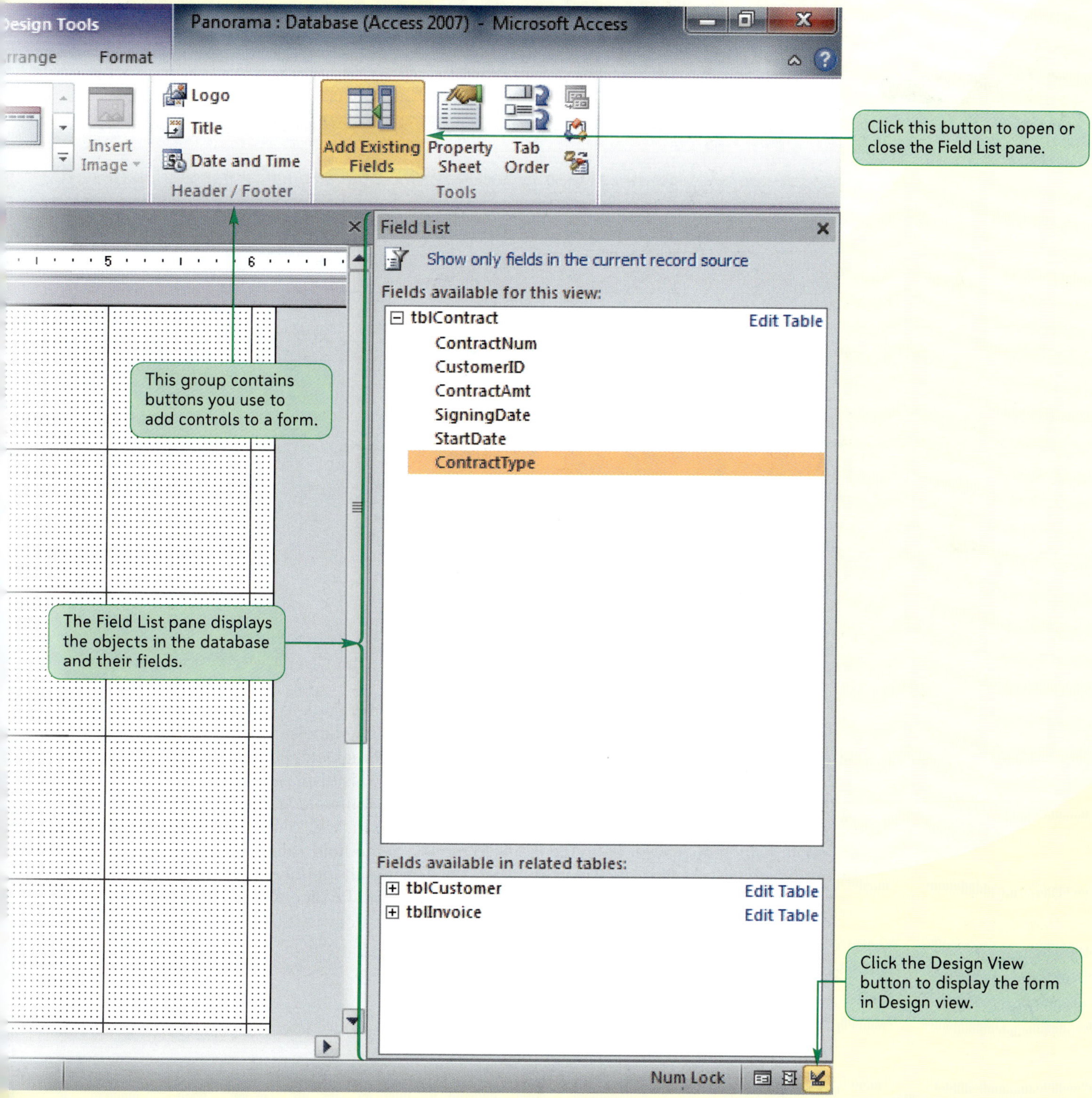

# Planning and Designing a Custom Form

Sarah needs a form to enter and view information about Belmont Landscapes contracts and their related invoices. She wants the information in a single form, and she asks Lucia to design a form for her review.

After several discussions with Sarah and her staff, Lucia prepared a paper design for a custom form to display a contract and its related invoices. Lucia then used her paper design to create the form shown in Figure 6-17.

**Figure 6-17** Lucia's design for the custom form

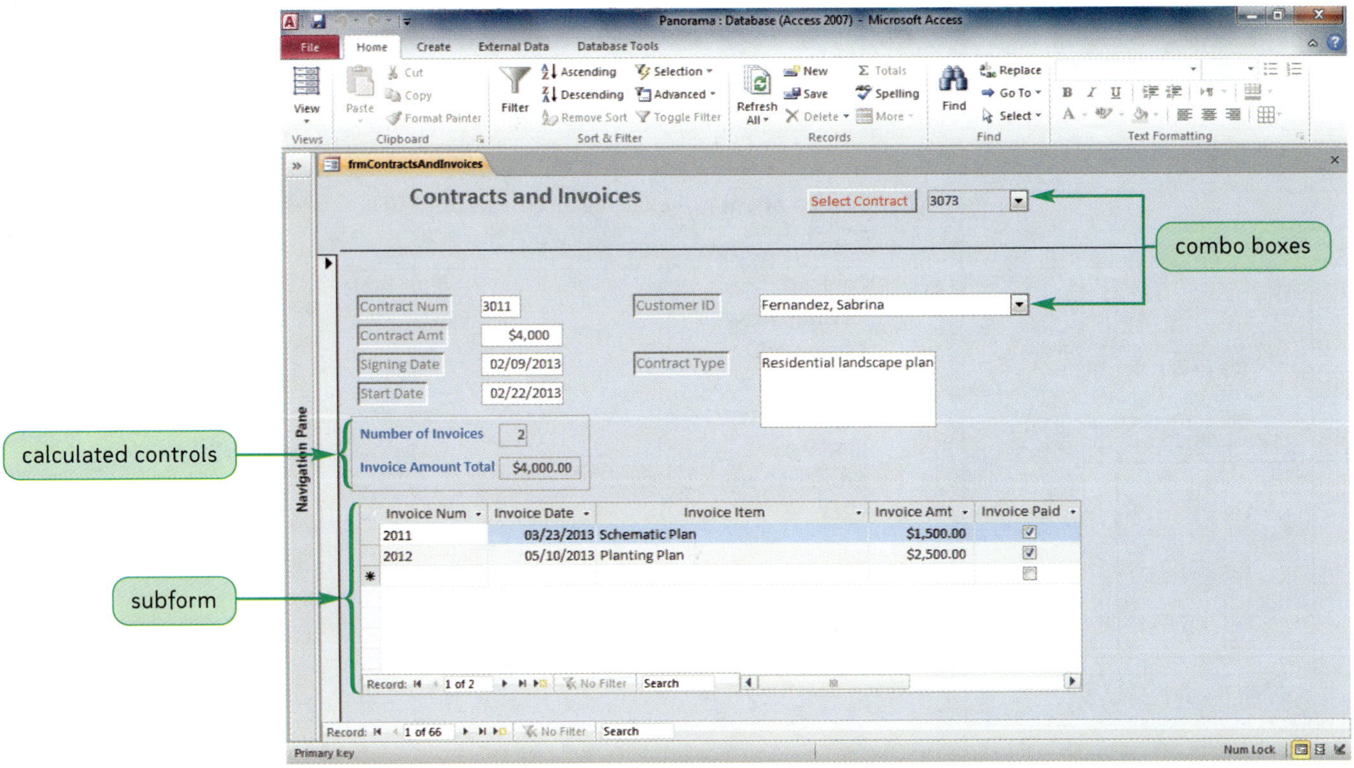


Notice that the top of the form displays a title and a combo box to select a contract record. Below these items are six field values with identifying labels from the tblContract table; these fields are the ContractNum, ContractAmt, SigningDate, StartDate, CustomerID, and ContractType fields. The CustomerID field is displayed in a combo box and the other field values are displayed in text boxes. The tblInvoice table fields appear in a subform, a separate form contained within another form. Unlike the tblContract table data, which displays identifying labels to the left of the field values in text boxes, the tblInvoice table data is displayed in datasheet format with identifying column headings above the field values. Finally, Number of Invoices and Invoice Amount Total in the main form display calculated controls based on the content of the subform.

# Creating a Custom Form in Design View

To create Lucia's custom form, you could use the Form Wizard to create a basic version of the form and then customize it in Layout and Design views. However, to create Lucia's form, you would need to make many modifications to a basic form created by a wizard, so you will create the form directly in Design view. Creating forms in Design view is easy once you've done one form, and Design view allows you more control, precision, and options than creating forms in Layout view. You'll also find that you'll create forms more productively if you switch between Design view and Layout view because some design modifications are easier to make in one of the two views than in the other view.

## The Form Window in Design View

You can use the Form window in Design view to create and modify forms. To create the custom form based on Lucia's design, you'll create a blank form, add the fields from the tblContract and tblInvoice tables, and then add other controls and make other form modifications.

REFERENCE

### *Creating a Form in Design View*

- Click the Create tab on the Ribbon.
- In the Forms group, click the Blank Form button.
- Click the Design View button on the status bar.
- Make sure the Field List pane is open, and then add the required fields to the form.
- Add other required controls to the form.
- Modify the size, position, and other properties as necessary for the fields and other controls in the form.
- Save the form.

The form you'll create will be a bound form. A **bound form** is a form that has a table or query as its record source. You use bound forms for maintaining and displaying table data. **Unbound forms** are forms that do not have a record source and are usually used for forms that help users navigate among the objects in a database. Now you'll create a blank bound form based on the tblContract table.

**To create a blank form in Design view:**

1. If you took a break after the previous session, make sure that the Panorama database is open and the Navigation Pane is open.
2. Click the **Create** tab on the Ribbon and then, in the Forms group on the Create tab, click the **Blank Form** button. Access opens the Form window in Layout view.
3. Click the **Design View** button on the status bar to switch to Design view, and then close the Navigation Pane. See Figure 6-18.

**Figure 6-18** **Blank form in Design view**

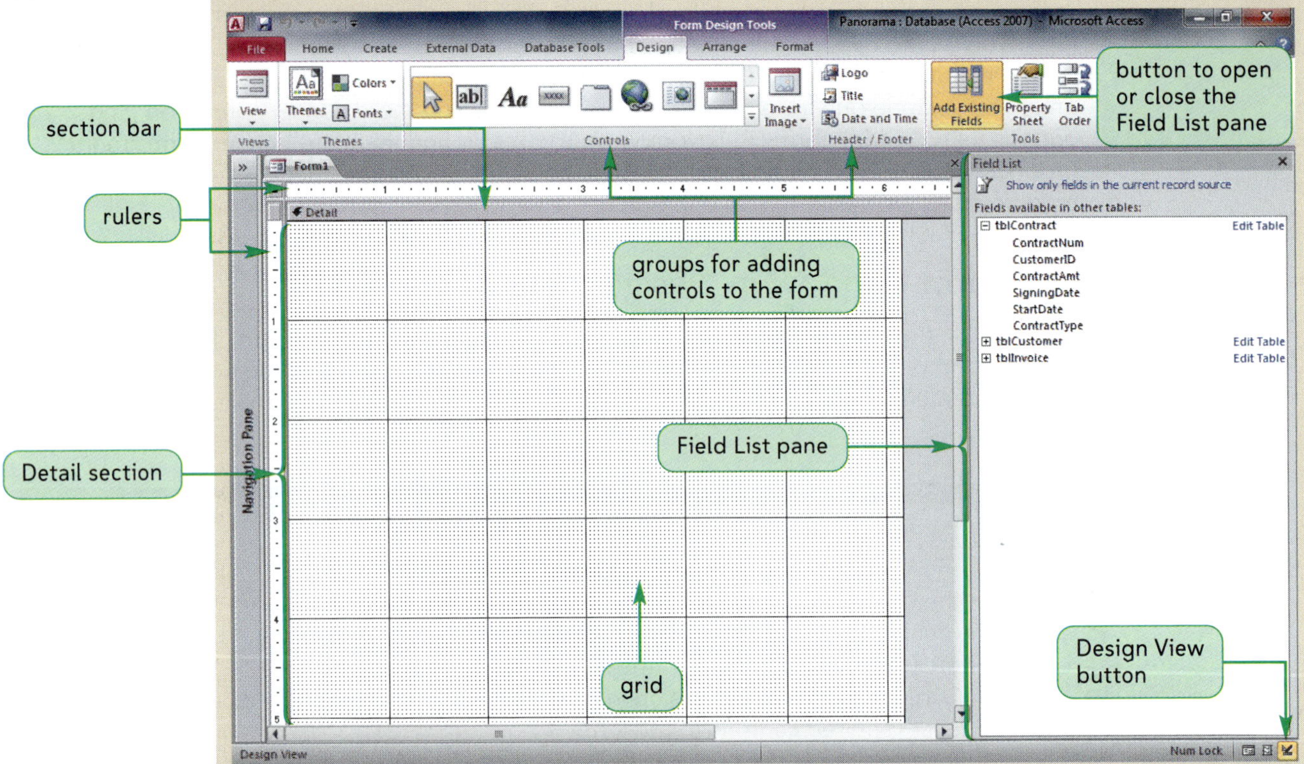


**Trouble?** If the Field List pane displays the "No fields available to be added to the current view" message, click the "Show all tables" link to display the tables in the Panorama database, and then click the plus sign next to tblContract in the Field List pane to display the fields in the table.

**Trouble?** If the tblContract table in the Field List pane is not expanded to show the fields in the table, click the plus sign next to tblContract to display the fields.

Design view contains the tools necessary to create a custom form. You create the form by placing controls in the blank form. You can place three kinds of controls in a form:

- A bound control is connected, or bound, to a field in the database based on the record source, or the underlying table or query. You use bound controls to display and maintain table field values.
- An **unbound control** is not connected to a field in the database. You use unbound controls to display text, such as a form title or instructions; to display lines, rectangles, and other objects; or to display graphics and pictures created using other software programs. An unbound control that displays text is called a **label**.
- A **calculated control** displays a value that is the result of an expression. The expression usually contains one or more fields, and the calculated control is recalculated each time any value in the expression changes.

To create a bound control, you add fields from the Field List pane to the Form window, and position the bound controls where you want them to appear in the form. To place other controls in a form or a report, you use the tools in the Controls and Header/Footer groups on the Design tab; ScreenTips are available for each control in these groups. The tools in the Controls group let you add to the form controls such as lines, rectangles, images, buttons, check boxes, and list boxes.

As noted earlier, Design view for a form contains a Detail section, which is a rectangular area consisting of a grid with a section bar above the grid. You click the section bar to select the section in preparation for setting properties for the entire section. The grid consists of the area with dotted and solid lines that help you position controls precisely in a form. In the Detail section, you place bound controls, unbound controls, and calculated controls in your form. You can change the size of the Detail section by dragging its edges. Rulers at the top and left edges of the Detail section define the horizontal and vertical dimensions of the form and serve as guides for placing controls in a form.

Your first task is to add bound controls to the Detail section for the six fields from the tblContract table.

## Adding Fields to a Form

When you add a bound control to a form, Access adds a text box and, to its left, an attached label. The text box displays a field value from the record source. The attached label displays either the Caption property value for the field, if the Caption property value has been set, or the field name. To create a bound control, you first display the Field List pane by clicking the Add Existing Fields button in the Tools group on the Design tab. Then you double-click a field in the Field List pane to add the bound control to the Detail section. You can also drag a field from the Field List pane to the Detail section.

Next, you'll add bound controls to the Detail section for the six fields in the Field List pane. The Field List pane displays the three tables in the Panorama database, and the six fields in the tblContract table.

### To add bound controls from the tblContract table to the grid:

1. Double-click **ContractNum** in the Field List pane. Access adds a bound control in the Detail section of the form, removes the tblCustomer and tblInvoice tables from the "Fields available for this view" section of the Field List pane, and places the two tables in the "Fields available in related tables" section of the Field List pane.
2. Repeat Step 1 for the **ContractAmt**, **SigningDate**, **StartDate**, **CustomerID**, and **ContractType** fields, in this order, in the Field List pane. Six bound controls—one for each of the six fields in the Field List pane—have been added in the Detail section of the form. See Figure 6-19.

**Figure 6-19** **Adding text boxes and attached labels as bound controls to a form**

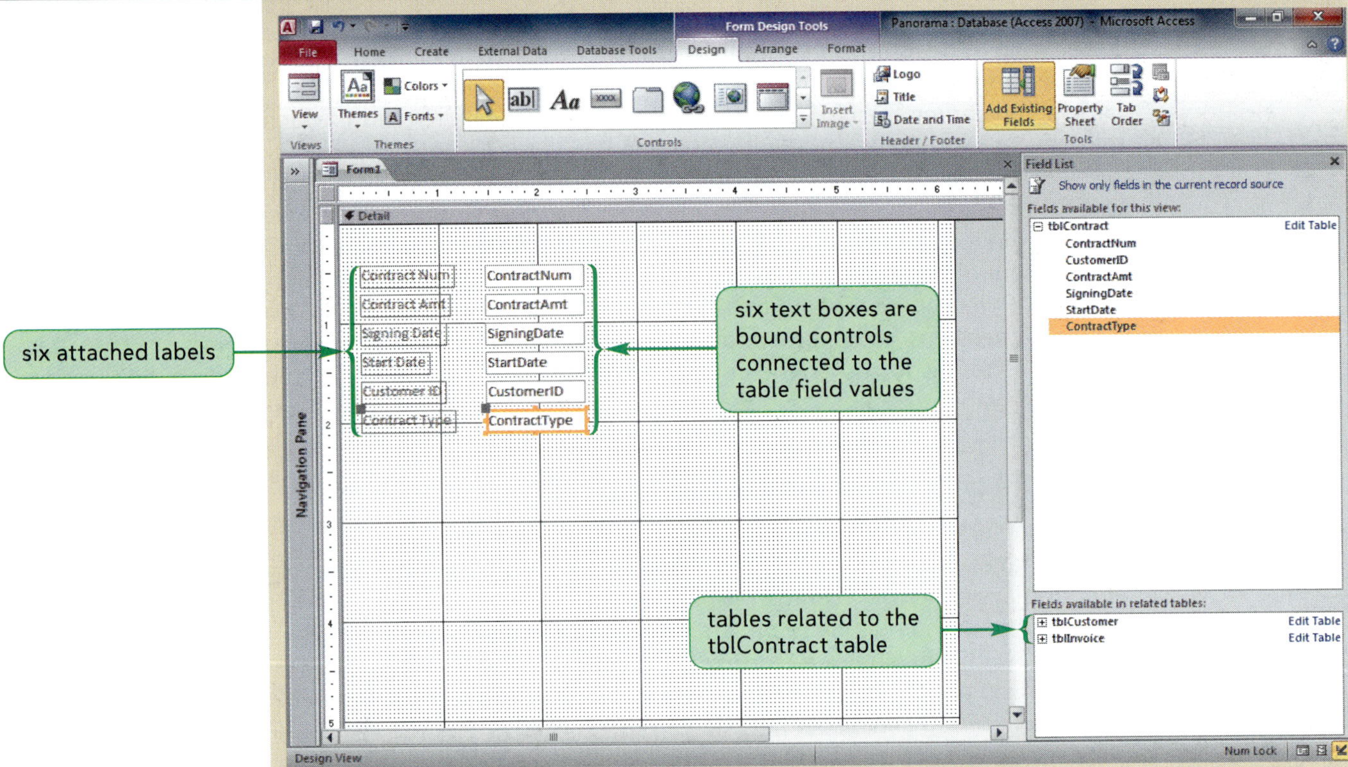


You should periodically save your work as you create a form, so you'll save the form now.

3. Click the **Save** button on the Quick Access Toolbar. The Save As dialog box opens.

4. With the default name Form1 (your name might be different) selected in the Form Name box, type **frmContractsAndInvoices**, and then press the **Enter** key. The tab for the form now displays the form name, and the form design is saved in the Panorama database.

You've added the fields you need to the grid, so you can close the Field List pane.

5. In the Tools group on the Design tab, click the **Add Existing Fields** button to close the Field List pane.

Creating and modifying a form in Design view might seem awkward at first. With practice you will become comfortable working with custom forms.

INSIGHT

*Suggestions for Creating a Form Productively*

To design a form productively, you should keep in mind the following suggestions:

- You can click the Undo button one or more times immediately after you make one or more errors or make undesired form adjustments.
- You should back up your database frequently, especially before you create new objects or customize existing objects. If you run into difficulty, you can revert to your most recent backup copy of the database.
- You should save your form after you've completed a portion of your work successfully and before you need to perform steps you've never done before. If you're not satisfied with subsequent steps, close the form without saving the changes you made since your last save, and then open the form and perform the steps again.
- You can always close the form, make a copy of the form in the Navigation Pane, and practice with the copy.
- Adding controls, setting properties, and performing other tasks in Access in the correct way should work all the time with consistent results, but in rare instances, you might find a feature doesn't work properly. If a feature you've previously used successfully suddenly doesn't work, you should save your work, close the database, make a backup copy of the database, open the database, and then compact and repair the database. Performing a compact and repair resolves most of these types of problems.

Compare your form's Detail section with Lucia's design, and notice that you need to move the ContractType bound control up and to the right. To do so, you must select and move the bound control.

## Selecting, Moving, and Aligning Controls

Six text boxes now appear in the form's Detail section, one below the other. Each text box is a bound control connected to a field in the underlying table. Each text box has an attached label to its left. Each text box and attached label pair is a control in the form, and each individual text box is also a control in the form, as is each individual label. When you select a control, the control becomes outlined in orange, and eight squares, called handles, appear on its four corners and at the midpoints of its four edges. The larger handle in a control's upper-left corner is its **move handle**, which you use to move the control. You use the other seven handles, called **sizing handles**, to resize the control. When you work in Design view, controls you place in the form do not become part of a control layout, so you can individually select, move, resize, and otherwise manipulate one control without also changing the other controls. However, at any time you can select a group of controls and place them in a control layout—either a stacked layout or a tabular layout.

REFERENCE

*Selecting and Moving Controls*

- Click the control to select it. To select several controls at once, press and hold down the Shift key while clicking each control. Handles appear around all selected controls.
- To move a single selected control, drag the control's move handle, which is the handle in the upper-left corner, to its new position.
- To move a group of selected controls, point to any selected control until the pointer changes to a move pointer, and then drag the group of selected controls to its new position.
- To move selected controls in small increments, press the appropriate arrow key.
- To move selected controls to the next nearest grid dot, hold down the Ctrl key and press the appropriate arrow key.

Based on Lucia's design for the custom form, you must select the ContractType bound control and move it up and to the right in the Detail section. The ContractType bound control consists of a field-value text box, labeled ContractType, and an attached label, labeled Contract Type, to its left.

## To select the ContractType bound control:

1. If necessary, click the **ContractType** text box to select it. Move handles, which are the larger handles, appear on the upper-left corners of the selected text box control and its attached label. Sizing handles also appear, but only on the text box. See Figure 6-20.

**Figure 6-20** **Selecting the ContractType bound control**

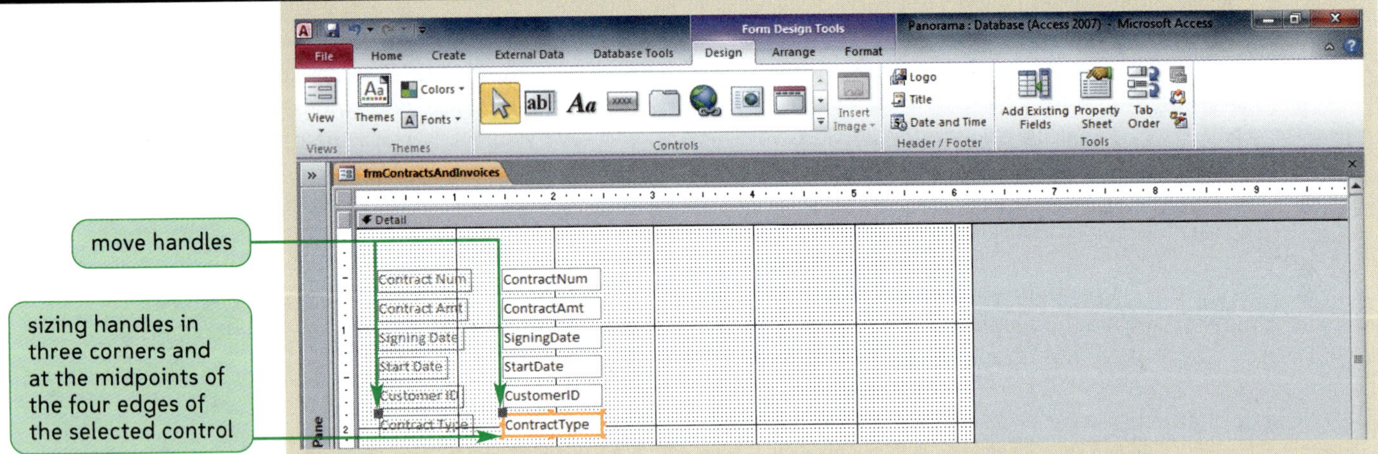


You can move a text box and its attached label together. To move them, place the pointer anywhere on the border of the text box, but not on a move handle or a sizing handle. When the pointer changes to a ✥ shape, you can drag the text box and its attached label to the new location. As you move a control, an outline of the control moves on the rulers to indicate the current position of the control as you drag it. To move a group of selected controls, point to any selected control until the pointer changes to a ✥ shape, and then drag the group of selected controls to its new position. You can move controls with more precision when you use the arrow keys instead of the mouse. To move selected controls in small increments, press the appropriate arrow key. To move selected controls to the next nearest grid dot, hold down the Ctrl key and press the appropriate arrow key.

You can also move either a text box or its label individually. If you want to move the text box but not its label, for example, place the pointer on the text box's move handle. When the pointer changes to a ✥ shape, drag the text box to the new location. You use the label's move handle in a similar way to move only the label.

You'll now arrange the controls to match Lucia's design.

## To move the ContractType bound control:

1. Position the pointer on one of the edges of the ContractType text box, but not on a move handle or a sizing handle. When the pointer changes to a ✥ shape, drag the control to the right until the left edge of the highlight on the horizontal ruler is at the 3-inch mark, drag the control up until the top of the highlight on the vertical ruler is just below the top of the SigningDate bound control, and then release the mouse button. See Figure 6-21.

**Figure 6-21** **After moving the ContractType bound control**

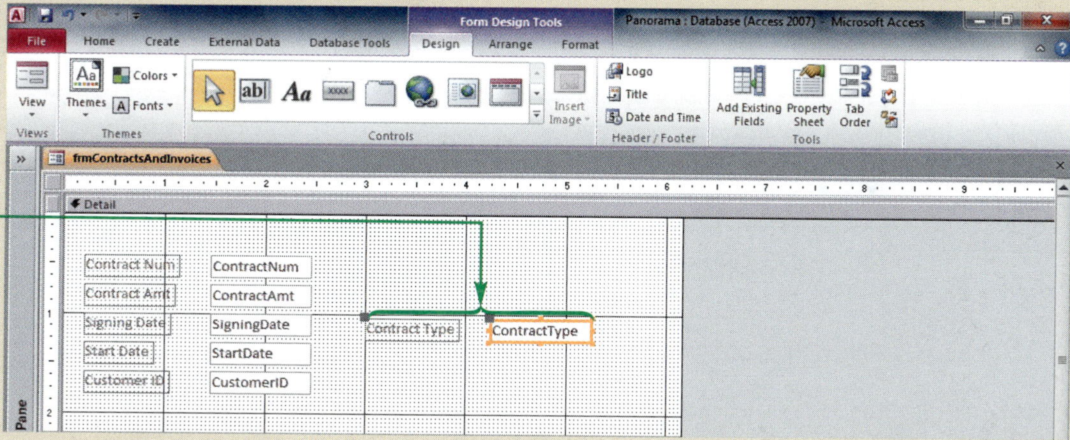


**Trouble?** If you need to make major adjustments to the placement of the ContractType bound control, click the Undo button on the Quick Access Toolbar one or more times until the bound control is back to its starting position, and then repeat Step 1. If you need to make minor adjustments to the placement of the ContractType bound control, use the arrow keys.

Now you need to align the ContractType and SigningDate bound controls on their top edges. If you've selected a column of controls, you can align the left edges or the right edges of the controls. If you've selected a row of controls, you can align the top edges or the bottom edges of the controls. A fifth alignment option, To Grid, aligns selected controls with the dots in the grid. You can find the five alignment options on the Arrange tab of the Ribbon or on the shortcut menu for the selected controls. You'll use the shortcut menu to align the two bound controls. Then you'll save the modified form and review your work in Form view.

### To align the ContractType and SigningDate bound controls:

1. Make sure the ContractType bound control is selected, hold down the **Shift** key, click the **Contract Type** label, click the **SigningDate** text box, click the **Signing Date** label, and then release the **Shift** key. This action selects the four controls; each selected control has an orange border.
2. Right-click one of the selected controls, point to **Align** on the shortcut menu, and then click **Top**. The four selected controls are aligned on their top edges. See Figure 6-22.

**Figure 6-22** **After top-aligning four controls in the Detail section**

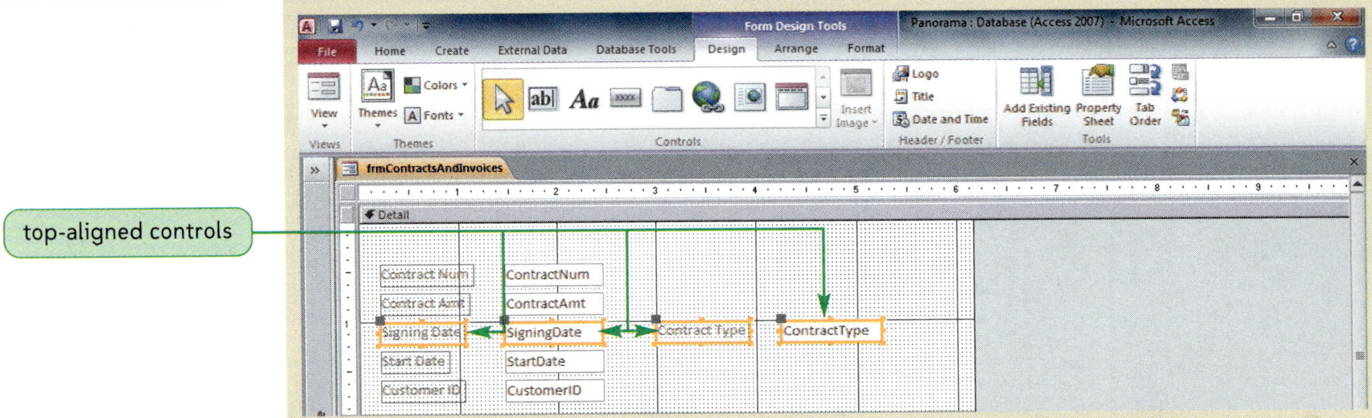


As you create a form, you should periodically save your modifications to the form and review your progress in Form view.

3. Save your form design changes, and then switch to Form view. See Figure 6-23.

**Figure 6-23** **Form displayed in Form view**

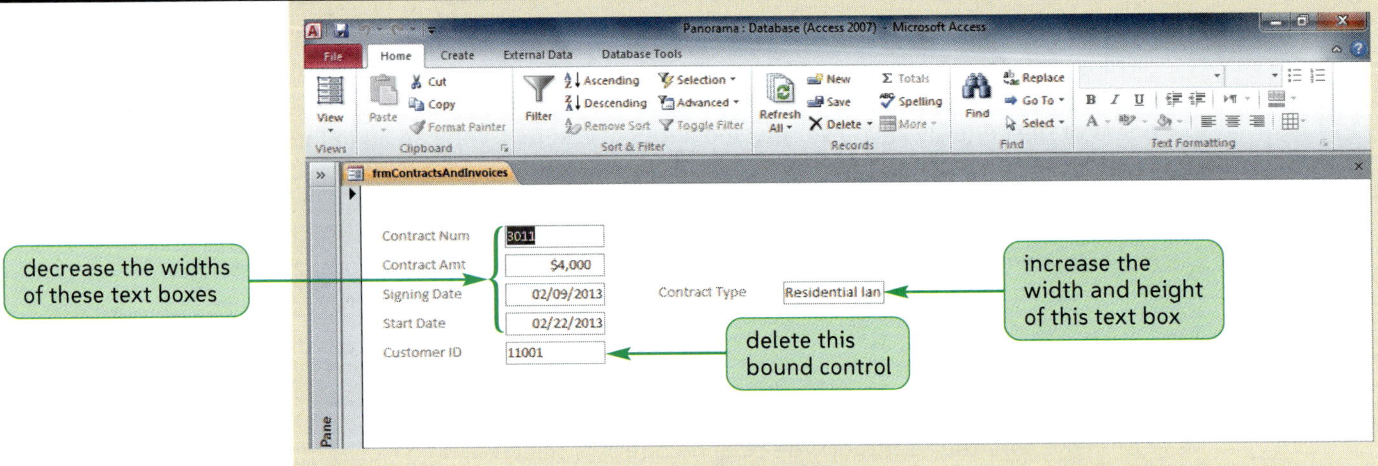


The value in the ContractType text box is not fully displayed, so you need to increase the size of the text box. The widths of the other four text boxes are wider than necessary, so you'll reduce their widths. Also, the CustomerID bound control consists of a label and a text box, but the plan for the form shows a combo box for the CustomerID positioned above the ContractType bound control. You'll delete the CustomerID bound control in preparation for adding it to the form as a combo box.

## Resizing and Deleting Controls

A selected control displays seven sizing handles: four at the midpoints on each edge of the control and one at each corner except the upper-left corner. Recall that the upper-left corner displays the move handle. Positioning the pointer over a sizing handle changes the pointer to a two-headed arrow; the directions in which the arrows point indicate in which direction you can resize the selected control. When you drag a sizing handle, you resize the control. As you resize the control, a thin line appears inside the sizing handle to guide you in completing the task accurately, as do the outlines that appear on the horizontal and vertical rulers.

**REFERENCE**

### *Resizing a Control in Design View*

- Click the control to select it and display the sizing handles.
- Place the pointer over the sizing handle you want, and then drag the edge of the control until it is the size you want.
- To resize selected controls in small increments, hold down the Shift key and press the appropriate arrow key. This technique applies the resizing to the right edge and the bottom edge of the control.

You'll begin by deleting the CustomerID bound control. Then you'll resize the ContractType text box, which is too narrow and too short to display ContractType field values. Then you'll resize the remaining four text boxes to reduce their widths.

### To delete a bound control and resize the text boxes:

1. Switch to Design view, click an unused portion of the grid, or to the right of the grid, to deselect all controls, and then click the **CustomerID** text box to select it.
2. Right-click the **CustomerID** text box to open the shortcut menu, and then click **Delete**. The label and the text box for the CustomerID bound control are deleted.
3. Click the **ContractType** text box to select it.
4. Place the pointer on the middle-right handle of the ContractType text box. When the pointer changes to a ↔ shape, drag the right border horizontally to the right to the 6-inch mark on the horizontal ruler.
5. Place the pointer on the middle-bottom handle of the ContractType text box. When the pointer changes to a ↕ shape, drag the bottom border down to the 1.75-inch mark on the vertical ruler. See Figure 6-24.

**TIP**

If you want to delete a label but not its associated text box, right-click the label, and then click Delete on the shortcut menu.

**Figure 6-24** **After resizing the ContractType text box**

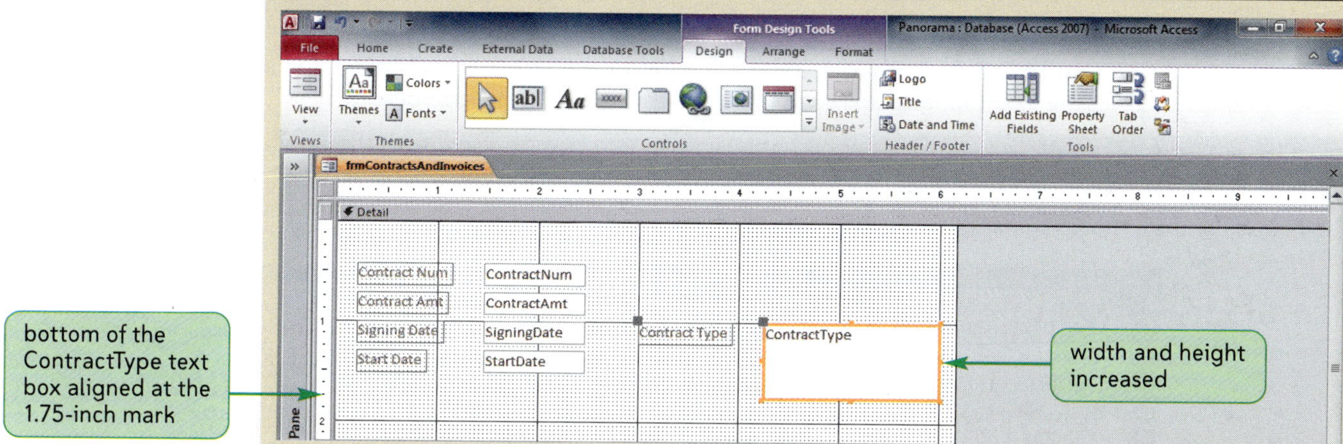


Resizing controls in Design view is a trial-and-error process, in which you resize a control in Design view, switch to Form view to observe the effect of the resizing, switch back to Design view to make further refinements to the control's size, and continue until the control is sized correctly. It's easier to resize controls in Layout view because you can see actual field values while you resize the controls. You'll resize the other four text boxes in Layout view.

6. Switch to Layout view, and then click the **ContractNum** text box (if necessary) to select it.

7. Position the pointer on the right edge of the **ContractNum** text box. When the pointer changes to a ↔ shape, drag the right border horizontally to the left until the text box is slightly wider than the field value it contains. See Figure 6-25.

   The sizes of the ContractAmt, SigningDate, and StartDate text boxes will look fine if you reduce them to have the same widths, so you'll select all three text boxes and resize them as a group.

**TIP**

If you select a control by mistake, hold down the Shift key, and then click the selected control to deselect it.

8. Select the **ContractAmt**, **SigningDate**, and **StartDate** text boxes.
9. Position the pointer on the right edge of any of the three selected controls. When the pointer changes to a ↔ shape, drag the right border horizontally to the left until the SigningDate and StartDate text boxes are slightly wider than the field values they contain. See Figure 6-25.

**Figure 6-25** **After resizing text boxes in Layout view**

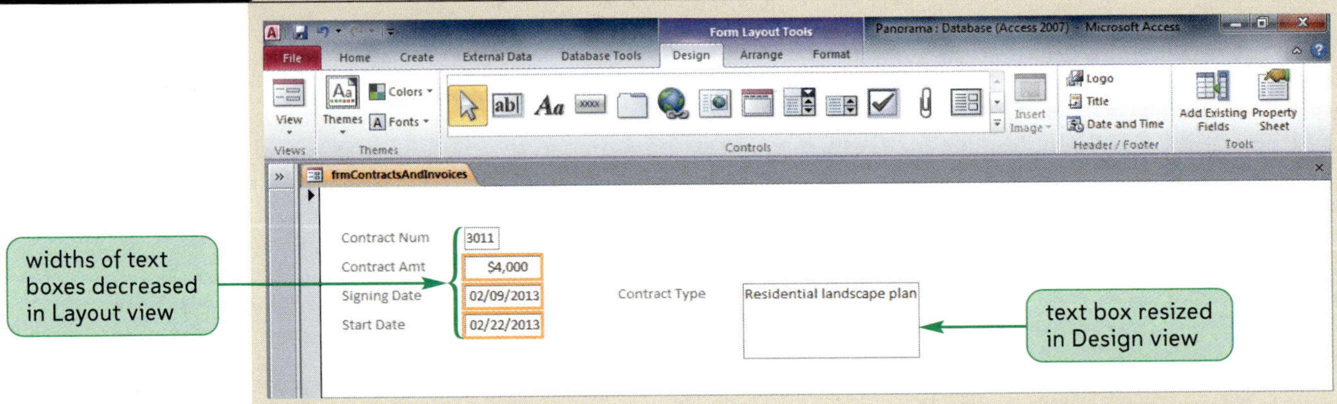


**Trouble?** If you resized the text boxes too far to the left, number signs will be displayed inside the SigningDate and StartDate text boxes. Drag the right edge of the text boxes slightly to the right and repeat the process until the date values are visible inside the text boxes.

10. Navigate through the first several records to make sure the five text boxes are sized properly and display the full field values. If any text box is too small, select the text box and increase its width the appropriate amount.
11. Save your form design changes, switch to Design view, and then deselect all controls by clicking in an unused portion of the grid.

**INSIGHT**

*Making Form Design Modifications*

When you design forms and other objects, you'll find it helpful to switch frequently between Design view and Layout view. Some form modifications are easier to make in Layout view, other form modifications are easier to make in Design view, and still other form modifications can be made only in Design view. You should check your progress frequently in either Layout view or Form view, and you should save your modifications after completing a set of changes successfully.

Recall that you removed the lookup feature from the CustomerID field because a combo box provides the same lookup capability in a form. Next, you'll add a combo box for the CustomerID field to the custom form.

# Adding a Combo Box to a Form

The Customer and Contract tables are related in a one-to-many relationship. The CustomerID field in the Contract table is a foreign key to the Customer table, and you can use a combo box in the custom form to view and maintain CustomerID field values more easily and accurately than using a text box. Recall that a combo box is a control that provides the features of a text box and a list box; you can choose a value from the list or type an entry.

PROSKILLS

## *Problem Solving: Using Combo Boxes for Foreign Keys*

When you design forms, combo boxes are a natural choice for foreign keys because foreign key values must match one of the primary key values in the related primary table. If you do not use combo boxes for foreign keys, you force users to type values in the text box; when they make typing mistakes, Access rejects the values and displays frustrating non-matching error messages. Combo boxes allow users to select from a list of only valid foreign key values, so non-matching situations are eliminated. At the same time, combo boxes allow users who are skilled at data entry to more rapidly type the values, instead of using the more time-consuming technique of choosing a value from the combo box list. Whenever you use an Access feature such as combo boxes for foreign keys, it takes extra time during development to add the feature, but you save users time and improve their accuracy for the many months or years they use the database.

You use the **Combo Box tool** in Design view to add a combo box to a form. If you want help when adding the combo box, you can select one of the Control Wizards. A **Control Wizard** asks a series of questions and then uses your answers to create a control in a form or report. Access offers Control Wizards for the Combo Box, List Box, Option Group, Command Button, Subform/Subreport, and other control tools.

You will use the Combo Box Wizard to add a combo box to the form for the CustomerID field.

### To add a combo box to the form:

1. In the Controls group on the Design tab, click the **More** button to open the Controls gallery. See Figure 6-26.

**Figure 6-26** Controls gallery

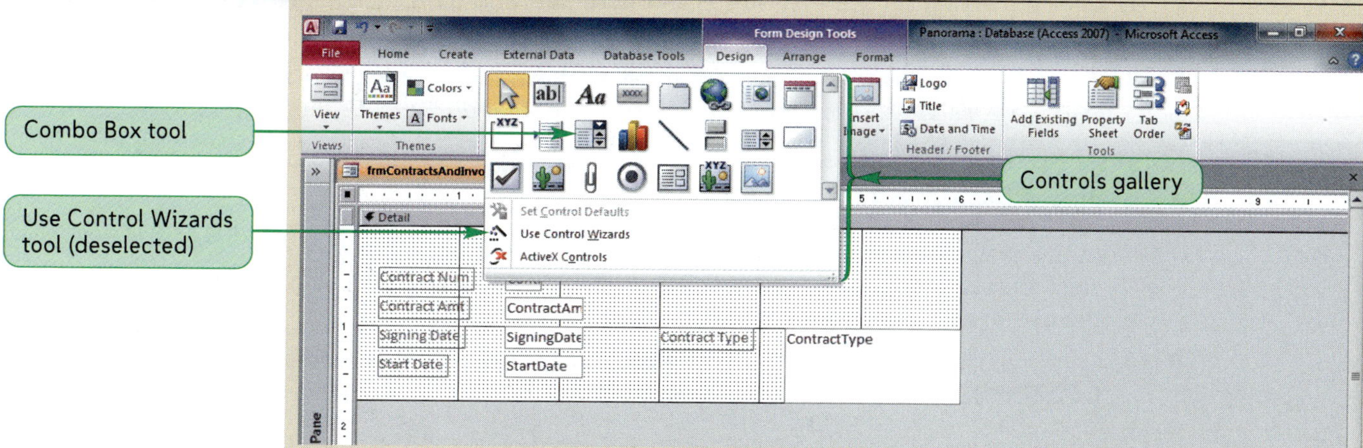

The Controls gallery contains 23 tools that allow you to add controls (such as text boxes, lines, charts, and labels) to a form. You drag a control from the Controls gallery and place it in position in the grid.

2. In the gallery, make sure the Use Control Wizards tool is selected (with an orange background) in the Controls gallery. If the tool is not selected, click the **Use Control Wizards** tool to select it, and then click the **More** button to open the Controls gallery again.

3. In the Controls gallery, click the **Combo Box** tool. The Controls gallery closes. After you click the Combo Box tool or most other tools in the Controls gallery, nothing happens until you move the pointer over the form. When you move the pointer over the form, the pointer changes to a shape that is unique for the control with a plus symbol in its upper-left corner. You position the plus symbol in the location where you want to place the upper-left corner of the control.

   You'll place the combo box near the top of the form, above the ContractType bound control, and then position it more precisely after you've finished the wizard.

4. Position the + portion of the pointer three grid dots below the top of the grid and at the 4-inch mark on the horizontal ruler, and then click the mouse button. Access places a combo box control in the form and opens the first Combo Box Wizard dialog box.

   You can use an existing table or query as the source for a new combo box or type the values for the combo box. In this case, you'll use the qryCustomersByName query as the basis for the new combo box. This query includes the Customer calculated field, whose value equals the Company field value, if it's nonnull, or the concatenation of the LastName and FirstName field values in all other cases.

5. Click the **I want the combo box to get the values from another table or query** option button (if necessary), click the **Next** button to open the next Combo Box Wizard dialog box, click the **Queries** option button in the View group, click **Query: qryCustomersByName**, and then click the **Next** button. Access opens the third Combo Box Wizard dialog box. This dialog box lets you select the fields from the query to appear as columns in the combo box. You'll select the first two fields.

6. Double-click **Customer** to move this field to the Selected Fields box, double-click **CustomerID**, and then click the **Next** button. This dialog box lets you choose a sort order for the combo box entries. Lucia wants the entries to appear in ascending Customer order.

7. Click the **arrow** for the first box, click **Customer**, and then click the **Next** button to open the next Combo Box Wizard dialog box.

8. Resize the columns to their best fit, scrolling down the columns to make sure all values are visible and resizing again if they're not, and then click the **Next** button.

   In this dialog box, you select the foreign key, which is the CustomerID field.

9. Click **CustomerID** and then click the **Next** button.

   In this dialog box, you specify the field in the tblContract table where you will store the selected CustomerID value from the combo box. You'll store the value in the CustomerID field in the tblContract table.

10. Click the **Store that value in this field** option button, click its **arrow**, click **CustomerID**, and then click the **Next** button.

**Trouble?** If CustomerID doesn't appear in the list, click the Cancel button, press the Delete key to delete the combo box, click the Add Existing Fields button in the Tools group on the Design tab, double-click CustomerID in the Field List pane, press the Delete key to delete CustomerID, close the Field List pane, and then repeat Steps 1-10.

In this dialog box, you specify the name for the combo box control. You'll use the field name of CustomerID.

11. Type **CustomerID** and then click the **Finish** button. The completed CustomerID combo box appears in the form.

You need to position and resize the combo box control, but first you'll change the text for the attached label from CustomerID to Customer ID to match the format used for other label controls in the form. To change the text for a label control, you set the control's Caption property value.

REFERENCE

*Changing a Label's Caption*

- Right-click the label to select it and to display the shortcut menu, and then click Properties to display the property sheet.
- If necessary, click the All tab to display the All page in the property sheet.
- Edit the existing text in the Caption box; or click the Caption box and press the F2 key to select the current value, and then type a new caption.
- In the Tools group on the Design tab, click the Property Sheet button to close the property sheet.

Next, you'll change the text that displays in the combo box label.

**To set the Caption property value for the CustomerID label:**

1. Right-click the **CustomerID** label, which is the control to the left of the CustomerID text box, to select it and to display the shortcut menu, and then click **Properties** on the shortcut menu. The property sheet for the CustomerID label opens.
2. If necessary, click the **All** tab to display all properties for the selected CustomerID label.

   **Trouble?** If the Selection type entry below the Property Sheet title bar is not "Label," then you selected the wrong control in Step 1. Click the CustomerID label to change to the property sheet for this control.
3. Click before the "ID" in the Caption box, press the **spacebar**, and then press the **Tab** key to move to the next property in the property sheet. The Caption property value should now be Customer ID and the label for the CustomerID bound control now displays Customer ID. See Figure 6-27.

**TIP**

After selecting a control, you can press the F4 key to open and close the property sheet for the control.

**TIP**

You won't see the effects of the new property setting until you select another property, select another control, or close the property sheet.

**Figure 6-27** CustomerID combo box added to the form

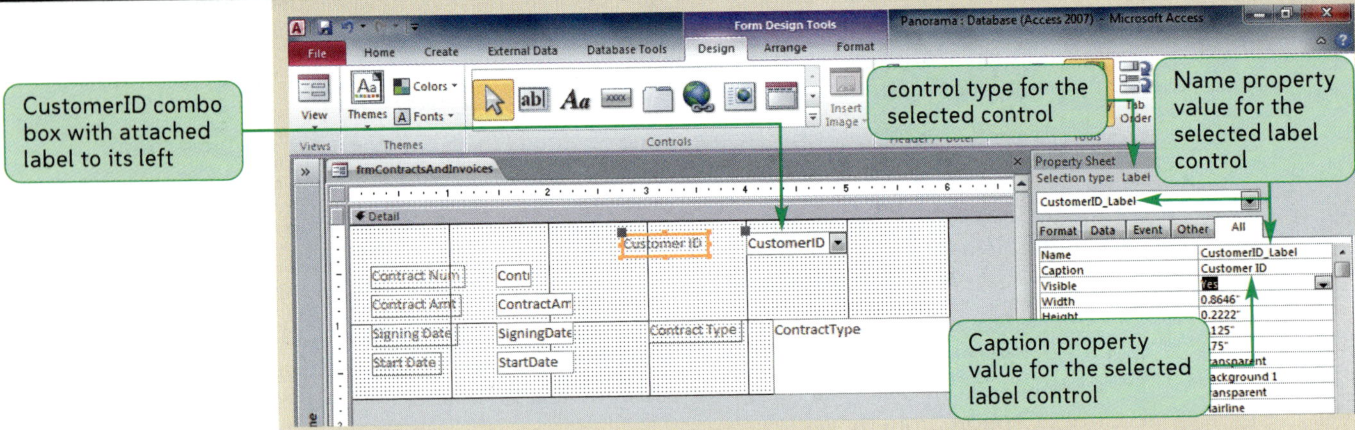


**Trouble?** Some property values in your property sheet, such as the Width and Top property values, might differ if your label's position slightly differs from the label position used as the basis for Figure 6-27. These differences cause no problems.

**TIP**

Always be sure to confirm that the Selection type entry displays the correct control type and the Control box displays the correct control name.

The Selection type entry, which appears below the property sheet title bar, displays the control type (Label in this case) for the selected control. Below the Selection type entry in the property sheet is the Control box, which you can use to select another control in the form and then change its properties in the property sheet. Or you can simply click the control in the form to change to its properties in the property sheet. The first property in the property sheet, the **Name property**, is the property that specifies the name of a control, section, or object (CustomerID_Label in this case). The Name property value is the same as the value displayed in the Control box. For bound controls, the Name property value matches the field name. For unbound controls, Access adds an underscore and a suffix of the control type (for example, Label) to the Name property setting. For unbound controls, you can set the Name property to another, more meaningful value at any time.

4. Close the property sheet, and then save your design changes.

Now that you've added the combo box to the form, you can position the combo box and its attached label and resize the combo box. You'll need to view the form in Form view to determine any fine tuning necessary for the width of the combo box.

### To modify the combo box in Design and Layout views:

1. Click the **CustomerID** combo box, hold down the **Shift** key, click the **Customer ID** label, and then release the **Shift** key to select both controls.

   First, you'll align the CustomerID combo box and its label with the ContractType and ContractNum bound controls. You'll move the selected controls to the right, align the Customer ID and Contract Type labels on their left edges, align the CustomerID combo box and the ContractType text box on their left edges, and then align the bottom edges of the combo box and its label with the bottom edges of the ContractNum bound control.

2. Drag the selected controls to the right until the left edge of the Customer ID label is approximately one-half inch to the right of the left edge of the Contract Type label, making sure the two controls remain above the ContractNum bound control.

3. Select the **Customer ID** label and the **Contract Type** label, click the **Arrange** tab on the Ribbon, and in the Sizing & Ordering group on the Arrange tab, click the **Align** button, and then click **Left**. The selected controls are aligned on their left edges.
4. Repeat Step 3 to align the **CustomerID** combo box and the **ContractType** text box on their left edges.
5. Select the **Contract Num** label, **ContractNum** text box, **Customer ID** label, and **CustomerID** combo box, and in the Sizing & Ordering group on the Arrange tab, click the **Align** button, and then click **Bottom**. The four selected controls are aligned on their bottom edges.
6. Switch to Form view, and then click the **CustomerID** arrow to open the control's list box. See Figure 6-28.

**Figure 6-28** **CustomerID combo box in Form view**

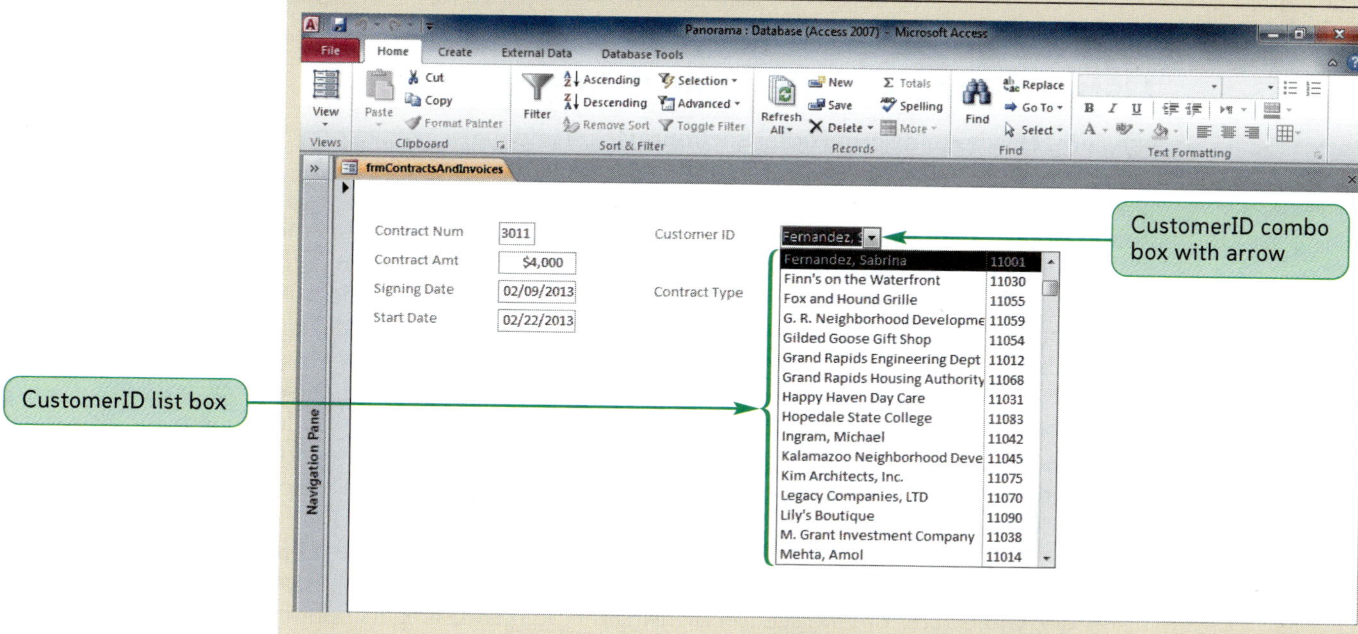


You need to widen the CustomerID combo box, so that the widest customer value in the list is displayed in the combo box. You can widen the combo box in Layout view or in Design view. Because Form view and Layout view display live data, you'll use Layout view instead of Design view to make this change because you can determine the proper width more accurately in Layout view.

7. Switch to Layout view, and then navigate to record 16. Weston Community Parks Foundation, which is the customer value for this record, is the widest value that is displayed in the combo box. You want to widen the combo box, so that the value in record 16 is completely visible.
8. Make sure that only the combo box is selected, and then pointing to the right edge, widen the combo box until the entire customer value is visible. See Figure 6-29.

**Figure 6-29** After resizing the CustomerID combo box in Layout view

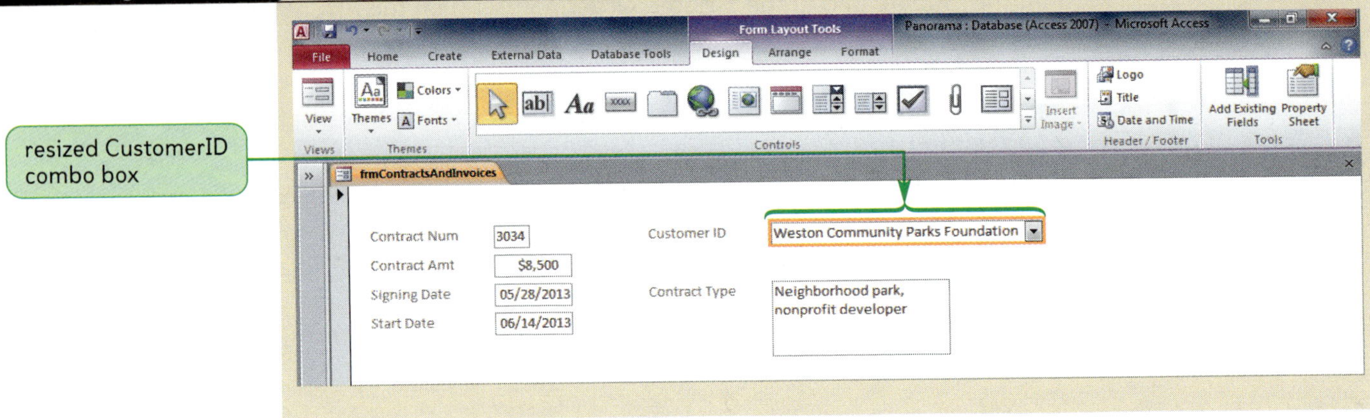


Now you'll add the title to the top of the form.

## Using Form Headers and Form Footers

The **Form Header** and **Form Footer sections** let you add titles, instructions, command buttons, and other controls to the top and bottom of your form, respectively. Controls placed in the Form Header or Form Footer sections remain on the screen whenever the form is displayed in Form view or Layout view; they do not change when the contents of the Detail section change as you navigate from one record to another record.

To add either a form header or footer to your form, you must first add both the Form Header and Form Footer sections as a pair to the form. If your form needs one of these sections but not the other, you can remove a section by setting its height to zero, which is the same method you would use to remove any form section. You can also prevent a section from appearing in Form view or in Print Preview by setting its Visible property to No. The **Visible property** determines if Access displays a control or section. Set the Visible property to Yes to display the control or section, and set the Visible property to No to hide it.

If you've set the Form Footer section's height to zero or set its Visible property to No and a future form design change makes adding controls to the Form Footer section necessary, you can restore the section by using the pointer to drag its bottom edge back down or by setting its Visible property to Yes.

You can add the Form Header and Form Footer sections as a pair to a form either directly or indirectly. The direct way to add these sections is to right-click the Detail section selector, and then click Form Header/Footer. This direct method is available only in Design view. The indirect way to add the Form Header and Form Footer sections in Layout view or Design view is to use one of these three buttons in the Header/Footer group on the Design tab: the Logo button, the Title button, or the Date and Time button. Clicking any of these three buttons causes Access to add the Form Header and Form Footer sections to the form and to place an appropriate control in the Form Header section. If you use the indirect method in Layout view, Access sets the Form Footer section's height to zero. In Design view, the indirect method creates a Form Footer section with the Height property set to one-quarter inch.

REFERENCE

### *Adding and Removing Form Header and Form Footer Sections*

- In Design view, right-click the Detail section selector, and then click Form Header/Footer on the shortcut menu.

*or*

- In Layout view or Design view, click a button in the Header/Footer group on the Design tab to add a logo, title, or date and time to the form.
- To remove a Form Header or Form Footer section, drag its bottom edge up until the section area disappears or set the section's Visible property to No.

Lucia's design includes a title at the top of the form. Because the title will not change as you navigate through the form records, you will add the title to the Form Header section in the form.

## Adding a Title to a Form

You'll add the title to Lucia's form in Layout view. When you add the title to the form in Layout view, Access adds the Form Header section to the form and places the title in the Form Header section. At the same time, Access adds the Page Footer section to the form and sets its height to zero.

### To add a title to the form:

1. In the Header/Footer group on the Design tab, click the **Title** button. Access adds the title to the form, displaying it in the upper-left of the form and using the form name as the title.

   You need to change the title. Because the title is already selected, you can type over or edit the selected title.

2. Press the **Home** key to move to the beginning of the title, press the **Delete** key three times to delete the first three characters, click before the word "And," press the **spacebar**, type the letter **a**, press the **Delete** key, press the → key twice, press the **spacebar**, and then press the **Enter** key. You've changed the title to "Contracts and Invoices." See Figure 6-30.

**Figure 6-30** **Title placed in the Form Header section**

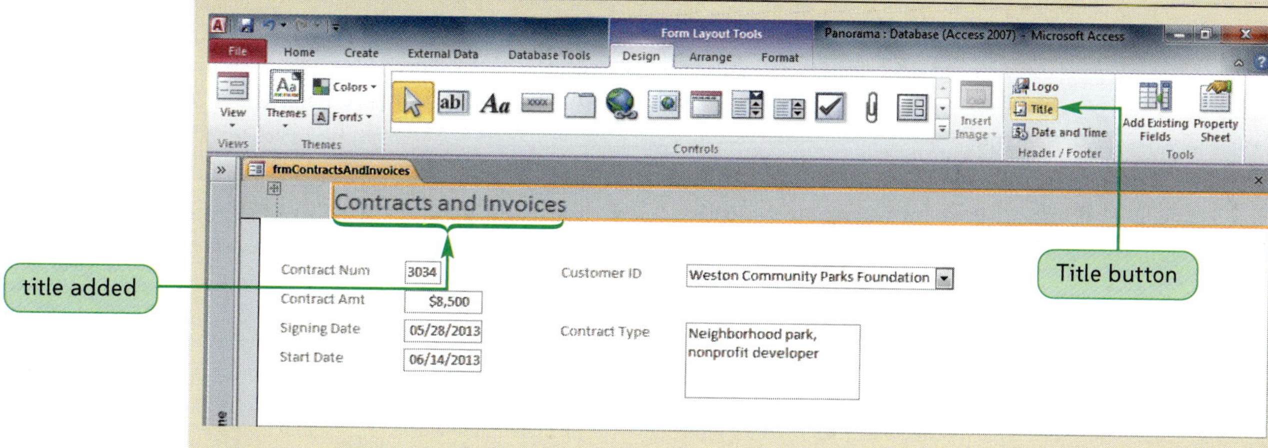

Lucia wants the title to be prominent in the form. The title is already a larger font size than the font used for the form's labels and text boxes, so you'll change the title's font weight to bold to increase its prominence.

3. Make sure the title control is still selected, click the **Format** tab, and then in the Font group on the Format tab, click the **Bold** button **B**. The title is displayed in 18-point, bold text.

   It is not obvious in Layout view that the title is displayed in the Form Header section, so you'll view the form design in Design view.

4. Switch to Design view, and then save your design changes. The title is displayed in the Form Header section. See Figure 6-31.

**Figure 6-31** **Form Header and Form Footer sections in Design view**

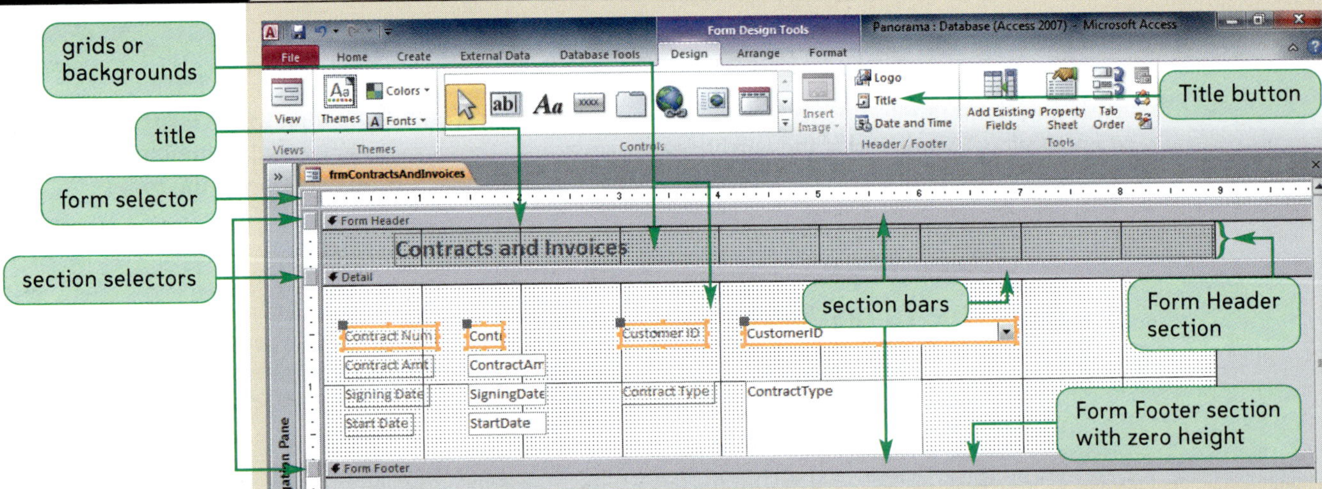


The form now contains a Form Header section that displays the title, a Detail section that displays the bound controls and combo box, and a Form Footer section that is set to a height of zero. Each section consists of a **section selector** and a section bar, either of which you can click to select and set properties for the entire section, and a grid or background, which is where you place controls that you want to display in the form. The **form selector** is the selector at the intersection of the horizontal and vertical rulers; you click the form selector when you want to select the form and set its properties. The vertical ruler is segmented into sections for the Form Header section, the Detail section, and the Form Footer section.

A form's total height includes the heights of the Form Header, Detail, and Form Footer sections. If you set the form's total height to more than the screen size, users will need to use scroll bars to view the content of your form, which is less productive for users and isn't good form design.

5. If you are not continuing on to the next session, close the Panorama database.

So far, you've added controls to the form and modified the controls by selecting, moving, aligning, resizing, and deleting them. You've added and modified a combo box and added a title in the Form Header section. In the next session, you will continue your work with the custom form by adding a combo box to find records, adding a subform, adding calculated controls, changing form and section properties, changing control properties, and using filters.

REVIEW

## *Session 6.2 Quick Check*

1. What is a bound form, and when do you use bound forms?
2. What is the difference between a bound control and an unbound control?
3. The ______________ consists of the dotted and solid lines that appear in the Detail section to help you position controls precisely in a form.
4. The handle in a selected object's upper-left corner is the ______________ handle.
5. How do you move a selected text box and its label at the same time?
6. How do you resize a control?
7. A(n) ______________ control provides the features of a text box and a list box.
8. How do you change a label's caption?
9. What is the Form Header section?

# SESSION 6.3 VISUAL OVERVIEW

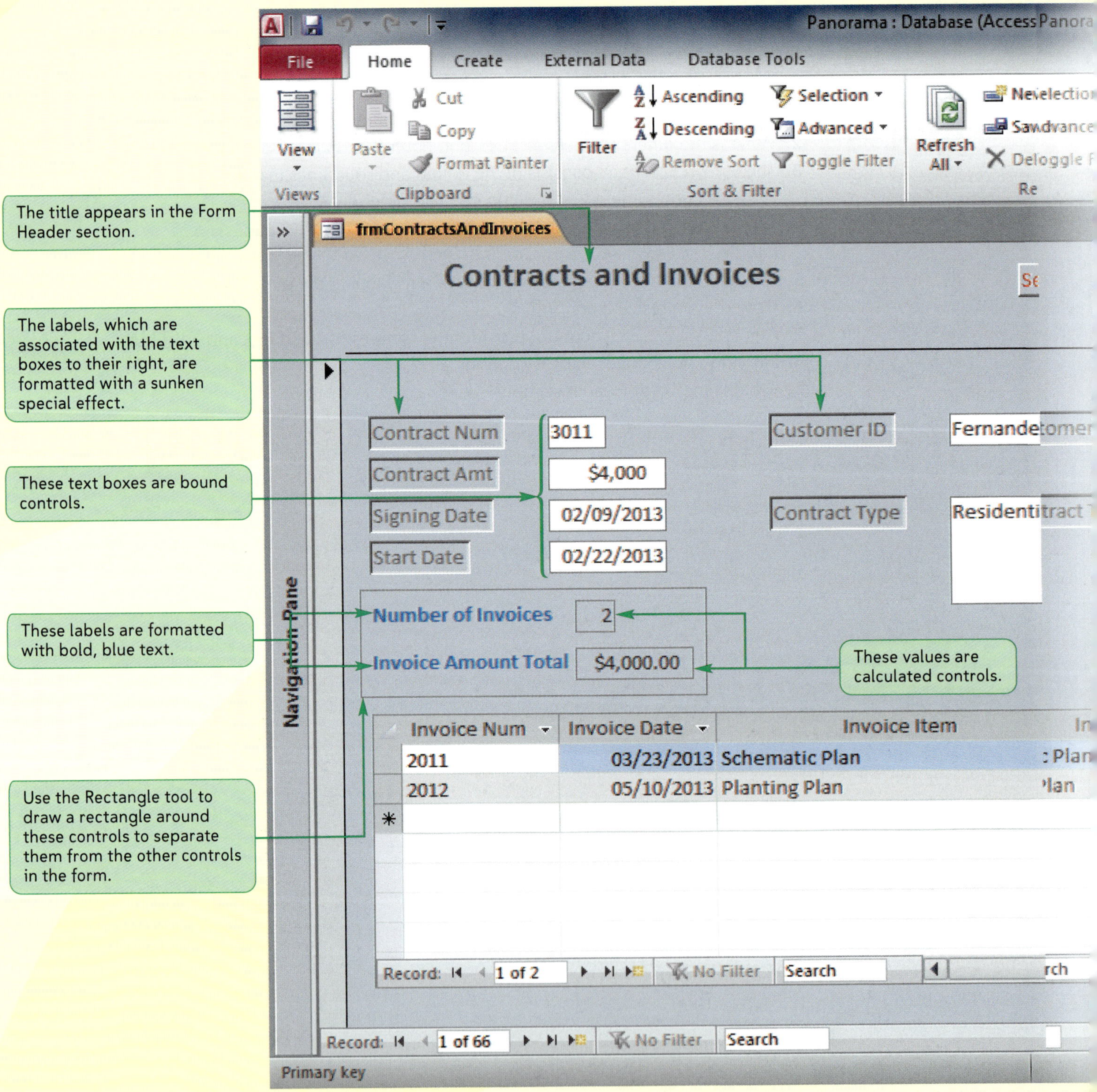

# CUSTOM FORM IN FORM VIEW

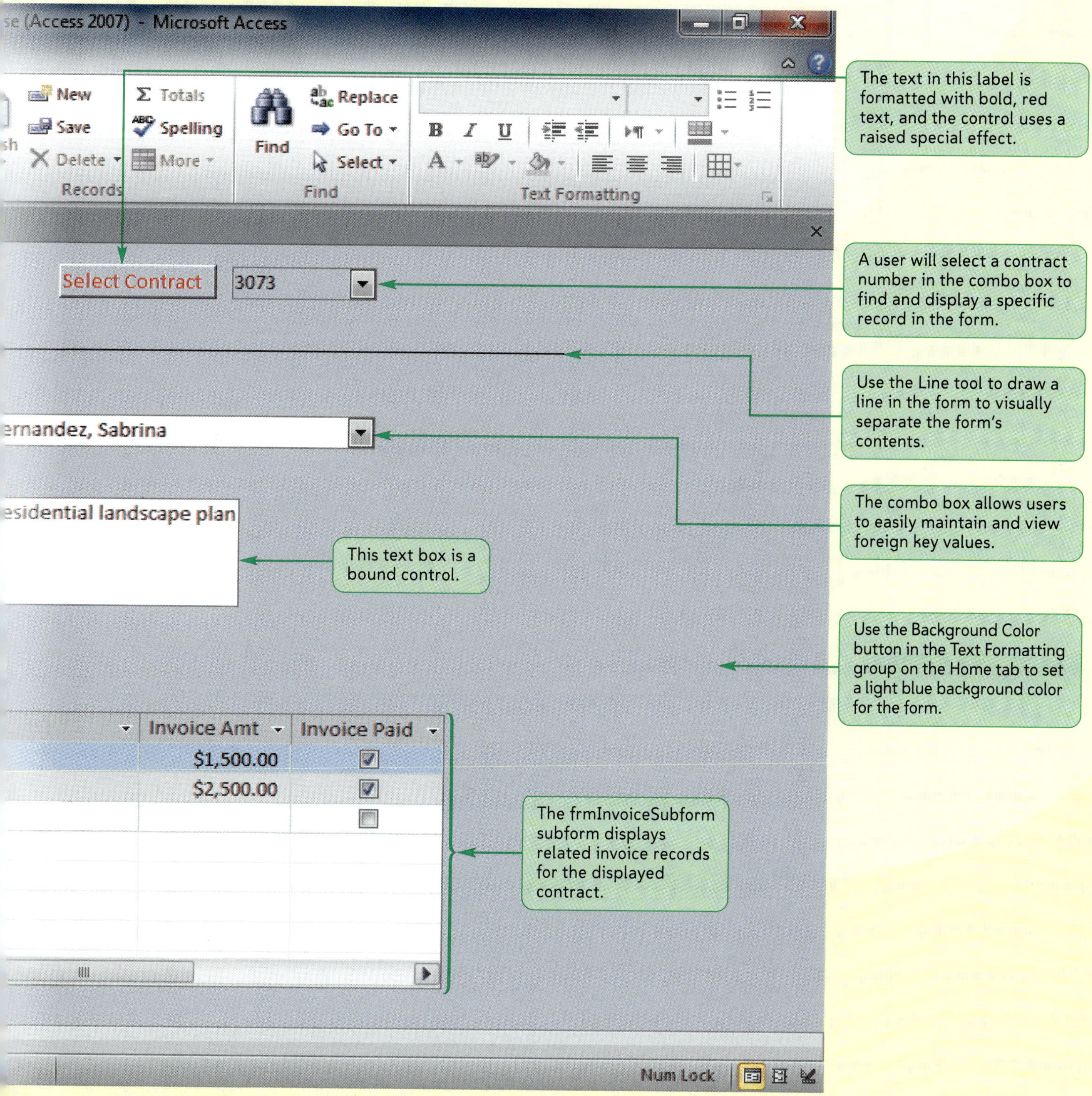

# Adding a Combo Box to Find Records

Most combo boxes are used to display and update data. You can also use combo boxes to find records. You will add a combo box to the Form Header section to find a specific record in the tblContract table to display in the form.

REFERENCE

*Adding a Combo Box to Find Records*

- Open the property sheet for the form in Design view, make sure the record source is a table or query, and then close the property sheet.
- In the Controls group on the Design tab, click the More button, click the Combo Box tool, and then click the position in the form where you want to place the control.
- Click the third option button (Find a record on my form based on the value I selected in my combo box) in the first Combo Box Wizard dialog box, and then complete the remaining Combo Box Wizard dialog boxes.

You can use the Combo Box Wizard to add a combo box to find records in a form. However, the Combo Box Wizard provides this find option only when the form's record source is a table or query. You'll view the property sheet for the form to view the Record Source property, and you'll change the property setting, if necessary.

### To add a combo box to find records to the form:

1. If you took a break after the previous session, make sure that the Panorama database is open, the frmContractsAndInvoices form is open in Design view, and the Navigation Pane is closed.
2. Click the **form selector** (located to the left of the horizontal ruler) to select the form, open the property sheet, and then click the **All** tab (if necessary). The property sheet displays the properties for the form. See Figure 6-32.

**Figure 6-32** Property sheet for the form

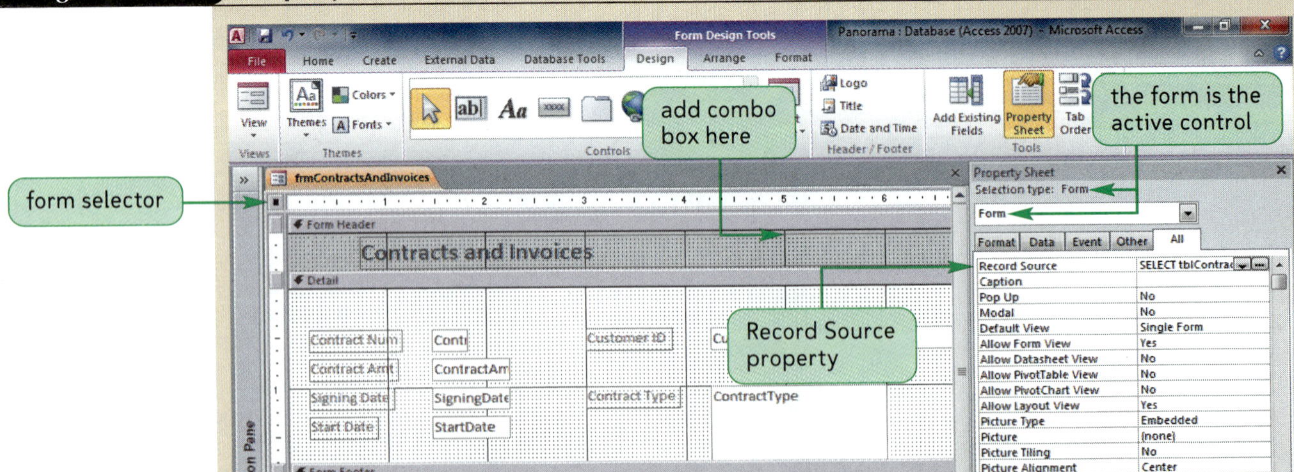


The Record Source property is set to an SQL SELECT statement. You need to change the Record Source property to a table or query, or the Combo Box Wizard will not present you with the option to find records in a form. You'll change the Record Source property to the tblContract table because this table is the record source for all the bound controls you added to the Detail section.

3. Click the **Record Source** box, press the **F2** key to select the entire property setting, type **t**, the AutoComplete feature fills in the rest of tblContract, press the **Tab** key to accept the entire entry of tblContract, and then close the property sheet.

   You'll now use the Combo Box Wizard to add a combo box to the form's Form Header section to find a record in the tblContract table to display in the form.

4. In the Controls group on the Design tab, click the **More** button to open the Controls gallery, make sure the Use Control Wizards tool is selected in the Controls gallery, click the **Combo Box** tool, position the + portion of the pointer at the top of the Form Header section and at the 5-inch mark on the horizontal ruler (see Figure 6-32), and then click the mouse button. Access places a combo box control in the form and opens the first Combo Box Wizard dialog box.

   The dialog box now displays a third option to "Find a record on my form based on the value I selected in my combo box," which you'll use for this combo box. You choose the first option, which you used for the CustomerID combo box, when you want to select a value from a list of foreign key values from an existing table or query. You choose the second option when you want users to select a value from a short fixed list of values that don't change. For example, if Belmont Landscapes wanted to include a field in the tblCustomer table to classify each customer, you could use a combo box with this second option to display a list of values such as Residential, Commercial, Nonprofit, and Government.

5. Click the **Find a record on my form based on the value I selected in my combo box** option button, and then click the **Next** button to open the next dialog box. This dialog box lets you select the fields from the tblContract table to appear as columns in the combo box. You'll select the first field.

6. Double-click **ContractNum** to move this field to the Selected Fields box, and then click the **Next** button.

7. Resize the column to its best fit, and then click the **Next** button.

   In this dialog box, you specify the name for the combo box's label. You'll use Select Contract as the label.

8. Type **Select Contract**, and then click the **Finish** button. The completed unbound combo box is displayed in the form. See Figure 6-33.

**Figure 6-33** Unbound combo box added to the form

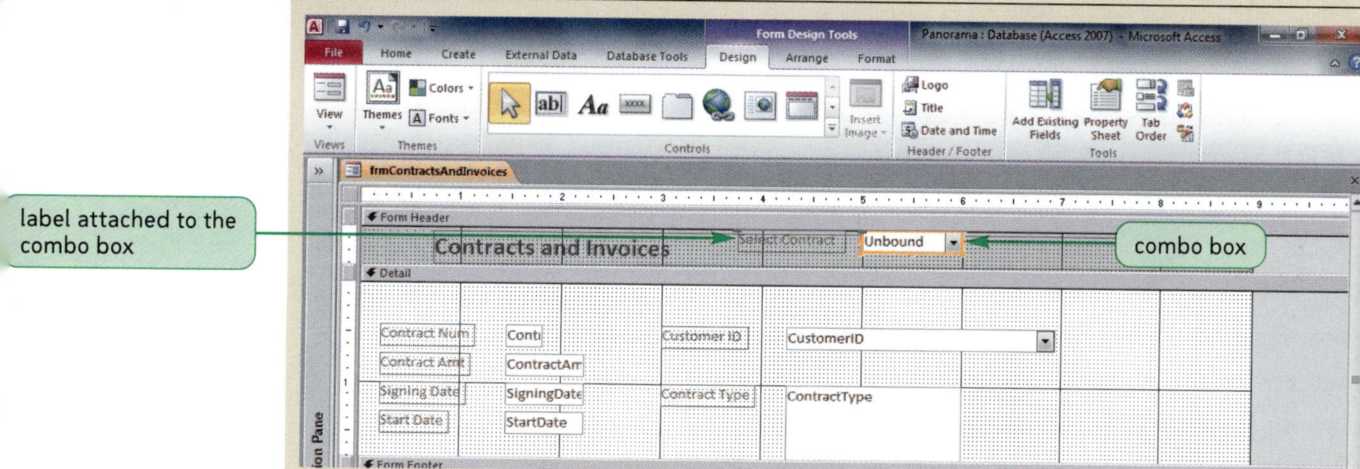

You'll align the right edges of the two combo boxes, move the attached label closer to the combo box, and then align the bottoms of the combo box and its attached label with the bottom of the title in the Form Header section.

9. Deselect all controls, select the two combo boxes (one in the Form Header section and the other in the Detail section), right-click one of the selected controls, point to **Align**, and then click **Right**. The two combo boxes are aligned on their right edges.
10. Click the **Select Contract** label, point to the label's move handle, and then drag the label to the right until it is two grid dots to the left of the combo box.
11. Select the combo box in the Form Header section, the **Select Contract** label, and the title, right-click one of the selected controls, point to **Align**, and then click **Bottom**. The three selected controls are aligned on their bottom edges. See Figure 6-34.

**Figure 6-34** After aligning the combo box control and the title

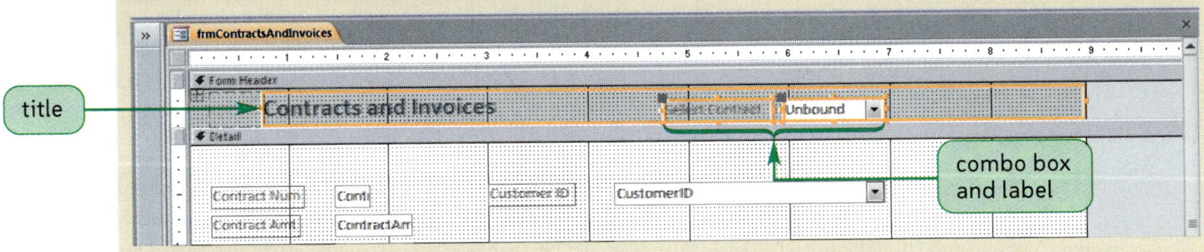


You'll save your form changes and view the new combo box in Form view.

## To find contract records using the combo box:

1. Save the form design changes, and then switch to Form view.
2. Click the **Select Contract** combo box arrow to open the list box. See Figure 6-35.

**Figure 6-35** Displaying the combo box's list of contract numbers

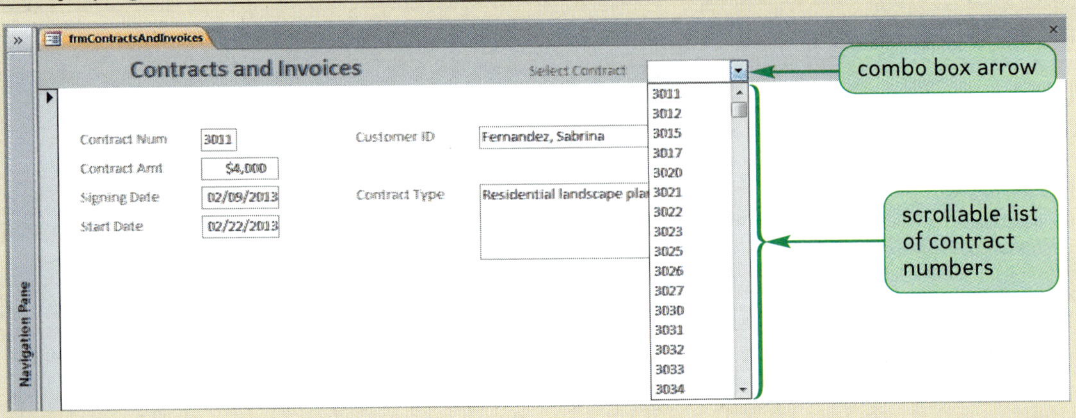

3. Scroll down the list, and then click **3073**. The current record changes from record 1 to record 41, which is the record for contract number 3073.

The form design is very plain at this point with no color, special effects, or visual contrast among the controls. Before making the form more attractive and useful, you'll add the remaining controls to the form: a subform and two calculated controls.

## Adding a Subform to a Form

Lucia's design for the form includes a subform that displays the related invoices for the displayed contract. The form you've been creating is the main form for records from the primary tblContract table (the "one" side of the one-to-many relationship), and the subform will display records from the related tblInvoice table (the "many" side of the one-to-many relationship). You use the **Subform/Subreport tool** in Design view to add a subform to a form. You can add the subform on your own, or you can get help adding the subform by using the SubForm Wizard.

You will use the SubForm Wizard to add the subform for the tblInvoice table records to the bottom of the form. First, you'll increase the height of the Detail section to make room for the subform.

**TIP**

Drag slightly beyond the desired ending position to expose the vertical ruler measurement, and then decrease the height back to the correct position.

### To add the subform to the form:

1. Switch to Design view.
2. Place the pointer on the bottom edge of the Detail section. When the pointer changes to a ✣ shape, drag the section's edge down until it is at the 4-inch mark on the vertical ruler.
3. In the Controls group on the Design tab, click the **More** button to open the Controls gallery, make sure the Control Wizards tool is selected, and then click the **Subform/Subreport** tool.
4. Position the + portion of the pointer in the Detail section at the 2.5-inch mark on the vertical ruler and at the 1-inch mark on the horizontal ruler, and then click the mouse button. Access places a subform control in the form's Detail section and opens the first SubForm Wizard dialog box.

You can use a table or query, or an existing form as the record source for a subform. In this case, you'll use the related tblInvoice table as the record source for a new subform.

### To use the SubForm Wizard to add the subform to the form:

1. Make sure the Use existing Tables and Queries option button is selected, and then click the **Next** button. Access opens the next SubForm Wizard dialog box, which lets you select a table or query as the record source for the subform and the fields from the selected table or query.
2. Click the **Tables/Queries arrow** to display the list of tables and queries in the Panorama database, scroll to the top of the list, and then click **Table: tblInvoice**. The Available Fields box shows the fields in the tblInvoice table.

Lucia's form design includes all fields from the tblInvoice table in the subform, except for the ContractNum field, which you already placed in the Detail section of the form from the tblContract table.

3. Click the >> button to move all available fields to the Selected Fields box, click **ContractNum** in the Selected Fields box, click the < button, and then click the **Next** button to open the next SubForm Wizard dialog box. See Figure 6-36.

**Figure 6-36 Selecting the linking field**

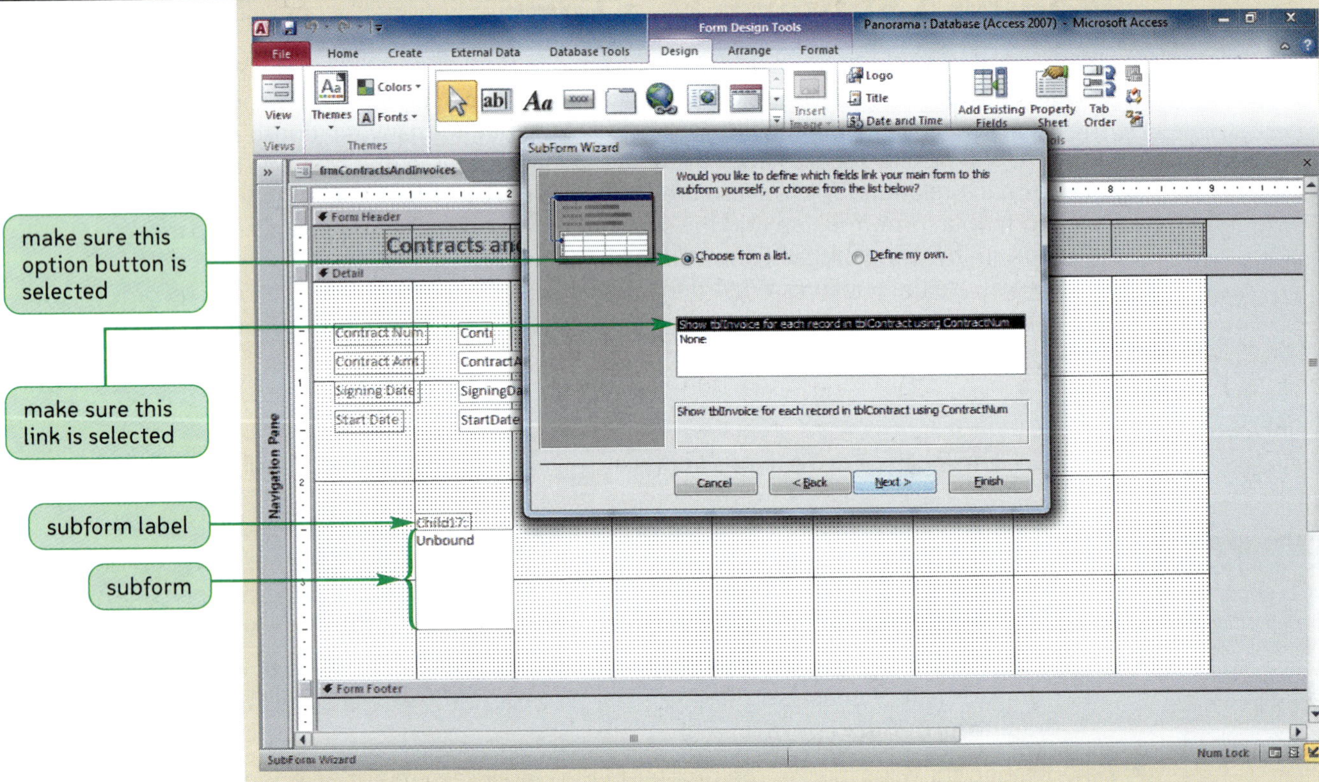


In this dialog box, you select the link between the primary tblContract table and the related tblInvoice table. The common field in the two tables, ContractNum, links the tables. Access uses the ContractNum field to display a record in the main form, which displays data from the primary tblContract table, and to select and display the related records for that contract in the subform, which displays data from the related tblInvoice table.

4. Make sure the Choose from a list option button is selected, make sure the first link is highlighted, and then click the **Next** button. The next SubForm Wizard dialog box lets you specify a name for the subform.

5. Type **frmInvoiceSubform** and then click the **Finish** button. Access increases the height and width of the subform in the form. The subform will display the related tblInvoice records; its label appears above the subform and displays the subform name.

6. Deselect all controls, save your form changes, switch to Form view, and then click the **ContractNum** text box to deselect the value. See Figure 6-37.

**Figure 6-37** Viewing the subform in Form view

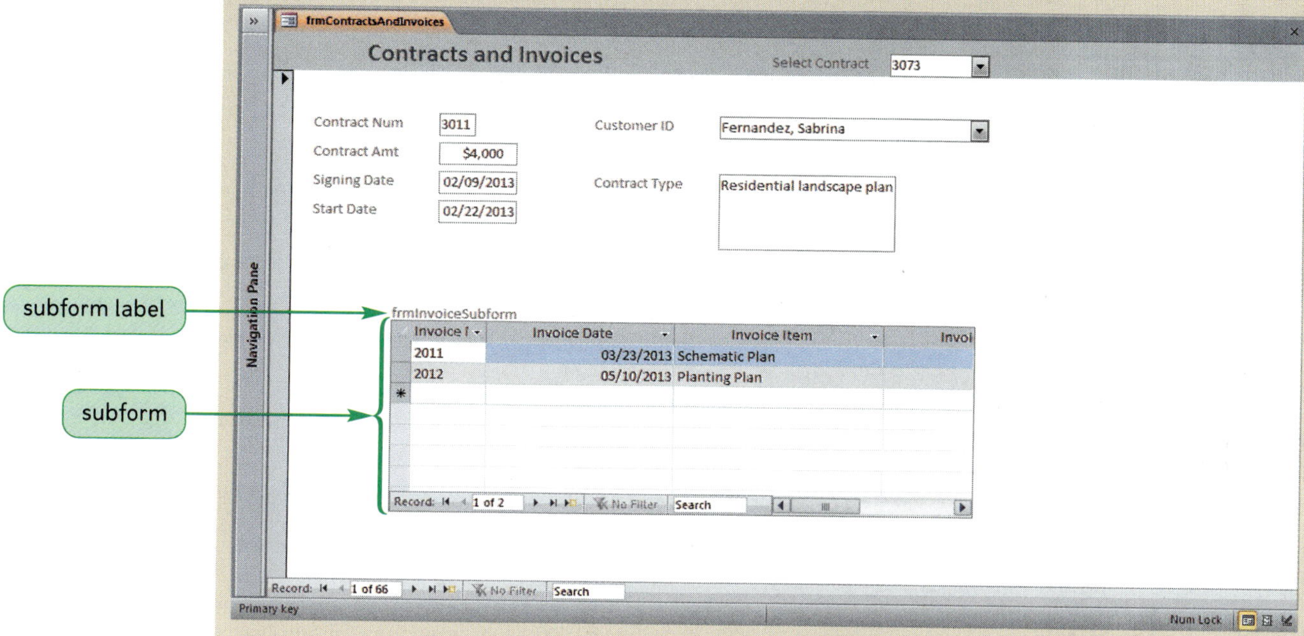


The subform displays the two invoices related to the first contract record for contract number 3011.

**Trouble?** If the widths of the columns in your datasheet differ or the position of your subform is different, don't worry. You'll resize all columns to their best fit and move the subform later.

After viewing the form, Lucia identifies some modifications she wants you to make. The subform is not properly sized and the columns in the subform are not sized to their best fit. She wants you to resize the subform and its columns, so that all columns in the subform are entirely visible. Also, she asks you to delete the subform label, because the label is unnecessary for identifying the subform contents. You'll use Design view and Layout view to make these changes.

## To modify the subform's design:

1. Switch to Design view. Notice that in Design view, the subform data does not appear in a datasheet format as it does in Form view. That difference causes no problem; you can ignore it.

   First, you'll delete the subform label.

2. Deselect all controls (if necessary), right-click the subform label to open the shortcut menu (make sure no other controls have handles), and then click **Cut**.

   Next, you'll move the subform by aligning it with the Start Date label.

3. Click the edge of the subform to select it (an orange border and handles appear on the subform's border when the subform is selected), hold down the **Shift** key, click the **Start Date** label, and then release the **Shift** key. The subform and the Start Date label are selected, and you'll align the two controls on their left edges.

4. Right-click the **Start Date** label, point to **Align** on the shortcut menu, and then click **Left**. The two controls are aligned on their left edges. You'll resize the subform in Layout view, so you can see your changes as you make them.

5. Switch to Layout view, click the edge of the subform to select it, and then drag the right edge of the subform to the right until all five datasheet columns are fully visible.

   Before resizing the columns in the subform, you'll display record 41 in the main form. The subform for this record contains the related records in the tblInvoice table with the longest field values.

6. Use the record navigation bar for the main form to display record 41, for contract number 3073, and then resize each column in the subform to its best fit.

   Next, you'll resize the subform again so its width matches the width of the five resized columns.

7. Resize the subform's right edge to the left, so it is aligned with the right edge of the Invoice Paid column. See Figure 6-38.

**Figure 6-38 After moving and resizing the subform**

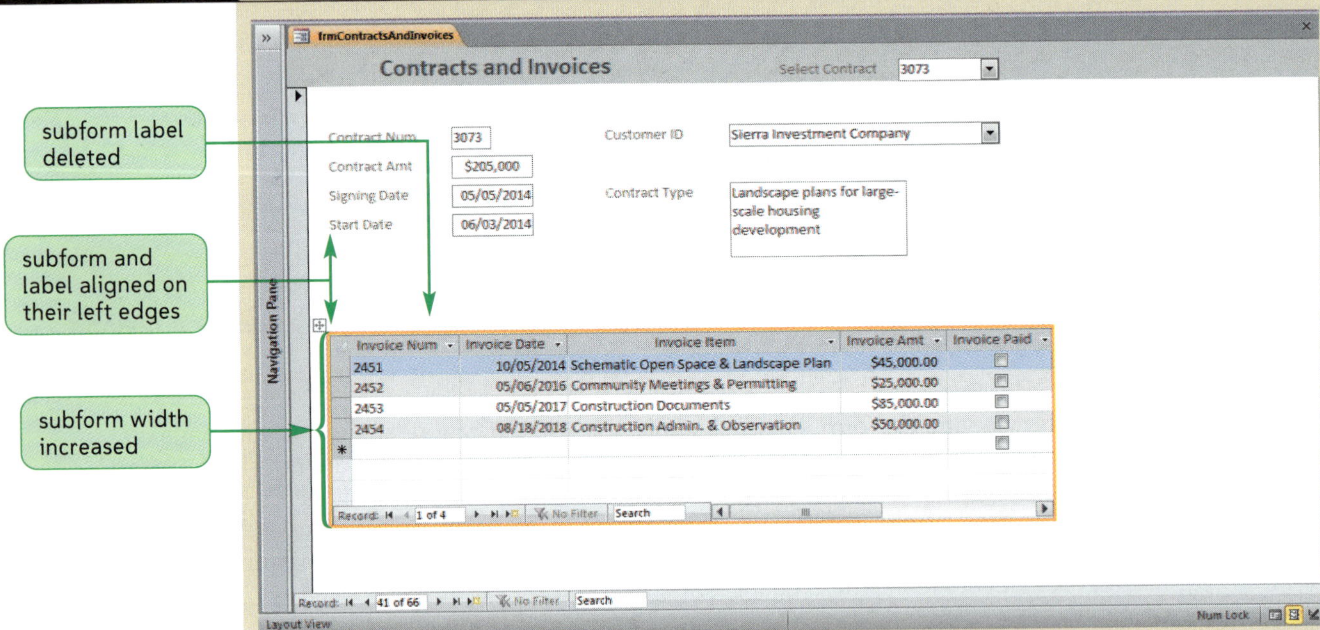


You've finished your work with the subform, and now you need to add two calculated controls to the main form.

## Displaying a Subform's Calculated Controls in the Main Form

For the invoices displayed in the subform, Lucia's form design includes the display of calculated controls in the main form for the number of invoices and for the total of the invoice amounts for the related records displayed in the subform. To display these calculated controls in a form or report, you use the Count and Sum functions. The **Count function** determines the number of occurrences of an expression, and its general format as a control in a form or report is =Count(*expression*). The **Sum function** calculates the total of an expression, and its general format as a control in a form or report is =Sum(*expression*). The invoices and invoice amounts are displayed in the subform's Detail section, so you'll need to place calculated controls for the number of invoices and the total invoice amounts in the subform's Form Footer section. However, your design has these two calculated controls displayed in the main form, not in the subform. Fortunately, the subform appears in Datasheet view, and Form Headers and Footers do not appear in Datasheet view, so the subform's calculated controls will not appear in the subform. Although the calculated controls are not displayed in the subform, the calculations occur, and you can add calculated controls in the main form that reference the subform's calculated controls and display these values.

## Adding Calculated Controls to a Subform's Form Footer Section

First, you'll open the subform in Design view in another window and add the calculated controls to the subform's Form Footer section.

### To add calculated controls to the subform's Form Footer section:

1. Save your form design changes, switch to Design view, click the subform border to select the subform, right-click the border, and then click **Subform in New Window** on the shortcut menu. The subform opens in Design view. See Figure 6-39.

**Figure 6-39** **Subform in Design view**

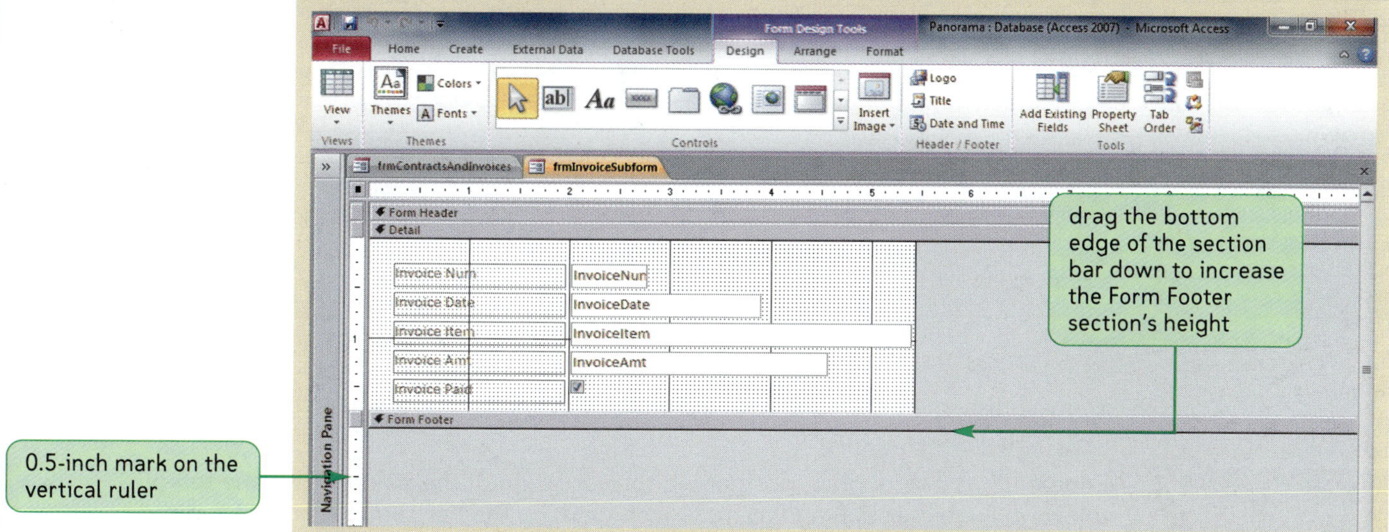


The subform's Detail section contains the tblInvoice table fields. As a subform in the main form, the fields appear in a datasheet even though the fields do not appear that way in Design view. The heights of the subform's Form Header and Form Footer sections are zero, meaning that these sections have been removed from the subform. You'll increase the height of the Form Footer section so that you can add the two calculated controls to the section.

2. Place the pointer at the bottom edge of the Form Footer section bar. When the pointer changes to a ‡ shape, drag the bottom edge of the section down to the 0.5-inch mark on the vertical ruler.

   Now you'll add the first calculated control to the Form Footer section. To create the text box for the calculated control, you use the **Text Box tool** in the Controls group on the Design tab. Because the Form Footer section is not displayed in a datasheet, you do not need to position the control precisely.

3. In the Controls group on the Design tab, click the **Text Box** tool ab|.

4. Position the + portion of the pointer near the top of the Form Footer section and at the 1-inch mark on the horizontal ruler, and then click the mouse button. Access places a text box control and an attached label control to its left in the Form Footer section.

**TIP**

You precede expressions with an equal sign to distinguish them from field names, which do not have an equal sign.

Next, you'll set the Name and Control Source properties for the text box. Recall that the Name property specifies the name of an object or control. Later, when you add the calculated control in the main form, you'll reference the subform's calculated control value by using its Name property value. The **Control Source property** specifies the source of the data that appears in the control; the Control Source property setting can be either a field name or an expression.

**TIP**

Read the Naming Conventions section in the appendix titled "Relational Databases and Database Design" for more information about naming conventions.

5. Open the property sheet for the text box in the Form Footer section (the word "Unbound" is displayed inside the text box), click the **All** tab (if necessary), select the entry in the Name box, type **txtInvoiceAmtSum** in the Name box, press the **Tab** key, type **=Sum(Inv** in the Control Source box, press the **Tab** key to accept the rest of the field name of InvoiceAmt suggested by Formula AutoComplete, type **)** (a right parenthesis), and then press the **Tab** key. InvoiceAmt is enclosed in brackets in the expression because it's a field name. See Figure 6-40.

**Figure 6-40 Setting properties for the subform calculated control**

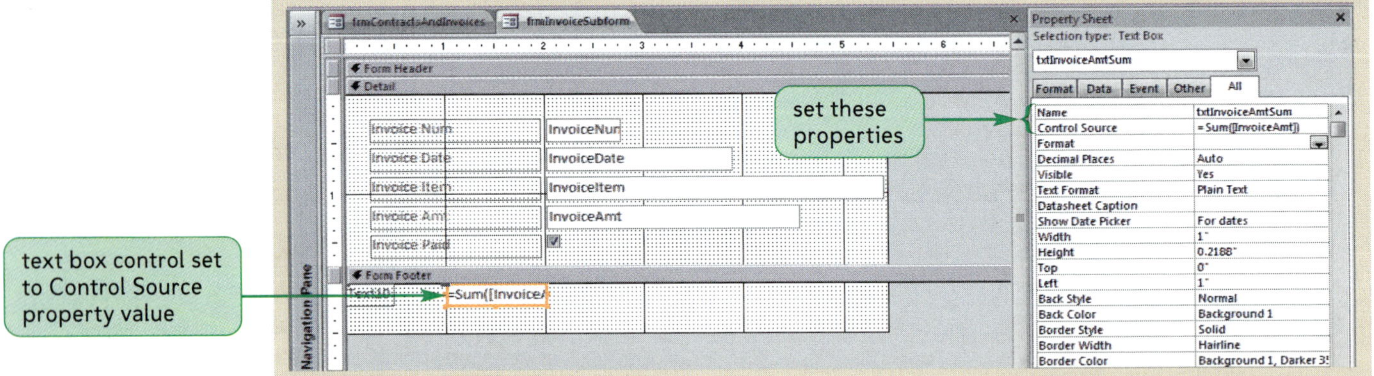


You've finished creating the first calculated control, and now you'll create the other calculated control.

**TIP**

In txtInvoiceAmtSum, txt identifies the control type (a text box), InvoiceAmt is the related field name, and Sum identifies the control as a summary control.

6. Repeat Steps 3 through 5, positioning the + portion of the pointer near the top of the Form Footer section and at the 4-inch mark on the horizontal ruler, setting the Name property value to **txtInvoiceNumCount**, and setting the Control Source property value to **=Count([InvoiceNum])**.

When you use the Count function, you are counting the number of displayed records—in this case, the number of records displayed in the subform. Instead of using InvoiceNum as the expression for the Count function, you could use any of the other fields displayed in the subform.

You've finished creating the subform's calculated controls, so you can close the property sheet, save your subform design changes, and return to the main form.

7. Close the property sheet, save your subform changes, and then close the subform. The active object is now the main form in Design view.

**Trouble?** The subform in the frmContractsAndInvoices form might appear to be blank after you close the frmInvoiceSubform form. This is a temporary effect; the subform's controls do still exist. Switch to Form view, and then back to Design view, to display the subform's controls.

8. Switch to Form view. The calculated controls you added in the subform's Form Footer section are not displayed in the subform.
9. Switch to Design view.

Next, you'll add two calculated controls in the main form to display the two calculated controls from the subform.

## Adding Calculated Controls to a Main Form

The subform's calculated controls now contain a count of the number of invoices and a total of the invoice amounts. You need to add two calculated controls in the main form that reference the values in the subform's calculated controls. Because it's easy to make a typing mistake with these references, you'll use Expression Builder to set the Control Source property for the two main form calculated controls.

### To add a calculated control to the main form's Detail section:

1. In the Controls group on the Design tab, click the **Text Box** tool, and then add the text box and its attached label in the Detail section, clicking the + portion of the pointer at the 2-inch mark on the horizontal ruler and the 2-inch mark on the vertical ruler. Don't be concerned about positioning the control precisely because you'll resize and move the label and text box later.
2. Select the label and open the property sheet, set its Caption property to **Number of Invoices**, right-click an edge of the label to open the shortcut menu, point to **Size**, and then click **To Fit**. Don't worry if the label now overlaps the text box.

   You'll use Expression Builder to set Control Source property for the text box.
3. Click the text box (the word "Unbound" is displayed inside the text box) to select it, click the **Control Source** box in the property sheet, and then click the property's **Build** button to open Expression Builder.
4. Click the **expand indicator** next to frmContractsAndInvoices in the Expression Elements box, click **frmInvoiceSubform** in the Expression Elements box, scroll down the Expression Categories box, and then double-click **txtInvoiceNumCount** in the Expression Categories box. See Figure 6-41.

**Figure 6-41** Text box control's expression in the Expression Builder dialog box

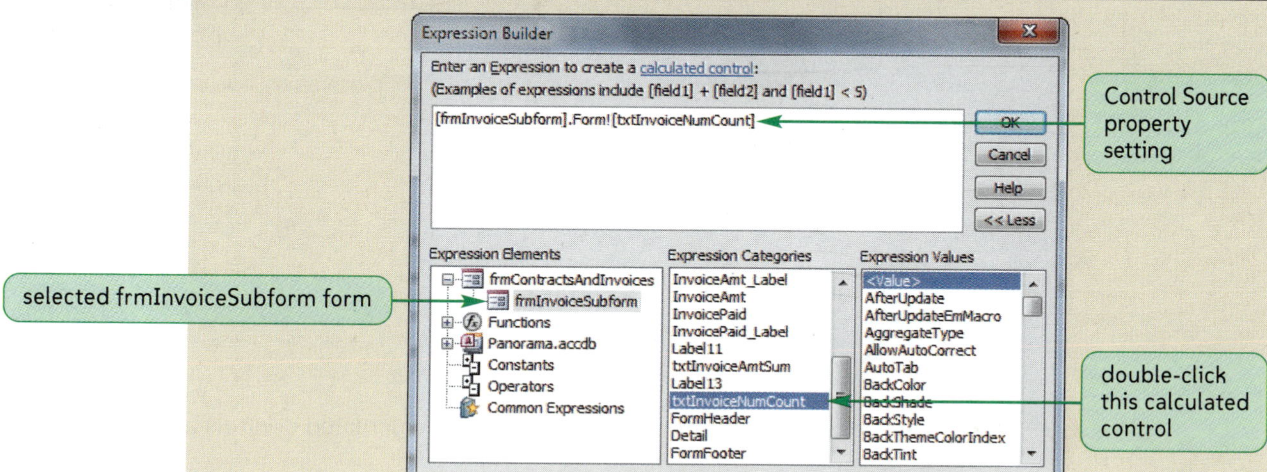

Instead of adding txtInvoiceNumCount to the expression box at the top, Access changed it to [frmInvoiceSubform].Form![txtInvoiceNumCount]. This expression asks Access to display the value of the txtInvoiceNumCount control that is located in the frmInvoiceSubform form, which is a form object.

You need to add an equal sign to the beginning of the expression.

5. Press the **Home** key, type **=** (an equal sign), and then click the **OK** button. Access closes the Expression Builder dialog box and sets the Control Source property.

Next, you'll add a second text box to the main form, set the Caption property for the label, and use Expression Builder to set the text box's Control Source property.

Be sure you resize the label to its best fit.

6. Repeat Steps 1 through 3 to add a text box to the main form, clicking the + portion of the pointer at the 5-inch mark on the horizontal ruler and the 2-inch mark on the vertical ruler, and setting the label's Caption property to **Invoice Amount Total**.

7. With the Expression Builder dialog box open for the new text box, type **=** (an equal sign), click the **expand indicator** next to frmContractsAndInvoices in the Expression Elements box, click **frmInvoiceSubform** in the Expression Elements box, scroll down the Expression Categories box, and then double-click **txtInvoiceAmtSum** in the Expression Categories box. Access changed the txtInvoiceAmtSum calculated field to the expression = [frmInvoiceSubform].Form![txtInvoiceAmtSum].

Next, you'll save your form changes and view the form in Layout view.

8. Click the **OK** button to accept the expression and close the Expression Builder dialog box, close the property sheet, save your form changes, and then switch to Layout view. See Figure 6-42.

**Figure 6-42** After adding two calculated controls

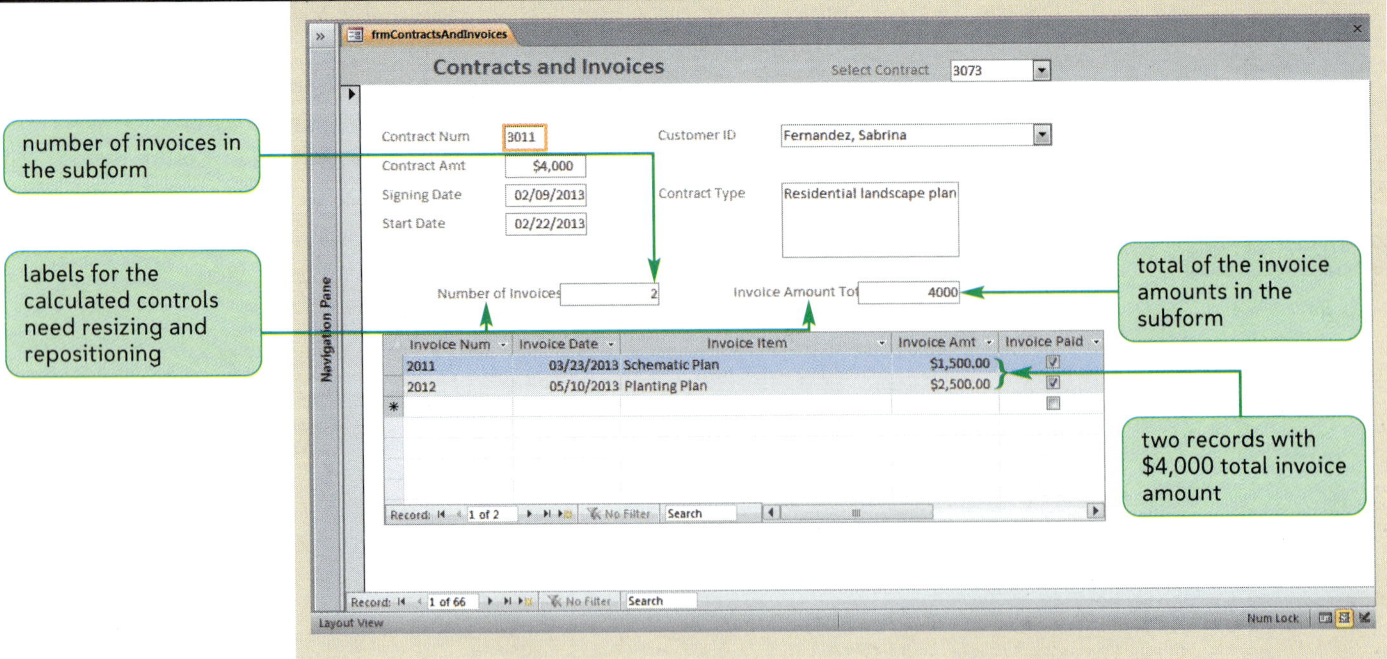


Next, you need to resize, move, and format the two calculated controls and their attached labels.

## Resizing, Moving, and Formatting Calculated Controls

In addition to resizing and repositioning the two calculated controls and their attached labels, you need to change the format of the rightmost calculated control to Currency and to set the following properties for both calculated controls:

- Set the Tab Stop property to a value of No. The **Tab Stop property** specifies whether users can use the Tab key to move to a control on a form. If the Tab Stop property is set to No, users can't tab to the control.
- Set the ControlTip Text property to a value of "Calculated total number of invoices for this contract" for the leftmost calculated control and "Calculated invoice total for this contract" for the rightmost calculated control. The **ControlTip Text property** specifies the text that appears in a ScreenTip when users hold the mouse pointer over a control in a form.

INSIGHT

### *Setting Properties in the Property Sheet*

You can set many properties in the property sheet by typing a value in the property's box, by clicking the arrow on the property and then selecting a value from the menu, or by double-clicking the property name. If you need to set a property by typing a long text entry, you can open the Zoom dialog box and type the entry in the dialog box. You can also use Expression Builder to help you enter expressions.

Now you'll resize, move, and format the calculated controls and their attached labels, and you'll set other properties for the calculated controls.

### To modify the calculated controls and their attached labels:

1. Right-click the rightmost calculated control, click **Properties** on the shortcut menu to open the property sheet, click the **All** tab in the property sheet (if necessary), set the Format property to **Currency**, and then close the property sheet. The value displayed in the calculated control changes from 4000 to $4,000.00.

   Now you'll resize the calculated controls, adjust the positions of each label and text box pair with respect to each other, and then move the controls into their final positions in the form.

2. Individually, reduce the widths of the two calculated controls from the left. See Figure 6-43.
3. Click the **Number of Invoices** label, use the → arrow key to move the label into position next to its related calculated control, repeat the process for the **Invoice Amount Total** label and its related calculated control, and then deselect all controls. See Figure 6-43.

**Figure 6-43** After modifying the calculated controls and their labels

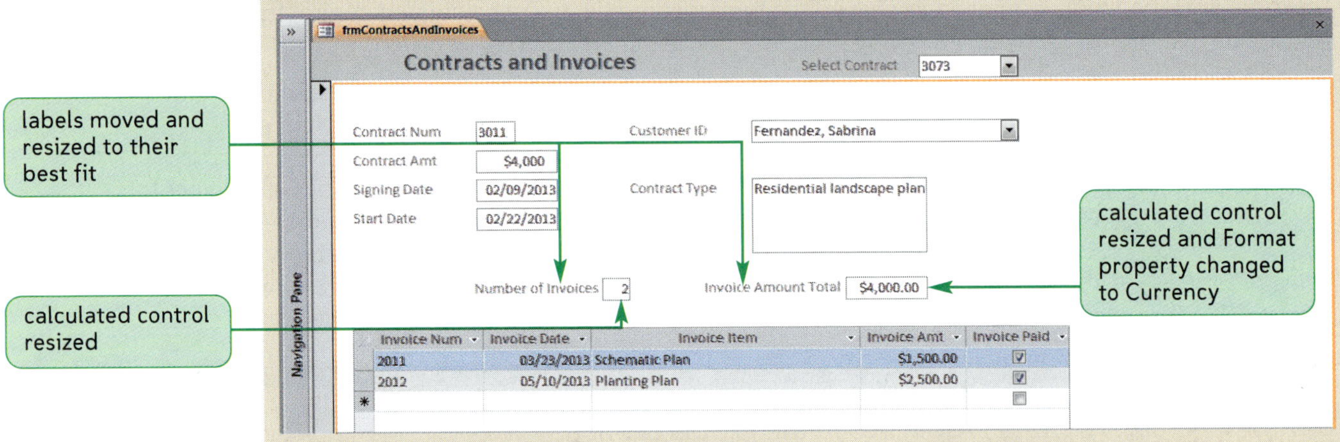


4. Switch to Design view, Use **Shift+Click** to select the **Start Date** label, the **Number of Invoices** label, and the related text box for the Number of Invoices label, right-click one of the selected controls to open the shortcut menu, point to **Align**, click **Left** to align the labels on their left edges, press the **Shift** key, click the **Start Date** label to deselect it, release the **Shift** key, and then use the arrow key to move the **Number of Invoices** label and its related text box up to the position shown in Figure 6-44.

**TIP**

In Design view you must use the move handle to move only a text box or its label, while in Layout view you can use either the move handle or the arrow keys.

5. Repeat Step 4 for the **Invoice Amount Total** label and its related calculated control. See Figure 6-44.

6. Use the move handle on the top calculated control text box to move it to the right, align the two calculated control text boxes on their left edges as shown in Figure 6-44, deselect all controls, and then switch to Layout view.

**Figure 6-44** After moving and aligning the calculated controls and their labels

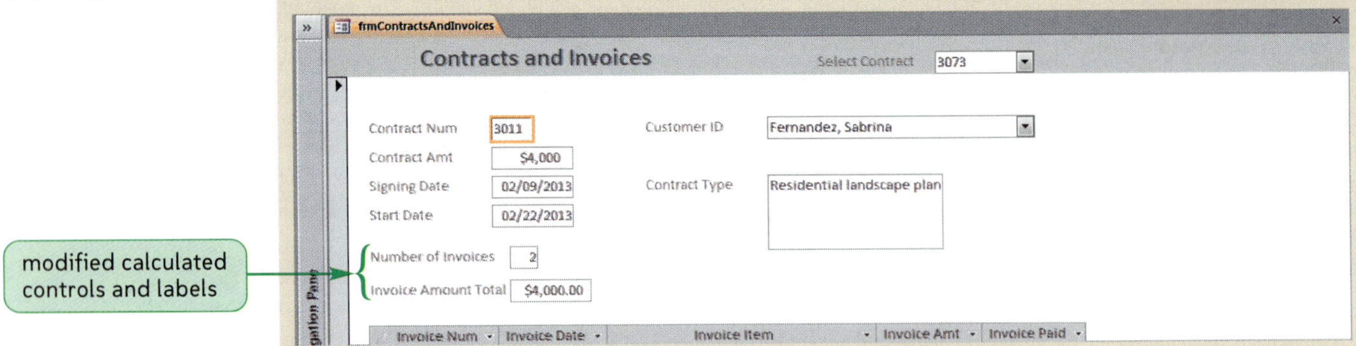


7. Right-click the bottom calculated control, click **Properties** on the shortcut menu, click the **Other** tab in the property sheet, set the Tab Stop property to **No**, and then set the ControlTip Text property to **Calculated invoice total for this contract**.

8. Click the top calculated control, set the Tab Stop property to **No**, set the ControlTip Text property to **Calculated total number of invoices for this contract**, close the property sheet, save your form design changes, and then switch to Form view.

**9.** Click the **Number of Invoices** text box, position the pointer on the Number of Invoices text box to display its ScreenTip, click the **Invoice Amount Total** text box, and then position the pointer on the Invoice Amount Total text box to display its ScreenTip. See Figure 6-45.

**Figure 6-45** Displaying a control's ScreenTip

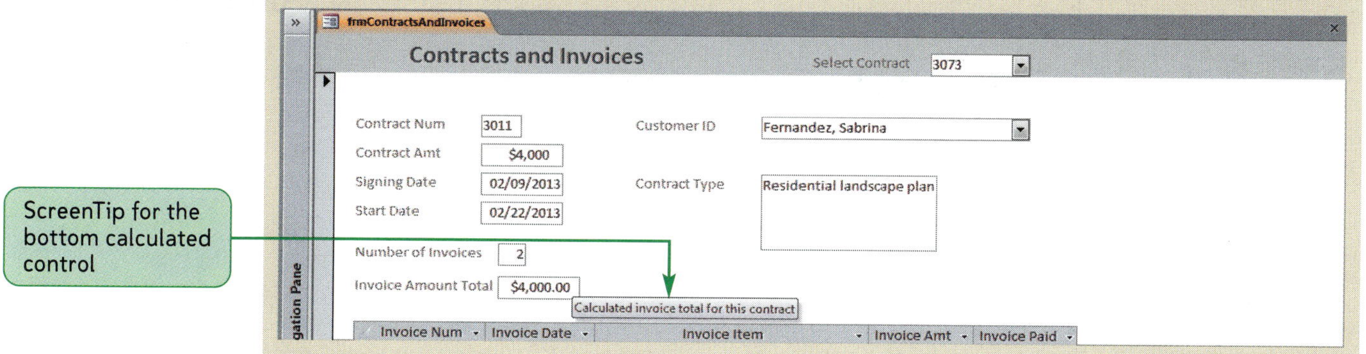


Lucia asks you to verify that users can't update the calculated controls in the main form and that users will tab in the correct order through the controls in the form.

## Changing the Tab Order in a Form

Pressing the Tab key in Form view moves the focus from one control to another. **Focus** refers to the control that is currently active and awaiting user action; focus also refers to the object and record that is currently active. The order in which you move from control to control, or change the focus, in a form when you press the Tab key is called the **tab order**. Lucia wants to verify that the tab order in the main form is top-to-bottom, left-to-right. First, you'll verify that users can't update the calculated controls.

### To test the calculated controls and modify the tab order:

**1.** Select **2** in the Number of Invoices text box, and then press the **8** key. The Number of Invoices value remains at 2, and a message is displayed on the status bar. See Figure 6-46.

**Figure 6-46** After attempting to update a calculated control

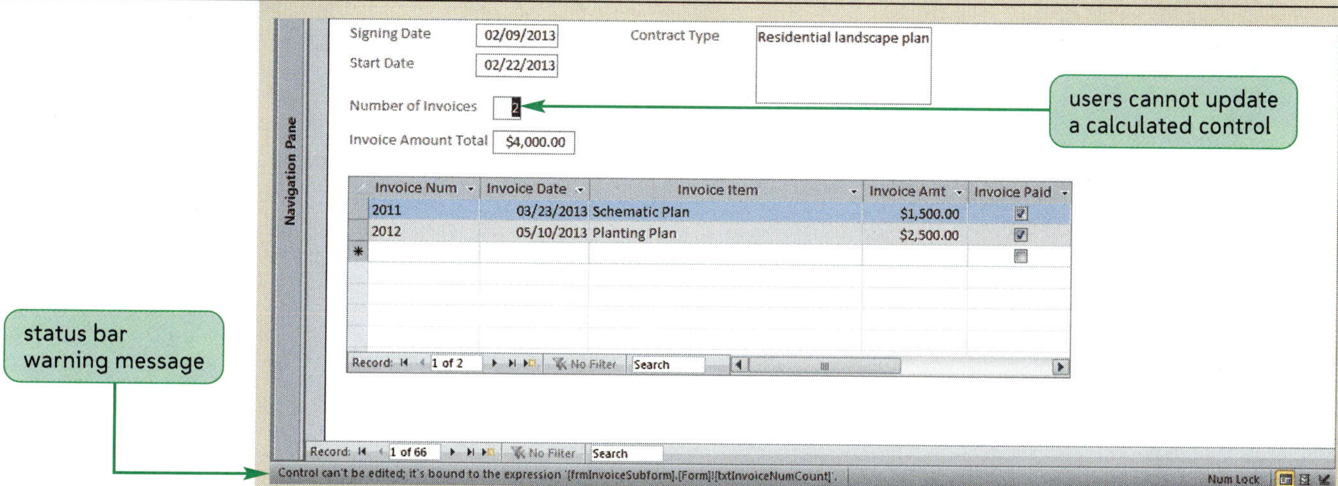

The status bar message warns you that you can't update, or edit, the calculated control because it's bound to an expression. The calculated control in the main form changes in value only when the value of the expression changes in the subform.

2. Click the **Invoice Amount Total** text box, and then press the **8** key. The value remains unchanged, and a message displays on the status bar because you cannot edit a calculated control.

   Next, you'll determine the tab order of the fields in the main form. Lucia wants the tab order to be down and then across.

3. Select **3011** in the ContractNum text box, press the **Tab** key to advance to the ContractAmt text box, and then press the **Tab** key five more times to advance to the SigningDate, StartDate, ContractType, CustomerID text boxes, in order, and then to the subform.

   Access sets the tab order in the same order in which you add controls to a form, so you should always check the form's tab order when you create a custom form in Layout or Design view. In this form, your testing reveals that you tab through the text boxes in a main form before tabbing through the fields in a subform. In the main form, tabbing bypasses the two calculated controls because you set their Tab Stop properties to No, and you bypass the Select Contract combo box because it's an unbound control. Also, you tab through only the text boxes in a form, not the labels.

   The tab order Lucia wants for the text boxes in the main form (top-to-bottom, left-to-right) is correct for the first four text boxes (ContractNum, ContractAmt, SigningDate, and StartDate text boxes). Then you should tab from the StartDate text box to the CustomerID text box and finally to the ContractType text box, but tabbing is reversed for the last two text boxes. The default tab order doesn't match the order Lucia wants, so you'll change the tab order. You must change the tab order in Design view.

4. Switch to Design view, and then in the Tools group on the Design tab, click the **Tab Order** button. The Tab Order dialog box opens. See Figure 6-47.

**Figure 6-47** **Changing the tab order for the Detail section in the main form**

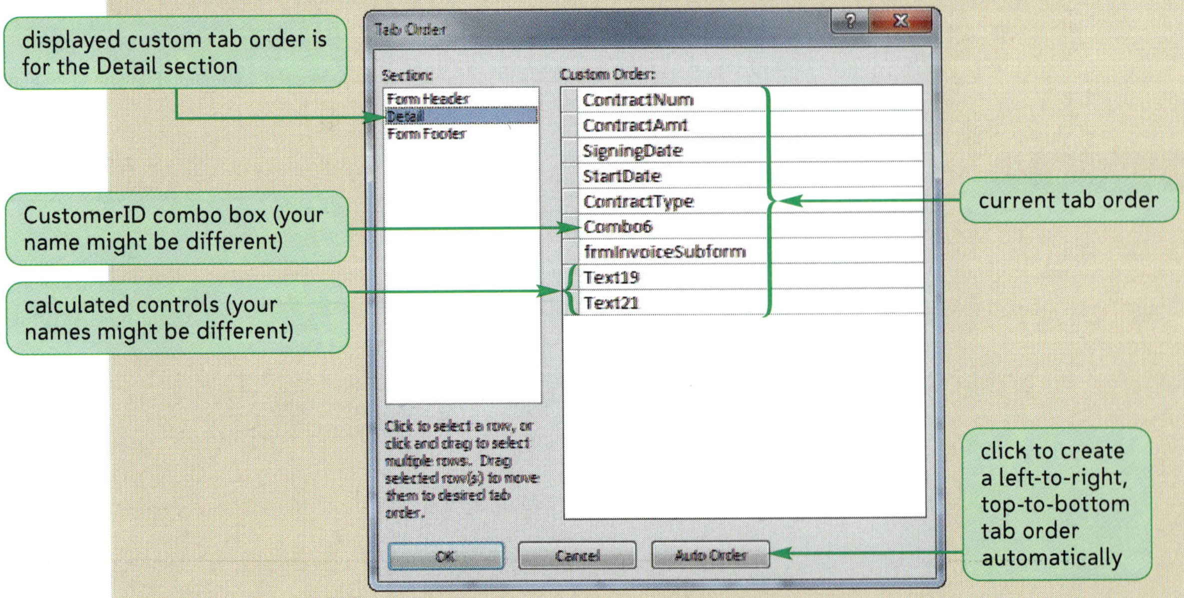

**TIP**

Setting the Name property for all your controls to meaningful names avoids having to guess which control a name references in this and similar situations.

Because you did not set the Name property for the combo box control and the calculated controls, Access assigned their names: Combo6 (your name might be different) for the CustomerID combo box, Text19 (your name might be different) for the Number of Invoices calculated control, and Text21 (your name might be different) for the Invoice Amount Total calculated control. The Auto Order button lets you create a left-to-right, top-to-bottom tab order automatically, which is not the order Lucia wants. You need to move the Combo6 entry above the ContractType entry.

5. Click the **row selector** to the left of Combo6, and then drag the row selector above the ContractType entry. The entries are now correct and in the correct order.

6. Click the **OK** button, save your form design changes, switch to Form view, and then tab through the controls in the main form to make sure the tab order is correct.

**Trouble?** If the tab order is incorrect, switch to Design view, click the Tab Order button in the Tools group on the Design tab, change your tab order in the Tab Order dialog box to match the one shown in Figure 6-47, and then repeat Step 6.

**PROSKILLS**

*Written Communication: Enhancing Information Using Calculated Controls*

For contracts with one or two invoices, it's easy for users to quickly count the number of invoices and to calculate the total invoice amount when the form doesn't display calculated controls. Similary, when students have completed few courses or when people have made few tax payments, it's easy for users to count the courses and calculate the student GPA or to count and total the tax payments. But for contracts with dozens or hundreds of invoices, for students with many courses, or for people with many tax payments, displaying summary calculated controls is mandatory. By adding a few simple calculated controls to forms and reports, you can increase the usefulness of the information presented and improve the ability of users to process the information, spot trends, and be more productive in their jobs.

You've finished adding controls to the form, but the form is plain looking and lacks visual clues for the different controls in the form. You'll complete the form by making it more attractive and easier for Sarah and her staff to use.

# Improving a Form's Appearance

The frmContractsAndInvoices form has four distinct areas: the Form Header section containing the title and the Select Contract combo box, the six bound controls in the Detail section, the two calculated controls in the Detail section, and the subform in the Detail section. To visually separate these four areas, you'll increase the height of the Form Header section, add a horizontal line at the bottom of the Form Header section, and draw a rectangle around the calculated controls.

## Adding a Line to a Form

You can use lines in a form to improve the form's readability, to group related information, or to underline important values. You use the **Line tool** in Design view to add a line to a form or report.

REFERENCE

*Adding a Line to a Form or Report*

- Display the form or report in Design view.
- In the Controls group on the Design tab, click the More button, and then click the Line tool.
- Position the pointer where you want the line to begin.
- Drag the pointer to the position for the end of the line, and then release the mouse button. If you want to ensure that you draw a straight horizontal or vertical line, hold down the Shift key before and during the drag operation.
- To make small adjustments to the line length, select the line, hold down the Shift key, and then press an arrow key. To make small adjustments in the placement of a line, select the line, hold down the Ctrl key, and then press an arrow key.

You will add a horizontal line to the Form Header section to separate the controls in this section from the controls in the Detail section.

## To add a line to the form:

1. Switch to Design view, and then drag down the bottom of the Form Header section to the 1-inch mark on the vertical ruler to make room to draw a horizontal line at the bottom of the Form Header section.
2. In the Controls group on the Design tab, click the **More** button to open the Controls gallery, and then click the **Line** tool.
3. Position the pointer's plus symbol (+) at the left edge of the Form Header section and at the 0.75-inch mark on the vertical ruler.
4. Hold down the **Shift** key, drag a horizontal line from left to right, so the end of the line ends at the 8.25-inch mark on the vertical ruler, release the mouse button, and then release the **Shift** key. See Figure 6-48.

**Figure 6-48** Adding a line to the form

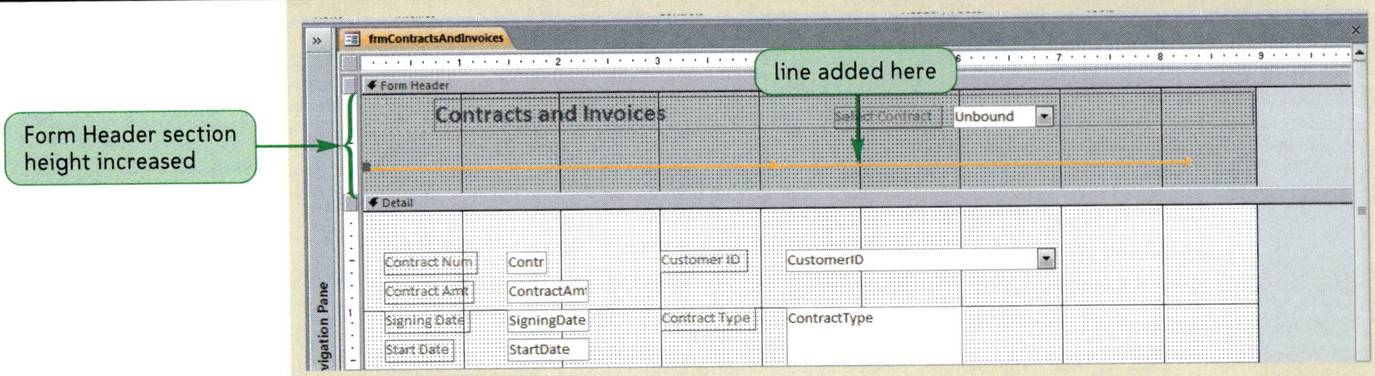


**Trouble?** If the line is not straight or not positioned correctly, click the Undo button on the Quick Access Toolbar, and then repeat Steps 2 through 4. If the line is not the correct length, be sure the line is selected, hold down the Shift key, and press one or more of the arrow keys until the line's length is the same as that of the line shown in Figure 6-48.

5. Drag up the bottom of the Form Header section to just below the line at the 0.75-inch mark on the vertical ruler.
6. Save your form design changes.

Next, you'll add a Rectangle around the calculated controls in the Detail section.

## Adding a Rectangle to a Form

You can use a rectangle in a form to group related controls and to separate the group from other controls. You use the **Rectangle tool** in Design view to add a rectangle to a form or report.

REFERENCE

### *Adding a Rectangle to a Form or Report*

- Display the form or report in Design view.
- In the Controls group on the Design tab, click the More button, and then click the Rectangle tool.
- Click in the form or report to create a default-sized rectangle, or drag a rectangle in the position and size you want.

You will add a rectangle around the calculated controls and their labels to separate them from the subform and from the other controls in the Detail section.

### To add a rectangle to the form:

1. In the Controls group on the Design tab, click the **More** button to open the Controls gallery, and then click the **Rectangle** tool.
2. Position the pointer's plus symbol (+) approximately two grid dots above and two grid dots to the left of the Number of Invoices label.
3. Drag a rectangle down and to the right until all four sides are approximately two grid dots from the two calculated controls and their labels. See Figure 6-49.

**Figure 6-49** Adding a rectangle to the form

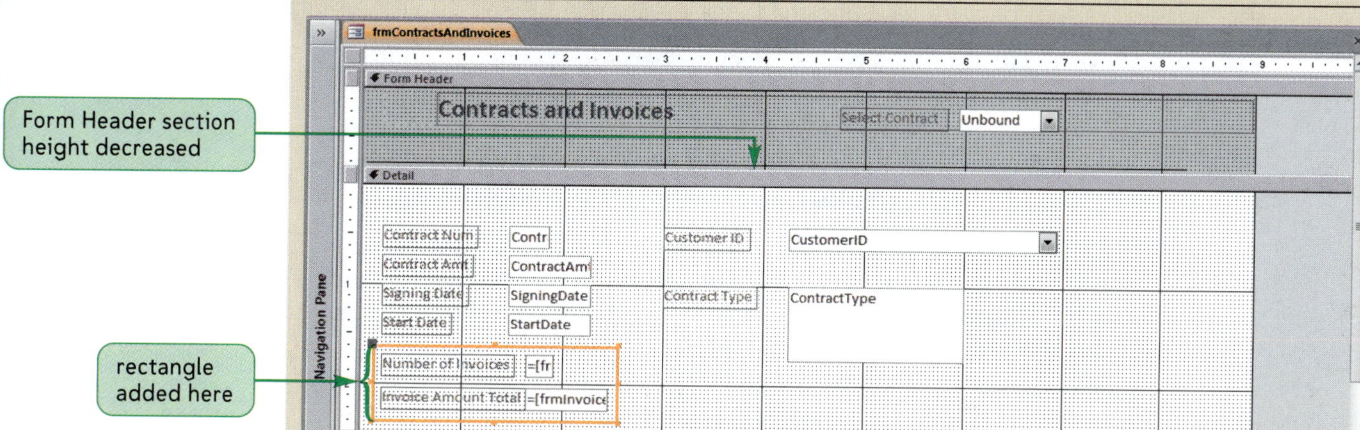

**Trouble?** If the rectangle is not sized or positioned correctly, use the sizing handles to adjust its size and the move handle to adjust its position.

Next, you'll set the thickness of the rectangle's lines.

4. Click the **Format** tab; in the Control Formatting group on the Format tab, click the **Shape Outline arrow**; point to **Line Thickness** at the bottom of the gallery; click the line with the ScreenTip **1 pt** in the list; and then deselect the control.

Next, you'll add color and visual effects to the form's controls.

**TIP**

Using a theme can improve a form's appearance, but a theme doesn't provide the control you can achieve by setting properties in Design or Layout view.

## Modifying the Visual Effects of the Controls in a Form

Distinguishing one group of controls in a form from other groups is an important visual cue to the users of the form. For example, users should be able to distinguish the bound controls in the form from the calculated controls and from the Select Contract control in the Form Header section. You'll now modify the controls in the form to provide these visual cues. You'll start by setting font properties for the calculated control's labels.

### To modify the controls in the form:

1. Select the **Number of Invoices** label and the **Invoice Amount Total** label; click the **Format** tab (if necessary); in the Font group on the Format tab, click the **Font Color button arrow** A; click the **Blue** color (row 7, column 8) in the Standard Colors palette; and then in the Font group on the Format tab, click the **Bold** button **B**. The labels' captions now use a bold, blue font.

   Next, you'll set properties for the Select Contract label in the Form Header section.

2. Select the **Select Contract** label in the Form Header section, set the label's font color to **Red** (row 7, column 2 in the Standard Colors palette), and then set the font style to bold.

   Next, you'll set the label's Special Effect property to a raised effect. The **Special Effect property** specifies the type of special effect applied to a control in a form or report. The choices for this property are Flat, Raised, Sunken, Etched, Shadowed, and Chiseled.

3. Open the property sheet for the Select Contract label, click the **All** tab (if necessary), and then set the Special Effect property to **Raised**. The label now has a raised special effect, and the label's caption now uses a bold, red font.

   Next, you'll set the Special Effect property for the bound control labels to a sunken effect.

4. Select the **Contract Num** label, **Contract Amt** label, **Signing Date** label, **Start Date** label, **Customer ID** label, and **Contract Type** label, set the controls' Special Effect property to **Sunken**, and then close the property sheet.

   Finally, you'll set the background color of the Form Header section, the Detail section, the Select Contract combo box, and the two calculated controls. You can use the **Background Color button** in the Font group on the Design tab to change the background color of a control, section, or object (form or report).

5. Click the Form Header's section bar, and in the Font group on the Format tab, click the **Background Color button arrow**; and then click the **Light Blue 2** color (row 3, column 5) in the Standard Colors palette. The Form Header's background color changes to the Light Blue 2 color.

6. Click the Detail section's section bar, and in the Font Group on the Format tab, click the **Background Color** button to change the Detail section's background color to the **Light Blue 2** color.
7. Select the **Select Contract** combo box, **Number of Invoices** text box, and the **Invoice Amount Total** text box, set the selected controls' background color to the **Light Blue 2** color, and then deselect all controls by clicking to the right of the Detail section's grid. See Figure 6-50.

**Figure 6-50 Completed custom form in Design view**

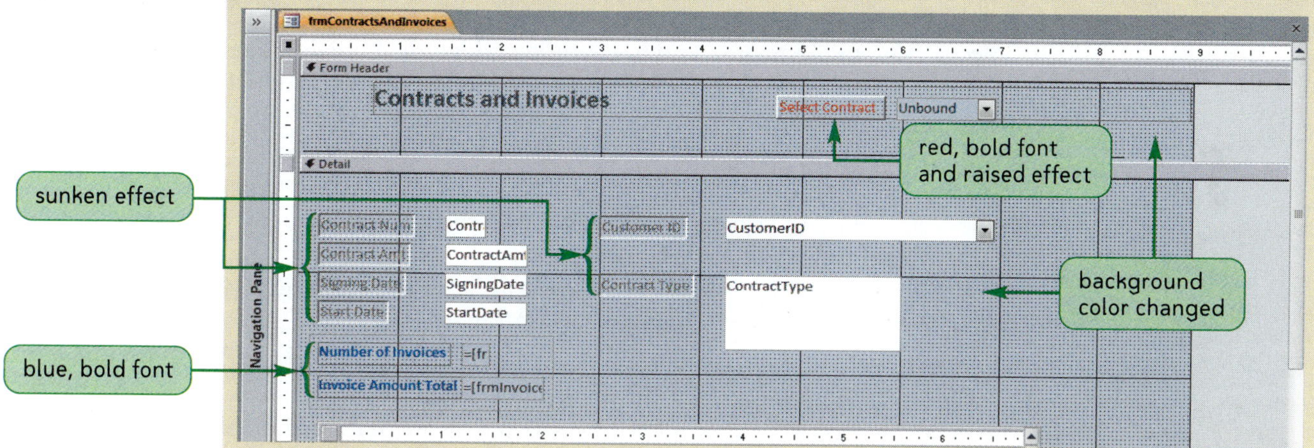


8. Switch to Form view, and then click the **ContractNum** text box to deselect the value. The Session 6.3 Visual Overview shows the completed form.
9. Test the form by tabbing between fields, navigating between records, and using the Select Contract combo box to find records, making sure you don't change any field values and observing that the calculated controls display the correct values.
10. Save your form design changes, close the form, make a backup copy of the database, compact and repair the database, and then close the database.

The completed custom form will make it easier for Sarah and her staff to work with contract and invoice data in the Panorama database.

REVIEW

## *Session 6.3 Quick Check*

1. To create a combo box to find records in a form with the Combo Box Wizard, the form's record source must be a(n) ______________.
2. You use the ______________ tool to add a subform to a form.
3. To calculate subtotals and overall totals in a form or report, you use the ______________ function.
4. The Control Source property setting can be either a(n) ______________ or a(n) ______________.
5. Explain the difference between the Tab Stop property and tab order.
6. What is focus?
7. The ______________ property has settings such as Raised and Sunken.

*Practice the skills you learned in the tutorial using the same case scenario.*

PRACTICE

## Review Assignments

**Data File needed for the Review Assignments: Products.accdb (*cont. from Tutorial 5*)**

Sarah wants you to create several forms, including a custom form that displays and updates companies and the products they offer. You'll do so by completing the following steps:

1. Open the **Products** database located in the Access2\Review folder provided with your Data Files.
2. Remove the lookup feature from the CompanyID field in the **tblProduct** table, and resize the Company ID column in the datasheet to its best fit. Save and close the table.
3. Edit the relationship between the primary tblCompany and related tblProduct tables to enforce referential integrity and to cascade update related fields. Create the relationship report, and then save the report as **rptRelationshipsForProducts**.
4. Use the Documenter to document the qryContactList query. Select all query options; use the Names, Data Types, and Sizes option for fields; and use the Names and Fields option for indexes. Print the report produced by the Documenter.
5. Use the Datasheet tool to create a form based on the tblProduct table, and then save the form as **frmProductDatasheet**.
6. Use the Multiple Items tool to create a form based on the qryCompanyList query, and then save the form as **frmCompanyListMultipleItems**.
7. Use the Split Form tool to create a split form based on the tblProduct table, and then make the following changes to the form in Layout view:
   a. Remove the two Unit controls from the stacked layout, reduce the width of the Unit text box by about half, and then anchor the two Unit controls to the bottom left.
   b. Remove the five control pairs in the right column from the stacked layout, and then anchor the group to the bottom right.
   c. Remove the ProductType and Price control pairs from the stacked layout, move them to the top right, and then anchor them to the top right.
   d. Reduce the widths of the ProductID and CompanyID text boxes to a reasonable size.
   e. Change the title to **Product**, and then save the modified form as **frmProductSplitForm**.
8. Use Figure 6-51 and the following steps to create a custom form named **frmCompaniesWithProducts** based on the tblCompany and tblProduct tables.
   a. Place the fields from the tblCompany table at the top of the Detail section. Delete the Contact Last Name label and change the caption for the Contact First Name label to **Contact**.
   b. Move the fields into two columns in the Detail section, as shown in Figure 6-51, resizing and aligning controls, as necessary.
   c. Add the title in the Form Header section.
   d. Make sure the form's Record Source property is set to tblCompany, and then add a combo box in the Form Header section to find CompanyName field values. In the wizard steps, select the CompanyName and CompanyID fields, and hide the key column. Resize and move the control.
   e. Add a subform based on the tblProduct table, include only the fields shown in Figure 6-51, link with CompanyID, name the subform **frmPartialProductSubform**, delete the subform label, resize the columns in the subform to their best fit, and resize and position the subform.
   f. Add a calculated control that displays the number of products displayed in the subform. Set the calculated control's Tab Stop property to No, and the ControlTip Text property to **Calculated number of products**.

**Figure 6-51** **Products database custom form design**

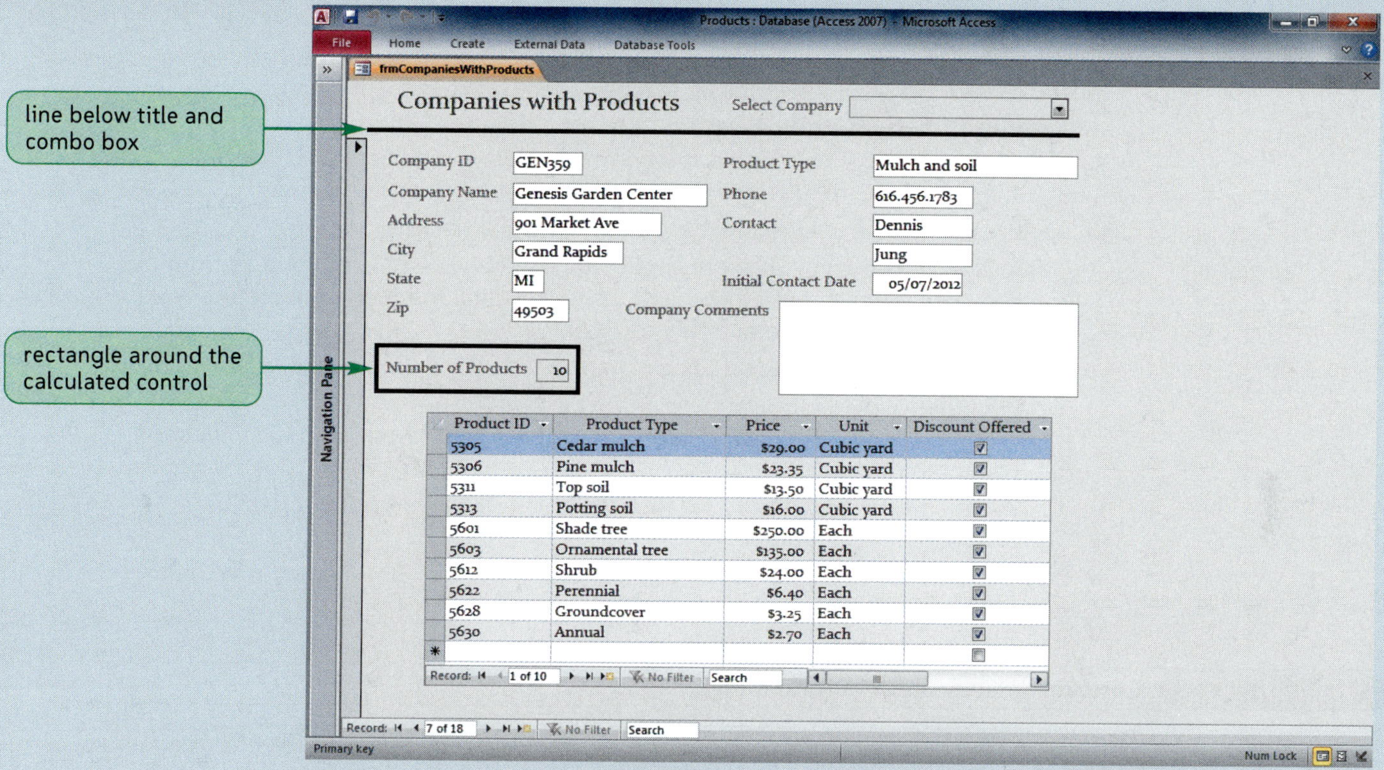


g. Add a line in the Form Header section, and add a rectangle around the calculated control and its label, setting the line thickness of both controls to the line style with the ScreenTip 3 pt. Use the Format Painter on the Format tab to paint the rectangle's color the same as the line's color.

h. In the main form, use the Black, Text 1 font color (row 1, column 2 in the Theme Colors palette) for all text boxes, and use the White, Background 1, Darker 5% fill color (row 2, column 1 in the Theme Colors palette) for the sections, the calculated control, and the Select Company combo box.

i. Make sure the tab order is top-to-bottom, left-to-right for the main form text boxes.

9. Make a backup copy of the database, compact and repair the database, and then close the database.

*Apply the skills you learned in the tutorial to create a custom form.*

CHALLENGE

## Case Problem 1

**Data File needed for this Case Problem: Contract.accdb (*cont. from Tutorial 5*)**

***Pine Hill Music School*** Yuka wants you to create several forms, including a custom form that displays and updates the school's music contracts with students. You'll do so by completing the following steps:

1. Open the **Contract** database located in the Access2\Case1 folder provided with your Data Files.
2. Remove the lookup feature from the TeacherID field in the **tblContract** table, and then resize the Teacher ID column to its best fit. Save and close the table.
3. Define a one-to-many relationship between the primary tblTeacher table and the related tblContract table. Select the referential integrity option and the cascade updates option for this relationship.

4. Use the Documenter to document the tblContract table. Select all table options; use the Names, Data Types, and Sizes option for fields; and use the Names and Fields option for indexes. Print the report produced by the Documenter.
5. Use the Multiple Items tool to create a form based on the qryLessonsByTeacher query, change the title to **Lessons by Teacher**, and then save the form as **frmLessonsByTeacherMultipleItems**.
6. Use the Split Form tool to create a split form based on the qryLessonsByTeacher query, and then make the following changes to the form in Layout view.
   a. Reduce the widths of all six text boxes to a reasonable size.
   b. Remove the LessonType, LessonLength, and MonthlyLessonCost controls from the stacked layout, move these three controls to the right and then to the top of the form, and then anchor them to the top right.
   c. Select the MonthlyLessonCost control and its label, and then anchor them to the bottom right.
   d. Remove the ContractEndDate control from the stacked layout, and then anchor the control to the bottom left.
   e. Change the title to **Lessons by Teacher**, and then save the modified form as **frmLessonsByTeacherSplitForm**.
7. Use Figure 6-52 and the following steps to create a custom form named **frmContract** based on the tblContract table.

**Figure 6-52 Contract database custom form design**

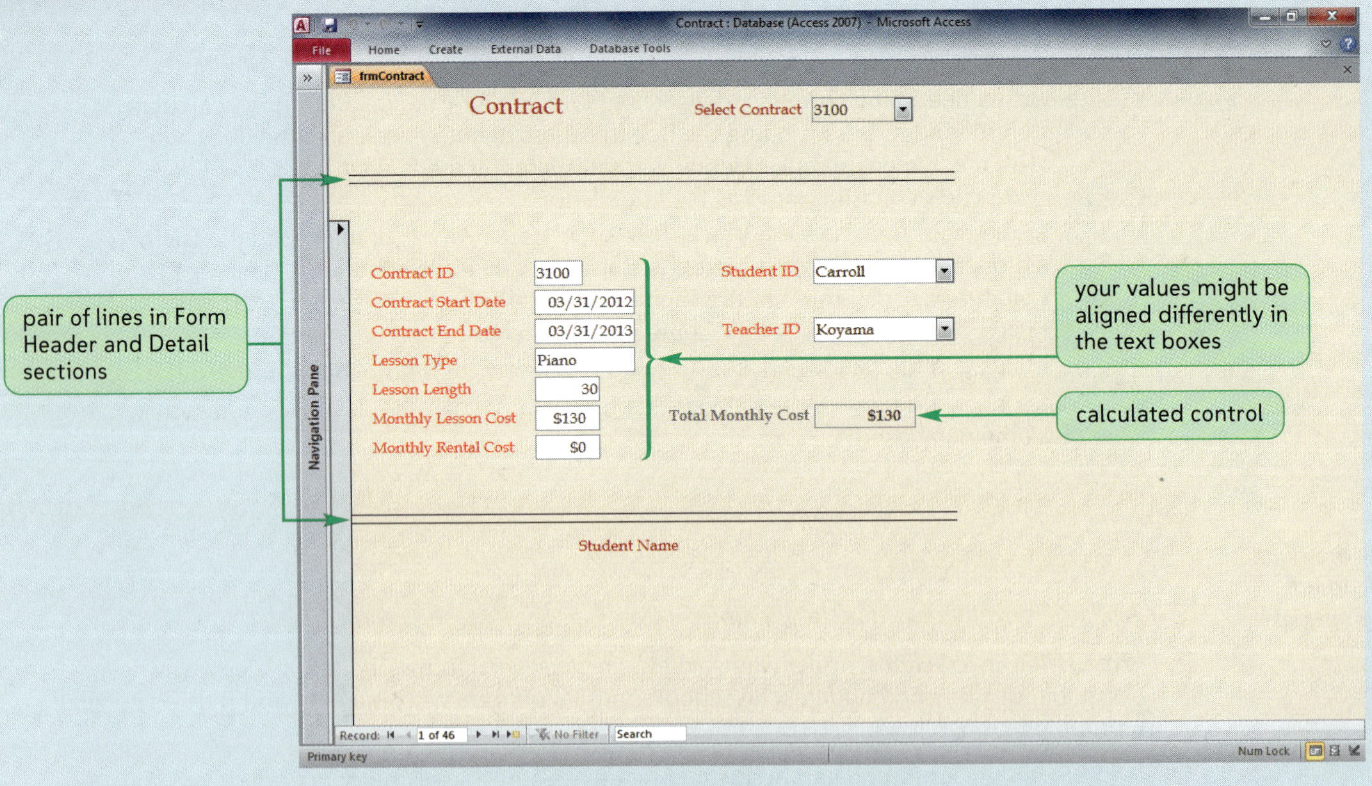


   a. For the StudentID combo box, select the LastName, FirstName, and StudentID fields from the tblStudent table, in order; and sort in ascending order by the LastName field and then by the FirstName field.
   b. For the TeacherID combo box, select the LastName, FirstName, and TeacherID fields from the tblTeacher table, in order; and sort in ascending order by the LastName field and then by the FirstName field.

c. Make sure the form's Record Source property is set to tblContract, and then add a combo box in the Form Header section to find ContractID field values.

EXPLORE

d. Add a calculated control that displays the total of the MonthlyLessonCost and MonthlyRentalCost fields. Set the calculated control's Tab Stop property to No and format the values as currency with no decimal places.

EXPLORE

e. Add a line in the Form Header section, and then add a second line below it, and then add a second pair of lines near the bottom of the Detail section. Set the line thickness of all lines to the line setting with the ScreenTip 1 pt.

EXPLORE

f. Use the Label tool to add your name below the pair of lines at the bottom of the Detail section.

g. For the labels in the Detail section, except for the Total Monthly Cost label and the label displaying your name, use the Red font color (row 7, column 2 in the Standard Colors palette).

h. For the title, Select Contract label, and the label displaying your name, use the Dark Red font color (row 7, column 1 in the Standard Colors palette).

i. For the calculated control and its label, bold the font.

j. For the background fill color of the sections, the calculated control, and the Select Contract combo box, use the Medium Gray color (row 1, column 3 in the Standard Colors palette).

k. Make sure the tab order is top-to-bottom, left-to-right for the main form text boxes.

8. Make a backup copy of the database, compact and repair the database, and then close the database.

*Use the skills you learned in the tutorial to create a custom form.*

CREATE

## Case Problem 2

**Data File needed for this Case Problem: Training.accdb (*cont. from Tutorial 5*)**

***Parkhurst Health & Fitness Center*** Martha Parkhurst wants you to create several forms, including two custom forms that display and update data in the Training database. You'll do so by completing the following steps:

1. Open the **Training** database located in the Access2\Case2 folder provided with your Data Files.
2. Use the Documenter to document the qryMemberNames query. Select all query options; use the Names, Data Types, and Sizes option for fields; and use the Names and Fields option for indexes. Print the first page of the report produced by the Documenter.
3. Use the Datasheet tool to create a form based on the tblProgram table, and then save the form as **frmProgramDatasheet**.

EXPLORE

4. Create a custom form based on the qryUpcomingExpirations query. Display all fields from the query in the form. Create your own design for the form. Add a label to the bottom of the Detail section that contains your first and last names. Change the label's font so that your name appears in bold, blue text. Change the ExpirationDate text box format so that the field value displays in bold, red text. Save the form as **frmUpcomingExpirations**.
5. Use Figure 6-53 and the following steps to create a custom form named **frmProgramsWithMembers** based on the tblProgram and tblMember tables.

**Figure 6-53** **Training database custom form design**

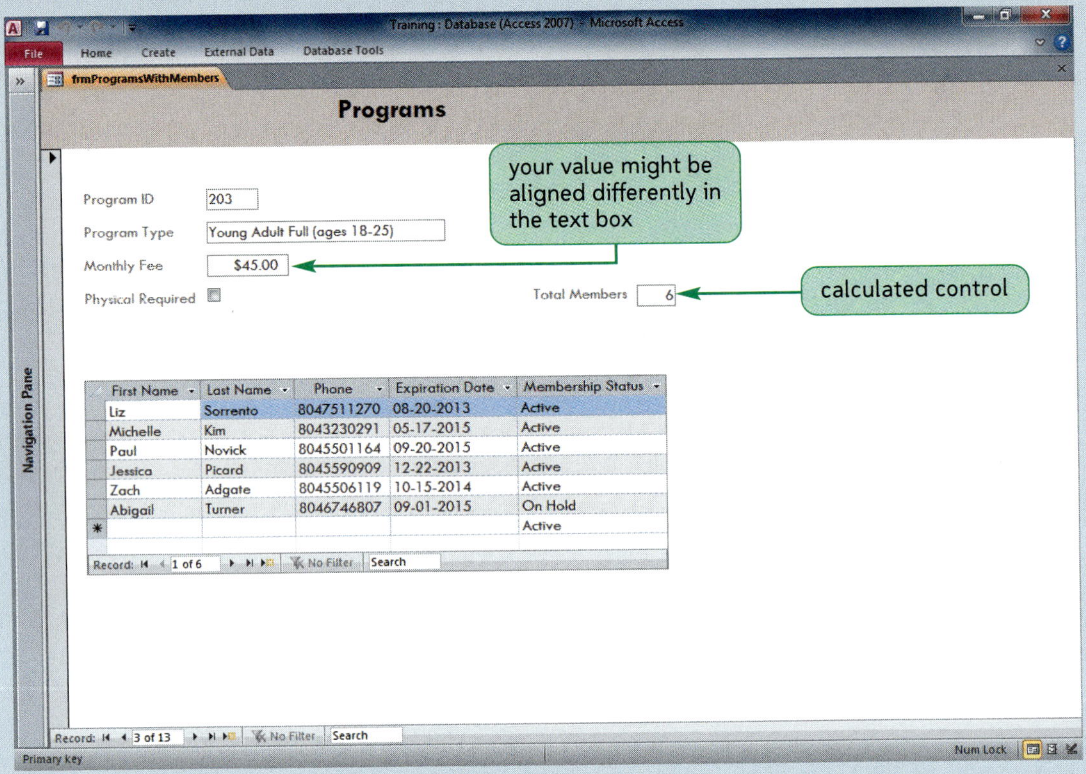


a. Selected fields from the tblMember table appear in a subform named **frmProgramMemberSubform**.

b. The calculated control displays the total number of records that appear in the subform. Set the calculated control's ControlTip Text property to **Total number of members in this program**. Set the calculated control's Tab Stop property to No.

c. Apply the Median theme to the form.

d. Save and view the form, and then print both pages for the first record.

6. Make a backup copy of the database, compact and repair the database, and then close the database.

*Use the skills you learned in the tutorial to create a custom form.*

CREATE

## Case Problem 3

**Data File needed for this Case Problem: Agency.accdb (*cont. from Tutorial 5*)**

***Rossi Recycling Group*** Mary Rossi asks you to create several forms, including a custom form for the Agency database so that she can better track donations for the agency. You'll do so by completing the following steps:

1. Open the **Agency** database located in the Access2\Case3 folder provided with your Data Files.
2. Use the Documenter to document the tblDonor table. Select all table options; use the Names, Data Types, and Sizes option for fields; and use the Names and Fields option for indexes. Print the report produced by the Documenter.
3. Use the Multiple Items tool to create a form based on the qryDonorPhoneList query, change the title to **Donor Phone List**, and then save the form as **frmDonorPhoneListMultipleItems**.

4. Use the Split Form tool to create a split form based on the tblDonor table, and then make the following changes to the form in Layout view.
   a. Reduce the widths of all five text boxes to a reasonable size.
   b. Remove the FirstName, LastName, and Phone controls from the stacked layout, move them to the top right, and then anchor them to the top right.
   c. Change the title to **Donor**, and then save the modified form as **frmDonorSplitForm**.
5. Use Figure 6-54 and the following steps to create a custom form named **frmDonorDonations** based on the tblDonor and tblDonation tables.

**Figure 6-54** **Agency database custom form design**

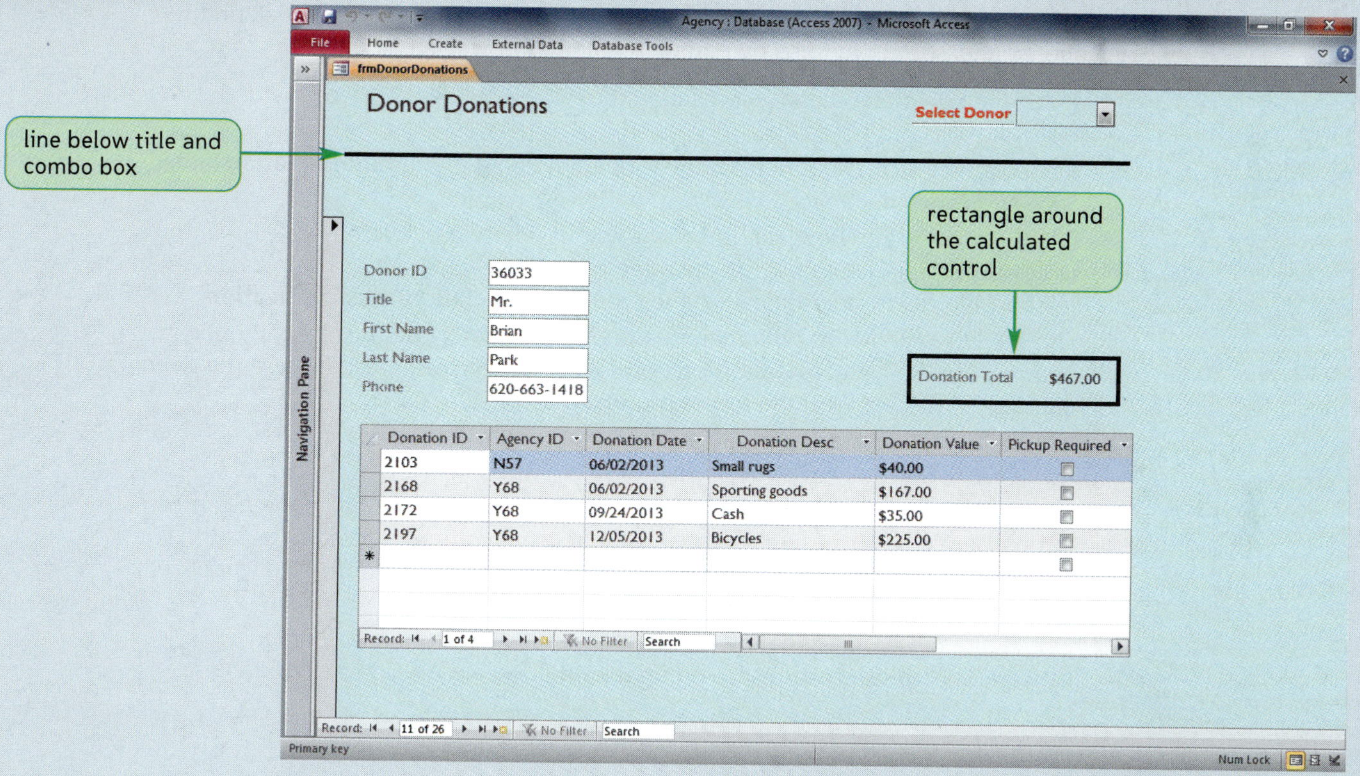


   a. Add the title in the Form Header section.
   b. Make sure the form's Record Source property is set to tblDonor, and then add a combo box in the Form Header section to find DonorID field values. In the wizard steps, select the DonorID field. Format the label using the Red font (row 7, column 2 in the Standard Colors palette), bold, and the Chiseled special effect.
   c. Add a subform based on the tblDonation table, name the subform **frmDonorDonationSubform**, delete the subform label, and resize the columns in the subform to their best fit and resize and position the subform.

EXPLORE

   d. Add a calculated control that displays the total of the DonationValue field displayed in the subform with the Currency format. Set the calculated control's Tab Stop property to No, and the Border Style property to Transparent.

EXPLORE

   e. Add a line in the Form Header section, and add a rectangle around the calculated control and its label, setting the line thickness of both controls to the line style with the ScreenTip 3 pt. Set the rectangle color to Black (row 1, column 2 in the Standard Colors section) using the Shape Outline button in the Control Formatting group on the Format tab.

f. Use the background color Aqua Blue 2 (row 3, column 9 in the Standard Colors palette) for the sections, the calculated control, and the Select Donor combo box.
g. Make sure the tab order is top-to-bottom for the main form text boxes.

6. Make a backup copy of the database, compact and repair the database, and then close the database.

*Use the skills you learned in the tutorial to create two custom forms.*

CREATE

## Case Problem 4

**Data File needed for this Case Problem: Vacation.accdb (*cont. from Tutorial 5*)**

***GEM Ultimate Vacations*** Griffin and Emma MacElroy want you to create several forms, including a custom form that displays and updates guest and reservation data in the Vacation database. You'll do so by completing the following steps:

1. Open the **Vacation** database located in the Access2\Case4 folder provided with your Data Files.
2. Remove the lookup feature from the PropertyID field in the **tblReservation** table. Save and close the table.
3. Edit the relationship between the primary tblProperty and related tblReservation tables to enforce referential integrity and to cascade update related fields. Create the relationship report, and then save the report as **rptRelationshipsForVacation**.
4. Use the Documenter to document the qryIllinoisGuests query. Select all query options; use the Names, Data Types, and Sizes option for fields; and use the Nothing option for indexes. Print the report produced by the Documenter.
5. Use the Datasheet tool to create a form based on the qryGuestTripDates query, and then save the form as **frmGuestTripDates**.
6. EXPLORE Create a custom form based on the qryRentalCost query. Display all fields in the form. Use your own design for the form, but use the title **Reserved Trips** in the Form Header section, and use the Label tool to add your name to the Form Header section. Save the form as **frmRentalCost**.
7. Use Figure 6-55 and the following steps to create a custom form named **frmGuestsWithReservations** based on the tblGuest and tblReservation tables.

**Figure 6-55** Vacation database custom form design

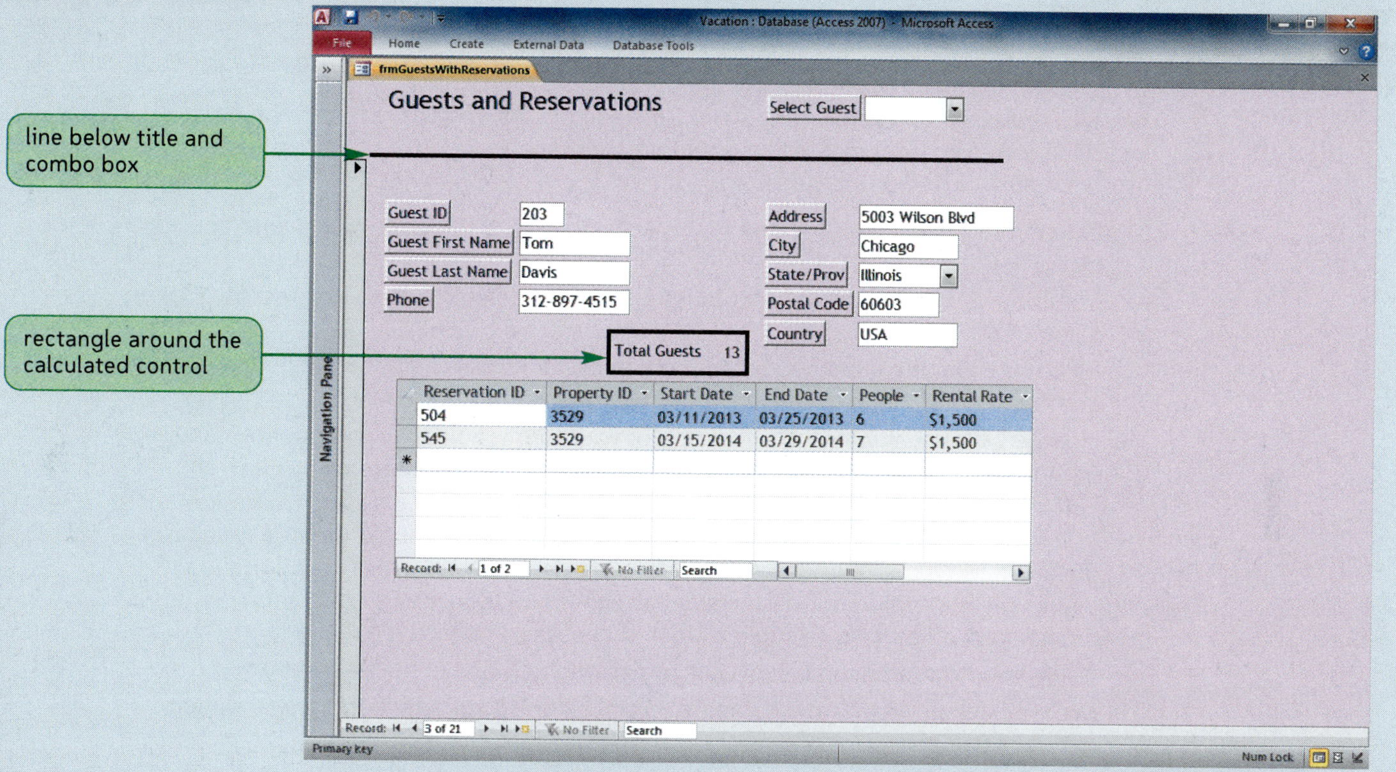


a. Add the title in the Form Header section.

b. Make sure the form's Record Source property is set to tblGuest and then add a combo box in the Form Header section to find GuestID field values.

c. Add a subform based on the tblReservation table, name the subform **frmGuestsWithReservationsSubform**, delete the subform label, and resize the columns in the subform to their best fit, and then resize and position the subform.

EXPLORE

d. Add a calculated control that displays the total of the People field displayed in the subform. Set the calculated control's Tab Stop property to No, and set the calculated control's Border Style property to Transparent.

EXPLORE

e. Add a line in the Form Header section, and add a rectangle around the calculated control and its label, setting the line thickness of both controls to the line style with the ScreenTip 3 pt. Set the rectangle color to Black (row 1, column 2 in the Standard Colors section) using the Shape Outline button in the Control Formatting group on the Format tab.

EXPLORE

f. Use black font color for all controls, including the controls in the subform.

g. Use the "Pink, Text 2, Lighter 80%" fill color (row 2, column 4 in the Theme Colors palette) for the sections and the calculated control.

h. Use the Raised special effect for the labels in the Detail section, except for the calculated control label, and the Form Header section, except for the title.

i. Make sure the tab order is top-to-bottom and left-to-right for the main form text boxes.

8. Make a backup copy of the database, compact and repair the database, and then close the database.

*Use the skills you learned in this tutorial to create a custom form.*

CREATE

## Case Problem 5

**Data File needed for this Case Problem: ACE.accdb (*cont. from Tutorial 5*)**

***Always Connected Everyday*** Chris and Pat Aquino want you to create several forms, including a custom form that displays and updates data in the ACE database. You'll do so by completing the following steps:

1. Open the **ACE** database located in the Access2\Case5 folder provided with your Data Files.
2. In Tutorial 5, you created a lookup field in the tblCustomer table. Remove the lookup feature from this field.
3. Make sure that the table relationship enforces referential integrity. Create the relationship report, and then save the report as **rptRelationshipsForACE**.
4. Use the Documenter to document one of your forms. Select all form options and use the Names option for sections and controls. Print the report produced by the Documenter.
5. In Tutorial 5, you created forms to display and update the data in the ACE database. Review these forms, and develop a consistent design strategy that you'll use to customize all the forms. Your design strategy should include the use of combo boxes for foreign keys and for searching, calculated controls, and visual effects.
6. Using your form design strategy, customize all the forms in the ACE database.
7. Make a backup copy of the database, compact and repair the database, and then close the database.

ASSESS

## SAM: Skills Assessment Manager

For current SAM information, including versions and content details, visit SAM Central (http://samcentral.course.com). If you have a SAM user profile, you may have access to hands-on instruction, practice, and assessment of the skills covered in this tutorial. Since various versions of SAM are supported throughout the life of this text, check with your instructor for the correct instructions and URL/Web site for accessing assignments.

### ENDING DATA FILES

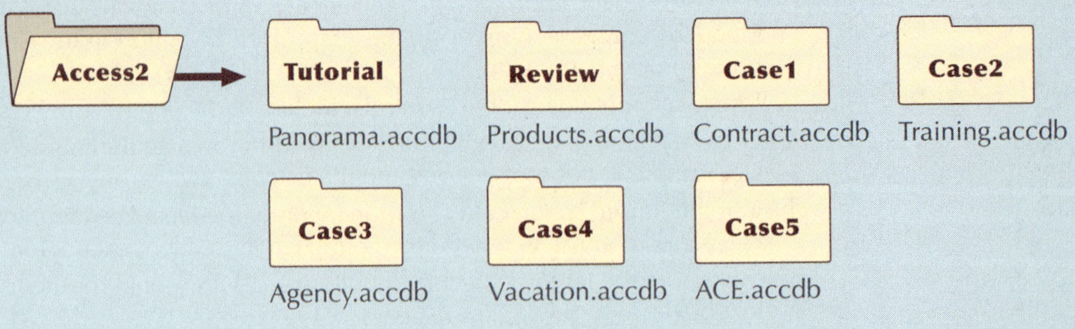

# Creating Custom Reports

*Creating Custom Reports for Belmont Landscapes*

## OBJECTIVES

**Session 7.1**
- View, filter, and copy report information in Report view
- Modify a report in Layout view
- Modify a report in Design view

**Session 7.2**
- Design and create a custom report
- Sort and group data in a report
- Add, move, resize, and align controls in a report
- Add lines to a report
- Hide duplicate values in a report

**Session 7.3**
- Add the date, page numbers, and title to a report
- Create and modify mailing labels

## Case | *Belmont Landscapes*

At a recent staff meeting, Sarah Fisher indicated that she would like to make some changes to an existing report in the database. She also requested a new report that she can use to produce a printed list of all invoices for all contracts.

In this tutorial, you will modify an existing report and create the new report for Sarah. In modifying and building these reports, you will use many Access report customization features, including grouping data, calculating totals, and adding lines to separate report sections. These features will enhance Sarah's reports and make them easier to read and use.

### STARTING DATA FILES

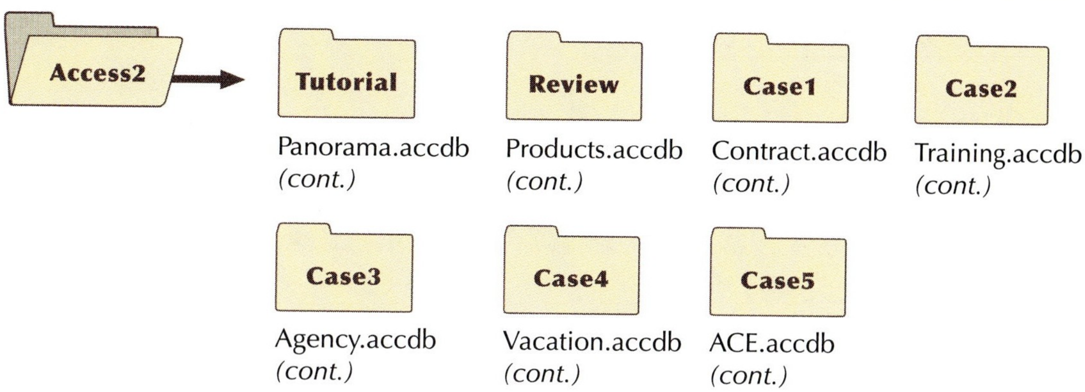

# SESSION 7.1 VISUAL OVERVIEW

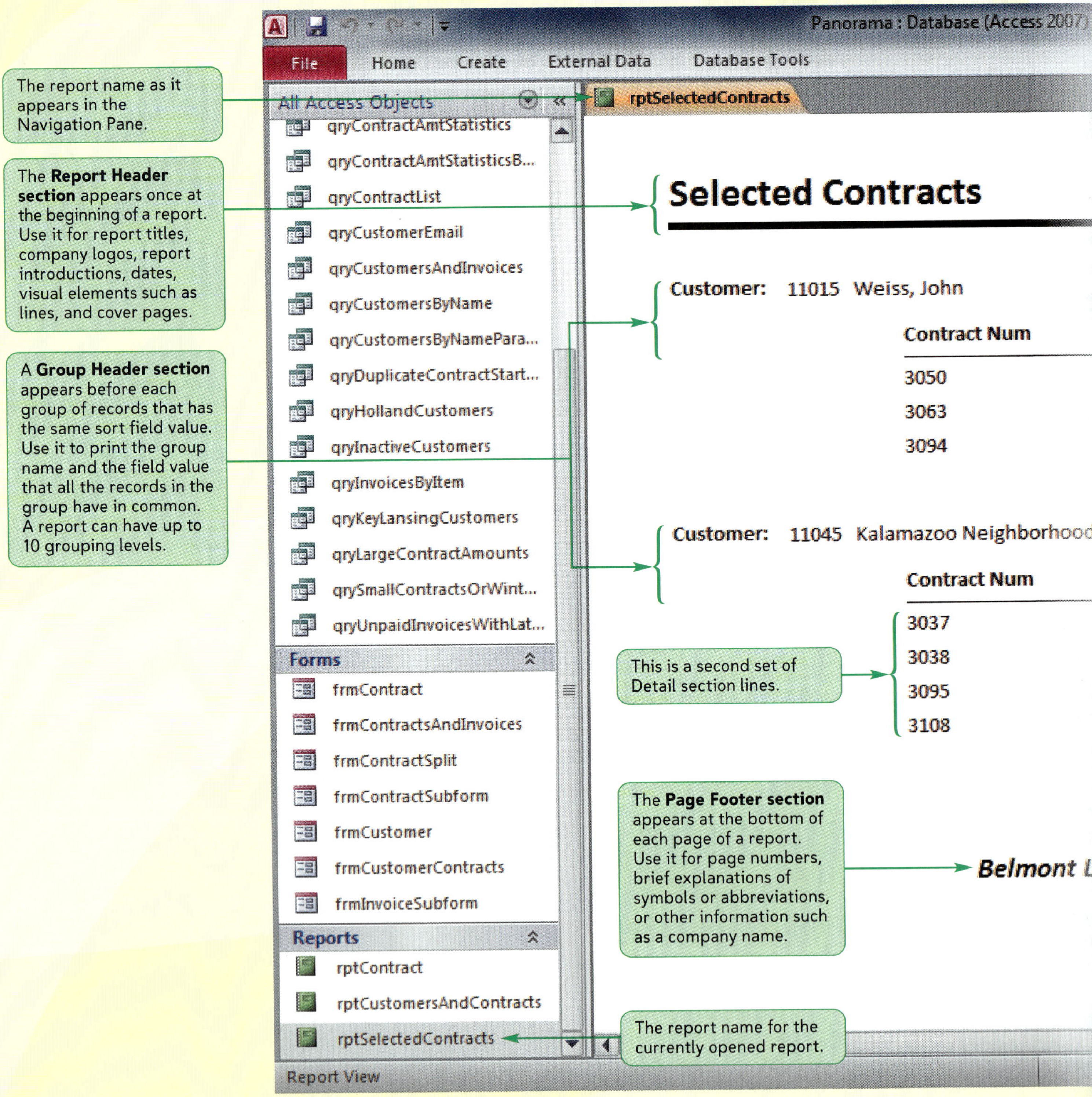

# REPORT SECTIONS

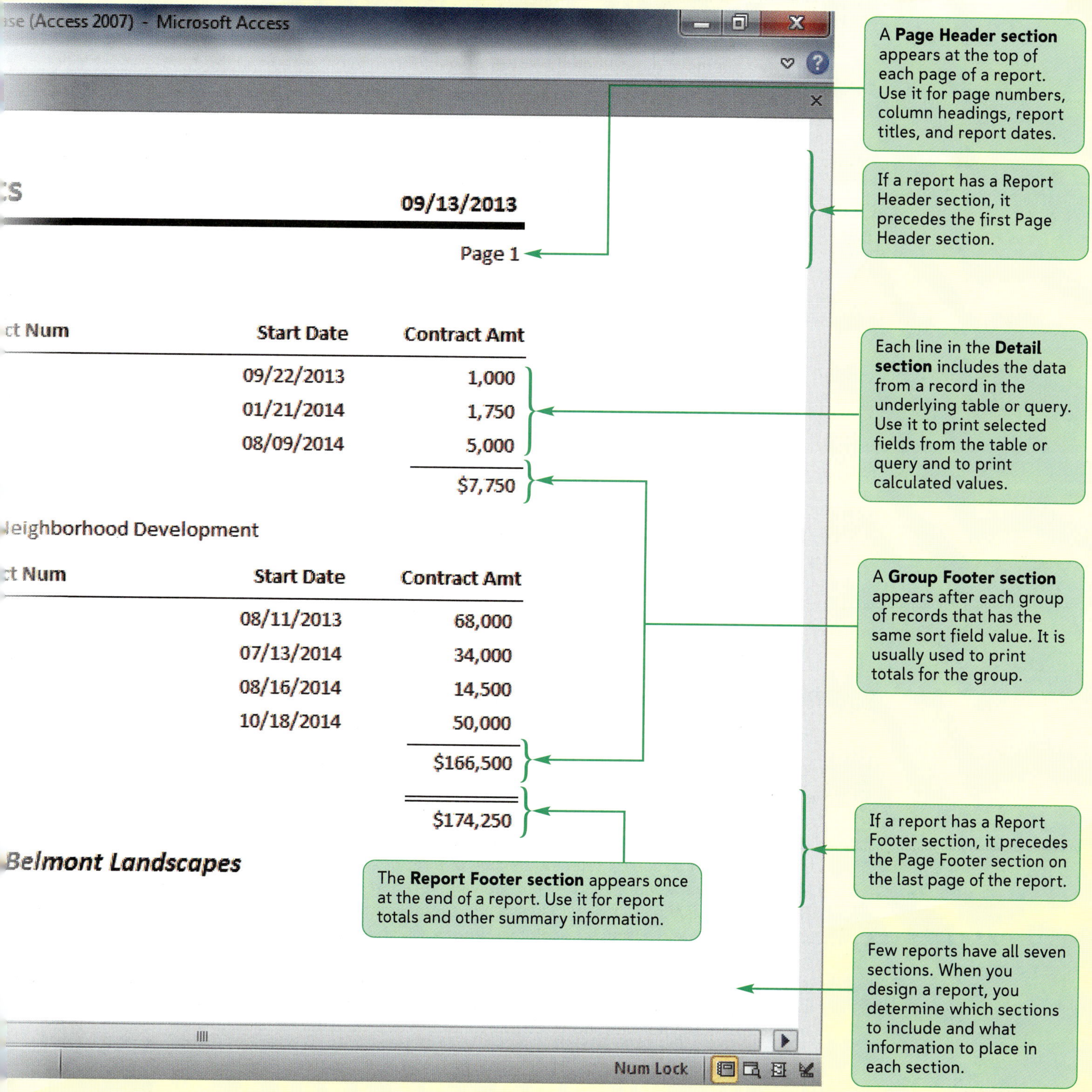

# Customizing Existing Reports

A report is a formatted printout (or screen display) of the contents of one or more tables in a database. Although you can format and print data using datasheets, queries, and forms, reports offer greater flexibility and provide a more professional, readable appearance. For example, the staff at Belmont Landscapes can create reports from the database for billing statements and mailing labels, but they cannot use datasheets, queries, and forms for the same purposes.

Before Lucia Perez joined Belmont Landscapes to enhance the Panorama database, Sarah Fisher and her staff created two reports. Sarah used the Report tool to create the rptContract report and the Report Wizard to create the rptCustomersAndContracts report. One of Sarah's staff members modified the rptCustomersAndContracts report in Layout view by modifying the title, moving and resizing fields, changing the font color of field names, and inserting a picture. The rptCustomersAndContracts report is an example of a custom report. When you modify a report created by the Report tool or the Report Wizard in Layout view or in Design view, or when you create a report from scratch in Layout view or in Design view, you produce a **custom report**. You need to produce a custom report whenever the Report tool or the Report Wizard cannot automatically create the specific report you need, or when you need to fine-tune an existing report to fix formatting problems or to add controls and special features.

Sarah asks Lucia to review the rptContract report, make improvements to it, and demonstrate features that Sarah's staff can use when working with reports.

## Viewing a Report in Report View

You can view reports on screen in Print Preview, Layout view, Design view, and Report view. You've already viewed and worked with reports in Print Preview and Layout view, and you'll find that making modifications in Design view for reports is similar to making changes in Design view for forms. **Report view** provides an interactive view of a report. You can use Report view to view the contents of a report and to apply a filter to the data in a report. You can also copy selected portions of the report to the Clipboard and use the selected data in another program.

INSIGHT

### *Choosing the View to Use for a Report*

You can view a report on screen using Report view, Print Preview, Layout view, or Design view. Which view you choose depends on what you intend to do with the report and its data.

- Use Report view when you want to filter the report data before printing a report, or when you want to copy a selected portion of a report.
- Use Print Preview when you want to see what a report will look like when it is printed. Print Preview is the only view in which you can navigate the pages of a report, zoom in or out, and view a **multiple-column report**, which is a report that prints the same collection of field values in two or more sets across the page.
- Use Layout view when you want to modify a report while seeing actual report data.
- Use Design view when you want to fine-tune a report's design, or when you want to add lines, rectangles, and other controls that are available only in Design view.

You'll open the rptContract report in Report view and show Sarah how she can interact with the report in this view.

## To interact with the rptContract report in Report view:

1. Start Access, and then open the **Panorama** database in the Access2\Tutorial folder provided with your Data Files.

   **Trouble?** If the Security Warning is displayed below the Ribbon, either the Panorama database is not located in the Access2\Tutorial folder or you did not designate that folder as a trusted folder. Make sure you opened the database in the Access2\Tutorial folder, and make sure that it's designated as a trusted folder.

2. Open the Navigation Pane, scroll down the Navigation Pane (if necessary), double-click **rptContract**, and then close the Navigation Pane. The rptContract report opens in Report view and the Navigation Pane closes.

   In Report view, you can view the live version of the report prior to printing it, just as you can do in Print Preview. Unlike in Print Preview, you can apply filters to the report before printing it. You'll show Sarah how to apply filters to the rptContract report.

3. In the first report detail line for Contract Num 3011, right-click **Residential landscape plan** in the Contract Type column to open the shortcut menu, and then point to **Text Filters**. A submenu of filter options for the Text field opens. See Figure 7-1.

**Figure 7-1 Filter options for a Text field in Report view**

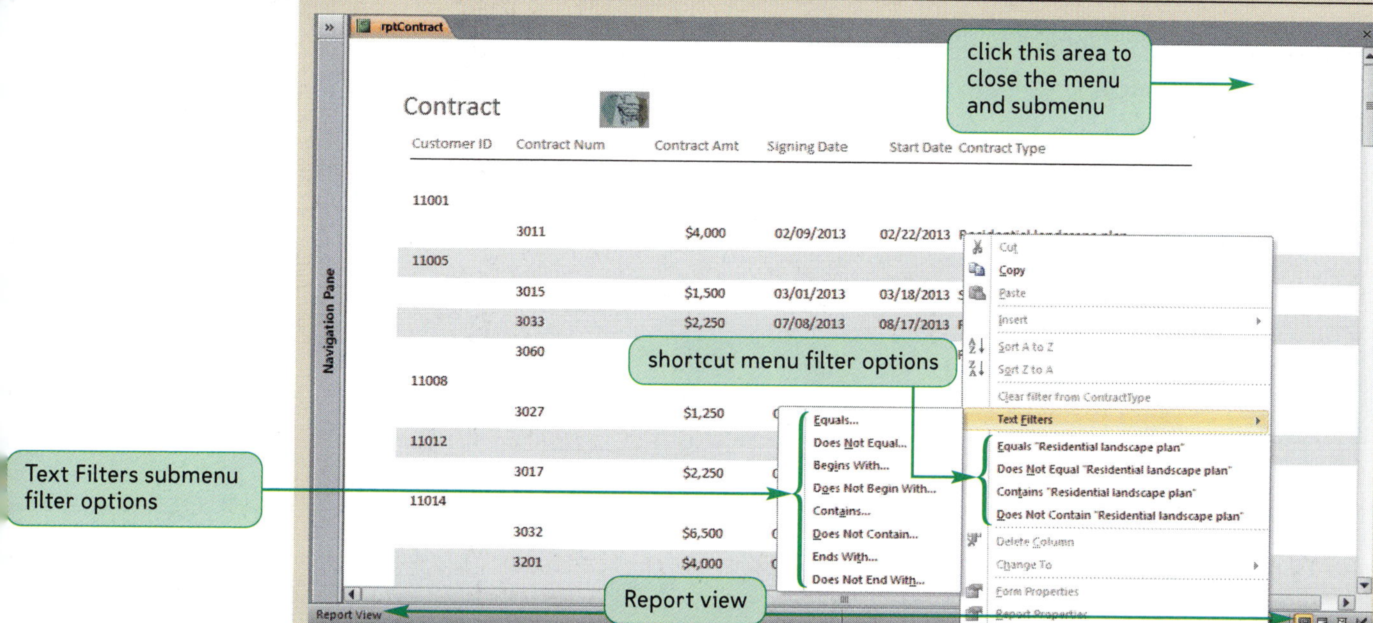


**Trouble?** Your Text Filters submenu will open to the left of the shortcut menu when you click the right side of the text in the Contract Type column.

The filter options that appear on the shortcut menu depend on the selected field's data type and the selected value. Because you clicked the ContractType field value without selecting a portion of the value, the shortcut menu displays filter options—various conditions using the value "Residential landscape plan"—for the entire ContractType field value. You'll close the menus and select a portion of the Contract Type column value to show Sarah a different way of filtering the report.

4. Click a blank area in the report (see Figure 7-1) to close the menus, and in the report detail line for Contract Num 3011, double-click **Residential** in the Contract

Type column to select it, right-click **Residential**, and then point to **Text Filters** on the shortcut menu. The filter options now apply to the selected text.

Notice that the filter options on the shortcut menu and on the Text Filters submenu include options such as "Begins With" and "Does Not Begin With" because the text you selected is at the beginning of the field value in the Contract Type column.

5. Click **Contains "Residential"** on the shortcut menu. The report content changes to display only those contracts that contain the word "residential" anywhere in the Contract Type column.
6. Double-click the word **residential** in the Contract Type column for the report detail line for Contract Num 3015 to select it, right-click **residential** to open the shortcut menu, and then point to **Text Filters**. The filter options now include the "Ends With" and "Does Not End With" options because the text you selected is at the end of the field value in the Contract Type column.

Sarah wants to view only those contracts that contain the phrase "residential landscape plan" in the Contract Type column.

7. Click a blank area in the report to close the menus, and in the report detail line for Contract Num 3011, right-click **Residential landscape plan** in the Contract Type column, and then click **Equals "Residential landscape plan"** on the shortcut menu. Only the five contracts that contain the selected phrase are displayed in the report. See Figure 7-2.

**Figure 7-2** **Filter applied to the report in Report view**

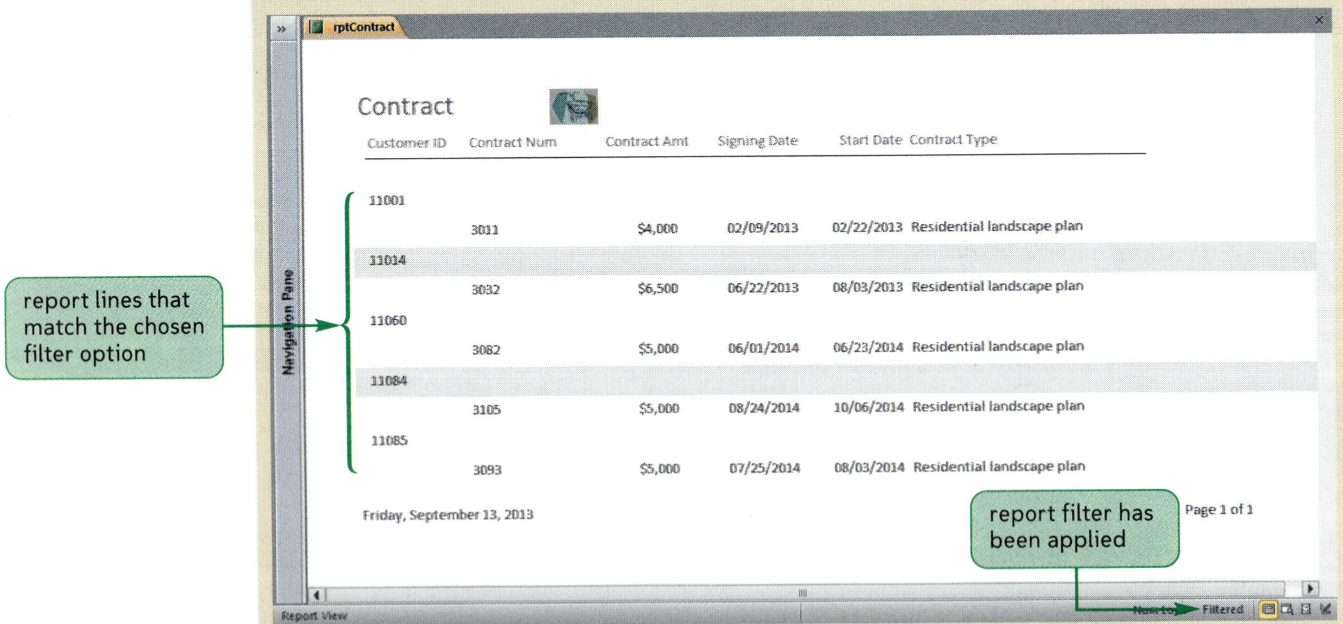


Sarah can print the filtered report, or she can select the entire filtered report or a portion of the filtered report. Then she can copy the selection to the Clipboard and paste it into another file, such as a Word document or an Excel spreadsheet. You'll show Sarah how to copy the entire filtered report to the Clipboard.

**TIP**

To select a portion of the report, click to the left of the top of the selection and drag down to the bottom of the selection.

8. Click to the left of the Contract title at the top of the report (but don't click in the Navigation Pane), drag down to the bottom of the report, release the mouse button to select the entire report, and then in the Clipboard group on the Home tab, point to the **Copy** button. See Figure 7-3.

**Trouble?** If you selected nothing, you clicked above the Contract title. Make sure the mouse pointer is to the left of the Contract title, but not above it, and then repeat Step 8.

**Trouble?** If you selected only a portion of the report, press the Esc key to deselect your selection, and then repeat Step 8.

**Figure 7-3** **After selecting the filtered report in Report view**

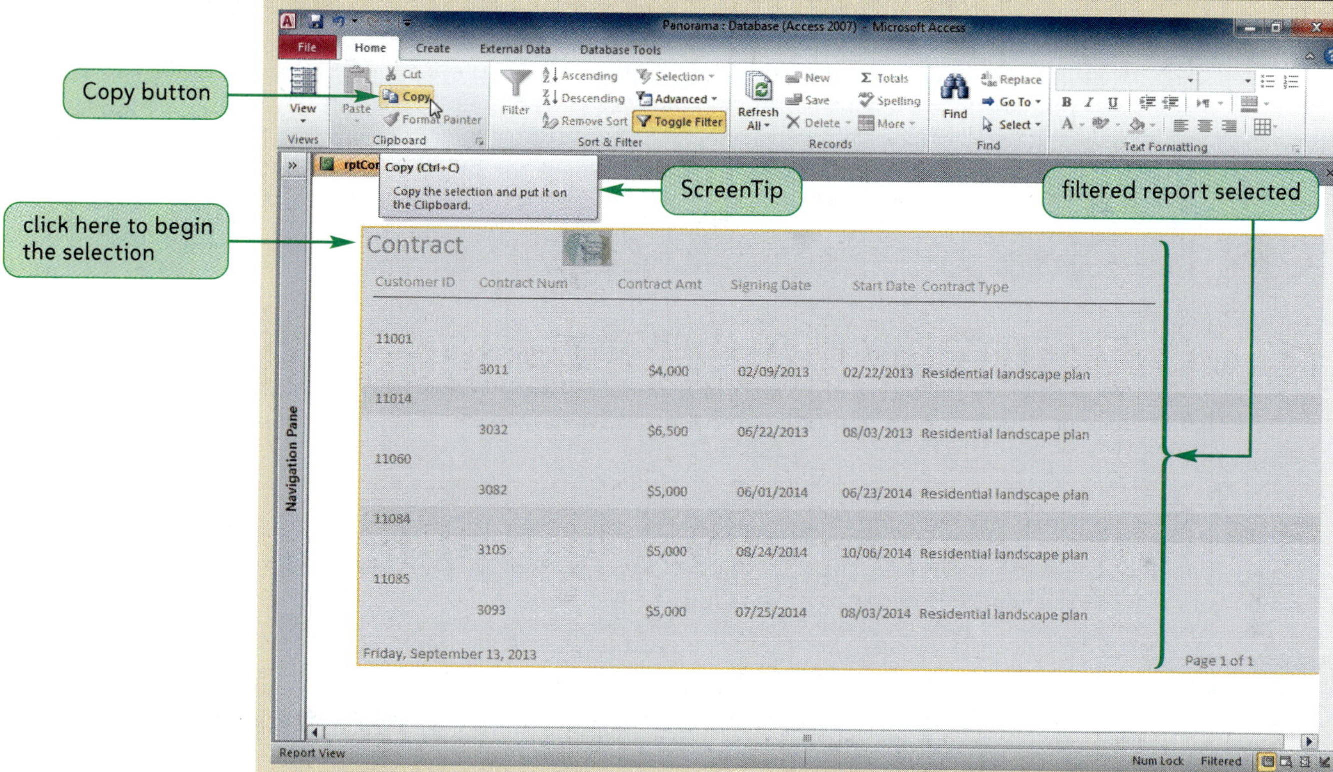


If you needed to copy the selection to the Clipboard, you would click the Copy button (see Figure 7-3). Sarah doesn't need to copy the selection, so you'll show her how to remove the filter from the report.

9. In the Sort & Filter group on the Home tab, click the **Toggle Filter** button. Access removes the filter and displays the complete report, which is still selected from the top to the bottom of the report.

10. Scroll down the report, and notice that some field values in the Contract Type column are not fully displayed and that no grand total of the ContractAmt field values is displayed at the end of the report.

Sarah wants you to modify the Contract Type column in the rptContract report so that all field values are fully displayed, while decreasing the width of other columns. She also wants you to rename some of the column headings, format the ContractAmt field values using the Standard format, resize the column headings, delete the picture from the Report Header section, remove the alternate row color from the detail and group header lines, and add a grand total of the ContractAmt field values. These changes will make the report more useful for Sarah.

PROSKILLS

### *Written Communication: Enhancing Reports Created by the Report Tool and the Report Wizard*

Creating a report using the Report tool or the Report Wizard can save time, but you should review the report to determine if you need to make any of the following types of common enhancements and corrections:

- Change the report title from the report object name (with an rpt prefix and no spaces) to one that has meaning to the users.
- Reduce the widths of the date and page number controls, and move the controls so that they are not printed on a separate page.
- Review the report in Print Preview and, if the report displays excess pages, adjust the page margins and the placement of controls.
- Verify that all controls are large enough to fully display their values.

Some of the report adjustments you need to make are subtle ones, so you need to carefully review all report controls to ensure the report is completely readable and usable for those using the report.

## Modifying a Report in Layout View

You can make the report changes Sarah wants in Layout view. Modifying a report in Layout view is similar to modifying a form in Layout view.

### To view the report in Layout view:

1. On the status bar, click the **Layout View** button, and then scroll to the top of the report (if necessary). See Figure 7-4.

**Figure 7-4 Viewing the report in Layout view**

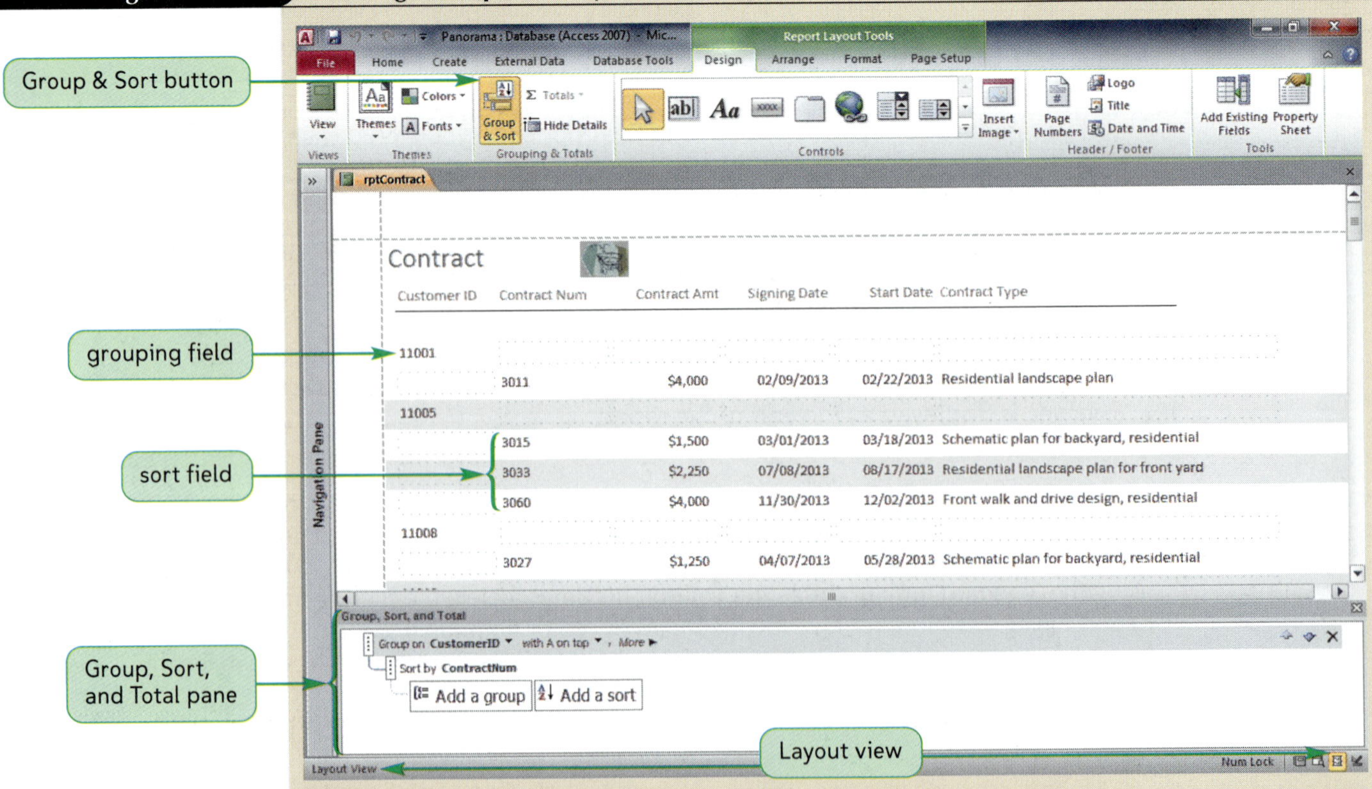

**Trouble?** If the Group, Sort, and Total pane is not open at the bottom of the screen, click the Group & Sort button in the Grouping & Totals group on the Design tab.

**TIP**

You can click the Group & Sort button in the Grouping & Totals group to open and close the Group, Sort, and Total pane.

The rptContract report has a grouping field (the CustomerID field) and a sort field (the ContractNum field). At the bottom of the screen, the **Group, Sort, and Total pane** provides you with the options to modify the report's grouping fields and sort fields, and the report calculations for the groups. A **grouping field** is a report sort field that includes a Group Header section before a group of records having the same sort field value and a Group Footer section after the group of records. A Group Header section usually displays the group name and the sort field value for the group. A Group Footer section usually displays subtotals or counts for the records in that group. The rptContract report's grouping field is the CustomerID field, which is displayed in a Group Header section that precedes the set of contracts for the customer; the grouping field does not have a Group Footer section. The ContractNum field is a secondary sort key, as shown in the Group, Sort, and Total pane.

Because you don't need to change the grouping or sort fields for the report, you'll close the pane and then make Sarah's modifications to the report.

### To modify the report in Layout view:

1. In the Grouping & Totals group on the Design tab, click the **Group & Sort** button to close the Group, Sort, and Total pane.

   First, you'll change the column headings for the first three columns to Cust ID, Contract#, and Amount. Sarah prefers to see all the detail data on one line, even when it means abbreviating column headings for columns whose headings are wider than the data. After reducing the column headings, you can reduce the column widths, freeing up space on the detail lines to widen the Contract Type column.

2. Double-click the **Customer ID** column heading to change to editing mode, change it to **Cust ID**, and then press the **Enter** key.
3. Repeat Step 2 to change the second column heading to **Contract#** and the third column heading to **Amount**.

   Next, you'll change the format of the field values in the Amount column to Standard.

4. Right-click any value in the **Amount** column to open the shortcut menu, click **Properties** to open the property sheet, set the Format property to **Standard**, and then close the property sheet.

   Now you'll increase the width of the Contract Type column after first reducing the widths of the first three columns.

5. Click the **Cust ID** column heading, move the pointer to the right edge of the column heading, and when the pointer changes to a ↔ shape, drag the right edge to the left. See Figure 7-5.
6. Repeat Step 5 to reduce the width of the **Contract#** column and then the width of the **Amount** column. See Figure 7-5.

**Figure 7-5** After resizing columns in Layout view

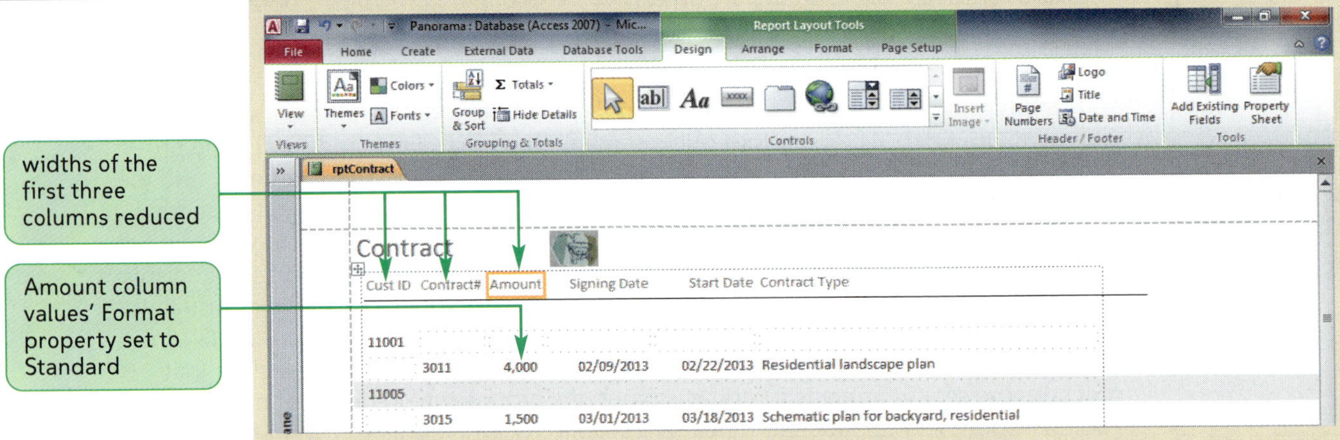


7. Scroll down the report to CustomerID 11083 and ContractNum 3043, which has the longest field value in the Contract Type column, click the **ContractType** field value for ContractNum 3043, move the pointer to the right edge of the selected value, and when the pointer changes to a ↔ shape, drag the right edge to the right until the entire field value is visible. See Figure 7-6.

**Figure 7-6** After resizing columns in Layout view

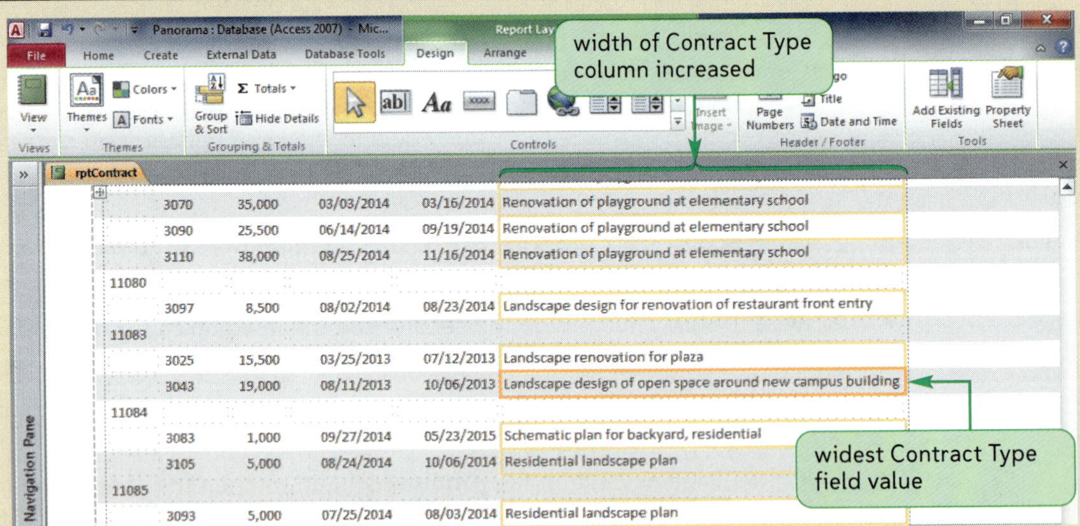


Sarah notes that the picture at the top of the report isn't necessary, so you'll delete it.

8. Scroll to the top of the report, right-click the picture at the top of the report to open the shortcut menu, and then click **Delete** to remove the picture.

Sarah notices the alternate row color setting in the group header and detail lines, finds it distracting, and asks you to remove this feature.

9. Click to the left of the outer vertical dashed line to the left of 3011 in the Contract# column to select the detail lines, click the **Format** tab, in the Background group click the **Alternate Row Color arrow** to display the gallery of available colors, and then at the bottom of the gallery, click **No Color**. The alternate row color is removed from the detail lines in the report.

You've removed the alternate row color from the detail lines in the report, and next you'll remove the alternate row color from the group header lines. Because the Alternate Row Color button is now set to "No Color," you can just click the button to remove the color.

10. Click to the left of the vertical dashed line to the left of 11005 in the Cust ID column to select the group header lines, and then click the **Alternate Row Color** button in the Background group to remove the alternate row color from the group header lines.

Sarah's last change to the report is to add a grand total of the ContractAmt field values. First, you must select the Amount column or one of the values in the column.

### To add a grand total to the report in Layout view:

1. In the detail line for ContractNum 3011, click **4,000** in the Amount column, click the **Design** tab, and then in the Grouping & Totals group, click the **Totals** button to display the Totals menu. See Figure 7-7.

**Figure 7-7** Displaying options on the Totals menu

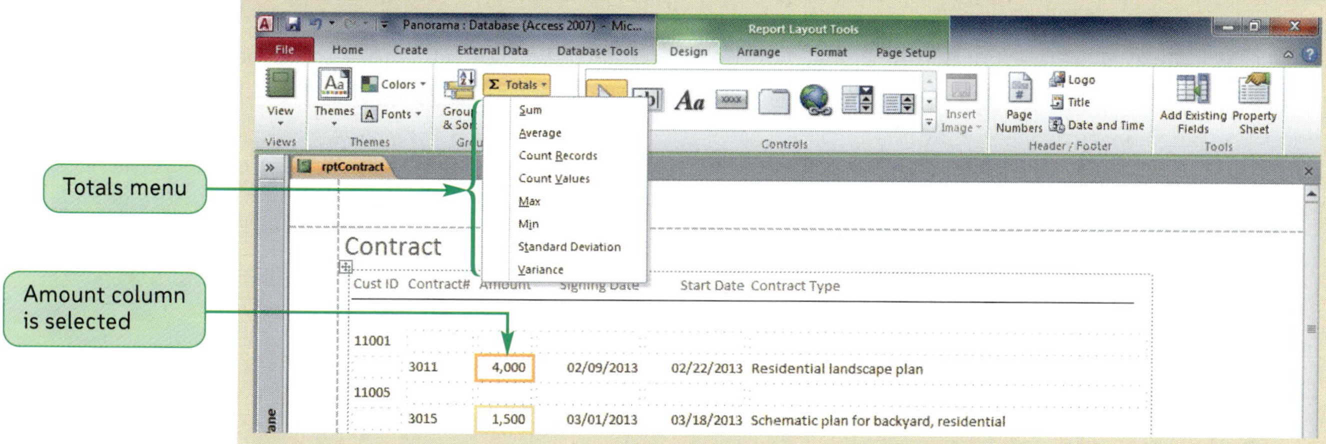


You select one of the eight aggregate functions on the Totals menu to summarize values in the selected column. To calculate and display the grand total contract amount, you'll select the Sum aggregate function.

**TIP**

A text box displays pound signs when the text box is too narrow to display the full field value.

2. Click **Sum** in the Totals menu, scroll to the bottom of the report, click **19,000** in the Amount column, and widen the Amount column to the right until the ###### changes to the correct grand total value of 1,758,075. In addition to the grand total, subtotals for each group of contracts are displayed for each CustomerID field value (19,000 for the last customer). See Figure 7-8.

**Trouble?** The commas in your subtotal and grand total might not be fully visible. You'll fix this problem in another step.

**Figure 7-8** After adding subtotals and a grand total of the ContractAmt field values

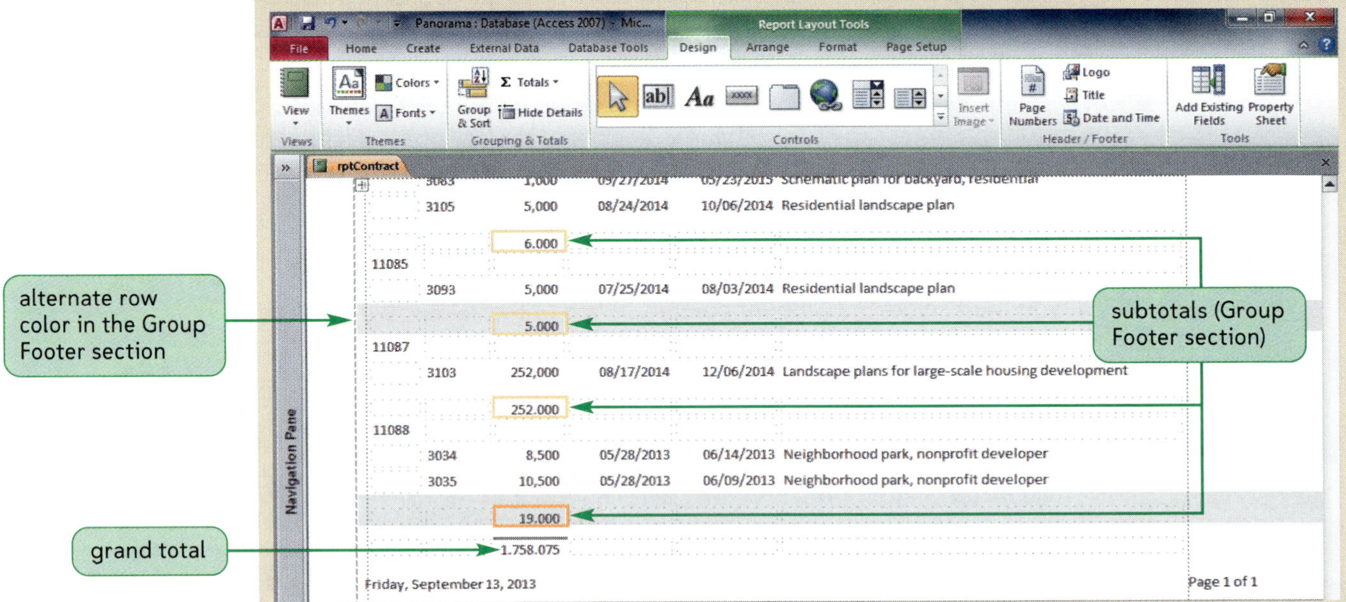


When you select an aggregate function in Layout view, Access adds the results of the function to the end of the report and adds subtotals for each grouping field. Because each customer has few contracts, Sarah asks you to remove the subtotals from the report.

3. Right-click the **19,000** subtotal to open the shortcut menu, click **Delete** to remove the subtotals, and then scroll to the end of the report. You deleted the subtotals, but the grand total still appears at the end of the report.

   Although you deleted the subtotals, the Group Footer section remains, and Sarah wants you to delete the section with its alternate row color.

4. Click to the left of the vertical dashed line on the left for one of the Group Footer lines, right-click one of the selected lines to open the shortcut menu, and then click **Delete** to remove the selected lines from the report.

   Sarah notices that the commas in the grand total value are not fully visible. You'll increase the height of the grand total next.

5. Click the grand total **1,758,075** to select it, and then use the ↕ pointer to drag the bottom edge of the grand total down slightly so the commas in the grand total are fully visible.

   Sarah wants to review the rptContract report in Print Preview.

6. Save your report changes, switch to Print Preview, and then page through the report, ending on the last page of the report.

   You can use the Zoom control on the status bar to zoom in or out pointer the report view in 10% increments (using the Zoom In or Zoom Out buttons) or in variable increments (by dragging the Zoom slider control).

7. Click the **Zoom In** button ⊕ on the status bar to increase the zoom percentage to 110%. See Figure 7-9.

**Figure 7-9** Viewing the rptContract report in Print Preview

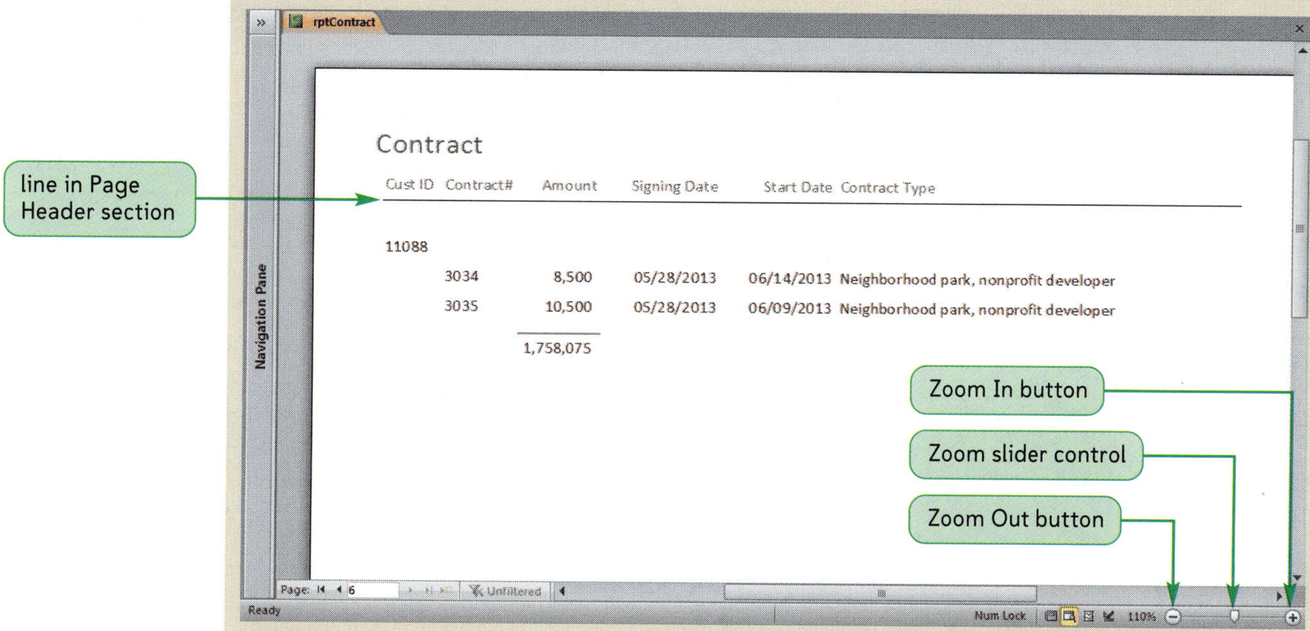


**Trouble?** Depending on the printer you are using, the last page of your report might differ. If so, don't worry. Different printers format reports in different ways, sometimes affecting the total number of pages and the number of records printed per page.

8. Click the **Zoom Out** button on the status bar to decrease the zoom percentage to 100%, and then close Print Preview for the report.

Sarah identifies two additional modifications she wants you to make to the report. She wants you to increase the length of the line below the column heading labels to better match the widths of the detail lines, and she wants you to move the page number at the bottom of each page to the left, so that its right edge is aligned with the right edge of ContractType text box in the Detail section.

## Modifying a Report in Design View

Although you can make Sarah's modifications in Layout view, you'll make them in Design view. Design view for reports is similar to Design view for forms, which you used in Tutorial 6 to customize forms.

### To view the report in Design view:

1. Switch to display the report in Design view. See Figure 7-10.

**Figure 7-10** rptContract report in Design view

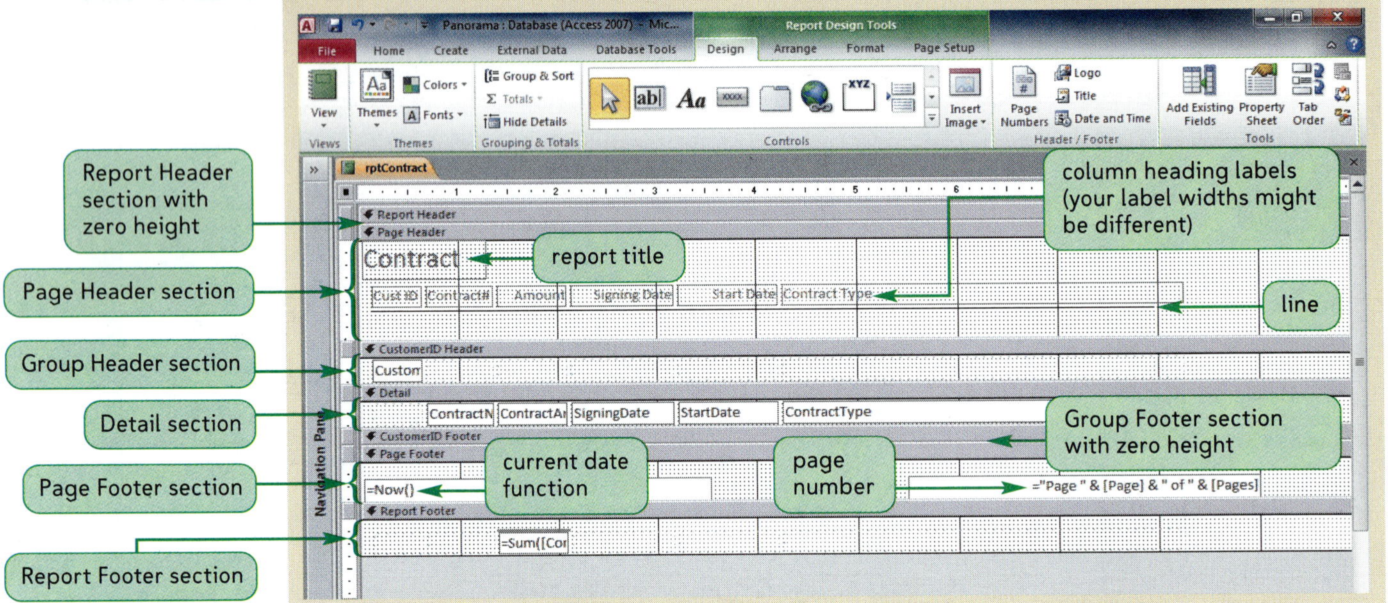


Notice that Design view for a report has most of the same components as Design view for a form. For example, Design view for forms and reports includes horizontal and vertical rulers, grids in each section, and similar buttons in the groups on the Design tab.

Design view for the rptContract report displays seven sections: the Report Header has zero height and isn't displayed in the report; the Page Header section contains the report title, column heading labels, and a horizontal line below the labels; the Group Header section (CustomerID Header) contains the CustomerID grouping field; the Detail section contains the bound controls to display the field values for each record in the record source (tblContract); the Group Footer section (CustomerID Footer) isn't displayed in the report; the Page Footer section contains the current date and the page number; and the Report Footer section contains a horizontal line above the Sum function, which calculates the grand total of the ContactAmt field values.

Refer to the Session 7.1 Visual Overview for a sample report from the Panorama database and descriptions of the seven sections in a report, all of which appear in the report shown in the Visual Overview.

To make Sarah's changes to the report, you need to extend the line control below the column headings in the Page Header section to the right, and then move the page number control in the Page Footer section to the left. Then you will align the right edges of both controls with the right edge of the ContractType text box in the Detail section.

### To modify the report in Design view:

1. Click the **Page Number** text box, and then press the ← key to move the text box to the left until the right edge of the text box is to the left of the right edge of the ContractType text box in the Detail section.
2. With the Page Number text box still selected, hold down the **Shift** key, click the **ContractType** text box, and then release the **Shift** key. Both controls are now selected.

3. Right-click one of the selected controls, point to **Align** on the shortcut menu, and then click **Right**. Both controls are now aligned on their right edges.

   Finally, you'll extend the line in the Page Header section to the right.

4. Click the **line** in the Page Header section to select the line as the current control.
5. Hold down the **Shift** key, and then position the pointer on the right end of the line. When the pointer changes to a shape, drag the end of the line to the right until it is right-aligned with the Contract Type label above it, release the mouse button, and then release the **Shift** key. See Figure 7-11.

**TIP**

To draw or extend a straight line, press the Shift key before dragging the line and release the Shift key after releasing the mouse button.

**Figure 7-11 After modifying the rptContract report in Design view**

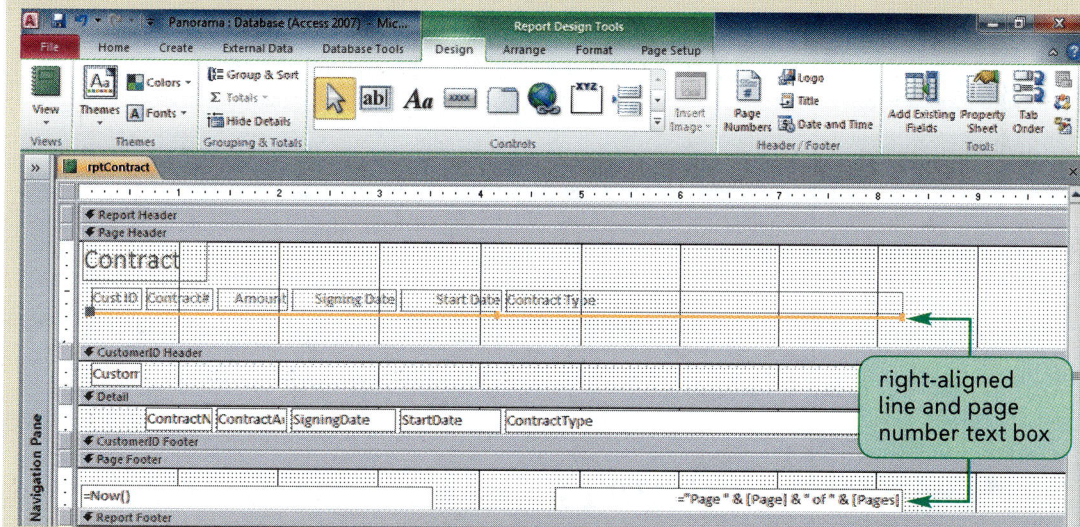


6. Save your report changes, switch to Print Preview, and then scroll and page through the report, paying particular attention to the placement of the line in the Page Header section and the page number in the Page Footer section.
7. Close the report.
8. If you are not continuing on to the next session, close the Panorama database.

Now that you have completed the changes to the rptContract report, you'll create a custom report for Sarah in the next session.

REVIEW

## *Session 7.1 Quick Check*

1. What is a custom report?
2. You can view a report in Report view. What other actions can you perform in Report view?
3. What is a grouping field?
4. Describe the seven sections of an Access report.

# SESSION 7.2 VISUAL OVERVIEW

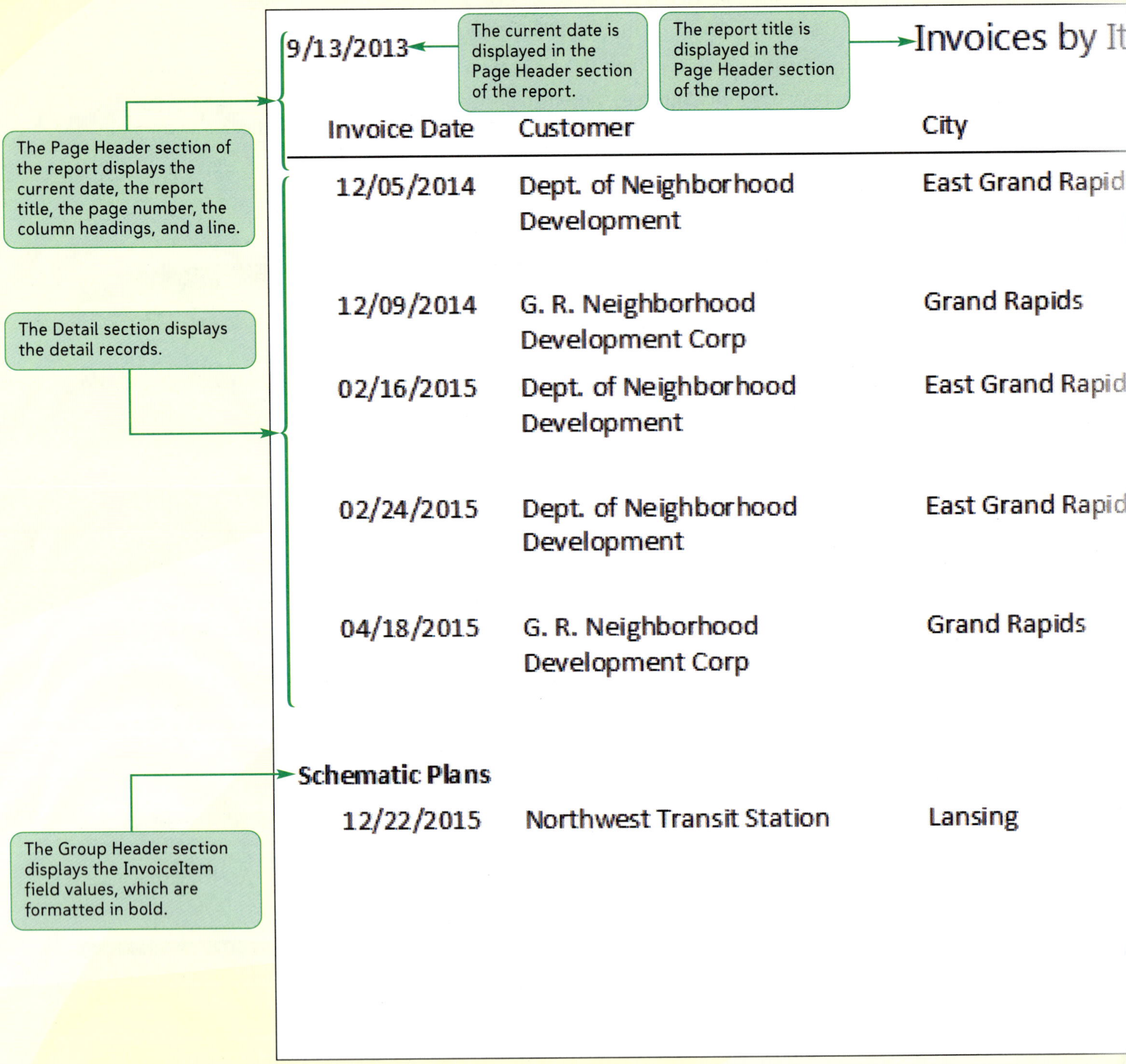

# CUSTOM REPORT DESIGN

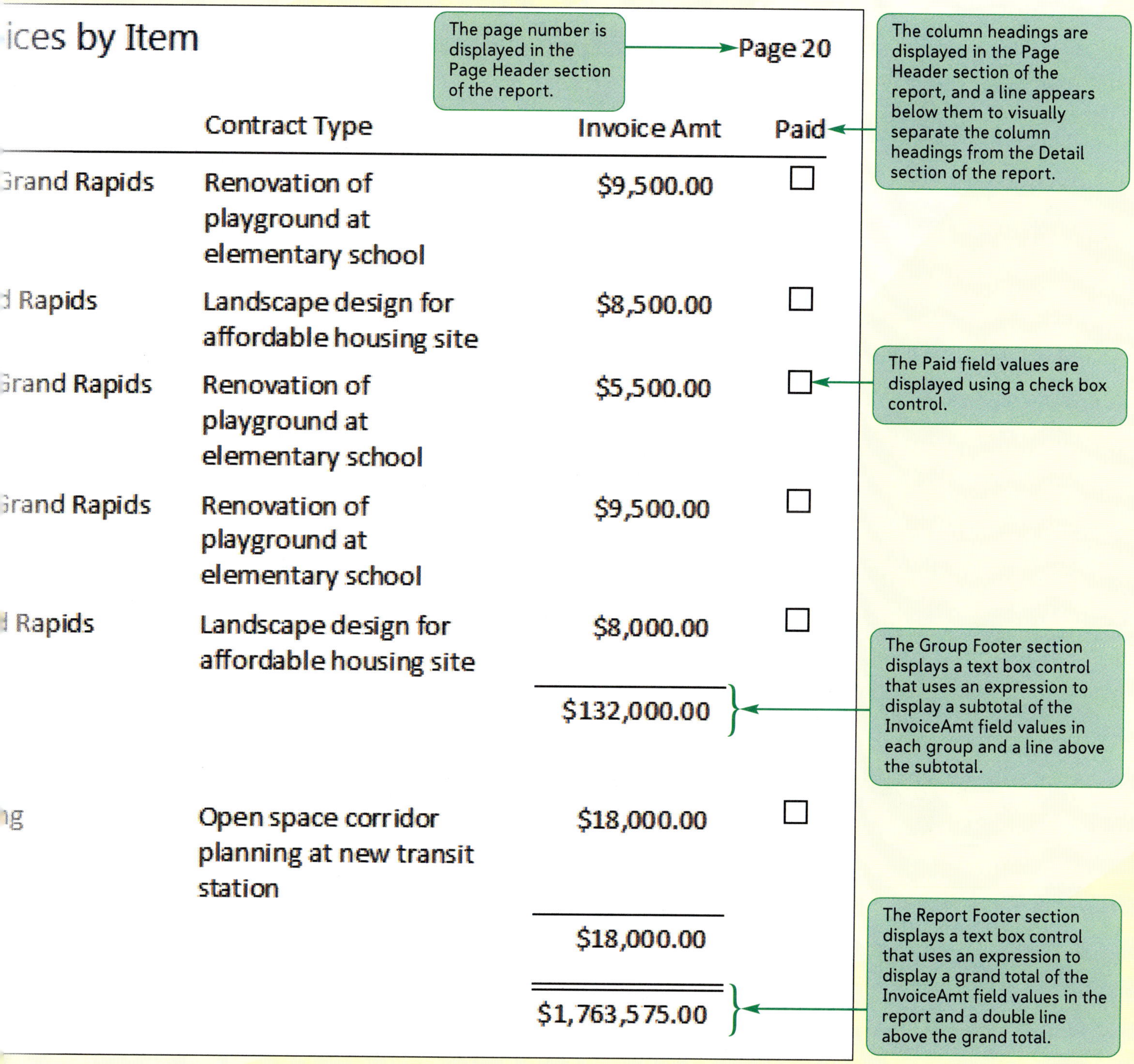

# Designing a Custom Report

Before you create a custom report, you should first plan the report's contents and appearance.

PROSKILLS

### *Decision Making: Guidelines for Designing a Report*

When you plan a report, you should keep in mind the following report design guidelines:

- Determine the purpose of and record source for the report. Recall that the record source is a table or query that provides the fields for a report. If the report displays detailed information (a **detail report**), such as a list of all contracts, then the report will display fields from the record source in the Detail section. If the report displays only summary information (a **summary report**), such as total contracts by city, then no detailed information appears; only grand totals and possibly subtotals appear based on calculations using fields from the record source.
- Determine the sort order for the information in the report.
- Identify any grouping fields in the report.

At the same time you are designing a report, you should keep in mind the following report formatting guidelines:

- Balance the report's attractiveness against its readability and economy. Keep in mind that an attractive, readable, two-page report is more economical than a report of three pages or more. Unlike forms, which usually display one record at a time in the main form, reports display multiple records. Instead of arranging fields vertically as you do in a form, you usually position fields horizontally across the page in a report. Typically, you single space the detail lines in a report. At the same time, make sure to include enough white space between columns so the values do not overlap or run together.
- Group related fields and position them in a meaningful, logical order. For example, position identifying fields, such as names and codes, on the left. Group together all location fields, such as street and city, and position them in their customary order.
- Identify each column of field values with a column heading label that names the field.
- Include the report title, page number, and date on every page of the report.
- Identify the end of a report either by displaying grand totals or an end-of-report message.
- Use few colors, fonts, and graphics to keep the report uncluttered and to keep the focus on the information.
- Use a consistent style for all reports in a database.

By following these report design and formatting guidelines, you create reports that make it easier for users to conduct their daily business and to make better decisions.

After working with Sarah and her staff to determine their requirements for a new report, Lucia prepared a paper design for a custom report to display invoices grouped by invoice item. Refer to the Session 7.2 Visual Overview for Lucia's design of the report.

The custom report will list the records for all invoices and will contain five sections:

- The Page Header section contains the report title ("Invoices by Item") centered between the current date on the left and the page number on the right. A horizontal line separates the column heading labels from the rest of the report page. From your work with the Report tool and the Report Wizard, you know that, by default, Access places the report title in the Report Header section and the date and page number in the Page Footer section. Sarah prefers the date, report title, and page number to appear at the top of each page, so you need to place this information in the custom report's Page Header section.
- The InvoiceItem field value from the tblInvoice table is displayed in a Group Header section.

- The Detail section contains the InvoiceDate, InvoiceAmt, and InvoicePaid field values from the tblInvoice table; the ContractType field value from the tblContract table; the City field value from the tblCustomer table; and the Customer calculated field value from the qryCustomersByName query. The detail records are sorted in ascending value by the InvoiceDate field.
- A subtotal of the InvoiceAmt field values is displayed below a line in the Group Footer section.
- The grand total of the InvoiceAmt field values is displayed below a double line in the Report Footer section.

Before you start creating the custom report, you need to create a query that'll serve as the record source for the report.

## Creating a Query for a Custom Report

**TIP**

Create queries to serve as the record source for forms and reports. As requirements change, you can easily add fields, including calculated fields, to the queries.

The data for a report can come from a single table, from a single query based on one or more tables, or from multiple tables and/or queries. Lucia's report will contain data from the tblInvoice, tblContract, and tblCustomer tables, and from the qryCustomersByName query. You'll use the Simple Query Wizard to create a query to retrieve all the data required for the custom report and to serve as the report's record source.

### To create the query using the Simple Query Wizard:

1. If you took a break after the previous session, make sure that the Panorama database is open and the Navigation Pane is closed.
2. Click the **Create** tab on the Ribbon, in the Queries group click the **Query Wizard** button, make sure **Simple Query Wizard** is selected, and then click the **OK** button. The first Simple Query Wizard dialog box opens.

   You need to select fields from the tblInvoice, tblContract, and tblCustomer tables, and from the qryCustomersByName query, in that order.
3. Select **Table: tblInvoice** in the Tables/Queries box, and then move the **InvoiceItem**, **InvoiceDate**, **InvoiceAmt**, and **InvoicePaid** fields, in that order, to the Selected Fields box.
4. Select **Table: tblContract** in the Tables/Queries box, and then move the **ContractType** field to the Selected Fields box.
5. Select **Table: tblCustomer** in the Tables/Queries box, and then move the **City** field to the Selected Fields box.
6. Select **Query: qryCustomersByName** in the Tables/Queries box, move the **Customer** calculated field to the Selected Fields box, and then click the **Next** button.
7. Make sure the **Detail (shows every field of every record)** option button is selected, and then click the **Next** button to open the final Simple Query Wizard dialog box.

   After entering the query name and creating the query, you'll need to set the sort fields for the query.
8. Change the query name to **qryInvoicesByItem**, click the **Modify the query design** option button, and then click the **Finish** button.

   The InvoiceItem field will be a grouping field, which means it's the primary sort field, and the InvoiceDate field is the secondary sort field.

9. Set the InvoiceItem Sort box to **Ascending**, set the InvoiceDate Sort box to **Ascending**, save your query changes, and then click below the field lists and above the design grid to deselect all values. The completed query contains seven fields from three tables and one query and has two sort fields, the InvoiceItem primary sort field and the InvoiceDate secondary sort field. See Figure 7-12.

**Figure 7-12** **Finished qryInvoicesByItem query in Design view**

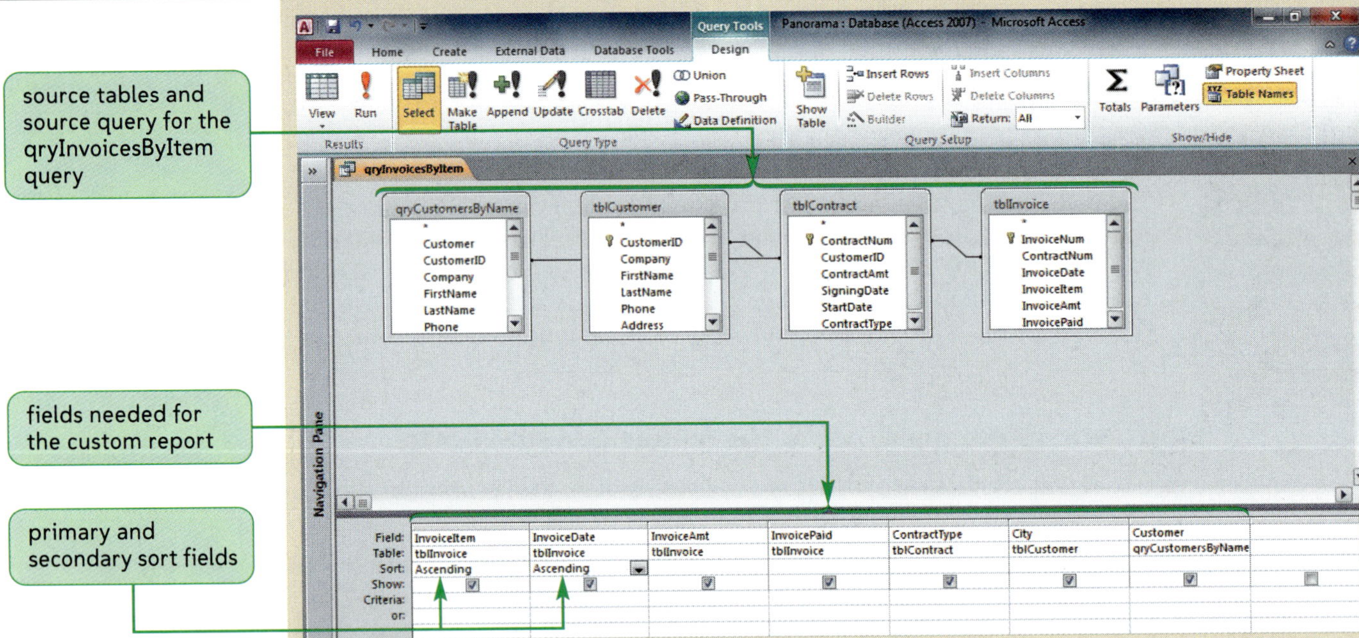


**Trouble?** After you've finished creating the query and close it, if you later open the query in Design view, you'll see the thicker join lines with referential integrity enforced, connecting the tblCustomer and tblContract table field lists and the tblContract and tblInvoice table field lists.

Before closing the query, you'll run it to view the query recordset.

10. Run the query, which displays 172 records, and then close the query.

You'll use the qryInvoicesByItem query as the record source for Lucia's custom report.

## Creating a Custom Report

You could use the Report Wizard to create the report and then modify it to match the report design. However, because you need to customize several components of the report, you will create a custom report in Layout view, and then switch between Layout and Design view to fine-tune the report. As the first step to creating the report, you need to create a blank report in Layout view.

REFERENCE

## *Creating a Blank Report in Layout View*

- Click the Create tab on the Ribbon.
- In the Reports group on the Create tab, click the Blank Report button to open a blank report in Layout view.

INSIGHT

## *Making Report Design Modifications*

You perform operations in Layout and Design views for reports the same as you perform operations in these views for forms. These operations become easier with practice. Remember to use the Undo button, back up your database frequently, save your report changes frequently, work from a copy of the report for complicated design changes, and compact and repair the database on a regular basis. You can also display the report in Print Preview at any time to view your progress on the report.

The record source for the report will be the qryInvoicesByItem query. You'll set the record source after you create a blank report in Layout view.

### To create a blank report and add bound controls in Layout view:

1. Click the **Create** tab on the Ribbon, and then in the Reports group, click the **Blank Report** button. A new report opens in Layout view with the Field List pane open. See Figure 7-13.

**Figure 7-13** **Blank report in Layout view**

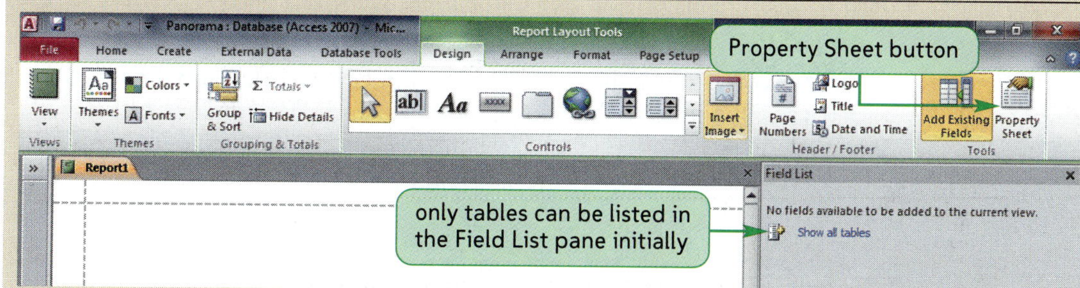


2. In the Tools group on the Design tab, click the **Property Sheet** button to open the property sheet for the report.
3. In the property sheet, click the **All** tab (if necessary), click the **Record Source** arrow, click **qryInvoicesByItem**, and then close the property sheet.
4. In the Tools group on the Design tab, click the **Add Existing Fields** button to open the Field List pane. The Field List pane displays the seven fields in the qryInvoicesByItem query, which is the record source for the report.

   Referring to Lucia's report design, you'll add six of the seven fields to the report in a tabular layout, which is the default control layout when you add fields to a report in Layout view.

5. Double-click **InvoiceDate** in the Field List pane, and then in order, double-click **Customer**, **City**, **ContractType**, **InvoiceAmt**, and **InvoicePaid** in the Field List pane. The six bound controls are displayed in a tabular layout in the report. See Figure 7-14.

**Figure 7-14** After adding fields to the report in Layout view

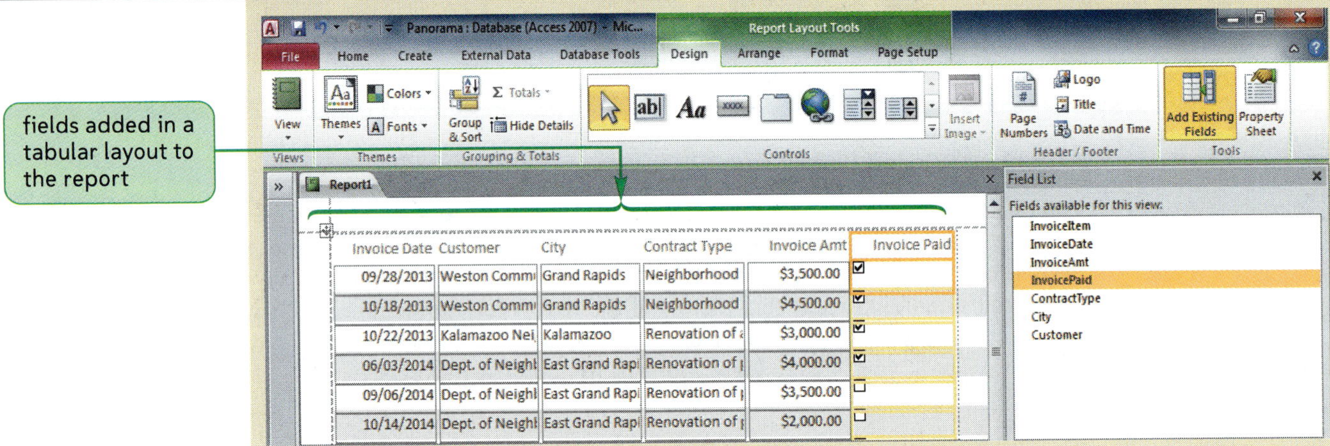


**Trouble?** If you add the wrong field to the report, click the field's column heading, press and hold the Shift key, click one of the field values in the column to select the column, release the Shift key, click the Home tab on the Ribbon, and then click the Delete button in the Records group to delete the field. If you add a field in the wrong order, click the column heading in the tabular layout, press and hold the Shift key, click one of the field values in the column, release the Shift key, and then drag the column to its correct columnar position.

You'll add the seventh field, the InvoiceItem field, as a grouping field, so you are done working with the Field List pane.

6. Close the Field List pane, and then save the report as **rptInvoicesByItem**.

Next, you'll adjust the column widths in Layout view, and then fine-tune the adjustments and the spacing between columns later in Design view. Also, because the Invoice Amt and Invoice Paid columns are adjacent, you can change the rightmost column heading to Paid without losing any meaning and to save space.

### To resize and rename columns in Layout view:

1. Click **Customer** to select the column, and then drag the right edge of the control to the right to increase its width, as shown in Figure 7-15.
2. Repeat Step 1 to resize the **City** and **Contract Type** columns, as shown in Figure 7-15.
3. Double-click **Invoice Paid** in the rightmost column, delete **Invoice** and the following space, and then press the **Enter** key.
4. Drag the right edge of the **Paid** control to the left to decrease the column's width, as shown in Figure 7-15.

Figure 7-15 After resizing and renaming columns in Layout view

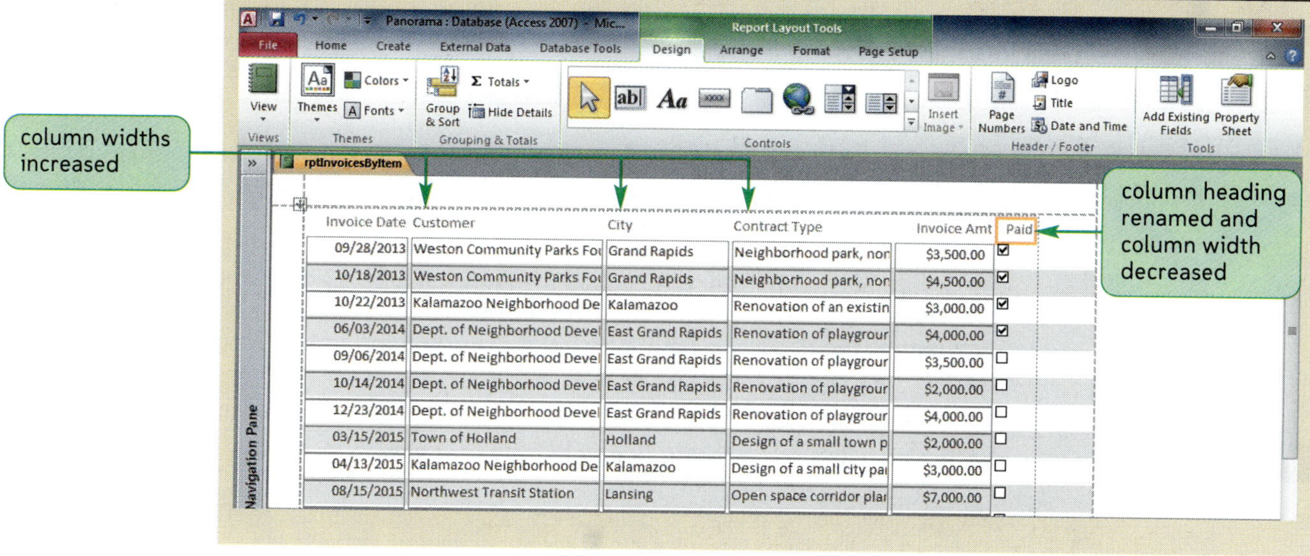


According to Lucia's plan for the report (see the Session 7.2 Visual Overview), the InvoiceItem field is a grouping field that is displayed in a Group Header section. Subtotals for the InvoiceAmt field are displayed in a Group Footer section for each InvoiceItem field value.

## Sorting and Grouping Data in a Report

Access lets you organize records in a report by sorting them using one or more sort fields. Each sort field can also be a grouping field. If you specify a sort field as a grouping field, you can include a Group Header section and a Group Footer section for the group. A Group Header section typically includes the name of the group, and a Group Footer section typically includes a count or subtotal for records in that group. Some reports have a Group Header section but not a Group Footer section, some reports have a Group Footer section but not a Group Header section, and some reports have both sections or have neither section.

You use the Group, Sort, and Total pane to select sort fields and grouping fields for a report. Each report can have up to 10 sort fields, and any of its sort fields can also be grouping fields.

REFERENCE

### *Sorting and Grouping Data in a Report*

- Display the report in Layout or Design view.
- If necessary, click the Group & Sort button in the Grouping & Totals group on the Design tab to display the Group, Sort, and Total pane.
- To select a grouping field, click the Add a group button in the Group, Sort, and Total pane, and then click the grouping field in the list. To set additional properties for the grouping field, click the More button on the group field band.
- To select a sort field that is not a grouping field, click the Add a sort button in the Group, Sort, and Total pane, and then click the sort field in the list. To set additional properties for the sort field, click the More button on the sort field band.

In Lucia's report design, the InvoiceItem field is a grouping field, and the InvoiceDate field is a sort field. The InvoiceItem field value is displayed in a Group Header section, but not its label. The sum of the InvoiceAmt field values is displayed in the Group Footer section for the InvoiceItem grouping field. Next, you'll select the grouping field and the sort field and set their properties.

## To select and set the properties for the grouping field and the sort field:

1. In the Grouping & Totals group, click the **Group & Sort** button to open the Group, Sort, and Total pane.
2. In the Group, Sort, and Total pane, click the **Add a group** button, and then click **InvoiceItem** in the list. Access adds a Group Header section to the report with InvoiceItem as the grouping field, and adds a group band in the Group, Sort, and Total pane. See Figure 7-16.

**Figure 7-16** **After selecting InvoiceItem as a grouping field in Layout view**

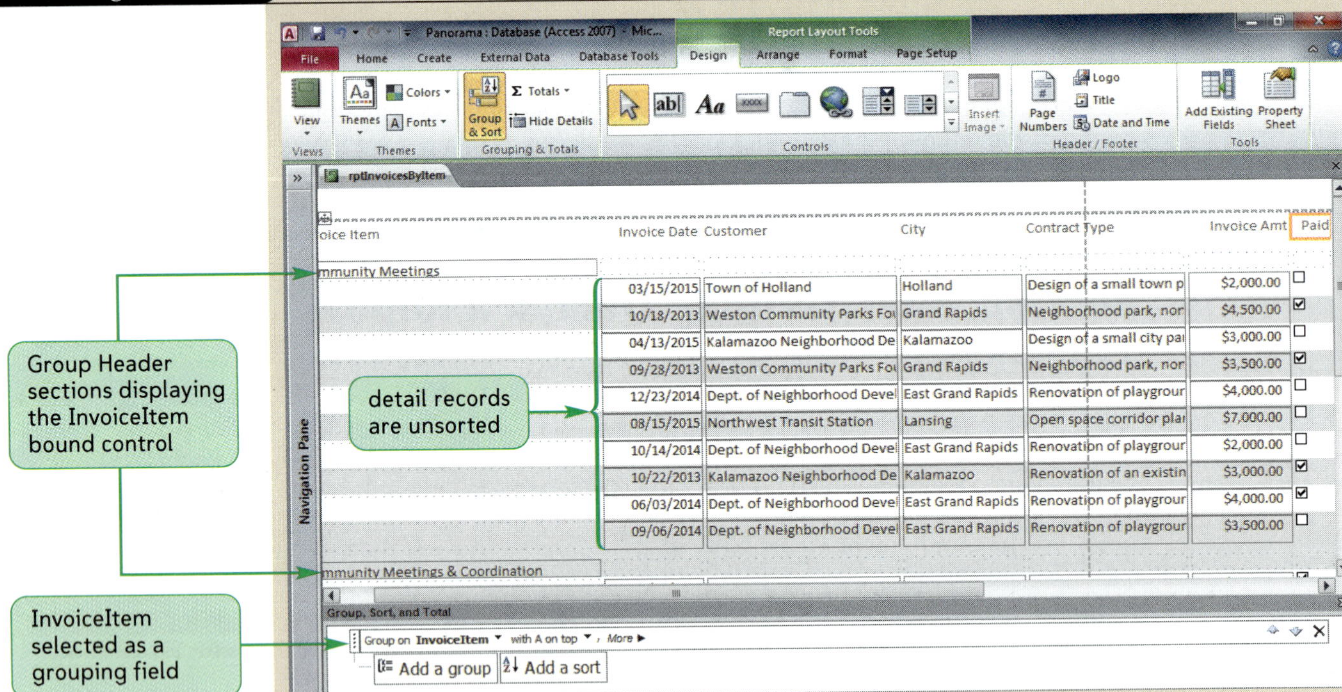


InvoiceItem is now a bound control in the report in a Group Header section that displays a field value text box and its attached label. The group band in the Group, Sort, and Total pane contains the name of the grouping field (InvoiceItem), the sort order ("with A on top" to indicate ascending), and the More option, which you click to display more options for the grouping field. You can click the "with A on top" arrow to change to descending sort order ("with Z on top").

Notice that the addition of the grouping field has moved the detail records to the right; you'll move them back to the left later in this tutorial. Also, notice that the detail records are unsorted, and Lucia's design specifies an ascending sort on the InvoiceDate field. Next, you'll select this field as a secondary sort field; the InvoiceItem grouping field is the primary sort field.

3. In the Group, Sort, and Total pane, click the **Add a sort** button, and then click **InvoiceDate** in the list. Access displays the detail records in ascending InvoiceDate order, and adds a sort band for the InvoiceDate field in the Group, Sort, and Total pane.

   Next, you'll display all the options for the InvoiceItem grouping field, and set grouping options as shown in Lucia's report design.

4. Click ⁝ to the left of the group band to select it, and then click **More** to expand the band and display all group options. See Figure 7-17.

**Figure 7-17** **After expanding the group band**

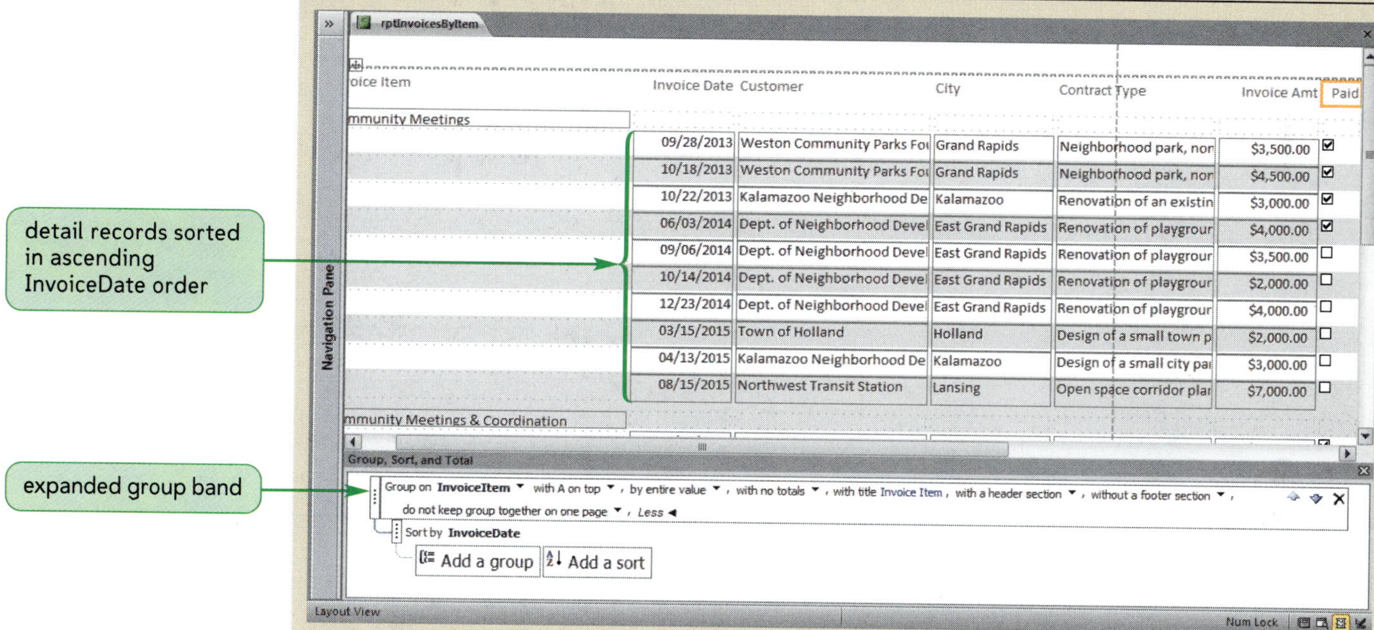


Reviewing Lucia's report design (see the Session 7.2 Visual Overview), you need to delete the Invoice Item label, add a Group Footer section with a subtotal for the InvoiceAmt field values, add a grand total for the InvoiceAmt field values to the Report Footer section, and set the Keep Together property. The **Keep Together property** prints a group header on a page only if there is enough room on the page to print the first detail record for the group; otherwise, the group header prints at the top of the next page.

5. In the "with title Invoice Item" option, click the **Invoice Item** link to open the Zoom dialog box, press the **Delete** key to delete the expression, and then click the **OK** button. The Invoice Item label is deleted from the report, and the option in the group band changes to "with title click to add."

6. In the group band, click the **do not keep group together on one page** arrow, and then click **keep header and first record together on one page**.

7. In the group band, click **More** to expand the band (if necessary), click the **without a footer section** arrow, and then click **with a footer section**. Access adds a Group Footer section for the InvoiceItem grouping field, but the report doesn't display this new section until you add controls to it.

8. In the group band, click **More** to expand the band (if necessary), click the **with no totals** arrow to open the Totals menu, click the **Total On** arrow, click **InvoiceAmt**, make sure **Sum** is selected in the Type box, and then click the **Show Grand Total** check box. The group band collapses.
9. In the group band, click **More** to expand the band (if necessary), click the **with InvoiceAmt totaled** arrow, click the **Total On** arrow, click **InvoiceAmt**, and then click the **Show subtotal in group footer** check box. The group band collapses.
10. In the group band, click **More** to expand the band (if necessary). The group band shows the InvoiceAmt subtotals and a grand total added to the report. See Figure 7-18.

**Figure 7-18** After setting properties in the group band

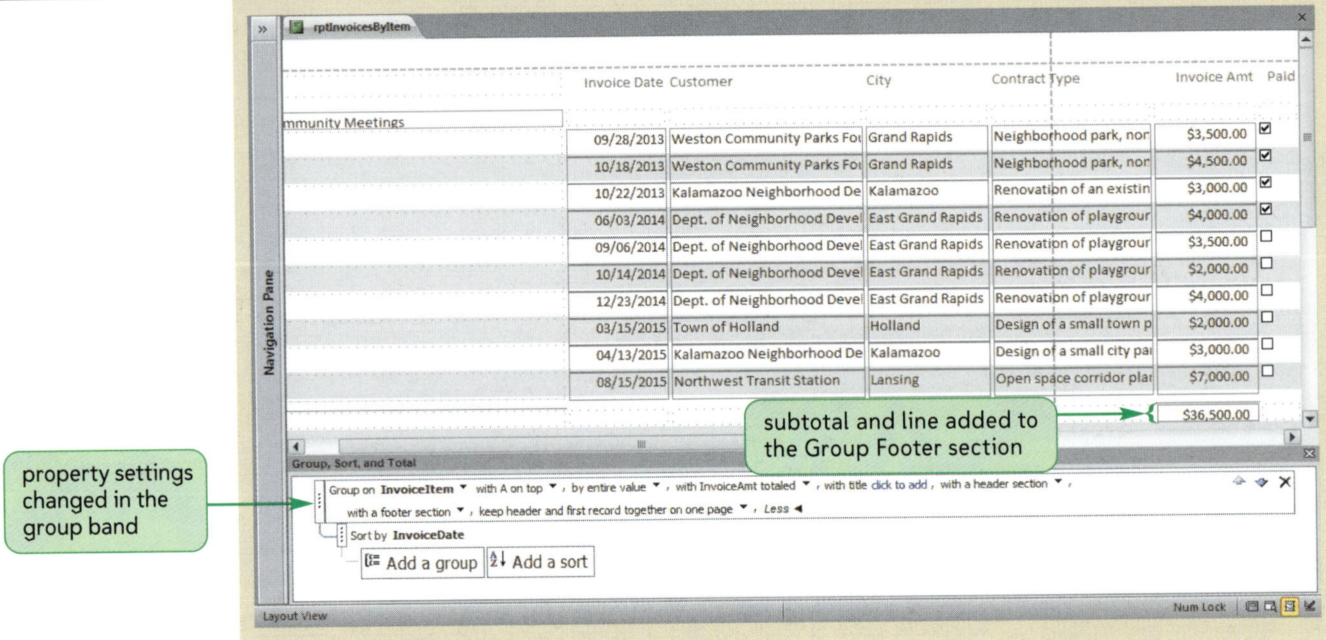


Similar to the sound form design strategy you followed in the previous tutorial, you should frequently save your report changes and review the report in Print Preview.

11. Save your report changes, switch to Print Preview, and review every page until you reach the end of the report—noticing in particular the details of the report format and the effects of the Keep Together property. Also, notice that because the grouping field forces the detail values to the right, the current report design prints the detail values across two pages.

Before you can move the detail values to the left onto one page, you need to remove all controls from the control layout.

**To remove controls from a control layout in Layout view:**

1. Switch to Layout view.
2. Click the **layout selector**, which is located at the top-left corner of the column heading line, to select the entire control layout. An orange outline, which identifies the controls that you've selected, appears around the labels and text boxes in the report.
3. Right-click one of the selected controls to open the shortcut menu, point to **Layout**, and then click **Remove Layout**.

   You'll next move all the controls to the left except for the InvoiceItem text box. You have to be careful when you move the remaining controls to the left. If you try to select all the column headings and the text boxes, you're likely to miss the subtotal and grand total controls. The safest technique is to select all controls in the report, and then remove the InvoiceItem text box from the selection. This latter step, removing individual controls from a selection, must be done in Design view because it doesn't work in Layout view.

4. Switch to Design view, click the **Format** tab, and then in the Selection group, click the **Select All** button. All controls in the report are now selected.
5. Hold down the **Shift** key, click the **InvoiceItem** text box in the InvoiceItem Header section to remove this control from the selection, and then release the **Shift** key.
6. Hold down the ← key to move the selected controls rapidly to the left edge of the report, and then release the ← key. See Figure 7-19.

**Figure 7-19** After moving all controls to the left in the report

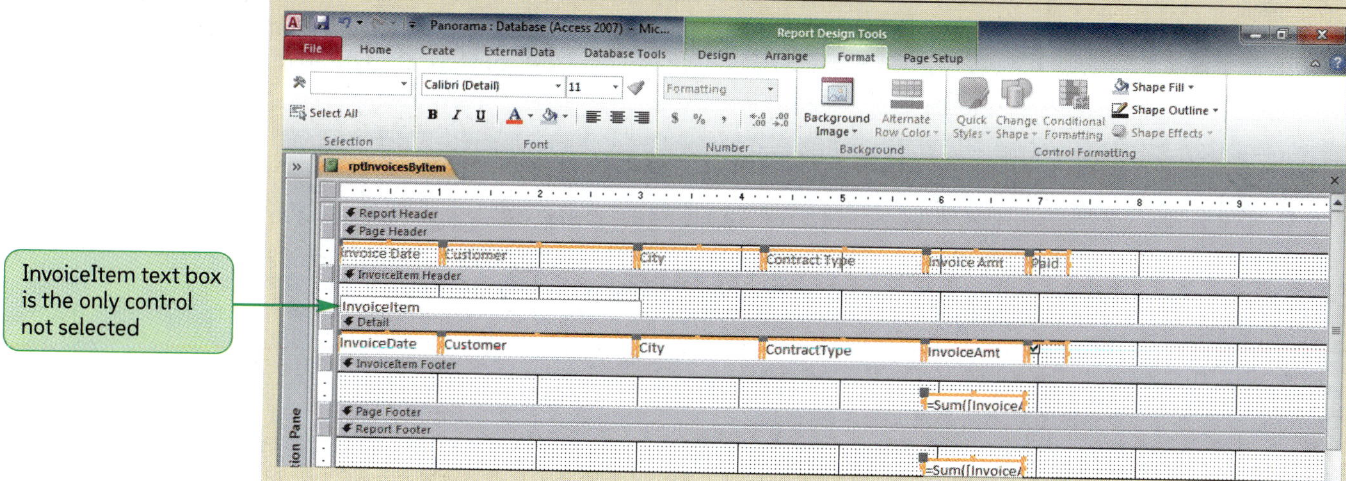


The grand total of the InvoiceAmt field values is displayed at the end of the report, and subtotals are displayed for each unique InvoiceItem field value in the Group Footer section. It's possible for subtotals to appear in an orphaned footer section. An **orphaned footer section** appears by itself at the top of a page, and the detail lines for the section appear on the previous page. When you set the Keep Together property for the grouping field, you set it to keep the group and the first detail record together on one page to prevent an **orphaned header section**, which is a section that appears by itself at the bottom of a page. To prevent both types of orphaned sections, you'll set the Keep Together property to keep the whole group together on one page.

In addition, you need to fine-tune the sizes of the text boxes in the Detail section, adjust the spacing between columns, and make other adjustments to the current content of the report design before adding a report title, the date, and page number to the Page Header section. You'll make most of these report design changes in Design view.

## Working with Controls in Design View

Compared to Layout view, Design view gives you greater control over the placement and sizing of controls, and lets you add and manipulate many more controls, but at the expense of not being able to see live data in the controls to guide you as you make changes.

The rptInvoicesByItem report has five sections: the Page Header section contains the six column heading labels, the InvoiceItem Header section (a Group Header section) contains the InvoiceItem text box, the Detail section contains the six bound controls, the InvoiceItem Footer section (a Group Footer section) contains a line and the subtotal text box, and the Report Footer section contains a line and the grand total text box.

You'll move and resize controls in the report in Design view. The Group, Sort, and Total pane is still open, so first you'll change the Keep Together property setting.

### To move and resize controls in the report:

1. In the Group, Sort, and Total pane, click ⁝ to the left of the group band to select it, click **More** to expand the band and display all group options, click the **keep header and first record together on one page** arrow, and then click **keep whole group together on one page**, and then close the Group, Sort, and Total pane.

   You'll start improving the report by setting the InvoiceItem text box font to bold.

2. Select the **InvoiceItem** text box in the InvoiceItem Header section, and then in the Font group on the Format tab, click the **Bold** button **B**. The InvoiceItem text box is displayed as bold text.

   The report's width is approximately 16 inches, which is much wider than the width of the contents of the report, so you'll reduce its width.

3. Scroll to the right until you see the right edge of the report (the point where the dotted grid ends), move the pointer to the right edge of the report, and when the pointer changes to a ↔ shape, drag to the left to the 7.5-inch mark on the horizontal ruler, and then scroll to the left to display the entire report from the left (if necessary). See Figure 7-20.

**Figure 7-20** After reducing the width of the report

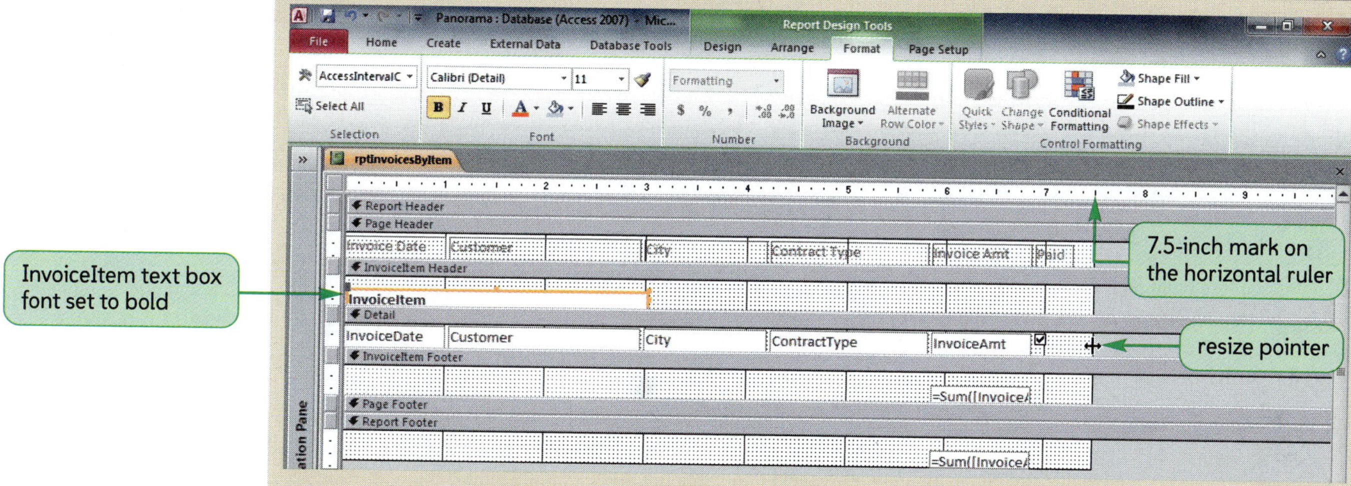


Now you'll check the report's page orientation and margins.

> **TIP**
> You usually determine page setup properties when you design a report or, as for this report, after you've placed the controls in the Detail section.

4. Click the **Page Setup** tab on the Ribbon.
5. In the Page Layout group, make sure the **Portrait** button is selected, click the **Page Setup** button, set the Top and Bottom margin properties to **0.7** and the Left and Right margin properties to **0.5**, and then click the **OK** button.

   The text boxes in the Detail section are crowded together with little space between them. Your reports shouldn't have too much space between columns, but reports are easier to read when the columns are separated more than they are in the rptInvoicesByItem report. Sometimes the amount of spacing is dictated by the users of the report, but mostly it's the report designer's choice to make. First, you'll resize the Paid label and the InvoicePaid check box, and move them to the right.

> **TIP**
> You can resize labels and controls added with the Label tool to fit, but you can't resize text boxes to fit.

6. Right-click the **Paid** label in the Page Header section, point to **Size**, click **To Fit**, hold down the **Shift** key, click the **InvoicePaid** check box in the Detail section, release the **Shift** key, and then move both controls to the right until the label's right edge is one column of grid dots to the left of the 7.5-inch mark on the horizontal ruler.

   You'll now resize the remaining labels to fit in the Page Header section.

7. Select the **Invoice Date** label in the Page Header section, the **Customer** label, the **City** label, the **Contract Type** label, and the **Invoice Amt** label, right-click one of the selected labels, point to **Size** on the shortcut menu, and then click **To Fit**.

   Because the InvoiceAmt text box and its subtotal and grand total text boxes are Number fields, you'll align the Invoice Amt label on its right edge with the text boxes.

8. Select the **Invoice Amt** label and the **InvoiceAmt** text box, right-click one of the selected controls, point to **Align**, and then click **Right**. See Figure 7-21.

**Figure 7-21** **After resizing and moving controls in Design view**

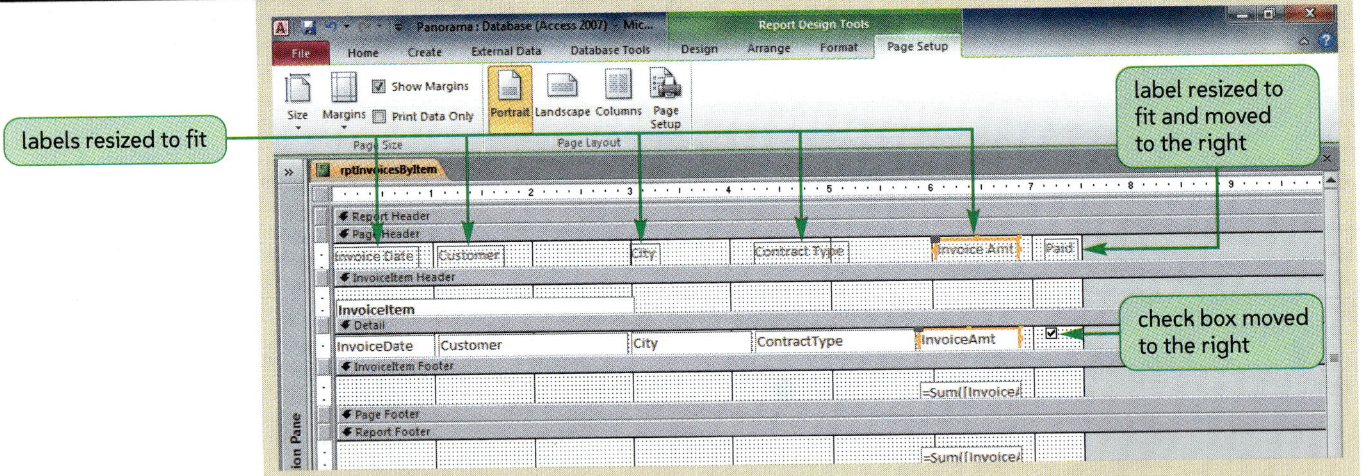


You resized the Customer and ContractType text boxes in Layout view, but you did not resize them wide enough to display the entire field value in all cases. For the Customer and ContractType text boxes, you'll set their Can Grow property to Yes. The **Can Grow property**, when set to Yes, expands a text box vertically to fit the field value when the report is printed, previewed, or viewed in Layout and Report views.

**TIP**

You can select two or more controls, and then set common properties for the selected controls, instead of setting them one control at a time.

9. Click the **Design** tab on the Ribbon, select the **Customer** and **ContractType** text boxes in the Detail section, open the property sheet, click the **Format** tab in the property sheet, scroll down the property sheet, make sure the Can Grow property is set to **Yes**, close the property sheet, and then save your report changes.

   **Trouble?** By default, the Can Grow property should be set to No. If the Can Grow property in your property sheet is already set to Yes, set the property to No, and then set it back to Yes.

10. Switch to Print Preview, and review every page of the report, ending on the last page of the report. See Figure 7-22.

**Figure 7-22** **Reviewing the report changes in Print Preview**

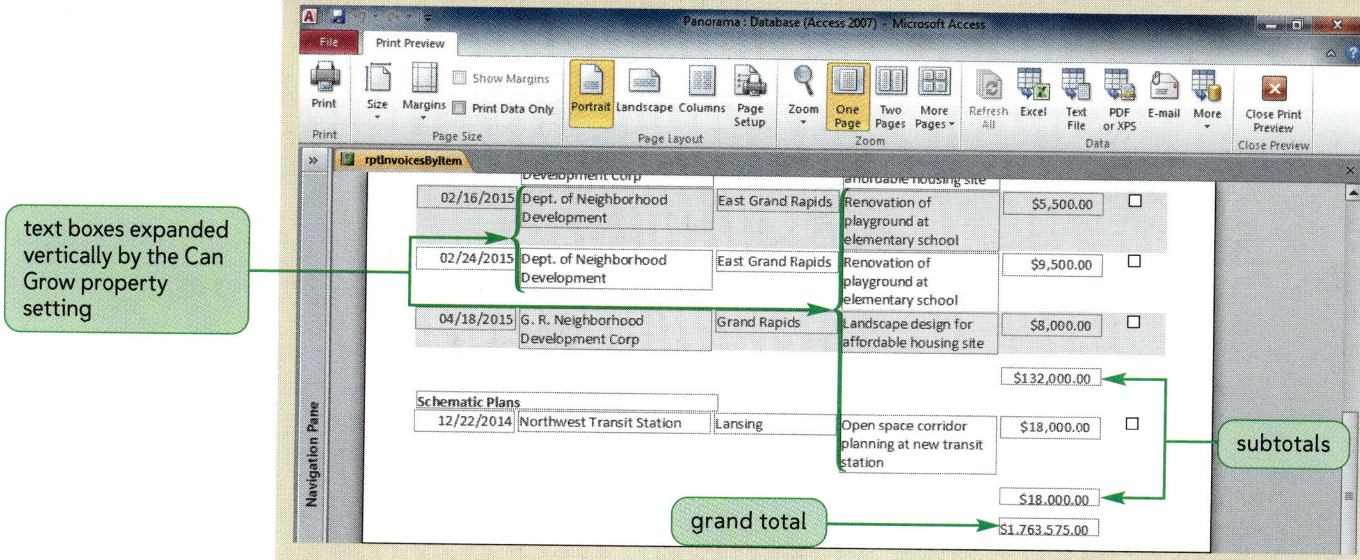


The groups stay together on one page, except for the groups that have too many detail lines to fit on one page. The Can Grow property correctly expands the height of the Customer and ContractType text boxes.

Also, the lines that were displayed above the subtotals and grand total are no longer displayed, and the commas in the values are not fully visible. You'll add those lines back in the report and resize the text boxes. First, Lucia thinks the borders around the text boxes and the alternate row color are too distracting, so you'll remove them from the report.

## To remove the borders and alternate row color:

1. Switch to Design view.
2. Click the **Format** tab, and then in the Selection group, click the **Select All** button.
3. Right-click one of the selected controls, and then click **Properties** on the shortcut menu to open the property sheet.
4. Click the **Format** tab (if necessary) in the property sheet, click the right side of the **Border Style** box, and then click **Transparent**. The transparent setting will remove the boxes from the report by making them transparent.
5. Click the **InvoiceItem Header** section bar, click the right side of the **Alternate Back Color** box in the property sheet, and then click **No Color** at the bottom of the gallery. This setting removes the alternate row color from the InvoiceItem Header section.

   You can set the Alternate Back Color property setting to the same No Color value for the Detail and InvoiceItem Footer sections by repeating Step 5 for each section, or by selecting each section and then clicking the Alternate Row Color button on the Ribbon because the two options set the same property.
6. Click the **Detail** section bar, and then in the Background group on the Ribbon, click the **Alternate Row Color** button. The Alternate Back Color property setting in the property sheet is now set to No Color.
7. Repeat Step 6 for the **InvoiceItem Footer** section.

8. Close the property sheet, save your report changes, switch to Print Preview, and review every page of the report, ending on the last page of the report. See Figure 7-23.

**Figure 7-23** After removing borders and the alternate row color

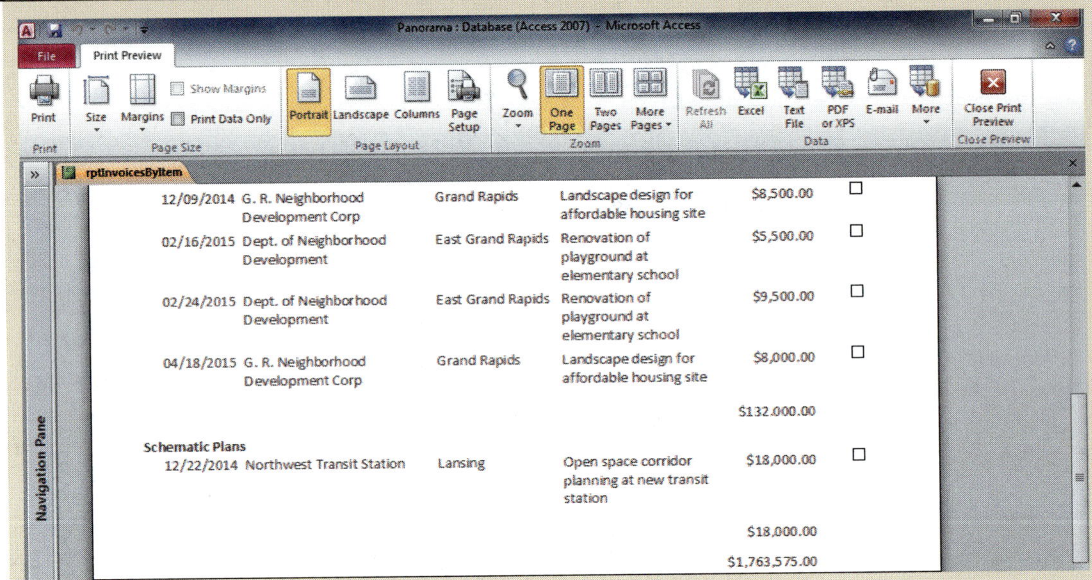


Next, you'll add lines to the report.

## Adding Lines to a Report

You've used the Line tool to add lines to a form. You can also use the Line tool to add lines to a report. You'll switch to Design view and use the Line tool to add a single line above the subtotal control and a double line above the grand total control. First, you'll resize the subtotal and grand total text boxes.

### To add lines to the report:

1. Switch to Design view.
2. In the InvoiceItem Footer section, click the text box control to select it, and then resize the control from the top so its height increases by one row of grid dots.
3. Repeat Step 2 to resize the text box control in the Report Footer section.
4. In the Controls group on the Design tab, click the **More** button to open the Controls gallery.
5. Click the **Line** tool, position the pointer's plus symbol (+) at the upper-left corner of the subtotal text box in the InvoiceItem Footer section, hold down the **Shift** key, drag a horizontal line from left to right, so the end of the line aligns with the upper-right corner of the subtotal text box, release the mouse button, and then release the **Shift** key.

6. Click the **grand total** text box in the Report Footer section, and then press the ↓ key four times to move the control down slightly in the section, and then deselect all controls.
7. In the Controls group on the Design tab, click the **More** button, click the **Line** tool, position the pointer's plus symbol (+) at the grid dot just above the upper-left corner of the grand total text box in the Report Footer section, hold down the **Shift** key, drag a horizontal line from left to right, so the end of the line aligns with the right edge of the grand total text box, release the mouse button, and then release the **Shift** key.

   Next, you'll copy and paste the line in the Report Footer section, and then align the copied line into position.
8. Right-click the selected line in the Report Footer section, and then click **Copy** on the shortcut menu.
9. Right-click the **Report Footer** section bar, and then click **Paste** on the shortcut menu. A copy of the line is pasted in the upper-left corner of the Report Footer section.
10. Press the ↓ key four times to move the copied line down in the section, hold down the **Shift** key, click the original line in the Report Footer section to select both lines, release the **Shift** key, right-click the copied line to open the shortcut menu, point to **Align**, and then click **Right**. A double line is now positioned above the grand total text box.
11. Save your report changes, switch to Print Preview, and then navigate to the last page of the report. See Figure 7-24.

**Figure 7-24** After adding lines to the report

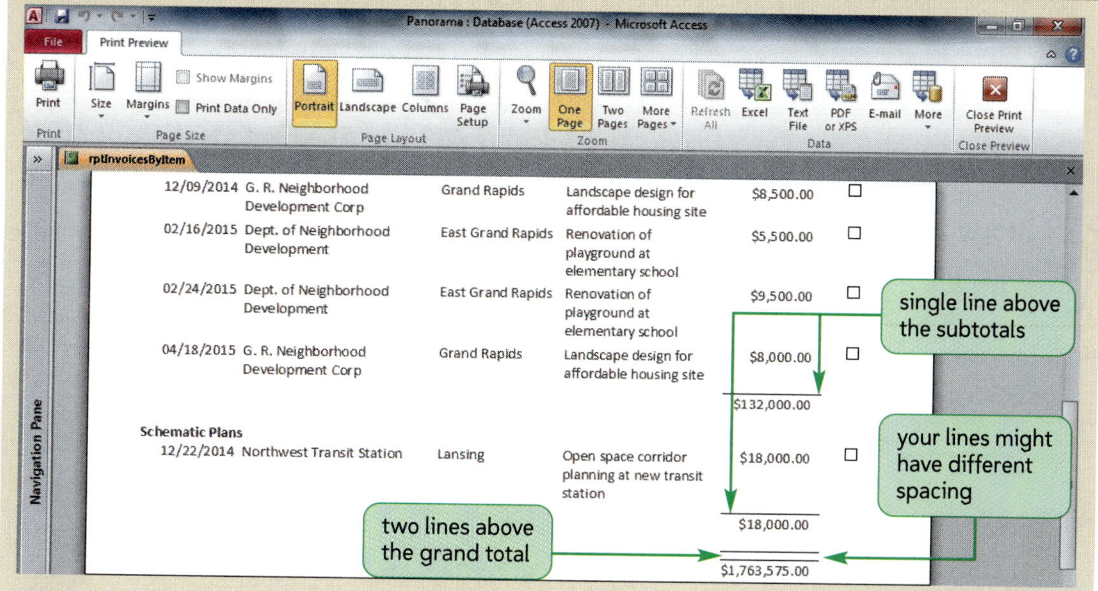

For the rptInvoicesByItem report, the InvoiceDate field is a sort field. Two or more consecutive detail report lines can have the same InvoiceDate field value. In these cases, Lucia wants the InvoiceDate field value printed for the first detail line but not for subsequent detail lines because she believes it makes the printed information easier to read.

## Hiding Duplicate Values in a Report

You use the **Hide Duplicates property** to hide a control in a report when the control's value is the same as that of the preceding record in the group.

REFERENCE

*Hiding Duplicate Values in a Report*

- Display the report in Layout or Design view.
- Open the property sheet for the field whose duplicate values you want to hide, set the Hide Duplicates property to Yes, and then close the property sheet.

Your next design change to the report is to hide duplicate InvoiceDate field values in the Detail section. This change will make the report easier to read.

**To hide the duplicate InvoiceDate field values:**

1. Switch to Design view, and then click below the Report Footer grid to deselect all controls.
2. Open the property sheet for the **InvoiceDate** text box in the Detail section.
3. Click the **Format** tab (if necessary), scroll down the property sheet (if necessary), click the right side of the **Hide Duplicates** box, and then click **Yes**.
4. Close the property sheet, save your report changes, switch to Print Preview, navigate to page 5 (the actual page you view might vary depending on your printer) to the Construction Observation group to see the two invoice records for 03/30/2015. The InvoiceDate field value is hidden for the second of the two consecutive records with a 03/30/2015 date. See Figure 7-25.

**TIP**

For properties offering a list of choices, you can double-click the property name repeatedly to cycle through the options in the list.

**Figure 7-25** **Report in Print Preview with hidden duplicate values**

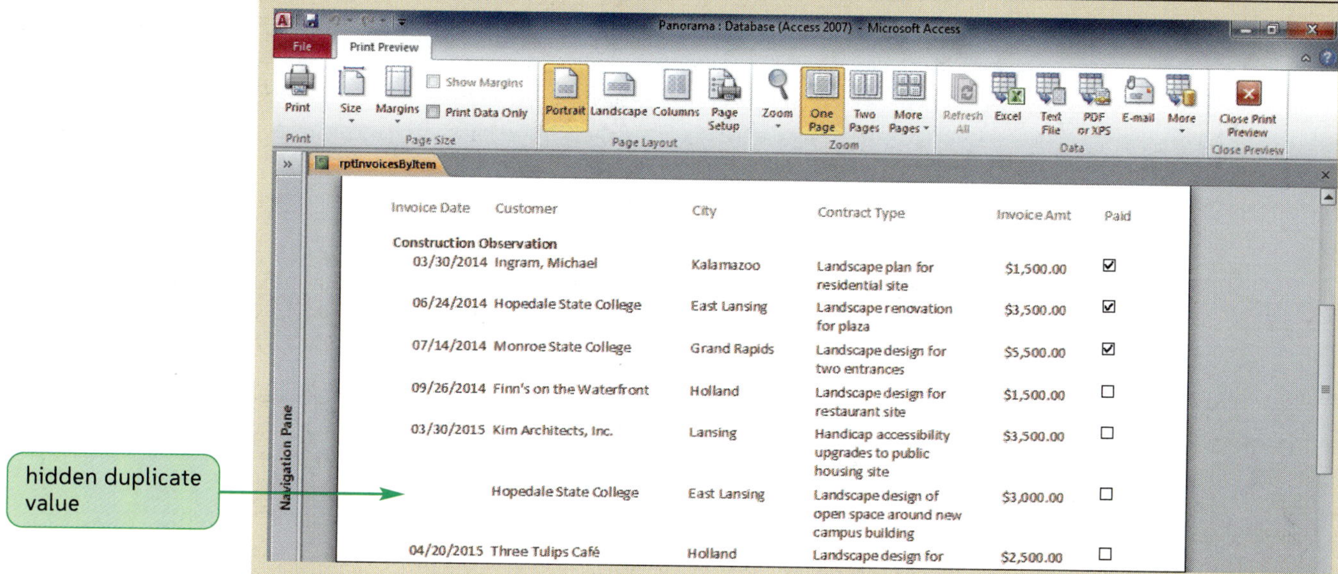


**5.** If you are not continuing on to the next session, close the Panorama database.

You have completed the Detail section, the Group Header section, and the Group Footer section of the custom report. In the next session, you will complete the custom report according to Lucia's design by adding controls to the Page Header section.

REVIEW

## *Session 7.2 Quick Check*

1. What is a detail report? a summary report?
2. The ______________ property prints a group header on a page only if there is enough room on the page to print the first detail record for the group; otherwise, the group header prints at the top of the next page.
3. A(n) ______________ section appears by itself at the top of a page, and the detail lines for the section appear on the previous page.
4. The ______________ property, when set to Yes, expands a text box vertically to fit the field value when a report is printed, previewed, or viewed in Layout and Report views.
5. Why might you want to hide duplicate values in a report?

# SESSION 7.3 VISUAL OVERVIEW

The Report Header section does not appear in the report; its height is zero.

The Page Header section contains today's date, the report title, the page number, column headings, and a line below the column headings.

The InvoiceItem Header section is a Group Header section that appears every time the value of the InvoiceItem field changes.

The Detail section contains the InvoiceDate, Customer, City, ContractType, InvoiceAmt, and InvoicePaid field values.

The InvoiceItem Footer section is a Group Footer section that appears every time the value of the InvoiceItem field changes.

The Report Footer section prints the grand total InvoiceAmt field value at the end of the report with a double line above the grand total.

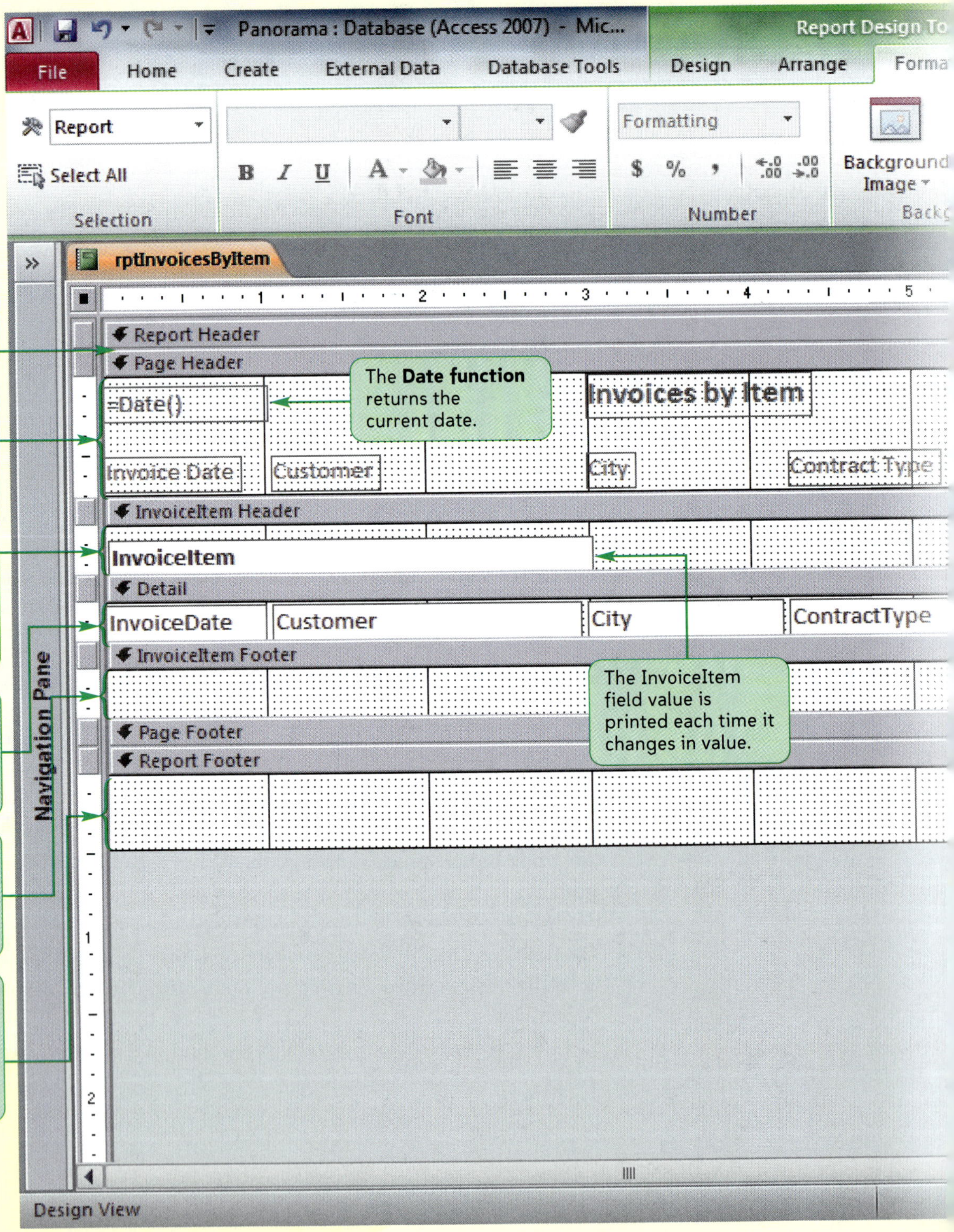


The **Date function** returns the current date.

The InvoiceItem field value is printed each time it changes in value.

# CUSTOM REPORT DESIGN

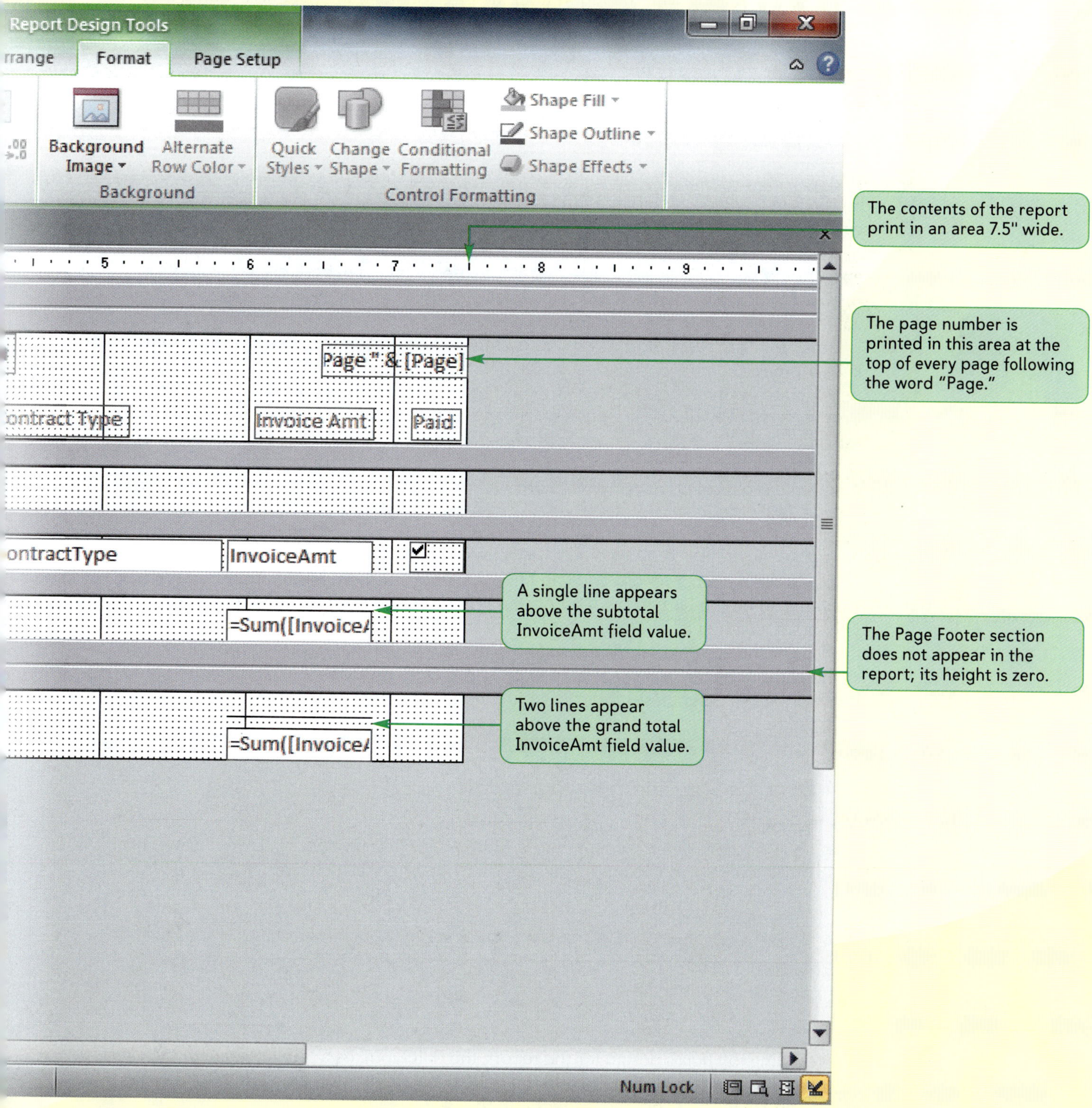

# Adding the Date to a Report

According to Lucia's design, the rptInvoicesByItem report includes the date in the Page Header section, along with the report title, the page number, the column heading labels, and a line below the labels.

PROSKILLS

### *Written Communication: Placing the Report Title, Date, and Page Number in the Page Header Section*

When you use the Report tool or the Report Wizard to create a report, the report title is displayed in the Report Header section and the page number is displayed in the Page Footer section. However, the date (and time) is displayed in the Report Header section when you use the Report tool and in the Page Footer section when you use the Report Wizard. Because report formatting guidelines require that all the reports in a database display controls in consistent positions, you have to move the date control for reports created by the Report tool or by the Report Wizard so the date is displayed in the same section for all reports.

Although company standards vary, a common report standard places the report title, date, and page number on the same line in the Page Header section. Using one line saves vertical space in the report compared to placing some controls in the Page Header section and others in the Page Footer section. Placing the report title in the Page Header section, instead of in the Report Header section, allows users to identify the report name on any page without having to turn to the first page. When you develop reports with a consistent format, the report users become more productive and more confident working with the information in the reports.

To add the date to a report, you can click the Date and Time button in the Header/Footer group on the Design tab, and Access will insert the Date function in a text box without an attached label at the right edge of the Report Header section. The Date function returns the current date. The format of the Date function is *=Date()*. The equal sign (=) indicates that what follows it is an expression; *Date* is the name of the function; and the empty set of parentheses indicates a function rather than simple text.

REFERENCE

### *Adding the Date and Time to a Report*

- Display the report in Layout or Design view.
- In the Header/Footer group on the Design tab in Design view or in Layout view, click the Date and Time button to open the Date and Time dialog box.
- To display the date, click the Include Date check box, and then click one of the three date option buttons.
- To display the time, click the Include Time check box, and then click one of the three time option buttons.
- Click the OK button.

According to Lucia's design for the report, the date appears at the left edge of the Page Header section, so you'll need to add the date to the report, and then cut the date from the Report Header section and paste it into the Page Header section.

### To add the date to the Page Header section:

1. If you took a break after the previous session, make sure that the Panorama database is open, that the rptInvoicesByItem report is open in Print Preview, and that the Navigation Pane is closed.

   You can add the current date in Layout or Design view. Because you can't cut and paste controls between sections in Layout view, you'll add the date in Design view. First, you'll move the column heading labels down in the Page Header section to make room for the controls you'll be adding above them.

2. Switch to Design view, increase the height of the Page Header section until the bottom edge of the section is at the 1-inch mark on the vertical ruler, select all six labels in the Page Header section, and then move the labels down until the tops of the labels are at the 0.5-inch mark on the vertical ruler.

   Lucia's report design has a horizontal line below the labels that you'll add next.

3. In the Controls group on the Design tab, click the **More** button, click the **Line** tool, position the pointer's plus symbol (+) at the lower-left corner of the Invoice Date label in the Page Header section, hold down the **Shift** key, drag a horizontal line from left to right so the end of the line aligns with the right edge of the Paid label, release the mouse button, and then release the **Shift** key.
4. Reduce the height of the Page Header section by dragging the bottom of the section up until it touches the bottom of the line you just added.
5. In the Header/Footer group on the Design tab, click the **Date and Time** button to open the Date and Time dialog box, make sure the **Include Date** check box is checked and the **Include Time** check box is unchecked, and then click the third date option button. See Figure 7-26.

**Figure 7-26** **Completed Date and Time dialog box**

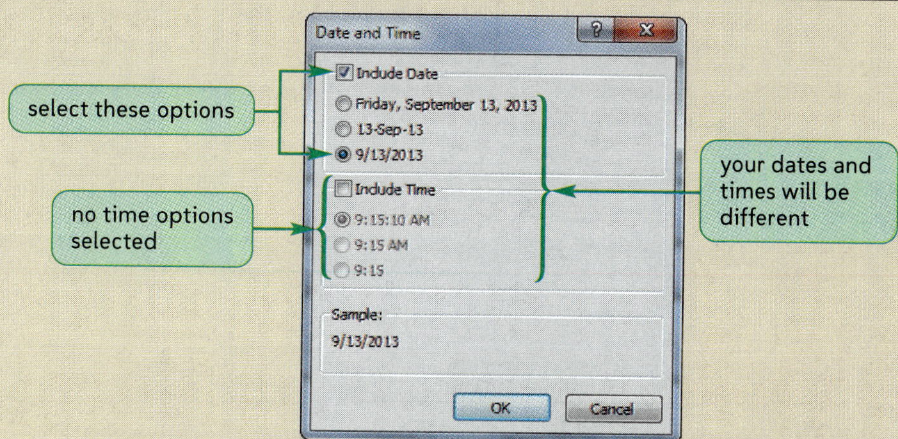


6. Click the **OK** button. The Date function is added to the Report Header section.
7. Click the **Date function** text box, and then click the **layout selector** in the upper-left corner of the Report Header section. The Date function text box is part of a control layout with three additional boxes, which are empty cells. See Figure 7-27.

**Figure 7-27** **Date function added to the Report Header section**

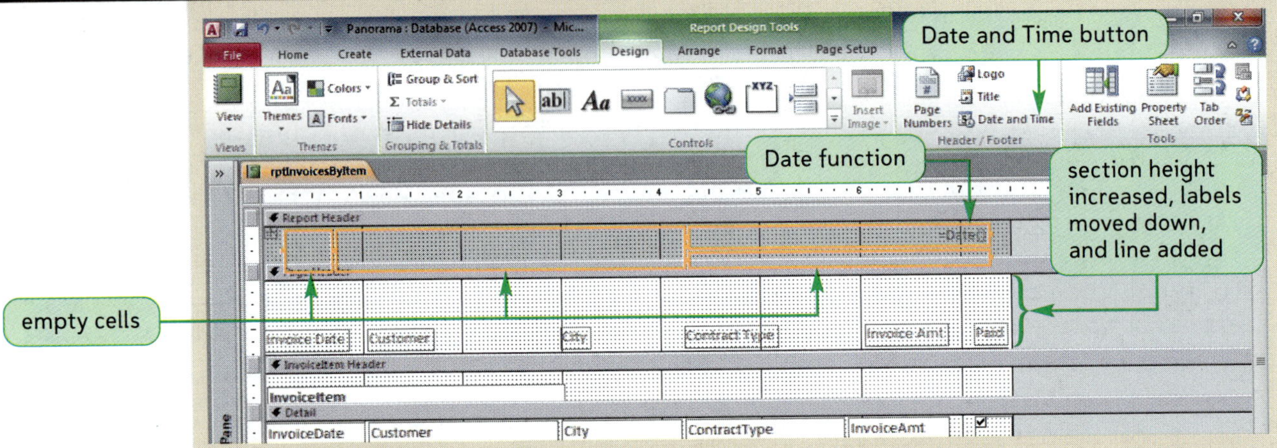


You need to remove these controls from the control layout before you work further with the Date function text box.

8. Right-click one of the selected controls, point to **Layout** on the shortcut menu, and then click **Remove Layout**. The three empty cells are deleted, and the Date function text box remains selected.

   The default size for the Date function text box must accommodate long dates and long times, so the text box is much wider than needed for the date that'll appear in the custom report. You'll decrease its width before moving it to the Page Header section.

9. Decrease the width of the Date function text box from the left to one inch total, right-click an edge of the **Date function** text box to open the shortcut menu, click **Cut** to delete the control, right-click the **Page Header** section bar to select that section and open the shortcut menu, and then click **Paste**. The Date function text box is pasted in the upper-left corner of the Page Header section.

10. Save your report changes, and then switch to Print Preview to view the date in the Page Header section. See Figure 7-28.

**Figure 7-28** **Viewing the date in Print Preview**

**TIP**

Notice that the current date is displayed instead of the Date function that appears in the text box in Design view.

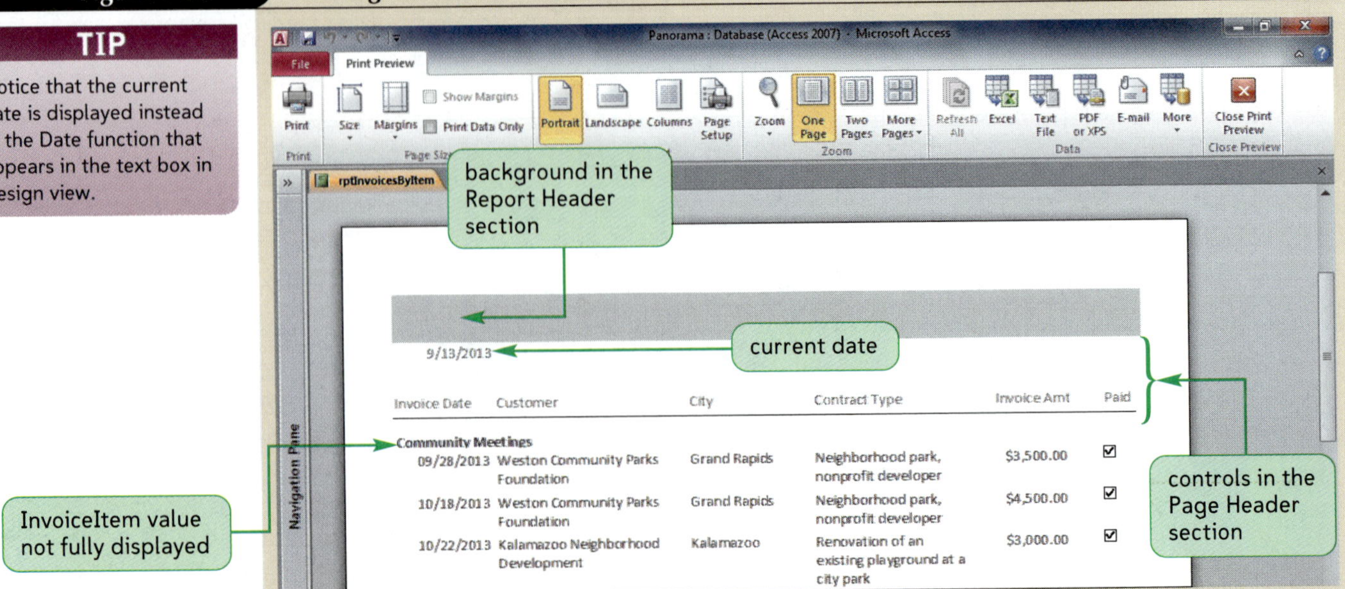

**Trouble?** Your year might appear with two digits instead of four digits as shown in Figure 7-28. Your date format might also differ, depending on your computer's date settings. These differences do not cause any problems.

You'll left-align the date in the text box in Design view. Also, notice that when you bolded the font in the InvoiceItem text box, you increased the size of the characters, so you need to increase the height of the text boxes to fully display all characters in the text box.

11. Switch to Design view, make sure the Date function text box is selected, click the **Format** tab, and then in the Font group, click the **Align Text Left** button.
12. Click the **InvoiceItem** text box, and then increase the height of the text box from the top by one row of grid dots.

INSIGHT

*Choosing a Theme for a Database*

Access has 40 themes that you can use to set the font type and size and the color and other effects for the objects in a database. The default theme is the Office theme, which uses Calibri 11 font. You should either use the default theme or choose a theme immediately after creating the first table in the database. If you wait to choose a theme until after you've created a large number of objects in the database, the theme you choose will probably have a font different from Calibri 11, and you'll have to go back and resize the table and query datasheets and the form and report text boxes and labels.

You are now ready to add page numbers to the Page Header section. You'll also delete the empty Report Header section by decreasing its height to zero.

## Adding Page Numbers to a Report

You can display page numbers in a report by including an expression in the Page Header or Page Footer section. You can click the Page Numbers button in the Header/Footer group in Layout or Design view to add a page number expression to a report. The inserted page number expression automatically displays the correct page number on each page of a report.

REFERENCE

*Adding Page Numbers to a Report*

- Display the report in Layout or Design view.
- In the Header/Footer group on the Design tab in Design view or in Layout view, click the Page Numbers button to open the Page Numbers dialog box.
- Select the format, position, and alignment options you want.
- Select whether you want to display the page number on the first page.
- Click the OK button to place the page number expression in the report.

Lucia's design shows the page number displayed on the right side of the Page Header section, bottom aligned with the date.

### To add page numbers to the Page Header section:

1. Delete the Report Header section by reducing its height to zero.
2. Click the **Design** tab, and then in the Header/Footer group, click the **Page Numbers** button. The Page Numbers dialog box opens.

   You use the Format options to specify the format of the page number. Lucia wants page numbers to appear as Page 1, Page 2, and so on. This is the "Page N" format option. You use the Position options to place the page numbers at the top of the page in the Page Header section or at the bottom of the page in the Page Footer section. Lucia's design shows page numbers at the top of the page.
3. Make sure that the **Page N** option button in the Format section and that the **Top of Page [Header]** option button in the Position section are both selected.

   The report design shows page numbers at the right side of the page. You can specify this placement in the Alignment box.
4. Click the **Alignment** arrow, and then click **Right**.
5. Make sure the **Show Number on First Page** check box is checked, so the page number prints on the first page and all other pages as well. See Figure 7-29.

**Figure 7-29** **Completed Page Numbers dialog box**

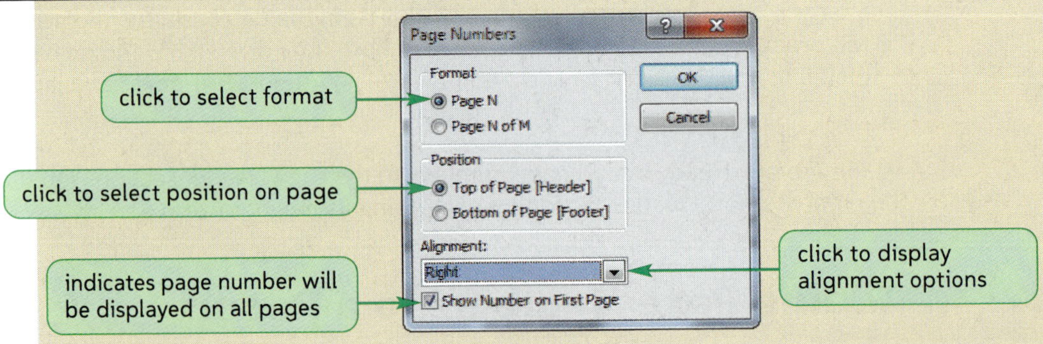


6. Click the **OK** button. The text box shown in Figure 7-30 appears in the upper-right corner of the Page Header section. The expression *="Page " & [Page]* in the text box means that the printed report will show the word "Page" followed by a space and the page number.

**Figure 7-30** **Page number expression added to the Page Header section**

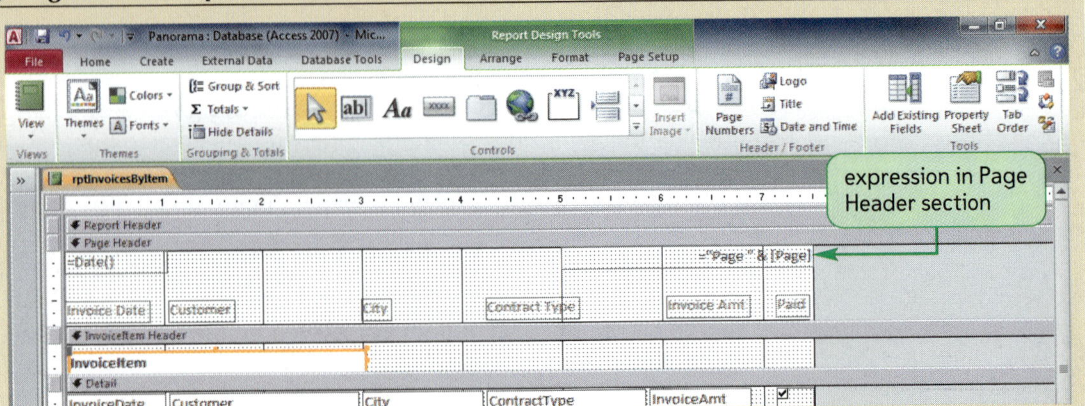

The page number text box is much wider than needed for the page number expression that'll appear in the custom report. You'll decrease its width.

7. Click the **Page Number** text box, and then decrease its width from the left to one inch total.
8. Save your report changes, and then switch to Print Preview. See Figure 7-31.

**Figure 7-31** Date and page number in the Page Header section

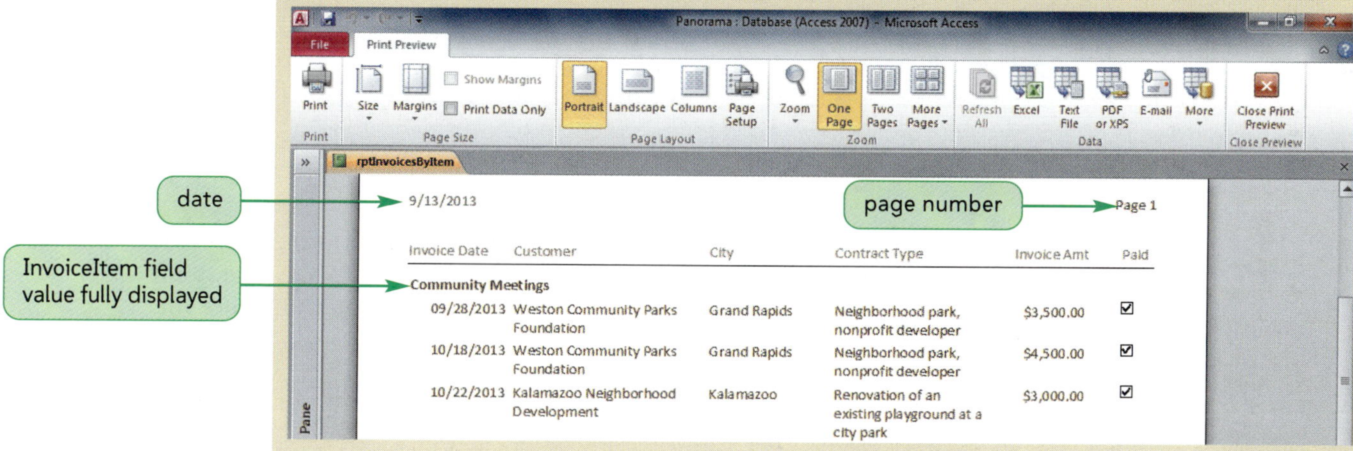


Now you are ready to add the title to the Page Header section.

## Adding a Title to a Report

Lucia's report design includes the title "Invoices by Item," which you'll add to the Page Header section centered between the date and the page number. You could use the Title button in the Header/Footer group on the Design tab to add the report title, but Access adds the title to the Report Header section, and Lucia's design positions the title in the Page Header section. It'll be easier to use the Label tool to add the title directly in the Page Header section.

### To add the title to the Page Header section:

1. Switch to Design view.
2. In the Controls group on the Design tab, click the **Label** tool, position the pointer's plus symbol (+) at the top of the Page Header section at the 3-inch mark on the horizontal ruler, and then click the mouse button. The insertion point flashes inside a narrow box, which will expand as you type the report title.

   To match Lucia's design, you need to type the title as "Invoices by Item," and change its font size to 14 points and its style to bold.

3. Type **Invoices by Item**, and then press the **Enter** key.
4. Click the **Format** tab, in the Font group click the **Font Size** arrow, click **14**, and then click the **Bold** button.

   The Error Checking Options button appears to the left of the report title.

5. Point to the **Error Checking Options** button. A ScreenTip describes the potential error. See Figure 7-32.

**Figure 7-32** **Report title in the Page Header section**

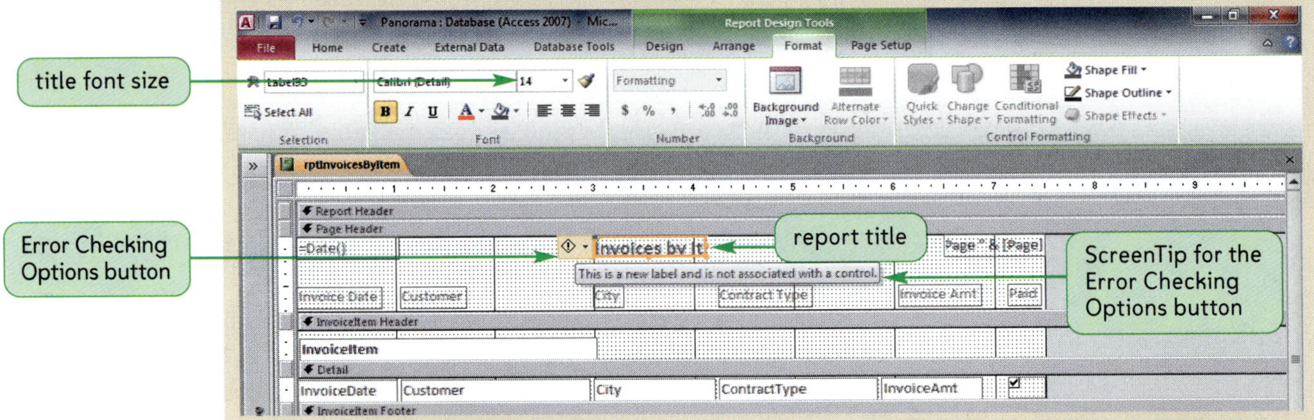


The ScreenTip indicates that the report title, which is a label control, is not associated with any bound or calculated control. Because you don't want a label that contains a report title to be associated with another control, you can ignore this potential error.

6. Click the **Error Checking Options** button, and then click **Ignore Error**.

   The report title is still selected, so you can resize it to fit.

7. Right-click an edge of the title to open the shortcut menu, point to **Size**, and then click **To Fit**.

   Finally, you'll align the date, report title, and page number controls on their bottom edges.

8. Select the date, report title, and page number controls in the Page Header section, right-click one of the selected controls, point to **Align**, and then click **Bottom**.

9. Save your report changes. You have completed the design of the custom report. See the Session 7.3 Visual Overview.

10. Switch to Print Preview to review the completed report, and then navigate to the top of the last page of the report to view your changes. See Figure 7-33.

**Figure 7-33** Completed rptInvoicesByItem report in Print Preview

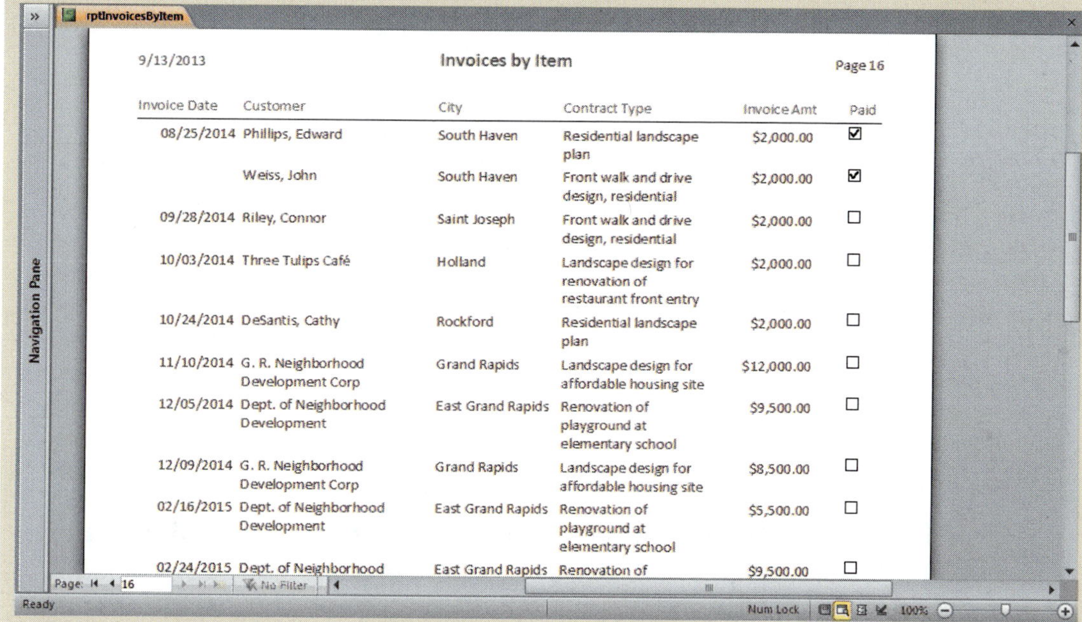


**11.** Close the report.

Next, Sarah wants you to create mailing labels that she can use to address materials to Belmont Landscapes customers.

# Creating Mailing Labels

Sarah needs a set of mailing labels printed for all customers so she can mail a marketing brochure and other materials to them. The tblCustomer table contains the name and address information that will serve as the record source for the labels. Each mailing label will have the same format: first name and last name on the first line; company name (if it exists for the customer) on the second line; address on the third line; and city, state, and zip code on the fourth line.

You could create a custom report to produce the mailing labels, but using the Label Wizard is an easier and faster way to produce them. The **Label Wizard** provides templates for hundreds of standard label formats, each of which is uniquely identified by a label manufacturer's name and number. These templates specify the dimensions and arrangement of labels on each page. Standard label formats can have between one and five labels across a page; the number of labels printed on a single page also varies. Sarah's mailing labels are Avery number C2163; each sheet has 12 1.5-inch by 3.9-inch labels arranged in two columns and six rows on the page.

REFERENCE

## *Creating Mailing Labels and Other Labels*

- In the Navigation Pane, click the table or query that'll serve as the record source for the labels.
- In the Reports group on the Create tab, click the Labels button to start the Label Wizard and open its first dialog box.
- Select the label manufacturer and its product number, and then click the Next button.
- Select the label font, color, and style, and then click the Next button.
- Construct the label content by selecting the fields from the record source and specifying their placement and spacing on the label, and then click the Next button.
- Select one or more optional sort fields, click the Next button, specify the report name, and then click the Finish button.

You'll use the Label Wizard to create a report to produce mailing labels for all customers.

### To use the Label Wizard to create the mailing label report:

1. Open the Navigation Pane, click **tblCustomer** to make it the current object that'll serve as the record source for the labels, close the Navigation Pane, and then click the **Create** tab on the Ribbon.
2. In the Reports group, click the **Labels** button. The first Label Wizard dialog box opens and asks you to select the standard or custom label you'll use.
3. Make sure that the **English** option button is selected in the Unit of Measure section, that the **Sheet feed** option button is selected in the Label Type section, and that **Avery** is selected in the Filter by manufacturer box, and then click **C2163** in the Product number box. See Figure 7-34.

**Figure 7-34 Selecting a standard label**

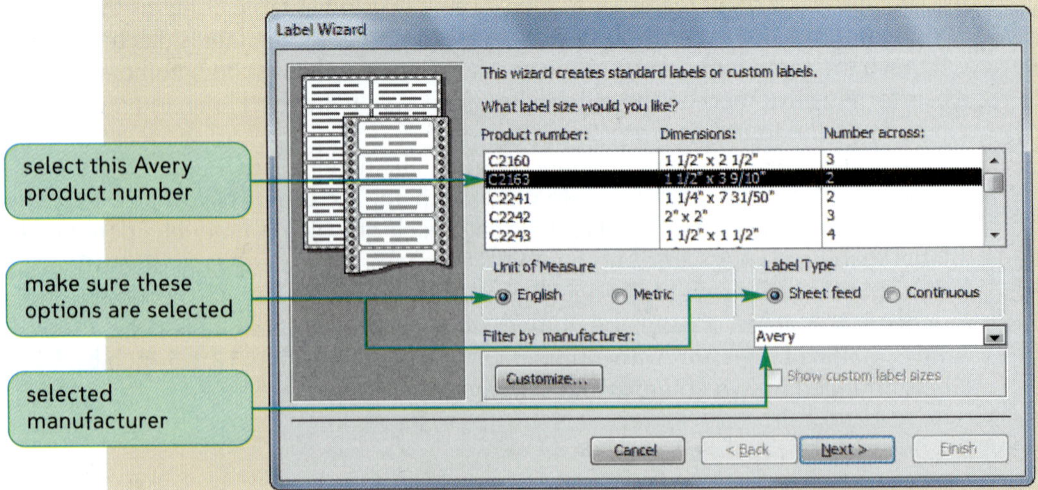


TIP

If your label manufacturer or its labels do not appear in the box, you can create your own custom format for them.

Because the labels are already filtered for the Avery manufacturer, the top box shows the Avery product number, dimensions, and number of labels across the page for each of its standard label formats. You can display the dimensions in the list in either inches or millimeters by choosing the appropriate option in the Unit of Measure section. You can also specify in the Label Type section whether the labels are on individual sheets or are continuous forms.

4. Click the **Next** button to open the second Label Wizard dialog box, in which you choose font specifications for the labels.

   Sarah wants the labels to use 10-point Arial with a medium font weight and without italics or underlines. The font weight determines how light or dark the characters will print; you can choose from nine values ranging from thin to heavy.

5. If necessary, select **Arial** for the font name, **10** for the font size, and **Medium** for the font weight; make sure the Italic and the Underline check boxes are not checked and that black is the text color; and then click the **Next** button to open the third Label Wizard dialog box, from which you select the data to appear on the labels.

   Sarah wants the mailing labels to print the FirstName and LastName fields on the first line; the Company field on the second line; the Address field on the third line; and the City, State, and Zip fields on the fourth line. One space will separate the FirstName and LastName fields, the City and State fields, and the State and Zip fields.

**TIP**

As you select fields from the Available fields box or type text for the label, the Prototype label box shows the format for the label.

6. Click **FirstName** in the Available fields box, click the > button to move the field to the Prototype label box, press the **spacebar**, click **LastName** in the Available fields box (if necessary), and then click the > button. The braces around the field names in the Prototype label box indicate that the name represents a field rather than text that you entered.

   **Trouble?** If you select the wrong field or type the wrong text, click the incorrect item in the Prototype label box, press the Delete key to remove the item, and then select the correct field or type the correct text.

7. Press the **Enter** key to move to the next line in the Prototype label box, and then use Figure 7-35 to complete the entries in the Prototype label box. Make sure you press the spacebar after selecting the City field and the State field.

**Figure 7-35 Completed label prototype**

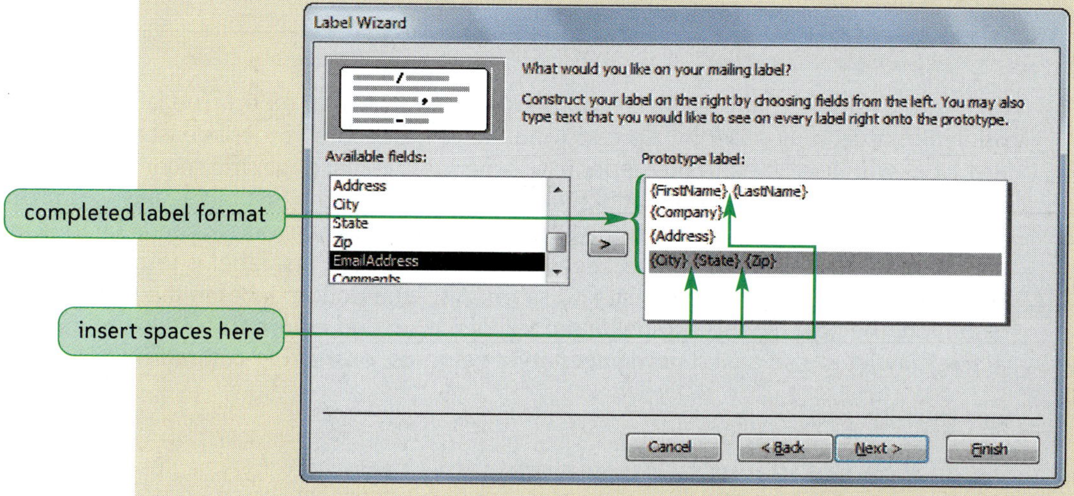


If a Company field value is null in the second line, Access moves up the third and fourth lines when you print or preview the label report to eliminate the blank line on the label.

8. Click the **Next** button to open the fourth Label Wizard dialog box, in which you choose the sort fields for the labels.

Sarah wants Zip to be the primary sort field and LastName to be the secondary sort field.

9. Scroll down the list and select the **Zip** field as the primary sort field, select the **LastName** field as the secondary sort field, and then click the **Next** button to open the last Label Wizard dialog box, in which you enter a name for the report.

10. Change the report name to **rptCustomerMailingLabels**, and then click the **Finish** button. Access saves the report as rptCustomerMailingLabels and then opens the first page of the report in Print Preview. Note that two columns of labels appear across the page. See Figure 7-36.

Figure 7-36 **Previewing the label content and sequence**

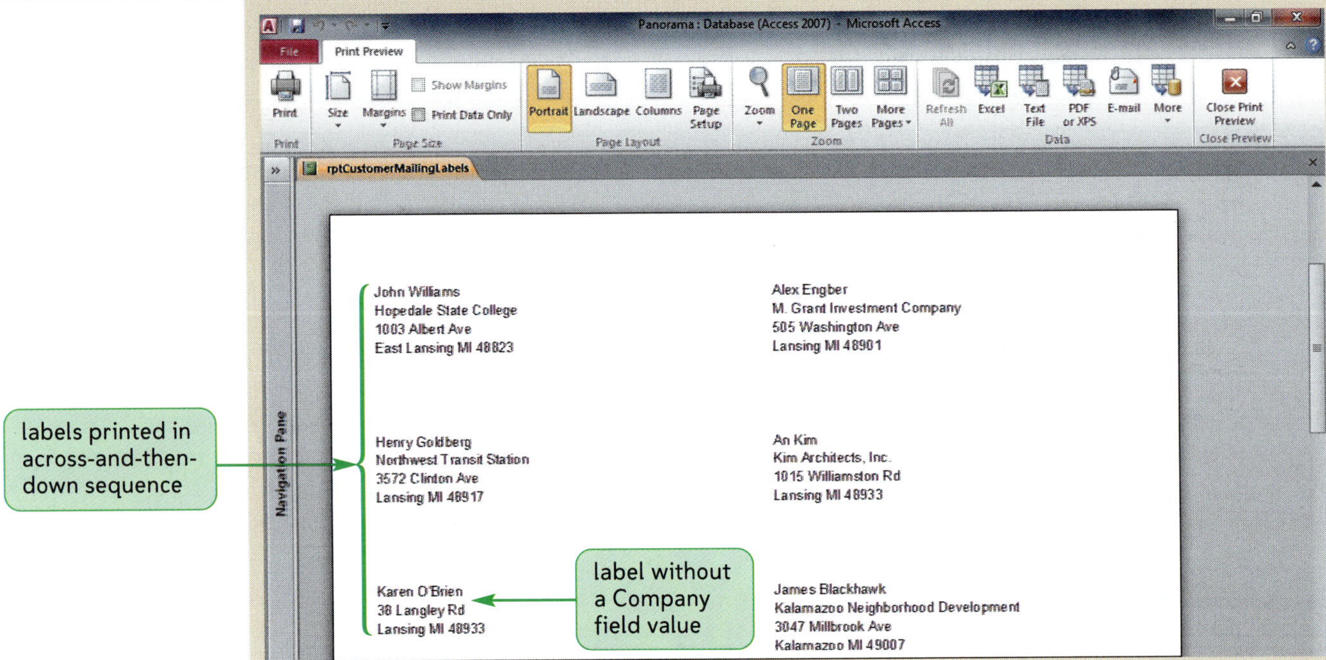


The rptCustomerMailingLabels report is a multiple-column report. The labels will be printed in ascending order by zip code and then in ascending order by last name. The first label will be printed in the upper-left corner on the first page, the second label will be printed to its right, the third label will be printed below the first label, and so on. This style of multiple-column report is the across-and-then-down layout. Instead, Sarah wants the labels to print with the "down, then across" layout—the first label is printed, the second label is printed below the first, and so on. After the bottom label in the first column is printed, the next label is printed at the top of the second column. The "down, then across" layout is also called **newspaper-style columns**, or **snaking columns**.

## To change the layout to the mailing label report:

1. Switch to Design view. The Detail section, the only section in the report, is sized for a single label.

   First, you'll change the layout to snaking columns.

2. Click the **Page Setup** tab on the Ribbon, click the **Page Setup** button in the Page Layout group, and then click the **Columns** tab. The Page Setup dialog box displays the column options for the report. See Figure 7-37.

**Figure 7-37** **Column options in the Page Setup dialog box**

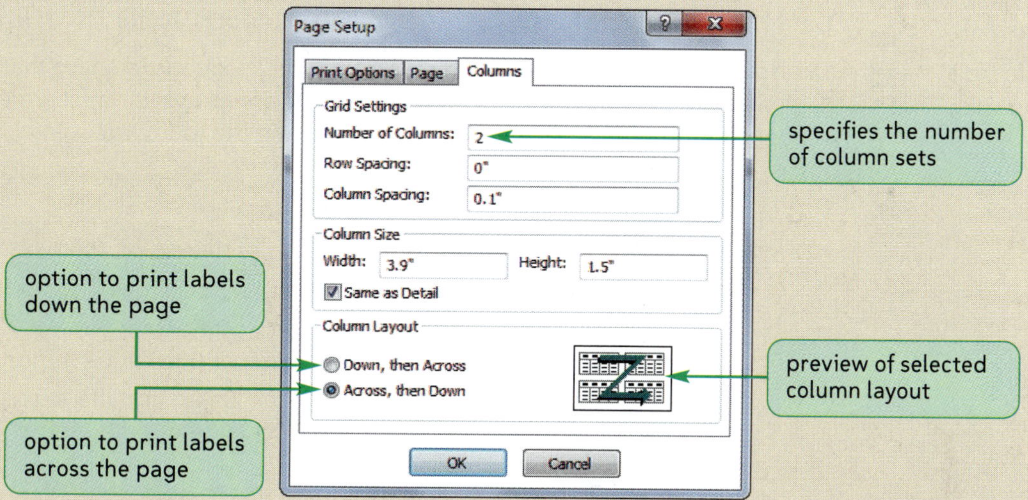


**TIP**

When you select a label using a manufacturer's name and product code, the options in the dialog box are set automatically.

The options in the Page Setup dialog box let you change the properties of a multiple-column report. In the Grid Settings section, you specify the number of column sets and the row and column spacing between the column sets. In the Column Size section, you specify the width and height of each column set. In the Column Layout section, you select between the "down, then across" and the "across, then down" layouts.

You can now change the layout for the labels.

3. Click the **Down, then Across** option button, and then click the **OK** button.

   You've finished the report changes, so you can now save and preview the report.

4. Save your report design changes, and then switch to Print Preview. The labels appear in the snaking-columns layout.

   You've finished all work on Sarah's reports.

5. Close the report, make a backup copy of the database, and compact and repair and then close the Panorama database.

Sarah is very pleased with the modified report and the two new reports, which will provide her with improved information and help expedite her written communications with customers.

REVIEW

## *Session 7.3 Quick Check*

1. What is the function and its format to print the current date in a report?
2. How do you insert a page number in the Page Header section?
3. Clicking the Title button in the Header/Footer group on the Design tab adds a report title to the ______________ section.
4. What is a multiple-column report?

*Practice the skills you learned in the tutorial using the same case scenario.*

PRACTICE

## Review Assignments

**Data File needed for the Review Assignments: Products.accdb (*cont. from Tutorial 6*)**

Sarah wants you to create a custom report for the Products database that prints all companies and the products they offer. She also wants you to customize an existing report. You will perform the tasks for Sarah by completing the following steps:

1. Open the **Products** database located in the Access2\Review folder provided with your Data Files.
2. Modify the **rptCompanyProducts** report by completing the following steps:
   a. Delete the picture at the top of the report.
   b. Change the report title to **Belmont Supplier Products**.
   c. Remove the alternate row color from the detail lines in the report.
   d. Change the second column heading to First Name and the third column heading to Last Name, and then resize the column headings with their text boxes to make sure all values are fully visible.
   e. In the Report Footer section, add a grand total count of the number of products that appear in the report, make sure the control has a transparent border, and left-align the count with the left edge of the ContactLastName text box.
   f. Add a label that contains the text **total products** to the right of the count of the total number of products.
   g. Left-align the page number text box with the left edge of the Price text box.
3. After you've completed and saved your modifications to the rptCompanyProducts report, filter the report in Report view, selecting all records that contain the word "table" in the ProductType field. Copy the entire filtered report and paste it into a new Word document, and then change the report orientation to landscape. Save the document as **Tables** in the Access2\Review folder. Close Word, and then close the Access report without saving changes.
4. Create a query that displays the ProductType and CompanyName fields from the tblCompany table, and the ProductType, Price, and Unit fields from the tblProduct table. Sort in ascending order by the first three fields in the query, and then save the query as **qryCompanyProducts**.
5. Create a custom report based on the qryCompanyProducts query. Figure 7-38 shows a sample of the last page of the completed report. Refer to the figure as you create the report.

**Figure 7-38 Products database custom report**

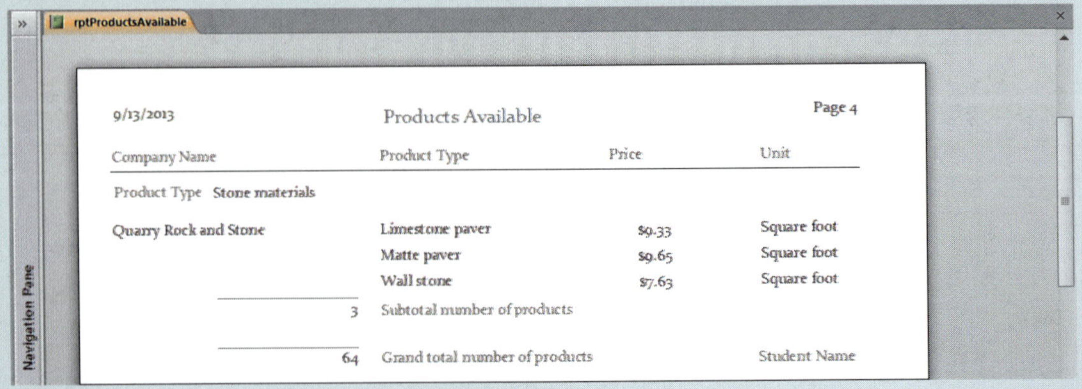


   a. Save the report as **rptProductsAvailable**.
   b. Use the ProductType field (from the tblCompany table) as a grouping field, and use the ProductType field (from the tblProduct table) as a sort field.

c. Hide duplicate values for the CompanyName field.
d. Add labels for the subtotals, the grand total, and your name.
e. Keep the whole group together on one page.
f. Remove the text box borders.
g. Remove the alternate row color from the group header and detail lines.

6. Create a mailing label report according to the following instructions:
   a. Use the tblCompany table as the record source.
   b. Use Avery C2160 labels, and use the default font, size, weight, and color.
   c. For the prototype label, add the ContactFirstName, a space, and ContactLastName on the first line; the CompanyName on the second line; the Address on the third line; and the City, a space, State, a space, and Zip on the fourth line.
   d. Sort by Zip and then by CompanyName, and then enter the report name **rptCompanyMailingLabels**.
7. Make a backup copy of the database, compact and repair, and then close the Products database.

*Apply the skills you learned in the tutorial to create a custom report.*

CHALLENGE

## Case Problem 1

### Data File needed for this Case Problem: Contract.accdb *(cont. from Tutorial 6)*

***Pine Hill Music School*** Yuka Koyama wants you to modify an existing report and to create a custom report and mailing labels for the Contract database. You'll do so by completing the following steps:

1. Open the **Contract** database located in the Access2\Case1 folder provided with your Data Files.
2. Modify the **rptStudentContracts** report. Figure 7-39 shows a sample of the last page of the completed report. Refer to the figure as you modify the report.

**Figure 7-39 Contract database enhanced report**

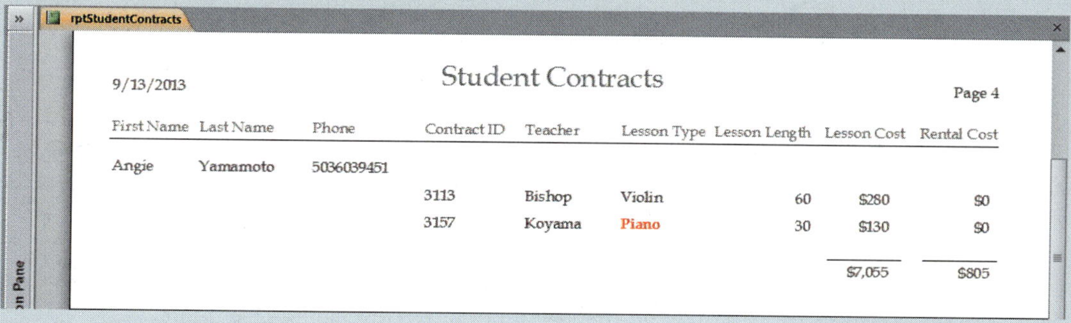


   a. Delete the picture at the top of the report.
   b. Center the report title.
   c. Remove the alternate row color from the group header and detail lines in the report.

EXPLORE

   d. Change the page number format from "Page n of m" to "Page n."
   e. Move the date, report title, and page number to the Page Header section.
   f. Add grand total controls that calculate the total monthly lesson cost and total monthly rental cost.

EXPLORE

   g. Add a conditional formatting rule for the LessonType field to display all values of Piano in red, bold font.

3. Create a query that displays, in order, the LastName and FirstName fields from the tblTeacher table, the LessonType field from the tblContract table, the FirstName and LastName fields from the tblStudent table, and the MonthlyLessonCost and MonthlyRentalCost fields from the tblContract table. Sort in ascending order by the first three fields in the query, and then save the query as **qryTeacherLessons**.
4. Create a custom report based on the qryTeacherLessons query. Figure 7-40 shows a sample of the last page of the completed report. Refer to the figure as you create the report.

**Figure 7-40 Contract database custom report**

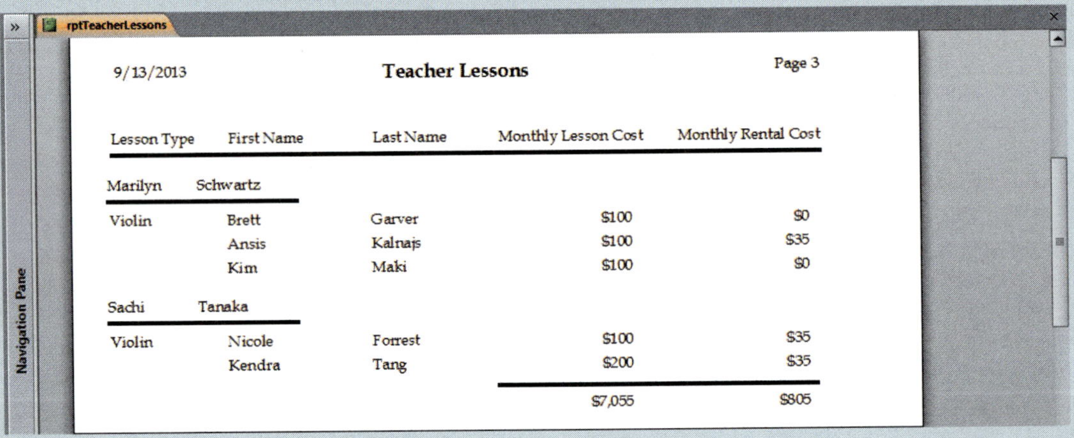


a. Save the report as **rptTeacherLessons**.
b. The LastName field (from the tblTeacher table) is a grouping field, and the FirstName field also appears in the Group Header section.
c. The LessonType field is a sort field, and the LastName field (from the tblStudent table) is a sort field.
d. Hide duplicate values for the LessonType field.
e. Use black font for all the controls, setting the lines' thickness to 3 pt.

5. Create a mailing label report according to the following instructions:
a. Use the tblStudent table as the record source.

**EXPLORE**

b. Use Avery C2160 labels, use a larger font size and a heavier font weight, and use the other default font and color options.
c. For the prototype label, place FirstName, a space, and LastName on the first line; Address on the second line; and City, a space, State, a space, and Zip on the third line.
d. Sort by Zip and then by LastName, and then enter the report name **rptStudentMailingLabels**.
e. Change the mailing label layout to snaking columns.

6. Make a backup copy of the database, compact and repair, and then close the Contract database.

*Apply what you learned in the tutorial to create a custom report.*

APPLY

## Case Problem 2

**Data File needed for this Case Problem: Training.accdb (*cont. from Tutorial 6*)**

***Parkhurst Health & Fitness Center*** Martha Parkhurst wants you to create a custom report and mailing labels for the Training database. The custom report will be based on the results of a query you will create. You will create the query, the custom report, and the mailing labels by completing the following steps:

1. Open the **Training** database located in the Access2\Case2 folder provided with your Data Files.
2. Create a query that displays the ProgramID, ProgramType, and MonthlyFee fields from the tblProgram table, and the MembershipStatus, FirstName, and LastName fields from the tblMember table. Sort in ascending order by the ProgramID, MembershipStatus, and LastName fields, and then save the query as **qryProgramMembership**.
3. Create a custom report based on the qryProgramMembership query. Figure 7-41 shows a sample of the last page of the completed report. Refer to the figure as you create the report.

**Figure 7-41 Training database custom report**

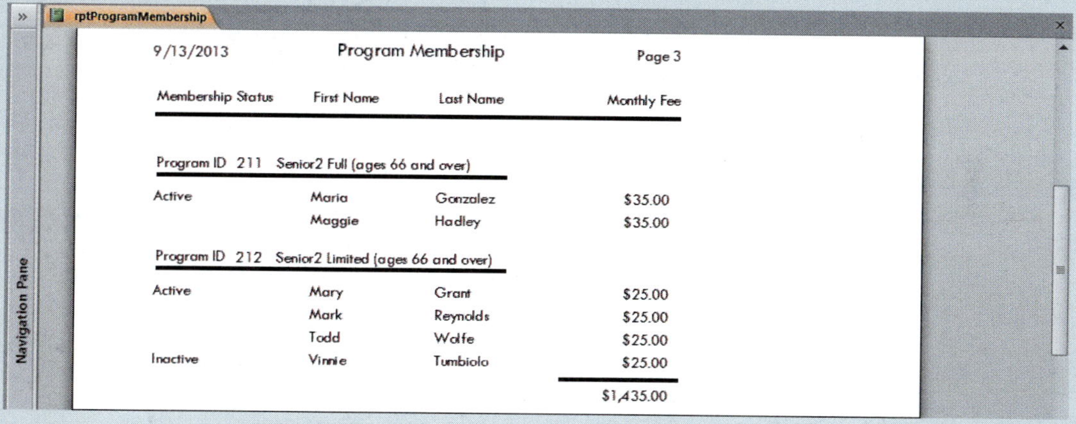


   a. Save the report as **rptProgramMembership**.
   b. Use the ProgramID field as a grouping field.
   c. Select the MembershipStatus field as a sort field, and the LastName field as a secondary sort field.
   d. Hide duplicate values for the MembershipStatus field.
   e. Add the ProgramType field to the Group Header section, and then delete its attached label.
   f. Keep the whole group together on one page.
   g. Use black font for all the controls, and set the lines' thickness to 3 pt.
4. Use the following instructions to create the mailing labels:
   a. Use the tblMember table as the record source for the mailing labels.
   b. Use Avery C2160 labels, and use the default font, size, weight, and color.

c. For the prototype label, place FirstName, a space, and LastName on the first line; Street on the second line; and City, a space, State, a space, and Zip on the third line.

d. Sort by Zip and then by LastName, and then type the report name **rptMemberLabels**.

5. Make a backup copy of the database, compact and repair, and then close the Training database.

*Apply what you learned in the tutorial to create a custom report.*

APPLY

## Case Problem 3

**Data File needed for this Case Problem: Agency.accdb (*cont. from Tutorial 6*)**

***Rossi Recycling Group*** Mary Rossi asks you to create a custom report for the Agency database so that she can better track donations made by donors and to create mailing labels. You'll do so by completing the following steps:

1. Open the **Agency** database located in the Access2\Case3 folder provided with your Data Files.
2. Create a query that displays the DonationDesc, DonationDate, and DonationValue fields from the tblDonation table, and the FirstName and LastName fields from the tblDonor table. Sort in ascending order by the DonationDesc, DonationDate, and LastName fields, and then save the query as **qryDonorDonations**.
3. Create a custom report based on the qryDonorDonations query. Figure 7-42 shows a sample of the last page of the completed report. Refer to the figure as you create the report.

**Figure 7-42** **Agency database custom report**

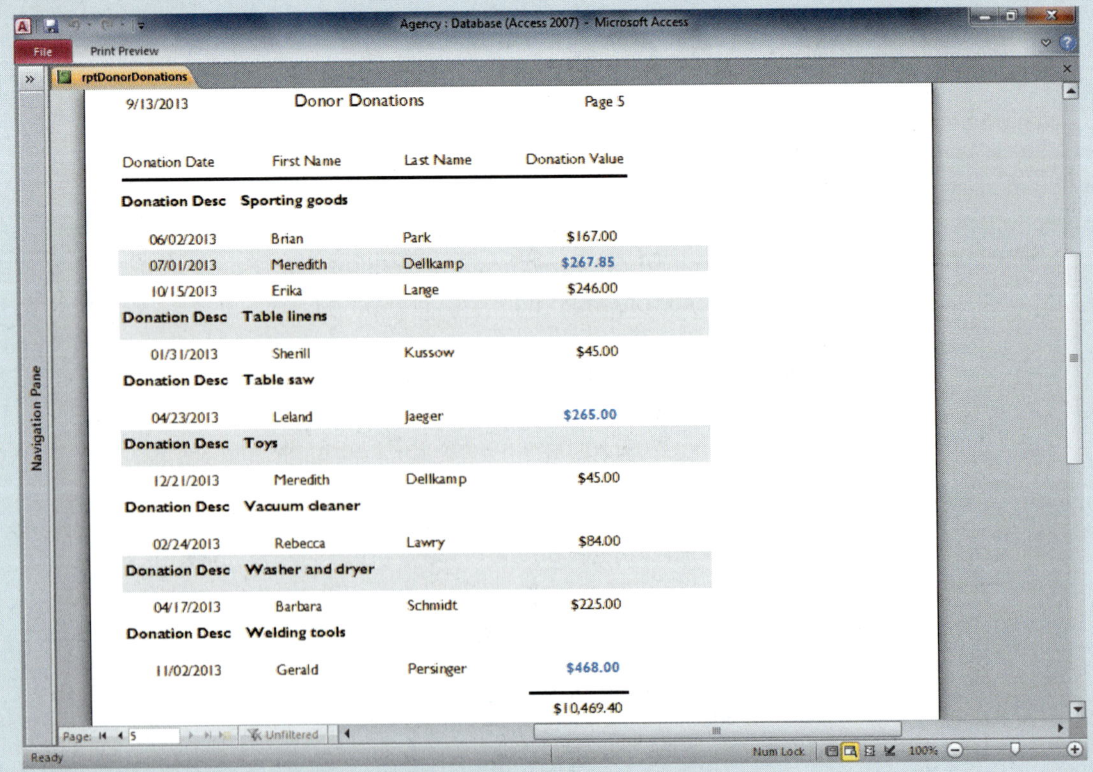

a. Save the report as **rptDonorDonations**.
b. Use the DonationDesc field as a grouping field.
c. Select the DonationDate field as a sort field, and the LastName field as a secondary sort field.
d. Hide duplicate values for the DonationDate field.
e. Use black font for all the controls, and set the lines' thickness to 2 pt.
f. Keep the whole group together on one page.

EXPLORE

g. Create a conditional formatting rule for the DonationValue field to display the value in blue, bold font when the amount is more than $250.

4. After you've created and saved the rptDonorDonations report, filter the report in Report view, selecting all records that contain the name "Park" in the LastName field. Copy the entire filtered report and paste it into a new Word document, and then change the report orientation to landscape. Save the document as **DonorPark** in the Access2\Case3 folder. Close Word, and then close the Access report without saving it.
5. Use the following instructions to create the mailing labels:
   a. Use the tblAgency table as the record source for the mailing labels.
   b. Use Avery C2160 labels, and use the default font, size, weight, and color.
   c. For the prototype label, place ContactFirstName, a space, and ContactLastName on the first line; AgencyName on the second line; Address on the third line; and City, a space, State, a space, and Zip on the fourth line.
   d. Sort by Zip and then by ContactLastName, and then type the report name **rptAgencyLabels**.
   e. Change the mailing label layout to snaking columns.
6. Make a backup copy of the database, compact and repair, and then close the Agency database.

*Use the skills you've learned in this tutorial to create a custom report.*

CREATE

## Case Problem 4

**Data File needed for this Case Problem: Vacation.accdb (*cont. from Tutorial 6*)**

***GEM Ultimate Vacations*** Griffin and Emma MacElroy want you to create a custom report and mailing labels for the Vacation database. You will create the custom report and the mailing labels by completing the following steps:

1. Open the **Vacation** database located in the Access2\Case4 folder provided with your Data Files.
2. Create a query that displays the PropertyName and Country fields from the tblProperty table, the StateProv field from the tblGuest table, and the StartDate, EndDate, and People fields from the tblReservation table. Sort in ascending order by the PropertyName, StateProv, and StartDate fields, and then save the query as **qryPropertyReservations**.
3. Create a custom report based on the qryPropertyReservations query. Figure 7-43 shows a sample of the last page of the completed report. Refer to the figure as you create the report.

**Figure 7-43** **Vacation database custom report**

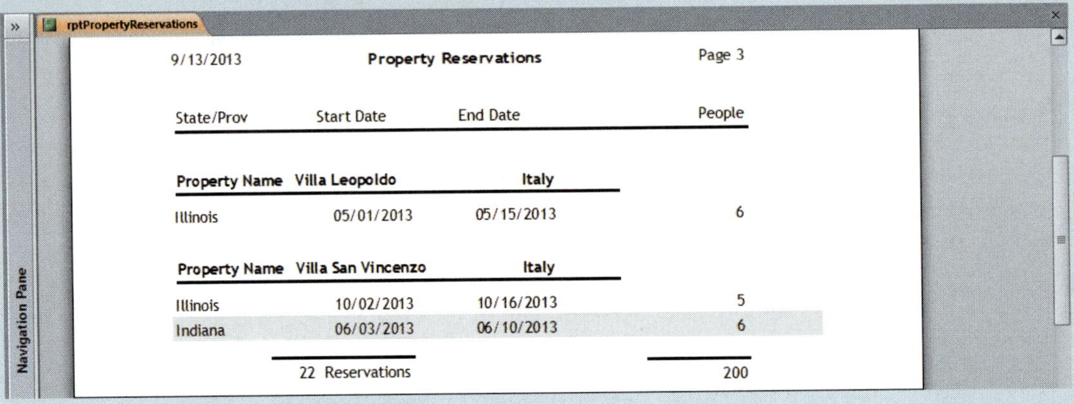


a. Save the report as **rptPropertyReservations**.
b. Use the PropertyName field as a grouping field.
c. Select the StateProv field as a sort field, and the StartDate field as a secondary sort field.
d. Hide duplicate values for the StateProv field.
e. Use black font for all the controls, and set the lines' thickness to 2 pt.
f. Keep the whole group together on one page.

**EXPLORE**

g. Add the Country field to the Group Header section.

4. Use the following instructions to create the mailing labels:
   a. Use the tblGuest table as the record source for the mailing labels.
   b. Use Avery C2163 labels, with the default font, size, weight, and color settings.
   c. For the prototype label, place GuestFirstName, a space, and GuestLastName on the first line; Address on the second line; City, a space, StateProv, a space, and PostalCode on the third line; and Country on the fourth line.
   d. Sort by PostalCode, then by GuestLastName, and then enter the report name **rptGuestLabels**.
   e. Change the mailing label layout to snaking columns.

**EXPLORE**

5. Make a copy of the rptPropertyReservations report, using the name **rptPropertyReservationsSummary** for the copy. Read Access Help to find out how to create a summary report. Modify the rptPropertyReservationsSummary report as follows to create the report shown in Figure 7-44:

**Figure 7-44** **Vacation database custom summary report**

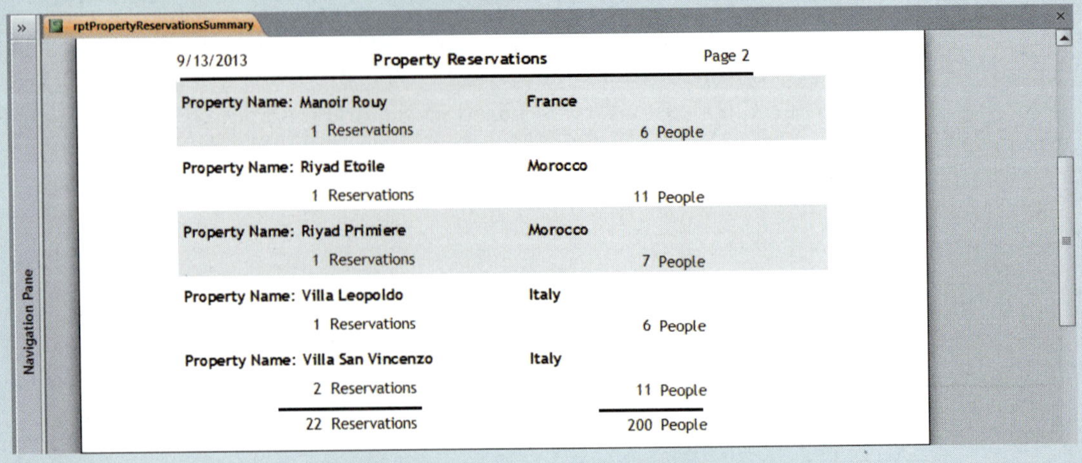

a. Delete the column heading labels, move up the line in the Page Header section to just below the remaining controls, and then reduce the height of the section.
b. Add subtotals for the number of reservations and number of people.
c. Change the report to a summary report.

6. Make a backup copy of the database, compact and repair, and then close the Vacation database.

*Work with the skills you've learned in the tutorial to create a custom report.*

CREATE

## Case Problem 5

**Data File needed for this Case Problem: ACE.accdb (*cont. from Tutorial 6*)**

***Always Connected Everyday*** Chris and Pat Dixon want you to create a custom report and mailing labels for the ACE database. You'll do so by completing the following steps:

1. Open the **ACE** database located in the Access2\Case5 folder provided with your Data Files.
2. Create a query to serve as the record source for the custom report shown in Figure 7-45, and then save the query as **qryAccessPlanCustomers**.
3. Create a custom report based on the qryAccessPlanCustomers query. Figure 7-45 shows a sample of the completed report. Refer to the figure as you create the report. Save the report as **rptAccessPlanCustomers**.

**Figure 7-45** ACE database custom report

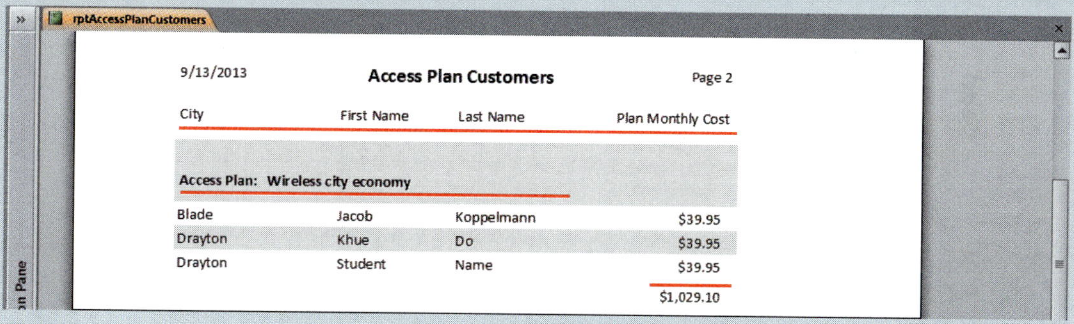


4. After you've created the rptAccessPlanCustomers report, filter the report in Report view, selecting all records that contain a specific value in the city field. Copy the entire filtered report and paste it into a new Word document. Save the document as **City** in the Access2\Case5 folder.
5. Use the tblCustomer table as the record source for the mailing labels. Choose appropriate options in the Label Wizard, change the mailing label layout to snaking columns, and save the report as **rptCustomerLabels**.
6. Make a backup copy of the database, compact and repair, and then close the ACE database.

ASSESS

## SAM: Skills Assessment Manager

For current SAM information, including versions and content details, visit SAM Central (http://samcentral.course.com). If you have a SAM user profile, you may have access to hands-on instruction, practice, and assessment of the skills covered in this tutorial. Since various versions of SAM are supported throughout the life of this text, check with your instructor for the correct instructions and URL/Web site for accessing assignments.

### ENDING DATA FILES

Access2 →

- **Tutorial**: Panorama.accdb
- **Review**: Products.accdb, Tables.docx
- **Case1**: Contract.accdb
- **Case2**: Training.accdb
- **Case3**: Agency.accdb, DonorPark.docx
- **Case4**: Vacation.accdb
- **Case5**: ACE.accdb, City.docx

TUTORIAL 8

# Sharing, Integrating, and Analyzing Data

## *Importing, Exporting, Linking, and Analyzing Data in the Panorama Database*

ACCESS

### OBJECTIVES

**Session 8.1**

- Export an Access table to an HTML document and view the document
- Import a CSV file as an Access table
- Use the Table Analyzer
- Import and export XML files
- Save and run import and export specifications

**Session 8.2**

- Create a multi-page form using a tab control
- Embed a chart in a form
- Create and modify PivotTables and PivotCharts
- Link data from an Excel workbook

## Case | ***Belmont Landscapes***

Oren Belmont, Sarah Fisher, and Taylor Sico are pleased with the design and contents of the Panorama database. Oren feels that other employees would benefit from gaining access to the Panorama database and by sharing data among the different programs employees use. Oren and Sarah would also like to be able to analyze the data in the database.

In this tutorial, you will show Oren and Sarah how to import, export, link, and embed data. You will also introduce them to the charting, PivotTable, and PivotChart features of Access.

### STARTING DATA FILES

**Access2** → 

**Tutorial**
BelmName.gif
BelmTemp.htm
Billing.csv
Panorama.accdb *(cont.)*
Products.xlsx
Prospect.xml

**Review**
Ads.xlsx
BelmName.gif
BelmTemp.htm
Payables.csv
Payments.xml
Products.accdb *(cont.)*

**Case1**
Contract.accdb *(cont.)*
Instrument.csv
Room.xlsx

**Case2**
CreditCard.xml
ParkName.gif
ParkTemp.htm
Schedule.xlsx
Training.accdb *(cont.)*

**Case3**
Agency.accdb *(cont.)*
Facility.csv

**Case4**
Personnel.xlsx
Vacation.accdb *(cont.)*
Works.xml

**Case5**
ACE.accdb *(cont.)*

# SESSION 8.1 VISUAL OVERVIEW

An **HTML template** is a file that contains HTML instructions for creating a Web page with both text and graphics, together with special instructions that tell Access where to place the Access data in the Web page.

When Access uses a template to format an exported HTML document, it places the object's name in the <TITLE> and </TITLE> tags.

The .htm (and .html) filename extensions identify a file as an HTML document.

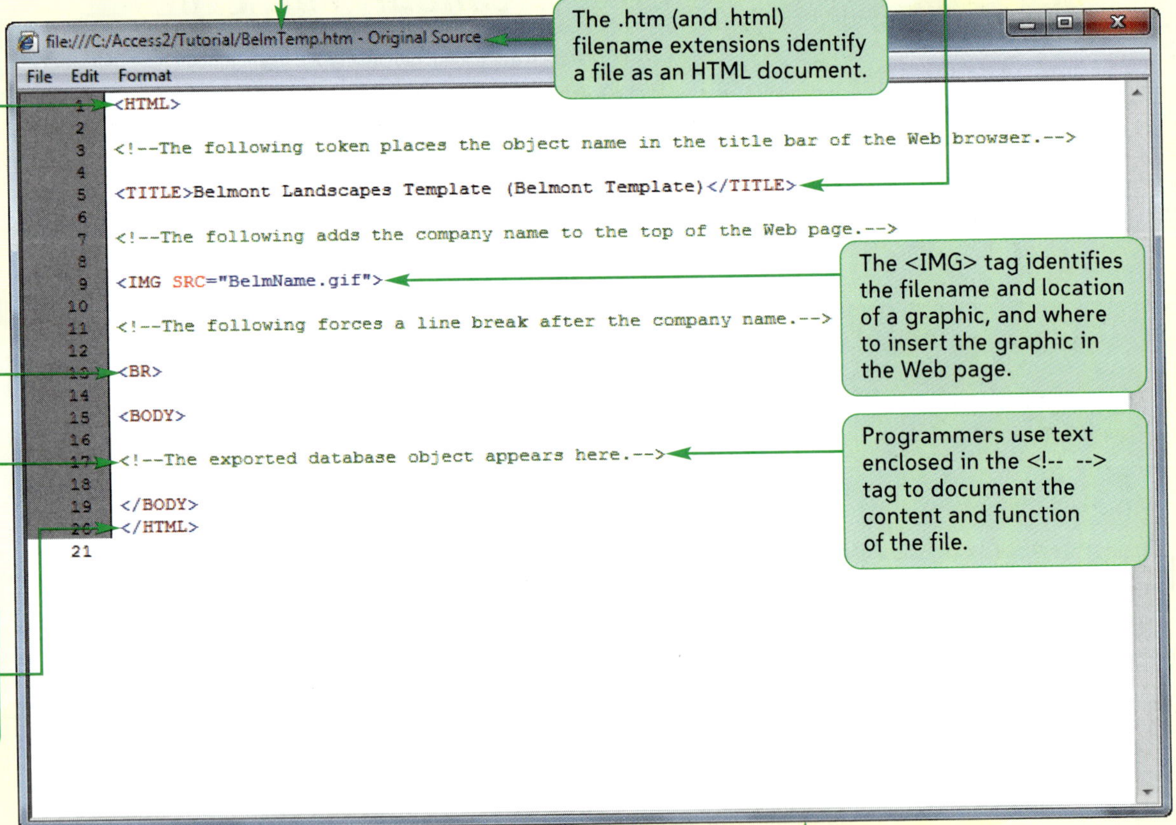


The opening <HTML> tag indicates the beginning of the HTML document.

The <BR> tag creates a blank line in a page.

The database object is inserted here, in the body of the Web page.

The closing </HTML> tag indicates the end of the HTML document.

The <IMG> tag identifies the filename and location of a graphic, and where to insert the graphic in the Web page.

Programmers use text enclosed in the <!-- --> tag to document the content and function of the file.

An **HTML document** contains tags and other instructions that a **Web browser**, such as Microsoft Internet Explorer or Mozilla Firefox, processes and displays as a Web page.

You will use the BelmTemp.htm template to format the HTML documents you export in this tutorial using objects in the Panorama database.

# HTML SOURCE AND WEB PAGE

A **Uniform Resource Locator (URL)** identifies where the Web page is stored. A URL can be an Internet Web server or a location on a hard drive. In this case, the Web page is stored on drive C, in a subfolder named Tutorial, of the main folder named Access2. The filename of the HTML document is Crosstab.html.

The title of a Web page appears in the browser's title bar.

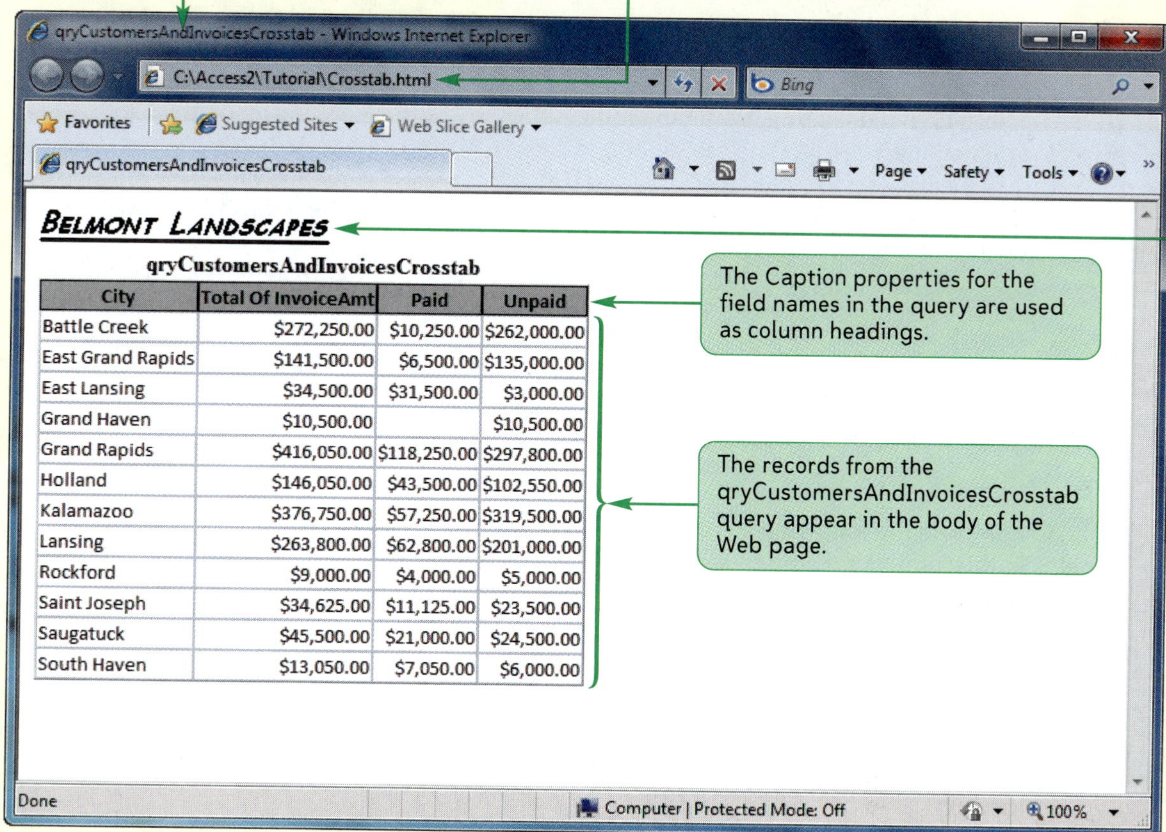


| City | Total Of InvoiceAmt | Paid | Unpaid |
|---|---|---|---|
| Battle Creek | $272,250.00 | $10,250.00 | $262,000.00 |
| East Grand Rapids | $141,500.00 | $6,500.00 | $135,000.00 |
| East Lansing | $34,500.00 | $31,500.00 | $3,000.00 |
| Grand Haven | $10,500.00 | | $10,500.00 |
| Grand Rapids | $416,050.00 | $118,250.00 | $297,800.00 |
| Holland | $146,050.00 | $43,500.00 | $102,550.00 |
| Kalamazoo | $376,750.00 | $57,250.00 | $319,500.00 |
| Lansing | $263,800.00 | $62,800.00 | $201,000.00 |
| Rockford | $9,000.00 | $4,000.00 | $5,000.00 |
| Saint Joseph | $34,625.00 | $11,125.00 | $23,500.00 |
| Saugatuck | $45,500.00 | $21,000.00 | $24,500.00 |
| South Haven | $13,050.00 | $7,050.00 | $6,000.00 |

This graphic was inserted by the HTML template, using the file saved as BelmName.gif

The Caption properties for the field names in the query are used as column headings.

The records from the qryCustomersAndInvoicesCrosstab query appear in the body of the Web page.

This Web page was created using the qryCustomersAndInvoicesCrosstab query. The formatting in the Web page uses the instructions in the BelmTemp.htm template on the left.

# Exporting an Access Query to an HTML Document

Oren wants to display the summary data in the qryCustomersAndInvoicesCrosstab query on the company's intranet so that all employees working in the office are able to access it. To store the data on the company's intranet, you'll create a Web page version of the qryCustomersAndInvoicesCrosstab query.

Creating the necessary HTML document to provide Oren with the information he wants is not as difficult as it might appear at first. You can use Access to export the query and convert it to an HTML document automatically.

REFERENCE

*Exporting an Access Object to an HTML Document*

- In the Navigation Pane, right-click the object (table, query, form, or report) you want to export, point to Export on the shortcut menu, and then click HTML Document.
  *or*
  In the Navigation Pane, click the object (table, query, form, or report) you want to export, click the External Data tab on the Ribbon, click the More button in the Export group on the External Data tab, and then click HTML Document.
- Click the Browse button in the Export – HTML Document dialog box, select the location where you want to save the file, enter the filename in the File name box, and then click the Save button.
- Click the Export data with formatting and layout check box to retain most formatting and layout information, and then click the OK button.
- If using a template, click the Select a HTML Template check box in the HTML Output Options dialog box, click the Browse button, select the location for the template, click the template filename, and then click the OK button.
- Click the OK button.

To complete the following steps, you need to use Access and a Web browser. The steps in this tutorial are written for Internet Explorer, the Web browser used at Belmont Landscapes. If you use another browser, the steps you need to complete might be slightly different.

You'll export the qryCustomersAndInvoicesCrosstab query as an HTML document.

**To export the qryCustomersAndInvoicesCrosstab query as an HTML document:**

1. Start Access, and then open the **Panorama** database in the Access2\Tutorial folder provided with your Data Files.
2. Open the Navigation Pane (if necessary), right-click **qryCustomersAndInvoicesCrosstab** to display the shortcut menu, point to **Export**, and then click **HTML Document**. The Export - HTML Document dialog box opens.
3. Click the **Browse** button to open the File Save dialog box, navigate to the **Access2\Tutorial** folder, select the text in the File name box, type **Crosstab**, and then click the **Save** button. The File Save dialog box closes, and the Export – HTML Document dialog box is the active window. See Figure 8-1.

**Figure 8-1** Export - HTML Document dialog box

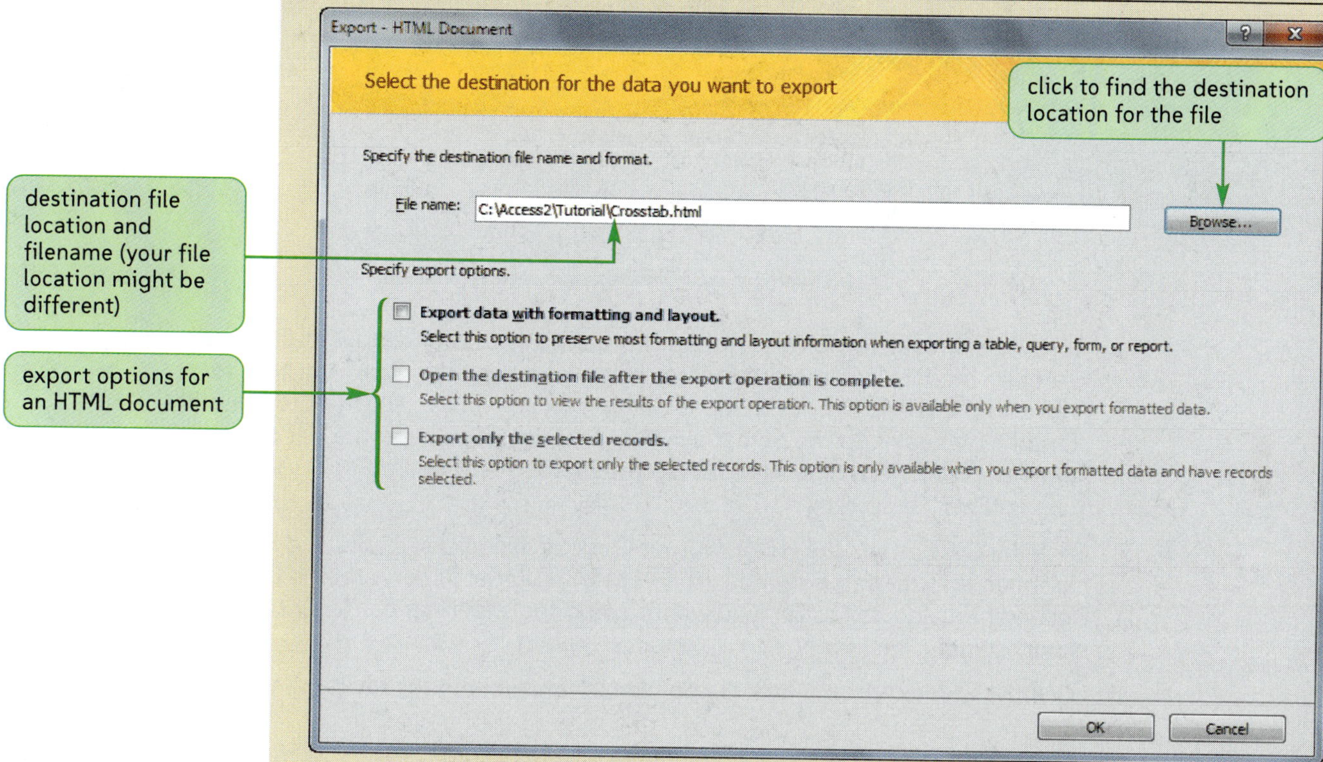


**TIP**

Always select the "Export data with formatting and layout" option, or the HTML document you create will be poorly formatted and difficult to read.

The dialog box provides options for exporting the data with formatting and layout, opening the exported file after the export operation is complete, and exporting selected records from the source object (available only when you select records in an object instead of the object in the Navigation Pane). You need to select the option for exporting the data with formatting and layout.

4. Click the **Export data with formatting and layout** check box to select it, and then click the **OK** button. The Export - HTML Document dialog box closes and the HTML Output Options dialog box opens.

   This dialog box lets you specify an HTML template or use the default format when saving the object. Lucia used a text-editing program to create the HTML template named BelmTemp, which is shown in the Visual Overview for Session 8.1. You'll use this template to create the Crosstab HTML document. The template will automatically insert a Belmont Landscapes logo in all Web pages created with it. You need to locate Lucia's template file in your Data Files.

5. If necessary, click the **Select a HTML Template** check box to select it.

6. Click the **Browse** button to open the HTML Template to Use dialog box, navigate to the **Access2\Tutorial** folder, click **BelmTemp**, and then click the **OK** button. Access closes the HTML Template to Use dialog box, returns to the HTML Output Options dialog box, and displays the location and filename for the HTML template. See Figure 8-2.

**Figure 8-2** **HTML Output Options dialog box**

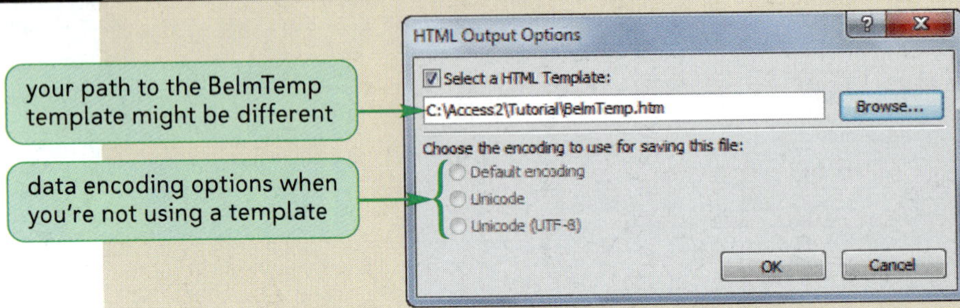


**Trouble?** If BelmTemp does not appear in the Access2\Tutorial folder when you open the HTML Template to Use dialog box, click the Cancel button to return to the HTML Output Options dialog box so you can specify the template filename manually. In the Select a HTML Template box, type the full path to the BelmTemp.htm file in the Access2\Tutorial folder—for example, C:\Access2\Tutorial\BelmTemp.htm.

7. Click the **OK** button. The HTML Output Options dialog box closes, the HTML document named Crosstab is saved in the Access2\Tutorial folder, and the Export - HTML Document dialog box asks if you want to save the export steps. You won't save these export steps.
8. Click the **Close** button in the dialog box to close it without saving the steps.

Now you can view the Web page.

## Viewing an HTML Document Using Internet Explorer

**TIP**

**HTML (Hypertext Markup Language)** is a programming language used to create Web pages.

Oren asks to see the Web page you created. You can view the HTML document that you created using any Web browser. You'll view it using Internet Explorer.

**To view the Crosstab Web page:**

1. Open Windows Explorer, and then navigate to and open the **Access2\Tutorial** folder, which is where you saved the exported HTML document.
2. Right-click **Crosstab** in the file list to open the shortcut menu, click **Open with**, click **Internet Explorer**, and then click the **OK** button (if necessary). Internet Explorer starts and opens the Crosstab Web page. See the Session 8.1 Visual Overview.

   **Trouble?** If Internet Explorer does not appear in the program list but another Web browser does appear, click the name of that browser. When you use another Web browser, your screens might look slightly different from the screen shown in the figure.

Changes that employees make to the Panorama database will not appear in the Crosstab Web page that you created because it is a **static Web page**—that is, it reflects the state of the qryCustomersAndInvoicesCrosstab query in the Panorama database at the time you created it. If data in the qryCustomersAndInvoicesCrosstab query changes, you will need to export the query as an HTML document again.

Because this static Web page is not linked to the qryCustomersAndInvoicesCrosstab query on which it is based, you cannot use your browser to make changes to its data. Before closing the Crosstab Web page, you'll try to change one of its field values.

**To attempt to change a field value, and then close the browser:**

1. Double-click **Holland** in the City column for the sixth record, and then type **D**. The value of Holland remains highlighted and unchanged because the Crosstab Web page is a static page.
2. Click the **Close** button on the Internet Explorer window title bar to close it and to return to Windows Explorer.
3. Click the **Close** button on the Windows Explorer window title bar to close it and to return to Access.

   **Trouble?** If the Access window is not active on your screen, click the Microsoft Access program button on the taskbar.

Sarah has a file containing customer billing addresses that she needs to add to the Panorama database. Instead of typing these billing addresses into new records, she asks you to import the data into the Panorama database.

## Importing a CSV File as an Access Table

For most customers, the Address, City, State, and Zip fields in the tblCustomer table identify both the customer's location and billing address, which is where Belmont Landscapes sends the customer's invoices. In a few cases, however, the billing address is different from the location address; additionally, the company name used for billing purposes might be different from the company name stored in the tblCustomer table. Sarah has been maintaining an Excel workbook containing customer billing data, and she's exported the data to a CSV file. A **CSV (comma-separated values) file** is a text file in which commas separate values, and each line is a record containing the same number of values in the same positions.

REFERENCE

*Importing a CSV File as an Access Table*

- In the Import & Link group on the External Data tab on the Ribbon, click the Text File button to open the Get External Data - Text File dialog box.
- Click the Browse button in the dialog box, navigate to the location where the file to import is stored, click the filename, and then click the Open button.
- Click the Import the source data into a new table in the current database option button, and then click the OK button.
- In the Import Text Wizard dialog box, click the Delimited option button, and then click the Next button.
- Make sure the Comma option button is selected. If appropriate, click the First Row Contains Field Names check box to select it, and then click the Next button.
- For each field, if necessary, select the column, type its field name and select its data type, and then click the Next button.
- Choose the appropriate option button to let Access create a primary key, to choose your own primary key, or to avoid setting a primary key, click the Next button, type the table name in the Import to Table box, and then click the Finish button.

Access can import data from a CSV file directly into a database table. Sarah's CSV file is named Billing, and you'll import it as a table into the Panorama database.

## To import the CSV file as an Access table:

1. Click the **External Data** tab on the Ribbon, and then in the Import & Link group, click the **Text File** button (with the ScreenTip "Import text file") to open the Get External Data - Text File dialog box.
2. Click the **Browse** button, navigate to the **Access2\Tutorial** folder, click **Billing**, click the **Open** button, and then click the **Import the source data into a new table in the current database** option button (if necessary). The selected path and filename appear in the File name box. See Figure 8-3.

**Figure 8-3** Get External Data - Text File dialog box

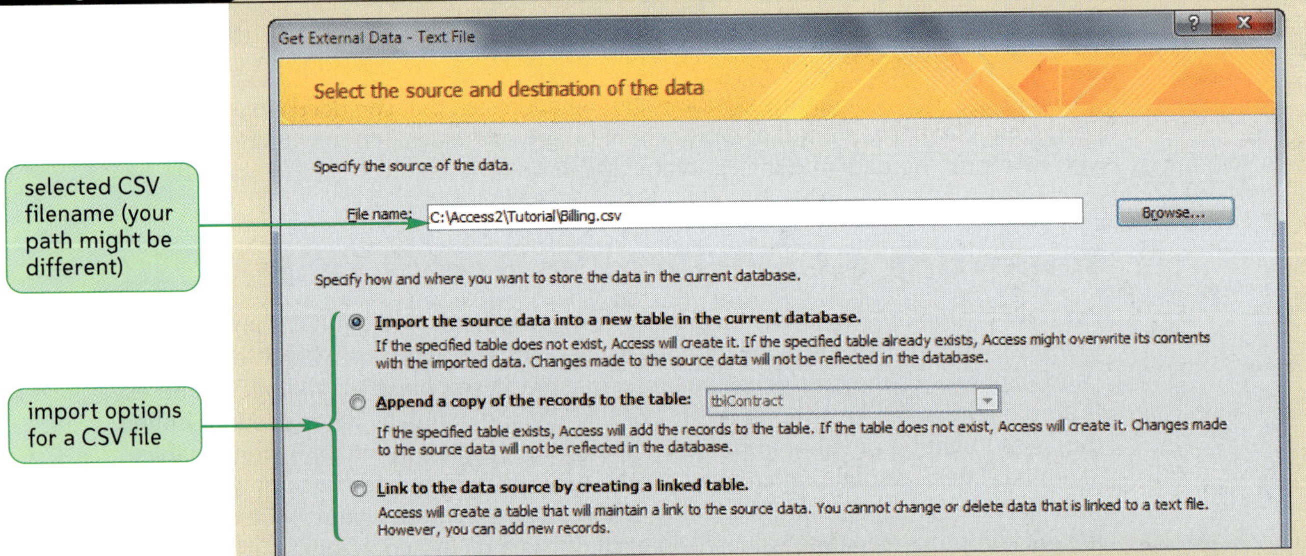


The dialog box provides options for importing the data into a new table in the database, appending a copy of the data to an existing table in the database, and linking to the source data. In the future, Sarah wants to maintain the customer billing data in the Panorama database, instead of using her Excel workbook, so you'll import the data into a new table.

3. Click the **OK** button to open the first Import Text Wizard dialog box, in which you designate how to identify the separation between field values in each line in the source data. The choices are the use of commas, tabs, or another character to separate, or delimit, the values, or the use of fixed width columns with spaces between each column. The wizard has correctly identified that values are delimited by commas.
4. Click the **Next** button to open the second Import Text Wizard dialog box, in which you verify the delimiter for values in each line. See Figure 8-4.

**Figure 8-4** Verifying the delimiter for values in the CSV file

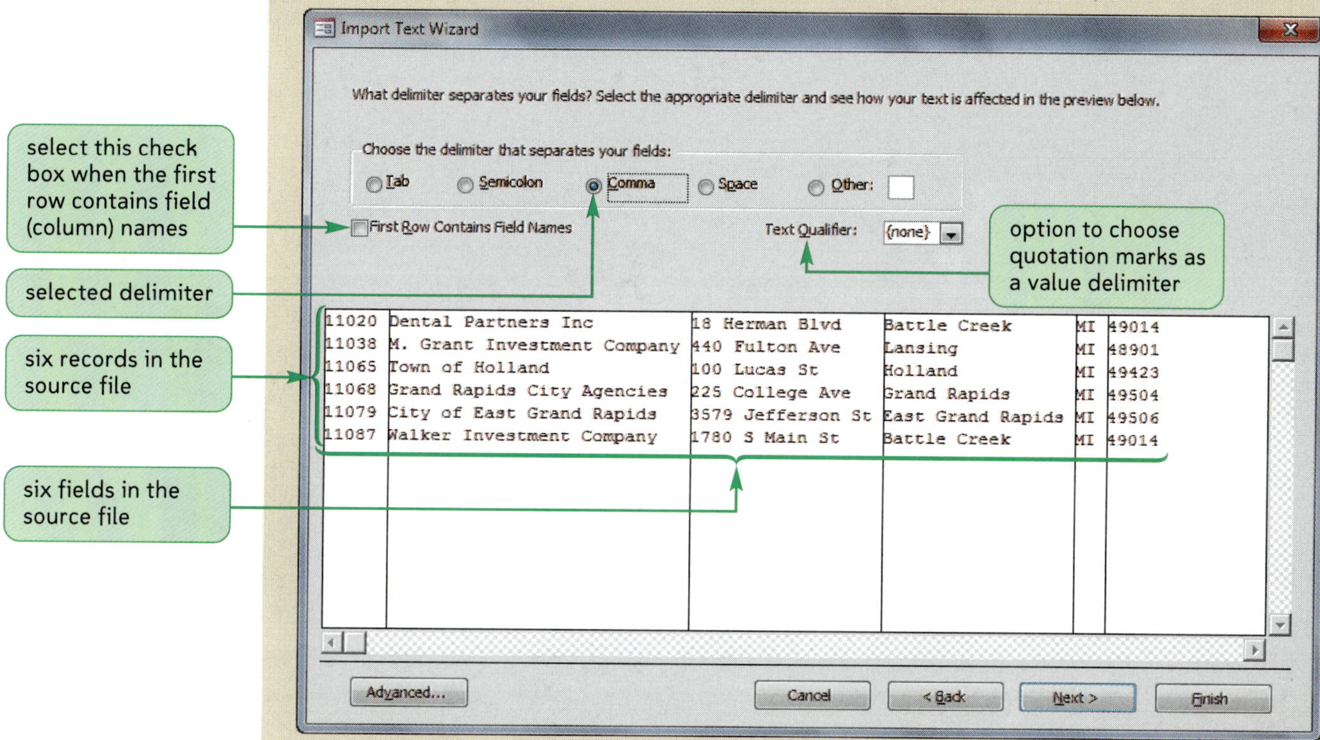


The CSV source file contains six records with six fields in each record. A comma serves as the delimiter for values in each line, so the Comma option button is selected. The first row in the source file contains the first record, not field names, so the First Row Contains Field Names check box is not checked. If the source file uses either single or double quotation marks to enclose values, you would click the Text Qualifier arrow to choose the appropriate option.

5. Click the **Next** button to open the third Import Text Wizard dialog box, in which you enter the field name and set other properties for the imported fields. You will import all fields from the source file and use the default data type and indexed settings for each field, except for the first field's data type.

6. Type **CustomerID** in the Field Name box, click the **Data Type** arrow, click **Text** in the list, and then click **Field2** in the table list. CustomerID (partially hidden) is the heading for the first column in the table list, and the second column is selected.

7. Repeat Step 6 for the rightmost five columns, making sure Text is the data type for all fields, typing **BillingCompany**, **BillingAddress**, **BillingCity**, **BillingState**, and **BillingZip** in the Field Name box. See Figure 8-5.

**Figure 8-5** After setting field names for the six fields in the source file

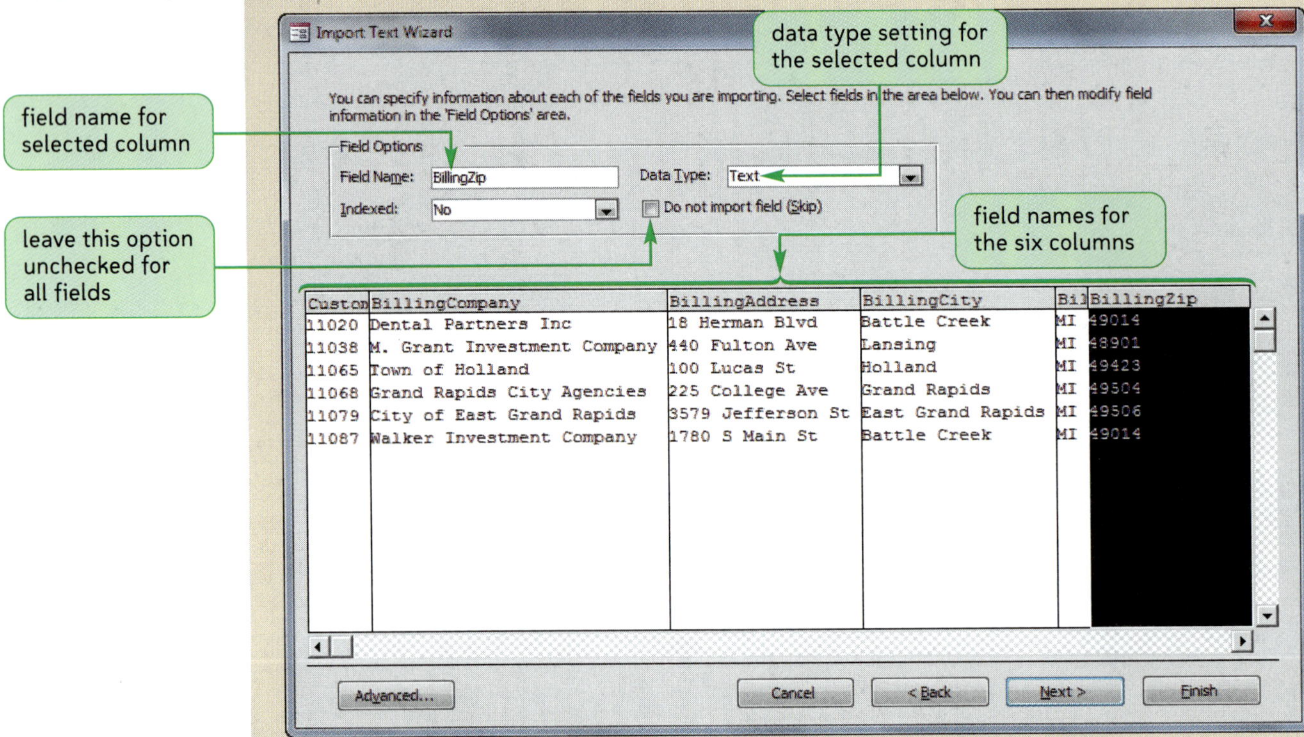


8. Click the **Next** button to open the fourth Import Text Wizard dialog box, in which you select the primary key for the imported table. CustomerID, the first column, will be the primary key. When you select this column as the table's primary key, Access will delete the ID column it created.

9. Click the **Choose my own primary key** option button, make sure **CustomerID** appears in the box for the option, click the **Next** button, type **tblCustomerBilling** as the table name in the Import to Table, click the **I would like a wizard to analyze my table after importing the data** check box to select it, and then click the **Finish** button. An Import Text Wizard dialog box opens asking if you want to analyze the table.

After importing data and creating a new table, you can use the Import Text Wizard to analyze the imported table. When you choose this option, you start the Table Analyzer.

## Analyzing a Table with the Table Analyzer

**TIP**

Read the Normalization section in the appendix titled "Relational Databases and Database Design" for more information about normalization and third normal form.

The **Table Analyzer** analyzes a single table and, if necessary, splits it into two or more tables that are in third normal form. The Table Analyzer looks for redundant data in the table. When the Table Analyzer encounters redundant data, it removes redundant fields from the table and then places the redundant fields in new tables.

**TIP**

You can start the Table Analyzer directly by clicking the Database Tools tab, and then clicking the Analyze Table button in the Analyze group.

### To use the Table Analyzer to analyze the imported table:

1. Click the **Yes** button to close the dialog box and to open the first Table Analyzer Wizard dialog box. The diagram and explanation in this dialog box describe the problem when duplicate data is stored in a table.
2. Click the first **Show me an example** button [»], read the explanation, close the example box, click the second **Show me an example** button [»], read the explanation, close the example box, and then click the **Next** button to open the second Table Analyzer Wizard dialog box. The diagram and explanation in this dialog box describe how the Table Analyzer solves the duplicate data problem.
3. Click the first **Show me an example** button [»], read the explanation, close the example box, click the second **Show me an example** button [»], read the explanation, close the example box, and then click the **Next** button to open the third Table Analyzer Wizard dialog box. In this dialog box, you choose whether to let the wizard decide which fields go in what tables, if the table is not already normalized. You'll let the wizard decide.
4. Make sure the **Yes, let the wizard decide** option button is selected, and then click the **Next** button. A message box informs you that the wizard does not recommend splitting the table because the table is normalized and does not contain redundant data.
5. Click the **Cancel** button to close the message box, exit the wizard, and return to the Get External Data - Text File dialog box, in which you are asked if you want to save the import steps. You don't need to save these steps because you're importing the data only this one time.
6. Click the **Close** button to close the dialog box.

The tblCustomerBilling table is now listed in the Tables section in the Navigation Pane. You'll open the table to verify the import results.

### To open the imported tblCustomerBilling table:

1. Double-click **tblCustomerBilling** in the Navigation Pane to open the table datasheet, resize all columns to their best fit, and then click **11020** in the first row in the CustomerID column to deselect all values. See Figure 8-6.

Figure 8-6 **Imported tblCustomerBilling table datasheet**

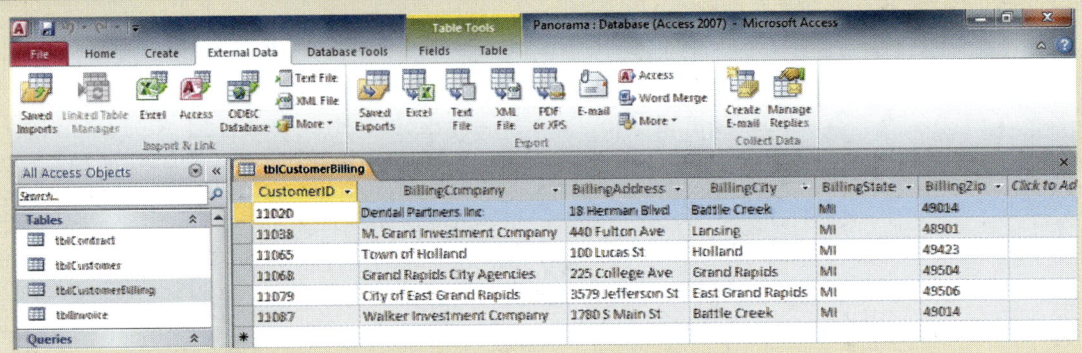

2. Save and close the table.

Sarah has some additional data that she wants to import into the Panorama database. The data is stored in XML format.

# Using XML

Belmont Landscapes has contacts in the building trade industry and gets customer leads from builders when they sell new homes. One of the builders has stored data about several prospective customers available to Sarah in an XML document, which she wants to add to the Panorama database. **XML** (**Extensible Markup Language**) is a programming language that is similar in format to HTML, but is more customizable and suited to the exchange of data between different programs. Unlike HTML, which uses a fixed set of tags to describe the appearance of a Web page, developers can customize XML to describe the data it contains and how that data should be structured.

PROSKILLS

### *Decision Making: Exchanging Data Between Programs*

XML files are used to exchange data between companies, and they are also used to exchange data between programs within a company. For example, you can store data either in an Excel workbook or in an Access table or query, depending on which program works best for the personnel working with the data and the business requirements of the company. Because the XML file format is a common file format for Excel and Access, whenever the data is needed in the other program, you can export the data as an XML file and import the file into the other program. You should consider the needs of the users and the characteristics of the programs they use when deciding the best means for exchanging data between programs.

## Importing an XML File as an Access Table

Access can import data from an XML file directly into a database table. Sarah's XML file is named Prospect, and you'll import it as a table into the Panorama database.

REFERENCE

*Importing an XML File as an Access Table*

- In the Import & Link group on the External Data tab on the Ribbon, click the XML File button to open the Get External Data - XML File dialog box.
- Click the Browse button, navigate to the location for the XML file, click the XML filename, and then click the Open button.
- Click the OK button in the Get External Data - XML File dialog box, click the table name in the Import XML dialog box, click the appropriate option button in the Import Options section, and then click the OK button.
- Click the Close button.

  *or*

  If you need to save the import steps, click the Save import steps check box, enter a name for the saved steps in the Save as box, and then click the Save Import button.

Now you will import the Prospect XML document as an Access database table.

## To import the XML document as an Access table:

1. Click the **External Data** tab on the Ribbon (if necessary), and then in the Import & Link group, click the **XML File** button (with the ScreenTip "Import XML file"). The Get External Data - XML File dialog box opens.
2. Click the **Browse** button, navigate to the **Access2\Tutorial** folder, click **Prospect**, and then click the **Open** button. The selected path and filename now appear in the File name box.
3. Click the **OK** button. The Import XML dialog box opens. See Figure 8-7.

**Figure 8-7** **Import XML dialog box**

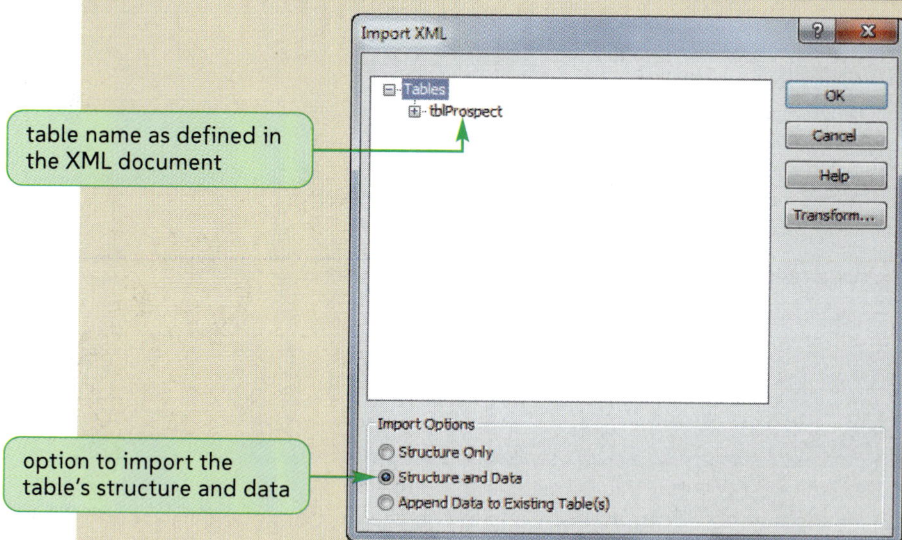


From the XML file, you can import only the table structure to a new table, import the table structure and data to a new table, or append the data in the XML file to an existing table. You'll import the table structure and data to a new table named tblProspect.

4. Make sure the **Structure and Data** option button is selected, click **tblProspect** in the box, and then click the **OK** button. The Import XML dialog box closes, and the last Get External Data - XML File dialog box is displayed.

Before reviewing the imported table, you'll save the import steps.

## Saving and Running Import Specifications

If you need to repeat the same import procedure many times, you can save the steps for the procedure and expedite future imports by running the saved import steps without using a wizard. Because the builder intends to send Sarah additional lists of prospective customers in the future, you'll save the import steps for Sarah.

### To save and run the XML file import steps:

1. Click the **Save import steps** check box to select it. The dialog box displays additional options for the save operation. See Figure 8-8.

**Figure 8-8** Saving the import steps

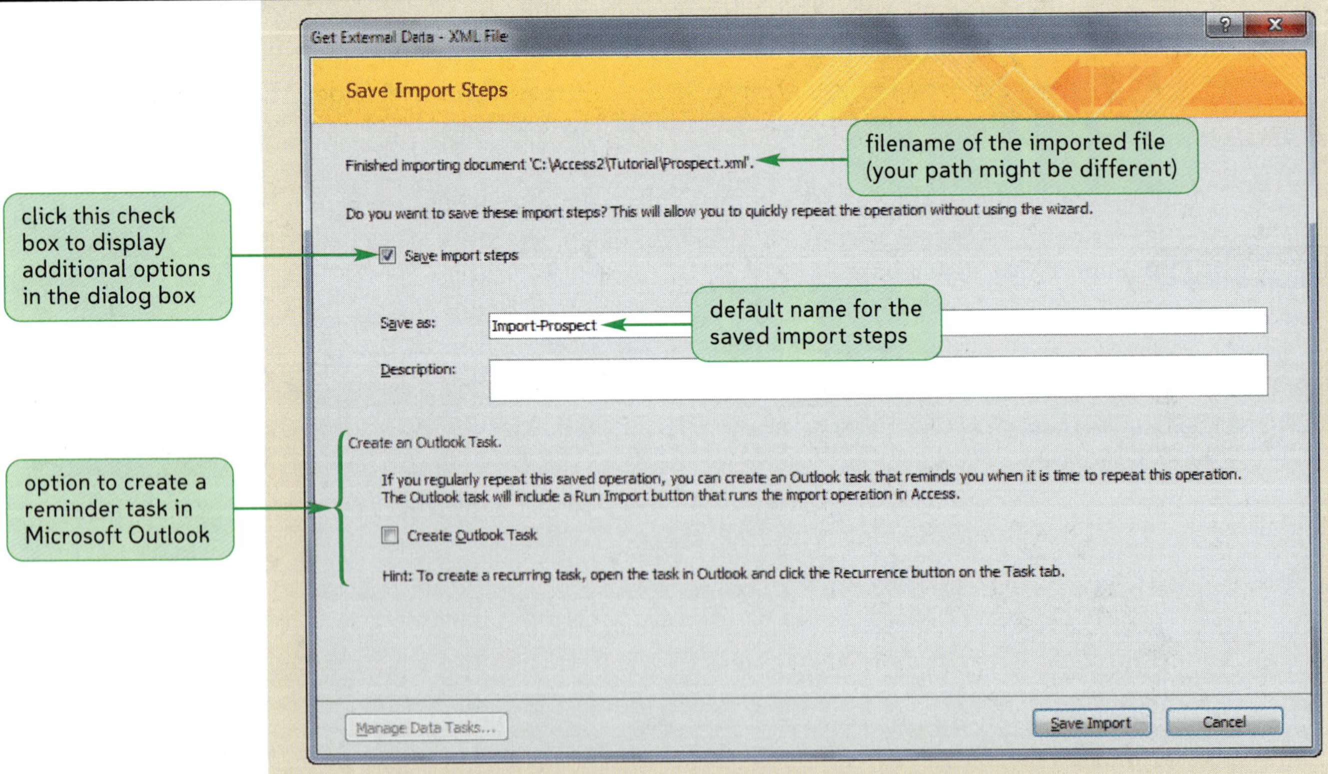


After displaying additional options in the dialog box, you can accept the default name for the saved import steps or choose one that you create, and you can enter an optional description. If the import will occur on a set schedule, you can also create a reminder task in Microsoft Outlook. You'll accept the default name for the saved steps, and you won't enter a description or schedule an Outlook task.

**TIP**

The table name is tblProspect, not Prospect, because the table name is tblProspect within the XML file.

2. Click the **Save Import** button. The import steps are saved as Import-Prospect, the Get External Data - XML File dialog box closes, the tblProspect table is imported into the Panorama database, and the table is now listed in the Navigation Pane.

   You'll now show Sarah how she can run the saved steps when she receives customer prospects from the builder in the future.

3. In the Import & Link group on the External Data tab, click the **Saved Imports** button. The Manage Data Tasks dialog box opens. See Figure 8-9.

**Figure 8-9** Manage Data Tasks dialog box

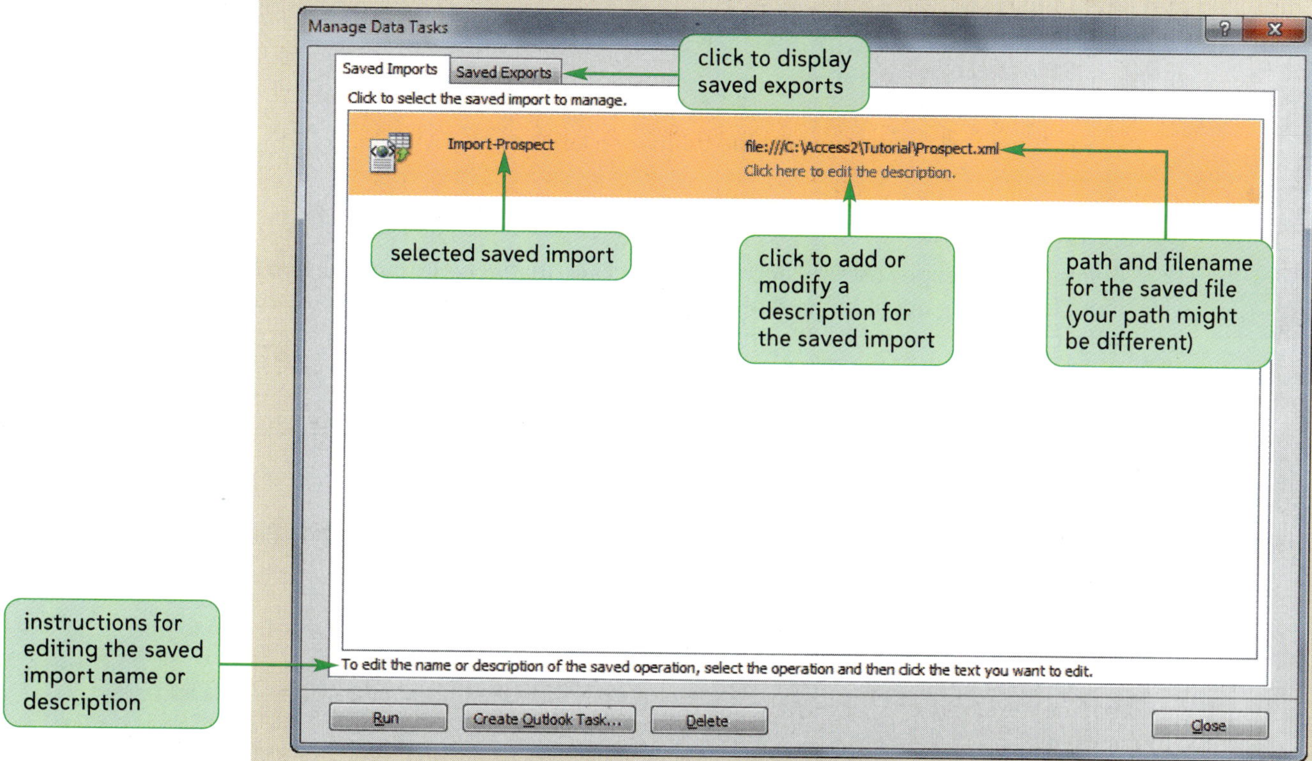


In this dialog box, you can change the saved import name, add or change its description, create an Outlook task for the saved import, run a saved import, or delete a saved import. You can also manage any saved export by clicking the Saved Exports tab. You'll add a description for the saved procedure and review the list of saved exports.

4. Click the **Click here to edit the description** text to open a box that contains the insertion point, type **Builder's XML file of customer prospects**, click an unused portion of the orange selection band to close the box and accept the typed description, and then click the **Saved Exports** tab. You have not saved any export steps, so no saved exports are displayed.
5. Click the **Close** button to close the Manage Data Tasks dialog box.
6. Double-click the **tblProspect** table in the Navigation Pane to open the table datasheet, close the Navigation Pane, resize all columns to their best fit, and then click **12001** in the first row in the CustomerID column to deselect all values. See Figure 8-10.

**Figure 8-10** Imported tblProspect table datasheet

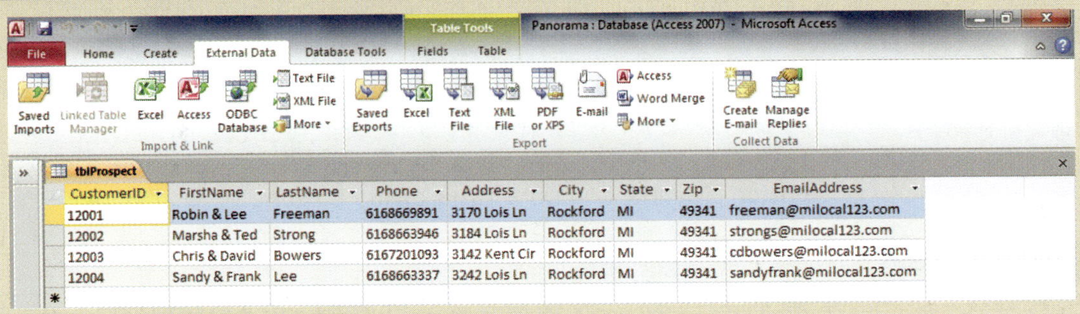


7. Save and close the table.

Sarah next asks you to export the tblInvoice table as an XML file.

## Exporting an Access Table as an XML File

Belmont Landscapes uses an accounting package that accepts the data in XML files as input for making accounting entries. Sarah wants to test this capability by exporting the tblInvoice table as an XML file and giving the XML file to the company's accounting manager for testing with the accounting package.

REFERENCE

### *Exporting an Access Object as an XML File*

- Right-click the object (table, query, form, or report) in the Navigation Pane, point to Export, and then click XML File.
  *or*
  Click the object (table, query, form, or report) in the Navigation Pane. In the Export group on the External Data tab, click XML File button.
- Click the Browse button in the Export - XML File dialog box, navigate to the location where you will save the XML file, and then click the Save button.
- Click the OK button in the dialog box, select the options in the Export XML dialog box or click the More Options button and select the options in the expanded Export XML dialog box, and then click the OK button.
- Click the Close button.
  *or*
  If you need to save the export steps, click the Save export steps check box, enter a name for the saved steps in the Save as box, and then click the Save Export button.

You can now export the tblInvoice table as an XML file.

**To export the tblInvoice table as an XML file:**

1. Open the Navigation Pane, right-click **tblInvoice** in the Navigation Pane, point to **Export** on the shortcut menu, and then click **XML File**. The Export - XML File dialog box opens.
2. Click the **Browse** button, navigate to the **Acess2\Tutorial** folder, change the name in the File name box to **Invoice**, and then click the **Save** button. The selected path and filename now appear in the File name box in the Export - XML File dialog box.

3. Click the **OK** button. The Export XML dialog box opens.

   Clicking the More Options button in the Export XML dialog box expands the dialog box and lets you view and change detailed options for exporting a database object to an XML file.

4. Click the **More Options** button to reveal detailed export options in the Export XML dialog box. See Figure 8-11.

**Figure 8-11 Data tab in the Export XML dialog box**

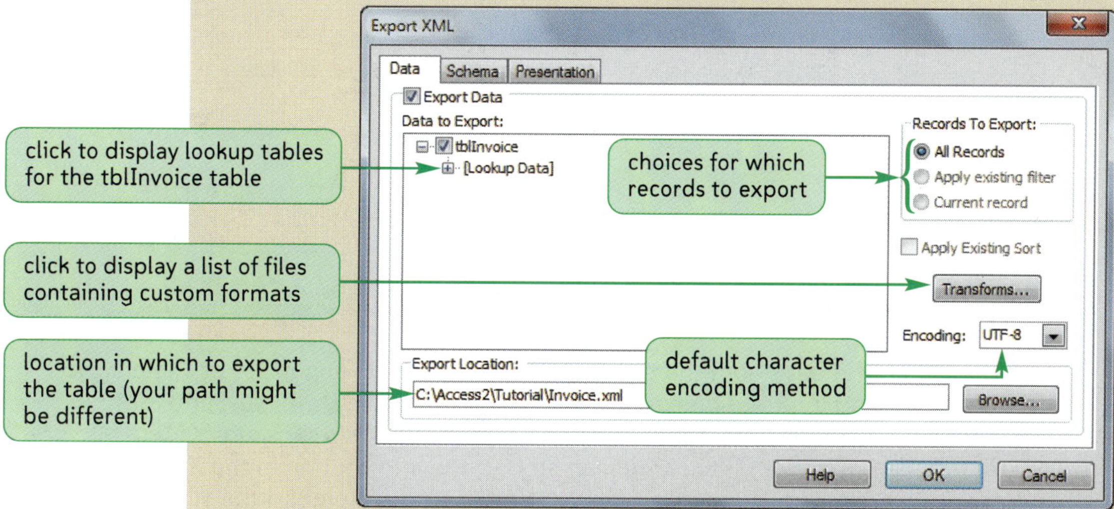


The Export Data check box, the Export Location box, and the Records To Export option group display the selections you made in the previous step. You're exporting all records from the tblInvoice table, including the data in the records and the structure of the table, to the Invoice.xml file in the Access2\Tutorial folder. The encoding option determines how characters will be represented in the exported XML file. The encoding choices are UTF-8, which uses 8 bits to represent each character, and UTF-16, which uses 16 bits to represent each character. You can also click the Transforms button if you have a special file that contains instructions for changing the exported data.

The accounting package doesn't have a transform file and requires the default encoding, but Sarah wants to review the tables that contain lookup data.

5. Click the plus box to the left of [Lookup Data]. The tblContract table contains lookup data because it's the primary table in the one-to-many relationship with the related tblInvoice table. The accounting package requirements don't include any lookup data from the tblContract table, so make sure the tblContract check box is not checked.

The Data tab settings are correct, so you'll verify the Schema tab settings.

6. Click the **Schema** tab. See Figure 8-12.

**Figure 8-12** **Schema tab in the Export XML dialog box**

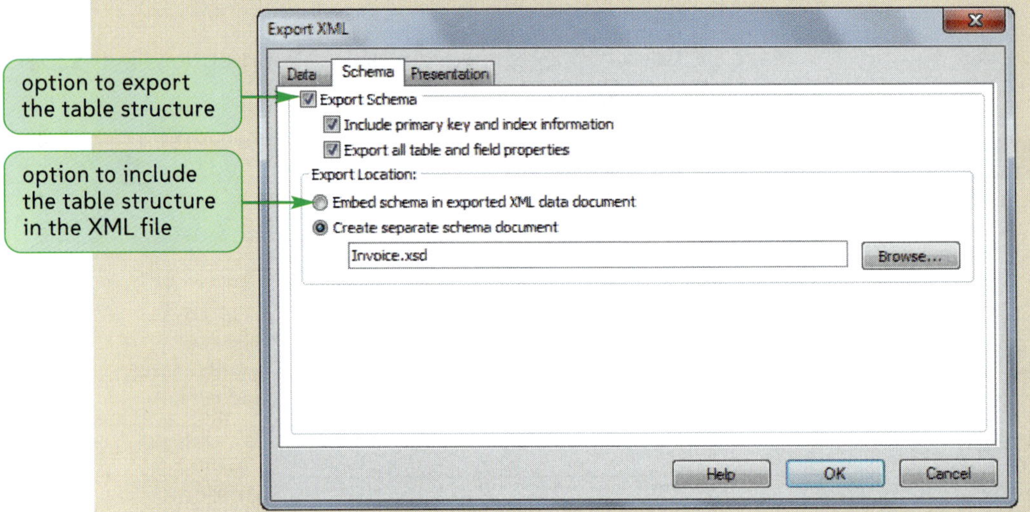


Along with the data from the tblInvoice table, you'll be exporting its table structure, including information about the table's primary key, indexes, and table and field properties. You can include this information in a separate **XSD** (**XML Structure Definition**) file, or you can embed the information in the XML file. The accounting package expects a single XML file, so you'll embed the structure information in the XML file.

7. Click the **Embed schema in exported XML data document** option button to select that option and to dim the "Create separate schema document" option, and then click the **Presentation** tab. See Figure 8-13.

**Figure 8-13** **Presentation tab in the Export XML dialog box**

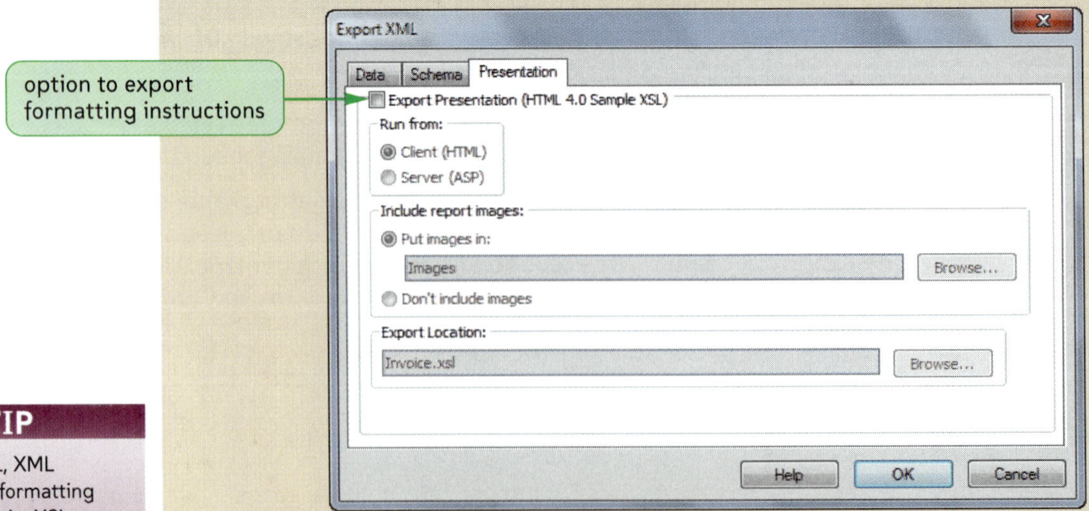


**TIP**

Unlike HTML, XML provides no formatting information. An XSL file provides formatting instructions so that a browser or another program can display the XML data file in a readable way.

The Presentation tab options let you export a separate **XSL** (**Extensible Stylesheet Language**) file containing the format specifications for the tblInvoice table data. The accounting package will import the tblInvoice table data directly into its computer program, which contains its own formatting instructions, so you will not export an XSL file.

8. Make sure that the **Export Presentation (HTML 4.0 Sample XSL)** check box is not checked, and then click the **OK** button. Access closes the Export XML dialog box, exports the data in the tblInvoice table as an XML file in the Access2\Tutorial folder, and returns you to the final Export - XML File dialog box.

Sarah plans to make further tests exporting the tblInvoice table as an XML file, so you'll save the export steps.

INSIGHT

*Importing and Exporting Data*

You've imported data from an Excel workbook and a text file (.txt extension) in Tutorial 2 and from a text file (.csv extension) and an XML file in this tutorial. Additional Access options include importing an object from another Access database, importing data from other databases (dBASE and ODBC databases such as SQL Server), and importing an HTML document, an Outlook folder, or a SharePoint list.

In addition to exporting Access objects as an XML file or an HTML document, Access includes options for exporting data to another Access database, other databases (ODBC database or dBASE), an Excel workbook, a text file, a Word document, a SharePoint list, or a PDF or XPS file. You can also "export" table or query data to Word's mail merge feature, or export an object to an e-mail message.

The steps you follow for all import and export options work similar to the import and export steps you've used in this tutorial and in Tutorial 2. For example, to save an object as an XPS file, right-click the name of the object you want to export in the Navigation Pane, point to Export on the shortcut menu, click PDF or XPS, navigate to the folder where you want to store the file, click the Save as type arrow, click XPS Document, click the Publish button, and then click the Close button.

## Saving and Running Export Specifications

Saving the steps to export the tblInvoice table as an XML file will save time and eliminate errors when Sarah repeats the export procedure. You'll save the export steps and then show Sarah how to run the saved export steps.

### To save and run the XML file export steps:

1. Click the **Save export steps** check box. The dialog box displays additional options for the save operation.

   The dialog box has the same options you saw earlier when you saved the XML import steps. You'll enter a description, and you won't create an Outlook task because Sarah will be running the saved export steps on an as needed basis.

2. In the Description box, type **XML file accounting entries from the tblInvoice table**. See Figure 8-14.

**Figure 8-14** Saving the export steps

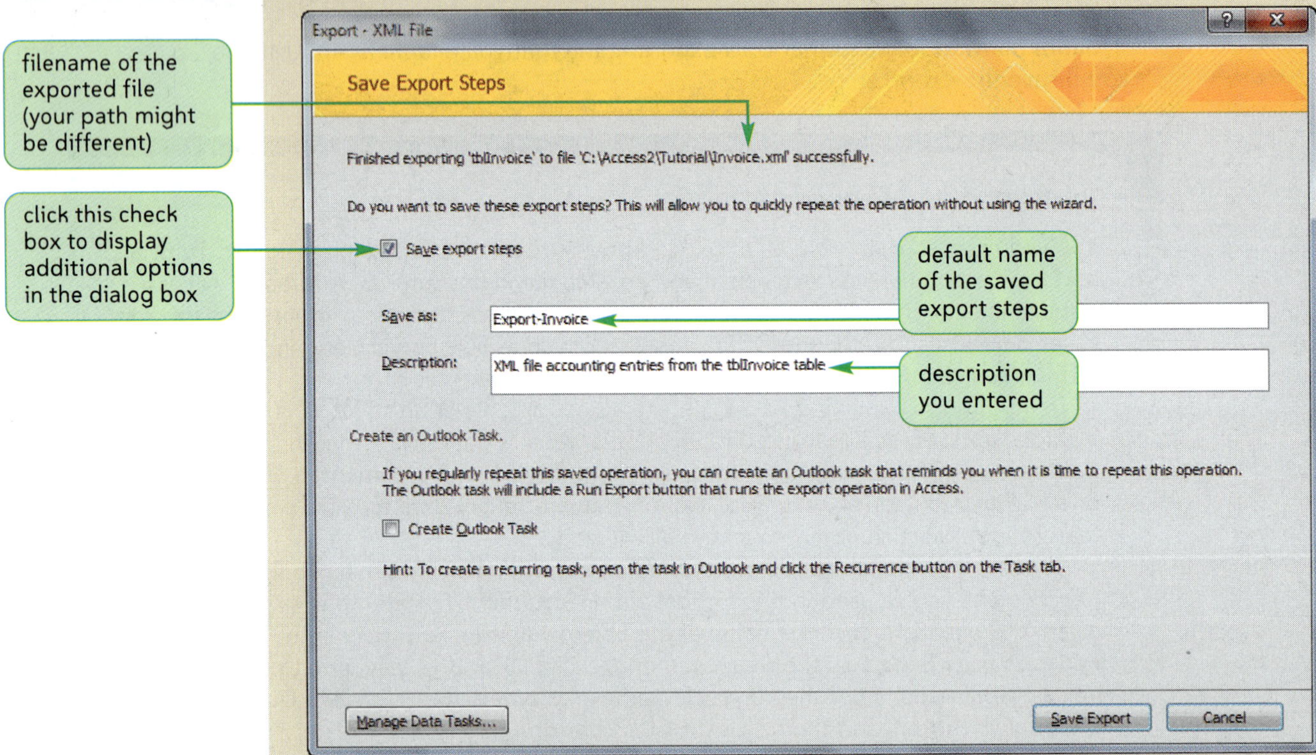


3. Click the **Save Export** button. The export steps are saved as Export-Invoice, the Export - XML File dialog box closes, and the tblInvoice table is exported as an XML file named Invoice.

   You'll now show Sarah how she can run the saved steps.

4. Click the **External Data** tab on the Ribbon (if necessary), and in the Export group, click the **Saved Exports** button. The Manage Data Tasks dialog box opens. See Figure 8-15.

**Figure 8-15** Manage Data Tasks dialog box

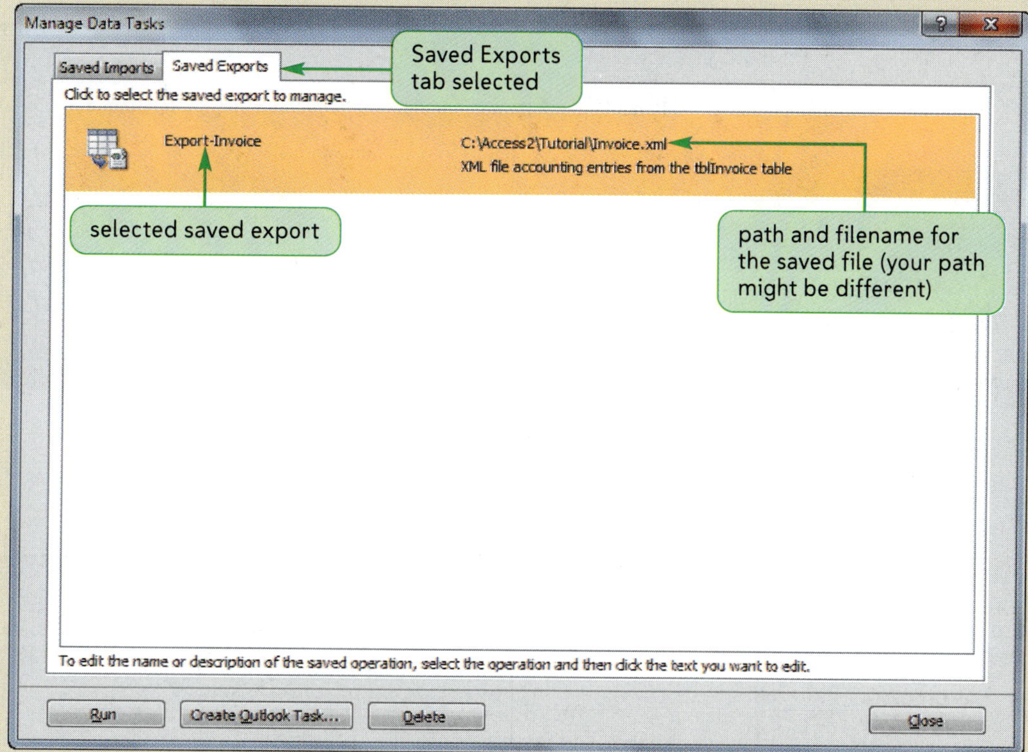


5. Click the **Run** button. The saved procedure runs, and a message box opens, asking if you want to replace the existing XML file you created earlier.
6. Click the **Yes** button to replace the existing XML file. A message box informs you that the export was completed successfully.
7. Click the **OK** button to close the message box, and then click the **Close** button to close the Manage Data Tasks dialog box.
8. If you are not continuing on to the next session, close the Panorama database.

You've imported and exported data, analyzed a table's design, and saved and run import and export specifications. In the next session, you will analyze data by working with a chart, PivotTable, PivotChart, and linked data, and you will add a tab control to a form.

REVIEW

## *Session 8.1 Quick Check*

1. What is HTML?
2. What is an HTML template?
3. What is a static Web page?
4. What is a CSV file?
5. What is the Table Analyzer?
6. ______________ is a programming language that describes data and its structure.

# SESSION 8.2 VISUAL OVERVIEW

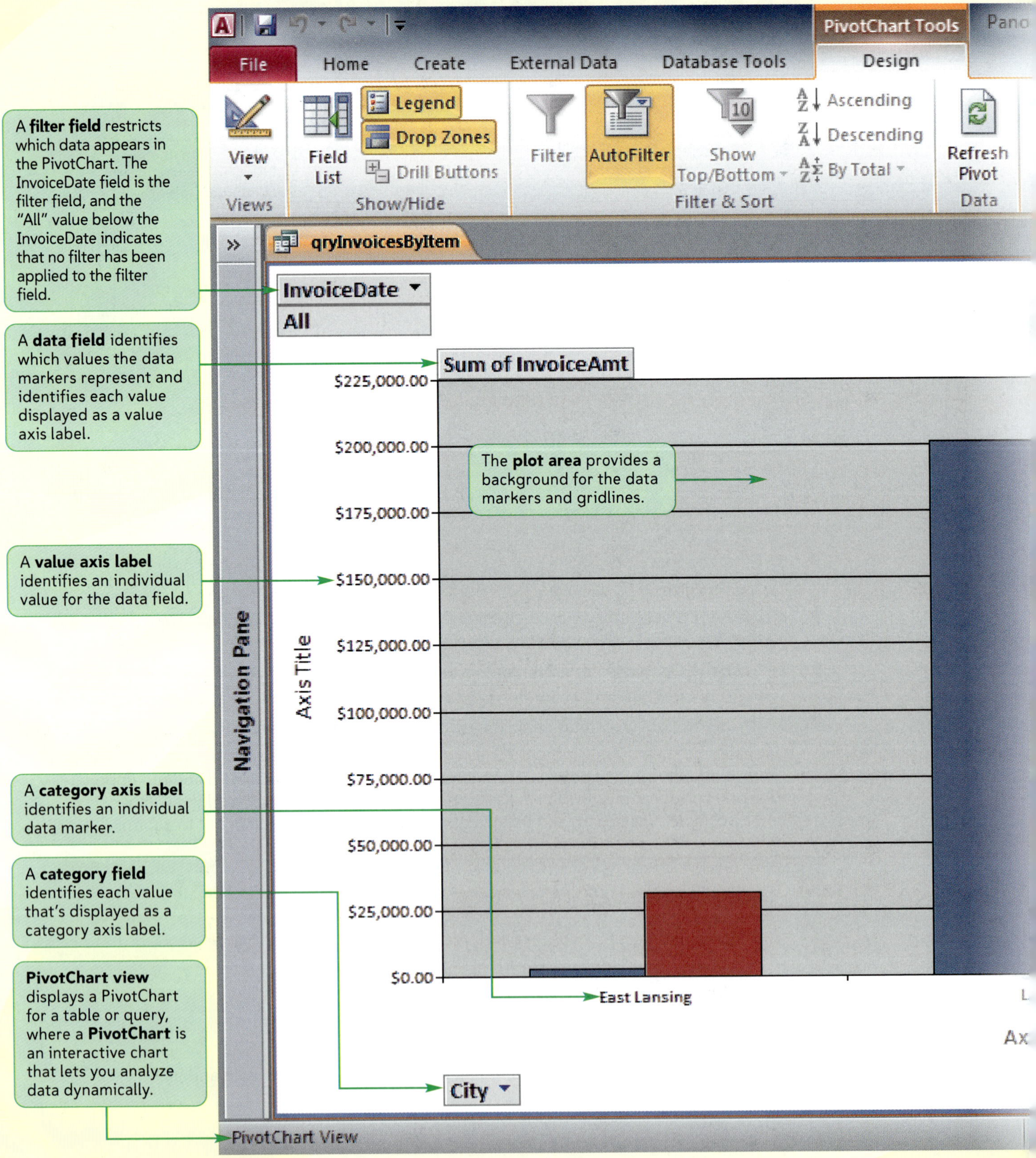

# FILTERED PIVOTCHART

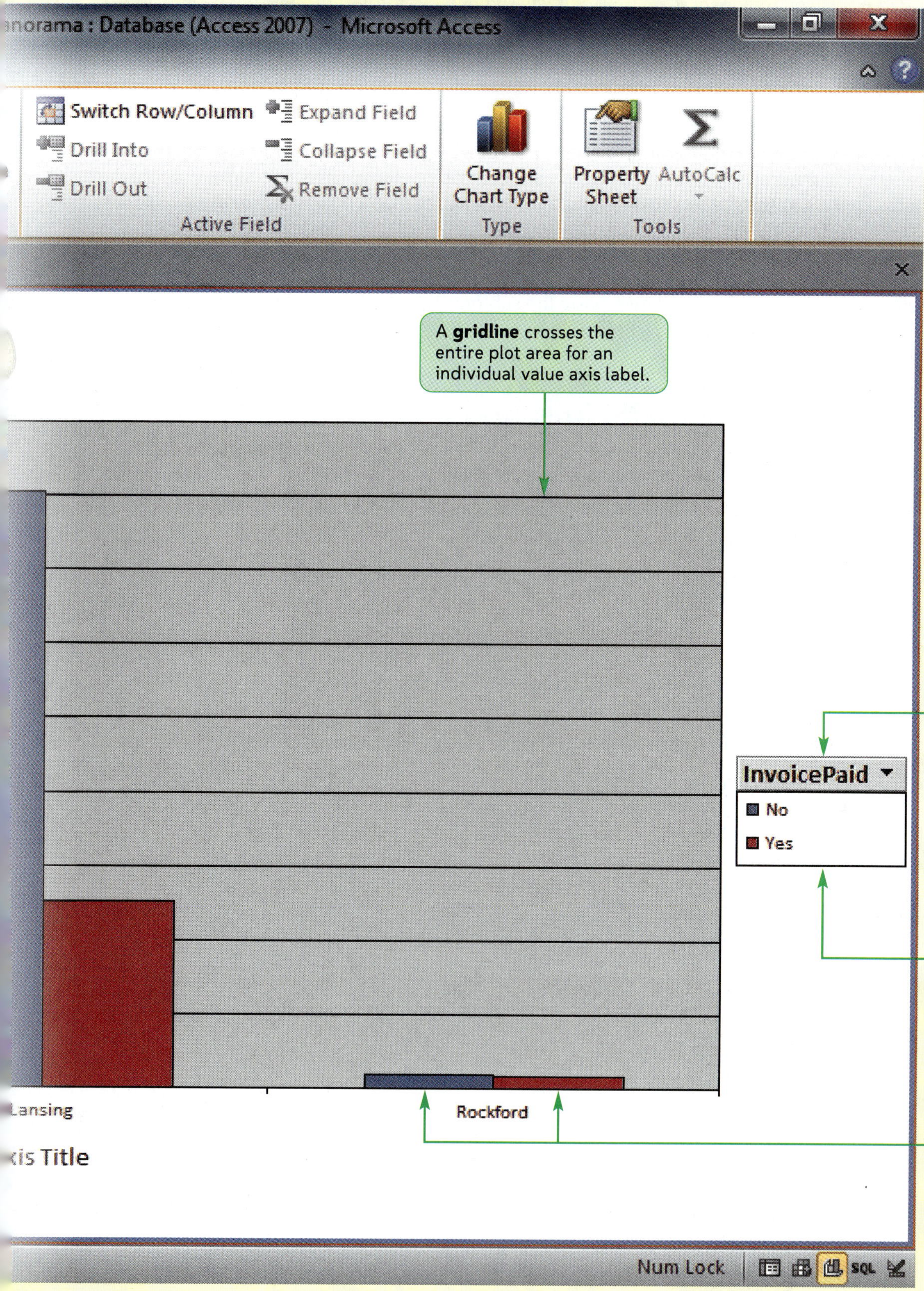


A **gridline** crosses the entire plot area for an individual value axis label.

A **series field** identifies the data markers' subdivisions or splits. The InvoicePaid field is the current series field, and each pair of markers represents the two values for the InvoicePaid field.

The **legend** is an optional list of the series field values, identifying how these values are identified on the data markers. The blue bars represent unpaid invoices (No value), and the red bars represent paid invoices (Yes value).

A **data marker** is a bar, dot, segment, or other symbol that represents a single data value.

# Creating a Multi-page Form Using a Tab Control

Sarah wants you to enhance the frmContractsAndInvoices form to display two pages—with the form on one page, and a chart on the other page—to create a multi-page form. The first page will contain the frmInvoiceSubform subform that is currently positioned at the bottom of the frmContractsAndInvoices form. The second page will contain a chart showing the invoice amounts for the invoices associated with the displayed contract.

You can create a multi-page form in two ways: use the **Page Break tool** to insert a page break control in the form, or use the **Tab Control tool** to insert a control that's called a tab control. If you insert a page break control in a form, users can move between the form pages by pressing the Page Up and Page Down keys. If you use a tab control, the control appears with tabs at the top, with one tab for each page. Users can switch between pages by clicking the tabs.

To expedite placing the subform in the tab control, you'll cut the subform from the form, add the tab control, and then paste the subform into the left tab on the tab control. You need to perform these steps in Design view.

### To add the tab control to the form:

1. If you took a break after the previous session, make sure that the Panorama database is open and the Navigation Pane is open.
2. Open the **frmContractsAndInvoices** form in Design view, and then close the Navigation Pane.
3. Right-click the top edge of the subform control to open the shortcut menu, and then click **Cut** to delete the subform control and place it on the Clipboard.

   **Trouble?** If you do not see Subform in New Window as one of the options on the shortcut menu, you did not click the top edge of the subform control correctly. Right-click the top edge of the subform control until you see this option on the shortcut menu, and then click Cut.
4. In the Controls group on the Design tab, click the **Tab Control** tool .
5. Position the + portion of the pointer in the Detail section three grid dots from the left edge of the grid and at the 2.5-inch mark on the vertical ruler, and then click the mouse button. Access places a tab control with two pages in the form.
6. Right-click in the middle of the tab control, and when an orange outline appears inside the tab control, click **Paste** on the shortcut menu. The subform is pasted in the tab control. See Figure 8-16.

**Figure 8-16** **Subform on the tab control in the Detail section**

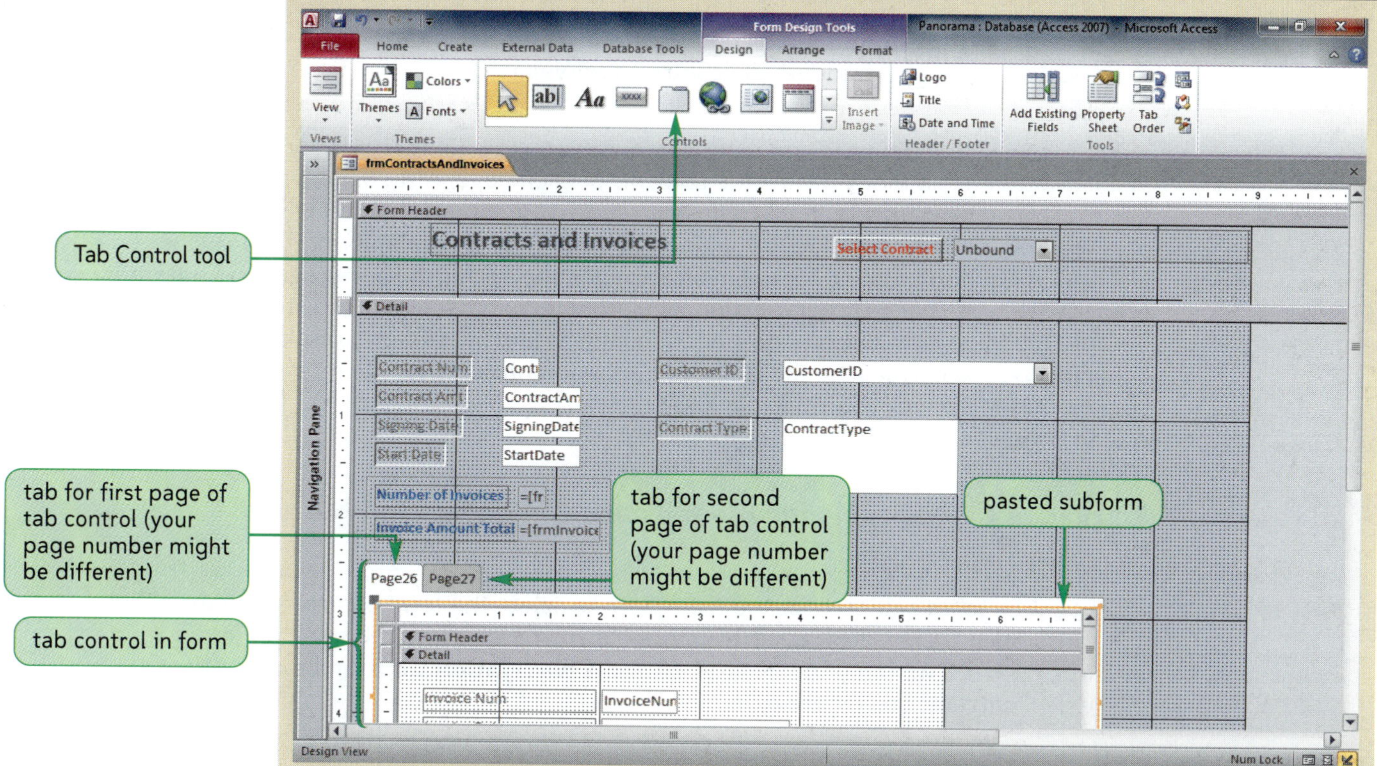


7. Switch to Form view, and then click **3011** in the ContractNum text box to deselect all controls. The left tab, which represents the first page in the tab control, is the active tab. See Figure 8-17.

**Figure 8-17** **Subform on the tab control in Form view**

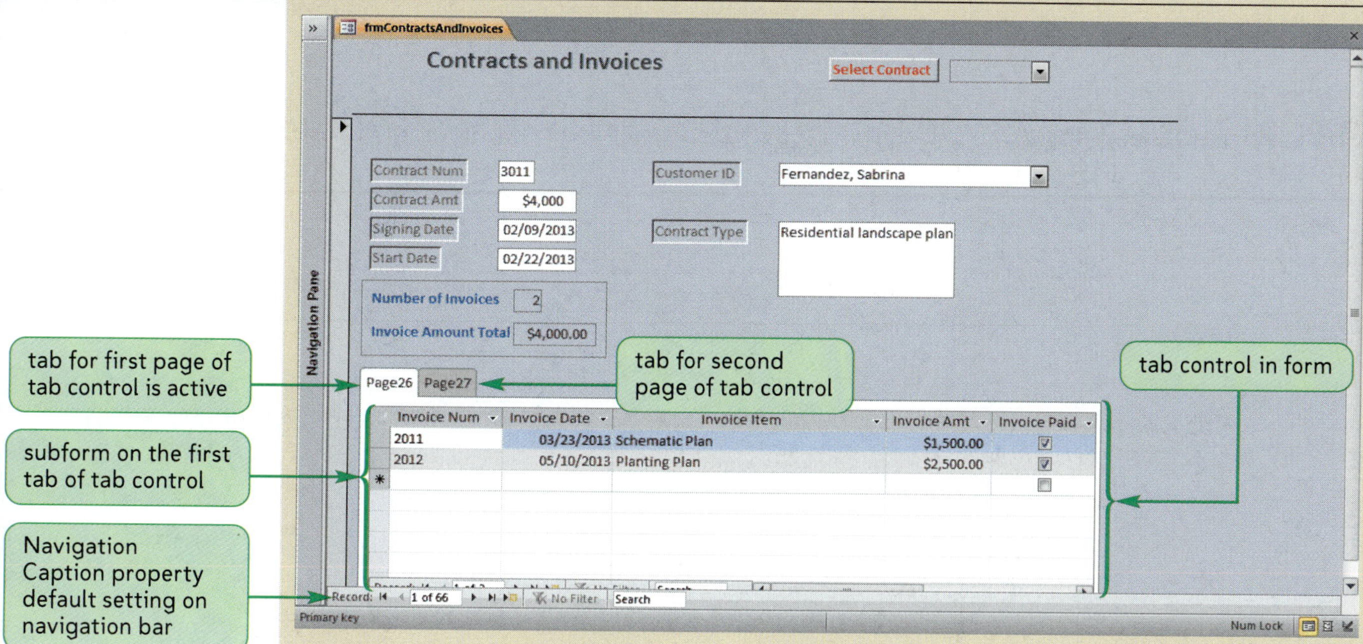

The subform is now displayed on the first page of the tab control and its design is the same as it was before you cut and pasted it to the tab control.

8. Click the **right tab** of the tab control to display the second page, which is empty because you haven't added any controls to it yet.

After viewing the form in Form view, Sarah asks you to edit the labels for the tabs in the tab control, so they indicate the contents of each page. Also, Sarah's staff finds the two sets of navigation buttons confusing—they waste time determining which set of navigation buttons applies to the subform and which to the main form. You'll set the Navigation Caption property for the main form and the subform. The **Navigation Caption property** lets you change the navigation label from the word "Record" to another value. Because the main form displays data about contracts and the subform displays data about invoices, you'll change the Navigation Caption property for the main form to "Contract" and for the subform to "Invoice."

### To change the captions for the tabs and the navigation buttons:

1. Switch to Design view.
2. Click the **form selector** for the main form to select the form control in the main form, open the property sheet to display the properties for the selected form control, click the **All** tab (if necessary), click the **Navigation Caption** box, and then type **Contract**. See Figure 8-18.

**Figure 8-18** Setting the Navigation Caption property for the main form

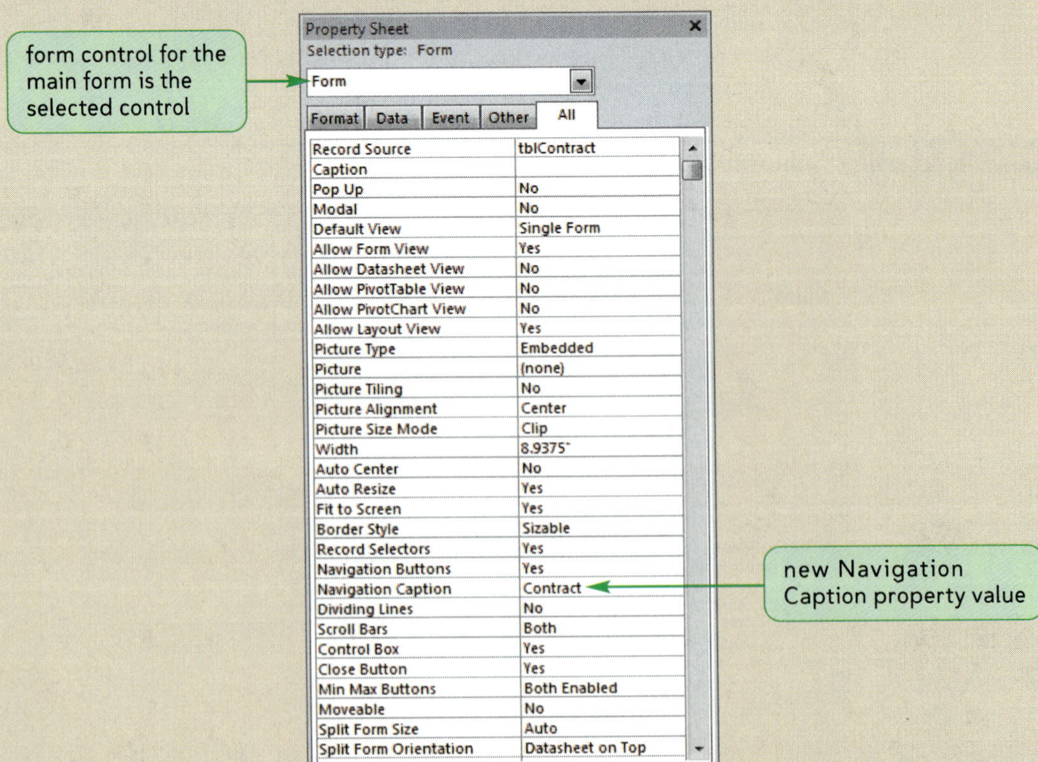

3. Click the **form selector** for the subform to select the subform, click the **form selector** for the subform again to select the form control in the subform and display the properties for the selected form control, click the **Navigation Caption** box, and then type **Invoice**. Navigation buttons don't appear in Design view, so you won't see the effects of the Navigation Caption property settings until you switch to Form view.
4. Click the **left tab** in the subform, click the **left tab** in the subform again to select it, type **Invoice Data** in the Caption box on the property sheet, and then press the **Tab** key. The Caption property value now appears in the left tab. See Figure 8-19.

**Figure 8-19** Setting the Caption property for the left tab

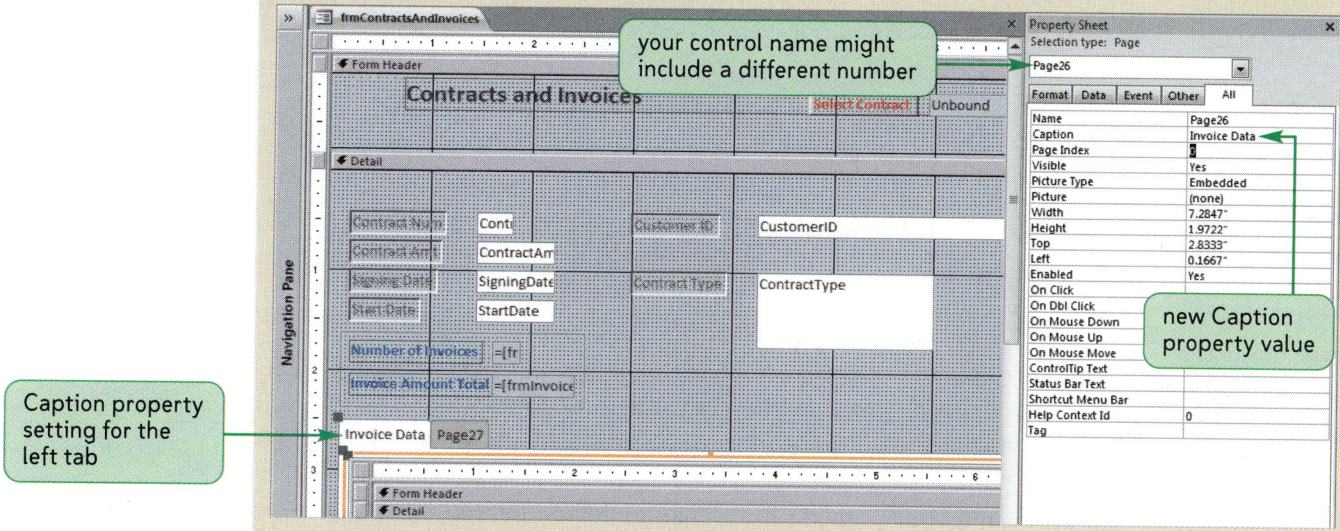


5. Click the **right tab** in the subform to select it, type **Invoice Chart** in the Caption box, and then close the property sheet.
6. Save your form design changes, switch to Form view, click **3011** in the ContractNum text box to deselect all controls, and then scroll to the bottom of the form. The tabs and the navigation buttons now display the new caption values. See Figure 8-20.

**Figure 8-20** **Subform on the tab control in Form view**

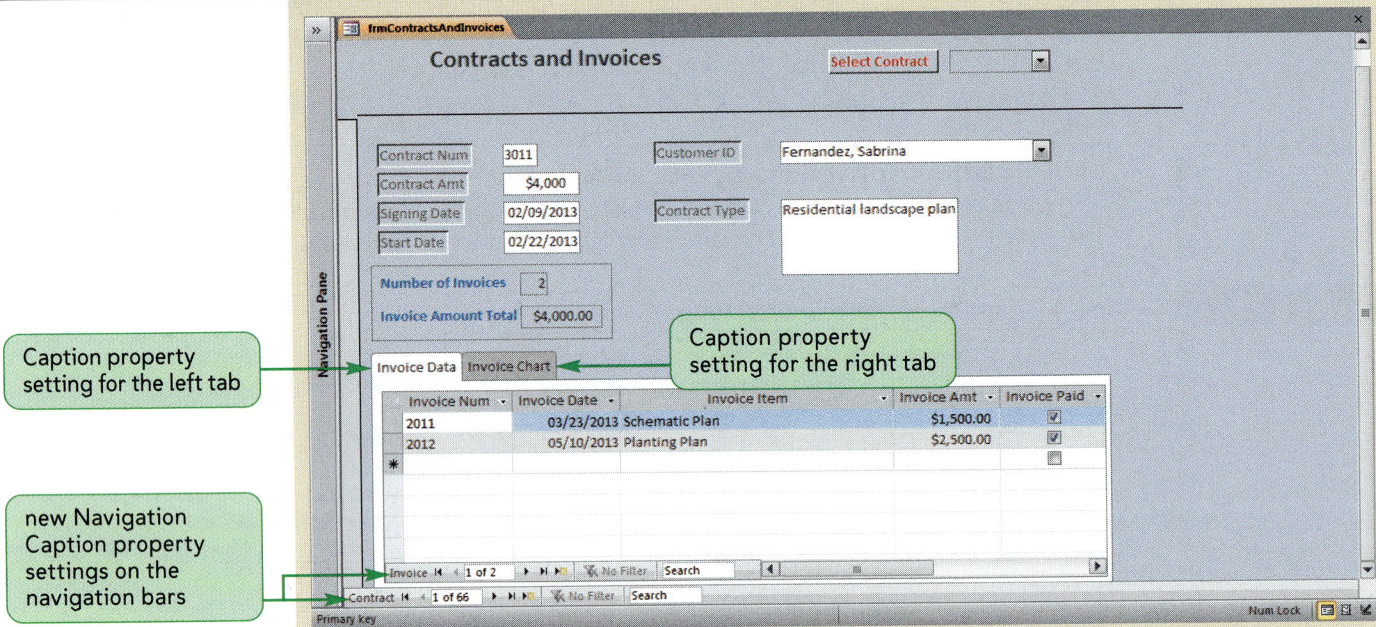


The tab control's height has increased the form's height, so you no longer can view the entire form on screen without scrolling. You can either decrease the tab control's height, or view the form with a minimized Ribbon. Until you finish the contents of the right tab, you won't decide which approach works best.

Sarah wants you to add a simple chart to the second page of the tab control.

## Integrating Access with Other Programs

When you create a form or report in Access, you include more than just the data from the record source table or query. You've added controls such as lines, rectangles, tab controls, and graphics in your forms and reports to improve their appearance and usability. You can also add charts, drawings, and other objects to your forms and reports, but Access doesn't have the capability to create them. Instead, you create these other objects using other programs and then place them in a form or report using the appropriate integration method.

When you integrate information between programs, the program containing the original information, or object, is called the **source program**, and the program in which you place the information created by the source program is called the **destination program**. Access offers three ways for you to integrate objects created by other programs.

- **Importing**. When you import an object, you include the contents of a file in a new table or append it to an existing table, or you include the contents of the file in a form, report, or field. For example, in Tutorial 2 you added a picture to a form, or imported it into the form, and in this tutorial you imported CSV and XML files as new tables in the Panorama database. The imported picture is a file with a .bmp extension that was created by a graphics program, and the CSV and XML files were created by other programs. After importing an object, it no longer has a connection to the program that created it. Any subsequent changes you make to the object using the source program are not reflected in the imported object.

- **Embedding**. When you embed an object in a form, report, or field, you preserve its connection to the source program, which enables you to edit the object, if necessary, using the features of the source program. Any changes you make to the object are reflected only in the form, report, or field in which it is embedded; the changes do not affect the original object in the file from which it was embedded. Likewise, if you start the source program outside Access and make any changes to the original object, these changes are not reflected in the embedded object.
- **Linking**. When you link an object to a form, report, or field, you include a connection in the destination program to the original file maintained by the source program; you do not store data from the file in the destination program. Any changes you make to the original file using the source program are reflected in the linked file version in the destination program.

PROSKILLS

*Decision Making: Importing, Embedding, and Linking Data*

How do you decide which method to use when you need to include in an Access database data that is stored in another file or format? When you intend to use Access to maintain the data and no longer need an updated version of the data with the source program, you can import a file as a new table or append the records in the file to an existing table. You link to the data when the source program will continue to maintain the data in the file, and you need to use an updated version of the file at all times in the destination program. When linking to the data, you can also maintain the data using the destination program, and the source program will always use the updated version of the file.

For objects in forms or reports, you import an object (such as a picture) when you want a copy of the object in your form or report and you don't intend to make any changes to the object. You embed or link an object when you want a copy of the object in your form or report and you intend to edit the object using the source program in the future. You embed the object when you do not want your edits to the object in the destination program to affect any other copies of the object used by other programs. You link the object when you want your edits to the object in the destination program to affect the object used by other programs.

The decision to import, embed, or link to data depends on how you will use the data in your database, and what connection is required to the original data. You should carefully consider the effect of changes to the original data and to the copied data before choosing which method to use.

Sarah wants you to embed a chart on the second page of the tab control.

## Embedding a Chart in a Form

The Chart Wizard in Access helps you to embed a chart in a form or report. The chart is actually created by another program, Microsoft Graph, but the Chart Wizard does the work of embedding the chart. After embeddng the chart in a form or report, you can edit it using the Microsoft Graph program.

REFERENCE

*Embedding a Chart in a Form or Report*

- In the Controls group on the Design tab in Design view, click the More button, and then click the Chart tool.
- Position the + portion of the pointer where you want to position the upper-left corner of the chart, and then click the mouse button to start the Chart Wizard.
- Select the record source, fields, and chart type.
- Edit the chart contents, and select the fields that link the object and chart, if necessary.
- Enter a chart title, select whether to include a legend, and then click the Finish button.

The tblInvoice table contains the information needed for the chart Sarah wants you to include in the form's right tab in the tab control.

**To add a chart in the tab control and start the Chart Wizard:**

1. Switch to Design view, and then click the **Invoice Chart** tab on the tab control, if necessary.
2. In the Controls group on the Design tab, click the **More** button, click the **Chart** tool, and then move the pointer to the tab control. When the pointer is inside the tab control, the rectangular portion of the tab control you can use to place controls is filled in black.
3. Position the + portion of the pointer in the upper-left corner of the black portion of the tab control, and then click the mouse button. Access places a chart control in the form and opens the first Chart Wizard dialog box, in which you select the source record for the chart.

Sarah wants the chart to provide her staff with a simple visual display of the relative proportions of the invoice amounts for the invoices for the currently displayed contract. You'll use the tblInvoice table as the record source for the chart and select the InvoiceDate and InvoiceAmt fields as the fields to use in the chart.

**To create the chart with the Chart Wizard:**

1. Click **Table: tblInvoice** in the box, and then click the **Next** button to display the second Chart Wizard dialog box.
2. Select the **InvoiceDate** and the **InvoiceAmt** fields, and then click the **Next** button to display the third Chart Wizard dialog box, in which you choose the chart type.
3. Click the **Pie Chart** button (row 4, column 1) to select the pie chart as the chart type to use for Sarah's chart. See Figure 8-21.

**TIP**

The box on the right displays a brief description of the selected chart type.

Figure 8-21 Selecting the chart type

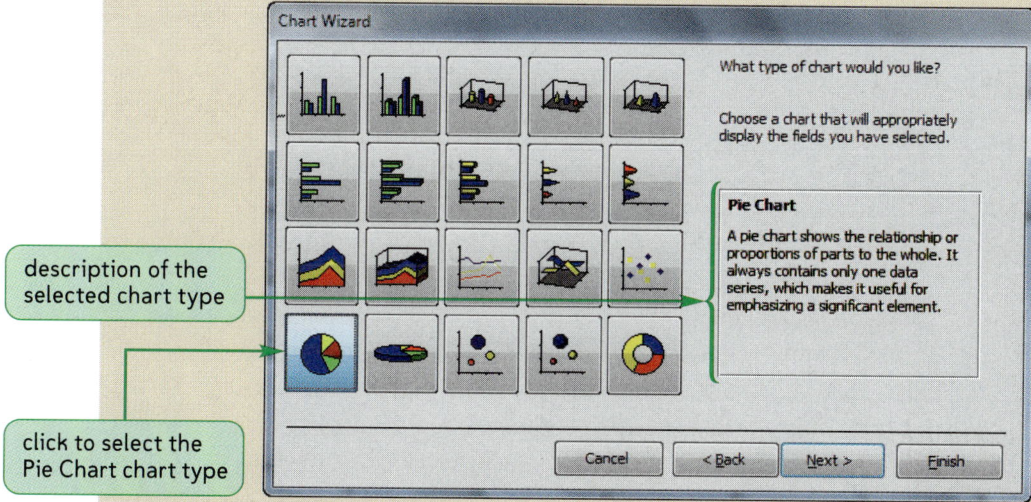


4. Click the **Next** button to display the next Chart Wizard dialog box, in which you preview the chart and modify the data and its placement in the chart. Because visualizing the chart from the displayed preview is difficult, you'll use the default layout based on the two selected fields. You can easily modify the chart after you create it.
5. Click the **Next** button to display the next Chart Wizard dialog box, in which you choose the fields that link records in the main form (the main form uses the tblContract table as its record source) to records in the chart (the chart uses the tblInvoice table as its record source). ContractNum is the common field linking these two tables, and you can use that field as the linking field even though you didn't select it as a field for the chart.
6. Click the **Next** button to display the final dialog box, in which you enter the title that will appear at the top of the chart and choose whether to include a legend in the chart.
7. Type **Invoices for this Contract**, make sure the **Yes, display a legend** option button is selected, and then click the **Finish** button. The completed chart appears in the tab control.

   You'll view the form in Form view, where it's easier to assess the chart's appearance.
8. Save your form design changes, switch to Form view, scroll down to the bottom of the form (if necessary), navigate to record 5 in the main form, notice the four contracts displayed in the subform, click the **Invoice Chart** tab to display the chart, and then scroll down to the bottom of the form (if necessary). See Figure 8-22.

**Figure 8-22** Embedded chart in Form view

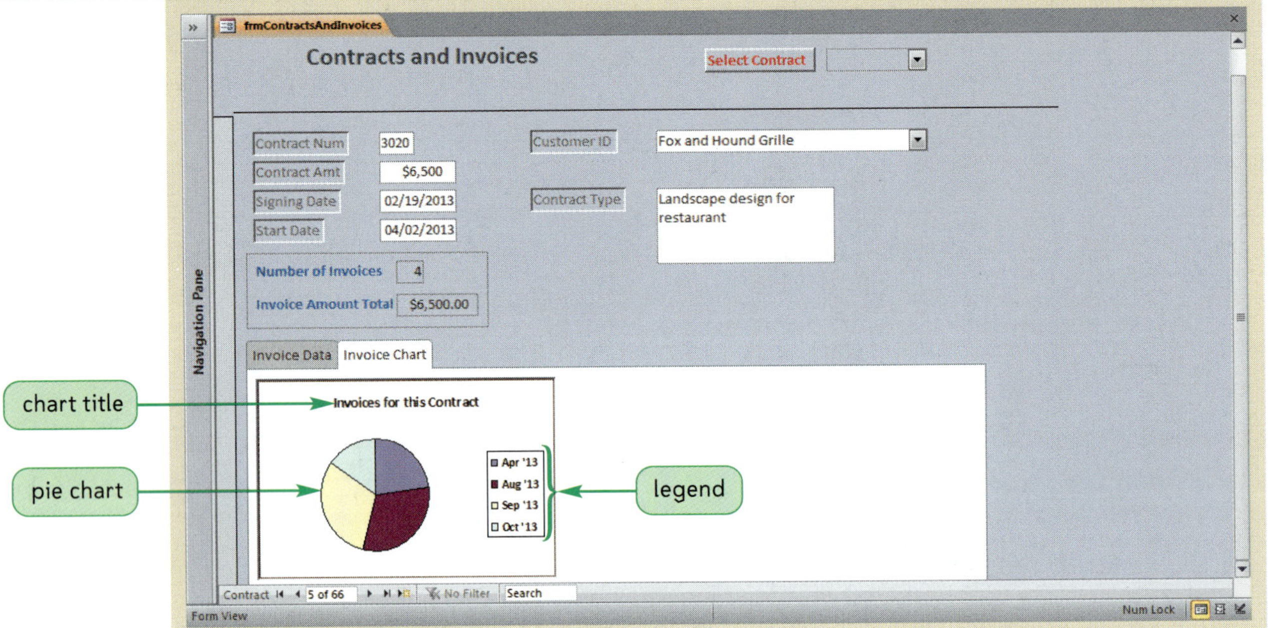


## INSIGHT

### *Linking Record Sources*

The record source for a primary main form must have a one-to-many relationship to the record source for a related subform or chart. The subform or chart object has its Link Master Fields property set to the primary key in the record source to the main form and its Link Child Fields property set to the foreign key in the record source to the subform or chart.

After viewing the chart, Sarah decides it needs some modificiations. She wants you to change the chart type from a pie chart to a bar chart, remove the legend, and modify the chart's background color. You'll make these changes by switching to Design view, and then you'll start Microsoft Graph so you can edit the chart.

### To edit the chart using Microsoft Graph:

If Chart Object doesn't appear on the shortcut menu, right-click the edge until it does.

1. Switch to Design view, right-click an edge of the chart object to open the shortcut menu, point to **Chart Object**, and then click **Open**. Microsoft Graph starts and displays the chart. See Figure 8-23.

**Figure 8-23** Editing the chart with Microsoft Graph

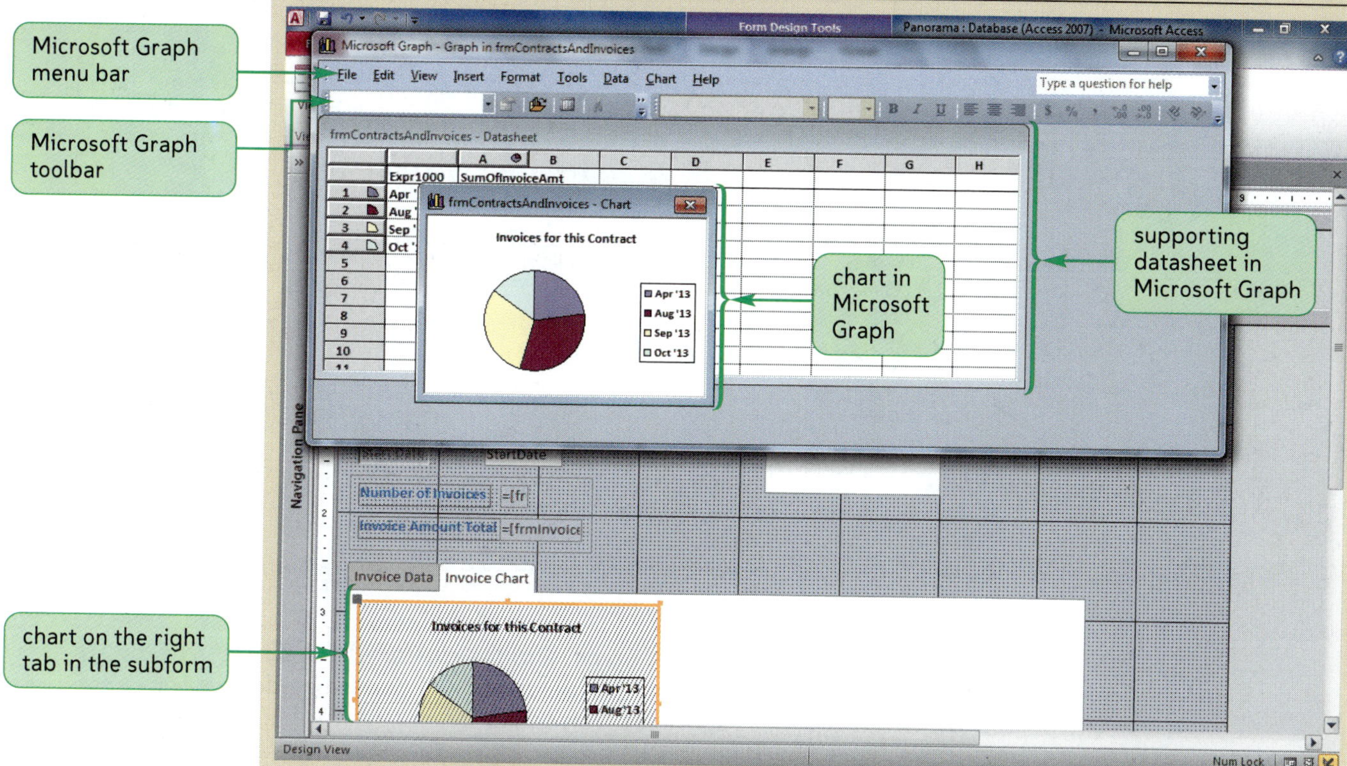


Microsoft Graph is the source program that the Chart Wizard used to create the chart. Because the chart was embedded in the form, editing the chart object starts Graph and allows you to edit the chart using the Graph menu bar and toolbar. In addition to displaying the selected chart, the Graph window displays a datasheet, which contains the data on which the chart is based. You'll now make Sarah's chart changes using Graph.

2. Click **Chart** on the Graph menu bar, click **Chart Type** to open the Chart Type dialog box, and then click **Column** in the Chart type box to display the types of column charts. See Figure 8-24.

**Figure 8-24** **Chart Type dialog box**

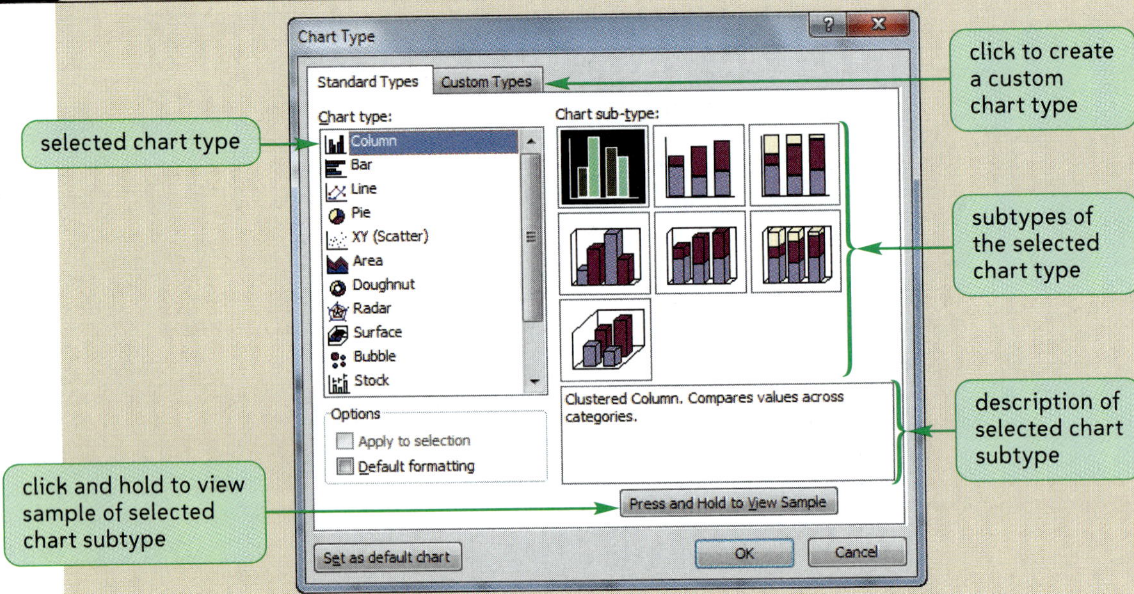


The column chart is the selected chart type, and the clustered column chart is the default chart subtype (row 1, column 1). A description of the selected chart subtype appears below the chart subtypes. You can create a custom chart by clicking the Custom Types tab. If you click and hold down the Press and Hold to View Sample button, you'll see a sample of the selected subtype.

3. Click the **Press and Hold to View Sample** button to view a sample of the chart, release the mouse button, and then click the **OK** button to close the dialog box and change the chart to a column chart in the Graph window and in the form.
4. Click **Chart** on the Graph menu bar, click **Chart Options** to open the Chart Options dialog box, click the **Legend** tab to display the chart's legend options, click the **Show legend** check box to clear it, and then click the **OK** button. The legend is removed from the chart object in the Graph window and in the form.

To change the color or other properties of a chart control—the chart background (or chart area), axes, labels to the left of the y-axis, labels below the x-axis, or data markers (columnar bars for a column chart)—you need to double-click the control.

5. In the Chart window, double-click one of the blue data markers inside the chart to open the Format Data Series dialog box, and then click the orange box (row 2, column 2) in the color palette in the Area section. See Figure 8-25.

**TIP**

A data marker is a bar, dot, segment, or other symbol that represents a single data value.

**Figure 8-25** **Format Data Series dialog box**

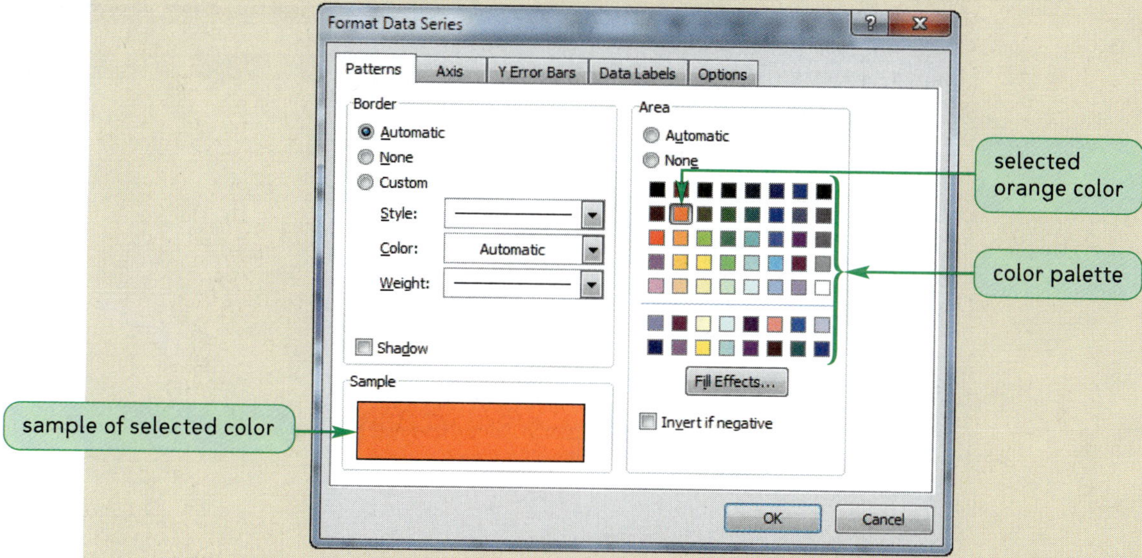


The sample color in the dialog box changes to orange to match the selected color in the color palette.

6. Click the **OK** button to close the dialog box and to change the color of the data markers in the chart in the Graph window and in the form to orange.
7. In the Chart window, double-click the white chart background to the left of the title to open the Format Chart Area dialog box, click the light orange box (row 5, column 2) in the color palette in the Area section, and then click the **OK** button. The chart's background color changes from white to light orange in the chart in the Graph window and in the form.
8. Click **File** on the Graph menu bar, and then click **Exit & Return to frmContractsAndInvoices** to exit Graph and return to the form.
9. Save your form design changes, switch to Form view, double-click the **Home** tab to minimize the Ribbon, navigate to record 5 in the main form, and then click the **Invoice Chart** tab to display the chart. See Figure 8-26.

Figure 8-26 **Completed chart in Form view**

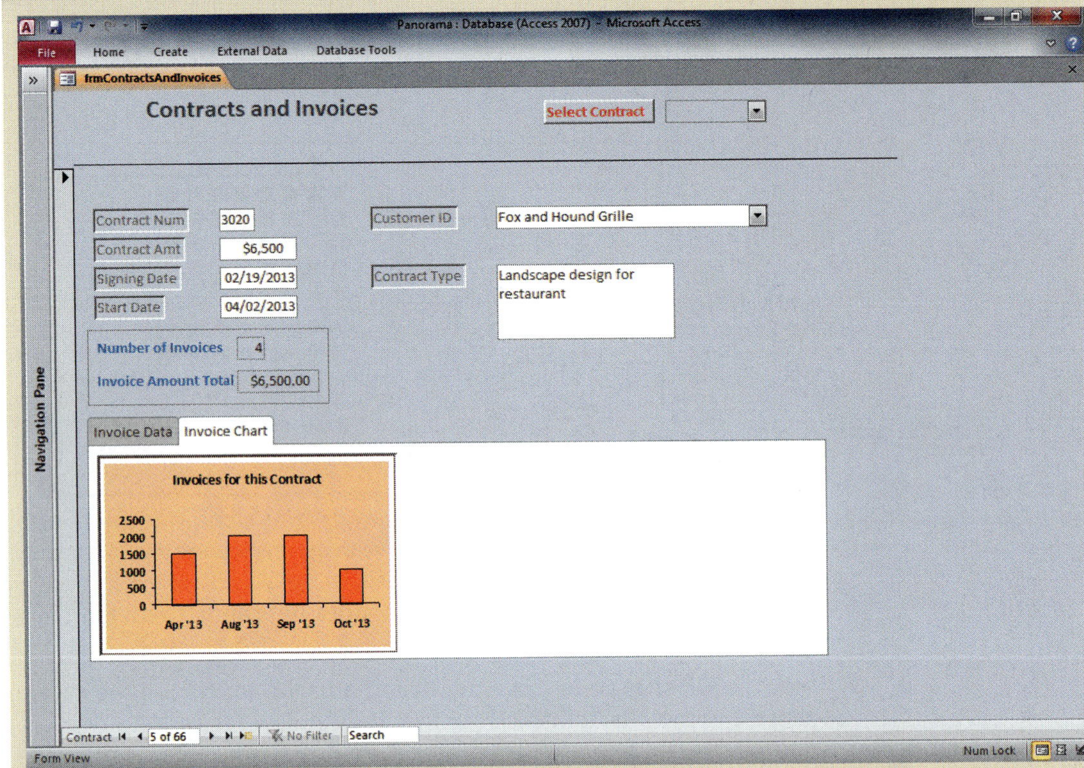


10. Close the form, and then double-click the **Home** tab to restore the Ribbon.

Sarah wants to know if Access has other charting and data analysis tools. You'll show her how to create a PivotTable and a PivotChart.

# Creating and Using a PivotTable

Sarah wants to be able to analyze data in a flexible way. You can use PivotTables to provide the flexible analysis that Sarah needs. A **PivotTable** is an interactive table that lets you analyze data dynamically. You can use a PivotTable to view and organize data from a database, look for summary or detail information, and dynamically change the contents and organization of the table. Figure 8-27 shows a PivotTable.

**Figure 8-27** **Sample PivotTable**

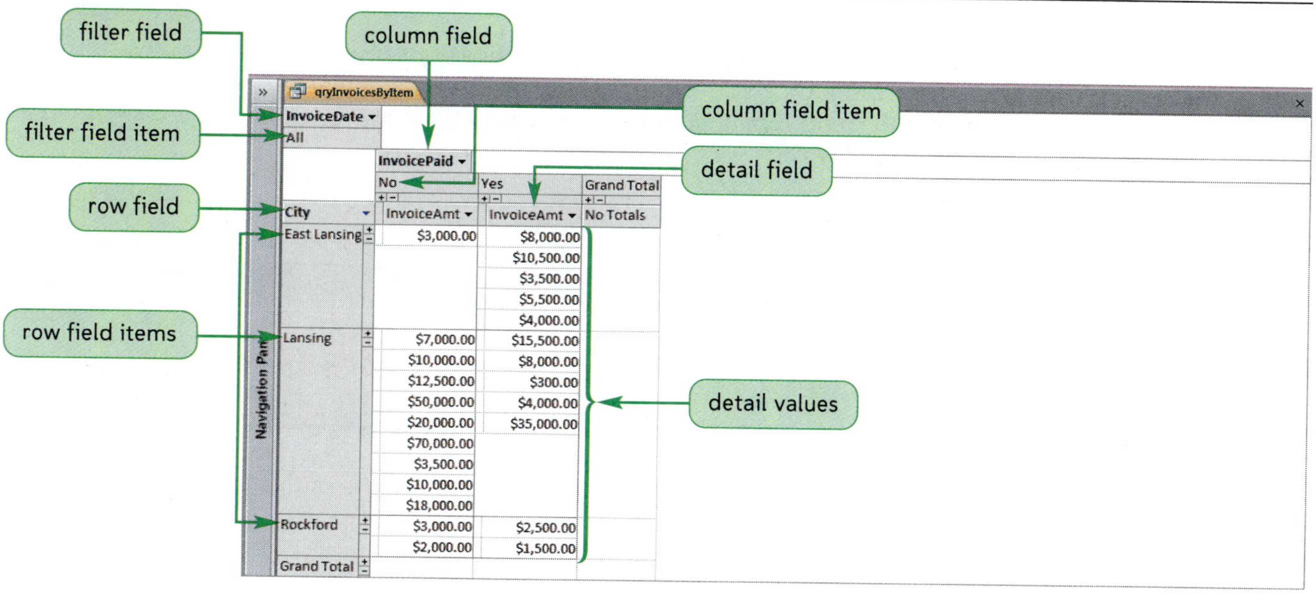


A PivotTable contains the following basic components:

- The **total/detail area**, consisting of a **detail field** and **detail values**, provides details and optional totals from a database table or query. In Figure 8-27, the detail field is the InvoiceAmt field from the tblInvoice table, and the detail values are the InvoiceAmt field values.
- The **row area**, consisting of a **row field** and **row field items**, provides row groupings in the PivotTable. In Figure 8-27, the row field is the City field from the tblCustomer table, and the row field items are the City field values.
- The **column area**, consisting of a **column field** and **column field items**, provides column groupings in the PivotTable. In Figure 8-27, the column field is the InvoicePaid field from the tblInvoice table, and the column field items are the InvoicePaid field values.
- The **filter area**, consisting of a **filter field** and **filter field items**, lets you restrict which data appears in the PivotTable. In Figure 8-27, the filter field is the InvoiceDate field from the tblInvoice table, and the filter field item is "All" dates, which means that all InvoiceDate field values are represented in the PivotTable.
- All the PivotTable areas—detail area, row area, column area, and filter area—can have multiple fields with multiple field items.

When you work with PivotTables, you use another program, the **Office PivotTable Component**, which is one of the **Office Web Components** that are part of Office 2010. Therefore, you can use PivotTables with other programs such as Excel. You can create PivotTables with Access tables and queries; the PivotTable view with these Access objects provides this capability.

## Creating a PivotTable

Sarah wants to analyze invoice amounts by city and by invoice date in various ways. You'll create a PivotTable using the qryInvoicesByItem query to let her perform this analysis.

## To create a PivotTable using a query:

1. Open the Navigation Pane, open the **qryInvoicesByItem** query datasheet to display the 172 records in the query, close the Navigation Pane, right-click the **qryInvoicesByItem** tab, and then click **PivotTable View** to switch to PivotTable view. See Figure 8-28.

**Figure 8-28** PivotTable view for the qryInvoicesByItem query

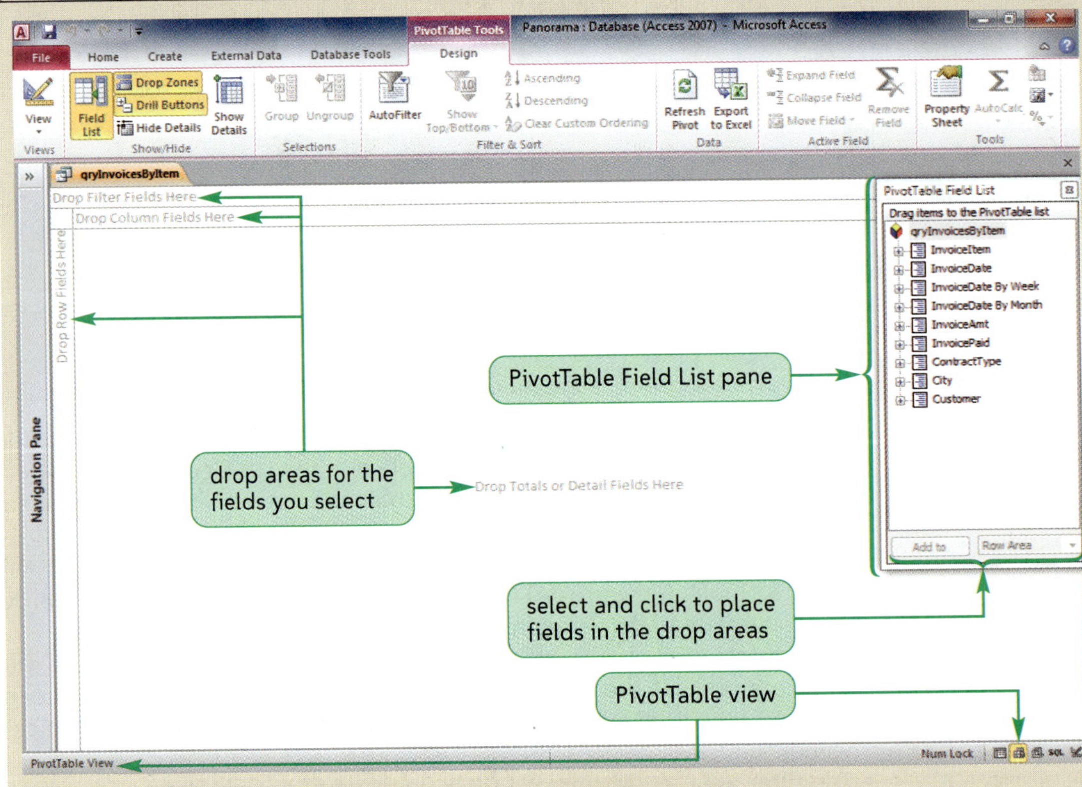


To create a PivotTable, you click a field in the PivotTable Field List pane to select it, and then drag it to one of the four drop areas—row, column, filter, or total/detail—or click the Add to button at the bottom of the PivotTable Field List pane after selecting one of the four drop areas in the list to the right of the Add to button.

Sarah wants to use the InvoicePaid field as the column field, the City field as the row field, the InvoiceDate field as the filter field, and the InvoiceAmt field as the detail field.

2. Click **InvoiceDate** in the PivotTable Field List pane, click the **Add to arrow** at the bottom of the PivotTable Field List pane, click **Filter Area** in the list, and then click the **Add to** button. Access places the InvoiceDate field and its field values in the filter drop area.

   **Trouble?** If you receive an error when you try to add a field to the PivotTable, switch to Design view, right-click the qryInvoicesByItem tab, click PivotTable View on the shortcut menu, and then repeat Step 2.

3. Repeat Step 2 to add the **City** field to the row drop area, the **InvoicePaid** field to the column drop area, and the **InvoiceAmt** field to the detail drop area. The four selected fields are bold in the PivotTable Field List pane and appear as components in the PivotTable. See Figure 8-29.

**Figure 8-29** After adding the four fields to the PivotTable

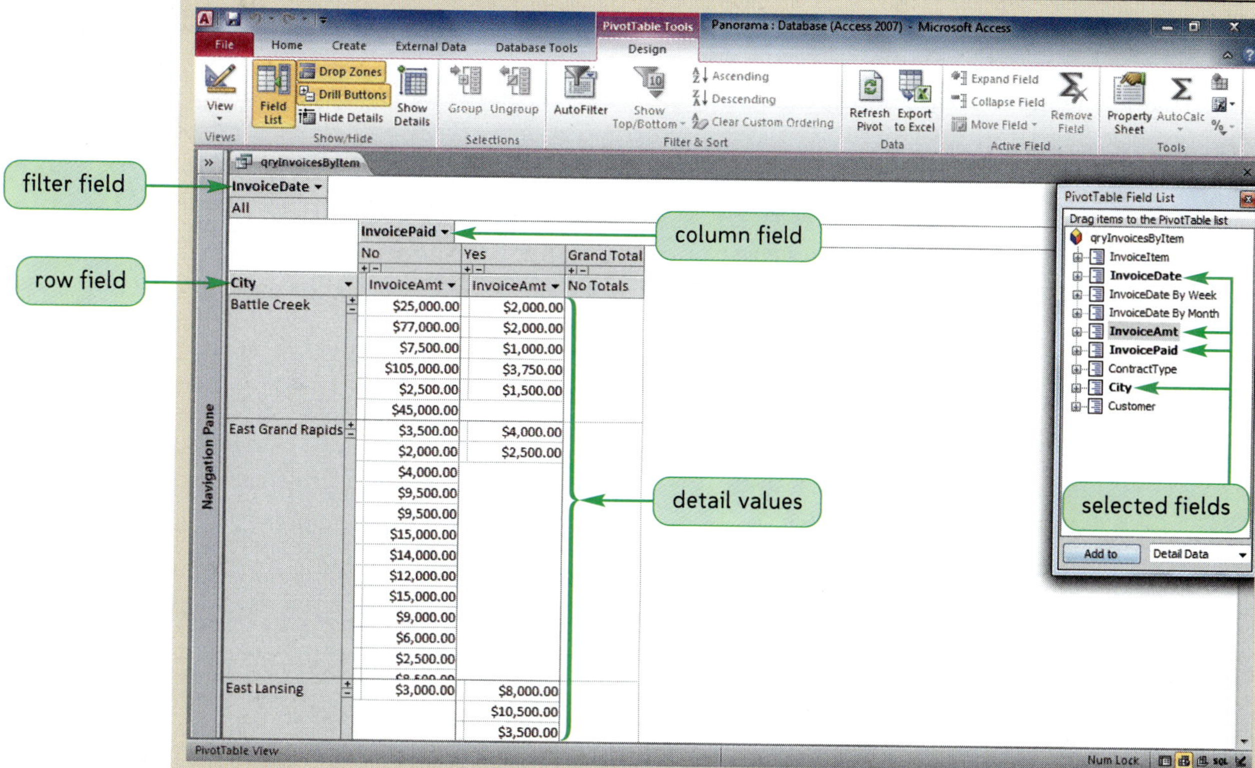


The PivotTable displays all the InvoiceAmt field values from the source query organized by city and invoice status (unpaid or paid).

4. Close the PivotTable Field List pane.

Sarah can filter the PivotTable using one or more of the four selected fields. She can also add total fields and hide the detail values in the PivotTable.

## Filtering and Summarizing Data in a PivotTable

A **total field** summarizes values from a source field. For example, Sarah can add subtotals and a grand total of the InvoiceAmt field values to the PivotTable. You'll show Sarah how to filter data in the PivotTable and how to add subtotals by city and a grand total for the InvoiceAmt field values.

**TIP**

You've applied a filter to the row field. In a similar way, you can apply filters to the column, filter, and detail fields.

### To filter data and add a total field in a PivotTable:

1. Click the **City** arrow, click the **All** check box to clear all the selections, click the **East Lansing** check box, click the **Lansing** check box, click the **Rockford** check box, and then click the **OK** button. Access applies the City filter and displays total invoice amounts for the three selected cities. See Figure 8-30.

**Figure 8-30** Filtering data for three cities

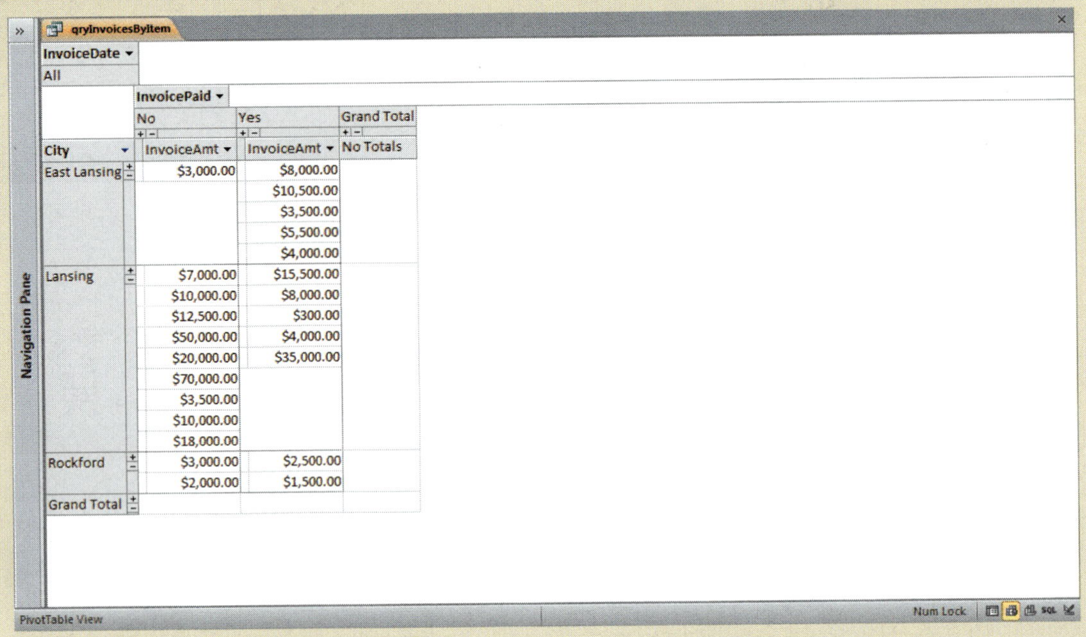


The applied City filter displays all the InvoiceAmt field values from the source query for the cities of East Lansing, Lansing, and Rockford.

2. Click one of the **InvoiceAmt** column heading labels to select the InvoiceAmt columns in the PivotTable; in the Tools group on the Design tab, click the **AutoCalc** button, click **Sum**, and then click to the right of the PivotTable to deselect all values. Access adds a new row for each city in the PivotTable that displays the city's InvoiceAmt total and a new row at the bottom of the PivotTable that displays the grand total for the displayed InvoiceAmt values. See Figure 8-31.

**Figure 8-31** After adding the total field to the PivotTable

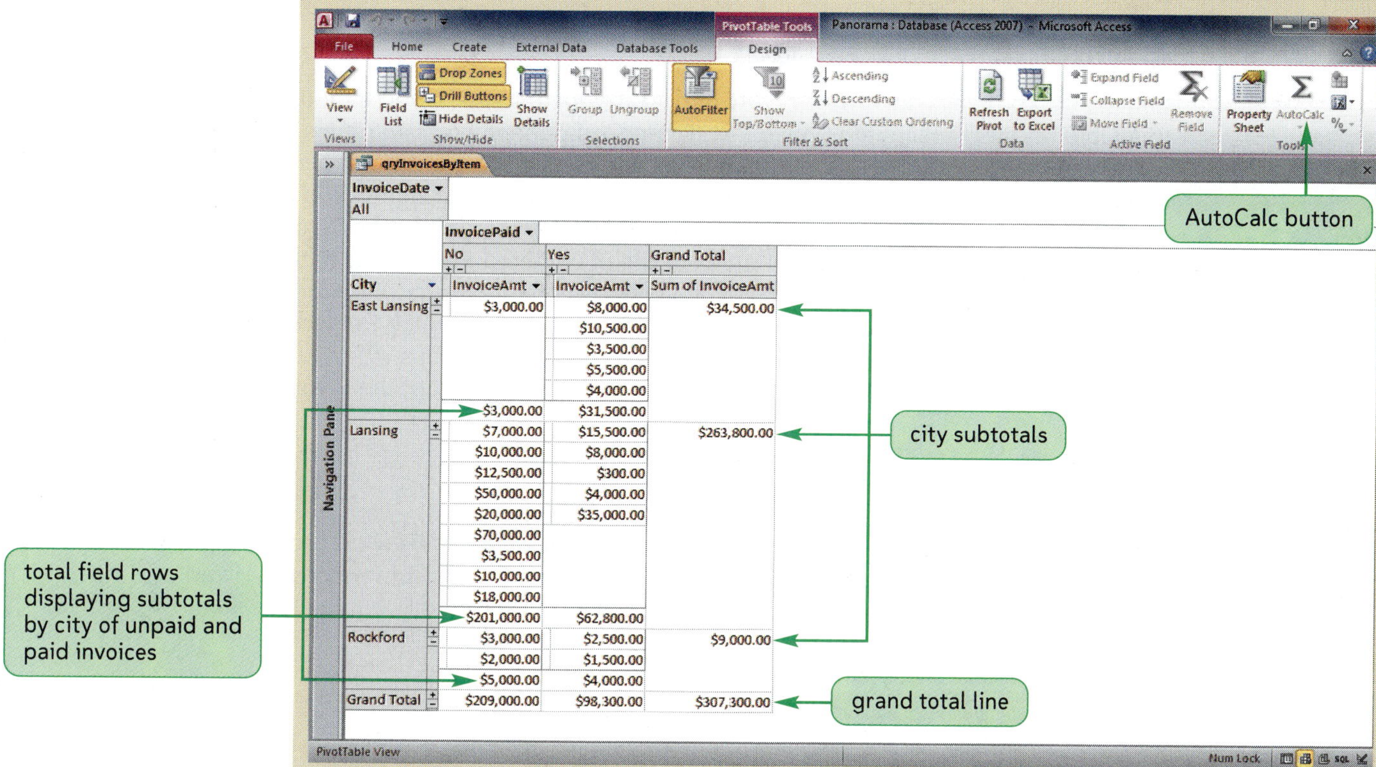


3. In the Show/Hide group on the Design tab, click the **Hide Details** button. Access hides the detail lines and displays only the subtotal and grand total lines in the PivotTable. See Figure 8-32.

**Figure 8-32** Subtotals and grand totals displayed in the PivotTable

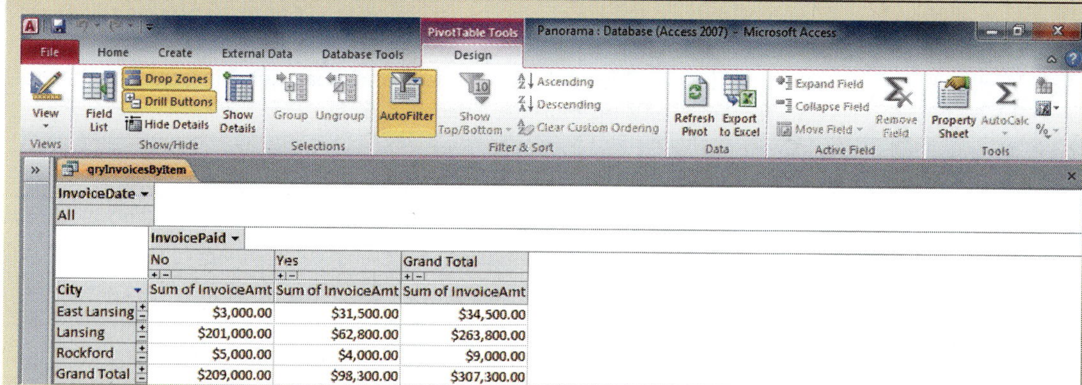


4. In the Show/Hide group on the Design tab, click the **Show Details** button. Access shows the detail lines and the subtotal and grand total lines in the PivotTable for the cities of East Lansing, Lansing, and Rockford.

Sarah asks if you can display the filtered PivotTable data in a chart. You'll switch to PivotChart view to satisfy Sarah's request.

## Creating a PivotChart

Office 2010 provides the **Office PivotChart Component** to assist you in adding a chart to a table or query. Using the Office PivotChart Component, you can create a PivotChart, an interactive chart that provides capabilities similar to a PivotTable. You can open a table or query, switch to PivotChart view, add fields to the PivotChart's drop areas, just as you did when you created the PivotTable, and then filter the data in the PivotChart. See the Session 8.2 Visual Overview for an example of a filtered PivotChart. When you create a PivotChart, you can switch to PivotTable view to view and further filter the charted data in a PivotTable. Likewise, after creating a PivotTable, you can switch to PivotChart view to view and further filter the tabular data in a PivotChart.

You'll switch to PivotChart view to show Sarah the PivotChart of the PivotTable data.

### To switch to PivotChart view:

1. Right-click the **qryInvoicesByItem** tab, click **PivotChart View** on the shortcut menu to switch to PivotChart view, close the Chart Field List (if necessary), and then in the Show/Hide group, click the **Legend** button to display the legend. See the Session 8.2 Visual Overview to become familiar with the contents of the PivotChart for the qryInvoicesByItem query.

Next, you'll show Sarah how to modify the PivotChart. First, Sarah wants to change the City filter to display data for Grand Rapids, Holland, Kalamazoo, and Lansing.

**TIP**

If you hover the mouse pointer on any PivotChart component, a ScreenTip displays information about that component.

### To modify the PivotChart:

1. Click the **City** arrow, click the **East Lansing** check box to clear it, click the **Rockford** check box to clear it, click the **Grand Rapids** check box to select it, click the **Holland** check box to select it, click the **Kalamazoo** check box to select it, and then click the **OK** button. Access applies the City filter, displays total invoice amounts for the four selected cities, and changes the scale of the horizontal axis and its value axis labels. See Figure 8-33.

**Figure 8-33** **After changing the City filter**

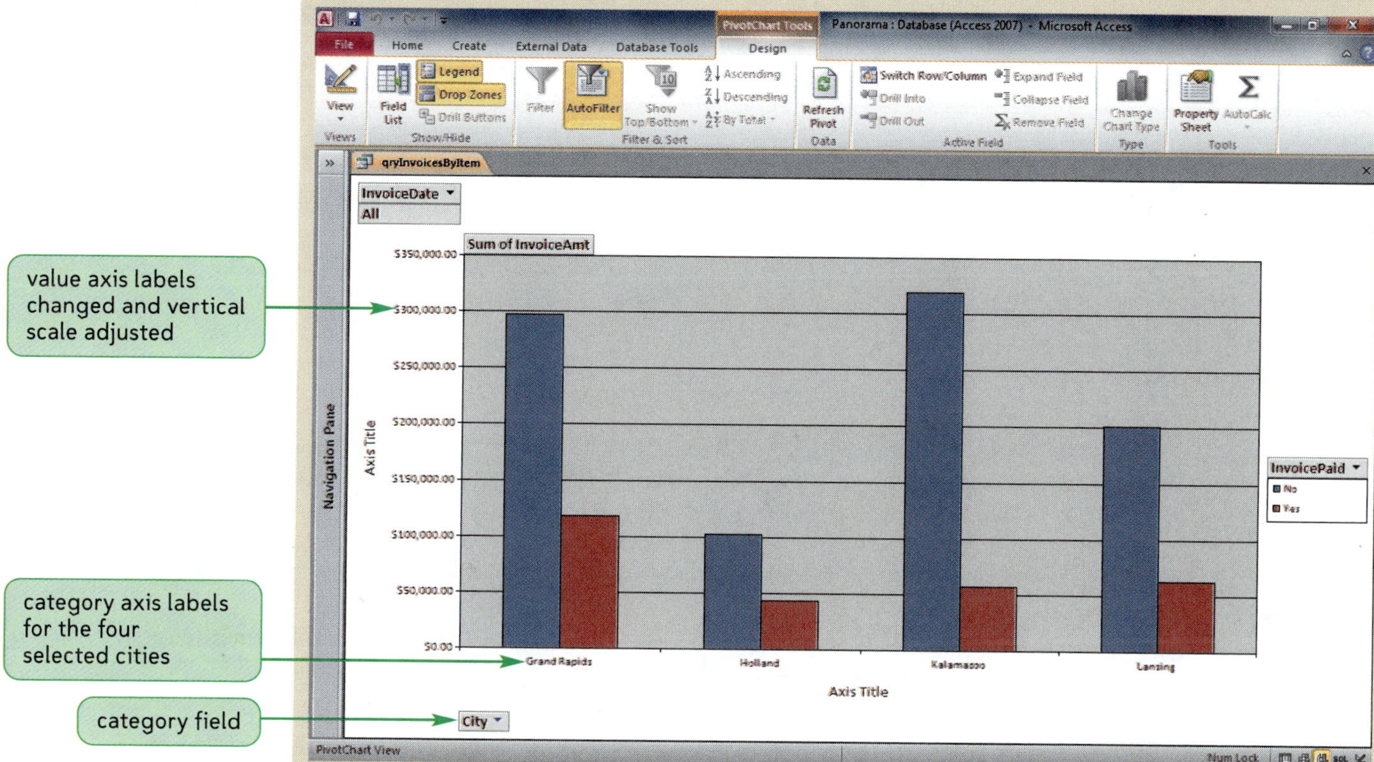


Sarah wants to change the PivotChart from a column chart to a bar chart, and she wants to change the colors of the data markers.

2. Click in the white portion of the chart (if necessary) to deselect any chart control, and then in the Type group on the Design tab, click the **Change Chart Type** button, click **Bar** in the left list, and then click the **Stacked Bar** chart (row 1, column 2) in the right list. The chart changes from a clustered column chart to a stacked bar chart.

3. In the chart, click the red data marker for Grand Rapids, hold down the **Shift** key, click the red data marker for Grand Rapids a second time, and then release the **Shift** key. All red data markers are now selected, and any property change you make in the Properties dialog box will apply to all four red data markers.

4. Click the **Border/Fill** tab in the Properties dialog box, click the **Fill Color** button, and then click the **DodgerBlue** color (row 3, column 4) in the color palette. The four selected data markers change to the selected DodgerBlue color. See Figure 8-34.

5. Repeat Steps 3 and 4, selecting the other four data markers (the leftmost data marker in each set), and clicking the **Tomato** color (row 8, column 13), and then click the **Fill Color** button to display the color palette. The four selected data markers change to the Tomato color. See Figure 8-34.

**Figure 8-34** After changing the chart type and data marker colors

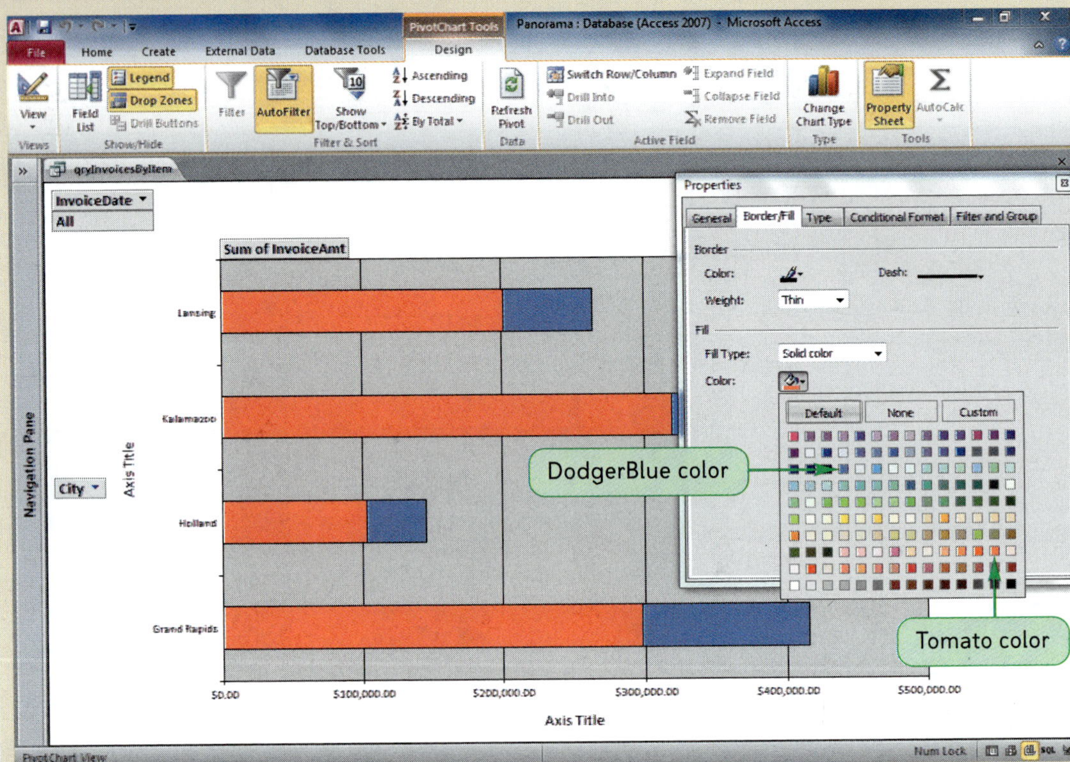


6. Close the Properties dialog box, save your PivotTable and PivotChart changes, and then close the query.
7. Open the Navigation Pane, open the **qryInvoicesByItem** query datasheet to display the 172 records in the query, switch to PivotChart view to display the saved PivotChart, switch to PivotTable view to display the saved PivotTable, and then close the query.

Sarah's staff mainatins an Excel workbook that tracks the products Belmont Landscapes has used for its landscaping projects. Sarah want to use the product data in the Panorama database.

## Linking Data from an Excel Worksheet

Sarah's staff has extensive experience working with Excel and prefers to maintain the landscaping product data in the Products workbook using Excel. However, Sarah needs to reference the product data in the Panorama database, and the data she's referencing must always be the current version of the worksheet data. Importing the Excel workbook data as an Access table would provide Sarah with data that's quickly out of date unless she repeats the import steps each time the data in the Excel workbook changes. Because Sarah doesn't need to update the product data in the Panorama database, you'll link to the workbook from the database. When the staff changes the Products workbook, the changes will be reflected automatically in the linked version of the database table. At the same time, Sarah won't be able to update the product data from the Panorama database, which ensures that only the staff members responsible for maintaining the workbook can update the data.

You'll now link to the data in the workbook.

## To link to the data in the Excel workbook:

1. Click the **External Data** tab on the Ribbon, and then in the Import & Link group, click the **Excel** button (with the ScreenTip "Import Excel spreadsheet"). The Get External Data - Excel Spreadsheet dialog box opens.
2. Click the **Browse** button, navigate to the **Access2\Tutorial** folder, click **Products**, click the **Open** button, and then click the **Link to the data source by creating a linked table** option button. The selected path and filename now appear in the File name box, and you've set the option to link to the data instead of importing or appending the data. See Figure 8-35.

**Figure 8-35** **Linking to data in an Excel workbook**

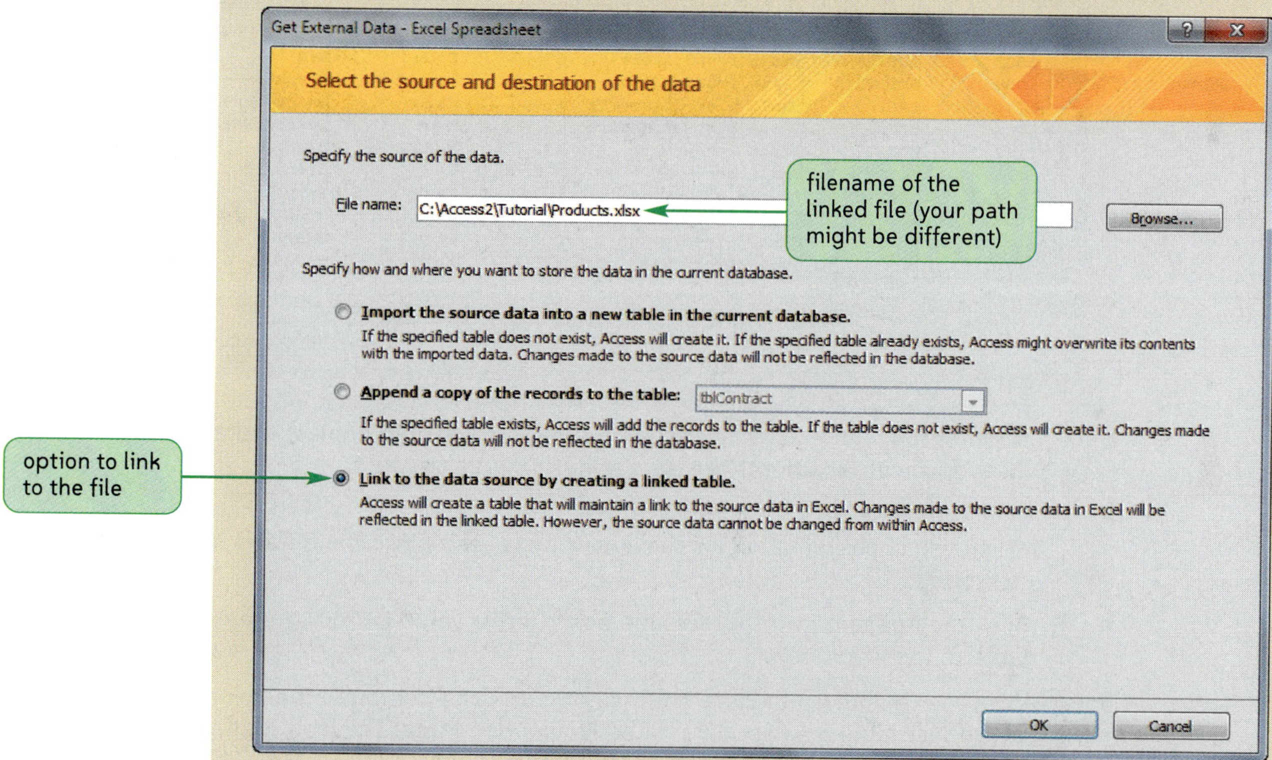


3. Click the **OK** button. The Link Spreadsheet Wizard dialog box opens. See Figure 8-36.

**Figure 8-36** **Linking to data in an Excel worksheet**

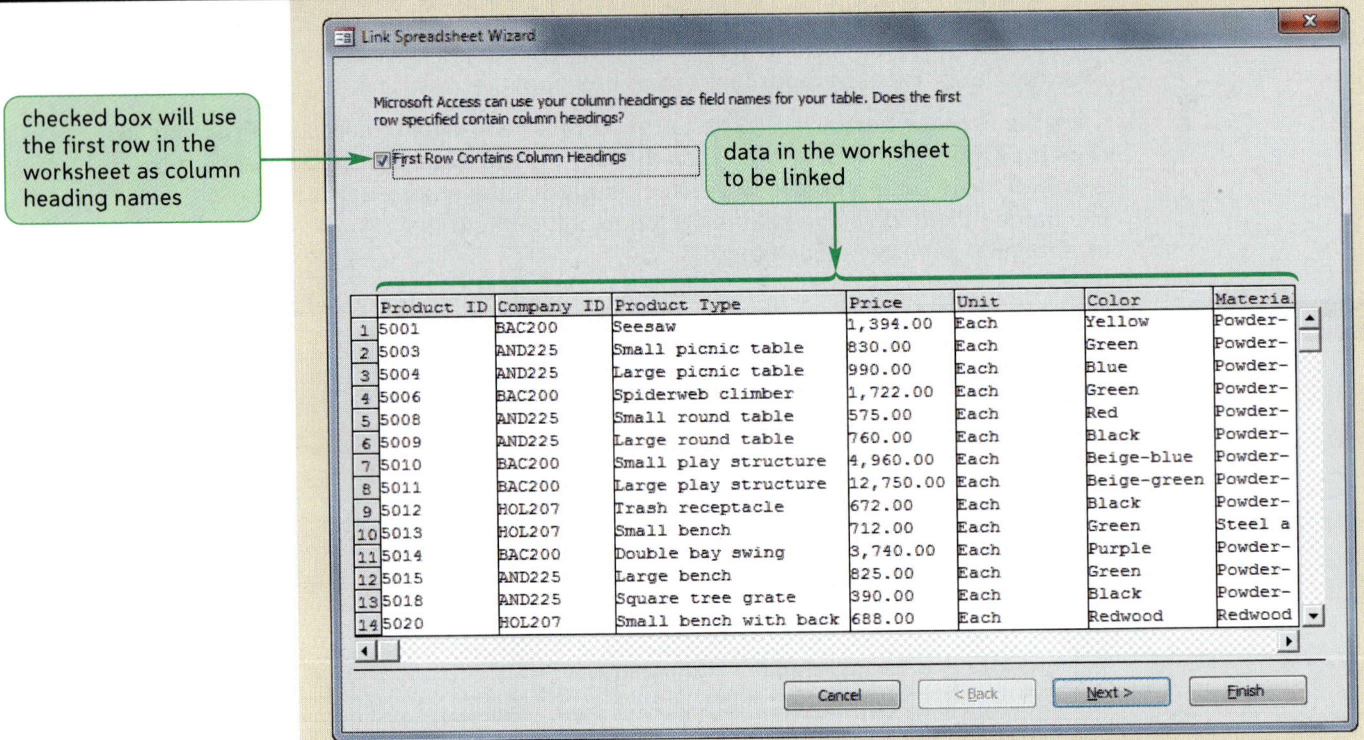


The first row in the worksheet contains column heading names, and each row in the worksheet represents the data about a single product.

4. Click the **Next** button to open the final Link Spreadsheet Wizard dialog box, in which you choose a name for the linked table. You'll use the default table name tblProduct.
5. Click the **Finish** button. A message box informs you that you've created a linking table to the workbook.
6. Click the **OK** button to close the message box and complete the linking steps. The tblProduct table now appears in the Navigation Pane. The icon to the left of the table name identifies the table as a linked table.

You can open and view the tblProduct table and use fields from the linked table in queries, forms, and reports, but you can't update the products data using the Panorama database. You can update the products data only from the Excel workbook.

Next, you'll show Sarah how the workbook and the linked table interact.

## To update the Excel workbook and view the data in the linked table:

1. Open Windows Explorer, navigate to and open the **Access2\Tutorial** folder, right-click **Products**, and then open the file using **Microsoft Excel**. The Products workbook opens and displays the tblProduct worksheet.

   **Trouble?** If you attempt to open the table in Access before you open the workbook in Excel, you'll get an error message and won't be able to open the workbook. Make sure you always open the workbook or other source file before you open a linked table.

2. Click the **Microsoft Access** program button on the taskbar to switch to the Panorama database, and then open the **tblProduct** datasheet. The fields and records in the tblProduct table display the same data as the tblProduct worksheet.
3. Select **Yellow** in the first record's Color column, and then type **G**. A warning sound chimes, the message "This Recordset is not updateable" is displayed on the status bar, and the value is not changed.

   **Trouble?** The Yellow value might change to another color value. Don't be concerned because this is a temporary aberration.
4. Click the **Microsoft Excel** program button on the taskbar to switch to the Products workbook, select **Yellow** in cell F2, type **Green**, and then press the **Enter** key. The value in cell F2 changes from Yellow to Green.
5. Click the **Microsoft Access** program button on the taskbar to switch to the Panorama database. The first row's Color field value is now Green because this is the updated value in the worksheet.

   When the Excel workbook and the linked Access table are open at the same time, you must first close the linked table in Access before closing the Excel workbook, or Access will display error values in the linked file.

   You've completed your work for Sarah and her staff.
6. Close the tblProduct table in Access.
7. Click the **Microsoft Excel** program button on the taskbar to switch to the Products workbook, save your worksheet change, and then exit Excel.
8. Make a backup copy of the database, compact and repair the Panorama database, and then close the database.

Knowing how to create charts, PivotTables, and PivotCharts and how to link to data maintained by other programs will make it easier for Sarah and her staff to anlayze their operations and to work efficiently in managing data.

REVIEW

## *Session 8.2 Quick Check*

1. The ______________ property lets you change the default navigation label from the word "Record" to another value.
2. When you use the Microsoft Graph program to create and change charts in a form or report, you must ______________ the chart.
3. What is a PivotTable?
4. Within a PivotTable you can choose fields from the field list to be a column field, a row field, a detail field, or a(n) ______________ field.
5. In a PivotChart, the ______________ field identifies which values are shown as value axis labels.
6. You can show or hide a legend for the ______________ field in a PivotChart.

*Practice the skills you learned in the tutorial to integrate data.*

PRACTICE

## Review Assignments

**Data Files needed for the Review Assignments: Ads.xlsx, BelmName.gif, BelmTemp.htm, Payables.csv, Payments.xml, and Products.accdb (*cont. from Tutorial 7*)**

Sarah wants you to integrate the data in the Products database with other programs and she wants to be able to analyze the data in the database. You'll help her achieve these goals by completing the following steps:

1. Open the **Products** database located in the Access2\Review folder provided with your Data Files.
2. Export the qryCompanyList query as an HTML document to the Access2\Review folder, using the HTML template file named BelmTemp, which is located in the Access2\Review folder, and saving the file as **Company**. Do not save the export steps.
3. Import the CSV file named Payables, which is located in the Access2\Review folder, as a new table in the database. Use the names in the first row as field names, use Currency as the data type for the numeric fields, choose your own primary key, name the table **tblPayable**, run the Table Analyzer, and record the Table Analyzer's recommendation. Do not save the import steps.
4. Import the data and structure from the XML file named Payments, which is located in the Access2\Review folder, as a new table named **tblPayments** in the database. Save the import steps, and then rename the table **tblPayment**.
5. Export the tblCompany table as an XML file named **Company** to the Access2\Review folder; do not create a separate XSD file. Save the export steps.
6. Link to the Ads workbook, which is located in the Access2\Review folder, using **tblAd** as the table name. Change the cost of the flyer for Ad Num 5 to **$300** and save the workbook.
7. Modify the **frmCompaniesWithProducts** form in the following ways:
   a. Add a tab control to the bottom of the Detail section, and place the existing subform on the first page of the tab control.
   b. Change the caption for the left tab to **Product Data** and for the right tab to **Product Chart**.
   c. Change the caption for the main form's navigation buttons to **Company** and for the subform's navigation buttons to **Product**.
   d. Add a chart to the second page of the tab control. Use the tblProduct table as the record source, select the ProductType, Price, and Unit fields, use the 3-D Column Chart type, include a legend, and use **Products Offered** as the chart title.
   e. Change the chart to a Clustered Column chart, and change the blue colored data markers to pink.
8. Open the **tblPayment** table and create a PivotTable with PaymentAmt as the detail field, PaymentDate as the column field, CompanyID as the row field, and PaymentID as the filter field. Add subtotals and a grand total for the PaymentAmt field values.
9. Switch to PivotChart view. Filter the CompanyID field, selecting BAC200, BEL273, and CHE802, make sure the legend is displayed, and then save the table.
10. Make a backup copy of the database, compact and repair the Products database, and then close the database.

*Apply the skills you learned in the tutorial to integrate data.*

APPLY

## Case Problem 1

**Data Files needed for this Case Problem: Contract.accdb (*cont. from Tutorial 7*), Instrument.csv, and Room.xlsx**

***Pine Hill Music School*** Yuka wants you to integrate the data in the Contract database with other programs, and she wants to be able to analyze the data in the database. You'll help her achieve these goals by completing the following steps:

1. Open the **Contract** database located in the Access2\Case1 folder provided with your Data Files.
2. EXPLORE Export the rptTeacherLessons report as an HTML document with a filename of **Less** to the Access2\Case1 folder; do not use a template or save the export steps. Use your Web browser to open the **Less** HTML document. Then scroll to the bottom of the page; use the First, Previous, Next, and Last links to navigate through the document.
3. Import the CSV file named Instrument, which is located in the Access2\Case1 folder, as a new table in the database. Use the names in the first row as field names, set the third column's data type to Currency and the other fields' data type to Text, choose your own primary key, name the table **tblInstrument**, run the Table Analyzer, and record the Table Analyzer's recommendation, but do not accept the recommendation. Do not save the import steps.
4. Export the tblTeacher table as an XML file named **Teacher** to the Access2\Case1 folder; do not create a separate XSD file. Save the export steps.
5. Link to the Room workbook, which is located in the Access2\Case1 folder, using **tblRoom** as the table name. Add a new record to the Room workbook as follows: Room Num **5**, Rental Cost **$25**, and Type **Private**.
6. Open the **qryLessonsByTeacher** query, and create a PivotTable with MonthlyLessonCost as the detail field, LessonType as the column field, LastName as the row field, and LessonLength as the filter field. Filter the LessonType field, selecting Guitar, Piano, and Saxophone. Add subtotals and a grand total for the MonthlyLessonCost field values.
7. Switch to PivotChart view. Display the legend (if necessary), change the color of the Saxophone data markers to yellow, and then save the query.
8. Make a backup copy of the database, compact and repair the Contract database, and then close the database.

*Use the skills you learned in the tutorial to integrate data.*

APPLY

## Case Problem 2

**Data Files needed for this Case Problem: CreditCard.xml, ParkName.gif, ParkTemp.htm, Schedule.xlsx, and Training.accdb (*cont. from Tutorial 7*)**

***Parkhurst Health & Fitness Center*** Martha Parkhurst wants you to integrate the data in the Training database with other programs, and she wants to be able to analyze the data in the database. You'll help her achieve these goals by completing the following steps:

1. Open the **Training** database located in the Access2\Case2 folder provided with your Data Files.
2. Export the qryPhysicalsNeeded query as an HTML document to the Access2\Case2 folder using a filename of **Physicals** and using the HTML template file named ParkTemp, which is located in the Access2\Case2 folder. Save the export steps.

EXPLORE

3. Export the rptProgramMembership report as an HTML document with a filename of **Program** to the Access2\Case2 folder; do not use a template or save the export steps. Use your Web browser to open the **Program** HTML document. Then scroll to the bottom of the page; use the First, Previous, Next, and Last links to navigate through the document.
4. Import the the data and structure from the XML file named CreditCard, which is located in the Access2\Case2 folder, as a new table. Rename the table as **tblCreditCard**. Save the import steps.
5. Export the tblProgram table as an XML file named **Program** to the Access2\Case2 folder; do not create a separate XSD file. Save the export steps.
6. Link to the Schedule workbook, which is located in the Access2\Case2 folder, using **tblSchedule** as the table name. For ClassID 301, change the ClassDay value to **F**.
7. Modify the **frmProgramsAndMembers** form in the following ways:
   a. Add a tab control to the bottom of the Detail section, and place the existing subform on the first page of the tab control.
   b. Change the caption for the left tab to **Member Data** and for the right tab to **Member Chart**.
   c. Change the caption for the main form's navigation buttons to **Program** and for the subform's navigation buttons to **Member**.
   d. Add a chart to the second page of the tab control. Use the tblMember table as the record source, select the ProgramID and MembershipStatus fields, use the Column Chart chart type, include a legend, and use **Membership Status** as the chart title.
   e. Change the color of the right data marker (or the middle data marker, depending on whether you see two or three data markers) to red.
8. Open the **qryMonthlyFeeStatus** query and create a PivotTable with MonthlyFee as the detail field, MonthlyFeeStatus as the column field, LastName as the row field, and ProgramType as the filter field. Add subtotals and a grand total of the MonthlyFee values, hide the details, and filter the ProgramType field to display only programs for juniors.
9. Switch to PivotChart view for the qryMonthlyFeeStatus query. Change the chart type to Clustered Bar, display the legend, change the data markers to colors of your choice, and then save the query.
10. Make a backup copy of the database, compact and repair the Training database, and then close the database.

*Use the skills you learned in the tutorial to integrate data.*

CHALLENGE

## Case Problem 3

**Data Files needed for this Case Problem: Agency.accdb (*cont. from Tutorial 7*) and Facility.csv**

***Rossi Recycling Group*** Mary Rossi wants you to integrate the data in the Agency database with other programs, and she wants to be able to analyze the data in the database. You'll help her achieve these goals by completing the following steps:

1. Open the **Agency** database located in the Access2\Case3 folder provided with your Data Files.
2. Export the qryNetDonationsCrosstab query as an HTML document named **Crosstab** to the Access2\Case3 folder; do not use a template. Save the export steps.

EXPLORE

3. Export the frmDonation form as an HTML document named **Donation** to the Access2\Case3 folder; do not use a template or save the export steps. Use your Web browser to open the HTML document and review its contents.

EXPLORE

4. Import the CSV file named Facility, which is located in the Access2\Case3 folder, as a new table in the database. Use the Text data type for all fields, choose your own primary key, name the table **tblTemporary**, and run the Table Analyzer. Accept the Table Analyzer's recommendations, rename the tables as **tblStorage** and **tblFacility**, make sure each table has the correct primary key, and let the Table Analzyer create a query. Do not save the import steps. Review the tblTemporary query, review the tblTemporary table (it might be named tblTemporary_OLD), and then review the tblStorage and tblFacility tables.
5. Export the tblDonation table as an XML file named **Donation** to the Access2\Case3 folder; do not create a separate XSD file. Save the export steps.
6. Modify the **frmDonorDonations** form in the following ways:
   a. Add a tab control to the bottom of the Detail section, and place the existing subform on the first page of the tab control.
   b. Change the caption for the left tab to **Donation Data** and for the right tab to **Donation Chart**.
   c. Change the caption for the main form's navigation buttons to **Donor** and for the subform's navigation buttons to **Donation**.
   d. Add a chart to the second page of the tab control. Use the tblDonation table as the record source; select the AgencyID, DonationValue, PickupRequired, and DonationDate fields; use the 3-D Column Chart type; include a legend; and use **Donations by Agency** as the chart title.
   e. Change the chart to a Clustered Bar chart, and change the color of the maroon data marker to red.
7. Open the **qryNetDonations** query and create a PivotTable with NetDonation as the data field, AgencyName as the column field, DonationDesc as the row field, and PickupRequired as the filter field. Filter the DonationDesc field to display only cash donations.
8. Switch to PivotChart view. Filter the AgencyName by removing the first five agencies, leaving the data for five agencies in the chart, display the legend, change the chart type to Clustered Bar, and then save the query.
9. Make a backup copy of the database, compact and repair the Agency database, and then close the database.

*Use the skills you learned in the tutorial to analyze data.*

CREATE

## Case Problem 4

**Data Files needed for this Case Problem: Personnel.xlsx, Vacation.accdb (*cont. from Tutorial 7*), and Works.xml**

***GEM Ultimate Vacations*** Griffin and Emma MacElroy want you to integrate the data in the Vacation database with other programs, and they want to be able to analyze the data in the database. You'll help them achieve these goals by completing the following steps:

1. Open the **Vacation** database located in the Access2\Case4 folder provided with your Data Files.
2. Export the qryPropertiesByRate query as an HTML document named **Property** to the Access2\Case4 folder; do not use a template. Save the export steps.
3. Import the data and structure from the XML file named Works, which is located in the Access2\Case4 folder, as a new table in the database. Rename the table as **tblWork**. Save the import steps.
4. Export the qryPropertyReservations query as an XML file named **Property** to the Access2\Case4 folder; do not create a separate XSD file. Do not save the export steps.

5. Link to the Personnel workbook, which is located in the Access2\Case4 folder, using **tblPersonnel** as the table name. Change the name in the fourth record from Edward Leary to **Marie Leary**.
6. Modify the **frmGuestsWithReservations** form in the following ways:
   a. Add a tab control to the bottom of the Detail section, and place the existing subform on the first page of the tab control.
   b. Change the caption for the left tab to **Reservation Data** and for the right tab to **Reservation Chart**.
   c. Change the caption for the main form's navigation buttons to **Guest** and for the subform's navigation buttons to **Reservation**.
   d. Add a chart to the second page of the tab control. Use the tblReservation table as the record source, select the StartDate, PropertyID, and RentalRate fields, use the Column Chart chart type, include a legend, and use **Reservations** as the chart title.

EXPLORE

7. Open the **qryGuestsAndReservations** query, and create a PivotTable with RentalRate as the detail field, StateProv as the column field, the Quarters component of the StartDate By Month entry in the PivotTable Field List as the row field, and PropertyID as the filter field. Add subtotals and a grand total of the RentalRate field, and then hide the details.
8. Switch to PivotChart view. Display the legend, change the green color to yellow, and then save the query.
9. Make a backup copy of the database, compact and repair the Vacation database, and then close the database.

*Use the skills you learned in this tutorial to integrate data.*

CREATE

## Case Problem 5

**Data File needed for this Case Problem: ACE.accdb (*cont. from Tutorial 7*)**

***Always Connected Everyday*** Chris and Pat Aquino want you to integrate the data in the ACE database with other programs, and they want to be able to analyze the data in the database. You'll help them achieve these goals by completing the following steps:

1. Open the **ACE** database located in the Access2\Case5 folder provided with your Data Files.
2. Export the tblAccessPlan table as an HTML document named **Plan** to the Access2\Case5 folder; do not use a template or save the import steps.

EXPLORE

3. Export the rptAccessPlanCustomers report as an HTML document named **Customers** to the Access2\Case5 folder; do not use a template or save the export steps. Use your Web browser to open and review the HTML document.
4. Export the tblCustomer table as an XML file named **Customer** to the Access2\Case5 folder; do not create a separate XSD file. Save the export steps.
5. Modify one of the existing forms or create a new form so that the form uses a tab control. Change the caption for the navigation buttons, and set the captions for the tab labels.
6. For one of the existing queries (or a new query you create), create a PivotTable, add subtotals and a grand total, apply a filter, and hide details. In PivotChart view, display the legend and make any other appropriate changes.
7. Make a backup copy of the database, compact and repair the ACE database, and then close the database.

ASSESS

## SAM: Skills Assessment Manager

For current SAM information, including versions and content details, visit SAM Central (http://samcentral.course.com). If you have a SAM user profile, you may have access to hands-on instruction, practice, and assessment of the skills covered in this tutorial. Since various versions of SAM are supported throughout the life of this text, check with your instructor for the correct instructions and URL/Web site for accessing assignments.

### ENDING DATA FILES

**Access2** → 

**Tutorial**
- Crosstab.html
- Invoice.xml
- Panorama.accdb
- Products.xlsx

**Review**
- Ads.xlsx
- Company.html
- Company.xml
- Products.accdb

**Case1**
- Contract.accdb
- Less.html
- LessPage2.html
- LessPage3.html
- Room.xlsx
- Teacher.xml

**Case2**
- Physicals.html
- Program.html
- ProgramPage2.html
- ProgramPage3.html
- Program.xml
- Schedule.xlsx
- Training.accdb

**Case3**
- Agency.accdb
- Crosstab.html
- Donation.html
- Donation.xml

**Case4**
- Personnel.xlsx
- Property.html
- Property.xml
- Vacation.accdb

**Case5**
- ACE.accdb
- Customer.xml
- Customers.html
- CustomersPage2.html
- Plan.html

ProSkills

# Decision Making

## Deciding When to Create a Personal Database

Decision making is a process of choosing between alternative courses of action. When you make decisions, you normally follow these steps:

1. Gather information relevant to the decision
2. Consider viable alternatives
3. Select the best alternative
4. Prepare an implementation action plan
5. Take action and monitor results
6. Verify the accuracy of the decision

For some decisions, you might combine some steps, and you might even skip steps for the simplest decisions.

## Gathering Information, Considering Alternatives, and Selecting the Best Alternative

To complete this ProSkills exercise, you'll create a personal database with any content of your choice. To get you started, however, you'll follow through the decision-making steps in creating a sample database. For example, you might now, or in the future, be charged with tracking volunteers and their jobs for a service organization or other entity that requires coordination of a large group of people. The first step in decision making—gathering relevant information—starts with the choice of how to organize the people and their jobs. For example, if your information shows that each person completes only one job, few people are involved in the process, and volunteers all report to the same coordinator, then you could use a Word document or an Excel workbook to manage the volunteers and their jobs. Documents and workbooks are easy to use for most people and can store the data you need in a useful and efficient format.

However, what if your information shows a very large number of volunteers, and many volunteers work in multiple jobs and report to more than one coordinator? Consider the efforts of a volunteer coordinator for parents who volunteer at a local elementary school. Some parents volunteer their time in multiple classrooms (one classroom for each of their children); others volunteer as needed in ways that contribute to fundraising efforts, leadership, and special events such as school plays or concerts. When the relevant information changes so that one parent is no longer completing only one job and no longer reporting to a single coordinator, managing the data in a Word document or Excel workbook becomes problematic—having multiple worksheets or documents to list all of the volunteers, jobs, and coordinators is almost guaranteed to result in problems related to data redundancy, data anomalies, and errors.

When making the decision to use a database to manage your data, at first you might find that some data exists in another format, such as in an Excel workbook. After considering the data that you have already collected (such as in a workbook) or data that you will collect in the future, consider the types of decisions you need to make. These decisions might include determining whether a database will effectively and efficiently manage your data, deciding which DBMS you will use, and evaluating the ability of users to manage and use the database to get the information they need. These decisions usually have

ProSkills

an immediate impact—the decision to use a DBMS has an upfront cost, requires someone with knowledge of database development and the selected DBMS to create it, and involves training users to access the database. It's also important to consider the long-term impact of your decision, such as whether future volunteer coordinators will have the ability and interest to continue using the DBMS you selected. In other words, part of the decision-making process needs to consider the impact of your decision both now and in the future. Being able to predict an organization's short-term and long-term needs can be difficult, but it's important to consider many possible outcomes when making your decision.

## Preparing an Implementation Action Plan

Once you have made the choice to use a DBMS, determine the steps you need to take to design and create the database. The first step is to analyze the data you have collected or will collect and start compiling it into tables. Then, you can begin identifying the primary and foreign keys in the tables to create the relationships between those tables. Finally, you can determine the field properties in anticipation of making data entry easier and reducing the likelihood of errors. For example, you might use the Default Value property to enter a city or state field value if all of your volunteers reside in the same geographic area, or use the AutoNumber data type to assign a primary key value to a table automatically when there is no natural primary key available.

## Taking Action and Monitoring Results

The next step in decision making involves implementation, which includes creating the database, defining the tables, and entering the data. After designing and installing the database, you need to make decisions about the types of queries, forms, and reports to create to produce the data in the format that users need. After implementation, you should make decisions about how the database will be updated so it remains current and ready for any future decisions you need to make.

## Verifying the Accuracy of the Decision

At the end of your decision-making process, review your steps and evaluate how well they worked. Did you discover data you wish you had originally collected and stored in the database, but didn't have available? How did that limitation affect your ability to make a good decision? What changes do you need to make to your database so that it will provide better information for future decisions? As you review your decisions, be sure to document any changes you need to make to enhance or reorganize the database so it provides greater usefulness for future decisions.

PROSKILLS

### Create a Personal Database

Most businesses use databases for decision making, and you can also use databases to track data in your personal life. Examples of personal database use include tracking personal collections, such as songs or books; hobby data, such as crafts or antiques; or items related to sports teams, theater clubs, or other organizations to which you might belong. In this exercise, you'll use Access to create a database that will contain information of your choice, using the Access skills and features you've learned in these tutorials.

# ProSkills

**Note:** Please be sure *not* to include any personal information of a sensitive nature in the database you create to be submitted to your instructor for this exercise. Later on, you can update the data in your database with such information for your own personal use.

1. Consider your personal interests and activities, school-related functions, and work-related duties, and select from them one set of requirements that includes data that is best tracked using a DBMS. (If you completed Tutorials 1-4 of this book and the ProSkills Exercise at the end of Tutorial 4, you can use and enhance the database you've already created, and you can skip this step and the next step.) Make sure the data is sufficiently complex that a Word document or Excel workbook would not be viable alternatives to store and manage the data.
2. Create a new Access database to contain the data you want to track. The database must include two or more tables that you can join through one-to-many relationships. Define the properties for each field in each table. Make sure you include a mix of data types for the fields (for example, do not include only Text fields in each table). Specify a primary key for each table, define the table relationships with referential integrity enforced, and enter records in each table.
3. Create queries that include at least the following: pattern query match, list-of-values match, parameter, crosstab, find duplicates, find unmatched, and the use of a conditional value in a calculated field.
4. For one or more fields, apply an input mask and specify field validation rules.
5. Create a split form and modify the form.
6. Create a custom form that uses at least the following: combo box for a lookup, combo box to find records, subform, lines and rectangles, and a tab control. Add one or more calculated controls to the main form based on the subform's calculated control(s), and add a chart, if appropriate. Check the main form's tab order, and improve the form's appearance.
7. Create a custom report that uses at least the following: grouping field, sort field(s), lines, and rectangles. Hide duplicates; and add the date, page numbers, and a report title.
8. Export two or more objects in different formats, and save the step specifications.
9. Create a PivotTable and PivotChart for one of the tables or queries.
10. Designate a trusted folder, make a backup copy of the database, and compact and repair the database.
11. Submit your completed database to your instructor as requested. Include printouts of any database objects, if required. Also, prepare a document that addresses the specific data you selected to store and track and why a DBMS was the best alternative choice.

APPENDIX A

# Relational Databases and Database Design

ACCESS

## OBJECTIVES

- Learn the characteristics of a table
- Learn about primary, candidate, alternate, composite, and foreign keys
- Study one-to-one, one-to-many, and many-to-many relationships
- Learn to describe tables and relationships with entity-relationship diagrams and with a shorthand method
- Study database integrity constraints for primary keys, referential integrity, and domains
- Learn about determinants, functional dependencies, anomalies, and normalization
- Understand the differences among natural, artificial, and surrogate keys
- Learn about naming conventions

This appendix introduces you to the basics of database design. Before trying to master this material, be sure you understand the following concepts: data, information, field, field value, record, table, relational database, common field, database management system (DBMS), and relational database management system (RDBMS).

## STARTING DATA FILES

There are no starting Data Files needed for this appendix.

# Tables

A relational database stores its data in tables. A **table** is a two-dimensional structure made up of rows and columns. The terms table, **record** (row), and **field** (column) are the popular names for the more formal terms **relation** (table), **tuple** (row), and **attribute** (column), as shown in Figure A-1.

**Figure A-1** **A table (relation) consisting of records and fields**

table name → Employee

| EmployeeNum | FirstName | LastName | DeptNum |
|---|---|---|---|
| 2173 | Barbara | Hennessey | 27 |
| 4519 | Lee | Noordsy | 31 |
| 8005 | Pat | Amidon | 27 |
| 8112 | Chris | Wandzell | 24 |

field names

records (rows or tuples)

fields (columns or attributes)

The Employee table shown in Figure A-1 is an example of a relational database table, a two-dimensional structure with the following characteristics:

- Each row is unique. Because no two rows are the same, you can easily locate and update specific data. For example, you can locate the row for EmployeeNum 8005 and change the FirstName value, Pat, the LastName value, Amidon, or the DeptNum value, 27.
- The order of the rows is unimportant. You can add or view rows in any order. For example, you can view the rows in LastName order instead of EmployeeNum order.
- Each table entry contains a single value. At the intersection of each row and column, you cannot have more than one value. For example, each row in Figure A-1 contains one EmployeeNum value, one FirstName value, one LastName value, and one DeptNum value.
- The order of the columns is unimportant. You can add or view columns in any order.
- Each column has a unique name called the **field name**. The field name allows you to access a specific column without needing to know its position within the table.
- Each row in a table describes, or shows the characteristics of, an **entity**. An entity is a person, place, object, event, or idea for which you want to store and process data. For example, EmployeeNum, FirstName, LastName, and DeptNum are characteristics of the employees of a company. The Employee table represents all the employee entities and their characteristics. That is, each row of the Employee table describes a different employee of the company using the characteristics of EmployeeNum, FirstName, LastName, and DeptNum. The Employee table includes only characteristics of employees. Other tables would exist for the company's other entities. For example, a Department table would describe the company's departments and a Position table would describe the company's job positions.

Knowing the characteristics of a table leads directly to a definition of a relational database. A **relational database** is a collection of tables (relations).

Note that this book uses singular table names, such as Employee and Department, but some people use plural table names, such as Employees and Departments. You can use either singular table names or plural table names, as long as you consistently use the style you choose.

## Keys

Primary keys ensure that each row in a table is unique. A **primary key** is a column, or a collection of columns, whose values uniquely identify each row in a table. In addition to being *unique*, a primary key must be *minimal* (that is, contain no unnecessary extra columns) and must not change in value. For example, in Figure A-2 the State table contains one record per state and uses the StateAbbrev column as its primary key.

**Figure A-2** **A table and its keys**

alternate keys

primary key

State

| StateAbbrev | StateName | EnteredUnionOrder | StateBird | StatePopulation |
|---|---|---|---|---|
| CT | Connecticut | 5 | American robin | 3,518,288 |
| MI | Michigan | 26 | robin | 9,969,727 |
| SD | South Dakota | 40 | pheasant | 812,383 |
| TN | Tennessee | 16 | mockingbird | 6,296,254 |
| TX | Texas | 28 | mockingbird | 24,782,302 |

Could any other column, or collection of columns, be the primary key of the State table?

- Could the StateBird column serve as the primary key? No, because the StateBird column does not have unique values (for example, the mockingbird is the state bird of more than one state).
- Could the StatePopulation column serve as the primary key? No, because the StatePopulation column values change periodically and are not guaranteed to be unique.
- Could the StateAbbrev and StateName columns together serve as the primary key? No, because the combination of these two columns is not minimal. Something less, such as the StateAbbrev column by itself, can serve as the primary key.
- Could the StateName column serve as the primary key? Yes, because the StateName column has unique values. In a similar way, you could select the EnteredUnionOrder column as the primary key for the State table. One column, or a collection of columns, that can serve as a primary key is called a **candidate key**. The candidate keys for the State table are the StateAbbrev column, the StateName column, and the EnteredUnionOrder column. You choose one of the candidate keys to be the primary key, and each remaining candidate key is called an **alternate key**. The StateAbbrev column is the State table's primary key in Figure A-2, so the StateName and EnteredUnionOrder columns become alternate keys in the table.

Figure A-3 shows a City table containing the fields StateAbbrev, CityName, and CityPopulation.

**Figure A-3** **A table with a composite key**

primary key

City

| StateAbbrev | CityName | CityPopulation |
|---|---|---:|
| CT | Hartford | 124,062 |
| CT | Madison | 18,803 |
| CT | Portland | 9,551 |
| MI | Lansing | 119,128 |
| SD | Madison | 6,482 |
| SD | Pierre | 13,899 |
| TN | Nashville | 569,462 |
| TX | Austin | 757,688 |
| TX | Portland | 16,490 |

What is the primary key for the City table? The values for the CityPopulation column periodically change and are not guaranteed to be unique, so the CityPopulation column cannot be the primary key. Because the values for each of the other two columns are not unique, the StateAbbrev column alone cannot be the primary key and neither can the CityName column (for example, there are two cities named Madison and two cities named Portland). The primary key is the combination of the StateAbbrev and CityName columns. Both columns together are needed to identify—uniquely and minimally—each row in the City table. A multiple-column primary key is called a **composite key** or a **concatenated key**.

The StateAbbrev column in the City table is also a foreign key. A **foreign key** is a column, or a collection of columns, in one table in which each column value must match the value of the primary key of some table or must be null. A **null** is the absence of a value in a particular table entry. A null value is not blank, nor zero, nor any other value. You give a null value to a column value when you do not know its value or when a value does not apply. As shown in Figure A-4, the values in the City table's StateAbbrev column match the values in the State table's StateAbbrev column. Thus, the StateAbbrev column, the primary key of the State table, is a foreign key in the City table. Although the field name StateAbbrev is the same in both tables, the names could be different. However, all experts use the same name for a field stored in two or more tables to broadcast clearly that they store similar values.

**Figure A-4** StateAbbrev as a primary key (State table) and a foreign key (City table)

primary key (State table)

State

| StateAbbrev | StateName | EnteredUnionOrder | StateBird | StatePopulation |
|---|---|---|---|---|
| CT | Connecticut | 5 | American robin | 3,518,288 |
| MI | Michigan | 26 | robin | 9,969,727 |
| SD | South Dakota | 40 | pheasant | 812,383 |
| TN | Tennessee | 16 | mockingbird | 6,296,254 |
| TX | Texas | 28 | mockingbird | 24,782,302 |

composite primary key (City table)

foreign key

City

| StateAbbrev | CityName | CityPopulation |
|---|---|---|
| CT | Hartford | 124,062 |
| CT | Madison | 18,803 |
| CT | Portland | 9,551 |
| MI | Lansing | 119,128 |
| SD | Madison | 6,482 |
| SD | Pierre | 13,899 |
| TN | Nashville | 596,462 |
| TX | Austin | 757,688 |
| TX | Portland | 16,490 |

A **nonkey field** is a field that is not part of the primary key. In the two tables shown in Figure A-4, all fields are nonkey fields except the StateAbbrev field in the State and City tables and the CityName field in the City table. *Key* is an ambiguous word because it can refer to a primary, candidate, alternate, or foreign key. When the word key appears alone, however, it means primary key and the definition for a nonkey field consequently makes sense.

# Relationships

In a database, a table can be associated with another table in one of three ways: a one-to-many relationship, a many-to-many relationship, or a one-to-one relationship.

## One-to-Many Relationship

The Department and Employee tables, shown in Figure A-5, have a one-to-many relationship. A **one-to-many relationship** (abbreviated **1:M** or **1:N**) exists between two tables when each row in the first table (sometimes called the **primary table**) matches many rows in the second table and each row in the second table (sometimes called the **related**

**table**) matches at most one row in the first table. "Many" can mean zero rows, one row, or two or more rows. The DeptNum field, which is a foreign key in the Employee table and the primary key in the Department table, is the common field that ties together the rows of the two tables. Each department has many employees; and each employee works in exactly one department or hasn't been assigned to a department, if the DeptNum field value for that employee is null.

**Figure A-5** **A one-to-many relationship**

primary key for the one-to-many relationship

Department

| DeptNum | DeptName | DeptHead |
|---|---|---|
| 24 | Finance | 8112 |
| 27 | Marketing | 2173 |
| 31 | Technology | 4519 |

foreign key for the one-to-many relationship

primary key

Employee

| EmployeeNum | FirstName | LastName | DeptNum |
|---|---|---|---|
| 2173 | Barbara | Hennessey | 27 |
| 4519 | Lee | Noordsy | 31 |
| 8005 | Pat | Amidon | 27 |
| 8112 | Chris | Wandzell | 24 |

## Many-to-Many Relationship

In Figure A-6, the Employee table (with the EmployeeNum field as its primary key) and the Position table (with the PositionID field as its primary key) have a many-to-many relationship. A **many-to-many relationship** (abbreviated as **M:N**) exists between two tables when each row in the first table matches many rows in the second table and each row in the second table matches many rows in the first table. In a relational database, you must use a third table (often called an **intersection table**, **junction table**, or **link table**) to serve as a bridge between the two many-to-many tables; the third table has the primary keys of the two many-to-many tables as its primary key. The original tables now each have a one-to-many relationship with the new table. The EmployeeNum and PositionID fields represent the primary key of the Employment table that is shown in Figure A-6. The EmployeeNum field, which is a foreign key in the Employment table and the primary key in the Employee table, is the common field that ties together the rows of the Employee and Employment tables. Likewise, the PositionID field is the common field for the Position and Employment tables. Each employee has served in many different positions within the company over time, and each position in the company has been filled by many different employees over time.

**Figure A-6** A many-to-many relationship

Employee

primary key (Employee table)

| EmployeeNum | FirstName | LastName | DeptNum |
|---|---|---|---|
| 2173 | Barbara | Hennessey | 27 |
| 4519 | Lee | Noordsy | 31 |
| 8005 | Pat | Amidon | 27 |
| 8112 | Chris | Wandzell | 24 |

Position

primary key (Position table)

| PositionID | PositionDesc | PayGrade |
|---|---|---|
| 1 | Director | 45 |
| 2 | Manager | 40 |
| 3 | Analyst | 30 |
| 4 | Clerk | 20 |

Employment

composite key of the intersection table

foreign keys related to the Employee and Position tables

| EmployeeNum | PositionID | StartDate | EndDate |
|---|---|---|---|
| 2173 | 2 | 12/14/2011 | |
| 4519 | 1 | 04/23/2013 | |
| 4519 | 3 | 11/11/2007 | 04/22/2013 |
| 8005 | 3 | 06/05/2012 | 08/25/2013 |
| 8005 | 4 | 07/02/2010 | 06/04/2012 |
| 8112 | 1 | 12/15/2012 | |
| 8112 | 2 | 10/04/2011 | 12/14/2012 |

## One-to-One Relationship

In Figure A-5, recall that there's a one-to-many relationship between the Department table (the primary table) and the Employee table (the related table). Each department has many employees, and each employee works in one department. The DeptNum field in the Employee table serves as a foreign key to connect records in that table to records with matching DeptNum field values in the Department table.

Furthermore, each department has a single employee who serves as the head of the department, and each employee either serves as the head of a department or simply works in a department without being the department head. Therefore, the Department and Employee tables not only have a one-to-many relationship, but these two tables also have a second relationship, a one-to-one relationship. A **one-to-one relationship** (abbreviated **1:1**) exists between two tables when each row in each table has at most one matching row in the other table. As shown in Figure A-7, each DeptHead field value in the Department table represents the employee number in the Employee table of the employee who heads the department. In other words, each DeptHead field value in the Department table matches exactly one EmployeeNum field value in the Employee table. At the same time, each EmployeeNum field value in the Employee table matches at most one DeptHead field value in the Department table—matching one DeptHead field value if the employee is a department head, or matching zero DeptHead field values if the employee is not a department head. For this one-to-one relationship, the EmployeeNum field in the

Employee table and the DeptHead field in the Department table are the fields that link the two tables, with the DeptHead field serving as a foreign key in the Department table and the EmployeeNum field serving as a primary key in the Employee table.

Some database designers might use EmployeeNum instead of DeptHead as the field name for the foreign key in the Department table because they both represent the employee number for the employees of the company. However, DeptHead better identifies the purpose of the field and would more commonly be used as the field name.

**Figure A-7** **A one-to-one relationship**

primary key (Department table) → DeptNum

foreign key for the one-to-one relationship → DeptHead

Department

| DeptNum | DeptName | DeptHead |
|---|---|---|
| 24 | Finance | 8112 |
| 27 | Marketing | 2173 |
| 31 | Technology | 4519 |

primary key for the one-to-one relationship → EmployeeNum

Employee

| EmployeeNum | FirstName | LastName | DeptNum |
|---|---|---|---|
| 2173 | Barbara | Hennessey | 27 |
| 4519 | Lee | Noordsy | 31 |
| 8005 | Pat | Amidon | 27 |
| 8112 | Chris | Wandzell | 24 |

## Entity Subtype

Suppose the company awards annual bonuses to a small number of employees who fill director positions in selected departments. As shown in Figure A-8, you could store the Bonus field in the Employee table because a bonus is an attribute associated with employees. The Bonus field would contain either the amount of the employee's bonus (record 4 in the Employee table) or a null value for employees without bonuses (records 1 through 3 in the Employee table).

**Figure A-8** **Bonus field added to the Employee table**

Employee

| EmployeeNum | FirstName | LastName | DeptNum | Bonus |
|---|---|---|---|---|
| 2173 | Barbara | Hennessey | 27 | |
| 4519 | Lee | Noordsy | 31 | |
| 8005 | Pat | Amidon | 27 | |
| 8112 | Chris | Wandzell | 24 | $20,000 |

nulls for these Bonus field values

Bonus field value for the fourth record

Figure A-9 shows an alternative approach, in which the Bonus field is placed in a separate table, the EmployeeBonus table. The EmployeeBonus table's primary key is the EmployeeNum field, and the table contains one row for each employee earning a bonus. Because some employees do not earn a bonus, the EmployeeBonus table has fewer rows than the Employee table. However, each row in the EmployeeBonus table has a matching row in the Employee table, with the EmployeeNum field serving as the common field; the EmployeeNum field is the primary key in the Employee table and is a foreign key in the EmployeeBonus table.

**Figure A-9** **Storing Bonus values in a separate table, an entity subtype**

Employee

| EmployeeNum | FirstName | LastName | DeptNum |
|---|---|---|---|
| 2173 | Barbara | Hennessey | 27 |
| 4519 | Lee | Noordsy | 31 |
| 8005 | Pat | Amidon | 27 |
| 8112 | Chris | Wandzell | 24 |

EmployeeBonus

| EmployeeNum | Bonus |
|---|---|
| 8112 | $20,000 |

primary key (Employee table)
primary key (EmployeeBonus table)
foreign key
entity subtype

The EmployeeBonus table, in this situation, is called an **entity subtype**, a table whose primary key is a foreign key to a second table and whose fields are additional fields for the second table. Database designers create an entity subtype in two situations. In the first situation, some users might need access to all employee fields, including employee bonuses, while other employees might need access to all employee fields except bonuses. Because most DBMSs allow you to control which tables a user can access, you can specify that some users can access both tables and that other users can access the Employee table but not the EmployeeBonus table, keeping the employee bonus information hidden from the latter group. In the second situation, you can create an entity subtype when a table has fields that could have nulls, as was the case for the Bonus field stored in the Employee table in Figure A-8. You should be aware that database experts are currently debating the validity of the use of nulls in relational databases, and many experts insist that you should never use nulls. This warning against nulls is partly based on the inconsistent way different RDBMSs treat nulls and partly due to the lack of a firm theoretical foundation for how to use nulls. In any case, entity subtypes are an alternative to the use of nulls.

## Entity-Relationship Diagrams

A common shorthand method for describing tables is to write the table name followed by its fields in parentheses, underlining the fields that represent the primary key and identifying the foreign keys for a table immediately after the table. Using this method, the tables that appear in Figures A-5 through A-7 and Figure A-9 are described in the following way:

Department (DeptNum, DeptName, DeptHead)
    Foreign key: DeptHead to Employee table
Employee (EmployeeNum, FirstName, LastName, DeptNum)
    Foreign key: DeptNum to Department table
Position (PositionID, PositionDesc, PayGrade)
Employment (EmployeeNum, PositionID, StartDate, EndDate)
    Foreign key: EmployeeNum to Employee table
    Foreign key: PositionID to Position table
EmployeeBonus (EmployeeNum, Bonus)
    Foreign key: EmployeeNum to Employee table

Another popular way to describe tables *and their relationships* is with entity-relationship diagrams. An **entity-relationship diagram (ERD)** shows a database's entities and the relationships among the entities in a symbolic, visual way. In an ERD, an entity and a table are equivalent. Figure A-10 shows an entity-relationship diagram for the tables that appear in Figures A-5 through A-7 and Figure A-9.

**Figure A-10** **An entity-relationship diagram (ERD)**

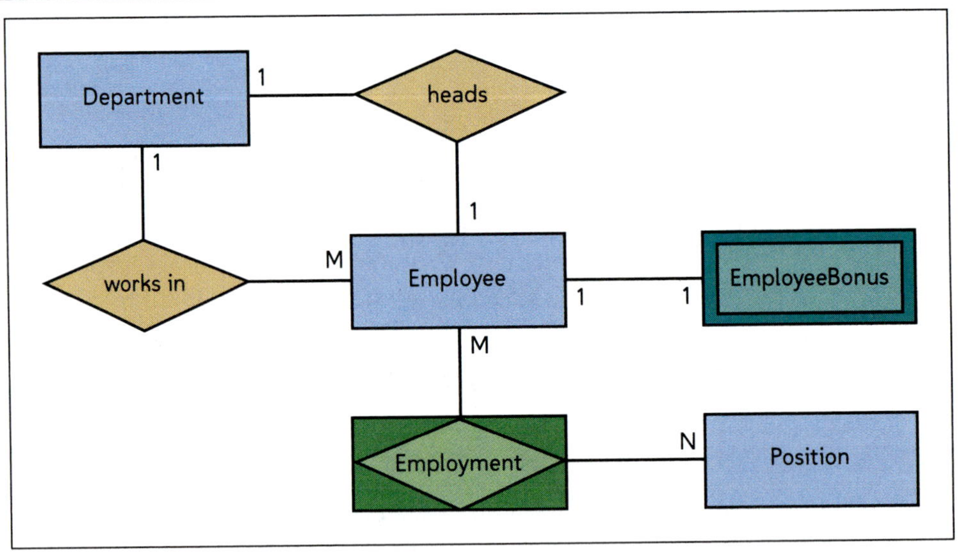


ERDs have the following characteristics:

- Entities, or tables, appear in rectangles, and relationships appear in diamonds. The entity name appears inside the rectangle, and a verb describing the relationship appears inside the diamond. For example, the Employee rectangle is connected to the Department rectangle by the "works in" diamond and is read: "an employee works in a department."
- The 1 by the Department entity and the M by the Employee entity identify a one-to-many relationship between these two entities. In a similar manner, a many-to-many relationship exists between the Employee and Position entities and one-to-one relationships exist between the Department and Employee entities and between the Employee and EmployeeBonus entities.

- A diamond inside a rectangle defines a composite entity. A **composite entity** is a relationship that has the characteristics of an entity. For example, Employment connects the Employee and Position entities in a many-to-many relationship and acts as an entity by containing the StartDate and EndDate fields, along with the composite key of the EmployeeNum and PositionID fields.
- An entity subtype, for example, EmployeeBonus, appears in a double rectangle and is connected without an intervening diamond directly to its related entity, Employee.

You can also show fields in an ERD by placing each individual field in a bubble connected to its entity or relationship. However, typical ERDs have large numbers of entities and relationships, so including the fields might confuse rather than clarify the ERD.

## Integrity Constraints

A database has **integrity** if its data follows certain rules; each rule is called an **integrity constraint**. The ideal is to have the DBMS enforce all integrity constraints. If a DBMS can enforce some integrity constraints but not others, the other integrity constraints must be enforced by other programs or by the people who use the DBMS. Integrity constraints can be divided into three groups: primary key constraints, foreign key constraints, and domain integrity constraints.

- One primary key constraint is inherent in the definition of a primary key, which says that the primary key must be unique. The **entity integrity constraint** says that the primary key cannot be null. For a composite key, none of the individual fields can be null. The uniqueness and nonnull properties of a primary key ensure that you can reference any data value in a database by supplying its table name, field name, and primary key value.
- Foreign keys provide the mechanism for forming a relationship between two tables, and referential integrity ensures that only valid relationships exist. **Referential integrity** is the constraint specifying that each nonnull foreign key value must match a primary key value in the primary table. Specifically, referential integrity means that you cannot add a row with an unmatched foreign key value. Referential integrity also means that you cannot change or delete the related primary key value and leave the foreign key orphaned. In some RDBMSs, if you try to change or delete a primary key value, you can specify one of these options: restricted, cascades, or nullifies. If you specify **restricted**, the DBMS updates or deletes the value only if there are no matching foreign key values. If you choose **cascades** and then change a primary key value, the DBMS changes the matching foreign key values to the new primary key value, or, if you delete a primary key value, the DBMS also deletes the matching foreign key rows. If you choose **nullifies** and then change or delete a primary key value, the DBMS sets all matching foreign key values to null.
- Recall that a domain is a set of values from which one or more fields draw their actual values. A **domain integrity constraint** is a rule you specify for a field. By choosing a data type for a field, you impose a constraint on the set of values allowed for the field. You can create specific validation rules for a field to limit its domain further. As you make a field's domain definition more precise, you exclude more and more unacceptable values for the field. For example, in the State table, shown in Figures A-2 and A-4, you could define the domain for the EnteredUnionOrder field to be a unique integer between 1 and 50 and the domain for the StateBird field to be any name containing 25 or fewer characters.

# Dependencies and Determinants

Tables are related to other tables. Fields are also related to other fields. Consider the modified Employee table shown in Figure A-11. Its description is:

Employee (<u>EmployeeNum</u>, <u>PositionID</u>, LastName, PositionDesc, StartDate, HealthPlan, PlanDesc)

**Figure A-11 A table combining fields from three tables**

primary key

Employee

| EmployeeNum | PositionID | LastName | PositionDesc | StartDate | HealthPlan | PlanDesc |
|---|---|---|---|---|---|---|
| 2173 | 2 | Hennessey | Manager | 12/14/2011 | B | Managed HMO |
| 4519 | 1 | Noordsy | Director | 04/23/2013 | A | Managed PPO |
| 4519 | 3 | Noordsy | Analyst | 11/11/2007 | A | Managed PPO |
| 8005 | 3 | Amidon | Analyst | 06/05/2012 | C | Health Savings |
| 8005 | 4 | Amidon | Clerk | 07/02/2010 | C | Health Savings |
| 8112 | 1 | Wandzell | Director | 12/15/2012 | A | Managed PPO |
| 8112 | 2 | Wandzell | Manager | 10/04/2011 | A | Managed PPO |

The modified Employee table combines several fields from the Employee, Position, and Employment tables that appeared in Figure A-6. The EmployeeNum and LastName fields are from the Employee table. The PositionID and PositionDesc fields are from the Position table. The EmployeeNum, PositionID, and StartDate fields are from the Employment table. The HealthPlan and PlanDesc fields are new fields for the Employee table, whose primary key is now the combination of the EmployeeNum and PositionID fields.

In the Employee table, each field is related to other fields. To determine field relationships, you ask "Does a value for a particular field give me a single value for another field?" If the answer is Yes, then the two fields are related. For example, a value for the EmployeeNum field determines a single value for the LastName field, and a value for the LastName field depends on the value of the EmployeeNum field. In database discussions, the word *functionally* is used, as in: "EmployeeNum functionally determines LastName" and "LastName is functionally dependent on EmployeeNum." In this case, EmployeeNum is called a determinant. A **determinant** is a field, or a collection of fields, whose values determine the values of another field. A field is functionally dependent on another field (or a collection of fields) if that other field is a determinant for it.

You can graphically show a table's functional dependencies and determinants in a **bubble diagram**; a bubble diagram is also called a **data model diagram** and a **functional dependency diagram**. Figure A-12 shows the bubble diagram for the Employee table shown in Figure A-11.

Figure A-12 **A bubble diagram for the modified Employee table**

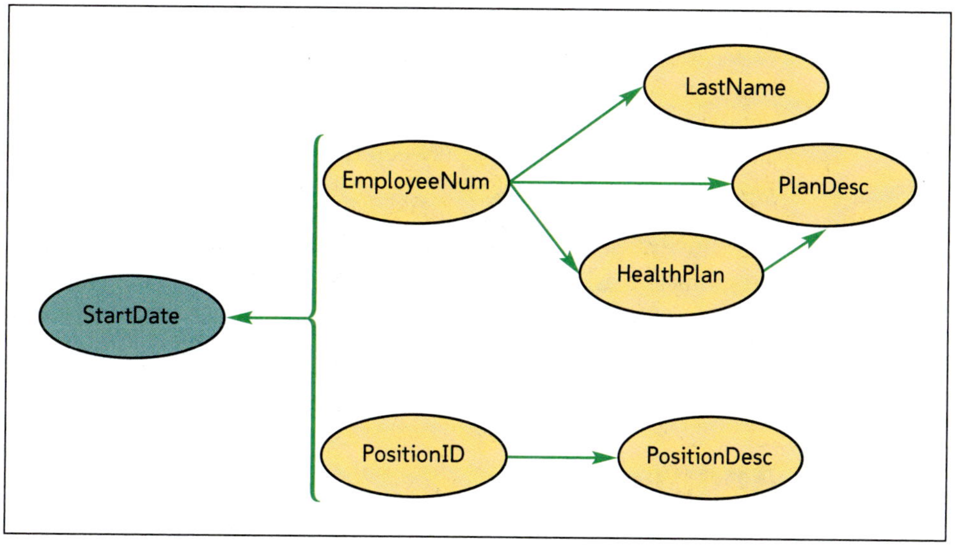


You can read the bubble diagram in Figure A-12 as follows:

- The EmployeeNum field is a determinant for the LastName, HealthPlan, and PlanDesc fields.
- The PositionID field is a determinant for the PositionDesc field.
- The StartDate field is functionally dependent on the EmployeeNum and PositionID fields together.
- The HealthPlan field is a determinant for the PlanDesc field.

Note that EmployeeNum and PositionID together is a determinant for the StartDate field and for all fields that depend on the EmployeeNum field alone and the PositionID field alone. Some experts include these additional fields and some don't. The previous list of determinants does not include these additional fields.

An alternative way to show determinants is to list the determinant, a right arrow, and then the dependent fields, separated by commas. Using this alternative, the determinants shown in Figure A-12 are:

EmployeeNum → LastName, HealthPlan, PlanDesc
PositionID → PositionDesc
EmployeeNum, PositionID → StartDate
HealthPlan → PlanDesc

Only the StartDate field is functionally dependent on the table's full primary key, the EmployeeNum and PositionID fields. The LastName, HealthPlan, and PlanDesc fields have partial dependencies because they are functionally dependent on the EmployeeNum field, which is part of the primary key. A **partial dependency** is a functional dependency on part of the primary key, instead of the entire primary key. Does another partial dependency exist in the Employee table? Yes, the PositionDesc field has a partial dependency on the PositionID field.

Because the EmployeeNum field is a determinant of both the HealthPlan and PlanDesc fields, and the HealthPlan field is a determinant of the PlanDesc field, the HealthPlan and PlanDesc fields have a transitive dependency. A **transitive dependency** is a functional dependency between two nonkey fields, which are both dependent on a third field.

How do you know which functional dependencies exist among a collection of fields, and how do you recognize partial and transitive dependencies? The answers lie with the questions you ask as you gather the requirements for a database application. For each field and entity, you must gain an accurate understanding of its meaning and relationships in the context of the application. **Semantic object modeling** is an entire area of study within the database field devoted to the meanings and relationships of data.

## Anomalies

When you use a DBMS, you are more likely to get results you can trust if you create your tables carefully. For example, problems might occur with tables that have partial and transitive dependencies, whereas you won't have as much trouble if you ensure that your tables include only fields that are directly related to each other. Also, when you remove data redundancy from a table, you improve that table. **Data redundancy** occurs when you store the same data in more than one place.

The problems caused by data redundancy and by partial and transitive dependencies are called **anomalies** because they are undesirable irregularities of tables. Anomalies are of three types: insertion, deletion, and update.

To examine the effects of these anomalies, consider the modified Employee table that is shown again in Figure A-13.

**Figure A-13** **A table with insertion, deletion, and update anomalies**

primary key

Employee

| EmployeeNum | PositionID | LastName | PositionDesc | StartDate | HealthPlan | PlanDesc |
|---|---|---|---|---|---|---|
| 2173 | 2 | Hennessey | Manager | 12/14/2011 | B | Managed HMO |
| 4519 | 1 | Noordsy | Director | 04/23/2013 | A | Managed PPO |
| 4519 | 3 | Noordsy | Analyst | 11/11/2007 | A | Managed PPO |
| 8005 | 3 | Amidon | Analyst | 06/05/2012 | C | Health Savings |
| 8005 | 4 | Amidon | Clerk | 07/02/2010 | C | Health Savings |
| 8112 | 1 | Wandzell | Director | 12/15/2012 | A | Managed PPO |
| 8112 | 2 | Wandzell | Manager | 10/04/2011 | A | Managed PPO |

- An **insertion anomaly** occurs when you cannot add a record to a table because you do not know the entire primary key value. For example, you cannot add the new employee Cathy Corbett with an EmployeeNum of 3322 to the Employee table if you do not know her position in the company. Entity integrity prevents you from leaving any part of a primary key null. Because the PositionID field is part of the primary key, you cannot leave it null. To add the new employee, your only option is to make up a PositionID field value, until you determine the correct position. This solution misrepresents the facts and is unacceptable, if a better approach is available.

- A **deletion anomaly** occurs when you delete data from a table and unintentionally lose other critical data. For example, if you delete EmployeeNum 2173 because Hennessey is no longer an employee, you also lose the only instance of HealthPlan B in the database. Thus, you no longer know that HealthPlan B is the "Managed HMO" plan.
- An **update anomaly** occurs when you change one field value and either the DBMS must make more than one change to the database or else the database ends up containing inconsistent data. For example, if you change a LastName, HealthPlan, or PlanDesc field value for EmployeeNum 8005, the DBMS must change multiple rows of the Employee table. If the DBMS fails to change all the rows, the LastName, HealthPlan, or PlanDesc field now has different values in the database and is inconsistent.

# Normalization

**Database design** is the process of determining the content and structure of data in a database in order to support some activity on behalf of a user or group of users. After you have determined the collection of fields users need to support an activity, you need to determine the precise tables needed for the collection of fields and then place those fields into the correct tables. Crucial to good database design is understanding the functional dependencies of all fields; recognizing the anomalies caused by data redundancy, partial dependencies, and transitive dependencies when they exist; and knowing how to eliminate the anomalies. Failure to eliminate anomalies leads to data redundancy and can cause data integrity and other problems as your database grows in size.

The process of identifying and eliminating anomalies is called **normalization**. Using normalization, you start with a collection of tables, apply sets of rules to eliminate anomalies, and produce a new collection of problem-free tables. The sets of rules are called **normal forms**. Of special interest for our purposes are the first three normal forms: first normal form, second normal form, and third normal form. First normal form improves the design of your tables, second normal form improves the first normal form design, and third normal form applies even more stringent rules to produce an even better design. Note that normal forms beyond third normal form exist; these higher normal forms can improve a database design in some situations but won't be covered in this section.

## First Normal Form

Consider the Employee table shown in Figure A-14. For each employee, the table contains EmployeeNum, which is the primary key; the employee's first name, last name, health plan code and description; and the ID, description, pay grade, and start date of each position held by the employee. For example, Barbara Hennessey has held one position, while the other three employees have held two positions. Because each entry in a table must contain a single value, the structure shown in Figure A-14 does not meet the requirements for a table, or relation; therefore, it is called an **unnormalized relation**. The set of fields that includes the PositionID, PositionDesc, PayGrade, and StartDate fields, which can have more than one value, is called a **repeating group**.

**Figure A-14** **Repeating groups of data in an unnormalized Employee table**



| EmployeeNum | PositionID | FirstName | LastName | PositionDesc | PayGrade | StartDate | HealthPlan | PlanDesc |
|---|---|---|---|---|---|---|---|---|
| 2173 | 2 | Barbara | Hennessey | Manager | 40 | 12/14/2011 | B | Managed HMO |
| 4519 | 1<br>3 | Lee | Noordsy | Director<br>Analyst | 45<br>30 | 04/23/2013<br>11/11/2007 | A | Managed PPO |
| 8005 | 3<br>4 | Pat | Amidon | Analyst<br>Clerk | 30<br>20 | 06/05/2012<br>07/02/2010 | C | Health Savings |
| 8112 | 1<br>2 | Chris | Wandzell | Director<br>Manager | 45<br>40 | 12/15/2012<br>10/04/2011 | A | Managed PPO |

First normal form addresses this repeating-group situation. A table is in **first normal form (1NF)** if it does not contain repeating groups. To remove a repeating group and convert to first normal form, you expand the primary key to include the primary key of the repeating group, forming a composite key. Performing the conversion step produces the 1NF table shown in Figure A-15.

**Figure A-15** **After conversion to 1NF**



| EmployeeNum | PositionID | FirstName | LastName | PositionDesc | PayGrade | StartDate | HealthPlan | PlanDesc |
|---|---|---|---|---|---|---|---|---|
| 2173 | 2 | Barbara | Hennessey | Manager | 40 | 12/14/2011 | B | Managed HMO |
| 4519 | 1 | Lee | Noordsy | Director | 45 | 04/23/2013 | A | Managed PPO |
| 4519 | 3 | Lee | Noordsy | Analyst | 30 | 11/11/2007 | A | Managed PPO |
| 8005 | 3 | Pat | Amidon | Analyst | 30 | 06/05/2012 | C | Health Savings |
| 8005 | 4 | Pat | Amidon | Clerk | 20 | 07/02/2010 | C | Health Savings |
| 8112 | 1 | Chris | Wandzell | Director | 45 | 12/15/2012 | A | Managed PPO |
| 8112 | 2 | Chris | Wandzell | Manager | 40 | 10/04/2011 | A | Managed PPO |

The alternative way to describe the 1NF table is:

Employee (<u>EmployeeNum</u>, <u>PositionID</u>, FirstName, LastName, PositionDesc, PayGrade, StartDate, HealthPlan, PlanDesc)

The Employee table is now a true table and has a composite key. The table, however, suffers from insertion, deletion, and update anomalies. (As an exercise, find examples of the three anomalies in the table.) The EmployeeNum field is a determinant for the FirstName, LastName, HealthPlan, and PlanDesc fields, so partial dependencies exist in the Employee table. It is these partial dependencies that cause the anomalies in the Employee table, and second normal form addresses the partial-dependency problem.

## Second Normal Form

A table in 1NF is in **second normal form (2NF)** if it does not contain any partial dependencies. To remove partial dependencies from a table and convert it to second normal form, you perform two steps. First, identify the functional dependencies for every field in the table. Second, if necessary, create new tables and place each field in a table, so that the field is functionally dependent on the entire primary key, not part of the primary key. If you need to create new tables, restrict them to ones with a primary key that is a subset of the original composite key. Note that partial dependencies occur only when you have a composite key; a table in first normal form with a single-field primary key is automatically in second normal form.

First, identifying the functional dependencies leads to the following determinants for the Employee table:

EmployeeNum → FirstName, LastName, HealthPlan, PlanDesc
PositionID → PositionDesc, PayGrade
EmployeeNum, PositionID → StartDate
HealthPlan → PlanDesc

The EmployeeNum field is a determinant for the FirstName, LastName, HealthPlan, and PlanDesc fields. The PositionID field is a determinant for the PositionDesc and PayGrade fields. The HealthPlan field is a determinant for the PlanDesc field. The composite key EmployeeNum and PositionID is a determinant for the StartDate field. Performing the second step in the conversion from first normal form to second form produces the three 2NF tables shown in Figure A-16.

**Figure A-16** After conversion to 2NF

Employee (primary key: EmployeeNum)

| EmployeeNum | FirstName | LastName | HealthPlan | PlanDesc |
|---|---|---|---|---|
| 2173 | Barbara | Hennessey | B | Managed HMO |
| 4519 | Lee | Noordsy | A | Managed PPO |
| 8005 | Pat | Amidon | C | Health Savings |
| 8112 | Chris | Wandzell | A | Managed PPO |

Position (primary key: PositionID)

| PositionID | PositionDesc | PayGrade |
|---|---|---|
| 1 | Director | 45 |
| 2 | Manager | 40 |
| 3 | Analyst | 30 |
| 4 | Clerk | 20 |

Employment (primary key: EmployeeNum, PositionID)

| EmployeeNum | PositionID | StartDate |
|---|---|---|
| 2173 | 2 | 12/14/2011 |
| 4519 | 1 | 04/23/2013 |
| 4519 | 3 | 11/11/2007 |
| 8005 | 3 | 06/05/2012 |
| 8005 | 4 | 07/02/2010 |
| 8112 | 1 | 12/15/2012 |
| 8112 | 2 | 10/04/2011 |

The alternative way to describe the 2NF tables is:

Employee (<u>EmployeeNum</u>, FirstName, LastName, HealthPlan, PlanDesc)
Position (<u>PositionID</u>, PositionDesc, PayGrade)
Employment (<u>EmployeeNum</u>, <u>PositionID</u>, StartDate)
    Foreign key: EmployeeNum to Employee table
    Foreign key: PositionID to Position table

All three tables are in second normal form. Do anomalies still exist? The Position and Employment tables show no anomalies, but the Employee table suffers from anomalies caused by the transitive dependency between the HealthPlan and PlanDesc fields. (As an exercise, find examples of the three anomalies caused by the transitive dependency.) That is, the HealthPlan field is a determinant for the PlanDesc field, and the EmployeeNum field is a determinant for the HealthPlan and PlanDesc fields. Third normal form addresses the transitive-dependency problem.

## Third Normal Form

A table in 2NF is in **third normal form (3NF)** if every determinant is a candidate key. This definition for 3NF is referred to as **Boyce-Codd normal form (BCNF)** and is an improvement over the original version of 3NF. What are the determinants in the Employee table? The EmployeeNum and HealthPlan fields are the determinants; however, the EmployeeNum field is a candidate key because it's the table's primary key, and the HealthPlan field is not a candidate key. Therefore, the Employee table is in second normal form, but it is not in third normal form.

To convert a table to third normal form, remove the fields that depend on the non-candidate-key determinant and place them into a new table with the determinant as the primary key. For the Employee table, the PlanDesc field depends on the HealthPlan field, which is a non-candidate-key determinant. Thus, you remove the PlanDesc field from the table, create a new HealthBenefits table, place the PlanDesc field in the HealthBenefits table, and then make the HealthPlan field the primary key of the HealthBenefits table. Note that only the PlanDesc field is removed from the Employee table; the HealthPlan field remains as a foreign key in the Employee table. Figure A-17 shows the database design for the four 3NF tables.

**Figure A-17** After conversion to 3NF

Employee

primary key → EmployeeNum

| EmployeeNum | FirstName | LastName | HealthPlan |
|---|---|---|---|
| 2173 | Barbara | Hennessey | B |
| 4519 | Lee | Noordsy | A |
| 8005 | Pat | Amidon | C |
| 8112 | Chris | Wandzell | A |

HealthBenefits

primary key → HealthPlan

| HealthPlan | PlanDesc |
|---|---|
| A | Managed PPO |
| B | Managed HMO |
| C | Health Savings |

Position

primary key → PositionID

| PositionID | PositionDesc | PayGrade |
|---|---|---|
| 1 | Director | 45 |
| 2 | Manager | 40 |
| 3 | Analyst | 30 |
| 4 | Clerk | 20 |

Employment

primary key → EmployeeNum, PositionID

| EmployeeNum | PositionID | StartDate |
|---|---|---|
| 2173 | 2 | 12/14/2011 |
| 4519 | 1 | 04/23/2013 |
| 4519 | 3 | 11/11/2007 |
| 8005 | 3 | 06/05/2012 |
| 8005 | 4 | 07/02/2010 |
| 8112 | 1 | 12/15/2012 |
| 8112 | 2 | 10/04/2011 |

The alternative way to describe the 3NF relations is:

HealthBenefits (HealthPlan, PlanDesc)
Employee (EmployeeNum, FirstName, LastName, HealthPlan)
    Foreign key: HealthPlan to HealthBenefits table
Position (PositionID, PositionDesc, PayGrade)
Employment (EmployeeNum, PositionID, StartDate)
    Foreign key: EmployeeNum to Employee table
    Foreign key: PositionID to Position table

The four tables have no anomalies because you have eliminated all the data redundancy, partial dependencies, and transitive dependencies. Normalization provides the framework for eliminating anomalies and delivering an optimal database design, which you should always strive to achieve. You should be aware, however, that experts sometimes denormalize tables to improve database performance—specifically, to decrease the time it takes the database to respond to a user's commands and requests. Typically, when you denormalize tables, you combine separate tables into one table to reduce the need for the DBMS to join the separate tables to process queries and other informational requests. When you denormalize a table, you reintroduce redundancy to the table. At the same time, you reintroduce anomalies. Thus, improving performance exposes a database to potential integrity problems. Only database experts should denormalize tables, but even experts first complete the normalization of their tables.

# Natural, Artificial, and Surrogate Keys

When you complete the design of a database, your tables should be in third normal form, free of anomalies and redundancy. Some tables, such as the State table (see Figure A-2), have obvious third normal form designs with obvious primary keys. The State table's description is:

State (StateAbbrev, StateName, EnteredUnionOrder, StateBird, StatePopulation)

Recall that the candidate keys for the State table are StateAbbrev, StateName, and EnteredUnionOrder. Choosing the StateAbbrev field as the State table's primary key makes the StateName and EnteredUnionOrder fields alternate keys. Primary keys such as the StateAbbrev field are sometimes called natural keys. A **natural key** (also called a **logical key** or an **intelligent key**) is a primary key that consists of a field, or a collection of fields, that is an inherent characteristic of the entity described by the table and that is visible to users. Other examples of natural keys are the ISBN (International Standard Book Number) for a book, the SSN (Social Security number) for a U.S. individual, the UPC (Universal Product Code) for a product, and the VIN (vehicle identification number) for a vehicle.

Is the PositionID field, which is the primary key for the Position table (see Figure A-17), a natural key? No, the PositionID field is not an inherent characteristic of a position. Instead, the PositionID field has been added to the Position table only as a way to identify each position uniquely. The PositionID field is an **artificial key**, which is a field that you add to a table to serve solely as the primary key and that is visible to users.

Another reason for using an artificial key arises in tables that allow duplicate records. Although relational database theory and most experts do not allow duplicate records in a table, consider a database that tracks donors and their donations. Figure A-18 shows a Donor table with an artificial key of DonorID and with the DonorFirstName and DonorLastName fields. Some cash donations are anonymous, which accounts for the fourth record in the Donor table. Figure A-18 also shows the Donation table with the DonorID field, a foreign key to the Donor table, and the DonationDate and DonationAmt fields.

**Figure A-18** Donor and Donation tables

primary key → DonorID

Donor

| DonorID | DonorFirstName | DonorLastName |
|---|---|---|
| 1 | Christina | Chang |
| 2 | Franco | Diaz |
| 3 | Angie | Diaz |
| 4 | | Anonymous |
| 5 | Tracy | Burns |

Donation

| DonorID | DonationDate | DonationAmt |
|---|---|---|
| 1 | 10/12/2013 | $50.00 |
| 1 | 09/30/2014 | $50.00 |
| 2 | 10/03/2014 | $75.00 |
| 4 | 10/10/2014 | $50.00 |
| 4 | 10/10/2014 | $50.00 |
| 4 | 10/11/2014 | $25.00 |
| 5 | 10/13/2014 | $50.00 |

duplicate records (the two DonorID 4, 10/10/2014, $50.00 rows)

What is the primary key of the Donation table? No single field is unique, and neither is any combination of fields. For example, on 10/10/2014, two anonymous donors (DonorID value of 4) donated $50 each. You need to add an artificial key, DonationID for example, to the Donation table. The addition of the artificial key makes every record in the Donation table unique, as shown in Figure A-19.

**Figure A-19** Donation table after adding DonationID, an artificial key

artificial key → DonationID

Donation

| DonationID | DonorID | DonationDate | DonationAmt |
|---|---|---|---|
| 1 | 1 | 10/12/2013 | $50.00 |
| 2 | 1 | 09/30/2014 | $50.00 |
| 3 | 2 | 10/03/2014 | $75.00 |
| 4 | 4 | 10/10/2014 | $50.00 |
| 5 | 4 | 10/10/2014 | $50.00 |
| 6 | 4 | 10/11/2014 | $25.00 |
| 7 | 5 | 10/13/2014 | $50.00 |

The descriptions of the Donor and Donation tables now are:

Donor (<u>DonorID</u>, DonorFirstName, DonorLastName)
Donation (<u>DonationID</u>, DonorID, DonationDate, DonationAmt)
    Foreign key: DonorID to Donor table

For another common situation, consider the 3NF tables you reviewed in the previous section (see Figure A-17) that have the following descriptions:

HealthBenefits (<u>HealthPlan</u>, PlanDesc)
Employee (<u>EmployeeNum</u>, FirstName, LastName, HealthPlan)
    Foreign key: HealthPlan to HealthBenefits table
Position (<u>PositionID</u>, PositionDesc, PayGrade)
Employment (<u>EmployeeNum</u>, <u>PositionID</u>, StartDate)
    Foreign key: EmployeeNum to Employee table
    Foreign key: PositionID to Position table

Recall that a primary key must be unique, must be minimal, and must not change in value. In theory, primary keys don't change in value. However, in practice, you might have to change EmployeeNum field values that you incorrectly entered in the Employment table. Further, if you need to change an EmployeeNum field value in the Employee table, the change must cascade to the EmployeeNum field values in the Employment table. Also, changes to a PositionID field value in the Position table must cascade to the Employment table. For these and other reasons, many experts add surrogate keys to their tables. A **surrogate key** (also called a **synthetic key**) is a system-generated primary key that is hidden from users. Usually you can use an automatic numbering data type, such as the Access AutoNumber data type, for a surrogate key. Figure A-20 shows the four tables with surrogate keys added to each table.

**Figure A-20** Using surrogate keys

foreign key (HealthSK)

surrogate key (EmployeeSK)

Employee

| EmployeeSK | EmployeeNum | FirstName | LastName | HealthSK |
|---|---|---|---|---|
| 1 | 2173 | Barbara | Hennessey | 2 |
| 2 | 4519 | Lee | Noordsy | 1 |
| 3 | 8005 | Pat | Amidon | 3 |
| 4 | 8112 | Chris | Wandzell | 1 |

surrogate key (HealthSK)

HealthBenefits

| HealthSK | HealthPlan | PlanDesc |
|---|---|---|
| 1 | A | Managed PPO |
| 2 | B | Managed HMO |
| 3 | C | Health Savings |

artificial key (PositionID)

Position

| PositionID | PositionDesc | PayGrade |
|---|---|---|
| 1 | Director | 45 |
| 2 | Manager | 40 |
| 3 | Analyst | 30 |
| 4 | Clerk | 20 |

foreign key (EmployeeSK)

foreign key (PositionID)

surrogate key (EmploymentSK)

Employment

| EmploymentSK | EmployeeSK | PositionID | StartDate |
|---|---|---|---|
| 1 | 1 | 2 | 12/14/2011 |
| 2 | 2 | 1 | 04/23/2013 |
| 3 | 2 | 3 | 11/11/2007 |
| 4 | 3 | 3 | 06/05/2012 |
| 5 | 3 | 4 | 07/02/2010 |
| 6 | 4 | 1 | 12/15/2012 |
| 7 | 4 | 2 | 10/04/2011 |

The HealthSK field replaces the HealthPlan field as a foreign key in the Employee table, and the EmployeeSK field replaces the EmployeeNum field in the Employment table. When you change an incorrectly entered EmployeeNum field value in the Employee table, you don't need to cascade the change to the Employment table. When you change an incorrectly entered HealthPlan field value in the HealthBenefits table, you don't need to cascade the change to the Employee table.

As you design a database, you should *not* consider the use of surrogate keys, and you should use an artificial key only for the rare table that has duplicate records. At the point when you implement a database, you might choose to use artificial and surrogate keys, but be aware that database experts debate their use and effectiveness. Some of the tradeoffs between natural and surrogate keys that you need to consider are:

- Use surrogate keys to avoid cascading updates to foreign key values. Surrogate keys can also replace lengthier foreign keys when those foreign keys reference composite fields.
- You don't need a surrogate key for a table whose primary key is not used as a foreign key in another table because cascading updates is not an issue.
- Tables with surrogate keys require more joins than do tables with natural keys. For example, if you need to know all employees with a HealthPlan field value of A, the surrogate key in Figure A-20 requires that you join the Employee and HealthBenefits tables to answer the question. Using natural keys as shown in Figure A-17, the HealthPlan field appears in the Employee table, so no join is necessary.
- Although surrogate keys are meant to be hidden from users, they cannot be hidden from users who create SQL statements and use other ad hoc tools.
- Because you need a unique index for the natural key and a unique index for the surrogate key, your database size is larger and index maintenance takes more time when you use a surrogate key. On the other hand, a foreign key using a surrogate key is usually smaller than a foreign key using a natural key, especially when the natural key is a composite key, so those indexes are smaller and faster to access for lookups and joins.

# Microsoft Access Naming Conventions

In the early 1980s, Microsoft's Charles Simonyi introduced an identifier naming convention that became known as Hungarian notation. Microsoft and other companies use this naming convention for variable, control, and other object naming in Basic, Visual Basic, and other programming languages. When Access was introduced in the early 1990s, Stan Leszynski and Greg Reddick adapted Hungarian notation for Microsoft Access databases; their guidelines became known as the Leszynski/Reddick naming conventions. In recent years, the Leszynski naming conventions, the Reddick naming conventions, and other naming conventions have been published. Individuals and companies have created their own Access naming conventions, but many are based on the Leszynski/Reddick naming conventions, as are the naming conventions covered in this section.

An Access database can contain thousands of objects, fields, controls, and other items, and keeping track of their names and what they represent is a difficult task. Consequently, you should use naming conventions that identify the type and purpose of each item in an Access database. You can use naming conventions that identify items generally or very specifically.

For objects, include a prefix tag to identify the type of object, as shown in Figure A-21. In each example in Figure A-21, the final object name consists of a three-character tag prefixed to the base object name. For example, the form name of frmEmployeesAndPositions consists of the frm tag and the EmployeesAndPositions base form name.

**Figure A-21** **Object naming tags**

| Object type | Tag | Example |
|---|---|---|
| Form | frm | frmEmployeesAndPositions |
| Macro | mcr | mcrSwitchboard |
| Module | bas | basCalculations |
| Query | qry | qryEmployee |
| Report | rpt | rptEmployeesAndPositions |
| Table | tbl | tblEmployee |

The tags in Figure A-21 identify each object type in general. If you want to identify object types more specifically, you could expand Figure A-21 to include tags such as fsub for a subform, qxtb for a crosstab query, tlkp for a lookup table, rsub for a subreport, and so on.

For controls in forms and reports, a general naming convention uses lbl as a prefix tag for labels and ctl as a prefix tag for other types of controls. For more specific naming conventions for controls, you'd use a specific prefix tag for each type of control. Figure A-22 shows the prefix tag for some common controls in forms and reports.

**Figure A-22** **Control naming tags**

| Control type | Tag |
|---|---|
| Check box | chk |
| Combo box | cbo |
| Command button | cmd |
| Image | img |
| Label | lbl |
| Line | lin |
| List box | lst |
| Option button | opt |
| PivotTable | pvt |
| Rectangle | shp |
| Subform/Subreport | sub |
| Text box | txt |

Some database developers use a prefix tag for each field name to identify the field's data type (for example, dtm for Date/Time, num for Number, and chr for Text or Character), others use a prefix tag for each field name to identify in which table the field is located (for example, emp for the Employee table and pos for the Position table), and still others don't use a prefix tag for field names.

You might use suffix tags for controls that might otherwise have identical names. For example, if you have two text boxes in a form for calculated controls that display the average and the sum of the OrderAmt field, both could legitimately be named txtOrderAmt unless you used suffix tags to name them txtOrderAmtAvg and txtOrderAmtSum.

You should ensure that any name you use does not duplicate a property name or any keyword Access reserves for special purposes. In general, you can avoid property and keyword name conflicts by using two-word field, control, and object names. For example, use StudentName instead of Name, and use OrderDate instead of Date to avoid name conflicts.

All database developers avoid spaces in names, mainly because spaces are not allowed in server DBMSs, such as SQL Server, Oracle, and DB2. If you are prototyping a Microsoft Access database that you'll migrate to one of these server DBMSs, or if future requirements might force a migration, you should restrict your Access identifier names so that they conform to the rules common to them all. Figure A-23 shows the identifier naming rules for Access, SQL Server, Oracle, and DB2.

**Figure A-23** **Identifier naming rules for common database management systems**

| Identifier naming rule | Access | SQL Server | Oracle | DB2 |
|---|---|---|---|---|
| Maximum character length | 64 | 30 | 30 | 30 |
| Allowable characters | Letters, digits, space, and special characters, except for period (.), exclamation point (!), accent grave (`), and square brackets ([ ]) | Letters, digits, dollar sign ($), underscore (_), number symbol (#), and at symbol (@) | Letters, digits, dollar sign ($), underscore (_), and number symbol (#) | Letters, digits, at symbol (@), dollar sign ($), underscore (_), and number symbol (#) |
| Special rules | | No spaces; first character must be a letter or at symbol (@) | No spaces; first character must be a letter; stored in the database in uppercase | No spaces; first character must be a letter, at symbol (@), dollar sign ($), or number symbol (#); stored in the database in uppercase |

PRACTICE

## Review Assignments

1. What are the formal names for a table, for a row, and for a column? What are the popular names for a row and for a column?
2. What is a domain?
3. What is an entity?
4. What is the relationship between a primary key and a candidate key?
5. What is a composite key?
6. What is a foreign key?
7. Look for an example of a one-to-one relationship, an example of a one-to-many relationship, and an example of a many-to-many relationship in a newspaper, magazine, book, or everyday situation you encounter. For each one, name the entities and select the primary and foreign keys.
8. When do you use an entity subtype?
9. What is a composite entity in an entity-relationship diagram?
10. What is the entity integrity constraint?
11. What is referential integrity?
12. What does the cascades option, which is used with referential integrity, accomplish?
13. What are partial and transitive dependencies?
14. What three types of anomalies can be exhibited by a table, and what problems do they cause?
15. Figure A-24 shows the Employee, Position, and Employment tables with primary keys EmployeeNum, PositionID, and both EmployeeNum and PositionID, respectively. Which two integrity constraints do these tables violate and why?

**Figure A-24** **Integrity constraint violations**

Employee

| EmployeeNum | FirstName | LastName | HealthPlan |
|---|---|---|---|
| 2173 | Barbara | Hennessey | B |
| 4519 | Lee | Noordsy | A |
| 8005 | Pat | Amidon | C |
| 8112 | Chris | Wandzell | A |

Position

| PositionID | PositionDesc | PayGrade |
|---|---|---|
| 1 | Director | 45 |
| 2 | Manager | 40 |
| 3 | Analyst | 30 |
| 4 | Clerk | 20 |

Employment

| EmployeeNum | PositionID | StartDate |
|---|---|---|
| 2173 | 2 | 12/14/2011 |
| 4519 | 1 | 04/23/2013 |
| 4519 | | 11/11/2007 |
| 8005 | 3 | 06/05/2012 |
| 8005 | 4 | 07/02/2010 |
| 8112 | 1 | 12/15/2012 |
| 9876 | 2 | 10/04/2011 |

16. The State and City tables, shown in Figure A-4, are described as follows:
State (<u>StateAbbrev</u>, StateName, EnteredUnionOrder, StateBird, StatePopulation)
City (<u>StateAbbrev</u>, <u>CityName</u>, CityPopulation)
Foreign key: StateAbbrev to State table
Add the field named CountyName for the county or counties in a state containing the city to this database, justify where you placed it (that is, in an existing table or in a new one), and draw the entity-relationship diagram for all the entities. Counties for some of the cities shown in Figure A-4 are Travis and Williamson counties for Austin TX; Hartford county for Hartford CT; Clinton, Eaton, and Ingham counties for Lansing MI; Davidson county for Nashville TN; Hughes county for Pierre SD; and Nueces and San Patricio counties for Portland TX.

17. Suppose you have a table for a dance studio. The fields are dancer's identification number, dancer's name, dancer's address, dancer's telephone number, class identification number, day that the class meets, time that the class meets, instructor name, and instructor identification number. Assume that each dancer takes one class, each class meets only once a week and has one instructor, and each instructor can teach

more than one class. In what normal form is the table currently, given the following alternative description?

Dancer (<u>DancerID</u>, DancerName, DancerAddr, DancerPhone, ClassID, ClassDay, ClassTime, InstrName, InstrID)

Convert this relation to 3NF and represent the design using the alternative description method.

18. Store the following fields for a library database: AuthorCode, AuthorName, BookTitle, BorrowerAddress, BorrowerName, BorrowerCardNumber, CopiesOfBook, ISBN (International Standard Book Number), LoanDate, PublisherCode, PublisherName, and PublisherAddress. A one-to-many relationship exists between publishers and books. Many-to-many relationships exist between authors and books and between borrowers and books.
    a. Name the entities for the library database.
    b. Create the tables for the library database and describe them using the alternative method. Be sure the tables are in third normal form.
    c. Draw an entity-relationship diagram for the library database.
19. In the database shown in Figure A-25, which consists of the Department and Employee tables, add one record to the end of the Employee table that violates both the entity integrity constraint and the referential integrity constraint.

**Figure A-25 Creating integrity constraint violations**

Department

| DeptID | DeptName | Location |
|---|---|---|
| M | Marketing | New York |
| R | Research | Houston |
| S | Sales | Chicago |

Employee

| EmployeeID | EmployeeName | DeptID |
|---|---|---|
| 1111 | Sue | R |
| 2222 | Pam | M |
| 3333 | Bob | S |
| 4444 | Chris | S |
| 5555 | Pat | R |
| 6666 | Meg | R |
| | | |

20. Consider the following table:

    Patient (PatientID, PatientName, BalanceOwed, DoctorID, DoctorName, ServiceCode, ServiceDesc, ServiceFee, ServiceDate)

    This is a table concerning data about patients of doctors at a clinic and the services the doctors perform for their patients. The following dependencies exist in the Patient table:

    PatientID → PatientName, BalanceOwed

    DoctorID → DoctorName

    ServiceCode → ServiceDesc, ServiceFee

    PatientID, DoctorID, ServiceCode → PatientName, BalanceOwed, DoctorName, ServiceDesc, ServiceFee, ServiceDate

    a. Based on the dependencies, convert the Patient table to first normal form.
    b. Next, convert the Patient table to third normal form.
21. Suppose you need to track data for mountain climbing expeditions. Each member of an expedition is called a climber, and one of the climbers is named to lead an expedition. Climbers can be members of many expeditions over time. The climbers in each expedition attempt to ascend one or more peaks by scaling one of the many faces of the peaks. The data you need to track includes the name of the expedition, the leader of the expedition, and comments about the expedition; the first name, last name, nationality, birth date, death date, and comments about each climber; the name, location, height, and comments about each peak; the name and comments about each face of a peak; comments about each climber for each expedition; and the highest height reached and the date for each ascent attempt by a climber on a face with commentary.
    a. Create the tables for the expedition database and describe them using the alternative method. Be sure the tables are in third normal form.
    b. Draw an entity-relationship diagram for the expedition database.
22. What is the difference among natural, artificial, and surrogate keys?
23. Why should you use naming conventions for the identifiers in a database?

## ENDING DATA FILES

There are no ending Data Files for this appendix.

POWERPOINT

TUTORIAL 3

# Adding and Customizing Media and Charts

*Preparing a Sales Presentation*

## OBJECTIVES

**Session 3.1**

- Insert slides from another presentation
- Insert and format a video on a slide
- Trim a video clip
- Set a poster frame
- Insert a sound clip
- Create and format a table
- Create and format a chart
- Apply a second animation to an object
- Change the speed of an animation

**Session 3.2**

- Change theme fonts
- Change theme colors
- Reset slides
- Apply a gradient background
- Add a picture to the background
- Add a textured background
- Customize bullets
- Create and apply a custom theme
- Apply a second theme to a presentation

## Case | *Classic Flowers, Inc.*

Sophie De Graff is a horticulturalist who works as the sales manager at Classic Flowers, Inc., in Bainbridge, Georgia. Classic Flowers grows and distributes flowers to retail stores throughout the state. One of Sophie's responsibilities is to obtain and manage new accounts. This involves giving sales presentations to large retail stores (Sam's Club, Costco, Wal-Mart, Piggly Wiggly, Kroger, and so forth) that have floral departments. Sophie asks you to help her prepare the PowerPoint presentation. She emphasizes the importance of preparing a high-quality presentation that includes a custom theme, video, graphics, sound effects, animations, charts, and other elements to maximize the visual effects.

In this tutorial, you'll insert slides from one presentation into another presentation, add video and sound, examine and modify the animation settings for video and sound, create a table and a chart, animate a chart, and apply a second animation to an object. You will also change theme fonts and create custom theme colors, modify the background and bullets, create a custom theme, and apply a second theme to a presentation.

## STARTING DATA FILES

**PowerPoint3** →

**Tutorial**
CFISound.wav
CFSales.pptx
Flowers.pptx
PinkFlower.jpg
Vases.avi

**Review**
Bulbs.avi
Farm.avi
HotSprings.pptx
HSProposal.pptx
Knock.wav
PurpleFlowers.jpg

**Case1**
Case.pptx
CompCase.avi
JustInCase.pptx

**Case2**
Wedding01.jpg
...
Wedding10.jpg
(10 photos)

**Case3**
MntHike.wmv
MntMap.jpg
MntPlateau1.jpg
MntPlateau2.jpg

**Case4**
(none)

# SESSION 3.1 VISUAL OVERVIEW

Click the Volume button to adjust the volume or mute the video.

Click the Trim Video button to open the Trim Video dialog box.

Use the Trim Video dialog box to trim the beginning and end of a video.

To trim a video, drag the green Start Time slider and the red End Time slider to specify the points at which the video will start and stop playing.

# WORKING WITH VIDEO

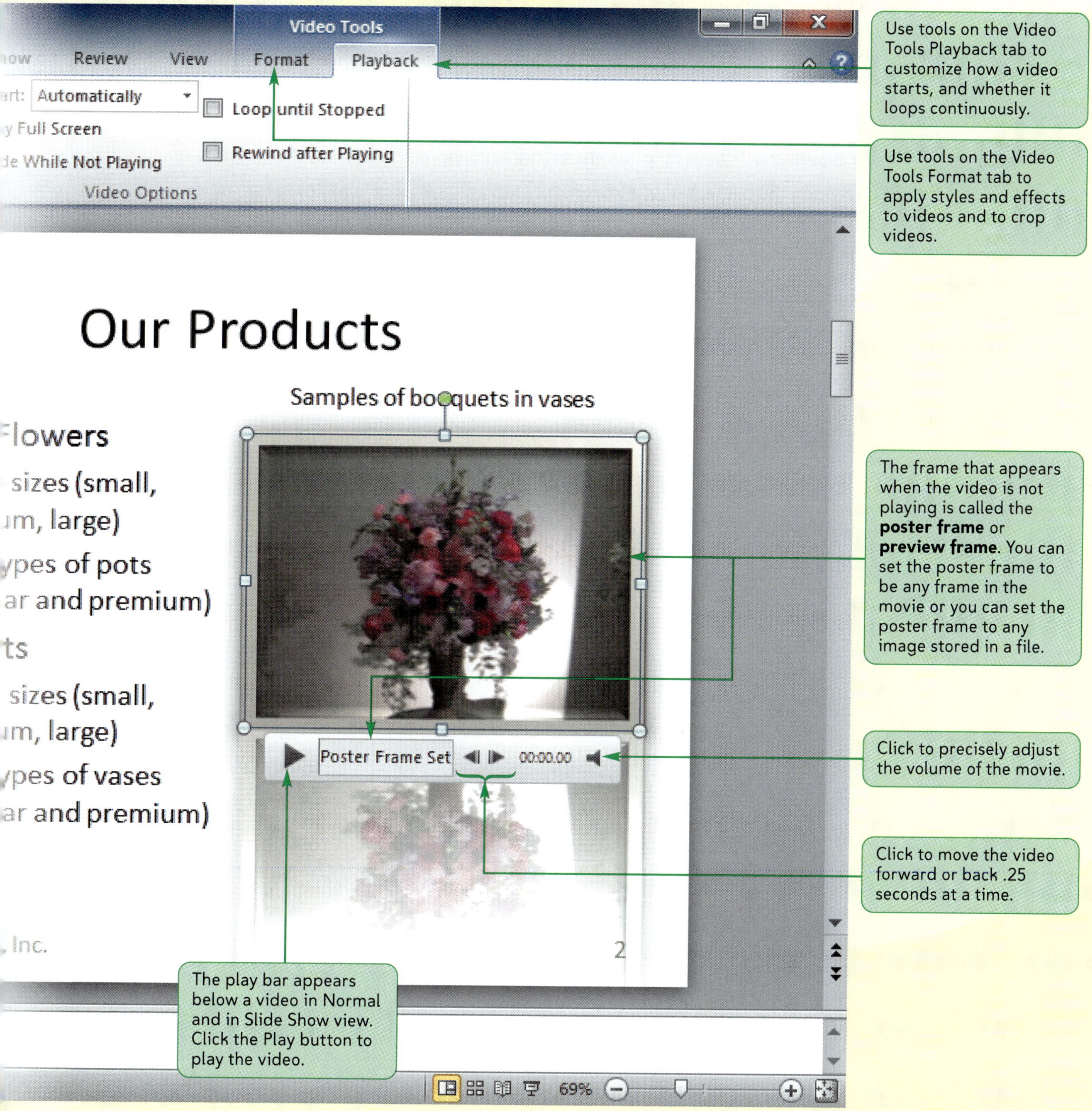

# Inserting Slides from Another Presentation

You can combine slides from two presentations to create one presentation. Sophie gives you two presentation files: Flowers, which contains text and pictures to describe the products and services, and CFSales, a presentation that includes additional information about Classic Flowers' sales. First, you'll open the Flowers presentation, and then, you'll add slides to it from the CFSales presentation.

### To open the Flowers presentation and save it with a new name:

1. Open the presentation **Flowers** located in the PowerPoint3\Tutorial folder included with your Data Files, and then save the presentation file as **Flower Sales** in the same folder. See Figure 3-1.

**Figure 3-1** Slide 1 of Flower Sales

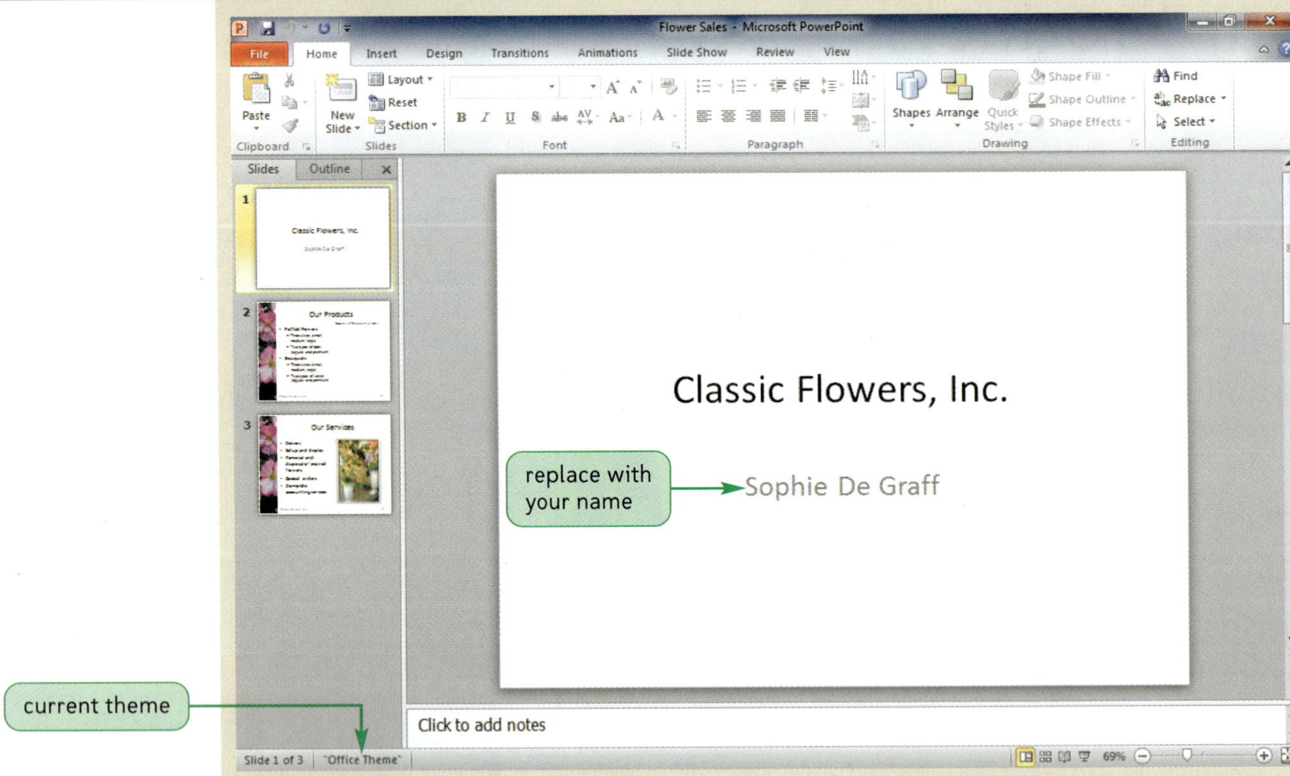


2. Change the subtitle ("Sophie De Graff") to your name, and then look through the three slides of the presentation so you have an idea of its content. Notice that the Office theme is applied and there is a long, slender photograph ("panel") of pink flowers on the slides with bulleted lists.

You use the Reuse Slides command on the New Slide menu to insert specific slides from any other presentation. If the inserted slides have a different design than the current presentation, the design of the current presentation will override the design of the inserted slides by default.

REFERENCE

*Inserting Slides from Another Presentation*

- Display the slide after which you want to insert slides from another presentation.
- In the Slides group on the Home tab, click the New Slide button arrow, and then click Reuse Slides to display the Reuse Slides task pane.
- In the task pane, click the Browse button, and then click Browse File to open the Browse dialog box.
- Navigate to the location of the presentation that contains the slides you want to insert, click the file, and then click the Open button.
- In the task pane, make sure the Keep source formatting check box is *not* selected, to force the inserted slides to use the theme in the current presentation or click the Keep source formatting check box to retain the theme of the slides you want to import.
- In the task pane, click each slide that you want to insert into the current presentation.

Sophie asks you to insert all six slides from the CFSales presentation into the Flower Sales presentation.

**To insert slides from the CFSales presentation:**

1. Display **Slide 3** ("Our Services") in the Slide pane.
2. In the Slides group on the Home tab, click the **New Slide button arrow**. The gallery of available layouts opens with a menu below the gallery.
3. On the menu, click **Reuse Slides**. The Reuse Slides task pane opens on the right side of the window.
4. Click the **Browse** button in the task pane, and then click **Browse File**. The Browse dialog box opens.
5. Navigate to the PowerPoint3\Tutorial folder, and then double-click **CFSales**. Thumbnails of the five slides from the CFSales presentation appear in the Reuse Slides task pane. The Apex theme is applied to these slides. See Figure 3-2. At the bottom of the task pane, the Keep source formatting check box is unchecked. You don't want to keep the formatting of the inserted slides, but rather you want the new slides to take on the theme and modifications of the slide master of the current Flower Sales presentation, so you will keep this unchecked.

**Figure 3-2** **CFSales presentation slides in the Reuse Slides task pane**

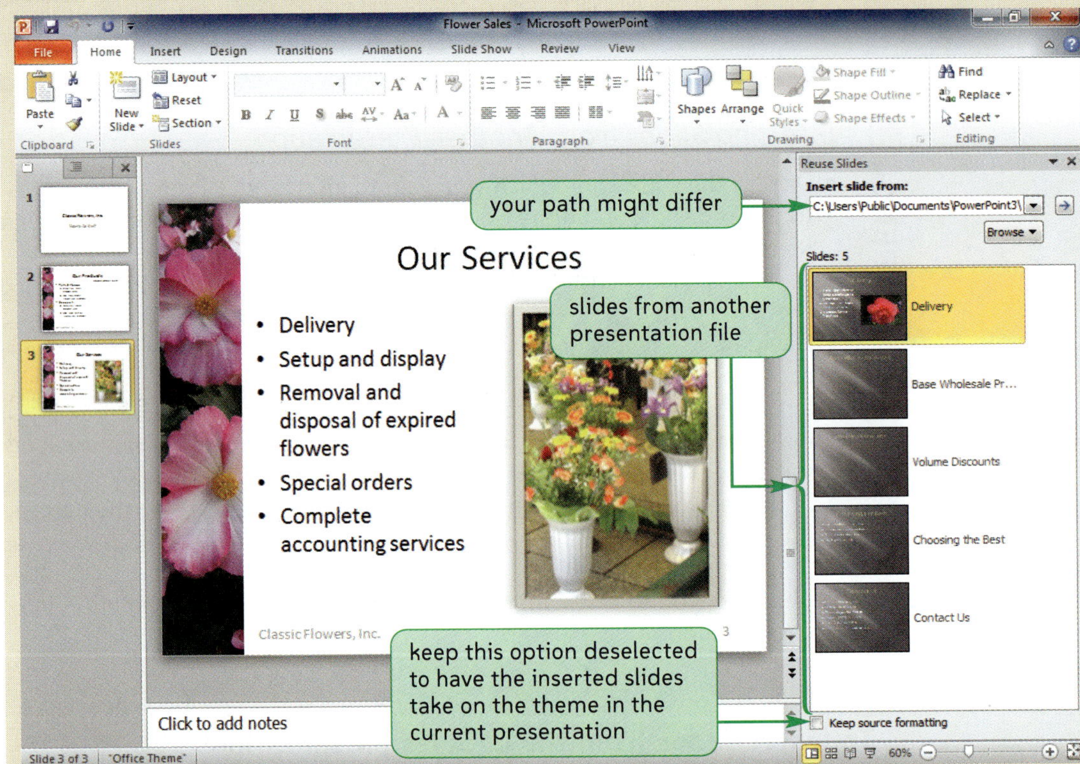


6. In the task pane, point to the first slide, "Delivery." The slide increases in size so that you can read its content.
7. Click the **Delivery** slide. It is inserted into the Flower Sales presentation after the current slide (Slide 3), and the Office Theme is applied instead of the Apex theme used in CFSales.
8. Insert the other four slides, one at a time. When you are finished, the presentation will have eight slides, and the last slide inserted, "Contact Us," will be displayed in the Slide pane.
9. In the Reuse Slides task pane title bar, click the **Close** button.
10. Save your changes.

The five slides from CFSales are now Slides 4 through 8 of the Flower Sales presentation. One of the new slides contains text and a photo; the rest contain only text.

# Adding Video

You can insert digital video in slides or in slide masters. PowerPoint supports various file formats, but the most commonly used are the Audio Visual Interleave format (listed in Explorer windows as the Video Clip file type), which uses the filename extension ".avi," and the Windows Media Video format, which uses the filename extension ".wmv." After you insert a video, you can modify it by changing the length of time the video plays, changing playback options, and applying formats and styles to the video.

## Inserting a Video in a Slide

You can insert a video clip in two different ways. You can change the layout to one of the content layouts, and then click the Insert Media Clip button, or you can use the Video button in the Media group on the Insert tab. If you want to add a video to a slide master, you must use the Video button on the Insert tab; otherwise you will replace the content placeholder on all slides using that master. You'll add the video now using the Insert Media Clip button in a content layout.

REFERENCE

### *Inserting a Video into a Presentation*

- In Normal view, display the slide in which you want to insert the video in the Slide pane; or in Slide Master view, display the layout master in which you want to insert the video.
- In Normal view, in a content placeholder, click the Insert Media Clip button; or in Normal or Slide Master view, click the Insert tab on the Ribbon, and then in the Media group, click the Video button.
- In the Insert Video dialog box, navigate to the folder containing the video, click the video file, and then click the Insert button.

Sophie wants you to insert a short video showing some of the vase arrangements that Classic Flowers sells as part of Slide 2, "Our Products."

### To add a video to Slide 2:

1. Display **Slide 2** ("Our Products") in the Slide pane. The Two Content layout is applied to this slide. Notice that there is a text box above the content placeholder.
2. In the content placeholder on the right, click the **Insert Media Clip** button. The Insert Video dialog box opens.
3. Navigate to the PowerPoint3\Tutorial folder included with your Data Files, click **Vases**, and then click the **Insert** button. The movie is inserted in place of the content placeholder. See Figure 3-3.

**Figure 3-3** Slide 2 with video

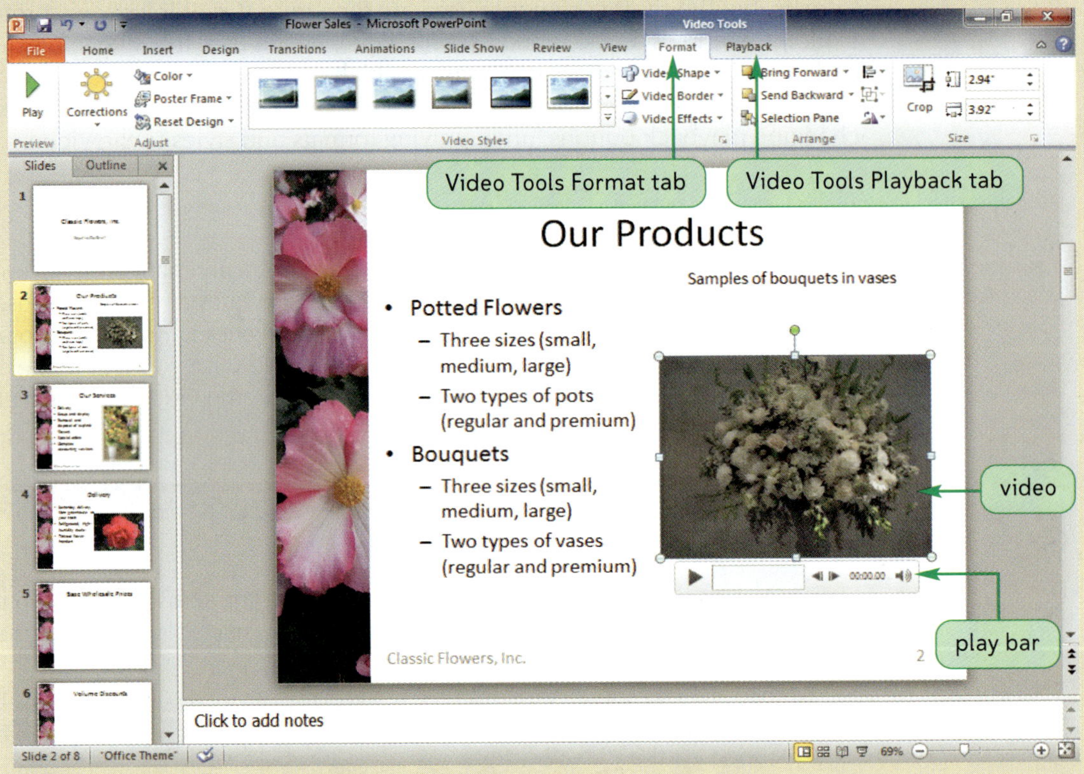


4. On the play bar below the movie, click the **Play** button ▶, and then watch the video.

INSIGHT

*Inserting a Video Behind Objects on a Slide*

You can insert videos behind other objects on a slide. Video added to a slide background can add visual interest to your presentation for audiences that are accustomed to multimedia. To do this, insert the video as usual. On the Video Tools Format tab, in the Arrange group, click the Send Backward button arrow, and then click Send to Back. The video object will move behind the rest of the objects on the slide; for example, if the slide contains a bulleted list, the bulleted list will appear on top of the video. If you choose to add a video to the background, it should not include too much action, or your audience will have difficulty making out the text or images in the foreground. Sometimes, applying a washout or gray color effect to background video produces the effect you need.

## Changing Video Playback Options

You can change several options for how a video plays. These options are listed in Figure 3-4.

**Figure 3-4** Video Playback options

| Video Option | Function |
|---|---|
| Volume | Change the volume of the video from high to medium or low or mute it. |
| Start | Change how the video starts, either when the presenter advances the slide show (On Click) or automatically when the slide appears during the slide show. |
| Play Full Screen | The video fills the screen during the slide show. |
| Hide While Not Playing | The video does not appear on the slide when it is not playing; make sure the video is set to play automatically if this option is selected. |
| Loop until Stopped | The video plays continuously until the next slide appears during the slide show. |
| Rewind after Playing | The video rewinds after it plays so that the first frame or the poster frame appears again. |

When you insert a video, the default is for it to play On Click. You can change this by changing the Start setting on the Video Tools Playback tab to Automatically. When you set a video to play automatically, you can override this, or after the video has played once, you can play it again by clicking the video or clicking the Play button under the video to start playback.

Sophie wants the video you inserted on Slide 2 to play automatically when the slide appears during the slide show. You'll change the start setting now.

### To change video options to play the video automatically:

1. With the movie selected, click the **Video Tools Playback** tab. The options for changing how the video plays are in the Video Options group. See Figure 3-5.

**Figure 3-5** Video Tools Playback tab

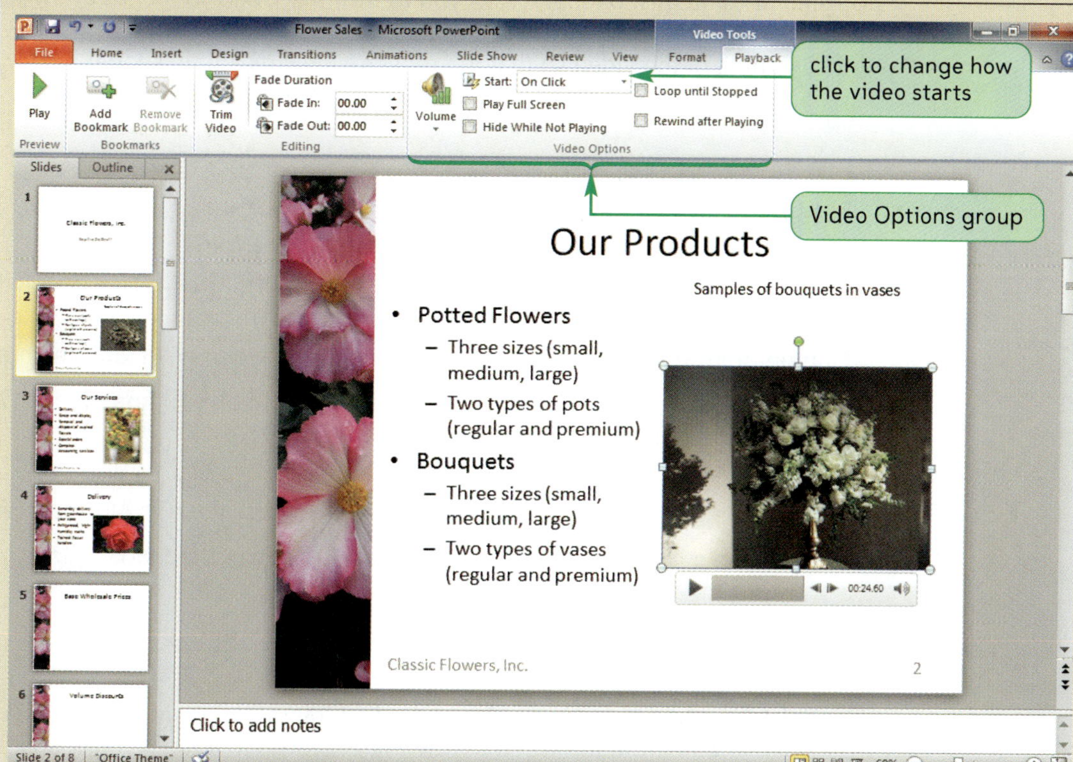

2. In the Video Options group, click the **Start** arrow, and then click **Automatically**. Now the video will play automatically when the slide appears during the slide show.

You can also set volume options for video. The video was filmed in a noisy atmosphere. Sophie thinks the background noise in the video will be distracting during her presentation, so she asks you to set the volume to mute while the video is playing.

**TIP**

To play the movie so that it fills the entire screen, select the Play Full Screen check box in the Video Options group on the Video Tools Playback tab.

**To adjust the volume of the video:**

1. In the Video Options group, click the **Volume** button. A menu opens with four options for adjusting the volume.
2. Click **Mute**. The menu closes. You can check the options you set in Slide Show view.
3. On the status bar, click the **Slide Show** button. The video plays automatically and the background noise is muted.
4. After the video is finished playing, press the **Esc** key to end the slide show.

## Trimming a Video

If a video is too long, or if there are parts you don't want to show during the slide show, you can trim it. To do this, you click the Trim Video button in the Editing group on the Video Tools Playback tab, and then, in the Trim Video dialog box, drag the sliders to indicate where you want the video to start and stop. Refer to the Session 3.1 Visual Overview for more information about using the Trim Video dialog box.

After reviewing the video, Sophie decides that the last bouquet in the video clip looks too similar to the first one. She asks you to trim the video so it ends at the point where the camera zooms in on the pink bouquet. She also wants you to trim a few seconds off the beginning of the video so that the movement starts a little sooner.

**To trim the video:**

1. In the Editing group on the Video Tools Playback tab, click the **Trim Video** button. The Trim Video dialog box opens.
2. On the bar below the video, drag the red **End Time slider** to the left to approximately the 19-second mark. The time in the End Time box changes to match the time point that you dragged the slider to. The video will stop playing at this point.
3. Drag the green **Start Time slider** to the right to approximately the 3-second mark. The time in the Start Time box changes to match the time point that you dragged the slider to. The video will now start playing at this point.
4. Click the **OK** button. You can watch the trimmed video in Normal view.
5. On the play bar, click the **Play** button. The trimmed video plays.

## Setting a Poster Frame

The default poster frame for a video is the first frame of the video. You can change this so that any frame from the video or any image stored in a file is the poster frame. Sophie wants the poster frame to show one of the pink bouquets.

**To set a poster frame for the video:**

1. In the Slide pane, position the pointer on top of the play bar so that you see a ScreenTip identifying the time at the point where the pointer is positioned.
2. Move the pointer until it is at approximately the 14-second mark, and then click. The gray indicator in the play bar moves back to the 14-second mark, and the bouquet with pink flowers appears.
3. Click the **Video Tools Format** tab.
4. In the Adjust group, click the **Poster Frame** button. A menu opens.
5. Click **Current Frame**. The menu closes and a note appears in the Play bar indicating that this will be the poster frame. See Figure 3-6. This frame will now be the poster frame for this video clip.

**Figure 3-6** Video after the poster frame is set

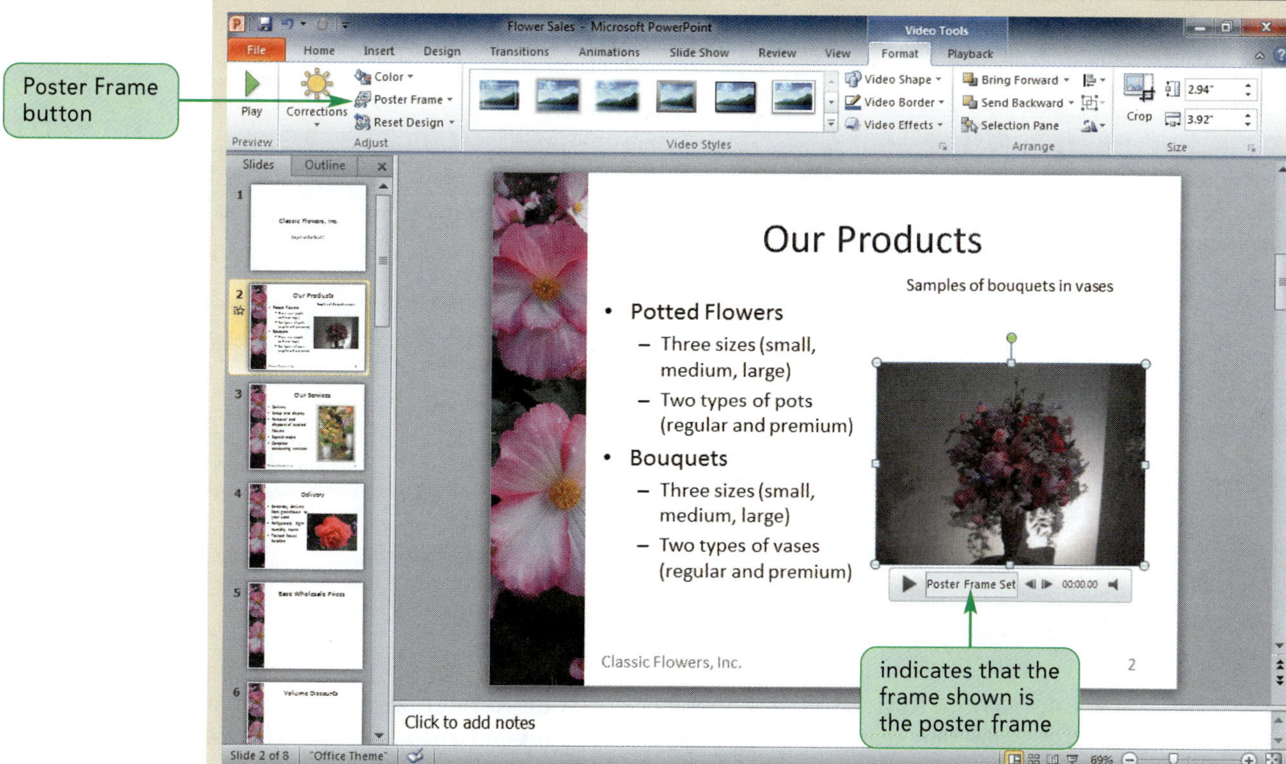


## Formatting a Video

You can format videos just like you format pictures. For example, you can crop the sides of a video, or you can resize it by dragging the sizing handles. You should be careful doing this. Normally, you don't want to change the proportions of a video because it will distort the image. You can also apply styles and special effects to videos.

The photograph on Slide 3 has the Metal Frame style applied to it, so Sophie asks you to apply the same style to the video on Slide 2. She also wants you to add a reflection effect to the video clip. When you apply a style or add an effect to a video, you see the style and effect when the video plays.

## To apply a style and a reflection effect to the video:

1. In the Video Styles group on the Video Tools Format tab, click the **More** button. The gallery opens.
2. Click the **Metal Frame** style (the last style in the gallery). See Figure 3-7. Now the frame around the movie photo matches the frame around the picture on Slide 3. Next, you can apply the reflection effect.

**Figure 3-7** Metal Frame style applied to the video

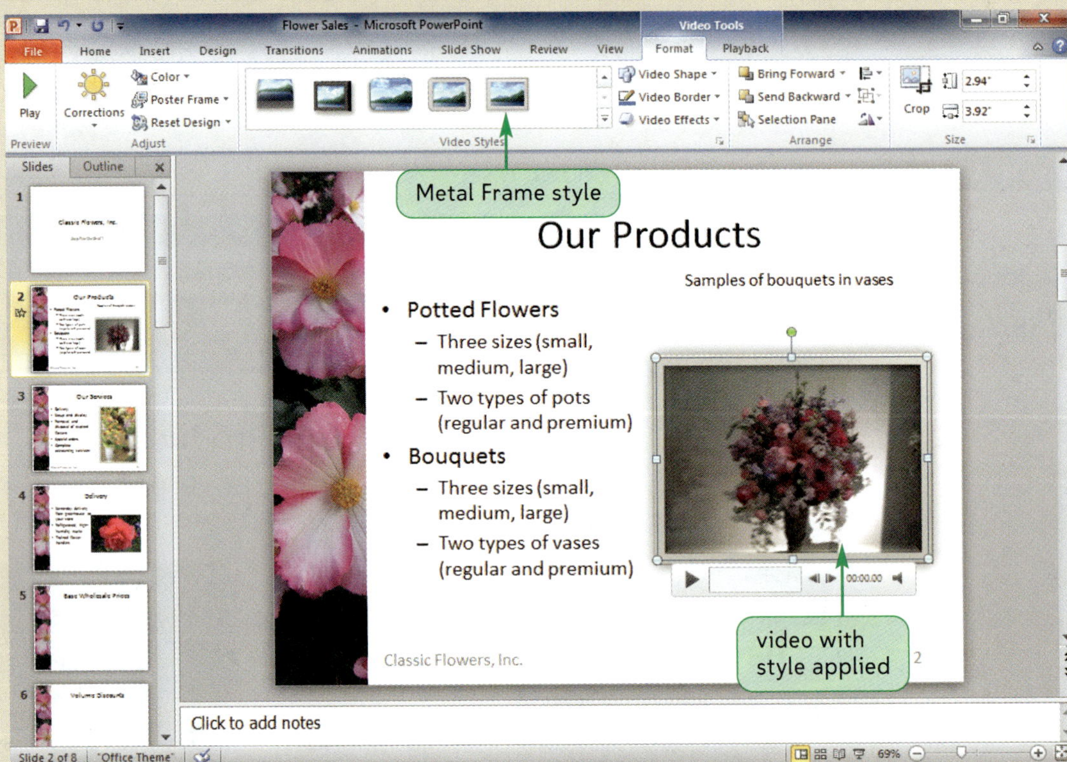


3. In the Video Styles group, click the **Video Effects** button. A menu appears listing special effects that you can apply to a video.
4. Point to **Reflection**, and then click the **Full Reflection, touching** style (the last reflection style in the first row under Reflection Variations). A reflection of the poster frame appears under the video. Now you will reposition the video a little higher on the slide.
5. Position the pointer on the selected video so that it changes to ✥, and then drag the video up so that the top of the video is approximately aligned with the "Potted Flowers" bullet, and then click a blank area of the slide. See Figure 3-8. Next, you'll check the effects you applied in Slide Show view.

**Figure 3-8** Reflection effect applied to the video

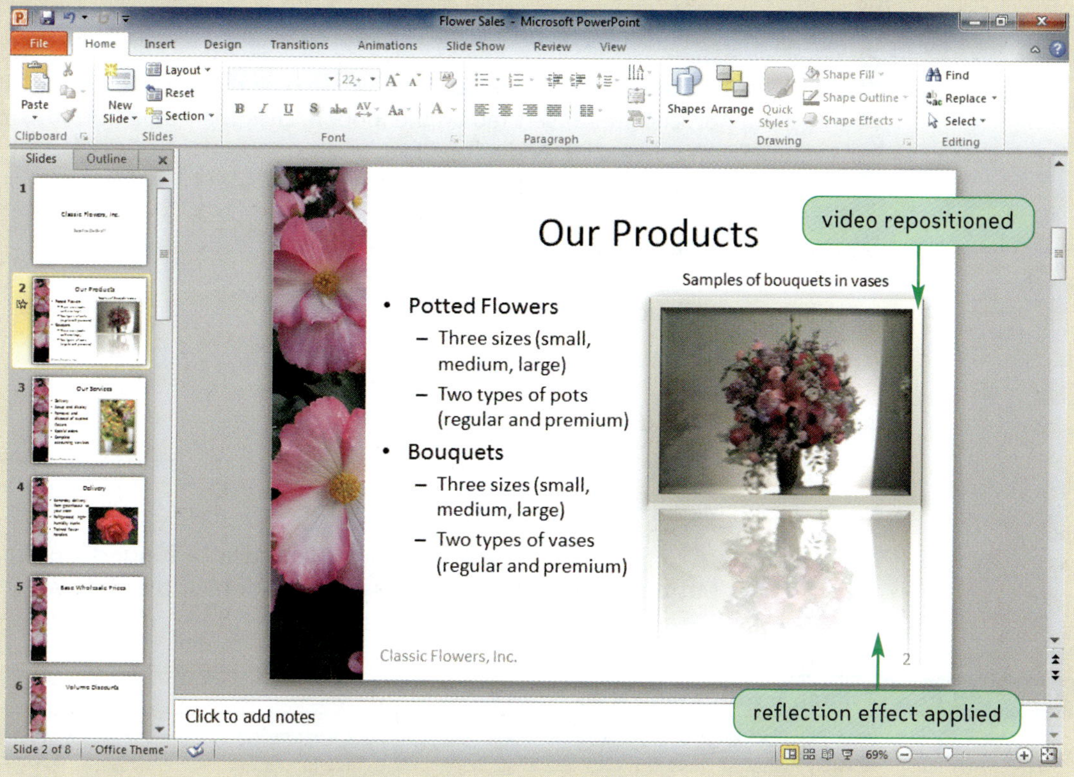


6. On the status bar, click the **Slide Show** button. Slide 2 appears in Slide Show view, and the video clip plays. Notice that the video played in the reflection as well.
7. Press the **[Esc]** key to end the slide show, and then save your changes.

PROSKILLS

*Decision Making: Choosing Video to Enhance Your Message*

Inserting and manipulating video in PowerPoint slides is easy to do. A video can convey information in a way that bulleted items can't match. Video in the background can add a powerful visual punch to a presentation. However, the content of video in a presentation should clearly convey, illustrate, or support your message. Always carefully consider the purpose of a video, and evaluate the video to make sure it enhances rather than distracts from your presentation.

In addition to inserting a video, you can insert a sound clip on a slide. You'll do this next.

## Inserting a Sound Clip

Sophie wants you to add two sound clips to the presentation—a recording of a welcome message on Slide 1 and a sound clip of music that will play across all the slides in the presentation except the first one. The recorded message is a Wave file, which is the most common file format for short sound clips. (Wave files use the filename extension ".wav.") The music you will insert is an MP3 file, another sound file format that PowerPoint supports.

To add a sound clip to a slide, use the Audio button in the Media group on the Insert tab.

REFERENCE

### *Inserting a Sound into a Presentation*

- In Normal view, display the slide in which you want to insert the sound in the Slide pane.
- Click the Insert tab on the Ribbon, and then click the Audio button in the Media group; or, click the Insert tab on the Ribbon, click the Audio button arrow in the Media group, and then click Audio from File.
- In the Insert Audio dialog box, navigate to the folder containing the sound clip, click the audio file, and then click the Insert button.

First, you will add a welcome message to Slide 1.

## To add a sound clip to Slide 1:

1. Display **Slide 1** in the Slide pane, and then click the **Insert** tab on the Ribbon.
2. In the Media group, click the **Audio** button. The Insert Audio dialog box opens.
3. Navigate to the PowerPoint3\Tutorial folder, click **CFISound**, and then click the **Insert** button. A sound icon appears in the middle of the slide with a play bar below it. See Figure 3-9.

**Figure 3-9** **Slide 1 with sound icon**

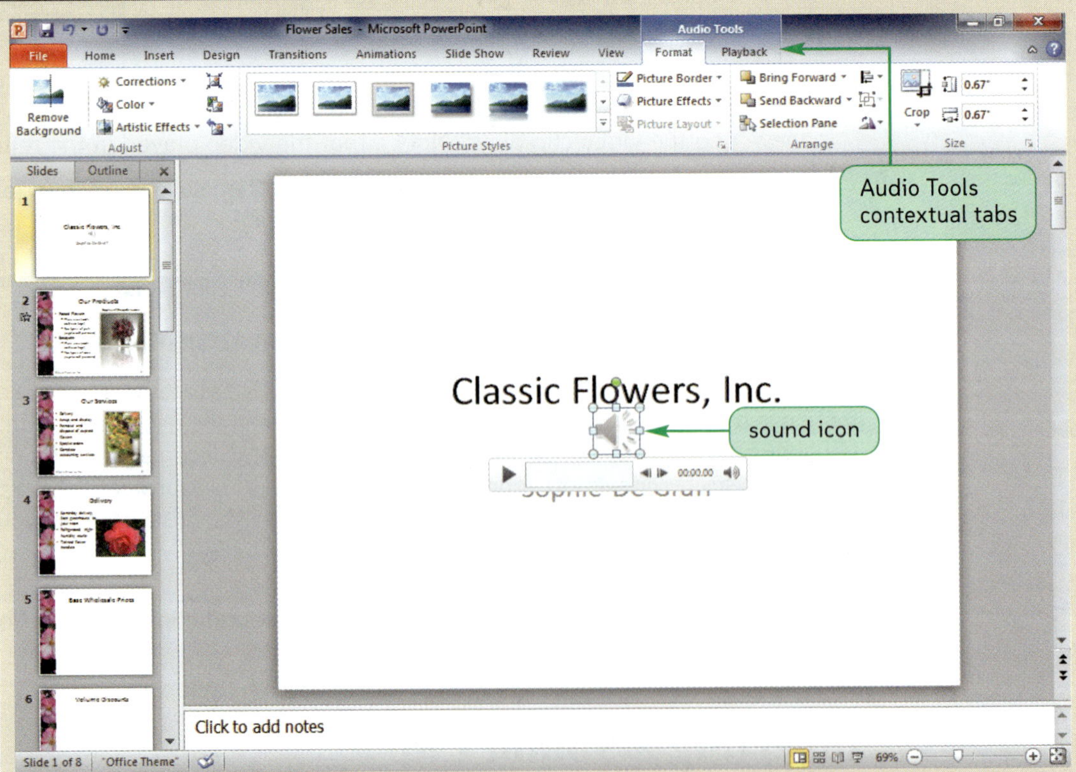


4. On the play bar, click the **Play** button ▶. You hear the sound clip, which is a welcome message. As with videos, the default start setting is On Click. You can verify this.
5. Click the **Audio Tools Playback** tab.

6. In the Audio Options group, confirm that the Start box displays On Click as the current setting.
7. Position the pointer on top of the border of the sound icon so that it changes to ✥, and then drag the sound icon to the lower-right corner of the slide.

Sophie wants you to keep the sound icon visible on Slide 1 because she will need to click it to play the message during the slide show. If you don't need to click the icon to play the sound—that is, if you set it to play automatically—you can hide the icon on the slide.

Sophie wants you to insert another clip to play soft music in the background throughout the rest of the slides in the slide show.

### To add a sound clip to Slide 2:

1. Display **Slide 2** ("Our Products") in the Slide pane. You'll insert one of the sample songs provided with Windows.
2. Click the **Insert** tab.
3. In the Media group, click the **Audio** button.
4. In the navigation pane on the left, click **Music**, and then double-click the **Sample Music** folder.

   **Trouble?** If you are using Windows Vista or XP, navigate to the Music or the Public Music folder, and then double-click the Sample Music folder.
5. Click **Sleep Away**, and then click the **Insert** button. The sound icon and play bar appear in the middle of the slide.

   **Trouble?** If you are using Windows Vista or XP, select any music in the Sample Music folder. Try to choose one that has no vocals.

To have this sound play throughout the rest of the slide show, you need to change the Start setting. You also will set the sound icon to be hidden during the slide show. Similar to videos, the options for changing how the sound plays during the slide show appear on the Audio Tools Playback tab. They are the same options that appear on the Video Tools Playback tab, except there is no option to play full screen.

### To change playback options for the sound clip on Slide 2:

1. Click the **Audio Tools Playback** tab on the Ribbon.
2. In the Audio Options group, click the **Start arrow**. You can choose to play the sound On Click, automatically, or across slides.
3. Click **Play across slides**. Because you want the sound clip to start over if it ends before the slide show is finished, you will set the sound clip to play continuously.
4. In the Audio Options group, click the **Loop until Stopped** check box. Now you will set the option to hide the icon during the slide show.
5. In the Audio Options group, click the **Hide During Show** check box to select it. See Figure 3-10. Because this is supposed to be quiet background music, you will adjust the volume to low.

**Figure 3-10** Audio Options set for sound clip

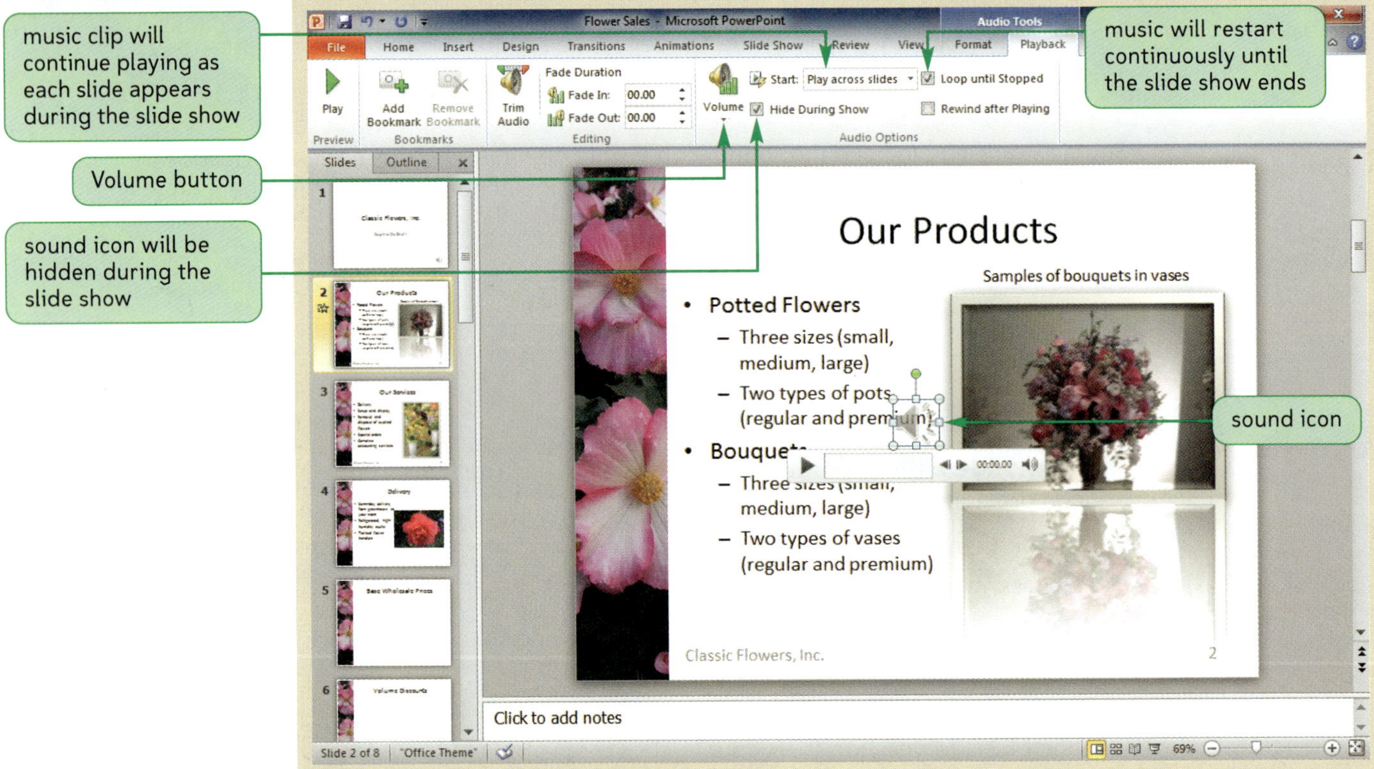


6. In the Audio Options group, click the **Volume** button, and then click **Low**. Now you can test your settings.
7. On the status bar, click the **Slide Show** button. Slide 2 appears in Slide Show view, and the flower video plays. When the video of the flowers finishes, the sound starts playing.
8. Advance the slide show. Slide 3 appears on the screen and the music keeps playing.
9. Advance through the rest of the slides until you reach Slide 8 ("Contact Us"). The music continues playing as each slide appears.
10. Wait until the music clip ends. The Sleep Away clip is three minutes and 20 seconds long. When the song is finished, there is silence for a moment, and then it starts again because you set it to Loop until Stopped.
11. End the slide show.

## Understanding Video and Audio Animation Effects

Why did the music audio not start until the flower video was over? When you insert video and audio clips, Media animation effects are applied to the clip automatically, and the start setting of these animation effects is tied to the Start setting of the media clip. When you insert a media clip, the default Start setting is On Click. A Play animation is also automatically applied to the clip and it too is set to start On Click. To fix the music clip settings so that it starts playing when the slide appears, as Sophie wants, you'll first examine the animation settings applied to the media clips you inserted.

**To examine the Media animation effects for the sound and video clips:**

1. Display **Slide 1** in the Slide pane, and then click the **sound icon** in the lower-right corner.
2. Click the **Animations** tab on the Ribbon. As shown in Figure 3-11, the Play animation is selected in the Animation gallery, and the Pause and Stop animations appear in the gallery as well. In the Timing group, the start of the selected animation is set to On Click.

**Figure 3-11** Animations tab when a sound clip is selected

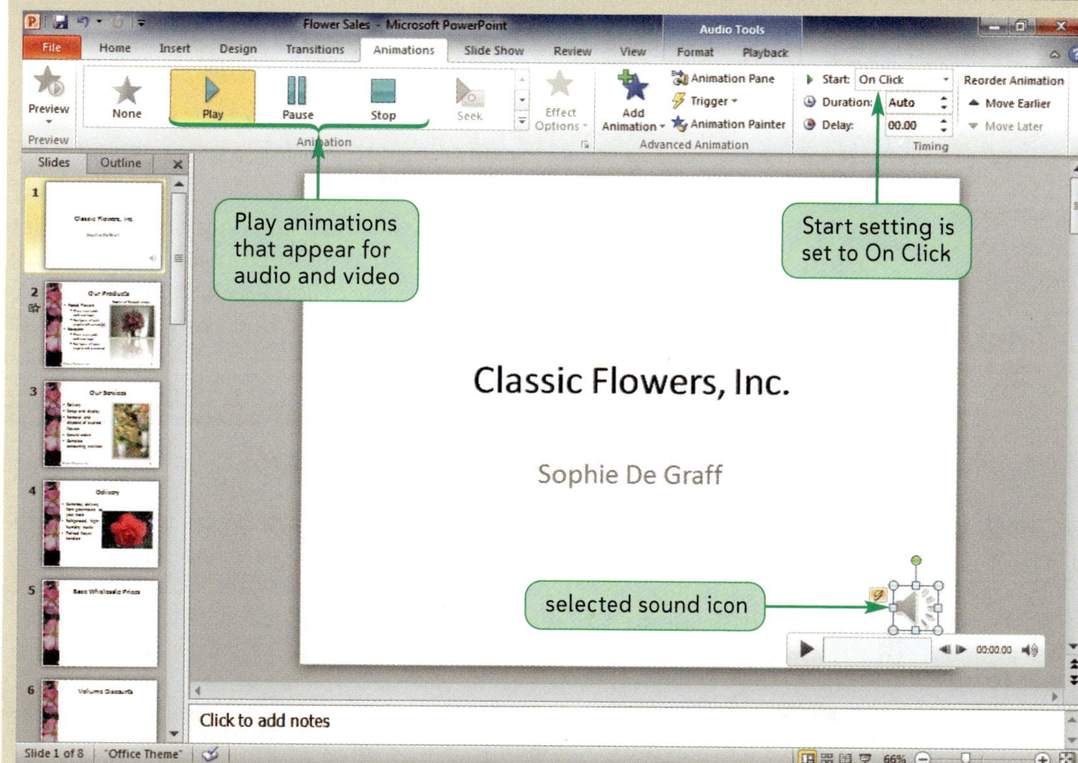


3. In the Animation group, click the **More** button. Notice that a new Media category is listed in the gallery. The Media category appears in the Animation gallery only when an audio or media clip is inserted.
4. Press the **Esc** key to close the gallery, display **Slide 2** ("Our Products") in the Slide pane, and then click the **sound icon** in the middle of the slide. The Play animation is selected in the Animation gallery again, and After Previous appears in the Start box. When you set a sound to play across slides, the Play animation setting changes from On Click to After Previous.
5. In the Slide pane, click the **flower video**. Multiple is selected in the Animation gallery.
6. Click the **0 animation sequence icon** to the left of the flower video. Play is selected in the Animation gallery, and After Previous appears in the Start box. The Start setting changes from On Click to After Previous when you change the Playback setting from On Click to Automatically.

Remember that if you want an animation to play at the same time as the previous animation or when the slide transitions, you can change the play animation start setting to With Previous. You'll do this now, so the music starts playing when the Vases video starts playing.

**To change the start setting for the Play animation applied to the sound clip on Slide 2:**

1. In the Slide pane, click the **sound icon** in the middle of Slide 2.
2. In the Timing group on the Animations tab, click the **Start** arrow, and then click **With Previous**. Next you will check the setting in Slide Show view.
3. On the status bar, click the **Slide Show** button. Slide 2 appears in Slide Show view, the video starts, and the music starts playing.
4. After the video finishes, advance the slide show to Slide 3. The music continues playing.
5. End the slide show.

## Creating a Table on a Slide

Sophie wants you to add a table of the base wholesale prices of Classic Flowers' products to Slide 5. A **table** is information arranged in horizontal rows and vertical columns. The area where a row and column intersect is called a **cell**. Each cell contains one piece of information. A table's structure is indicated by borders, which are lines that outline the rows and columns.

REFERENCE

*Inserting a Table*

- Switch to a layout that includes a content placeholder, and then click the Insert Table button in the content placeholder; or, click the Insert tab on the Ribbon, click the Table button in the Tables group, and then click Insert Table.
- Specify the desired table size—the numbers of columns and rows—and then click the OK button.

*or*

- Click the Insert tab on the Ribbon, and then in the Tables group, click the Table button.
- Click a box in the grid that opens to create a table of that size.

The table of wholesale prices that you'll create will have three columns—one for the type of arrangement, one for the size of the arrangement, and one for the price. The table needs to have seven rows—one row for column labels and six rows for data.

**To create a table on Slide 5:**

1. Display **Slide 5** ("Base Wholesale Prices") in the Slide pane.
2. In the content placeholder, click the **Insert Table** button. The Insert Table dialog box opens.
3. In the Number of columns box, type **3**.
4. Press the **Tab** key to move to the Number of rows box, and then type **7**.
5. Click the **OK** button. The dialog box closes, a table with three columns and seven rows appears on the slide, and the Table Tools contextual tabs appear on the Ribbon. The insertion point is blinking in the first cell. See Figure 3-12.

**Figure 3-12** Slide 5 with table

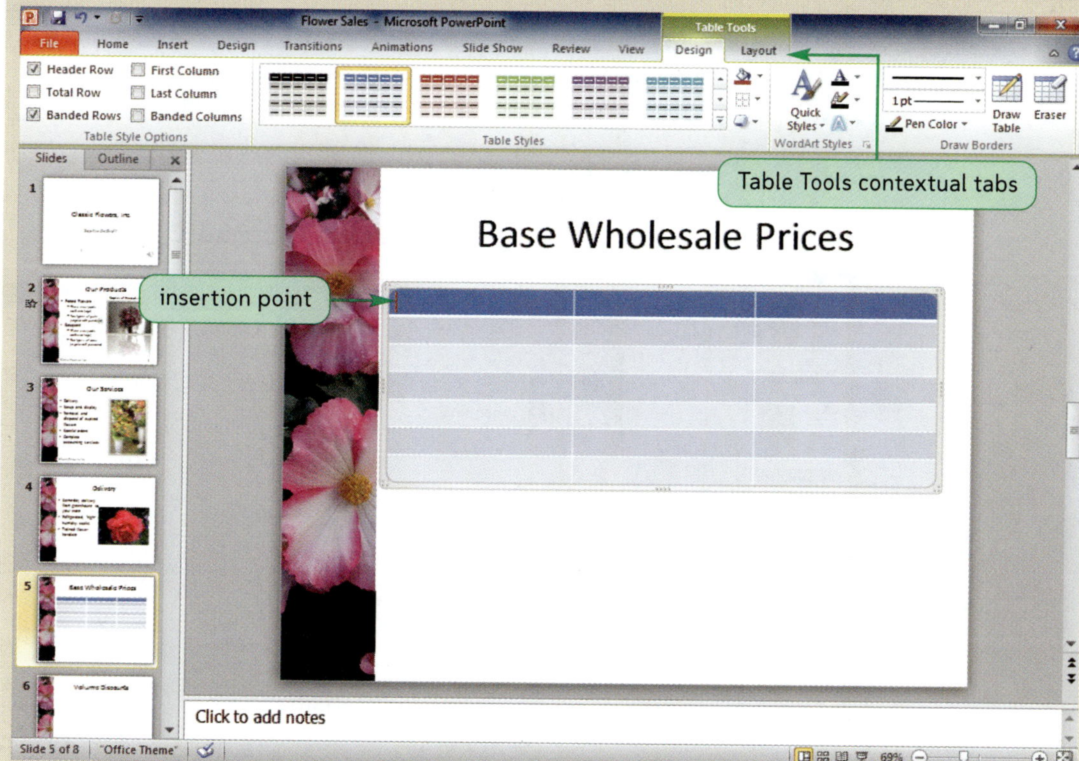


Now you're ready to fill the blank cells with the information about the available arrangements. To enter data in a table, you click in the cell in which you want to enter data. Use the Tab and arrow keys to move from one cell to another.

**To add information to the table:**

1. With the insertion point blinking in the upper-left cell, type **Type**, and then press the **Tab** key. The insertion point moves to the second cell in the first row.
2. Type **Size**, press the **Tab** key to move to the third cell in the first row, and then type **Price**. These are the column labels.
3. Press the **Tab** key again. The insertion point moves to the first cell in the second row.
4. Type **Potted**, press the **Tab** key, type **Small**, press the **Tab** key, and then type **$3.85**. This completes the first row of data.
5. In the third row, click in the **second cell** (the cell under "Small") to place the insertion point in that cell.
6. Type **Medium**, press the **Tab** key, and then type **$5.25**.
7. Press the **Tab** key twice, type **Large**, press the **Tab** key, and then type **$6.75**.
8. In the next row, starting with the first cell, type **Bouquets**, **Small**, **$6.95**.
9. In the next row, skip the first cell in the row, and then type **Medium**, **$8.50**.
10. In the last row, skip the first cell in the row, and then type **Large**, **$10.25**. The table should look like Figure 3-13.

**TIP**

To add new rows and columns to the table, use the buttons in the Rows & Columns group on the Table Tools Layout tab.

**Figure 3-13** Completed table

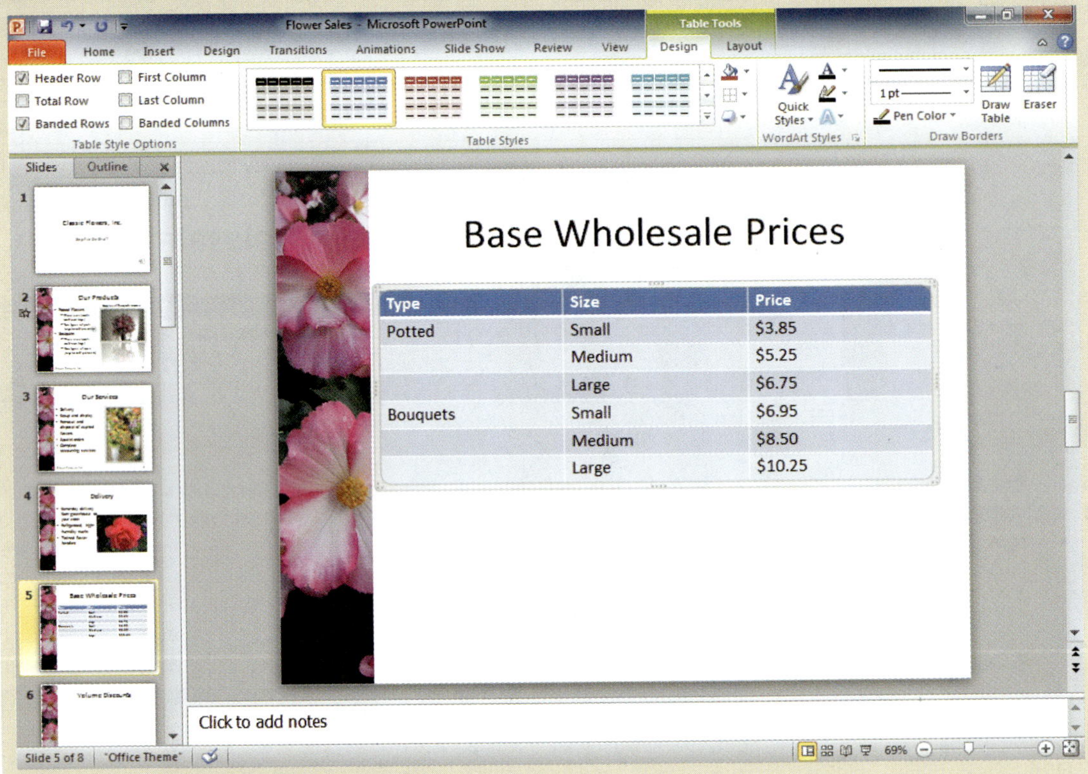


**Trouble?** If you have a blank row at the bottom of your table, you probably pressed the Tab key after entering the data in the last cell, which inserted a new, blank row at the bottom of the table. On the Quick Access Toolbar, click the Undo button to undo the creation of the extra row.

## Changing the Table Style

PowerPoint comes with built-in table styles for each theme. Table styles include the borders around the table and cells and color schemes. You can use Live Preview to see how your table will look with different table styles. Sophie wants you to add color and borders to the table, so you will apply a style with a header row (for the column labels), horizontal borders, and some color to add visual interest.

### To change the table style:

1. If necessary, click the **Table Tools Design** tab on the Ribbon.

   **Trouble?** If the Table Tools contextual tabs are not on the Ribbon, click anywhere in the table.

   **Trouble?** If you see presentation themes on the Ribbon instead of table styles, you clicked the Design tab next to the Insert tab. Click the Design tab farther to the right under the Table Tools label.

2. In the Table Style Options group, make sure the **Header Row** check box is selected, click the **Banded Rows** check box to deselect it, and then make sure the rest of the check boxes in the Table Style Options group are not selected.

3. In the Table Styles group, click the **More** button. Notice that the default style is the second style in the second row under Medium.
4. In the Medium section, click the **Medium Style 2 – Accent 4** style (the fifth style in the second row under Medium). The style you selected is applied, and the first row is formatted in bold because the Header Row check box was selected. See Figure 3-14.

**Figure 3-14** Table with a table style applied

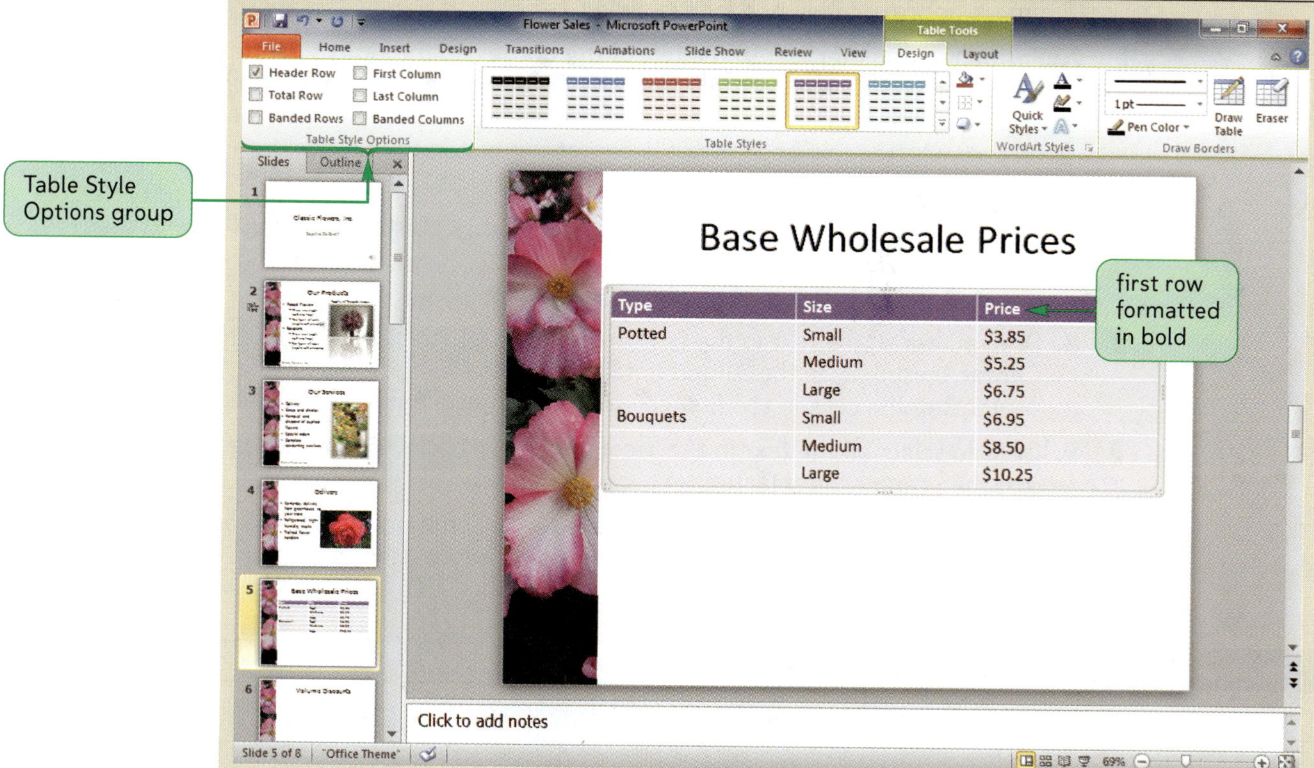


## Changing the Table Layout

After you insert data into a table, you usually need to adjust the layout so it fits nicely on the slide and is readable. Commands on the Table Tools Layout tab on the Ribbon let you remove rows, add and remove columns, combine cells, split cells, position text in cells, and perform other modifications to the table. As you can see, all three columns of the table are of equal width. All of the columns could be narrower, and the column labels might be clearer if the numbers were centered in the cells. Before making these changes, you will merge the cells containing the "Potted" and "Bouquet" labels with the empty cells beneath them, and then vertically center the labels in the merged cells.

### To change the table layout:

1. Click the **Table Tools Layout** tab on the Ribbon.
2. Click in the first cell in the second row (the cell containing "Potted"), press and hold the mouse button, and then drag down to the fourth row to select the first cells in rows 2, 3, and 4. These are the cells you want to merge.
3. In the Merge group on the Layout tab, click the **Merge Cells** button. The cells are merged into one cell.

4. Merge the cell containing "Bouquets" and the two cells under it. Next, you will resize the columns to better fit the data.
5. Position the pointer on the divider between the first two columns so that the pointer changes to +||+, and then double-click. The first column shrinks so that it is just wide enough to fit the widest entry in the column.
6. Position the pointer on the divider between the last two columns so that the pointer changes to +||+, and then drag the border to the left until the second column is approximately two inches wide.
7. Position the pointer just to the left of the border on the right side of the table so that the pointer changes to +||+, and then drag to the left until the third column is approximately two inches wide. Next, you will horizontally center the text in the first row in the table and vertically center the text in the first column of the table.

   **Trouble?** If the entire table moved, you dragged the table border instead of the column border. On the Quick Access Toolbar, click the Undo button, and then repeat Step 7, taking care to position the pointer just to the left of the table border so that it changes to +||+.
8. Drag across all the text in the first row of the table to select it, and then click the **Center** button in the Alignment group on the Table Tools Layout tab. The contents of the cells in the first column are center-aligned in the cells.
9. Drag to select all the text in the second and third columns below the header row, and then center the selected text.
10. Drag to select the text in the two merged cells containing "Potted" and "Bouquets," and then click the **Center Vertically** button in the Alignment group. See Figure 3-15.

**Figure 3-15** Table after changing the layout

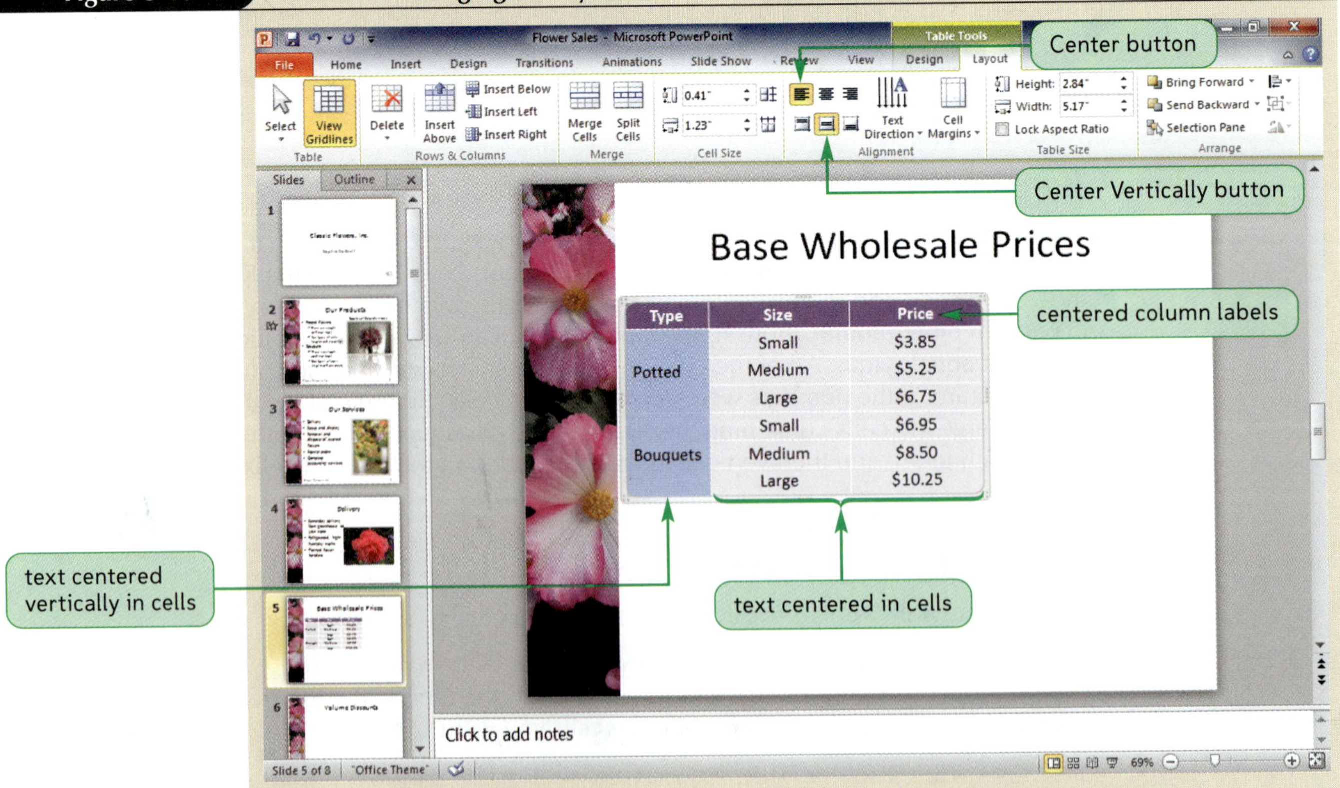

The font size of the text in the table is a little small, so Sophie asks you to increase it. You will also make the entire table larger, and then center it on the slide.

## To resize and reposition the table:

1. Position the pointer on one of the table borders so that it changes to , and then click the **border** to select the entire table.
2. Click the **Home** tab on the Ribbon.
3. In the Font group, click the **Increase Font Size** button twice to change the font size to 24 points.
4. Position the pointer on the lower-right corner of the table border so that the pointer changes to , and then drag the lower-right corner of the table down and to the right until the table is approximately 6½ inches wide and 4½ inches tall and the right side of the table is aligned with the right side of the title.
5. Drag the table to position it approximately in the center of the white space on the slide. Compare your finished table to Figure 3-16.

**Figure 3-16** Finished table

6. Save your work.

Sophie likes the way the table looks on the slide. Next, she wants you to create a chart on Slide 6.

# Creating a Chart

A **chart** is a visual depiction of data in a spreadsheet. A **spreadsheet**, called a worksheet in Microsoft Excel, is a grid of cells that contain numbers and text. When you create a chart in a slide, a Microsoft Excel program window opens with a worksheet containing sample data that you can change to the data to be depicted in your chart. As in a table, the intersection of a row and a column is a **cell**, and you add data and labels in cells. The columns are labeled A, B, C, and so on, and the rows are numbered 1, 2, 3, and so forth. You can use a chart to show an audience data trends and patterns or to visually compare data.

REFERENCE

*Creating a Chart*

- Change the slide layout to one of the content layouts, and then click the Insert Chart button in the content placeholder to open the Insert Chart dialog box; or click the Insert tab, and then, in the Illustrations group, click the Chart button to open the Insert Chart dialog box.
- Click one of the chart icons in the Insert Chart gallery, and then click the OK button.
- In the Excel worksheet that opens, edit the information in the worksheet for the data that you want to plot.
- In the Excel window, click the Close button.

Sophie wants you to create a chart in Slide 6 to show the volume discount prices from the base wholesale prices given in Slide 5.

**To insert a chart on Slide 6:**

1. Display **Slide 6** ("Volume Discounts") in the Slide pane.
2. In the content placeholder, click the **Insert Chart** button. The Insert Chart dialog box opens, displaying a gallery of charts. See Figure 3-17.

**Figure 3-17** **Insert Chart dialog box**

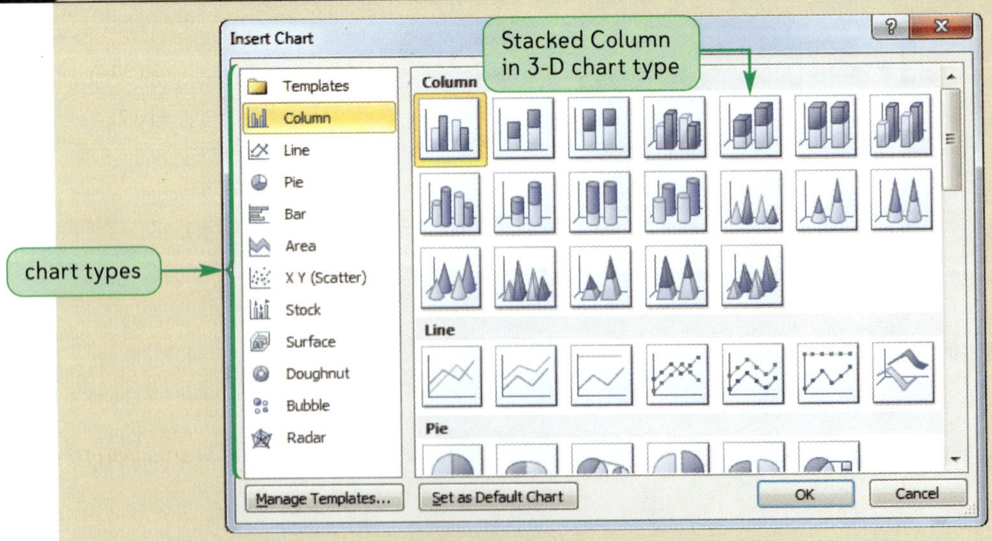

3. Click the **Stacked Column in 3-D** chart type, which is the fifth chart in the first row in the gallery, and then click the **OK** button. A sample chart is inserted in Slide 6, the PowerPoint program window is resized to fit half of the screen, and a Microsoft Excel worksheet opens on the right side of the screen with sample data. See Figure 3-18. Notice that some of the groups on the Home tab on the Ribbon in both windows are collapsed into buttons.

**Figure 3-18** Excel spreadsheet with data for chart

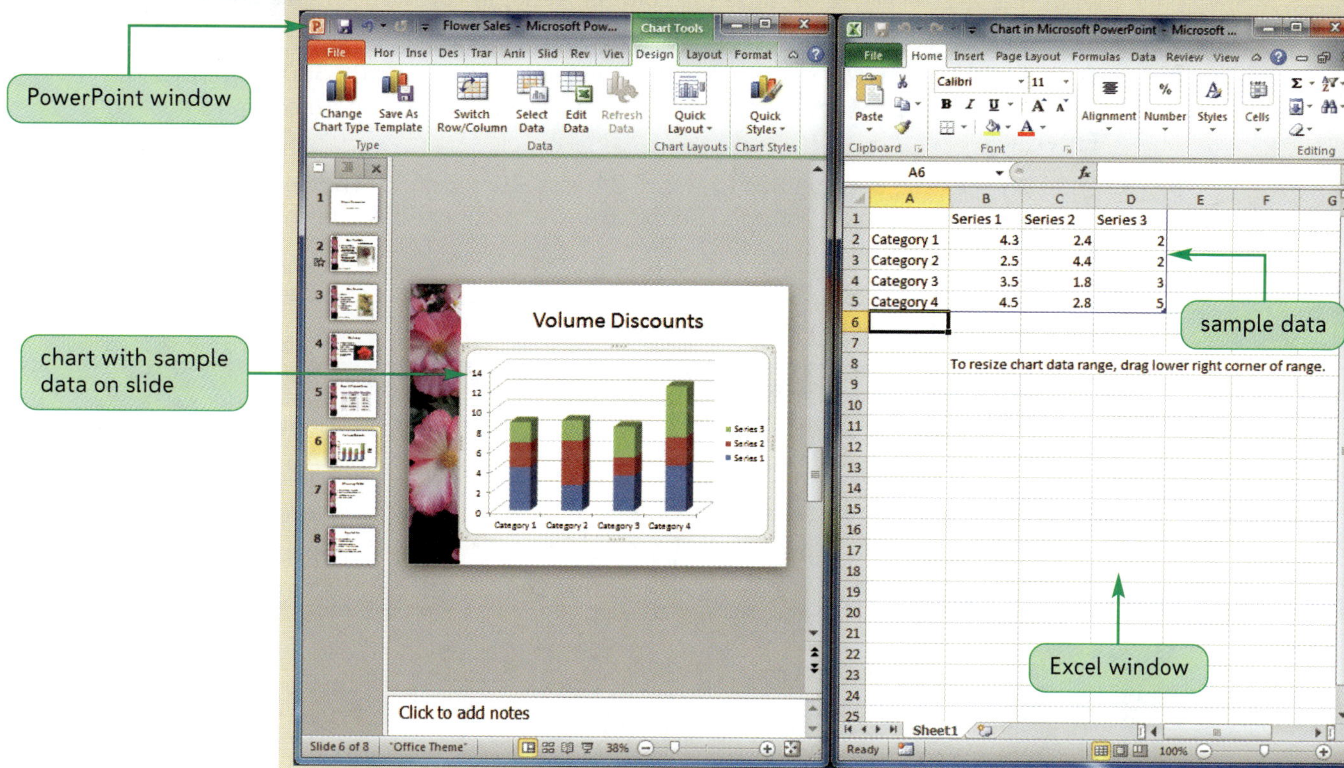


To create the chart for Sophie's presentation, you simply edit the information in the sample worksheet in the Excel window. When you work with a worksheet, the cell in which you are entering data is the **active cell**. The active cell has a thick black border around it. In this chart, Sophie wants only two columns, one with the number of units ordered (per month) and one with the percent discount. You'll begin by deleting the third and fourth columns of data in the worksheet.

## To enter the data for the chart:

1. In the Excel worksheet, click anywhere in column D. Notice the blue border around the sample data.
2. On the Home tab in the Excel worksheet, click the **Cells** button, click the **Delete button arrow**, and then click **Delete Table Columns**. Column D is deleted from the worksheet, the blue border adjusts to exclude column D, and the chart in the slide is redrawn to match the worksheet.

   **Trouble?** If you see the Cells group instead of the Cells button on the Home tab, click the Delete button arrow located in that group.

3. Delete column C. The blue border adjusts again.
4. Click cell **B1**, which currently contains the column label "Series 1."
5. Type **Discount %**, and then press the **Enter** key. The text you typed replaces the text in cell B1. Notice that the legend and the title in the chart in the PowerPoint window change as well.
6. Click cell **A2** ("Category 1"), type **11-50 Units/Mo**, and then press the **Enter** key. The text is entered into cell A2, and cell A3 becomes the active cell. You can't see all of the text in cell A2 because the column is too narrow to fit it. This doesn't matter because the worksheet will not appear on the slide.
7. Type **51-100 Units/Mo** in cell A3, press the **Enter** key, type **101-300 Units/Mo** in cell A4, press the **Enter** key, type **>300 Units/Mo** in cell A5, and then press the **Enter** key.
8. Enter **3** in cell B2, **8** in cell B3, **15** in cell B4, and **20** in cell B5. The new values appear in cells B2 through B5 in Excel and are reflected in the chart in PowerPoint. See Figure 3-19.

**TIP**

If you want to widen the columns in the Excel window, double-click the column divider to resize the column to fit the widest entry or drag the column divider to resize the column to a specific width.

**Figure 3-19 Completed Excel worksheet with data for chart**

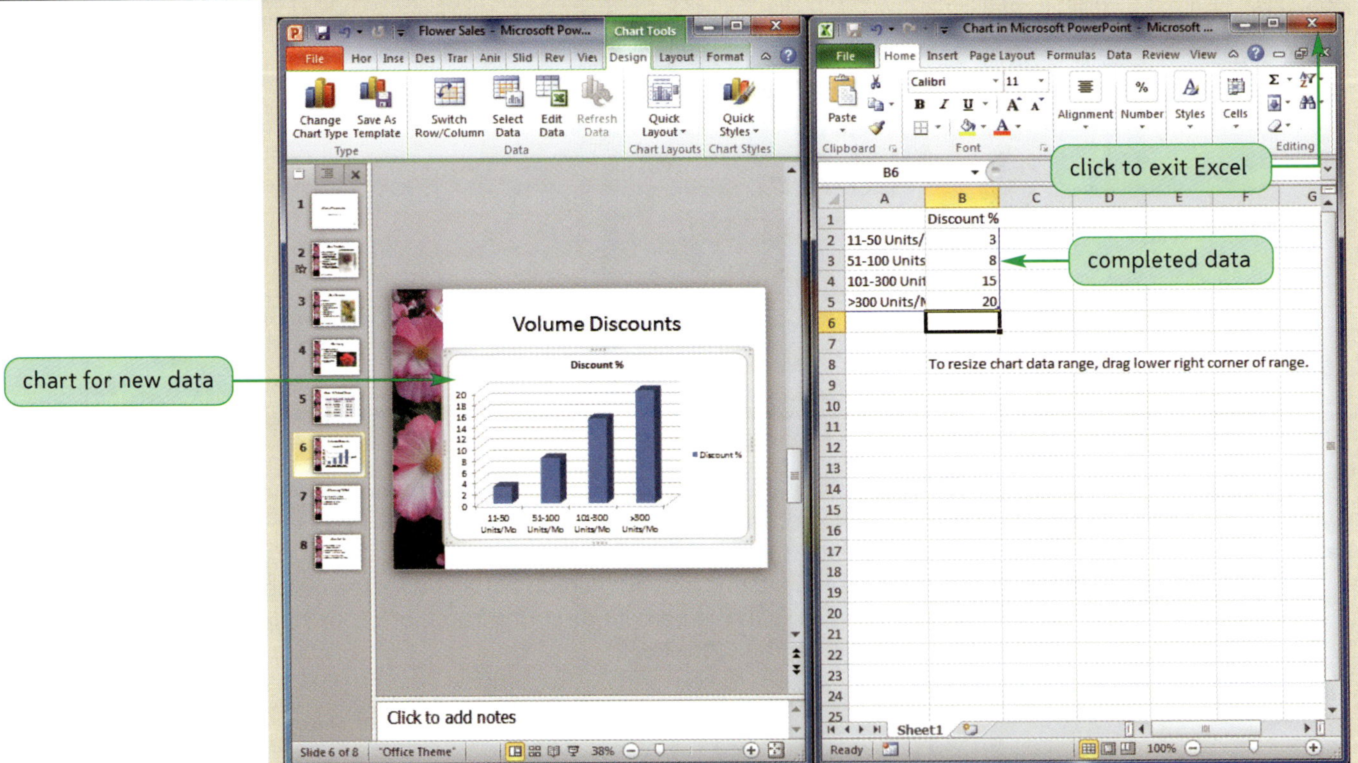


9. In the Excel window, click the **Close** button on the Excel title bar. The Excel window closes, the Excel data is saved in the PowerPoint presentation, and the PowerPoint window expands to fill the full screen. The new chart is selected in Slide 6, as shown in Figure 3-20, and three Chart Tools contextual tabs appear on the Ribbon.

**Figure 3-20** Slide 6 with chart

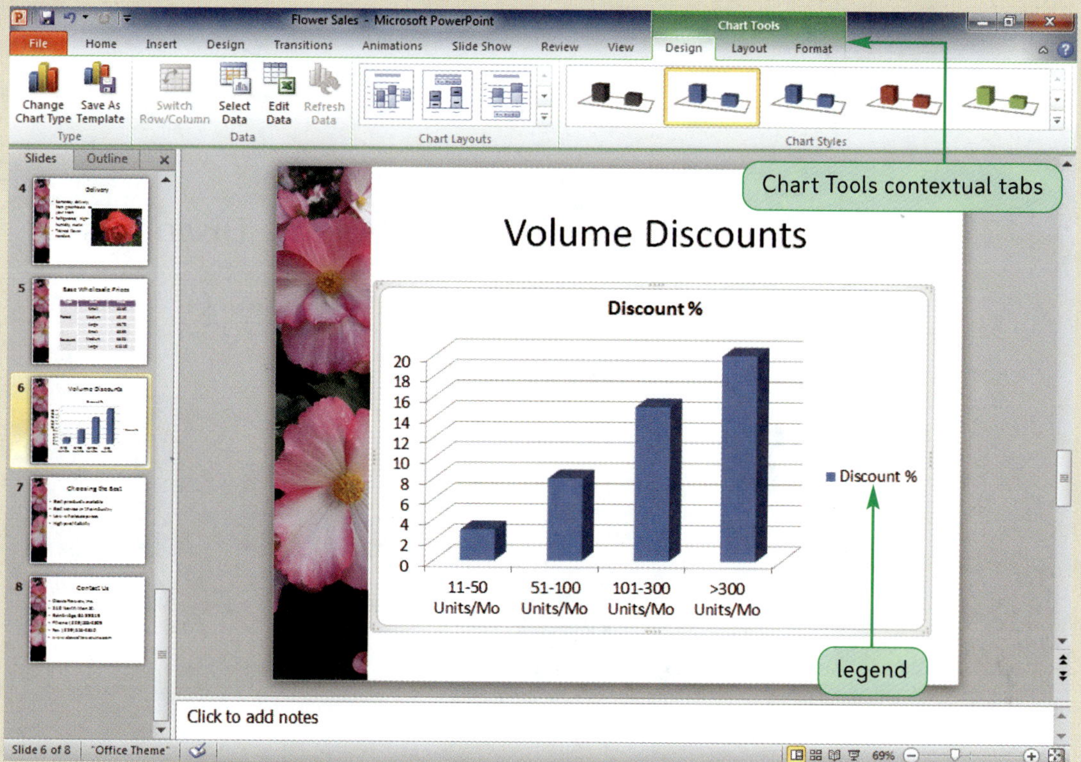


## Modifying a Chart

Once the chart is on the slide, you can modify it by changing or formatting the various elements of the chart. For example, the legend on the right side of the chart is unnecessary because all the columns in the chart refer to the discount percentage, so you can choose to delete it. You can apply a chart style to your chart to change its look. You can also add gridlines and labels or edit or remove a chart's title.

Sophie wants you to modify the chart by deleting the legend, applying a style, and adding gridlines and labels. You'll do this now.

**TIP**

You can also delete the legend by clicking the Chart Tools Layout tab on the Ribbon, clicking the Legend button in the Labels group, and then clicking None.

### To edit and format the chart:

1. Click the **legend** to select it, and then press the **Delete** key. The legend is removed from the chart, and the chart expands to fill the space that was occupied by the text box you deleted. You can also change the chart style.
2. If necessary, click the **Chart Tools Design** tab on the Ribbon.
3. In the Chart Styles group, click the **More** button, and then click **Style 14**, the purple style in the second row in the gallery. The column colors change from blue to purple. See Figure 3-21.

**Figure 3-21** Chart after deleting legend and applying a style

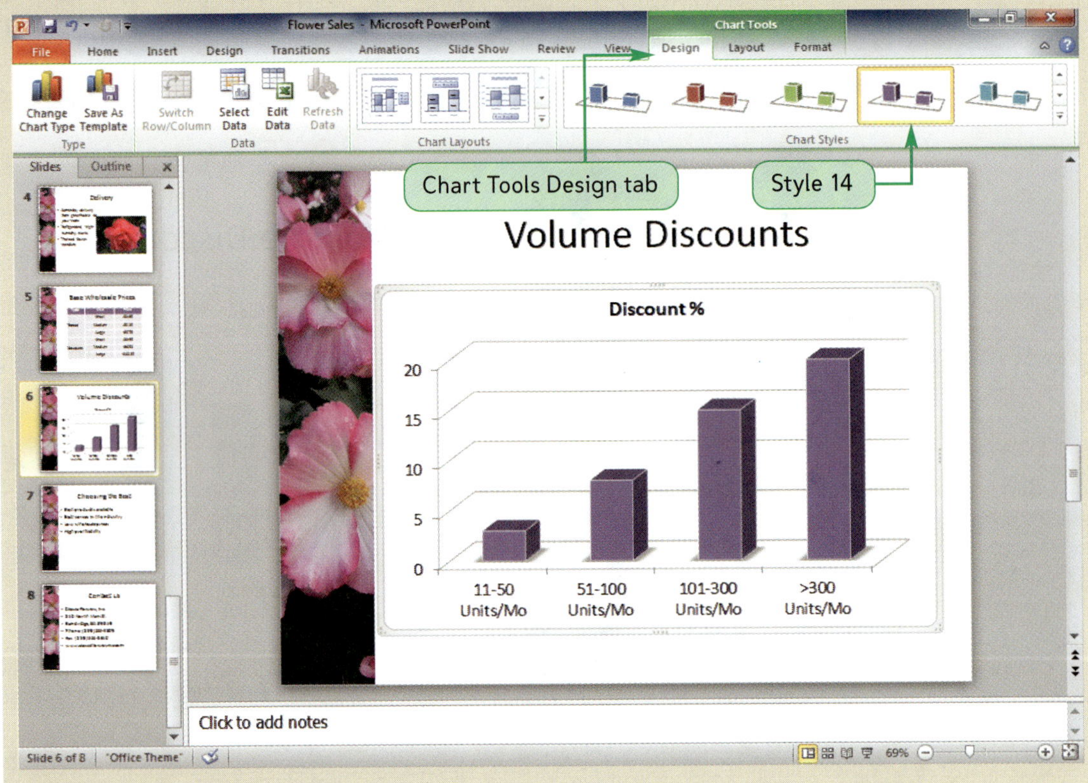


4. Click the **Chart Tools Layout** tab on the Ribbon.
5. In the Labels group, click the **Data Labels** button, and then click **Show**. Now the actual values of the discount percent appear on the columns in the chart. Next, you'll add vertical gridlines to the chart.
6. In the Axes group, click the **Gridlines** button, point to **Primary Vertical Gridlines**, and then click **Major Gridlines**. Now you can see not only horizontal but also vertical gridlines. See Figure 3-22. Next, Sophie wants you to add a label to the vertical axis on the left. You'll add rotated text along that axis.

**Figure 3-22** Chart after displaying column values and gridlines

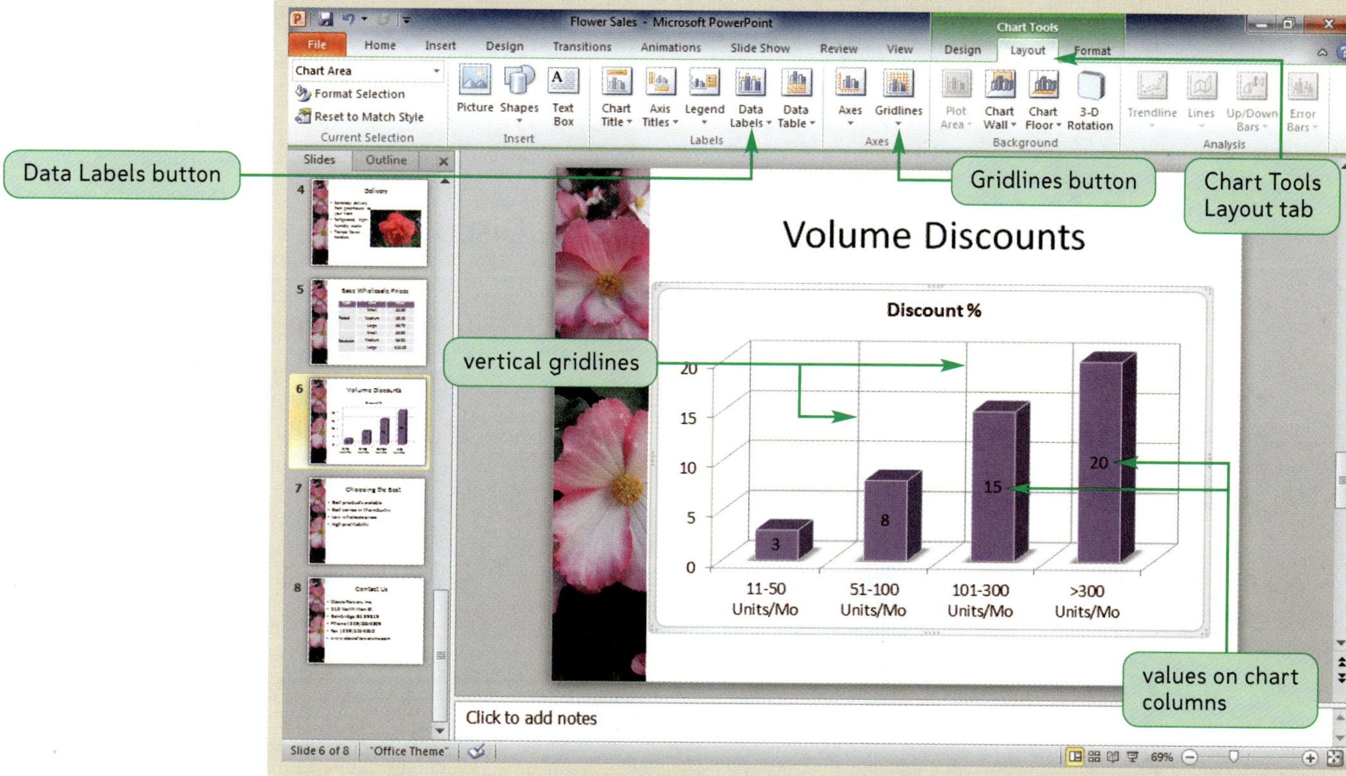


7. In the Labels group, click the **Axis Titles** button, point to **Primary Vertical Axis Title**, and then click **Rotated Title**. A text box, rotated so it reads bottom to top parallel to the vertical axis, appears on the chart with the text "Axis Title." The new text box is selected, so you can just start typing to replace the temporary axis title.
8. Type **Percent Discount**. The text "Axis Title" is changed to "Percent Discount." The slide title describes the chart, so you will delete the chart title.
9. In the Labels group, click the **Chart Title** button, and then click **None**. Compare your chart to the one shown in Figure 3-23.

Figure 3-23 Completed chart

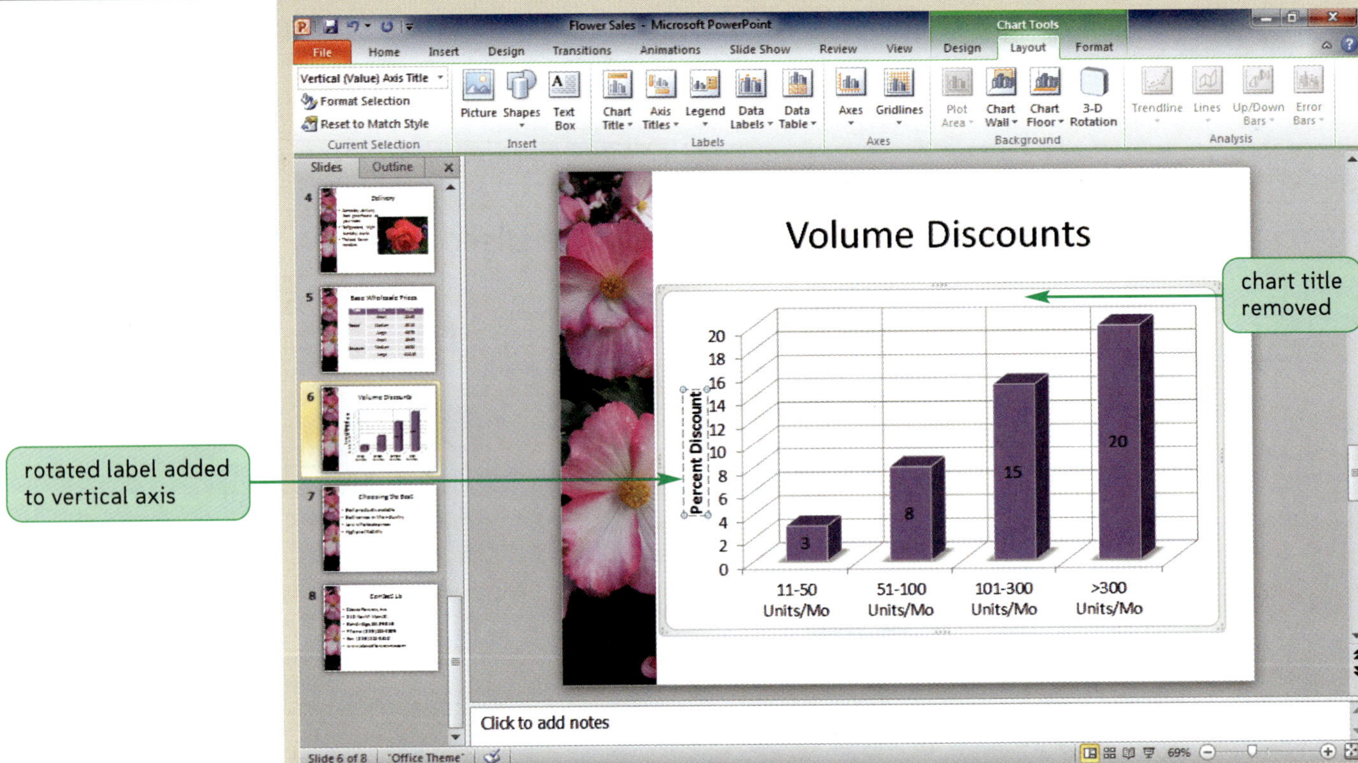


**10.** Save your changes.

## Animating a Chart

Sophie now wants you to apply an entrance animation effect to the chart in Slide 6. To apply an animation to a chart, you use the same technique as animating any other object on a slide.

### To animate the chart:

1. Click the **Animations** tab on the Ribbon. The chart should still be selected.
2. In the Animations gallery, click the **More** button, and then in the second row under Entrance, click **Random Bars**. The animation previews. One animation sequence icon appears next to the chart. The default is for the chart to animate as one object (the same as SmartArt), but you want each bar to appear one after the other.
3. In the Animation group, click the **Effect Options** button. Notice that there are five options under Sequence.
4. Click **By Element in Series**. The animation previews with the chart appearing with the Random Bars effect followed by each bar, one after the other. Five animation sequence icons now appear next to the chart; the first icon, number 1, is for the chart grid, and numbers 2 through 5 are associated with each bar.

## Adding a Second Animation to an Object

After Sophie spends some time discussing the information on this slide during her presentation, she wants to draw her audience's attention back to the chart. To do this, she asks you to apply an emphasis animation to occur after the entrance animation.

### To add a second animation to the chart and change its speed:

1. Make sure the chart is still selected.
2. In the Advanced Animation group, click the **Add Animation** button. The same gallery that opens when you click the More button in the Animation group appears.
3. In the first row under Emphasis, click **Pulse**. This effect causes the object to pulse—that is, to zoom in slightly and then shrink back. Notice the additional five animation sequence icons next to the chart. See Figure 3-24. Although the default for charts is to animate as one object, because you changed the Entrance animation so that each bar in the chart animates one series at a time, the default for this second animation that you applied to the chart is By Element in Series as well. It's too distracting to have the chart pulse one bar at a time, so Sophie suggests that since both animations must have the same sequence effect, it would be better to have them animate as one object.

**Figure 3-24** Chart with two animations set to animate by element in series

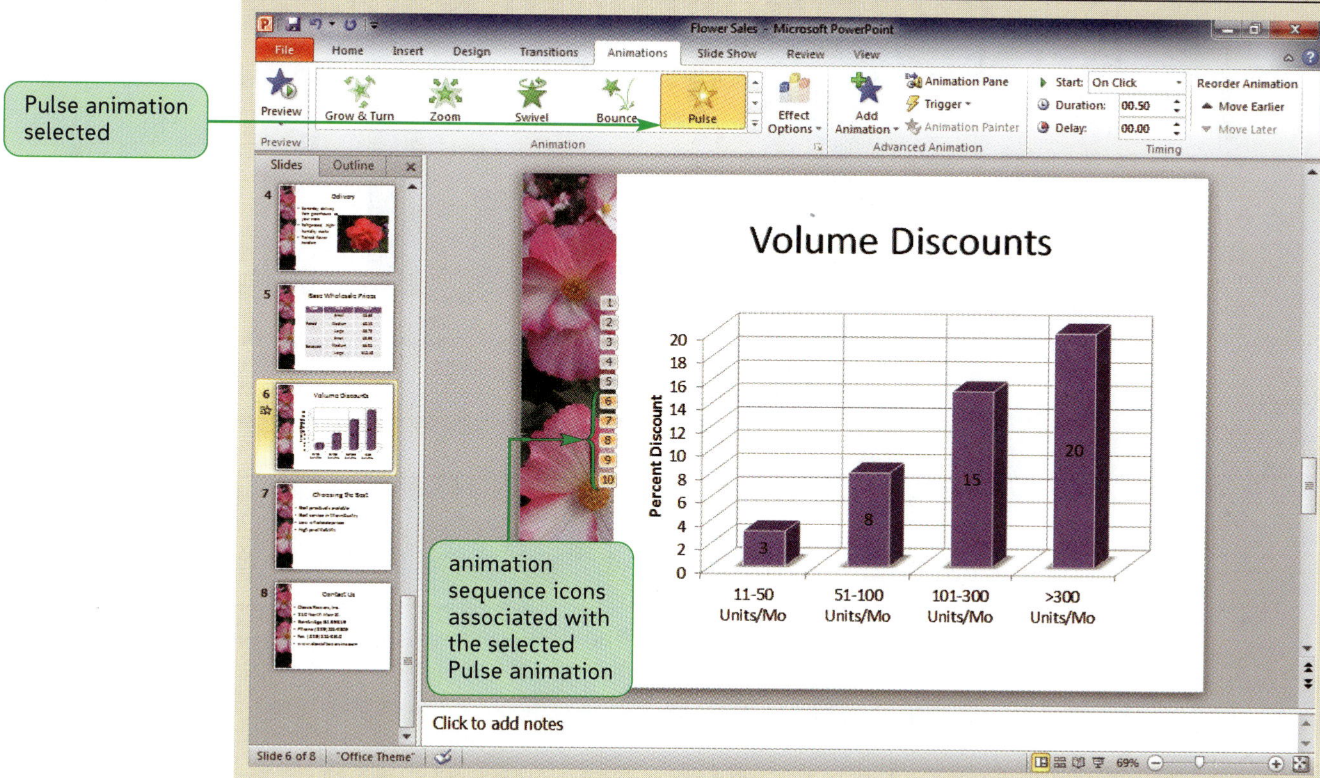


4. In the Animation group, click the **Effect Options** button, and then click **As One Object**. Now just two animation sequence icons appear next to the chart.

# Changing the Speed of Animations

You can adjust the speed of animations. For the chart, Sophie wants the entrance animation to progress more slowly than the default setting of one-half second, and she wants the Pulse animation to occur more quickly. To change the speed of an animation, you change the time in the Duration box in the Timing group on the Animations tab.

## To change the speed of the chart animations:

1. Click the animation sequence icon with the number 1 in it. Random Bars is selected in the Animation group on the Animations tab.
2. In the Timing group, click the **Duration up arrow** twice. See Figure 3-25. The Random Bars animation will now take one second instead of one-half second.

**Figure 3-25** Speed of the Random Bars animation modified

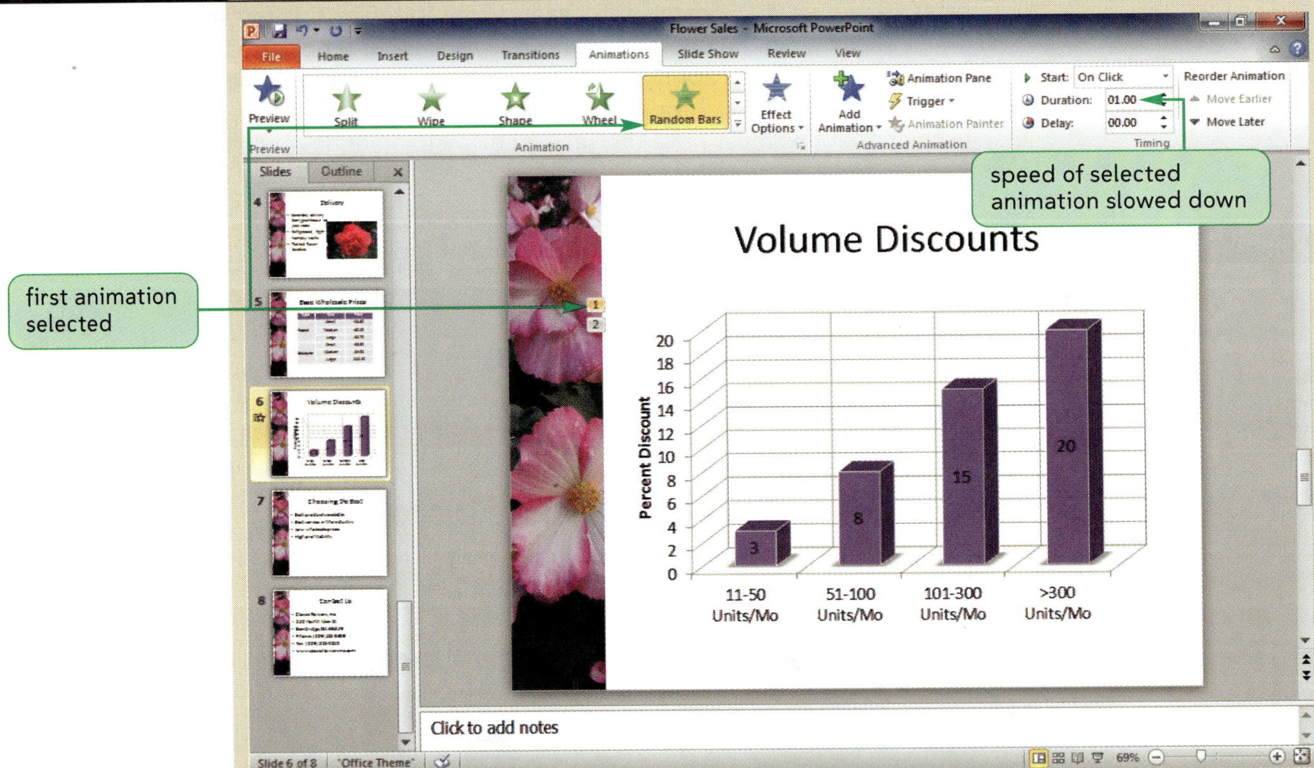


3. Click the animation sequence icon with the number 2 in it. Pulse is selected in the Animation group.
4. In the Timing group, click the **Duration down arrow** to change the Duration to .25 seconds.
5. In the Preview group, click the **Preview** button to preview the chart animations.
6. Save your changes.

You have created content for Sophie's sales presentation by inserting slides from another presentation and adding video, sound, a table, and a chart. You have also added a second animation to an object and changed the speed of animations. In the next session, you will customize the theme by changing the theme fonts and colors and modifying the slide background and bullet styles, and then save the modified theme as a custom theme. You will also apply a different theme to one slide in the presentation.

REVIEW

## *Session 3.1 Quick Check*

1. Describe how you insert slides from one presentation into another.
2. What happens when you add a reflection effect to a video?
3. How do you shorten a video's playback?
4. True or False. You cannot set a sound clip to play across multiple slides.
5. When you apply a table style, how do you quickly identify columns or rows that should be formatted differently?
6. What program opens when you insert a chart on a slide?
7. True or False. To add a second animation to an object, you click the second animation in the Animation gallery.
8. How do you change the speed of an animation?

# SESSION 3.2 VISUAL OVERVIEW

Each color on the left corresponds to an element in the sample. The sample shows you how the colors look together.

These four colors provide you with two alternatives for light text on a dark background and two alternatives for dark text on a light background. The default text color is the first color, and the default background color is the second color.

The six Accent colors are used for lines, shapes, charts, tables, shadows, picture borders, and other objects on your presentation slides.

These colors are used for hyperlinks and hyperlinks after they have been followed (clicked to jump to the hyperlinked location).

Click the Reset button if you change your mind and want to restore the colors to the default colors for the currently applied theme.

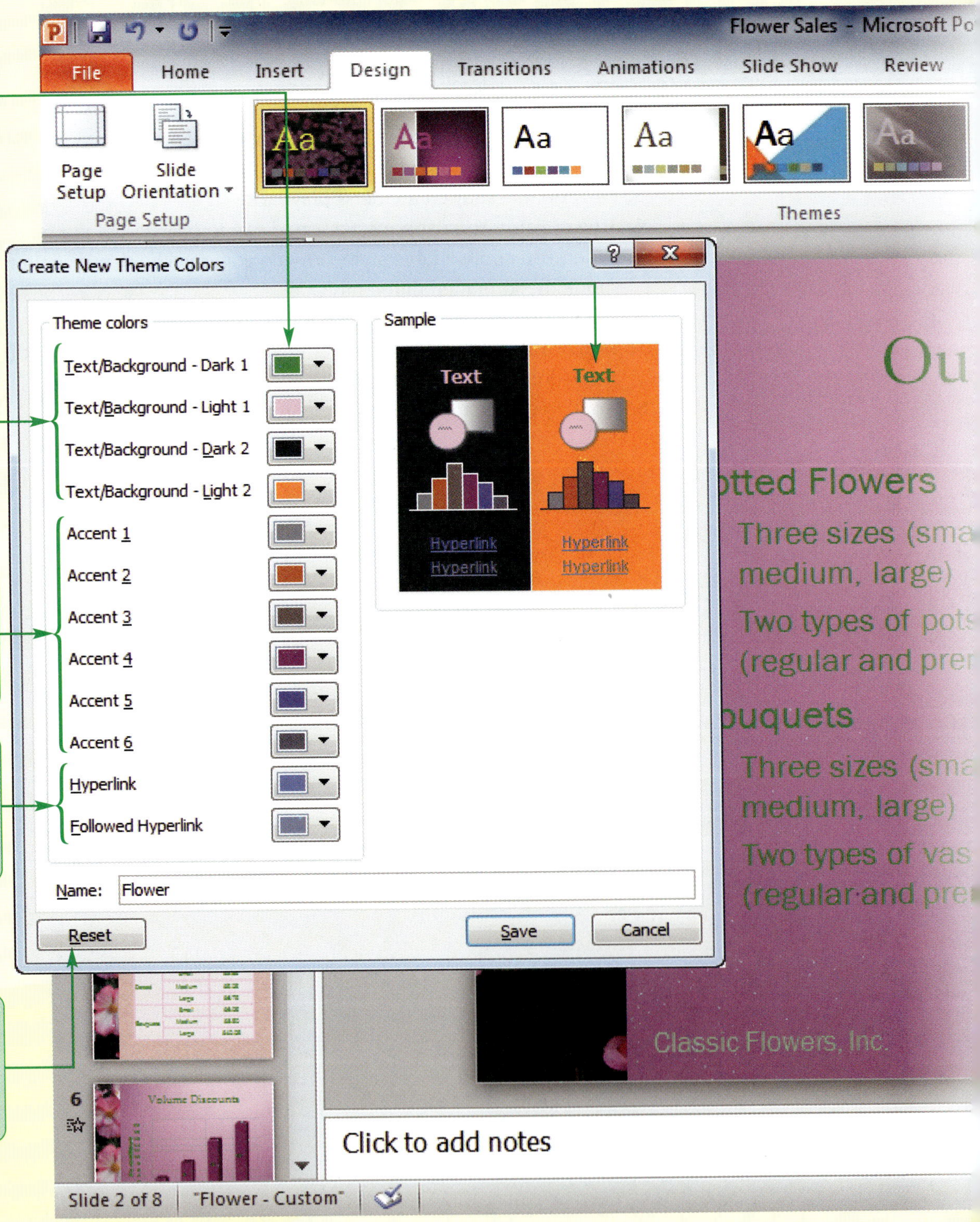

# THEME COLORS AND BACKGROUNDS

A **gradient fill** is a type of shading in which one color blends into another or varies from one shade to another. This background varies from dark pink (or violet) in the lower-left corner to light pink in the upper-right corner.

To change the background style or color, add a picture to the background, or apply a textured background, click the Background Styles button in the Background group on the Design tab or on the Slide Master tab.

Custom theme color palettes are listed at the top of the Colors gallery.

Built-in theme color palettes are listed in alphabetical order after the Office Theme and Grayscale theme color palettes.

Click Create New Theme Colors to open the dialog box.

# Changing Theme Fonts and Colors

The 20 built-in themes provide many choices for personalizing the design of a presentation. However, if you don't like the specific colors or fonts that come with a theme, you can change them easily. You could change the fonts used for the slide titles and content and the colors used for elements shown in the slide masters, but this would not change the default font used for text boxes you draw, the text used in shapes and tables, the text used for labels in charts, and so on. Instead, you can change the set of theme fonts and theme colors.

## Changing Theme Fonts

Recall from Tutorial 1 that theme fonts are two coordinating fonts or font styles, one for the titles (or headings) and one for text in content placeholders and other text elements on a slide. To change the theme fonts, you click the Fonts button in the Themes group on the Design tab, and then select the coordinating set of fonts from another theme.

The Flower Sales presentation is based on the Office theme, and the font used for all the text in the presentation is Calibri. Sophie would like to use a different set of theme fonts in the Flower Sales presentation. You'll change the theme fonts now.

**To change the theme fonts:**

1. If you took a break after the last session, make sure the **Flower Sales** presentation you created in Session 3.1 is open in the PowerPoint window in Normal view.
2. Display **Slide 1** in the Slide pane, and then click the **Design** tab on the Ribbon.
3. In the Themes group, click the **Fonts** button. The gallery of theme fonts opens.
4. Scroll down the alphabetical list, and then point to **Pushpin**. Live Preview shows the fonts change from Calibri, used in the Office theme, to Constantia for the slide titles and Franklin Gothic Book for text in the content text boxes, the fonts used in the Pushpin theme. See Figure 3-26.

Figure 3-26 Fonts gallery

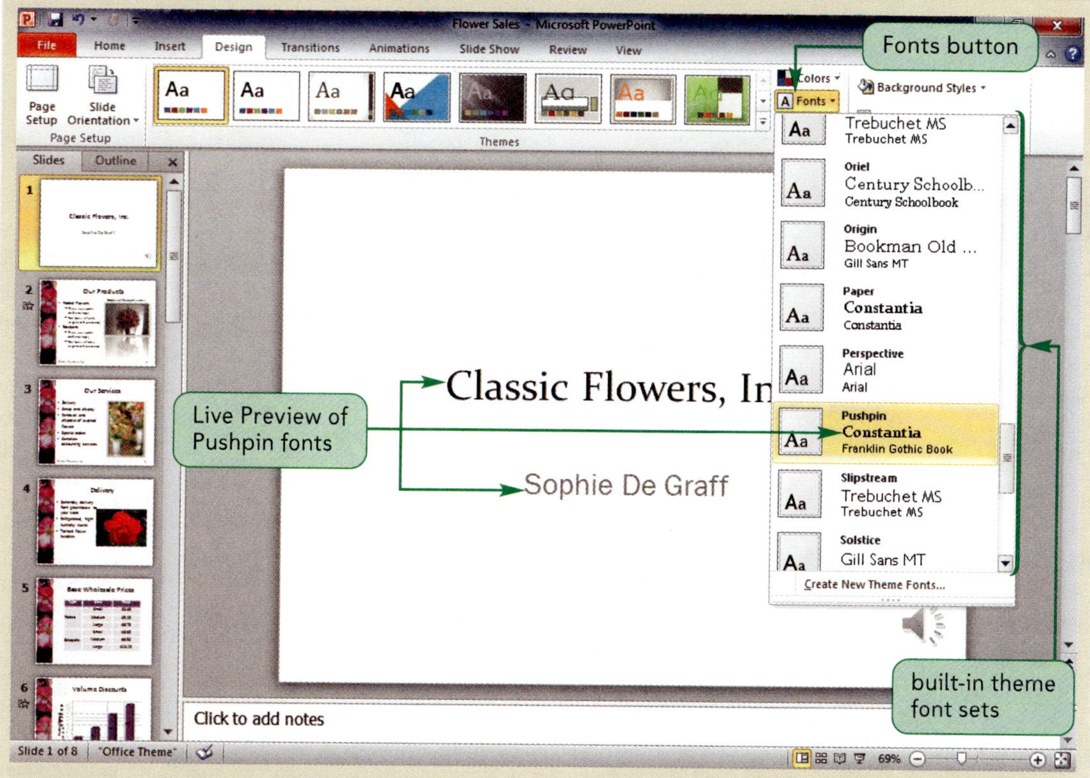


5. Click **Pushpin**. The menu closes and the fonts in the presentation are changed to the fonts used with the Pushpin theme.
6. Save your changes.

You can also customize a theme by choosing a different set of theme colors.

## Changing Theme Colors

Each of the built-in PowerPoint themes, including the default Office theme, has a set of 12 theme colors associated with it. Recall that theme colors are the coordinating colors used for the background, title fonts, body fonts, and other elements of the presentation. Refer to the Session 3.2 Visual Overview for more information about theme colors.

The current presentation uses the color theme called "Office," which is the default set of colors used when the Office theme is applied. The default background color is white and the default text color is black (except for the gray subtitle on the title slide). Sophie feels that this simple theme doesn't fit well with the sales presentation on potted flowers and bouquets. She would like you to choose a theme that uses a brighter set of theme colors.

You choose a different set of theme colors using the Colors button in the Themes group on the Design tab.

**To change the theme colors in the presentation:**

1. In the Themes group on the Design tab, click the **Colors** button to display the Colors gallery. See Figure 3-27. Office and Grayscale appear at the top of the list, followed by an alphabetical list of theme color sets. Grayscale is not a theme, but is available as a set of theme colors if you want to create a presentation using only shades of gray.

**Figure 3-27** **Colors gallery**

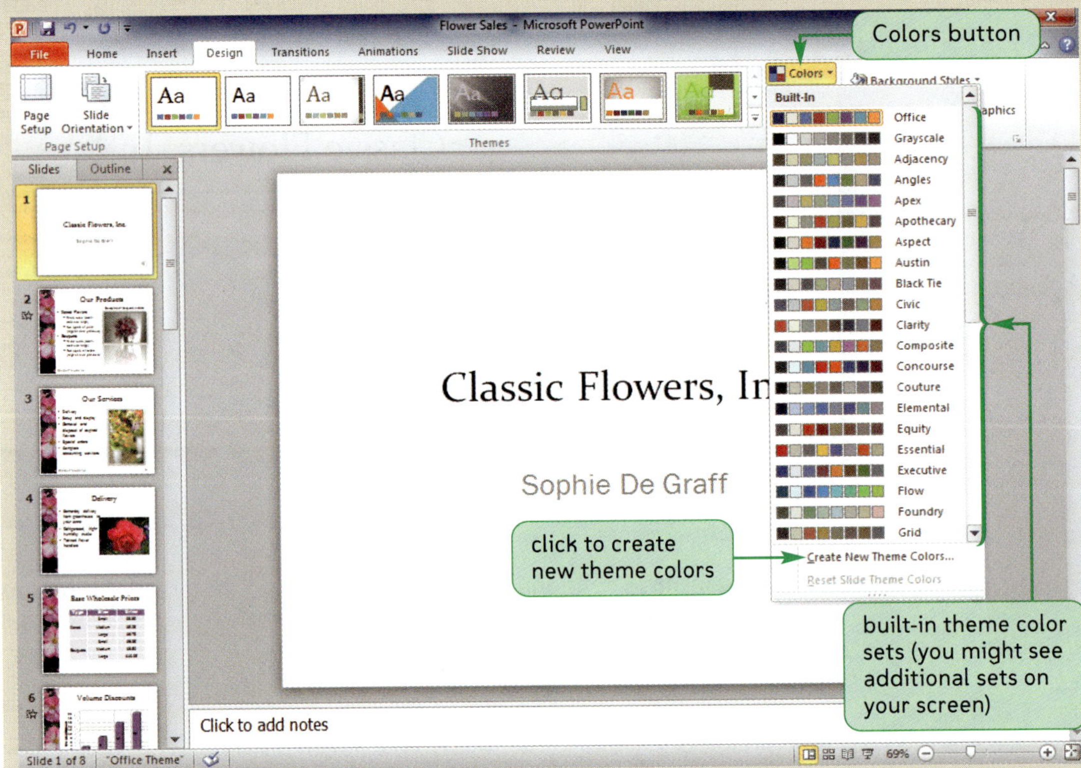


2. Scroll down the list, and then click **Perspective**. This set of theme colors uses brighter colors than those used in the Office theme. Because the text and background colors for the Perspective theme are also black and white, the only change that happens in the presentation is that the table and chart on Slides 5 and 6 changed color slightly.

## Customizing Theme Colors

The color change was not as dramatic as Sophie had hoped. She decides she would like you to customize the theme colors by changing the color of text to green and the color of the background to pink. To do this, you need to create a new, custom set of theme colors. Refer back to the Session 3.2 Visual Overview for more information about how each color is assigned to an element and how to change these colors.

### To create custom theme colors:

1. In the Themes group, click the **Colors** button, and then at the bottom of the gallery, click **Create New Theme Colors**. The Create New Theme Colors dialog box opens. You want to change the color of text from black to green.
2. Click the **Text/Background – Dark 1** button to display the complete Theme Colors and Standard Colors palettes. Because no dark-green tile appears in the palette, you'll look at more colors.
3. At the bottom of the palette, click **More Colors** to display the Colors dialog box, and then, if necessary, click the **Standard** tab. See Figure 3-28.

**Figure 3-28** Standard tab in the Colors dialog box

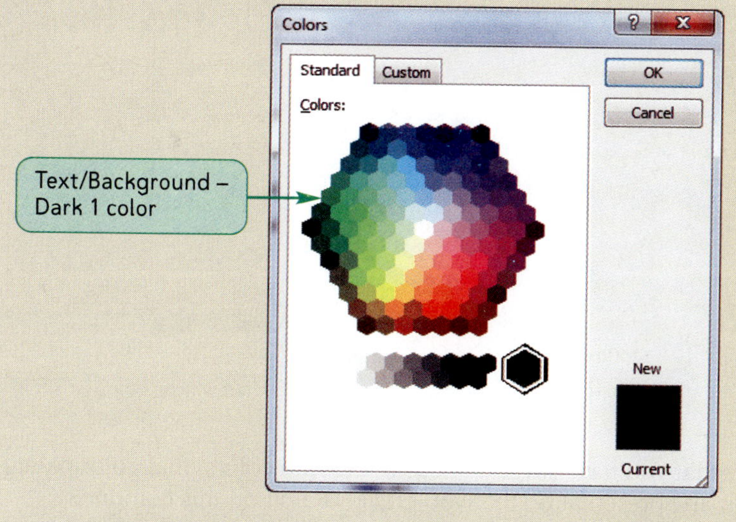


4. Refer to Figure 3-28, click the dark green tile labeled **Text/Background – Dark 1** in the figure, and then click the **OK** button. The Colors dialog box closes. The Text/Background – Dark 1 color changes from black to dark green, and the text in the panel on the right in the Sample area of the Create New Theme Colors dialog box changes to dark green also. Next, you'll change the color of the light color background.
5. Click the **Text/Background – Light 1** button to display the Colors gallery.
6. Under Theme Colors, click the **Dark Purple, Accent 4, Lighter 80%** color (the pink color in the eighth column, second row). The text in the panel on the left in the Sample area changes to light pink. Even though the text in the left panel changed, the Text/Background – Light 1 color will be applied to the slide background. Since you created a new set of theme colors, you need to save them in order to apply them to the presentation.
7. In the **Name** box, delete the text "**Custom 1**," and then type **Flower**.
8. Click the **Save** button. The dialog box closes and the custom theme colors are applied to the presentation. As you can see in Slide 1, the title text is now dark green and the background is light pink. The subtitle text changed to a complementary color to the title text. See Figure 3-29.

**TIP**

Never select dark text on dark background or light text on light background.

Figure 3-29 New theme colors applied to the presentation

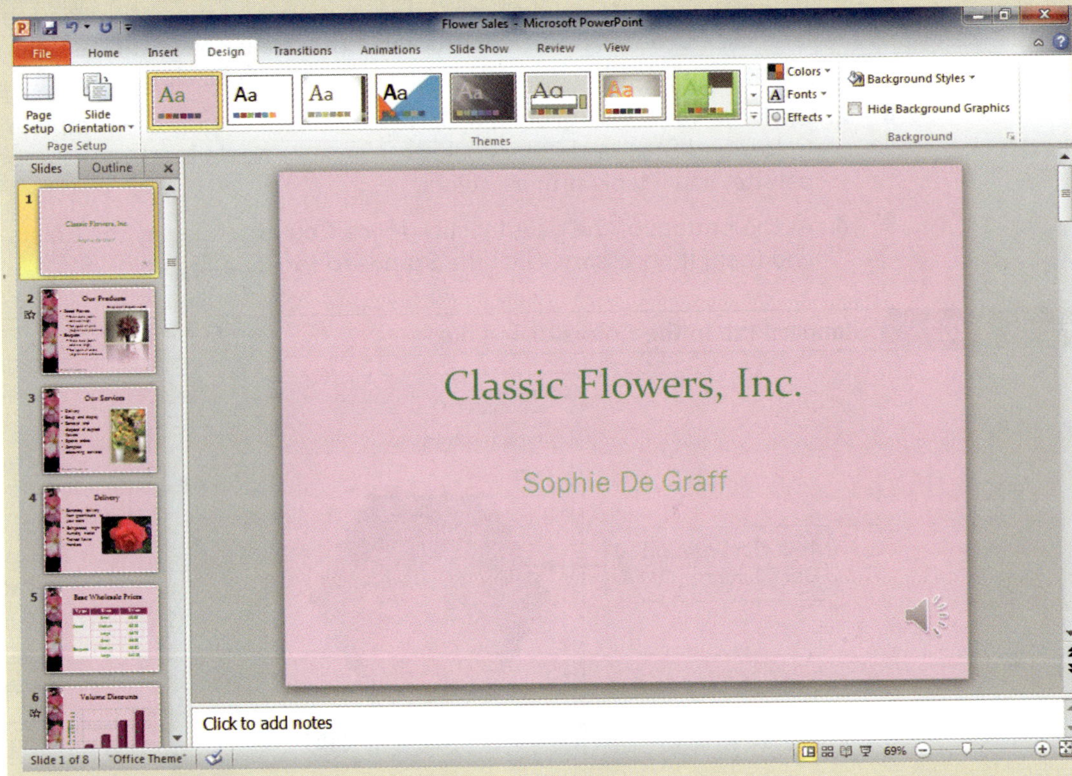


Now that you have saved the custom theme colors, that color palette is available to apply to any presentation that you create or edit on this computer.

INSIGHT

### *Choosing Custom Theme Colors*

When creating custom theme colors, you need to be wary of selecting colors that don't match or make text illegible; for example, red text on a blue background might seem like a good combination, but it's actually difficult to read for an audience at a distance from the screen. It's usually safer, therefore, to select one of the built-in theme color sets and stick with it, or make only minor modifications. If you do create a new set of theme colors, select colors that go well together and that maximize legibility of your slides.

## Deleting Custom Theme Colors

You can delete a custom theme or theme colors. If you've applied the theme or the theme colors to a presentation, and then saved that presentation, the theme and colors will still be applied to that presentation even if you delete the theme or theme colors from the hard drive. You'll delete the custom theme color palette you created from the computer you are using.

**TIP**

To access the Colors menu, a presentation must be open.

**To delete the custom theme colors:**

1. In the Themes group, click the **Colors** button. The Flower custom color theme you created appears at the top of the Colors gallery under "Custom."
2. Right-click the **Flower** theme color palette, and then click **Delete** on the shortcut menu. A dialog box opens asking if you want to delete these theme colors.
3. Click the **Yes** button. The dialog box closes and the custom theme colors are deleted.
4. In the Themes group, click the **Colors** button, and confirm that the Flower theme color palette is deleted.
5. Click a blank area of the window to close the menu without making a selection.
6. Save your changes.

## Resetting Slides

When you create custom theme colors or change the theme fonts, you should examine the slides to make sure they look as you expect. When you change theme or slide master elements in a presentation, you sometimes need to reset the slides so that they pick up the new formatting. In this case, the new text color did not get picked up by the existing slides in the presentation. You can fix this by resetting the slides. When you reset slides, you reset every object on the slides, so you might need to reposition objects or reapply styles. Slide 1 is fine and does not need to be reset.

**To reset the slides:**

1. Display **Slide 8** ("Contact Us") in the Slide pane. The text on this slide did not change to the new green color.
2. Click the **Home** tab on the Ribbon.
3. In the Slides group, click the **Reset** button. The text changes to the green color you selected.
4. Reset **Slide 7** ("Choosing the Best"), **Slide 6** ("Volume Discounts"), and **Slide 5** ("Best Wholesale Prices"). When you reset Slide 5, the table moved back to its original position on the slide.
5. Drag the **table** to position it approximately in the center of the pink area of the slide below the slide title.
6. Reset **Slide 4** ("Delivery"). The text changed to green, and the flower picture on the slide moved down. You'll leave this as it is for now.
7. Reset **Slide 3** ("Our Services"). In addition to the text changing to green, the Metal Frame style is removed from the picture. You'll reapply that style.
8. Select the picture, click the **Picture Tools Format** tab, and then in the Picture Styles group, click the **Metal Frame** style (the third style in the gallery).
9. Reset **Slide 2** ("Our Products"). The text changed to green, but the reflection effect and the Metal Frame style are removed from the video and the video moved back down to its original position on the slide. This is a case where resetting the slide made the problem worse, not better. You can undo your change.

10. On the Quick Access Toolbar, click the **Undo** button. The changes made to the image are undone, but the text in the title and content text boxes is still green. This is because the color of the text is directly connected to the theme, and therefore the slide master and the Reset command simply fixed something that should have been changed when the theme changes were made.
11. In the text box above the image, drag across the text to select it.
12. In the Font group on the Home tab, click the **Font Color button arrow**, and then click the **Green, Text 1** color in the first row under Theme Colors—even if it is already selected.
13. Click a blank area of the slide, and then save your changes.

Now that you've created a new set of theme colors for the presentation, you'll change the background style of the slides.

## Modifying the Slide Background

The background of a slide can be as important as the foreground when you are creating a presentation with a strong visual impact. You can modify the background style and colors, add a picture or even video as the slide background, or add a textured background. You can change the background from the Design tab or from the Slide Master tab.

### Adding a Gradient

You can change the background for one or all slides using the Background Styles gallery, which lists the four colors used for the Text/Background colors in the Create New Theme Colors dialog box. Gradient shading added to the background of slides can add interest and a professional touch to the presentation. You can make this change in Normal or Slide Master view.

You changed the background color to a light pink. Sophie thinks that a gradient background will look a little more interesting, so you'll add a gradient fill.

**TIP**

To change the background style on only one slide, right-click the style you want to apply, and then on the shortcut menu, click Apply to Selected Slides.

**To change the background style to a gradient fill:**

1. Click the **Design** tab on the Ribbon.
2. In the Background group, click the **Background Styles** button. The Background Styles gallery opens. See Figure 3-30. The Background Styles gallery includes 12 styles—four solid colors along the top row corresponding to the four Text/Background theme colors and two gradient styles for each of those colors.

**Figure 3-30** Background Styles gallery

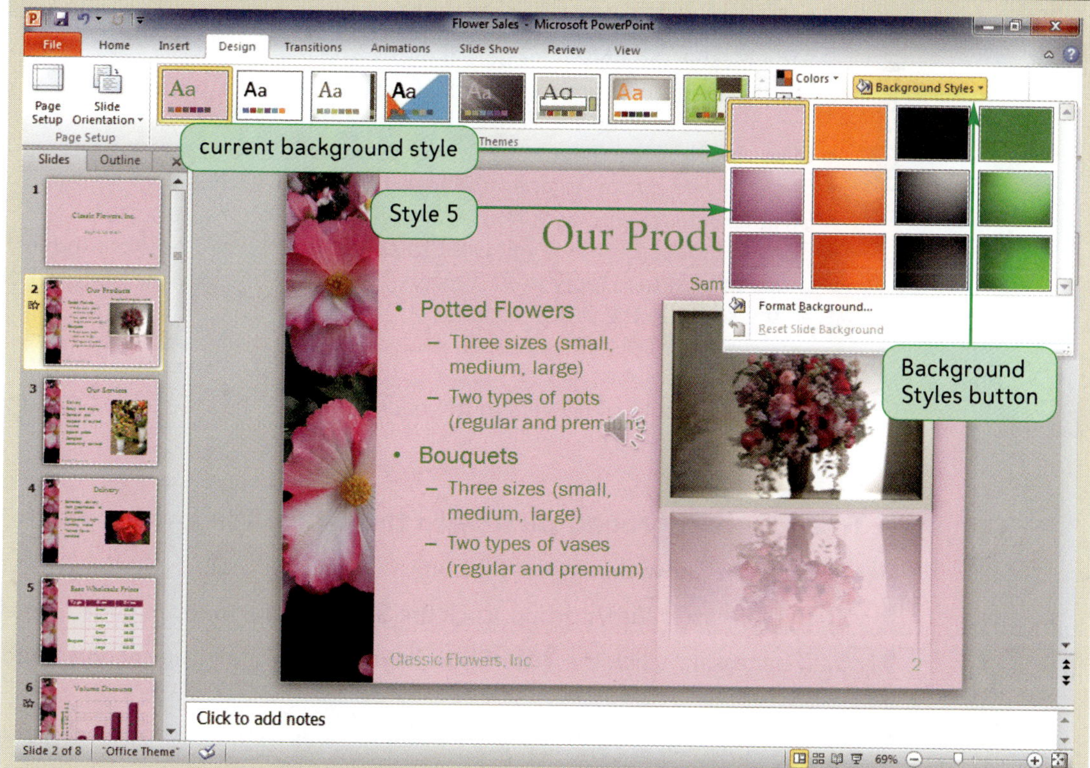


3. Click **Style 5**, which is the first background style in the second row. The background of the slides now vary from dark pink (or violet) in the lower-left corner to light pink in the upper-right corner.

As you can see from the Slide pane and the slide thumbnails in the pane on the left, all of the slides now have a background with a gradient fill. You'll now add a picture to the background of Slide 1.

## Adding a Background Picture

Sophie wants you to add a photo of a bed of flowers to the background of Slide 1. Although you can change the background style in Normal or Slide Master view, if you want a background picture to become part of the theme, you need to add it to the slide background in Slide Master view. You want to be able to apply the formatting changes you made in this presentation to future presentations, so you'll add the picture to the Title Slide Layout master. Recall that the slide master contains the objects that appear on the slide layouts, and the Title Slide layout master contains the objects that appear only on the title slide.

REFERENCE

## *Adding a Picture to a Background*

- Click the Design tab on the Ribbon; or, switch to Slide Master view, and then click the Slide Master tab on the Ribbon, if necessary.
- In the Background group, click the Background Styles button, and then click Format Background to open the Format Background dialog box.
- Click the Picture or texture fill option button.
- Click the File button to open the Insert Picture dialog box.
- Click the image you want to use, and then click the Insert button.
- Click the Close button if you want to apply the textured background just to the current slide, or click the Apply to All button if you want to apply the textured background to all the slides in the presentation.

You'll add a photo of flowers to the background of the Title Slide Layout master now.

**To add a background picture to the Title Slide Layout master:**

1. Click the **View** tab on the Ribbon.
2. In the Master Views group, click the **Slide Master** button. Slide Master view opens.
3. If necessary, click the **Title Slide Layout** thumbnail (the second thumbnail from the top in the pane on the left).
4. In the Background group on the Slide Master tab, click the **Background Styles** button. The Background Styles gallery opens.
5. Below the gallery in the menu, click **Format Background**. The Format Background dialog box opens with Fill selected in the left pane.
6. Click the **Picture or texture fill** option button. The dialog box changes to display commands for customizing a background with a texture or a picture. See Figure 3-31. The default background for this option—the Papyrus textured background—appears on the slide behind the dialog box.

**TIP**

If you decide you do not want a picture or a textured background, click the Reset Background button in the Format Background dialog box.

**Figure 3-31** Format Background dialog box with Fill options

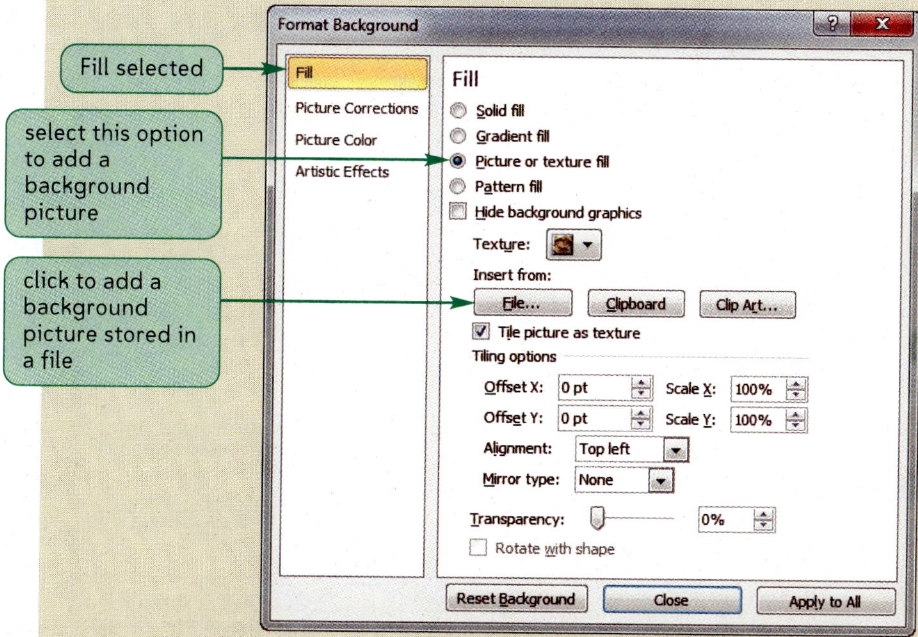


7. In the Insert from section in the center of the dialog box, click the **File** button. The Insert Picture dialog box opens.
8. Navigate to the PowerPoint3\Tutorial folder, click the picture file **PinkFlower**, and then click the **Insert** button. The Insert Picture dialog box closes and the picture is inserted into the background of the Title Slide Layout, which is visible behind the Format Background dialog box.

The new background makes it difficult to read the text on the slide, so Sophie asks you to adjust the brightness and contrast. Because the image is part of the background, you must adjust the brightness and contrast in the Format Background dialog box; you cannot adjust it on the Picture Tools Format tab.

**TIP**

You can also open the Format Background dialog box by right-clicking a blank area of the slide, and then clicking Format Background.

### To change the brightness and contrast of the background image:

1. In the left pane of the Format Background dialog box, click **Picture Corrections**. The dialog box changes to include commands for modifying the picture on the background. See Figure 3-32.

**Figure 3-32** Format Background dialog box with Picture Corrections options

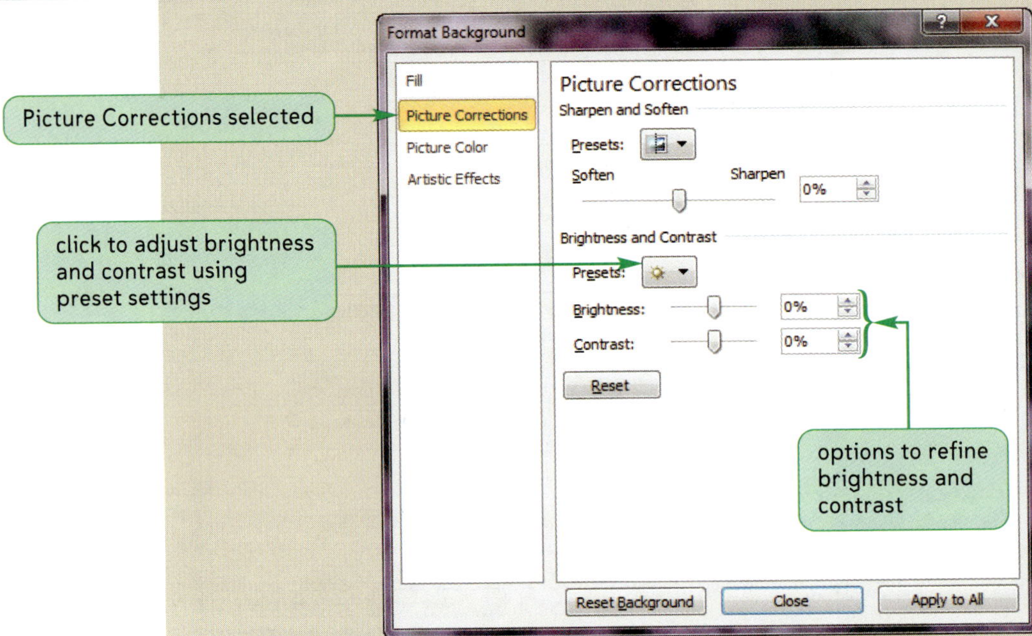


2. In the Brightness and Contrast section, click the **Presets** button. The Brightness and Contrast gallery opens.

   **Trouble?** If you see only one row of styles, you clicked the Presets button in the Sharpen and Soften section. Click the Presets button to close the gallery without selecting anything, and then repeat Step 2.

3. In the first row, click the **second style** (its ScreenTip is Brightness -20% Contrast -40%). The brightness and contrast of the image changes behind the Format Background dialog box. You want the image to be a little darker.

4. Drag the **Brightness** slider to the left until the box indicates **-30%**. The picture behind the dialog box darkens slightly.

   **Trouble?** If you can't position the slider exactly, click the up or down arrow in the box containing the percentage as needed, or drag to select the percentage and then type -30.

5. Click the **Close** button in the dialog box.

The backgrounds appear as Sophie wants them, but she now wants you to make the title text on the slides stand out more. You'll modify the color of the text.

### To change the color of the presentation title and subtitle:

1. With the Title Slide Layout master still selected, click the border of the title text placeholder, which currently contains dark-green text.

2. Click the **Home** tab on the Ribbon.

3. In the Font group, click the **Font Color button arrow** to display the theme colors palette.

4. Under Standard Colors, click the **Yellow** color (the fourth color in the row).

   **Trouble?** If the title text color did not change, you probably clicked inside the title text placeholder instead of directly on the border. Click directly on the border to select the entire placeholder, and then repeat Steps 3 and 4.

5. Change the color of the subtitle text to the Standard Color **Orange** (the third color in the row under Standard Colors).

6. Deselect the text box. See Figure 3-33.

**Figure 3-33** **Title Slide Layout master with modified title text**

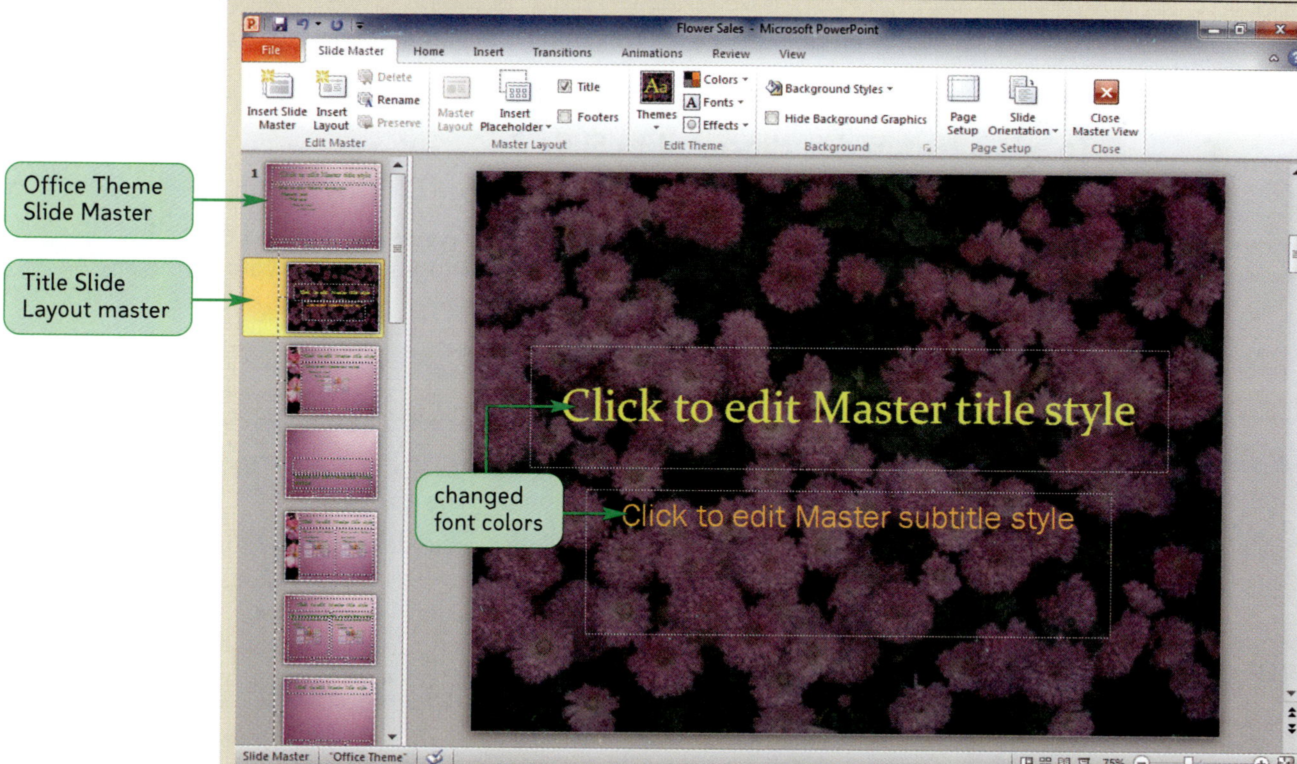


7. Close Slide Master view, and then display **Slide 1** (the title slide) in the Slide pane so that you can examine the changes you made.

8. Save your changes.

## Adding a Textured Background

In addition to changing the background style and adding a picture to the background, you can apply a textured background to a slide. Sophie asks you to change the background of Slide 5, which contains a table of the base wholesale prices of Classic Flowers' products, to highlight that slide. Because this change will highlight Slide 5 only—not all the slides with the Title and Content Layout master applied—you'll make this change in Normal view.

REFERENCE

### Applying a Textured Background

- Click the Design tab on the Ribbon.
- In the Background group, click the Background Styles button, and then click Format Background to open the Format Background dialog box.
- Click the Picture or texture fill option button.
- Click the Texture button to display a gallery of textured backgrounds.
- Click the desired texture and then click the Close button if you want to apply the textured background just to the current slide, or click the Apply to All button if you want to apply the textured background to all the slides in the presentation.

You'll now apply a "pink tissue paper" texture to the background of Slide 5.

### To add a textured background to Slide 5:

1. Display **Slide 5** ("Base Wholesale Prices"), and then click the **Design** tab.
2. In the Background group, click the **Background Styles** button, and then click **Format Background**. The Format Background dialog box opens with Fill selected on the left.
3. Click the **Picture or texture fill** option button. The dialog box changes to include commands for inserting a picture or a fill.
4. Click the **Texture** button. A gallery of textured backgrounds appears.
5. Click the **Pink tissue paper** texture, located in row 4, column 3. The background of the slide changes to pink tissue paper behind the dialog box.
6. Click the **Close** button. The pink tissue paper texture is applied to the current slide. See Figure 3-34.

**Figure 3-34** Slide 5 with textured background

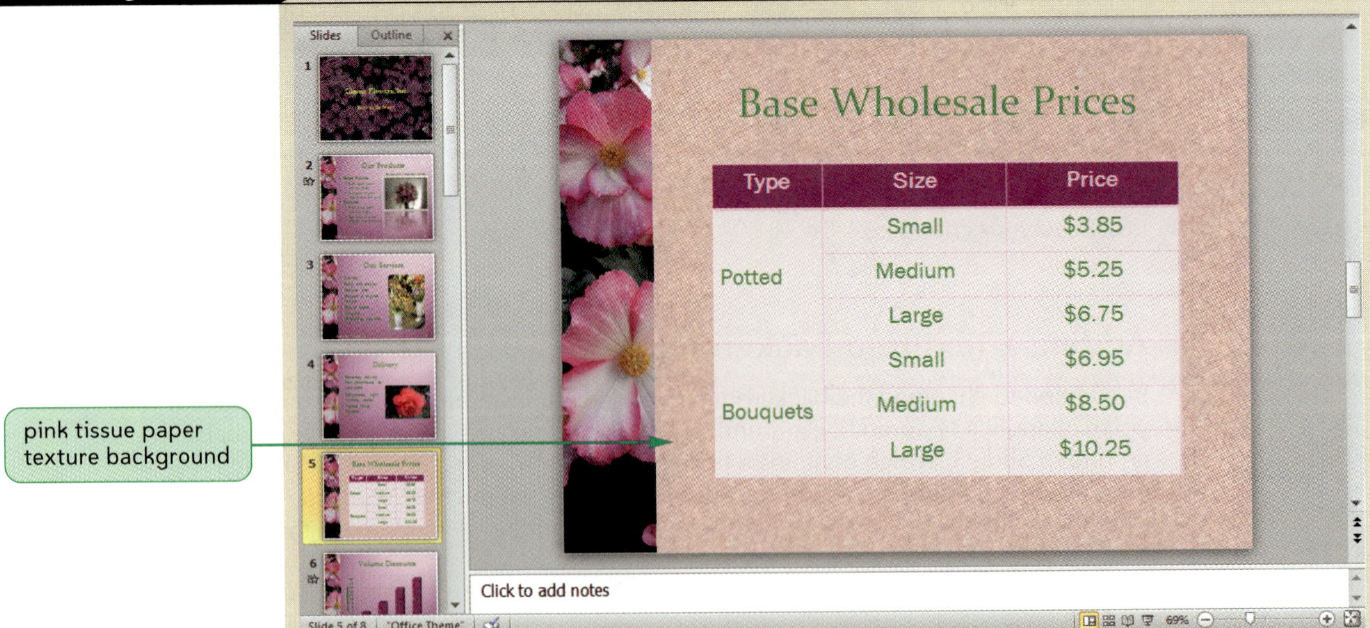


7. Save your changes.

Sophie looks over the presentation, and asks you to change the bullets to a more distinctive style. You'll do this next.

## Modifying Bullet Styles

You can change the style, size, and color of bullets. Like font changes, this change should be made in the slide master so that all the bullets in the presentation look the same.

First, you'll change the first-level bullets to a picture bullet that looks a little like the yellow center of a flower. You want the new bullet style to be applied to all the content text boxes in the presentation, so you'll make this change in Slide Master view.

### To change the first-level bullets to a picture bullet:

1. Switch to Slide Master view.
2. In the pane on the left, scroll up, and then click the **Office Theme Slide Master** thumbnail to display the Slide Master in the slide pane.
3. Click anywhere in the first bulleted item, which says "Click to edit Master text styles."
4. Click the **Home** tab on the Ribbon.
5. In the Paragraph group, click the **Bullets button arrow** to display the Bullets gallery.
6. Click **Bullets and Numbering** at the bottom of the Bullets gallery to display the Bullets and Numbering dialog box with the Bulleted tab on top.
7. Click the **Picture** button. The Picture Bullet dialog box opens.
8. Scroll down until the scroll box is about one-third the way down the scroll bar, so that you see the picture bullet shown in Figure 3-35.

**Figure 3-35** Picture Bullet dialog box

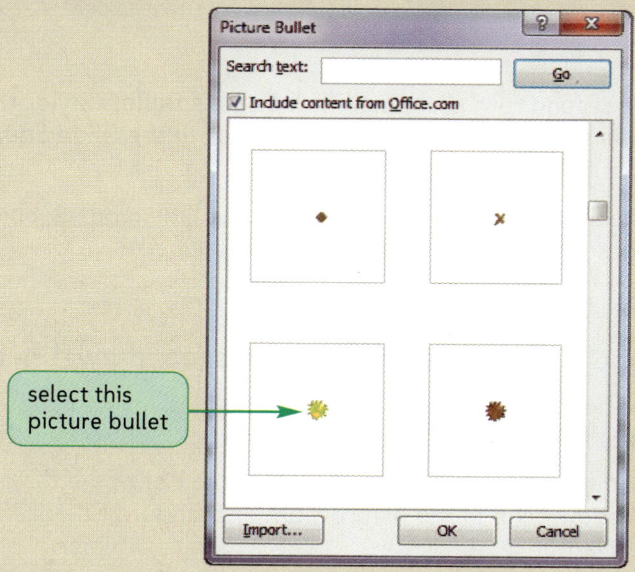


9. Click the bullet indicated in Figure 3-35, and then click the **OK** button. Both dialog boxes close, and the picture bullet you selected becomes the first-level bullet in the content placeholder.

Now you'll change the second-level bullet. For this bullet, Sophie asks you to use one of the standard bullet styles.

### To change the second-level bullets to a standard bullet symbol:

1. Click anywhere in the "Second level" bulleted item.
2. Click the **Bullets button arrow** [button]. The Bullets gallery opens. See Figure 3-36.

**Figure 3-36** **Bullets gallery**

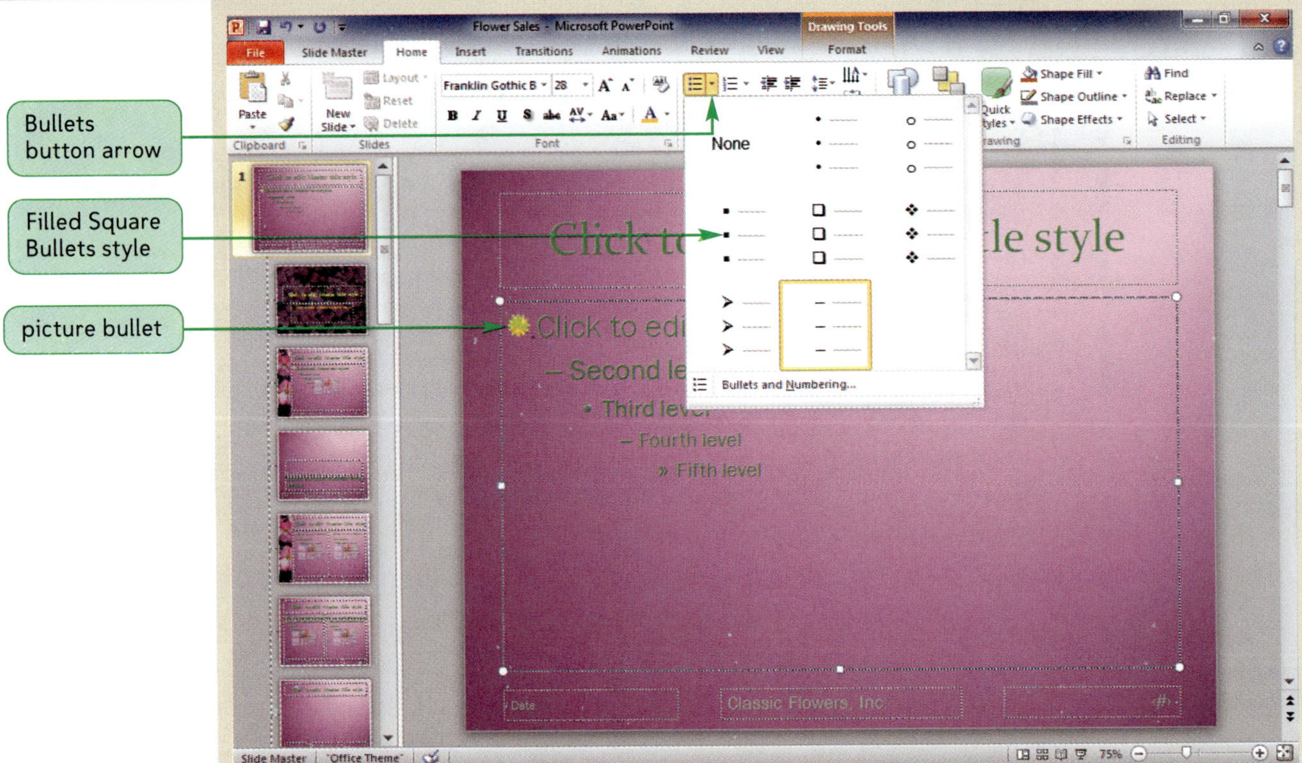


3. In the second row, click the **Filled Square Bullets** style. The Bullets gallery closes, and the second-level item bullet changes to the Filled Square Bullet style.

To make the second-level bullet stand out a little more, Sophie asks you to change the color of these bullets to yellow and increase their size.

### To change the color and size of the second-level bullets:

1. With the insertion point still in the "Second level" bulleted item, click the **Bullets button arrow** [button], and then click **Bullets and Numbering**.
2. Click the **Color** button in the lower-left corner of the dialog box, and then click the **Yellow** color in the first row under Standard Colors. You want the bullet to be a little larger.
3. In the Size box, drag to select **100**, and then type **120**. The bullet will be 120% of the size of the text. See Figure 3-37.

**Figure 3-37** **Bullet tab in the Bullets and Numbering dialog box**

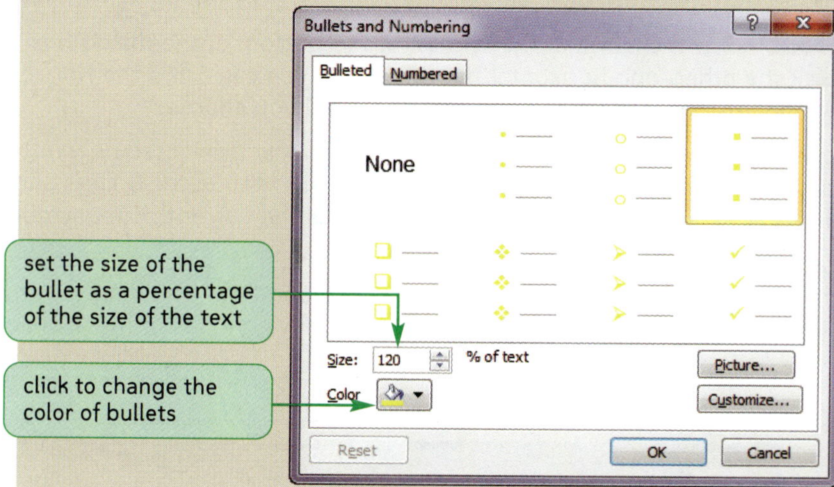


4. Click the **OK** button to close the dialog box.

Now you will change the third-level bullets. For this bullet, you use a bullet symbol in the Symbol dialog box.

## To change the third-level bullets to a nonstandard bullet symbol:

1. Click anywhere in the "Third level" bulleted item, and then open the Bulleted tab in the Bullets and Numbering dialog box. You want to use a bullet symbol, but you want to use a dash, which does not appear in the gallery of standard bullet symbols.
2. Click the **Customize** button. The Symbol dialog box opens. The bullet symbol is selected and is identified at the bottom-left of the dialog box. See Figure 3-38.

**Figure 3-38** **Symbol dialog box**

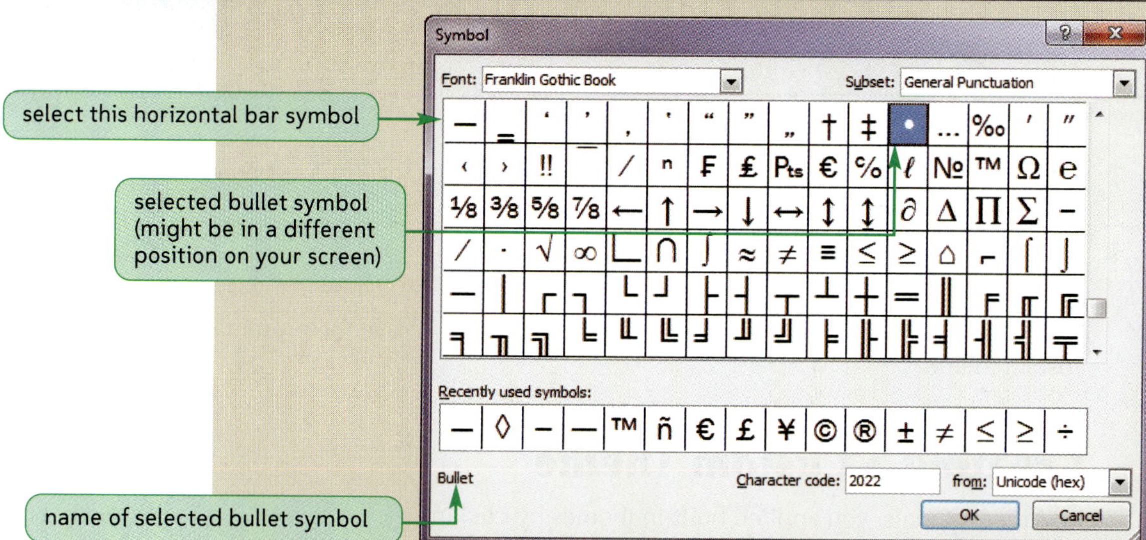

**TIP**

You can scroll through the entire list of symbols, or you can click the Subset arrow to move to a subset of symbols. You can also change the symbols shown by using the Font arrow to change the current font.

3. Scroll up or down a few rows to locate and then click the **Horizontal Bar** symbol. At the bottom of the dialog box, the name of the symbol, Horizontal Bar, appears.

   **Trouble?** If the name of the symbol at the bottom of the dialog box is Em Dash, click the other long horizontal bar symbol. If you can't find the Horizontal Bar symbol, use the Em Dash or any other symbol you choose.

4. Click the **OK** button. The horizontal bar symbol you selected now appears as the last symbol in the Bullets gallery on the Bulleted tab in the Bullets and Numbering box, and it is highlighted to indicate that it is the current bullet symbol.

5. Click the **OK** button. The dialog box closes and the new symbol appears next to the "Third level" item. See Figure 3-39. You don't have any fourth- or fifth-level bulleted items, so you do not need to make any changes to these bullet styles.

**Figure 3-39** Slide Master with modified bullets

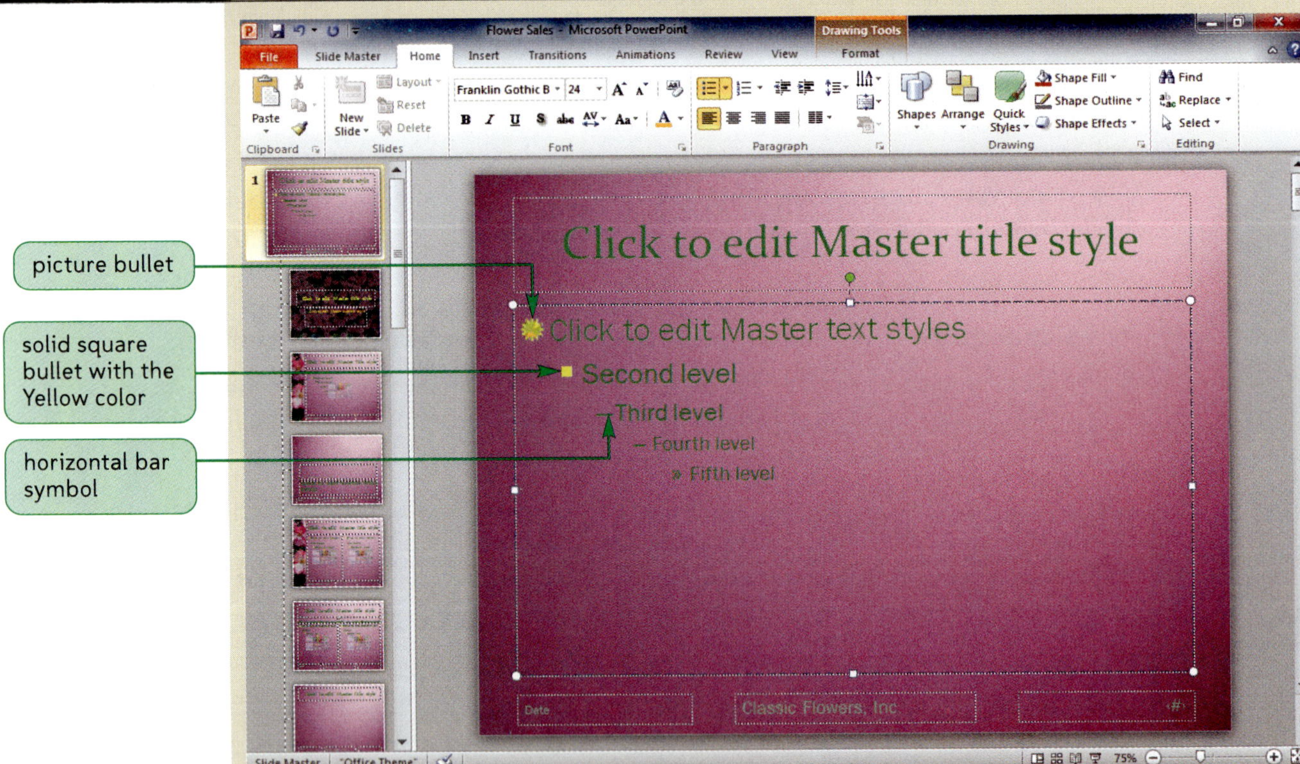


6. Close Slide Master view, and then display **Slide 2** ("Our Products") in the Slide pane. You see the new first- and second-level bullets on Slide 2.

7. Save your changes.

Sophie likes the way the new bullets look. She wants to save the presentation as a custom theme.

## Creating a Custom Theme

In earlier tutorials, you applied built-in themes by clicking the Design tab on the Ribbon to display the Themes group, and then selecting the desired theme. For this presentation, you started with a presentation using the Office theme, and then made changes to customize the theme colors, theme fonts, slide background, and bullet styles—essentially creating a custom theme to suit your needs. You can save this custom theme so that you can apply it to other presentations.

Sophie wants you to save the formatting changes you made to the Flower Sales presentation as a custom theme. When you do so, the custom theme becomes an **Office theme file**, with the filename extension ".thmx". You can use an Office theme file to apply a custom theme to an existing PowerPoint presentation, or you can create a new presentation based on the custom theme.

INSIGHT

### *Understanding the Difference Between a Theme and a Template*

When you save a PowerPoint presentation as a theme, only the design elements (including background graphics) are saved, not the content, that is, not the text or objects applied to the slides. If you want to save a theme with the contents for use in other presentations, you would instead save the presentation as a PowerPoint template.

The default location for saving a custom theme is the Document Themes folder located in the Templates folder, but you can save a theme in any folder. If you save a custom theme in the Document Themes folder, it will appear in the Themes gallery. If you save a theme to a different folder, you can apply it to a presentation by clicking the More button in the Themes group on the Design tab, and then clicking Browse for Themes. You can also use this command to apply a theme from any existing presentation, not just a theme file.

REFERENCE

### *Saving a Custom Theme*

- Click the Design tab on the Ribbon.
- In the Themes group, click the More button, and then click Save Current Theme to open the Save Current Theme dialog box with Office Theme already selected in the Save as type box; or click the File tab, in the navigation bar click Save As to open the Save As dialog box, click the Save as type arrow, and then click Office Theme.
- Navigate to the desired location, type a filename, and then click the Save button.

You've saved your work as a normal PowerPoint presentation. Now you'll save it as a custom theme as Sophie requested, and then test it by creating a new presentation based on this theme.

**To save the presentation as a theme:**

1. Click the **Design** tab on the Ribbon.
2. In the Themes group, click the **More** button, and then below the gallery, click **Save Current Theme**. The Save Current Theme dialog box opens with Office Theme selected as the Save as type, and the current folder in the Address bar changes to Document Themes. See Figure 3-40.

**Figure 3-40** Save Current Theme dialog box

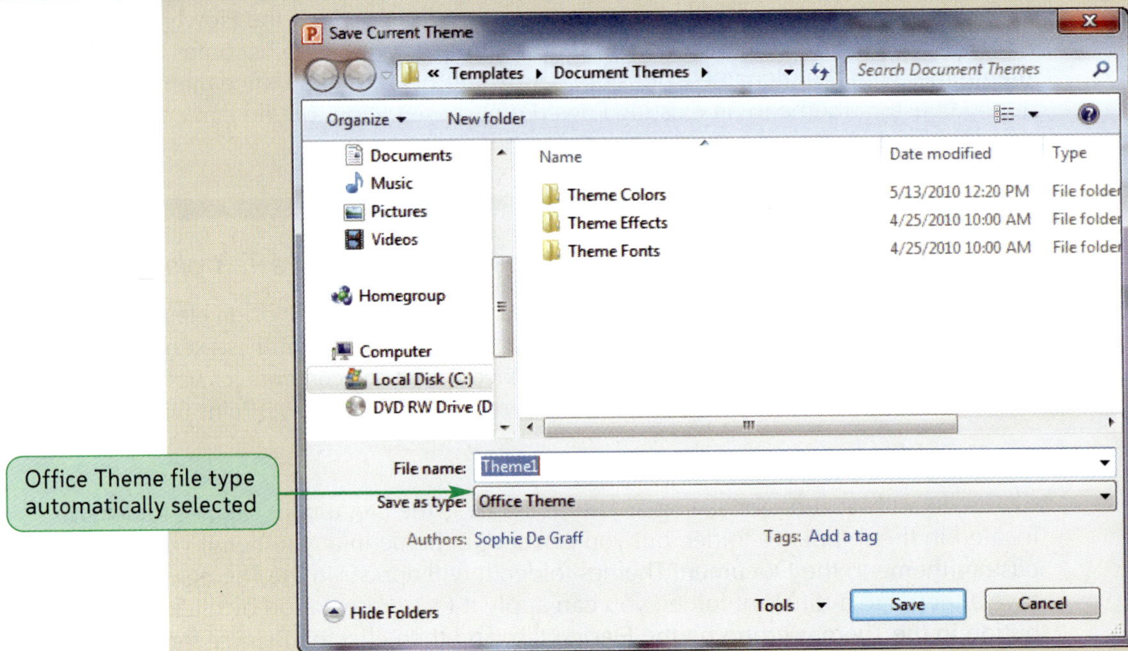


3. Click the **Save as type** arrow. The Save as type list opens. The list shows only one file type because by clicking the Save Current Theme command, you restricted the file type to the Office Theme file type.
4. Edit the text in the File name box to **Flower – Custom**, and then click the **Save** button. Because you didn't change the default folder, the theme will be listed as a Custom theme in the Themes gallery. Now you will save the theme file in the same location where you saved the Flower Sales presentation (in the PowerPoint3\Tutorial folder included with your Data Files). This time, you will use the Save As command to save the theme.
5. Click the **File** tab, and then click **Save As** in the navigation bar. The Save As dialog box opens.
6. Click the **Save as type** arrow. A list of file types opens. See Figure 3-41.

**Figure 3-41** Save as type list in the Save As dialog box

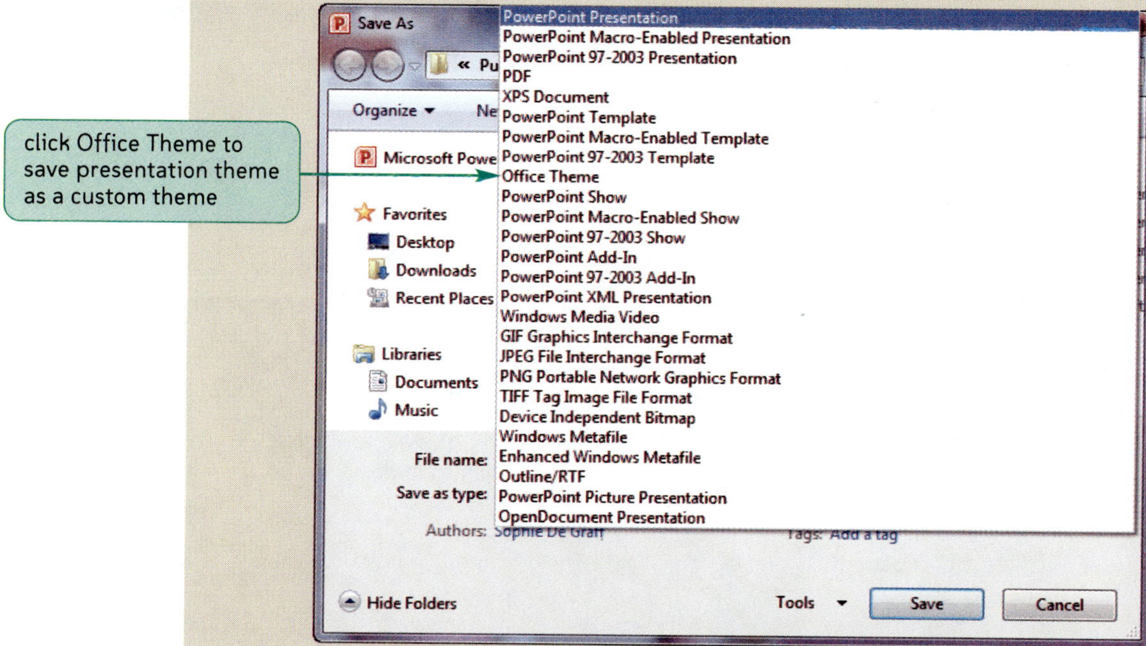


7. In the list, click **Office Theme**. The current folder changes to the Document Themes folder.
8. Navigate to the PowerPoint3\Tutorial folder included with your Data Files, edit the text in the File name box to **Flower**, and then click the **Save** button. PowerPoint saves the file as a theme in the folder you specified.

You have now created a custom theme that Sophie and others can use with any new presentation. You decide to apply the saved theme to the Flower Sales presentation so that the custom theme name appears in the status bar.

**To apply the custom theme in the Themes gallery to the presentation:**

1. Click the **Design** tab on the Ribbon.
2. In the Themes group, click the **More** button. The Themes gallery opens. A new section labeled Custom appears above the Built-In section, and the custom theme you created and saved in the Document Themes folder appears in this section.
3. In the Custom section, point to the theme. The ScreenTip identifies this theme as Flower – Custom. See Figure 3-42.

**Figure 3-42** Custom theme in the Themes gallery

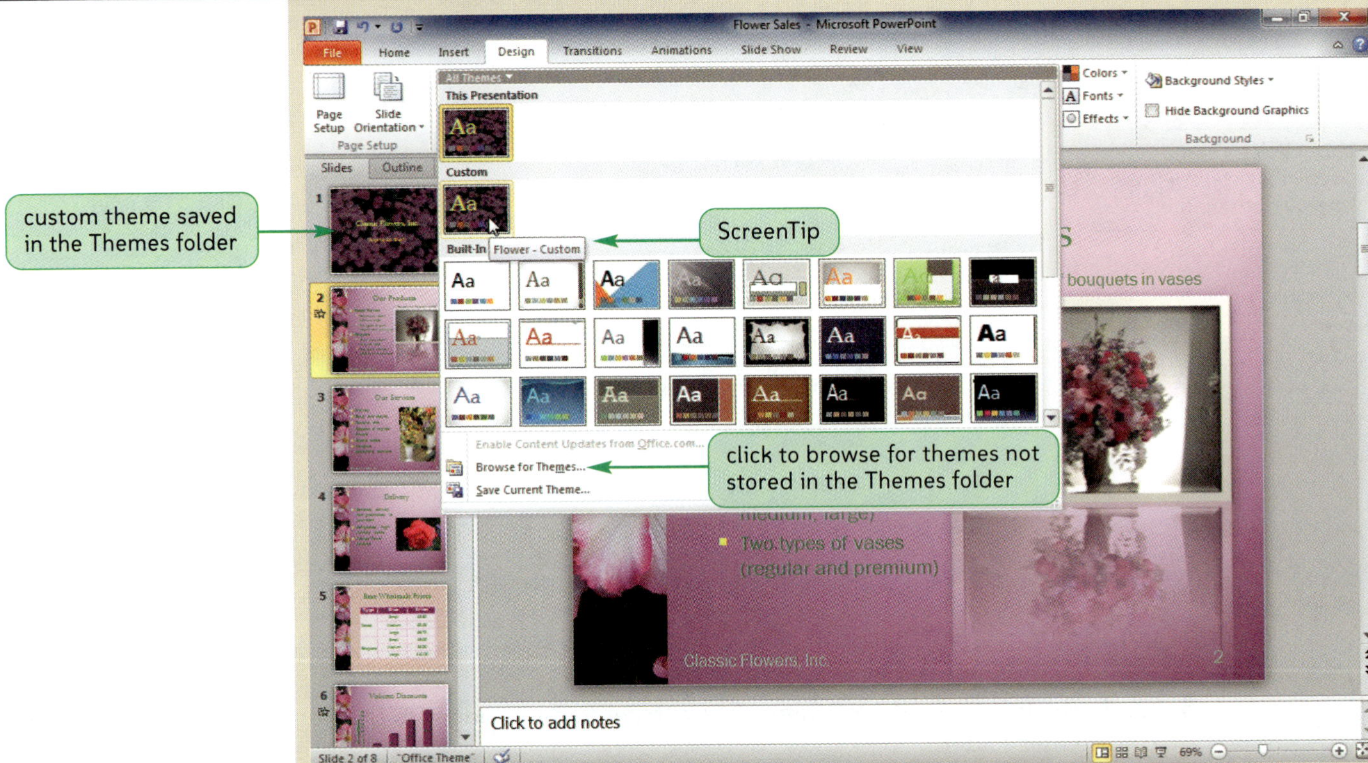


4. Click the **Flower – Custom** theme. The Flower theme is applied to the presentation. The slides don't change much, because you had already applied the changes to the slides, but the theme name in the status bar now is Flower – Custom. See Figure 3-43.

**Figure 3-43** Custom theme applied to the presentation

5. Save your changes.

PROSKILLS

## *Problem Solving: How Should You Create Your Own Theme?*

PowerPoint comes with professional designed themes, theme colors, and theme fonts. The various combinations give you hundreds of professional designs from which to choose. If you decide you need to create a custom theme, you can start "from scratch" and assign every theme color and create your own combination of fonts. But unless you are a graphics designer, consider creating a custom theme as was done in this tutorial—by starting with a theme or theme colors that most closely match the colors you want to use, and then selectively customize some of the colors, fonts, or styles. By creating a theme this way, you can take advantage of the professional designs available in PowerPoint to create your own custom look.

You decide to test your new custom theme on a new presentation. This time, you'll apply the theme you saved to the PowerPoint3\Tutorial folder.

**To create a new presentation using the custom theme:**

1. Click the **File** tab to open Backstage view.
2. Click **New** in the navigation bar, and then with the Blank presentation button selected in the Available Templates and Themes section, click the **Create** button. PowerPoint creates a new presentation with the default Office Theme applied.
3. Click the **Design** tab on the Ribbon.
4. In the Themes group, click the **More** button. You could click the custom theme in the Custom section of the gallery, but instead, you'll apply the theme that you saved to the PowerPoint3\Tutorial folder.
5. Below the Themes gallery, click **Browse for Themes**. The Choose Theme or Themed Document dialog box opens listing presentations, templates, and theme files stored in this folder. You can choose any of the PowerPoint file types to apply the theme used in that presentation.
6. Navigate to the PowerPoint3\Tutorial folder included with your Data Files, and then double-click the Office Theme file **Flower**. The custom theme Flower is applied to the new presentation.
7. Close the presentation without saving it. Keep Flower Sales open in PowerPoint.

When you save a theme to the Document Themes folder, it is available to anyone who works on that computer. You can easily delete a custom theme.

**To delete the custom theme from the Themes gallery:**

1. In the Themes group, click the **More** button. The Themes gallery opens again.
2. Right-click the **Flower – Custom** theme, and then click **Delete** on the shortcut menu. A warning dialog box opens asking if you want to delete this theme.
3. Click the **Yes** button. The dialog box closes.
4. In the Themes group, click the **More** button. The custom theme you saved to the Document Themes folder is no longer listed.
5. Click a blank area of the window to close the gallery without making a selection.

## Applying a Different Theme to Individual Slides

Normally, all your slides in one presentation will have the same theme. On occasion, however, you might want to apply a different theme to only one, or a few, of the slides in your presentation. Sophie wants you to change the theme for Slide 8, "Contact Us," so that this slide stands out from the others because it lists the contact information.

### To apply a different theme to Slide 8:

1. Display **Slide 8** ("Contact Us") in the Slide pane.
2. In the Themes group on the Design tab, click the **More** button.
3. Right-click the **Opulent** theme (the third theme in the fourth row under "Built-In"), and then click **Apply to Selected Slides**. Because Slide 8 is the only selected slide, the Opulent design theme is applied only to that slide. The title text overlaps the panel of flowers on the slide master. You can change the layout to one that doesn't have the flower panel on its master. Remember, the photo panel appears only on the Title and Content and Two Content slides.
4. Click the **Home** tab on the Ribbon.
5. In the Slides group, click the **Layout** button. The Layout gallery appears. Notice that it now contains two sections, one for each theme used in the presentation. See Figure 3-44.

**Figure 3-44** Layout menu when two themes are applied to a presentation

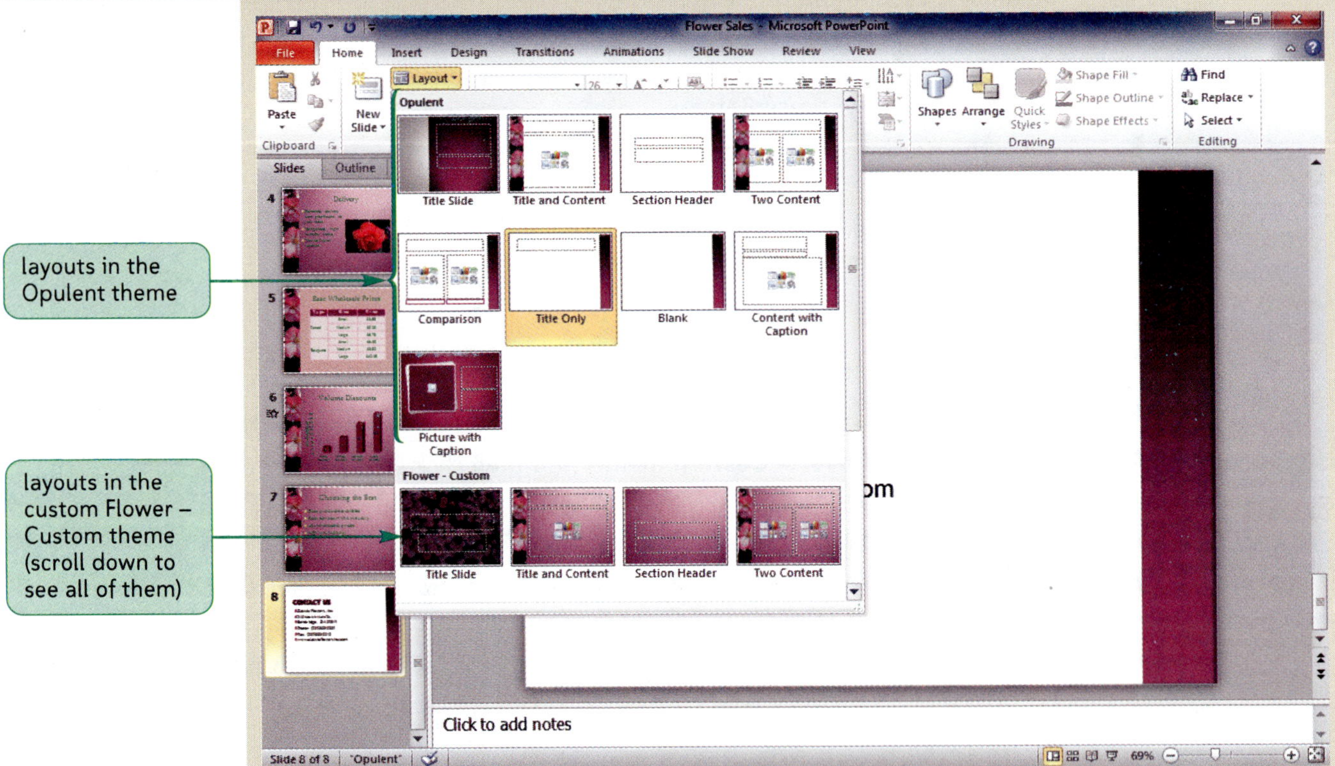


6. In the Opulent section, click the **Title Only** layout. The Opulent Title Only layout is applied to the current slide, and the flower panel photo is removed.
7. Click anywhere on the bulleted list, and then drag the left middle sizing handle to the right approximately one-half inch so that the left edge of the content text box is aligned with the left edge of the slide title.
8. Save your changes.

If you apply a second theme to a presentation, slide masters for that theme are applied to the presentation. You can see the second set of masters if you switch to Slide Master view.

### To examine the slide masters for the second theme:

1. Switch to Slide Master view. In the pane on the left, the Title Only Layout master is selected, and "Opulent" appears in the status bar.
2. In the pane on the left, drag the scroll box about halfway up in the scroll bar, and then click the **Opulent Slide Master** thumbnail. See Figure 3-45. The number 2 next to the Opulent Slide Master indicates that the masters following this slide are associated with the second theme used in the presentation.

**Figure 3-45** Slide Master view when two themes are applied to a presentation

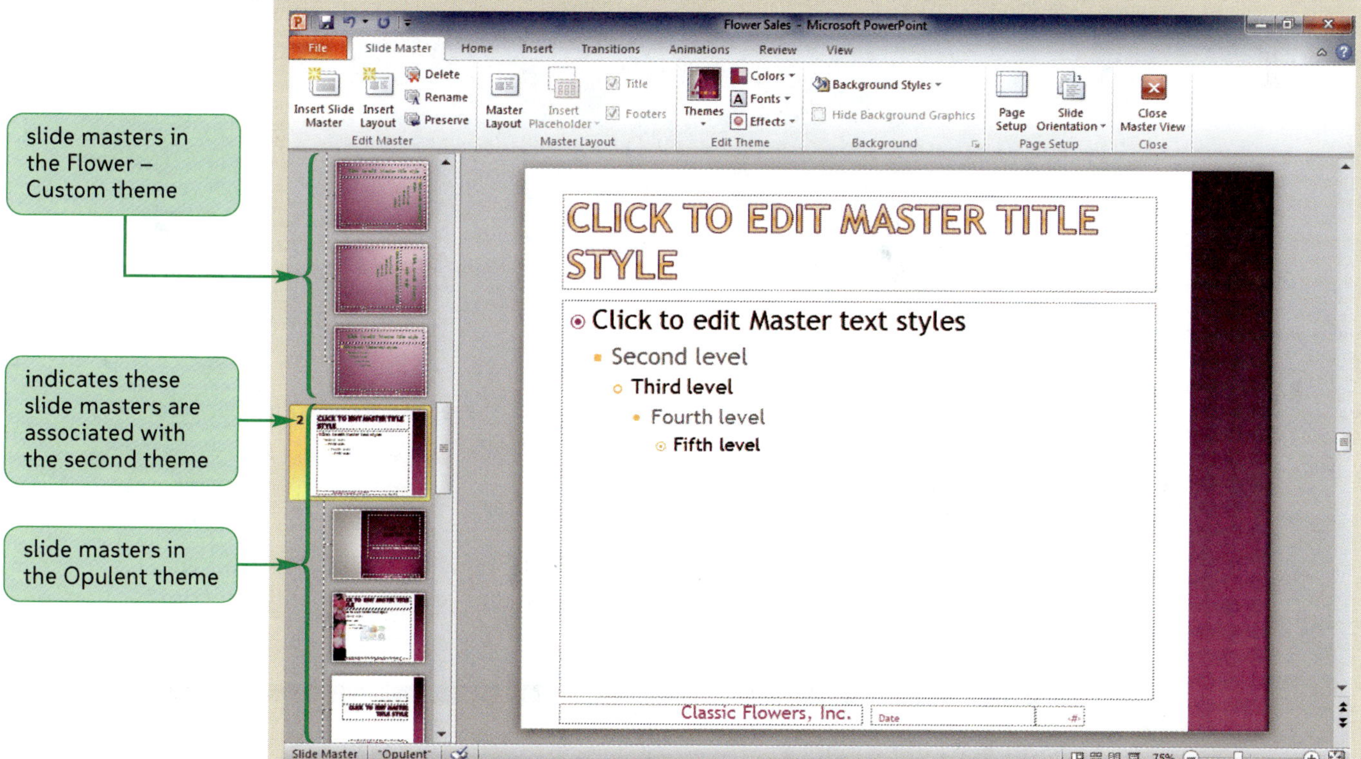


3. Scroll to the top of the left pane, and then click the **Flower – Custom Slide Master** thumbnail. Notice that the number 1 appears next to this Slide Master. When a presentation uses multiple themes, the themes are listed in Slide Master view in alphabetical order.
4. Scroll back down until the **Opulent Slide Master** is the top thumbnail in the left pane, and then click and examine, in turn, the **Title Slide Layout** master, the **Title and Content Layout** master, and the **Two Content Layout** master. Notice that the flower panel was picked up from the Flowers – Custom theme, but the text boxes were not resized. Since none of the slides in the presentation use these layouts, you don't need to fix these masters.
5. Close Slide Master view.
6. Display the presentation in Slide Sorter view at 90% zoom. Compare your screen to Figure 3-46.

**Figure 3-46** **Final presentation in Slide Sorter view**

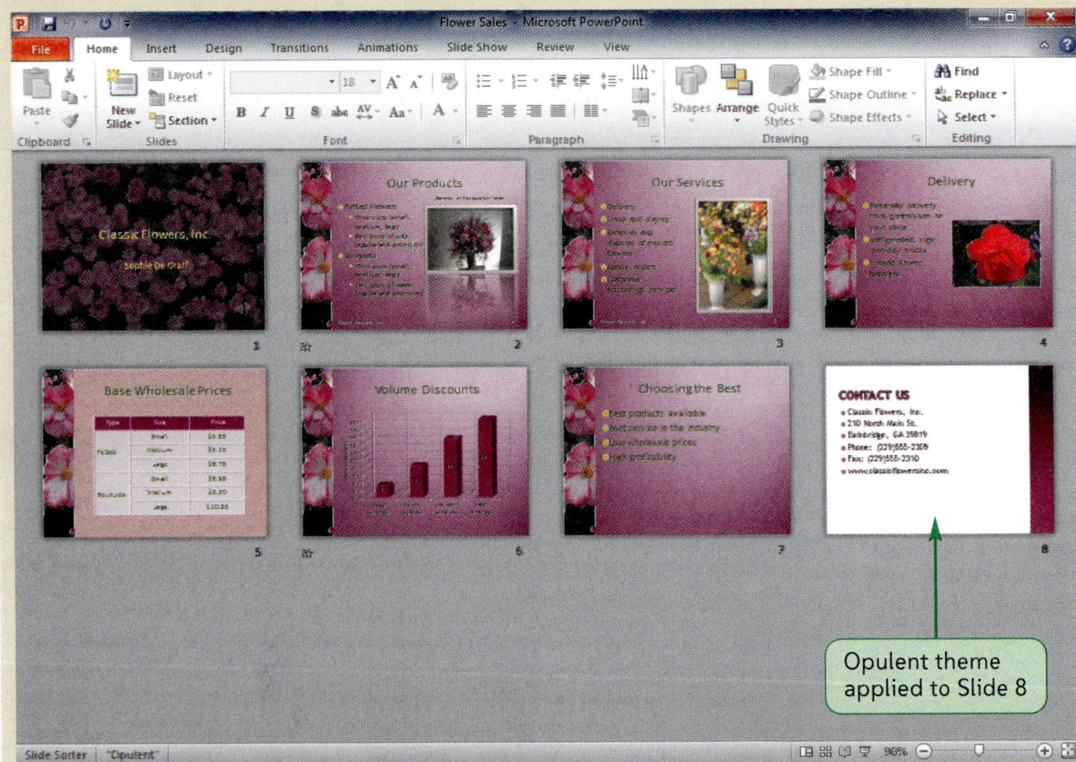


7. Save your changes, and then submit the finished presentation to your instructor, either in printed or electronic form, as requested.
8. Close the presentation.

Sophie looked over your presentation, and she is happy with it. She thinks that the customized theme elements enhance her presentation and will help identify her company for her audience.

REVIEW

## *Session 3.2 Quick Check*

1. How do you change theme fonts?
2. Once you have created a set of theme colors in the Create New Theme Colors dialog box, what should you do so that they are available for applying to other presentations?
3. True or False. You can delete a custom theme color set.
4. How do you apply a textured background to a slide?
5. True or False. You can change a bullet to a picture bullet.
6. Describe how you save a custom theme as an Office Theme file.
7. True or False. You can apply only one theme at a time to a presentation.

*Practice the skills you learned in the tutorial using the same case scenario.*

PRACTICE

## Review Assignments

**Data Files needed for the Review Assignments: Bulbs.avi, Farm.avi, HotSprings.pptx, HSProposal.pptx, Knock.wav, PurpleFlowers.jpg**

The chief horticulturalist for Classic Flowers, Inc., Kathleen Bahlmann, recently became aware that a particular farm in southern Georgia is for sale. The farm is special because it has a natural hot spring on its premises. The farm owner has set up a system to use water from the spring to heat his barns during the winter. Now that the farm is for sale, Kathleen sees this as an opportunity to improve the profitability of Classic Flowers by purchasing the farm, converting the barns to greenhouses, and using the water from the hot spring to heat the greenhouses. This has the potential of saving millions of dollars on heating expenses over the next several years. Kathleen wants to present her idea to the board of directors of Classic Flowers, and she has asked you to help her create the PowerPoint presentation. She has already created a couple of PowerPoint presentation files; one contains a title slide with some elements that she wants to use for a design theme, and the other contains some of the text that she wants in the final presentation. Complete the following steps:

1. Open the file **HSProposal**, located in the PowerPoint3\Review folder included with your Data Files, change the subtitle from "Kathleen Bahlmann" to your name, and then save the file as **Hot Springs Proposal** in the same PowerPoint3\Review folder.
2. Insert Slides 2 through 8 (that is, all but the first slide) from the file **HotSprings**, located in the PowerPoint3\Review folder.
3. In Slide 8 ("Farm for Sale"), add the movie **Farm** located in the PowerPoint3\Review folder. Set it to start Automatically, and loop until stopped, and set the poster frame to the frame at the three-second mark.
4. Apply the Rounded Diagonal Corner, White style to the video, and then apply the Half Reflection, touching reflection effect.
5. In Slide 7 ("Sample Bulbs"), add the movie **Bulbs**, located in the PowerPoint3\Review folder. Trim the video so that it starts at the 3-second mark and ends at the 24-second mark. Mute the volume.
6. In Slide 2 ("Opportunity Knocks"), insert the sound clip **Knock**, located in the PowerPoint3\Review folder. Set it to start automatically, and hide the icon during the slide show.
7. In Slide 3 ("Problem with a Solution"), insert the music file **Maid with the Flaxen Hair** from the Sample Music folder included with Windows 7. (*Hint:* If you are using Windows Vista or XP, insert any music file from the Sample Music folder. Try to find one without vocals.) Set the music to play across slides, set it to loop until it is stopped, change the volume to low, and hide the icon during the slide show.
8. In Slide 8 ("Farm For Sale"), change the Play animation so that it starts with the previous action. (*Hint:* Click the zero animation sequence icon.)
9. In Slide 6 ("Proposed Flats For Sale") insert a table with three columns and seven rows. Insert the following labels and data in the table:

| Type | Size | Price |
|---|---|---|
| Flowers | Small flat | $5.29 |
| | Large flat | $8.49 |
| Vegetables | Small flat | $6.59 |
| | Large flat | $9.69 |
| Herbs | Small flat | $5.99 |
| | Large flat | $8.99 |

10. Apply the Dark Style 1 – Accent 1 table style with a header row and banded rows, and then change the color of the text in all the rows except the header row to Dark Green, Text 1.
11. Modify the table layout by changing the width of each column in the table to approximately two inches wide and merging the cells containing "Flowers," "Vegetables," and "Herbs" with the empty cells below each of them.
12. Resize the table so it is approximately eight inches wide and four-and-a-half inches high, change the font size of the text in the table to 28 points, and then drag the table to center it on the slide.
13. Center the text in the cells in the first row, and then vertically center the text in the cells in the first column in all the rows except the first one.
14. In Slide 5 ("Heating Costs and Profits over Five Years"), insert a chart using the 3-D Clustered Column style.
15. In the Excel spreadsheet for the PowerPoint chart, do the following:
    a. Delete column D.
    b. Change cell B1 to **Heating Costs (in millions)**.
    c. Change cell C1 to **Profits (in millions)**.
    d. Change the labels in cells A2 through A5 to the years **2009** through **2012**, and then add **2013** in cell A6. Click the OK button in the warning dialog box that appears.
    e. In cells B2 through B6 (below Heating Costs), replace the current cell contents with **1.8**, **2.2**, **2.7**, **3.3**, **4.1**.
    f. In cells C2 through C6 (below Profits), replace the current cell contents with **3.2**, **3.1**, **2.9**, **2.7**, **2.5**.
    g. Drag to select cells B2 through C6. On the Home tab in the Excel window, click the Number button, and then click the Accounting Number Format button to format these numbers as currency.
16. Close the Excel window, and then in the chart, show the data labels, and add vertical major gridlines.
17. Animate the chart with the entrance animation Split, and then add the Teeter emphasis animation to the chart.
18. Increase the speed of the Split animation so it takes .25 seconds, and then increase the speed of the Teeter animation so it takes .5 seconds.
19. Change the theme fonts to the Solstice fonts and the Theme colors to the Perspective colors.
20. Modify the theme colors by changing the Text/Background – Light 1 color to the Dark Purple, Accent 4, Darker 25% theme color, and changing the Text/Background – Light 2 color to the White, Text 1 color. Save the new color set using the name **HotSprings**.
21. Change the background style so it has a gradient by applying the background style Style 9.
22. Apply the Stationery textured background to Slide 5 ("Heating Costs and Profits over Five Years").
23. Add the PurpleFlowers picture located in the PowerPoint3\Review folder to the background of the Title Slide Layout master. Adjust the brightness to -40% and the contrast to +40%, and change the color of the subtitle to Yellow.
24. In the Office Theme Slide Master, do the following:
    a. Change the first-level bullet to a picture of a yellow-gold square.
    b. Change the second-level bullet to the Arrow Bullets symbol, and then change the color of the bullet to Brown, Accent 2.
    c. Change the third-level bullet to the Lozenge symbol—a diamond outline located in the last visible row in the Symbol dialog box—and change the size of the bullet to 90% of the size of the text.

25. Save your changes to the presentation, and then save the theme to the PowerPoint3\Review folder using the filename **Flower2**.
26. Apply the custom theme Flower2 to the presentation.
27. Change the theme of Slide 4 ("The Culprit") to the Executive theme.
28. View the slide show in Slide Show view. Remember to click the Bulbs video on Slide 7 to play it. If you see any errors in the presentation, press the Esc key to end the slide show, fix the error, and then start the slide show again from the current slide.
29. Delete the custom color set HotSprings.
30. Submit the presentation in printed or electronic format, as directed by your instructor.

*Apply the skills you learned to create a presentation for an eBay store.*

APPLY

## Case Problem 1

**Data Files needed for this Case Problem: Case.pptx, CompCase.avi, JustInCase.pptx**

***Just in Case*** Jergen Oleson is a small-electronics aficionado. He had the latest in electronic gadgets—MP3 player, cell phone, palm computer, laptop, GPS receiver, digital camera, and so forth. But he was always frustrated in trying to find proper cases for these items. He was surprised, in fact, by the dearth of companies that sold cases for electronic gadgets. So he decided to start his own company, which he called Just in Case, and to sell his products through his own eBay store. He now asks you to help him create a theme for his PowerPoint presentations and to start creating a presentation that he will give to potential manufacturers of his cases. Complete the following steps:

1. Open the presentation file **JustInCase**, located in the PowerPoint3\Case1 folder included with your Data Files. This is a file with the Just in Case logo placed on three of the slide masters and with modifications to the size, location, and text justification of some of the placeholders. You'll continue creating the Office Theme file from here.
2. Change the theme fonts to the Apex fonts, and change the theme colors to the Elemental theme colors.
3. Create a new set of theme colors by changing the Text/Background – Dark 1 color to White, Text 1, and then changing the Text/Background – Light 1 color to a Dark Blue color by using the More Colors command, and selecting the last cell in the top row of the color diagram in the Colors dialog box. Save the theme colors using the name **JustInCase**.
4. Change the background style to Style 5.
5. In the Office Theme Slide Master, do the following:
   a. Change the first-level bullet to a yellow filled-square bullet.
   b. Change the second-level bullet to a filled round bullet colored Teal, Accent 5 and sized 110% of the size of the normal bullet.
   c. Change the third-level bullet to a white, hollow, round bullet.
   d. Change the second-level text color to Yellow.
6. Save the presentation as an Office Theme file to the PowerPoint3\Case1 folder using the filename **Just in Case**. Close the file without saving it.
7. Open a new, blank presentation and apply the Just in Case theme. Delete the JustInCase theme color set.
8. On the title page, insert the title **Case Manufacturing and Order Fulfillment Services**. Insert your name as the subtitle.
9. Save the presentation in the PowerPoint3\Case1 folder using the filename **Case Manufacturing**.
10. Insert into this presentation file all six slides from the file **Case**, located in the PowerPoint3\Case1 folder.

11. In Slide 3, insert the movie **CompCase**, so that it plays when clicked during a slide show, and then apply the video style Reflected Rounded Rectangle. Set the poster frame to the frame at the .5-second mark, and rewind the video when it is finished playing.
12. In Slide 6, insert a chart as follows:
    a. Insert the Line with Markers chart, in the Line section in the Insert Chart dialog box.
    b. Change "Category 1" through "Category 4" to **2010**, **2011**, **2012**, and **2013** to represent the years.
    c. Change "Series 1" to **Sales (in $Thousands)** and "Series 2" to **Profits (in $Thousands)**.
    d. In the Sales column (cells B2 through B5), insert the values **850**, **1000**, **1100**, **1250**.
    e. In the Profits column (cells C2 through C5), insert the values **80**, **180**, **280**, **400**.
    f. Delete column D.
13. Change the Chart Style to Style 28.
14. In Slide 7, add the Denim textured background.
15. In Slide 2, animate the picture to enter the screen using the Fly In entrance effect, then add the Teeter emphasis effect.
16. Change the speed of the Fly In animation to .75 seconds.
17. To all the slides, apply the Push slide transition.
18. Run the slide show, and make any needed corrections. Save your changes.
19. Submit the presentation in printed or electronic format, as directed by your instructor.

*Go beyond the skills you've learned to create a self-running presentation for a photographer.*

CHALLENGE

## Case Problem 2

### Data Files needed for this Case Problem: Wedding01.jpg through Wedding10.jpg

***Ultimate Slideshows*** Sharah-Renae Wabbinton has a home business shooting or scanning photos for special occasions—primarily graduations, weddings, family reunions, and religious events—and preparing self-running, animated slide shows using the Photo Album feature in PowerPoint. She gives you 10 photographs from a recent wedding, and has asked you to prepare not only a PowerPoint presentation using those photos but also a custom Office theme for her business.

Complete the following steps:

1. Start a new, blank presentation (using the Office theme).
2. **EXPLORE** Change the background style to a gradient fill, with the preset colors design called Peacock. Apply this background to all slides. (*Hint*: Use the Preset colors button in the Format Background dialog box.)
3. Change the theme fonts to the Waveform theme font set.
4. **EXPLORE** In the Office Theme Slide Master, change all the text placeholders to white text, and then draw a rectangle that is the same shape and almost the same size as the entire slide, so that a white border appears between the rectangle and the outer edges of the slide approximately one-quarter of an inch from the edge of the slides. (*Hint*: Use the rectangle Shape tool to draw the rectangle so that it completely covers the slide of the Slide Master, and then, while holding down the Alt key, drag the resize handles to slightly reduce the size of the rectangle on all four sides.)
5. **EXPLORE** Set the Shape Fill of the rectangle to No Fill, and set the Shape Outline to a white, 3-point line.
6. **EXPLORE** With the Slide Master still in the slide pane, set the slide transition to any transition in the Exciting section.
7. **EXPLORE** Set up the slide show to advance automatically from one slide to the next, with about 5 seconds for each slide. (*Hint*: With the Slide Master still in the slide pane, on

the Transitions tab in the Timing group, deselect the On Mouse Click check box, and then select the After check box. Change the After time from 00:00.00 to 00:05.00)

8. In Normal view, save the presentation as an Office theme named **Wedding** in the PowerPoint3\Case2 folder included with the Data Files. Save the presentation again as an Office theme named **Wedding** in the default Document Themes folder.
9. Close the current presentation without saving it, and then create a new, blank presentation.
10. **EXPLORE** In the Images group on the Insert tab, use the Photo Album button to insert all 10 photographs, **Wedding01** through **Wedding10**, located in the PowerPoint3\Case2 folder. Do not close the Photo Album dialog box. (*Hint*: In the Photo Album dialog box, click the File/Disk button, navigate to the folder containing the pictures, select all the pictures, and then click the Insert button.)
11. **EXPLORE** With the Photo Album dialog box still open, in the Album Layout section, set the Picture layout to 1 picture (meaning, 1 picture per slide). Set the Frame shape to Simple Frame, White. Apply the Wedding theme you created and saved in the PowerPoint3\Case2 folder. Click the Create button at the bottom of the Photo Album dialog box to create the photo album. (*Hint*: If you already closed the Photo Album dialog box, click the Photo Album button arrow, and then click Edit Photo Album.)
12. In Slide 1, change the title to **Curtis and Cassandra**. The name in the subtitle is the name of the registered user on your computer. If your name does not appear as the subtitle, change the name in the subtitle to your own.
13. In Slides 2 through 11, apply a different Entrance animation effect to each photograph. Change the Start setting for each animation to With Previous, and change the duration to two seconds.
14. **EXPLORE** Set up the presentation to loop automatically so that it starts over when it reaches the end. (*Hint*: On the Slide Show tab, in the Set Up group, click the Set Up Slide Show button, and then click the Loop continuously until 'Esc' check box.)
15. Start the slide show and make sure that it runs on its own and continues to run until you press the Esc key.
16. Save the presentation as **Wedding Slideshow** in the PowerPoint3\Case2 folder.
17. Delete the Wedding custom theme from the Themes gallery.
18. Submit the presentation in printed or electronic format, as directed by your instructor.

*Use the skills you learned to create a custom theme and presentation for a cartography company.*

CREATE

## Case Problem 3

**Data Files needed for this Case Problem: MntHike.avi, MntMap.jpg, MntPlateau1.jpg, MntPlateau2.jpg**

***Cartography Research Systems*** Barrett Worthington is founder and president of Cartography Research Systems (CRS), a company that maps geological formations and nearby areas. Sample geological areas include glaciers, caves, canyons, river beds, and wilderness sites. CRS clients mostly are energy and mineral exploration companies, but they also include the National Parks Service and land developers. Barrett has asked you to create and save a design theme that his company can use for their presentations to clients. He then asks you to help him prepare a portion of a presentation to one of his clients, Eckstein Energy.

Complete the following steps:

1. Create a new presentation, change the theme colors to Flow, and then modify them as shown in Figure 3-47. Your colors don't have to be exactly the same as those shown in the figure. Just try to select each theme color as close as you can. Save the theme colors as **CRScolors**.

**Figure 3-47** **Selections for custom theme colors**

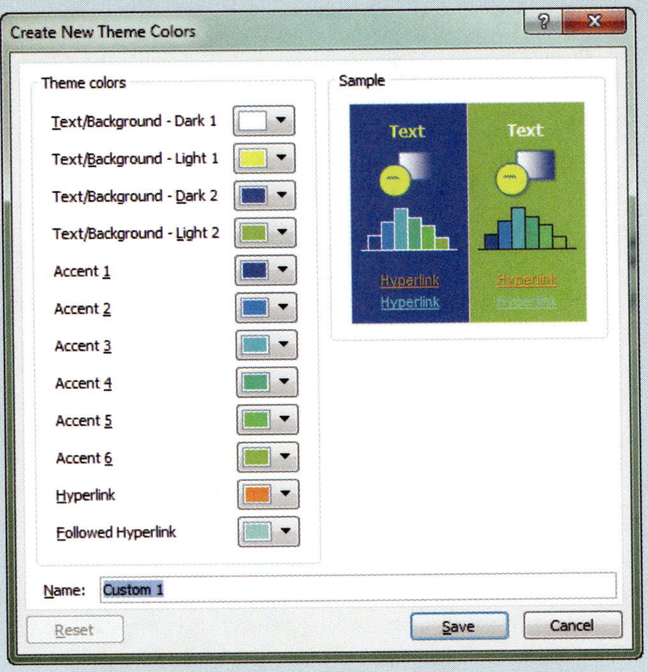


2. Use the slide masters to apply the background style, font attributes, and bullets shown in Figure 3-48. If you're not sure of a particular color, just pick any theme color that is close.

**Figure 3-48** **Selections for background style, font attributes, and bullets**

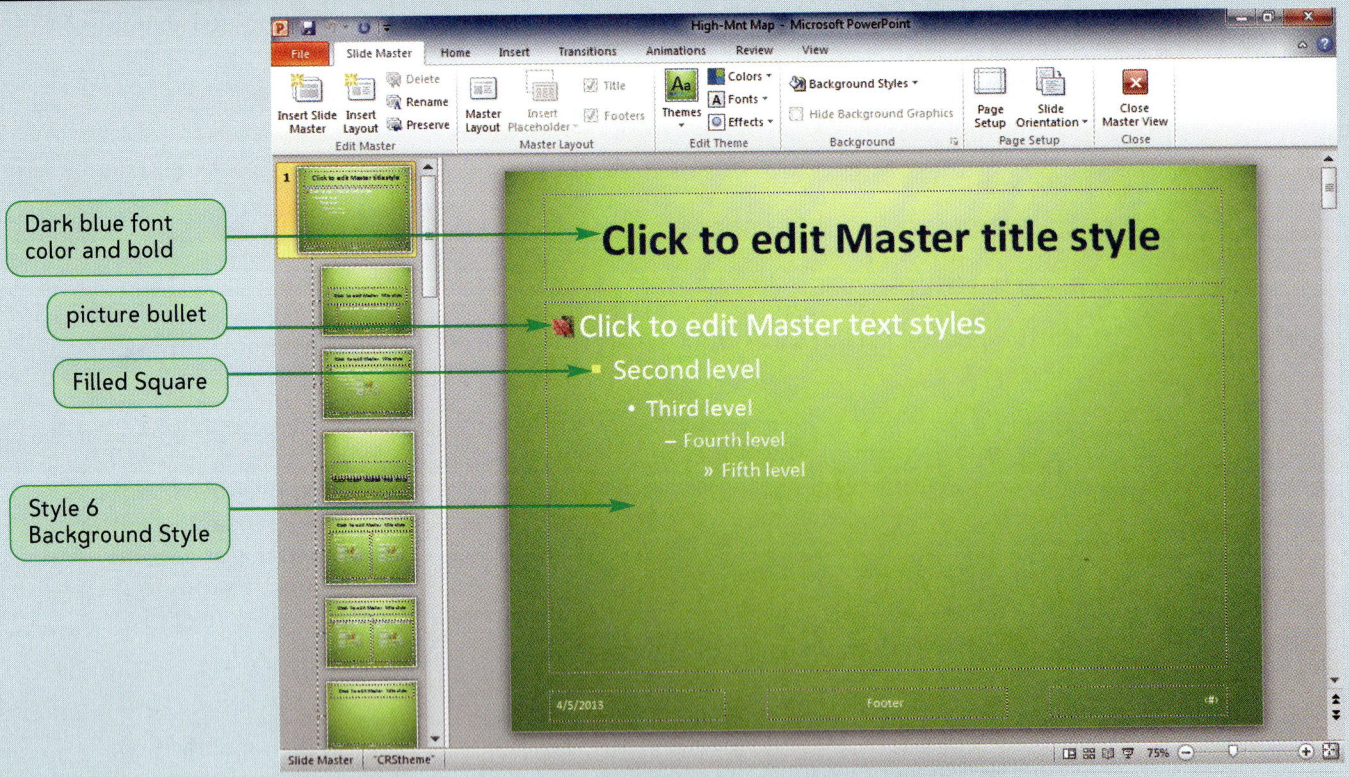

3. Save the file as an Office Theme file in the PowerPoint3\Case3 folder using the filename **CRStheme**, and then close the presentation without saving changes.
4. Start a new PowerPoint presentation, and then apply the CRStheme you created. Save the presentation in the PowerPoint3\Case3 folder using the filename **High-Mnt Map**. Delete the CRScolors theme color set.
5. Add content to the new presentation, as shown in Figure 3-49. Refer to the following as you add the content:
   a. In Slide 1, add the title shown, but use your own name for the subtitle.
   b. In Slide 2, insert the photos **MntPlateau1** and **MntPlateau2**, and then apply the picture style called Snip Diagonal Corner, White.
   c. In Slide 3, add the video **MntHike**. Set the poster frame to the frame at the 13-second mark. Trim the video so that it ends just before it fades to black, at approximately the 18-second mark. Set the video to play automatically, and to play full screen.

EXPLORE

   d. Crop off the black borders on the video. To do this, select the video, and then in the Size group on the Video Tools Format tab, click the Crop button. Drag the middle crop handles on the top, bottom, and sides of the video to remove the black borders.
   e. In Slide 4, insert the picture **MntMap**, and then apply the picture style called Metal Frame.
   f. In Slide 4, insert, rotate, and then color the text boxes that label the reservoir, springs, creeks, and trails, as shown.
   g. In Slide 5, create an elevation chart using the Line type chart format called Line with Markers. In the Excel window, first, delete columns C and D, then drag the lower right corner of the blue border down so the blue border surrounds cells A1 through B16. Enter the following data in this table:

| | **Altitude feet** | | **Altitude feet** |
|---|---|---|---|
| 0 | 6800 | 8 | 8200 |
| 1 | 7400 | 9 | 8800 |
| 2 | 8200 | 10 | 8400 |
| 3 | 9500 | 11 | 9400 |
| 4 | 8800 | 12 | 7600 |
| 5 | 8000 | 13 | 7200 |
| 6 | 7400 | 14 | 6800 |
| 7 | 7700 | | |

   h. Remove the legend, and then add axis titles to the horizontal and vertical axes, as shown on Slide 5 in Figure 3-49. Along the primary horizontal (x) axis, the text is **Miles from Trailhead**, and along the primary vertical (y) axis, the text is **Elevation above Sea Level (feet)**.
   i. In Slide 6, after you enter the information, apply the textured background called Medium Wood.

**Figure 3-49** CRS presentation content

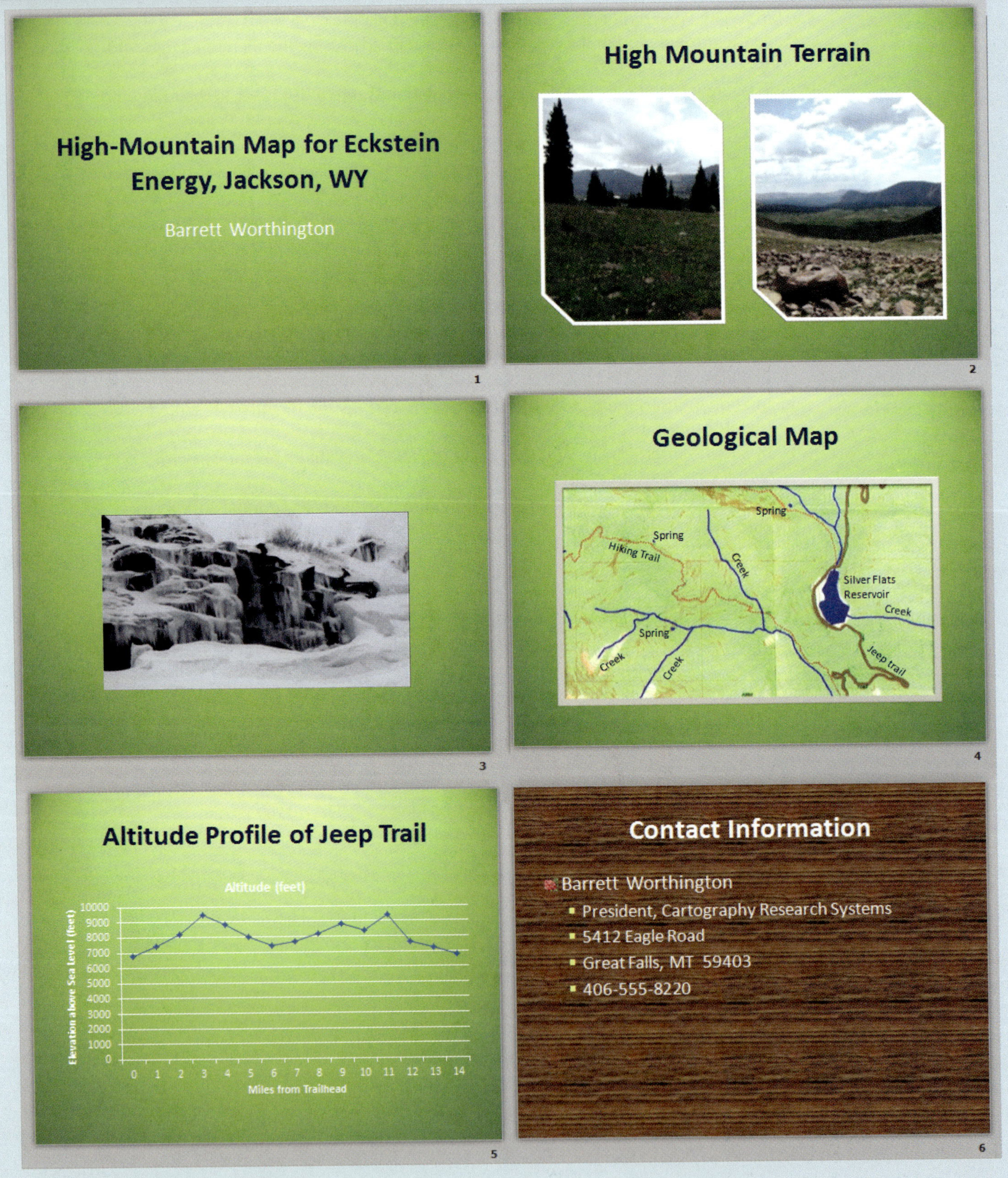

6. Animate all the text boxes on Slide 4 using the Appear entrance effect.
7. On Slide 2 ("High Mountain Terrain"), apply an entrance animation to each photograph.

**EXPLORE**

8. On Slide 2 ("High Mountain Terrain"), add audio clip art of a camera shutter sound. (*Hint:* In the Media group on the Insert tab, click the Audio button arrow, and then click Clip Art Audio. To find a camera sound, you need to be connected to the Internet, and the Include Office.com content check box must be selected. If you are not connected to the Internet, use another sound.)

**EXPLORE**

9. Change the Start setting for the Play animation of the camera sound to With Previous, and then change the order of the selected animation so it has the same animation sequence number as the first photograph. (*Hint:* With the animation selected, click the Move Earlier button in the Timing group on the Animations tab as many times as needed.)
10. Select the sound icon, and then add a second Play animation. Change its start to With Previous.
11. Run the slide show, and correct any errors.
12. Save your changes, and then submit the presentation in electronic or printed form, as requested.

*Use the skills you learned to create a presentation about a collection for a volunteer group.*

**CREATE**

## Case Problem 4

**There are no Data Files needed for this Case Problem.**

***Cabot Collectibles*** Cabot Collectibles is a group of volunteer collectors who create PowerPoint presentations about personal collections. They make these presentations available to anyone who wants to present information on collectibles to schools, churches, civic organizations, clubs, and so forth. They rely on collectors to prepare the PowerPoint presentations. Complete the following steps

1. Select a type of collectible—stamps, coins, foreign currency, baseball cards, jewelry, comic books, artwork, rocks, dolls, figurines, chess sets, or almost anything else.
2. Plan your presentation so the audience learns basic information about your chosen collectible and sees pictures, with descriptions, of sample items from the collection.
3. Acquire pictures or a video of sample items. You can take the pictures yourself with a digital camera, take the pictures with a film camera and scan the photographs, scan flat items directly (stamps, bills, cards, book covers, and so forth), or get pictures from the Web.
4. Gather information about the items depicted in your graphics. You might want to include some of the following—name of item, age of item, origin (purchase location or place of manufacture), date of purchase, dimensions, and special characteristics (handmade, natural dyes, first edition, and so forth).
5. Create a custom theme appropriate for your presentation. In selecting theme fonts and theme colors, take into account the nature of the collection and the common colors found in the graphics that you're going to include. Your theme should include the following:
   a. Custom theme colors
   b. At least one graphic—logo, picture, ready-made shape (rectangle, circle, triangle, and so forth), or textured background
   c. A custom set of bullets, including a picture bullet for the first-level bulleted items
   d. Progressive disclosure, with dimming, of the bulleted lists
6. Create a new presentation based on your custom theme.

7. Include a title slide, at least two slides with bulleted lists, and at least six slides with pictures of collectibles.
8. Apply slide transitions to your slide presentation.
9. Animate at least one graphic with two animations.

**EXPLORE**

10. If you have access to a microphone on your computer, create at least one sound clip and insert it in your presentation. Keep the recording shorter than three seconds. For example, record your voice saying a hard-to-pronounce noun or a foreign word associated with a collectible item, or record a sound effect, like a knock on the door, a bell, or a whistle. (*Hint*: Use the Sound Recorder installed with Windows. Click the Start button, point to All Programs, click Accessories, and then click Sound Recorder. With your microphone ready, click the Start Recording button. When you're finished recording, click the Stop Recording button.)
11. Save the presentation in the PowerPoint3\Case4 folder using the filename **Collection**.
12. Save the theme in the PowerPoint3\Case4 folder using the filename **Collectible**.
13. Run the slide show and correct any errors. Save your changes.
14. Submit your presentation in electronic or printed form, as requested by your instructor.

ASSESS

## SAM: Skills Assessment Manager

For current SAM information, including versions and content details, visit SAM Central (http://samcentral.course.com). If you have a SAM user profile, you may have access to hands-on instruction, practice, and assessment of the skills covered in this tutorial. Since various versions of SAM are supported throughout the life of this text, check with your instructor for the correct instructions and URL/Web site for accessing assignments.

## ENDING DATA FILES

**PowerPoint3** →

**Tutorial**

Flower Sales.pptx
Flower.thmx

**Review**

Flower2.thmx
Hot Springs Proposal.pptx

**Case1**

Just in Case.thmx
Case Manufacturing.pptx

**Case2**

Wedding Slideshow.pptx
Wedding.thmx

**Case3**

CRStheme.thmx
High-Mnt Map.pptx

**Case4**

Collectible.thmx
Collection.pptx

TUTORIAL 4

# Integrating PowerPoint and Collaborating with Others

*Presenting Clinical Trial Results*

POWERPOINT

## OBJECTIVES

**Session 4.1**
- Import, modify, and export a Word outline
- Import graphics
- Copy an object from another presentation
- Remove the background from photographs
- Embed and modify a table from Word
- Link and modify an Excel chart
- Create and edit hyperlinks
- Add action buttons

**Session 4.2**
- Apply a dynamic content transition
- Customize handout masters
- Mark slides during a slide show
- Work with comments and compare presentations
- Inspect documents for private or hidden data
- Identify features not supported by previous versions of PowerPoint
- Mark a presentation as final
- Save a presentation in other formats

## Case | *Landon Pharmaceuticals Testing*

Alyssa Byington is director of customer service at Landon Pharmaceuticals Testing (LPT), a company that performs clinical trial testing of medicinal drugs developed by other pharmaceutical companies. Alyssa asks you to help create a PowerPoint presentation on the results of a clinical trial for a client, Pamerleau Biotechnologies. Pamerleau has developed a drug, with the code name Asperitol and code number PB0182, for the treatment of autoimmune diseases such as rheumatoid arthritis and lupus.

In this tutorial, you'll add data from Word and Excel files and hyperlinks to a presentation. You'll also apply dynamic content transitions, customize handout masters, and mark slides during a slide show. Finally, you'll learn how to add and review comments, compare presentations, and save a presentation in other formats.

## STARTING DATA FILES

PowerPoint4 →

**Tutorial**
Chart.xlsx
Clinical.pptx
ClinOutline.docx
Demogr.docx
DJ Review.pptx
Landon.pptx

**Review**
Company.pptx
Hospitals.docx
Landon2.pptx
LPTChart.xlsx
LPTInfo.docx
LT Review.pptx

**Case1**
Branches.docx
DH Review.pptx
FLCU.pptx
FLCUchart.xlsx
FLCUOutline.docx
FLCUPhotos.pptx

**Case2**
Bird.jpg
Flower.jpg
WMCchart.xlsx
WMCDesign.pptx
WMCOutline.docx

**Case3**
72HrKit.jpg
EPR.pptx
EPRChart.xlsx
EPROutline.docx
Flood.jpg
Phone Table.docx
Wheat.jpg

**Case4**
Wetland1.jpg
Wetland2.jpg
Wetland3.jpg
Wetland4.jpg
Wetland5.jpg

# SESSION 4.1 VISUAL OVERVIEW

## source file (Word outline)

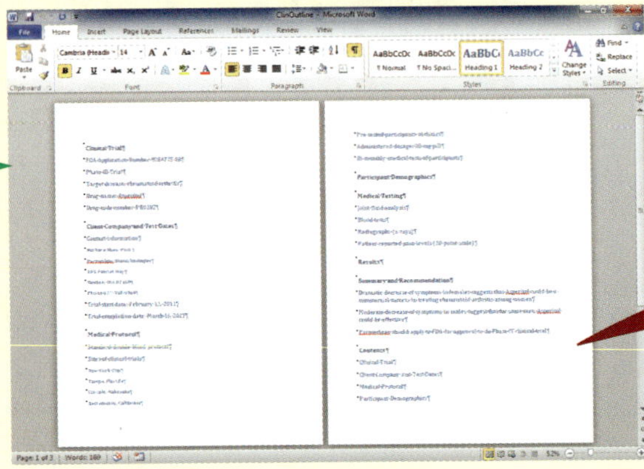

The program used to create the object is called the **source program**; the file that initially contains the object is called the **source file**.

When you **import** an object, a copy of an object created in the source program becomes part of the destination file; you can edit the object with the tools available in the destination program.

## source file (Word table)

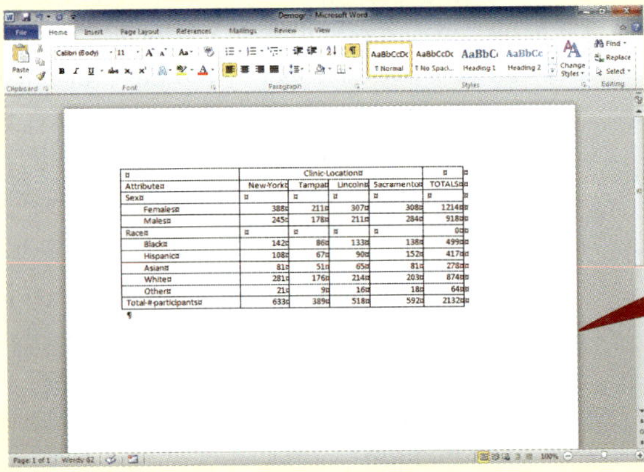

| | Clinic Location | | | | |
|---|---|---|---|---|---|
| Attribute | New York | Tampa | Lincoln | Sacramento | TOTALS |
| Sex | | | | | |
| Females | 388 | 211 | 307 | 308 | 1214 |
| Males | 245 | 178 | 211 | 284 | 918 |
| Race | | | | | 0 |
| Black | 142 | 86 | 133 | 138 | 499 |
| Hispanic | 108 | 67 | 90 | 152 | 417 |
| Asian | 81 | 51 | 65 | 81 | 278 |
| White | 281 | 176 | 214 | 203 | 874 |
| Other | 21 | 9 | 16 | 18 | 64 |
| Total # participants | 633 | 389 | 518 | 592 | 2132 |

When you **embed** an object, a copy of the object along with a one-way connection to the source program become part of the destination file, and you can edit the object using the source program's commands. Changes made do not appear on the source file.

## source program

You must have access to the source program to edit an embedded object; however, you do not need access to the source file.

## source file (Excel chart)

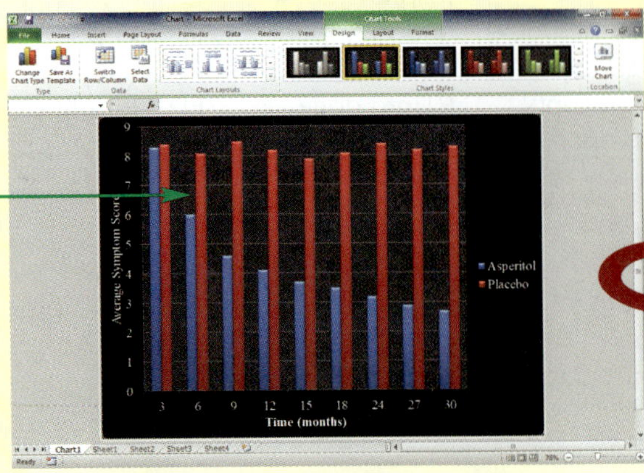


When linking an object, you must have access to the source file if you want to make changes to the source object.

# SHARING DATA

## destination file (Powerpoint presentation)

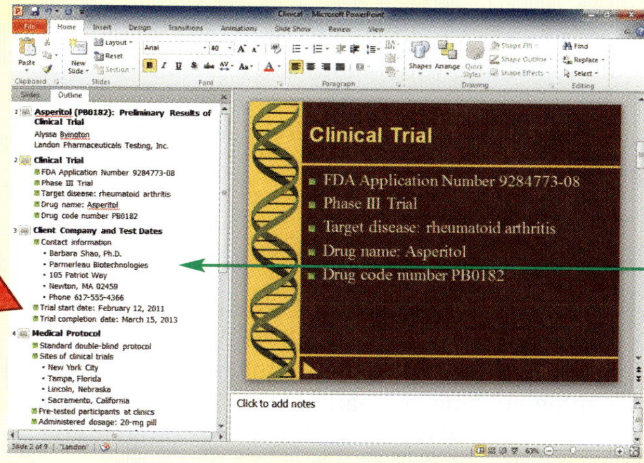


The program used to create the file where you want to insert the object is called the **destination program**; the file where you want to insert the object is called the **destination file**.

## destination file (Powerpoint presentation)

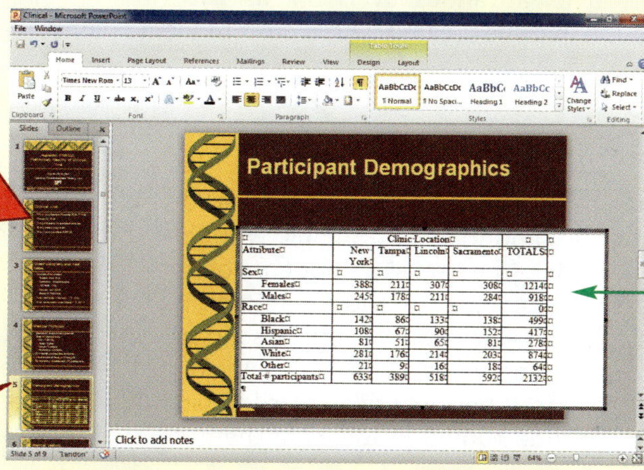


There is no connection between an embedded object and its source file; therefore, changes made to the object in the source file do not appear in the destination file.

When you **link** an object, a direct connection is created between the source and destination programs, so that the object exists in only one place—the source file—but the link displays the object in the destination file as well.

## destination file (Powerpoint presentation)

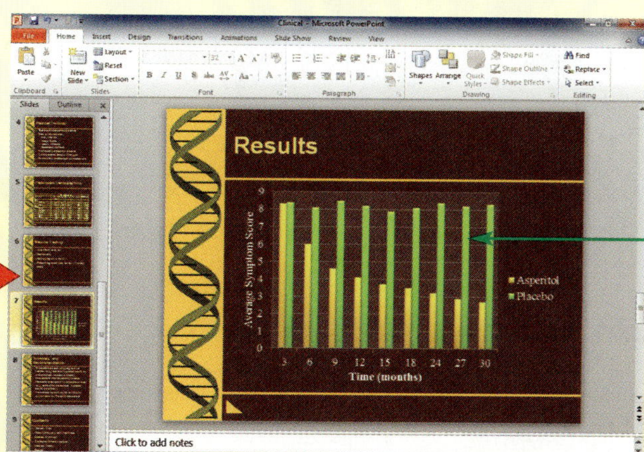


If you edit a linked object in the source file, the link ensures that the changes appear in the destination file.

# Importing and Exporting a Word Outline

If your presentation contains quite a bit of text, it might be easier to create the outline of your presentation in Word, so that you can take advantage of the extensive text-editing features available in that program. Fortunately, if you create an outline in a Word document, you don't need to retype it in PowerPoint. You can import it directly into your presentation.

You can also use Word to create handouts. Although you can create handouts in PowerPoint, sometimes you might want to take advantage of Word's formatting commands to make the text easier to read. You might also want to use the presentation outline as the basis for a more detailed document. To do this, you can export the outline to a Word document.

## Importing a Word Outline

As you know, when you work in the Outline tab in PowerPoint, each level-one heading (also called Heading 1 or A head) automatically becomes a slide title; each level-two heading (a Heading 2 or B head) automatically becomes a level-one bulleted paragraph; each level-three heading (a Heading 3 or C head) automatically becomes a level-two bulleted paragraph, and so forth. Similarly, Word lets you assign heading levels to text. To create text at the first level, you apply the built-in Heading 1 style; to create text at the second level, you apply the built-in Heading 2 style, and so forth.

Alyssa created a Word document in which she applied heading styles to create an outline with text at various levels. She asks you to import her outline into a PowerPoint presentation that she created with a custom theme named Landon.

### To import the Word outline:

1. Open the file **Clinical** from the PowerPoint4\Tutorial folder included with your Data Files, and then save the file with the new filename **Clinical Report** to the same folder. The title slide appears on the screen with the name of the presenter, Alyssa Byington, in the subtitle text box. See Figure 4-1. Alyssa's custom theme includes the color scheme with a solid brown background, yellow title text, white body text, and a background graphic of a DNA double helix. Notice that the presentation includes only this one slide, and a footer identifying the company name and the slide number appears at the bottom of the slide.

**Figure 4-1** Title slide of Clinical Report presentation

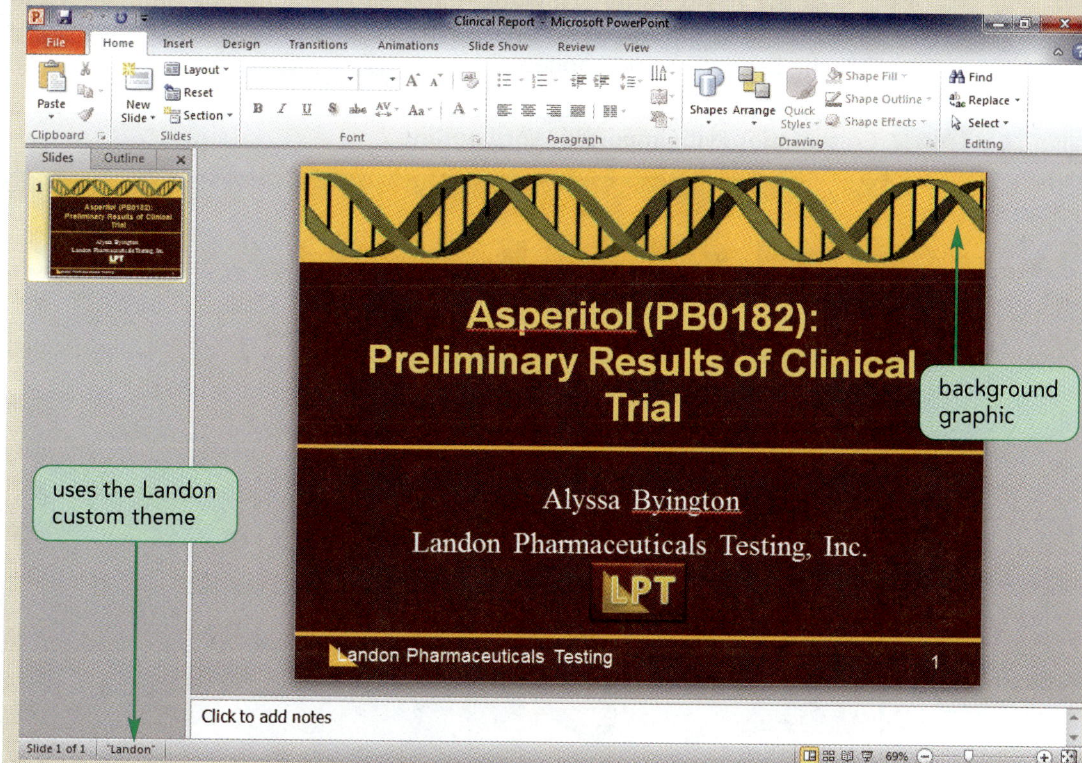


2. In the Slides group on the Home tab, click the **New Slide button arrow**, and then click **Slides from Outline**. The Insert Outline dialog box opens.
3. Navigate to the PowerPoint4\Tutorial folder included with your Data Files, click **ClinOutline**, and then click the **Insert** button. The Word outline is inserted as new slides after the current slide in the PowerPoint presentation, with all the level-one text becoming new slide titles. Slide 2 appears in the Slide pane and is currently selected in the Slides tab. Notice that PowerPoint applies the fonts and text colors of the outline document rather than of the presentation theme. A new layout, Title and Text, was created and applied to all of the slides that were inserted. You need to apply the Title and Content layout and then reset the slides.
4. Press and hold the **Shift** key, scroll down the Slides tab, and then click **Slide 9** (the last slide) to select Slides 2 through 9.
5. In the Slides group, click the **Layout** button, and then click **Title and Content**. The Title and Content layout is applied to the selected slides. Now you need to reset the slides to the default settings from the Slide Master.
6. In the Slides group, click the **Reset** button. The font style and color are reset to the presentation theme. The slide number and footer that appeared on Slide 1, however, do not appear on all the slides.
7. Click the **Insert** tab on the Ribbon.
8. In the Text group, click the **Header & Footer** button to display the Header and Footer dialog box. The footer that appears on Slide 1 is in the Footer box, but the Slide number and Footer check boxes are not selected.

9. Click the **Slide number** check box, click the **Footer** check box, and then click the **Apply to All** button. Now the footer and page number appear on all the slides. See Figure 4-2. The imported Word outline is now in the PowerPoint slides with the Landon theme applied.

**Figure 4-2** **Presentation with imported Word outline**

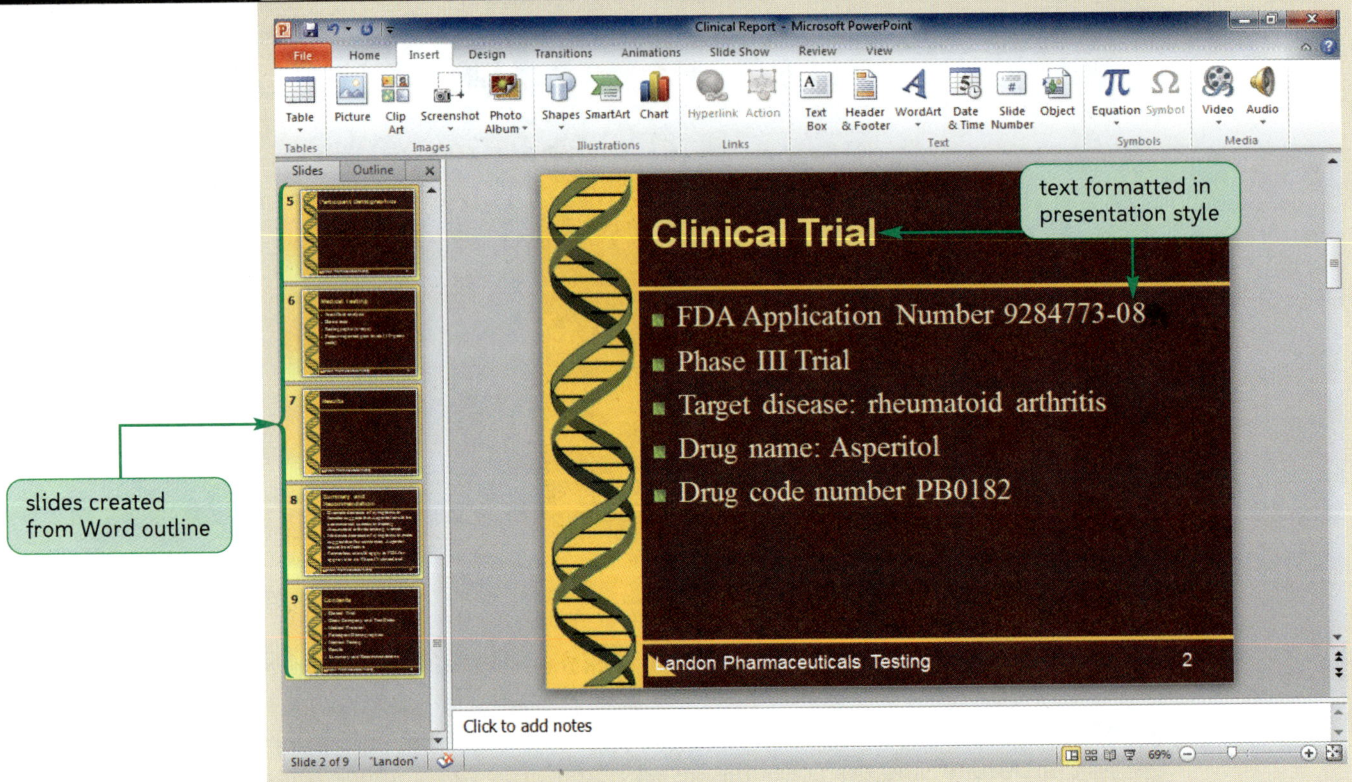


Because you imported the outline, the text is now part of PowerPoint and has no relationship with the Word file ClinOutline. Any changes you make to the PowerPoint presentation will have no effect on the ClinOutline file.

## Exporting an Outline to Word

After looking over the presentation, Alyssa decides that she wants Slide 9 ("Contents") to become Slide 2, so that her audience gets an overview of the presentation contents near the beginning. She then wants you to export the revised text as a Word document so that she can create a written report based on the revised outline. You'll do this now.

### To modify the presentation outline in Slide Sorter view:

1. Switch to Slide Sorter view.
2. Drag the **Slide 9** thumbnail to the right of the Slide 1 thumbnail (and to the left of the Slide 2 thumbnail). The Contents slide becomes the new Slide 2.
3. Double-click **Slide 1** to return to Normal view, and then click the **Outline** tab in the pane on the left so you can see the text of the outline. See Figure 4-3.

**Figure 4-3** Presentation outline after "Contents" slide is moved

Contents slide

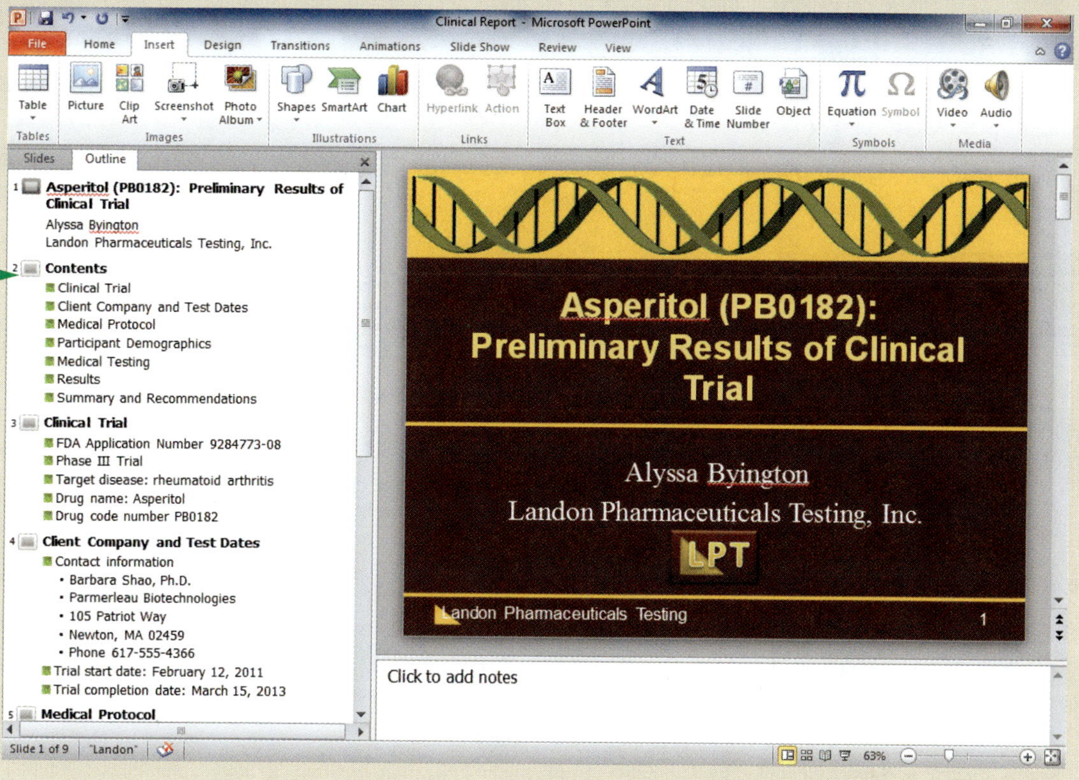


Now you'll export the revised outline to a Word file.

## To export the outline to Word:

1. Click the **File** tab, and then click the **Save As** command in the navigation bar. The Save As dialog box opens.
2. Click the **Save as type** arrow, and then click **Outline/RTF**. "RTF" stands for Rich Text Format, which is a text format that preserves most formatting and can be read by most word processors.
3. Navigate to the PowerPoint4\Tutorial folder, if necessary, change the filename to **Report Outline**, and then click the **Save** button. PowerPoint saves the text of the PowerPoint file as an RTF file.
4. Start Microsoft Word 2010, and then open the document **Report Outline**, located in the PowerPoint4\Tutorial folder. The text is barely visible because PowerPoint created the RTF file using the same font sizes and colors as in the presentation, so in this case, it is yellow or white text on a white background. You'll make the text more visible.
5. Press the **Ctrl+A** keys to select all the text in the document.
6. Change the font to **Calibri**, change the font size to **12**, and then change the font color to **Automatic** (black).

   **Trouble?** If you are unfamiliar with Microsoft Word 2010, skip Steps 6 and 7.
7. Click anywhere to deselect the text. Now you can read the text. See Figure 4-4.

**TIP**

You can also click the File tab, click Save & Send in the navigation bar, click Create Handouts, and then click the Create Handouts button. In the Send To Microsoft Word dialog box, click the Outline Only option button.

**Figure 4-4** Exported outline in Microsoft Word

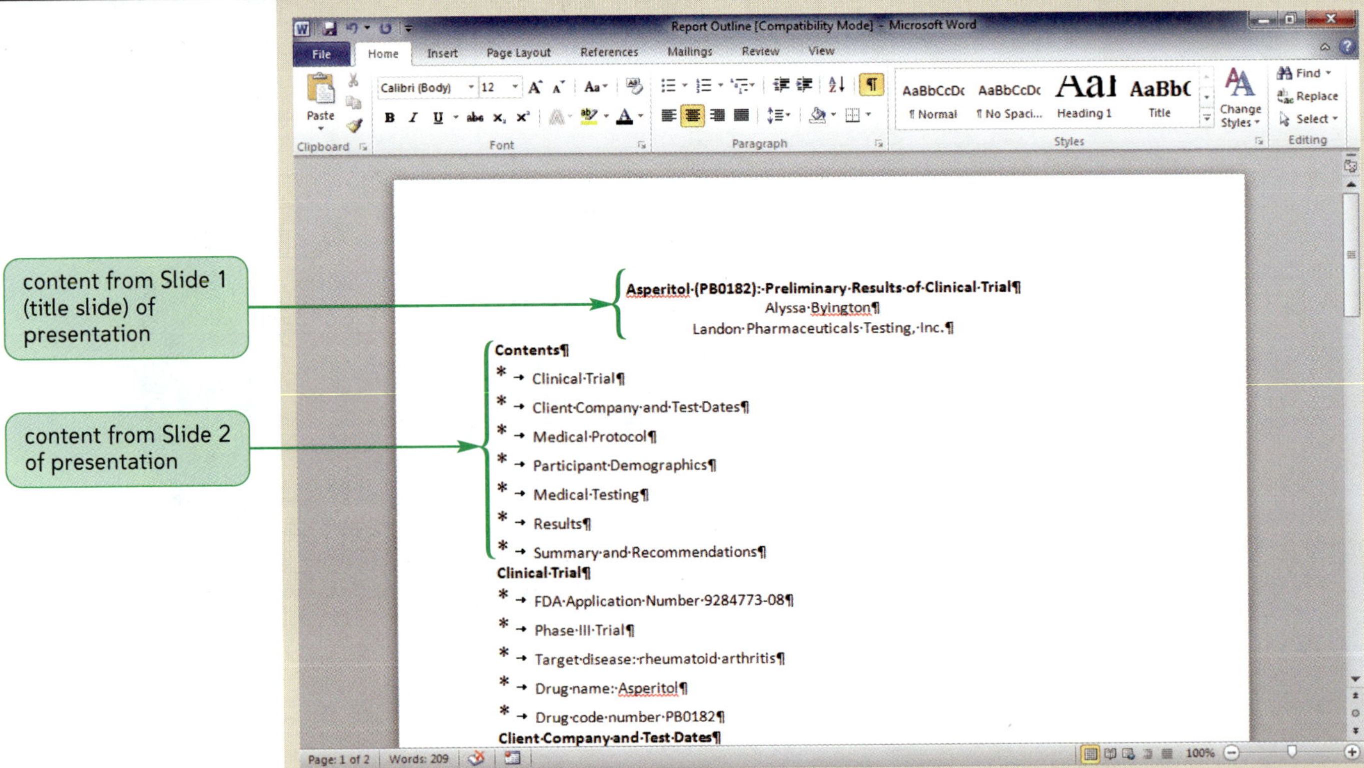


8. Click the **File** tab, and then click **Save As** in the navigation bar. The Save As dialog box opens with Rich Text Format listed in the Save as type box.
9. Click the **Save as type** arrow, and then click **Word Document**.
10. Click the **Save** button. A dialog box opens indicating that you are about to save the document to one of the new file formats.
11. Click the **OK** button. Word saves the Report Outline document as a Word document.
12. Exit Word. PowerPoint is the active window again.
13. Click the **Slides** tab. The slide thumbnails appear in the pane on the left.

Next Alyssa wants you to insert a photograph into the presentation by copying it from another presentation.

## Copying an Object from a Different Presentation

You can copy an object from one presentation and paste it into another using the Copy and Paste commands and the Clipboard. A photograph of Asperitol pills is included in a short presentation that Alyssa's assistant created. Alyssa asks you to copy that photograph to Slide 3 in the Clinical Report presentation.

## To copy an object from the Landon presentation:

1. With the Clinical Report presentation open in the PowerPoint window, open the presentation **Landon**, which is located in the PowerPoint4\Tutorial folder.
2. Display **Slide 3** ("Latest Phase III Trial: Asperitol") in the Slide pane, and then click the photo of the pills to select it.
3. In the Clipboard group, click the **Copy** button. The photo is copied to the Clipboard.
4. In the title bar, click the **Close** button to close the Landon presentation and return to the Clinical Report presentation.
5. Display **Slide 3** ("Clinical Trial") in the Slide pane, and then change the layout to the **Two Content** layout. The bulleted list appears in the content text box on the left and a content placeholder appears on the right.
6. In the Clipboard group, click the **Paste** button. The photograph of the pills appears in the center of the slide. It did not replace the content placeholder.
7. Click the border of the content placeholder on the right, and then press the **Delete** key. The content placeholder on the right is deleted.
8. Drag the photograph to approximately center it in the area to the right of the bulleted list, and then click a blank area of the slide to deselect the pasted object. See Figure 4-5.

**Figure 4-5** Slide 3 with pasted photograph

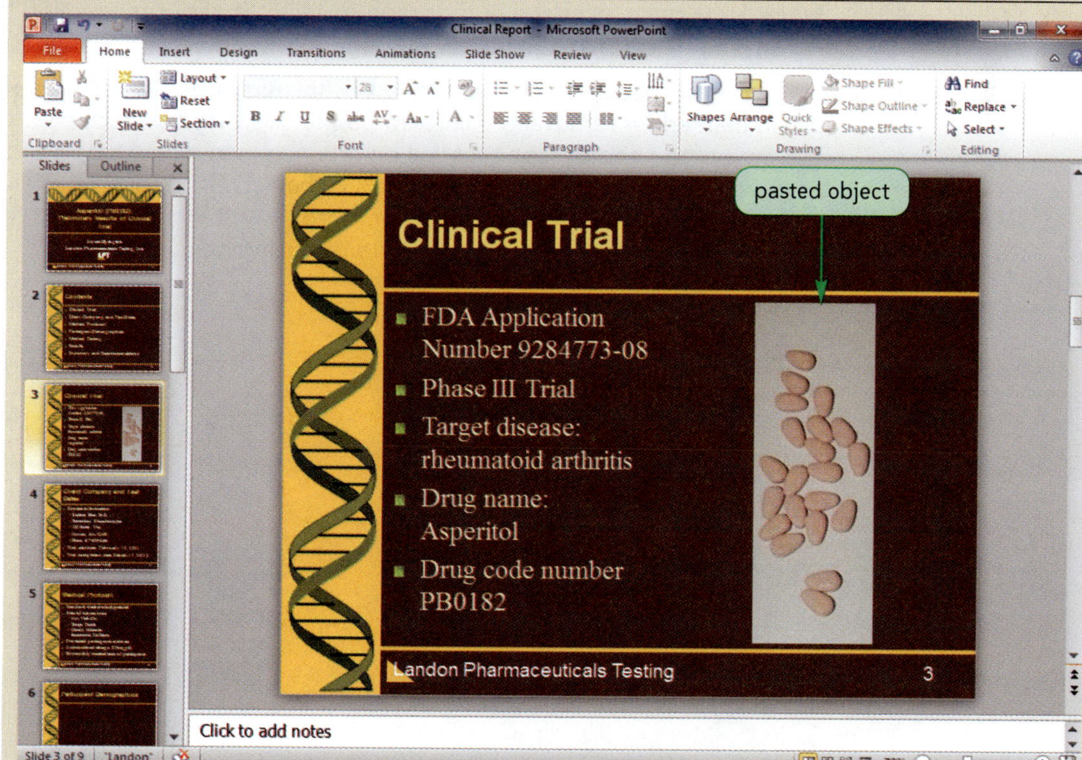


9. Save your changes.

Next, you'll modify the photograph you pasted by removing its background.

# Removing the Background from Photographs

Alyssa thinks that the photograph of the pills on Slide 3 would look better without the gray background. You can remove the background in photographs with the Remove Background tool. When you click the Remove Background button, the photograph is analyzed; part of it is marked to be removed and part of it is marked to be retained.

REFERENCE

*Removing the Background of a Photograph*

- Click the photograph, and then click the Picture Tools Format tab on the Ribbon.
- In the Adjust group, click the Remove Background button.
- Drag the sizing handles on the remove background border to make broad adjustments to the area marked for removal.
- In the Refine group on the Background Removal tab, click the Mark Areas to Keep or the Mark Areas to Remove button, and then click or drag through an area of the photo that you want marked to keep or remove.
- Click a blank area of the slide or click the Keep Changes button in the Close group to accept the changes.

You'll remove the background on the photograph now.

**To remove the background of the photograph:**

1. In the Slide pane, click the photograph to select it, if necessary, and then click the **Picture Tools Format** tab on the Ribbon.
2. In the Adjust group, click the **Remove Background** button. The areas of the photograph marked for removal are colored purple. A sizing box appears around the general area of the photograph that will be retained, and a new tab, the Background Removal tab, appears on the Ribbon and is the active tab. See Figure 4-6. Notice several of the pills are marked to be removed as well. You can adjust the area of the photograph that is retained by dragging the sizing handles.

**Figure 4-6** Photograph after clicking the Remove Background button

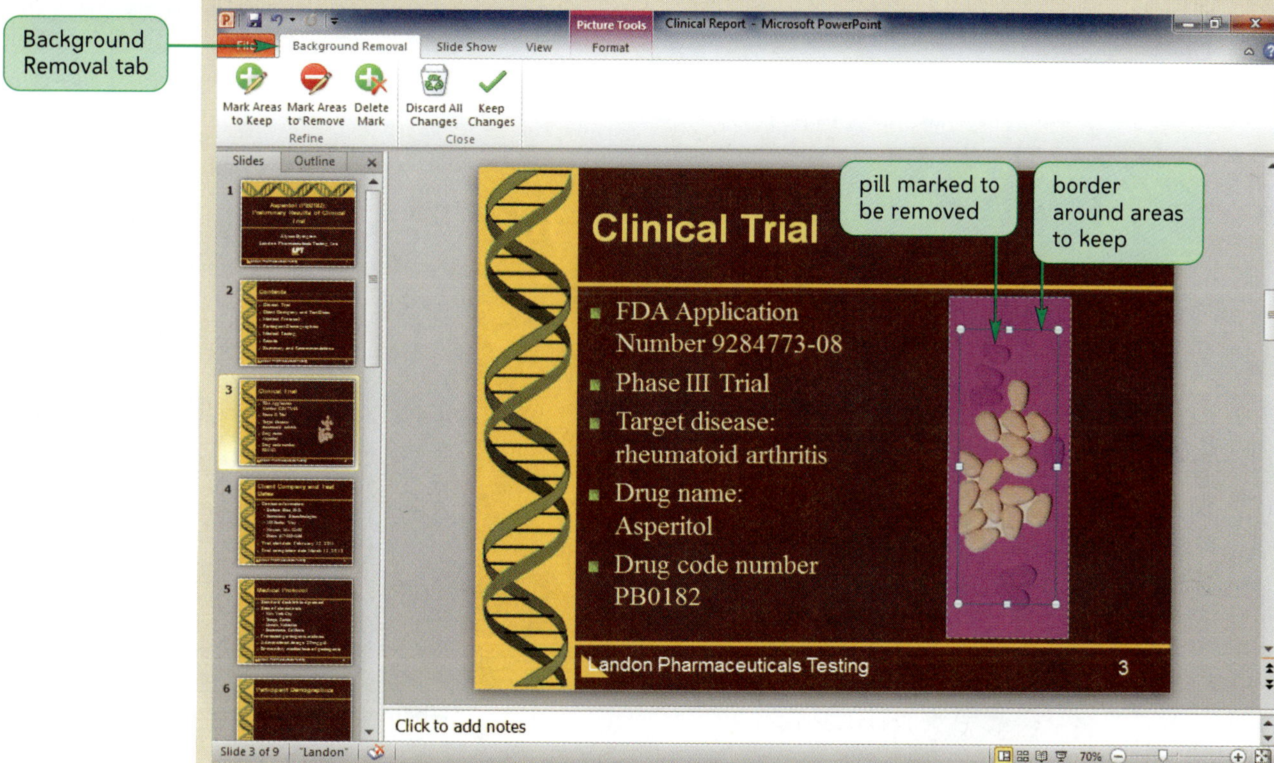


3. Drag the **right middle sizing handle** to the right edge of the photograph. The pill on the right that had been marked for removal is colored normally again.
4. Drag the **left middle sizing handle** to the left edge of the photograph. The pills on the left that had been cut off are colored normally. There are still three pills at the top and two pills at the bottom that are marked for removal.
5. Drag the **bottom middle sizing handle** down to about halfway between the bottom pill in the photograph and the bottom border of the photograph. Now all the pills are inside the border, but one at the top and two at the bottom are still marked for removal. Also, some of the gray background is visible again. See Figure 4-7. You can fine tune the removal if adjusting the sizing handles doesn't work.

   **Trouble?** If your photograph doesn't look exactly like the one in Figure 4-7, don't be concerned. You will adjust it in the next few steps.

**Figure 4-7** **Border resized around area to keep**

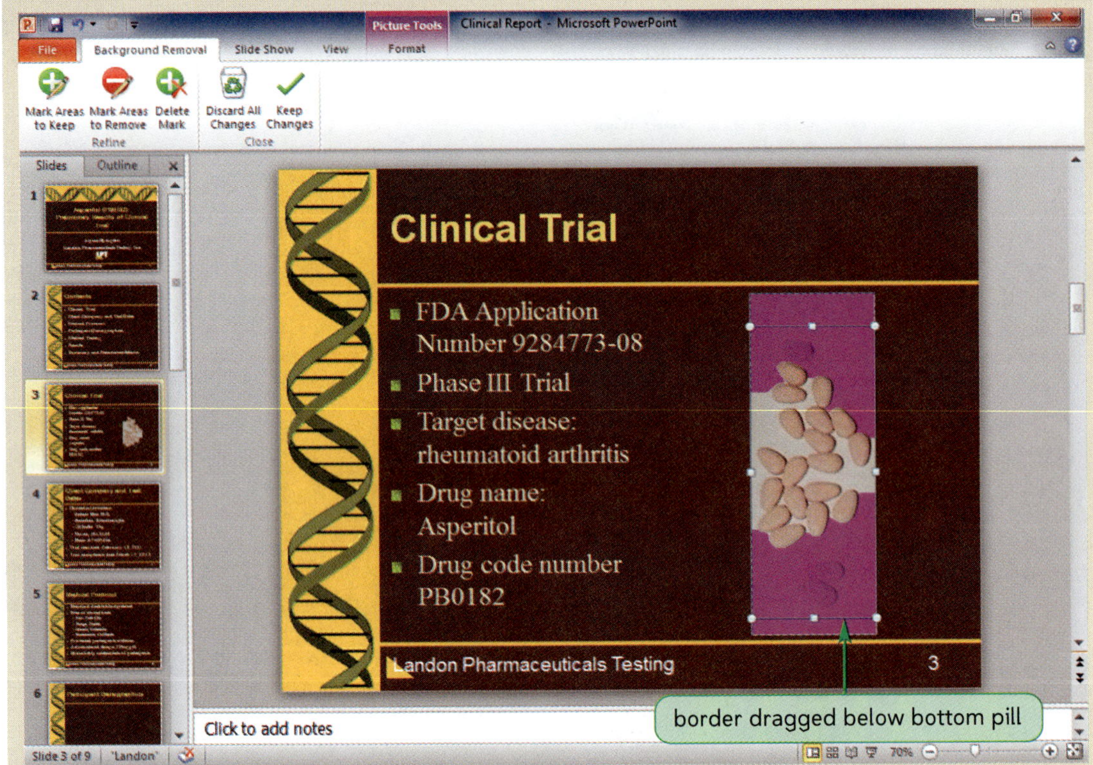


6. In the Refine group on the Background Removal tab, click the **Mark Areas to Remove** button, and then position the pointer on top of the photo. The pointer changes to ✎.

7. On the right side of the photograph, click in the gray area below the rightmost pill. A circle with a minus sign appears, and a portion of the gray area near where you clicked might be marked for removal. If you drag through an area that you want to remove or keep, you provide more information about the exact portions to keep or remove. To see the difference, first, you'll undo the change you just made.

8. On the Quick Access Toolbar, click the **Undo** button.

9. In the Refine Group, click the **Mark Areas to Remove** button again, and then on the right side of the photograph, drag down from between the cluster of pills on the right to the bottom part of the gray area, taking care not to touch any of the pills. The gray area you dragged through is marked for removal, and a dotted line indicating the path you dragged through appears on either side of the circle with the minus sign. See Figure 4-8.

**Figure 4-8** Photograph after marking a specific area to remove

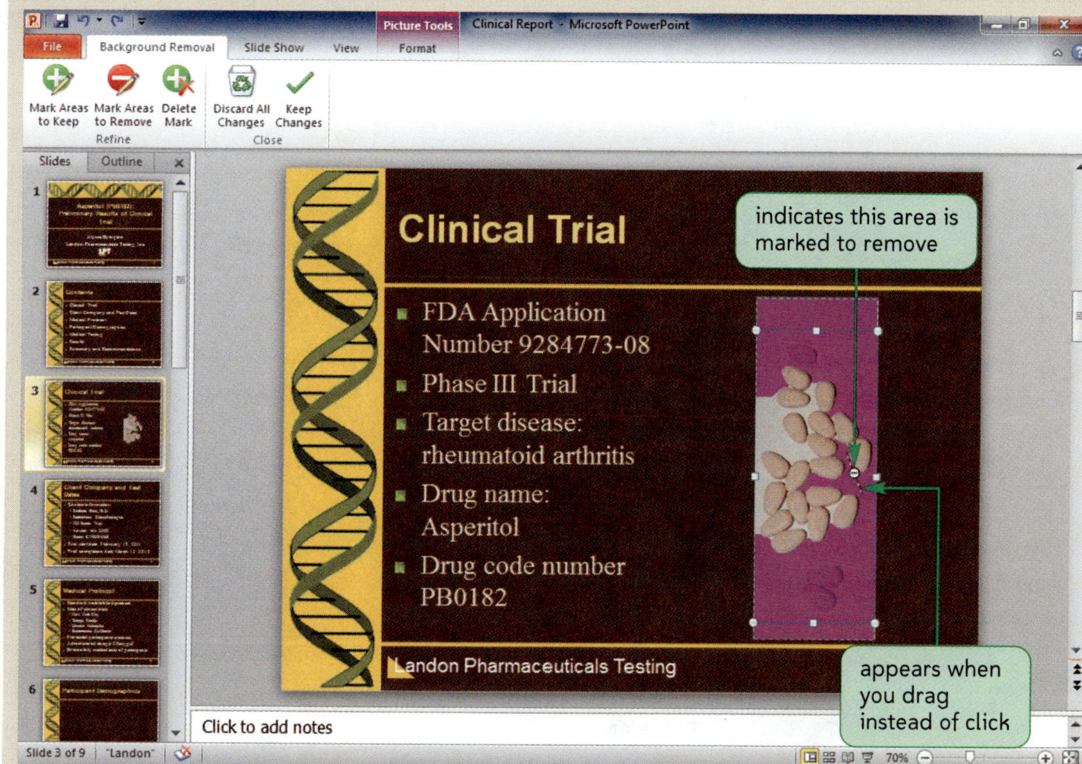


10. On the left side of the photograph, click in the gray area to the left of the pills, and then click the other gray areas in the photograph. The gray areas are now all marked for removal.

    **Trouble?** If a pill is marked for removal, don't be concerned. In the next step, you will mark areas to keep.

11. In the Refine group, click the **Mark Areas to Keep** button, and then click the top pill. The top three pills are now marked to appear in the final photo.

    **Trouble?** If there are still pills at the top of the photograph that are marked for removal, make sure the Mark Areas to Keep button is still selected, and then click them.

12. At the bottom of the photograph, click one of the two pills marked for removal, and then click any other pills that are marked for removal. All the pills are now colored normally and most of the gray background is marked for removal.

    **Trouble?** If any pills are still marked for removal, click them with the Mark Areas to Keep pointer.

13. In the Close group, click the **Keep Changes** button. The changes you made are applied to the photograph, and the Background Removal tab disappears from the Ribbon. See Figure 4-9.

**Figure 4-9** Photograph of pills with the background removed

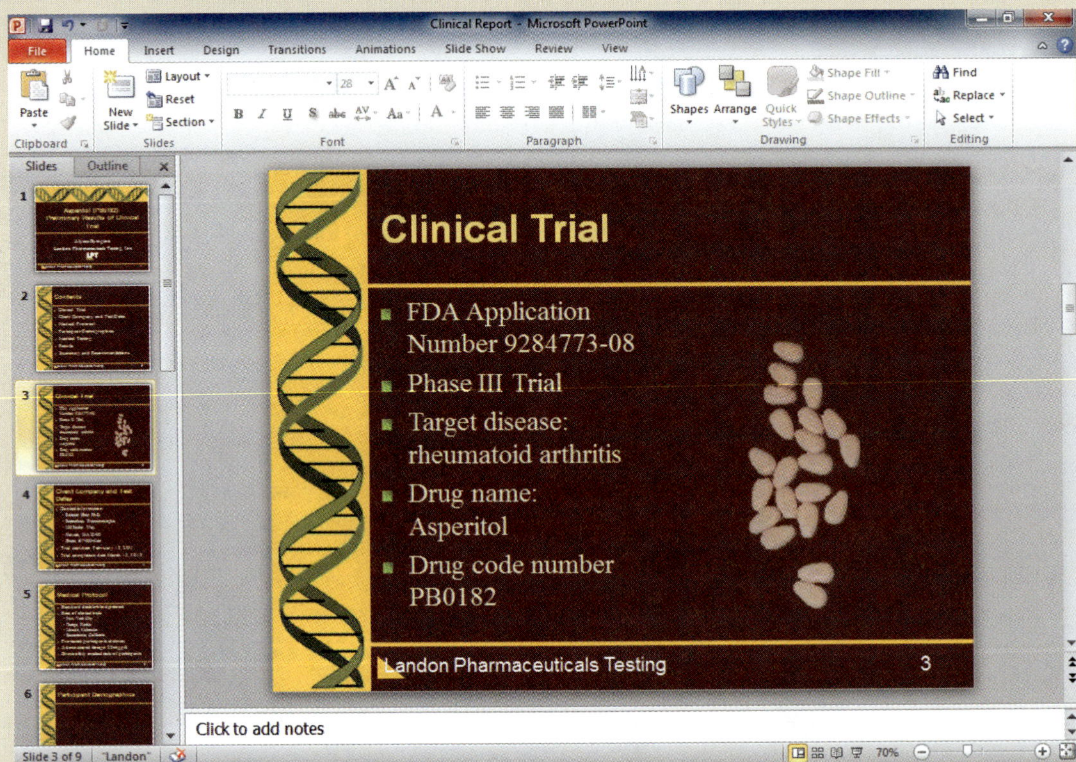


**14.** Save your changes.

**TIP**

You can also click a blank area of the slide to accept the changes.

If you change your mind and decide that you want the background after all, you can click the Reset Picture button in the Adjust group on the Picture Tools Format tab. Alyssa likes the way the photograph looks without the gray background.

## Embedding and Modifying a Word Table

You know how to use PowerPoint commands to create a table in a slide, but what if you've already created a table using Word? You don't have to re-create it in PowerPoint; instead, you can copy the table and paste it in a slide. If you embed the table, you can then edit it using Word table commands. You can use copy and paste commands to embed a Word table, but if the Word file contains only the Word table, you can use the Object command instead. The Object command inserts the entire file in a slide.

**REFERENCE**

*Embedding a Word Table in a Slide Using the Object Command*

- Click the Insert tab, and then click the Object button in the Text group to open the Insert Object dialog box.
- Click the Create from file option button.
- Click the Browse button to open the Browse dialog box, navigate to the drive and folder containing the file with the table, and then click the OK button.
- Make sure the Link check box is deselected in the Insert Object dialog box.
- Click the OK button.

Alyssa created a table in a Word document that lists the demographics of the participants in the trials, and she asks you to embed the table in Slide 6 in her presentation. Alyssa created the table with a black font on a white background, so it is legible in a Word document. But as you'll see, it's not legible against the dark background in the PowerPoint presentation.

### To embed a Word file in the presentation:

1. Display **Slide 6** ("Participant Demographics") in the Slide pane, and then click the **Insert** tab on the Ribbon.
2. In the Text group, click the **Object** button. The Insert Object dialog box opens. You can create a new embedded file or use an existing one. You'll use the existing file that Alyssa created.
3. Click the **Create from file** option button, and then click the **Browse** button to open the Browse dialog box.
4. Navigate to the PowerPoint4\Tutorial folder included with your Data Files, click **Demogr**, and then click the **OK** button. The Browse dialog box closes, and the path and filename of the file you selected appear in the File box in the Insert Object dialog box. See Figure 4-10.

**Figure 4-10** Insert Object dialog box

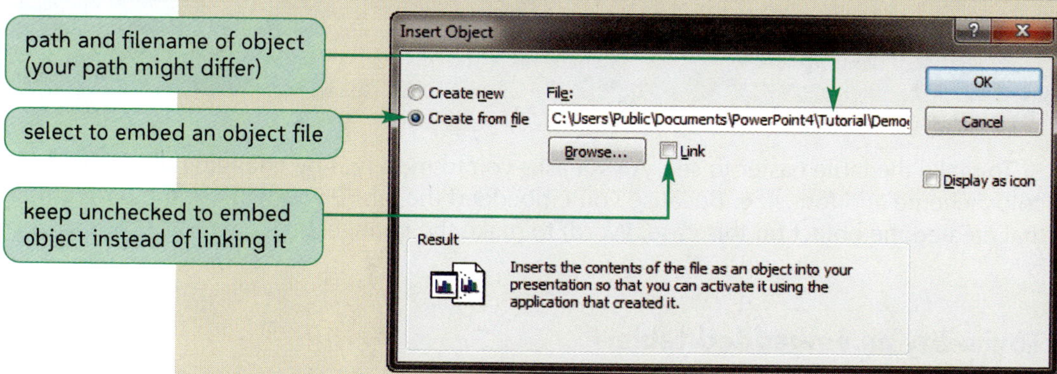


5. Make sure the **Link** check box is not selected, as shown in Figure 4-10, and then click the **OK** button. The embedded table appears in Slide 6.
6. Resize the table by dragging the corner sizing handles so that the table is as large as possible and still fits on the middle of the slide without overlapping background objects. You will have to drag the object border beyond the edges of the slide to make the table as big as possible. See Figure 4-11.

**Figure 4-11** Slide 6 with embedded Word table

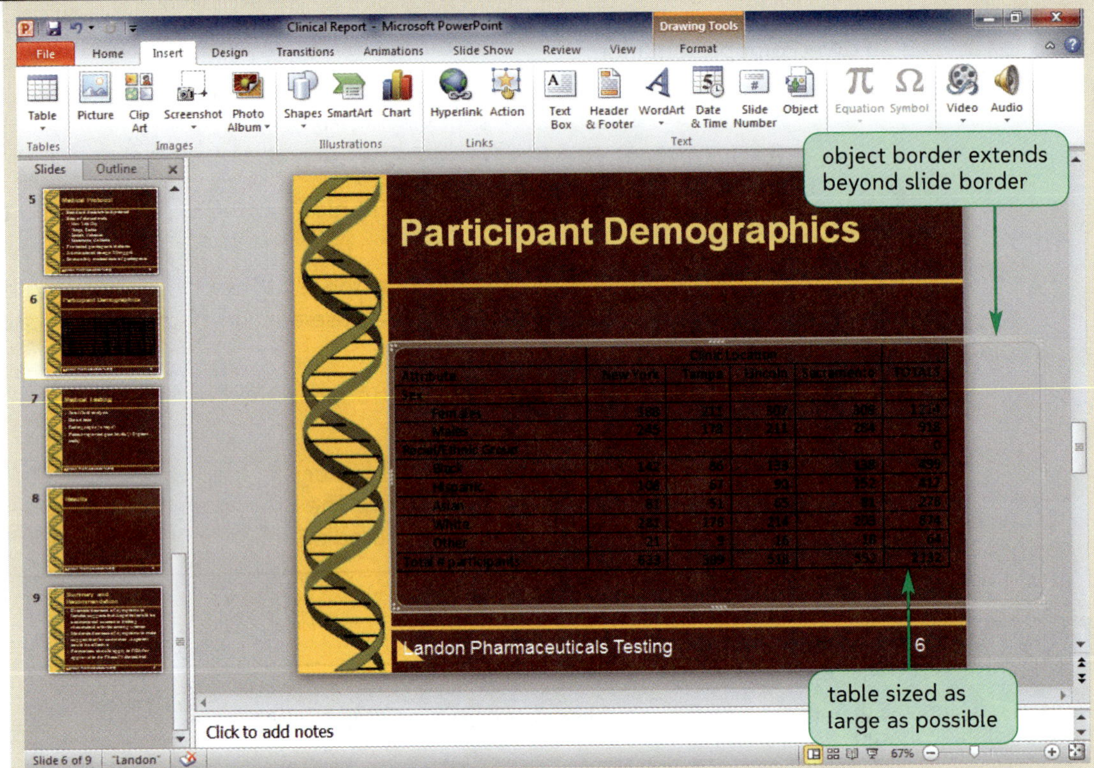


To make the table easier to see, Alyssa asks you to modify it by changing the table color scheme and font size. Because you embedded the table, you will use the program that created the object (in this case, Word) to make the changes.

## To modify an embedded table:

1. Double-click anywhere in the table in Slide 6. The embedded table object becomes active in Word, and the Word Ribbon replaces the PowerPoint Ribbon. See Figure 4-12.

**Figure 4-12** Slide 6 with embedded Word table made active

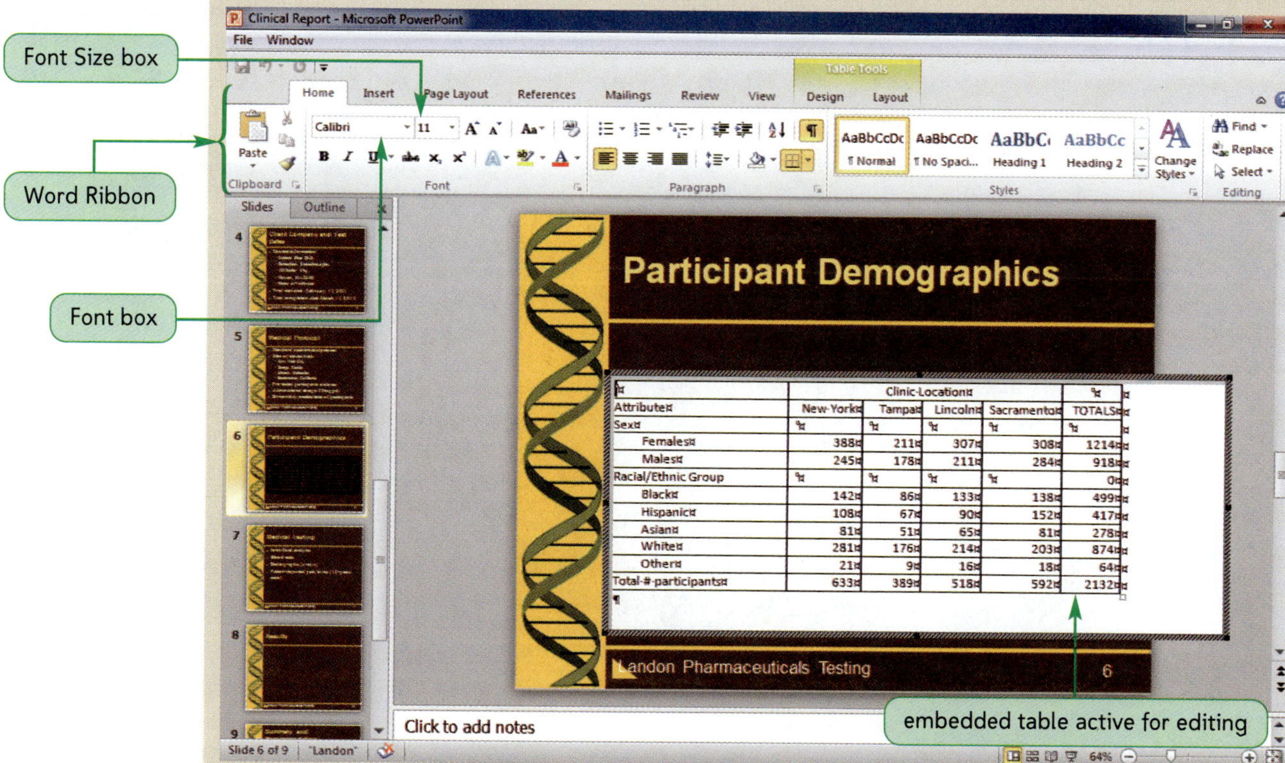


2. Drag the mouse pointer from the upper-left cell to the bottom-right cell to select the entire table.
3. In the Font group on the Home tab, click the **Font box arrow**, and then scroll to locate and select **Times New Roman**.
4. Click in the **Font Size** box, type **13**, and then press the **Enter** key. The text of the table is now 13-point Times New Roman.
5. Click the **Font Color button arrow**, and click the **White, Background 1** color. The font in the Word window seems to disappear, because it is white on a white background. On Slide 6, which has a dark brown background, the text will show up nicely.
6. In the Paragraph group, click the **Borders button arrow**, and then click **Borders and Shading** at the bottom of the gallery. The Borders and Shading dialog box opens.
7. Click the **Color** arrow, and then click the **Yellow** color under Standard Colors to change the table grid lines to yellow.
8. Click the **OK** button, click a blank area of the slide to exit Word and return to PowerPoint, and then click a blank area again to deselect the table. See Figure 4-13.

**TIP**

Use the Shading button in the Table Styles group on the Table Tools Design tab to fill a cell with gradient color, a texture, or a picture.

**Figure 4-13** Slide 6 with modified table

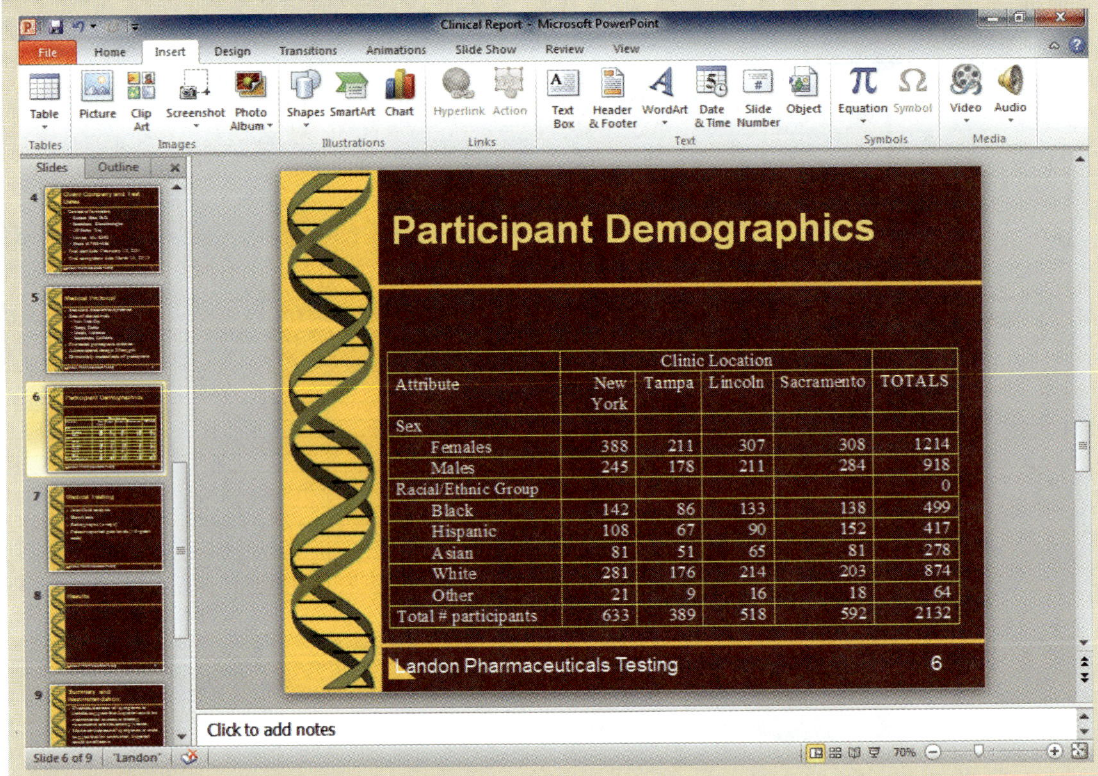


**Trouble?** If your table doesn't look similar to the one in Figure 4-13, make any adjustments now.

9. Save your changes.

Keep in mind that the changes you made to the embedded object did not change the original table in the Word document because embedding maintains a connection only with the program that was used to create the object, not with the original object itself.

Next, you'll link an Excel chart to the presentation.

## Linking and Modifying an Excel Chart

Now you know how to insert objects into a PowerPoint slide by importing them and by embedding them. What if you needed to include in your presentation data that might change? For example, you might need data from an Excel worksheet, but you know that the final numbers won't be available for a while or that the numbers will change over time. In this case, you can link the data. Then, when the source file is updated, you can automatically update the linked object in the destination file so that it reflects the changes made to the source file.

REFERENCE

### *Linking an Excel Chart to a Slide Using Copy and Paste*

- Start Excel (the source program), open the file containing the chart to be linked, select the chart you want to link to the destination program, and then in the Clipboard group on the Home tab, click the Copy button.
- In the PowerPoint file that will contain the linked chart (the destination file), in the Clipboard group on the Home tab, click the Paste button, click the Paste Options button, and then click the Use Destination Theme & Link Data button or click the Keep Source Formatting & Link Data button; or click the Paste button arrow, and then click the Use Destination Theme & Link Data or Keep Source Formatting & Link Data button.

Alyssa wants to include a bar chart of the results of the drug clinical trial in the presentation. She wants to use a bar chart because it emphasizes the effects of the drug on trial participants. The bar chart was created using Excel, based on data in an Excel workbook, but Alyssa anticipates that she will have to modify the chart after she creates the PowerPoint presentation because some of the trial results were incomplete. Alyssa wants any changes made to the chart to be reflected in the PowerPoint file, so she asks you to link the Excel chart to the PowerPoint presentation.

### To insert a chart linked to an Excel worksheet:

1. Display **Slide 8** ("Results") in the Slide pane, and then change the slide layout to **Title Only**.
2. Start Microsoft Office Excel 2010, open the file **Chart** located in the PowerPoint4\Tutorial folder, and then save it as **Clinical Chart** in the same folder. Now you can make changes to the chart without modifying the original document.
3. Click the edge of the chart to select it, click the **Home** tab, and then click the **Copy** button in the Clipboard group to copy the chart to the Clipboard.
4. On the taskbar, click the **PowerPoint** button. The Clinical Report presentation appears with Slide 8 in the Slide pane.

In order for link commands to appear as paste options, do not exit Excel.

5. In the Clipboard group, click the **Paste** button to paste the chart into Slide 8. The chart is pasted in the slide.
6. Below the lower-right corner of the chart, click the **Paste Options** button (Ctrl). Notice that the default selected button is the Use Destination Theme & Link Data button. This is what you want, so you don't need to select a different option on the menu.
7. Click the **Paste Options** button (Ctrl) to close the menu without making a selection.
8. Resize the chart so it fits within the large blank region of the slide, and then drag the entire chart to approximately center it in the blank area of the slide. Compare your screen to Figure 4-14.

**TIP**

When you copy and paste an object from another program into a PowerPoint presentation, the object is normally imported, not embedded or linked, except when you copy and paste a chart from Excel into PowerPoint; in this case, the chart is linked.

Figure 4-14 Slide 8 with linked Excel chart

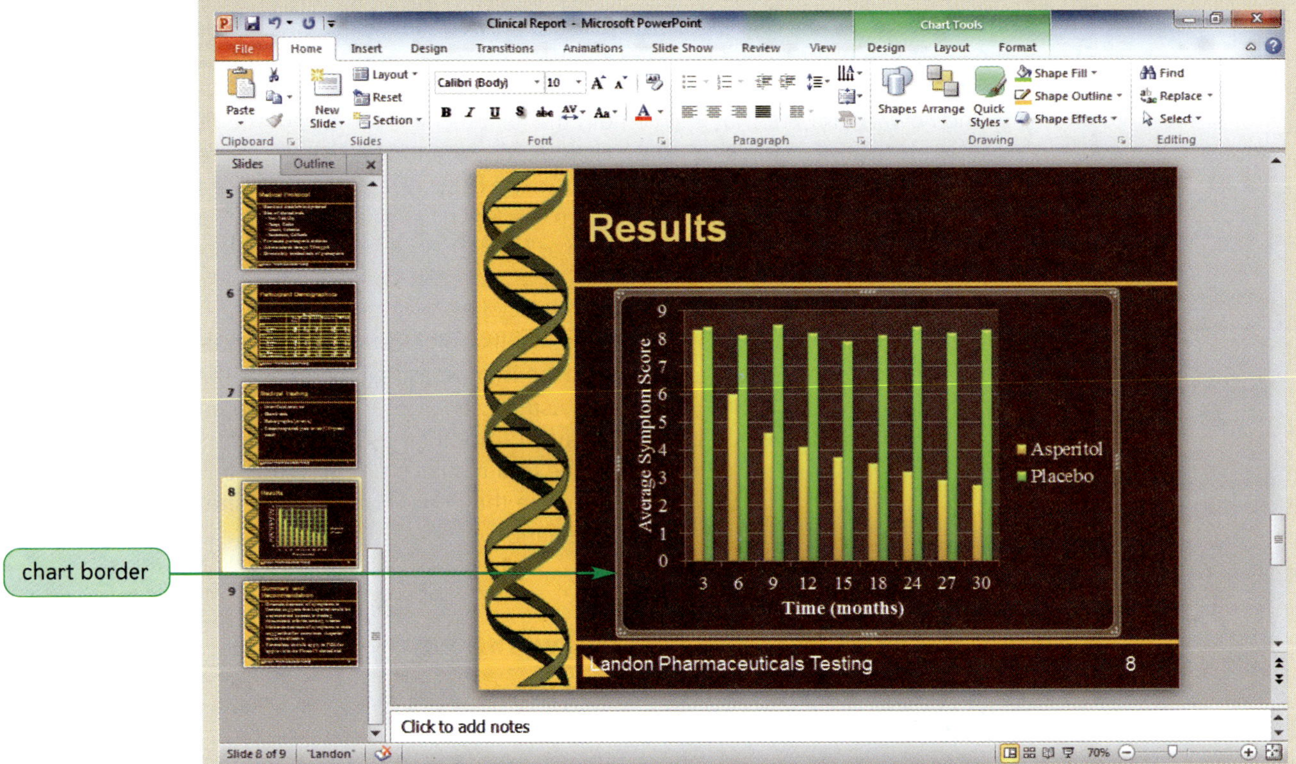


After you linked the chart, Alyssa received updated information about one of the results in the clinical trial report. The scientists at Landon had estimated that the average symptom score after 30 months would be 2.7, but after all the data was collected, the value was actually 3.1. Alyssa asks you to make changes to the Excel worksheet data, which will then be reflected in the chart, both in the Excel and PowerPoint files.

## To modify the linked chart:

1. Click the **Chart Tools Design** tab on the Ribbon.
2. In the Data group, click the **Edit Data** button. The PowerPoint program window is resized to fit in the left half of the screen, and the Excel window containing the linked chart appears on the right. See Figure 4-15.

**Figure 4-15** **Adding a chart in Slide 8**

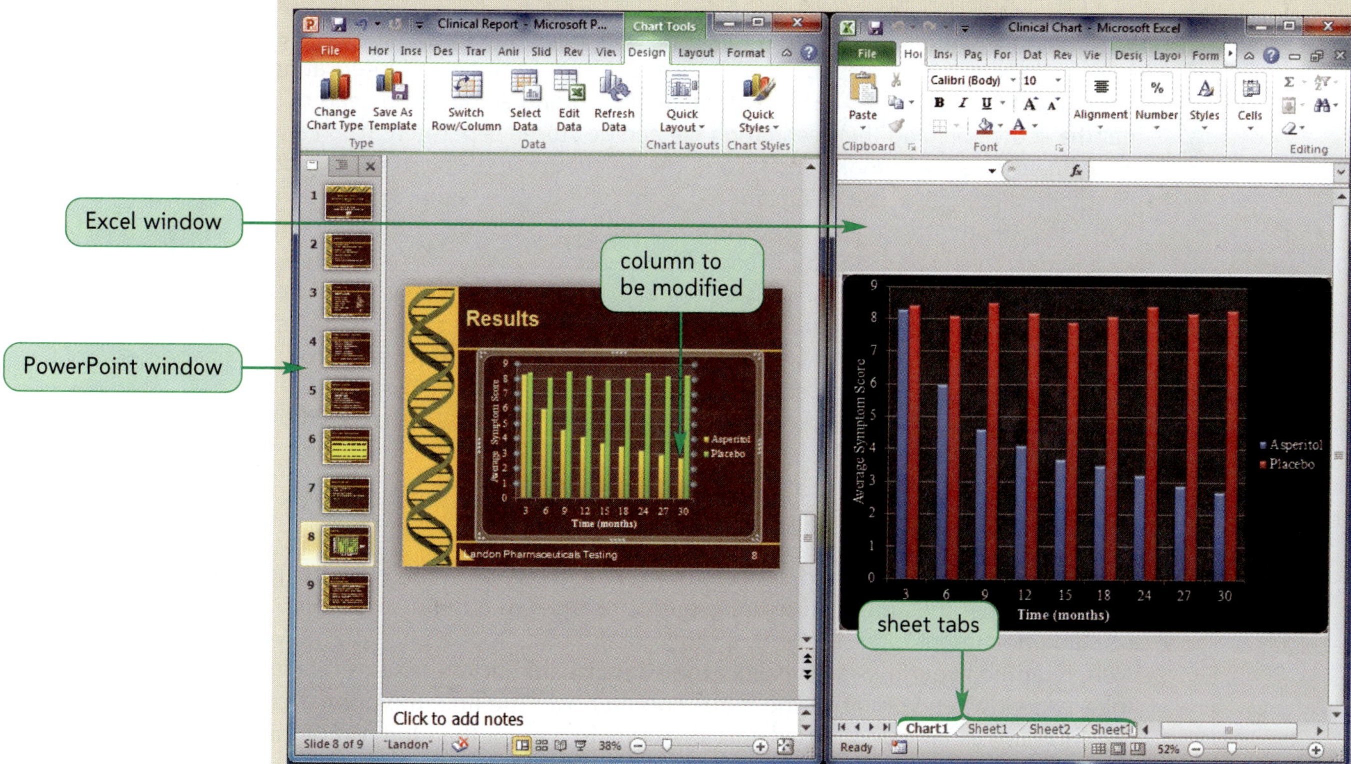


3. In the Excel window, click the **Sheet1** tab at the bottom of the window, and then click cell **B10** (the intersection of column B and row 10).
4. Type **3.1**, but don't press the Enter key yet. Look at the chart in the PowerPoint window on the left. Focus on the rightmost yellow bar, which indicates the average symptom score at 30 months.
5. Press the **Enter** key. The rightmost yellow bar in the chart in the PowerPoint window changed.
6. In the Excel window, click the **Close** button, and then click the **Save** button when asked if you want to save the changes to the Excel file. PowerPoint now fills the screen again.
7. Save your changes to the presentation.

You have now linked and edited an Excel chart in a PowerPoint presentation. If you decide later to make further changes to the chart, you can do so either by directly starting Excel and opening the Clinical Chart workbook, or accessing the workbook by clicking the Edit Data button in PowerPoint. Either way, any changes made to the workbook will be reflected in the linked object in the PowerPoint slide.

PROSKILLS

### *Decision Making: Comparing Import, Embed, and Linking Options*

Both linking and embedding involve inserting an object into a destination file; the difference lies in where their respective objects are stored. Each type of integration has advantages and disadvantages. The advantage of embedding an object instead of linking it is that the source file and the destination file can be stored separately. You can use the source program commands to make changes to the object in the destination file, and the source file will be unaffected. The disadvantage is that the destination file size is somewhat larger than it would be if the object were simply imported as a picture or text or linked. The advantage of linking an object instead of embedding it is that the object remains identical in the source and destination files, and the destination file size does not increase as much as if the object were embedded. The disadvantage is that the source and destination files must be stored together. When you need to copy information from one program to another, consider which option is the best choice for your needs.

# Creating and Editing Hyperlinks

A **hyperlink** (or **link**) is a word, phrase, or graphic image that you click to "jump to" (or display) another location, called the **target**. The target of a link can be a location within the same document (presentation), a different document, or a page on the World Wide Web. Graphic hyperlinks are visually indistinguishable from graphics that are not hyperlinks, except when you move the mouse pointer over the link, the pointer changes to 👆. Text links are usually underlined and are a different color than the rest of the text. After clicking a text link during a slide show, the link changes to another color to reflect the fact that it has been clicked, or **followed**.

## Formatting Text as a Hyperlink

Alyssa is expecting that some in her audience will be eager to see the results of the clinical trial, before the details of the trial are presented. Therefore, she wants to be able to easily move from Slide 2, which lists the presentation contents, to Slide 8 showing the chart summarizing the trial results. Therefore, she asks you to create a hyperlink between the Results bullet in Slide 2 and the corresponding Slide 8 in the presentation, and then to create a hyperlink from Slide 8 back to Slide 2.

REFERENCE

### *Creating a Hyperlink to Another Slide in a Presentation*

- Select the text or object from which you want to create the hyperlink.
- Click the Insert tab, and then click the Hyperlink button in the Links group.
- In the Insert Hyperlink dialog box, under Link to, click Place in This Document.
- In the Select a place in this document list, click the slide to which you want to link.
- Click the OK button.

You will create this hyperlink next.

### To create a hyperlink from text on Slide 2 to Slide 8:

1. Display **Slide 2** ("Contents") in the Slide pane.
2. In the bulleted list, select the text **Results**.
3. Click the **Insert** tab, and then click the **Hyperlink** button in the Links group. The Insert Hyperlink dialog box opens. See Figure 4-16. You need to identify the file or location to which you want to link. In this case, you're going to link to a place in the existing document, so you'll want to select that option in the Link to panel on the left side of the dialog box.

**Figure 4-16** **Insert Hyperlink dialog box**

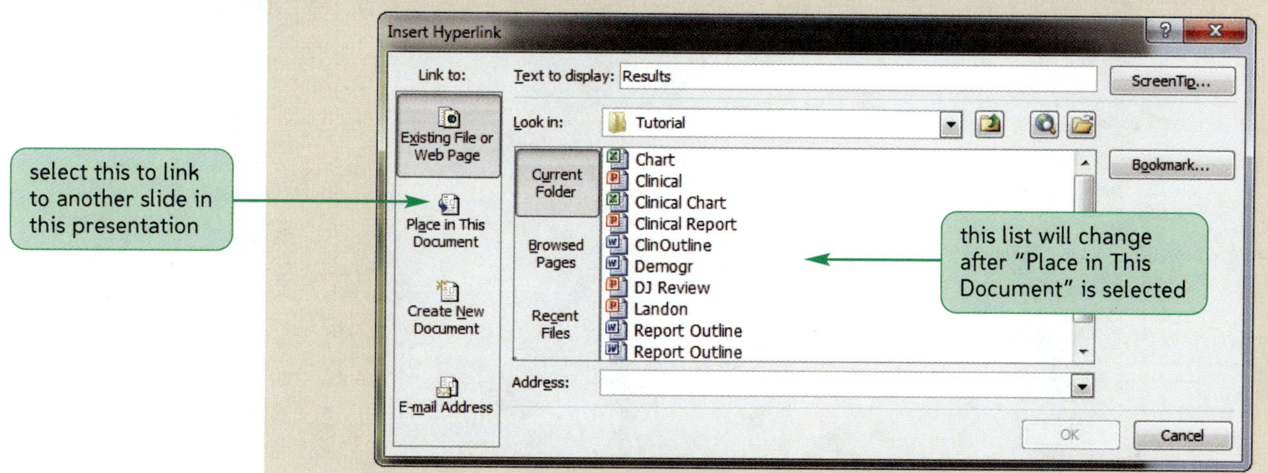


4. In the Link to panel on the left side of the dialog box, click **Place in This Document**. The dialog box changes to list all of the slides in the presentation.
5. In the Select a place in this document list, click **8. Results**. The Slide preview area on the right side of the dialog box displays Slide 8. This is the slide to which the text will be linked. See Figure 4-17.

**Figure 4-17** **Insert Hyperlink dialog box after selecting a slide in the current document**

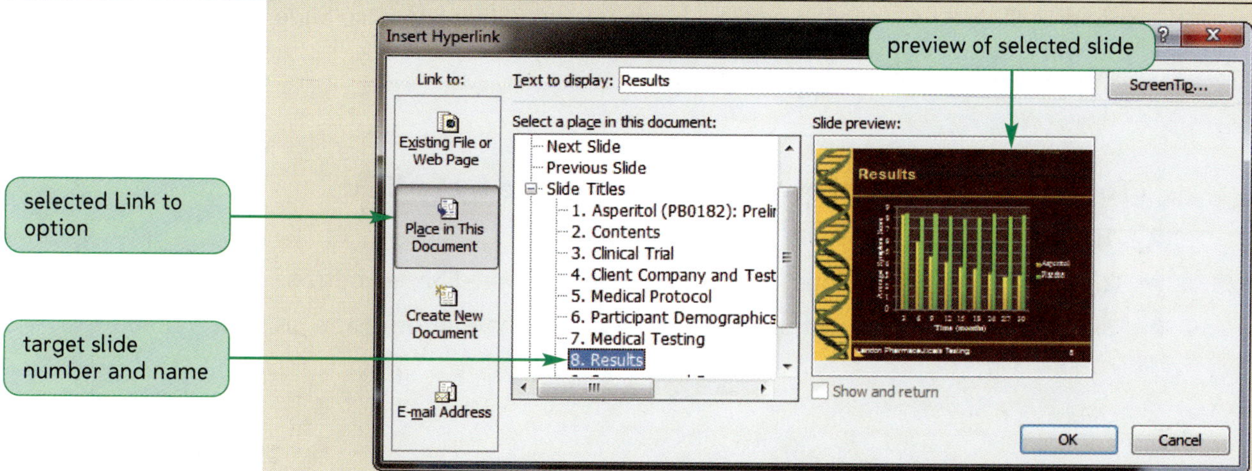

6. Click the **OK** button, and then click a blank area of the slide to deselect the text. The text "Results" is now a hyperlink, and it is now formatted as green and underlined. (Recall that you can specify the hyperlink color when you customize the theme colors.) See Figure 4-18.

**Figure 4-18** Slide 2 with a hyperlink to Slide 8

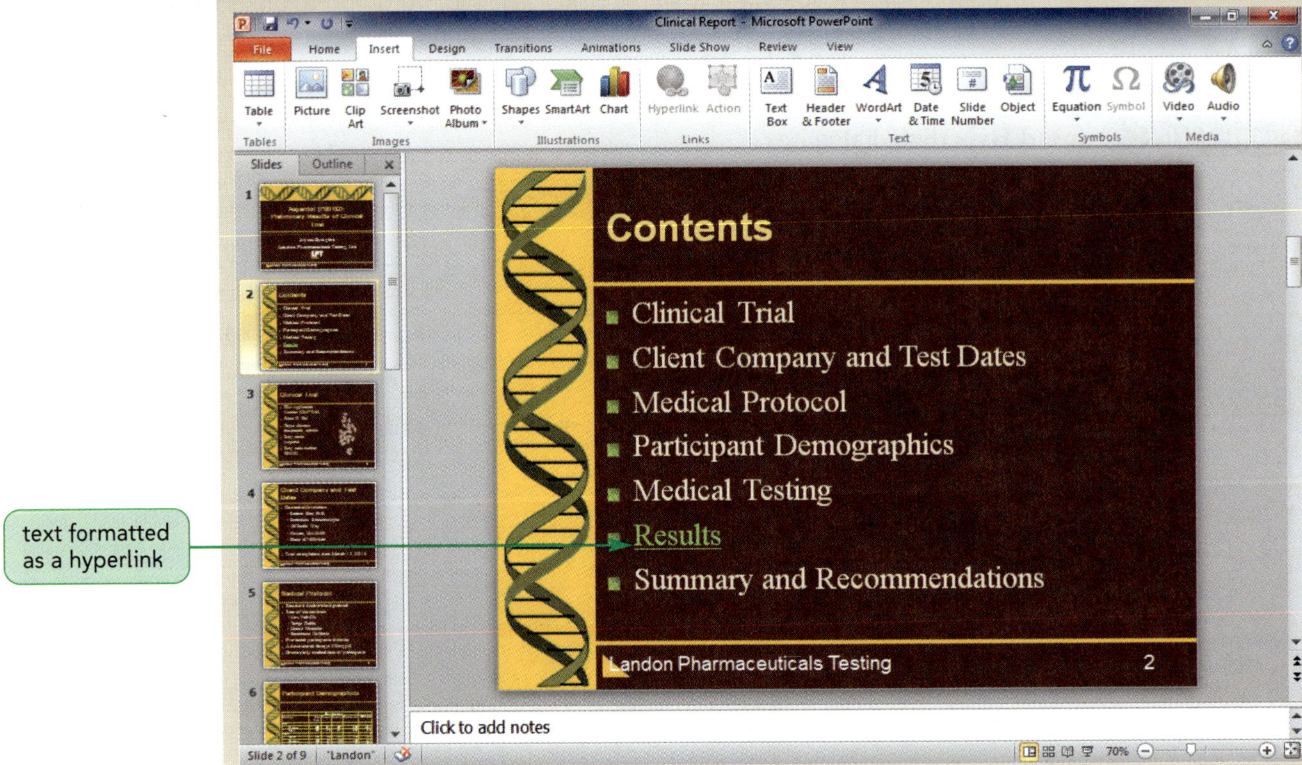


## Formatting a Shape as a Hyperlink

Now that you have formatted the Results bullet in Slide 2 as a hyperlink to the corresponding Slide 8, you need to create a hyperlink from Slide 8 back to Slide 2. To do this, you will create a shape to format as a hyperlink.

You'll first create the shape.

**To insert the shape that you will format as a hyperlink:**

1. Display **Slide 8** ("Results") in the Slide pane.
2. In the Illustrations group on the Insert tab, click the **Shapes** button.
3. In the Basic Shapes section of the gallery, click the **Plaque** shape, as indicated in Figure 4-19.

**Figure 4-19** Slide 8 with the Shapes gallery open

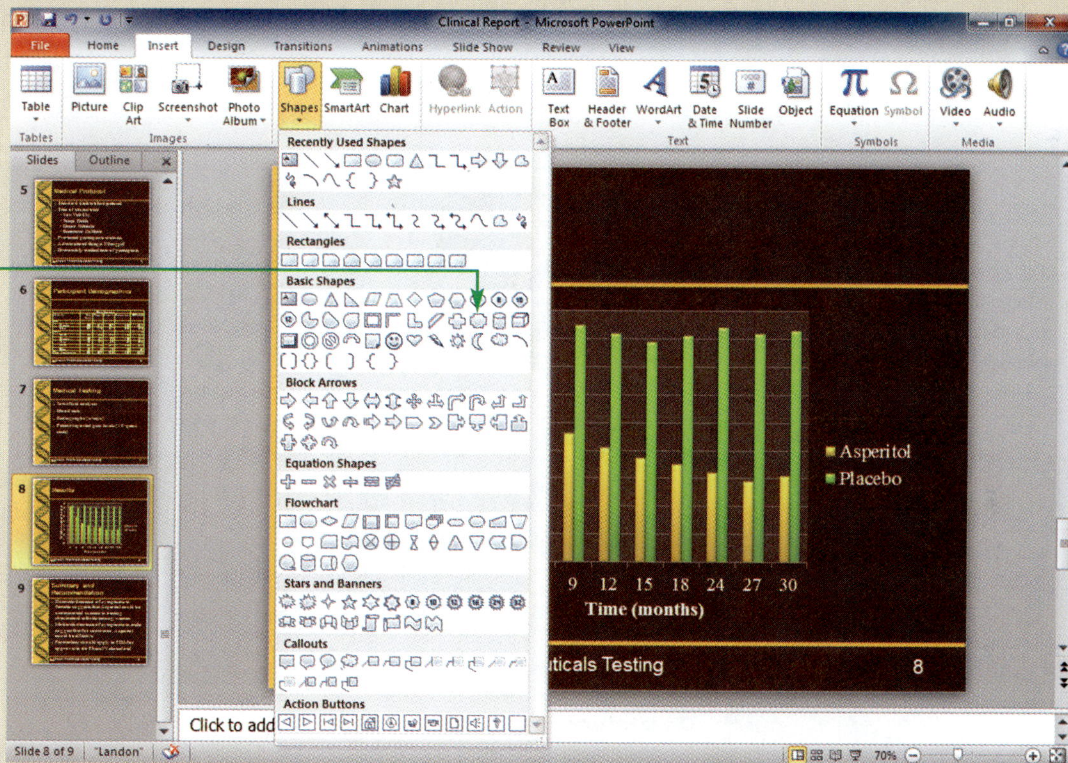


4. Position the pointer between the footer and the slide number near the bottom of the slide, and then drag down and to the right to make the shape shown in Figure 4-20. Don't worry about the exact location and size of the shape; you can fix it later.

**Figure 4-20** Slide 8 after the plaque shape is inserted

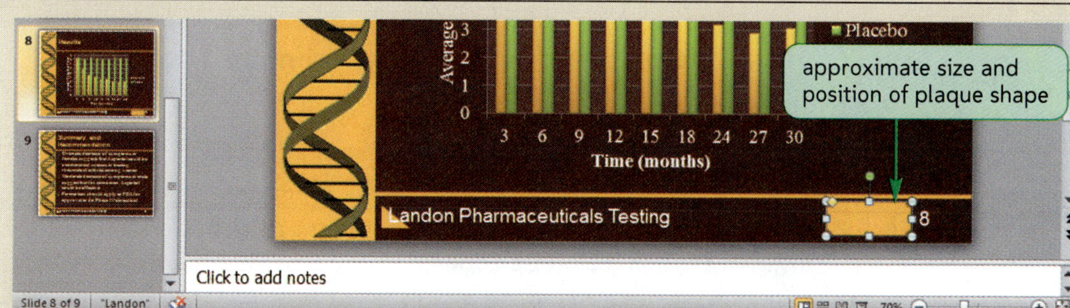


5. Click the **Drawing Tools Format** tab on the Ribbon.
6. In the Shape Styles group, click the **More** button, and then in the Shape Styles gallery, click the **Intense Effect – Orange, Accent 6** style (last column and the last row). Alyssa wants you to add text to the shape to remind her that clicking this shape will display the Contents slide.
7. With the shape still selected, type **Contents**.
8. If necessary, drag the middle sizing handle on the left or right edge of the shape until the shape is big enough to fit the word "Contents" on one line, and then deselect the shape. See Figure 4-21.

**Figure 4-21** Slide 8 with formatted shape

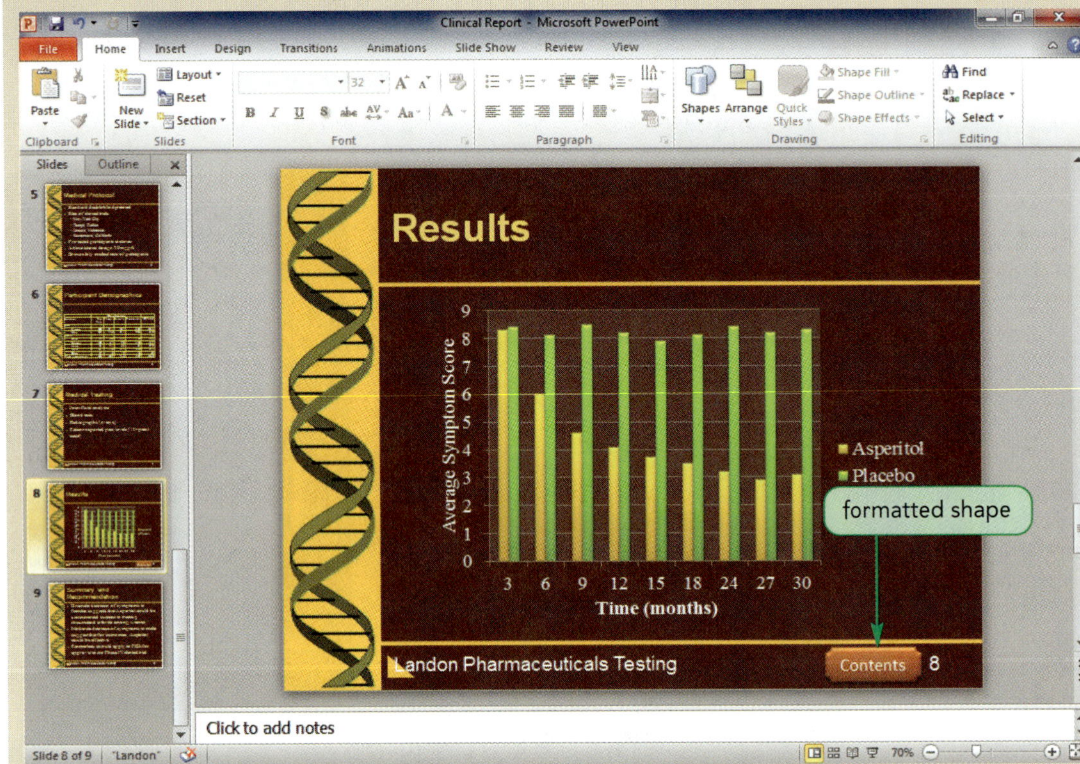


**Trouble?** If the size and position of the shape in your slide doesn't look like Figure 4-21, make any adjustments now.

You're now ready to make the Contents shape a hyperlink.

### To format the plaque shape as a hyperlink to Slide 2:

1. Click the edge of the plaque shape to select it.

   **Trouble?** If the insertion point is blinking in the text "Contents" you clicked inside the shape. Click the border of the shape to select the entire shape.

2. Click the **Insert** tab, and then click the **Hyperlink** button in the Links group. The Insert Hyperlink dialog box opens.

3. In the Link to panel on the left side of the dialog box, make sure **Place in This Document** is selected, and then click **2. Contents**. This is the target of the hyperlink.

4. Click the **OK** button. The dialog box closes and the shape is formatted as a hyperlink to Slide 2. Because you selected the shape, the entire shape is the hyperlink, not just the text inside the shape, and therefore, the text doesn't change to the green hyperlink color. Shapes and other non-text objects don't change color when they are converted to a hyperlink.

   **Trouble?** If the text "Contents" changed so that it is green and underlined, you did not select the entire shape. On the Quick Access Toolbar, click the Undo button, and then repeat Steps 1 through 4.

Now you're ready to test the results. You need to test the hyperlinks in Slide Show view because they aren't active in Normal view.

**To test the hyperlinks:**

1. Display **Slide 2** ("Contents") in the Slide pane, and then on the status bar, click the **Slide Show** button.
2. Click the **Results** hyperlink. PowerPoint displays Slide 8 ("Results").
3. Click the **Contents** hyperlink on Slide 8. PowerPoint again displays Slide 2. See Figure 4-22. The Results link text is now yellow, indicating that the hyperlink was followed.

**Figure 4-22** Slide 2 in Slide Show view with followed hyperlink

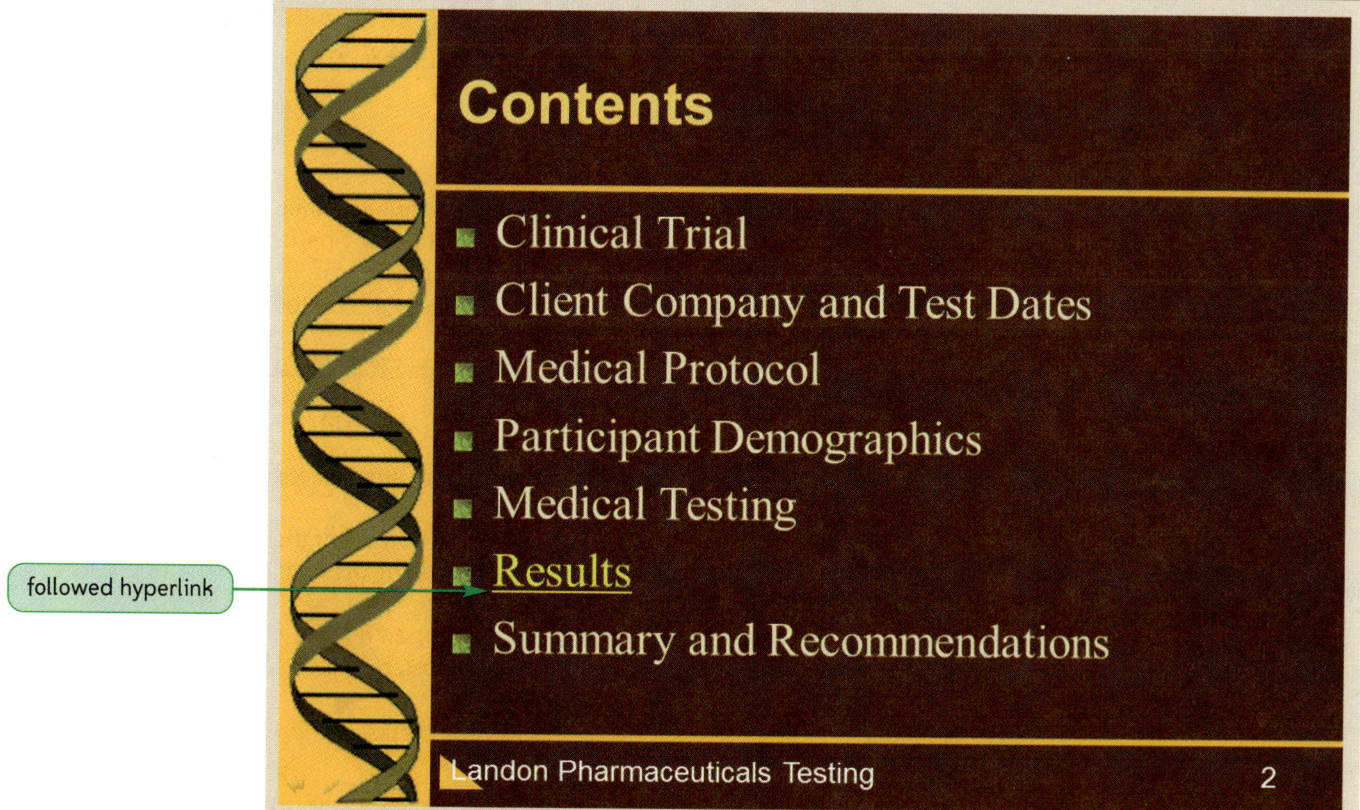


4. End the slide show to return to Slide 2 in Normal view.

In addition to creating hyperlinks on slides, you can add action buttons that have essentially the same effect. Alyssa wants you to insert an action button that will add a link to another presentation.

INSIGHT

### *Viewing a Slide Show with Linked Objects*

When you present a slide show using a presentation that contains a linked file, a copy of the linked file is not included within the PowerPoint file itself; only the path and filename for accessing the linked file are there. Any linked files in a presentation must be available on a disk so that PowerPoint can access them, so you should view the presentation on the system that will be used for running the slide show to make sure it has the necessary files and that the hyperlinks are set up properly. The links include the original path and filename to the files on the hard drive of the computer where you created the links. If linked objects don't work when you run the slide show, you'll have to edit the path so that PowerPoint can find the objects on your disk. To update the link path to a linked object in a presentation, click the File tab, click the Info tab in the navigation bar, and then under Related Documents in the right pane, click Edit Links to Files. In the Links dialog box that opens, click the Change Source button. If a hyperlink or an action button opens another file, you should check that path as well by right-clicking the hyperlink or action button, and then clicking Edit Hyperlink.

## Adding Action Buttons

An **action button** is a ready-made shape intended to be a hyperlink to other slides or documents. You can use one of the 12 action buttons available in the Shapes gallery, such as Action Button: Home or Action Button: Sound. Each action button can link to any slide or presentation; the various shapes simply offer variety in the way the buttons look.

REFERENCE

### *Adding an Action Button as a Link to Another Presentation*

- Click the Insert tab, and then click the Shapes button in the Illustrations group to open the Shapes gallery.
- Click an action button in the Action Buttons section at the bottom of the gallery.
- Position the pointer at the location in the slide where you want the action button to appear.
- In the Action Settings dialog box, click the Hyperlink to option button, click the Hyperlink to arrow, and then click Other PowerPoint Presentation to open the Hyperlink to Other PowerPoint Presentation dialog box.
- Select the presentation to which you want to link, and then click the OK button.
- Click the OK button in the Action Settings dialog box.
- Resize and reposition the action button icon as desired.

Alyssa wants you to add a hyperlink between her presentation and the Landon presentation, which gives the mission statement and contact information of Landon Pharmaceuticals Testing. You'll create a hyperlink to that presentation by adding an action button.

### To add an action button to link to the Landon presentation:

1. In the Illustrations group on the Insert tab, click the **Shapes** button. The gallery of shapes appears with the action buttons at the bottom.
2. Click the **Action Button: Document** button located fourth from the right in the bottom row of the gallery. The gallery closes and the pointer changes to +.

3. Click to the left of the slide number near the bottom of Slide 2, at about the same location where you placed the plaque shape on Slide 8. A large button with a document icon appears on the slide, and the Action Settings dialog box opens. See Figure 4-23.

**Figure 4-23** Action Settings dialog box

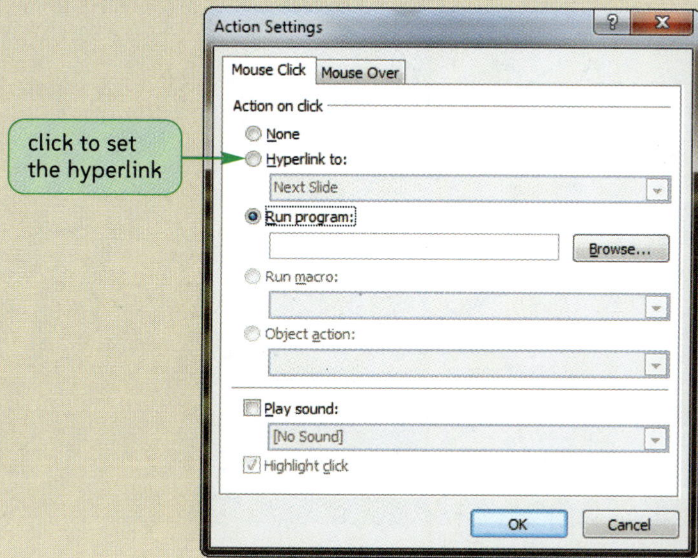


4. In the dialog box, click the **Hyperlink to** option button, click the **Hyperlink to** arrow, scroll down, and then click **Other PowerPoint Presentation**. The Hyperlink to Other PowerPoint Presentation dialog box opens.

5. Navigate to the PowerPoint4\Tutorial folder, if necessary, click **Landon**, and then click the **OK** button. The Hyperlink to Slide dialog box opens listing the four slides in the Landon presentation. See Figure 4-24. Alyssa wants to display Slide 2 of this presentation, which contains the company mission statement, when she clicks the Action Button.

**Figure 4-24** Hyperlink to Slide dialog box

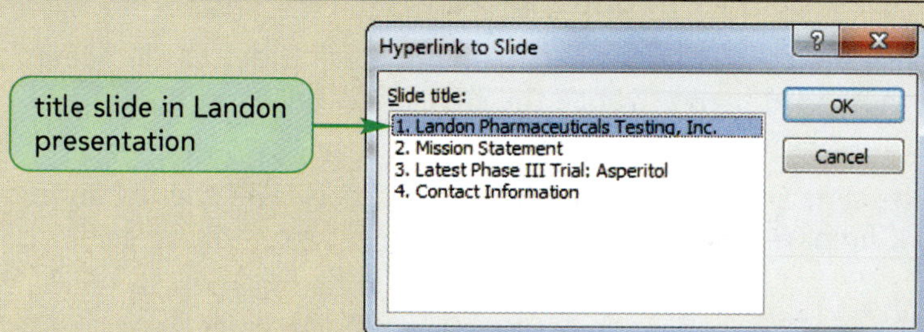


6. Click **2. Mission Statement**, click the **OK** button, and then click **OK** in the Actions Settings dialog box.

7. Adjust the size and position of the action button, as shown in Figure 4-25.

**Figure 4-25** Slide 2 with resized Action Button

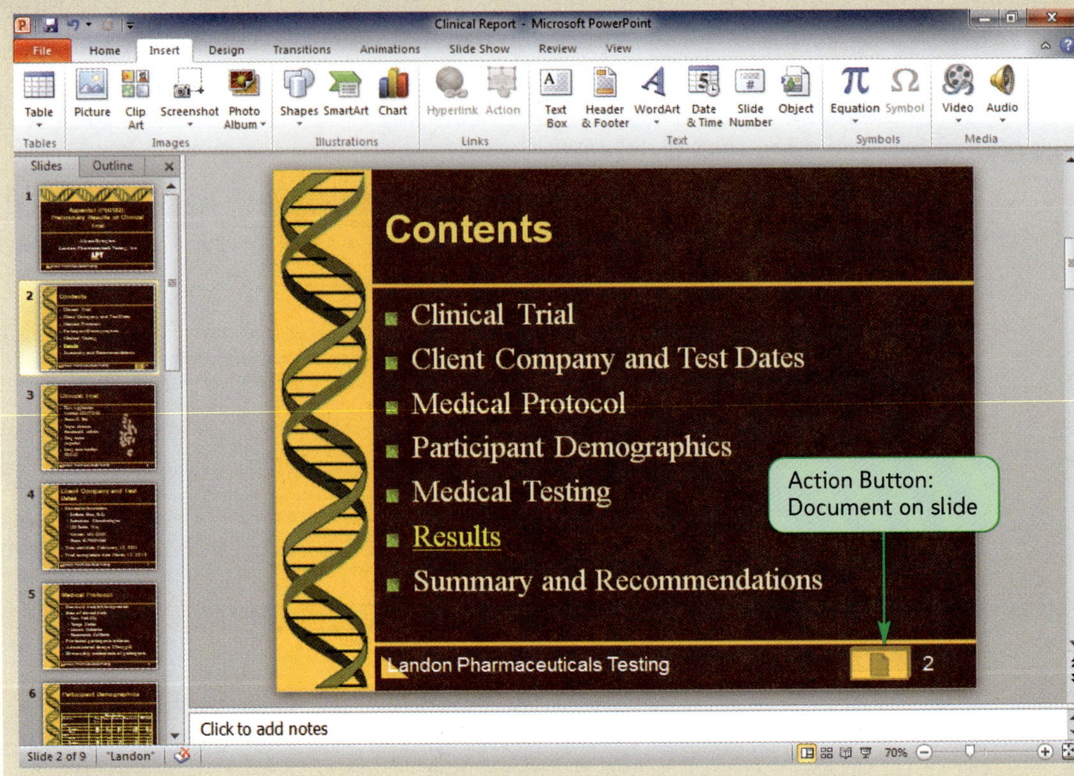


Now you need to test the action button.

**To test the action button:**

1. Switch to Slide Show view with Slide 2 ("Contents"), on the screen, and then click the **action button**. Slide 2 of the Landon presentation appears on the screen. Alyssa wants to jump to Slide 4, which contains contact information.
2. Right-click anywhere on the slide, point to **Go to Slide** on the shortcut menu, and then click **4 Contact Information**.
3. Advance the presentation to display the black slide that indicates the end of the slide show, and then advance the slide show once more. Slide 2 of the Clinical Report presentation appears again.
4. End the slide show, switch to Slide Sorter view, and then change the zoom level to **90%**. Compare your final presentation to Figure 4-26.

**TIP**

To return to the original presentation from a linked presentation, press the Esc key or right-click any slide, and then click End Show on the shortcut menu.

**Figure 4-26** **Presentation in Slide Sorter view**

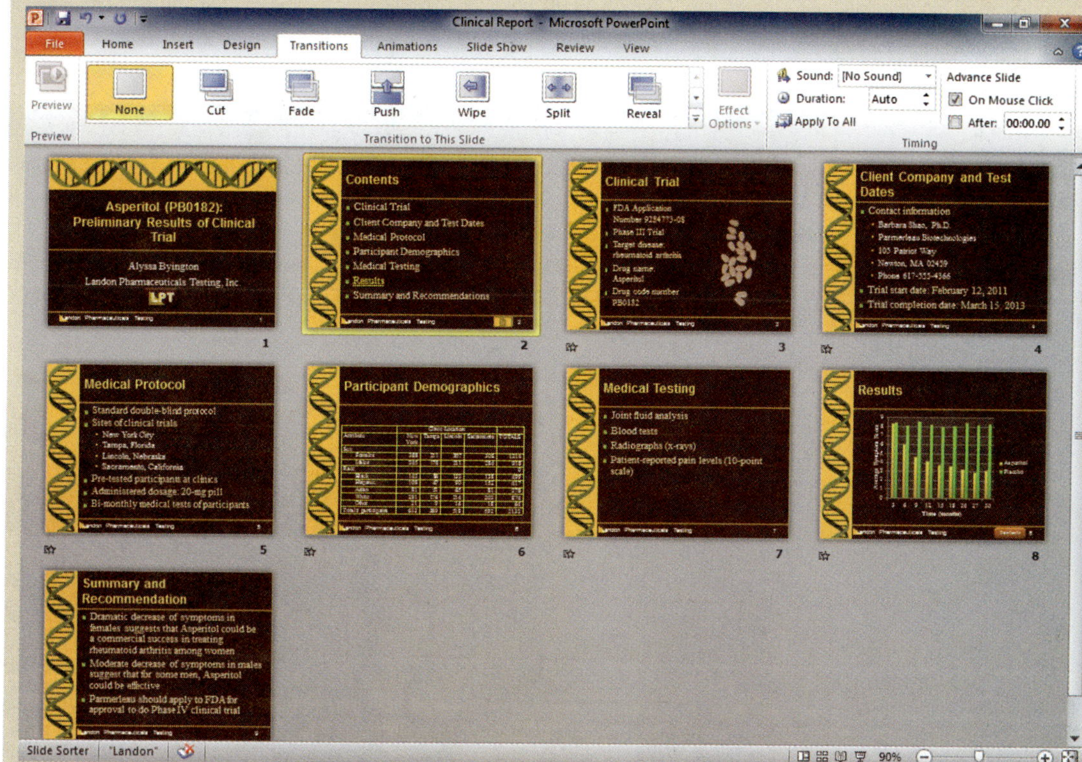


5. Save your changes.

Alyssa is pleased with the completed content of the presentation, which now includes an imported table from Word, an Excel chart, hyperlinks to other slides in the presentation, and an action button with a link to another presentation. In the next session you will get the presentation ready for delivery by checking and adjusting the slide transitions. You will customize handout masters and mark slides during a slide show, collaborate with others, and save the presentation in formats for distribution.

REVIEW

## *Session 4.1 Quick Check*

1. Describe how you use a Word outline to create slides in PowerPoint.
2. What does it mean to embed an object in a presentation?
3. If you modify the source file of a linked object, such as an Excel chart linked to a PowerPoint slide, what happens to the linked object in the PowerPoint slide?
4. Why would you link an object rather than embed it?
5. True or False. You can create a hyperlink to any other slide in a presentation.
6. What is a hyperlink?
7. What is an action button?

# SESSION 4.2 VISUAL OVERVIEW

Click the Show Markup button to hide or display comment thumbnails.

Comments are indicated by **comment thumbnails**, which contain the initials of the person who made the comment. Each person's comments appear in a different color in a comment thumbnail, which are numbered to indicate the order in which the comments were inserted by each person.

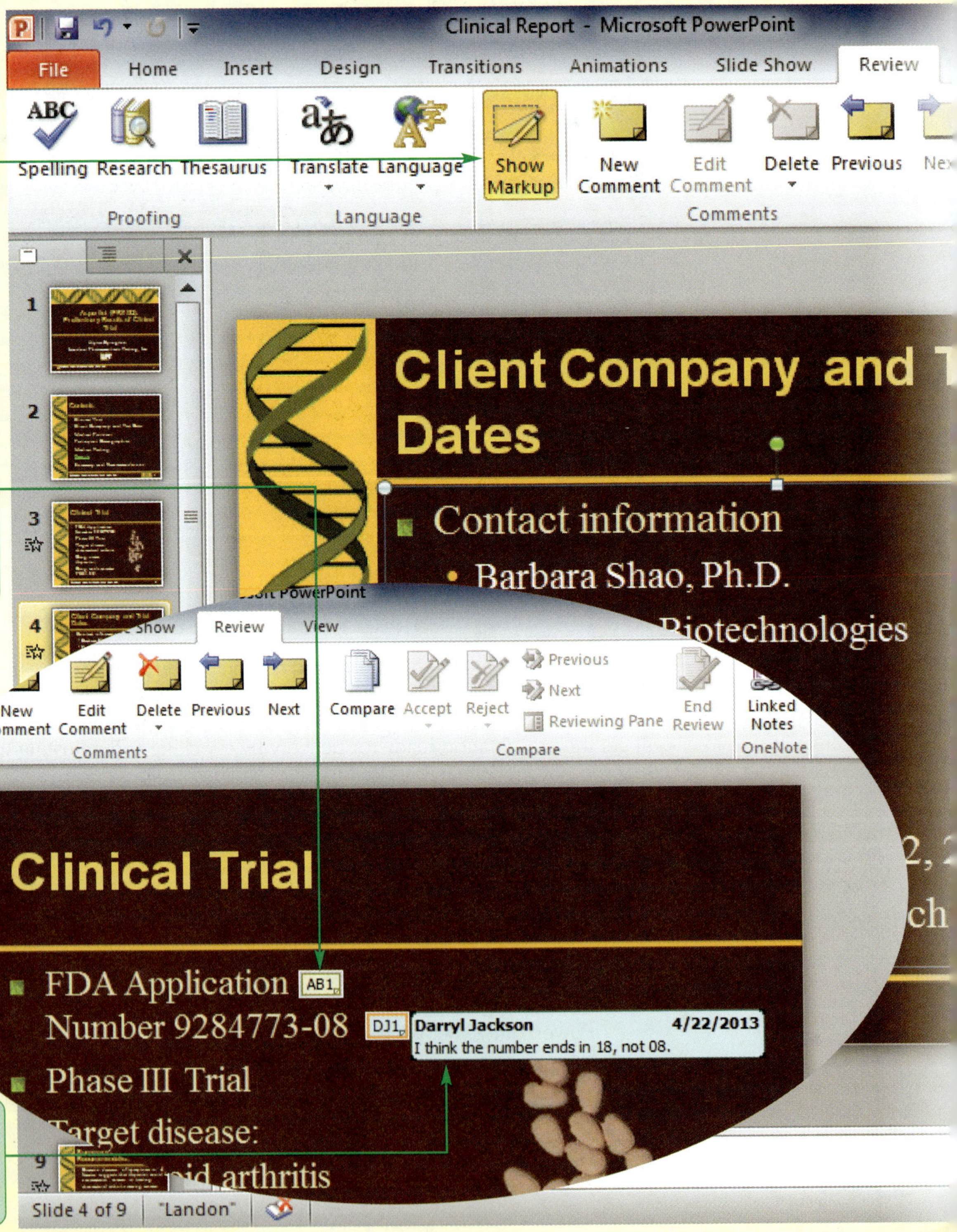


The **comment box** displays the comment, the name of the person who made the comment, and the date the comment was inserted.

# COMPARING AND COMMENTING

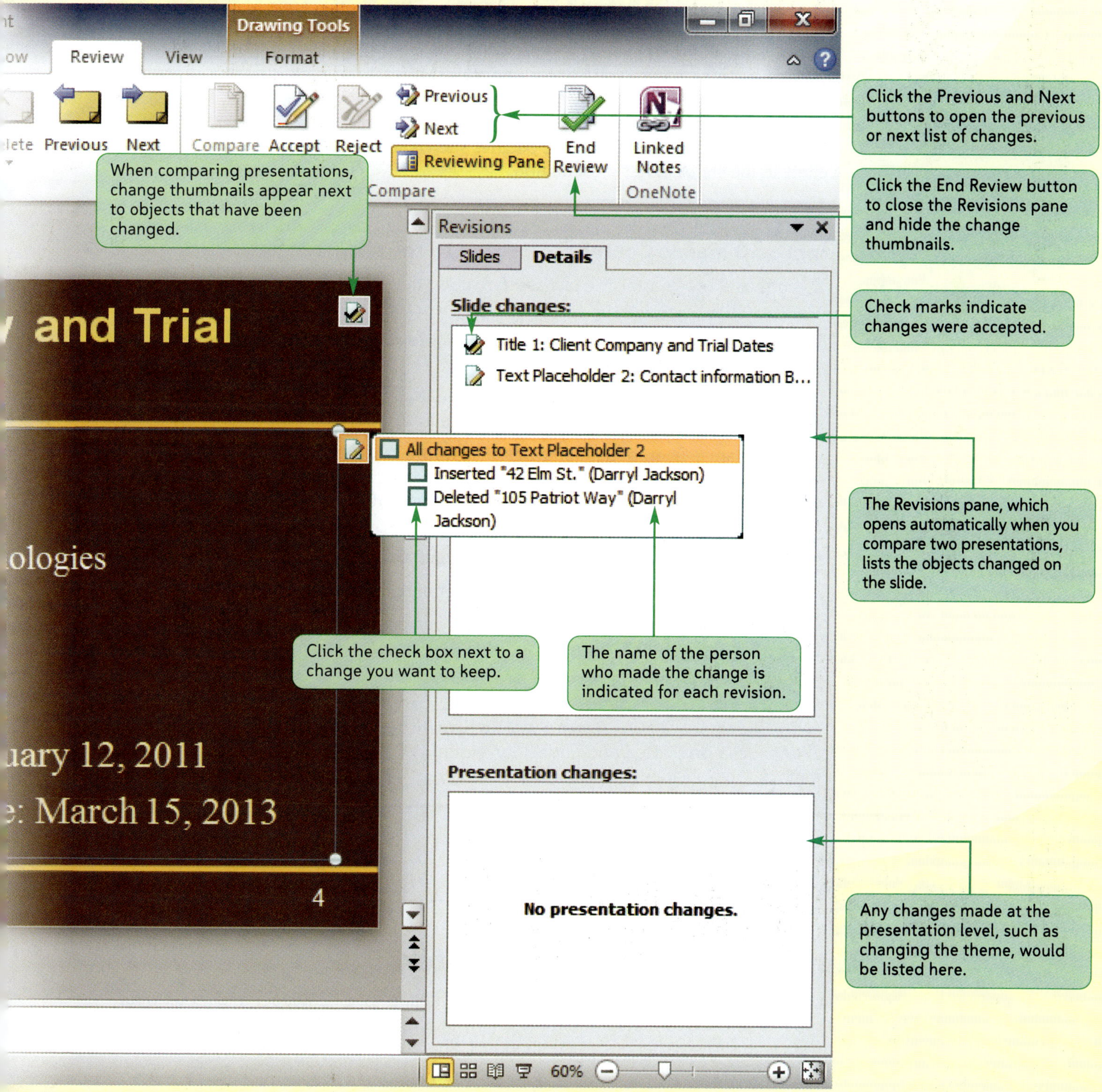

## Applying a Dynamic Content Transition

Most transitions make the slides appear as if they were in motion as they display during the slide show. To make only the slide content appear as if it were in motion, you can apply one of the transitions in the Dynamic Content section of the Transitions gallery. When an ordinary transition is applied to slides, the entire slide moves onto the screen with the selected transition. When a dynamic content transition is applied to slides, the content on the current slide transitions off the screen using the effect you chose, and at the same time, the slide background fades out. Then the slide background for the next slide fades in as the content for the next slide transitions onto the screen using the selected transition effect you chose. When slides have the same background, it appears as if the content transitions, but the slide background does not change.

Alyssa reviews the presentation and decides she wants you to add a dynamic transition effect to the slides in her presentation.

### To apply a Dynamic Content transition to the slides:

1. If you took a break after the last session, open the **Clinical Report** presentation located in the PowerPoint4\Tutorial folder included with your Data Files.
2. Switch to Normal view, if necessary, select **Slides 2-9** in the Slides tab, and then click the **Transitions** tab on the Ribbon.
3. In the Transition to This Slide group, click the **More** button. The Dynamic Content section is at the bottom of the Transitions gallery.
4. In the Dynamic Content section, click the **Rotate** transition. The transition previews by briefly displaying Slide 1 in the Slide pane, and then fading in the slide background of Slide 2 before rotating the content of Slide 2 onto the screen.
5. Click the **Slide Show** tab on the Ribbon, and then click the **From Beginning** button in the Start Slide Show group. Slide 1 appears in Slide Show view.
6. Advance the slide show. You see the same effect you saw in the preview.
7. Advance the slide show to display Slide 3 ("Clinical Trial") on the screen. Because Slide 3 has the same background as Slide 2, it appeared as if only the text were moving onto the screen.
8. Press the **Esc** key to end the slide show, and then display **Slide 2** ("Contents") in the Slide pane. Alyssa doesn't want a dynamic content transition applied to Slide 2 because Slide 2 and Slide 1 have different backgrounds, so she asks you to remove the transition from that slide.
9. Click the **Transitions** tab, click the **More** button in the Transition to This Slide group, and then click the **None** transition.

Next, you'll customize the handout masters.

## Customizing Handout Masters

You can customize handouts and notes pages to include specific header and footer information. You can also format handout masters with background styles and color.

Alyssa wants to give her audience handouts. She asks you to customize the Handout Masters.

**To customize the Handout Masters:**

1. Click the **Insert** tab on the Ribbon.
2. In the Text group, click the **Header & Footer** button, and then click the **Notes and Handouts** tab in the Header and Footer dialog box. The Page number check box is selected by default.
3. Click the **Footer** check box to select it, and then in the Footer box, type **Clinical Report of Asperitol**.
4. Click the **Apply to All** button, and then click the **View** tab on the Ribbon.
5. In the Master Views group, click the **Handout Master** button. The Handouts Master tab appears and becomes the active tab on the Ribbon, and the handout master appears in the window. Notice that the four options in the Placeholders group are selected, and in the handout master, placeholders appear in each corner of the master. The Footer placeholder contains the text you typed in the Header and Footer dialog box. See Figure 4-27.

**Figure 4-27** Handout master

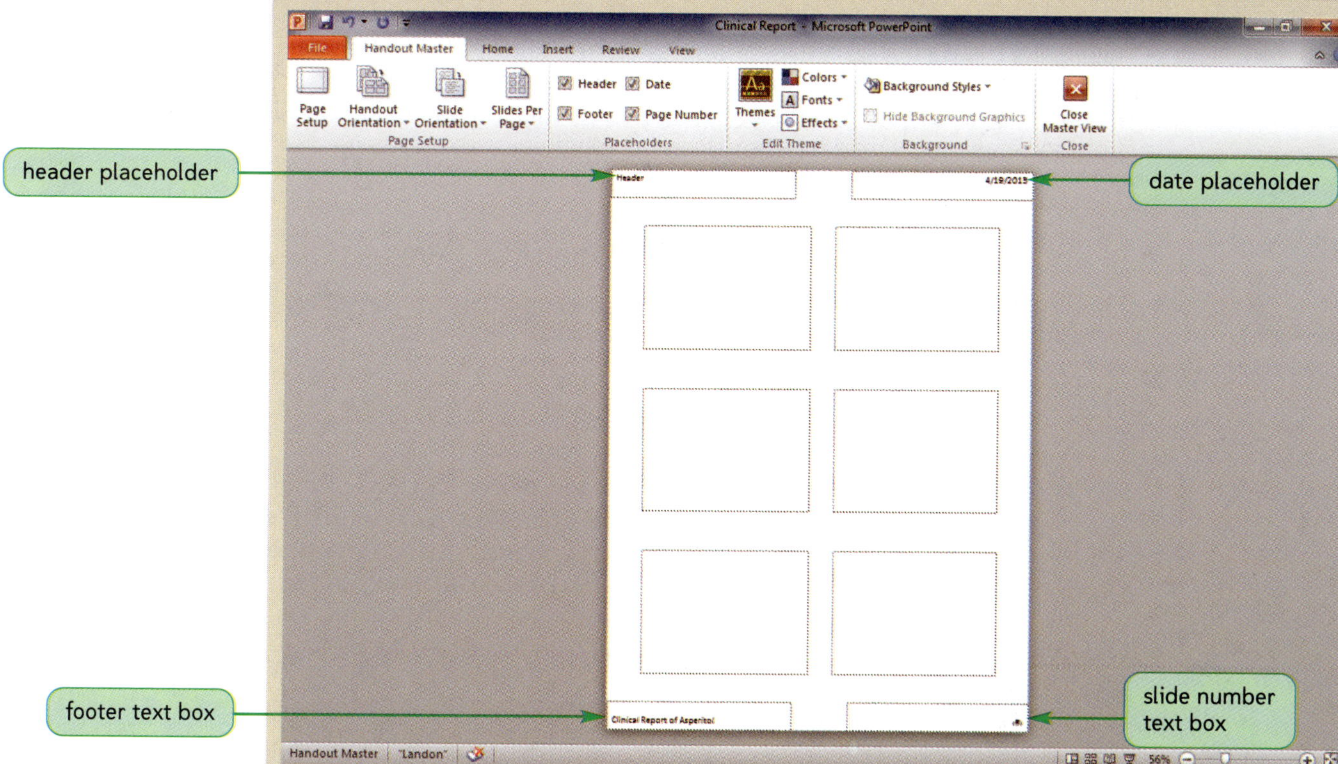


6. In the Placeholders group, click the **Header** check box to deselect it, and then click the **Date** check box to deselect it. The Header placeholder in the upper-left corner and the Date placeholder in the upper-right corner are removed from the master. The Footer and Page Number check boxes are still selected, and the corresponding text boxes still appear at the bottom of the master.

7. In the Background group, click the **Background Styles** button, and then click **Style 2** in the gallery. The gallery closes and the page background changes from white to light gray.

8. In the Close group, click the **Close Master View** button, and then save your changes.

Alyssa likes the customized handouts and makes printed color copies of them with nine slides per page so that all the presentation slides fit on one page.

Alyssa wants to be able to mark important information on a slide during the slide show. She can do this using the pointer as a pen.

## Marking Slides During a Slide Show

During a slide show, you can mark the slides to emphasize a point. The **pen** is a pointer that allows you to draw lines on the screen during a slide show. For example, you might use it to underline a word or phrase that you want to emphasize, or to circle a graphic that you want to point out. PowerPoint gives you the option of three pen types: Ballpoint Pen (draws thin, usually blue lines), Felt Tip Pen (draws thicker, usually red lines), and Highlighter (draws thick, usually yellow, transparent lines). You can change the ink color of any of the pens you select. You can also select the Eraser tool to remove pen lines that you've already drawn. After you go through a presentation and mark it, you have the choice of keeping the markings or discarding them.

**To use the pen to mark slides during the slide show:**

1. Display **Slide 8** ("Results") in the Slide pane, and then on the status bar, click the **Slide Show** button. Slide 8 appears in Slide Show view.

2. Move the mouse until you see the mouse pointer. The pointer appears on the screen, but it will disappear again if you don't move the mouse for a couple seconds.

3. Right-click anywhere on the screen, point to **Pointer Options** on the shortcut menu, and then click **Pen**. You can use the Pointer Options shortcut menu to select the type of pen, ink color, and other options. After you have selected the Pen, the mouse pointer becomes a small, red dot. By clicking and dragging the pen on the screen, you can draw lines.

4. Click and drag to draw a circle around the last set of columns to draw attention to it. See Figure 4-28.

**Figure 4-28** Slide 8 in Slide Show view with Pen mark

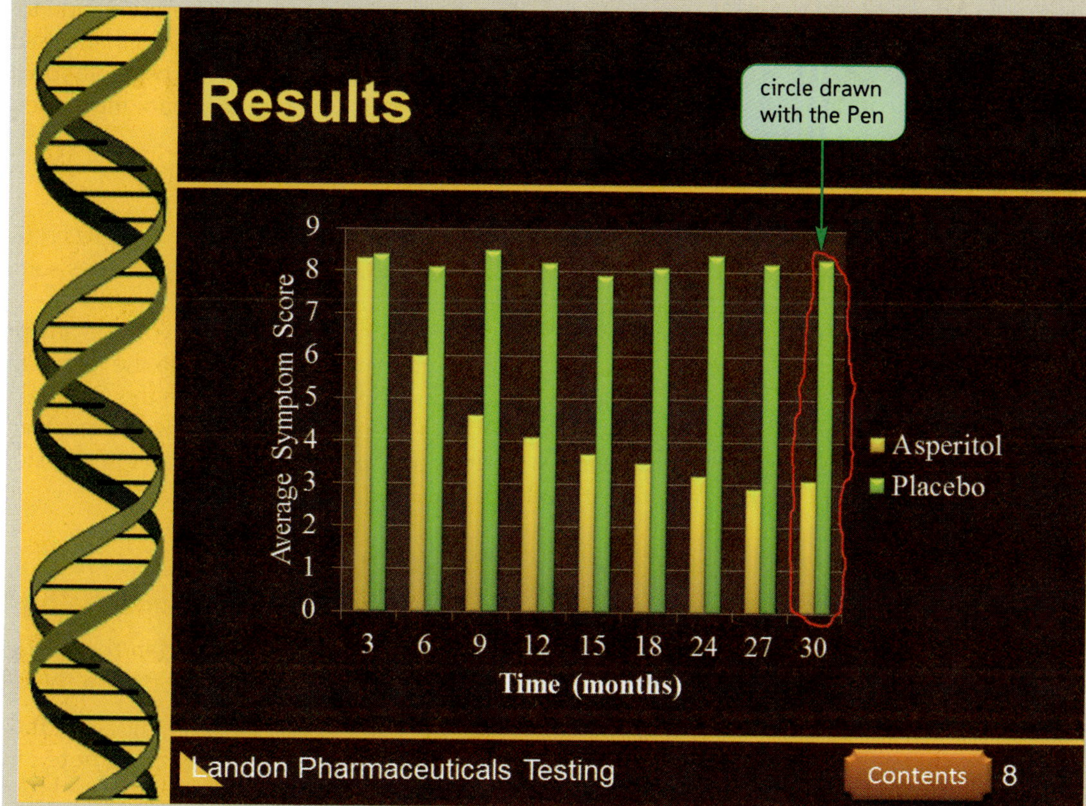


5. Press the **spacebar** to move to Slide 9. Note that you can't click the mouse button to proceed through the slide show while a pointer pen is selected.
6. Repeat Step 3 to select the Pen again, and then starting in the yellow panel on the left, draw an arrow pointing to the first bulleted item.
7. Right-click anywhere on the slide, point to **Pointer Options** on the shortcut menu, and then click **Arrow**. The mouse pointer changes back to the arrow pointer. Now you can click the mouse button to advance the slide show.
8. Click the mouse button to end the slide show and display the black screen, and then click again to return to Normal view. A dialog box opens asking if you want to keep your ink annotations.
9. Click the **Keep** button. Slide 8 ("Results") appears in Normal view. Because you chose to keep the annotations, the red circle you drew around the last set of columns is on the slide. The marks you drew in Slide Show view can be deleted just like any object on a slide.
10. Click the red circle you drew to select it, and then press the **Delete** key. The circle is deleted.
11. Display **Slide 9** ("Summary and Recommendation") in the Slide pane. Notice that the arrow that you drew is on the slide. You'll keep this annotation in the presentation for now.
12. Save your changes.

**TIP**

If you want to skip a slide during a slide show, in Normal view, click the Slide Show tab, and then click the Hide Slide button in the Set Up group.

# Sharing and Collaborating with Others

You can send a presentation to colleagues for review. They can make changes and add comments that you can then review. You can also examine a presentation to make sure it doesn't contain private information or to see if it contains features that are supported by previous versions of PowerPoint. Finally, if you want to send a presentation for review but do not want to allow anyone to make any changes, you can mark the presentation as final.

## Adding Comments to a Presentation

It can be helpful to have colleagues review your presentation and give you suggestions on how to improve it or to check it for accuracy. If a colleague notices something, he or she can insert a comment describing the issue.

Alyssa asks you to review her presentation and comment if you see any problems. When you insert a comment in a presentation, it is labeled with the name and initials of the person listed in the User Name and in the Initials box on the General tab in the PowerPoint Options dialog box. You can change this to your own name. You'll do this now.

*Note*: If you are working in a lab or on a public computer, get permission from your instructor before completing the following steps.

**To change the user name in the PowerPoint Options dialog box:**

1. Click the **File** tab, and then click the **Options** command in the navigation bar. The PowerPoint Options dialog box opens with General selected in the left panel.
2. Note the name currently in the User name box and the initials in the Initials box. If the name and initials in these boxes are not yours, make a note of them as you will need to restore these later.
3. If necessary, click in the **User name** box, delete the current name, and then type your name.
4. If necessary, click in the **Initials** box, delete the current initials, and then type your initials.
5. Click the **OK** button to close the dialog box.

Now that your name and initials are listed in the PowerPoint Options dialog box, you can insert a comment.

**To insert a comment in Slide 3:**

1. Display **Slide 3** ("Clinical Trial") in the Slide pane, and then click the **Review** tab on the Ribbon.
2. In the Comments group, click the **New Comment** button. A blank comment box is inserted in the document with the insertion point inside it. See Figure 4-29. The current date appears in the upper-right of the comment box. The name in the User name box in the General tab in the PowerPoint Options dialog box appears in the upper-left of the comment box. (If you performed the previous set of steps, then this should be your name.) Also, a comment thumbnail to the left of the comment box contains your initials. The number 1 in the comment thumbnail indicates that this is the first comment inserted in this presentation.

**Figure 4-29** New blank comment inserted in Slide 3

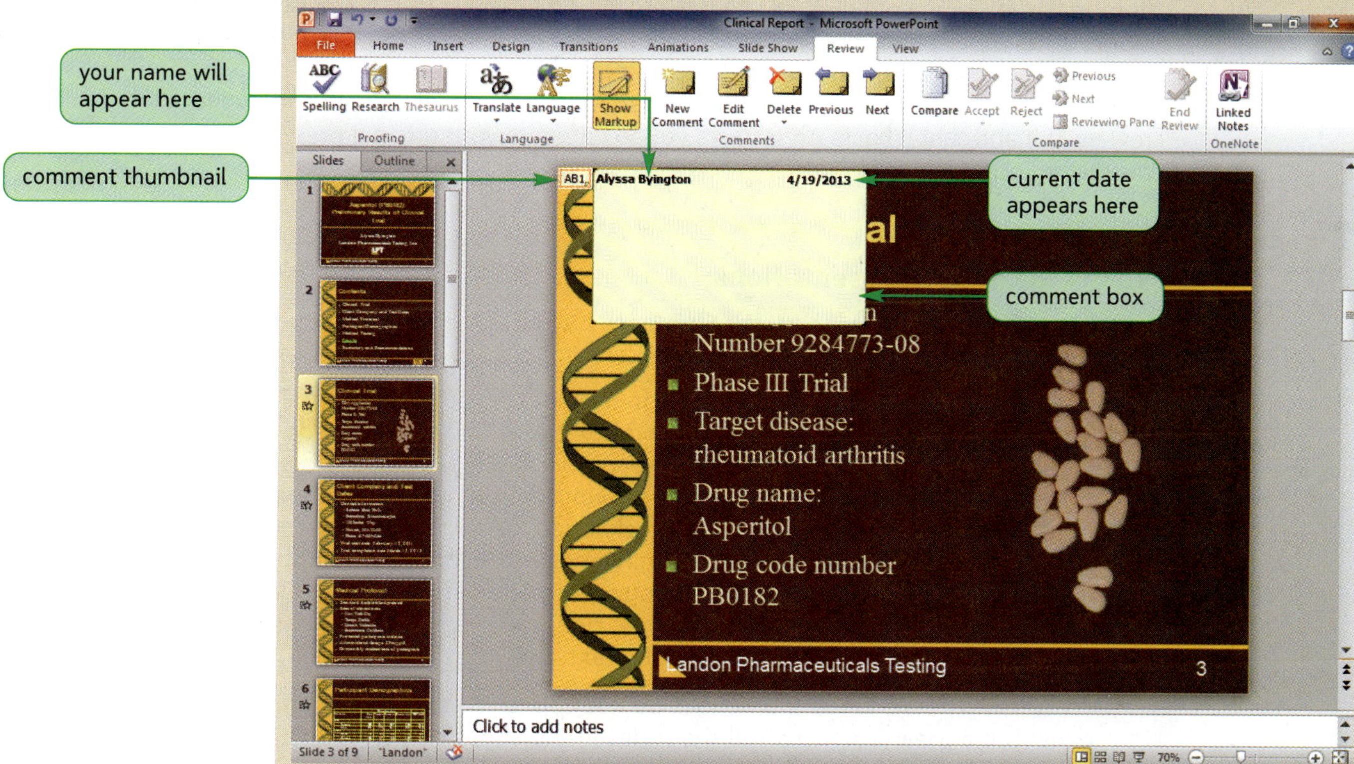


3. Type **Is the number correct?**
4. Click outside the comment box. The comment box closes and you see only the comment thumbnail.

You realize that there are two numbers on Slide 3—the FDA Application Number and the drug code number. Alyssa suggests you edit the comment to make it clearer, and then position it next to the bulleted item it references. You'll edit the comment and then reposition the comment thumbnail.

**TIP**

You can also right-click a comment thumbnail, and then click Edit Comment on the shortcut menu.

## To edit and position the comment in Slide 3:

1. Click the comment thumbnail. A comment balloon opens displaying the comment you typed.
2. In the Comments group, click the **Edit Comment** button. The comment box appears with the insertion point in it.
3. Position the insertion point immediately before the word "number," type **FDA Application**, and then press the **spacebar**.
4. Click outside the comment box to close it.
5. Drag the **comment** thumbnail to position it to the right of "FDA Application" in the first bulleted item.
6. Save your changes.

The Compare process (in the next set of steps) can be unpredictable so save before proceeding.

## Comparing Presentations

After a colleague reviews a presentation, you can compare it to your original presentation using the Compare button on the Review tab. After you select the revised presentation, a Revisions pane appears on the right listing the changes. You can select each insertion and deletion and decide whether to accept it.

Alyssa sent the presentation to Darryl Jackson, the lead researcher at Landon. He reviewed it and sent it back. Alyssa asks you to compare your original presentation with his revised presentation.

### To compare two presentations:

1. In the Compare group, click the **Compare** button. The Choose File to Merge with Current Presentation dialog box opens.
2. Navigate to the PowerPoint4\Tutorial folder, if necessary, click **DJ Review**, and then click the **Merge** button. The dialog box closes and the first slide that contains a difference between the two presentations, Slide 4 ("Client Company and Test Dates"), appears in the Slide pane. Two change thumbnails appear on the slide, one next to each object that was changed by Darryl. The changes associated with the first thumbnail are listed in a changes box next to the thumbnail. Darryl's name—the person who made the change—appears in parentheses after each change. The Revisions pane opens on the right. See Figure 4-30. Alyssa agrees with the change Darryl made to the title text.

   **Trouble?** If the change thumbnails do not appear on the slide in the Slide pane, but appear instead on all the slides in the Slides tab, close the presentation without saving changes, open the presentation DJ Review, located in the PowerPoint4\Tutorial folder, and then save it as DJ Review Copy to the same folder. Re-open the Clinical Report presentation, and then repeat Steps 1 and 2, but this time in Step 2, click DJ Review Copy. You might need to do this any time you compare files so that both files were saved on the same machine.

   **Trouble?** If the change icons don't appear on your screen, click the Show Markup button in the Comments group to select it.

   **Trouble?** If Slide 3 appears in the Slide pane listing the comments in the Revisions pane, click the Slide 4 thumbnail in the Slides tab, and then, if necessary, click the top change thumbnail to display the list of changes.

**Figure 4-30** Changes listed on Slide 4

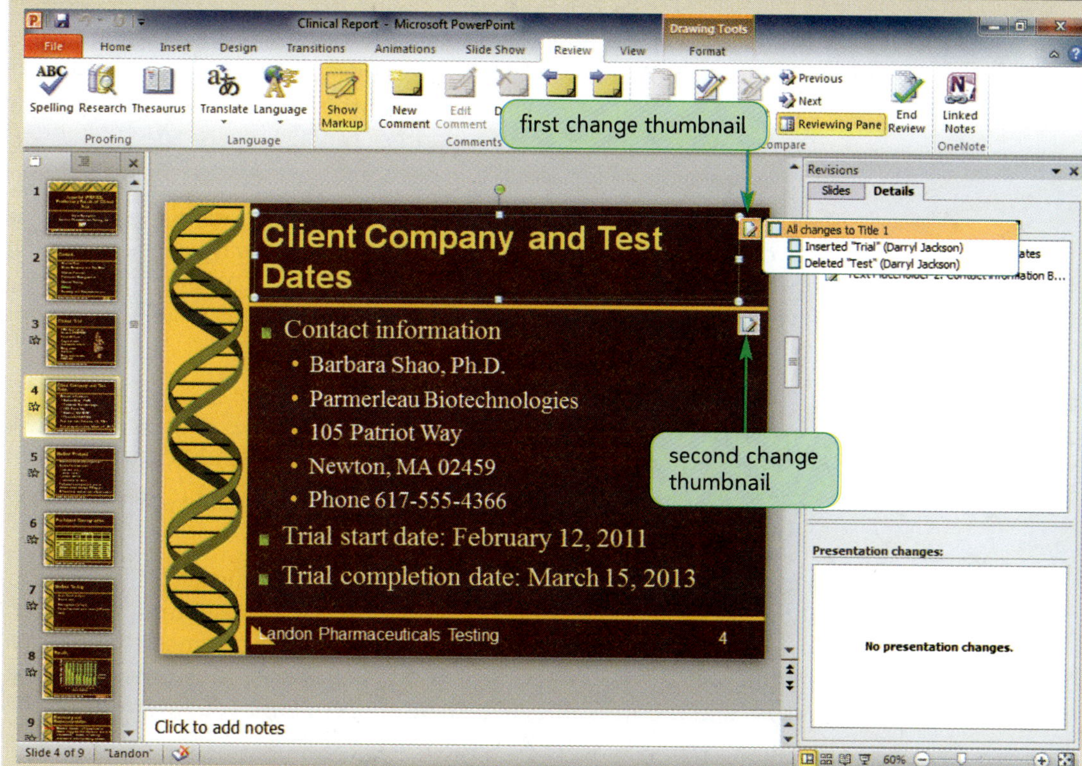


3. In the change box, click the **Inserted "Trial" (Darryl Jackson)** check box to select it. The word "Trial" appears in the title text box.
4. In the change box, click the **Deleted "Test" (Darryl Jackson)** check box. The word "Test" in the title text box is deleted. Notice that the check box next to All changes to Title 1 is also selected, and the change thumbnail now has a check mark on it. Now you'll examine the next change on the slide.

**TIP**

You can also click a change thumbnail to open the change box.

5. In the Compare group, click the **Next** button. The change box next to the title text box closes. The next change box, in this case adjacent to the content text box, opens. Now you can see the changes listed in the Revision pane.

   **Trouble?** If Slide 3 appears in the Slide pane listing comments in the Revisions pane, you clicked the Next button in the Comments group instead of clicking the Next comment in the Compare group. Repeat Step 5 two or three times as needed to display Slide 4 in the Slide pane with the list of changes associated with the second change thumbnail displayed, and then continue with Step 6.
6. Click the **All changes to Text Placeholder 2** check box. In the slide, "105 Patriot Way" changes to "42 Elm St." In this case, Darryl is mistaken; Parmerleau Technologies recently moved to Patriot Way.
7. Click the **All changes to Text Placeholder 2** check box to deselect it and undo the change on the slide.
8. In the Compare group, click the **Next** button. A dialog box opens stating that there are no more changes and asking if you want to continue from the beginning of the change list. You don't need to review the changes again.
9. Click the **Cancel** button. You are finished reviewing the changes in the presentation.

10. In the Compare group, click the **End Review** button. A dialog box opens confirming that you want to end the review and warning that any unapplied changes will be discarded.
11. Click the **Yes** button. The dialog box closes, the Revisions pane closes, and the change icons disappear. The change to the title that you accepted appears in the title text object, and the street address remains unchanged.

The Compare command does not list comments that are in the revised presentation, so after you compare two presentations, you should always check to see if the person who reviewed the presentation inserted any comments. You can decide what to do based on the comments, and then you can delete the comments when you are finished. Alyssa asks you to review the comments in the presentation next.

### To review and delete a comment in the presentation:

1. Display **Slide 1** (the title slide) in the Slide pane. You'll start your search for comments from the beginning of the presentation.
2. In the Comments group, click the **Next** button. Slide 3 ("Clinical Trial") appears in the Slide pane, and the first comment in the presentation, the comment you inserted next to "FDA Application," is open in a comment balloon. Notice that another comment appears on this slide as well. The comment contains Darryl's initials and is a different color than the comment you inserted.
3. Click the **DJ1** comment thumbnail. The comment balloon for your comment closes and the comment balloon for Darryl's comment opens. Alyssa double-checked the number and tells you that it is correct.
4. In the Comments group, click the **Delete** button. The selected comment is deleted.
5. In the Comments group, click the **Next** button. The comment balloon associated with your comment opens again.
6. In the Comments group, click the **Next** button. A dialog box opens asking if you want to continue from the beginning of the change list.
7. Click the **Cancel** button. The dialog box closes.

Now you need to change the user name and initials back to their original values.

### To change the user name in the PowerPoint Options dialog box back to its original value:

1. Click the **File** tab, and then click the **Options** command in the navigation bar.
2. If necessary, click in the **User name** box, delete the current name, and then type the name that was originally in this box.
3. If necessary, click in the **Initials** box, delete the current initials, and then type the initials originally in this box.
4. Click the **OK** button to close the dialog box.

## Using the Document Inspector

The **Document Inspector** is a tool you can use to check a presentation for hidden data, such as the author's name and other personal information, as well as comments, objects that are in the presentation but don't appear on a slide, hidden objects on slides, speaker notes, and custom data used for labeling objects and text in the presentation. Alyssa wants you to check the Clinical Report presentation for hidden data.

### To check the document using the Document Inspector:

1. Click the **File** tab. Backstage view appears with the Info tab selected in the navigation bar. Backstage view displays information about the presentation. In the right pane, you see the file properties, including the number of slides and the author name. In the left pane, under Information about Clinical Report, in the Prepare for Sharing section, a bulleted list identifies hidden information and potential problems for people with vision disabilities. The types of hidden data found in the presentation are listed in the Prepare for Sharing section. See Figure 4-31.

**Figure 4-31** Info tab in Backstage view

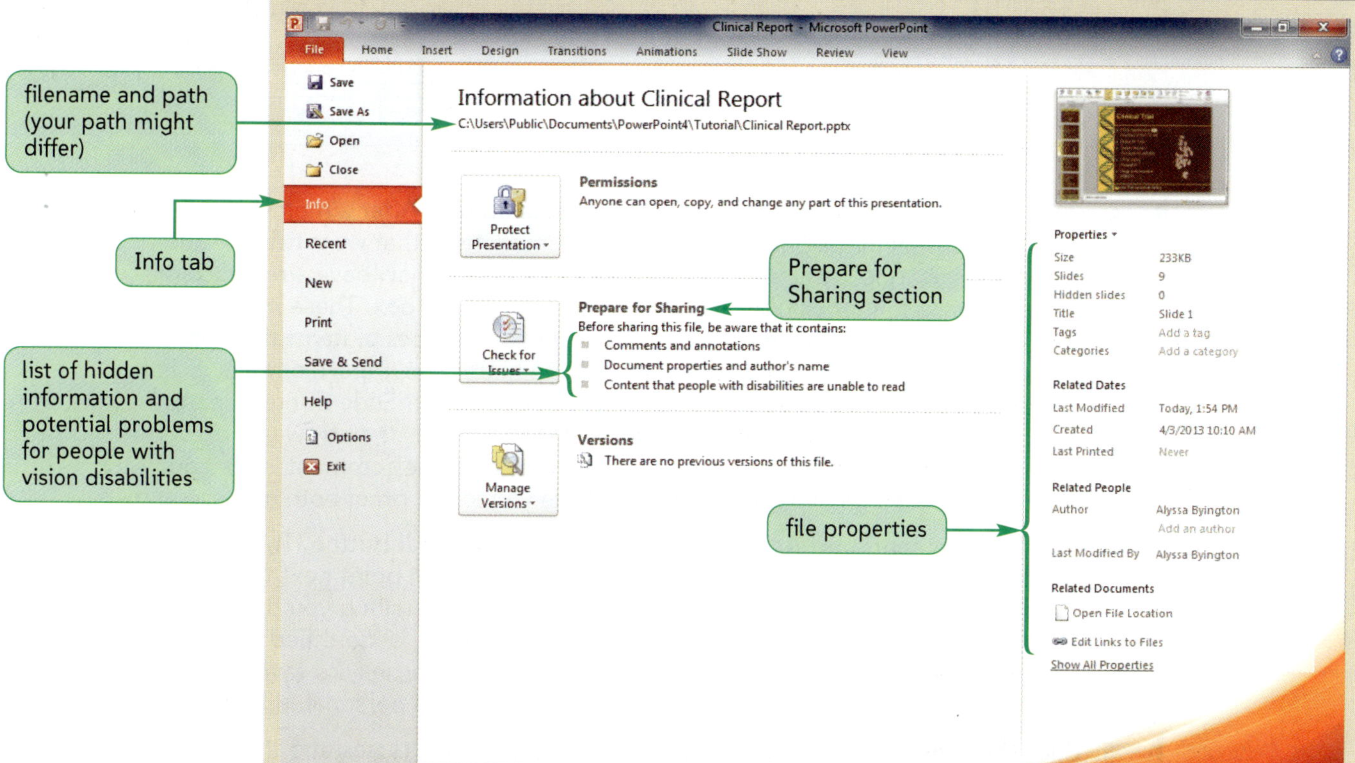


2. In the Prepare for Sharing section, click the **Check for Issues** button, and then click **Inspect Document**. The Document Inspector dialog box opens.
3. Click any of the check boxes in this dialog box that are not checked. See Figure 4-32.

**Figure 4-32** Document Inspector dialog box

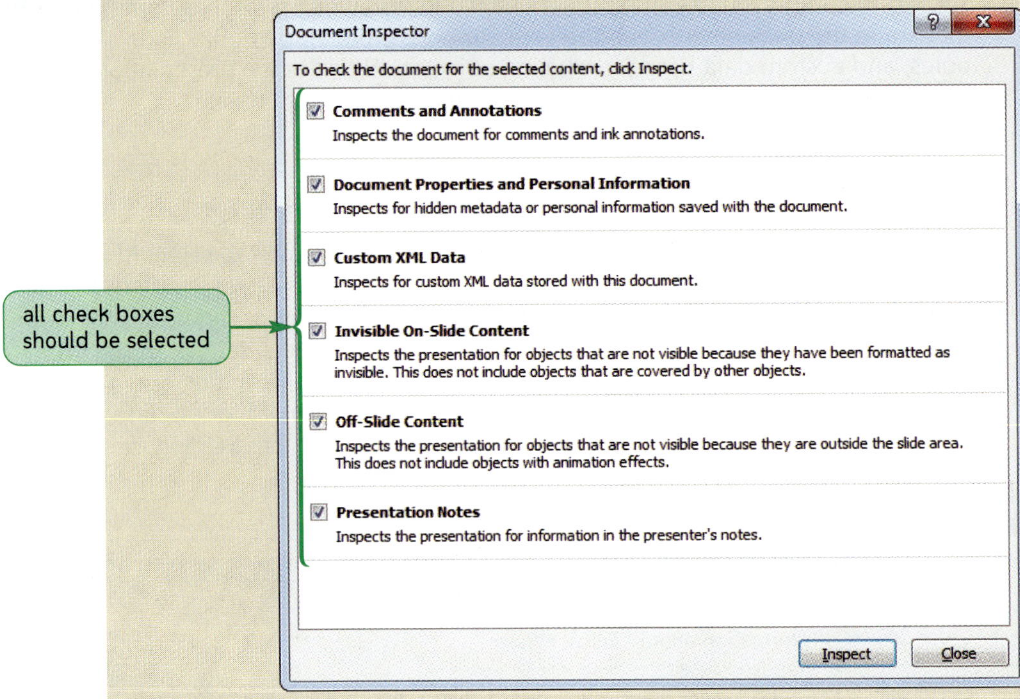


4. Click the **Inspect** button at the bottom of the dialog box. After a moment, the Document Inspector displays the results. The same items that were listed in the Prepare for Sharing section on the Info tab in Backstage view have a red exclamation point next to them in the Document Inspector dialog box. These items have a Remove All button next to them. Look over the other types of items that the Document Inspector checks. For example, if you happen to import, embed, or link an object that extends beyond the edges of a slide, the Off-Slide Content feature would have detected the problem. The annotation found is the arrow you drew on Slide 9 when you used the pen in Slide Show view, and the comment is the comment you inserted on Slide 3. Alyssa would like you to get rid of both of these items.
5. Next to Comments and Annotations, click the **Remove All** button. The button disappears, a blue check mark replaces the red exclamation point next to Comments and Annotations, and a message appears in that section telling you that all items were successfully removed. Alyssa doesn't mind that she is identified as the author of the presentation or that other document properties are saved with the file, so you will not remove the document properties and personal information.
6. Click the **Close** button in the dialog box. The dialog box closes and the Info tab in Backstage view is visible again.
7. Click the **File** tab to exit Backstage view. Slide 3 ("Clinical Trial") appears again. The comment you made no longer appears on this slide.

8. Display **Slide 9** ("Summary and Recommendation") in the Slide pane. The arrow that you drew using the Pen in Slide Show view is no longer on the slide.
9. Save your changes.

INSIGHT

### *Making a Presentation Accessible to People with Vision Disabilities*

The Accessibility Checker allows you to check a presentation for content that someone with a vision disability would have trouble seeing or reading. It lists each error and offers suggestions on how to fix it. To check the presentation for content that is difficult for people with a vision disability to read, display the Info tab in Backstage view. In the Prepare for Sharing section, click the Check for Issues button, and then click Check Accessibility. Backstage view will close, and the presentation appears in Normal view with the Accessibility Checker pane open on the right displaying a list of the errors found. Click each error to see an explanation of the problem in the bottom part of the pane, along with instructions on how to fix it.

## Identifying Features Not Supported by Previous Versions

Alyssa realizes that some of her clients and colleagues haven't yet upgraded to PowerPoint 2010, so she asks you to check the Clinical Report presentation for features not supported by previous versions. For this purpose, you'll use the Microsoft PowerPoint Compatibility Checker.

**To check for features not supported by previous versions of PowerPoint:**

1. Click the **File** tab on the Ribbon to display the Info tab in Backstage view.
2. In the Prepare for Sharing section, click the **Check for Issues** button, and then click **Check Compatibility**. Backstage view closes, and after a moment, the Microsoft PowerPoint Compatibility Checker dialog box opens listing features that aren't supported by earlier versions of PowerPoint. See Figure 4-33. Look over the features in the dialog box. Most of the incompatible features would probably show up properly; you just wouldn't be able to edit them. The last issue listed warns you that the transition effect you selected will not appear in earlier versions of PowerPoint. You inform Alyssa of these incompatibilities so she can decide later if she wants to save the presentation in an earlier format. Notice also that the Check compatibility when saving in PowerPoint 97-2003 formats check box is selected. This means that if you save the presentation in the format compatible with PowerPoint versions 97 through 2003, the Compatibility Checker will run automatically.

**Figure 4-33** Microsoft PowerPoint Compatibility Checker dialog box

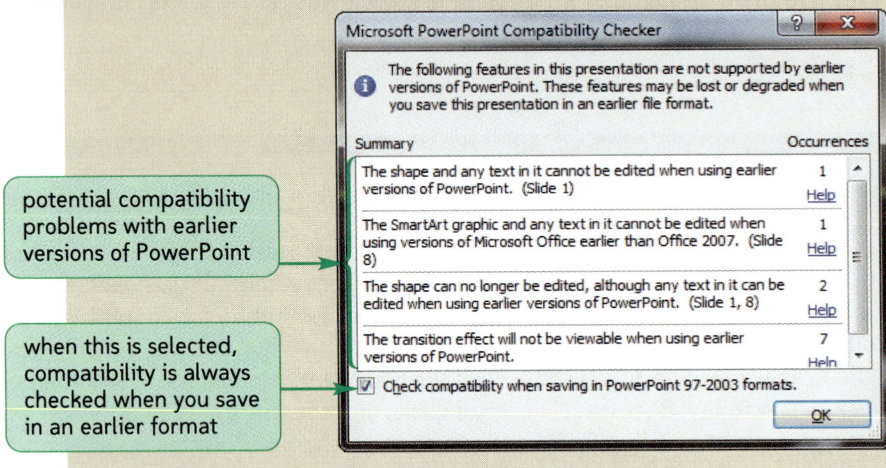


3. Click the **OK** button. The dialog box closes.

## Marking the Presentation as Final

Alyssa wants to send a preview of the presentation to her colleagues at Landon, but she does not want them to make changes. One way to prevent people from making changes to a presentation is to mark it as final. This makes the presentation "read-only," which means that others can read but not modify it. After you mark a presentation as final, you can turn off this status, and then edit the presentation, but this will remove the Marked as Final status. You'll mark Clinical Report as final for Alyssa. First, you'll change the name in the subtitle text box to your own name.

**To mark the presentation as final:**

1. Display **Slide 1** (the title slide) in the Slide pane, and then replace "Alyssa Byington" with your name.
2. Click the **File** tab. Backstage view appears again with the Info tab selected. In the Permissions section, the message tells you that anyone can open, copy, and change the presentation.
3. In the Permissions section, click the **Protect Presentation** button, and then click **Mark as Final**. A dialog box opens stating that the presentation will be marked as final and then saved.
4. Click the **OK** button. The dialog box closes and another dialog box opens telling you that the document has been marked as final.

   **Trouble?** If the dialog box stating that the document has been marked as final does not appear, someone clicked the Don't show this message again check box in that dialog box. Skip Step 5.

5. Click the **OK** button. The Permissions section now indicates that the presentation has been marked as final. See Figure 4-34.

**Figure 4-34 Info tab after presentation is marked as final**

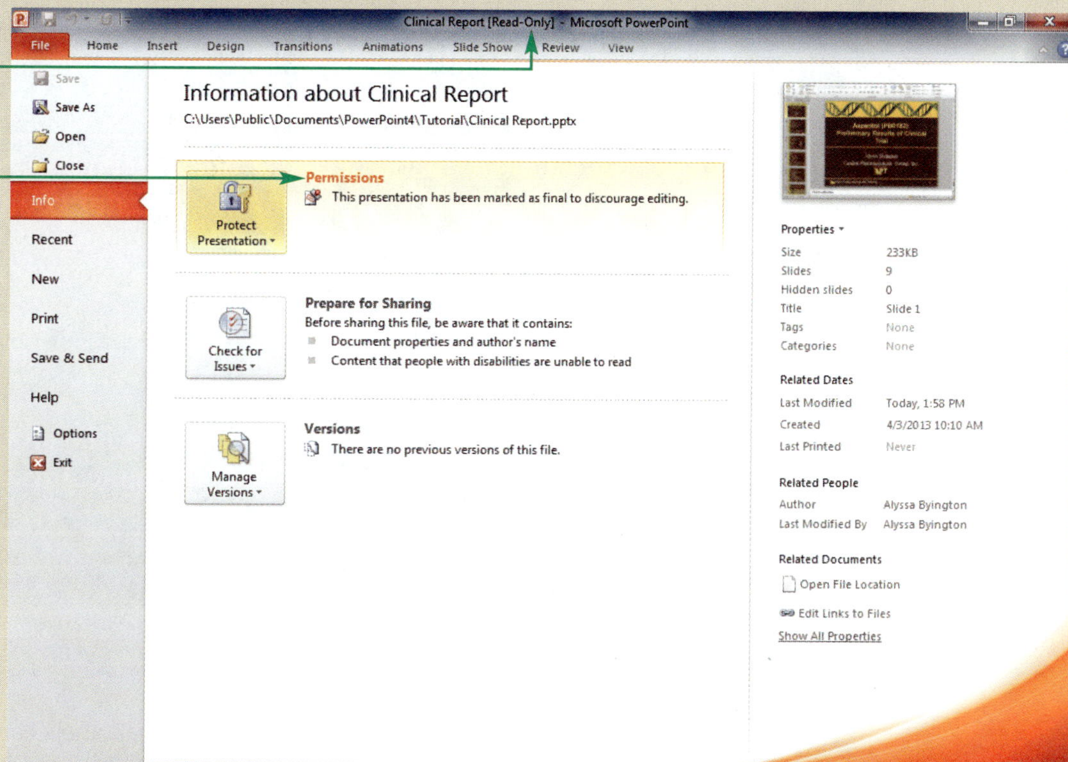


6. Click the **File** tab on the Ribbon. Backstage view closes and the presentation appears in Normal view. A yellow Marked as Final bar appears in place of the Ribbon, the Marked as Final icon appears in the status bar, and "Read-Only" appears in the title bar. See Figure 4-35.

**Figure 4-35** **Presentation in Normal view after it is marked as final**

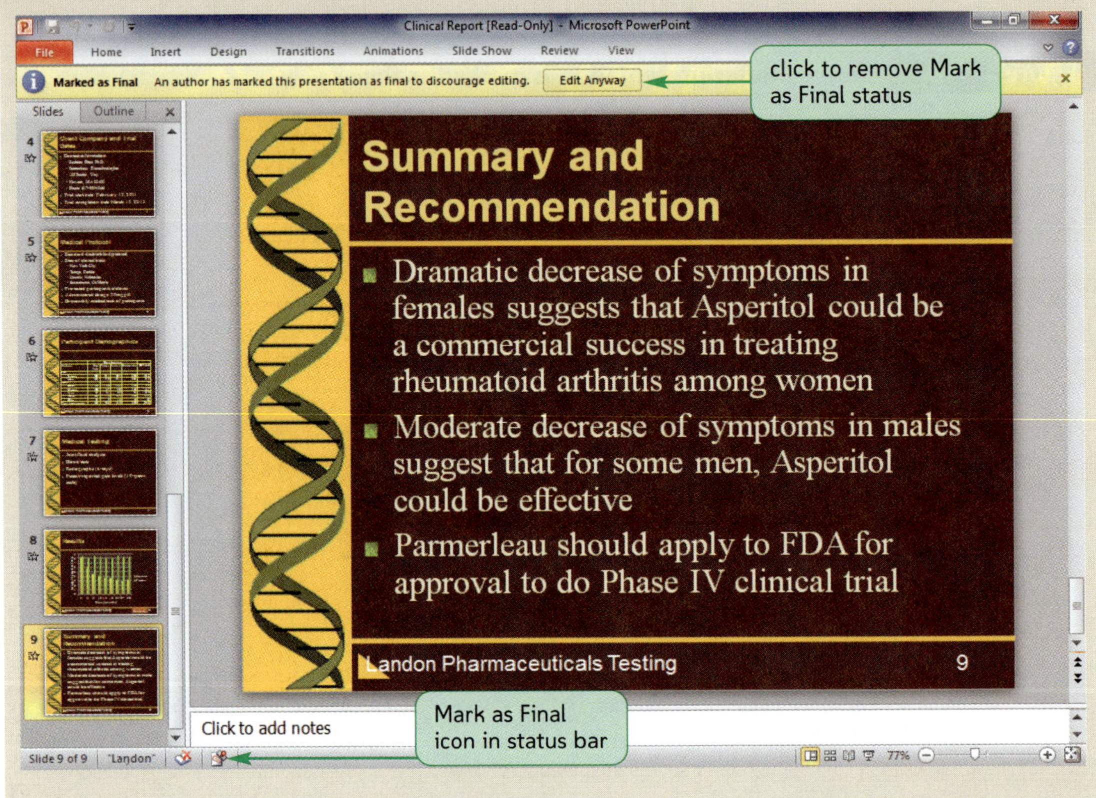


Next, you'll save the presentation using various methods so that others can easily view it.

PROSKILLS

### *Teamwork: Virtual Teams and Technology*

A virtual team is one whose members rarely, if ever, meet in person to work on team tasks or build a corporate culture or team camaraderie. Instead, technology makes it possible for members to be geographically distant yet work as if everyone was in the same room. Virtual team members use technologies such as email and voice mail, file transfer protocol (FTP) sites, telephone, Web conferencing software, and groupware and collaboration software tools, such as those found in Office 2010.

Virtual teams often must work rapidly and cohesively to accomplish tasks, so knowing how best to use these technologies is critical. To make virtual teams function well, team leaders must spend extra time ensuring that each member is equipped to work together in a virtual environment. This means leaders need to build trust early and quickly figure out the best way to communicate with team members. The leader must also find a way to let individuals get to know one another. Since the team can't all gather at a local restaurant after work on Thursdays, for example, using technology to help socialize, share photos, and build community can make a difference in team productivity. Effectively using digital communication tools also can increase team member connection and the ability to get work done efficiently.

# Saving the Presentation for Distribution

PowerPoint lets you save presentations in several formats that allow others to view the presentation, but does not allow them to make any changes to it. You can save the presentation as a picture presentation, create a video from a presentation, and save the presentation in PDF format. Each method produces a different type of file for you to distribute. First, you'll save the presentation as a picture presentation.

## Saving the Presentation as a Picture Presentation

If you want to distribute your presentation to others so they can see it but prevent them from modifying it or copying complex animations, backgrounds, or other features, you can save the presentation as a picture presentation. When you save a presentation as a picture presentation, each slide is saved as an image file in the JPEG format, and then that image is placed on a slide in a new presentation so that it fills the entire slide.

Alyssa wants to give her presentation to the management team at Pamerleau Biotechnologies so that they can make it available to their employees. However, she doesn't want them to be able to modify it or copy the slide background. She asks you to save the presentation as a picture.

### To save the presentation as a picture:

1. Click the **File** tab, and then click the **Save & Send** tab in the navigation bar.
2. In the File Types section in the left pane, click **Change File Type**. The right pane of the Save & Send tab changes to list various file type options that you can save the presentation as. See Figure 4-36.

**Figure 4-36** Change File Type selected on Save & Send tab in Backstage view

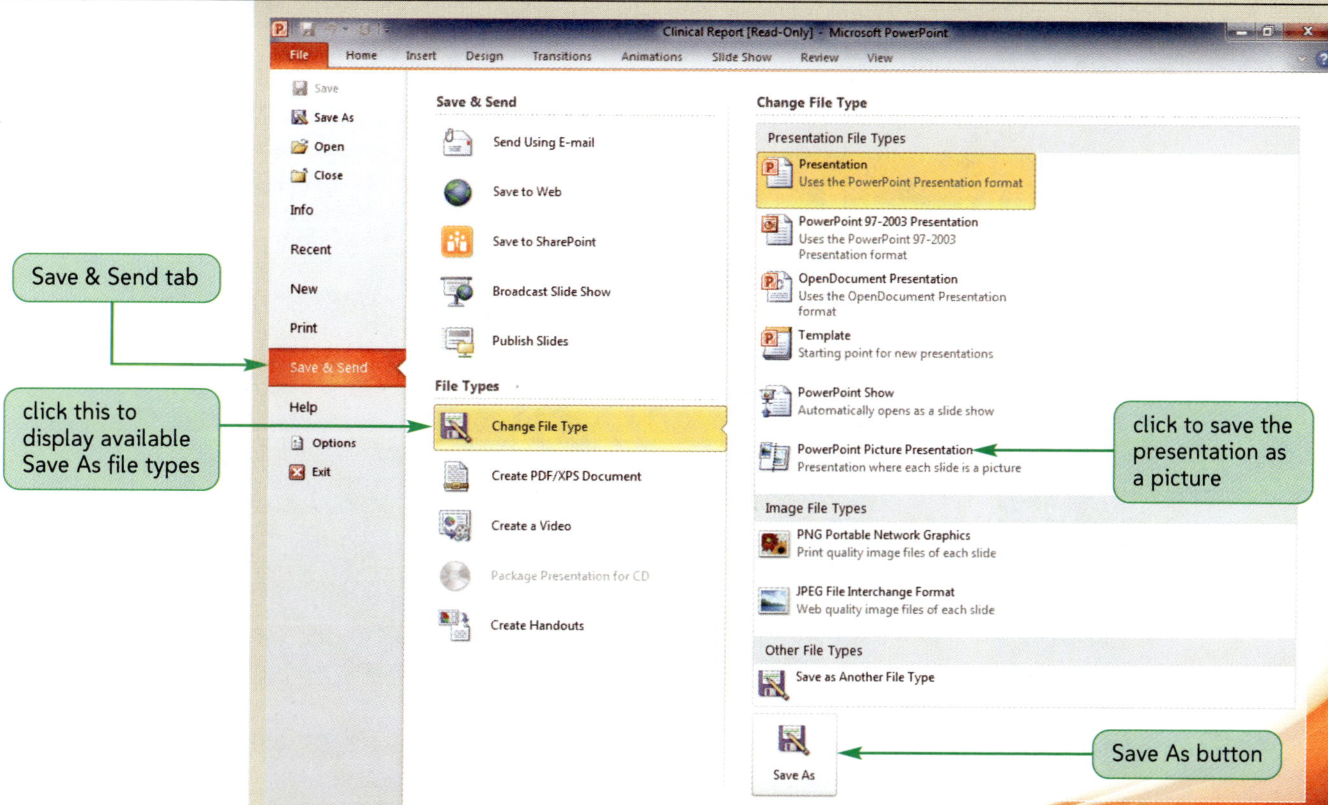

**TIP**

You can also save the slides as individual image files by selecting one of the file types under Image File Types on the Save & Send tab or by selecting GIF, JPEG, PNG, or TIFF as the file type in the Save As dialog box.

3. In the Presentation File Types section in the right pane, click **PowerPoint Picture Presentation**, and then click the **Save As** button. Backstage view closes and the Save As dialog box opens with PowerPoint Picture Presentation in the Save as type box. The name in the File name box is the same as the presentation filename.
4. If necessary, navigate to the PowerPoint4\Tutorial folder, change the filename to **Landon Report**, and then click the **Save** button. The Save As dialog box closes and, after a moment, another dialog box opens telling you that a copy of the presentation has been saved.
5. Click the **OK** button. The dialog box closes.

You can open the picture presentation in the same way you normally open a presentation. You'll do this now.

### To open the picture presentation:

1. Click the **File** tab, and then click the **Open** command in the navigation bar. The Open dialog box opens.
2. Navigate to the PowerPoint4\Tutorial folder, if necessary, and then double-click **Landon Report**. The Landon Report opens in Normal view.
3. In the Slide pane, click anywhere on the slide. Notice that sizing handles appear around the edges of the Slide pane. This is because the objects in the original slide were converted to a single JPEG file. See Figure 4-37.

**Figure 4-37** JPEG image on Slide 1 selected in the picture presentation

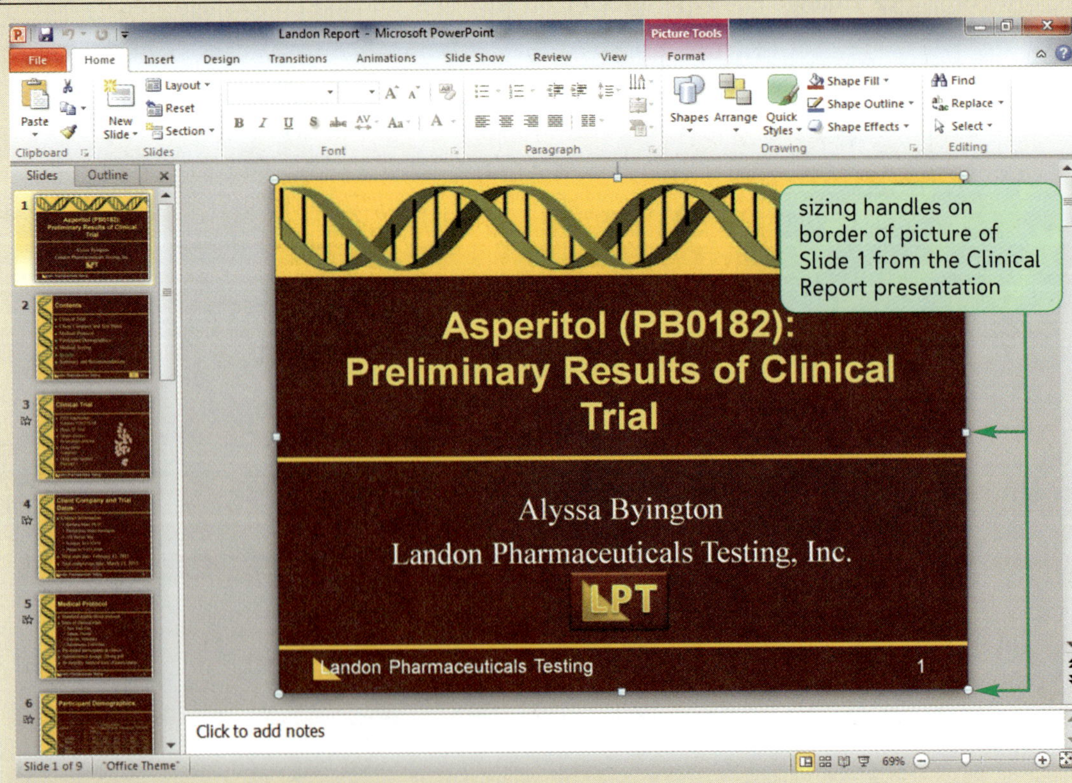


4. Display **Slide 2** ("Contents") in the Slide pane, and then click the action button. The whole image of Slide 2 is selected, not the action button.

5. On the status bar, click the **Slide Show** button. Slide 2 appears in Slide Show view.
6. Click the **Results** link. The slide show transitions to Slide 3 instead of jumping to Slide 8 ("Results"). The Results link does not function because this is just a picture of the original Slide 2.
7. Advance the slide show. Slide 4 transitions onto the screen with the Rotate transition. Recall that in the original presentation, the Rotate transition rotated the text and objects onto the screen while keeping the slide background static. In this presentation, the Rotate transition was retained, but it appears as if the entire slide rotates because the picture of each slide is the content on the slide that rotates.
8. Press the **Esc** key to end the slide show, and then close the **Landon Report** presentation. The Clinical Report presentation appears again.

## Saving a Presentation as a Video

You can also save a presentation as a Windows Media Video file (with a .wmv filename extension). When you save it, you can choose the resolution of the video and how long each slide will appear on the screen. After you have created the video, you can play it in Windows Media Player or any other video player.

Alyssa wants you to save a presentation as a video so she can distribute it to Landon shareholders who do not know how to use PowerPoint.

### To save the presentation as a video:

1. Click the **File** tab, and then in the navigation bar, click the **Save & Send** tab. The Save & Send tab appears in Backstage view.
2. In the File Types section, click **Create a Video**. The right pane of Backstage view changes to show options for creating a video. See Figure 4-38. First, you need to select the quality of the video you want to create. Alyssa wants people to be able to play this presentation on their MP3 players, cell phones, or other portable devices.

**Figure 4-38** Save & Send tab in Backstage view with Create a Video selected

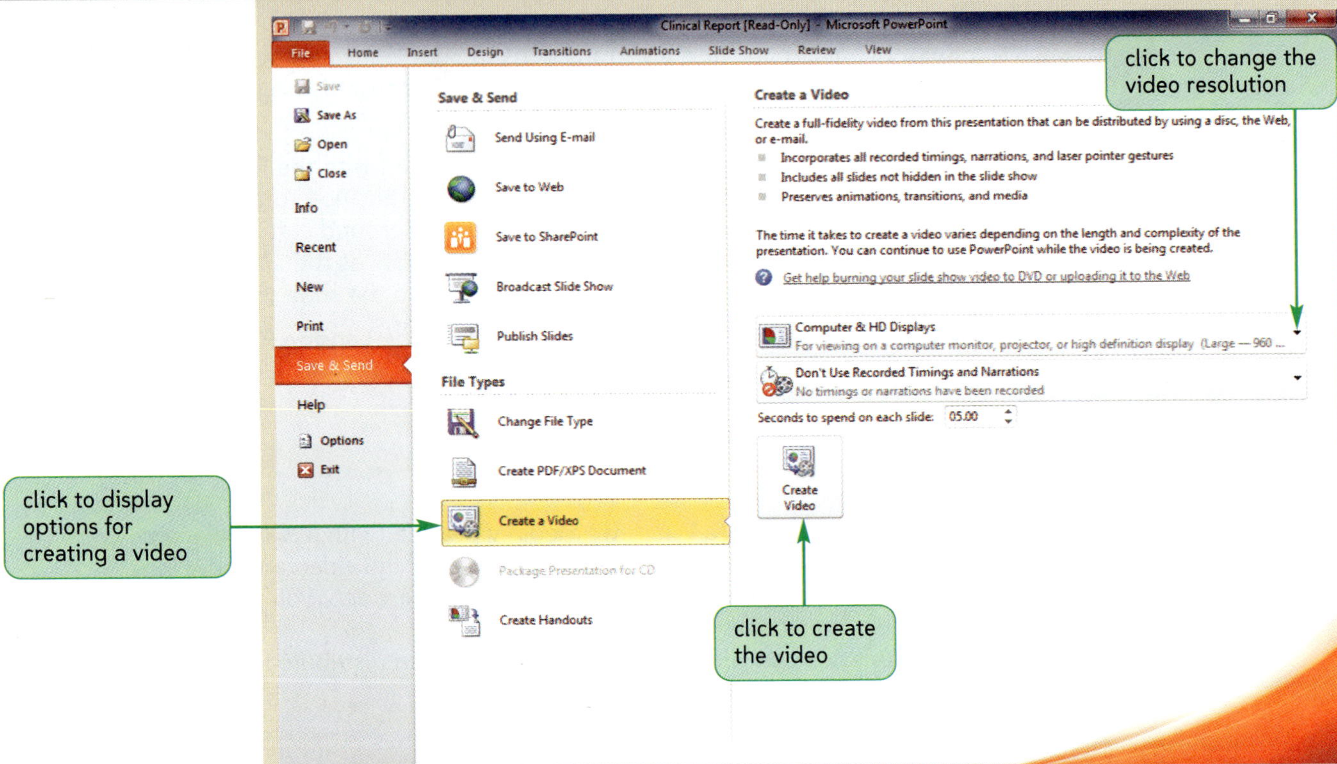


**TIP**

If a presentation has automatic timing set, or has recorded narrations, you could choose to include them here.

3. Click the **Computer & HD Displays** button, and then click **Portable Devices**. Next, you need to choose the number of seconds for each slide to be displayed.
4. In the Seconds to spend on each slide box, click the **down arrow** twice. The number of seconds to spend on each slide is changed to 3.
5. Click the **Create Video** button. Backstage view closes and the Save As dialog box opens with Windows Media Video selected in the Save as type box.
6. Change the name in the File name box to **Clinical Report video**, and then click the **Save** button. The dialog box closes and a progress bar labeled Creating video Clinical Report video.wmv appears in the status bar. After a moment, the progress bar disappears.

Now that you've created the video, you can use Windows Media Player to watch it.

## To watch the movie:

1. On the taskbar, click the **Start** button, and then on the right side of the Start menu, click **Documents**.
2. Navigate to the PowerPoint4\Tutorial folder. The Clinical Report video file is included in the file list.

3. Double-click **Clinical Report video**. Windows Media Player starts and the video you created starts playing. Figure 4-39 shows the title slide in the maximized Media Player window. Each slide displays for three seconds. Notice that the video retained the transitions you applied. After the last slide appears, the video ends, and options to restart the video and other Media Player commands appear in the Media Player window.

   **Trouble?** If a Welcome screen appears, click the Recommended settings option button, click the Finish button, and then repeat Step 3.

   **Trouble?** If your Media Player window is not maximized, you can click the Maximize button in the title bar.

**Figure 4-39** **Video in maximized Media Player window**

4. On the Media Player title bar, click the **Close** button.
5. In the Windows Explorer title bar, click the **Close** button. The PowerPoint window is displayed again.

## Saving a Presentation as a PDF

**Portable Document File (PDF)** format is a file format that can be opened on any make or model of computer, as long as the computer has installed the free, downloadable program Adobe Reader. Because most computers have Adobe Reader installed, and any computer connected to the Internet can easily get it installed at no cost, a PDF is an important file format for sharing documents.

INSIGHT

### *Saving a Presentation as an XPS Document*

You can also publish a presentation as an **XPS document**, which is a Microsoft electronic paper format that you can view in a Web browser. When you double-click the filename of an XPS document in Windows Explorer, the document opens and shows the slides as a list that you can scroll through. You can publish to an XPS document using essentially the same method you use to publish in PDF format; the only exception is that you need to click the Save as type arrow and then click XPS Document in the Publish as PDF or XPS dialog box.

The executives at Pamerleau asked Alyssa to email the presentation to several of their sales representatives so that they would have the latest information about the clinical trial. Alyssa knows that anyone can download and install Adobe Reader, so she asks you to save the presentation as a PDF file.

## To publish the presentation in PDF format:

1. Click the **File** tab, and then click the **Save & Send** tab in the navigation bar.
2. In the File Types section, click **Create PDF/XPS Document**. The right pane of the Save & Send tab changes to describe the PDF and XPS file types.
3. Click the **Create PDF/XPS** button. Backstage view closes, and the Publish as PDF or XPS dialog box opens with PDF listed in the Save as type box. See Figure 4-40.

   **Trouble?** If XPS appears in the Save as type box instead of PDF, click the Save as type arrow, and then click PDF.

**Figure 4-40** Publish as PDF or XPS dialog box

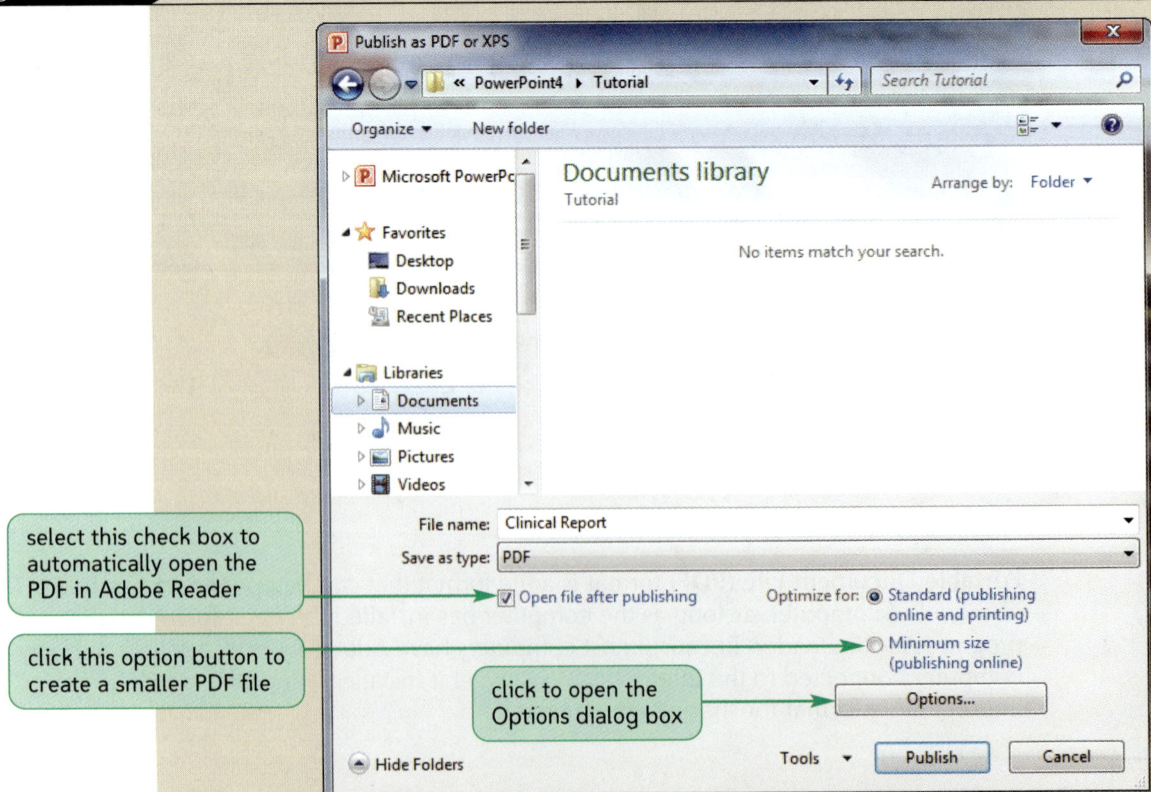

4. Navigate to the PowerPoint4\Tutorial folder, if necessary, and then change the filename to **Clinical Report PDF**. You want to create a smaller file size suitable for attaching to an email message.
5. Click the **Minimum size** (publishing online) option button. You can change the options for the PDF file.
6. Click the **Options** button. The Options dialog box opens. See Figure 4-41. Alyssa doesn't want the document properties to be included, as she expects this file to be widely distributed.

**Figure 4-41** **Options dialog box for saving a presentation as a PDF file**

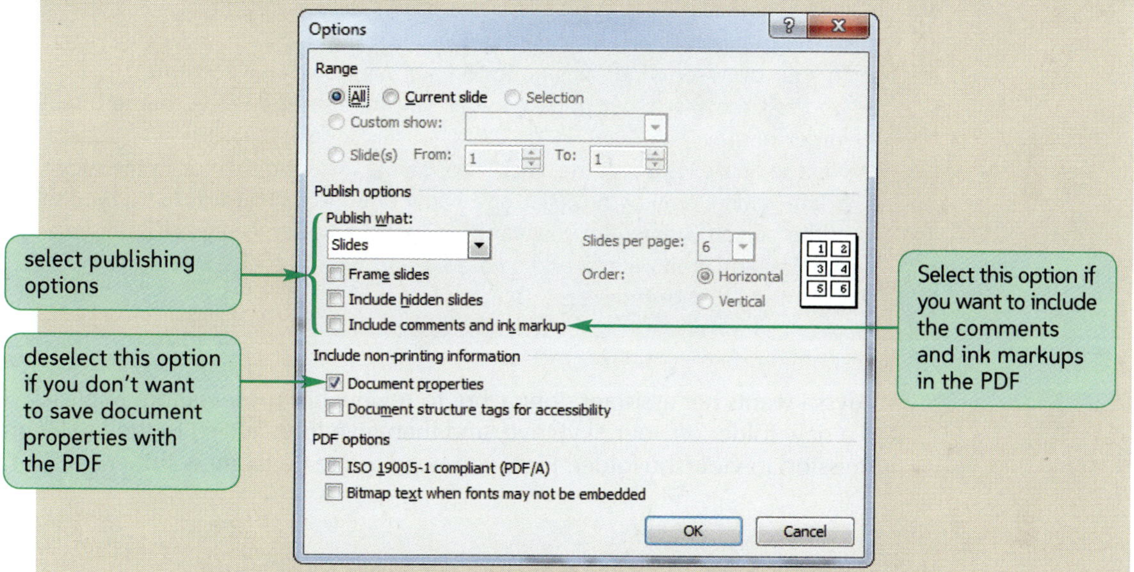


7. In the Include non-printing information section, click the **Document properties** check box to deselect it.
8. Click the **OK** button. You want to review the PDF file after saving it.
9. In the Publish as PDF or XPS dialog box, click the **Open file after publishing** check box to select it, if necessary, and then click the **Publish** button. Your presentation is saved in PDF format, and Adobe Reader automatically opens displaying Clinical Report PDF file in the Adobe Reader window.

   **Trouble?** If the Open file after publishing check box and label are dimmed, Adobe Reader is not installed on your computer. Click the Publish button to save the file as a PDF document, and then skip Steps 10 through 12.
10. In the vertical scroll bar, click the down scroll arrow to view each slide as a page in the PDF file.
11. In the title bar, click the **Close** button to exit the Adobe Reader program.
12. In the PowerPoint window, close the Clinical Report presentation.

**TIP**

If Adobe Reader is not installed on your computer, start your Web browser, and then go to Adobe's Web site at www.adobe.com. Look for a link to get the free Adobe Reader.

## Saving a Presentation to SkyDrive

**TIP**

**Cloud computing** refers to data, applications, and even resources that are stored on servers that you access over the Internet rather than on your own computer.

Another way to make a presentation available to others is to save it to SkyDrive. **SkyDrive** is an online storage and file sharing service. When you create a Windows Live ID, you are also given a SkyDrive account. You can upload files to folders on your SkyDrive and then give others permission to access your folders to view or edit your files.

**REFERENCE**

*Creating a New folder on SkyDrive and Granting Permission for Access*

- Click the File tab, and then click Save & Send in the navigation bar.
- Under Save & Send, click Save to Web.
- In the pane on the right, click the Sign In button, and then sign in to your Windows Live account.
- In the pane on the right, click the New button.
- In your browser window, sign in to your Windows Live account.
- On the Create a folder page on your SkyDrive, in the Folder name box, type the new folder name.
- Next to Share with Just me, click the Change link, and then drag the slider to the appropriate option; or click in the Enter a name or an e-mail address box, type the email address of the person with whom you want to share the folder, press the Enter key, and then click the Can add, edit details, and delete files arrow and click Can view files, if desired.
- Click the Next button.

Alyssa wants her assistant, John Cho, to review her presentation. She asks you to post it to a new folder on your SkyDrive, and then give John access to the file by granting him permission to view the folder. First, you need to create the new folder.

### To create a new, shared folder on your SkyDrive:

1. Click the **File** tab, click **Save & Send** in the navigation bar, and then click **Save to Web** under Save & Send.

   The right pane changes to display a Sign In button that you can use to sign in to your Windows Live account. See Figure 4-42.

**Figure 4-42** Save & Send tab in Backstage view after clicking Save to Web

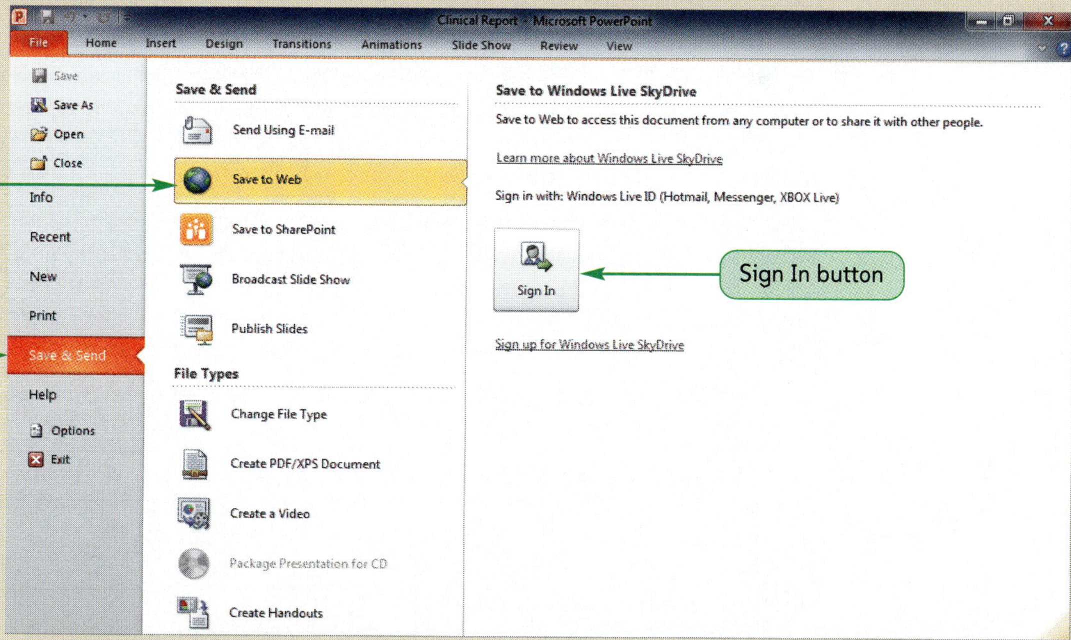


**Trouble?** If you are already signed into Windows Live, you will see the folders in your SkyDrive account listed instead, as shown in Figure 4-43. Skip Steps 3-6 and continue with Step 7.

3. Click the **Sign In** button. The Connecting to docs.live.net dialog box opens.
4. In the E-mail address box, type the email address associated with your Windows Live ID account.
5. Press the **Tab** key, and then type the password associated with your Windows Live account in the Password box.
6. Click the **OK** button. The dialog box closes, and another dialog box appears briefly while you connect to the Windows Live server. After you connect, the right pane in Backstage view changes to list the folders on your SkyDrive account. See Figure 4-43. You want to create a new folder on your SkyDrive.

**Figure 4-43** Save & Send tab after connecting to Windows Live

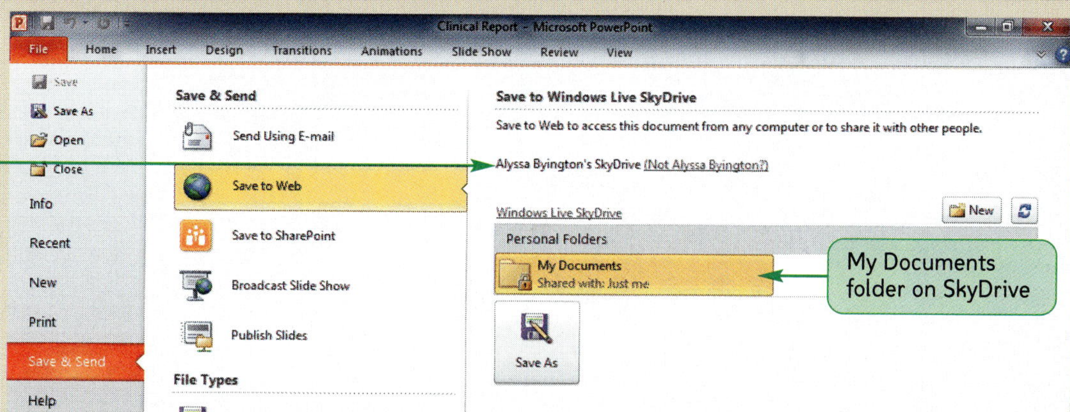

7. In the right pane, click the **New** button. Your browser starts, or if your browser is already open, a new tab opens, and the page to sign in to your Windows Live account appears.
8. In the Windows Live ID box, type the email address associated with your Windows Live ID account, click in the **Password** box, type your password, and then click the **Sign in** button. The Create a folder page on your SkyDrive appears. The temporary name New folder is selected in the Name box.

   **Trouble?** If there is an email address listed under sign in and it is not your email address, click the Sign in with a different Windows Live ID link, and then complete Step 8. If there is an email address listed under sign in and it is your email address, point to it, click the Sign in button, type your password in the box below your email address, click the Sign in button again, and then continue with Step 9.
9. In the Name box, type **Landon**. This is the name of your new folder. Under the Name box, Just me appears next to Share with.
10. Next to Just me, click the **Change** link. A list with a slider bar next to it opens and the Add specific people section appears at the bottom of the window. You can use the slider bar to make the contents of the new folder public by sharing it with everyone, your friends as listed on your Windows Live ID account and their friends, just your friends, or only some friends. You can also share it only with specific people that you list. Alyssa wants to share this folder with her assistant, John.
11. Under Add specific people, click in the **Enter a name or an e-mail address** box, and then type **cho_john@live.com**. This is the email address associated with John's Windows Live account.
12. Press the **Enter** key. John's email address appears below the Enter a name or an e-mail address box next to a check box with a check mark in it, and a list box to the right identifies the level of access. Alyssa wants John to have more limited access, where he can view files in this folder, but not change the folder's contents. See Figure 4-44.

Figure 4-44 Create a folder page on SkyDrive after granting permission to John Cho

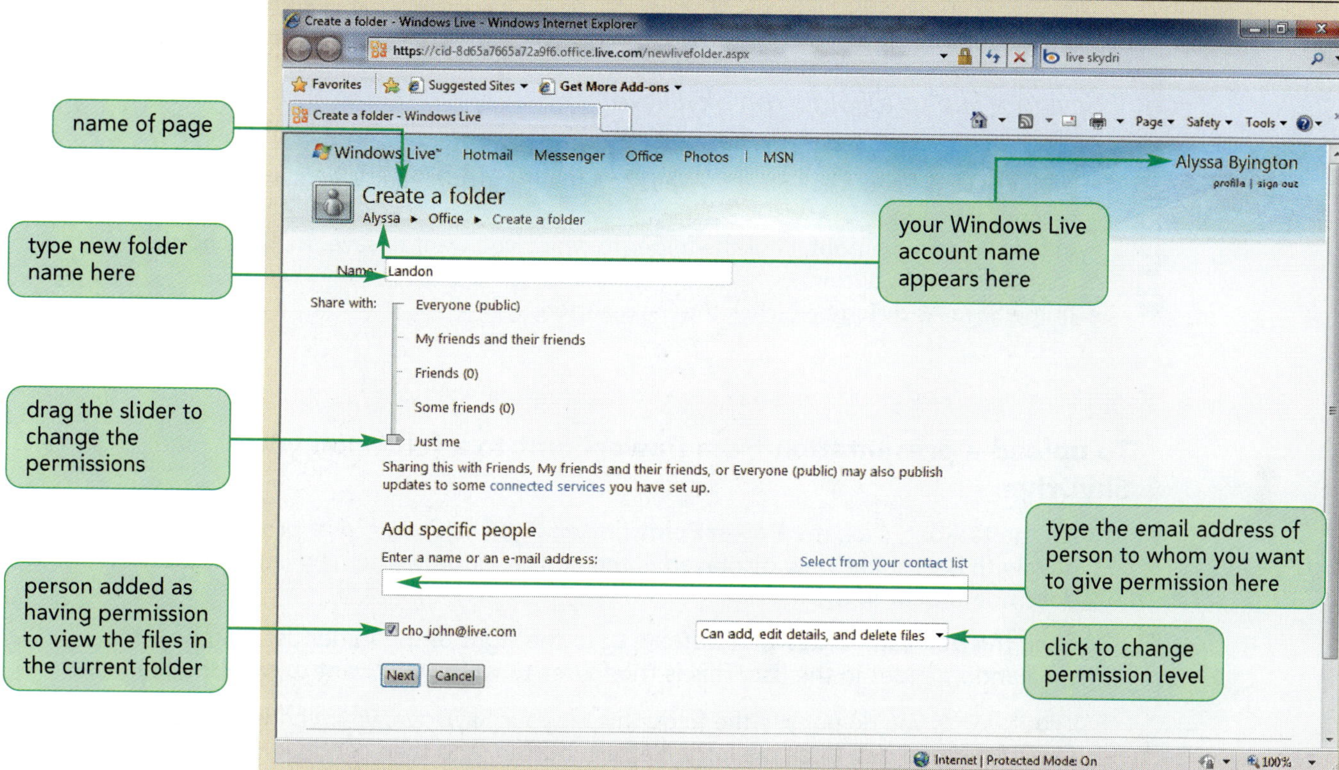


13. Click the **Can add, edit details, and delete files** arrow, and then click **Can view files**.

**Trouble?** If Can view files already appears in the box, skip Step 13.

14. Click the **Next** button. The Landon folder page on your SkyDrive account appears. See Figure 4-45.

Figure 4-45 Landon folder page on SkyDrive

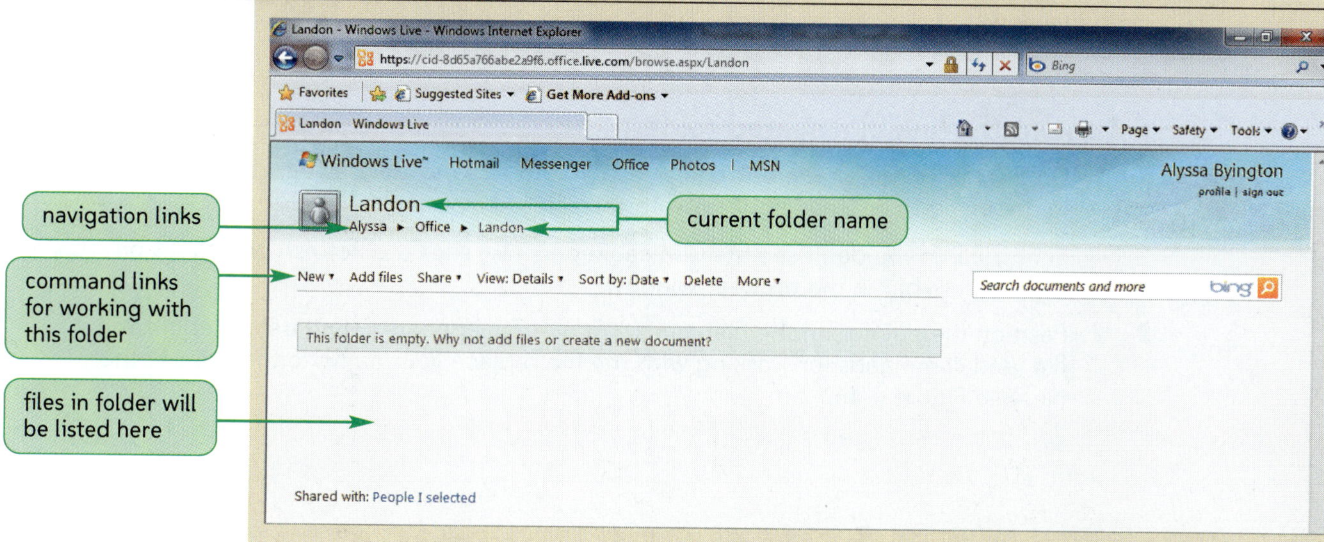

Now that the new folder is created, Alyssa needs you to upload the file to it. You can do this from the SkyDrive folder in the browser window or you can do this from Backstage view in the PowerPoint window.

REFERENCE

*Saving a File to a Folder on SkyDrive*

- Click the File tab, and then click Save & Send in the navigation bar.
- Under Save & Send, click Save to Web, and then sign into your Windows Live ID account if necessary.
- In the pane on the right, click the folder to which you want to save the file, and then click the Save As button.
- In the Save As dialog box, click the Save button.

**To upload a presentation from PowerPoint to a folder on your SkyDrive:**

1. On the taskbar, click the **PowerPoint** button. The PowerPoint program window with Backstage view displayed is the active window. The new Landon folder does not appear in the list.
2. Click the **Refresh Folder List** button to the right of the folder list. You now see the Landon folder in the list. This is the folder to which you want to save the file.

   **Trouble?** If you do not see the folder list on your SkyDrive, your connection to your SkyDrive timed out. Click the large Refresh button, and then continue with Step 3.
3. In the folder list, click the **Landon** folder.
4. Click the **Save As** button. Backstage view closes, and then after a few moments, the Save As dialog box opens.
5. Click the **Save** button. The Clinical Report file is saved to the Landon folder on your SkyDrive.

When you grant permission for other people to access a folder on your SkyDrive, you need to send them the link to the folder so that they can find it. Alyssa asks you to do this now.

**To send the link of a shared folder:**

1. On the taskbar, click the button corresponding to your browser. The Landon folder on your SkyDrive appears with the Clinical Report file listed.

   **Trouble?** If you don't see the Clinical Report file, click the Refresh button on the Address bar in the browser window.
2. Position the pointer on the filename. A ScreenTip appears listing details about the file, and commands for working with the file replace your name to the right of the file. See Figure 4-46.

**Figure 4-46** Clinical Report file in the Landon folder on SkyDrive

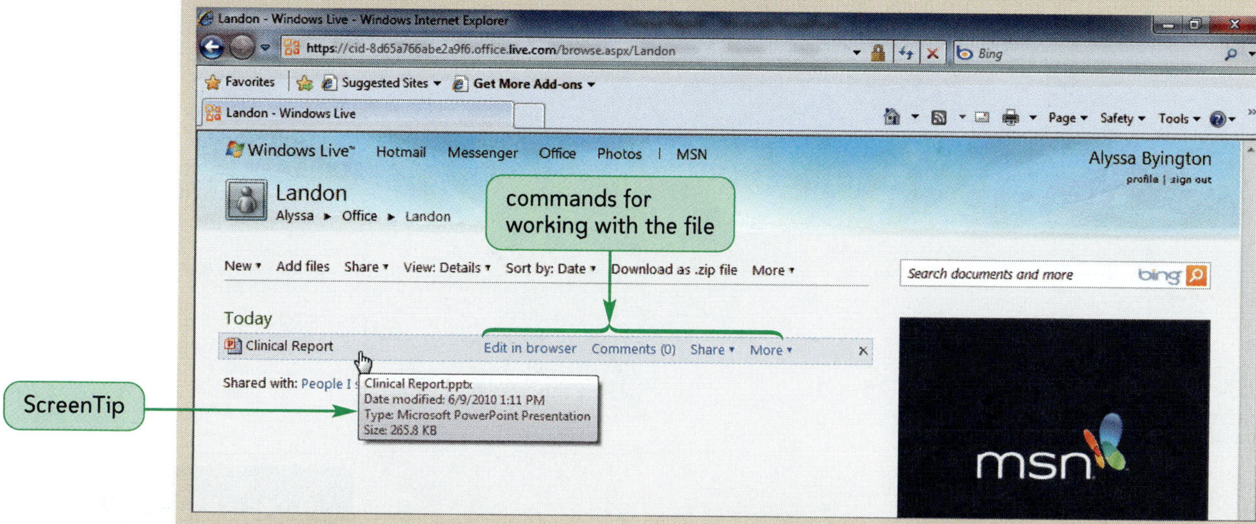


3. In the list of commands that appear, click the **Share** link, and then click **Send a link**. The Permissions for Clinical Report.pptx page appears with a message that tells you that permission for the Clinical Report file comes from the Landon folder. See Figure 4-47. Permission is not granted to individual files on SkyDrive; it is granted to folders at the same level as the My Documents and the Public folder.

**Figure 4-47** Permissions for Clinical Report.pptx page on SkyDrive

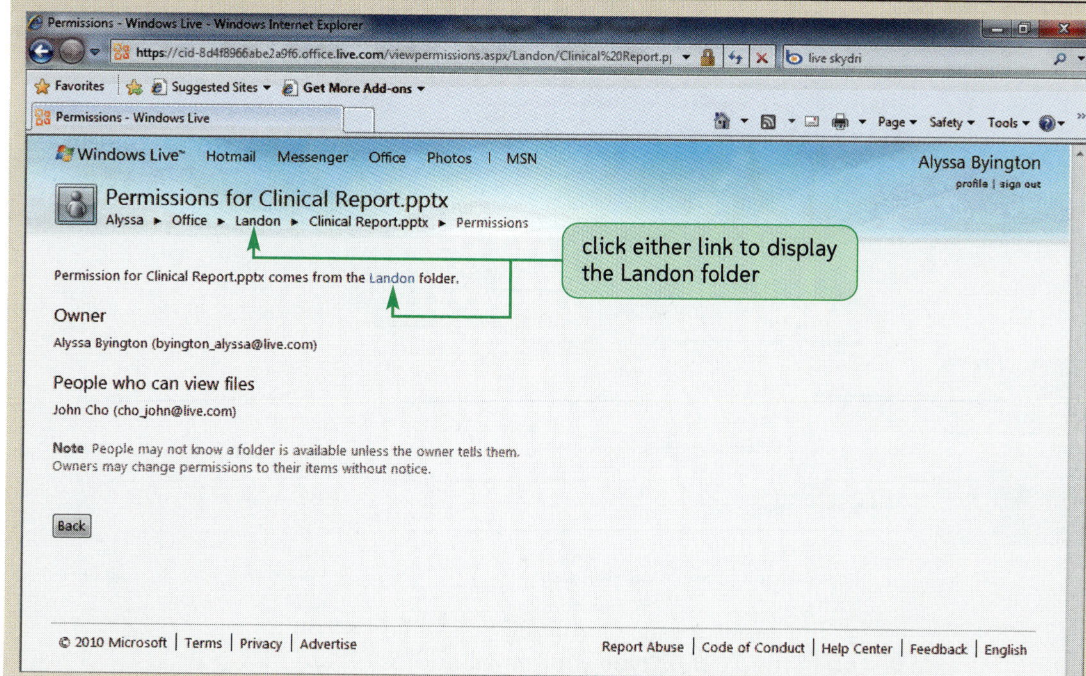


4. Click the **Landon** link. The Landon folder page appears. See Figure 4-48.

**Figure 4-48** Landon folder page on SkyDrive

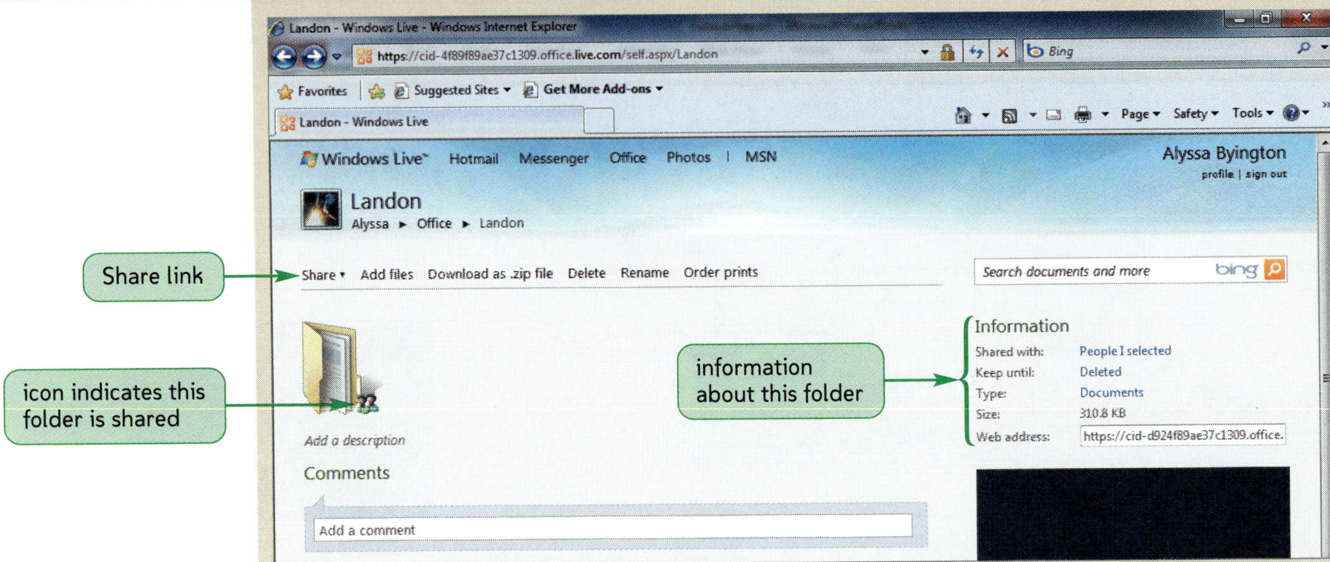


5. In the list of command links, click the **Share** link, and then click **Send a link**. The Send a link page appears. See Figure 4-49. Because you already granted John permission to access the folder, his email address appears in the To box. Alyssa wants you to send a copy of the message to yourself so that you have a record of it.

**Figure 4-49** Send a link page on SkyDrive

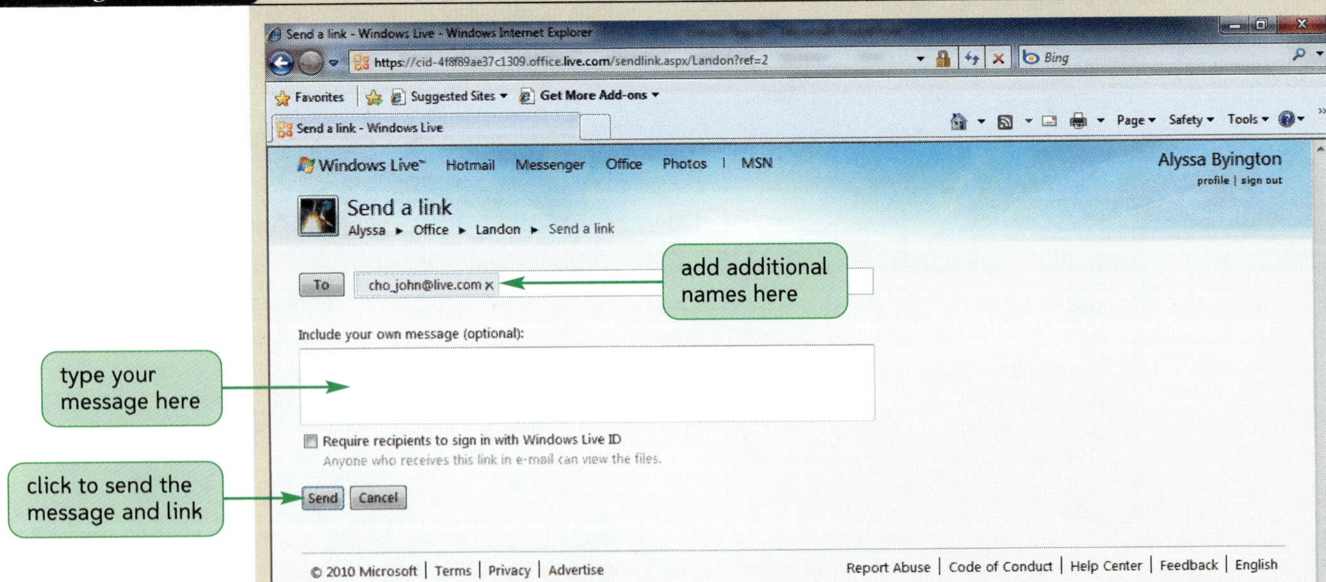


6. In the To box, type your email address.
7. Click in the **Include your own message (optional)** box, and then type **Here is the link to the Landon folder on my SkyDrive**.
8. Click the **Send** button. The Send a link page closes and the Landon folder page appears again.

If you had added additional names in the To box on the Send a link page, those people would have automatically been granted permission to access the Landon folder.

You will receive an email message in your Inbox with the subject "<*Your Name*> has shared documents with you." In the message, there is a View folder button that you can click to go directly to the Landon folder on your SkyDrive.

Once a file is stored on SkyDrive, you can download it to your hard drive if you need to by pointing to the filename to display the links for working with the file, clicking the More link, and then clicking Download.

Alyssa is pleased to have several options for distributing the presentation file to others without allowing them to modify the presentation.

REVIEW

## *Session 4.2 Quick Check*

1. How is a dynamic content transition different from an ordinary transition?
2. True or False. When you mark a slide with the Pen during a slide show, you cannot save your annotations.
3. What appears in the comment thumbnail when you insert a comment?
4. What does the Document Inspector reveal?
5. In Normal view, how do you know if a presentation is marked as final?
6. What happens when a presentation is saved as a picture presentation?
7. What is the file type of a presentation that you save as a video?

*Practice the skills you learned in the tutorial using the same case scenario.*

PRACTICE

## Review Assignments

**Data Files needed for the Review Assignments: Company.pptx, Hospitals.docx, Landon2.pptx, LPTChart.xlsx, LPTInfo.docx, LT Review.pptx**

Alyssa not only gives reports on clinical trials to clients of Landon Pharmaceuticals Testing, she also gives presentations to prospective clients. She now asks you to help prepare an information presentation on Landon Pharmaceuticals Testing. Complete the following steps:

1. Open the file **Company**, located in the PowerPoint4\Review folder included with your Data Files, and then save the presentation to the same folder as **Landon Info**.
2. Import the Word outline **LPTInfo**, located in the PowerPoint4\Review folder, after Slide 2.
3. Apply the Title and Content layout to all of the new slides except Slides 5 and 9. Apply the Two Content layout to Slide 5 and the Title Only layout to Slide 9.
4. Reset the slides, and then turn on slide numbering and apply the footer in the Header and Footer dialog box to all the slides, including the title slide.
5. Export the outline to a Rich Text file named **Landon Info Outline** in the PowerPoint4\Review folder.
6. Start Word, open the **Landon Info Outline** file you just exported, and then change all the text to 11-point, black Calibri. Save the document as a Word document to the same folder using the same filename. Exit Word.
7. Open the **Landon2** presentation located in the PowerPoint4\Review folder, and then copy the picture of the pill bottles on Slide 4 ("Previous Trials") to the Clipboard.
8. Switch back to the Landon Info presentation. Paste the picture of the pill bottles in Slide 5 ("What Our Subcontractors Do"), and then delete the content placeholder on Slide 5. Position the picture approximately centered in the blank area on the right side of the slide. Close the Landon2 presentation.
9. Remove the background from the picture of the pill bottles. Make sure all parts of the pill bottles are marked to keep and all of the gray background is marked for removal.
10. In Slide 8, use the Object command to embed the Word table from the Word file **Hospitals**, located in the PowerPoint4\Review folder.
11. Make the Word program active, change the font size for all the text in the table to 16 points, change the style of all the text in the first row to bold, change the font color for all the text in the table to white, and then change the border color to Orange, Accent 6. Click a blank area of the slide and return to PowerPoint, and then drag the table to position it in the center of the area below the title on the slide.
12. Start Excel, open the Excel file **LPTChart**, located in the PowerPoint4\Review folder, and then save it as **Landon Cost Chart** in the same folder.
13. Copy the chart, and then return to the Landon Info presentation (but do not close the Landon Cost Chart workbook). Use the Paste command to paste the chart as a link on Slide 9 ("Costs per Phase III Patient 2007 to 2013") using the theme from the presentation. Resize the chart so it fits in the blank area of the slide.
14. Use the Edit Data command to display the PowerPoint and the Excel windows side by side, go to Sheet1 in the Excel window, edit the cost per patient in 2009 to $3417, and then save the file and exit Excel.
15. In Slide 3 ("What We Will Cover"), create a hyperlink to Slide 5 ("What Our Subcontractors Do") from the second bulleted item.

16. In Slide 3 ("What We Will Cover"), create a Plaque shape in the lower-right corner of the slide. Add the text **Mission Statement** to the shape, and then resize and reposition the shape so that it fits to the left of the slide number and below the yellow horizontal line, and so the text fits inside the shape on one line. Make the shape a hyperlink to Slide 2.
17. In Slide 5, insert the Action Button: Home at the bottom of the slide, between the footer and slide number. Use the Hyperlink to list in the Action Settings dialog box to link to Slide 3 in the presentation. (*Hint*: Click Slide in the Hyperlink to list.)
18. Adjust the size of the action button so that it fits between the yellow line at the bottom of the slide just to the left of the slide number, and then change the shape style of the action button to Intense Effect – Orange, Accent 6.
19. Apply the Conveyor transition in the Dynamic Content section of the Transitions gallery to Slides 3 through 10.
20. Customize the Handout Master so that it displays only the date and the page number. Change the background style of the Handout Master to Style 6.
21. Run the slide show. Verify that the links on Slide 3 and the action button on Slide 5 work. On Slide 5, circle the third bulleted item ("Prepare matching placebos"), and then underline the slide title. When the slide show is finished, save the annotations.
22. Change the name and initials on the General tab in the PowerPoint Options dialog box to your name and initials, if necessary. On Slide 8 ("Associated Hospitals and Clinics"), insert the following as a new comment: **Please verify that the contact names are up-to-date.**
23. Edit the comment you just inserted by inserting **and email addresses** after "names," and then position the comment thumbnail above the third column in the table.
24. Compare your presentation to the presentation **LT Review**, located in the PowerPoint4\Review folder. Accept all the changes to the title text box on Slide 8, do not accept the second change on Slide 8, and then delete the LT1 comment.
25. Change the name and initials on the General tab in the PowerPoint Options dialog box back to their original values, if necessary, and then add your name as the subtitle on Slide 1.
26. Save your changes, and then, if necessary, change the user name and initials on the General tab in the PowerPoint Options dialog box back to their original values.
27. Inspect the document for hidden and private data. Remove the document properties and personal information. Do not remove the comments and annotations. Save the file again.
28. Check the file to see if there are any features not supported by earlier versions of PowerPoint.
29. Mark the presentation as final.
30. Post the file to a new folder named Landon Info on your SkyDrive, giving permission to Alyssa's assistant John Cho using the email address cho_john@live.com.
31. Save the presentation as a picture presentation named **Info Pictures** in the PowerPoint4\Review folder.
32. Save the presentation as a video named **Landon Info video** in the PowerPoint4\Review folder. Set the resolution for Portable Devices, and change the seconds to spend on each slide to four.
33. Save the presentation as a PDF file named **Landon Info PDF** in the PowerPoint4\Review folder using Standard optimization. Do not change any of the options.
34. Submit the completed presentation and other files in printed or electronic form, as requested by your instructor, and then close all open files.

*Apply your skills to create a presentation to recruit new customers for a credit union.*

APPLY

## Case Problem 1

**Data Files needed for this Case Problem: Branches.docx, DH Review.pptx, FLCU.pptx, FLCUChart.xlsx, FLCUOutline.docx, FLCUPhotos.pptx**

***Flat Lake Credit Union*** Dwayne Harris is the manager of the Flat Lake Credit Union in Safford, Arizona. One of his responsibilities is to give presentations to potential customers about the services and benefits of membership in the credit union. Complete the following steps:

1. Open the presentation **FLCU**, located in the PowerPoint4\Case1 folder included with your Data Files, and then save the presentation to the same folder with the filename **FLCU Services**.
2. Replace "Flat Lake Credit Union" in the title in the title slide with **Services and Benefits of Credit Union Membership** (leave "Safford Arizona" as part of the title), and then type your name as the subtitle.
3. Import the Word outline **FLCUOutline**, located in the PowerPoint4\Case1 folder after Slide 1.
4. Apply the Title and Content layout to all of the new slides except Slides 3, 7, and 9, apply the Two Content layout to Slides 3 and 7, apply the Title Only layout to Slide 9, and then reset the new slides.
5. Display the footer and slide numbers on all the slides except the title slide.
6. Open the presentation **FLCUPhotos**, and then copy the photo of money in Slide 2. Paste this photo in Slide 3 ("Loans") of the FLCU Services presentation. Remove the background of the photo.
7. In FLCUPhotos, copy the photo of the building on Slide 3. In Slide 7 ("Special Member Discounts") of the FLCU Services presentation, resize the text placeholder that contains the bulleted list so it is double its current width, and then delete the content placeholder. Paste the photo of the building you copied to Slide 7, and then position it below the bulleted list.
8. In Slide 8 ("Credit Union Branches"), embed a Word table from the file **Branches**, located in the PowerPoint4\Case1 folder. Resize the table so it appears as large as possible.
9. Edit the table so that the text is yellow and the borders are white.
10. In Slide 9 ("Credit Union Earnings"), link the chart in the Excel worksheet **FLCUChart** (located in the PowerPoint4\Case1 folder), and then resize the chart so it fits in the blank area of the slide. Exit Excel when you are finished.
11. In Slide 10, insert the Action Button: Home, and make it a hyperlink to the first slide in the presentation. (*Hint*: Change the "Hyperlink to" value to First Slide.)
12. Resize the action button to 0.75 by 0.75 inches. (*Hint*: With the action button selected, click the Drawing Tools Format tab, and then use the Shape Height and Shape Width boxes in the Size group.)
13. Move the action button to the lower-left corner of the slide, so it's near the bottom of the picture panel of Flat Lake, and then change the shape style to Intense Effect – Green, Accent 1.
14. View the slide show in Slide Show view. On Slide 2, use the Pen to circle each instance of the word "Free." Test the action button that you inserted on Slide 10. Keep the annotations.
15. Compare the presentation with the presentation **DH Review**, located in the PowerPoint4\Case1 folder. Locate and accept the suggested change (reject the change to the subtitle text on the title slide), and then locate and delete both comments. Do not delete the annotations. (*Hint*: When you accept the change, the check mark might not appear in the change thumbnail.)

16. Inspect the document for private or hidden data. Remove all of the annotations and document properties and personal information.
17. Save your changes, and then mark the presentation as final.
18. Post the presentation to a new folder named FLCU on your SkyDrive. Do not grant permission to anyone to view or edit the files in this folder.
19. Save the presentation as a video named **FLCU video** in the PowerPoint4\Case1 folder. Set the resolution to Portable Devices and set the time to spend on each slide to three seconds.
20. Submit the completed presentation and video in printed or electronic form as instructed, and then close the presentation.

*Expand your skills to create a presentation for a wildlife management company.*

CHALLENGE

## Case Problem 2

**Data Files needed for this Case Problem: Bird.jpg, Flower.jpg, WMCchart.xlsx, WMCDesign.pptx, WMCOutline.docx**

***Wildlife Management Consultants*** Hillary Trejo of DeForest, Wisconsin, is president of Wildlife Management Consultants (WMC), a small company that contracts with the Wisconsin Division of Natural Resources and the Bureau of Wildlife Management to manage wildlife (plants and animals) in refuges and state forests. Hillary asks you to help her prepare and publish a presentation on the services offered by WMC. She wants you to modify this file so you can use it in other presentations as a design theme. Complete the following steps:

1. Open the presentation file **WMCDesign** located in the PowerPoint4\Case2 folder included with your Data Files. Replace the name in the subtitle with your name, and then save the presentation as **WMC Services** in the same folder.
2. Switch to Slide Master view, and then click the Office Theme Slide Master at the top of the pane on the left side of the window.

EXPLORE

3. Click the placeholder text of the level-1 (top) bullet, and change the bullet to the picture **Bird**, located in the PowerPoint4\Case2 folder. (*Hint*: Open the Picture Bullet dialog box, and then click the Import button.) Make the second-level bullet the picture **Flower**, located in the PowerPoint4\Case2 folder.
4. After Slide 1, import the Word outline in the file **WMCOutline**, located in the PowerPoint4\Case2 folder. Apply the Title and Content layout to all of the inserted slides, and then reset the slides to follow the default design theme.
5. Make each of the bulleted items in Slide 2 ("Services") a link to the corresponding slide in the presentation.

EXPLORE

6. Format the background image Wilderness (text with overlaid plants and animals) as a hyperlink to Slide 2. (*Hint*: Switch to Slide Master view.)
7. In Slide 8, change the layout to Title Only, and then link the Excel chart **WMCchart**, located in the PowerPoint4\Case2 folder. Resize the chart so it fits in the blank area in the slide.

EXPLORE

8. Change the chart design to Style 45. (*Hint*: Click the Chart Tools Design tab, click the Chart Styles More button, and then use the ScreenTips to locate the correct style.)

EXPLORE

9. Customize the Handout Master in the following ways:
   a. Change the font size of the header, date, footer, and page number to 20 points.
   b. Add the header text **WMC Services**.
   c. Add the footer text **Wildlife Management Consultants**, and then increase the width of the footer so the text fits all on one line.

d. Set the background to the lightest Olive Green color in the theme colors. (*Hint*: Click Format Background located at the bottom of the Background Style gallery, set the Fill to Solid fill, and then click the Color button. Click the Close button in the dialog box, not the Apply to All button, or you will apply the background style to all the slides, not just to the Handout Master.)

10. Apply the Dynamic Content Fly Through transition to every slide in the presentation.
11. EXPLORE Add the Wind sound to the transitions. (*Hint*: Click the Sound arrow in the Timing group on the Transitions tab.)
12. EXPLORE Separate the presentation into sections. Put Slides 1 and 2 in the first section, Slides 3 and 4 in the second section, Slides 5, 6, and 7 in the third section, and Slides 8, 9, and 10 in the fourth section. (*Hint*: Click Slide 1 in the Slides tab, and then click the Section command in the Slides group. Then click the first slide in the next section, and repeat.)
13. EXPLORE Name the first section **Introduction**, name the second section **Management**, name the third section **Monitoring**, and name the fourth section **Programs**. (*Hint*: Right-click the Untitled Section bar, and then click Rename Section.)
14. Run the slide show, making sure you test all the hyperlinks.
15. Check the presentation for features not supported by earlier versions of PowerPoint. Make a note of these features.
16. Export the outline to an RTF file named **WMC Outline New**. Start Word, and then open the file you created. Reformat the text so that it is 10-point, black Calibri. Go to the end of the document, and then add text describing the features of the presentation that are not supported in earlier versions of PowerPoint. Save your changes, and then exit Word.
17. Save your changes to the presentation, mark the presentation as final, and then save it as a PDF file named **WMC Services PDF** in the PowerPoint4\Case2 folder. Use the Standard optimization, and do not change any of the default options.
18. Submit the completed presentation and PDF file in printed or electronic form, as requested by your instructor, and then close all open files.

*Create a presentation for a company that sells emergency preparedness products.*

CREATE

## Case Problem 3

**Data Files needed for this Case Problem: 72HrKit.jpg, EPR.pptx, EPRChart.xlsx, EPROutline.docx, Flood.jpg, Phone Table.docx, Wheat.jpg**

***Emergency Preparedness Resources*** Emergency Preparedness Resources (EPR) is a growing business in West Wendover, Nevada. The owner and president of EPR, Parker Salvatore, gives presentations on his company's products at emergency preparedness seminars, conferences, and trade shows. Parker asks you to set up a PowerPoint presentation on his company's products. Create the finished presentation, as shown in Figure 4-50, and then create a Web page of the presentation. Read all the steps before you start creating your presentation.

1. The presentation is created from the **EPR** presentation, located in the PowerPoint4\Case3 folder included with your Data Files. Change the name "Parker Salvatore" on Slide 1 to your name, and save it as **EPR Products**.
2. The text for the subsequent slides in the presentation comes from the Word outline file **EPROutline**, located in the PowerPoint4\Case3 folder. Don't forget to apply slide layouts and reset the slides. Make sure the current date, footer, and slide number appear on all the slides.
3. Images that appear in Slides 2 through 4 are **Flood**, **72HrKit**, and **Wheat**, respectively, located in the PowerPoint4\Case3 folder. Remove the background from the Wheat photo on Slide 4.

4. In Slide 5, because the double-columned bulleted list appears as a single list when you first import the outline, change the slide layout to Two Content and use a cut-and-paste operation to move the last seven bulleted items to the second content placeholder.
5. The table of contact numbers on Slide 7 comes from the file **Phone Table**, located in the PowerPoint4\Case3 folder. Format the table by applying the Colorful List – Accent 2 table style.
6. The linked pie chart in Slide 8 comes from the Excel file **EPRChart**, located in the PowerPoint4\Case3 folder.
7. The Action Button: Home buttons shown in the upper-right corner of Slide 2 through 9 are hyperlinked to Slide 1 and are formatted with a shape style. (*Hint*: Insert and format the action button on Slide 2, and then copy it to the other slides.)
8. Apply the Dynamic Content Orbit transition to all the slides except Slides 1 and 2.
9. Add a comment to Slide 8 suggesting that the slide might not be appropriate for this presentation. Position the comment above the slide title.
10. Save your changes, and then save the presentation as a picture presentation named **EPR Pictures** to the PowerPoint4\Case3 folder.
11. Post the presentation to a new folder on your SkyDrive named EPR, granting permission to a friend or colleague to view and edit the files in the folder.
12. Submit the completed presentations in printed or electronic form, as requested by your instructor, and then close the file.

**Figure 4-50** **Final EPR Products presentation**

*Apply your skills to create a presentation about wetlands.*

CREATE

## Case Problem 4

**Data Files needed for this Case Problem: Wetland1.jpg, Wetland2.jpg, Wetland3.jpg, Wetland4.jpg, Wetland5.jpg**

***Campus Conservation Consortium*** The Campus Conservation Consortium (CCC) is an organization of college students that gives presentations to other students on conserving America's wetlands. Prepare a presentation to your classmates on information about wetlands. You might choose a topic such as grants and scholarships on wetland conservation, analysis and information about wetlands in a particular state, legislation on wetland conservation, description of wetland types (saltwater habitats, freshwater habitats, and upland habitat), use of wetlands by migratory birds or other animals, information about an organization involved in wetland conservation, conservation plans for private owners of wetlands, or other related topics. Complete the following steps:

EXPLORE

1. Using Microsoft Word, create an outline of your presentation on wetland conservation. Include at least six titles, which will become slide titles. (Remember to switch to Outline view in Word to type your slide titles, which will be formatted with the Heading 1 style.) Under each title, add information (content) items (formatted in the Heading 2 style), which will become the bulleted lists on each slide. Use books and magazines from your college library, encyclopedia, the Internet, or other sources of information to get the necessary information on wetland conservation. If you haven't covered Microsoft Word in your courses and don't know how to create an outline with heading styles, use the Help feature in Word.
2. Save the Word file using the filename **Wetlands Outline** to the PowerPoint4\Case4 folder included with your Data Files.
3. In another Word document, create a table. Your table might list various wetland preserves, their total area, examples of major wildlife in the area, or other information. You might be able to find a table on the Internet from which you can extract the data.
4. Save the Word file with the table using the filename **Wetlands Table** to the PowerPoint4\Case4 folder.
5. Open a new, blank presentation, and enter an appropriate title of your choosing and a subtitle with your name as the presenter. Save the presentation as **Wetlands** in the PowerPoint4\Case4 folder.
6. Import the Word outline into PowerPoint.
7. Apply the built-in theme Flow.
8. Apply appropriate slide layouts to the new slides, and reset the slides, as needed, so they have the proper format.
9. Embed your table into one of the slides in your presentation. Resize, reposition, and reformat it as needed to maximize its readability.
10. Include a text box either on the first slide or the last slide acknowledging the sources of your information.
11. Insert at least one action button into your presentation with a link to another slide within your presentation.
12. Include at least two text hyperlinks in your presentation, with links to other slides. The text of the hyperlinks can be bulleted items, text in a table cell, or text boxes.

13. Add graphics to the slide show, as desired. If you want, you can use any of the pictures **Wetland1** through **Wetland5** located in the PowerPoint4\Case4 folder.
14. Apply a Dynamic Content transition to all the slides except Slides 1 and 2.
15. Save your changes, and then save the presentation as a picture presentation named **Wetlands Picture** to the PowerPoint4\Case4 folder.
16. Submit the completed presentations in printed or electronic form, as requested by your instructor, and then close the file.

ASSESS

## SAM: Skills Assessment Manager

For current SAM information, including versions and content details, visit SAM Central (http://samcentral.course.com). If you have a SAM user profile, you may have access to hands-on instruction, practice, and assessment of the skills covered in this tutorial. Since various versions of SAM are supported throughout the life of this text, check with your instructor for the correct instructions and URL/Web site for accessing assignments.

## ENDING DATA FILES

**PowerPoint4** →

**Tutorial**
- Clinical Chart.xlsx
- Clinical Report.pptx
- Clinical Report PDF.pdf
- Clinical Report video.wmv
- Landon Report.pptx
- Report Outline.docx
- Report Outline.rtf

**Review**
- Info Pictures.pptx
- Landon Cost Chart.xlsx
- Landon Info Outline.docx
- Landon Info Outline.rtf
- Landon Info.pptx
- Landon Info PDF.pdf
- Landon Info video.wmv

**Case1**
- FLCU Services.pptx
- FLCU video.wmv

**Case2**
- WMC Outline New.rtf
- WMC Services PDF.pdf
- WMC Services.pptx

**Case3**
- EPR Pictures.pptx
- EPR Products.pptx

**Case4**
- Wetlands.pptx
- Wetlands Outline.docx
- Wetlands Picture.pptx
- Wetlands Table.docx

ProSkills

# Teamwork

## What Is a Team?

The American Heritage Dictionary describes a team as a "group organized to work together." More than just people thrown together, teams consist of individuals who have skills, talents, and abilities that complement each other and, when joined, produce synergy—results greater than those a single individual could achieve. It is this sense of shared mission and responsibility for results that makes a team successful in its efforts to reach organizational goals.

## Characteristics of Teams

Have you ever heard someone described as a "team player"? Members on a team get to know how the others work, so they can make contributions where they'll count most. On a football team, not everyone plays the role of quarterback; the team needs other positions working with the quarterback if touchdowns are to be scored. However, before the first play is ever made, the members bring their skills to the team and spend time learning each others' moves so they can catch the pass, block, or run toward the goal line together. Similarly, in a professional environment, the best teams have members whose background, skills, and abilities complement each other.

## Managing Workflow on a Team

When team members collaborate on a project, someone needs to manage the workflow. This is especially important if team members are all contributing to a shared file stored on a server or a shared folder on the Internet. Some businesses have the capability to allow team members to co-author a presentation stored on a server. If this capability is not available, however, the team will need to create a strategy for managing the file to make sure that one person's changes do not get overwritten.

One way to manage workflow is to create an ordered list of team members assigned to work on a presentation file, and have team members access and edit the file only after the person preceding them on the list is finished with it. Another way is to allow anyone to access the presentation, but to have each team member save their version of the presentation with a different name—for example, they can add their initials to the end of the filename—and then each person can make their version available for the team member who has been designated to compare all the presentations to create one final version.

ProSkills

PROSKILLS

## Create a Collaborative Presentation

Many people volunteer for a program that requires them to work collaboratively. For example, you might be a coach of a youth sports program, a Boy Scout leader, or a member of a local historical society. Often, volunteer groups require their members to meet occasionally to share ideas and information. PowerPoint is a useful tool for collecting notes, data, and images that you can then show everyone all at once. One way to do this could be to create a presentation for the group, post it to a shared folder on the World Wide Web, such as a Windows Live SkyDrive folder, and each person in the group can add slides containing the information they want to share. Additionally, other group members can add comments to slides if something is unclear or if they have a question. In this exercise, you'll use PowerPoint to create a presentation for an upcoming meeting for a group of which you are a member, using the skills and features presented in Tutorials 3 and 4.

**Note:** Please be sure *not* to include any personal information of a sensitive nature in the documents you create to be submitted to your instructor for this exercise. Later on, you can update the documents with such information for your own personal use.

1. Start a new, blank PowerPoint presentation, and apply a theme appropriate for the group. It is probably best to apply a theme that does not have a busy background design.
2. Modify the theme colors to match the colors used by your group or association. Add the group's logo or a photo appropriate to the group to the slide master. Consider modifying the background style and using picture bullets for the bulleted lists to add interest. Save the file as an Office Theme so that you can use it for future presentations.
3. Start a new presentation using the theme that you created. Save it with an appropriate name.
4. On Slide 1, type an informative title for your presentation, and add the name of the group as a subtitle.
5. Create a slide that lists the group members who will contribute to the presentation. As group members add to the presentation, they can add their names to the list on this slide.
6. Create at least six slides for the presentation. Consider the purpose of the group as well as the purpose of the upcoming meeting. If you know others have information to share, add slides with titles to help guide them.
7. Add video clips from past group events and recorded sounds to your presentation if you have any.
8. Add interesting slide transitions and custom animations to your presentation. Customize the start timing and the speed of the animations. If appropriate, add a second animation to items.
9. If you have any data to share, consider adding a table or chart that you create in PowerPoint, or consider embedding a Word table or linking to a chart that already exists in an Excel workbook.
10. Decide how you want to manage the workflow, and communicate this process to the group.

ProSkills

11. Save the presentation to your Windows Live SkyDrive folder, and give group members permission to view the file. Send them the link, and ask them to download the file to their own computers. (*Hint*: To do this, point to the file, and then click the Download link.)
12. After group members have made their modifications and added comments to the presentation, compare the presentations or review the single presentation that members took turns modifying. Accept any changes you wish to accept, and decide whether to delete comments.
13. Consider saving the presentation as a picture presentation, a video, or a PDF file if that will make it easier for the entire group to access. Save this file to the group folder on your SkyDrive account.
14. Submit the completed presentation in printed or electronic form, as requested by your instructor, and then close the file.

# GLOSSARY/INDEX

## SPECIAL CHARACTERS



## A



## B

## E

## G



## H

## I

## K



## L

## M



## N

**normal forms** The sets of rules applied to a collection of tables during normalization to eliminate anomalies and to produce a new collection of problem-free tables. AC A15
first normal form, AC A15–A17
second normal form, AC A17–A19
third normal form, AC A19–A21

**normalization** The process of identifying and eliminating anomalies in a collection of tables. AC A15–A21

**Normal template** The default template for new Word documents. WD 220

**Not logical operator** A logical operator that negates a criterion or selects records for which the designated field does not match the criterion. AC 225–226

**null** The absence of a value in a particular table entry. AC A4

**nullifies** A referential integrity option in which the DBMS, when you change or delete a primary key value, automatically sets all matching foreign key values to null. AC A11

**number format** Formatting that displays values in a way that makes it easy for the reader to understand and interpret them.
custom, EX A11–A13

number sign (#)
error values, EX 394
input masks, AC 260

## O

Object command, embedding Word tables in sides, PPT 204–206

**Object Dependencies task pane** A task pane that displays a collapsible list of the dependencies among the objects in an Access database; you click the list's expand indicators to show or hide different levels of dependencies. AC 262–264

**object dependency** A relationship that exists between two objects when a change to the properties of data in one object affects the properties of data in the other object. AC 262–264

**object linking and embedding (OLE)** A technology that allows you to share information among the Office programs. WD 340

object naming convention, AC A25–A26

**Office PivotChart Component** One of the Office Web Components that provides support for PivotCharts in Office programs such as Access and Excel. AC 458

**Office PivotTable Component** One of the Office Web Components that provides support for PivotTables in Office programs such as Access and Excel. AC 453

**Office theme file** A PowerPoint file with the filename extension ."thmx" that is used to apply a custom theme to an existing PowerPoint presentation, or to create a new presentation based on the custom theme. PPT 173

**Office Web Apps** Web-based versions of Microsoft Excel, Word, PowerPoint, and OneNote that allow you to create, view, and edit Office files directly from a Web browser as well as share files and collaborate with other users online. EX 348

**Office Web Components** A Microsoft Office program that provides support for features such as PivotTables and PivotCharts in Access, Excel, and other Office programs. AC 453

**one-to-many relationship (1:M)** A relationship between two tables in which each row in the first table matches many rows in the second table and each row in the second table matches at most one row in the first table. AC A5–A6

**one-to-one relationship (1:1)** A relationship between two tables in which each row in each table has at most one matching row in the other table. AC A7–A8

opening
documents based on templates, WD 262
reopening main documents, WD 292–293
workbooks created in earlier versions of Excel, EX A2–A3
workbooks with macros, EX 472

**& operator** The operator that concatenates or joins the contents of two or more cells; also called the Concatenation operator. EX A6

Options dialog box, PPT 245

Oracle naming rule, AC A27

**OR function** A logical function that returns a TRUE value if any of the logical conditions are true, and a FALSE value if none of the logical conditions are true. EX 365, EX 374–376

**orphaned footer section** A report footer section that appears by itself at the top of a page; the detail lines for the section appear on the previous page. AC 385

**orphaned header section** A report header section that appears by itself at the bottom of a page. The first detail record that follows the orphaned header section appears at the top of the next page. AC 385

outline
exporting to Word, PPT 196–198
Word, importing, PPT 194–196

## P

**Page Break tool** An Access tool that you use to place a page break in a form so that users can move between the form pages by pressing the Page Up and Page Down keys. AC 440

**Page Footer section** A section that appears at the bottom of each page of a report and is used for page numbers, brief explanations of symbols or abbreviations, or other information such as a company name. AC 360, AC 395

**Page Header section** A section that appears at the top of each page of a report and is used for page numbers, column headings, report titles, and report dates. AC 361, AC 374, AC 394, AC 396

page numbering, reports, AC 399–401

Page Numbers dialog box, AC 400

**pane** A section of a window; In Excel, you can split the worksheet window into two or four resizable panes. EX 251
splitting worksheet window into panes, EX 261–263

**paragraph spacing** The space, measured in points, that appears directly above and below a paragraph. WD 234–235

**paragraph style** A style with formatting options that affect the paragraph's appearance, including line spacing, text alignment, tab stops, and borders. WD 236

**parameter query** A query that displays a dialog box that prompts the user to enter one or more criteria values when the query is run. AC 233–237

password protection, EX 446

Paste Names command, EX 428

Paste Options menu, WD 346–347

Paste Special dialog box, WD 344

Paste Values command, EX A5

**pattern match** A selection of records with a value for the designated field that matches the pattern of a simple condition value. AC 221–223

**pen** A pointer that allows you to draw lines on the screen during a slide show. PPT 226–227

**Personal Macro workbook** A hidden workbook named Personal.xlsb that opens whenever you start Excel, making the macros you stored there available any time you use Excel. EX 458

## Q



## R

## T

## U

## X

# TASK REFERENCE

| TASK | PAGE # | RECOMMENDED METHOD |
|---|---|---|
| **3-D reference, use** | EX 313 | *See* Reference box: Entering a Function That Contains a 3-D Reference |
| **Action button, add** | PPT 218 | *See* Reference box: Adding an Action Button as a Link to Another Presentation |
| **Advanced filter, clear** | EX B7 | Click Clear button in Sort & Filter group on Data tab |
| **Advanced filter, create** | EX B4 | Click Advanced button in Sort & Filter group on Data tab, set filter options, data, and criteria ranges in Advanced Filter dialog box, click OK |
| **Animation, add a second one to an object** | PPT 151 | Click Animations tab, click Add Animation button in Advanced Animation group, click desired animation |
| **Animation, change speed of** | PPT 152 | Click Animations tab, click in Duration box in Timing group, type new time for animation, press Enter |
| **AutoFilter, use in a table or query datasheet** | AC 227 | Click arrow on column heading, click filter option |
| **Background, add a texture to** | PPT 168 | *See* Reference box: Applying a Textured Background |
| **Background, add picture to** | PPT 164 | *See* Reference box: Adding a Picture to a Background |
| **Bookmark, create** | WD 361 | Select text, click Insert tab, click Bookmark button in Links group, type bookmark name, click Add |
| **Bullet, change to picture bullet** | PPT 169 | Click Home tab, click Bullets button arrow in Paragraph group, click Bullets and Numbering, click Picture, click desired picture, click OK |
| **Caption, change for a form's navigation bar** | AC 442 | Click the form selector, open the property sheet, type the value in the Navigation Caption box, press Enter |
| **Caption, change for a label** | AC 321 | *See* Reference box: Changing a Label's Caption |
| **Cell or range, create defined name** | EX 424 | *See* Reference box: Creating a Defined Name for a Cell or Range |
| **Cell or range, select by defined name** | EX 426 | Click Name box arrow, click defined name |
| **Cells, lock or unlock** | EX 445 | Select cell or range, click Dialog Box Launcher in Font group on Home tab, click Protection tab, check or uncheck Locked check box, click OK |
| **Cells, reference in other worksheets** | EX 310 | Enter reference in the format =*SheetName*!*CellRange* |
| **Character spacing, adjust** | WD 232 | Select text, click Dialog Box Launcher in Font group on Home tab, click Advanced tab, click Spacing arrow, select spacing option, type point measurement in By box, click OK |
| **Chart, create on a slide** | PPT 144 | *See* Reference box: Creating a Chart |
| **Chart, edit with Microsoft Graph** | AC 448 | In Design view, right-click the chart's edge, point to Chart Object, click Open, make desired changes, click File, click Exit & Return |
| **Chart, embed in a form or report** | AC 446 | *See* Reference box: Embedding a Chart in a Form or Report |
| **Color, change an object's background** | AC 348 | Click the object, click  arrow, click the desired color |
| **Combo box, add to a form** | AC 330 | *See* Reference box: Adding a Combo Box to Find Records |
| **Comment, delete** | EX 450 | Click cell with comment, click Delete button in Comments group on Review tab |
| **Comment, delete single** | WD 336 | Click in comment balloon, click Review tab, click Delete button in Comments group |

| TASK | PAGE # | RECOMMENDED METHOD |
|---|---|---|
| **Comment, insert** | EX 449 | *See* Reference box: Inserting a Comment |
| **Comment, insert on a slide** | PPT 228 | Click Review tab, click New Comment button in Comments group, type comment in balloon |
| **Comment, show or hide** | EX 450 | Click cell with comment, click Show/Hide Comment button in Comments group on Review tab |
| **Comments, delete all in document** | WD 336 | Click in comment balloon, click Review tab, click Delete button arrow in Comments group, click Delete All Comments in Document |
| **Comments, insert** | WD 330 | *See* Reference box: Inserting Comments |
| **Conditional formatting rule, edit** | EX 402 | *See* Reference box: Entering a Conditional Formatting Rule |
| **Control layout, remove control from in a form** | AC 301 | In Layout view, right-click the control, point to Layout, click Remove Layout |
| **Control tip property, set for a form control** | AC 342 | In Layout view, right-click the control, click Properties, click Other tab, type the tip in the ControlTip Text property, press Enter |
| **Control, anchor in a form** | AC 302 | In Layout view, select the control to anchor, click Arrange tab, click Anchoring button in Position group, click option in gallery |
| **Control, apply special effect to** | AC 348 | Select the control, open property sheet, set the Special Effect property |
| **Control, delete** | AC 317 | Right-click the control, click Delete |
| **Control, move in a form** | AC 313 | *See* Reference box: Selecting and Moving Controls |
| **Control, resize in a form** | AC 317 | *See* Reference box: Resizing a Control in Design View |
| **Control, select** | AC 313 | *See* Reference box: Selecting and Moving Controls |
| **Controls, align selected** | AC 315 | Right-click one of the selected controls, point to Align, click desired alignment |
| **Criteria filter, specify complex criteria** | EX 256 | Click filter arrow, point to Number Filters, Text Filters, or Date Filters, specify filter criteria, click OK |
| **Crosstab query, create** | AC 242 | *See* Reference box: Using the Crosstab Query Wizard |
| **CSV file, import as an Access table** | AC 423 | *See* Reference box: Importing a CSV File as an Access Table |
| **Custom format, create** | EX A11 | Select range, click Dialog Box Launcher in Number group on Home tab, click Number tab, click Custom in Category box, enter format codes in Type box, click OK |
| **Data, create input message, error alert message, or validation rule** | EX 438 | *See* Reference box: Validating Data |
| **Data, group in a report** | AC 381 | *See* Reference box: Sorting and Grouping Data in a Report |
| **Data, sort in a report** | AC 381 | *See* Reference box: Sorting and Grouping Data in a Report |
| **Data, split from one column into separate columns** | EX A7 | Select range, click Text to Columns button in Data Tools group on Data tab, follow steps in wizard. |
| **Date and time, add to a report** | AC 396 | *See* Reference box: Adding the Date and Time to a Report |
| **Defined name, create for cell or range** | EX 424 | *See* Reference box: Creating a Defined Name for a Cell or Range |
| **Defined name, edit or delete** | EX 427 | Click Name Manager button in Defined Names group on Formulas tab, select name, click Edit and modify or click Delete, click OK |
| **Defined names, add to existing formulas** | EX 433 | *See* Reference Window: Adding Defined Names to Existing Formulas |

| TASK | PAGE # | RECOMMENDED METHOD |
|---|---|---|
| **Defined names, paste list in worksheet** | EX 428 | Click cell, click Use in Formula button in Defined Names group on Formulas tab, click Paste Names, click Paste List button |
| **Definition, look up in dictionary** | WD 253 | Right-click word or selected text, point to Look up, click Encarta Dictionary: English (North America) |
| **Developer tab, display or hide** | EX 454 | Click File tab, click Options button, click Customize Ribbon, check or uncheck Developer check box, click OK |
| **Documenter, use** | AC 291 | *See* Reference box: Using the Documenter |
| **Documents, compare or combine** | WD 333 | *See* Reference box: Comparing and Combining Documents |
| **Duplicate values, hide** | AC 392 | *See* Reference box: Hiding Duplicate Values in a Report |
| **Duplicate values, highlight** | EX 400 | *See* Reference box: Highlighting Duplicate Values |
| **Embedded object, modify** | WD 345 | Double-click object, use commands and tools of source program to modify object, click outside embedded object |
| **Error Alert message, create** | EX 438 | *See* Reference box: Validating Data |
| **Excel chart, link to a slide using copy and paste** | PPT 209 | *See* Reference box: Linking an Excel Chart to a Slide Using Copy and Paste |
| **Excel table, add a record** | EX 242 | *See* Reference box: Adding a Record to an Excel Table |
| **Excel table, add a record** | EX 242 | *See* Reference box: Adding a Record to an Excel Table |
| **Excel table, create** | EX 239 | Click Table button in Tables group on Insert tab, verify range of data, click OK |
| **Excel table, format** | EX 241 | Click options in Table Style Options group on Table Tools Design tab |
| **Excel table, rename** | EX 240 | Click Excel table, select name in Table Name box in Properties group on Table Tools Design tab, type name |
| **Excel worksheet, link data from** | AC 460 | Click External Data tab, click Excel button in Import & Link group, click Browse, select the workbook, click Open, click Link to the data source by creating a linked table, click OK, follow the steps in the Link Spreadsheet Wizard |
| **Export steps, save** | AC 435 | Click Save export steps check box in Export dialog box, enter description, click Save Export |
| **External reference formula, create** | EX 325 | Click cell in destination file, type =, click cell in source file, complete formula as usual |
| **Field, add to a form or report** | AC 311 | In Design view, click Add Existing Fields button in Tools group, click the record source, double-click the field |
| **File, insert into a Word document** | WD 225 | Click Insert tab, click Object button arrow in Text group, click Text from File, click file, click Insert |
| **File shared on SkyDrive, send link** | PPT 250 | In SkyDrive in browser, display folder page, click Share, click Send a link, click folder name, click Share, click Send a link, type email addresses in To box, type message, click Send |
| **Filter, clear from column** | EX 255 | Click filter arrow, click Clear Filter From *column* |
| **Filter, clear from Excel table** | EX 259 | Click Clear button in Sort & Filter group on Data tab |
| **Filter, select multiple items** | EX 255 | Click filter arrow, check two or more items, click OK |
| **Filter, use multiple columns** | EX 254 | Filter for one column, repeat to filter for additional columns |
| **Filter, use one column** | EX 252 | Click filter arrow, check item to filter by, click OK |

| TASK | PAGE # | RECOMMENDED METHOD |
|---|---|---|
| **Filter arrows, display or hide** | EX 252 | In Sort & Filter group on Data tab, click Filter button |
| **Find duplicates query, create** | AC 246 | *See* Reference box: Using the Find Duplicates Query Wizard |
| **Find unmatched query, create** | AC 248 | *See* Reference box: Using the Find Unmatched Query Wizard |
| **Folder, create on SkyDrive and grant permission for access** | PPT 246 | *See* Reference box: Creating a New Folder on SkyDrive and Granting Permission for Access |
| **Form Footer, add** | AC 325 | *See* Reference box: Adding and Removing Form Header and Form Footer Sections |
| **Form Footer, remove** | AC 325 | *See* Reference box: Adding and Removing Form Header and Form Footer Sections |
| **Form Header, add** | AC 325 | *See* Reference box: Adding and Removing Form Header and Form Footer Sections |
| **Form Header, remove** | AC 325 | *See* Reference box: Adding and Removing Form Header and Form Footer Sections |
| **Form, create a custom** | AC 309 | *See* Reference box: Creating a Form in Design View |
| **Form, create using the Datasheet tool** | AC 294 | Select record source in Navigation Pane, click Create tab, click More Forms button in Forms group, click Datasheet |
| **Form, create using the Multiple Items tool** | AC 296 | Select record source in Navigation Pane, click Create tab, click More Forms button in Forms group, click Multiple Items button |
| **Form, create using the Split Form tool** | AC 298 | Select record source in Navigation Pane, click Create tab, click More Forms button in Forms group, click Split Form button |
| **Form, select in Design view** | AC 326 | Click the form selector |
| **Formula, reference another worksheet** | EX 311 | *See* Reference box: Entering a Formula with References to Another Worksheet |
| **Formula results, copy and paste as values** | EX A5 | Copy range with formula results, click first cell in paste location, click Paste button arrow in Clipboard group on Home tab, click Values button |
| **Handout Master, customize** | PPT 225 | Click View tab, click Handout Master in Master Views group, customize master, click Close Master View button in Close group |
| **Horizontal line, insert** | WD 371 | Click Borders and Shading button arrow on Home tab in Paragraph group, click Borders and Shading, click Horizontal Line, click a line style, click OK |
| **HTML document, export an Access object as** | AC 420 | *See* Reference box: Exporting an Access Object to an HTML Document |
| **Hyperlink, create** | EX 338 | *See* Reference box: Inserting a Hyperlink |
| **Hyperlink, create to another slide** | PPT 212 | *See* Reference box: Creating a Hyperlink to Another Slide in a Presentation |
| **Hyperlink, edit** | WD 373 | Right-click hyperlink, click Edit Hyperlink, select option in Link to pane, select document or Web page, click OK |
| **Hyperlink, edit** | EX 340 | Right-click cell with hyperlink, click Edit Hyperlink, make edits in Edit Hyperlink dialog box, click OK |
| **Hyperlink to a location in the same document, create** | WD 362 | *See* Reference box: Creating a Hyperlink to a Location in the Same Document |
| **Hyperlink to another file or Web page, create** | WD 364 | *See* Reference box: Creating a Hyperlink to Another Document |

| TASK | PAGE # | RECOMMENDED METHOD |
|---|---|---|
| **Import steps, save** | AC 430 | Click Save import steps check box in Import dialog box, enter description, click Save Import |
| **Input Mask Wizard, activate** | AC 258 | Click the field's Input Mask box, click [...], specify your choices in the Input Mask Wizard dialog boxes |
| **Input message, create** | EX 438 | *See* Reference box: Validating Data |
| **Invalid data, circle** | EX 444 | Click Data Validation button arrow in Data Tools group on Data tab, click Circle Invalid Data |
| **Legend, add to PivotChart** | AC 458 | Click Design tab, click Legend button in Show/Hide group |
| **Line, add to a form or report** | AC 346 | *See* Reference box: Adding a Line to a Form or Report |
| **Link, break** | WD 351–352 | *See* Reference box: Breaking a Link to a Source File |
| **Linked workbooks, update** | EX 329 | Click in source file, edit as usual |
| **Links, manage** | EX 332 | Click Edit Links button in Connections group on Data tab, select option, click OK |
| **Lookup field, change to Text field** | AC 288 | Display the table in Design view, select the field, click the Lookup tab, set the Display Control property to Text Box |
| **Lookup field, create** | AC 254 | Click the Data Type arrow, click Lookup Wizard, specify your choices in the Lookup Wizard dialog boxes |
| **Macro, edit** | EX 464 | *See* Reference box: Editing a Macro |
| **Macro, record** | EX 458 | *See* Reference box: Recording a Macro |
| **Macro, run** | EX 461 | *See* Reference box: Running a Macro |
| **Macro, set security level for** | EX 456 | *See* Reference box: Setting Macro Security in Excel |
| **Macro, view code** | EX 464 | *See* Reference box: Editing a Macro |
| **Macro button, create** | EX 468 | *See* Reference box: Creating a Macro Button |
| **Macro button, move** | EX 470 | Right-click macro button, press Esc, drag button by its selection box to new location |
| **Macro button, resize** | EX 470 | Right-click macro button, press Esc, drag sizing handle |
| **Mail merge data source, create** | WD 275 | *See* Reference box: Creating A Data Source for a Mail Merge |
| **Mail merge data source, edit in Word** | WD 293 | *See* Reference box: Editing a Data Source in Word |
| **Mail merge data source, filter** | WD 297–298 | Select type of main document, select or create data source, click Edit Recipient List button in Start Mail Merge group on Mailings tab, click arrow button in column header for field you want to filter by, click field entry |
| **Mail merge data source, sort** | WD 296 | *See* Reference box: Sorting a Data Source by Multiple Fields |
| **Mail merge main document, select type of** | WD 272–273 | Click Mailings tab, click Start Mail Merge button in the Start Mail Merge group, click type of main document |
| **Mail merge, finish by merging to new document** | WD 287 | Click Mailings tab, click Finish & Merge button in Finish group, click Edit Individual Documents, click OK |
| **Mail merge, finish by merging to printer** | WD 287 | Click Mailings tab, click Finish & Merge button in Finish group, click Print Documents, click OK |
| **Mail merge, insert merge fields in main document for** | WD 281–282 | Click Mailings tab, click Insert Merge Field button arrow in Write & Insert Fields group, click merge field |

| TASK | PAGE # | RECOMMENDED METHOD |
|---|---|---|
| **Mail merge, preview merged document for** | WD 285 | Click Review tab, click Preview Results button in Preview Results group |
| **Mailing labels, create** | WD 299–300 | Click Mailings tab, click Start Mail Merge button in Start Mail Merge group, click Labels, click Label vendors arrow, click vendor, click option in Product number box, click OK, select data source, insert merge fields, click Update Labels in the Write & Insert Fields group, finish merge |
| **Mailing labels, create** | AC 404 | *See* Reference box: Creating Mailing Labels and Other Labels |
| **Memo field, change properties of** | AC 269 | Display the table in Design view, select the Memo field, click the Text Format box or click the Append Only box |
| **Mini Translator, display** | WD 261 | Click Review tab, select translation languages, click Translate button in Language group, click Mini Translator, select text, point to selected text, move mouse pointer over Mini Translator |
| **Multilevel list style, apply** | WD 312 | Format text as bulleted or numbered list, select list, click , click style |
| **Multiple-column report, modify** | AC 406 | In Design view, click Page Setup tab, click Page Setup button, click the Columns tab, set the column options, click OK |
| **Object dependencies, identify** | AC 262 | Click Database Tools tab, click Object Dependencies button in Relationships group, click the object, click |
| **Object, embed in Word document** | WD 343 | Select and copy object in source program, return to Word, click destination location, click Paste button arrow in Clipboard group on Home tab, click Paste Special, in As list box select option that will paste object as an Object, click OK |
| **Object, link to Word document** | WD 346–347 | Select and copy object in source program, return to Word, click destination location, click Paste button arrow in Clipboard group on Home tab, click Link & Keep Source Formatting or click Link & Use Destination Styles |
| **Outline, export to Word** | PPT 197 | Click File tab, click Save As, click Save as type arrow, click Outline/RTF, type filename, click Save |
| **Outline, import from Word** | PPT 194 | Click Home tab, click New Slide button arrow in Slides group, click Slides from Outline, click outline file, click Insert |
| **Padding, change in a form control** | AC 302 | In Layout view, click the control, click Arrange tab, click Control Padding button in Position group, click the desired setting |
| **Page Color gradient, add** | WD 369–370 | Click Page Layout tab, click Page Color button in Page Background group, click Fill Effects, click Gradient tab, click One color or Two colors, select colors and shading style, click OK |
| **Page Color, add** | WD 369–370 | Click Page Layout tab, click Page Color button in Page Background group, click color |
| **Page numbers, add to a report** | AC 399 | *See* Reference box: Adding Page Numbers to a Report |
| **Parameter query, create** | AC 234 | *See* Reference box: Creating a Parameter Query |
| **Photograph, remove background from** | PPT 200 | *See* Reference box: Removing the Background of a Photograph |
| **PivotChart, add to a table or query** | AC 458 | Open the table or query in Datasheet view, right-click the object tab, click PivotChart View, drag the fields from the Field List pane into the PivotChart |
| **PivotTable, add a total field** | AC 455 | Click a detail field's column heading, click Design tab, click AutoCalc button in Tools group, click an aggregate option |

| TASK | PAGE # | RECOMMENDED METHOD |
|---|---|---|
| **PivotTable, add to a table or query** | AC 453 | Open the table or query in Datasheet view, right-click the object tab, click PivotTable View, drag the fields from the Field List pane into the PivotTable |
| **PivotChart, create** | EX 291 | Click PivotChart button in Tools group on PivotTable Tools Options tab, complete Insert Chart dialog box, click OK |
| **PivotTable, create** | EX 272 | *See* Reference box: Creating a PivotTable |
| **PivotTable, filter using slicer** | EX 286 | Click slicer button |
| **PivotTable, rearrange** | EX 277 | Drag field buttons in PivotTable Field List |
| **PivotTable, refresh** | EX 287 | click Refresh button in Data group on PivotTable Tools Options tab |
| **PivotTable, show or hide details** | AC 457 | Click Design tab, click Show Details or Hide Details in Show/Hide group |
| **PivotTable field, remove** | EX 284 | Uncheck items in field area of PivotTable Field List |
| **PivotTable fields, filter** | EX 281 | Click the column or row label filter arrow in PivotTable for data to filter, check and uncheck items |
| **PivotTable items, group** | EX 288 | Click Group Field button in Group group on PivotTable Tools Options tab, select options in Grouping dialog box, click OK |
| **PivotTable report filter, add** | EX 279 | Drag field button from PivotTable Field List to Report Filter box |
| **PivotTable report filter, modify** | EX 280 | Click report filter arrow, click filter items |
| **PivotTable report layout, change** | EX 278 | Click Report Layout button in Layout group on PivotTable Tools Design tab, click layout |
| **PivotTable slicer, create** | EX 285 | Click Insert Slicer button in Sort & Filter group on PivotTable Tools Options tab, click field check box, click OK |
| **PivotTable style, apply** | EX 276 | Click More button in PivotTable Styles group on PivotTable Tools Design tab, click style |
| **PivotTable value fields, format** | EX 276 | Click cell in PivotTable, click Field Settings button in Active Field group on PivotTable Tools Options tab, click Number Format button, select format, click OK |
| **Presentation, save to SkyDrive** | PPT 250 | *See* Reference box: Saving a File to a Folder on SkyDrive |
| **Presentations, compare** | PPT 230 | Click Review tab, click Compare button in Compare group, click presentation to compare to, click Merge, click check boxes to accept changes, click End Review button in Compare group, click Yes |
| **Property sheet, open or close for a field or control** | AC 232 | Select the field or control, click Design tab, click Property Sheet button in Show/Hide group |
| **Record, delete from Excel table** | EX 244 | Select the record, click Delete button arrow in Cells group on Home tab, click Delete Table Rows |
| **Records, find and replace in Excel table** | EX 243 | Click Excel table, click the Find & Select button in Editing group on Home tab, use Find and Replace dialog box |
| **Rectangle, add to a form or report** | AC 347 | *See* Reference box: Adding a Rectangle to a Form or Report |
| **Report, create a custom** | AC 379 | *See* Reference box: Creating a Blank Report in Layout View |
| **Report, filter in Report view** | AC 363 | Right-click the value to filter, point to Text Filters, click filter option |
| **Report, select and copy data in Report view** | AC 364 | Click the top of the selection, drag to the end of the selection, click Home tab, click  in Clipboard group |
| **Research task pane, open** | WD 253 | Right-click text in document, point to Look up, click option; or, click Review tab, click Research button in Proofing group |

| TASK | PAGE # | RECOMMENDED METHOD |
|---|---|---|
| **Reveal Formatting pane, open** | WD 245 | Click [icon] at bottom of Styles pane, click [icon] in Style Inspector |
| **Ribbon, minimize or maximize** | EX 473 | Click [icon] or [icon], or double-click any tab |
| **Row(s) and column(s), freeze** | EX 238 | Click cell below and to right of row(s) and column(s) to freeze, click Freeze Panes button in Window group on View tab, click option |
| **Row(s) and column(s), unfreeze** | EX 239 | Click Freeze Panes button in Window group on View tab, click Unfreeze Panes |
| **Saved export, run** | AC 435 | Click External Data tab, click Saved Exports button in Export group, click the saved export, click Run |
| **Saved import, run** | AC 430 | Click External Data tab, click Saved Imports button in Import & Link group, click the saved import, click Run |
| **SkyDrive, access files on** | WD 358 | *See* Reference box: Accessing Files Stored on Sky Drive |
| **SkyDrive, create shared folder on** | WD 358 | Start Internet Explorer, sign into Windows Live, display your Sky Drive folders, click New, click Folder, type a name for new folder, click Change, select sharing options, click Next, click Add files, click select document from your computer to begin uploading document you want to share |
| **SkyDrive, email URL of file saved in Public folder** | WD 358 | Start Internet Explorer, sign into Windows Live, display document on your SkyDrive, right-click URL in browser's Address bar, click Copy, open email program and paste URL into a new email |
| **SkyDrive, save document to** | WD 356–357 | Click File tab, click Save & Send tab, click Save to Web, click Sign In button and sign into Windows Live if necessary, click SkyDrive folder you want to save document to, click Save As, type file name in Save As dialog box, click Save |
| **Slides, mark during slide show** | PPT 226 | Start slide show, right-click, point to Pointer Options, click Pen, write on slide |
| **Slides, reset** | PPT 161 | Click Home tab, click Reset button in Slides group |
| **Sort, create a custom list** | EX 248 | *See* Reference box: Creating a Custom List |
| **Sort, multiple columns** | EX 245 | *See* Reference box: Sorting Data Using Multiple Sort Fields |
| **Sort, one column** | EX 244 | Click [icon] or [icon] |
| **Sound clip, insert** | PPT 134 | *See* Reference box: Inserting a Sound into a Presentation |
| **Spacing, change in a form control** | AC 301 | In Layout view, click the control, click Arrange tab, click Control Margins button in Position group, click the desired setting |
| **Special format, apply to data** | EX A10 | Select range, click Dialog Box Launcher in Number group on Home tab, click Number tab, click Special in Category box, click special format, click OK |
| **Split panes, create or remove** | EX 261 | Click Split button in Window group on View tab |
| **Style, create a new** | WD 242 | *See* Reference box: Creating a New Style |
| **Style, modify** | WD 226 | *See* Reference box: Modifying Styles Using the Style pane |
| **Style Inspector, open** | WD 245–246 | Click [icon] at bottom of Styles pane |
| **Style Set, select** | WD 231 | Click Home tab, click Change Styles button in Styles group, point to Style Set, click style set |
| **Styles pane, change way styles are displayed in** | WD 237 | Click Options in bottom-right corner of the Styles pane, select style pane options, click OK |

| TASK | PAGE # | RECOMMENDED METHOD |
|---|---|---|
| **Styles pane, open** | WD 236 | In Styles group on Home tab, click Styles Dialog Box Launcher |
| **Synonym, replace selected word or text with** | WD 254 | Right-click word or selected text, point to Synonyms, click synonym |
| **Subform, open in a new window** | AC 337 | Right-click the subform border, click Subform in New Window |
| **Subform/Subreport Wizard, activate** | AC 333 | Click in Controls group, make sure is selected, click , click in the grid at the upper-left corner for the subform/subreport |
| **Subtotal Outline view, use** | EX 266 | Click outline button to show or hide the selected outline level |
| **Subtotals, insert** | EX 263 | *See* Reference box: Calculating Subtotals for a Range of Data |
| **Subtotals, remove** | EX 266 | Click Subtotal button in Outline group on Data tab, click Remove All button |
| **Tab Control, add to a form** | AC 440 | Click Design tab, click Tab Control tool in Controls group, click in the grid at the upper-left corner for the tab control |
| **Tab order, change in a form** | AC 343 | In Design view, click the Design tab, click Tab Order button in Tools group, drag the rows into the desired order, click OK |
| **Tab Stop property, change for a form control** | AC 342 | In Layout view, right-click the control, click Properties, click Other tab, set the Tab Stop property |
| **Table, align text in cells** | PPT 142 | Click Table Tools Layout tab, click an alignment button in Alignment group |
| **Table, analyze** | AC 426 | Select the table, click Database Tools tab, click Analyze Table button in Analyze group |
| **Table, insert on slide** | PPT 138 | *See* Reference box: Inserting a Table |
| **Table, merge cells** | PPT 141 | Click Table Tools Layout tab, select cells to merge, click Merge Cells button in Merge group |
| **Table, resize column** | PPT 142 | Drag column divider line, or double-click column divider line to autofit contents |
| **Table of Contents, add text to** | WD 251 | Select text, click References tab, click Add Text button in Table of Contents group, click level |
| **Table of Contents, create** | WD 248 | *See* Reference box: Creating a Table of Contents |
| **Table of Contents, update** | WD 252 | Click References tab, click Update Table button in Table of Contents group, click Update entire table option button, click OK |
| **Table, convert to text** | WD 311 | Select table, click Table Tools Layout tab, click Convert to Text in Data group, select separator character, click OK |
| **Tabs, clear all from document** | WD 305 | Click Dialog Box Launcher in Paragraph group on Home tab, click Tabs, click Clear all, click OK |
| **Template, create custom** | EX 344 | *See* Reference box: Creating a Custom Template |
| **Template, use an HTML** | AC 421 | Click the Export data with formatting and layout check box in the Export - HTML Document dialog box, click the Select a HTML Template check box, click Browse, select template, click OK |
| **Template from Office.com, create a new document from** | WD 224 | Click File tab, click New tab, click option under "Office.com Tempates," click template, click Download |
| **Template installed with Word, create a new document from** | WD 224 | Click File tab, click New tab, click Sample templates, click template, click Create |

| TASK | PAGE # | RECOMMENDED METHOD |
|---|---|---|
| **Template saved to folder other than Templates folder, create new document from** | WD 262 | Click File tab, click New tab, click New from existing, navigate to correct location, click template, click Create New |
| **Template saved to Templates folder, create new document from** | WD 262 | Click File tab, click New tab, click My Templates, click template, click OK |
| **Template, saving a document as** | WD 259 | *See* Reference box: Saving a Document as a Template |
| **Text, convert to table** | WD 307–308 | Set up text with consistent separator characters, select text, click Insert tab, click Tables button in Tables group, click Convert Text to Table, click appropriate option button under "Separate text at," click OK |
| **Theme, create custom** | PPT 173 | *See* Reference box: Saving a Custom Theme |
| **Theme colors, customize** | WD 229 | Click Page Layout tab, click in Themes group, click Create New Theme Colors, select theme colors, type theme name in Name box, click Save |
| **Theme colors, change** | PPT 159 | Click Design tab, click Colors button in Themes group, click desired color set |
| **Theme colors, select** | WD 227 | Click Page Layout tab, click in Themes group, click set of theme colors |
| **Theme fonts, customize** | WD 229 | Click Page Layout tab, click in Themes group, click Create New Theme Fonts, select heading and body font, type name for theme fonts in Name box, click Save |
| **Theme fonts, select** | WD 228 | Click Page Layout tab, click in Themes group, click set of theme fonts |
| **Theme, create a custom** | WD 229 | Click Page Layout tab, click Themes button in Themes group, click Save Current Theme, navigate to new location if necessary, type theme name in File name box, click Save |
| **Title, add to a form or report** | AC 325 | In Header/Footer group, click Title button, type the title, press Enter |
| **Top values query, create** | AC 249 | In the Query Setup group on the Design tab, enter the number of or percentage of records to select in the Return (Top Values) box |
| **Total, calculate in a report** | AC 369 | In Layout view, click any value in the column to calculate, click Design tab, click Totals button in Grouping & Totals group, click desired function |
| **Total row, add or remove from Excel table** | EX 259 | Check or uncheck Total Row check box in Table Style Options group on Table Tools Design tab |
| **Total row, select summary statistics** | EX 260 | Click arrow button in Total row cell, click summary function |
| **Translation language, select** | WD 256–257 | Click Review tab, click Translate button in Language group, click Choose Translation Language, select language for Mini Translator and document translation, click OK |
| **Translation of current document, display** | WD 258 | Click Review tab, select translation language, click Translate button in Proofing group, click Translate Document |
| **Trusted folder, create** | AC 270 | Click File tab, click Options, click Trust Center, click Trust Center Settings, click Trusted Locations, click Add new location, click Browse, navigate to the desired folder, click OK four times |
| **User name and initials, change** | WD 326 | Click Review tab, click Track Changes button arrow in Tracking group, click Change User Name, type new user name and initials, click OK |

| TASK | PAGE # | RECOMMENDED METHOD |
|---|---|---|
| **Validation circle, clear from a cell** | EX 444 | Enter valid data |
| **Validation circles, clear all** | EX 444 | Click Data Validation button arrow in Data Tools group on Data tab, click Clear Validation Circles |
| **Validation circles, create** | EX 444 | Click Data Validation button arrow in Data Tools group on Data tab, click Circle Invalid Data |
| **Validation rule, create** | EX 438 | *See* Reference box: Validating Data |
| **Validation Rule property, set** | AC 264 | Display the table in Design view, select the field, enter the rule in the Validation Rule box |
| **Validation Text property, set** | AC 265 | Display the table in Design view, select the field, enter the text in the Validation Text box |
| **VBA code, view** | EX 454 | *See* Reference box: Editing a Macro |
| **Video, adjust volume** | PPT 130 | Click Video Tools Playback tab, click Volume button in Video Options group, click desired volume |
| **Video, insert in a presentation** | PPT 127 | *See* Reference box: Inserting a Video into a Presentation |
| **Video, set poster frame** | PPT 131 | Play video to desired frame, click Video Tools Format tab, click Poster Frame button in Adjust group, click Current Frame |
| **Video, set to play automatically** | PPT 129 | Click Video Tools Playback tab, click Start arrow in Video Options group, click Automatically |
| **Video, trim** | PPT 130 | Click Video Tools Playback tab, click Trim Video button in Editing group, drag Start and End sliders, click OK |
| **Visual Basic Editor, open or close** | EX 454 | *See* Reference box: Editing a Macro |
| **Web page, open in Internet Explorer** | WD 373 | Start Internet Explorer, right-click blank area of Favorites bar and click Menu Bar to insert a check if necessary, click File, click Open, select Web page, click OK |
| **Web page, save document as** | WD 367 | *See* Reference box: Saving a Word Document as a Web Page |
| **Word table, embed using Object command** | PPT 204 | *See* Reference box: Embedding a Word Table in a Slide Using the Object Command |
| **Workbook, create from template** | EX 342 | *See* Reference box: Creating a Workbook Based on a Template |
| **Workbook, protect** | EX 448 | *See* Reference box: Protecting a Workbook |
| **Workbook, save earlier Excel file format in current format** | EX A2 | In Save As dialog box, click Save as type button, click Excel Workbook |
| **Workbook, save in earlier Excel file format** | EX A14 | In Save As dialog box, click Save as type button, click Excel 97-2003 Workbook, click Save, click Continue or Cancel in Compatibility Checker |
| **Workbook, save to SkyDrive** | EX 349 | *See* Reference box: Saving a Workbook to SkyDrive |
| **Workbook, save with macros** | EX 471 | In Save As dialog box, select save location, enter filename, click the Save as type button, click Excel Macro-Enabled Workbook, click Save |
| **Workbooks, arrange** | EX 324 | *See* Reference box: Arranging Workbooks |
| **Workbooks, link** | EX 322 | Enter formula in the format =[*WorkbookName*]*WorksheetName*!*CellRange* |
| **Workbooks, switch between** | EX 324 | Click Switch Windows button in Window group on View tab, click workbook to make active |

| TASK | PAGE # | RECOMMENDED METHOD |
|---|---|---|
| **Worksheet, protect** | EX 446 | *See* Reference box: Protecting a Worksheet |
| **Worksheet, unprotect** | EX 449 | Make worksheet active, click Unprotect Sheet button in Changes group on Review tab |
| **Worksheet group, print** | EX 317 | Create worksheet group, apply page layout settings, print as usual |
| **Worksheets, copy to another workbook** | EX 310 | *See* Reference box: Copying Worksheets to Another Workbook |
| **Worksheets, group or ungroup** | EX 305 | *See* Reference box: Grouping and Ungrouping Worksheets |
| **Workspace, create** | EX 333 | Open and arrange workbooks as desired, click Save Workspace button in Window group on View tab, save as usual |
| **XML file, export an Access object to an** | AC 432 | *See* Reference box: Exporting an Access Object as an XML File |
| **XML file, import as an Access table** | AC 429 | *See* Reference box: Importing an XML File as an Access Table |